CUMULATIVE PROBABILITIES FOR THE STANDARD NORMAL DISTRIBUTION

W9-AHI-177

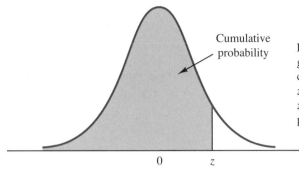

Cumulative probability

Entries in the table give the area under the curve to the left of the z value. For example, for $z = 1.25$, the cumulative probability is .8944.

z	.00	.01	.02	.03	.04	.05	.06	.07	.08	.09
.0	.5000	.5040	.5080	.5120	.5160	.5199	.5239	.5279	.5319	.5359
.1	.5398	.5438	.5478	.5517	.5557	.5596	.5636	.5675	.5714	.5753
.2	.5793	.5832	.5871	.5910	.5948	.5987	.6026	.6064	.6103	.6141
.3	.6179	.6217	.6255	.6293	.6331	.6368	.6406	.6443	.6480	.6517
.4	.6554	.6591	.6628	.6664	.6700	.6736	.6772	.6808	.6844	.6879
.5	.6915	.6950	.6985	.7019	.7054	.7088	.7123	.7157	.7190	.7224
.6	.7257	.7291	.7324	.7357	.7389	.7422	.7454	.7486	.7517	.7549
.7	.7580	.7611	.7642	.7673	.7704	.7734	.7764	.7794	.7823	.7852
.8	.7881	.7910	.7939	.7967	.7995	.8023	.8051	.8078	.8106	.8133
.9	.8159	.8186	.8212	.8238	.8264	.8289	.8315	.8340	.8365	.8389
1.0	.8413	.8438	.8461	.8485	.8508	.8531	.8554	.8577	.8599	.8621
1.1	.8643	.8665	.8686	.8708	.8729	.8749	.8770	.8790	.8810	.8830
1.2	.8849	.8869	.8888	.8907	.8925	.8944	.8962	.8980	.8997	.9015
1.3	.9032	.9049	.9066	.9082	.9099	.9115	.9131	.9147	.9162	.9177
1.4	.9192	.9207	.9222	.9236	.9251	.9265	.9279	.9292	.9306	.9319
1.5	.9332	.9345	.9357	.9370	.9382	.9394	.9406	.9418	.9429	.9441
1.6	.9452	.9463	.9474	.9484	.9495	.9505	.9515	.9525	.9535	.9545
1.7	.9554	.9564	.9573	.9582	.9591	.9599	.9608	.9616	.9625	.9633
1.8	.9641	.9649	.9656	.9664	.9671	.9678	.9686	.9693	.9699	.9706
1.9	.9713	.9719	.9726	.9732	.9738	.9744	.9750	.9756	.9761	.9767
2.0	.9772	.9778	.9783	.9788	.9793	.9798	.9803	.9808	.9812	.9817
2.1	.9821	.9826	.9830	.9834	.9838	.9842	.9846	.9850	.9854	.9857
2.2	.9861	.9864	.9868	.9871	.9875	.9878	.9881	.9884	.9887	.9890
2.3	.9893	.9896	.9898	.9901	.9904	.9906	.9909	.9911	.9913	.9913
2.4	.9918	.9920	.9922	.9925	.9927	.9929	.9931	.9932	.9934	.9936
2.5	.9938	.9940	.9941	.9943	.9945	.9946	.9948	.9949	.9951	.9952
2.6	.9953	.9955	.9956	.9957	.9959	.9960	.9961	.9962	.9963	.9964
2.7	.9965	.9966	.9967	.9968	.9969	.9970	.9971	.9972	.9973	.9974
2.8	.9974	.9975	.9976	.9977	.9977	.9978	.9979	.9979	.9980	.9981
2.9	.9981	.9982	.9982	.9983	.9984	.9984	.9985	.9985	.9986	.9986
3.0	.9986	.9987	.9987	.9988	.9988	.9989	.9989	.9989	.9990	.9990

Essentials of Modern Business Statistics

With Microsoft® Office Excel®

David R. Anderson
University of Cincinnati

Dennis J. Sweeney
University of Cincinnati

Thomas A. Williams
Rochester Institute of Technology

Essentials of Modern Business Statistics

With Microsoft® Office Excel®

4e

David R. Anderson
University of Cincinnati

Dennis J. Sweeney
University of Cincinnati

Thomas A. Williams
Rochester Institute of Technology

SOUTH-WESTERN
CENGAGE Learning™

Australia • Brazil • Japan • Korea • Mexico • Singapore • Spain • United Kingdom • United States

SOUTH-WESTERN
CENGAGE Learning

Essentials of Modern Business Statistics With Microsoft® Office Excel®, Fourth Edition
David R. Anderson, Dennis J. Sweeney, Thomas A. Williams

Editorial Director: Jack W. Calhoun

Editor-in-Chief: Alex von Rosenberg

Senior Acquisitions Editor:
    Charles McCormick, Jr.

Developmental Editor: Margaret Kubale

Marketing Communications Manager:
    Libby Shipp

Marketing Manager: Bryant Chrzan

Content Project Manager:
    Jacquelyn K Featherly

Media Editor: Chris Valentine

Senior Manufacturing Coordinator:
    Diane Gibbons

Production House/Compositor:
    ICC Macmillan Inc.

Art Director: Stacy Jenkins Shirley

Internal Designer:
    Michael Stratton/cmiller design

Cover Designer: Craig Ramsdell

Cover Images:
    Getty Images/GlowImages

Photo Manager: John Hill

© 2009, 2007 South-Western, a part of Cengage Learning

ALL RIGHTS RESERVED. No part of this work covered by the copyright herein may be reproduced, transmitted, stored or used in any form or by any means graphic, electronic, or mechanical, including but not limited to photocopying, recording, scanning, digitizing, taping, Web distribution, information networks, or information storage and retrieval systems, except as permitted under Section 107 or 108 of the 1976 United States Copyright Act, without the prior written permission of the publisher.

For product information and technology assistance, contact us at **Cengage Learning Customer & Sales Support, 1-800-354-9706**

For permission to use material from this text or product, submit all requests online at **www.cengage.com/permissions**
Further permissions questions can be emailed to **permissionrequest@cengage.com**

ExamView® and ExamView Pro® are registered trademarks of FSCreations, Inc. Windows is a registered trademark of the Microsoft Corporation used herein under license. Macintosh and Power Macintosh are registered trademarks of Apple Computer, Inc. used herein under license.

Library of Congress Control Number: 2008927533

Student Edition Package 13: 978-0-324-78351-3

Student Edition Package 10: 0-324-78351-5

Student Edition ISBN 13: 978-0-324-59004-3

Student Edition ISBN 10: 0-324-59004-0

South-Western Cengage Learning
5191 Natorp Boulevard
Mason, OH 45040
USA

Cengage Learning products are represented in Canada by Nelson Education, Ltd.

For your course and learning solutions, visit
academic.cengage.com

Purchase any of our products at your local college store or at our preferred online store **www.ichapters.com**

Printed in China by China Translation & Printing Services Limited
2 3 4 5 6 7 12 11 10

Dedicated to
Krista, Justin, Mark, and Colleen
Mark, Linda, Brad, Tim, Scott, and Lisa
Cathy, David, and Kristin

Brief Contents

Contents

Chapter 3   Descriptive Statistics: Numerical Measures   93

Chapter 5   Discrete Probability Distributions   200

Chapter 10 Comparisons Involving Means, Experimental Design, and Analysis of Variance 395

Chapter 14 Statistical Methods for Quality Control 610

The purpose of *Essentials of Modern Business Statistics with Microsoft® Office Excel®* is to give students, primarily those in the fields of business administration and economics, a conceptual introduction to the field of statistics and its many applications. The text is applications oriented and written with the needs of the nonmathematician in mind; the mathematical prerequisite is knowledge of algebra.

Applications of data analysis and statistical methodology are an integral part of the organization and presentation of the text material. The discussion and development of each technique is presented in an applications setting, with the statistical results providing insights to decisions and solutions to problems.

Although the book is applications oriented, we have taken care to provide sound methodological development and to use notation that is generally accepted for the topic being covered. Hence, students will find that this text provides good preparation for the study of more advanced statistical material. A bibliography to guide further study is included as an appendix.

Use of Microsoft Excel for Statistical Analysis

Essentials of Modern Business Statistics with Microsoft Excel is first and foremost a statistics textbook that emphasizes statistical concepts and applications. But, since most practical problems are too large to be solved using hand calculations, some type of statistical software package is required to solve these problems. There are several excellent statistical packages available today. However, because most students and potential employers value spreadsheet experience, many schools now use a spreadsheet package in their statistics courses. Microsoft Excel is the most widely used spreadsheet package in business as well as in colleges and universities. We have written *Essentials of Modern Business Statistics with Microsoft Excel* especially for statistics courses in which Microsoft Excel is used as the software package.

Excel has been integrated within each of the chapters and plays an integral part in providing an application orientation. Although we assume that readers using this text are familiar with Excel basics such as selecting cells, entering formulas, copying, and so on, we do not assume that readers are familiar with Excel 2007. As a result, we have included Appendix E, which provides an introduction to Excel 2007 and tools for statistical analysis, including the use of Excel 2007 functions and data analysis tools.

Throughout the text, the discussion of using Excel to perform a statistical procedure appears in a subsection immediately following the discussion of the statistical procedure. We believe that this style enables us to fully integrate the use of Excel throughout the text but still maintain the primary emphasis on the statistical methodology being discussed. In each of these subsections, we use a standard format for setting up a worksheet for statistical analysis. There are three primary tasks: Enter Data, Enter Functions and Formulas, and Apply Tools. We believe a consistent framework for applying Excel helps users to focus on the statistical methodology without getting bogged down in the details of using Excel.

In presenting worksheet figures we often use a nested approach in which the worksheet shown in the background of the figure displays the formulas and the worksheet

FIGURE 2.1   FREQUENCY DISTRIBUTION FOR SOFT DRINK PURCHASES CONSTRUCTED USING EXCEL'S COUNTIF FUNCTION

	A	B	C	D	E
1	**Brand Purchased**		**Soft Drink**	**Frequency**	
2	Coke Classic		Coke Classic	=COUNTIF($A$2:$A$51,C2)	
3	Diet Coke		Diet Coke	=COUNTIF($A$2:$A$51,C3)	
4	Pepsi		Dr. Pepper	=COUNTIF($A$2:$A$51,C4)	
5	Diet Coke		Pepsi	=COUNTIF($A$2:$A$51,C5)	
6	Coke Classic		Sprite	=COUNTIF($A$2:$A$51,C6)	
7	Coke Classic				
8	Dr. Pepper				
9	Diet Coke				
10	Pepsi				
11	Pepsi				
12	Coke Classic				
13	Dr. Pepper				
14	Sprite				
15	Coke Classic				
16	Diet Coke				
17	Coke Classic				
18	Coke Classic				
19	Sprite				
20	Coke Classic				
50	Pepsi				
51	Sprite				
52					

	A	B	C	D	E
1	**Brand Purchased**		**Soft Drink**	**Frequency**	
2	Coke Classic		Coke Classic	19	
3	Diet Coke		Diet Coke	8	
4	Pepsi		Dr. Pepper	5	
5	Diet Coke		Pepsi	13	
6	Coke Classic		Sprite	5	
7	Coke Classic				
8	Dr. Pepper				
9	Diet Coke				
10	Pepsi				
11	Pepsi				
12	Coke Classic				
13	Dr. Pepper				
14	Sprite				
15	Coke Classic				
16	Diet Coke				
17	Coke Classic				
18	Coke Classic				
19	Sprite				
20	Coke Classic				
50	Pepsi				
51	Sprite				
52					

Note: Rows 21–49 are hidden.

shown in the foreground shows the values computed using the formulas. Above is Figure 2.1 from the text, which is displayed to explain the use of color in Excel figures. We use lavender to highlight the data from the sample (soft drink purchases in this figure) and green to highlight the cells containing Excel functions and formulas. The green cells show the functions and formulas in the background worksheet and they show the values obtained using the formulas in the foreground worksheet. A third color (gold) is used in certain figures to highlight the material that is printed by Excel as a result of using one of the data analysis tools.

Changes in the Fourth Edition

We appreciate the acceptance and positive response to the previous editions of *Essentials of Modern Business Statistics with Microsoft Excel*. Accordingly, in making modifications for this new edition, we have maintained the presentation style and readability of those editions. The significant changes in the new edition are summarized here.

- **Microsoft Excel 2007.** Step-by-step instructions and screen captures show how to use the latest version of Excel 2007 to implement statistical procedures. More extensive use of Excel's PivotTable report and Excel's chart tools is also provided.

- **Change in Terminology for Data.** In the previous edition, nominal and ordinal data were classified as qualitative; interval and ratio data were classified as quantitative. In this edition, nominal and ordinal data are referred to as categorical data. Nominal and ordinal data use labels or names to identify categories of like items. Thus, we believe that the term categorical is more descriptive of this type of data.

- **Revised Sampling Material.** In the previous edition, Chapter 7 included a discussion of selecting a simple random sample from a finite and from an infinite population. We now focus on sampling from a finite population and sampling from a process. A practical advice subsection has been added on using good judgment to obtain a close correspondence between the target population and the sampled population.

- **p-Values.** In the previous edition, we emphasized the use of p-values as the preferred approach to hypothesis testing. We continue this approach in the new edition. However, we have eased the introduction to p-values by simplifying the conceptual definition for the student. We now say, "A p-value is a probability that provides a measure of the evidence against the null hypothesis provided by the sample. The smaller the p-value, the more evidence there is against H_0." After this conceptual definition, we provide operational definitions that make it clear how the p-value is computed for a lower tail test, an upper tail test, and a two-tail test. Based on our experience, we have found that separating the conceptual definition from the operational definitions is helpful to the novice student trying to digest difficult new material.

- **Experimental Design and Analysis of Variance.** In Section 10.4 we introduce the basic principles of an experimental study and show how they are used in a completely randomized design. We also provide a conceptual overview of the statistical procedure called analysis of variance (ANOVA). In Section 10.5 we show how ANOVA can be used to test for the equality of k population means using data obtained from a completely randomized design as well as data obtained from an observational study.

- **StatTools Add-In.** Excel 2007 does not contain statistical functions or data analysis tools to perform all of the statistical procedures discussed in the text. StatTools is a commercial Excel 2007 add-in, developed by Palisades Corporation, that extends the range of statistical options for Excel users. In an appendix to Chapter 1 we show how to download and install StatTools, and most chapters include a chapter appendix that shows the steps required to accomplish a statistical procedure using StatTools.

  We have been very careful to make the use of StatTools completely optional so users who want to teach using the standard tools available in Excel 2007 can continue to do so. But users who want additional statistical capabilities not available in standard Excel 2007 now have access to an industry standard statistics add-in that students will be able to continue to use in the workplace.

- **Other Content Revisions.** Two additional content revisions appear in the new edition. New examples of time series data are provided in Chapter 1. The Solutions Manual now provides more details in the explanations about how to compute p-values for hypothesis testing.

- **New Examples and Exercises Based on Real Data.** We have added over 180 new examples and exercises based on real data and recent reference sources of statistical information. Using data obtained from various data collection organizations and other sources, such as *The Wall Street Journal*, *USA Today*, *Fortune*, *Barron's*, and so on, we have drawn upon actual studies to develop explanations and to create exercises that demonstrate many uses of statistics in business and economics. We believe the use of real data helps generate more student interest in the material and enables the student to learn about both the statistical methodology and its application.
- **New Case Problems.** We have added four new case problems to this edition. The new case problems appear in the chapters on descriptive statistics, interval estimation, and regression. The 22 case problems in the text provide students with the opportunity to analyze somewhat larger data sets and prepare managerial reports based on the results of the analysis.

Features and Pedagogy

Authors Anderson, Sweeney, and Williams have continued many of the features that appeared in previous editions. Important ones for students are noted here.

Statistics in Practice

Each chapter begins with a Statistics in Practice article that describes an application of the statistical methodology to be covered in the chapter.

Methods Exercises and Applications Exercises

The end-of-section exercises are split into two parts, Methods and Applications. The Methods exercises require students to use the formulas and make the necessary computations. The Applications exercises require students to use the chapter material in real-world situations. Thus, students first focus on the computational "nuts and bolts" and then move on to the subtleties of statistical application and interpretation.

Self-Test Exercises

Certain exercises are identified as self-test exercises. Completely worked-out solutions for those exercises are provided in Appendix D at the back of the book. Students can attempt the self-test exercises and immediately check the solution to evaluate their understanding of the concepts presented in the chapter.

Margin Annotations and Notes and Comments

Margin annotations that highlight key points and provide additional insights for the students are a key feature of this text. These annotations are designed to provide emphasis and enhance understanding of the terms and concepts being presented in the text.

At the end of many sections, we provide Notes and Comments designed to give the student additional insights about the statistical methodology and its application. Notes and Comments include warnings about or limitations of the methodology, recommendations for application, brief descriptions of additional technical considerations, and other matters.

Data Files Accompany the Text

Approximately 200 data files are available on the website that accompanies this text. The data sets are available in Excel 2007 format. Data set logos are used in the text to identify the data sets that are available on the website. Data sets for all case problems as well as data sets for larger exercises are included.

Get Choice and Flexibility with CengageNOW™

You envisioned it, we developed it. Designed *by* instructors and students *for* instructors and students, *CengageNOW for ASW's Essentials of Modern Business Statistics with Microsoft® Office Excel®* is the most reliable, flexible, and easy-to-use online suite of services and resources. With efficient and immediate paths to success, CengageNow delivers the results you expect.

- **Personalized learning plans.** For every chapter, personalized learning plans allow students to focus on what they still need to learn and to select the activities that best match their learning styles (such as the relevant EasyStat tutorials, animations, step-by-step problem demonstrations, and text pages).
- **More study options.** Students can choose how they read the textbook—via integrated digital eBook or by reading the print version.

Ancillary Learning Materials for Students

- The website that accompanies the text contains approximately 200 data files in Excel format. Data sets for all case problems, as well as data sets for larger exercises, are included.
- **EasyStat Digital Tutor for Microsoft® Excel 2007, Version 3.** These focused online tutorials will make it easier for students to learn how to use one of these well-known software products to perform statistical analysis. Each digital video demonstrates how the software can be used to perform a particular statistical procedure.

  The EasyStat for Excel versions 2.0 (for Excel 2003) and 3.0 (for Excel 2007) are included in the CengageNOW package described earlier. Students may purchase an online subscription for EasyStat Digital Tutor at **http://www.academic.cengage.com/bstatistics.easystat.com**.

Acknowledgments

A special thanks goes to our associates from business and industry who supplied the Statistics in Practice features. We recognize them individually by a credit line in each of the articles. We are also indebted to our senior acquisitions editor Charles McCormick Jr., our developmental editor Margaret Kubale, our content project manager Jacquelyn K Featherly, our marketing manager Bryant Chrzan, and others at South-Western Cengage Learning for their editorial counsel and support during the preparation of this text.

We would like to acknowledge the work of our reviewers who provided comments and suggestions of ways to continue to improve our text. Thanks to:

James Bang, Virginia Military Institute

Robert J. Banis, University of Missouri-St. Louis

Timothy M. Bergquist, Northwest Christian College

William Bleuel, Pepperdine University

Derrick Boone, Wake Forest University

Lawrence J. Bos, Cornerstone University

Sheng-Kai Chang, Wayne State University

Robert D. Collins, Marquette University

Philip A. Gibbs, Washington & Lee University

Daniel L. Gilbert, Tennessee Wesleyan College

Michael Gorman, University of Dayton

Erick Hofacker, University of Wisconsin, River Falls

David Juriga, St. Louis Community College

Tenpao Lee, Niagara University

Ying Liao, Meredith College

Daniel Light, Northwest State College

Ralph Maliszewski, Waynesburg University

Patricia A. Mullins, University of Wisconsin-Madison

Jack Muryn, Cardinal Stritch University

Anthony Narsing, Macon State College

Robert M. Nauss, University of Missouri-St. Louis

Elizabeth L. Rankin, Centenary College of Louisiana

Surekha Rao, Indiana University, Northwest

Susan Sandblom, Scottsdale Community College

Robert Scott, Monmouth University

Toni Somers, Wayne State University

Jordan H. Stein, University of Arizona

Bruce Thompson, Milwaukee School of Engineering

Ahmad Vessal, California State University, Northridge

Dave Vinson, Pellissippi State

Daniel B. Widdis, Naval Postgraduate School

We would like to recognize the following individuals who have helped us in the past and continue to influence our writing.

Glen Archibald, University of Mississippi

Darl Bien, University of Denver

Thomas W. Bolland, Ohio University

Mike Bourke, Houston Baptist University

Peter Bryant, University of Colorado

Terri L. Byczkowski, University of Cincinnati

Robert Carver, Stonehill College

Ying Chien, University of Scranton

Robert Cochran, University of Wyoming

Murray Côté, University of Florida

David W. Cravens, Texas Christian University

Eddine Dahel, Monterey Institute of International Studies

Tom Dahlstrom, Eastern College

Terry Dielman, Texas Christian University

Joan Donohue, University of South Carolina

Jianjun Du, University of Houston–Victoria

Thomas J. Dudley, Pepperdine University

Swarna Dutt, University of West Georgia

Ronald Ehresman, Baldwin-Wallace College

Mohammed A. El-Saidi, Ferris State University

Robert Escudero, Pepperdine University

Stacy Everly, Delaware County Community College

Soheila Kahkashan Fardanesh, Towson University

Nicholas Farnum, California State University–Fullerton

Abe Feinberg, California State University, Northridge

Michael Ford, Rochester Institute of Technology

Phil Fry, Boise State University

V. Daniel Guide, Duquesne University

Paul Guy, California State University-Chico

Charles Harrington, University of Southern Indiana

Carl H. Hess, Marymount University

Woodrow W. Hughes, Jr., Converse College

Alan Humphrey, University of Rhode Island

Ann Hussein, Philadelphia College of Textiles and Science

Ben Isselhardt, Rochester Institute of Technology

Jeffery Jarrett, University of Rhode Island

Barry Kadets, Bryant College

Homayoun Khamooshi, George Washington University

Kenneth Klassen, California State University Northridge

David Krueger, St. Cloud State University

June Lapidus, Roosevelt University

Martin S. Levy, University of Cincinnati

Daniel M. Light, Northwest State College

Ka-sing Man, Georgetown University

Don Marx, University of Alaska, Anchorage

Tom McCullough, University of California–Berkeley

Timothy McDaniel, Buena Vista University

Mario Miranda, The Ohio State University

Barry J. Monk, Macon State College

Mitchell Muesham, Sam Houston State University

Richard O'Connell, Miami University of Ohio

Alan Olinsky, Bryant College

Lynne Pastor, Carnegie Mellon University

Von Roderick Plessner, Northwest State University

Robert D. Potter, University of Central Florida

Tom Pray, Rochester Institute of Technology

Harold Rahmlow, St. Joseph's University

Derrick Reagle, Fordham University

Avuthu Rami Reddy, University of Wisconsin–Platteville

Tom Ryan, Case Western Reserve University

Ahmad Saranjam, Bridgewater State College

Bill Seaver, University of Tennessee

Alan Smith, Robert Morris College

William Struning, Seton Hall University

Ahmad Syamil, Arkansas State University

David Tufte, University of New Orleans

Jack Vaughn, University of Texas–El Paso

Elizabeth Wark, Springfield College

Ari Wijetunga, Morehead State University

Nancy A. Williams, Loyola College in Maryland

J. E. Willis, Louisiana State University

Larry Woodward, University of Mary Hardin-Baylor

Mustafa Yilmaz, Northeastern University

David R. Anderson
Dennis J. Sweeney
Thomas A. Williams

David R. Anderson   David R. Anderson is Professor of Quantitative Analysis in the College of Business Administration at the University of Cincinnati. Born in Grand Forks, North Dakota, he earned his B.S., M.S., and Ph.D. degrees from Purdue University. Professor Anderson has served as Head of the Department of Quantitative Analysis and Operations Management and as Associate Dean of the College of Business Administration. In addition, he was the coordinator of the College's first Executive Program.

At the University of Cincinnati, Professor Anderson has taught introductory statistics for business students as well as graduate-level courses in regression analysis, multivariate analysis, and management science. He has also taught statistical courses at the Department of Labor in Washington, D.C. He has been honored with nominations and awards for excellence in teaching and excellence in service to student organizations.

Professor Anderson has coauthored 10 textbooks in the areas of statistics, management science, linear programming, and production and operations management. He is an active consultant in the field of sampling and statistical methods.

Dennis J. Sweeney   Dennis J. Sweeney is Professor of Quantitative Analysis and Founder of the Center for Productivity Improvement at the University of Cincinnati. Born in Des Moines, Iowa, he earned a B.S.B.A. degree from Drake University and his M.B.A. and D.B.A. degrees from Indiana University, where he was an NDEA Fellow. During 1978–1979, Professor Sweeney worked in the management science group at Procter & Gamble; during 1981–1982, he was a visiting professor at Duke University. Professor Sweeney served as Head of the Department of Quantitative Analysis and as Associate Dean of the College of Business Administration at the University of Cincinnati.

Professor Sweeney has published more than 30 articles and monographs in the area of management science and statistics. The National Science Foundation, IBM, Procter & Gamble, Federated Department Stores, Kroger, and Cincinnati Gas & Electric have funded his research, which has been published in *Management Science*, *Operations Research*, *Mathematical Programming*, *Decision Sciences*, and other journals.

Professor Sweeney has coauthored 10 textbooks in the areas of statistics, management science, linear programming, and production and operations management.

Thomas A. Williams   Thomas A. Williams is Professor of Management Science in the College of Business at Rochester Institute of Technology. Born in Elmira, New York, he earned his B.S. degree at Clarkson University. He did his graduate work at Rensselaer Polytechnic Institute, where he received his M.S. and Ph.D. degrees.

Before joining the College of Business at RIT, Professor Williams served for seven years as a faculty member in the College of Business Administration at the University of Cincinnati, where he developed the undergraduate program in Information Systems and then served as its coordinator. At RIT he was the first chairman of the Decision Sciences Department. He teaches courses in management science and statistics, as well as graduate courses in regression and decision analysis.

Professor Williams is the coauthor of 11 textbooks in the areas of management science, statistics, production and operations management, and mathematics. He has been a consultant for numerous *Fortune* 500 companies and has worked on projects ranging from the use of data analysis to the development of large-scale regression models.

Essentials of Modern Business Statistics

With Microsoft® Office Excel®

CHAPTER 1

Data and Statistics

STATISTICS *in* PRACTICE

BUSINESSWEEK*
NEW YORK, NEW YORK

With a global circulation of more than 1 million, *BusinessWeek* is the most widely read business magazine in the world. More than 200 dedicated reporters and editors in 26 bureaus worldwide deliver a variety of articles of interest to the business and economic community. Along with feature articles on current topics, the magazine contains regular sections on International Business, Economic Analysis, Information Processing, and Science & Technology. Information in the feature articles and the regular sections helps readers stay abreast of current developments and assess the impact of those developments on business and economic conditions.

Most issues of *BusinessWeek* provide an in-depth report on a topic of current interest. Often, the in-depth reports contain statistical facts and summaries that help the reader understand the business and economic information. For example, the January 8, 2007, issue contained a feature article about business travel, the November 29, 2007, issue included a discussion of the impact of diminished oil supplies on the U.S. economy, and the February 18, 2008, issue had a special report on the credit crisis. In addition, the weekly *BusinessWeek Investor* provides statistics about the state of the economy, including production indexes, stock prices, mutual funds, and interest rates.

BusinessWeek also uses statistics and statistical information in managing its own business. For example, an annual survey of subscribers helps the company learn about subscriber demographics, reading habits, likely purchases, lifestyles, and so on. *BusinessWeek* managers use statistical summaries from the survey to provide better services to subscribers and advertisers. One recent North

BusinessWeek uses statistical facts and summaries in many of its articles. © Terri Miller/E-Visual Communications, Inc.

American subscriber survey indicated that 90% of *BusinessWeek* subscribers use a personal computer at home and that 64% of *BusinessWeek* subscribers are involved with computer purchases at work. Such statistics alert *BusinessWeek* managers to subscriber interest in articles about new developments in computers. The results of the survey are also made available to potential advertisers. The high percentage of subscribers using personal computers at home and the high percentage of subscribers involved with computer purchases at work would be an incentive for a computer manufacturer to consider advertising in *BusinessWeek*.

In this chapter, we discuss the types of data available for statistical analysis and describe how the data are obtained. We introduce descriptive statistics and statistical inference as ways of converting data into meaningful and easily interpreted statistical information.

*The authors are indebted to Charlene Trentham, Research Manager at *BusinessWeek*, for providing this Statistics in Practice.

Frequently, we see the following types of statements in newspapers and magazines:

- The National Association of Realtors said Wednesday that the median price for an existing home decreased a record 5.1% last month to $207,800 because many buyers are having trouble getting financing (*USA Today,* November 28, 2007).
- Anheuser-Busch, the biggest U.S. brewer and third worldwide by volume, said that it received an unsolicited $46.3 billion takeover bid from Belgium-based InBev (*USA Today,* June 12, 2008).
- Crude oil prices surged nearly $11 on Friday to close at a record of $138.54 per barrel (*The Wall Street Journal,* June 9, 2008).

- With a 24% annual return over the past decade, Ken Heebner is arguably the best fund manager of our time (*Fortune,* June 9, 2008).
- The average amount banks charge to let you overdraw your checking account, a service known as "courtesy overdraft loan," is $34 (*Money,* September 2007).
- According to the China Banking Regulatory Commission, nonperforming loans as a percentage of total loans at Chinese commercial banks dropped from 12.4% in March 2005 to 6.2% in September 2007 (*The New York Times,* November 29, 2007).
- The Dow Jones Industrial Average closed at 12,210 (*Barron's,* June 9, 2008).

The numerical facts in the preceding statements (5.1%; $207,800; $46.3 billion; $11; $138.54; 24%; $34; 12.4%; 6.2%; and 12,210) are called statistics. In this usage, the term *statistics* refers to numerical facts such as averages, medians, percents, and index numbers that help us understand a variety of business and economic conditions. However, as you will see, the field, or subject, of statistics involves much more than numerical facts. In a broader sense, statistics is defined as the art and science of collecting, analyzing, presenting, and interpreting data. Particularly in business and economics, the information provided by collecting, analyzing, presenting, and interpreting data gives managers and decision makers a better understanding of the business and economic environment and thus enables them to make more informed and better decisions. In this text, we emphasize the use of statistics for business and economic decision making.

Chapter 1 begins with some illustrations of the applications of statistics in business and economics. In Section 1.2 we define the term *data* and introduce the concept of a data set. This section also introduces key terms such as *variables* and *observations,* discusses the difference between quantitative and categorical data, and illustrates the uses of cross-sectional and time series data. Section 1.3 discusses how data can be obtained from existing sources or through survey and experimental studies designed to obtain new data. The important role that the Internet now plays in obtaining data is also highlighted. The uses of data in developing descriptive statistics and in making statistical inferences are described in Sections 1.4 and 1.5. Section 1.6 discusses statistical analysis using Microsoft Excel, and Section 1.7 discusses ethical guidelines for statistical practice.

1.1   Applications in Business and Economics

In today's global business and economic environment, anyone can access vast amounts of statistical information. The most successful managers and decision makers understand the information and know how to use it effectively. In this section, we provide examples that illustrate some of the uses of statistics in business and economics.

Accounting

Public accounting firms use statistical sampling procedures when conducting audits for their clients. For instance, suppose an accounting firm wants to determine whether the amount of accounts receivable shown on a client's balance sheet fairly represents the actual amount of accounts receivable. Usually the large number of individual accounts receivable makes reviewing and validating every account too time-consuming and expensive. As common practice in such situations, the audit staff selects a subset of the accounts called a sample. After reviewing the accuracy of the sampled accounts, the auditors draw a conclusion as to whether the accounts receivable amount shown on the client's balance sheet is acceptable.

Finance

Financial analysts use a variety of statistical information to guide their investment recommendations. In the case of stocks, the analysts review a variety of financial data including price/earnings ratios and dividend yields. By comparing the information for an individual stock with information about the stock market averages, a financial analyst can begin to draw a conclusion as to whether an individual stock is over- or underpriced. For example, *Barron's* (February 18, 2008) reported that the average dividend yield for the 30 stocks in the Dow Jones Industrial Average was 2.45%. Altria Group showed a dividend yield of 3.05%. In this case, the statistical information on dividend yield indicates a higher dividend yield for Altria Group than the average for the Dow Jones stocks. Therefore, a financial analyst might conclude that Altria Group was underpriced. This and other information about Altria Group would help the analyst make a buy, sell, or hold recommendation for the stock.

Marketing

Electronic scanners at retail checkout counters collect data for a variety of marketing research applications. For example, data suppliers such as ACNielsen and Information Resources, Inc., purchase point-of-sale scanner data from grocery stores, process the data, and then sell statistical summaries of the data to manufacturers. Manufacturers spend hundreds of thousands of dollars per product category to obtain this type of scanner data. Manufacturers also purchase data and statistical summaries on promotional activities such as special pricing and the use of in-store displays. Brand managers can review the scanner statistics and the promotional activity statistics to gain a better understanding of the relationship between promotional activities and sales. Such analyses often prove helpful in establishing future marketing strategies for the various products.

Production

Today's emphasis on quality makes quality control an important application of statistics in production. A variety of statistical quality control charts are used to monitor the output of a production process. In particular, an x-bar chart can be used to monitor the average output. Suppose, for example, that a machine fills containers with 12 ounces of a soft drink. Periodically, a production worker selects a sample of containers and computes the average number of ounces in the sample. This average, or x-bar value, is plotted on an x-bar chart. A plotted value above the chart's upper control limit indicates overfilling, and a plotted value below the chart's lower control limit indicates underfilling. The process is termed "in control" and allowed to continue as long as the plotted x-bar values fall between the chart's upper and lower control limits. Properly interpreted, an x-bar chart can help determine when adjustments are necessary to correct a production process.

Economics

Economists frequently provide forecasts about the future of the economy or some aspect of it. They use a variety of statistical information in making such forecasts. For instance, in forecasting inflation rates, economists use statistical information on such indicators as the Producer Price Index, the unemployment rate, and manufacturing capacity utilization. Often these statistical indicators are entered into computerized forecasting models that predict inflation rates.

Applications of statistics such as those described in this section are an integral part of this text. Such examples provide an overview of the breadth of statistical applications. To supplement these examples, practitioners in the fields of business and economics provided chapter-opening Statistics in Practice articles that introduce the material covered in each chapter. The Statistics in Practice applications show the importance of statistics in a wide variety of business and economic situations.

1.2 Data

Data are the facts and figures collected, analyzed, and summarized for presentation and interpretation. All the data collected in a particular study are referred to as the **data set** for the
study. Table 1.1 shows a data set containing information for 25 mutual funds that are part
of the *Morningstar Funds500* for 2008. Morningstar is a company that tracks over 7000
mutual funds and prepares in-depth analyses of 2000 of these. Their recommendations are
followed closely by financial analysts and individual investors.

Elements, Variables, and Observations

Elements are the entities on which data are collected. For the data set in Table 1.1 each individual mutual fund is an element: the element names appear in the first column. With 25
mutual funds, the data set contains 25 elements.

A **variable** is a characteristic of interest for the elements. The data set in Table 1.1 includes the following five variables:

- *Fund Type:* The type of mutual fund, labeled DE (Domestic Equity), IE (International Equity), and FI (Fixed Income)
- *Net Asset Value ($):* The closing price per share on December 31, 2007

TABLE 1.1   DATA SET FOR 25 MUTUAL FUNDS

Fund Name	Fund Type	Net Asset Value ($)	5-Year Average Return (%)	Expense Ratio (%)	Morningstar Rank
American Century Intl. Disc	IE	14.37	30.53	1.41	3-Star
American Century Tax-Free Bond	FI	10.73	3.34	0.49	4-Star
American Century Ultra	DE	24.94	10.88	0.99	3-Star
Artisan Small Cap	DE	16.92	15.67	1.18	3-Star
Brown Cap Small	DE	35.73	15.85	1.20	4-Star
DFA U.S. Micro Cap	DE	13.47	17.23	0.53	3-Star
Fidelity Contrafund	DE	73.11	17.99	0.89	5-Star
Fidelity Overseas	IE	48.39	23.46	0.90	4-Star
Fidelity Sel Electronics	DE	45.60	13.50	0.89	3-Star
Fidelity Sh-Term Bond	FI	8.60	2.76	0.45	3-Star
Gabelli Asset AAA	DE	49.81	16.70	1.36	4-Star
Kalmar Gr Val Sm Cp	DE	15.30	15.31	1.32	3-Star
Marsico 21st Century	DE	17.44	15.16	1.31	5-Star
Mathews Pacific Tiger	IE	27.86	32.70	1.16	3-Star
Oakmark I	DE	40.37	9.51	1.05	2-Star
PIMCO Emerg Mkts Bd D	FI	10.68	13.57	1.25	3-Star
RS Value A	DE	26.27	23.68	1.36	4-Star
T. Rowe Price Latin Am.	IE	53.89	51.10	1.24	4-Star
T. Rowe Price Mid Val	DE	22.46	16.91	0.80	4-Star
Thornburg Value A	DE	37.53	15.46	1.27	4-Star
USAA Income	FI	12.10	4.31	0.62	3-Star
Vanguard Equity-Inc	DE	24.42	13.41	0.29	4-Star
Vanguard Sht-Tm TE	FI	15.68	2.37	0.16	3-Star
Vanguard Sm Cp Idx	DE	32.58	17.01	0.23	3-Star
Wasatch Sm Cp Growth	DE	35.41	13.98	1.19	4-Star

Source: Morningstar Funds500 (2008).

WEB file

Morningstar

- *5-Year Average Return (%):* The average annual return for the fund over the past 5 years
- *Expense Ratio:* The percentage of assets deducted each fiscal year for fund expenses
- *Morningstar Rank:* The overall risk-adjusted star rating for each fund; Morningstar ranks go from a low of 1-Star to a high of 5-Stars

Measurements collected on each variable for every element in a study provide the data. The set of measurements obtained for a particular element is called an **observation**. Referring to Table 1.1 we see that the set of measurements for the first observation (American Century Intl. Disc) is IE, 14.37, 30.53, 1.41, and 3-Star. The set of measurements for the second observation (American Century Tax-Free Bond) is FI, 10.73, 3.34, 0.49, and 4-Star, and so on. A data set with 25 elements contains 25 observations.

Scales of Measurement

Data collection requires one of the following scales of measurement: nominal, ordinal, interval, or ratio. The scale of measurement determines the amount of information contained in the data and indicates the most appropriate data summarization and statistical analyses.

When the data for a variable consist of labels or names used to identify an attribute of the element, the scale of measurement is considered a **nominal scale.** For example, referring to the data in Table 1.1, we see that the scale of measurement for the Fund Type variable is nominal because DE, IE, and FI are labels used to identify the category or type of fund. In cases where the scale of measurement is nominal, a numeric code as well as non-numeric labels may be used. For example, to facilitate data collection and to prepare the data for entry into a computer database, we might use a numeric code by letting 1 denote Domestic Equity, 2 denote International Equity, and 3 denote Fixed Income. In this case the numeric values 1, 2, and 3 identify the category of fund. The scale of measurement is nominal even though the data appear as numeric values.

The scale of measurement for a variable is called an **ordinal scale** if the data exhibit the properties of nominal data and the order or rank of the data is meaningful. For example, Eastside Automotive sends customers a questionnaire designed to obtain data on the quality of its automotive repair service. Each customer provides a repair service rating of excellent, good, or poor. Because the data obtained are the labels—excellent, good, or poor—the data have the properties of nominal data. In addition, the data can be ranked, or ordered, with respect to the service quality. Data recorded as excellent indicate the best service, followed by good and then poor. Thus, the scale of measurement is ordinal. As another example, note that the Morningstar Rank for the data in Table 1.1 is ordinal data. It provides a rank from 1 to 5-Stars based on Morningstar's assessment of the fund's risk-adjusted return. Ordinal data can also be provided using a numeric code, for example, your class rank in school.

The scale of measurement for a variable is an **interval scale** if the data have all the properties of ordinal data and the interval between values is expressed in terms of a fixed unit of measure. Interval data are always numeric. Scholastic Aptitude Test (SAT) scores are an example of interval-scaled data. For example, three students with SAT math scores of 620, 550, and 470 can be ranked or ordered in terms of best performance to poorest performance. In addition, the differences between the scores are meaningful. For instance, student 1 scored $620 - 550 = 70$ points more than student 2, while student 2 scored $550 - 470 = 80$ points more than student 3.

The scale of measurement for a variable is a **ratio scale** if the data have all the properties of interval data and the ratio of two values is meaningful. Variables such as distance, height, weight, and time use the ratio scale of measurement. This scale requires that a zero value be included to indicate that nothing exists for the variable at the zero point. For example, consider the cost of an automobile. A zero value for the cost would indicate that the automobile has no cost and is free. In addition, if we compare the cost of $30,000 for one automobile to the cost of $15,000 for a second automobile, the ratio property shows that the first automobile is $30,000/$15,000 = 2 times, or twice, the cost of the second automobile.

Categorical and Quantitative Data

Categorical data are often referred to as qualitative data.

Data can be classified as either categorical or quantitative. Data that can be grouped by specific categories are referred to as **categorical data.** Categorical data use either the nominal or ordinal scale of measurement. Data that use numeric values to indicate how much or how many are referred to as **quantitative data.** Quantitative data are obtained using either the interval or ratio scale of measurement.

The statistical method appropriate for summarizing data depends upon whether the data are categorical or quantitative.

A **categorical variable** is a variable with categorical data, and a **quantitative variable** is a variable with quantitative data. The statistical analysis appropriate for a particular variable depends upon whether the variable is categorical or quantitative. If the variable is categorical, the statistical analysis is limited. We can summarize categorical data by counting the number of observations in each category or by computing the proportion of the observations in each category. However, even when the categorical data are identified by a numerical code, arithmetic operations such as addition, subtraction, multiplication, and division do not provide meaningful results. Section 2.1 discusses ways for summarizing categorical data.

Arithmetic operations provide meaningful results for quantitative variables. For example, quantitative data may be added and then divided by the number of observations to compute the average value. This average is usually meaningful and easily interpreted. In general, more alternatives for statistical analysis are possible when data are quantitative. Section 2.2 and Chapter 3 provide ways of summarizing quantitative data.

Cross-Sectional and Time Series Data

For purposes of statistical analysis, distinguishing between cross-sectional data and time series data is important. Cross-sectional data are data collected at the same or approximately the same point in time. The data in Table 1.1 are cross-sectional because they describe the five variables for the 25 mutual funds at the same point in time. Time series data are data collected over several time periods. For example, Figure 1.1 provides a graph of the U.S. average price per gallon for conventional regular gasoline. The graph shows gasoline price rising in the first half of 2006 and then falling in the second half of 2006. Gasoline price then steadily increased until June 2007 and then began to decrease until October 2007. In 2008 prices steadily increased, reaching a value of over $4.00 per gallon in June.

Graphs of time series data are frequently found in business and economic publications. Such graphs help analysts understand what happened in the past, identify any trends over time, and project future levels for the time series. The graphs of time series data can take on a variety of forms, as shown in Figure 1.2. With a little study, these graphs are usually easy to understand and interpret.

For example, Panel (A) in Figure 1.2 is a graph showing the interest rate for student Stafford Loans between 2000 and 2006. After 2000, the interest rate declined and reached its lowest level of 3.2% in 2004. However, after 2004, the interest rate for student loans showed a steep increase, reaching 6.8% in 2006. With the U.S. Department of Education estimating that more than 50% of undergraduate students graduate with debt, this increasing interest rate places a greater financial burden on many new college graduates.

FIGURE 1.1   U.S. AVERAGE PRICE PER GALLON FOR CONVENTIONAL
REGULAR GASOLINE

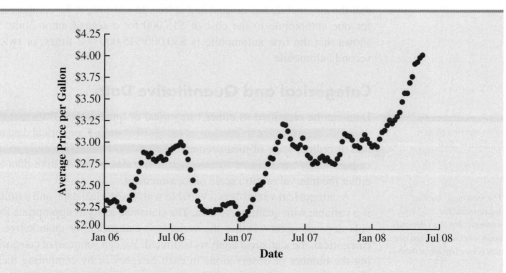

Source: U.S. Department of Energy, Energy Information Administration, February 2008.

The graph in Panel (B) shows a rather disturbing increase in the average credit card debt per household over the 10-year period from 1995 to 2005. Notice how the time series shows an almost steady annual increase in the average credit card debt per household from $4500 in 1995 to $9500 in 2005. In 2005, an average credit card debt per household of $10,000 appeared not far off. Most credit card companies offer relatively low introductory interest rates. After this initial period, however, annual interest rates of 18%, 20%, or more are common. These rates make the credit card debt difficult for households to handle.

Panel (C) shows a graph of the time series for the occupancy rate of hotels in South Florida during a typical one-year period. The highest occupancy rates of 95% to 98% occur during the months of February and March when the climate of South Florida is attractive to tourists. In fact, January to April is the typical high occupancy season for South Florida hotels. On the other hand, note the low occupancy rates in August to October, the lowest occupancy of 50% occurring in September. Higher temperatures and the hurricane season are the primary reasons for the drop in hotel occupancy during this period.

NOTES AND COMMENTS

1. An observation is the set of measurements obtained for each element in a data set. Hence, the number of observations is always the same as the number of elements. The number of measurements obtained for each element equals the number of variables. Hence, the total number of data items can be determined by multiplying the number of observations by the number of variables.

2. Quantitative data may be discrete or continuous. Quantitative data that measure how many (e.g., number of calls received in 5 minutes) are discrete. Quantitative data that measure how much (e.g., weight or time) are continuous because no separation occurs between the possible data values.

FIGURE 1.2   A VARIETY OF GRAPHS OF TIME SERIES DATA

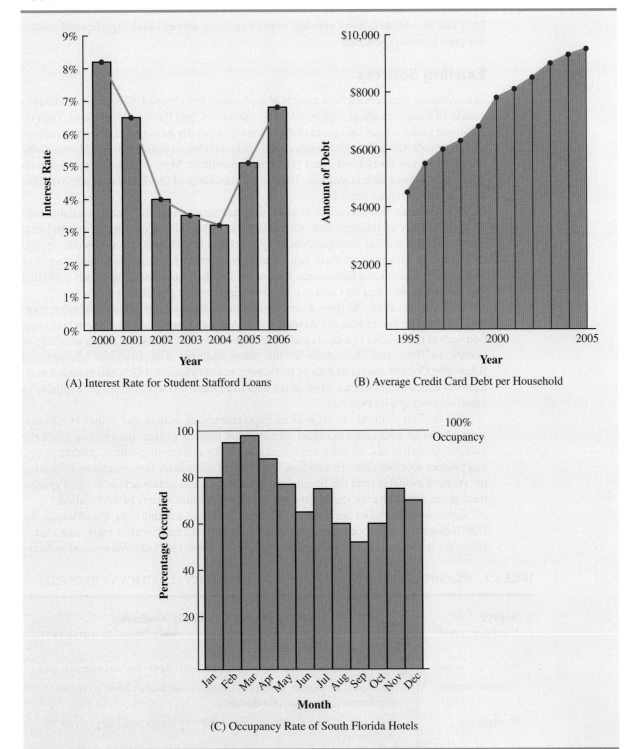

(A) Interest Rate for Student Stafford Loans

(B) Average Credit Card Debt per Household

(C) Occupancy Rate of South Florida Hotels

1.3 Data Sources

Data can be obtained from existing sources or from surveys and experimental studies designed to collect new data.

Existing Sources

In some cases, data needed for a particular application already exist. Companies maintain a variety of databases about their employees, customers, and business operations. Data on employee salaries, ages, and years of experience can usually be obtained from internal personnel records. Other internal records contain data on sales, advertising expenditures, distribution costs, inventory levels, and production quantities. Most companies also maintain detailed data about their customers. Table 1.2 shows some of the data commonly available from internal company records.

Organizations that specialize in collecting and maintaining data make available substantial amounts of business and economic data. Companies access these external data sources through leasing arrangements or by purchase. Dun & Bradstreet, Bloomberg, and Dow Jones & Company are three firms that provide extensive business database services to clients. ACNielsen and Information Resources, Inc., built successful businesses collecting and processing data that they sell to advertisers and product manufacturers.

Data are also available from a variety of industry associations and special interest organizations. The Travel Industry Association of America maintains travel-related information such as the number of tourists and travel expenditures by states. Such data would be of interest to firms and individuals in the travel industry. The Graduate Management Admission Council maintains data on test scores, student characteristics, and graduate management education programs. Most of the data from these types of sources are available to qualified users at a modest cost.

The Internet continues to grow as an important source of data and statistical information. Almost all companies maintain websites that provide general information about the company as well as data on sales, number of employees, number of products, product prices, and product specifications. In addition, a number of companies now specialize in making information available over the Internet. As a result, one can obtain access to stock quotes, meal prices at restaurants, salary data, and an almost infinite variety of information.

Government agencies are another important source of existing data. For instance, the U.S. Department of Labor maintains considerable data on employment rates, wage rates, size of the labor force, and union membership. Table 1.3 lists selected governmental agencies

TABLE 1.2   EXAMPLES OF DATA AVAILABLE FROM INTERNAL COMPANY RECORDS

Source	Some of the Data Typically Available
Employee records	Name, address, social security number, salary, number of vacation days, number of sick days, and bonus
Production records	Part or product number, quantity produced, direct labor cost, and materials cost
Inventory records	Part or product number, number of units on hand, reorder level, economic order quantity, and discount schedule
Sales records	Product number, sales volume, sales volume by region, and sales volume by customer type
Credit records	Customer name, address, phone number, credit limit, and accounts receivable balance
Customer profile	Age, gender, income level, household size, address, and preferences

TABLE 1.3   EXAMPLES OF DATA AVAILABLE FROM SELECTED GOVERNMENT AGENCIES

Government Agency	Some of the Data Available
Census Bureau *http://www.census.gov*	Population data, number of households, and household income
Federal Reserve Board *http://www.federalreserve.gov*	Data on the money supply, installment credit, exchange rates, and discount rates
Office of Management and Budget *http://www.whitehouse.gov/omb*	Data on revenue, expenditures, and debt of the federal government
Department of Commerce *http://www.doc.gov*	Data on business activity, value of shipments by industry, level of profits by industry, and growing and declining industries
Bureau of Labor Statistics *http://www.bls.gov*	Consumer spending, hourly earnings, unemployment rate, safety records, and international statistics

FIGURE 1.3   U.S. CENSUS BUREAU HOMEPAGE

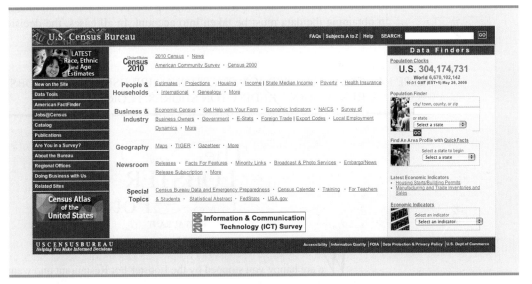

and some of the data they provide. Most government agencies that collect and process data also make the results available through a website. For instance, the U.S. Census Bureau has a wealth of data at its website, *http://www.census.gov*. Figure 1.3 shows the homepage for the U.S. Census Bureau.

Statistical Studies

Sometimes the data needed for a particular application are not available through existing sources. In such cases, the data can often be obtained by conducting a statistical study. Statistical studies can be classified as either *experimental* or *observational*.

In an experimental study, a variable of interest is first identified. Then one or more other variables are identified and controlled so that data can be obtained about how they influence the variable of interest. For example, a pharmaceutical firm might be interested in conducting an experiment to learn about how a new drug affects blood pressure. Blood pressure is the variable of interest in the study. The dosage level of the new drug is another variable that is hoped to have a causal effect on blood pressure. To obtain data about the effect of the

The largest experimental statistical study ever conducted is believed to be the 1954 Public Health Service experiment for the Salk polio vaccine. Nearly 2 million children in grades 1, 2, and 3 were selected from throughout the United States.

new drug, researchers select a sample of individuals. The dosage level of the new drug is controlled, as different groups of individuals are given different dosage levels. Before and after data on blood pressure are collected for each group. Statistical analysis of the experimental data can help determine how the new drug affects blood pressure.

Nonexperimental, or observational, statistical studies make no attempt to control the variables of interest. A survey is perhaps the most common type of observational study. For instance, in a personal interview survey, research questions are first identified. Then a questionnaire is designed and administered to a sample of individuals. Some restaurants use observational studies to obtain data about their customers' opinions of the quality of food, service, atmosphere, and so on. A questionnaire used by the Lobster Pot Restaurant in Redington Shores, Florida, is shown in Figure 1.4. Note that the customers completing the questionnaire are asked to provide ratings for five variables: food quality, friendliness of service, promptness of service, cleanliness, and management. The response categories of excellent, good, satisfactory, and unsatisfactory provide ordinal data that enable Lobster Pot's managers to assess the quality of the restaurant's operation.

Managers wanting to use data and statistical analysis as aids to decision making must be aware of the time and cost required to obtain the data. The use of existing data sources is desirable when data must be obtained in a relatively short period of time. If important data are not readily available from an existing source, the additional time and cost involved in obtaining the data must be taken into account. In all cases, the decision maker should

Studies of smokers and nonsmokers are observational studies because researchers do not determine or control who will smoke and who will not smoke.

FIGURE 1.4   CUSTOMER OPINION QUESTIONNAIRE USED BY THE LOBSTER POT RESTAURANT, REDINGTON SHORES, FLORIDA

The
LOBSTER
Pot
RESTAURANT

*W*e are happy you stopped by the Lobster Pot Restaurant and want to make sure you will come back. So, if you have a little time, we will really appreciate it if you will fill out this card. Your comments and suggestions are extremely important to us. Thank you!

Server's Name _____

	Excellent	Good	Satisfactory	Unsatisfactory
Food Quality	❏	❏	❏	❏
Friendly Service	❏	❏	❏	❏
Prompt Service	❏	❏	❏	❏
Cleanliness	❏	❏	❏	❏
Management	❏	❏	❏	❏

Comments _____

_____

What prompted your visit to us? _____

_____

Please drop in suggestion box at entrance. Thank you.

consider the contribution of the statistical analysis to the decision-making process. The cost of data acquisition and the subsequent statistical analysis should not exceed the savings generated by using the information to make a better decision.

Data Acquisition Errors

Managers should always be aware of the possibility of data errors in statistical studies. Using erroneous data can be worse than not using any data at all. An error in data acquisition occurs whenever the data value obtained is not equal to the true or actual value that would be obtained with a correct procedure. Such errors can occur in a number of ways. For example, an interviewer might make a recording error, such as a transposition in writing the age of a 24-year-old person as 42, or the person answering an interview question might misinterpret the question and provide an incorrect response.

Experienced data analysts take great care in collecting and recording data to ensure that errors are not made. Special procedures can be used to check for internal consistency of the data. For instance, such procedures would indicate that the analyst should review the accuracy of data for a respondent shown to be 22 years of age but reporting 20 years of work experience. Data analysts also review data with unusually large and small values, called outliers, which are candidates for possible data errors. In Chapter 3 we present some of the methods statisticians use to identify outliers.

Errors often occur during data acquisition. Blindly using any data that happen to be available or using data that were acquired with little care can result in misleading information and bad decisions. Thus, taking steps to acquire accurate data can help ensure reliable and valuable decision-making information.

1.4 Descriptive Statistics

Most of the statistical information in newspapers, magazines, company reports, and other publications consists of data that are summarized and presented in a form that is easy for the reader to understand. Such summaries of data, which may be tabular, graphical, or numerical, are referred to as descriptive statistics.

Refer again to the data set in Table 1.1 showing data on 25 mutual funds. Methods of descriptive statistics can be used to provide summaries of the information in this data set. For example, a tabular summary of the data for the categorical variable Fund Type is shown in Table 1.4. A graphical summary of the same data, called a bar chart, is shown in Figure 1.5. These types of tabular and graphical summaries generally make the data easier to interpret. Referring to Table 1.4 and Figure 1.5, we can see easily that the majority of the mutual funds are of the Domestic Equity type. On a percentage basis, 64% are of the Domestic Equity type, 16% are of the International Equity type, and 20% are of the Fixed Income type.

TABLE 1.4   FREQUENCIES AND PERCENT FREQUENCIES FOR MUTUAL FUND TYPE

Mutual Fund Type	Frequency	Percent Frequency
Domestic Equity	16	64
International Equity	4	16
Fixed Income	5	20
Totals	**25**	**100**

FIGURE 1.5   BAR CHART FOR MUTUAL FUND TYPE

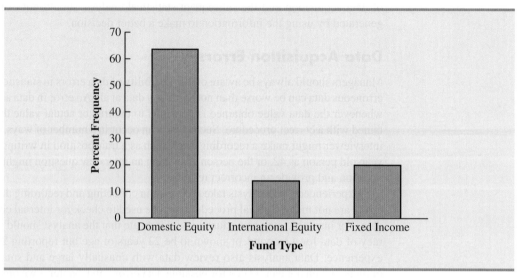

A graphical summary of the data for the quantitative variable Net Asset Value, called a histogram, is provided in Figure 1.6. The histogram makes it easy to see that the net asset values range from $0 to $75, with the highest concentration between $15 and $30. Only one of the net asset values is greater than $60.

In addition to tabular and graphical displays, numerical descriptive statistics are used to summarize data. The most common numerical descriptive statistic is the average, or

FIGURE 1.6   HISTOGRAM OF NET ASSET VALUE FOR 25 MUTUAL FUNDS

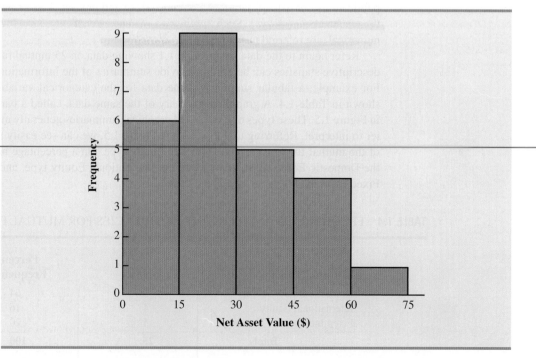

mean. Using the data on 5-Year Average Return for the mutual funds in Table 1.1, we can compute the average by adding the returns for all 25 mutual funds and dividing the sum by 25. Doing so provides a 5-year average return of 16.50%. This average demonstrates a measure of the central tendency, or central location, of the data for that variable.

There is a great deal of interest in effective methods for developing and presenting descriptive statistics. Chapters 2 and 3 devote attention to the tabular, graphical, and numerical methods of descriptive statistics.

1.5   Statistical Inference

Many situations require information about a large group of elements (individuals, companies, voters, households, products, customers, and so on). But, because of time, cost, and other considerations, data can be collected from only a small portion of the group. The larger group of elements in a particular study is called the **population**, and the smaller group is called the **sample**. Formally, we use the following definitions.

> **POPULATION**
>
> A population is the set of all elements of interest in a particular study.

> **SAMPLE**
>
> A sample is a subset of the population.

The U.S. government conducts a census every 10 years. Market research firms conduct sample surveys every day.

The process of conducting a survey to collect data for the entire population is called a **census**. The process of conducting a survey to collect data for a sample is called a **sample survey**. As one of its major contributions, statistics uses data from a sample to make estimates and test hypotheses about the characteristics of a population through a process referred to as **statistical inference**.

As an example of statistical inference, let us consider the study conducted by Norris Electronics. Norris manufactures a high-intensity lightbulb used in a variety of electrical products. In an attempt to increase the useful life of the lightbulb, the product design group developed a new lightbulb filament. In this case, the population is defined as all lightbulbs that could be produced with the new filament. To evaluate the advantages of the new filament, 200 bulbs with the new filament were manufactured and tested. Data collected from this sample showed the number of hours each lightbulb operated before filament burnout. See Table 1.5.

Suppose Norris wants to use the sample data to make an inference about the average hours of useful life for the population of all lightbulbs that could be produced with the new filament. Adding the 200 values in Table 1.5 and dividing the total by 200 provides the sample average lifetime for the lightbulbs: 76 hours. We can use this sample result to estimate that the average lifetime for the lightbulbs in the population is 76 hours. Figure 1.7 provides a graphical summary of the statistical inference process for Norris Electronics.

Whenever statisticians use a sample to estimate a population characteristic of interest, they usually provide a statement of the quality, or precision, associated with the estimate.

**TABLE 1.5   HOURS UNTIL BURNOUT FOR A SAMPLE OF 200 LIGHTBULBS
FOR THE NORRIS ELECTRONICS EXAMPLE**

Norris

107	73	68	97	76	79	94	59	98	57
54	65	71	70	84	88	62	61	79	98
66	62	79	86	68	74	61	82	65	98
62	116	65	88	64	79	78	79	77	86
74	85	73	80	68	78	89	72	58	69
92	78	88	77	103	88	63	68	88	81
75	90	62	89	71	71	74	70	74	70
65	81	75	62	94	71	85	84	83	63
81	62	79	83	93	61	65	62	92	65
83	70	70	81	77	72	84	67	59	58
78	66	66	94	77	63	66	75	68	76
90	78	71	101	78	43	59	67	61	71
96	75	64	76	72	77	74	65	82	86
66	86	96	89	81	71	85	99	59	92
68	72	77	60	87	84	75	77	51	45
85	67	87	80	84	93	69	76	89	75
83	68	72	67	92	89	82	96	77	102
74	91	76	83	66	68	61	73	72	76
73	77	79	94	63	59	62	71	81	65
73	63	63	89	82	64	85	92	64	73

**FIGURE 1.7   THE PROCESS OF STATISTICAL INFERENCE FOR THE NORRIS
ELECTRONICS EXAMPLE**

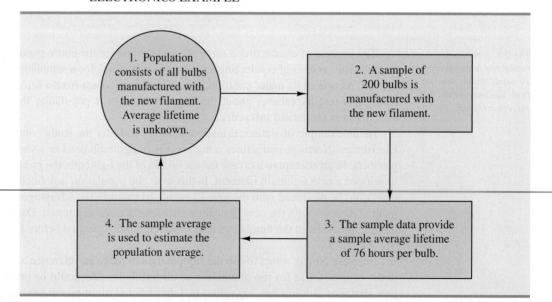

For the Norris example, the statistician might state that the point estimate of the average lifetime for the population of new lightbulbs is 76 hours with a margin of error of ±4 hours.
Thus, an interval estimate of the average lifetime for all lightbulbs produced with the new
filament is 72 hours to 80 hours. The statistician can also state how confident he or she is
that the interval from 72 hours to 80 hours contains the population average.

1.6 Statistical Analysis Using Microsoft Excel

Because statistical analysis typically involves working with large amounts of data, computer software is frequently used to conduct the analysis. Often the data to be analyzed reside in a spreadsheet. Given the data management, data analysis, and presentation capabilities of modern spreadsheet packages, it is now possible to conduct statistical analyses using them. In this book we show how statistical analysis can be performed using Microsoft Excel. In selected cases where Excel does not contain statistical analysis functions or data analysis tools that can be used to perform a statistical procedure discussed in the text, we have included chapter appendixes that show how to use StatTools, an add-in for Excel that provides an extended range of statistical and graphical options. The appendix to Chapter 1 provides an introduction to StatTools.

We want to emphasize that this book is about statistics; it is not a book about spreadsheets. Thus, our focus is on showing the appropriate statistical procedures for collecting, analyzing, presenting, and interpreting data. Because Excel is widely available in business organizations, you can expect to put the knowledge gained here to use in the setting where you currently, or soon will, work. If, in the process of studying this material, you become more proficient in Excel, so much the better.

We begin most sections with an application scenario in which a statistical procedure is useful. After showing what the statistical procedure is and how it is used, we turn to showing how to implement the procedure using Excel. Thus, you should gain an understanding of what the procedure is, the situations in which it is useful, and how to implement it using the capabilities of Excel.

Data Sets and Excel Worksheets

Data sets are organized in Excel worksheets in much the same way as the data set for the 25 mutual fund companies that appears in Table 1.1. Figure 1.8 shows an Excel worksheet for that data set. Note that row 1 and column A contain labels. Cells B1:F1 contain the variable names and cells A2:A26 contain the observation names. Cells B2:F26 contain the data that were collected. A purple screen highlights the data. The data are the focus of the statistical analysis. Except for the headings in row 1, each row in the worksheet corresponds to an observation and each column corresponds to a variable. For instance, row 2 of the worksheet contains the data for the first observation, American Century Intl. Disc; row 3 contains the data for the second observation, American Century Tax-Free Bond; and so on. Thus, the names in column A provide a convenient way to refer to each of the 25 observations in the study. Note that column B of the worksheet contains the data for the variable Fund Type, column C contains the data for the variable Net Asset Value ($), and so on.

Suppose now that we want to use Excel to analyze the Norris Electronics data shown in Table 1.5. The data in Table 1.5 are organized into 10 columns with 20 data values in each column so that it would fit nicely on a single page of the text. Even though the table has several columns, it shows data for only one variable (hours until burnout). In statistical worksheets, it is customary to put all the data for each variable in a single column. Refer to the Excel worksheet shown in Figure 1.9. To make it easier to identify each observation in the data set, we entered the heading Observation into cell A1 and the numbers 1–200 into cells A2:A201. The heading Hours until Burnout has been entered into cell B1, and the data for the 200 observations have been entered into cells B2:B201. Displaying a worksheet with this many rows on a single page of a textbook is not practical. In such cases we will hide selected rows to conserve space. In the Excel worksheet for the Norris Electronics problem we have hidden rows 7 through 195 (observations 6 through 194) to conserve space.[1]

---

[1]To hide rows 7 through 195 in the Excel worksheet, first select rows 7 through 195. Then, right-click and choose the Hide option. To redisplay rows 7 through 195, just select rows 6 and 196, right-click, and select the Unhide option.

FIGURE 1.8   EXCEL WORKSHEET FOR THE 25 MUTUAL FUNDS DATA SET

	A	B	C	D	E	F	G
		Fund	Net Asset	5 Year Average	Expense	Morningstar	
1	Fund Name	Type	Value ($)	Return (%)	Ratio (%)	Rank	
2	American Century Intl. Disc	IE	14.37	30.53	1.41	3-Star	
3	American Century Tax-Free Bond	FI	10.73	3.34	0.49	4-Star	
4	American Century Ultra	DE	24.94	10.88	0.99	3-Star	
5	Artisan Small Cap	DE	16.92	15.67	1.18	3-Star	
6	Brown Cap Small	DE	35.73	15.85	1.20	4-Star	
7	DFA U.S. Micro Cap	DE	13.47	17.23	0.53	3-Star	
8	Fidelity Contrafund	DE	73.11	17.99	0.89	5-Star	
9	Fidelity Overseas	IE	48.39	23.46	0.90	4-Star	
10	Fidelity Sel Electronics	DE	45.60	13.50	0.89	3-Star	
11	Fidelity Sh-Term Bond	FI	8.60	2.76	0.45	3-Star	
12	Gabelli Asset AAA	DE	49.81	16.70	1.36	4-Star	
13	Kalmar Gr Val Sm Cp	DE	15.30	15.31	1.32	3-Star	
14	Marsico 21st Century	DE	17.44	15.16	1.31	5-Star	
15	Mathews Pacific Tiger	IE	27.86	32.70	1.16	3-Star	
16	Oakmark I	DE	40.37	9.51	1.05	2-Star	
17	PIMCO Emerg Mkts Bd D	FI	10.68	13.57	1.25	3-Star	
18	RS Value A	DE	26.27	23.68	1.36	4-Star	
19	T. Rowe Price Latin Am.	IE	53.89	51.10	1.24	4-Star	
20	T. Rowe Price Mid Val	DE	22.46	16.91	0.80	4-Star	
21	Thornburg Value A	DE	37.53	15.46	1.27	4-Star	
22	USAA Income	FI	12.10	4.31	0.62	3-Star	
23	Vanguard Equity-Inc	DE	24.42	13.41	0.29	4-Star	
24	Vanguard Sht-Tm TE	FI	15.68	2.37	0.16	3-Star	
25	Vanguard Sm Cp Idx	DE	32.58	17.01	0.23	3-Star	
26	Wasatch Sm Cp Growth	DE	35.41	13.98	1.19	4-Star	
27							

FIGURE 1.9   EXCEL WORKSHEET FOR THE NORRIS ELECTRONICS DATA SET

Note: Rows 7–195 are hidden.

	A	B	C
1	Observation	Hours until Burnout	
2	1	107	
3	2	54	
4	3	66	
5	4	62	
6	5	74	
196	195	45	
197	196	75	
198	197	102	
199	198	76	
200	199	65	
201	200	73	
202			

Using Excel for Statistical Analysis

In this text, we are careful to separate the discussion of a statistical procedure from the discussion of using Excel to implement the procedure. The material that discusses the use of Excel will usually be set apart in sections with headings such as Using Excel's COUNTIF Function to Construct a Frequency Distribution, Using Excel's Chart Tools to Construct Bar Charts and Pie Charts, and so on. In using Excel for statistical analysis, three tasks may be needed: Enter Data; Enter Functions and Formulas; and Apply Tools.

Enter Data: Select cell locations for the data and enter the data along with appropriate descriptive labels.

Enter Functions and Formulas: Select cell locations, enter Excel functions and formulas, and provide descriptive material to identify the results.

Apply Tools: Use Excel's tools for data management, data analysis, and presentation.

Our approach will be to describe how these tasks are performed each time we use Excel to implement a statistical procedure. It will always be necessary to enter data. But, depending upon the complexity of the statistical analysis, only one of the last two tasks may be needed.

To illustrate how the discussion of using Excel will appear throughout the book, we will show how to use Excel's AVERAGE function to compute the average lifetime for the 200 burnout times in Table 1.5. Refer to Figure 1.10 as we describe the tasks involved. The worksheet shown in the foreground of Figure 1.10 displays the data for the problem and shows the results of the analysis. It is called a value worksheet. The worksheet shown in the background displays the Excel formula used to compute the average lifetime and is called the formula worksheet. A purple screen is used to highlight the data in both worksheets. In addition, a green screen is used to highlight functions and formulas in the formula worksheet and the corresponding results in the value worksheet.

Enter Data: The labels Observation and Hours until Burnout are entered into cells A1:B1. The numbers 1–200 are entered into cells A2:A201 to identify each of the observations, and

FIGURE 1.10   COMPUTING THE AVERAGE LIFETIME OF LIGHTBULBS FOR NORRIS ELECTRONICS USING EXCEL'S AVERAGE FUNCTION

	A	B	C	D	E	F
1	**Observation**	**Hours until Burnout**				
2	1	107		**Average Lifetime**	=AVERAGE(B2:B201)	
3	2	54				
4	3	66				
5	4	62				
6	5	74				
196	195	45				
197	196	75				
198	197	102				
199	198	76				
200	199	65				
201	200	73				
202						

Note: Rows 7–195 are hidden.

	A	B	C	D	E	F
1	**Observation**	**Hours until Burnout**				
2	1	107		**Average Lifetime**	76	
3	2	54				
4	3	66				
5	4	62				
6	5	74				
196	195	45				
197	196	75				
198	197	102				
199	198	76				
200	199	65				
201	200	73				
202						

the data showing the hours until burnout for each observation are entered into cells B2:B201 of the worksheet.

Enter Functions and Formulas: Excel's AVERAGE function can be used to compute the average lifetime for the 200 lightbulbs. We can compute the average lifetime by entering the following formula into cell E2:

$$=\text{AVERAGE(B2:B201)}$$

To identify the result, the label Average Lifetime is entered into cell D2. Note that for this problem, the Apply Tools task was not required. The value worksheet shows that the value computed using the AVERAGE function is 76 hours.

1.7   Ethical Guidelines for Statistical Practice

Ethical behavior is something we should strive for in all that we do. Ethical issues arise in statistics because of the important role statistics plays in the collection, analysis, presentation, and interpretation of data. In a statistical study, unethical behavior can take a variety of forms including improper sampling, inappropriate analysis of the data, development of misleading graphs, use of inappropriate summary statistics, and/or a biased interpretation of the statistical results.

As you begin to do your own statistical work, we encourage you to be fair, thorough, objective, and neutral as you collect data, conduct analyses, make oral presentations, and present written reports containing information developed. As a consumer of statistics, you should also be aware of the possibility of unethical statistical behavior by others. When you see statistics in newspapers, on television, on the Internet, and so on, it is a good idea to view the information with some skepticism, always being aware of the source as well as the purpose and objectivity of the statistics provided.

The American Statistical Association, the nation's leading professional organization for statistics and statisticians, developed the report "Ethical Guidelines for Statistical Practice"[2] to help statistical practitioners make and communicate ethical decisions and assist students in learning how to perform statistical work responsibly. The report contains 67 guidelines organized into eight topic areas: Professionalism; Responsibilities to Funders, Clients, and Employers; Responsibilities in Publications and Testimony; Responsibilities to Research Subjects; Responsibilities to Research Team Colleagues; Responsibilities to Other Statisticians or Statistical Practitioners; Responsibilities Regarding Allegations of Misconduct; and Responsibilities of Employers Including Organizations, Individuals, Attorneys, or Other Clients Employing Statistical Practitioners.

One of the ethical guidelines in the professionalism area addresses the issue of running multiple tests until a desired result is obtained. Let us consider an example. In Section 1.5 we discussed a statistical study conducted by Norris Electronics involving a sample of 200 high-intensity lightbulbs manufactured with a new filament. The average lifetime for the sample, 76 hours, provided an estimate of the average lifetime for all lightbulbs produced with the new filament. However, consider this. Because Norris selected a sample of bulbs, it is reasonable to assume that another sample would have provided a different average lifetime.

Suppose Norris's management had hoped the sample results would enable them to claim that the average lifetime for the new lightbulbs was 80 hours or more. Suppose further that Norris's management decides to continue the study by manufacturing and testing repeated samples of 200 lightbulbs with the new filament until a sample mean of 80 hours

[2]American Statistical Association (1999), "Ethical Guidelines for Statistical Practice," *http://www.amstat.org/profession/index.cfm?fuseaction=ethicalstatistics.*

or more is obtained. If the study is repeated enough times, a sample may eventually be obtained—by chance alone—that would provide the desired result and enable Norris to make such a claim. In this case, consumers would be misled into thinking the new product is better than it actually is. Clearly, this type of behavior is unethical and represents a gross misuse of statistics in practice.

Several ethical guidelines in the responsibilities and publications and testimony area deal with issues involving the handling of data. For instance, a statistician must account for all data considered in a study and explain the sample(s) actually used. In the Norris Electronics study the average lifetime for the 200 bulbs in the original sample is 76 hours; this is considerably less than the 80 hours or more that management hoped to obtain. Suppose now that after reviewing the results showing a 76 hour average lifetime, Norris discards all the observations with 70 or fewer hours until burnout, allegedly because these bulbs contain imperfections caused by startup problems in the manufacturing process. After discarding these lightbulbs, the average lifetime for the remaining lightbulbs in the sample turns out to be 82 hours. Would you be suspicious of Norris's claim that the lifetime for their lightbulbs is 82 hours?

If the Norris lightbulbs showing 70 or fewer hours until burnout were discarded to simply provide an average lifetime of 82 hours, there is no question that discarding the lightbulbs with 70 or fewer hours until burnout is unethical. But, even if the discarded lightbulbs contain imperfections due to startup problems in the manufacturing process—and, as a result, should not have been included in the analysis—the statistician who conducted the study must account for all the data that were considered and explain how the sample actually used was obtained. To do otherwise is potentially misleading and would constitute unethical behavior on the part of both the company and the statistician.

A guideline in the shared values section of the American Statistical Association report states that statistical practitioners should avoid any tendency to slant statistical work toward predetermined outcomes. This type of unethical practice is often observed when unrepresentative samples are used to make claims. For instance, in many areas of the country smoking is not permitted in restaurants. Suppose, however, a lobbyist for the tobacco industry interviews people in restaurants where smoking is permitted in order to estimate the percentage of people who are in favor of allowing smoking in restaurants. The sample results show that 90% of the people interviewed are in favor of allowing smoking in restaurants. Based upon these sample results, the lobbyist claims that 90% of all people who eat in restaurants are in favor of permitting smoking in restaurants. In this case we would argue that only sampling persons eating in restaurants that allow smoking has biased the results. If only the final results of such a study are reported, readers unfamiliar with the details of the study (i.e., that the sample was collected only in restaurants allowing smoking) can be misled.

The scope of the American Statistical Association's report is broad and includes ethical guidelines that are not only appropriate for a statistician, but also for consumers of statistical information. We encourage you to read the report to obtain a better perspective of ethical issues as you continue your study of statistics and to gain the background for determining how to ensure that ethical standards are met when you start to use statistics in practice.

Summary

Statistics is the art and science of collecting, analyzing, presenting, and interpreting data. Nearly every college student majoring in business or economics is required to take a course in statistics. We began the chapter by describing typical statistical applications for business and economics.

Data consist of the facts and figures that are collected and analyzed. Four scales of measurement used to obtain data on a particular variable include nominal, ordinal, interval, and ratio. The scale of measurement for a variable is nominal when the data are labels or names used to identify an attribute of an element. The scale is ordinal if the data demonstrate the properties of nominal data and the order or rank of the data is meaningful. The scale is interval if the data demonstrate the properties of ordinal data and the interval between values is expressed in terms of a fixed unit of measure. Finally, the scale of measurement is ratio if the data show all the properties of interval data and the ratio of two values is meaningful.

For purposes of statistical analysis, data can be classified as categorical or quantitative. Categorical data use labels or names to identify an attribute of each element. Categorical data use either the nominal or ordinal scale of measurement and may be nonnumeric or numeric. Quantitative data are numeric values that indicate how much or how many. Quantitative data use either the interval or ratio scale of measurement. Ordinary arithmetic operations are meaningful only if the data are quantitative. Therefore, statistical computations used for quantitative data are not always appropriate for categorical data.

In Sections 1.4 and 1.5 we introduced the topics of descriptive statistics and statistical inference. Descriptive statistics are the tabular, graphical, and numerical methods used to summarize data. The process of statistical inference uses data obtained from a sample to make estimates or test hypotheses about the characteristics of a population. In Section 1.6 we provided an introduction to the use of Excel for statistical analysis. In the last section of the chapter we discussed ethical guidelines for statistical practice.

Glossary

Statistics The art and science of collecting, analyzing, presenting, and interpreting data.

Data The facts and figures collected, analyzed, and summarized for presentation and interpretation.

Data set All the data collected in a particular study.

Elements The entities on which data are collected.

Variable A characteristic of interest for the elements.

Observation The set of measurements obtained for a particular element.

Nominal scale The scale of measurement for a variable when the data are labels or names used to identify an attribute of an element. Nominal data may be nonnumeric or numeric.

Ordinal scale The scale of measurement for a variable if the data exhibit the properties of nominal data and the order or rank of the data is meaningful. Ordinal data may be nonnumeric or numeric.

Interval scale The scale of measurement for a variable if the data demonstrate the properties of ordinal data and the interval between values is expressed in terms of a fixed unit of measure. Interval data are always numeric.

Ratio scale The scale of measurement for a variable if the data demonstrate all the properties of interval data and the ratio of two values is meaningful. Ratio data are always numeric.

Categorical data Labels or names used to identify an attribute of each element. Categorical data use either the nominal or ordinal scale of measurement and may be nonnumeric or numeric.

Quantitative data Numeric values that indicate how much or how many of something. Quantitative data are obtained using either the interval or ratio scale of measurement.

Categorical variable A variable with categorical data.

Quantitative variable A variable with quantitative data.

Cross-sectional data Data collected at the same or approximately the same point in time.

Time series data Data collected over several time periods.

Descriptive statistics Tabular, graphical, and numerical summaries of data.

Population The set of all elements of interest in a particular study.

Sample A subset of the population.

Census A survey to collect data on the entire population.

Sample survey A survey to collect data on a sample.

Statistical inference The process of using data obtained from a sample to make estimates or test hypotheses about the characteristics of a population.

Supplementary Exercises

1. Discuss the differences between statistics as numerical facts and statistics as a discipline or field of study.

2. The U.S. Department of Energy's Fuel Economy Guide provides fuel efficiency data for cars and trucks. Table 1.6 shows data for a sample of 10 cars (*http://www.fueleconomy.gov*, February 22, 2008). The column labeled Class shows the car size (compact, midsize, and large), the column labeled Cylinders specifies the number of cylinders the engine has, the column labeled City MPG shows the fuel efficiency rating for city driving in terms of miles per gallon (mpg), the column labeled Highway MPG shows the fuel efficiency rating for highway driving in terms of miles per gallon (mpg), and the column labeled Fuel Type specifies whether the car uses premium or regular fuel.
   a. How many elements are in this data set? 10
   b. How many variables are in this data set? 5
   c. Which variables are categorical and which variables are quantitative?
   d. What type of measurement scale is used for each of the variables?

3. Refer to Table 1.6.
   a. What is the average fuel efficiency rating for city driving?
   b. On average, how much higher is the fuel efficiency rating for highway driving as compared to city driving?
   c. What percentage of the cars have four-cylinder engines?
   d. What percentage of the cars will run on regular fuel?

TABLE 1.6   FUEL EFFICIENCY RATINGS FOR 10 CARS

Car	Class	Cylinders	City MPG	Highway MPG	Fuel Type
Audi A8	Large	12	13	19	Premium
BMW 328Xi	Compact	6	17	25	Premium
Cadillac CTS	Midsize	6	16	25	Regular
Chevrolet Malibu	Midsize	6	17	26	Regular
Chrysler 300	Large	8	13	18	Premium
Ford Focus	Compact	4	24	33	Regular
Hyundai Elantra	Midsize	4	25	33	Regular
Pontiac G6	Compact	6	15	22	Regular
Toyota Camry	Midsize	4	21	31	Regular
Volkswagen Jetta	Compact	5	21	29	Regular

TABLE 1.7   DATA FOR SEVEN ELITE COLLEGES AND UNIVERSITIES

School	State	Campus Setting	Endowment ($ billions)	% Applicants Admitted	NCAA Division
Amherst College	Massachusetts	Town: Fringe	1.7	18	III
Duke	North Carolina	City: Midsize	5.9	21	I-A
Harvard University	Massachusetts	City: Midsize	34.6	9	I-AA
Swarthmore College	Pennsylvania	Suburb: Large	1.4	18	III
University of Pennsylvania	Pennsylvania	City: Large	6.6	18	I-AA
Williams College	Massachusetts	Town: Fringe	1.9	18	III
Yale University	Connecticut	City: Midsize	22.5	9	I-AA

4. Table 1.7 shows data for seven elite colleges and universities. The endowment (in billions of dollars) and the percentage of applicants admitted appeared in *USA Today* (February 5, 2008); the state each college and university is located in, the campus setting, and the NCAA Division for varsity teams were obtained from the National Center of Education Statistics (*http://nces.ed.gov/collegenavigator/*, February 22, 2008).
   a. How many elements does this data set contain?
   b. How many variables are in the data set?
   c. Which of the variables are quantitative and which are categorical?

5. Consider the data set in Table 1.7
   a. Compute the average endowment for the sample.
   b. Compute the average percentage of applicants admitted.
   c. What percentage of the colleges and universities has NCAA Division III varsity teams?
   d. What percentage of the colleges and universities has a City: Midsize campus setting?

6. *Foreign Affairs* conducted a survey to develop a profile of its subscribers (*http:// www.foreignaffairs.org/advertising/download/FA_media_kit_2008.pdf*, February 23, 2008). Some of the following questions were asked.
   a. How many nights have you stayed in a hotel in the past 12 months?
   b. Where do you purchase books? Three options were listed: Bookstore, Internet, and Book Club.
   c. Do you own or lease a luxury vehicle? (Yes or No)
   d. What is your age?
   e. For foreign trips taken in the past three years, what was your destination? Seven international destinations were listed.
   Comment on whether each question provides categorical or quantitative data.

7. The Ritz-Carlton Hotel used a customer opinion questionnaire to obtain performance data about its dining and entertainment services (The Ritz-Carlton Hotel, Naples, Florida, February 2006). Customers were asked to rate six factors: Welcome, Service, Food, Menu Appeal, Atmosphere, and Overall Experience. Data were recorded for each factor with 1 for Fair, 2 for Average, 3 for Good, and 4 for Excellent.
   a. The customer responses provided data for six variables. Are the variables categorical or quantitative?
   b. What measurement scale is used?

8. The *FinancialTimes*/Harris Poll is a monthly online poll of adults from six countries in Europe and the United States. The *FT*/Harris Poll conducted between January 10, 2008, and January 21, 2008, included 1015 adults (aged 18–64) in the United States. One of

the questions asked was, "How would you rate the Federal Bank in handling the credit problems in the financial markets?" Possible responses were Excellent, Good, Fair, Bad, and Terrible (*http://www.harrisinteractive.com*).

    a.   What was the sample size for this survey?

    b.   Are the data categorical or quantitative?

    c.   Would it make more sense to use averages or percentages as a summary of the data for this question?

    d.   Suppose the responses were recorded as 1 if Terrible, 2 if Bad, 3 if Fair, 4 if Good, and 5 if Excellent? Would your answers to parts (b) and (c) change?

    e.   Of the respondents in the United States, 10% said the Federal Bank is doing a good job. How many individuals provided this response?

9. The Commerce Department reported receiving the following applications for the Malcolm Baldrige National Quality Award: 23 from large manufacturing firms, 18 from large service firms, and 30 from small businesses.

    a.   Is type of business a categorical or quantitative variable?

    b.   What percentage of the applications came from small businesses?

10. *The Wall Street Journal (WSJ)* subscriber survey (October 13, 2003) asked 46 questions about subscriber characteristics and interests. State whether each of the following questions provided categorical or quantitative data and indicate the measurement scale appropriate for each.

    a.   What is your age?

    b.   Are you male or female?

    c.   When did you first start reading the *WSJ*? High school, college, early career, mid-career, late career, or retirement?

    d.   How long have you been in your present job or position?

    e.   What type of vehicle are you considering for your next purchase? Nine response categories include sedan, sports car, SUV, minivan, and so on.

11. State whether each of the following variables is categorical or quantitative and indicate its measurement scale.

    a.   Annual sales

    b.   Soft drink size (small, medium, large)

    c.   Employee classification (GS1 through GS18)

    d.   Earnings per share

    e.   Method of payment (cash, check, credit card)

12. The Hawaii Visitors Bureau collects data on visitors to Hawaii. The following questions were among 16 asked in a questionnaire handed out to passengers during incoming airline flights in June 2003.

    •   This trip to Hawaii is my: 1st, 2nd, 3rd, 4th, etc.

    •   The primary reason for this trip is: (10 categories including vacation, convention, honeymoon)

    •   Where I plan to stay: (11 categories including hotel, apartment, relatives, camping)

    •   Total days in Hawaii

    a.   What is the population being studied?

    b.   Is the use of a questionnaire a good way to reach the population of passengers on incoming airline flights?

    c.   Comment on each of the four questions in terms of whether it will provide categorical or quantitative data.

13. Figure 1.11 provides a bar chart showing the amount of federal spending for the years 2002 to 2009 (*USA Today,* February 5, 2008).

    a.   Are the data categorical or quantitative?

    b.   Are the data time series or cross-sectional?

    c.   What is the variable of interest?

    d.   Comment on the trend in federal spending over time.

FIGURE 1.11   FEDERAL SPENDING

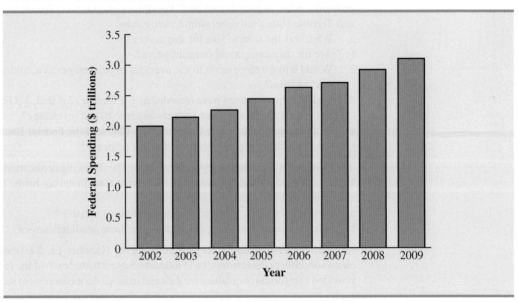

14. CSM Worldwide forecasts global production for all automobile manufacturers. The following CSM data show the forecast of global auto production for General Motors, Ford, DaimlerChrysler, and Toyota for the years 2004 to 2007 (*USA Today*, December 21, 2005). Data are in millions of vehicles.

Manufacturer	2004	2005	2006	2007
General Motors	8.9	9.0	8.9	8.8
Ford	7.8	7.7	7.8	7.9
DaimlerChrysler	4.1	4.2	4.3	4.6
Toyota	7.8	8.3	9.1	9.6

a. Construct a time series graph for the years 2004 to 2007 showing the number of vehicles manufactured by each automotive company. Show the time series for all four manufacturers on the same graph.

b. General Motors has been the undisputed production leader of automobiles since 1931. What does the time series graph show about who is the world's biggest car company? Discuss.

c. Construct a bar graph showing vehicles produced by automobile manufacturer using the 2007 data. Is this graph based on cross-sectional or time series data?

15. The Food and Drug Administration (FDA) reported the number of new drugs approved over an eight-year period (*The Wall Street Journal*, January 12, 2004). Figure 1.12 provides a bar chart summarizing the number of new drugs approved each year.

a. Are the data categorical or quantitative?

b. Are the data time series or cross-sectional?

c. How many new drugs were approved in 2003?

d. In what year were the fewest new drugs approved? How many?

e. Comment on the trend in the number of new drugs approved by the FDA over the eight-year period.

FIGURE 1.12 NUMBER OF NEW DRUGS APPROVED BY THE FOOD AND DRUG ADMINISTRATION

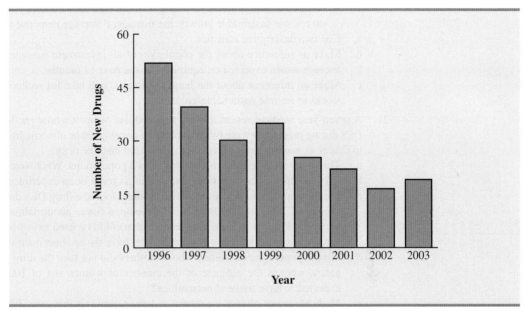

16. The marketing group at your company developed a new diet soft drink that it claims will capture a large share of the young adult market.
   a. What data would you want to see before deciding to invest substantial funds in introducing the new product into the marketplace?
   b. How would you expect the data mentioned in part (a) to be obtained?

17. A manager of a large corporation recommends a $10,000 raise be given to keep a valued subordinate from moving to another company. What internal and external sources of data might be used to decide whether such a salary increase is appropriate?

18. A survey of 430 business travelers found 155 business travelers used a travel agent to make the travel arrangements (*USA Today,* November 20, 2003).
   a. Develop a descriptive statistic that can be used to estimate the percentage of all business travelers who use a travel agent to make travel arrangements.
   b. The survey reported that the most frequent way business travelers make travel arrangements is by using an online travel site. If 44% of business travelers surveyed made their arrangements this way, how many of the 430 business travelers used an online travel site?
   c. Are the data on how travel arrangements are made categorical or quantitative?

19. A *BusinessWeek* North American subscriber study collected data from a sample of 2861 subscribers. Fifty-nine percent of the respondents indicated an annual income of $75,000 or more, and 50% reported having an American Express credit card.
   a. What is the population of interest in this study?
   b. Is annual income a categorical or quantitative variable?
   c. Is ownership of an American Express card a categorical or quantitative variable?
   d. Does this study involve cross-sectional or time series data?
   e. Describe any statistical inferences *BusinessWeek* might make on the basis of the survey.

20. A survey of 131 investment managers in *Barron's* Big Money poll revealed the following (*Barron's,* October 28, 2002):
   - 43% of managers classified themselves as bullish or very bullish on the stock market.
   - The average expected return over the next 12 months for equities was 11.2%.

- 21% selected health care as the sector most likely to lead the market in the next 12 months.
- When asked to estimate how long it would take for technology and telecom stocks to resume sustainable growth, the managers' average response was 2.5 years.

a. Cite two descriptive statistics.

b. Make an inference about the population of all investment managers concerning the average return expected on equities over the next 12 months.

c. Make an inference about the length of time it will take for technology and telecom stocks to resume sustainable growth.

21. A seven-year medical research study reported that women whose mothers took the drug DES during pregnancy were twice as likely to develop tissue abnormalities that might lead to cancer as were women whose mothers did not take the drug.

   a. This study involved the comparison of two populations. What were the populations?

   b. Do you suppose the data were obtained in a survey or an experiment?

   c. For the population of women whose mothers took the drug DES during pregnancy, a sample of 3980 women showed 63 developed tissue abnormalities that might lead to cancer. Provide a descriptive statistic that could be used to estimate the number of women out of 1000 in this population who have tissue abnormalities.

   d. For the population of women whose mothers did not take the drug DES during pregnancy, what is the estimate of the number of women out of 1000 who would be expected to have tissue abnormalities?

   e. Medical studies often use a relatively large sample (in this case, 3980). Why?

22. The Nielsen Company surveyed consumers in 47 markets from Europe, Asia-Pacific, the Americas, and the Middle East to determine which factors are most important in determining where they buy their groceries. Using a scale of 1 (low) to 5 (high), the highest rated factor was *good value for money*, with an average point score of 4.32. The second highest rated factor was *better selection of high-quality brands and products,* with an average point score of 3.78, and the lowest rated factor was *uses recyclable bags and packaging*, with an average point score of 2.71 (*http://www.acnielsen.com,* February 24, 2008). Suppose that you have been hired by a grocery store chain to conduct a similar study to determine what factors customers at the chain's stores in Charlotte, North Carolina, think are most important in determining where they buy their groceries.

   a. What is the population for the survey that you will be conducting?

   b. How would you collect the data for this study?

23. Nielsen Media Research conducts weekly surveys of television viewing throughout the United States, publishing both rating and market share data. The Nielsen rating is the percentage of households with televisions watching a program, while the Nielsen share is the percentage of households watching a program among those households with televisions in use. For example, Nielsen Media Research results for the 2003 Baseball World Series between the New York Yankees and the Florida Marlins showed a rating of 12.8% and a share of 22% (Associated Press, October 27, 2003). Thus, 12.8% of households with televisions were watching the World Series and 22% of households with televisions in use were watching the World Series. Based on the rating and share data for major television programs, Nielsen publishes a weekly ranking of television programs as well as a weekly ranking of the four major networks: ABC, CBS, NBC, and Fox.

   a. What is Nielsen Media Research attempting to measure?

   b. What is the population?

   c. Why would a sample be used in this situation?

   d. What kinds of decisions or actions are based on the Nielsen rankings?

24. A sample of midterm grades for five students showed the following results: 72, 65, 82, 90, 76. Which of the following statements are correct, and which should be challenged as being too generalized?

TABLE 1.8 DATA SET FOR 25 SHADOW STOCKS

Company	Exchange	Ticker Symbol	Market Cap ($ millions)	Price/ Earnings Ratio	Gross Profit Margin (%)
DeWolfe Companies	AMEX	DWL	36.4	8.4	36.7
North Coast Energy	OTC	NCEB	52.5	6.2	59.3
Hansen Natural Corp.	OTC	HANS	41.1	14.6	44.8
MarineMax, Inc.	NYSE	HZO	111.5	7.2	23.8
Nanometrics Incorporated	OTC	NANO	228.6	38.0	53.3
TeamStaff, Inc.	OTC	TSTF	92.1	33.5	4.1
Environmental Tectonics	AMEX	ETC	51.1	35.8	35.9
Measurement Specialties	AMEX	MSS	101.8	26.8	37.6
SEMCO Energy, Inc.	NYSE	SEN	193.4	18.7	23.6
Party City Corporation	OTC	PCTY	97.2	15.9	36.4
Embrex, Inc.	OTC	EMBX	136.5	18.9	59.5
Tech/Ops Sevcon, Inc.	AMEX	TO	23.2	20.7	35.7
ARCADIS NV	OTC	ARCAF	173.4	8.8	9.6
Qiao Xing Universal Tele.	OTC	XING	64.3	22.1	30.8
Energy West Incorporated	OTC	EWST	29.1	9.7	16.3
Barnwell Industries, Inc.	AMEX	BRN	27.3	7.4	73.4
Innodata Corporation	OTC	INOD	66.1	11.0	29.6
Medical Action Industries	OTC	MDCI	137.1	26.9	30.6
Instrumentarium Corp.	OTC	INMRY	240.9	3.6	52.1
Petroleum Development	OTC	PETD	95.9	6.1	19.4
Drexler Technology Corp.	OTC	DRXR	233.6	45.6	53.6
Gerber Childrenswear Inc.	NYSE	GCW	126.9	7.9	25.8
Gaiam, Inc.	OTC	GAIA	295.5	68.2	60.7
Artesian Resources Corp.	OTC	ARTNA	62.8	20.5	45.5
York Water Company	OTC	YORW	92.2	22.9	74.2

WEB file

Shadow02

    a. The average midterm grade for the sample of five students is 77.
    b. The average midterm grade for all students who took the exam is 77.
    c. An estimate of the average midterm grade for all students who took the exam is 77.
    d. More than half of the students who take this exam will score between 70 and 85.
    e. If five other students are included in the sample, their grades will be between 65 and 90.

25. Table 1.8 shows a data set containing information for 25 of the shadow stocks tracked by the American Association of Individual Investors (*http://www.aaii.com,* February 2002). Shadow stocks are common stocks of smaller companies that are not closely followed by Wall Street analysts. The data set is also on the website that accompanies the text in the file named Shadow02.

    a. How many variables are in the data set?
    b. Which of the variables are categorical and which are quantitative?
    c. For the Exchange variable, show the frequency and the percent frequency for AMEX, NYSE, and OTC. Construct a bar graph similar to Figure 1.5 for the Exchange variable.
    d. Show the frequency distribution for the Gross Profit Margin using the five intervals: 0–14.9, 15–29.9, 30–44.9, 45–59.9, and 60–74.9. Construct a histogram similar to Figure 1.6.
    e. What is the average price/earnings ratio?

Appendix   An Introduction to StatTools

Excel 2007 does not contain statistical functions or data analysis tools to perform all the statistical procedures discussed in the text. StatTools is a Microsoft Excel statistics add-in that extends the range of statistical and graphical options for Excel users. Most chapters include a chapter appendix that shows the steps required to accomplish a statistical procedure using StatTools. For those students who want to make more extensive use of the software, StatTools offers an excellent Help facility. The StatTools Help system includes detailed explanations of the statistical and data analysis options available, as well as descriptions and definitions of the types of output provided.

Installing and Opening StatTools

Instructions for downloading and installing the StatTools software on your computer are provided on the website that accompanies the text. After installing the StatTools software, perform the following steps to use it as an Excel add-in.

Step 1. Click the **Start** button on the taskbar and then point to **All Programs**
Step 2. Point to the folder entitled **Palisade Decision Tools**
Step 3. Click **StatTools for Excel**

These steps will open Excel and add the StatTools tab next to the Add-Ins tab on the Excel Ribbon. Alternately, if you are already working in Excel, these steps will make StatTools available.

Using StatTools

Before conducting any statistical analysis, we must create a StatTools data set using the StatTools Data Set Manager. Let us use the Excel worksheet for the mutual funds data set in Table 1.1 to show how this is done. The following steps show how to create a StatTools data set for the mutual funds data.

Step 1. Open the Excel file named Morningstar
Step 2. Select any cell in the data set (for example, cell A1)
Step 3. Click the **StatTools** tab on the Ribbon
Step 4. In the **Data** group, click **Data Set Manager**
Step 5. When StatTools asks if you want to add the range $A$1:$F$26 as a new StatTools data set, click **Yes**
Step 6. When the StatTools—Data Set Manager dialog box appears, Click **OK**

Figure 1.13 shows the StatTools—Data Set Manager dialog box that appears in step 6. By default, the name of the new StatTools data set is Data Set #1. You can replace the name Data Set #1 in step 6 with a more descriptive name. And, if you select the Apply Cell Format option, the column labels will be highlighted in blue and the entire data set will have outside and inside borders. You can always select the Data Set Manager at any time in your analysis to make these types of changes.

Recommended Application Settings

StatTools allows the user to specify some of the application settings that control such things as where statistical output is displayed and how calculations are performed. The following steps show how to access the StatTools—Application Settings dialog box.

Step 1. Click the **StatTools** tab on the Ribbon
Step 2. In the **Tools Group**, click **Utilities**
Step 3. Choose **Application Settings** from the list of options

FIGURE 1.13   THE STATTOOLS—DATA SET MANAGER DIALOG BOX

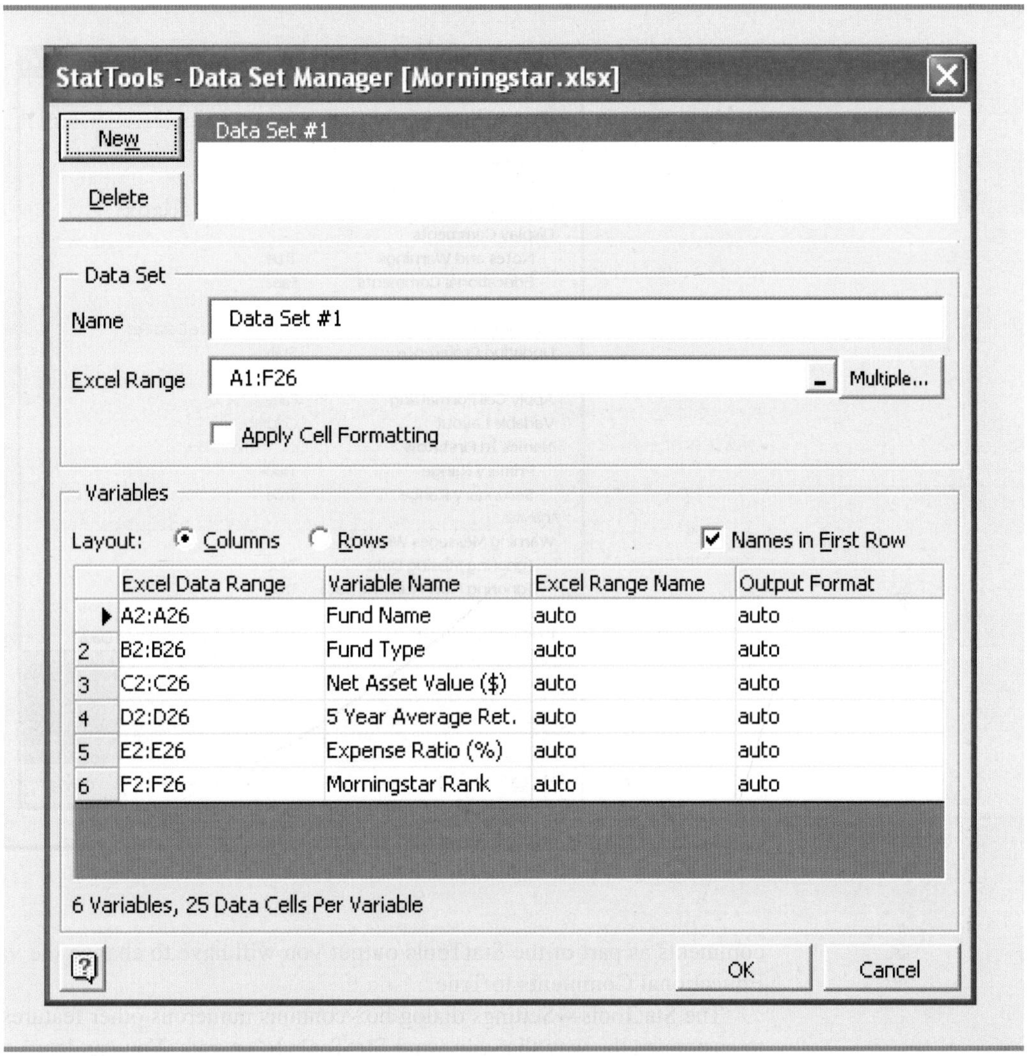

Figure 1.14 shows that the StatTools—Application Settings dialog box has five sections: General Settings; Reports; Utilities; Data Set Defaults; and Analyses. Let's see how we can make changes in the Reports section of this dialog box.

Figure 1.14 shows that the Placement option currently selected is **New Workbook**. Using this option, the StatTools output will be placed in a new workbook. But, suppose you would like to place the StatTools output in the current (active) workbook. If you click the words **New Workbook**, a downward-pointing arrow will appear to the right. Clicking this arrow will display a list of all the placement options, including **Active Workbook**; we recommend using this option. Figure 1.14 also shows that the Updating Preferences option in the Reports section is currently **Live—Linked to Input Data**. With live updating anytime one or more data values are changed StatTools will automatically change the output previously produced; we also recommend using this option. Note that there are two options available under Display Comments: **Notes and Warnings**; and **Educational Comments**. Because these options provide useful notes and information regarding the output, we recommend using both options. Thus, to include educational

FIGURE 1.14   THE STATTOOLS—APPLICATION SETTINGS DIALOG BOX

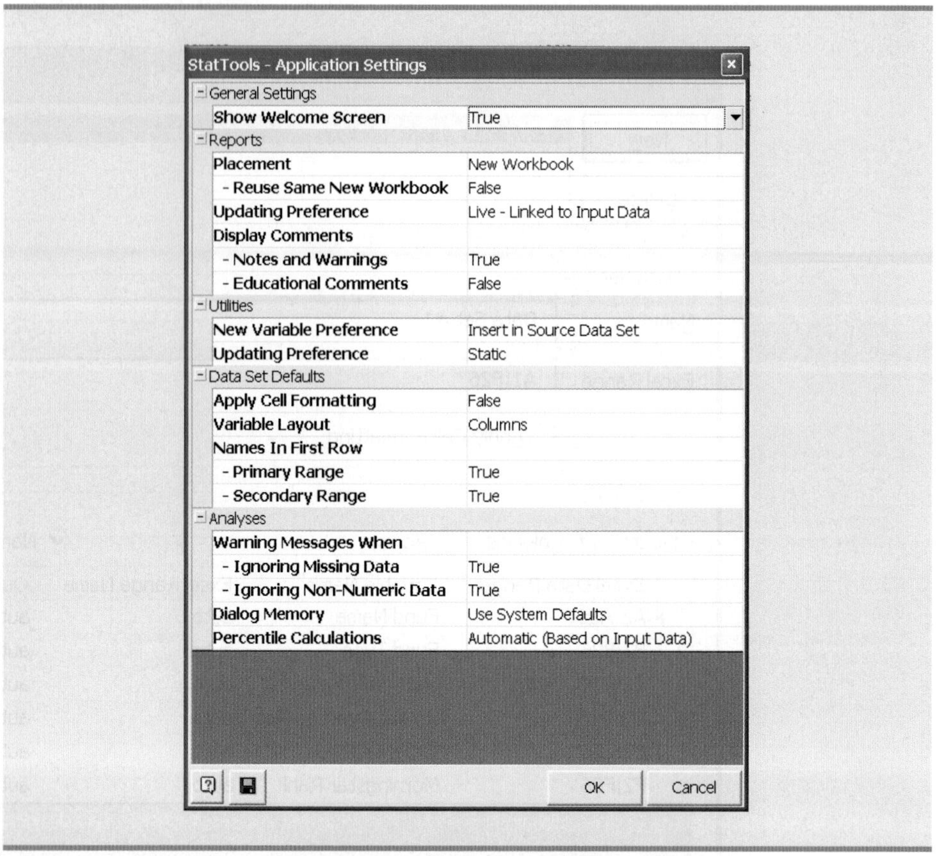

comments as part of the StatTools output you will have to change the value of False for Educational Comments to True.

The StatTools—Settings dialog box contains numerous other features that enable you to customize the way that you want StatTools to operate. You can learn more about all of these features by selecting the Help option located in the Tools group, or by clicking the Help icon located in the lower left-hand corner of the dialog box. When you are done making changes in the application settings, click OK at the bottom of the dialog box and then click Yes when StatTools asks you if you want to save the new application settings.

CHAPTER 2

Descriptive Statistics: Tabular and Graphical Presentations

CONTENTS

STATISTICS *in* PRACTICE

COLGATE-PALMOLIVE COMPANY*
NEW YORK, NEW YORK

The Colgate-Palmolive Company started as a small soap and candle shop in New York City in 1806. Today, Colgate-Palmolive employs more than 40,000 people working in more than 200 countries and territories around the world. Although best known for its brand names of Colgate, Palmolive, Ajax, and Fab, the company also markets Mennen, Hill's Science Diet, and Hill's Prescription Diet products.

The Colgate-Palmolive Company uses statistics in its quality assurance program for home laundry detergent products. One concern is customer satisfaction with the quantity of detergent in a carton. Every carton in each size category is filled with the same amount of detergent by weight, but the volume of detergent is affected by the density of the detergent powder. For instance, if the powder density is on the heavy side, a smaller volume of detergent is needed to reach the carton's specified weight. As a result, the carton may appear to be under-filled when opened by the consumer.

To control the problem of heavy detergent powder, limits are placed on the acceptable range of powder density. Statistical samples are taken periodically, and the density of each powder sample is measured. Data summaries are then provided for operating personnel so that corrective action can be taken if necessary to keep the density within the desired quality specifications.

A frequency distribution for the densities of 150 samples taken over a one-week period and a histogram are shown in the accompanying table and figure. Density levels above .40 are unacceptably high. The frequency distribution and histogram show that the operation is meeting its quality guidelines with all of the densities less than or equal to .40. Managers viewing these statistical summaries would be pleased with the quality of the detergent production process.

In this chapter, you will learn about tabular and graphical methods of descriptive statistics such as frequency distributions, bar charts, histograms, stem-and-leaf

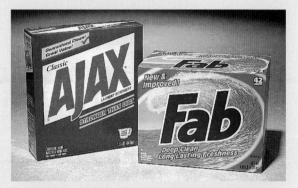

Statistical summaries help maintain the quality of these Colgate-Palmolive products. © Joe Higgins/South-Western.

displays, crosstabulations, and others. The goal of these methods is to summarize data so that the data can be easily understood and interpreted.

Frequency Distribution of Density Data

Density	Frequency
.29–.30	30
.31–.32	75
.33–.34	32
.35–.36	9
.37–.38	3
.39–.40	1
Total	150

Histogram of Density Data

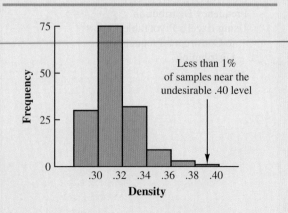

Less than 1% of samples near the undesirable .40 level

*The authors are indebted to William R. Fowle, Manager of Quality Assurance, Colgate-Palmolive Company, for providing this Statistics in Practice.

As indicated in Chapter 1, data can be classified as either categorical or quantitative. **Categorical data** use labels or names to identify categories of like items. **Quantitative data** are numerical values that indicate how much or how many.

This chapter introduces tabular and graphical methods commonly used to summarize both categorical and quantitative data. Tabular and graphical summaries of data can be found in annual reports, newspaper articles, and research studies. Everyone is exposed to these types of presentations. Hence, it is important to understand how they are prepared and how they should be interpreted. We begin with tabular and graphical methods for summarizing data concerning a single variable. The last section introduces methods for summarizing data when the relationship between two variables is of interest.

Excel's wide variety of statistical functions and tools will be used extensively in this chapter. We will find the chart tools and PivotTable tools to be especially helpful. These tools can be used to provide tabular and graphical summaries for a single categorical or quantitative variable as well as provide crosstabulations and graphical presentations for data sets involving more than one variable.

2.1 Summarizing Categorical Data

Frequency Distribution

We begin the discussion of how tabular and graphical methods can be used to summarize categorical data with the definition of a **frequency distribution**.

> FREQUENCY DISTRIBUTION
>
> A frequency distribution is a tabular summary of data showing the number (frequency) of items in each of several nonoverlapping classes.

The following example demonstrates the construction and interpretation of a frequency distribution for categorical data. Coke Classic, Diet Coke, Dr. Pepper, Pepsi, and Sprite are five popular soft drinks. Assume that the data in Table 2.1 show the soft drink selected in a sample of 50 soft drink purchases.

TABLE 2.1   DATA FROM A SAMPLE OF 50 SOFT DRINK PURCHASES

WEB file

SoftDrink

Coke Classic	Sprite	Pepsi
Diet Coke	Coke Classic	Coke Classic
Pepsi	Diet Coke	Coke Classic
Diet Coke	Coke Classic	Coke Classic
Coke Classic	Diet Coke	Coke Classic
Coke Classic	Coke Classic	Pepsi
Dr. Pepper	Sprite	Dr. Pepper
Diet Coke	Pepsi	Coke Classic
Pepsi	Coke Classic	Diet Coke
Pepsi	Coke Classic	Pepsi
Coke Classic	Coke Classic	Pepsi
Dr. Pepper	Pepsi	Pepsi
Sprite	Coke Classic	Coke Classic
Coke Classic	Sprite	Dr. Pepper
Diet Coke	Dr. Pepper	Pepsi
Coke Classic	Pepsi	Sprite
Coke Classic	Diet Coke	

TABLE 2.2

FREQUENCY
DISTRIBUTION OF
SOFT DRINK
PURCHASES

Soft Drink	Frequency
Coke Classic	19
Diet Coke	8
Dr. Pepper	5
Pepsi	13
Sprite	5
Total	50

To develop a frequency distribution for these data, we count the number of times each soft drink appears in Table 2.1. Coke Classic appears 19 times, Diet Coke appears 8 times, Dr. Pepper appears 5 times, Pepsi appears 13 times, and Sprite appears 5 times. These counts are summarized in the frequency distribution in Table 2.2.

This frequency distribution provides a summary of how the 50 soft drink purchases are distributed across the five soft drinks. This summary offers more insight than the original data shown in Table 2.1. Viewing the frequency distribution, we see that Coke Classic is the leader, Pepsi is second, Diet Coke is third, and Sprite and Dr. Pepper are tied for fourth. The frequency distribution summarizes information about the popularity of the five soft drinks.

Let us examine how Excel can be used to count the frequencies and construct a frequency distribution for the soft drink data in Table 2.1.

Using Excel's COUNTIF Function to Construct a Frequency Distribution

Two tasks are involved in using Excel's COUNTIF function to construct a frequency distribution: Enter Data and Enter Functions and Formulas. Refer to Figure 2.1 as we describe the tasks involved. The formula worksheet is in the background; the value worksheet is in the foreground.

Enter Data: The label "Brand Purchased" and the data for the 50 soft drink purchases are entered into cells A1:A51.

Enter Functions and Formulas: Excel's COUNTIF function can be used to count the number of times each soft drink appears in cells A2:A51. We first entered a label and the soft drink names into cells C1:C6 and D1. Then, to count the number of times that Coke Classic appears, we entered the following formula into cell D2:

$$=\text{COUNTIF}(\$A\$2:\$A\$51,C2)$$

Appendix 2.1 shows how to use Excel's PivotTable Report to construct a frequency distribution for categorical data.

To count the number of times the other soft drinks appear, we copied the same formula into cells D3:D6.

The value worksheet, in the foreground of Figure 2.1, shows the values computed using these cell formulas; we see that the Excel worksheet shows the same frequency distribution that we developed in Table 2.2.

Relative Frequency and Percent Frequency Distributions

A frequency distribution shows the number (frequency) of items in each of several nonoverlapping classes. However, we are often interested in the proportion, or percentage, of items in each class. The *relative frequency* of a class equals the fraction or proportion of items belonging to a class. For a data set with *n* observations, the relative frequency of each class can be determined as follows:

RELATIVE FREQUENCY

$$\text{Relative frequency of a class} = \frac{\text{Frequency of the class}}{n} \qquad (2.1)$$

The *percent frequency* of a class is the relative frequency multiplied by 100.

A **relative frequency distribution** gives a tabular summary of data showing the relative frequency for each class. A **percent frequency distribution** summarizes the percent

	A	B	C	D	E
1	**Brand Purchased**		**Soft Drink**	**Frequency**	
2	Coke Classic		Coke Classic	=COUNTIF($A$2:$A$51,C2)	
3	Diet Coke		Diet Coke	=COUNTIF($A$2:$A$51,C3)	
4	Pepsi		Dr. Pepper	=COUNTIF($A$2:$A$51,C4)	
5	Diet Coke		Pepsi	=COUNTIF($A$2:$A$51,C5)	
6	Coke Classic		Sprite	=COUNTIF($A$2:$A$51,C6)	
7	Coke Classic				
8	Dr. Pepper				

	A	B	C	D	E
1	**Brand Purchased**		**Soft Drink**	**Frequency**	
2	Coke Classic		Coke Classic	19	
3	Diet Coke		Diet Coke	8	
4	Pepsi		Dr. Pepper	5	
5	Diet Coke		Pepsi	13	
6	Coke Classic		Sprite	5	
7	Coke Classic				
8	Dr. Pepper				
9	Diet Coke				
10	Pepsi				
11	Pepsi				
12	Coke Classic				
13	Dr. Pepper				
14	Sprite				
15	Coke Classic				
16	Diet Coke				
17	Coke Classic				
18	Coke Classic				
19	Sprite				
20	Coke Classic				
50	Pepsi				
51	Sprite				
52					

(Left worksheet continued)

	A
9	Diet Coke
10	Pepsi
11	Pepsi
12	Coke Classic
13	Dr. Pepper
14	Sprite
15	Coke Classic
16	Diet Coke
17	Coke Classic
18	Coke Classic
19	Sprite
20	Coke Classic
50	Pepsi
51	Sprite
52	

Note: Rows 21–49 are hidden.

frequency of the data for each class. Table 2.3 shows a relative frequency distribution and a percent frequency distribution for the soft drink data. In Table 2.3 we see that the relative frequency for Coke Classic is 19/50 = .38, the relative frequency for Diet Coke is 8/50 = .16, and so on. From the percent frequency distribution, we see that 38% of the purchases were Coke Classic, 16% of the purchases were Diet Coke, and so on. We can also note that 38% + 26% + 16% = 80% of the purchases were the top three soft drinks.

Using Excel to Construct Relative Frequency and Percent Frequency Distributions

Extending the worksheet shown in Figure 2.1, we can develop the relative frequency and percent frequency distributions shown in Table 2.3. Refer to Figure 2.2 as we describe the tasks involved. The formula worksheet is in the background; the value worksheet is in the foreground.

Enter Data: The label "Brand Purchased" and the data for the 50 soft drink purchases are entered into cells A1:A51.

TABLE 2.3   RELATIVE FREQUENCY AND PERCENT FREQUENCY DISTRIBUTIONS OF SOFT DRINK PURCHASES

Soft Drink	Relative Frequency	Percent Frequency
Coke Classic	.38	38
Diet Coke	.16	16
Dr. Pepper	.10	10
Pepsi	.26	26
Sprite	.10	10
Total	1.00	100

Enter Functions and Formulas: The information in cells C1:D6 is the same as in Figure 2.1. Excel's SUM function is used in cell D7 to compute the sum of the frequencies in cells D2:D6. The resulting value of 50 is the number of observations in the data set. To compute the relative frequency for Coke Classic using equation (2.1), we entered the formula =D2/$D$7 into cell E2; the result, 0.38, is the relative frequency for Coke Classic. Copying cell E2 to cells E3:E6 computes the relative frequencies for each of the other soft drinks.

To compute the percent frequency for Coke Classic we entered the formula =E2*100 into cell F2. The result, 38, indicates that 38% of the soft drink purchases were Coke

FIGURE 2.2   RELATIVE FREQUENCY AND PERCENT FREQUENCY DISTRIBUTIONS OF SOFT DRINK PURCHASES CONSTRUCTED USING EXCEL

	A	B	C	D	E	F	G
1	Brand Purchased		Soft Drink	Frequency	Relative Frequency	Percent Frequency	
2	Coke Classic		Coke Classic	=COUNTIF($A$2:$A$51,C2)	=D2/$D$7	=E2*100	
3	Diet Coke		Diet Coke	=COUNTIF($A$2:$A$51,C3)	=D3/$D$7	=E3*100	
4	Pepsi		Dr. Pepper	=COUNTIF($A$2:$A$51,C4)	=D4/$D$7	=E4*100	
5	Diet Coke		Pepsi	=COUNTIF($A$2:$A$51,C5)	=D5/$D$7	=E5*100	
6	Coke Classic		Sprite	=COUNTIF($A$2:$A$51,C6)	=D6/$D$7	=E6*100	
7	Coke Classic		Total	=SUM(D2:D6)	=SUM(E2:E6)	=SUM(F2:F6)	
8	Dr. Pepper						
9	Diet Coke						
10	Pepsi						
11	Pepsi						
12	Coke Classic						
13	Dr. Pepper						
14	Sprite						
15	Coke Classic						
16	Diet Coke						
17	Coke Classic						
18	Coke Classic						
19	Sprite						
20	Coke Classic						
50	Pepsi						
51	Sprite						
52							

	A	B	C	D	E	F	G
1	Brand Purchased		Soft Drink	Frequency	Relative Frequency	Percent Frequency	
2	Coke Classic		Coke Classic	19	0.38	38	
3	Diet Coke		Diet Coke	8	0.16	16	
4	Pepsi		Dr. Pepper	5	0.1	10	
5	Diet Coke		Pepsi	13	0.26	26	
6	Coke Classic		Sprite	5	0.1	10	
7	Coke Classic		Total	50	1.00	100	
8	Dr. Pepper						
9	Diet Coke						
10	Pepsi						
11	Pepsi						
12	Coke Classic						
13	Dr. Pepper						
14	Sprite						
15	Coke Classic						
16	Diet Coke						
17	Coke Classic						
18	Coke Classic						
19	Sprite						
20	Coke Classic						
50	Pepsi						
51	Sprite						
52							

Note: Rows 21–49 are hidden.

Classic. Copying cell F2 to cells F3:F6 computes the percent frequencies for each of the other soft drinks. Finally, copying cell D7 to cells E7:F7 computes the total of the relative frequencies (1.00) and the total of the percent frequencies (100).

Bar Charts and Pie Charts

A **bar chart** is a graph used to display categorical data summarized in a frequency, relative frequency, or percent frequency distribution. On one axis of the graph we specify the labels that are used for the classes (categories). A frequency, relative frequency, or percent frequency scale can be used for the other axis of the graph. Then, using a bar of fixed width drawn above each class label, we extend the length of the bar until we reach the frequency, relative frequency, or percent frequency of the class. Figure 2.3 shows a bar chart for the 50 soft drink purchases in which the vertical axis is used to display the frequencies. Note how the graphical presentation shows Coke Classic, Pepsi, and Diet Coke to be the most preferred brands.

In quality control applications, bar charts are used to identify the most important causes of problems. When the bars are arranged in descending order of height from left to right with the most frequently occurring cause appearing first, the bar chart is called a pareto diagram. This diagram is named for its founder, Vilfredo Pareto, an Italian economist.

The **pie chart** provides another graphical device for presenting relative frequency and percent frequency distributions for categorical data. To construct a pie chart, we first draw a circle to represent all the data. Then we use the relative frequencies to subdivide the circle into sectors, or parts, that correspond to the relative frequency for each class. For example, because a circle contains 360 degrees and Coke Classic shows a relative frequency of .38, the sector of the pie chart labeled Coke Classic consists of .38(360) = 136.8 degrees. The sector of the pie chart labeled Diet Coke consists of .16(360) = 57.6 degrees. Similar calculations for the other classes yield the pie chart in Figure 2.4. The numerical values shown for each sector can be frequencies, relative frequencies, or percent frequencies.

Using Excel's Chart Tools to Construct a Bar Chart and a Pie Chart

Excel's chart tools make it very easy to create a variety of graphical displays, including bar charts and pie charts. When such tools are used, a third task is needed for worksheet construction: **Apply Tools.** We illustrate by showing how to construct the bar chart for soft drink purchases. Refer to Figure 2.5 as we describe the tasks involved.

Enter Data: Same as in Figure 2.1

Enter Functions and Formulas: Same as in Figure 2.1

FIGURE 2.3 BAR CHART OF SOFT DRINK PURCHASES

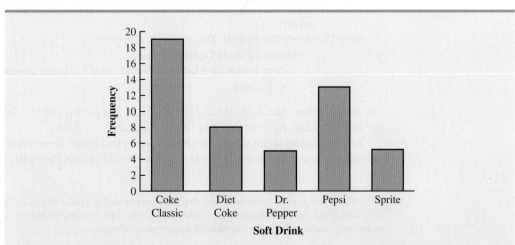

FIGURE 2.4   PIE CHART OF SOFT DRINK PURCHASES

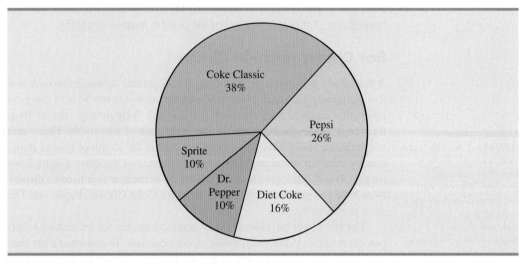

Apply Tools: The following steps describe how to use Excel's chart tools to construct a bar chart for the soft drink data using the frequency distribution appearing in cells C1:D6. The bar chart we will create uses the vertical axis to display the frequencies; in Excel this type of bar chart is referred to as a column chart.

Step 1. Select cells C2:D6
Step 2. Click the **Insert** tab on the Ribbon
Step 3. In the **Charts** group, click **Column**
Step 4. When the list of column chart subtypes appears,
    Go to the **2-D Column** section
    Click **Clustered Column** (the leftmost chart)
Step 5. In the **Chart Layouts** group, click the **More** button (the downward pointing arrow with a line over it) to display all the options
Step 6. Choose **Layout 9**
Step 7. Click the **Chart Title** and replace it with **Bar Chart of Soft Drink Purchases**
Step 8. Click the **Horizontal (Category) Axis Title** and replace it with **Soft Drink**
Step 9. Click the **Vertical (Value) Axis Title** and replace it with **Frequency**
Step 10. Right click the **Series 1 Legend Entry** and choose **Delete** from the list of options that appears
Step 11. Right-click the vertical axis and choose **Format Axis** from the options that appear
Step 12. When the Format Axis dialog box appears,
    Go to the **Axis Options** section
    Select **Fixed** for **Major Unit** and enter 5.0 in the corresponding box
    Click **Close**

The resulting bar chart is shown in Figure 2.5.[1] If you prefer, you can display the bars on the horizontal axis by choosing **Bar** in step 3 instead of Column.

Excel's chart tools can also be used to develop a pie chart for the soft drink data in a similar fashion. The major difference is that in step 3 we would choose **Pie** in the Charts group.

_____
[1]The bar chart in Figure 2.5 is slightly different than what was provided by Excel after clicking Close. Resizing an Excel chart is not difficult. First, select the chart. Small black squares, called sizing handles, will appear on the chart border. Click on the sizing handles and drag them to resize the figure to your preference.

FIGURE 2.5   BAR CHART OF SOFT DRINK PURCHASES CONSTRUCTED USING EXCEL'S CHART TOOLS

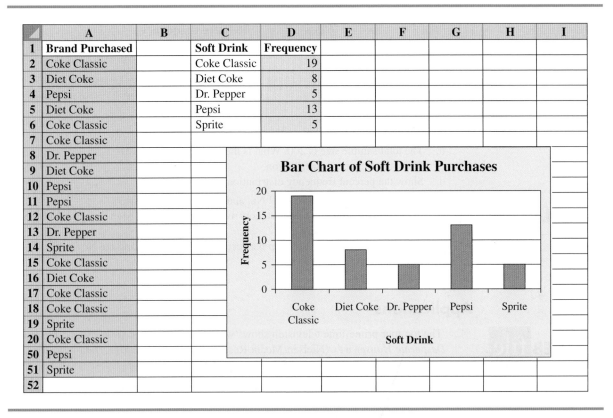

NOTES AND COMMENTS

1. Often the number of classes in a frequency distribution is the same as the number of categories found in the data, as is the case for the soft drink purchase data in this section. The data involve only five soft drinks, and a separate frequency distribution class was defined for each one. Data that included all soft drinks would require many categories, most of which would have a small number of purchases. Most statisticians recommend that classes with smaller frequencies be grouped into an aggregate class called "other." Classes with frequencies of 5% or less would most often be treated in this fashion.

2. The sum of the frequencies in any frequency distribution always equals the number of observations. The sum of the relative frequencies in any relative frequency distribution always equals 1.00, and the sum of the percentages in a percent frequency distribution always equals 100.

3. Excel's PivotChart Report is a valuable tool for summarizing data and preparing charts. In Appendix 2.1, we show how it can be used to construct a bar chart for categorical data.

Exercises

Methods

1. The response to a question has three alternatives: A, B, and C. A sample of 120 responses provides 60 A, 24 B, and 36 C. Show the frequency and relative frequency distributions.

2.   A partial relative frequency distribution is given.

Class	Relative Frequency
A	.22
B	.18
C	.40
D	

a.   What is the relative frequency of class D?
b.   The total sample size is 200. What is the frequency of class D?
c.   Show the frequency distribution.
d.   Show the percent frequency distribution.

3.   A questionnaire provides 58 Yes, 42 No, and 20 no-opinion answers.
a.   In the construction of a pie chart, how many degrees would be in the section of the pie showing the Yes answers?
b.   How many degrees would be in the section of the pie showing the No answers?
c.   Construct a pie chart.
d.   Construct a bar chart.

Applications

BestTV

4.   The top four prime-time television shows were *Law & Order, CSI, Without a Trace,* and *Desperate Housewives* (Nielsen Media Research, January 1, 2007). Data indicating the preferred shows for a sample of 50 viewers follow.

DH	CSI	DH	CSI	L&O
Trace	CSI	L&O	Trace	CSI
CSI	DH	Trace	CSI	DH
L&O	L&O	L&O	CSI	DH
CSI	DH	DH	CSI	CSI
DH	Trace	CSI	Trace	DH
DH	CSI	CSI	L&O	CSI
L&O	CSI	Trace	Trace	DH
L&O	CSI	CSI	CSI	DH
CSI	DH	Trace	Trace	L&O

a.   Are these data categorical or quantitative?
b.   Provide frequency and percent frequency distributions.
c.   Construct a bar chart and a pie chart.
d.   On the basis of the sample, which television show has the largest viewing audience? Which one is second?

5.   In alphabetical order, the six most common last names in the United States are Brown, Davis, Johnson, Jones, Smith, and Williams (*The World Almanac,* 2006). Assume that a sample of 50 individuals with one of these last names provided the following data.

Names

Brown	Williams	Williams	Williams	Brown
Smith	Jones	Smith	Johnson	Smith
Davis	Smith	Brown	Williams	Johnson
Johnson	Smith	Smith	Johnson	Brown
Williams	Davis	Johnson	Williams	Johnson
Williams	Johnson	Jones	Smith	Brown
Johnson	Smith	Smith	Brown	Jones
Jones	Jones	Smith	Smith	Davis
Davis	Jones	Williams	Davis	Smith
Jones	Johnson	Brown	Johnson	Davis

Summarize the data by constructing the following:

a.   Relative and percent frequency distributions

b.   A bar chart

c.   A pie chart

d.   Based on these data, what are the three most common last names?

6.   The Nielsen Media Research television rating measures the percentage of television owners who are watching a particular television program. The highest-rated television program
in television history was the *M*A*S*H Last Episode Special* shown on February 28, 1983.
A 60.2 rating indicated that 60.2% of all television owners were watching this program.
Nielsen Media Research provided the list of the 50 top-rated single shows in television
history (*The New York Times Almanac,* 2006). The following data show the television
network that produced each of these 50 top-rated shows.

Networks

ABC	ABC	ABC	NBC	CBS
ABC	CBS	ABC	ABC	NBC
NBC	NBC	CBS	ABC	NBC
CBS	ABC	CBS	NBC	ABC
CBS	NBC	NBC	CBS	NBC
CBS	CBS	CBS	NBC	NBC
FOX	CBS	CBS	ABC	NBC
ABC	ABC	CBS	NBC	NBC
NBC	CBS	NBC	CBS	CBS
ABC	CBS	ABC	NBC	ABC

a.   Construct a frequency distribution, percent frequency distribution, and bar chart for
the data.

b.   Which network or networks have done the best in terms of presenting top-rated television shows? Compare the performance of ABC, CBS, and NBC.

7.   Leverock's Waterfront Steakhouse in Maderia Beach, Florida, uses a questionnaire to ask
customers how they rate the server, food quality, cocktails, prices, and atmosphere at the
restaurant. Each characteristic is rated on a scale of outstanding (O), very good (V), good (G),
average (A), and poor (P). Use descriptive statistics to summarize the following data collected on food quality. What is your feeling about the food quality ratings at the restaurant?

G	O	V	G	A	O	V	O	V	G	O	V	A
V	O	P	V	O	G	A	O	O	O	G	O	V
V	A	G	O	V	P	V	O	O	G	O	O	V
O	G	A	O	V	O	O	G	V	A	G		

8.   Data for a sample of 55 members of the Baseball Hall of Fame in Cooperstown, New York,
are shown here. Each observation indicates the primary position played by the Hall of
Famers: pitcher (P), catcher (H), 1st base (1), 2nd base (2), 3rd base (3), shortstop (S), left
field (L), center field (C), and right field (R).

L	P	C	H	2	P	R	1	S	S	1	L	P	R	P
P	P	P	R	C	S	L	R	P	C	C	P	P	R	P
2	3	P	H	L	P	1	C	P	P	P	S	1	L	R
R	1	2	H	S	3	H	2	L	P					

a.   Use frequency and relative frequency distributions to summarize the data.

b.   What position provides the most Hall of Famers?

c.   What position provides the fewest Hall of Famers?

d.   What outfield position (L, C, or R) provides the most Hall of Famers?

e.   Compare infielders (1, 2, 3, and S) to outfielders (L, C, and R).

9.   About 60% of small and medium-sized businesses are family-owned. A TEC International
Inc. survey asked the chief executive officers (CEOs) of family-owned businesses how
they became the CEO (*The Wall Street Journal,* December 16, 2003). Responses were that
the CEO inherited the business, the CEO built the business, or the CEO was hired by the

family-owned firm. A sample of 26 CEOs of family-owned businesses provided the following data on how each became the CEO.

CEOs

Built	Built	Built	Inherited
Inherited	Built	Inherited	Built
Inherited	Built	Built	Built
Built	Hired	Hired	Hired
Inherited	Inherited	Inherited	Built
Built	Built	Built	Hired
Built	Inherited		

a. Provide a frequency distribution.
b. Provide a percent frequency distribution.
c. Construct a bar chart.
d. What percentage of CEOs of family-owned businesses became the CEO because they inherited the business? What is the primary reason a person becomes the CEO of a family-owned business?

10. The *Financial Times*/Harris Poll is a monthly online poll of adults from six countries in Europe and the United States. The *FT*/Harris Poll conducted between January 10, 2008, and January 21, 2008, included 1015 adults (aged 18–64) in the United States. One of the questions asked was, "How would you rate the Federal Bank in handling the credit problems in the financial markets?" Possible responses were Excellent, Good, Fair, Bad, and Terrible (*http://www.harrisinteractive.com*). The 1015 responses for this question can be found on the website that accompanies the text in the file named FedBank.

WEB file

FedBank

a. Construct a frequency distribution.
b. Construct a percent frequency distribution.
c. Construct a bar chart for the percent frequency distribution.
d. Comment on how adults in the United States think the Federal Bank is doing in handling the credit problems in the financial markets.
e. In Spain, 1114 adults were asked, "How would you rate the European Central Bank in handling the credit problems in the financial markets." The percent frequency distribution obtained follows:

Rating	Percent Frequency
Excellent	0
Good	4
Fair	46
Bad	40
Terrible	10

Compare the results obtained in Spain with the results obtained in the United States.

2.2 Summarizing Quantitative Data

Frequency Distribution

TABLE 2.4

YEAR-END AUDIT TIMES (IN DAYS)

12	14	19	18
15	15	18	17
20	27	22	23
22	21	33	28
14	18	16	13

As defined in Section 2.1, a frequency distribution is a tabular summary of data showing the number (frequency) of items in each of several nonoverlapping classes. This definition holds for quantitative as well as categorical data. However, with quantitative data we must be more careful in defining the nonoverlapping classes to be used in the frequency distribution.

For example, consider the quantitative data in Table 2.4. These data show the time in days required to complete year-end audits for a sample of 20 clients of Sanderson and

Clifford, a small public accounting firm. The three steps necessary to define the classes for a frequency distribution with quantitative data are

1. Determine the number of nonoverlapping classes.
2. Determine the width of each class.
3. Determine the class limits.

Audit

Let us demonstrate these steps by developing a frequency distribution for the audit time data in Table 2.4.

Number of classes   Classes are formed by specifying ranges that will be used to group the data. As a general guideline, we recommend using between 5 and 20 classes. For a small number of data items, as few as five or six classes may be used to summarize the data. For a larger number of data items, a larger number of classes is usually required. The goal is to use enough classes to show the variation in the data, but not so many classes that some contain only a few data items. Because the number of data items in Table 2.4 is relatively small ($n = 20$), we chose to develop a frequency distribution with five classes.

Making the classes the same width reduces the chance of inappropriate interpretations by the user.

Width of the classes   The second step in constructing a frequency distribution for quantitative data is to choose a width for the classes. As a general guideline, we recommend that the width be the same for each class. Thus the choices of the number of classes and the width of classes are not independent decisions. A larger number of classes means a smaller class width, and vice versa. To determine an approximate class width, we begin by identifying the largest and smallest data values. Then, with the desired number of classes specified, we can use the following expression to determine the approximate class width.

$$\text{Approximate class width} = \frac{\text{Largest data value } - \text{ Smallest data value}}{\text{Number of classes}} \quad \textbf{(2.2)}$$

The approximate class width given by equation (2.2) can be rounded to a more convenient value based on the preference of the person developing the frequency distribution. For example, an approximate class width of 9.28 might be rounded to 10 simply because 10 is a more convenient class width to use in presenting a frequency distribution.

For the data involving the year-end audit times, the largest data value is 33 and the smallest data value is 12. Because we decided to summarize the data with five classes, using equation (2.2) provides an approximate class width of $(33 - 12)/5 = 4.2$. We therefore decided to round up and use a class width of five days in the frequency distribution.

No single frequency distribution is best for a data set. Different people may construct different, but equally acceptable, frequency distributions. The goal is to reveal the natural grouping and variation in the data.

In practice, the number of classes and the appropriate class width are determined by trial and error. Once a possible number of classes is chosen, equation (2.2) is used to find the approximate class width. The process can be repeated for a different number of classes. Ultimately, the analyst uses judgment to determine the combination of the number of classes and class width that provides the best frequency distribution for summarizing the data.

For the audit time data in Table 2.4, after deciding to use five classes, each with a width of five days, the next task is to specify the class limits for each of the classes.

Class limits   Class limits must be chosen so that each data item belongs to one and only one class. The *lower class limit* identifies the smallest possible data value assigned to the class. The *upper class limit* identifies the largest possible data value assigned to the class. In developing frequency distributions for categorical data, we did not need to specify class limits because each data item naturally fell into a separate class. But with quantitative data, such as the audit times in Table 2.4, class limits are necessary to determine where each data value belongs.

Using the audit time data in Table 2.4, we selected 10 days as the lower class limit and 14 days as the upper class limit for the first class. This class is denoted 10–14 in Table 2.5. The smallest data value, 12, is included in the 10–14 class. We then selected 15 days as the lower class limit and 19 days as the upper class limit of the next class. We continued defining the lower and upper class limits to obtain a total of five classes: 10–14, 15–19, 20–24, 25–29, and 30–34. The largest data value, 33, is included in the 30–34 class. The difference between the lower class limits of adjacent classes is the class width. Using the first two lower class limits of 10 and 15, we see that the class width is $15 - 10 = 5$.

With the number of classes, class width, and class limits determined, a frequency distribution can be obtained by counting the number of data values belonging to each class. For example, the data in Table 2.4 show that four values—12, 14, 14, and 13—belong to the 10–14 class. Thus, the frequency for the 10–14 class is 4. Continuing this counting process for the 15–19, 20–24, 25–29, and 30–34 classes provides the frequency distribution in Table 2.5. Using this frequency distribution, we can observe the following:

1. The most frequently occurring audit times are in the class of 15–19 days. Eight of the 20 audit times belong to this class.
2. Only one audit required 30 or more days.

Other conclusions are possible, depending on the interests of the person viewing the frequency distribution. The value of a frequency distribution is that it provides insights about the data that are not easily obtained by viewing the data in their original unorganized form.

Class midpoint In some applications, we want to know the midpoints of the classes in a frequency distribution for quantitative data. The **class midpoint** is the value halfway between the lower and upper class limits. For the audit time data, the five class midpoints are 12, 17, 22, 27, and 32.

TABLE 2.5

FREQUENCY DISTRIBUTION FOR THE AUDIT TIME DATA

Audit Time (days)	Frequency
10–14	4
15–19	8
20–24	5
25–29	2
30–34	1
Total	20

Using Excel's PivotTable Report to Construct a Frequency Distribution

Excel's FREQUENCY function can also be used to construct a frequency distribution for quantitative data.

Excel's PivotTable report is a powerful tool for summarizing data. In this section we show how to use Excel's PivotTable report to construct a frequency distribution for quantitative data by showing how to construct a frequency distribution for the audit time data.

Enter Data: The label "Audit Time" and the 20 audit times are entered into cells A1:A21 of the Excel worksheet in Figure 2.6.

Enter Functions and Formulas: No functions and formulas are needed.

Apply Tools: The following steps describe how to use Excel's PivotTable report to construct a frequency distribution for the audit time data. When using Excel's PivotTable report, each column of data is referred to as a field. Thus, for the audit time example, the data appearing in cells A2:A21 and the corresponding label in cell A1 are referred to as the Audit Time field.

Step 1. Click the **Insert** tab on the Ribbon
Step 2. In the **Tables** group, click the icon above the word PivotTable
Step 3. When the **Create PivotTable** dialog box appears,
    Choose **Select a table or range**
    Enter A1:A21 in the **Table/Range** box
    Choose **Existing Worksheet** as the location for the PivotTable
    Enter C1 in the **Location** box
    Click **OK**

FIGURE 2.6   PIVOTTABLE FIELD LIST AND INITIAL PIVOTTABLE REPORT USED TO CONSTRUCT
A FREQUENCY DISTRIBUTION FOR THE AUDIT TIME DATA

	A	B	C	D	E	F	G	H	I	J
1	Audit Time		Row Labels ▾	Count of Audit Time						
2	12		12	1						
3	15		13	1						
4	20		14	2						
5	22		15	2						
6	14		16	1						
7	14		17	1						
8	15		18	3						
9	27		19	1						
10	21		20	1						
11	18		21	1						
12	19		22	2						
13	18		23	1						
14	22		27	1						
15	33		28	1						
16	16		33	1						
17	18		Grand Total	20						
18	17									
19	23									
20	28									
21	13									
22										

Step 4. In the **PivotTable Field List,** go to **Choose Fields to add to report,**
   Drag the **Audit Time** field to the **Row Labels** area
   Drag the **Audit Time** field to the **Values** area
Step 5. Click on **Sum of Audit Time** in the **Values** area
Step 6. Click **Value Field Settings** from the list of options that appears
Step 7. When the Value Field Settings dialog appears,
   Under **Summarize value field by,** choose **Count**
   Click **OK**

Figure 2.6 shows the resulting PivotTable Field List and the corresponding PivotTable report. To construct the frequency distribution for the audit time data we must group the rows containing audit times. The following steps accomplish this.

Step 1. Right-click cell C2 in the PivotTable report or any other cell containing an audit time
Step 2. Choose **Group** from the list of options that appears
Step 3. When the **Grouping** dialog box appears,
   Enter 10 in the **Starting at** box
   Enter 34 in the **Ending at** box
   Enter 5 in the **By** box
   Click **OK**

Figure 2.7 shows the completed PivotTable Field List and PivotTable report. We see that with the exception of the column headings, the PivotTable report provides the same information as the frequency distribution shown in Table 2.5. And, if desired, we can change the labels to match the labels in Table 2.5 by selecting the cell and typing in the new label.

FIGURE 2.7 FREQUENCY DISTRIBUTION FOR THE AUDIT TIME DATA CONSTRUCTED USING EXCEL'S PIVOTTABLE REPORT

	A	B	C	D	E	F	G	H	I	J
1	Audit Time		Row Labels ▾	Count of Audit Time						
2	12		10-14	4						
3	15		15-19	8		PivotTable Field List			▾ ×	
4	20		20-24	5		Choose fields to add to report:			⬚ ▾	
5	22		25-29	2		☑ Audit Time				
6	14		30-34	1						
7	14		Grand Total	20						
8	15					Drag fields between areas below:				
9	27					▼ Report Filter		▦ Column Labels		
10	21									
11	18					▦ Row Labels		Σ Values		
12	19					Audit Time ▾		Count of Audit Time ▾		
13	18					☐ Defer Layout Update		Update		
14	22									
15	33									
16	16									
17	18									
18	17									
19	23									
20	28									
21	13									
22										

Relative Frequency and Percent Frequency Distributions

We define the relative frequency and percent frequency distributions for quantitative data in the same manner as for categorical data. First, recall that the relative frequency is the proportion of the observations belonging to a class. With n observations,

$$\text{Relative frequency of class} = \frac{\text{Frequency of the class}}{n}$$

The percent frequency of a class is the relative frequency multiplied by 100.

Based on the class frequencies in Table 2.5 and with $n = 20$, Table 2.6 shows the relative frequency distribution and percent frequency distribution for the audit time data. Note that .40 of the audits, or 40%, required from 15 to 19 days. Only .05 of the audits, or 5%,

TABLE 2.6 RELATIVE FREQUENCY AND PERCENT FREQUENCY DISTRIBUTIONS FOR THE AUDIT TIME DATA

Audit Time (days)	Relative Frequency	Percent Frequency
10–14	.20	20
15–19	.40	40
20–24	.25	25
25–29	.10	10
30–34	.05	5
Total	1.00	100

FIGURE 2.8   DOT PLOT FOR THE AUDIT TIME DATA

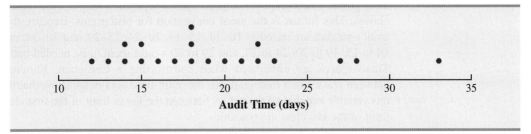

required 30 or more days. Again, additional interpretations and insights can be obtained by using Table 2.6.

Dot Plot

One of the simplest graphical summaries of data is a **dot plot**. A horizontal axis shows the range for the data. Each data value is represented by a dot placed above the axis. Figure 2.8 is the dot plot for the audit time data in Table 2.4. The three dots located above 18 on the horizontal axis indicate that an audit time of 18 days occurred three times. Dot plots show the details of the data and are useful for comparing the distribution of the data for two or more variables.

Histogram

A common graphical presentation of quantitative data is a **histogram**. This graphical summary can be prepared for data previously summarized in either a frequency, relative frequency, or percent frequency distribution. A histogram is constructed by placing the variable of interest on the horizontal axis and the frequency, relative frequency, or percent frequency on the vertical axis. The frequency, relative frequency, or percent frequency of each class is shown by drawing a rectangle whose base is determined by the class limits on the horizontal axis and whose height is the corresponding frequency, relative frequency, or percent frequency.

Figure 2.9 is a histogram for the audit time data. Note that the class with the greatest frequency is shown by the rectangle appearing above the class of 15–19 days. The height of the rectangle shows that the frequency of this class is 8. A histogram for the relative or percent frequency distribution of these data would look the same as the histogram in Figure 2.9 with the exception that the vertical axis would be labeled with relative or percent frequency values.

FIGURE 2.9   HISTOGRAM FOR THE AUDIT TIME DATA

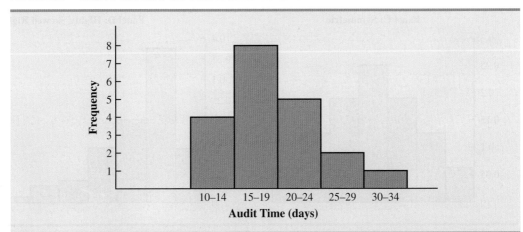

As Figure 2.9 shows, the adjacent rectangles of a histogram touch one another. Unlike a bar graph, a histogram contains no natural separation between the rectangles of adjacent classes. This format is the usual convention for histograms. Because the classes for the audit time data are stated as 10–14, 15–19, 20–24, 25–29, and 30–34, one-unit spaces of 14 to 15, 19 to 20, 24 to 25, and 29 to 30 would seem to be needed between the classes. These spaces are eliminated when constructing a histogram. Eliminating the spaces between classes in a histogram for the audit time data helps show that time is a continuous variable and that all the values between the lower limit of the first class and the upper limit of the last class are possible.

One of the most important uses of a histogram is to provide information about the shape, or form, of a distribution. Figure 2.10 contains four histograms constructed from relative frequency distributions. Panel A shows the histogram for a set of data moderately skewed to the left. A histogram is said to be skewed to the left if its tail extends farther to the left. This histogram is typical for exam scores, with no scores above 100%, most of the scores above 70%, and only a few really low scores. Panel B shows the histogram for a set of data moderately skewed to the right. A histogram is said to be skewed to the right if its tail extends farther to the right. An example of this type of histogram would be for data such as housing prices; a few expensive houses create the skewness in the right tail.

Panel C shows a symmetric histogram. In a symmetric histogram, the left tail mirrors the shape of the right tail. Histograms for data found in applications are never perfectly symmetric, but the histogram for many applications may be roughly symmetric. Data for SAT

FIGURE 2.10   HISTOGRAMS SHOWING DIFFERING LEVELS OF SKEWNESS

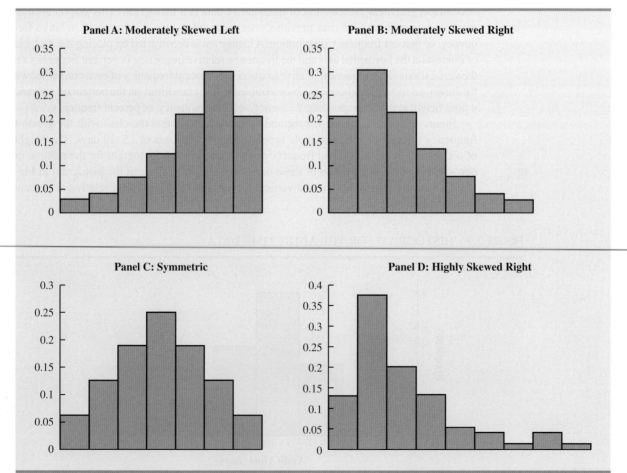

scores, heights and weights of people, and so on lead to histograms that are roughly symmetric. Panel D shows a histogram highly skewed to the right. This histogram was constructed from data on the amount of customer purchases over one day at a women's apparel store. Data from applications in business and economics often lead to histograms that are skewed to the right. For instance, data on housing prices, salaries, purchase amounts, and so on often result in histograms skewed to the right.

Using Excel's PivotChart Report to Construct a Frequency Distribution and a Histogram

We showed how Excel's PivotTable report can be used to construct a frequency distribution for quantitative data. Excel's PivotChart report can be used to develop both a frequency distribution and a histogram at the same time. We will illustrate the use of the PivotChart report using the audit time data in Table 2.4. Refer to Figure 2.11 as we describe the tasks involved.

Enter Data: The label "Audit Time" and the 20 audit times are entered into cells A1:A21 of an Excel worksheet.

Enter Functions and Formulas: No functions and formulas are needed.

Apply Tools: The following steps describe how to use Excel's PivotChart report to construct a frequency distribution and a histogram for the audit time data.

Step 1. Click the **Insert** tab on the Ribbon
Step 2. In the **Tables** group, click the word **PivotTable**
Step 3. Choose **PivotChart** from the options that appear

FIGURE 2.11 USING EXCEL'S PIVOTCHART REPORT TO CONSTRUCT A FREQUENCY DISTRIBUTION AND HISTOGRAM FOR THE AUDIT TIME DATA

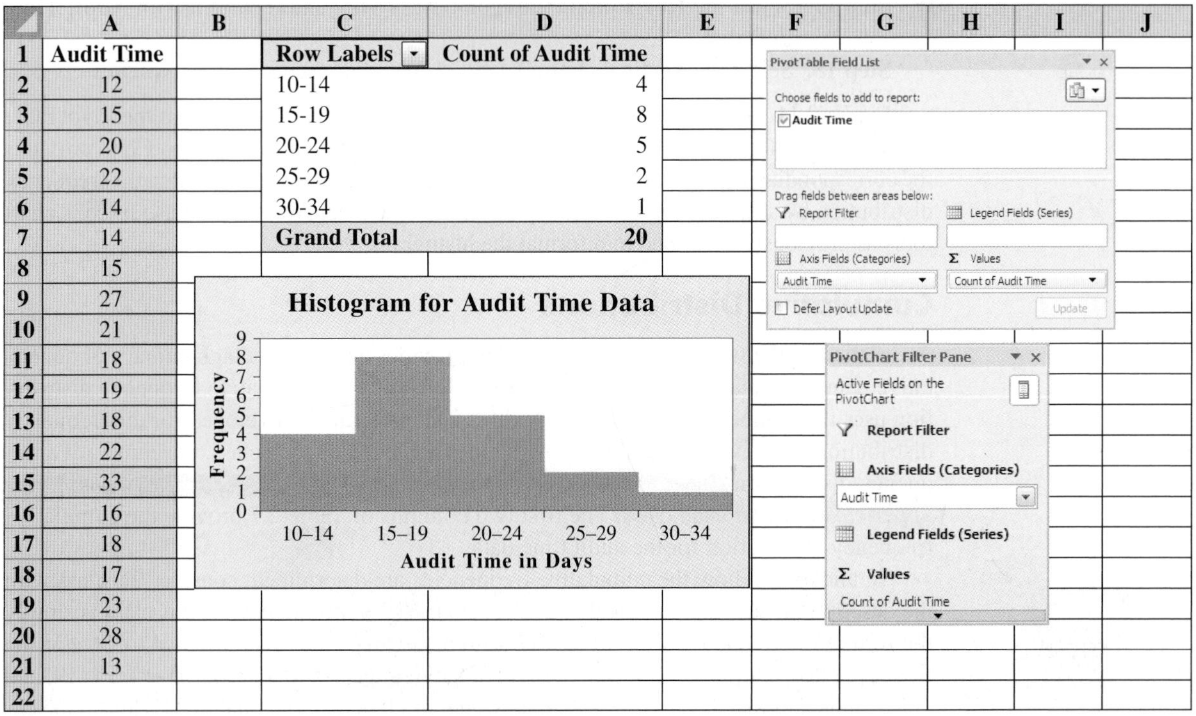

Step 4. When the **Create PivotTable with PivotChart** dialog box appears,

Choose **Select a table or range**

Enter A1:A21 in the **Table/Range** box

Choose **Existing Worksheet** as the location for the PivotTable and PivotChart

Enter C1 in the **Location** box

Click **OK**

Step 5. In the **PivotTable Field List,** go to **Choose Fields to add to report**

Drag the **Audit Time** field to the **Axis Fields (Categories)** area

Drag the **Audit Time** field to the **Values** area

Step 6. Click **Sum of Audit Time** in the **Values** area

Step 7. Click **Value Field Settings** from the list of options that appears

Step 8. When the Value Field Settings dialog appears,

Under **Summarize value field by,** choose **Count**

Click **OK**

Step 9. Right-click cell C2 in the PivotTable report or any other cell containing an audit time

Step 10. Choose **Group** from the list of options that appears

Step 11. When the **Grouping** dialog box appears,

Enter 10 in the **Starting at** box

Enter 34 in the **Ending at** box

Enter 5 in the **By** box

Click **OK** (a PivotChart will appear)

Step 12. Click inside the resulting PivotChart

Step 13. Click the **Design** tab on the Ribbon

Step 14. In the **Chart Layouts** group, click the **More** button (the downward pointing arrow with a line over it) to display all the options

Step 15. Choose **Layout 8**

Step 16. Select the **Chart Title** and replace it with **Histogram for Audit Time Data**

Step 17. Select the **Horizontal (Category) Axis Title** and replace it with **Audit Time in Days**

Step 18. Select the **Vertical (Value) Axis Title** and replace it with **Frequency**

Figure 2.11 shows the resulting PivotTable and PivotChart. We see that the PivotTable report provides the frequency distribution for the audit time data and the PivotChart provides the corresponding histogram. If desired, we can change the labels in any cell in the frequency distribution by selecting the cell and typing in the new label. We can also use Excel's chart tools as previously described to reformat the histogram.

Cumulative Distributions

A variation of the frequency distribution that provides another tabular summary of quantitative data is the **cumulative frequency distribution**. The cumulative frequency distribution uses the number of classes, class widths, and class limits developed for the frequency distribution. However, rather than showing the frequency of each class, the cumulative frequency distribution shows the number of data items with values *less than or equal to the upper class limit* of each class. The first two columns of Table 2.7 provide the cumulative frequency distribution for the audit time data.

To understand how the cumulative frequencies are determined, consider the class with the description "less than or equal to 24." The cumulative frequency for this class is simply the sum of the frequencies for all classes with data values less than or equal to 24. For the frequency distribution in Table 2.5, the sum of the frequencies for classes 10–14, 15–19, and 20–24 indicates that $4 + 8 + 5 = 17$ data values are less than or equal to 24. Hence, the cumulative frequency for this class is 17. In addition, the cumulative frequency distribution in

TABLE 2.7   CUMULATIVE FREQUENCY, CUMULATIVE RELATIVE FREQUENCY,
AND CUMULATIVE PERCENT FREQUENCY DISTRIBUTIONS
FOR THE AUDIT TIME DATA

Audit Time (days)	Cumulative Frequency	Cumulative Relative Frequency	Cumulative Percent Frequency
Less than or equal to 14	4	.20	20
Less than or equal to 19	12	.60	60
Less than or equal to 24	17	.85	85
Less than or equal to 29	19	.95	95
Less than or equal to 34	20	1.00	100

Table 2.7 shows that four audits were completed in 14 days or less and 19 audits were completed in 29 days or less.

As a final point, we note that a **cumulative relative frequency distribution** shows the proportion of data items, and a **cumulative percent frequency distribution** shows the percentage of data items with values less than or equal to the upper limit of each class. The cumulative relative frequency distribution can be computed either by summing the relative frequencies in the relative frequency distribution or by dividing the cumulative frequencies by the total number of items. Using the latter approach, we found the cumulative relative frequencies in column 3 of Table 2.7 by dividing the cumulative frequencies in column 2 by the total number of items ($n = 20$). The cumulative percent frequencies were again computed by multiplying the relative frequencies by 100. The cumulative relative and percent frequency distributions show that .85 of the audits, or 85%, were completed in 24 days or less, .95 of the audits, or 95%, were completed in 29 days or less, and so on.

Ogive

A graph of a cumulative distribution, called an **ogive**, shows data values on the horizontal axis and either the cumulative frequencies, the cumulative relative frequencies, or the cumulative percent frequencies on the vertical axis. Figure 2.12 illustrates an ogive for the cumulative frequencies of the audit time data in Table 2.7.

FIGURE 2.12   OGIVE FOR THE AUDIT TIME DATA

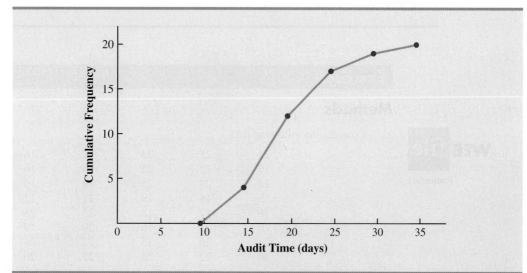

The ogive is constructed by plotting a point corresponding to the cumulative frequency of each class. Because the classes for the audit time data are 10–14, 15–19, 20–24, and so on, one-unit gaps appear from 14 to 15, 19 to 20, and so on. These gaps are eliminated by plotting points halfway between the class limits. Thus, 14.5 is used for the 10–14 class, 19.5 is used for the 15–19 class, and so on. The "less than or equal to 14" class with a cumulative frequency of 4 is shown on the ogive in Figure 2.12 by the point located at 14.5 on the horizontal axis and 4 on the vertical axis. The "less than or equal to 19" class with a cumulative frequency of 12 is shown by the point located at 19.5 on the horizontal axis and 12 on the vertical axis. Note that one additional point is plotted at the left end of the ogive. This point starts the ogive by showing that no data values fall below the 10–14 class. It is plotted at 9.5 on the horizontal axis and 0 on the vertical axis. The plotted points are connected by straight lines to complete the ogive.

NOTES AND COMMENTS

1. A bar chart and a histogram are essentially the same thing; both are graphical presentations of the data in a frequency distribution. A histogram is just a bar chart with no separation between bars. For some discrete quantitative data, a separation between bars is also appropriate. Consider, for example, the number of classes in which a college student is enrolled. The data may only assume integer values. Intermediate values such as 1.5, 2.73, and so on are not possible. With continuous quantitative data, however, such as the audit times in Table 2.4, a separation between bars is not appropriate.

2. The appropriate values for the class limits with quantitative data depend on the level of accuracy of the data. For instance, with the audit time data of Table 2.4 the limits used were integer values. If the data were rounded to the nearest tenth of a day (e.g., 12.3, 14.4, and so on), then the limits would be stated in tenths of days. For instance, the first class would be 10.0–14.9. If the data were recorded to the nearest hundredth

of a day (e.g., 12.34, 14.45, and so on), the limits would be stated in hundredths of days. For instance, the first class would be 10.00–14.99.

3. An *open-end* class requires only a lower class limit or an upper class limit. For example, in the audit time data of Table 2.4, suppose two of the audits had taken 58 and 65 days. Rather than continue with the classes of width 5 with classes 35–39, 40–44, 45–49, and so on, we could simplify the frequency distribution to show an open-end class of "35 or more." This class would have a frequency of 2. Most often the open-end class appears at the upper end of the distribution. Sometimes an open-end class appears at the lower end of the distribution, and occasionally such classes appear at both ends.

4. The last entry in a cumulative frequency distribution always equals the total number of observations. The last entry in a cumulative relative frequency distribution always equals 1.00 and the last entry in a cumulative percent frequency distribution always equals 100.

Exercises

Methods

Frequency

11. Consider the following data.

14	21	23	21	16
19	22	25	16	16
24	24	25	19	16
19	18	19	21	12
16	17	18	23	25
20	23	16	20	19
24	26	15	22	24
20	22	24	22	20

a.   Develop a frequency distribution using classes of 12–14, 15–17, 18–20, 21–23, and 24–26.
b.   Develop a relative frequency distribution and a percent frequency distribution using the classes in part (a).

12.   Consider the following frequency distribution.

Class	Frequency
10–19	10
20–29	14
30–39	17
40–49	7
50–59	2

Construct a cumulative frequency distribution and a cumulative relative frequency distribution.

13.   Construct a histogram and an ogive for the data in exercise 12.

14.   Consider the following data.

8.9	10.2	11.5	7.8	10.0	12.2	13.5	14.1	10.0	12.2
6.8	9.5	11.5	11.2	14.9	7.5	10.0	6.0	15.8	11.5

a.   Construct a dot plot.
b.   Construct a frequency distribution.
c.   Construct a percent frequency distribution.

Applications

15.   A doctor's office staff studied the waiting times for patients who arrive at the office with a request for emergency service. The following data with waiting times in minutes were collected over a one-month period.

2	5	10	12	4	4	5	17	11	8	9	8	12	21	6	8	7	13	18	3

Use classes of 0–4, 5–9, and so on in the following:
a.   Show the frequency distribution.
b.   Show the relative frequency distribution.
c.   Show the cumulative frequency distribution.
d.   Show the cumulative relative frequency distribution.
e.   What proportion of patients needing emergency service wait 9 minutes or less?

16.   A shortage of candidates has required school districts to pay higher salaries and offer extras to attract and retain school district superintendents. The following data show the annual base salary ($1000s) for superintendents in 20 districts in the greater Rochester, New York, area (*The Rochester Democrat and Chronicle,* February 10, 2008).

187	184	174	185
175	172	202	197
165	208	215	164
162	172	182	156
172	175	170	183

Use classes of 150–159, 160–169, and so on in the following.
a.   Show the frequency distribution.
b.   Show the percent frequency distribution.
c.   Show the cumulative percent frequency distribution.
d.   Develop a histogram for the annual base salary.
e.   Do the data appear to be skewed? Explain.
f.   What percentage of the superintendents make more than $200,000?

17. What is the typical price for a share of stock for the 30 Dow Jones Industrial Average companies? The following data show the price for a share of stock to the nearest dollar in January 2006 (*The Wall Street Journal,* January 16, 2006).

PriceShare

Company	$/Share	Company	$/Share
AIG	70	Home Depot	42
Alcoa	29	Honeywell	37
Altria Group	76	IBM	83
American Express	53	Intel	26
AT&T	25	Johnson & Johnson	62
Boeing	69	JPMorgan Chase	40
Caterpillar	62	McDonald's	35
Citigroup	49	Merck	33
Coca-Cola	41	Microsoft	27
Disney	26	3M	78
DuPont	40	Pfizer	25
ExxonMobil	61	Procter & Gamble	59
General Electric	35	United Technologies	56
General Motors	20	Verizon	32
Hewlett-Packard	32	Wal-Mart	45

a. Prepare a frequency distribution of the data.
b. Prepare a histogram of the data. Interpret the histogram, including a discussion of the general shape of the histogram, the mid-price per share range, the most frequent price per share range, and the high and low extreme prices per share.
c. What are the highest-priced and the lowest-priced stocks?
d. Use *The Wall Street Journal* to find the current price per share for these companies. Prepare a histogram of the data and discuss any changes since January 2006.

18. NRF/BIG research provided results of a consumer holiday spending survey (*USA Today,* December 20, 2005). The following data provide the dollar amount of holiday spending for a sample of 25 consumers.

WEB file
Holiday

1200	850	740	590	340
450	890	260	610	350
1780	180	850	2050	770
800	1090	510	520	220
1450	280	1120	200	350

a. What is the lowest holiday spending? The highest?
b. Use a class width of $250 to prepare a frequency distribution and a percent frequency distribution for the data.
c. Prepare a histogram and comment on the shape of the distribution.
d. What observations can you make about holiday spending?

19. Sorting through unsolicited e-mail and spam affects the productivity of office workers. An InsightExpress survey monitored office workers to determine the unproductive time per day devoted to unsolicited e-mail and spam (*USA Today,* November 13, 2003). The following data show a sample of time in minutes devoted to this task.

2	4	8	4
8	1	2	32
12	1	5	7
5	5	3	4
24	19	4	14

Using classes of 1–5, 6–10, 11–15, and so on, summarize the data by constructing the following:

a. A frequency distribution
b. A relative frequency distribution
c. A cumulative frequency distribution
d. A cumulative relative frequency distribution
e. An ogive
f. What percentage of office workers spend 5 minutes or less on unsolicited e-mail and spam? What percentage of office workers spend more than 10 minutes a day on this task?

20. The *Golf Digest 50* lists the 50 golfers with the highest total income. Total income is the sum of on-course income and off-course income, and the minimum needed to qualify for this year's list was $4 million. Tiger Woods was ranked first, with on-course earnings of more than $22 million and off-course earnings of almost $100 million. The 10 golfers with the highest off-course earnings are shown below.

Name	Off-Course Income ($1000s)
Tiger Woods	99,800
Phil Mickelson	40,200
Arnold Palmer	29,500
Vijay Singh	25,250
Ernie Els	24,500
Greg Norman	24,000
Jack Nicklaus	20,750
Sergio Garcia	14,500
Michelle Wie	12,500
Jim Furyk	11,000

WEB file
GolfIncome

The off-course earnings for the other 40 golfers in the *Golf Digest 50*, ranging from $10,550.000 for Padraig Harrington to $1,350,000 for Stephen Ames, can be found on the website that accompanies the text in the file named GolfIncome. Use classes of 1300–3299, 3300–5299, and so on, to answer the following questions.

a. Construct a frequency distribution and a percent frequency distribution.
b. For all the golfers who were ranked 11–50 in terms of off-course income, what percentage of golfers earned less than $5,300,000?
c. Construct a histogram.
d. Comment on the shape of the distribution.
e. Considering all golfers in the *Golf Digest 50*, what percentage earned less than $5,300,000?

21. The *Nielsen Home Technology Report* provided information about home technology and its usage. The following data are the hours of personal computer usage during one week for a sample of 50 persons.

WEB file
Computer

4.1	1.5	10.4	5.9	3.4	5.7	1.6	6.1	3.0	3.7
3.1	4.8	2.0	14.8	5.4	4.2	3.9	4.1	11.1	3.5
4.1	4.1	8.8	5.6	4.3	3.3	7.1	10.3	6.2	7.6
10.8	2.8	9.5	12.9	12.1	0.7	4.0	9.2	4.4	5.7
7.2	6.1	5.7	5.9	4.7	3.9	3.7	3.1	6.1	3.1

Summarize the data by constructing the following:

a. A frequency distribution (use a class width of three hours)
b. A relative frequency distribution

    c. A histogram
    d. An ogive
    e. Comment on what the data indicate about personal computer usage at home.

2.3 Exploratory Data Analysis: Stem-and-Leaf Display

The techniques of **exploratory data analysis** consist of simple arithmetic and easy-to-draw graphs that can be used to summarize data quickly. One technique—referred to as a **stem-and-leaf display**—can be used to show both the rank order and shape of a data set simultaneously.

To illustrate the use of a stem-and-leaf display, consider the data in Table 2.8. These data result from a 150-question aptitude test given to 50 individuals recently interviewed for a position at Haskens Manufacturing. The data indicate the number of questions answered correctly.

To develop a stem-and-leaf display, we first arrange the leading digits of each data value to the left of a vertical line. To the right of the vertical line, we record the last digit for each data value. Based on the top row of data in Table 2.8 (112, 72, 69, 97, and 107), the first five entries in constructing a stem-and-leaf display would be as follows:

```
 6 | 9
 7 | 2
 8 |
 9 | 7
10 | 7
11 | 2
12 |
13 |
14 |
```

For example, the data value 112 shows the leading digits 11 to the left of the line and the last digit 2 to the right of the line. Similarly, the data value 72 shows the leading digit 7 to the left of the line and last digit 2 to the right of the line. Continuing to place the last

TABLE 2.8 NUMBER OF QUESTIONS ANSWERED CORRECTLY ON AN APTITUDE TEST

WEB file

ApTest

112	72	69	97	107
73	92	76	86	73
126	128	118	127	124
82	104	132	134	83
92	108	96	100	92
115	76	91	102	81
95	141	81	80	106
84	119	113	98	75
68	98	115	106	95
100	85	94	106	119

digit of each data value on the line corresponding to its leading digit(s) provides the following:

```
 6 | 9  8
 7 | 2  3  6  3  6  5
 8 | 6  2  3  1  1  0  4  5
 9 | 7  2  2  6  2  1  5  8  8  5  4
10 | 7  4  8  0  2  6  6  0  6
11 | 2  8  5  9  3  5  9
12 | 6  8  7  4
13 | 2  4
14 | 1
```

   With this organization of the data, sorting the digits on each line into rank order is simple. Doing so provides the stem-and-leaf display shown here.

```
 6 | 8  9
 7 | 2  3  3  5  6  6
 8 | 0  1  1  2  3  4  5  6
 9 | 1  2  2  2  4  5  5  6  7  8  8
10 | 0  0  2  4  6  6  6  7  8
11 | 2  3  5  5  8  9  9
12 | 4  6  7  8
13 | 2  4
14 | 1
```

The numbers to the left of the vertical line (6, 7, 8, 9, 10, 11, 12, 13, and 14) form the *stem,* and each digit to the right of the vertical line is a *leaf.* For example, consider the first row with a stem value of 6 and leaves of 8 and 9.

```
6 | 8  9
```

This row indicates that two data values have a first digit of 6. The leaves show that the data values are 68 and 69. Similarly, the second row

```
7 | 2  3  3  5  6  6
```

indicates that six data values have a first digit of 7. The leaves show that the data values are 72, 73, 73, 75, 76, and 76.

   To focus on the shape indicated by the stem-and-leaf display, let us use a rectangle to contain the leaves of each stem. Doing so, we obtain the following.

```
 6 | 8  9
 7 | 2  3  3  5  6  6
 8 | 0  1  1  2  3  4  5  6
 9 | 1  2  2  2  4  5  5  6  7  8  8
10 | 0  0  2  4  6  6  6  7  8
11 | 2  3  5  5  8  9  9
12 | 4  6  7  8
13 | 2  4
14 | 1
```

Rotating this page counterclockwise onto its side provides a picture of the data that is similar to a histogram with classes of 60–69, 70–79, 80–89, and so on.

Although the stem-and-leaf display may appear to offer the same information as a histogram, it has two primary advantages.

1. The stem-and-leaf display is easier to construct by hand.
2. Within a class interval, the stem-and-leaf display provides more information than the histogram because the stem-and-leaf shows the actual data.

Just as a frequency distribution or histogram has no absolute number of classes, neither does a stem-and-leaf display have an absolute number of rows or stems. If we believe that our original stem-and-leaf display condensed the data too much, we can easily stretch the display by using two or more stems for each leading digit. For example, to use two stems for each leading digit, we would place all data values ending in 0, 1, 2, 3, and 4 in one row and all values ending in 5, 6, 7, 8, and 9 in a second row. The following stretched stem-and-leaf display illustrates this approach.

In a stretched stem-and-leaf display, whenever a stem value is stated twice, the first value corresponds to leaf values of 0–4, and the second value corresponds to leaf values of 5–9.

```
 6 | 8  9
 7 | 2  3  3
 7 | 5  6  6
 8 | 0  1  1  2  3  4
 8 | 5  6
 9 | 1  2  2  2  4
 9 | 5  5  6  7  8  8
10 | 0  0  2  4
10 | 6  6  6  7  8
11 | 2  3
11 | 5  5  8  9  9
12 | 4
12 | 6  7  8
13 | 2  4
13 |
14 | 1
```

Note that values 72, 73, and 73 have leaves in the 0–4 range and are shown with the first stem value of 7. The values 75, 76, and 76 have leaves in the 5–9 range and are shown with the second stem value of 7. This stretched stem-and-leaf display is similar to a frequency distribution with intervals of 65–69, 70–74, 75–79, and so on.

The preceding example showed a stem-and-leaf display for data with as many as three digits. Stem-and-leaf displays for data with more than three digits are possible. For example, consider the following data on the number of hamburgers sold by a fast-food restaurant for each of 15 weeks.

1565	1852	1644	1766	1888	1912	2044	1812
1790	1679	2008	1852	1967	1954	1733	

A stem-and-leaf display of these data follows.

Leaf unit = 10

```
15 | 6
16 | 4  7
17 | 3  6  9
18 | 1  5  5  8
19 | 1  5  6
20 | 0  4
```

A single digit is used to define each leaf in a stem-and-leaf display. The leaf unit indicates how to multiply the stem-and-leaf numbers in order to approximate the original data. Leaf units may be 100, 10, 1, 0.1, and so on.

Note that a single digit is used to define each leaf and that only the first three digits of each data value have been used to construct the display. At the top of the display we have specified Leaf unit = 10. To illustrate how to interpret the values in the display, consider the first stem, 15, and its associated leaf, 6. Combining these numbers, we obtain 156. To reconstruct an approximation of the original data value, we must multiply this number by 10, the value of the *leaf unit*. Thus, 156 × 10 = 1560 is an approximation of the original data value used to construct the stem-and-leaf display. Although it is not possible to reconstruct the exact data value from this stem-and-leaf display, the convention of using a single digit for each leaf enables stem-and-leaf displays to be constructed for data having a large number of digits. For stem-and-leaf displays where the leaf unit is not shown, the leaf unit is assumed to equal 1.

Exercises

Methods

22. Construct a stem-and-leaf display for the following data.

| 70 | 72 | 75 | 64 | 58 | 83 | 80 | 82 |
| 76 | 75 | 68 | 65 | 57 | 78 | 85 | 72 |

23. Construct a stem-and-leaf display for the following data.

| 11.3 | 9.6 | 10.4 | 7.5 | 8.3 | 10.5 | 10.0 |
| 9.3 | 8.1 | 7.7 | 7.5 | 8.4 | 6.3 | 8.8 |

24. Construct a stem-and-leaf display for the following data. Use a leaf unit of 10.

| 1161 | 1206 | 1478 | 1300 | 1604 | 1725 | 1361 | 1422 |
| 1221 | 1378 | 1623 | 1426 | 1557 | 1730 | 1706 | 1689 |

Applications

25. A psychologist developed a new test of adult intelligence. The test was administered to 20 individuals, and the following data were obtained.

| 114 | 99 | 131 | 124 | 117 | 102 | 106 | 127 | 119 | 115 |
| 98 | 104 | 144 | 151 | 132 | 106 | 125 | 122 | 118 | 118 |

Construct a stem-and-leaf display for the data.

26. The American Association of Individual Investors conducts an annual survey of discount brokers. The following prices charged are from a sample of 24 discount brokers (*AAII Journal,* January 2003). The two types of trades are a broker-assisted trade of 100 shares at $50 per share and an online trade of 500 shares at $50 per share.

WEB file

Broker

Broker	Broker-Assisted 100 Shares at $50/Share	Online 500 Shares at $50/Share	Broker	Broker-Assisted 100 Shares at $50/Share	Online 500 Shares at $50/Share
Accutrade	30.00	29.95	Merrill Lynch Direct	50.00	29.95
Ameritrade	24.99	10.99	Muriel Siebert	45.00	14.95
Banc of America	54.00	24.95	NetVest	24.00	14.00
Brown & Co.	17.00	5.00	Recom Securities	35.00	12.95
Charles Schwab	55.00	29.95	Scottrade	17.00	7.00
CyberTrader	12.95	9.95	Sloan Securities	39.95	19.95
E*TRADE Securities	49.95	14.95	Strong Investments	55.00	24.95
First Discount	35.00	19.75	TD Waterhouse	45.00	17.95
Freedom Investments	25.00	15.00	T. Rowe Price	50.00	19.95
Harrisdirect	40.00	20.00	Vanguard	48.00	20.00
Investors National	39.00	62.50	Wall Street Discount	29.95	19.95
MB Trading	9.95	10.55	York Securities	40.00	36.00

a.   Round the trading prices to the nearest dollar and develop a stem-and-leaf display for 100 shares at $50 per share. Comment on what you learned about broker-assisted trading prices.

b.   Round the trading prices to the nearest dollar and develop a stretched stem-and-leaf display for 500 shares online at $50 per share. Comment on what you learned about online trading prices.

27.   Most major ski resorts offer family programs that provide ski and snowboarding instruction for children. The typical classes provide four to six hours on the snow with a certified instructor. The daily rate for a group lesson at 15 ski resorts follows (*The Wall Street Journal,* January 20, 2006).

Resort	Location	Daily Rate	Resort	Location	Daily Rate
Beaver Creek	Colorado	$137	Okemo	Vermont	$ 86
Deer Valley	Utah	115	Park City	Utah	145
Diamond Peak	California	95	Butternut	Massachusetts	75
Heavenly	California	145	Steamboat	Colorado	98
Hunter	New York	79	Stowe	Vermont	104
Mammoth	California	111	Sugar Bowl	California	100
Mount Sunapee	New Hampshire	96	Whistler-Blackcomb	British Columbia	104
Mount Bachelor	Oregon	83			

a.   Develop a stem-and-leaf display for the data.

b.   Interpret the stem-and-leaf display in terms of what it tells you about the daily rate for these ski and snowboarding instruction programs.

28.   The 2004 Naples, Florida, mini marathon (13.1 miles) had 1228 registrants (*Naples Daily News,* January 17, 2004). Competition was held in six age groups. The following data show the ages for a sample of 40 individuals who participated in the marathon.

Marathon

49	33	40	37	56
44	46	57	55	32
50	52	43	64	40
46	24	30	37	43
31	43	50	36	61
27	44	35	31	43
52	43	66	31	50
72	26	59	21	47

a.   Show a stretched stem-and-leaf display.

b.   What age group had the largest number of runners?

c.   What age occurred most frequently?

d.   A *Naples Daily News* feature article emphasized the number of runners who were "20-something." What percentage of the runners were in the 20-something age group? What do you suppose was the focus of the article?

2.4   Crosstabulations and Scatter Diagrams

Crosstabulations and scatter diagrams are used to summarize data in a way that reveals the relationship between two variables.

Thus far in this chapter, we have focused on tabular and graphical methods used to summarize the data for *one variable at a time.* Often a manager or decision maker requires tabular and graphical methods that will assist in the understanding of the *relationship between two variables.* Crosstabulations and scatter diagrams are two such methods.

TABLE 2.9 QUALITY RATING AND MEAL PRICE FOR 300 LOS ANGELES RESTAURANTS

Restaurant	Quality Rating	Meal Price ($)
1	Good	18
2	Very Good	22
3	Good	28
4	Excellent	38
5	Very Good	33
6	Good	28
7	Very Good	19
8	Very Good	11
9	Very Good	23
10	Good	13
.	.	.
.	.	.
.	.	.

WEB file

Restaurant

Crosstabulation

A **crosstabulation** is a tabular summary of data for two variables. Let us illustrate the use of a crosstabulation by considering the following application based on data from Zagat's Restaurant Review. The quality rating and the meal price data were collected for a sample of 300 restaurants located in the Los Angeles area. Table 2.9 shows the data for the first 10 restaurants. Data on a restaurant's quality rating and typical meal price are reported. Quality rating is a categorical variable with rating categories of good, very good, and excellent. Meal price is a quantitative variable that ranges from $10 to $49.

A crosstabulation of the data for this application is shown in Table 2.10. The left and top margin labels define the classes for the two variables. In the left margin, the row labels (good, very good, and excellent) correspond to the three classes of the quality rating variable. In the top margin, the column labels ($10–19, $20–29, $30–39, and $40–49) correspond to the four classes of the meal price variable. Each restaurant in the sample provides a quality rating and a meal price. Thus, each restaurant in the sample is associated with a cell appearing in one of the rows and one of the columns of the crosstabulation. For example, restaurant 5 is identified as having a very good quality rating and a meal price of $33. This restaurant belongs to the cell in row 2 and column 3 of Table 2.10. In constructing a crosstabulation, we simply count the number of restaurants that belong to each of the cells in the crosstabulation table.

In reviewing Table 2.10, we see that the greatest number of restaurants in the sample (64) have a very good quality rating and a meal price in the $20–29 range. Only two restaurants have an excellent quality rating and a meal price in the $10–19 range. Similar interpretations of the other frequencies can be made. In addition, note that the right and bottom

TABLE 2.10 CROSSTABULATION OF QUALITY RATING AND MEAL PRICE FOR 300 LOS ANGELES RESTAURANTS

Quality Rating	Meal Price				Total
	$10–19	**$20–29**	**$30–39**	**$40–49**	
Good	42	40	2	0	84
Very Good	34	64	46	6	150
Excellent	2	14	28	22	66
Total	78	118	76	28	300

margins of the crosstabulation provide the frequency distributions for quality rating and meal price separately. From the frequency distribution in the right margin, we see that data on quality ratings show that 84 restaurants were rated good, 150 were rated very good, and 66 were rated excellent. Similarly, the bottom margin shows the frequency distribution for the meal price variable.

Dividing the totals in the right margin of the crosstabulation by the total for that column provides a relative and percent frequency distribution for the quality rating variable.

Quality Rating	Relative Frequency	Percent Frequency
Good	.28	28
Very Good	.50	50
Excellent	.22	22
Total	1.00	100

From the percent frequency distribution we see that 28% of the restaurants were rated good, 50% were rated very good, and 22% were rated excellent.

Dividing the totals in the bottom row of the crosstabulation by the total for that row provides a relative and percent frequency distribution for the meal price variable.

Meal Price	Relative Frequency	Percent Frequency
$10–19	.26	26
$20–29	.39	39
$30–39	.25	25
$40–49	.09	9
Total	1.00	100

Note that the sum of the values in each column does not add exactly to the column total, because the values being summed are rounded. From the percent frequency distribution we see that 26% of the meal prices are in the lowest price class ($10–19), 39% are in the next higher class, and so on.

The frequency and relative frequency distributions constructed from the margins of a crosstabulation provide information about each of the variables individually, but they do not shed any light on the relationship between the variables. The primary value of a crosstabulation lies in the insight it offers about the relationship between the variables. A review of the crosstabulation in Table 2.10 reveals that higher meal prices are associated with the higher quality restaurants, and the lower meal prices are associated with the lower quality restaurants.

Converting the entries in a crosstabulation into row percentages or column percentages can provide more insight into the relationship between the two variables. For row percentages, the results of dividing each frequency in Table 2.10 by its corresponding row total and multiplying by 100 are shown in Table 2.11. Each row of Table 2.11 is a percent frequency

TABLE 2.11   ROW PERCENTAGES FOR EACH QUALITY RATING CATEGORY

| Quality Rating | Meal Price | | | | Total |
	$10–19	$20–29	$30–39	$40–49	
Good	50.0	47.6	2.4	0.0	100
Very Good	22.7	42.7	30.6	4.0	100
Excellent	3.0	21.2	42.4	33.4	100

FIGURE 2.13 EXCEL COLUMN CHART SHOWING ROW PERCENTAGES FOR EACH QUALITY RATING CATEGORY

distribution of meal price for one of the quality rating categories. Of the restaurants with the lowest quality rating (good), we see that the greatest percentages are for the less expensive restaurants (50% have $10–19 meal prices and 47.6% have $20–29 meal prices). Of the restaurants with the highest quality rating (excellent), we see that the greatest percentages are for the more expensive restaurants (42.4% have $30–39 meal prices and 33.4% have $40–49 meal prices). Thus, we continue to see that the more expensive meals are associated with the higher quality restaurants.

A graph showing the information in a crosstabulation can also be developed to enhance the presentation. Figure 2.13 shows an Excel column chart for the results displayed in Table 2.11.

In practice, the final reports for many statistical studies include a large number of crosstabulations. In the Los Angeles restaurant survey, the crosstabulation is based on one categorical variable (quality rating) and one quantitative variable (meal price). Crosstabulations can also be developed when both variables are categorical and when both variables are quantitative. When quantitative variables are used, however, we must first create classes for the values of the variable. For instance, in the restaurant example we grouped the meal prices into four classes ($10–19, $20–29, $30–39, and $40–49).

Using Excel's PivotTable Report to Construct a Crosstabulation

Excel's PivotTable Report provides an excellent tool for summarizing the data for two or more variables simultaneously. We will illustrate the use of Excel's PivotTable Report by showing how to develop a crosstabulation of quality ratings and meal prices for the sample of 300 restaurants located in the Los Angeles area.

Enter Data: The labels "Restaurant," "Quality Rating," and "Meal Price ($)" have been entered into cells A1:C1 of the worksheet shown in Figure 2.14. The data for each of the 300 restaurants in the sample have been entered into cells B2:C301.

Enter Functions and Formulas: No functions and formulas are needed.

Apply Tools: To use the PivotTable report to create a crosstabulation, we need to perform three tasks: Display the Initial PivotTable Field List and PivotTable Report; Set Up the PivotTable Field List; Finalize the PivotTable Report.

FIGURE 2.14   EXCEL WORKSHEET CONTAINING RESTAURANT DATA

WEB file

Restaurant

Note: Rows 12–291 are hidden.

	A	B	C	D
1	**Restaurant**	**Quality Rating**	**Meal Price ($)**	
2	1	Good	18	
3	2	Very Good	22	
4	3	Good	28	
5	4	Excellent	38	
6	5	Very Good	33	
7	6	Good	28	
8	7	Very Good	19	
9	8	Very Good	11	
10	9	Very Good	23	
11	10	Good	13	
292	291	Very Good	23	
293	292	Very Good	24	
294	293	Excellent	45	
295	294	Good	14	
296	295	Good	18	
297	296	Good	17	
298	297	Good	16	
299	298	Good	15	
300	299	Very Good	38	
301	300	Very Good	31	
302				

Display the Initial PivotTable Field List and PivotTable Report: Three steps are needed to display the initial PivotTable Field List and PivotTable report.

Step 1. Click the **Insert** tab on the Ribbon
Step 2. In the **Tables** group, click the icon above the word PivotTable
Step 3. When the **Create PivotTable** dialog box appears,
Choose **Select a Table or Range**
Enter A1:C301 in the **Table/Range** box
Choose **New Worksheet** as the location for the PivotTable Report
Click **OK**

The resulting initial PivotTable Field List and PivotTable Report are shown in Figure 2.15.

Set Up the PivotTable Field List: Each of the three columns in Figure 2.14 (labeled Restaurant, Quality Rating, and Meal Price ($)) is considered a field by Excel. Fields may be chosen to represent rows, columns, or values in the body of the PivotTable Report. The following steps show how to use Excel's PivotTable Field List to assign the Quality Rating field to the rows, the Meal Price ($) field to the columns, and the Restaurant field to the body of the PivotTable report.

Step 1. In the **PivotTable Field List,** go to **Choose Fields to add to report**
Drag the **Quality Rating** field to the **Row Labels** area
Drag the **Meal Price ($)** field to the **Column Labels** area
Drag the **Restaurant** field to the **Values** area
Step 2. Click on **Sum of Restaurant** in the **Values** area
Step 3. Click **Value Field Settings** from the list of options that appear

FIGURE 2.15 INITIAL PIVOTTABLE FIELD LIST AND PIVOTTABLE FIELD REPORT FOR THE RESTAURANT DATA

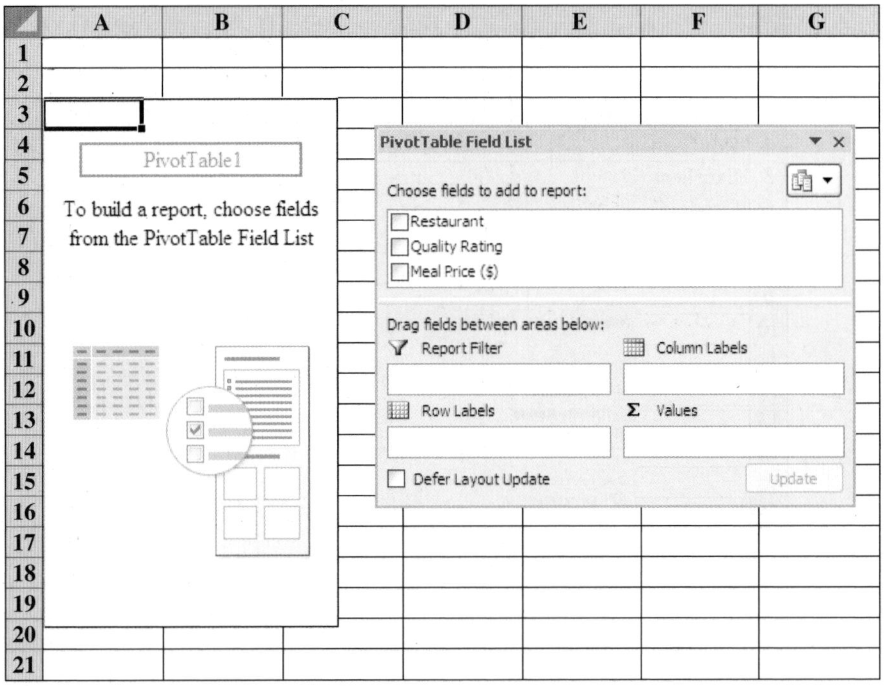

Step 4. When the Value Field Settings dialog appears,
    Under **Summarize value field by**, choose **Count**
    Click **OK**

Figure 2.16 shows the completed PivotTable Field List and a portion of the PivotTable worksheet as it now appears.

Finalize the PivotTable Report: To complete the PivotTable Report we need to group the columns representing meal prices and place the row labels for quality rating in the proper order. The following steps accomplish this.

Step 1. Right-click in cell B4 or any cell containing meal prices
Step 2. Choose **Group** from the list of options that appears
Step 3. When the **Grouping** dialog box appears,
    Enter 10 in the **Starting at** box
    Enter 49 in the **Ending at** box
    Enter 10 in the **By** box
    Click **OK**
Step 4. Right-click on **Excellent** in cell A5
Step 5. Choose **Move** and click **Move "Excellent" to End**

The final PivotTable Report is shown in Figure 2.17. Note that it provides the same information as the crosstabulation shown in Table 2.10. We can now use Excel's chart tools to construct the column chart shown in Figure 2.13. Alternatively, Excel's PivotChart report can be used to create both the crosstabulation and corresponding column chart at the same time.

FIGURE 2.16 COMPLETED PIVOTTABLE FIELD LIST AND A PORTION OF THE PIVOTTABLE REPORT FOR THE RESTAURANT DATA (COLUMNS H:AK ARE HIDDEN)

	A	B	C	D	E	F	G	AL	AM	AN	AO
1											
2											
3	Count of Restaurant	Column Labels ▾									
4	Row Labels ▾		10	11	12	13	14	15	47	48	Grand Total	
5	Excellent					1			2	2	66	
6	Good		6	4	3	3	2	4			84	
7	Very Good		1	4	3	5	6	1		1	150	
8	Grand Total		7	8	6	9	8	5	2	3	300	
9											
10											
11											
12											
13											
14											
15											
16											
17											
18											
19											
20											

PivotTable Field List

Choose fields to add to report:
☑ Restaurant
☑ Quality Rating
☑ Meal Price ($)

Drag fields between areas below:
- ▽ Report Filter
- ▦ Column Labels — Meal Price ($) ▾
- ▦ Row Labels — Quality Rating ▾
- Σ Values — Count of Restaurant ▾
- ☐ Defer Layout Update — Update

FIGURE 2.17 FINAL PIVOTTABLE REPORT FOR THE RESTAURANT DATA

	A	B	C	D	E	F	G
1							
2							
3	Count of Restaurant	Column Labels ▾					
4	Row Labels ▾	10–19	20–29	30–39	40–49	Grand Total	
5	Good		42	40	2	84	
6	Very Good		34	64	46	6	150
7	Excellent		2	14	28	22	66
8	Grand Total		78	118	76	28	300
9							
10							
11							
12							
13							
14							
15							
16							
17							
18							
19							
20							
21							

PivotTable Field List

Choose fields to add to report:
☑ Restaurant
☑ Quality Rating
☑ Meal Price ($)

Drag fields between areas below:
- ▽ Report Filter
- ▦ Column Labels — Meal Price ($) ▾
- ▦ Row Labels — Quality Rating ▾
- Σ Values — Count of Restaurant ▾
- ☐ Defer Layout Update — Update

As we have seen, Excel's PivotTable report and PivotChart report are very useful in summarizing univariate and bivariate data. Once you have used these tools to create tabular and graphical summaries for one or two data sets, we think you will find that both tools are not only very easy to use, but they provide a very powerful option for quickly summarizing very complex data sets as well.

Simpson's Paradox

The data in two or more crosstabulations are often combined or aggregated to produce a summary crosstabulation showing how two variables are related. In such cases, we must be careful in drawing conclusions about the relationship between the two variables in the aggregated crosstabulation. In some cases the conclusions based upon the aggregated crosstabulation can be completely reversed if we look at the unaggregated data, an occurrence known as **Simpson's paradox**. To provide an illustration of Simpson's paradox we consider an example involving the analysis of verdicts for two judges in two types of courts.

Judges Ron Luckett and Dennis Kendall presided over cases in Common Pleas Court and Municipal Court during the past three years. Some of the verdicts they rendered were appealed. In most of these cases the appeals court upheld the original verdicts, but in some cases those verdicts were reversed. For each judge a crosstabulation was developed based upon two variables: Verdict (upheld or reversed) and Type of Court (Common Pleas or Municipal). Suppose that the two crosstabulations were then combined by aggregating the type of court data. The resulting aggregated crosstabulation contains two variables: Verdict (upheld or reversed) and Judge (Luckett or Kendall). This crosstabulation shows the number of appeals in which the verdict was upheld and the number in which the verdict was reversed for both judges. The following crosstabulation shows these results along with the column percentages in parentheses next to each value.

Verdict	Judge		Total
	Luckett	**Kendall**	
Upheld	129 (86%)	110 (88%)	239
Reversed	21 (14%)	15 (12%)	36
Total (%)	150 (100%)	125 (100%)	275

A review of the column percentages shows that 14% of the verdicts were reversed for Judge Luckett, but only 12% of the verdicts were reversed for Judge Kendall. Thus, we might conclude that Judge Kendall is doing a better job because a higher percentage of his verdicts are being upheld. This conclusion, however, is faulty.

The following crosstabulations show the cases tried by Luckett and Kendall in the two courts; column percentages are also shown in parentheses next to each value.

Verdict	Judge Luckett				Verdict	Judge Kendall		
	Common Pleas	**Municipal Court**	**Total**			**Common Pleas**	**Municipal Court**	**Total**
Upheld	29 (91%)	100 (85%)	129		**Upheld**	90 (90%)	20 (80%)	110
Reversed	3 (9%)	18 (15%)	21		**Reversed**	10 (10%)	5 (20%)	15
Total (%)	32 (100%)	118 (100%)	150		**Total (%)**	100 (100%)	25 (100%)	125

From the crosstabulation and column percentages for Luckett, we see that his verdicts were upheld in 91% of the Common Pleas Court cases and in 85% of the Municipal Court cases. From the crosstabulation and column percentages for Kendall, we see that his verdicts were upheld in 90% of the Common Pleas Court cases and in 80% of the Municipal Court cases. Comparing the column percentages for the two judges, we see that Judge Luckett demonstrates a better record than Judge Kendall in both courts. This result contradicts the conclusion we reached when we aggregated the data across both courts for the original crosstabulation. It appeared then that Judge Kendall had the better record. This example illustrates Simpson's paradox.

The original crosstabulation was obtained by aggregating the data in the separate crosstabulations for the two courts. Note that for both judges the percentage of appeals that resulted in reversals was much higher in Municipal Court than in Common Pleas Court. Because Judge Luckett tried a much higher percentage of his cases in Municipal Court, the aggregated data favored Judge Kendall. When we look at the crosstabulations for the two courts separately, however, Judge Luckett clearly shows the better record. Thus, for the original crosstabulation, we see that the *type of court* is a hidden variable that cannot be ignored when evaluating the records of the two judges.

Because of Simpson's paradox, we need to be especially careful when drawing conclusions using aggregated data. Before drawing any conclusions about the relationship between two variables shown for a crosstabulation involving aggregated data, you should investigate whether any hidden variables could affect the results.

Scatter Diagram and Trendline

A **scatter diagram** is a graphical presentation of the relationship between two quantitative variables, and a **trendline** is a line that provides an approximation of the relationship. As an illustration, consider the advertising/sales relationship for a stereo and sound equipment store in San Francisco. On 10 occasions during the past three months, the store used weekend television commercials to promote sales at its stores. The managers want to investigate whether a relationship exists between the number of commercials shown and sales at the store during the following week. Sample data for the 10 weeks with sales in hundreds of dollars are shown in Table 2.12.

Figure 2.18 shows the scatter diagram and the trendline[2] for the data in Table 2.12. The number of commercials (x) is shown on the horizontal axis and the sales (y) are shown on

TABLE 2.12   SAMPLE DATA FOR THE STEREO AND SOUND EQUIPMENT STORE

Week	Number of Commercials x	Sales ($100s) y
1	2	50
2	5	57
3	1	41
4	3	54
5	4	54
6	1	38
7	5	63
8	3	48
9	4	59
10	2	46

WEB file
Stereo

---
[2]The equation of the trendline is $y = 36.15 + 4.95x$. The slope of the trendline is 4.95 and the y-intercept (the point where the line intersects the y-axis) is 36.15. We will discuss in detail the interpretation of the slope and y-intercept for a linear trendline in Chapter 12 when we study simple linear regression.

FIGURE 2.18   SCATTER DIAGRAM AND TRENDLINE FOR THE STEREO AND SOUND
EQUIPMENT STORE

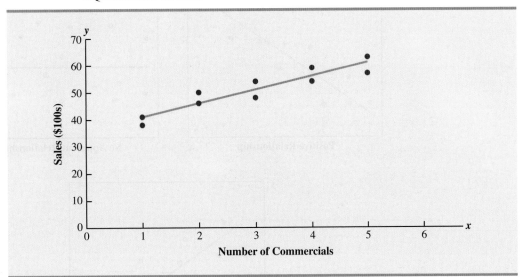

the vertical axis. For week 1, $x = 2$ and $y = 50$. A point with those coordinates is plotted on the scatter diagram. Similar points are plotted for the other nine weeks. Note that during two of the weeks one commercial was shown, during two of the weeks two commercials were shown, and so on.

The completed scatter diagram in Figure 2.18 indicates a positive relationship between the number of commercials and sales. Higher sales are associated with a higher number of commercials. The relationship is not perfect in that all points are not on a straight line. However, the general pattern of the points and the trendline suggest that the overall relationship is positive.

Some general scatter diagram patterns and the types of relationships they suggest are shown in Figure 2.19. The top left panel depicts a positive relationship similar to the one for the number of commercials and sales example. In the top right panel, the scatter diagram shows no apparent relationship between the variables. The bottom panel depicts a negative relationship where y tends to decrease as x increases.

Using Excel's Chart Tools to Construct a Scatter Diagram and a Trendline

We can use Excel's chart tools to construct a scatter diagram and a trendline for the stereo and sound equipment store data. Refer to Figures 2.20 and 2.21 as we describe the tasks involved.

Enter Data: Appropriate labels and the sample data have been entered into cells A1:C11 of the worksheet shown in Figure 2.20.

Enter Functions and Formulas: No functions and formulas are needed.

Apply Tools: The following steps describe how to use Excel's chart tools to produce a scatter diagram from the data in the worksheet.

Step 1. Select cells B2:C11
Step 2. Click the **Insert** tab on the Ribbon

FIGURE 2.19   TYPES OF RELATIONSHIPS DEPICTED BY SCATTER DIAGRAMS

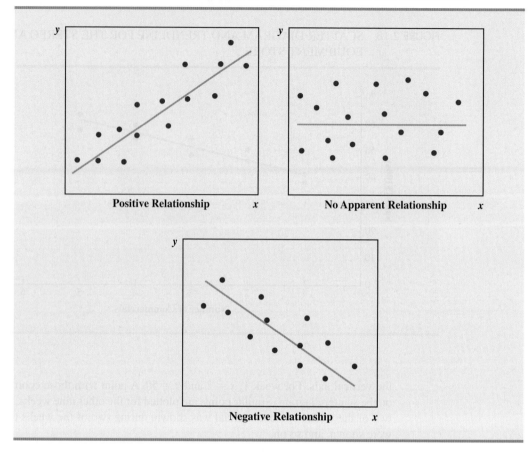

FIGURE 2.20   SCATTER DIAGRAM FOR THE STEREO AND SOUND EQUIPMENT STORE USING EXCEL'S CHART TOOLS

	A	B	C	D	E	F	G	H
1	Week	No. of Commercials	Sales Volume					
2	1	2	50					
3	2	5	57					
4	3	1	41					
5	4	3	54					
6	5	4	54					
7	6	1	38					
8	7	5	63					
9	8	3	48					
10	9	4	59					
11	10	2	46					
12								
13								
14								
15								
16								
17								
18								
19								
20								

FIGURE 2.21 SCATTER DIAGRAM AND TRENDLINE FOR THE STEREO AND SOUND EQUIPMENT STORE USING EXCEL'S CHART TOOLS

	A	B	C	D	E	F	G	H
1	Week	No. of Commercials	Sales Volume					
2	1	2	50					
3	2	5	57					
4	3	1	41					
5	4	3	54					
6	5	4	54					
7	6	1	38					
8	7	5	63					
9	8	3	48					
10	9	4	59					
11	10	2	46					
12								
13								
14								
15								
16								
17								
18								
19								
20								

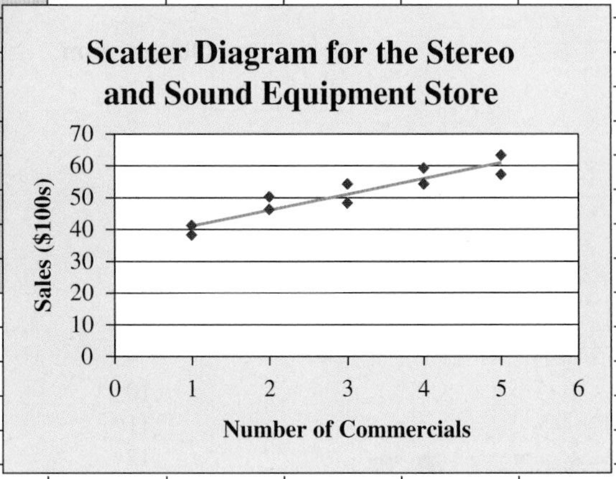

Step 3. In the **Charts** group, click **Scatter**

Step 4. When the list of scatter diagram subtypes appears, click **Scatter with only Markers** (the chart in the upper left corner)

Step 5. In the **Chart Layouts** group, click **Layout 1**

Step 6. Select the **Chart Title** and replace it with **Scatter Diagram for the Stereo and Sound Equipment Store**

Step 7. Select the **Horizontal (Value) Axis Title** and replace it with **Number of Commercials**

Step 8. Select the **Vertical (Value) Axis Title** and replace it with **Sales ($100s)**

Step 9. Right-click the **Series 1 Legend Entry** and click **Delete**

The worksheet displayed in Figure 2.20 shows the scatter diagram produced by Excel. The following steps describe how to add a trendline.

Step 1. Position the mouse pointer over any data point in the scatter diagram and right-click to display a list of options

Step 2. Choose **Add Trendline**

Step 3. When the **Format Trendline** dialog box appears,
Select **Trendline Options**
Choose **Linear** from the **Trend/Regression Type** list
Click **Close**

The worksheet displayed in Figure 2.21 shows the scatter diagram with the trendline added.

Exercises

Methods

29. The following data are for 30 observations involving two qualitative variables, x and y. The categories for x are A, B, and C; the categories for y are 1 and 2.

Crosstab

Observation	x	y	Observation	x	y
1	A	1	16	B	2
2	B	1	17	C	1
3	B	1	18	B	1
4	C	2	19	C	1
5	B	1	20	B	1
6	C	2	21	C	2
7	B	1	22	B	1
8	C	2	23	C	2
9	A	1	24	A	1
10	B	1	25	B	1
11	A	1	26	C	2
12	B	1	27	C	2
13	C	2	28	A	1
14	C	2	29	B	1
15	C	2	30	B	2

    a. Develop a crosstabulation for the data, with x as the row variable and y as the column variable.

    b. Compute the row percentages.

    c. Compute the column percentages.

    d. What is the relationship, if any, between x and y?

30. The following 20 observations are for two quantitative variables, x and y.

Scatter

Observation	x	y	Observation	x	y
1	−22	22	11	−37	48
2	−33	49	12	34	−29
3	2	8	13	9	−18
4	29	−16	14	−33	31
5	−13	10	15	20	−16
6	21	−28	16	−3	14
7	−13	27	17	−15	18
8	−23	35	18	12	17
9	14	−5	19	−20	−11
10	3	−3	20	−7	−22

    a. Develop a scatter diagram for the relationship between x and y.

    b. What is the relationship, if any, between x and y?

Applications

31. The following crosstabulation shows household income by educational level of the head of household (*Statistical Abstract of the United States: 2002*).

	Household Income ($1000s)					
Educational Level	**Under 25**	**25.0– 49.9**	**50.0– 74.9**	**75.0– 99.9**	**100 or more**	**Total**
Not H.S. graduate	9285	4093	1589	541	354	15862
H.S. graduate	10150	9821	6050	2737	2028	30786
Some college	6011	8221	5813	3215	3120	26380
Bachelor's degree	2138	3985	3952	2698	4748	17521
Beyond bach. deg.	813	1497	1815	1589	3765	9479
Total	28397	27617	19219	10780	14015	100028

a. Compute the row percentages and identify the percent frequency distributions of income for households in which the head is a high school graduate and in which the head holds a bachelor's degree.

b. What percentage of households headed by high school graduates earn $75,000 or more? What percentage of households headed by bachelor's degree recipients earn $75,000 or more?

c. Construct percent frequency histograms of income for households headed by persons with a high school diploma and for those headed by persons with a bachelor's degree. Is any relationship evident between household income and educational level?

32. Refer again to the crosstabulation of household income by educational level shown in exercise 31.

a. Compute column percentages and identify the percent frequency distributions displayed. What percentage of the heads of households did not graduate from high school?

b. What percentage of the households earning $100,000 or more were headed by a person having schooling beyond a bachelor's degree? What percentage of the households headed by a person with schooling beyond a bachelor's degree earned over $100,000? Why are these two percentages different?

c. Compare the percent frequency distributions for those households earning "Under 25," "100 or more," and for "Total." Comment on the relationship between household income and educational level of the head of household.

33. Recently, management at Oak Tree Golf Course received a few complaints about the condition of the greens. Several players complained that the greens are too fast. Rather than react to the comments of just a few, the Golf Association conducted a survey of 100 male and 100 female golfers. The survey results are summarized here.

Male Golfers

	Greens Condition	
Handicap	**Too Fast**	**Fine**
Under 15	10	40
15 or more	25	25

Female Golfers

	Greens Condition	
Handicap	**Too Fast**	**Fine**
Under 15	1	9
15 or more	39	51

a. Combine these two crosstabulations into one with Male and Female as the row labels and Too Fast and Fine as the column labels. Which group shows the higher percentage saying that the greens are too fast?

b. Refer to the initial crosstabulations. For those players with low handicaps (better players), which group (male or female) shows the higher percentage saying the greens are too fast?

c. Refer to the initial crosstabulations. For those players with higher handicaps, which group (male or female) shows the higher percentage saying the greens are too fast?

    d. What conclusions can you draw about the preferences of men and women concerning the speed of the greens? Are the conclusions you draw from part (a) as compared with parts (b) and (c) consistent? Explain any apparent inconsistencies.

34. Table 2.13 shows a data set containing information for 45 mutual funds that are part of the *Morningstar Funds500* for 2008. The data set includes the following five variables:

    Fund Type: The type of fund, labeled DE (Domestic Equity), IE (International Equity), and FI (Fixed Income)

    Net Asset Value ($): The closing price per share on December 31, 2007

    5-Year Average Return (%): The average annual return for the fund over the past 5 years

    Expense Ratio (%): The percentage of assets deducted each fiscal year for fund expenses

    Morningstar Rank: The risk adjusted star rating for each fund; Morningstar ranks go from a low of 1-Star to a high of 5-Stars

    a. Prepare a crosstabulation of the data on Fund Type (rows) and the average annual return over the past 5 years (columns). Use classes of 0–9.99, 10–19.99, 20–29.99, 30–39.99, 40–49.99, and 50–59.99 for the 5-Year Average Return (%).

    b. Prepare a frequency distribution for the data on Fund Type.

    c. Prepare a frequency distribution for the data on 5-Year Average Return (%).

    d. How has the crosstabulation helped in preparing the frequency distributions in parts (b) and (c)?

    e. What conclusions can you draw about the average return over the past 5 years and the type of fund?

35. Refer to the data in Table 2.13.

    a. Prepare a crosstabulation of the data on Fund Type (rows) and the expense ratio (columns). Use classes of .25–.49, .50–.74, .75–.99, 1.00–1.24, and 1.25–1.49 for Expense Ratio (%).

    b. Prepare a percent frequency distribution for Expense Ratio (%).

    c. What conclusions can you draw about the expense ratio and the type of fund?

36. Refer to the data in Table 2.13.

    a. Prepare a scatter diagram with 5-Year Average Return (%) on the horizontal axis and Net Asset Value ($) on the vertical axis.

    b. Comment on the relationship, if any, between the variables.

37. The U.S. Department of Energy's Fuel Economy Guide provides fuel efficiency data for cars and trucks (*http://www.fueleconomy.gov*, February 22, 2008). A portion of the data for 311 compact, midsize, and large cars is shown in Table 2.14. The data set contains the following variables:

FuelData

    Class: Compact, Midsize, and Large

    Displacement: Engine size in liters

    Cylinders: Number of cylinders in the engine

    Drive: Front wheel (F), rear wheel (R), and four wheel (4)

    Fuel Type: Premium (P) or regular (R) fuel

    City MPG: Fuel efficiency rating for city driving in terms of miles per gallon

    Hwy MPG: Fuel efficiency rating for highway driving in terms of miles per gallon

The complete data set is contained in the file named FuelData.

    a. Prepare a crosstabulation of the data on Class (rows) and Hwy MPG (columns). Use classes of 15–19, 20–24, 25–29, 30–34, and 35–39 for Hwy MPG.

    b. Comment on the relationship beween Class and Hwy MPG.

TABLE 2.13   FINANCIAL DATA FOR A SAMPLE OF 45 MUTUAL FUNDS

Fund Name	Fund Type	Net Asset Value ($)	5-Year Average Return (%)	Expense Ratio (%)	Morningstar Rank
Amer Cent Inc & Growth Inv	DE	28.88	12.39	0.67	2-Star
American Century Intl. Disc	IE	14.37	30.53	1.41	3-Star
American Century Tax-Free Bond	FI	10.73	3.34	0.49	4-Star
American Century Ultra	DE	24.94	10.88	0.99	3-Star
Ariel	DE	46.39	11.32	1.03	2-Star
Artisan Intl Val	IE	25.52	24.95	1.23	3-Star
Artisan Small Cap	DE	16.92	15.67	1.18	3-Star
Baron Asset	DE	50.67	16.77	1.31	5-Star
Brandywine	DE	36.58	18.14	1.08	4-Star
Brown Cap Small	DE	35.73	15.85	1.20	4-Star
Buffalo Mid Cap	DE	15.29	17.25	1.02	3-Star
Delafield	DE	24.32	17.77	1.32	4-Star
DFA U.S. Micro Cap	DE	13.47	17.23	0.53	3-Star
Dodge & Cox Income	FI	12.51	4.31	0.44	4-Star
Fairholme	DE	31.86	18.23	1.00	5-Star
Fidelity Contrafund	DE	73.11	17.99	0.89	5-Star
Fidelity Municipal Income	FI	12.58	4.41	0.45	5-Star
Fidelity Overseas	IE	48.39	23.46	0.90	4-Star
Fidelity Sel Electronics	DE	45.60	13.50	0.89	3-Star
Fidelity Sh-Term Bond	FI	8.60	2.76	0.45	3-Star
Fidelity	DE	39.85	14.40	0.56	4-Star
FPA New Income	FI	10.95	4.63	0.62	3-Star
Gabelli Asset AAA	DE	49.81	16.70	1.36	4-Star
Greenspring	DE	23.59	12.46	1.07	3-Star
Janus	DE	32.26	12.81	0.90	3-Star
Janus Worldwide	IE	54.83	12.31	0.86	2-Star
Kalmar Gr Val Sm Cp	DE	15.30	15.31	1.32	3-Star
Managers Freemont Bond	FI	10.56	5.14	0.60	5-Star
Marsico 21st Century	DE	17.44	15.16	1.31	5-Star
Mathews Pacific Tiger	IE	27.86	32.70	1.16	3-Star
Meridan Value	DE	31.92	15.33	1.08	4-Star
Oakmark I	DE	40.37	9.51	1.05	2-Star
PIMCO Emerg Mkts Bd D	FI	10.68	13.57	1.25	3-Star
RS Value A	DE	26.27	23.68	1.36	4-Star
T. Rowe Price Latin Am.	IE	53.89	51.10	1.24	4-Star
T. Rowe Price Mid Val	DE	22.46	16.91	0.80	4-Star
Templeton Growth A	IE	24.07	15.91	1.01	3-Star
Thornburg Value A	DE	37.53	15.46	1.27	4-Star
USAA Income	FI	12.10	4.31	0.62	3-Star
Vanguard Equity-Inc	DE	24.42	13.41	0.29	4-Star
Vanguard Global Equity	IE	23.71	21.77	0.64	5-Star
Vanguard GNMA	FI	10.37	4.25	0.21	5-Star
Vanguard Sht-Tm TE	FI	15.68	2.37	0.16	3-Star
Vanguard Sm Cp Idx	DE	32.58	17.01	0.23	3-Star
Wasatch Sm Cp Growth	DE	35.41	13.98	1.19	4-Star

WEB file

MutualFunds

TABLE 2.14   FUEL EFFICIENCY DATA FOR 311 CARS

FuelData

Car	Class	Displacement	Cylinders	Drive	Fuel Type	City MPG	Hwy MPG
1	Compact	3.1	6	4	P	15	25
2	Compact	3.1	6	4	P	17	25
3	Compact	3.0	6	4	P	17	25
•	•	•	•	•	•	•	•
•	•	•	•	•	•	•	•
•	•	•	•	•	•	•	•
161	Midsize	2.4	4	F	R	22	30
162	Midsize	2.0	4	F	P	19	29
•	•	•	•	•	•	•	•
•	•	•	•	•	•	•	•
•	•	•	•	•	•	•	•
310	Large	3.0	6	F	R	17	25
311	Large	3.0	6	F	R	18	25

    c. Prepare a crosstabulation of the data on Drive (rows) and City MPG (columns). Use classes of 5–9, 10–14, 15–19, 20–24, 25–29, 30–34, and 35–39 for City MPG.

    d. Comment on the relationship between Drive and City MPG.

    e. Prepare a crosstabulation of the data on Fuel Type (rows) and City MPG (columns). Use classes of 5–9, 10–14, 15–19, 20–24, 25–29, 30–34, and 35–39 for City MPG.

    f. Comment on the relationship between Fuel Type and City MPG.

38. Refer to exercise 37 and the data in the file named FuelData.

    a. Prepare a crosstabulation of the data on Displacement (rows) and Hwy MPG (columns). Use classes of 15–19, 20–24, 25–29, 30–34, and 35–39 for Hwy MPG.

    b. Comment on the relationship, if any, between Displacement and Hwy MPG.

    c. Develop a scatter diagram of the data on Displacement and Hwy MPG. Use the vertical axis for Hwy MPG.

    d. What does the scatter diagram developed in part (c) indicate about the relationship, if any, between Displacement and Hwy MPG?

    e. In investigating the relationship between Displacement and Hwy MPG you developed a tabular summary of the data (crosstabulation) and a graphical summary (scatter diagram). In this case which approach do you prefer? Explain.

Summary

A set of data, even if modest in size, is often difficult to interpret directly in the form in which it is gathered. Tabular and graphical methods provide procedures for organizing and summarizing data so that patterns are revealed and the data are more easily interpreted. Frequency distributions, relative frequency distributions, percent frequency distributions, bar graphs, and pie charts were presented as tabular and graphical procedures for summarizing categorical data. Frequency distributions, relative frequency distributions, percent frequency distributions, histograms, cumulative frequency distributions, cumulative relative frequency distributions, cumulative percent frequency distributions, and ogives were presented as ways of summarizing quantitative data. A stem-and-leaf display provides an exploratory data analysis technique that can be used to summarize quantitative data. Crosstabulation was presented as a tabular method for summarizing data for two variables. The scatter diagram was introduced as a graphical method for showing the relationship between two quantitative variables. Figure 2.22 shows the tabular and graphical methods presented in this chapter.

FIGURE 2.22   TABULAR AND GRAPHICAL METHODS FOR SUMMARIZING DATA

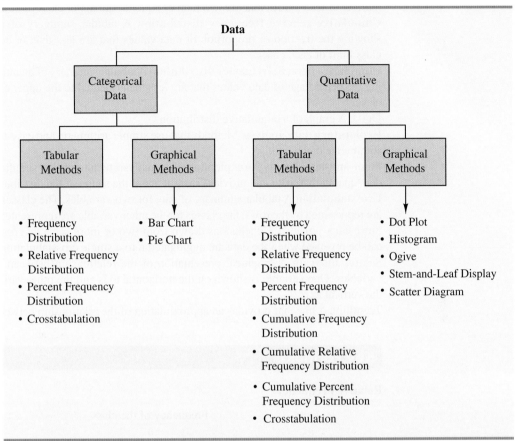

Categorical data Labels or names used to identify categories of like items.

Quantitative data Numerical values that indicate how much or how many.

Frequency distribution A tabular summary of data showing the number (frequency) of data values in each of several nonoverlapping classes.

Relative frequency distribution A tabular summary of data showing the fraction or proportion of data values in each of several nonoverlapping classes.

Percent frequency distribution A tabular summary of data showing the percentage of data values in each of several nonoverlapping classes.

Bar chart A graphical device for depicting categorical data that have been summarized in a frequency, relative frequency, or percent frequency distribution.

Pie chart A graphical device for presenting data summaries based on subdivision of a circle into sectors that correspond to the relative frequency for each class.

Class midpoint The value halfway between the lower and upper class limits.

Dot plot A graphical device that summarizes data by the number of dots above each data value on the horizontal axis.

Histogram A graphical presentation of a frequency distribution, relative frequency distribution, or percent frequency distribution of quantitative data constructed by placing the class intervals on the horizontal axis and the frequencies, relative frequencies, or percent frequencies on the vertical axis.

Cumulative frequency distribution A tabular summary of quantitative data showing the number of data values that are less than or equal to the upper class limit of each class.

Cumulative relative frequency distribution A tabular summary of quantitative data showing the fraction or proportion of data values that are less than or equal to the upper class limit of each class.

Cumulative percent frequency distribution A tabular summary of quantitative data showing the percentage of data values that are less than or equal to the upper class limit of each class.

Ogive A graph of a cumulative distribution.

Exploratory data analysis Methods that use simple arithmetic and easy-to-draw graphs to summarize data quickly.

Stem-and-leaf display An exploratory data analysis technique that simultaneously rank orders quantitative data and provides insight about the shape of the distribution.

Crosstabulation A tabular summary of data for two variables. The classes for one variable are represented by the rows; the classes for the other variable are represented by the columns.

Simpson's paradox Conclusions drawn from two or more separate crosstabulations that can be reversed when the data are aggregated into a single crosstabulation.

Scatter diagram A graphical presentation of the relationship between two quantitative variables. One variable is shown on the horizontal axis and the other variable is shown on the vertical axis.

Trendline A line that provides an approximation of the relationship between two variables.

Key Formulas

Relative Frequency

$$\frac{\text{Frequency of the class}}{n} \tag{2.1}$$

Approximate Class Width

$$\frac{\text{Largest data value} - \text{Smallest data value}}{\text{Number of classes}} \tag{2.2}$$

Supplementary Exercises

39. The Higher Education Research Institute at UCLA provides statistics on the most popular majors among incoming college freshmen. The five most popular majors are Arts and Humanities (A), Business Administration (B), Engineering (E), Professional (P), and Social Science (S) (*The New York Times Almanac*, 2006). A broad range of other (O) majors, including biological science, physical science, computer science, and education, are grouped together. The majors selected for a sample of 64 college freshmen follow.

WEB file

Major

S	P	P	O	B	E	O	E	P	O	O	B	O	O	O	A
O	E	E	B	S	O	B	O	A	O	E	O	E	O	B	P
B	A	S	O	E	A	B	O	S	S	O	O	E	B	O	B
A	E	B	E	A	A	P	O	O	E	O	B	B	O	P	B

a. Show a frequency distribution and percent frequency distribution.
b. Show a bar chart.
c. What percentage of freshmen selects one of the five most popular majors?
d. What is the most popular major for incoming freshmen? What percentage of freshmen select this major?

40. *Golf Magazine*'s Top 100 Teachers were asked the question, "What is the most critical area that prevents golfers from reaching their potential?" The possible responses were lack of accuracy, poor approach shots, poor mental approach, lack of power, limited practice, poor putting, poor short game, and poor strategic decisions. The data obtained follow (*Golf Magazine,* February 2002):

Golf

Mental approach	Mental approach	Short game	Short game	Short game
Practice	Accuracy	Mental approach	Accuracy	Putting
Power	Approach shots	Accuracy	Short game	Putting
Accuracy	Mental approach	Mental approach	Accuracy	Power
Accuracy	Accuracy	Short game	Power	Short game
Accuracy	Putting	Mental approach	Strategic decisions	Accuracy
Short game	Power	Mental approach	Approach shots	Short game
Practice	Practice	Mental approach	Power	Power
Mental approach	Short game	Mental approach	Short game	Strategic decisions
Accuracy	Short game	Accuracy	Mental approach	Short game
Mental approach	Putting	Mental approach	Mental approach	Putting
Practice	Putting	Practice	Short game	Putting
Power	Mental approach	Short game	Practice	Strategic decisions
Accuracy	Short game	Accuracy	Practice	Putting
Accuracy	Short game	Accuracy	Short game	Putting
Accuracy	Approach shots	Short game	Mental approach	Practice
Short game	Short game	Strategic decisions	Short game	Short game
Practice	Practice	Short game	Practice	Strategic decisions
Mental approach	Strategic decisions	Strategic decisions	Power	Short game
Accuracy	Practice	Practice	Practice	Accuracy

a. Develop a frequency and percent frequency distribution.
b. Which four critical areas most often prevent golfers from reaching their potential?

41. Dividend yield is the annual dividend paid by a company expressed as a percentage of the price of the stock (Dividend/Stock Price $\times$ 100). The dividend yield for the Dow Jones Industrial Average companies is shown in Table 2.15 (*The Wall Street Journal,* March 3, 2006).

TABLE 2.15   DIVIDEND YIELD FOR DOW JONES INDUSTRIAL AVERAGE COMPANIES

DivYield

Company	Dividend Yield %	Company	Dividend Yield %
AIG	0.9	Home Depot	1.4
Alcoa	2.0	Honeywell	2.2
Altria Group	4.5	IBM	1.0
American Express	0.9	Intel	2.0
AT&T	4.7	Johnson & Johnson	2.3
Boeing	1.6	JPMorgan Chase	3.3
Caterpillar	1.3	McDonald's	1.9
Citigroup	4.3	Merck	4.3
Coca-Cola	3.0	Microsoft	1.3
Disney	1.0	3M	2.5
DuPont	3.6	Pfizer	3.7
ExxonMobil	2.1	Procter & Gamble	1.9
General Electric	3.0	United Technologies	1.5
General Motors	5.2	Verizon	4.8
Hewlett-Packard	0.9	Wal-Mart Stores	1.3

a. Construct a frequency distribution and percent frequency distribution.
b. Construct a histogram.
c. Comment on the shape of the distribution.
d. What do the tabular and graphical summaries tell about the dividend yields among the Dow Jones Industrial Average companies?
e. What company has the highest dividend yield? If the stock for this company currently sells for $20 per share and you purchase 500 shares, how much dividend income will this investment generate in one year?

42. Approximately 1.5 million high school students take the Scholastic Aptitude Test (SAT) each year and nearly 80% of the college and universities without open admissions policies use SAT scores in making admission decisions (*College Board,* March 2006). A sample of SAT scores for the combined math and verbal portions of the test are as follows:

WEB file

SATScores

1025	1042	1195	880	945
1102	845	1095	936	790
1097	913	1245	1040	998
998	940	1043	1048	1130
1017	1140	1030	1171	1035

a. Show a frequency distribution and histogram for the SAT scores. Begin the first class with an SAT score of 750 and use a class width of 100.
b. Comment on the shape of the distribution.
c. What other observations can be made about SAT scores based on the tabular and graphical summaries?

43. Ninety-four shadow stocks were reported by the American Association of Individual Investors. The term *shadow* indicates stocks for small to medium-sized firms not followed closely by the major brokerage houses. Information on where the stock was traded—New York Stock Exchange (NYSE), American Stock Exchange (AMEX), and over-the-counter (OTC)—the earnings per share, and the price/earnings ratio was provided for the following sample of 20 shadow stocks.

WEB file

Shadow

Stock	Exchange	Earnings per Share ($)	Price/Earnings Ratio
Chemi-Trol	OTC	.39	27.30
Candie's	OTC	.07	36.20
TST/Impreso	OTC	.65	12.70
Unimed Pharm.	OTC	.12	59.30
Skyline Chili	AMEX	.34	19.30
Cyanotech	OTC	.22	29.30
Catalina Light.	NYSE	.15	33.20
DDL Elect.	NYSE	.10	10.20
Euphonix	OTC	.09	49.70
Mesa Labs	OTC	.37	14.40
RCM Tech.	OTC	.47	18.60
Anuhco	AMEX	.70	11.40
Hello Direct	OTC	.23	21.10
Hilite Industries	OTC	.61	7.80
Alpha Tech.	OTC	.11	34.60
Wegener Group	OTC	.16	24.50
U.S. Home & Garden	OTC	.24	8.70
Chalone Wine	OTC	.27	44.40
Eng. Support Sys.	OTC	.89	16.70
Int. Remote Imaging	AMEX	.86	4.70

a. Provide frequency and relative frequency distributions for the exchange data. Where are most shadow stocks listed?
b. Provide frequency and relative frequency distributions for the earnings per share and price/earnings ratio data. Use classes of 0.00–0.19, 0.20–0.39, and so on for the earnings per share data and classes of 0.0–9.9, 10.0–19.9, and so on for the price/earnings ratio data. What observations and comments can you make about the shadow stocks?

44. Data from the U.S. Census Bureau provides the population by state in millions of people (*The World Almanac,* 2006).

WEB file

Population

State	Population	State	Population	State	Population
Alabama	4.5	Louisiana	4.5	Ohio	11.5
Alaska	0.7	Maine	1.3	Oklahoma	3.5
Arizona	5.7	Maryland	5.6	Oregon	3.6
Arkansas	2.8	Massachusetts	6.4	Pennsylvania	12.4
California	35.9	Michigan	10.1	Rhode Island	1.1
Colorado	4.6	Minnesota	5.1	South Carolina	4.2
Connecticut	3.5	Mississippi	2.9	South Dakota	0.8
Delaware	0.8	Missouri	5.8	Tennessee	5.9
Florida	17.4	Montana	0.9	Texas	22.5
Georgia	8.8	Nebraska	1.7	Utah	2.4
Hawaii	1.3	Nevada	2.3	Vermont	0.6
Idaho	1.4	New Hampshire	1.3	Virginia	7.5
Illinois	12.7	New Jersey	8.7	Washington	6.2
Indiana	6.2	New Mexico	1.9	West Virginia	1.8
Iowa	3.0	New York	19.2	Wisconsin	5.5
Kansas	2.7	North Carolina	8.5	Wyoming	0.5
Kentucky	4.1	North Dakota	0.6		

a. Develop a frequency distribution, a percent frequency distribution, and a histogram. Use a class width of 2.5 million.
b. Discuss the skewness in the distribution.
c. What observations can you make about the population of the 50 states?

45. *Drug Store News* (September 2002) provided data on annual pharmacy sales for the leading pharmacy retailers in the United States. The following data are annual sales in millions.

Retailer	Sales	Retailer	Sales
Ahold USA	$ 1700	Medicine Shoppe	$ 1757
CVS	12700	Rite-Aid	8637
Eckerd	7739	Safeway	2150
Kmart	1863	Walgreens	11660
Kroger	3400	Wal-Mart	7250

a. Show a stem-and-leaf display.
b. Identify the annual sales levels for the smallest, medium, and largest drug retailers.
c. What are the two largest drug retailers?

46. The daily high and low temperatures for 20 cities follow (*USA Today,* March 3, 2006).

CityTemp

City	High	Low	City	High	Low
Albuquerque	66	39	Los Angeles	60	46
Atlanta	61	35	Miami	84	65
Baltimore	42	26	Minneapolis	30	11
Charlotte	60	29	New Orleans	68	50
Cincinnati	41	21	Oklahoma City	62	40
Dallas	62	47	Phoenix	77	50
Denver	60	31	Portland	54	38
Houston	70	54	St. Louis	45	27
Indianapolis	42	22	San Francisco	55	43
Las Vegas	65	43	Seattle	52	36

a. Prepare a stem-and-leaf display of the high temperatures.
b. Prepare a stem-and-leaf display of the low temperatures.
c. Compare the two stem-and-leaf displays and make comments about the difference between the high and low temperatures.
d. Provide a frequency distribution for both high and low temperatures.

47. Refer to the data set for high and low temperatures for 20 cities in exercise 46.
a. Develop a scatter diagram to show the relationship between the two variables, high temperature and low temperature.
b. Comment on the relationship between high and low temperatures.

48. One of the questions in a *Financial Times*/Harris Poll conducted online by Harris Interactive® between January 30 and February 8, 2008, was, "How much do you favor or oppose a higher tax on higher carbon emission cars?" Possible responses were strongly favor, favor more than oppose, oppose more than favor, and strongly oppose. The following crosstabulation shows the responses obtained for 5372 adults surveyed in four countries in Europe and the United States (*http://www.harrisinteractive.com/harris_poll/,* February 27, 2008).

	Country					
Level of Support	Great Britain	Italy	Spain	Germany	United States	Total
Strongly favor	337	334	510	222	214	1617
Favor more than oppose	370	408	355	411	327	1871
Oppose more than favor	250	188	155	267	275	1135
Strongly oppose	130	115	89	211	204	749
Total	1087	1045	1109	1111	1020	5372

a. Construct a percent frequency distribution for the level of support variable. Do you think the results show support for a higher tax on higher carbon emission cars?
b. Construct a percent frequency distribution for the country variable.
c. Does the level of support among adults in the European countries appear to be different than the level of support among adults in the United States? Explain.

49. A study of job satisfaction was conducted for four occupations. Job satisfaction was measured using an 18-item questionnaire with each question receiving a response score of 1 to 5 with higher scores indicating greater satisfaction. The sum of the 18 scores

provides the job satisfaction score for each individual in the sample. The data are as follows.

OccupSat

Occupation	Satisfaction Score	Occupation	Satisfaction Score	Occupation	Satisfaction Score
Lawyer	42	Physical Therapist	78	Systems Analyst	60
Physical Therapist	86	Systems Analyst	44	Physical Therapist	59
Lawyer	42	Systems Analyst	71	Cabinetmaker	78
Systems Analyst	55	Lawyer	50	Physical Therapist	60
Lawyer	38	Lawyer	48	Physical Therapist	50
Cabinetmaker	79	Cabinetmaker	69	Cabinetmaker	79
Lawyer	44	Physical Therapist	80	Systems Analyst	62
Systems Analyst	41	Systems Analyst	64	Lawyer	45
Physical Therapist	55	Physical Therapist	55	Cabinetmaker	84
Systems Analyst	66	Cabinetmaker	64	Physical Therapist	62
Lawyer	53	Cabinetmaker	59	Systems Analyst	73
Cabinetmaker	65	Cabinetmaker	54	Cabinetmaker	60
Lawyer	74	Systems Analyst	76	Lawyer	64
Physical Therapist	52				

a. Provide a crosstabulation of occupation and job satisfaction score.
b. Compute the row percentages for your crosstabulation in part (a).
c. What observations can you make concerning the level of job satisfaction for these occupations?

50. A survey of commercial buildings served by the Cincinnati Gas & Electric Company asked what main heating fuel was used and what year the building was constructed. A partial crosstabulation of the findings follows.

Year Constructed	Fuel Type				
	Electricity	Natural Gas	Oil	Propane	Other
1973 or before	40	183	12	5	7
1974–1979	24	26	2	2	0
1980–1986	37	38	1	0	6
1987–1991	48	70	2	0	1

a. Complete the crosstabulation by showing the row totals and column totals.
b. Show the frequency distributions for year constructed and for fuel type.
c. Prepare a crosstabulation showing column percentages.
d. Prepare a crosstabulation showing row percentages.
e. Comment on the relationship between year constructed and fuel type.

51. Table 2.16 contains a portion of the data on the file named Fortune. It provides data on stockholders' equity, market value, and profits for a sample of 50 *Fortune* 500 companies.
a. Prepare a crosstabulation for the variables Stockholders' Equity and Profit. Use classes of 0–200, 200–400, . . . , 1000–1200 for Profit, and classes of 0–1200, 1200–2400, . . . , 4800–6000 for Stockholders' Equity.
b. Compute the row percentages for your crosstabulation in part (a).
c. What relationship, if any, do you notice between Profit and Stockholders' Equity?

TABLE 2.16　　DATA FOR A SAMPLE OF 50 *FORTUNE* 500 COMPANIES

WEB file

Fortune

Company	Stockholders' Equity ($1000s)	Market Value ($1000s)	Profit ($1000s)
AGCO	982.1	372.1	60.6
AMP	2698.0	12017.6	2.0
Apple Computer	1642.0	4605.0	309.0
Baxter International	2839.0	21743.0	315.0
Bergen Brunswick	629.1	2787.5	3.1
Best Buy	557.7	10376.5	94.5
Charles Schwab	1429.0	35340.6	348.5
.	.	.	.
.	.	.	.
.	.	.	.
Walgreen	2849.0	30324.7	511.0
Westvaco	2246.4	2225.6	132.0
Whirlpool	2001.0	3729.4	325.0
Xerox	5544.0	35603.7	395.0

52. Refer to the data set in Table 2.16.
    a. Prepare a crosstabulation for the variables Market Value and Profit.
    b. Compute the row percentages for your crosstabulation in part (a).
    c. Comment on any relationship between the variables.

53. Refer to the data set in Table 2.16.
    a. Prepare a scatter diagram to show the relationship between the variables Profit and Stockholders' Equity.
    b. Comment on any relationship between the variables.

54. Refer to the data set in Table 2.16.
    a. Prepare a scatter diagram to show the relationship between the variables Market Value and Stockholders' Equity.
    b. Comment on any relationship between the variables.

Case Problem 1　　# Pelican Stores

Pelican Stores, a division of National Clothing, is a chain of women's apparel stores operating throughout the country. The chain recently ran a promotion in which discount coupons were sent to customers of other National Clothing stores. Data collected for a sample of 100 in-store credit card transactions at Pelican Stores during one day while the promotion was running are contained in the file named PelicanStores. Table 2.17 shows a portion of the data set. The Proprietary Card method of payment refers to charges made using a National Clothing charge card. Customers who made a purchase using a discount coupon are referred to as promotional customers and customers who made a purchase but did not use a discount coupon are referred to as regular customers. Because the promotional coupons were not sent to regular Pelican Stores customers, management considers the sales made to people presenting the promotional coupons as sales it would not otherwise make. Of course, Pelican also hopes that the promotional customers will continue to shop at its stores.

TABLE 2.17   DATA FOR A SAMPLE OF 100 CREDIT CARD PURCHASES AT P|

Customer	Type of Customer	Items	Net Sales	Method of Payment	Gender		
1	Regular	1	39.50	Discover	Male		
2	Promotional	1	102.40	Proprietary Card	Female	.	
3	Regular	1	22.50	Proprietary Card	Female	Married	32
4	Promotional	5	100.40	Proprietary Card	Female	Married	28
5	Regular	2	54.00	MasterCard	Female	Married	34
.	.	.	.	.	.	.	.
.	.	.	.	.	.	.	.
96	Regular	1	39.50	MasterCard	Female	Married	44
97	Promotional	9	253.00	Proprietary Card	Female	Married	30
98	Promotional	10	287.59	Proprietary Card	Female	Married	52
99	Promotional	2	47.60	Proprietary Card	Female	Married	30
100	Promotional	1	28.44	Proprietary Card	Female	Married	44

WEB file

PelicanStores

Most of the variables shown in Table 2.17 are self-explanatory, but two of the variables require some clarification.

Items	The total number of items purchased
Net Sales	The total amount ($) charged to the credit card

Pelican's management would like to use this sample data to learn about its customer base and to evaluate the promotion involving discount coupons.

Managerial Report

Use the tabular and graphical methods of descriptive statistics to help management develop a customer profile and to evaluate the promotional campaign. At a minimum, your report should include the following:

1. Percent frequency distribution for key variables.
2. A bar or pie chart showing the number of customer purchases attributable to the method of payment.
3. A crosstabulation of type of customer (regular or promotional) versus net sales. Comment on any similarities or differences present.
4. A scatter diagram to explore the relationship between net sales and customer age.

Case Problem 2 Motion Picture Industry

The motion picture industry is a competitive business. More than 50 studios produce a total of 300 to 400 new motion pictures each year, and the financial success of each motion picture varies considerably. The opening weekend gross sales ($millions), the total gross sales ($millions), the number of theaters the movie was shown in, and the number of weeks the motion picture was in the top 60 for gross sales are common variables used to measure the success of a motion picture. Data collected for a sample of 100 motion pictures produced in 2005 are contained in the file named Movies. Table 2.18 shows the data for the first 10 motion pictures in this file.

TABLE 2.18   PERFORMANCE DATA FOR 10 MOTION PICTURES

Motion Picture	Opening Weekend Gross Sales ($millions)	Total Gross Sales ($millions)	Number of Theaters	Weeks in Top 60
Coach Carter	29.17	67.25	2574	16
Ladies in Lavender	0.15	6.65	119	22
Batman Begins	48.75	205.28	3858	18
Unleashed	10.90	24.47	1962	8
Pretty Persuasion	0.06	0.23	24	4
Fever Pitch	12.40	42.01	3275	14
Harry Potter and the Goblet of Fire	102.69	287.18	3858	13
Monster-in-Law	23.11	82.89	3424	16
White Noise	24.11	55.85	2279	7
Mr. and Mrs. Smith	50.34	186.22	3451	21

WEB file

Movies

Managerial Report

Use the tabular and graphical methods of descriptive statistics to learn how these variables contribute to the success of a motion picture. Include the following in your report.

1. Tabular and graphical summaries for each of the four variables along with a discussion of what each summary tells us about the motion picture industry.
2. A scatter diagram to explore the relationship between Total Gross Sales and Opening Weekend Gross Sales. Discuss.
3. A scatter diagram to explore the relationship between Total Gross Sales and Number of Theaters. Discuss.
4. A scatter diagram to explore the relationship between Total Gross Sales and Number of Weeks in the Top 60. Discuss.

Appendix 2.1   Using Excel's PivotTable Report and PivotChart Report to Summarize Categorical Data

In Section 2.1 we showed how Excel's COUNTIF function can be used to develop a frequency distribution and how Excel's chart tools can be used to create bar and pie charts for categorical data. In Section 2.2 we showed how Excel's PivotTable and PivotChart reports can be used to develop a frequency distribution and a histogram for quantitative data. Excel's PivotTable and PivotChart reports can also be used to develop frequency distributions and graphical displays for categorical data.

First, we will show how Excel's PivotTable Report can be used to construct a frequency distribution for the soft drink data in Figure 2.1. We will then expand the discussion to show how the PivotChart report can be used to develop a frequency distribution and a bar chart at the same time.

Enter Data: Same as in Figure 2.1

Enter Functions and Formulas: No functions and formulas are needed.

FIGURE 2.23   INITIAL PIVOTTABLE FIELD LIST USED TO CONSTRUCT A FREQUENCY DISTRIBUTION OF SOFT DRINK PURCHASES

	A	B	C	D	E	F	G	H	I
1	**Brand Purchased**								
2	Coke Classic								
3	Diet Coke								
4	Pepsi								
5	Diet Coke								
6	Coke Classic								
7	Coke Classic								
8	Dr. Pepper								
9	Diet Coke								
10	Pepsi								
11	Pepsi								
12	Coke Classic								
13	Dr. Pepper								
14	Sprite								
15	Coke Classic								
16	Diet Coke								
17	Coke Classic								
18	Coke Classic								
19	Sprite								
20	Coke Classic								
50	Pepsi								
51	Sprite								
52									

PivotTable1

To build a report, choose fields from the PivotTable Field List

PivotTable Field List

Choose fields to add to report:
☐ Brand Purchased

Drag fields between areas below:
∇ Report Filter   ▦ Column Labels

▦ Row Labels   Σ Values

☐ Defer Layout Update   Update

Apply Tools: When using Excel's PivotTable report, each column of data is referred to as a field. Thus, for the soft drink purchase example, the label in cell A1 and the data appearing in cells A2:A51 are referred to as the Brand Purchased field.

Step 1. Click the **Insert** tab on the Ribbon
Step 2. In the **Tables** group, click the icon above the word PivotTable
Step 3. When the **Create PivotTable** dialog box appears,
   Choose **Select a table or range**
   Enter A1:A51 in the **Table/Range** box
   Choose **Existing Worksheet** as the location for the PivotTable
   Enter C1 in the **Location** box
   Click **OK** (Figure 2.23 shows the resulting worksheet)
Step 4. In the **PivotTable Field List,** go to **Choose Fields to add to report**
   Drag the **Brand Purchased** field to the **Row Labels** area
   Drag the **Brand Purchased** field to the **Values** area

Figure 2.24 shows the completed PivotTable Field List and the resulting PivotTable report. We see that with the exception of the column labels, the PivotTable report looks the same as the frequency distribution we developed previously. If desired, we can change the labels in any cell by selecting the cell and typing in a new label. We could now use Excel's chart tools as previously described to create a bar chart. Alternatively,

FIGURE 2.24 COMPLETED PIVOTTABLE FIELD LIST AND PIVOTTABLE REPORT USED TO CONSTRUCT A FREQUENCY DISTRIBUTION OF SOFT DRINK PURCHASES

	A	B	C	D	E
1	**Brand Purchased**		**Row Labels** ▾	**Count of Brand Purchased**	
2	Coke Classic		Coke Classic	19	
3	Diet Coke		Diet Coke	8	
4	Pepsi		Dr. Pepper	5	
5	Diet Coke		Pepsi	13	
6	Coke Classic		Sprite	5	
7	Coke Classic		**Grand Total**	**50**	
8	Dr. Pepper				
9	Diet Coke				
10	Pepsi				
11	Pepsi				
12	Coke Classic				
13	Dr. Pepper				
14	Sprite				
15	Coke Classic				
16	Diet Coke				
17	Coke Classic				
18	Coke Classic				
19	Sprite				
20	Coke Classic				
50	Pepsi				
51	Sprite				
52					

PivotTable Field List

Choose fields to add to report:
☑ Brand Purchased

Drag fields between areas below:
▽ Report Filter — Column Labels
Row Labels: Brand Purchased ▾
Σ Values: Count of Brand Purchased ▾
☐ Defer Layout Update — Update

we can use Excel's PivotChart report to construct both a frequency distribution and a bar graph at the same time by simply modifying the steps in the Apply Tools section.

Apply Tools: The following steps describe how to use Excel's PivotChart report to construct a frequency distribution and a bar chart for the soft drink data.

Step 1. Click the **Insert** tab on the Ribbon
Step 2. In the **Tables** group, click the word **PivotTable**
Step 3. Choose **PivotChart** from the options that appear
Step 4. When the **Create PivotTable with PivotChart** dialog box appears,
  Choose **Select a table or range**
  Enter A1:A51 in the **Table/Range** box
  Choose **Existing Worksheet** as the location for the PivotTable and PivotChart
  Enter C1 in the **Location** box
  Click **OK**
Step 5. In the **PivotTable Field List,** go to **Choose Fields to add to report**
  Drag the **Brand Purchased** field to the **Axis Fields (Categories)** area
  Drag the **Brand Purchased** field to the **Values** area

Figure 2.25 shows the resulting PivotTable and PivotChart. The PivotTable report provides the frequency distribution for the soft drink data and the PivotChart provides the corresponding bar chart. If desired, we can change the labels in any cell in the frequency distribution by selecting the cell and typing in the new label. We can also use Excel's chart tools to reformat the bar chart.

FIGURE 2.25   USING EXCEL'S PIVOTCHART REPORT TO CONSTRUCT A FREQUENCY DISTRIBUTION AND A BAR CHART OF SOFT DRINK PURCHASES

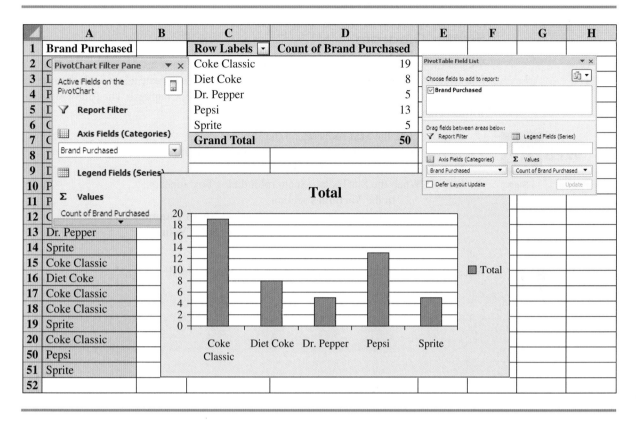

Appendix 2.2   Using StatTools for Tabular and Graphical Presentations

In this appendix we show how StatTools can be used to construct a histogram and a scatter diagram.

Histogram

We use the audit time data in Table 2.4 to illustrate. Begin by using the Data Set Manager to create a StatTools data set for these data using the procedure described in the appendix in Chapter 1. The following steps will generate a histogram.

Audit

Step 1. Click the **StatTools** tab on the Ribbon
Step 2. In the **Analyses Group,** click **Summary Graphs**
Step 3. Choose the **Histogram** option
Step 4. When the StatTools—Histogram dialog box appears,
   In the **Variables** section, select **Audit Time**
   In the **Options** section,
      Enter 5 in the **Number of Bins** box
      Enter 9.5 in the **Histogram Minimum** box
      Enter 34.5 in the **Histogram Maximum** box
      Choose **Categorical** in the **X-Axis** box
      Choose **Frequency** in the **Y-Axis** box
   Click **OK**

A histogram for the audit time data similar to the histogram shown in Figure 2.9 will appear. The only difference is the histogram developed using StatTools shows the class midpoints on the horizontal axis.

Scatter Diagram

We use the stereo and sound equipment data in Table 2.12 to demonstrate the construction of a scatter diagram. Begin by using the Data Set Manager to create a StatTools data set for these data using the procedure described in the appendix in Chapter 1. The following steps will generate a scatter diagram.

Stereo

Step 1. Click the **StatTools** tab on the Ribbon
Step 2. In the **Analyses Group,** click **Summary Graphs**
Step 3. Choose the **Scatterplot** option
Step 4. When the StatTools—Scatterplot dialog box appears,
　　　　In the **Variables** section,
　　　　　In the column labeled **X**, select **No. of Commercials**
　　　　　In the column labeled **Y**, select **Sales Volume**
　　　　Click **OK**

A scatter diagram similar to the one shown in Figure 2.20 will appear.

CHAPTER 3

Descriptive Statistics: Numerical Measures

SMALL FRY DESIGN*
SANTA ANA, CALIFORNIA

Small Fry Design is a toy and accessory company that designs and imports products for infants. The company's product line includes teddy bears, mobiles, musical toys, rattles, and security blankets and features high-quality soft toy designs with an emphasis on color, texture, and sound. The products are designed in the United States and manufactured in China.

Small Fry Design uses independent representatives to sell the products to infant furnishing retailers, children's accessory and apparel stores, gift shops, upscale department stores, and major catalog companies. Currently, Small Fry Design products are distributed in more than 1000 retail outlets throughout the United States.

Cash flow management is one of the most critical activities in the day-to-day operation of this company. Ensuring sufficient incoming cash to meet both current and ongoing debt obligations can mean the difference between business success and failure. A critical factor in cash flow management is the analysis and control of accounts receivable. By measuring the average age and dollar value of outstanding invoices, management can predict cash availability and monitor changes in the status of accounts receivable. The company set the following goals: the average age for outstanding invoices should not exceed 45 days, and the dollar value of invoices more than 60 days old should not exceed 5% of the dollar value of all accounts receivable.

In a recent summary of accounts receivable status, the following descriptive statistics were provided for the age of outstanding invoices:

Mean	40 days
Median	35 days
Mode	31 days

Small Fry Design's "King of the Jungle" mobile.
© Courtesy of Small Fry Design, Inc.

Interpretation of these statistics shows that the mean or average age of an invoice is 40 days. The median shows that half the invoices remain outstanding 35 days or more. The mode of 31 days, the most frequent invoice age, indicates that the most common length of time an invoice is outstanding is 31 days. The statistical summary also showed that only 3% of the dollar value of all accounts receivable was more than 60 days old. Based on the statistical information, management was satisfied that accounts receivable and incoming cash flow were under control.

In this chapter, you will learn how to compute and interpret some of the statistical measures used by Small Fry Design. In addition to the mean, median, and mode, you will learn about other descriptive statistics such as the range, variance, standard deviation, percentiles, and correlation. These numerical measures will assist in the understanding and interpretation of data.

*The authors are indebted to John A. McCarthy, President of Small Fry Design, for providing this Statistics in Practice.

In Chapter 2 we discussed tabular and graphical presentations used to summarize data. In this chapter, we present several numerical measures that provide additional alternatives for summarizing data.

We start by developing numerical summary measures for data sets consisting of a single variable. When a data set contains more than one variable, the same numerical measures can be computed separately for each variable. However, in the two-variable case, we will also develop measures of the relationship between the variables.

Numerical measures of location, dispersion, shape, and association are introduced. If the measures are computed for data from a sample, they are called **sample statistics**. If the measures are computed for data from a population, they are called **population parameters**. In statistical inference, a sample statistic is referred to as the **point estimator** of the corresponding population parameter. In Chapter 7 we will discuss in more detail the process of point estimation.

3.1   Measures of Location

Mean

Perhaps the most important measure of location is the **mean**, or average value, for a variable. The mean provides a measure of central location for the data. If the data are for a sample, the mean is denoted by $\bar{x}$; if the data are for a population, the mean is denoted by the Greek letter μ.

In statistical formulas, it is customary to denote the value of variable x for the first observation by x_1, the value of variable x for the second observation by x_2, and so on. In general, the value of variable x for the ith observation is denoted by x_i. For a sample with n observations, the formula for the sample mean is as follows.

The sample mean $\bar{x}$ is a sample statistic.

SAMPLE MEAN

$$\bar{x} = \frac{\Sigma x_i}{n} \tag{3.1}$$

In the preceding formula, the numerator is the sum of the values of the n observations. That is,

$$\Sigma x_i = x_1 + x_2 + \cdots + x_n$$

The Greek letter Σ is the summation sign.

To illustrate the computation of a sample mean, let us consider the following class size data for a sample of five college classes.

$$46 \quad 54 \quad 42 \quad 46 \quad 32$$

We use the notation x_1, x_2, x_3, x_4, x_5 to represent the number of students in each of the five classes.

$$x_1 = 46 \qquad x_2 = 54 \qquad x_3 = 42 \qquad x_4 = 46 \qquad x_5 = 32$$

Hence, to compute the sample mean, we can write

$$\bar{x} = \frac{\Sigma x_i}{n} = \frac{x_1 + x_2 + x_3 + x_4 + x_5}{5} = \frac{46 + 54 + 42 + 46 + 32}{5} = 44$$

The sample mean class size is 44 students.

Another illustration of the computation of a sample mean is given in the following situation. Suppose that a college placement office sent a questionnaire to a sample of business school graduates requesting information on monthly starting salaries. Table 3.1 shows the

TABLE 3.1   MONTHLY STARTING SALARIES FOR A SAMPLE OF 12 BUSINESS SCHOOL
GRADUATES

Graduate	Monthly Starting Salary ($)	Graduate	Monthly Starting Salary ($)
1	3450	7	3490
2	3550	8	3730
3	3650	9	3540
4	3480	10	3925
5	3355	11	3520
6	3310	12	3480

WEB file

StartSalary

collected data. The mean monthly starting salary for the sample of 12 business college
graduates is computed as

$$\bar{x} = \frac{\Sigma x_i}{n} = \frac{x_1 + x_2 + \cdots + x_{12}}{12}$$

$$= \frac{3450 + 3550 + \cdots + 3480}{12}$$

$$= \frac{42{,}480}{12} = 3540$$

Equation (3.1) shows how the mean is computed for a sample with n observations. The
formula for computing the mean of a population remains the same, but we use different
notation to indicate that we are working with the entire population. The number of observations in a population is denoted by N and the symbol for a population mean is μ.

The sample mean $\bar{x}$ is a
point estimator of the
population mean μ.

POPULATION MEAN

$$\mu = \frac{\Sigma x_i}{N} \tag{3.2}$$

Median

The **median** is another measure of central location. The median is the value in the middle
when the data are arranged in ascending order (smallest value to largest value). With an odd
number of observations, the median is the middle value. An even number of observations
has no single middle value. In this case, we follow convention and define the median as the
average of the values for the middle two observations. For convenience the definition of the
median is restated as follows.

MEDIAN

Arrange the data in ascending order (smallest value to largest value).

(a) For an odd number of observations, the median is the middle value.
(b) For an even number of observations, the median is the average of the two middle values.

Let us apply this definition to compute the median class size for the sample of five college classes. Arranging the data in ascending order provides the following list.

$$32 \quad 42 \quad 46 \quad 46 \quad 54$$

Because $n = 5$ is odd, the median is the middle value. Thus the median class size is 46 students. Even though this data set contains two observations with values of 46, each observation is treated separately when we arrange the data in ascending order.

Suppose we also compute the median starting salary for the 12 business college graduates in Table 3.1. We first arrange the data in ascending order.

3310   3355   3450   3480   3480   3490   3520   3540   3550   3650   3730   3925

Middle Two Values

Because $n = 12$ is even, we identify the middle two values: 3490 and 3520. The median is the average of these values.

$$\text{Median} = \frac{3490 + 3520}{2} = 3505$$

The median is the measure of location most often reported for annual income and property value data because a few extremely large incomes or property values can inflate the mean. In such cases, the median is the preferred measure of central location.

Although the mean is the more commonly used measure of central location, in some situations the median is preferred. The mean is influenced by extremely small and large data values. For instance, suppose that one of the graduates had a starting salary of $10,000 per month (maybe the individual's family owns the company). If we change the highest monthly starting salary in Table 3.1 from $3925 to $10,000 and recompute the mean, the sample mean changes from $3540 to $4046. The median of $3505, however, is unchanged, because $3490 and $3520 are still the middle two values. With the extremely high starting salary included, the median provides a better measure of central location than the mean. We can generalize to say that whenever a data set contains extreme values, the median is often the preferred measure of central location.

Mode

A third measure of location is the **mode**. The mode is defined as follows.

> **MODE**
>
> The mode is the value that occurs with greatest frequency.

To illustrate the identification of the mode, consider the sample of five class sizes. The only value that occurs more than once is 46. Because this value, occurring with a frequency of 2, has the greatest frequency, it is the mode. As another illustration, consider the sample of starting salaries for the business school graduates. The only monthly starting salary that occurs more than once is $3480. Because this value has the greatest frequency, it is the mode.

Situations can arise for which the greatest frequency occurs at two or more different values. In these instances more than one mode exists. If the data contain exactly two modes, we say that the data are *bimodal*. If data contain more than two modes, we say that the data are *multimodal*. In multimodal cases the mode is almost never reported because listing three or more modes would not be particularly helpful in describing a location for the data.

Using Excel to Compute the Mean, Median, and Mode

Excel provides functions for computing the mean, median, and mode. We illustrate the use of these Excel functions by computing the mean, median, and mode for the starting salary data in Table 3.1. Refer to Figure 3.1 as we describe the tasks involved. The formula worksheet is in the background; the value worksheet is in the foreground.

Enter Data: Labels and the starting salary data are entered into cells A1:B13 of the worksheet.

Enter Functions and Formulas: Excel's AVERAGE function can be used to compute the mean by entering the following formula into cell E1:

$$=AVERAGE(B2:B13)$$

If the data are bimodal or multimodal, Excel's MODE function will incorrectly identify a single mode.

Similarly, the formulas =MEDIAN(B2:B13) and =MODE(B2:B13) are entered into cells E2 and E3, respectively, to compute the median and the mode. The labels Mean, Median, and Mode are entered into cells D1:D3 to identify the output.

The formulas in cells E1:E3 are displayed in the formula worksheet in the background of Figure 3.1. The worksheet in the foreground shows the values computed using the Excel functions. Note that the mean (3540), median (3505), and mode (3480) are the same as we computed earlier.

Percentiles

A **percentile** provides information about how the data are spread over the interval from the smallest value to the largest value. For data that do not contain numerous repeated

---

FIGURE 3.1   EXCEL WORKSHEET USED TO COMPUTE THE MEAN, MEDIAN, AND MODE FOR STARTING SALARIES

	A	B	C	D	E	F
1	Graduate	Starting Salary		Mean	=AVERAGE(B2:B13)	
2	1	3450		Median	=MEDIAN(B2:B13)	
3	2	3550		Mode	=MODE(B2:B13)	
4	3	3650				
5	4	3480				
6	5	3355				
7	6	3310				
8	7	3490				
9	8	3730				
10	9	3540				
11	10	3925				
12	11	3520				
13	12	3480				
14						

	A	B	C	D	E	F
1	Graduate	Starting Salary		Mean	3540	
2	1	3450		Median	3505	
3	2	3550		Mode	3480	
4	3	3650				
5	4	3480				
6	5	3355				
7	6	3310				
8	7	3490				
9	8	3730				
10	9	3540				
11	10	3925				
12	11	3520				
13	12	3480				
14						

values, the pth percentile divides the data into two parts. Approximately p percent of the observations have values less than the pth percentile; approximately $(100 - p)$ percent of the observations have values greater than the pth percentile. The pth percentile is formally defined as follows.

> **PERCENTILE**
>
> The pth percentile is a value such that *at least* p percent of the observations are less than or equal to this value and *at least* $(100 - p)$ percent of the observations are greater than or equal to this value.

Colleges and universities frequently report admission test scores in terms of percentiles. For instance, suppose an applicant obtains a raw score of 54 on the verbal portion of an admission test. How this student performed in relation to other students taking the same test may not be readily apparent. However, if the raw score of 54 corresponds to the 70th percentile, we know that approximately 70% of the students scored lower than this individual and approximately 30% of the students scored higher than this individual.

The following procedure can be used to compute the pth percentile.

> **CALCULATING THE pTH PERCENTILE**
>
> *Following these steps makes it easy to calculate percentiles.*
>
> **Step 1.** Arrange the data in ascending order (smallest value to largest value).
> **Step 2.** Compute an index i
>
> $$i = \left(\frac{p}{100}\right)n$$
>
> where p is the percentile of interest and n is the number of observations.
> **Step 3.** (a) If i *is not an integer, round up.* The next integer *greater* than i denotes the position of the pth percentile.
> (b) If i *is an integer,* the pth percentile is the average of the values in positions i and $i + 1$.

As an illustration of this procedure, let us determine the 85th percentile for the starting salary data in Table 3.1.

Step 1. Arrange the data in ascending order.

3310   3355   3450   3480   3480   3490   3520   3540   3550   3650   3730   3925

Step 2.

$$i = \left(\frac{p}{100}\right)n = \left(\frac{85}{100}\right)12 = 10.2$$

Step 3. Because i is not an integer, *round up.* The position of the 85th percentile is the next integer greater than 10.2, the 11th position.

Returning to the data, we see that the 85th percentile is the data value in the 11th position, or 3730.

FIGURE 3.2   LOCATION OF THE QUARTILES

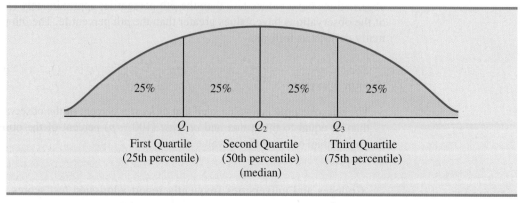

As another illustration of this procedure, let us consider the calculation of the 50th percentile for the starting salary data. Applying step 2, we obtain

$$i = \left(\frac{50}{100}\right)12 = 6$$

Because i is an integer, step 3(b) states that the 50th percentile is the average of the sixth and seventh data values; thus the 50th percentile is $(3490 + 3520)/2 = 3505$. Note that the *50th percentile is also the median.*

Quartiles

Quartiles are just specific percentiles; thus, the steps for computing percentiles can be applied directly in the computation of quartiles.

It is often desirable to divide data into four parts, with each part containing approximately one-fourth, or 25% of the observations. Figure 3.2 shows a data distribution divided into four parts. The division points are referred to as the **quartiles** and are defined as

Q_1 = first quartile, or 25th percentile

Q_2 = second quartile, or 50th percentile (also the median)

Q_3 = third quartile, or 75th percentile.

The starting salary data are again arranged in ascending order.

3310   3355   3450   3480   3480   3490   3520   3540   3550   3650   3730   3925

We already identified Q_2, the second quartile (median), as 3505. The computations of quartiles Q_1 and Q_3 require the use of the rule for finding the 25th and 75th percentiles. These calculations follow.

For Q_1,

$$i = \left(\frac{p}{100}\right)n = \left(\frac{25}{100}\right)12 = 3$$

Because i is an integer, step 3(b) indicates that the first quartile, or 25th percentile, is the average of the third and fourth data values; thus, $Q_1 = (3450 + 3480)/2 = 3465$.

For Q_3,

$$i = \left(\frac{p}{100}\right)n = \left(\frac{75}{100}\right)12 = 9$$

Again, because i is an integer, step 3(b) indicates that the third quartile, or 75th percentile, is the average of the ninth and tenth data values; thus, $Q_3 = (3550 + 3650)/2 = 3600$.

The quartiles divide the starting salary data into four parts, with each part containing 25% of the observations.

$$3310 \quad 3355 \quad 3450 \quad \bigg| \quad 3480 \quad 3480 \quad 3490 \quad \bigg| \quad 3520 \quad 3540 \quad 3550 \quad \bigg| \quad 3650 \quad 3730 \quad 3925$$

$$Q_1 = 3465 \qquad\qquad Q_2 = 3505 \qquad\qquad Q_3 = 3600$$
$$\text{(Median)}$$

We defined the quartiles as the 25th, 50th, and 75th percentiles. Thus, we computed the quartiles in the same way as percentiles. However, other conventions are sometimes used to compute quartiles, and the actual values reported for quartiles may vary slightly depending on the convention used. Nevertheless, the objective of all procedures for computing quartiles is to divide the data into four equal parts.

Using Excel's Rank and Percentile Tool to Compute Percentiles and Quartiles

Computer software packages do not all use the same method to compute percentiles and quartiles. The formula Excel uses to compute the location (L_p) of the pth percentile is

$$L_p = \left(\frac{p}{100} \right) n + \left(1 - \frac{p}{100} \right)$$

For instance, Excel would compute the location of the 85th percentile for the starting salary data as follows:

$$L_{85} = (.85)12 + (1 - .85) = 10.20 + .15 = 10.35$$

The value of $L_{85} = 10.35$ indicates that the 85th percentile is between the 10th and the 11th observations in rank order from the bottom up. It is the value of observation 10 (3650) plus .35 of the difference between observation 11 (3730) and observation 10. Therefore, the 85th percentile is $3650 + .35(3730 - 3650) = 3650 + .35(80) = 3678$.[1]

Computing percentiles and quartiles using Excel is easy. For instance, Excel's PERCENTILE function can be used to compute the 85th percentile for the starting salary data by entering the following formula into any empty cell of the worksheet shown in Figure 3.1:

$$=\text{PERCENTILE(B2:B13,.85)}$$

The value Excel provides is 3678. To compute a different percentile we simply change the value of .85. For instance, we can use Excel's PERCENTILE function to compute the quartiles for the starting salary data by replacing .85 with values of .25 (25th percentile or first quartile), .50 (50th percentile or second quartile), and .75 (75th percentile or third quartile).

Alternatively, we can use Excel's QUARTILE function to compute the quartiles. For example, to compute the first quartile for the starting salary data we would enter the following formula into an empty cell of the worksheet in Figure 3.1.

$$=\text{QUARTILE(B2:B13,1)}$$

---

[1]The value Excel computed for the 85th percentile does not strictly satisfy the definition of the 85th percentile because only 83% of the values are less than or equal to 3678. Our procedure would round up in this case to obtain 3730 as the value satisfying the definition of the 85th percentile. For larger data sets, the difference between the approximate value provided by Excel and the value computed using our three-step procedure is not of practical significance.

FIGURE 3.3   USING EXCEL'S RANK AND PERCENTILE TOOL FOR STARTING SALARIES

	A	B	C	D	E	F	G	H
1	Graduate	Starting Salary		Point	Starting Salary	Rank	Percent	
2	1	3450		10	3925	1	100.00%	
3	2	3550		8	3730	2	90.90%	
4	3	3650		3	3650	3	81.80%	
5	4	3480		2	3550	4	72.70%	
6	5	3355		9	3540	5	63.60%	
7	6	3310		11	3520	6	54.50%	
8	7	3490		7	3490	7	45.40%	
9	8	3730		4	3480	8	27.20%	
10	9	3540		12	3480	8	27.20%	
11	10	3925		1	3450	10	18.10%	
12	11	3520		5	3355	11	9.00%	
13	12	3480		6	3310	12	0.00%	
14								

If the value of 1 in the QUARTILE function is changed to 0, Excel computes the minimum value in the data set. If the value of 1 is changed to 4, Excel computes the maximum value.

The value Excel provides is 3472.5. We can compute the second quartile or median by replacing the value of 1 with 2, and the third quartile by replacing the value of 1 with 3.

Computing percentiles and quartiles is useful for a data analyst who is interested in getting a feel for how the values in a data set are distributed. However, if you are a student who wants to know how the starting salary you received ranks compared to all the other starting salaries, then what you would like to do is to take your salary and compute its rank and percentile. Or perhaps you know your raw score on an exam and would like to know its rank and percentile. Excel's Rank and Percentile tool can be used to provide this information for an entire data set.

We illustrate the use of Excel's Rank and Percentile tool by computing the ranks and percentiles for the starting salaries in Table 3.1. Refer to Figure 3.3 as we present the tasks involved.

Enter Data: Labels and the starting salary data are entered into cells A1:B13.

Enter Functions and Formulas: No functions and formulas are needed.

Apply Tools: The following steps will compute the rank and percentile for each observation.

Step 1. Click the **Data** tab on the Ribbon
Step 2. In the **Analysis** group, click **Data Analysis**
Step 3. Choose **Rank and Percentile** from the list of Analysis Tools
Step 4. When the Rank and Percentile dialog box appears,
Enter B1:B13 in the **Input Range** box
Select **Grouped by Columns**
Select **Labels in First Row**
Select **Output Range**
Enter D1 in the **Output Range** box
(Any cell where the upper left corner of the output is desired may be entered here.)
Click **OK**

The output from using the Rank and Percentile tool appears in cells D1:G13. Cells F2:F13 contain the rank of each observation. The highest salary is given a rank of 1 and the lowest salary is given a rank of 12. Cells G2:G13 show the percentile each salary represents. For instance, the percentile for 3450 is 18.1% because 2 of the other 11 salaries are smaller than 3450. The lowest salary is the 0th percentile and the highest salary is the 100th percentile. The percentiles increase by (1/11)100% as we move up from the lowest salary to the highest, except for ties. In the case of a tie, Excel gives the tied values the same rank and percentile. Note that the two observations with the same value (3480) both received a rank of 8 and a percentile of 27.20%.

NOTES AND COMMENTS

It is better to use the median than the mean as a measure of central location when a data set contains extreme values. Another measure, sometimes used when extreme values are present, is the *trimmed mean.* It is obtained by deleting a percentage of the smallest and largest values from a data set and then computing the mean of the remaining values. For example, the 5% trimmed mean is obtained by removing the smallest 5% and the largest 5% of the data values and then computing the mean of the remaining values. Using the sample with $n = 12$ starting salaries, $0.05(12) = 0.6$. Rounding this value to 1 indicates that the 5% trimmed mean would remove the 1 smallest data value and the 1 largest data value. The 5% trimmed mean using the 10 remaining observations is 3524.50.

Exercises

Methods

1. Consider a sample with data values of 10, 20, 12, 17, and 16. Compute the mean and median.

2. Consider a sample with data values of 10, 20, 21, 17, 16, and 12. Compute the mean and median.

3. Consider a sample with data values of 27, 25, 20, 15, 30, 34, 28, and 25. Compute the 20th, 25th, 65th, and 75th percentiles.

4. Consider a sample with data values of 53, 55, 70, 58, 64, 57, 53, 69, 57, 68, and 53. Compute the mean, median, and mode.

Applications

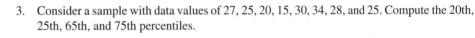

5. The Dow Jones Travel Index reported what business travelers pay for hotel rooms per night in major U.S. cities (*The Wall Street Journal,* January 16, 2004). The average hotel room rates for 20 cities are as follows:

Atlanta	$163	Minneapolis	$125
Boston	177	New Orleans	167
Chicago	166	New York	245
Cleveland	126	Orlando	146
Dallas	123	Phoenix	139
Denver	120	Pittsburgh	134
Detroit	144	San Francisco	167
Houston	173	Seattle	162
Los Angeles	160	St. Louis	145
Miami	192	Washington, D.C.	207

a. What is the mean hotel room rate?
b. What is the median hotel room rate?
c. What is the mode?
d. What is the first quartile?
e. What is the third quartile?

6. The National Association of Colleges and Employers compiled information about annual starting salaries for college graduates by major. The mean starting salary for business administration graduates was $39,850 (*http://CNNMoney.com*, February 15, 2006). Samples with annual starting data for marketing majors and accounting majors follow (data are in thousands):

BASalary

Marketing Majors

| 34.2 | 45.0 | 39.5 | 28.4 | 37.7 | 35.8 | 30.6 | 35.2 | 34.2 | 42.4 |

Accounting Majors

| 33.5 | 57.1 | 49.7 | 40.2 | 44.2 | 45.2 | 47.8 | 38.0 |
| 53.9 | 41.1 | 41.7 | 40.8 | 55.5 | 43.5 | 49.1 | 49.9 |

a. Compute the mean, median, and mode of the annual starting salary for both majors.
b. Compute the first and third quartiles for both majors.
c. Business administration students with accounting majors generally obtain the highest annual salary after graduation. What do the sample data indicate about the difference between the annual starting salaries for marketing and accounting majors?

7. The American Association of Individual Investors conducted an annual survey of discount brokers (*AAII Journal,* January 2003). The commissions charged by 24 discount brokers for two types of trades, a broker-assisted trade of 100 shares at $50 per share and an online trade of 500 shares at $50 per share, are shown in Table 3.2.
a. Compute the mean, median, and mode for the commission charged on a broker-assisted trade of 100 shares at $50 per share.
b. Compute the mean, median, and mode for the commission charged on an online trade of 500 shares at $50 per share.
c. Which costs more, a broker-assisted trade of 100 shares at $50 per share or an online trade of 500 shares at $50 per share?
d. Is the cost of a transaction related to the amount of the transaction?

TABLE 3.2   COMMISSIONS CHARGED BY DISCOUNT BROKERS

Broker

Broker	Broker-Assisted 100 Shares at $50/Share	Online 500 Shares at $50/Share	Broker	Broker-Assisted 100 Shares at $50/Share	Online 500 Shares at $50/Share
Accutrade	30.00	29.95	Merrill Lynch Direct	50.00	29.95
Ameritrade	24.99	10.99	Muriel Siebert	45.00	14.95
Banc of America	54.00	24.95	NetVest	24.00	14.00
Brown & Co.	17.00	5.00	Recom Securities	35.00	12.95
Charles Schwab	55.00	29.95	Scottrade	17.00	7.00
CyberTrader	12.95	9.95	Sloan Securities	39.95	19.95
E*TRADE Securities	49.95	14.95	Strong Investments	55.00	24.95
First Discount	35.00	19.75	TD Waterhouse	45.00	17.95
Freedom Investments	25.00	15.00	T. Rowe Price	50.00	19.95
Harrisdirect	40.00	20.00	Vanguard	48.00	20.00
Investors National	39.00	62.50	Wall Street Discount	29.95	19.95
MB Trading	9.95	10.55	York Securities	40.00	36.00

Source: AAII Journal, January 2003.

SELF test

WEB file

TaxCost

8.   The cost of consumer purchases such as single-family housing, gasoline, Internet services, tax preparation, and hospitalization were provided in *The Wall-Street Journal* (January 2, 2007). Sample data typical of the cost of tax-return preparation by services such as H&R Block are shown below.

120	230	110	115	160
130	150	105	195	155
105	360	120	120	140
100	115	180	235	255

   a.   Compute the mean, median, and mode.
   b.   Compute the first and third quartiles.
   c.   Compute and interpret the 90th percentile.

9.   J. D. Powers and Associates surveyed cell phone users in order to learn about the minutes of cell phone usage per month (Associated Press, June 2002). Minutes per month for a sample of 15 cell phone users are shown here.

615	135	395
430	830	1180
690	250	420
265	245	210
180	380	105

   a.   What is the mean number of minutes of usage per month?
   b.   What is the median number of minutes of usage per month?
   c.   What is the 85th percentile?
   d.   J. D. Powers and Associates reported that the average wireless subscriber plan allows up to 750 minutes of usage per month. What do the data suggest about cell phone subscribers' utilization of their monthly plan?

10.   A panel of economists provided forecasts of the U.S. economy for the first six months of 2007 (*The Wall Street Journal,* January 2, 2007). The percent changes in the gross domestic product (GDP) forecasted by 30 economists are as follows.

2.6	3.1	2.3	2.7	3.4	0.9	2.6	2.8	2.0	2.4
2.7	2.7	2.7	2.9	3.1	2.8	1.7	2.3	2.8	3.5
0.4	2.5	2.2	1.9	1.8	1.1	2.0	2.1	2.5	0.5

WEB file

Economy

   a.   What is the minimum forecast for the percent change in the GDP? What is the maximum?
   b.   Compute the mean, median, and mode.
   c.   Compute the first and third quartiles.
   d.   Did the economists provide an optimistic or pessimistic outlook for the U.S. economy? Discuss.

11.   In automobile mileage and gasoline-consumption testing, 13 automobiles were road tested for 300 miles in both city and highway driving conditions. The following data were recorded for miles-per-gallon performance.

   City: 16.2 16.7 15.9 14.4 13.2 15.3 16.8 16.0 16.1 15.3 15.2 15.3 16.2
   Highway: 19.4 20.6 18.3 18.6 19.2 17.4 17.2 18.6 19.0 21.1 19.4 18.5 18.7

   Use the mean, median, and mode to make a statement about the difference in performance for city and highway driving.

12.   Walt Disney Company bought Pixar Animation Studios, Inc., in a deal worth $7.4 billion (*http://CNNMoney.com,* January 24, 2006). The animated movies produced by Disney and Pixar during the previous 10 years are listed below. The box office revenues are in millions

of dollars. Compute the total revenue, the mean, the median, and the quartiles to compare the box office success of the movies produced by both companies. Do the statistics suggest at least one of the reasons Disney was interested in buying Pixar? Discuss.

Disney

Disney Movies	Revenue ($millions)	Pixar Movies	Revenue ($millions)
Pocahontas	346	*Toy Story*	362
Hunchback of Notre Dame	325	*A Bug's Life*	363
Hercules	253	*Toy Story 2*	485
Mulan	304	*Monsters, Inc.*	525
Tarzan	448	*Finding Nemo*	865
Dinosaur	354	*The Incredibles*	631
The Emperor's New Groove	169		
Lilo & Stitch	273		
Treasure Planet	110		
The Jungle Book 2	136		
Brother Bear	250		
Home on the Range	104		
Chicken Little	249		

(3.2) Measures of Variability

The variability in the delivery time creates uncertainty for production scheduling. Methods in this section help measure and understand variability.

In addition to measures of location, it is often desirable to consider measures of variability, or dispersion. For example, suppose that you are a purchasing agent for a large manufacturing firm and that you regularly place orders with two different suppliers. After several months of operation, you find that the mean number of days required to fill orders is 10 days for both of the suppliers. The histograms summarizing the number of working days required to fill orders from the suppliers are shown in Figure 3.4. Although the mean number of days is 10 for both suppliers, do the two suppliers demonstrate the same degree of reliability in terms of making deliveries on schedule? Note the dispersion, or variability, in delivery times indicated by the histograms. Which supplier would you prefer?

FIGURE 3.4   HISTORICAL DATA SHOWING THE NUMBER OF DAYS REQUIRED TO FILL ORDERS

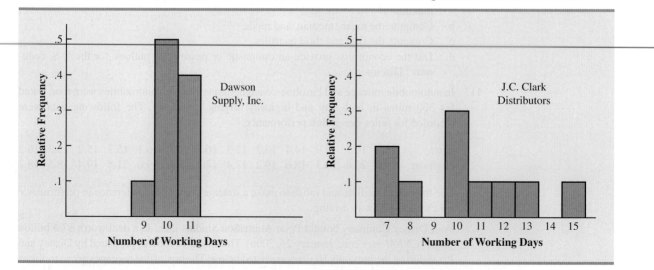

For most firms, receiving materials and supplies on schedule is important. The seven- or eight-day deliveries shown for J.C. Clark Distributors might be viewed favorably; however, a few of the slow 13- to 15-day deliveries could be disastrous in terms of keeping a workforce busy and production on schedule. This example illustrates a situation in which the variability in the delivery times may be an overriding consideration in selecting a supplier. For most purchasing agents, the lower variability shown for Dawson Supply, Inc., would make Dawson the preferred supplier.

We turn now to a discussion of some commonly used measures of variability.

Range

The simplest measure of variability is the **range**.

RANGE

$$\text{Range} = \text{Largest value} - \text{Smallest value}$$

Let us refer to the data on starting salaries for business school graduates in Table 3.1. The largest starting salary is 3925 and the smallest is 3310. The range is $3925 - 3310 = 615$.

Although the range is the easiest of the measures of variability to compute, it is seldom used as the only measure. The reason is that the range is based on only two of the observations and thus is highly influenced by extreme values. Suppose one of the graduates received a starting salary of $10,000 per month. In this case, the range would be $10,000 - 3310 = 6690$ rather than 615. This large value for the range would not be especially descriptive of the variability in the data because 11 of the 12 starting salaries are closely grouped between 3310 and 3730.

Interquartile Range

A measure of variability that overcomes the dependency on extreme values is the **interquartile range (IQR)**. This measure of variability is the difference between the third quartile, Q_3, and the first quartile, Q_1. In other words, the interquartile range is the range for the middle 50% of the data.

INTERQUARTILE RANGE

$$IQR = Q_3 - Q_1 \tag{3.3}$$

For the data on monthly starting salaries, the quartiles are $Q_3 = 3600$ and $Q_1 = 3465$. Thus, the interquartile range is $3600 - 3465 = 135$.

Variance

The **variance** is a measure of variability that utilizes all the data. The variance is based on the difference between the value of each observation (x_i) and the mean. The difference between each x_i and the mean ($\bar{x}$ for a sample, μ for a population) is called a *deviation about the mean*. For a sample, a deviation about the mean is written ($x_i - \bar{x}$); for a population, it is written ($x_i - \mu$). In the computation of the variance, the deviations about the mean are *squared*.

If the data are for a population, the average of the squared deviations is called the *population variance*. The population variance is denoted by the Greek symbol σ^2. For a population of N observations and with μ denoting the population mean, the definition of the population variance is as follows.

POPULATION VARIANCE

$$\sigma^2 = \frac{\Sigma(x_i - \mu)^2}{N} \tag{3.4}$$

In most statistical applications, the data being analyzed are for a sample. When we compute a sample variance, we are often interested in using it to estimate the population variance σ^2. Although a detailed explanation is beyond the scope of this text, it can be shown that if the sum of the squared deviations about the sample mean is divided by $n - 1$, and not n, the resulting sample variance provides an unbiased estimate of the population variance. For this reason, the *sample variance,* denoted by s^2, is defined as follows.

The sample variance s^2 is a point estimator of the population variance σ^2.

SAMPLE VARIANCE

$$s^2 = \frac{\Sigma(x_i - \bar{x})^2}{n - 1} \tag{3.5}$$

To illustrate the computation of the sample variance, we will use the data on class size for the sample of five college classes as presented in Section 3.1. A summary of the data, including the computation of the deviations about the mean and the squared deviations about the mean, is shown in Table 3.3. The sum of squared deviations about the mean is $\Sigma(x_i - \bar{x})^2 = 256$. Hence, with $n - 1 = 4$, the sample variance is

$$s^2 = \frac{\Sigma(x_i - \bar{x})^2}{n - 1} = \frac{256}{4} = 64$$

Before moving on, let us note that the units associated with the sample variance often cause confusion. Because the values being summed in the variance calculation, $(x_i - \bar{x})^2$, are squared, the units associated with the sample variance are also *squared*. For instance, the sample variance for the class size data is $s^2 = 64$ (students)^2. The squared units associated

TABLE 3.3   COMPUTATION OF DEVIATIONS AND SQUARED DEVIATIONS ABOUT THE MEAN FOR THE CLASS SIZE DATA

Number of Students in Class (x_i)	Mean Class Size ($\bar{x}$)	Deviation About the Mean ($x_i - \bar{x}$)	Squared Deviation About the Mean ($x_i - \bar{x})^2$
46	44	2	4
54	44	10	100
42	44	−2	4
46	44	2	4
32	44	−12	144
		0	256
		$\Sigma(x_i - \bar{x})$	$\Sigma(x_i - \bar{x})^2$

TABLE 3.4 COMPUTATION OF THE SAMPLE VARIANCE FOR THE STARTING SALARY DATA

Monthly Salary (x_i)	Sample Mean $(\bar{x})$	Deviation About the Mean $(x_i - \bar{x})$	Squared Deviation About the Mean $(x_i - \bar{x})^2$
3450	3540	−90	8,100
3550	3540	10	100
3650	3540	110	12,100
3480	3540	−60	3,600
3355	3540	−185	34,225
3310	3540	−230	52,900
3490	3540	−50	2,500
3730	3540	190	36,100
3540	3540	0	0
3925	3540	385	148,225
3520	3540	−20	400
3480	3540	−60	3,600
		0	301,850
		$\Sigma(x_i - \bar{x})$	$\Sigma(x_i - \bar{x})^2$

Using equation (3.5),

$$s^2 = \frac{\Sigma(x_i - \bar{x})^2}{n - 1} = \frac{301,850}{11} = 27,440.91$$

The variance is useful in comparing the variability of two or more variables.

with variance make it difficult to obtain an intuitive understanding and interpretation of the numerical value of the variance. We recommend that you think of the variance as a measure useful in comparing the amount of variability for two or more variables. In a comparison of the variables, the one with the largest variance shows the most variability. Further interpretation of the value of the variance may not be necessary.

As another illustration of computing a sample variance, consider the starting salaries listed in Table 3.1 for the 12 business school graduates. In Section 3.1, we showed that the sample mean starting salary was 3540. The computation of the sample variance ($s^2 = 27,440.91$) is shown in Table 3.4.

In Tables 3.3 and 3.4 we show both the sum of the deviations about the mean and the sum of the squared deviations about the mean. For any data set, the sum of the deviations about the mean will *always equal zero*. Note that in Tables 3.3 and 3.4, $\Sigma(x_i - \bar{x}) = 0$. The positive deviations and negative deviations cancel each other, causing the sum of the deviations about the mean to equal zero.

Standard Deviation

The **standard deviation** is defined to be the positive square root of the variance. Following the notation we adopted for a sample variance and a population variance, we use s to denote the sample standard deviation and σ to denote the population standard deviation. The standard deviation is derived from the variance in the following way.

The sample standard deviation s is a point estimator of the population standard deviation σ.

STANDARD DEVIATION

$$\text{Sample standard deviation} = s = \sqrt{s^2} \tag{3.6}$$

$$\text{Population standard deviation} = \sigma = \sqrt{\sigma^2} \tag{3.7}$$

Recall that the sample variance for the sample of class sizes in five college classes is $s^2 = 64$. Thus, the sample standard deviation is $s = \sqrt{64} = 8$. For the data on starting salaries, the sample standard deviation is $s = \sqrt{27,440.91} = 165.65$.

The standard deviation is easier to interpret than the variance because the standard deviation is measured in the same units as the data.

What is gained by converting the variance to its corresponding standard deviation? Recall that the units associated with the variance are squared. For example, the sample variance for the starting salary data of business school graduates is $s^2 = 27,440.91$ (dollars)^2. Because the standard deviation is the square root of the variance, the units of the variance, dollars squared, are converted to dollars in the standard deviation. Thus, the standard deviation of the starting salary data is $165.65. In other words, the standard deviation is measured in the same units as the original data. For this reason the standard deviation is more easily compared to the mean and other statistics that are measured in the same units as the original data.

Using Excel to Compute the Sample Variance and Sample Standard Deviation

Excel provides functions for computing the sample variance and sample standard deviation, which we will illustrate using the starting salary data. Refer to Figure 3.5 as we describe the steps involved. Figure 3.5 is an extension of Figure 3.1, where we showed how to use Excel functions to compute the mean, median, and mode. The formula worksheet is in the background; the value worksheet is in the foreground.

Enter Data: Labels and the starting salary data are entered into cells A1:B13 of the worksheet.

Enter Functions and Formulas: The Excel AVERAGE, MEDIAN, and MODE functions are entered into cells E1:E3 as described earlier. Excel's VAR function can be used to compute the sample variance by entering the following formula into cell E4:

$$=\text{VAR(B2:B13)}$$

FIGURE 3.5   EXCEL WORKSHEET USED TO COMPUTE THE SAMPLE VARIANCE AND THE SAMPLE STANDARD DEVIATION FOR STARTING SALARIES

	A	B	C	D	E	F
1	Graduate	Starting Salary		Mean	=AVERAGE(B2:B13)	
2	1	3450		Median	=MEDIAN(B2:B13)	
3	2	3550		Mode	=MODE(B2:B13)	
4	3	3650		Variance	=VAR(B2:B13)	
5	4	3480		Standard Deviation	=STDEV(B2:B13)	
6	5	3355				
7	6	3310				
8	7	3490				
9	8	3730				
10	9	3540				
11	10	3925				
12	11	3520				
13	12	3480				
14						

	A	B	C	D	E	F
1	Graduate	Starting Salary		Mean	3540	
2	1	3450		Median	3505	
3	2	3550		Mode	3480	
4	3	3650		Variance	27440.91	
5	4	3480		Standard Deviation	165.65	
6	5	3355				
7	6	3310				
8	7	3490				
9	8	3730				
10	9	3540				
11	10	3925				
12	11	3520				
13	12	3480				
14						

Similarly, the formula =STDEV(B2:B13) is entered into cell E5 to compute the sample standard deviation. Appropriate labels are entered into cells D1:D5 to identify the output.

The value worksheet, in the foreground, shows the values computed using the Excel functions. Note that the sample variance and sample standard deviation are the same as we computed earlier using the definitions.

Coefficient of Variation

The coefficient of variation is a relative measure of variability; it measures the standard deviation relative to the mean.

In some situations we may be interested in a descriptive statistic that indicates how large the standard deviation is relative to the mean. This measure is called the **coefficient of variation** and is usually expressed as a percentage.

COEFFICIENT OF VARIATION

$$\left(\frac{\text{Standard deviation}}{\text{Mean}} \times 100\right)\% \tag{3.8}$$

For the class size data, we found a sample mean of 44 and a sample standard deviation of 8. The coefficient of variation is $[(8/44) \times 100]\% = 18.2\%$. In words, the coefficient of variation tells us that the sample standard deviation is 18.2% of the value of the sample mean. For the starting salary data with a sample mean of 3540 and a sample standard deviation of 165.65, the coefficient of variation, $[(165.65/3540) \times 100]\% = 4.7\%$, tells us the sample standard deviation is only 4.7% of the value of the sample mean. In general, the coefficient of variation is a useful statistic for comparing the variability of variables that have different standard deviations and different means.

Using Excel's Descriptive Statistics Tool

As we have seen, Excel provides statistical functions to compute descriptive statistics for a data set. These functions can be used to compute one statistic at a time (e.g., mean, variance, etc.). Excel also provides a variety of data analysis tools. One of these, called Descriptive Statistics, allows the user to compute a variety of descriptive statistics at once. We show here how it can be used to compute descriptive statistics for the starting salary data in Table 3.1. Refer to Figure 3.6 as we describe the tasks involved.

Enter Data: Labels and the starting salary data are entered into cells A1:B13 of the worksheet.

Enter Functions and Formulas: No functions and formulas are needed.

Apply Analysis Tools: The following steps describe how to use Excel's Descriptive Statistics tool for these data:

Step 1. Click the **Data** tab on the Ribbon
Step 2. In the **Analysis** group, click **Data Analysis**
Step 3. Choose **Descriptive Statistics** from the list of **Analysis Tools**
Step 4. When the Descriptive Statistics dialog box appears (see Figure 3.7),
　　　　　　Enter B1:B13 in the **Input Range** box
　　　　　　Select **Grouped By Columns**
　　　　　　Select **Labels in First Row**
　　　　　　Select **Output Range**
　　　　　　Enter D1 in the **Output Range** box (to identify the upper left corner of the section of the worksheet where the descriptive statistics will appear)
　　　　　　Select **Summary Statistics**
　　　　　　Click **OK**

FIGURE 3.6   USING EXCEL TO COMPUTE DESCRIPTIVE STATISTICS FOR STARTING SALARIES

	A	B	C	D	E	F
1	Graduate	Starting Salary		*Starting Salary*		
2	1	3450				
3	2	3550		**Mean**	3540	
4	3	3650		Standard Error	47.8199	
5	4	3480		**Median**	3505	
6	5	3355		**Mode**	3480	
7	6	3310		**Standard Deviation**	165.653	
8	7	3490		**Sample Variance**	27440.91	
9	8	3730		Kurtosis	1.7189	
10	9	3540		Skewness	1.0911	
11	10	3925		**Range**	615	
12	11	3520		**Minimum**	3310	
13	12	3480		**Maximum**	3925	
14				**Sum**	42480	
15				**Count**	12	
16						

Cells D1:E15 of Figure 3.6 show the descriptive statistics provided by Excel. A yellow screen is used to highlight the results. The boldfaced entries are the descriptive statistics we have covered. The descriptive statistics that are not boldfaced are either covered subsequently in the text or discussed in more advanced texts.

FIGURE 3.7   DESCRIPTIVE STATISTICS DIALOG BOX FOR THE STARTING SALARY DATA

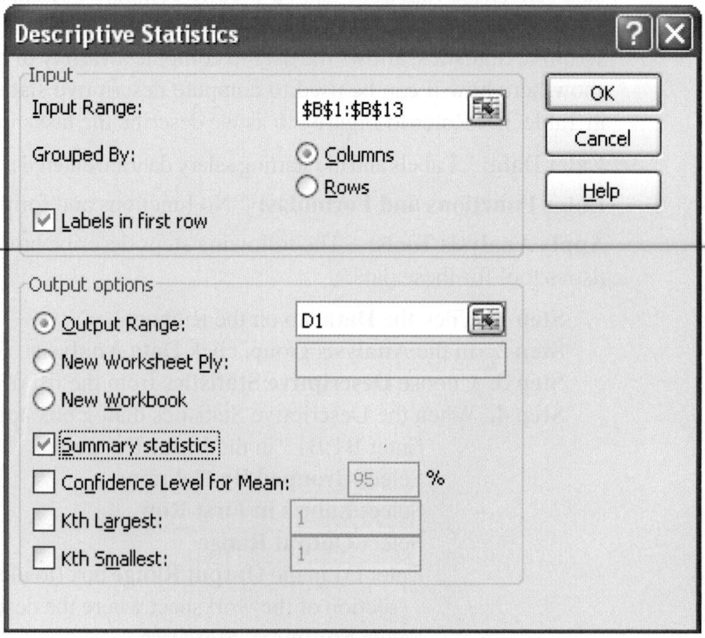

NOTES AND COMMENTS

1. The standard deviation is a commonly used measure of the risk associated with investing in stock and stock funds (*BusinessWeek,* January 17, 2000). It provides a measure of how monthly returns fluctuate around the long-run average return.

2. Rounding the value of the sample mean $\bar{x}$ and the values of the squared deviations $(x_i - \bar{x})^2$ may introduce errors when a calculator is used in the computation of the variance and standard deviation. To reduce rounding errors, we recommend carrying at least six significant digits during intermediate calculations. The resulting variance or standard deviation can then be rounded to fewer digits.

3. An alternative formula for the computation of the sample variance is

$$s^2 = \frac{\Sigma x_i^2 - n\bar{x}^2}{n - 1}$$

where $\Sigma x_i^2 = x_1^2 + x_2^2 + \cdots + x_n^2$.

Exercises

Methods

13. Consider a sample with data values of 10, 20, 12, 17, and 16. Compute the range and interquartile range.

14. Consider a sample with data values of 10, 20, 12, 17, and 16. Compute the variance and standard deviation.

15. Consider a sample with data values of 27, 25, 20, 15, 30, 34, 28, and 25. Compute the range, interquartile range, variance, and standard deviation.

Applications

16. A bowler's scores for six games were 182, 168, 184, 190, 170, and 174. Using these data as a sample, compute the following descriptive statistics.
    a. Range
    b. Variance
    c. Standard deviation
    d. Coefficient of variation

17. A home theater in a box is the easiest and cheapest way to provide surround sound for a home entertainment center. A sample of prices is shown here (*Consumer Reports Buying Guide,* 2004). The prices are for models with a DVD player and for models without a DVD player.

Models with DVD Player	Price	Models without DVD Player	Price
Sony HT-1800DP	$450	Pioneer HTP-230	$300
Pioneer HTD-330DV	300	Sony HT-DDW750	300
Sony HT-C800DP	400	Kenwood HTB-306	360
Panasonic SC-HT900	500	RCA RT-2600	290
Panasonic SC-MTI	400	Kenwood HTB-206	300

a. Compute the mean price for models with a DVD player and the mean price for models without a DVD player. What is the additional price paid to have a DVD player included in a home theater unit?

b. Compute the range, variance, and standard deviation for the two samples. What does this information tell you about the prices for models with and without a DVD player?

18. Car rental rates per day for a sample of seven Eastern U.S. cities are as follows (*The Wall Street Journal*, January 16, 2004).

City	Daily Rate
Boston	$43
Atlanta	35
Miami	34
New York	58
Orlando	30
Pittsburgh	30
Washington, D.C.	36

a. Compute the mean, variance, and standard deviation for the car rental rates.
b. A similar sample of seven Western U.S. cities showed a sample mean car rental rate of $38 per day. The variance and standard deviation were 12.3 and 3.5, respectively. Discuss any difference between the car rental rates in Eastern and Western U.S. cities.

19. The *Los Angeles Times* regularly reports the air quality index for various areas of Southern California. A sample of air quality index values for Pomona provided the following data: 28, 42, 58, 48, 45, 55, 60, 49, and 50.
a. Compute the range and interquartile range.
b. Compute the sample variance and sample standard deviation.
c. A sample of air quality index readings for Anaheim provided a sample mean of 48.5, a sample variance of 136, and a sample standard deviation of 11.66. What comparisons can you make between the air quality in Pomona and that in Anaheim on the basis of these descriptive statistics?

20. The following data were used to construct the histograms of the number of days required to fill orders for Dawson Supply, Inc., and J.C. Clark Distributors (see Figure 3.2).

Dawson Supply Days for Delivery: 11   10   9   10   11   11   10   11   10   10
Clark Distributors Days for Delivery: 8   10   13   7   10   11   10   7   15   12

Use the range and standard deviation to support the previous observation that Dawson Supply provides the more consistent and reliable delivery times.

21. How do grocery costs compare across the country? Using a market basket of 10 items including meat, milk, bread, eggs, coffee, potatoes, cereal, and orange juice, *Where to Retire* magazine calculated the cost of the market basket in six cities and in six retirement areas across the country (*Where to Retire,* November/December 2003). The data with market basket cost to the nearest dollar are as follows:

City	Cost	Retirement Area	Cost
Buffalo, NY	$33	Biloxi-Gulfport, MS	$29
Des Moines, IA	27	Asheville, NC	32
Hartford, CT	32	Flagstaff, AZ	32
Los Angeles, CA	38	Hilton Head, SC	34
Miami, FL	36	Fort Myers, FL	34
Pittsburgh, PA	32	Santa Fe, NM	31

a. Compute the mean, variance, and standard deviation for the sample of cities and the sample of retirement areas.
b. What observations can be made based on the two samples?

BackToSchool

22. The National Retail Federation reported that freshman students spend more on back-to-school items than any other college group (*USA Today*, August 4, 2006). Sample data comparing the back-to-school expenditures for 25 freshmen and 20 seniors are shown in the data file BackToSchool.
    a. What is the mean back-to-school expenditure for each group? Are the data consistent with the National Retail Federation's report?
    b. What is the range for the expenditures in each group?
    c. What is the interquartile range for the expenditures in each group?
    d. What is the standard deviation for expenditures in each group?
    e. Do freshmen or seniors have more variation in back-to-school expenditures?

23. Scores turned in by an amateur golfer at the Bonita Fairways Golf Course in Bonita Springs, Florida, during 2005 and 2006 are as follows:

2005 Season	74	78	79	77	75	73	75	77
2006 Season	71	70	75	77	85	80	71	79

   a. Use the mean and standard deviation to evaluate the golfer's performance over the two-year period.
   b. What is the primary difference in performance between 2005 and 2006? What improvement, if any, can be seen in the 2006 scores?

24. The following times were recorded by the quarter-mile and mile runners of a university track team (times are in minutes).

Quarter-Mile Times:	.92	.98	1.04	.90	.99
Mile Times:	4.52	4.35	4.60	4.70	4.50

   After viewing this sample of running times, one of the coaches commented that the quarter-milers turned in the more consistent times. Use the standard deviation and the coefficient of variation to summarize the variability in the data. Does the use of the coefficient of variation indicate that the coach's statement should be qualified?

(3.3) Measures of Distribution Shape, Relative Location, and Detecting Outliers

We have described several measures of location and variability for data. In addition, it is often important to have a measure of the shape of a distribution. In Chapter 2 we noted that a histogram provides a graphical display showing the shape of a distribution. An important numerical measure of the shape of a distribution is called **skewness**.

Distribution Shape

Shown in Figure 3.8 are four histograms constructed from relative frequency distributions. The histograms in Panels A and B are moderately skewed. The one in Panel A is skewed to the left; its skewness is $-.85$. The histogram in Panel B is skewed to the right; its skewness is $+.85$. The histogram in Panel C is symmetric; its skewness is zero. The histogram in Panel D is highly skewed to the right; its skewness is 1.62.

The formula used to compute skewness is somewhat complex.[2] However, the skewness can be easily computed using Excel. In Section 3.2 we showed how Excel's Descriptive

---

[2]The formula for the skewness of sample data:

$$\text{Skewness} = \frac{n}{(n-1)(n-2)} \sum \left(\frac{x_i - \bar{x}}{s} \right)^3$$

FIGURE 3.8   HISTOGRAMS SHOWING THE SKEWNESS FOR FOUR DISTRIBUTIONS

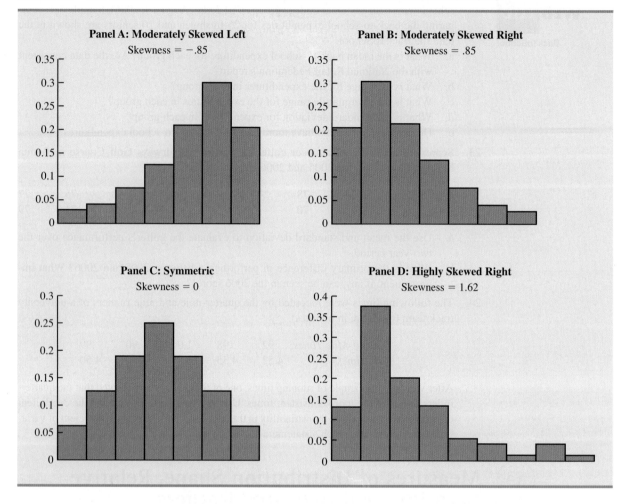

Statistics tool can be used to compute descriptive statistics for the starting salary data in Table 3.1; the results were shown in the worksheet in Figure 3.6. The label Skewness in cell D10 and the corresponding value of 1.0911 in cell E10 indicates that the starting salary data are moderately to highly skewed to the right.

Excel's SKEW function can also be used to compute the skewness by entering the following formula into any empty cell of the worksheet in Figure 3.6: =SKEW(B2:B13).

For a symmetric distribution, the mean and the median are equal. When the data are positively skewed, the mean will usually be greater than the median; when the data are negatively skewed, the mean will usually be less than the median. The data used to construct the histogram in Panel D are customer purchases at a women's apparel store. The mean purchase amount is $77.60 and the median purchase amount is $59.70. The relatively few large purchase amounts tend to increase the mean, while the median remains unaffected by the large purchase amounts. The median provides the preferred measure of location when the data are highly skewed.

z-Scores

In addition to measures of location, variability, and shape, we are also interested in the relative location of values within a data set. Measures of relative location help us determine how far a particular value is from the mean.

By using both the mean and standard deviation, we can determine the relative location of any observation. Suppose we have a sample of n observations, with the values denoted by $x_1, x_2, \ldots, x_n$. In addition, assume that the sample mean, $\bar{x}$, and the sample standard deviation, s, are already computed. Associated with each value, x_i, is another value called its z-**score**. Equation (3.9) shows how the z-score is computed for each x_i.

Excel's STANDARDIZE function can be used to compute the z-score. But it is just as easy to enter a cell formula to compute z_i.

z-SCORE

$$z_i = \frac{x_i - \bar{x}}{s} \tag{3.9}$$

where

$z_i = $ the z-score for x_i
$\bar{x} = $ the sample mean
$s = $ the sample standard deviation

The z-score is often called the *standardized value*. The z-score, z_i, can be interpreted as the *number of standard deviations x_i is from the mean $\bar{x}$*. For example, $z_1 = 1.2$ would indicate that x_1 is 1.2 standard deviations greater than the sample mean. Similarly, $z_2 = -.5$ would indicate that x_2 is .5, or 1/2, standard deviation less than the sample mean. A z-score greater than zero occurs for observations with a value greater than the mean, and a z-score less than zero occurs for observations with a value less than the mean. A z-score of zero indicates that the value of the observation is equal to the mean.

The z-score for any observation can be interpreted as a measure of the relative location of the observation in a data set. Thus, observations in two different data sets with the same z-score can be said to have the same relative location in terms of being the same number of standard deviations from the mean.

The z-scores for the class size data are computed in Table 3.5. Recall the previously computed sample mean, $\bar{x} = 44$, and sample standard deviation, $s = 8$. The z-score of -1.50 for the fifth observation shows it is farthest from the mean; it is 1.50 standard deviations below the mean.

Chebyshev's Theorem

Chebyshev's theorem enables us to make statements about the proportion of data values that must be within a specified number of standard deviations of the mean.

TABLE 3.5 z-SCORES FOR THE CLASS SIZE DATA

Number of Students in Class (x_i)	Deviation About the Mean $(x_i - \bar{x})$	z-Score $\left(\dfrac{x_i - \bar{x}}{s}\right)$
46	2	$2/8 = $ .25
54	10	$10/8 = $ 1.25
42	-2	$-2/8 = $ $-.25$
46	2	$2/8 = $ .25
32	-12	$-12/8 = -1.50$

> **CHEBYSHEV'S THEOREM**
>
> At least $(1 - 1/z^2)$ of the data values must be within z standard deviations of the mean, where z is any value greater than 1.

Some of the implications of this theorem, with $z = 2, 3$, and 4 standard deviations, follow.

- At least .75, or 75%, of the data values must be within $z = 2$ standard deviations of the mean.
- At least .89, or 89%, of the data values must be within $z = 3$ standard deviations of the mean.
- At least .94, or 94%, of the data values must be within $z = 4$ standard deviations of the mean.

For an example using Chebyshev's theorem, suppose that the midterm test scores for 100 students in a college business statistics course had a mean of 70 and a standard deviation of 5. How many students had test scores between 60 and 80? How many students had test scores between 58 and 82?

For the test scores between 60 and 80, we note that 60 is two standard deviations below the mean and 80 is two standard deviations above the mean. Using Chebyshev's theorem, we see that at least .75, or at least 75%, of the observations must have values within two standard deviations of the mean. Thus, at least 75% of the students must have scored between 60 and 80.

Chebyshev's theorem requires z > 1; but z need not be an integer.

For the test scores between 58 and 82, we see that $(58 - 70)/5 = -2.4$ indicates 58 is 2.4 standard deviations below the mean and that $(82 - 70)/5 = +2.4$ indicates 82 is 2.4 standard deviations above the mean. Applying Chebyshev's theorem with $z = 2.4$, we have

$$\left(1 - \frac{1}{z^2}\right) = \left(1 - \frac{1}{(2.4)^2}\right) = .826$$

At least 82.6% of the students must have test scores between 58 and 82.

Empirical Rule

The empirical rule is based on the normal probability distribution, which will be discussed in Chapter 6. The normal distribution is used extensively throughout the text.

One of the advantages of Chebyshev's theorem is that it applies to any data set regardless of the shape of the distribution of the data. Indeed, it could be used with any of the distributions in Figure 3.3. In many practical applications, however, data sets exhibit a symmetric mound-shaped or bell-shaped distribution like the one shown in Figure 3.9. When the data are believed to approximate this distribution, the **empirical rule** can be used to determine the percentage of data values that must be within a specified number of standard deviations of the mean.

> **EMPIRICAL RULE**
>
> For data having a bell-shaped distribution:
>
> - Approximately 68% of the data values will be within one standard deviation of the mean.
> - Approximately 95% of the data values will be within two standard deviations of the mean.
> - Almost all of the data values will be within three standard deviations of the mean.

FIGURE 3.9 A SYMMETRIC MOUND-SHAPED OR BELL-SHAPED DISTRIBUTION

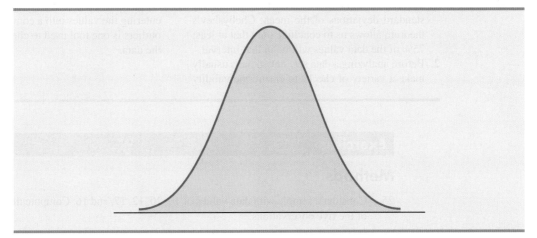

For example, liquid detergent cartons are filled automatically on a production line. Filling weights frequently have a bell-shaped distribution. If the mean filling weight is 16 ounces and the standard deviation is .25 ounces, we can use the empirical rule to draw the following conclusions.

- Approximately 68% of the filled cartons will have weights between 15.75 and 16.25 ounces (within one standard deviation of the mean).
- Approximately 95% of the filled cartons will have weights between 15.50 and 16.50 ounces (within two standard deviations of the mean).
- Almost all filled cartons will have weights between 15.25 and 16.75 ounces (within three standard deviations of the mean).

Detecting Outliers

Sometimes a data set will have one or more observations with unusually large or unusually small values. These extreme values are called **outliers**. Experienced statisticians take steps to identify outliers and then review each one carefully. An outlier may be a data value that has been incorrectly recorded. If so, it can be corrected before further analysis. An outlier may also be from an observation that was incorrectly included in the data set; if so, it can be removed. Finally, an outlier may be an unusual data value that has been recorded correctly and belongs in the data set. In such cases it should remain.

It is a good idea to check for outliers before making decisions based on data analysis. Errors are often made in recording data and entering data into the computer. Outliers should not necessarily be deleted, but their accuracy and appropriateness should be verified.

Standardized values (z-scores) can be used to identify outliers. Recall that the empirical rule allows us to conclude that for data with a bell-shaped distribution, almost all the data values will be within three standard deviations of the mean. Hence, in using z-scores to identify outliers, we recommend treating any data value with a z-score less than -3 or greater than $+3$ as an outlier. Such data values can then be reviewed for accuracy and to determine whether they belong in the data set.

Refer to the z-scores for the class size data in Table 3.5. The z-score of -1.50 shows the fifth class size is farthest from the mean. However, this standardized value is well within the -3 to $+3$ guideline for outliers. Thus, the z-scores do not indicate that outliers are present in the class size data.

NOTES AND COMMENTS

1. Chebyshev's theorem is applicable for any data set and can be used to state the minimum number of data values that will be within a certain number of standard deviations of the mean. If the data are known to be approximately bell-shaped, more can be said. For instance, the

(continued)

empirical rule allows us to say that *approximately* 95% of the data values will be within two standard deviations of the mean; Chebyshev's theorem allows us to conclude only that at least 75% of the data values will be in that interval.

2. Before analyzing a data set, statisticians usually make a variety of checks to ensure the validity of data. In a large study it is not uncommon for errors to be made in recording data values or in entering the values into a computer. Identifying outliers is one tool used to check the validity of the data.

Exercises

Methods

25. Consider a sample with data values of 10, 20, 12, 17, and 16. Compute the *z*-score for each of the five observations.

26. Consider a sample with a mean of 500 and a standard deviation of 100. What are the *z*-scores for the following data values: 520, 650, 500, 450, and 280?

27. Consider a sample with a mean of 30 and a standard deviation of 5. Use Chebyshev's theorem to determine the percentage of the data within each of the following ranges.
    a. 20 to 40
    b. 15 to 45
    c. 22 to 38
    d. 18 to 42
    e. 12 to 48

28. Suppose the data have a bell-shaped distribution with a mean of 30 and a standard deviation of 5. Use the empirical rule to determine the percentage of data within each of the following ranges.
    a. 20 to 40
    b. 15 to 45
    c. 25 to 35

Applications

29. The results of a national survey showed that on average, adults sleep 6.9 hours per night. Suppose that the standard deviation is 1.2 hours.
    a. Use Chebyshev's theorem to calculate the percentage of individuals who sleep between 4.5 and 9.3 hours.
    b. Use Chebyshev's theorem to calculate the percentage of individuals who sleep between 3.9 and 9.9 hours.
    c. Assume that the number of hours of sleep follows a bell-shaped distribution. Use the empirical rule to calculate the percentage of individuals who sleep between 4.5 and 9.3 hours per day. How does this result compare to the value that you obtained using Chebyshev's theorem in part (a)?

30. The Energy Information Administration reported that the mean retail price per gallon of regular grade gasoline was approximately $4.00 (U.S. Department of Energy, Energy Information Administration, June 17, 2008). Suppose that the standard deviation was $.10 and that the retail price per gallon has a bell-shaped distribution.
    a. What percentage of regular grade gasoline sold between $3.90 and $4.10 per gallon?
    b. What percentage of regular grade gasoline sold between $3.90 and $4.20 per gallon?
    c. What percentage of regular grade gasoline sold for more than $4.20 per gallon?

31. The national average for the verbal portion of the College Board's Scholastic Aptitude Test (SAT) is 507 (*The World Almanac*, 2006). The College Board periodically rescales the test scores such that the standard deviation is approximately 100. Answer the following questions using a bell-shaped distribution and the empirical rule for the verbal test scores.

a.   What percentage of students have an SAT verbal score greater than 607?
b.   What percentage of students have an SAT verbal score greater than 707?
c.   What percentage of students have an SAT verbal score between 407 and 507?
d.   What percentage of students have an SAT verbal score between 307 and 607?

32.   The high costs in the California real estate market have caused families who cannot afford to buy bigger homes to consider backyard sheds as an alternative form of housing expansion. Many are using the backyard structures for home offices, art studios, and hobby areas as well as for additional storage. The mean price of a customized wooden, shingled backyard structure is $3100 (*Newsweek,* September 29, 2003). Assume that the standard deviation is $1200.
a.   What is the *z*-score for a backyard structure costing $2300?
b.   What is the *z*-score for a backyard structure costing $4900?
c.   Interpret the *z*-scores in parts (a) and (b). Comment on whether either should be considered an outlier.
d.   The *Newsweek* article described a backyard shed-office combination built in Albany, California, for $13,000. Should this structure be considered an outlier? Explain.

33.   Florida Power & Light (FP&L) Company has enjoyed a reputation for quickly fixing its electric system after storms. However, during the hurricane seasons of 2004 and 2005, a new reality was that the company's historical approach to emergency electric system repairs was no longer good enough (*The Wall Street Journal,* January 16, 2006). Data showing the days required to restore electric service after seven hurricanes during 2004 and 2005 follow.

Hurricane	Days to Restore Service
Charley	13
Frances	12
Jeanne	8
Dennis	3
Katrina	8
Rita	2
Wilma	18

Based on this sample of seven, compute the following descriptive statistics:
a.   Mean, median, and mode
b.   Range and standard deviation
c.   Should Wilma be considered an outlier in terms of the days required to restore electric service?
d.   The seven hurricanes resulted in 10 million service interruptions to customers. Do the statistics show that FP&L should consider updating its approach to emergency electric system repairs? Discuss.

34.   A sample of 10 NCAA college basketball game scores provided the following data (*USA Today,* January 26, 2004).

NCAA

Winning Team	Points	Losing Team	Points	Winning Margin
Arizona	90	Oregon	66	24
Duke	85	Georgetown	66	19
Florida State	75	Wake Forest	70	5
Kansas	78	Colorado	57	21
Kentucky	71	Notre Dame	63	8
Louisville	65	Tennessee	62	3
Oklahoma State	72	Texas	66	6
Purdue	76	Michigan State	70	6
Stanford	77	Southern Cal	67	10
Wisconsin	76	Illinois	56	20

a. Compute the mean and standard deviation for the points scored by the winning team.
b. Assume that the points scored by the winning teams for all NCAA games follow a bell-shaped distribution. Using the mean and standard deviation found in part (a), estimate the percentage of all NCAA games in which the winning team scores 84 or more points. Estimate the percentage of NCAA games in which the winning team scores more than 90 points.
c. Compute the mean and standard deviation for the winning margin. Do the data contain outliers? Explain.

35. *Consumer Review* posts reviews and ratings of a variety of products on the Internet. The following is a sample of 20 speaker systems and their ratings (*http://www.audioreview.com*). The ratings are on a scale of 1 to 5, with 5 being best.

Speakers

Speaker	Rating	Speaker	Rating
Infinity Kappa 6.1	4.00	ACI Sapphire III	4.67
Allison One	4.12	Bose 501 Series	2.14
Cambridge Ensemble II	3.82	DCM KX-212	4.09
Dynaudio Contour 1.3	4.00	Eosone RSF1000	4.17
Hsu Rsch. HRSW12V	4.56	Joseph Audio RM7si	4.88
Legacy Audio Focus	4.32	Martin Logan Aerius	4.26
Mission 73li	4.33	Omni Audio SA 12.3	2.32
PSB 400i	4.50	Polk Audio RT12	4.50
Snell Acoustics D IV	4.64	Sunfire True Subwoofer	4.17
Thiel CS1.5	4.20	Yamaha NS-A636	2.17

a. Compute the mean and the median.
b. Compute the first and third quartiles.
c. Compute the standard deviation.
d. The skewness of this data is -1.67. Comment on the shape of the distribution.
e. What are the z-scores associated with Allison One and Omni Audio?
f. Do the data contain any outliers? Explain.

3.4 Exploratory Data Analysis

In Chapter 2 we introduced the stem-and-leaf display as a technique of exploratory data analysis. Recall that exploratory data analysis enables us to use simple arithmetic and easy-to-draw pictures to summarize data. In this section we continue exploratory data analysis by considering five-number summaries and box plots.

Five-Number Summary

In a **five-number summary**, the following five numbers are used to summarize the data.

1. Smallest value
2. First quartile (Q_1)
3. Median (Q_2)
4. Third quartile (Q_3)
5. Largest value

The easiest way to develop a five-number summary is to first place the data in ascending order. Then it is easy to identify the smallest value, the three quartiles, and the largest value. The monthly starting salaries shown in Table 3.1 for a sample of 12 business school graduates are repeated here in ascending order.

3310 3355 3450 | 3480 3480 3490 | 3520 3540 3550 | 3650 3730 3925

$$Q_1 = 3465 \qquad Q_2 = 3505 \qquad Q_3 = 3600$$
$$\text{(Median)}$$

The median of 3505 and the quartiles $Q_1 = 3465$ and $Q_3 = 3600$ were computed in Section 3.1. Reviewing the data shows a smallest value of 3310 and a largest value of 3925. Thus the five-number summary for the salary data is 3310, 3465, 3505, 3600, 3925. Approximately one-fourth, or 25%, of the observations are between adjacent numbers in a five-number summary.

Box Plot

A **box plot** is a graphical summary of data that is based on a five-number summary. A key to the development of a box plot is the computation of the median and the quartiles, Q_1 and Q_3. The interquartile range, IQR = $Q_3 - Q_1$, is also used. Figure 3.10 is the box plot for the monthly starting salary data. The steps used to construct the box plot follow.

Box plots provide another way to identify outliers. But they do not necessarily identify the same values as those with a z-score less than −3 or greater than +3. Either or both procedures may be used.

1. A box is drawn with the ends of the box located at the first and third quartiles. For the salary data, $Q_1 = 3465$ and $Q_3 = 3600$. This box contains the middle 50% of the data.
2. A vertical line is drawn in the box at the location of the median (3505 for the salary data).
3. By using the interquartile range, IQR = $Q_3 - Q_1$, *limits* are located. The limits for the box plot are 1.5(IQR) below Q_1 and 1.5(IQR) above Q_3. For the salary data, IQR = $Q_3 - Q_1$ = 3600 − 3465 = 135. Thus, the limits are 3465 − 1.5(135) = 3262.5 and 3600 + 1.5(135) = 3802.5. Data outside these limits are considered *outliers*.
4. The dashed lines in Figure 3.10 are called *whiskers*. The whiskers are drawn from the ends of the box to the smallest and largest values *inside the limits* computed in step 3. Thus, the whiskers end at salary values of 3310 and 3730.
5. Finally, the location of each outlier is shown with the symbol *. In Figure 3.10 we see one outlier, 3925.

In Figure 3.10 we included lines showing the location of the upper and lower limits. These lines were drawn to show how the limits are computed and where they are located

FIGURE 3.10 BOX PLOT OF THE STARTING SALARY DATA WITH LINES SHOWING THE LOWER AND UPPER LIMITS

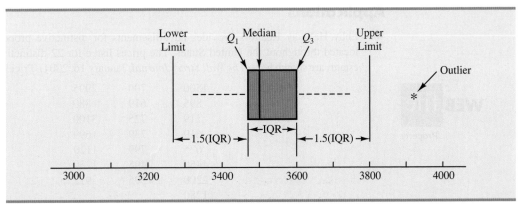

FIGURE 3.11   BOX PLOT OF THE STARTING SALARY DATA

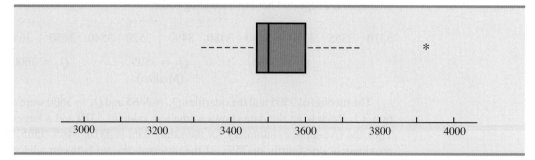

for the salary data. Although the limits are always computed, generally they are not drawn on the box plots. Figure 3.11 shows the usual appearance of a box plot for the salary data.

NOTES AND COMMENTS

1. An advantage of the exploratory data analysis procedures is that they are easy to use; few numerical calculations are necessary. We simply sort the data values into ascending order and identify the five-number summary. The box plot can then be constructed. It is not necessary to compute the mean and the standard deviation for the data.

2. In the chapter appendix, we show how to construct a box plot for the starting salary data using StatTools.

Exercises

Methods

36. Consider a sample with data values of 27, 25, 20, 15, 30, 34, 28, and 25. Provide the five-number summary for the data.

37. Show the box plot for the data in exercise 36.

38. Show the five-number summary and the box plot for the following data: 5, 15, 18, 10, 8, 12, 16, 10, 6.

39. A data set has a first quartile of 42 and a third quartile of 50. Compute the lower and upper limits for the corresponding box plot. Should a data value of 65 be considered an outlier?

Applications

40. Ebby Halliday Realtors provides advertisements for distinctive properties and estates located throughout the United States. The prices listed for 22 distinctive properties and estates are shown here (*The Wall Street Journal*, January 16, 2004). Prices are in thousands.

Property

1500	700	2995
895	619	880
719	725	3100
619	739	1699
625	799	1120
4450	2495	1250
2200	1395	912
1280		

a. Provide a five-number summary.
b. Compute the lower and upper limits.
c. The highest priced property, $4,450,000, is listed as an estate overlooking White Rock Lake in Dallas, Texas. Should this property be considered an outlier? Explain.
d. Should the second highest priced property, listed for $3,100,000, be considered an outlier? Explain.
e. Show a box plot.

41. Annual sales, in millions of dollars, for 21 pharmaceutical companies follow.

8408	1374	1872	8879	2459	11413
608	14138	6452	1850	2818	1356
10498	7478	4019	4341	739	2127
3653	5794	8305			

a. Provide a five-number summary.
b. Compute the lower and upper limits.
c. Do the data contain any outliers?
d. Johnson & Johnson's sales are the largest on the list at $14,138 million. Suppose a data entry error (a transposition) had been made and the sales had been entered as $41,138 million. Would the method of detecting outliers in part (c) identify this problem and allow for correction of the data entry error?
e. Show a box plot.

42. Major League Baseball payrolls continue to escalate. Team payrolls in millions are as follows (*USA Today* Online Database, March 2006).

Baseball

Team	Payroll	Team	Payroll
Arizona	$ 62	Milwaukee	$ 40
Atlanta	86	Minnesota	56
Baltimore	74	NY Mets	101
Boston	124	NY Yankees	208
Chi Cubs	87	Oakland	55
Chi White Sox	75	Philadelphia	96
Cincinnati	62	Pittsburgh	38
Cleveland	42	San Diego	63
Colorado	48	San Francisco	90
Detroit	69	Seattle	88
Florida	60	St. Louis	92
Houston	77	Tampa Bay	30
Kansas City	37	Texas	56
LA Angels	98	Toronto	46
LA Dodgers	83	Washington	49

a. What is the median team payroll?
b. Provide a five-number summary.
c. Is the $208 million payroll for the New York Yankees an outlier? Explain.
d. Show a box plot.

43. New York Stock Exchange (NYSE) Chairman Richard Grasso and NYSE Board of Directors came under fire for the large compensation package being paid to Grasso. When it comes to salary plus bonus, Grasso's $8.5 million outearned the top executives of all major financial services companies. The data that follow show total annual salary plus bonus

paid to the top executives of 14 financial services companies (*The Wall Street Journal,* September 17, 2003). Data are in millions.

Company	Salary/Bonus	Company	Salary/Bonus
Aetna	$3.5	Fannie Mae	$4.3
AIG	6.0	Federal Home Loan	0.8
Allstate	4.1	Fleet Boston	1.0
American Express	3.8	Freddie Mac	1.2
Chubb	2.1	Mellon Financial	2.0
Cigna	1.0	Merrill Lynch	7.7
Citigroup	1.0	Wells Fargo	8.0

a. Add Grasso's $8.5 million salary and bonus to the above data set. What is the median annual salary plus bonus paid to the 15 executives.
b. Provide a five-number summary.
c. Should Grasso's $8.5 million annual salary plus bonus be considered an outlier for this group of top executives? Explain.
d. Show a box plot.

Mutual

44. A listing of 46 mutual funds and their 12-month total return percentage is shown in Table 3.6 (*Smart Money,* February 2004).
a. What are the mean and median return percentages for these mutual funds?
b. What are the first and third quartiles?
c. Provide a five-number summary.
d. Do the data contain any outliers? Show a box plot.

TABLE 3.6   TWELVE-MONTH RETURN FOR MUTUAL FUNDS

Mutual Fund	Return (%)	Mutual Fund	Return (%)
Alger Capital Appreciation	23.5	Nations Small Company	21.4
Alger LargeCap Growth	22.8	Nations SmallCap Index	24.5
Alger MidCap Growth	38.3	Nations Strategic Growth	10.4
Alger SmallCap	41.3	Nations Value Inv	10.8
AllianceBernstein Technology	40.6	One Group Diversified Equity	10.0
Federated American Leaders	15.6	One Group Diversified Int'l	10.9
Federated Capital Appreciation	12.4	One Group Diversified Mid Cap	15.1
Federated Equity-Income	11.5	One Group Equity Income	6.6
Federated Kaufmann	33.3	One Group Int'l Equity Index	13.2
Federated Max-Cap Index	16.0	One Group Large Cap Growth	13.6
Federated Stock	16.9	One Group Large Cap Value	12.8
Janus Adviser Int'l Growth	10.3	One Group Mid Cap Growth	18.7
Janus Adviser Worldwide	3.4	One Group Mid Cap Value	11.4
Janus Enterprise	24.2	One Group Small Cap Growth	23.6
Janus High-Yield	12.1	PBHG Growth	27.3
Janus Mercury	20.6	Putnam Europe Equity	20.4
Janus Overseas	11.9	Putnam Int'l Capital Opportunity	36.6
Janus Worldwide	4.1	Putnam International Equity	21.5
Nations Convertible Securities	13.6	Putnam Int'l New Opportunity	26.3
Nations Int'l Equity	10.7	Strong Advisor Mid Cap Growth	23.7
Nations LargeCap Enhd. Core	13.2	Strong Growth 20	11.7
Nations LargeCap Index	13.5	Strong Growth Inv	23.2
Nation MidCap Index	19.5	Strong Large Cap Growth	14.5

Measures of Association Between Two Variables

Thus far we have examined numerical methods used to summarize the data for *one variable at a time*. Often a manager or decision maker is interested in the *relationship between two variables*. In this section we present covariance and correlation as descriptive measures of the relationship between two variables.

We begin by reconsidering the application concerning a stereo and sound equipment store in San Francisco as presented in Section 2.4. The store's manager wants to determine the relationship between the number of weekend television commercials shown and the sales at the store during the following week. Sample data with sales expressed in hundreds of dollars are provided in Table 3.7. It shows 10 observations ($n = 10$), one for each week. The scatter diagram in Figure 3.12 shows a positive relationship, with higher sales (y) associated with a greater number of commercials (x). In fact, the scatter diagram suggests that a straight line could be used as an approximation of the relationship. In the following discussion, we introduce **covariance** as a descriptive measure of the linear association between two variables.

Covariance

For a sample of size n with the observations (x_1, y_1), (x_2, y_2), and so on, the sample covariance is defined as follows:

SAMPLE COVARIANCE

$$s_{xy} = \frac{\Sigma(x_i - \bar{x})(y_i - \bar{y})}{n - 1} \tag{3.10}$$

This formula pairs each x_i with a y_i. We then sum the products obtained by multiplying the deviation of each x_i from its sample mean $\bar{x}$ by the deviation of the corresponding y_i from its sample mean $\bar{y}$; this sum is then divided by $n - 1$.

To measure the strength of the linear relationship between the number of commercials x and the sales volume y in the stereo and sound equipment store problem, we use equation (3.10) to compute the sample covariance. The calculations in Table 3.8 show the

TABLE 3.7   SAMPLE DATA FOR THE STEREO AND SOUND EQUIPMENT STORE

Week	Number of Commercials x	Sales Volume ($100s) y
1	2	50
2	5	57
3	1	41
4	3	54
5	4	54
6	1	38
7	5	63
8	3	48
9	4	59
10	2	46

WEB file

Stereo

FIGURE 3.12   SCATTER DIAGRAM FOR THE STEREO AND SOUND EQUIPMENT STORE

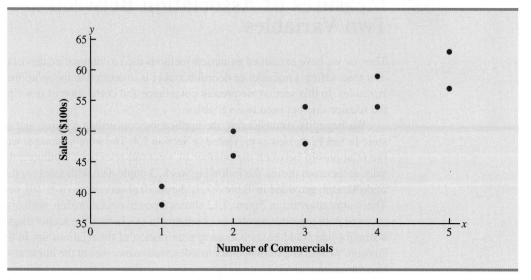

computation of $\Sigma(x_i - \bar{x})(y_i - \bar{y})$. Note that $\bar{x} = 30/10 = 3$ and $\bar{y} = 510/10 = 51$. Using equation (3.10), we obtain a sample covariance of

$$s_{xy} = \frac{\Sigma(x_i - \bar{x})(y_i - \bar{y})}{n - 1} = \frac{99}{9} = 11$$

The formula for computing the covariance of a population of size N is similar to equation (3.10), but we use different notation to indicate that we are working with the entire population.

POPULATION COVARIANCE

$$\sigma_{xy} = \frac{\Sigma(x_i - \mu_x)(y_i - \mu_y)}{N} \tag{3.11}$$

TABLE 3.8   CALCULATIONS FOR THE SAMPLE COVARIANCE

	x_i	y_i	$x_i - \bar{x}$	$y_i - \bar{y}$	$(x_i - \bar{x})(y_i - \bar{y})$
	2	50	-1	-1	1
	5	57	2	6	12
	1	41	-2	-10	20
	3	54	0	3	0
	4	54	1	3	3
	1	38	-2	-13	26
	5	63	2	12	24
	3	48	0	-3	0
	4	59	1	8	8
	2	46	-1	-5	5
Totals	30	510	0	0	99

$$s_{xy} = \frac{\Sigma(x_i - \bar{x})(y_i - \bar{y})}{n - 1} = \frac{99}{10 - 1} = 11$$

In equation (3.11) we use the notation μ_x for the population mean of the variable x and μ_y for the population mean of the variable y. The population covariance σ_{xy} is defined for a population of size N.

Interpretation of the Covariance

To aid in the interpretation of the sample covariance, consider Figure 3.13. It is the same as the scatter diagram of Figure 3.12 with a vertical dashed line at $\bar{x} = 3$ and a horizontal dashed line at $\bar{y} = 51$. The lines divide the graph into four quadrants. Points in quadrant I correspond to x_i greater than $\bar{x}$ and y_i greater than $\bar{y}$, points in quadrant II correspond to x_i less than $\bar{x}$ and y_i greater than $\bar{y}$, and so on. Thus, the value of $(x_i - \bar{x})(y_i - \bar{y})$ must be positive for points in quadrant I, negative for points in quadrant II, positive for points in quadrant III, and negative for points in quadrant IV.

The covariance is a measure of the linear association between two variables.

If the value of s_{xy} is positive, the points with the greatest influence on s_{xy} must be in quadrants I and III. Hence, a positive value for s_{xy} indicates a positive linear association between x and y; that is, as the value of x increases, the value of y increases. If the value of s_{xy} is negative, however, the points with the greatest influence on s_{xy} are in quadrants II and IV. Hence, a negative value for s_{xy} indicates a negative linear association between x and y; that is, as the value of x increases, the value of y decreases. Finally, if the points are evenly distributed across all four quadrants, the value of s_{xy} will be close to zero, indicating no linear association between x and y. Figure 3.14 shows the values of s_{xy} that can be expected with three different types of scatter diagrams.

Referring again to Figure 3.13, we see that the scatter diagram for the stereo and sound equipment store follows the pattern in the top panel of Figure 3.14. As we should expect, the value of the sample covariance indicates a positive linear relationship with $s_{xy} = 11$.

From the preceding discussion, it might appear that a large positive value for the covariance indicates a strong positive linear relationship and that a large negative value indicates a strong negative linear relationship. However, one problem with using

FIGURE 3.13   PARTITIONED SCATTER DIAGRAM FOR THE STEREO AND SOUND
EQUIPMENT STORE

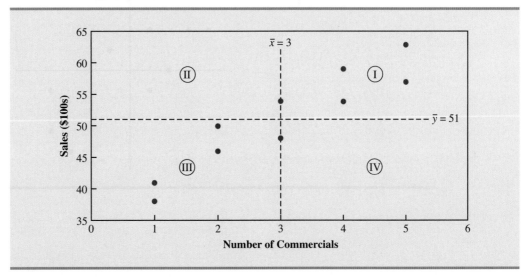

FIGURE 3.14   INTERPRETATION OF SAMPLE COVARIANCE

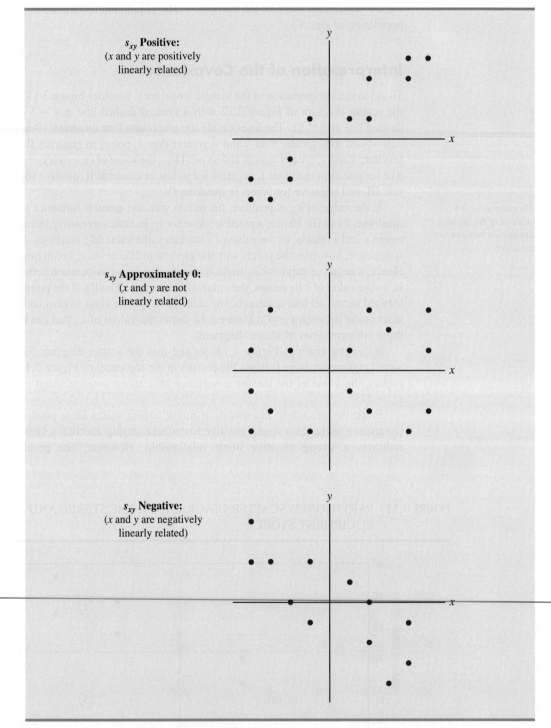

covariance as a measure of the strength of the linear relationship is that the value of the covariance depends on the units of measurement for x and y. For example, suppose we are interested in the relationship between height x and weight y for individuals. Clearly the strength of the relationship should be the same whether we measure height in feet or inches. Measuring the height in inches, however, gives us much larger numerical values for $(x_i - \bar{x})$ than when we measure height in feet. Thus, with height measured in inches, we would obtain a larger value for the numerator $\Sigma(x_i - \bar{x})(y_i - \bar{y})$ in equation (3.10)—and hence a larger covariance—when in fact the relationship does not change. A measure of the relationship between two variables that is not affected by the units of measurement for x and y is the **correlation coefficient**.

Correlation Coefficient

For sample data, the Pearson product moment correlation coefficient is defined as follows.

PEARSON PRODUCT MOMENT CORRELATION COEFFICIENT: SAMPLE DATA

$$r_{xy} = \frac{s_{xy}}{s_x s_y} \tag{3.12}$$

where

$$r_{xy} = \text{sample correlation coefficient}$$
$$s_{xy} = \text{sample covariance}$$
$$s_x = \text{sample standard deviation of } x$$
$$s_y = \text{sample standard deviation of } y$$

Equation (3.12) shows that the Pearson product moment correlation coefficient for sample data (commonly referred to more simply as the *sample correlation coefficient*) is computed by dividing the sample covariance by the product of the sample standard deviation of x and the sample standard deviation of y.

Let us now compute the sample correlation coefficient for the stereo and sound equipment store. Using the data in Table 3.8, we can compute the sample standard deviations for the two variables.

$$s_x = \sqrt{\frac{\Sigma(x_i - \bar{x})^2}{n - 1}} = \sqrt{\frac{20}{9}} = 1.49$$

$$s_y = \sqrt{\frac{\Sigma(y_i - \bar{y})^2}{n - 1}} = \sqrt{\frac{566}{9}} = 7.93$$

Now, because $s_{xy} = 11$, the sample correlation coefficient equals

$$r_{xy} = \frac{s_{xy}}{s_x s_y} = \frac{11}{(1.49)(7.93)} = +.93$$

The formula for computing the correlation coefficient for a population, denoted by the Greek letter ρ_{xy} (rho, pronounced "row"), follows.

PEARSON PRODUCT MOMENT CORRELATION COEFFICIENT: POPULATION DATA

The sample correlation coefficient r_{xy} is the estimator of the population correlation coefficient ρ_{xy}.

$$\rho_{xy} = \frac{\sigma_{xy}}{\sigma_x \sigma_y}$$

(3.13)

where

ρ_{xy} = population correlation coefficient
σ_{xy} = population covariance
σ_x = population standard deviation for x
σ_y = population standard deviation for y

The sample correlation coefficient r_{xy} provides an estimate of the population correlation coefficient ρ_{xy}.

Interpretation of the Correlation Coefficient

First let us consider a simple example that illustrates the concept of a perfect positive linear relationship. The scatter diagram in Figure 3.15 depicts the relationship between x and y based on the following sample data.

x_i	y_i
5	10
10	30
15	50

The straight line drawn through each of the three points shows a perfect linear relationship between x and y. In order to apply equation (3.12) to compute the sample correlation we

FIGURE 3.15   SCATTER DIAGRAM DEPICTING A PERFECT POSITIVE LINEAR RELATIONSHIP

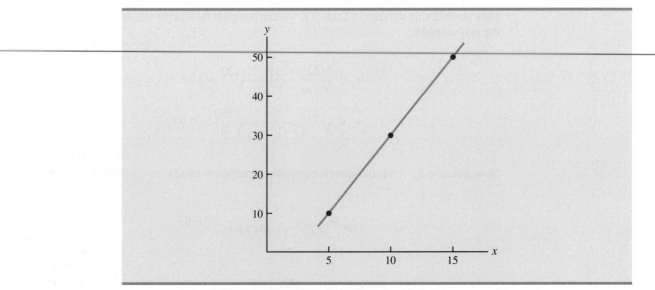

TABLE 3.9 COMPUTATIONS USED IN CALCULATING THE SAMPLE CORRELATION COEFFICIENT

	x_i	y_i	$x_i - \bar{x}$	$(x_i - \bar{x})^2$	$y_i - \bar{y}$	$(y_i - \bar{y})^2$	$(x_i - \bar{x})(y_i - \bar{y})$
	5	10	−5	25	−20	400	100
	10	30	0	0	0	0	0
	15	50	5	25	20	400	100
Totals	30	90	0	50	0	800	200

$$\bar{x} = 10 \quad \bar{y} = 30$$

must first compute s_{xy}, s_x, and s_y. Some of the computations are shown in Table 3.9. Using the results in Table 3.9, we find

$$s_{xy} = \frac{\Sigma(x_i - \bar{x})(y_i - \bar{y})}{n - 1} = \frac{200}{2} = 100$$

$$s_x = \sqrt{\frac{\Sigma(x_i - \bar{x})^2}{n - 1}} = \sqrt{\frac{50}{2}} = 5$$

$$s_y = \sqrt{\frac{\Sigma(y_i - \bar{y})^2}{n - 1}} = \sqrt{\frac{800}{2}} = 20$$

$$r_{xy} = \frac{s_{xy}}{s_x s_y} = \frac{100}{5(20)} = 1$$

The correlation coefficient ranges from −1 to +1. Values close to −1 or +1 indicate a strong linear relationship. The closer the correlation is to zero, the weaker the relationship.

Thus, we see that the value of the sample correlation coefficient is 1.

In general, it can be shown that if all the points in a data set fall on a positively sloped straight line, the value of the sample correlation coefficient is +1; that is, a sample correlation coefficient of +1 corresponds to a perfect positive linear relationship between x and y. Moreover, if the points in the data set fall on a straight line having negative slope, the value of the sample correlation coefficient is −1; that is, a sample correlation coefficient of −1 corresponds to a perfect negative linear relationship between x and y.

Let us now suppose that a certain data set indicates a positive linear relationship between x and y but that the relationship is not perfect. The value of r_{xy} will be less than 1, indicating that the points in the scatter diagram are not all on a straight line. As the points deviate more and more from a perfect positive linear relationship, the value of r_{xy} becomes smaller and smaller. A value of r_{xy} equal to zero indicates no linear relationship between x and y, and values of r_{xy} near zero indicate a weak linear relationship.

For the data involving the stereo and sound equipment store, recall that $r_{xy} = +.93$. Therefore, we conclude that a strong positive linear relationship occurs between the number of commercials and sales. More specifically, an increase in the number of commercials is associated with an increase in sales.

In closing, we note that correlation provides a measure of linear association and not necessarily causation. A high correlation between two variables does not mean that changes in one variable will cause changes in the other variable. For example, we may find that the quality rating and the typical meal price of restaurants are positively correlated. However, simply increasing the meal price at a restaurant will not cause the quality rating to increase.

Using Excel to Compute the Covariance and Correlation Coefficient

Excel's COVAR function is designed for a population and Excel's CORREL function is designed for a sample.

Excel provides functions that can be used to compute the covariance and correlation coefficient. But you must be careful when using these functions because the covariance function treats the data as a population and the correlation function treats the data as a sample.

FIGURE 3.16   EXCEL WORKSHEET USED TO COMPUTE THE COVARIANCE AND CORRELATION COEFFICIENT

	A	B	C	D	E	F	G
1	Week	Commercials	Sales Volume		Population Covariance	=COVAR(B2:B11,C2:C11)	
2	1	2	50		Sample Correlation	=CORREL(B2:B11,C2:C11)	
3	2	5	57				
4	3	1	41				
5	4	3	54				
6	5	4	54				
7	6	1	38				
8	7	5	63				
9	8	3	48				
10	9	4	59				
11	10	2	46				
12							

	A	B	C	D	E	F	G
1	Week	Commercials	Sales Volume		Population Covariance	9.9	
2	1	2	50		Sample Correlation	0.9305	
3	2	5	57				
4	3	1	41				
5	4	3	54				
6	5	4	54				
7	6	1	38				
8	7	5	63				
9	8	3	48				
10	9	4	59				
11	10	2	46				
12							

Thus, the result obtained using Excel's covariance function must be adjusted to provide the sample covariance. We show here how these functions can be used to compute the sample covariance and the sample correlation coefficient for the stereo and sound equipment store data. Refer to Figure 3.16 as we present the steps involved. The formula worksheet is in the background; the value worksheet is in the foreground.

Enter Data: Labels and data on commercials and sales are entered into cells A1:C11 of the worksheet.

Enter Functions and Formulas: Excel's covariance function, COVAR, can be used to compute the population covariance by entering the following formula into cell F1:

$$=COVAR(B2:B11,C2:C11)$$

Similarly, the formula =CORREL(B2:B11,C2:C11) is entered into cell F2 to compute the sample correlation coefficient. The labels Population Covariance and Sample Correlation are entered into cells E1 and E2 to identify the output.

The formulas in cells F1:F2 are displayed in the worksheet in the background of Figure 3.16. The worksheet in the foreground shows the values computed using the Excel functions. Note that, except for rounding, the value of the sample correlation coefficient (.9305) is the same as we computed earlier using equation (3.12). However, the result provided by the COVAR function, 9.9, was obtained by treating the data as a population. Thus, we must adjust the Excel result of 9.9 to obtain the sample covariance. The adjustment is rather simple. First, note that the formula for the population covariance, equation (3.11), requires dividing by the total number of observations in the data set. But the formula for the sample covariance, equation (3.10), requires dividing by the total number of observations minus 1. So to use the Excel result of 9.9 to compute the sample covariance, we simply multiply 9.9 by $n/(n-1)$. With $n = 10$, we obtain

$$s_{xy} = \left(\frac{10}{9}\right)9.9 = 11$$

Thus, the sample covariance for the stereo and sound equipment data is 11.

Exercises

Methods

45.   Five observations taken for two variables follow.

x_i	4	6	11	3	16
y_i	50	50	40	60	30

   a.   Develop a scatter diagram with x on the horizontal axis.
   b.   What does the scatter diagram developed in part (a) indicate about the relationship between the two variables?
   c.   Compute and interpret the sample covariance.
   d.   Compute and interpret the sample correlation coefficient.

46.   Five observations taken for two variables follow.

x_i	6	11	15	21	27
y_i	6	9	6	17	12

   a.   Develop a scatter diagram for these data.
   b.   What does the scatter diagram indicate about a relationship between x and y?
   c.   Compute and interpret the sample covariance.
   d.   Compute and interpret the sample correlation coefficient.

Applications

47.   Nielsen Media Research provides two measures of the television viewing audience: a television program *rating,* which is the percentage of households with televisions watching a program, and a television program *share,* which is the percentage of households watching a program among those with televisions in use. The following data show the Nielsen television ratings and share data for the Major League Baseball World Series over a nine-year period (Associated Press, October 27, 2003).

Rating	19	17	17	14	16	12	15	12	13
Share	32	28	29	24	26	20	24	20	22

   a.   Develop a scatter diagram with rating on the horizontal axis.
   b.   What is the relationship between rating and share? Explain.
   c.   Compute and interpret the sample covariance.
   d.   Compute the sample correlation coefficient. What does this value tell us about the relationship between rating and share?

48.   A department of transportation's study on driving speed and mileage for midsize automobiles resulted in the following data.

Driving Speed	30	50	40	55	30	25	60	25	50	55
Mileage	28	25	25	23	30	32	21	35	26	25

   Compute and interpret the sample correlation coefficient.

49.   *PC World* provided ratings for 15 notebook PCs (*PC World,* February 2000). The performance score is a measure of how fast a PC can run a mix of common business applications as compared to a baseline machine. For example, a PC with a performance score of 200 is twice as fast as the baseline machine. A 100-point scale was used to provide an overall rating for each notebook tested in the study. A score in the 90s is exceptional, while one in the 70s is good. Table 3.10 shows the performance scores and the overall ratings for the 15 notebooks.

TABLE 3.10   PERFORMANCE SCORES AND OVERALL RATINGS FOR 15 NOTEBOOK PCs

WEB file

PCs

Notebook	Performance Score	Overall Rating
AMS Tech Roadster 15CTA380	115	67
Compaq Armada M700	191	78
Compaq Prosignia Notebook 150	153	79
Dell Inspiron 3700 C466GT	194	80
Dell Inspiron 7500 R500VT	236	84
Dell Latitude Cpi A366XT	184	76
Enpower ENP-313 Pro	184	77
Gateway Solo 9300LS	216	92
HP Pavilion Notebook PC	185	83
IBM ThinkPad I Series 1480	183	78
Micro Express NP7400	189	77
Micron TransPort NX PII-400	202	78
NEC Versa SX	192	78
Sceptre Soundx 5200	141	73
Sony VAIO PCG-F340	187	77

a. Compute the sample correlation coefficient.
b. What does the sample correlation coefficient tell about the relationship between the performance score and the overall rating?

50. The Dow Jones Industrial Average (DJIA) and the Standard & Poor's 500 Index (S&P 500) are both used to measure the performance of the stock market. The DJIA is based on the price of stocks for 30 large companies; the S&P 500 is based on the price of stocks for 500 companies. If both the DJIA and S&P 500 measure the performance of the stock market, how are they correlated? The following data show the daily percent increase or daily percent decrease in the DJIA and S&P 500 for a sample of nine days over a three-month period (*The Wall Street Journal,* January 15 to March 10, 2006).

WEB file

StockMarket

DJIA	.20	.82	−.99	.04	−.24	1.01	.30	.55	−.25
S&P 500	.24	.19	−.91	.08	−.33	.87	.36	.83	−.16

a. Show a scatter diagram.
b. Compute the sample correlation coefficient for these data.
c. Discuss the association between the DJIA and S&P 500. Do you need to check both before having a general idea about the daily stock market performance?

51. The daily high and low temperatures for 12 U.S. cities are as follows (Weather Channel, January 25, 2004).

WEB file

Temperature

City	High	Low	City	High	Low
Albany	9	−8	Los Angeles	62	47
Boise	32	26	New Orleans	71	55
Cleveland	21	19	Portland	43	36
Denver	37	10	Providence	18	8
Des Moines	24	16	Raleigh	28	24
Detroit	20	17	Tulsa	55	38

a. What is the sample mean daily high temperature?
b. What is the sample mean daily low temperature?
c. What is the correlation between the high and low temperatures?

The Weighted Mean and Working with Grouped Data

In Section 3.1, we presented the mean as one of the most important measures of central location. The formula for the mean of a sample with n observations is restated as follows.

$$\bar{x} = \frac{\Sigma x_i}{n} = \frac{x_1 + x_2 + \cdots + x_n}{n} \tag{3.14}$$

In this formula, each x_i is given equal importance or weight. Although this practice is most common, in some instances, the mean is computed by giving each observation a weight that reflects its importance. A mean computed in this manner is referred to as a **weighted mean**.

Weighted Mean

The weighted mean is computed as follows:

WEIGHTED MEAN

$$\bar{x} = \frac{\Sigma w_i x_i}{\Sigma w_i} \tag{3.15}$$

where

x_i = value of observation i
w_i = weight for observation i

When the data are from a sample, equation (3.15) provides the weighted sample mean. When the data are from a population, μ replaces $\bar{x}$ and equation (3.15) provides the weighted population mean.

As an example of the need for a weighted mean, consider the following sample of five purchases of a raw material over the past three months.

Purchase	Cost per Pound ($)	Number of Pounds
1	3.00	1200
2	3.40	500
3	2.80	2750
4	2.90	1000
5	3.25	800

Note that the cost per pound varies from $2.80 to $3.40, and the quantity purchased varies from 500 to 2750 pounds. Suppose that a manager asked for information about the mean cost per pound of the raw material. Because the quantities ordered vary, we must use the formula for a weighted mean. The five cost-per-pound data values are $x_1 = 3.00, x_2 = 3.40, x_3 = 2.80$, $x_4 = 2.90$, and $x_5 = 3.25$. The weighted mean cost per pound is found by weighting each cost by its corresponding quantity. For this example, the weights are $w_1 = 1200$, $w_2 = 500$, $w_3 = 2750$, $w_4 = 1000$, and $w_5 = 800$. Based on equation (3.15), the weighted mean is calculated as follows:

$$\bar{x} = \frac{1200(3.00) + 500(3.40) + 2750(2.80) + 1000(2.90) + 800(3.25)}{1200 + 500 + 2750 + 1000 + 800}$$

$$= \frac{18,500}{6250} = 2.96$$

Thus, the weighted mean computation shows that the mean cost per pound for the raw material is $2.96. Note that using equation (3.14) rather than the weighted mean formula would have provided misleading results. In this case, the mean of the five cost-per-pound values is $(3.00 + 3.40 + 2.80 + 2.90 + 3.25)/5 = 15.35/5 = \$3.07$, which overstates the actual mean cost per pound purchased.

Computing a grade point average is a good example of the use of a weighted mean.

The choice of weights for a particular weighted mean computation depends upon the application. An example that is well known to college students is the computation of a grade point average (GPA). In this computation, the data values generally used are 4 for an A grade, 3 for a B grade, 2 for a C grade, 1 for a D grade, and 0 for an F grade. The weights are the number of credits hours earned for each grade. Exercise 54 at the end of this section provides an example of this weighted mean computation. In other weighted mean computations, quantities such as pounds, dollars, or volume are frequently used as weights. In any case, when observations vary in importance, the analyst must choose the weight that best reflects the importance of each observation in the determination of the mean.

Grouped Data

In most cases, measures of location and variability are computed by using the individual data values. Sometimes, however, data are available only in a grouped or frequency distribution form. In the following discussion, we show how the weighted mean formula can be used to obtain approximations of the mean, variance, and standard deviation for **grouped data**.

In Section 2.2 we provided a frequency distribution of the time in days required to complete year-end audits for the public accounting firm of Sanderson and Clifford. The frequency distribution of audit times based on a sample of 20 clients is shown again in Table 3.11. Based on this frequency distribution, what is the sample mean audit time?

To compute the mean using only the grouped data, we treat the midpoint of each class as being representative of the items in the class. Let M_i denote the midpoint for class i and let f_i denote the frequency of class i. The weighted mean formula is then used with the data values denoted as M_i and the weights given by the frequencies f_i. In this case, the denominator of equation (3.15) is the sum of the frequencies, which is the

TABLE 3.11   FREQUENCY DISTRIBUTION OF AUDIT TIMES

Audit Time (days)	Frequency
10–14	4
15–19	8
20–24	5
25–29	2
30–34	1
Total	20

sample size n. That is, $\Sigma f_i = n$. Thus, the equation for the sample mean for grouped data is as follows.

SAMPLE MEAN FOR GROUPED DATA

$$\bar{x} = \frac{\Sigma f_i M_i}{n} \qquad\qquad (3.16)$$

where

$$M_i = \text{the midpoint for class } i$$
$$f_i = \text{the frequency for class } i$$
$$n = \text{the sample size}$$

With the class midpoints, M_i, halfway between the class limits, the first class of 10–14 in Table 3.11 has a midpoint at $(10 + 14)/2 = 12$. The five class midpoints and the weighted mean computation for the audit time data are summarized in Table 3.12. As can be seen, the sample mean audit time is 19 days.

   To compute the variance for grouped data, we use a slightly altered version of the formula for the variance provided in equation (3.5). In equation (3.5), the squared deviations of the data about the sample mean $\bar{x}$ were written $(x_i - \bar{x})^2$. However, with grouped data, the values are not known. In this case, we treat the class midpoint, M_i, as being representative of the x_i values in the corresponding class. Thus, the squared deviations about the sample mean, $(x_i - \bar{x})^2$, are replaced by $(M_i - \bar{x})^2$. Then, just as we did with the sample mean calculations for grouped data, we weight each value by the frequency of the class, f_i. The sum of the squared deviations about the mean for all the data is approximated by $\Sigma f_i (M_i - \bar{x})^2$. The term $n - 1$ rather than n appears in the denominator in order to make the sample variance the estimate of the population variance. Thus, the following formula is used to obtain the sample variance for grouped data.

SAMPLE VARIANCE FOR GROUPED DATA

$$s^2 = \frac{\Sigma f_i (M_i - \bar{x})^2}{n - 1} \qquad\qquad (3.17)$$

TABLE 3.12   COMPUTATION OF THE SAMPLE MEAN AUDIT TIME FOR GROUPED DATA

Audit Time (days)	Class Midpoint (M_i)	Frequency (f_i)	$f_i M_i$
10–14	12	4	48
15–19	17	8	136
20–24	22	5	110
25–29	27	2	54
30–34	32	1	32
		20	380

$$\text{Sample mean } \bar{x} = \frac{\Sigma f_i M_i}{n} = \frac{380}{20} = 19 \text{ days}$$

TABLE 3.13   COMPUTATION OF THE SAMPLE VARIANCE OF AUDIT TIMES
FOR GROUPED DATA (SAMPLE MEAN $\bar{x} = 19$)

Audit Time (days)	Class Midpoint (M_i)	Frequency (f_i)	Deviation ($M_i - \bar{x}$)	Squared Deviation ($M_i - \bar{x})^2$	$f_i(M_i - \bar{x})^2$
10–14	12	4	−7	49	196
15–19	17	8	−2	4	32
20–24	22	5	3	9	45
25–29	27	2	8	64	128
30–34	32	1	13	169	169
		20			570

$$\Sigma f_i(M_i - \bar{x})^2$$

Sample variance $s^2 = \dfrac{\Sigma f_i(M_i - \bar{x})^2}{n - 1} = \dfrac{570}{19} = 30$

The calculation of the sample variance for audit times based on the grouped data from Table 3.11 is shown in Table 3.13. As can be seen, the sample variance is 30.

The standard deviation for grouped data is simply the square root of the variance for grouped data. For the audit time data, the sample standard deviation is $s = \sqrt{30} = 5.48$.

Before closing this section on computing measures of location and dispersion for grouped data, we note that formulas (3.16) and (3.17) are for a sample. Population summary measures are computed similarly. The grouped data formulas for a population mean and variance follow.

POPULATION MEAN FOR GROUPED DATA

$$\mu = \frac{\Sigma f_i M_i}{N} \tag{3.18}$$

POPULATION VARIANCE FOR GROUPED DATA

$$\sigma^2 = \frac{\Sigma f_i(M_i - \mu)^2}{N} \tag{3.19}$$

NOTES AND COMMENTS

In computing descriptive statistics for grouped data, the class midpoints are used to approximate the data values in each class. As a result, the descriptive statistics for grouped data approximate the descriptive statistics that would result from using the original data directly. We therefore recommend computing descriptive statistics from the original data rather than from grouped data whenever possible.

Exercises

Methods

52. Consider the following data and corresponding weights.

x_i	Weight (w_i)
3.2	6
2.0	3
2.5	2
5.0	8

    a. Compute the weighted mean.
    b. Compute the sample mean of the four data values without weighting. Note the difference in the results provided by the two computations.

53. Consider the sample data in the following frequency distribution.

Class	Midpoint	Frequency
3–7	5	4
8–12	10	7
13–17	15	9
18–22	20	5

    a. Compute the sample mean.
    b. Compute the sample variance and sample standard deviation.

Applications

54. The grade point average for college students is based on a weighted mean computation. For most colleges, the grades are given the following data values: A (4), B (3), C (2), D (1), and F (0). After 60 credit hours of course work, a student at State University earned 9 credit hours of A, 15 credit hours of B, 33 credit hours of C, and 3 credit hours of D.
    a. Compute the student's grade point average.
    b. Students at State University must maintain a 2.5 grade point average for their first 60 credit hours of course work in order to be admitted to the business college. Will this student be admitted?

55. Morningstar tracks the total return for a large universe of mutual funds. The following table shows the total return and the number of funds for several categories of mutual funds during 2007 (*Morningstar Funds500*, 2008).

Type of Fund	Total Return (%)	Number of Funds
Domestic Equity	4.65	9191
International Equity	18.15	2621
Specialty Stock	11.36	1419
Hybrid	6.75	2900

    a. Using the number of funds as weights, compute the weighted average total return for the universe of mutual funds covered by Morningstar.

b.   Is there any difficulty associated with using the "number of funds" as the weights in computing the weighted average total return for Morningstar in part (a)? Discuss. What else might be used for weights?

c.   Suppose you had invested $10,000 in mutual funds at the beginning of 2007 and diversified your investment by placing $2000 in Domestic Equity funds, $4000 in International Equity funds, $3000 in Specialty Stock funds, and $1000 in Hybrid funds. What could you expect as the return on your portfolio?

56.   A survey of subscribers to *Fortune* magazine asked the following question: "How many of the last four issues have you read?" Suppose that the following frequency distribution summarizes 500 responses.

Number Read	Frequency
0	15
1	10
2	40
3	85
4	350
Total	500

a.   What is the mean number of issues read by a *Fortune* subscriber?
b.   What is the standard deviation of the number of issues read?

57.   The following frequency distribution shows the price per share for the 30 companies in the Dow Jones Industrial Average (*The Wall Street Journal,* January 16, 2006).

Price per Share	Frequency
$20–29	7
$30–39	6
$40–49	6
$50–59	3
$60–69	4
$70–79	3
$80–89	1

Compute the mean price per share and the standard deviation of the price per share for the Dow Jones Industrial Average companies.

Summary

In this chapter we introduced several descriptive statistics that can be used to summarize the location, variability, and shape of a data distribution. Unlike the tabular and graphical procedures introduced in Chapter 2, the measures introduced in this chapter summarize the data in terms of numerical values. When the numerical values obtained are for a sample, they are called sample statistics. When the numerical values obtained are for a population, they are called population parameters. Some of the notation used for sample statistics and population parameters follow.

In statistical inference, a sample statistic is referred to as a point estimator of the population parameter.

	Sample Statistic	**Population Parameter**
Mean	$\bar{x}$	μ
Variance	s^2	σ^2
Standard deviation	s	σ
Covariance	s_{xy}	σ_{xy}
Correlation	r_{xy}	ρ_{xy}

As measures of central location, we defined the mean, median, and mode. Then the concept of percentiles was used to describe other locations in the data set. Next, we presented the range, interquartile range, variance, standard deviation, and coefficient of variation as measures of variability or dispersion. Our primary measure of the shape of a data distribution was the skewness. Negative values indicate a data distribution skewed to the left. Positive values indicate a data distribution skewed to the right. We then described how the mean and standard deviation could be used, applying Chebyshev's theorem and the empirical rule, to provide more information about the distribution of data and to identify outliers.

In Section 3.4 we showed how to develop a five-number summary and a box plot to provide simultaneous information about the location, variability, and shape of the distribution. In Section 3.5 we introduced covariance and the correlation coefficient as measures of association between two variables. In the final section, we showed how to compute a weighted mean and how to calculate a mean, variance, and standard deviation for grouped data.

Glossary

Sample statistic A numerical value used as a summary measure for a sample (e.g., the sample mean, $\bar{x}$, the sample variance, s^2, and the sample standard deviation, s).

Population parameter A numerical value used as a summary measure for a population (e.g., the population mean, μ, the population variance, σ^2, and the population standard deviation, σ).

Point estimator A sample statistic, such as $\bar{x}$, s^2, and s, that is used to estimate the corresponding population parameter.

Mean A measure of central location computed by summing the data values and dividing by the number of observations.

Median A measure of central location provided by the value in the middle when the data are arranged in ascending order.

Mode A measure of location, defined as the value that occurs with greatest frequency.

Percentile A value such that at least p percent of the observations are less than or equal to this value and at least $(100 - p)$ percent of the observations are greater than or equal to this value. The 50th percentile is the median.

Quartiles The 25th, 50th, and 75th percentiles, referred to as the first quartile, the second quartile (median), and third quartile, respectively. The quartiles can be used to divide a data set into four parts, with each part containing approximately 25% of the data.

Range A measure of variability, defined to be the largest value minus the smallest value.

Interquartile range (IQR) A measure of variability, defined to be the difference between the third and first quartiles.

Variance A measure of variability based on the squared deviations of the data values about the mean.

Standard deviation A measure of variability computed by taking the positive square root of the variance.

Coefficient of variation A measure of relative variability computed by dividing the standard deviation by the mean and multiplying by 100.

Skewness A measure of the shape of a data distribution. Data skewed to the left result in negative skewness; a symmetric data distribution results in zero skewness; and data skewed to the right result in positive skewness.

z-**score** A value computed by dividing the deviation about the mean $(x_i - \bar{x})$ by the standard deviation *s*. A *z*-score is referred to as a standardized value and denotes the number of standard deviations x_i is from the mean.

Chebyshev's theorem A theorem that can be used to make statements about the proportion of data values that must be within a specified number of standard deviations of the mean.

Empirical rule A rule that can be used to compute the percentage of data values that must be within one, two, and three standard deviations of the mean for data that exhibit a bell-shaped distribution.

Outlier An unusually small or unusually large data value.

Five-number summary An exploratory data analysis technique that uses five numbers to summarize the data: smallest value, first quartile, median, third quartile, and largest value.

Box plot A graphical summary of data based on a five-number summary.

Covariance A measure of linear association between two variables. Positive values indicate a positive relationship; negative values indicate a negative relationship.

Correlation coefficient A measure of linear association between two variables that takes on values between -1 and $+1$. Values near $+1$ indicate a strong positive linear relationship; values near -1 indicate a strong negative linear relationship; and values near zero indicate the lack of a linear relationship.

Weighted mean The mean obtained by assigning each observation a weight that reflects its importance.

Grouped data Data available in class intervals as summarized by a frequency distribution. Individual values of the original data are not available.

Key Formulas

Sample Mean

$$\bar{x} = \frac{\Sigma x_i}{n} \tag{3.1}$$

Population Mean

$$\mu = \frac{\Sigma x_i}{N} \tag{3.2}$$

Interquartile Range

$$\text{IQR} = Q_3 - Q_1 \tag{3.3}$$

Population Variance

$$\sigma^2 = \frac{\Sigma(x_i - \mu)^2}{N} \tag{3.4}$$

Sample Variance

$$s^2 = \frac{\Sigma(x_i - \bar{x})^2}{n - 1} \qquad (3.5)$$

Standard Deviation

$$\text{Sample standard deviation} = s = \sqrt{s^2} \qquad (3.6)$$

$$\text{Population standard deviation} = \sigma = \sqrt{\sigma^2} \qquad (3.7)$$

Coefficient of Variation

$$\left(\frac{\text{Standard deviation}}{\text{Mean}} \times 100\right)\% \qquad (3.8)$$

z-Score

$$z_i = \frac{x_i - \bar{x}}{s} \qquad (3.9)$$

Sample Covariance

$$s_{xy} = \frac{\Sigma(x_i - \bar{x})(y_i - \bar{y})}{n - 1} \qquad (3.10)$$

Population Covariance

$$\sigma_{xy} = \frac{\Sigma(x_i - \mu_x)(y_i - \mu_y)}{N} \qquad (3.11)$$

Pearson Product Moment Correlation Coefficient: Sample Data

$$r_{xy} = \frac{s_{xy}}{s_x s_y} \qquad (3.12)$$

Pearson Product Moment Correlation Coefficient: Population Data

$$\rho_{xy} = \frac{\sigma_{xy}}{\sigma_x \sigma_y} \qquad (3.13)$$

Weighted Mean

$$\bar{x} = \frac{\Sigma w_i x_i}{\Sigma w_i} \qquad (3.15)$$

Sample Mean for Grouped Data

$$\bar{x} = \frac{\Sigma f_i M_i}{n} \qquad (3.16)$$

Sample Variance for Grouped Data

$$s^2 = \frac{\Sigma f_i (M_i - \bar{x})^2}{n - 1} \qquad (3.17)$$

Population Mean for Grouped Data

$$\mu = \frac{\sum f_i M_i}{N} \qquad\qquad (3.18)$$

Population Variance for Grouped Data

$$\sigma^2 = \frac{\sum f_i (M_i - \mu)^2}{N} \qquad\qquad (3.19)$$

Supplementary Exercises

58. According to the 2003 Annual Consumer Spending Survey, the average monthly Bank of America Visa credit card charge was $1838 (*U.S. Airways Attaché Magazine,* December 2003). A sample of monthly credit card charges provides the following data.

Visa

236	1710	1351	825	7450
316	4135	1333	1584	387
991	3396	170	1428	1688

    a.   Compute the mean and median.
    b.   Compute the first and third quartiles.
    c.   Compute the range and interquartile range.
    d.   Compute the variance and standard deviation.
    e.   The skewness measure for these data is 2.12. Comment on the shape of this distribution. Is it the shape you would expect? Why or why not?
    f.   Do the data contain outliers?

59. The U.S. Census Bureau provides statistics on family life in the United States, including the age at the time of first marriage, current marital status, and size of household (*http://www.census.gov,* March 20, 2006). The following data show the age at the time of first marriage for a sample of men and a sample of women.

Ages

Men	26	23	28	25	27	30	26	35	28
	21	24	27	29	30	27	32	27	25
Women	20	28	23	30	24	29	26	25	
	22	22	25	23	27	26	19		

    a.   Determine the median age at the time of first marriage for men and women.
    b.   Compute the first and third quartiles for both men and women.
    c.   Twenty-five years ago the median age at the time of first marriage was 25 for men and 22 for women. What insight does this information provide about the decision of when to marry among young people today?

60. Dividend yield is the annual dividend per share a company pays divided by the current market price per share expressed as a percentage. A sample of 10 large companies provided the following dividend yield data (*The Wall Street Journal,* January 16, 2004).

Company	Yield %	Company	Yield %
Altria Group	5.0	General Motors	3.7
American Express	0.8	JPMorgan Chase	3.5
Caterpillar	1.8	McDonald's	1.6
Eastman Kodak	1.9	United Technology	1.5
ExxonMobil	2.5	Wal-Mart Stores	0.7

a. What are the mean and median dividend yields?
b. What are the variance and standard deviation?
c. Which company provides the highest dividend yield?
d. What is the z-score for McDonald's? Interpret this z-score.
e. What is the z-score for General Motors? Interpret this z-score.
f. Based on z-scores, do the data contain any outliers?

61. The U.S. Department of Education reports that about 50% of all college students use a student loan to help cover college expenses (National Center for Educational Studies, January 2006). A sample of students who graduated with student loan debt is shown here. The data, in thousands of dollars, show typical amounts of debt upon graduation.

    10.1   14.8   5.0   10.2   12.4   12.2   2.0   11.5   17.8   4.0

    a. For those students who use a student loan, what is the mean loan debt upon graduation?
    b. What is the variance? Standard deviation?

62. Small business owners often look to payroll service companies to handle their employee payroll. Reasons are that small business owners face complicated tax regulations and penalties for employment tax errors are costly. According to the Internal Revenue Service, 26% of all small business employment tax returns contained errors that resulted in a tax penalty to the owner (*The Wall Street Journal,* January 30, 2006). The tax penalty for a sample of 20 small business owners follows:

WEB file

Penalty

    | 820 | 270 | 450 | 1010 | 890 | 700 | 1350 | 350 | 300 | 1200 |
    | 390 | 730 | 2040 | 230 | 640 | 350 | 420 | 270 | 370 | 620 |

    a. What is the mean tax penalty for improperly filed employment tax returns?
    b. What is the standard deviation?
    c. Is the highest penalty, $2040, an outlier?
    d. What are some of the advantages of a small business owner hiring a payroll service company to handle employee payroll services, including the employment tax returns?

63. Public transportation and the automobile are two methods an employee can use to get to work each day. Samples of times recorded for each method are shown. Times are in minutes.

    Public Transportation: 28   29   32   37   33   25   29   32   41   34
    Automobile: 29   31   33   32   34   30   31   32   35   33

    a. Compute the sample mean time to get to work for each method.
    b. Compute the sample standard deviation for each method.
    c. On the basis of your results from parts (a) and (b), which method of transportation should be preferred? Explain.
    d. Develop a box plot for each method. Does a comparison of the box plots support your conclusion in part (c)?

64. The National Association of Realtors reported the median home price in the United States and the increase in median home price over a five-year period (*The Wall Street Journal,* January 16, 2006). Use the sample home prices shown here to answer the following questions.

WEB file

Homes

    | 995.9 | 48.8 | 175.0 | 263.5 | 298.0 | 218.9 | 209.0 |
    | 628.3 | 111.0 | 212.9 | 92.6 | 2325.0 | 958.0 | 212.5 |

    a. What is the sample median home price?
    b. In January 2001, the National Association of Realtors reported a median home price of $139,300 in the United States. What was the percentage increase in the median home price over the five-year period?
    c. What are the first quartile and the third quartile for the sample data?
    d. Provide a five-number summary for the home prices.
    e. Do the data contain any outliers?
    f. What is the mean home price for the sample? Why does the National Association of Realtors prefer to use the median home price in its reports?

65. The following data show the media expenditures ($ millions) and shipments in millions of barrels (bbls.) for 10 major brands of beer.

WEB file

Beer

Brand	Media Expenditures ($millions)	Shipments in bbls. (millions)
Budweiser	120.0	36.3
Bud Light	68.7	20.7
Miller Lite	100.1	15.9
Coors Light	76.6	13.2
Busch	8.7	8.1
Natural Light	0.1	7.1
Miller Genuine Draft	21.5	5.6
Miller High Life	1.4	4.4
Busch Lite	5.3	4.3
Milwaukee's Best	1.7	4.3

   a. What is the sample covariance? Does it indicate a positive or negative relationship?
   b. What is the sample correlation coefficient?

66. *Road & Track* provided the following sample of the tire ratings and load-carrying capacity of automobiles tires.

Tire Rating	Load-Carrying Capacity
75	853
82	1047
85	1135
87	1201
88	1235
91	1356
92	1389
93	1433
105	2039

   a. Develop a scatter diagram for the data with tire rating on the *x*-axis.
   b. What is the sample correlation coefficient, and what does it tell you about the relationship between tire rating and load-carrying capacity?

WEB file

FairValue

67. Morningstar tracks and evaluates a large number of common stocks and publishes its evaluations. For the stocks it follows, Morningstar publishes a Fair Value estimate along with a variety of other data. Data for 30 companies followed by Morningstar are contained in the website that accompanies the text in the file named FairValue. The data provided for each company include the Fair Value estimate, the stock's share price, and the stock's earnings per share (*Morningstar Stocks500*, 2008).
   a. Develop a scatter diagram for the data on Fair Value and Share Price with Share Price on the horizontal axis. What is the sample correlation coefficient, and what can you say about the relationship between the variables?
   b. Develop a scatter diagram for the data on Fair Value and Earnings per Share with Earnings per Share on the horizontal axis. What is the sample correlation coefficient, and what can you say about the relationship between the variables?

68. A forecasting technique referred to as moving averages uses the average or mean of the most recent *n* periods to forecast the next value for time series data. With a three-period moving average, the most recent three periods of data are used in the forecast computation. Consider a product with the following demand for the first three months of the current year: January (800 units), February (750 units), and March (900 units).

a. What is the three-month moving average forecast for April?

b. A variation of this forecasting technique is called weighted moving averages. The weighting allows the more recent time series data to receive more weight or more importance in the computation of the forecast. For example, a weighted three-month moving average might give a weight of 3 to data one month old, a weight of 2 to data two months old, and a weight of 1 to data three months old. Use the data given to provide a three-month weighted moving average forecast for April.

69. The days to maturity for a sample of five money market funds are shown here. The dollar amounts invested in the funds are provided. Use the weighted mean to determine the mean number of days to maturity for dollars invested in these five money market funds.

Days to Maturity	Dollar Value ($millions)
20	20
12	30
7	10
5	15
6	10

70. Automobiles traveling on a road with a posted speed limit of 55 miles per hour are checked for speed by a state police radar system. Following is a frequency distribution of speeds.

Speed (miles per hour)	Frequency
45–49	10
50–54	40
55–59	150
60–64	175
65–69	75
70–74	15
75–79	10
Total	475

a. What is the mean speed of the automobiles traveling on this road?

b. Compute the variance and the standard deviation.

Case Problem 1   Pelican Stores

Pelican Stores, a division of National Clothing, is a chain of women's apparel stores operating throughout the country. The chain recently ran a promotion in which discount coupons were sent to customers of other National Clothing stores. Data collected for a sample of 100 in-store credit card transactions at Pelican Stores during one day while the promotion was running are contained in the file named PelicanStores. Table 3.14 shows a portion of the data set. The proprietary card method of payment refers to charges made using a National Clothing charge card. Customers who made a purchase using a discount coupon are referred to as promotional customers and customers who made a purchase but did not use a discount coupon are referred to as regular customers. Because the promotional coupons were not sent to regular Pelican Stores customers, management considers the sales made to people presenting the promotional coupons as sales it would not otherwise make. Of course, Pelican also hopes that the promotional customers will continue to shop at its stores.

Most of the variables shown in Table 3.14 are self-explanatory, but two of the variables require some clarification.

Items   The total number of items purchased
Net Sales The total amount ($) charged to the credit card

Pelican's management would like to use this sample data to learn about its customer base and to evaluate the promotion involving discount coupons.

Managerial Report

Use the methods of descriptive statistics presented in this chapter to summarize the data and comment on your findings. At a minimum, your report should include the following:

1. Descriptive statistics on net sales and descriptive statistics on net sales by various classifications of customers.
2. Descriptive statistics concerning the relationship between age and net sales.

TABLE 3.14   SAMPLE OF 100 CREDIT CARD PURCHASES AT PELICAN STORES

WEB file

PelicanStores

Customer	Type of Customer	Items	Net Sales	Method of Payment	Gender	Marital Status	Age
1	Regular	1	39.50	Discover	Male	Married	32
2	Promotional	1	102.40	Proprietary Card	Female	Married	36
3	Regular	1	22.50	Proprietary Card	Female	Married	32
4	Promotional	5	100.40	Proprietary Card	Female	Married	28
5	Regular	2	54.00	MasterCard	Female	Married	34
6	Regular	1	44.50	MasterCard	Female	Married	44
7	Promotional	2	78.00	Proprietary Card	Female	Married	30
8	Regular	1	22.50	Visa	Female	Married	40
9	Promotional	2	56.52	Proprietary Card	Female	Married	46
10	Regular	1	44.50	Proprietary Card	Female	Married	36
.	.	.	.	.	.	.	.
.	.	.	.	.	.	.	.
.	.	.	.	.	.	.	.
96	Regular	1	39.50	MasterCard	Female	Married	44
97	Promotional	9	253.00	Proprietary Card	Female	Married	30
98	Promotional	10	287.59	Proprietary Card	Female	Married	52
99	Promotional	2	47.60	Proprietary Card	Female	Married	30
100	Promotional	1	28.44	Proprietary Card	Female	Married	44

Case Problem 2   # Motion Picture Industry

The motion picture industry is a competitive business. More than 50 studios produce a total of 300 to 400 new motion pictures each year, and the financial success of each motion picture varies considerably. The opening weekend gross sales, the total gross sales, the number of theaters the movie was shown in, and the number of weeks the motion picture was in the top 60 for gross sales are common variables used to measure the success of a motion picture. Data collected for a sample of 100 motion pictures produced in 2005 are contained in the file named Movies. Table 3.15 shows the data for the first 10 motion pictures in the file.

Managerial Report

Use the numerical methods of descriptive statistics presented in this chapter to learn how these variables contribute to the success of a motion picture. Include the following in your report.

1. Descriptive statistics for each of the four variables along with a discussion of what the descriptive statistics tell us about the motion picture industry.
2. What motion pictures, if any, should be considered high-performance outliers? Explain.
3. Descriptive statistics showing the relationship between total gross sales and each of the other variables. Discuss.

TABLE 3.15   PERFORMANCE DATA FOR 10 MOTION PICTURES

Movies

Motion Picture	Opening Gross Sales ($millions)	Total Gross Sales ($millions)	Number of Theaters	Weeks in Top 60
Coach Carter	29.17	67.25	2574	16
Ladies in Lavender	0.15	6.65	119	22
Batman Begins	48.75	205.28	3858	18
Unleashed	10.90	24.47	1962	8
Pretty Persuasion	0.06	0.23	24	4
Fever Pitch	12.40	42.01	3275	14
Harry Potter and the Goblet of Fire	102.69	287.18	3858	13
Monster-in-Law	23.11	82.89	3424	16
White Noise	24.11	55.85	2279	7
Mr. and Mrs. Smith	50.34	186.22	3451	21

Case Problem 3   # Business Schools of Asia-Pacific

WEB file

Asian

The pursuit of a higher education degree in business is now international. A survey shows that more and more Asians choose the Master of Business Administration degree route to corporate success. As a result, the number of applicants for MBA courses at Asia-Pacific schools continues to increase.

Across the region, thousands of Asians show an increasing willingness to temporarily shelve their careers and spend two years in pursuit of a theoretical business qualification. Courses in these schools are notoriously tough and include economics, banking, marketing, behavioral sciences, labor relations, decision making, strategic thinking, business law, and more. The data set in Table 3.16 shows some of the characteristics of the leading Asia-Pacific business schools.

TABLE 3.16   DATA FOR 25 ASIA-PACIFIC BUSINESS SCHOOLS

Business School	Full-Time Enrollment	Students per Faculty	Local Tuition ($)	Foreign Tuition ($)	Age	%Foreign	GMAT	English Test	Work Experience	Starting Salary ($)
Melbourne Business School	200	5	24,420	29,600	28	47	Yes	No	Yes	71,400
University of New South Wales (Sydney)	228	4	19,993	32,582	29	28	Yes	No	Yes	65,200
Indian Institute of Management (Ahmedabad)	392	5	4,300	4,300	22	0	No	No	No	7,100
Chinese University of Hong Kong	90	5	11,140	11,140	29	10	Yes	No	No	31,000
International University of Japan (Niigata)	126	4	33,060	33,060	28	60	Yes	Yes	No	87,000
Asian Institute of Management (Manila)	389	5	7,562	9,000	25	50	Yes	No	Yes	22,800
Indian Institute of Management (Bangalore)	380	5	3,935	16,000	23	1	Yes	No	No	7,500
National University of Singapore	147	6	6,146	7,170	29	51	Yes	Yes	Yes	43,300
Indian Institute of Management (Calcutta)	463	8	2,880	16,000	23	0	No	No	No	7,400
Australian National University (Canberra)	42	2	20,300	20,300	30	80	Yes	Yes	Yes	46,600
Nanyang Technological University (Singapore)	50	5	8,500	8,500	32	20	Yes	No	Yes	49,300
University of Queensland (Brisbane)	138	17	16,000	22,800	32	26	No	No	Yes	49,600
Hong Kong University of Science and Technology	60	2	11,513	11,513	26	37	Yes	No	Yes	34,000
Macquarie Graduate School of Management (Sydney)	12	8	17,172	19,778	34	27	No	No	Yes	60,100
Chulalongkorn University (Bangkok)	200	7	17,355	17,355	25	6	Yes	No	No	17,600
Monash Mt. Eliza Business School (Melbourne)	350	13	16,200	22,500	30	30	Yes	Yes	Yes	52,500
Asian Institute of Management (Bangkok)	300	10	18,200	18,200	29	90	No	Yes	Yes	25,000
University of Adelaide	20	19	16,426	23,100	30	10	No	No	Yes	66,000
Massey University (Palmerston North, New Zealand)	30	15	13,106	21,625	37	35	No	Yes	Yes	41,400
Royal Melbourne Institute of Technology Business Graduate School	30	7	13,880	17,765	32	30	No	Yes	Yes	48,900
Jamnalal Bajaj Institute of Management Studies (Bombay)	240	9	1,000	1,000	24	0	No	No	Yes	7,000
Curtin Institute of Technology (Perth)	98	15	9,475	19,097	29	43	Yes	No	Yes	55,000
Lahore University of Management Sciences	70	14	11,250	26,300	23	2.5	No	No	No	7,500
Universiti Sains Malaysia (Penang)	30	5	2,260	2,260	32	15	No	Yes	Yes	16,000
De La Salle University (Manila)	44	17	3,300	3,600	28	3.5	Yes	No	Yes	13,100

Managerial Report

Use the methods of descriptive statistics to summarize the data in Table 3.16. Discuss your findings.

1. Include a summary for each variable in the data set. Make comments and interpretations based on maximums and minimums, as well as the appropriate means and proportions. What new insights do these descriptive statistics provide concerning Asia-Pacific business schools?
2. Summarize the data to compare the following:
   a. Any difference between local and foreign tuition costs.
   b. Any difference between mean starting salaries for schools requiring and not requiring work experience.
   c. Any difference between starting salaries for schools requiring and not requiring English tests.
3. Do starting salaries appear to be related to tuition?
4. Present any additional graphical and numerical summaries that will be beneficial in communicating the data in Table 3.16 to others.

Appendix # Descriptive Statistics and Box Plot Using StatTools

In this appendix we show how StatTools can be used to develop descriptive statistics and construct a box plot.

Descriptive Statistics for One Variable

StartSalary

We use the starting salary data in Table 3.1 to illustrate. Begin by using the Data Set Manager to create a StatTools data set for these data using the procedure described in the appendix in Chapter 1. The following steps will generate a variety of descriptive statistics.

Step 1. Click the **StatTools** tab on the Ribbon
Step 2. In the **Analyses Group,** click **Summary Statistics**
Step 3. Choose the **One-Variable Summary** option
Step 4. When the One-Variable Summary Statistics dialog box appears,
   In the **Variables** section, select **Starting Salary**
   Click **OK**

A variety of summary statistics will appear.

Constructing a Box Plot

We use the starting salary data in Table 3.1 to illustrate. Begin by using the Data Set Manager to create a StatTools data set for these data using the procedure described in the appendix in Chapter 1. The following steps will create a box plot for these data.

StartSalary

Step 1. Click the **StatTools** tab on the Ribbon
Step 2. In the **Analyses Group,** click **Summary Graphs**
Step 3. Choose the **Box-Whisker Plot** option
Step 4. When the StatTools—Box-Whisker Plot dialog box appears,
   In the Variables section, select **Starting Salary**
   Click **OK**

A box plot similar to the one in Figure 3.11 will appear.

Covariance and Correlation

We use the stereo and sound equipment data in Table 3.7 to demonstrate the computation of the sample covariance and the sample correlation coefficient. Begin by using the Data Set Manager to create a StatTools data set for these data using the procedure described in the appendix in Chapter 1. The following steps will provide the sample covariance and sample correlation coefficient.

Stereo

Step 1. Click the **StatTools** tab on the Ribbon
Step 2. In the **Analyses Group,** click **Summary Statistics**
Step 3. Choose the **Correlation and Covariance** option
Step 4. When the StatTools—Correlation and Covariance dialog box appears,
    In the **Variables** section
      Select **No. of Commercials**
      Select **Sales Volume**
    In the **Tables to Create** section,
      Select **Table of Correlations**
      Select **Table of Covariances**
    In the **Table Structure** section select **Symmetric**
    Click **OK**

A table showing the correlation coefficient and the covariance will appear.

Introduction to Probability

STATISTICS *in* PRACTICE

ROHM AND HAAS COMPANY*
PHILADELPHIA, PENNSYLVANIA

Rohm and Haas is the world's leading producer of specialty materials, including electronic materials, polymers for paints, and personal care items. Company products enable the creation of leading-edge consumer goods in markets such as pharmaceuticals, retail food, building supplies, communication equipment, and household products. The company has a workforce of more than 17,000 and annual sales of $8 billion. A network of more than 100 manufacturing, technical research, and customer service sites provide Rohm and Haas products and services in 27 countries worldwide.

In the area of specialty chemical products, the company offers a variety of chemicals designed to meet the unique specifications of its customers. For one particular customer, the company produced an expensive catalyst used in the customer's chemical processing operation. Some, but not all, of the shipments from the company met the customer's specifications for the product. The contract called for the customer to test each shipment after receiving it and determine whether the catalyst would perform the desired function. Shipments that did not pass the customer's test would be returned. Over time, experience showed that the customer was accepting 60% of the shipments, but returning 40% of the shipments. Neither the customer nor the company was pleased with this level of service.

The company explored the possibility of duplicating the customer's test prior to shipment. However, the high cost of the special testing equipment that was required made this alternative infeasible. Company chemists working on the problem proposed a different but relatively low-cost test that could be conducted prior to shipment to the customer. The company believed that the new test would provide an indication of whether the catalyst would pass the customer's more sophisticated test.

A new test prior to shipment improved customer service. © Mason Morfit/Workbook Stock/Jupiter Images.

The probability question was: What is the probability that the catalyst would pass the customer's test given that it passed the new test prior to shipment?

A sample of the catalyst was produced and subjected to the new company test. Only samples of the catalyst that passed the new test were sent to the customer. Probability analysis of the data indicated that if the catalyst passed the new test prior to shipment, there was a .909 probability that the catalyst would pass the customer's test. Or, if the catalyst passed the new test prior to shipment, there was only a .091 probability that it would fail the customer's test and be returned. The probability analysis provided supporting evidence for the implementation of the testing procedure prior to shipment. This new test resulted in an immediate improvement in customer service and a substantial reduction in shipping and handling costs for the returned shipments.

The probability of a shipment being accepted by the customer given it had passed the new test is called a conditional probability. In this chapter, you will learn how to compute conditional and other probabilities that are helpful in decision making.

*The authors are indebted to Michael Haskell of the Rohm and Haas subsidiary Morton International for providing this statistics in practice.

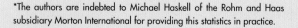

Managers often base their decisions on an analysis of uncertainties such as the following:

1. What are the chances that sales will decrease if we increase prices?
2. What is the likelihood a new assembly method will increase productivity?
3. How likely is it that the project will be finished on time?
4. What is the chance that a new investment will be profitable?

FIGURE 4.1 PROBABILITY AS A NUMERICAL MEASURE OF THE LIKELIHOOD OF AN EVENT OCCURRING

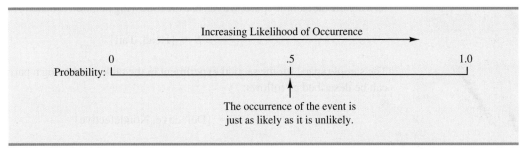

Some of the earliest work on probability originated in a series of letters between Pierre de Fermat and Blaise Pascal in the 1650s.

Probability is a numerical measure of the likelihood that an event will occur. Thus, probabilities can be used as measures of the degree of uncertainty associated with the four events previously listed. If probabilities are available, we can determine the likelihood of each event occurring.

Probability values are always assigned on a scale from 0 to 1. A probability near zero indicates an event is unlikely to occur; a probability near 1 indicates an event is almost certain to occur. Other probabilities between 0 and 1 represent degrees of likelihood that an event will occur. For example, if we consider the event "rain tomorrow," we understand that when the weather report indicates "a near-zero probability of rain," it means almost no chance of rain. However, if a .90 probability of rain is reported, we know that rain is likely to occur. A .50 probability indicates that rain is just as likely to occur as not. Figure 4.1 depicts the view of probability as a numerical measure of the likelihood of an event occurring.

4.1 Experiments, Counting Rules, and Assigning Probabilities

In discussing probability, we define an **experiment** as a process that generates well-defined outcomes. On any single repetition of an experiment, one and only one of the possible experimental outcomes will occur. Several examples of experiments and their associated outcomes follow.

Experiment	**Experimental Outcomes**
Toss a coin	Head, tail
Select a part for inspection	Defective, nondefective
Conduct a sales call	Purchase, no purchase
Roll a die	1, 2, 3, 4, 5, 6
Play a football game	Win, lose, tie

By specifying all possible experimental outcomes, we identify the **sample space** for an experiment.

> **SAMPLE SPACE**
>
> The sample space for an experiment is the set of all experimental outcomes.

Experimental outcomes are also called sample points.

An experimental outcome is also called a **sample point** to identify it as an element of the sample space.

Consider the first experiment in the preceding table—tossing a coin. The upward face of the coin—a head or a tail—determines the experimental outcome (sample point). If we let S denote the sample space, we can use the following notation to describe the sample space:

$$S = \{\text{Head, Tail}\}$$

The sample space for the second experiment in the table—selecting a part for inspection—can be described as follows:

$$S = \{\text{Defective, Nondefective}\}$$

Both of the experiments just described have two experimental outcomes (sample points). However, suppose we consider the fourth experiment listed in the table—rolling a die. The possible experimental outcomes, defined as the number of dots appearing on the upward face of the die, are the six points in the sample space for this experiment:

$$S = \{1, 2, 3, 4, 5, 6\}$$

Counting Rules, Combinations, and Permutations

Being able to identify and count the experimental outcomes is a necessary step in assigning probabilities. We now discuss three useful counting rules.

Multiple-step experiments The first counting rule applies to multiple-step experiments. Consider the experiment of tossing two coins. Let the experimental outcomes be defined in terms of the pattern of heads and tails appearing on the upward faces of the two coins. How many experimental outcomes are possible for this experiment? The experiment of tossing two coins can be thought of as a two-step experiment in which step 1 is the tossing of the first coin and step 2 is the tossing of the second coin. If we use H to denote a head and T to denote a tail, (H, H) indicates the experimental outcome with a head on the first coin and a head on the second coin. Continuing this notation, we can describe the sample space (S) for this coin-tossing experiment as follows:

$$S = \{(H, H), (H, T), (T, H), (T, T)\}$$

Thus, we see that four experimental outcomes are possible. In this case, we can easily list all the experimental outcomes.

The counting rule for multiple-step experiments makes it possible to determine the number of experimental outcomes without listing them.

COUNTING RULE FOR MULTIPLE-STEP EXPERIMENTS

If an experiment can be described as a sequence of k steps with n_1 possible outcomes on the first step, n_2 possible outcomes on the second step, and so on, then the total number of experimental outcomes is given by $(n_1) (n_2) \ldots (n_k)$.

Viewing the experiment of tossing two coins as a sequence of first tossing one coin ($n_1 = 2$) and then tossing the other coin ($n_2 = 2$), we can see from the counting rule that $(2)(2) = 4$ distinct experimental outcomes are possible. As shown, they are $S = \{(H, H), (H, T), (T, H), (T, T)\}$. The number of experimental outcomes in an experiment involving tossing six coins is $(2)(2)(2)(2)(2)(2) = 64$.

FIGURE 4.2   TREE DIAGRAM FOR THE EXPERIMENT OF TOSSING TWO COINS

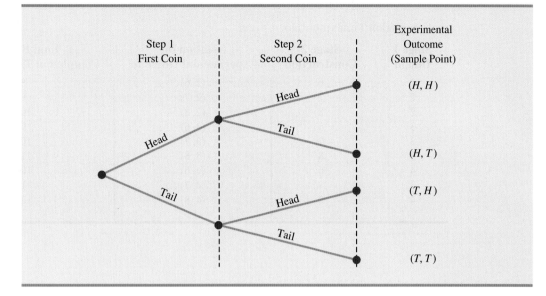

Without the tree diagram, one might think only three experimental outcomes are possible for two tosses of a coin: 0 heads, 1 head, and 2 heads.

A **tree diagram** is a graphical representation that helps in visualizing a multiple-step experiment. Figure 4.2 shows a tree diagram for the experiment of tossing two coins. The sequence of steps moves from left to right through the tree. Step 1 corresponds to tossing the first coin, and step 2 corresponds to tossing the second coin. For each step, the two possible outcomes are head or tail. Note that for each possible outcome at step 1 two branches correspond to the two possible outcomes at step 2. Each of the points on the right end of the tree corresponds to an experimental outcome. Each path through the tree from the leftmost node to one of the nodes at the right side of the tree corresponds to a unique sequence of outcomes.

Let us now see how the counting rule for multiple-step experiments can be used in the analysis of a capacity expansion project for the Kentucky Power & Light Company (KP&L). KP&L is starting a project designed to increase the generating capacity of one of its plants in northern Kentucky. The project is divided into two sequential stages or steps: stage 1 (design) and stage 2 (construction). Even though each stage will be scheduled and controlled as closely as possible, management cannot predict beforehand the exact time required to complete each stage of the project. An analysis of similar construction projects revealed possible completion times for the design stage of 2, 3, or 4 months and possible completion times for the construction stage of 6, 7, or 8 months. In addition, because of the critical need for additional electrical power, management set a goal of 10 months for the completion of the entire project.

Because this project has three possible completion times for the design stage (step 1) and three possible completion times for the construction stage (step 2), the counting rule for multiple-step experiments can be applied here to determine a total of $(3)(3) = 9$ experimental outcomes. To describe the experimental outcomes, we use a two-number notation; for instance, (2, 6) indicates that the design stage is completed in 2 months and the construction stage is completed in 6 months. This experimental outcome results in a total of $2 + 6 = 8$ months to complete the entire project. Table 4.1 summarizes the nine experimental outcomes for the KP&L problem. The tree diagram in Figure 4.3 shows how the nine outcomes (sample points) occur.

The counting rule and tree diagram help the project manager identify the experimental outcomes and determine the possible project completion times. From the information in

TABLE 4.1   EXPERIMENTAL OUTCOMES (SAMPLE POINTS) FOR THE KP&L PROJECT

Completion Time (months)			
Stage 1 Design	**Stage 2 Construction**	**Notation for Experimental Outcome**	**Total Project Completion Time (months)**
2	6	(2, 6)	8
2	7	(2, 7)	9
2	8	(2, 8)	10
3	6	(3, 6)	9
3	7	(3, 7)	10
3	8	(3, 8)	11
4	6	(4, 6)	10
4	7	(4, 7)	11
4	8	(4, 8)	12

FIGURE 4.3   TREE DIAGRAM FOR THE KP&L PROJECT

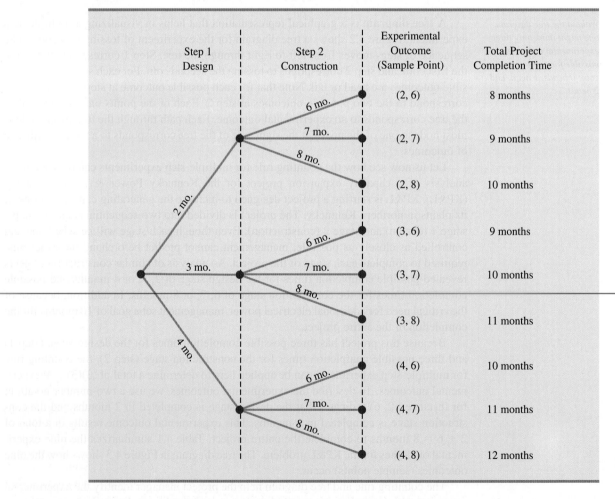

Figure 4.3, we see that the project will be completed in 8 to 12 months, with six of the nine experimental outcomes providing the desired completion time of 10 months or less. Even though identifying the experimental outcomes may be helpful, we need to consider how probability values can be assigned to the experimental outcomes before making an assessment of the probability that the project will be completed within the desired 10 months.

Combinations A second useful counting rule allows one to count the number of experimental outcomes when the experiment involves selecting n objects from a (usually larger) set of N objects. It is called the counting rule for combinations.

COUNTING RULE FOR COMBINATIONS

The number of combinations of N objects taken n at a time is

$$C_n^N = \binom{N}{n} = \frac{N!}{n!(N-n)!} \tag{4.1}$$

where

$$N! = N(N-1)(N-2)\cdots(2)(1)$$
$$n! = n(n-1)(n-2)\cdots(2)(1)$$

and, by definition,

$$0! = 1$$

In sampling from a finite population of size N, the counting rule for combinations is used to find the number of different samples of size n that can be selected.

The notation ! means *factorial;* for example, 5 factorial is $5! = (5)(4)(3)(2)(1) = 120$.

As an illustration of the counting rule for combinations, consider a quality control procedure in which an inspector randomly selects two of five parts to test for defects. In a group of five parts, how many combinations of two parts can be selected? The counting rule in equation (4.1) shows that with $N = 5$ and $n = 2$, we have

$$C_2^5 = \binom{5}{2} = \frac{5!}{2!(5-2)!} = \frac{(5)(4)(3)(2)(1)}{(2)(1)(3)(2)(1)} = \frac{120}{12} = 10$$

Thus, 10 outcomes are possible for the experiment of randomly selecting two parts from a group of five. If we label the five parts as A, B, C, D, and E, the 10 combinations or experimental outcomes can be identified as AB, AC, AD, AE, BC, BD, BE, CD, CE, and DE.

As another example, consider that the Florida lottery system uses the random selection of six integers from a group of 53 to determine the weekly winner. The counting rule for combinations, equation (4.1), can be used to determine the number of ways six different integers can be selected from a group of 53.

$$\binom{53}{6} = \frac{53!}{6!(53-6)!} = \frac{53!}{6!47!} = \frac{(53)(52)(51)(50)(49)(48)}{(6)(5)(4)(3)(2)(1)} = 22{,}957{,}480$$

The counting rule for combinations shows that the chance of winning the lottery is very unlikely.

The counting rule for combinations tells us that almost 23 million experimental outcomes are possible in the lottery drawing. An individual who buys a lottery ticket has 1 chance in 22,957,480 of winning.

Permutations A third counting rule that is sometimes useful is the counting rule for permutations. It allows one to compute the number of experimental outcomes when n objects are to be selected from a set of N objects where the order of selection is important. The same n objects selected in a different order are considered a different experimental outcome.

COUNTING RULE FOR PERMUTATIONS

The number of permutations of N objects taken n at a time is given by

$$P_n^N = n!\binom{N}{n} = \frac{N!}{(N-n)!} \tag{4.2}$$

The counting rule for permutations closely relates to the one for combinations; however, an experiment results in more permutations than combinations for the same number of objects because every selection of n objects can be ordered in $n!$ different ways.

As an example, consider again the quality control process in which an inspector selects two of five parts to inspect for defects. How many permutations may be selected? The counting rule in equation (4.2) shows that with $N = 5$ and $n = 2$, we have

$$P_2^5 = \frac{5!}{(5-2)!} = \frac{5!}{3!} = \frac{(5)(4)(3)(2)(1)}{(3)(2)(1)} = \frac{120}{6} = 20$$

Thus, 20 outcomes are possible for the experiment of randomly selecting two parts from a group of five when the order of selection must be taken into account. If we label the parts A, B, C, D, and E, the 20 permutations are AB, BA, AC, CA, AD, DA, AE, EA, BC, CB, BD, DB, BE, EB, CD, DC, CE, EC, DE, and ED.

Assigning Probabilities

Now let us see how probabilities can be assigned to experimental outcomes. The three approaches most frequently used are the classical, relative frequency, and subjective methods. Regardless of the method used, two **basic requirements for assigning probabilities** must be met.

BASIC REQUIREMENTS FOR ASSIGNING PROBABILITIES

1. The probability assigned to each experimental outcome must be between 0 and 1, inclusively. If we let E_i denote the ith experimental outcome and $P(E_i)$ its probability, then this requirement can be written as

$$0 \le P(E_i) \le 1 \text{ for all } i \tag{4.3}$$

2. The sum of the probabilities for all the experimental outcomes must equal 1.0. For n experimental outcomes, this requirement can be written as

$$P(E_1) + P(E_2) + \cdots + P(E_n) = 1 \tag{4.4}$$

The **classical method** of assigning probabilities is appropriate when all the experimental outcomes are equally likely. If n experimental outcomes are possible, a probability of $1/n$ is assigned to each experimental outcome. When using this approach, the two basic requirements for assigning probabilities are automatically satisfied.

For an example, consider the experiment of tossing a fair coin; the two experimental outcomes—head and tail—are equally likely. Because one of the two equally likely outcomes is a head, the probability of observing a head is 1/2, or .50. Similarly, the probability of observing a tail is also 1/2, or .50.

As another example, consider the experiment of rolling a die. It would seem reasonable to conclude that the six possible outcomes are equally likely, and hence each outcome is assigned a probability of 1/6. If $P(1)$ denotes the probability that one dot appears on the upward face of the die, then $P(1) = 1/6$. Similarly, $P(2) = 1/6, P(3) = 1/6, P(4) = 1/6, P(5) = 1/6,$ and $P(6) = 1/6$. Note that these probabilities satisfy the two basic requirements of equations (4.3) and (4.4) because each of the probabilities is greater than or equal to zero and they sum to 1.0.

The **relative frequency method** of assigning probabilities is appropriate when data are available to estimate the proportion of the time the experimental outcome will occur if the experiment is repeated a large number of times. As an example, consider a study of waiting times in the X-ray department for a local hospital. A clerk recorded the number of patients waiting for service at 9:00 A.M. on 20 successive days and obtained the following results.

Number Waiting	Number of Days Outcome Occurred
0	2
1	5
2	6
3	4
4	3
Total	20

These data show that on 2 of the 20 days, zero patients were waiting for service; on 5 of the days, one patient was waiting for service; and so on. Using the relative frequency method, we would assign a probability of 2/20 = .10 to the experimental outcome of zero patients waiting for service, 5/20 = .25 to the experimental outcome of one patient waiting, 6/20 = .30 to two patients waiting, 4/20 = .20 to three patients waiting, and 3/20 = .15 to four patients waiting. As with the classical method, using the relative frequency method automatically satisfies the two basic requirements of equations (4.3) and (4.4).

The **subjective method** of assigning probabilities is most appropriate when one cannot realistically assume that the experimental outcomes are equally likely and when little relevant data are available. When the subjective method is used to assign probabilities to the experimental outcomes, we may use any information available, such as our experience or intuition. After considering all available information, a probability value that expresses our *degree of belief* (on a scale from 0 to 1) that the experimental outcome will occur is specified. Because subjective probability expresses a person's degree of belief, it is personal. Using the subjective method, different people can be expected to assign different probabilities to the same experimental outcome.

The subjective method requires extra care to ensure that the two basic requirements of equations (4.3) and (4.4) are satisfied. Regardless of a person's degree of belief, the probability value assigned to each experimental outcome must be between 0 and 1, inclusive, and the sum of all the probabilities for the experimental outcomes must equal 1.0.

Consider the case in which Tom and Judy Elsbernd make an offer to purchase a house. Two outcomes are possible:

$$E_1 = \text{their offer is accepted}$$
$$E_2 = \text{their offer is rejected}$$

Judy believes that the probability their offer will be accepted is .8; thus, Judy would set $P(E_1) = .8$ and $P(E_2) = .2$. Tom, however, believes that the probability that their offer will be accepted is .6; hence, Tom would set $P(E_1) = .6$ and $P(E_2) = .4$. Note that Tom's probability estimate for E_1 reflects a greater pessimism that their offer will be accepted.

Bayes' theorem (see Section 4.5) provides a means for combining subjectively determined prior probabilities with probabilities obtained by other means to obtain revised, or posterior, probabilities.

Both Judy and Tom assigned probabilities that satisfy the two basic requirements. The fact that their probability estimates are different emphasizes the personal nature of the subjective method.

Even in business situations where either the classical or the relative frequency approach can be applied, managers may want to provide subjective probability estimates. In such cases, the best probability estimates are often obtained by combining the estimates from the classical or relative frequency approach with subjective probability estimates.

Probabilities for the KP&L Project

To perform further analysis on the KP&L project, we must develop probabilities for each of the nine experimental outcomes listed in Table 4.1. On the basis of experience and judgment, management concluded that the experimental outcomes were not equally likely. Hence, the classical method of assigning probabilities could not be used. Management then decided to conduct a study of the completion times for similar projects undertaken by KP&L over the past three years. The results of a study of 40 similar projects are summarized in Table 4.2.

After reviewing the results of the study, management decided to employ the relative frequency method of assigning probabilities. Management could have provided subjective probability estimates but felt that the current project was quite similar to the 40 previous projects. Thus, the relative frequency method was judged best.

In using the data in Table 4.2 to compute probabilities, we note that outcome (2, 6)—stage 1 completed in 2 months and stage 2 completed in 6 months—occurred six times in the 40 projects. We can use the relative frequency method to assign a probability of $6/40 = .15$ to this outcome. Similarly, outcome (2, 7) also occurred in six of the 40 projects, providing a $6/40 = .15$ probability. Continuing in this manner, we obtain the probability assignments for the sample points of the KP&L project shown in Table 4.3. Note that $P(2, 6)$ represents the probability of the sample point (2, 6), $P(2, 7)$ represents the probability of the sample point (2, 7), and so on.

TABLE 4.2   COMPLETION RESULTS FOR 40 KP&L PROJECTS

Completion Time (months)			Number of Past Projects Having These Completion Times
Stage 1 Design	**Stage 2 Construction**	**Sample Point**	
2	6	(2, 6)	6
2	7	(2, 7)	6
2	8	(2, 8)	2
3	6	(3, 6)	4
3	7	(3, 7)	8
3	8	(3, 8)	2
4	6	(4, 6)	2
4	7	(4, 7)	4
4	8	(4, 8)	6
		Total	40

TABLE 4.3   PROBABILITY ASSIGNMENTS FOR THE KP&L PROJECT BASED ON THE RELATIVE FREQUENCY METHOD

Sample Point	Project Completion Time	Probability of Sample Point
(2, 6)	8 months	$P(2, 6) = 6/40 = .15$
(2, 7)	9 months	$P(2, 7) = 6/40 = .15$
(2, 8)	10 months	$P(2, 8) = 2/40 = .05$
(3, 6)	9 months	$P(3, 6) = 4/40 = .10$
(3, 7)	10 months	$P(3, 7) = 8/40 = .20$
(3, 8)	11 months	$P(3, 8) = 2/40 = .05$
(4, 6)	10 months	$P(4, 6) = 2/40 = .05$
(4, 7)	11 months	$P(4, 7) = 4/40 = .10$
(4, 8)	12 months	$P(4, 8) = 6/40 = .15$
		Total 1.00

NOTES AND COMMENTS

1. In statistics, the notion of an experiment differs somewhat from the notion of an experiment in the physical sciences. In the physical sciences, researchers usually conduct an experiment in a laboratory or a controlled environment in order to learn about cause and effect. In statistical experiments, probability determines outcomes. Even though the experiment is repeated in exactly the same way, an entirely different outcome may occur. Because of this influence of probability on the outcome, the experiments of statistics are sometimes called *random experiments.*

2. When drawing a random sample without replacement from a population of size N, the counting rule for combinations is used to find the number of different samples of size n that can be selected.

Exercises

Methods

1.   An experiment has three steps with three outcomes possible for the first step, two outcomes possible for the second step, and four outcomes possible for the third step. How many experimental outcomes exist for the entire experiment?

2.   How many ways can three items be selected from a group of six items? Use the letters A, B, C, D, E, and F to identify the items, and list each of the different combinations of three items.

3.   How many permutations of three items can be selected from a group of six? Use the letters A, B, C, D, E, and F to identify the items, and list each of the permutations of items B, D, and F.

4.   Consider the experiment of tossing a coin three times.
  a.   Develop a tree diagram for the experiment.
  b.   List the experimental outcomes.
  c.   What is the probability for each experimental outcome?

5.   Suppose an experiment has five equally likely outcomes: E_1, E_2, E_3, E_4, E_5. Assign probabilities to each outcome and show that the requirements in equations (4.3) and (4.4) are satisfied. What method did you use?

6.   An experiment with three outcomes has been repeated 50 times, and it was learned that E_1 occurred 20 times, E_2 occurred 13 times, and E_3 occurred 17 times. Assign probabilities to the outcomes. What method did you use?

7. A decision maker subjectively assigned the following probabilities to the four outcomes of an experiment: $P(E_1) = .10$, $P(E_2) = .15$, $P(E_3) = .40$, and $P(E_4) = .20$. Are these probability assignments valid? Explain.

Applications

8. In the city of Milford, applications for zoning changes go through a two-step process: a review by the planning commission and a final decision by the city council. At step 1 the planning commission reviews the zoning change request and makes a positive or negative recommendation concerning the change. At step 2 the city council reviews the planning commission's recommendation and then votes to approve or to disapprove the zoning change. Suppose the developer of an apartment complex submits an application for a zoning change. Consider the application process as an experiment.
   a. How many sample points are there for this experiment? List the sample points.
   b. Construct a tree diagram for the experiment.

9. Simple random sampling uses a sample of size n from a population of size N to obtain data that can be used to make inferences about the characteristics of a population. Suppose that, from a population of 50 bank accounts, we want to take a random sample of 4 accounts in order to learn about the population. How many different random samples of 4 accounts are possible?

10. Many students have accumulated a large amount of debt by the time they graduate from college. Shown below is the percentage of students graduating with debt and the average amount of debt for students graduating with debt at four national universities and at four liberal arts colleges (*U.S. News and World Report, America's Best Colleges,* 2008).

National University	% with Debt	Amount($)	Liberal Arts College	% with Debt	Amount($)
Pace	72	32,980	Wartburg	83	28,758
Iowa State	69	32,130	Morehouse	94	27,000
Massachusetts	55	11,227	Wellesley	55	10,206
SUNY–Albany	64	11,856	Wofford	49	11,012

   a. If you randomly choose a graduate of Morehouse, what is the probability this individual will have graduated with debt?
   b. If you randomly choose one of these institutions for a follow-up study on student loans, what is the probability you will choose an institution from which over 60% of the students graduated with debt?
   c. If you randomly choose one of these institutions for a follow-up study on student loans, what is the probability you will choose an institution in which the average amount of debt is greater than $30,000 per student graduating with debt?
   d. What is the probability a student graduates from Pace without any debt?
   e. For Pace University, what is the average amount of debt owed per graduating student?
   f. In making probability calculations above, were you using the classical, relative frequency, or subjective method?

11. The National Highway Traffic Safety Administration (NHTSA) conducted a survey to learn about how drivers throughout the United States are using seat belts (Associated Press, August 25, 2003). Sample data consistent with the NHTSA survey are as follows.

| | Driver Using Seat Belt? | |
Region	Yes	No
Northeast	148	52
Midwest	162	54
South	296	74
West	252	48
Total	858	228

a. For the United States, what is the probability that a driver is using a seat belt?
b. The seat belt usage probability for a U.S. driver a year earlier was .75. NHTSA chief Dr. Jeffrey Runge had hoped for a .78 probability in 2003. Would he have been pleased with the 2003 survey results?
c. What is the probability of seat belt usage by region of the country? What region has the highest seat belt usage?
d. What proportion of the drivers in the sample came from each region of the country? What region had the most drivers selected? What region had the second most drivers selected?
e. Assuming the total number of drivers in each region is the same, do you see any reason why the probability estimate in part (a) might be too high? Explain.

12. The Powerball lottery is played twice each week in 28 states, the Virgin Islands, and the District of Columbia. To play Powerball a participant must purchase a ticket and then select five numbers from the digits 1 through 55 and a Powerball number from the digits 1 through 42. To determine the winning numbers for each game, lottery officials draw five white balls out of a drum with 55 white balls, and one red ball out of a drum with 42 red balls. To win the jackpot, a participant's numbers must match the numbers on the five white balls in any order and the number on the red Powerball. Eight coworkers at the ConAgra Foods plant in Lincoln, Nebraska, claimed the record $365 million jackpot on February 18, 2006, by matching the numbers 15-17-43-44-49 and the Powerball number 29. A variety of other cash prizes are awarded each time the game is played. For instance, a prize of $200,000 is paid if the participant's five numbers match the numbers on the five white balls (*http://www.powerball.com,* March 19, 2006).
a. Compute the number of ways the first five numbers can be selected.
b. What is the probability of winning a prize of $200,000 by matching the numbers on the five white balls?
c. What is the probability of winning the Powerball jackpot?

13. A company that manufactures toothpaste is studying five different package designs. Assuming that one design is just as likely to be selected by a consumer as any other design, what selection probability would you assign to each of the package designs? In an actual experiment, 100 consumers were asked to pick the design they preferred. The following data were obtained. Do the data confirm the belief that one design is just as likely to be selected as another? Explain.

Design	Number of Times Preferred
1	5
2	15
3	30
4	40
5	10

4.2   Events and Their Probabilities

In the introduction to this chapter we used the term *event* much as it would be used in every-day language. Then, in Section 4.1 we introduced the concept of an experiment and its associated experimental outcomes or sample points. Sample points and events provide the foundation for the study of probability. As a result, we must now introduce the formal definition of an **event** as it relates to sample points. Doing so will provide the basis for determining the probability of an event.

> **EVENT**
>
> An event is a collection of sample points.

For an example, let us return to the KP&L project and assume that the project manager is interested in the event that the entire project can be completed in 10 months or less. Referring to Table 4.3, we see that six sample points—(2, 6), (2, 7), (2, 8), (3, 6), (3, 7), and (4, 6)—provide a project completion time of 10 months or less. Let C denote the event that the project is completed in 10 months or less; we write

$$C = \{(2, 6), (2, 7), (2, 8), (3, 6), (3, 7), (4, 6)\}$$

Event C is said to occur if *any one* of these six sample points appears as the experimental outcome.

Other events that might be of interest to KP&L management include the following.

L = The event that the project is completed in *less* than 10 months
M = The event that the project is completed in *more* than 10 months

Using the information in Table 4.3, we see that these events consist of the following sample points.

$$L = \{(2, 6), (2, 7), (3, 6)\}$$
$$M = \{(3, 8), (4, 7), (4, 8)\}$$

A variety of additional events can be defined for the KP&L project, but in each case the event must be identified as a collection of sample points for the experiment.

Given the probabilities of the sample points shown in Table 4.3, we can use the following definition to compute the probability of any event that KP&L management might want to consider.

> **PROBABILITY OF AN EVENT**
>
> The probability of any event is equal to the sum of the probabilities of the sample points in the event.

Using this definition, we calculate the probability of a particular event by adding the probabilities of the sample points (experimental outcomes) that make up the event. We can now compute the probability that the project will take 10 months or less to complete. Because this event is given by $C = \{(2, 6), (2, 7), (2, 8), (3, 6), (3, 7), (4, 6)\}$, the probability of event C, denoted $P(C)$, is given by

$$P(C) = P(2, 6) + P(2, 7) + P(2, 8) + P(3, 6) + P(3, 7) + P(4, 6)$$

Refer to the sample point probabilities in Table 4.3; we have

$$P(C) = .15 + .15 + .05 + .10 + .20 + .05 = .70$$

Similarly, because the event that the project is completed in less than 10 months is given by $L = \{(2, 6), (2, 7), (3, 6)\}$, the probability of this event is given by

$$P(L) = P(2, 6) + P(2, 7) + P(3, 6)$$
$$= .15 + .15 + .10 = .40$$

Finally, for the event that the project is completed in more than 10 months, we have $M = \{(3, 8), (4, 7), (4, 8)\}$ and thus

$$P(M) = P(3, 8) + P(4, 7) + P(4, 8)$$
$$= .05 + .10 + .15 = .30$$

Using these probability results, we can now tell KP&L management that there is a .70 probability that the project will be completed in 10 months or less, a .40 probability that the project will be completed in less than 10 months, and a .30 probability that the project will be completed in more than 10 months. This procedure of computing event probabilities can be repeated for any event of interest to the KP&L management.

Any time that we can identify all the sample points of an experiment and assign probabilities to each, we can compute the probability of an event using the definition. However, in many experiments the large number of sample points makes the identification of the sample points, as well as the determination of their associated probabilities, extremely cumbersome, if not impossible. In the remaining sections of this chapter, we present some basic probability relationships that can be used to compute the probability of an event without knowledge of all the sample point probabilities.

NOTES AND COMMENTS

1. The sample space, S, is an event. Because it contains all the experimental outcomes, it has a probability of 1; that is, $P(S) = 1$.
2. When the classical method is used to assign probabilities, the assumption is that the experimental outcomes are equally likely. In such cases, the probability of an event can be computed by counting the number of experimental outcomes in the event and dividing the result by the total number of experimental outcomes.

Exercises

Methods

14. An experiment has four equally likely outcomes: E_1, E_2, E_3, and E_4.
    a. What is the probability that E_2 occurs?
    b. What is the probability that any two of the outcomes occur (e.g., E_1 or E_3)?
    c. What is the probability that any three of the outcomes occur (e.g., E_1 or E_2 or E_4)?

15. Consider the experiment of selecting a playing card from a deck of 52 playing cards. Each card corresponds to a sample point with a 1/52 probability.
    a. List the sample points in the event an ace is selected.
    b. List the sample points in the event a club is selected.
    c. List the sample points in the event a face card (jack, queen, or king) is selected.
    d. Find the probabilities associated with each of the events in parts (a), (b), and (c).

16. Consider the experiment of rolling a pair of dice. Suppose that we are interested in the sum of the face values showing on the dice.
    a. How many sample points are possible? (*Hint:* Use the counting rule for multiple-step experiments.)
    b. List the sample points.
    c. What is the probability of obtaining a value of 7?
    d. What is the probability of obtaining a value of 9 or greater?
    e. Because each roll has six possible even values (2, 4, 6, 8, 10, and 12) and only five possible odd values (3, 5, 7, 9, and 11), the dice should show even values more often than odd values. Do you agree with this statement? Explain.
    f. What method did you use to assign the probabilities requested?

Applications

17. Refer to the KP&L sample points and sample point probabilities in Tables 4.2 and 4.3.
    a. The design stage (stage 1) will run over budget if it takes 4 months to complete. List the sample points in the event the design stage is over budget.
    b. What is the probability that the design stage is over budget?
    c. The construction stage (stage 2) will run over budget if it takes 8 months to complete. List the sample points in the event the construction stage is over budget.
    d. What is the probability that the construction stage is over budget?
    e. What is the probability that both stages are over budget?

18. To investigate how often we eat at home as a family during the week, Harris Interactive surveyed 496 adults living with children under the age of 18 (*USA Today*, January 3, 2007). The survey results are shown in the following table.

Number of Family Meals	Number of Times Outcome Occurred
0	11
1	11
2	30
3	36
4	36
5	119
6	114
7 or more	139

For a randomly selected family with children under the age of 18, compute the following.
    a. The probability the family eats no meals at home during the week.
    b. The probability the family eats at least four meals at home during the week.
    c. The probability the family eats two or fewer meals at home during the week.

19. The National Sporting Goods Association conducted a survey of persons 7 years of age or older about participation in sports activities (*Statistical Abstract of the United States: 2002*). The total population in this age group was reported at 248.5 million, with 120.9 million male and 127.6 million female. The number of participants for the top five sports activities appears here.

Activity	Participants (millions)	
	Male	**Female**
Bicycle riding	22.2	21.0
Camping	25.6	24.3
Exercise walking	28.7	57.7
Exercising with equipment	20.4	24.4
Swimming	26.4	34.4

   a.   For a randomly selected female, estimate the probability of participation in each of the sports activities.
   b.   For a randomly selected male, estimate the probability of participation in each of the sports activities.
   c.   For a randomly selected person, what is the probability the person participates in exercise walking?
   d.   Suppose you just happen to see an exercise walker going by. What is the probability the walker is a woman? What is the probability the walker is a man?

20.   *Fortune* magazine publishes an annual list of the 500 largest companies in the United States. The following data show the five states with the largest number of *Fortune* 500 companies (*The New York Times Almanac,* 2006).

State	Number of Companies
New York	54
California	52
Texas	48
Illinois	33
Ohio	30

   Suppose a *Fortune* 500 company is chosen for a follow-up questionnaire. What are the probabilities of the following events?
   a.   Let N be the event the company is headquartered in New York. Find $P(N)$.
   b.   Let T be the event the company is headquartered in Texas. Find $P(T)$.
   c.   Let B be the event the company is headquartered in one of these five states. Find $P(B)$.

21.   The U.S. population by age is as follows (*The World Almanac,* 2004). The data are in millions of people.

Age	Number
19 and under	80.5
20 to 24	19.0
25 to 34	39.9
35 to 44	45.2
45 to 54	37.7
55 to 64	24.3
65 and over	35.0

   Assume that a person will be randomly chosen from this population.
   a.   What is the probability the person is 20 to 24 years old?
   b.   What is the probability the person is 20 to 34 years old?
   c.   What is the probability the person is 45 years or older?

Some Basic Relationships of Probability

Complement of an Event

Given an event A, the **complement of** A is defined to be the event consisting of all sample points that are *not* in A. The complement of A is denoted by A^c. Figure 4.4 is a diagram, known as a **Venn diagram**, which illustrates the concept of a complement. The rectangular area represents the sample space for the experiment and as such contains all possible

FIGURE 4.4   COMPLEMENT OF EVENT *A* IS SHADED

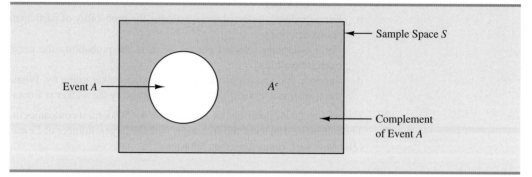

sample points. The circle represents event *A* and contains only the sample points that be-long to *A*. The shaded region of the rectangle contains all sample points not in event *A* and is by definition the complement of *A*.

In any probability application, either event *A* or its complement A^c must occur. There-fore, we have

$$P(A) + P(A^c) = 1$$

Solving for $P(A)$, we obtain the following result.

COMPUTING PROBABILITY USING THE COMPLEMENT

$$P(A) = 1 - P(A^c) \tag{4.5}$$

Equation (4.5) shows that the probability of an event *A* can be computed easily if the proba-bility of its complement, $P(A^c)$, is known.

As an example, consider the case of a sales manager who, after reviewing sales reports, states that 80% of new customer contacts result in no sale. By allowing *A* to denote the event of a sale and A^c to denote the event of no sale, the manager is stating that $P(A^c) = .80$. Using equation (4.5), we see that

$$P(A) = 1 - P(A^c) = 1 - .80 = .20$$

We can conclude that a new customer contact has a .20 probability of resulting in a sale.

In another example, a purchasing agent states a .90 probability that a supplier will send a shipment that is free of defective parts. Using the complement, we can conclude that there is a $1 - .90 = .10$ probability that the shipment will contain defective parts.

Addition Law

The addition law is helpful when we are interested in knowing the probability that at least one of two events occurs. That is, with events *A* and *B* we are interested in knowing the probability that event *A* or event *B* or both occur.

Before we present the addition law, we need to discuss two concepts related to the com-bination of events: the *union* of events and the *intersection* of events. Given two events *A* and *B*, the **union of *A* and *B*** is defined as follows.

UNION OF TWO EVENTS

The *union* of *A* and *B* is the event containing *all* sample points belonging to *A or B or both*. The union is denoted by $A \cup B$.

FIGURE 4.5   UNION OF EVENTS *A* AND *B* IS SHADED

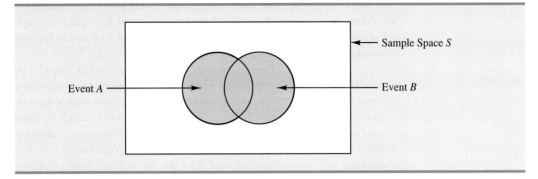

The Venn diagram in Figure 4.5 depicts the union of events *A* and *B*. Note that the two circles contain all the sample points in event *A* as well as all the sample points in event *B*. The fact that the circles overlap indicates that some sample points are contained in both *A* and *B*.

The definition of the **intersection of *A* and *B*** follows.

INTERSECTION OF TWO EVENTS

Given two events *A* and *B*, the *intersection* of *A* and *B* is the event containing the sample points belonging to *both A and B*. The intersection is denoted by $A \cap B$.

The Venn diagram depicting the intersection of events *A* and *B* is shown in Figure 4.6. The area where the two circles overlap is the intersection; it contains the sample points that are in both *A* and *B*.

Let us now continue with a discussion of the addition law. The **addition law** provides a way to compute the probability that event *A* or event *B* or both occur. In other words, the addition law is used to compute the probability of the union of two events. The addition law is written as follows.

ADDITION LAW

$$P(A \cup B) = P(A) + P(B) - P(A \cap B) \qquad \textbf{(4.6)}$$

FIGURE 4.6   INTERSECTION OF EVENTS *A* AND *B* IS SHADED

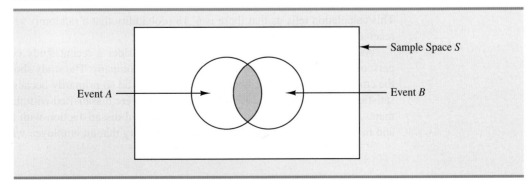

To understand the addition law intuitively, note that the first two terms in the addition law, $P(A) + P(B)$, account for all the sample points in $A \cup B$. However, because the sample points in the intersection $A \cap B$ are in both A and B, when we compute $P(A) + P(B)$, we are in effect counting each of the sample points in $A \cap B$ twice. We correct for this overcounting by subtracting $P(A \cap B)$.

As an example of an application of the addition law, let us consider the case of a small assembly plant with 50 employees. Each worker is expected to complete work assignments on time and in such a way that the assembled product will pass a final inspection. On occasion, some of the workers fail to meet the performance standards by completing work late or assembling a defective product. At the end of a performance evaluation period, the production manager found that 5 of the 50 workers completed work late, 6 of the 50 workers assembled a defective product, and 2 of the 50 workers both completed work late *and* assembled a defective product.

Let

$$L = \text{the event that the work is completed late}$$
$$D = \text{the event that the assembled product is defective}$$

The relative frequency information leads to the following probabilities.

$$P(L) = \frac{5}{50} = .10$$

$$P(D) = \frac{6}{50} = .12$$

$$P(L \cap D) = \frac{2}{50} = .04$$

After reviewing the performance data, the production manager decided to assign a poor performance rating to any employee whose work was either late or defective; thus the event of interest is $L \cup D$. What is the probability that the production manager assigned an employee a poor performance rating?

Note that the probability question is about the union of two events. Specifically, we want to know $P(L \cup D)$. Using equation (4.6), we have

$$P(L \cup D) = P(L) + P(D) - P(L \cap D)$$

Knowing values for the three probabilities on the right side of this expression, we can write

$$P(L \cup D) = .10 + .12 - .04 = .18$$

This calculation tells us that there is a .18 probability that a randomly selected employee received a poor performance rating.

As another example of the addition law, consider a recent study conducted by the personnel manager of a major computer software company. The study showed that 30% of the employees who left the firm within two years did so primarily because they were dissatisfied with their salary, 20% left because they were dissatisfied with their work assignments, and 12% of the former employees indicated dissatisfaction with *both* their salary and their work assignments. What is the probability that an employee who leaves within two years does so because of dissatisfaction with salary, dissatisfaction with the work assignment, or both?

Let

$$S = \text{the event that the employee leaves because of salary}$$
$$W = \text{the event that the employee leaves because of work assignment}$$

We have $P(S) = .30$, $P(W) = .20$, and $P(S \cap W) = .12$. Using equation (4.6), the addition law, we have

$$P(S \cup W) = P(S) + P(W) - P(S \cap W) = .30 + .20 - .12 = .38.$$

We find a .38 probability that an employee leaves for salary or work assignment reasons.

Before we conclude our discussion of the addition law, let us consider a special case that arises for **mutually exclusive events**.

MUTUALLY EXCLUSIVE EVENTS

Two events are said to be mutually exclusive if the events have no sample points in common.

Events A and B are mutually exclusive if, when one event occurs, the other cannot occur. Thus, a requirement for A and B to be mutually exclusive is that their intersection must contain no sample points. The Venn diagram depicting two mutually exclusive events A and B is shown in Figure 4.7. In this case $P(A \cap B) = 0$ and the addition law can be written as follows.

ADDITION LAW FOR MUTUALLY EXCLUSIVE EVENTS

$$P(A \cup B) = P(A) + P(B)$$

FIGURE 4.7   MUTUALLY EXCLUSIVE EVENTS

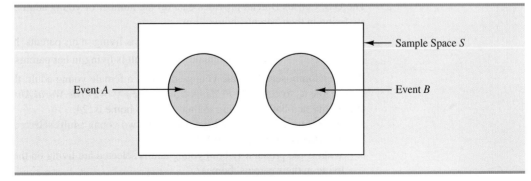

Exercises

Methods

22. Suppose that we have a sample space with five equally likely experimental outcomes: E_1, E_2, E_3, E_4, E_5. Let

$$A = \{E_1, E_2\}$$
$$B = \{E_3, E_4\}$$
$$C = \{E_2, E_3, E_5\}$$

a. Find $P(A)$, $P(B)$, and $P(C)$.
b. Find $P(A \cup B)$. Are A and B mutually exclusive?
c. Find A^c, C^c, $P(A^c)$, and $P(C^c)$.
d. Find $A \cup B^c$ and $P(A \cup B^c)$.
e. Find $P(B \cup C)$.

23. Suppose that we have a sample space $S = \{E_1, E_2, E_3, E_4, E_5, E_6, E_7\}$, where E_1, E_2, ..., E_7 denote the sample points. The following probability assignments apply: $P(E_1) = .05$, $P(E_2) = .20$, $P(E_3) = .20$, $P(E_4) = .25$, $P(E_5) = .15$, $P(E_6) = .10$, and $P(E_7) = .05$. Let

$$A = \{E_1, E_4, E_6\}$$
$$B = \{E_2, E_4, E_7\}$$
$$C = \{E_2, E_3, E_5, E_7\}$$

a. Find $P(A)$, $P(B)$, and $P(C)$.
b. Find $A \cup B$ and $P(A \cup B)$.
c. Find $A \cap B$ and $P(A \cap B)$.
d. Are events A and C mutually exclusive?
e. Find B^c and $P(B^c)$.

Applications

24. Clarkson University surveyed alumni to learn more about what they think of Clarkson. One part of the survey asked respondents to indicate whether their overall experience at Clarkson fell short of expectations, met expectations, or surpassed expectations. The results showed that 4% of the respondents did not provide a response, 26% said that their experience fell short of expectations, and 65% of the respondents said that their experience met expectations (*Clarkson Magazine,* Summer 2001).
a. If we chose an alumnus at random, what is the probability that the alumnus would say their experience surpassed expectations?
b. If we chose an alumnus at random, what is the probability that the alumnus would say their experience met or surpassed expectations?

25. The U.S. Census Bureau provides data on the number of young adults, ages 18–24, who are living in their parents' home.[1] Let

M = the event a male young adult is living in his parents' home

F = the event a female young adult is living in her parents' home

If we randomly select a male young adult and a female young adult, the Census Bureau data enable us to conclude $P(M) = .56$ and $P(F) = .42$ (*The World Almanac,* 2006). The probability that both are living in their parents' home is .24.
a. What is the probability at least one of the two young adults selected is living in his or her parents' home?
b. What is the probability both young adults selected are living on their own (neither is living in their parents' home)?

[1] The data include single young adults who are living in college dormitories because it is assumed these young adults will return to their parents' home when school is not in session.

26. Data on 25 mutual funds followed by Morningstar are shown in Table 1.1. The data are also on the website that accompanies this text. One of these funds will be randomly selected to learn about its investment strategy.
    a. What is the probability of selecting a fund with a 4- or 5-star rating?
    b. What is the probability of selecting a Domestic Equity fund?
    c. What is the probability of selecting a fund that is both a Domestic Equity fund and a fund having a 4- or 5-star rating?
    d. What is the probability of selecting a fund that is either a Domestic Equity fund or a fund having a 4- or 5-star rating?

27. A 2001 preseason NCAA football poll asked respondents to answer the question, "Will the Big Ten or the Pac-10 have a team in this year's national championship game, the Rose Bowl?" Of the 13,429 respondents, 2961 said the Big Ten would, 4494 said the Pac-10 would, and 6823 said neither the Big Ten nor the Pac-10 would have a team in the Rose Bowl (*http://www.yahoo.com*, August 30, 2001).
    a. What is the probability that a respondent said neither the Big Ten nor the Pac-10 would have a team in the Rose Bowl?
    b. What is the probability that a respondent said either the Big Ten or the Pac-10 would have a team in the Rose Bowl?
    c. Find the probability that a respondent said both the Big Ten and the Pac-10 would have a team in the Rose Bowl.

SELF test

28. A survey of magazine subscribers showed that 45.8% rented a car during the past 12 months for business reasons, 54% rented a car during the past 12 months for personal reasons, and 30% rented a car during the past 12 months for both business and personal reasons.
    a. What is the probability that a subscriber rented a car during the past 12 months for business or personal reasons?
    b. What is the probability that a subscriber did not rent a car during the past 12 months for either business or personal reasons?

29. High school seniors with strong academic records apply to the nation's most selective colleges in greater number each year. Because the number of slots remains relatively stable, some colleges reject more early applicants. The University of Pennsylvania (Penn) received 2851 applications for early admission. Of this group, it admitted 1033 students early, rejected 854 outright, and deferred 964 to the regular admission pool for further consideration. In the past, Penn has admitted about 18% of the deferred early admission applicants during the regular admission process. Counting the additional students who were admitted during the regular admission process, the total class size was 2375 (*USA Today*, January 24, 2001). Let E, R, and D represent the events that a student who applies for early admission is admitted early, rejected outright, or deferred to the regular admissions pool.
    a. Use the data to estimate $P(E)$, $P(R)$, and $P(D)$.
    b. Are events E and D mutually exclusive? Find $P(E \cap D)$.
    c. For the 2375 students admitted to Penn, what is the probability that a randomly selected student was accepted for early admission?
    d. Suppose a student applies to Penn for early admission. What is the probability the student will be admitted for early admission or be deferred and later admitted during the regular admission process?

(4.4) Conditional Probability

Often, the probability of an event is influenced by whether a related event already occurred. Suppose we have an event A with probability $P(A)$. If we obtain new information and learn that a related event, denoted by B, already occurred, we will want to take advantage of this information by calculating a new probability for event A. This new probability of event A is called a **conditional probability** and is written $P(A \mid B)$. We use the vertical line | to indicate that we are considering the probability of event A *given* the condition that event B has occurred. Hence, the notation $P(A \mid B)$ reads "the probability of A given B."

As an illustration of the application of conditional probability, consider the situation of the promotion record of male and female officers of a major metropolitan police force in the eastern United States. The police force consists of 1200 officers, 960 men and 240 women. Over the past two years, 324 officers on the police force received promotions. The specific breakdown of promotions for male and female officers is shown in Table 4.4.

After reviewing the promotion record, a committee of female officers raised a discrimination case on the basis that 288 male officers had received promotions but only 36 female officers had received promotions. The police administration argued that the relatively low number of promotions for female officers was due not to discrimination, but to the fact that relatively few females are members of the police force. Let us show how conditional probability could be used to analyze the discrimination charge.

Let

$$M = \text{event an officer is a man}$$
$$W = \text{event an officer is a woman}$$
$$A = \text{event an officer is promoted}$$
$$A^c = \text{event an officer is not promoted}$$

Dividing the data values in Table 4.4 by the total of 1200 officers enables us to summarize the available information with the following probability values.

$P(M \cap A) = 288/1200 = .24 =$ probability that a randomly selected officer is a man *and* is promoted

$P(M \cap A^c) = 672/1200 = .56 =$ probability that a randomly selected officer is a man *and* is not promoted

$P(W \cap A) = 36/1200 = .03 =$ probability that a randomly selected officer is a woman *and* is promoted

$P(W \cap A^c) = 204/1200 = .17 =$ probability that a randomly selected officer is a woman *and* is not promoted

Because each of these values gives the probability of the intersection of two events, the probabilities are called **joint probabilities**. Table 4.5, which provides a summary of the probability information for the police officer promotion situation, is referred to as a *joint probability table.*

The values in the margins of the joint probability table provide the probabilities of each event separately. That is, $P(M) = .80$, $P(W) = .20$, $P(A) = .27$, and $P(A^c) = .73$. These probabilities are referred to as **marginal probabilities** because of their location in the

TABLE 4.4   PROMOTION STATUS OF POLICE OFFICERS OVER THE PAST TWO YEARS

	Men	Women	Total
Promoted	288	36	324
Not Promoted	672	204	876
Total	960	240	1200

TABLE 4.5   JOINT PROBABILITY TABLE FOR PROMOTIONS

Joint probabilities appear in the body of the table.	Men (*M*)	Women (*W*)	Total
Promoted (*A*)	.24	.03	.27
Not Promoted (*A^c*)	.56	.17	.73
Total	.80	.20	1.00

Marginal probabilities appear in the margins of the table.

margins of the joint probability table. We note that the marginal probabilities are found by summing the joint probabilities in the corresponding row or column of the joint probability table. For instance, the marginal probability of being promoted is $P(A) = P(M \cap A) + P(W \cap A) = .24 + .03 = .27$. From the marginal probabilities, we see that 80% of the force is male, 20% of the force is female, 27% of all officers received promotions, and 73% were not promoted.

Let us begin the conditional probability analysis by computing the probability that an officer is promoted given that the officer is a man. In conditional probability notation, we are attempting to determine $P(A \mid M)$. To calculate $P(A \mid M)$, we first realize that this notation simply means that we are considering the probability of the event A (promotion) given that the condition designated as event M (the officer is a man) is known to exist. Thus $P(A \mid M)$ tells us that we are now concerned only with the promotion status of the 960 male officers. Because 288 of the 960 male officers received promotions, the probability of being promoted given that the officer is a man is 288/960 = .30. In other words, given that an officer is a man, that officer had a 30% chance of receiving a promotion over the past two years.

This procedure was easy to apply because the values in Table 4.4 show the number of officers in each category. We now want to demonstrate how conditional probabilities such as $P(A \mid M)$ can be computed directly from related event probabilities rather than the frequency data of Table 4.4.

We have shown that $P(A \mid M) = 288/960 = .30$. Let us now divide both the numerator and denominator of this fraction by 1200, the total number of officers in the study.

$$P(A \mid M) = \frac{288}{960} = \frac{288/1200}{960/1200} = \frac{.24}{.80} = .30$$

We now see that the conditional probability $P(A \mid M)$ can be computed as .24/.80. Refer to the joint probability table (Table 4.5). Note in particular that .24 is the joint probability of A and M; that is, $P(A \cap M) = .24$. Also note that .80 is the marginal probability that a randomly selected officer is a man; that is, $P(M) = .80$. Thus, the conditional probability $P(A \mid M)$ can be computed as the ratio of the joint probability $P(A \cap M)$ to the marginal probability $P(M)$.

$$P(A \mid M) = \frac{P(A \cap M)}{P(M)} = \frac{.24}{.80} = .30$$

The fact that conditional probabilities can be computed as the ratio of a joint probability to a marginal probability provides the following general formula for conditional probability calculations for two events A and B.

CONDITIONAL PROBABILITY

$$P(A \mid B) = \frac{P(A \cap B)}{P(B)} \tag{4.7}$$

or

$$P(B \mid A) = \frac{P(A \cap B)}{P(A)} \tag{4.8}$$

The Venn diagram in Figure 4.8 is helpful in obtaining an intuitive understanding of conditional probability. The circle on the right shows that event B has occurred; the portion of the circle that overlaps with event A denotes the event ($A \cap B$). We know that once event B has occurred, the only way that we can also observe event A is for the event ($A \cap B$) to occur. Thus, the ratio $P(A \cap B)/P(B)$ provides the conditional probability that we will observe event A given that event B has already occurred.

Let us return to the issue of discrimination against the female officers. The marginal probability in row 1 of Table 4.5 shows that the probability of promotion of an officer is $P(A) = .27$ (regardless of whether that officer is male or female). However, the critical issue in the discrimination case involves the two conditional probabilities $P(A \mid M)$ and $P(A \mid W)$. That is, what is the probability of a promotion *given* that the officer is a man, and what is the probability of a promotion *given* that the officer is a woman? If these two probabilities are equal, a discrimination argument has no basis because the chances of a promotion are the same for male and female officers. However, a difference in the two conditional probabilities will support the position that male and female officers are treated differently in promotion decisions.

We already determined that $P(A \mid M) = .30$. Let us now use the probability values in Table 4.5 and the basic relationship of conditional probability in equation (4.7) to compute

FIGURE 4.8   CONDITIONAL PROBABILITY $P(A \mid B) = P(A \cap B)/P(B)$

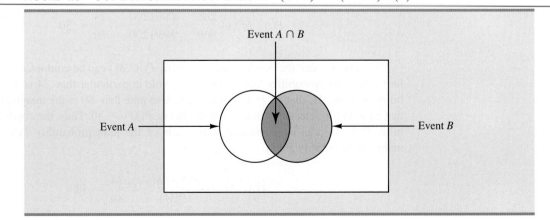

the probability that an officer is promoted given that the officer is a woman; that is, $P(A \mid W)$. Using equation (4.7), with W replacing B, we obtain

$$P(A \mid W) = \frac{P(A \cap W)}{P(W)} = \frac{.03}{.20} = .15$$

What conclusion do you draw? The probability of a promotion given that the officer is a man is .30, twice the .15 probability of a promotion given that the officer is a woman. Although the use of conditional probability does not in itself prove that discrimination exists in this case, the conditional probability values support the argument presented by the female officers.

Independent Events

In the preceding illustration, $P(A) = .27$, $P(A \mid M) = .30$, and $P(A \mid W) = .15$. We see that the probability of a promotion (event A) is affected or influenced by whether the officer is a man or a woman. Particularly, because $P(A \mid M) \neq P(A)$, we would say that events A and M are dependent events. That is, the probability of event A (promotion) is altered or affected by knowing that event M (the officer is a man) exists. Similarly, with $P(A \mid W) \neq P(A)$, we would say that events A and W are *dependent events.* However, if the probability of event A is not changed by the existence of event M—that is, $P(A \mid M) = P(A)$—we would say that events A and M are **independent events**. This situation leads to the following definition of the independence of two events.

INDEPENDENT EVENTS

Two events A and B are independent if

$$P(A \mid B) = P(A) \tag{4.9}$$

or

$$P(B \mid A) = P(B) \tag{4.10}$$

Otherwise, the events are dependent.

Multiplication Law

Whereas the addition law of probability is used to compute the probability of a union of two events, the multiplication law is used to compute the probability of the intersection of two events. The multiplication law is based on the definition of conditional probability. Using equations (4.7) and (4.8) and solving for $P(A \cap B)$, we obtain the **multiplication law**.

MULTIPLICATION LAW

$$P(A \cap B) = P(B)P(A \mid B) \tag{4.11}$$

or

$$P(A \cap B) = P(A)P(B \mid A) \tag{4.12}$$

To illustrate the use of the multiplication law, consider a newspaper circulation department where it is known that 84% of the households in a particular neighborhood subscribe to the daily edition of the paper. If we let D denote the event that a household subscribes to the daily edition, $P(D) = .84$. In addition, it is known that the probability that a household that already holds a daily subscription also subscribes to the Sunday edition (event S) is .75; that is, $P(S \mid D) = .75$.

What is the probability that a household subscribes to both the Sunday and daily editions of the newspaper? Using the multiplication law, we compute the desired $P(S \cap D)$ as

$$P(S \cap D) = P(D)P(S \mid D) = .84(.75) = .63$$

We now know that 63% of the households subscribe to both the Sunday and daily editions.

Before concluding this section, let us consider the special case of the multiplication law when the events involved are independent. Recall that events A and B are independent whenever $P(A \mid B) = P(A)$ or $P(B \mid A) = P(B)$. Hence, using equations (4.11) and (4.12) for the special case of independent events, we obtain the following multiplication law.

MULTIPLICATION LAW FOR INDEPENDENT EVENTS

$$P(A \cap B) = P(A)P(B) \tag{4.13}$$

To compute the probability of the intersection of two independent events, we simply multiply the corresponding probabilities. Note that the multiplication law for independent events provides another way to determine whether A and B are independent. That is, if $P(A \cap B) = P(A)P(B)$, then A and B are independent; if $P(A \cap B) \neq P(A)P(B)$, then A and B are dependent.

As an application of the multiplication law for independent events, consider the situation of a service station manager who knows from past experience that 80% of the customers use a credit card when they purchase gasoline. What is the probability that the next two customers purchasing gasoline will each use a credit card? If we let

A = the event that the first customer uses a credit card

B = the event that the second customer uses a credit card

then the event of interest is $A \cap B$. Given no other information, we can reasonably assume that A and B are independent events. Thus,

$$P(A \cap B) = P(A)P(B) = (.80)(.80) = .64$$

To summarize this section, we note that our interest in conditional probability is motivated by the fact that events are often related. In such cases, we say the events are dependent and the conditional probability formulas in equations (4.7) and (4.8) must be used to compute the event probabilities. If two events are not related, they are independent; in this case neither event's probability is affected by whether the other event occurred.

NOTES AND COMMENTS

Do not confuse the notion of mutually exclusive events with that of independent events. Two events with nonzero probabilities cannot be both mutually exclusive and independent. If one mutually exclusive event is known to occur, the other cannot occur; thus, the probability of the other event occurring is reduced to zero. They are therefore dependent.

Exercises

Methods

30. Suppose that we have two events, A and B, with $P(A) = .50$, $P(B) = .60$, and $P(A \cap B) = .40$.
    a. Find $P(A \mid B)$.
    b. Find $P(B \mid A)$.
    c. Are A and B independent? Why or why not?

31. Assume that we have two events, *A* and *B*, that are mutually exclusive. Assume further that we know $P(A) = .30$ and $P(B) = .40$.
    a. What is $P(A \cap B)$?
    b. What is $P(A \mid B)$?
    c. A student in statistics argues that the concepts of mutually exclusive events and independent events are really the same, and that if events are mutually exclusive they must be independent. Do you agree with this statement? Use the probability information in this problem to justify your answer.
    d. What general conclusion would you make about mutually exclusive and independent events given the results of this problem?

Applications

32. Due to rising health insurance costs, 43 million people in the United States go without health insurance (*Time*, December 1, 2003). Sample data representative of the national health insurance coverage are shown here.

		Health Insurance	
		Yes	**No**
Age	**18 to 34**	750	170
	35 and older	950	130

    a. Develop a joint probability table for these data and use the table to answer the remaining questions.
    b. What do the marginal probabilities tell you about the age of the U.S. population?
    c. What is the probability that a randomly selected individual does not have health insurance coverage?
    d. If the individual is between the ages of 18 and 34, what is the probability that the individual does not have health insurance coverage?
    e. If the individual is age 35 or older, what is the probability that the individual does not have health insurance coverage?
    f. If the individual does not have health insurance, what is the probability that the individual is in the 18 to 34 age group?
    g. What does the probability information tell you about health insurance coverage in the United States?

33. In a survey of MBA students, the following data were obtained on "students' first reason for application to the school in which they matriculated."

		Reason for Application			
		School Quality	**School Cost or Convenience**	**Other**	**Totals**
Enrollment Status	**Full Time**	421	393	76	890
	Part Time	400	593	46	1039
	Totals	821	986	122	1929

    a. Develop a joint probability table for these data.
    b. Use the marginal probabilities of school quality, school cost or convenience, and other to comment on the most important reason for choosing a school.
    c. If a student goes full time, what is the probability that school quality is the first reason for choosing a school?

d.   If a student goes part time, what is the probability that school quality is the first reason for choosing a school?

e.   Let *A* denote the event that a student is full time and let *B* denote the event that the student lists school quality as the first reason for applying. Are events *A* and *B* independent? Justify your answer.

34. The U.S. Department of Transportation reported that during November, 83.4% of Southwest Airlines' flights, 75.1% of US Airways' flights, and 70.1% of JetBlue's flights arrived on time (*USA Today*, January 4, 2007). Assume that this on-time performance is applicable for flights arriving at concourse A of the Rochester International Airport, and that 40% of the arrivals at concourse A are Southwest Airlines flights, 35% are US Airways flights, and 25% are JetBlue flights.

a.   Develop a joint probability table with three rows (airlines) and two columns (on-time arrivals vs. late arrivals).

b.   An announcement has just been made that Flight 1424 will be arriving at gate 20 in concourse A. What is the most likely airline for this arrival?

c.   What is the probability that Flight 1424 will arrive on time?

d.   Suppose that an announcement is made saying that Flight 1424 will be arriving late. What is the most likely airline for this arrival? What is the least likely airline?

35. The U.S. Bureau of Labor Statistics collected data on the occupations of workers 25 to 64 years old. The following table shows the number of male and female workers (in millions) in each occupation category (*Statistical Abstract of the United States: 2002*).

Occupation	Male	Female
Managerial/Professional	19079	19021
Tech./Sales/Administrative	11079	19315
Service	4977	7947
Precision Production	11682	1138
Operators/Fabricators/Labor	10576	3482
Farming/Forestry/Fishing	1838	514

a.   Develop a joint probability table.

b.   What is the probability of a female worker being a manager or professional?

c.   What is the probability of a male worker being in precision production?

d.   Is occupation independent of gender? Justify your answer with a probability calculation.

36. Reggie Miller of the Indiana Pacers is the National Basketball Association's best career free throw shooter, making 89% of his shots (*USA Today*, January 22, 2004). Assume that late in a basketball game, Reggie Miller is fouled and is awarded two shots.

a.   What is the probability that he will make both shots?

b.   What is the probability that he will make at least one shot?

c.   What is the probability that he will miss both shots?

d.   Late in a basketball game, a team often intentionally fouls an opposing player in order to stop the game clock. The usual strategy is to intentionally foul the other team's worst free-throw shooter. Assume that the Indiana Pacers' center makes 58% of his free-throw shots. Calculate the probabilities for the center as shown in parts (a), (b), and (c), and show that intentionally fouling the Indiana Pacers' center is a better strategy than intentionally fouling Reggie Miller.

37. Visa Card USA studied how frequently young consumers, ages 18 to 24, use plastic (debit and credit) cards in making purchases (Associated Press, January 16, 2006). The results of the study provided the following probabilities.

•   The probability that a consumer uses a plastic card when making a purchase is .37.

•   Given that the consumer uses a plastic card, there is a .19 probability that the consumer is 18 to 24 years old.

•   Given that the consumer uses a plastic card, there is a .81 probability that the consumer is more than 24 years old.

U. S. Census Bureau data show that 14% of the consumer population is 18 to 24 years old.

a. Given the consumer is 18 to 24 years old, what is the probability that the consumer use a plastic card?

b. Given the consumer is over 24 years old, what is the probability that the consumer uses a plastic card?

c. What is the interpretation of the probabilities shown in parts (a) and (b)?

d. Should companies such as Visa, MasterCard, and Discover make plastic cards available to the 18- to 24-year-old age group before these consumers have had time to establish a credit history? If no, why? If yes, what restrictions might the companies place on this age group?

38. A Morgan Stanley Consumer Research Survey sampled men and women and asked each whether they preferred to drink plain bottled water or a sports drink such as Gatorade or Propel Fitness water (*The Atlanta Journal-Constitution,* December 28, 2005). Suppose 200 men and 200 women participated in the study, and 280 reported they preferred plain bottled water. Of the group preferring a sports drink, 80 were men and 40 were women.

Let

M = the event the consumer is a man
W = the event the consumer is a woman
B = the event the consumer preferred plain bottled water
S = the event the consumer preferred sports drink

a. What is the probability a person in the study preferred plain bottled water?

b. What is the probability a person in the study preferred a sports drink?

c. What are the conditional probabilities $P(M \mid S)$ and $P(W \mid S)$?

d. What are the joint probabilities $P(M \cap S)$ and $P(W \cap S)$?

e. Given a consumer is a man, what is the probability he will prefer a sports drink?

f. Given a consumer is a woman, what is the probability she will prefer a sports drink?

g. Is preference for a sports drink independent of whether the consumer is a man or a woman? Explain using probability information.

(4.5) Bayes' Theorem

In the discussion of conditional probability, we indicated that revising probabilities when new information is obtained is an important phase of probability analysis. Often, we begin the analysis with initial or **prior probability** estimates for specific events of interest. Then, from sources such as a sample, a special report, or a product test, we obtain additional information about the events. Given this new information, we update the prior probability values by calculating revised probabilities, referred to as **posterior probabilities. Bayes' theorem** provides a means for making these probability calculations. The steps in this probability revision process are shown in Figure 4.9.

As an application of Bayes' theorem, consider a manufacturing firm that receives shipments of parts from two different suppliers. Let A_1 denote the event that a part is from supplier 1 and A_2 denote the event that a part is from supplier 2. Currently, 65% of the parts purchased by the company are from supplier 1 and the remaining 35% are from supplier 2. Hence, if a part is selected at random, we would assign the prior probabilities $P(A_1)$ = .65 and $P(A_2)$ = .35.

FIGURE 4.9 PROBABILITY REVISION USING BAYES' THEOREM

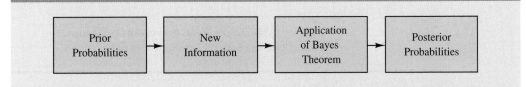

TABLE 4.6   HISTORICAL QUALITY LEVELS OF TWO SUPPLIERS

	Percentage Good Parts	Percentage Bad Parts
Supplier 1	98	2
Supplier 2	95	5

The quality of the purchased parts varies with the source of supply. Historic data suggest that the quality ratings of the two suppliers are as shown in Table 4.6. If we let G denote the event that a part is good and B denote the event that a part is bad, the information in Table 4.6 provides the following conditional probability values.

$$P(G \mid A_1) = .98 \quad P(B \mid A_1) = .02$$
$$P(G \mid A_2) = .95 \quad P(B \mid A_2) = .05$$

The tree diagram in Figure 4.10 depicts the process of the firm receiving a part from one of the two suppliers and then discovering that the part is good or bad as a two-step experiment. We see that four experimental outcomes are possible; two correspond to the part being good and two correspond to the part being bad.

Each of the experimental outcomes is the intersection of two events, so we can use the multiplication rule to compute the probabilities. For instance,

$$P(A_1, G) = P(A_1 \cap G) = P(A_1)P(G \mid A_1)$$

The process of computing these joint probabilities can be depicted in what is called a probability tree (see Figure 4.11). From left to right through the tree, the probabilities for each branch at step 1 are prior probabilities and the probabilities for each branch at step 2 are conditional probabilities. To find the probabilities of each experimental outcome, we simply multiply the probabilities on the branches leading to the outcome. Each of these joint probabilities is shown in Figure 4.11 along with the known probabilities for each branch.

FIGURE 4.10   TREE DIAGRAM FOR TWO-SUPPLIER EXAMPLE

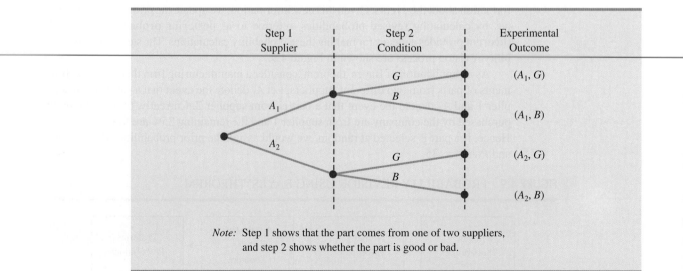

Note: Step 1 shows that the part comes from one of two suppliers, and step 2 shows whether the part is good or bad.

FIGURE 4.11   PROBABILITY TREE FOR TWO-SUPPLIER EXAMPLE

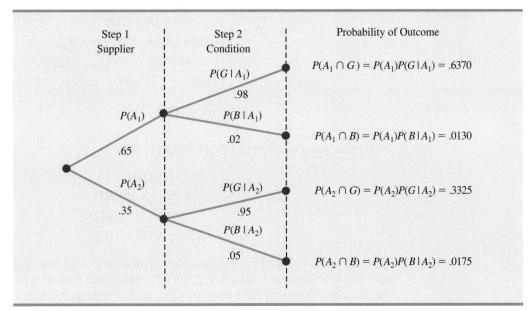

Suppose now that the parts from the two suppliers are used in the firm's manufacturing process and that a machine breaks down because it attempts to process a bad part. Given the information that the part is bad, what is the probability that it came from supplier 1 and what is the probability that it came from supplier 2? With the information in the probability tree (Figure 4.11), Bayes' theorem can be used to answer these questions.

Letting B denote the event that the part is bad, we are looking for the posterior probabilities $P(A_1 \mid B)$ and $P(A_2 \mid B)$. From the law of conditional probability, we know that

$$P(A_1 \mid B) = \frac{P(A_1 \cap B)}{P(B)} \tag{4.14}$$

Referring to the probability tree, we see that

$$P(A_1 \cap B) = P(A_1)P(B \mid A_1) \tag{4.15}$$

To find $P(B)$, we note that event B can occur in only two ways: $(A_1 \cap B)$ and $(A_2 \cap B)$. Therefore, we have

$$\begin{aligned}P(B) &= P(A_1 \cap B) + P(A_2 \cap B) \\ &= P(A_1)P(B \mid A_1) + P(A_2)P(B \mid A_2)\end{aligned} \tag{4.16}$$

Substituting from equations (4.15) and (4.16) into equation (4.14) and writing a similar result for $P(A_2 \mid B)$, we obtain Bayes' theorem for the case of two events A_1 and A_2.

The Reverend Thomas Bayes (1702–1761), a Presbyterian minister, is credited with the original work leading to the version of Bayes' theorem in use today.

BAYES' THEOREM (TWO-EVENT CASE)

$$P(A_1 \mid B) = \frac{P(A_1)P(B \mid A_1)}{P(A_1)P(B \mid A_1) + P(A_2)P(B \mid A_2)} \tag{4.17}$$

$$P(A_2 \mid B) = \frac{P(A_2)P(B \mid A_2)}{P(A_1)P(B \mid A_1) + P(A_2)P(B \mid A_2)} \tag{4.18}$$

Using equation (4.17) and the probability values provided in the example, we have

$$P(A_1 \mid B) = \frac{P(A_1)P(B \mid A_1)}{P(A_1)P(B \mid A_1) + P(A_2)P(B \mid A_2)}$$

$$= \frac{(.65)(.02)}{(.65)(.02) + (.35)(.05)} = \frac{.0130}{.0130 + .0175}$$

$$= \frac{.0130}{.0305} = .4262$$

In addition, using equation (4.18), we find $P(A_2 \mid B)$.

$$P(A_2 \mid B) = \frac{(.35)(.05)}{(.65)(.02) + (.35)(.05)}$$

$$= \frac{.0175}{.0130 + .0175} = \frac{.0175}{.0305} = .5738$$

Note that in this application we started with a probability of .65 that a part selected at random was from supplier 1. However, given information that the part is bad, the probability that the part is from supplier 1 drops to .4262. In fact, if the part is bad, it has better than a 50/50 chance that it came from supplier 2; that is, $P(A_2 \mid B) = .5738$.

Bayes' theorem is applicable when the events for which we want to compute posterior probabilities are mutually exclusive and their union is the entire sample space.[2] For the case of n mutually exclusive events $A_1, A_2, \ldots, A_n$, whose union is the entire sample space, Bayes' theorem can be used to compute any posterior probability $P(A_i \mid B)$ as shown here.

BAYES' THEOREM

$$P(A_i \mid B) = \frac{P(A_i)P(B \mid A_i)}{P(A_1)P(B \mid A_1) + P(A_2)P(B \mid A_2) + \cdots + P(A_n)P(B \mid A_n)} \quad \text{(4.19)}$$

With prior probabilities $P(A_1), P(A_2), \ldots, P(A_n)$ and the appropriate conditional probabilities $P(B \mid A_1), P(B \mid A_2), \ldots, P(B \mid A_n)$, equation (4.19) can be used to compute the posterior probability of the events $A_1, A_2, \ldots, A_n$.

Tabular Approach

A tabular approach is helpful in conducting the Bayes' theorem calculations. Such an approach is shown in Table 4.7 for the parts supplier problem. The computations shown there are done in the following steps.

Step 1. Prepare the following three columns:
    Column 1—The mutually exclusive events A_i for which posterior probabilities are desired
    Column 2—The prior probabilities $P(A_i)$ for the events
    Column 3—The conditional probabilities $P(B \mid A_i)$ of the new information B given each event
Step 2. In column 4, compute the joint probabilities $P(A_i \cap B)$ for each event and the new information B by using the multiplication law. These joint probabilities are found by multiplying the prior probabilities in column 2 by the

[2]If the union of events is the entire sample space, the events are said to be *collectively exhaustive*.

TABLE 4.7   TABULAR APPROACH TO BAYES' THEOREM CALCULATIONS
FOR THE TWO-SUPPLIER PROBLEM

(1) Events A_i	(2) Prior Probabilities $P(A_i)$	(3) Conditional Probabilities $P(B \mid A_i)$	(4) Joint Probabilities $P(A_i \cap B)$	(5) Posterior Probabilities $P(A_i \mid B)$
A_1	.65	.02	.0130	.0130/.0305 = .4262
A_2	.35	.05	.0175	.0175/.0305 = .5738
	1.00		$P(B)$ = .0305	1.0000

corresponding conditional probabilities in column 3; that is, $P(A_i \cap B) = P(A_i)P(B \mid A_i)$.

Step 3. Sum the joint probabilities in column 4. The sum is the probability of the new information, $P(B)$. Thus we see in Table 4.7 that there is a .0130 probability that the part came from supplier 1 and is bad and a .0175 probability that the part came from supplier 2 and is bad. Because these are the only two ways in which a bad part can be obtained, the sum .0130 + .0175 shows an overall probability of .0305 of finding a bad part from the combined shipments of the two suppliers.

Step 4. In column 5, compute the posterior probabilities using the basic relationship of conditional probability.

$$P(A_i \mid B) = \frac{P(A_i \cap B)}{P(B)}$$

Note that the joint probabilities $P(A_i \cap B)$ are in column 4 and the probability $P(B)$ is the sum of column 4.

Using Excel to Compute Posterior Probabilities

The tabular approach to Bayes' theorem can be easily implemented within an Excel worksheet. In this subsection we show how the Bayes' theorem calculations shown in Table 4.7 can be made. Refer to Figure 4.12 as we describe the tasks involved. The formula worksheet is in the background; the value worksheet is in the foreground.

Enter Data: Labels are placed in rows 1 and 2 and the two mutually exclusive events are identified in cells A3:A4. The prior probabilities were entered into cells B3:B4 and the conditional probabilities were entered into cells C3:C4.

FIGURE 4.12   EXCEL WORKSHEET FOR COMPUTING POSTERIOR PROBABILITIES

	A	B	C	D	E	F
1		Prior	Conditional	Joint	Posterior	
2	Events	Probabilities	Probabilities	Probabilities	Probabilities	
3	A1	0.65	0.02	=B3*C3	=D3/$D$5	
4	A2	0.35	0.05	=B4*C4	=D4/$D$5	
5		=SUM(B3:B4)		=SUM(D3:D4)	=SUM(E3:E4)	
6						

	A	B	C	D	E	F
1		Prior	Conditional	Joint	Posterior	
2	Events	Probabilities	Probabilities	Probabilities	Probabilities	
3	A1	0.65	0.02	0.0130	0.4262	
4	A2	0.35	0.05	0.0175	0.5738	
5		1		0.0305	1.0000	
6						

Enter Functions and Formulas: The formulas in cells D3:D4 show that the joint probabilities are the product of the prior probabilities in column B and the conditional probabilities in column C. The results, shown in cells D3:D4 of the value worksheet, are the same as those shown in Table 4.7. The sum in cell D5 shows that the probability of finding a bad part is .0305. This probability is the denominator in Bayes' theorem. The formulas in cells E3:E4 provide the posterior probabilities. From the value worksheet we see that they are the same as the posterior probabilities in Table 4.7.

Note that the same worksheet could be used to find the posterior probabilities of the two suppliers given a good part is found. The prior probabilities in cells B3:B4 would not change. But we would replace the conditional probabilities in cells C3:C4 with the values .98 and .95, respectively. Doing so would provide $P(A_1 \mid G) = .6570$ and $P(A_2 \mid G) = .3430$ in cells E3:E4.

This worksheet can also be modified to handle Bayes' theorem calculations for more than two events. Just add a row for each additional event and move the sum row down.

NOTES AND COMMENTS

1. Bayes' theorem is used extensively in decision analysis. The prior probabilities are often subjective estimates provided by a decision maker. Sample information is obtained and posterior probabilities are computed for use in choosing the best decision.

2. An event and its complement are mutually exclusive, and their union is the entire sample space. Thus, Bayes' theorem is always applicable for computing posterior probabilities of an event and its complement.

Exercises

Methods

39. The prior probabilities for events A_1 and A_2 are $P(A_1) = .40$ and $P(A_2) = .60$. It is also known that $P(A_1 \cap A_2) = 0$. Suppose $P(B \mid A_1) = .20$ and $P(B \mid A_2) = .05$.
    a. Are A_1 and A_2 mutually exclusive? Explain.
    b. Compute $P(A_1 \cap B)$ and $P(A_2 \cap B)$.
    c. Compute $P(B)$.
    d. Apply Bayes' theorem to compute $P(A_1 \mid B)$ and $P(A_2 \mid B)$.

40. The prior probabilities for events $A_1, A_2,$ and A_3 are $P(A_1) = .20, P(A_2) = .50,$ and $P(A_3) = .30$. The conditional probabilities of event B given $A_1, A_2,$ and A_3 are $P(B \mid A_1) = .50,$ $P(B \mid A_2) = .40,$ and $P(B \mid A_3) = .30$.
    a. Compute $P(B \cap A_1), P(B \cap A_2),$ and $P(B \cap A_3)$.
    b. Apply Bayes' theorem, equation (4.19), to compute the posterior probability $P(A_2 \mid B)$.
    c. Use the tabular approach to applying Bayes' theorem to compute $P(A_1 \mid B), P(A_2 \mid B),$ and $P(A_3 \mid B)$.

Applications

41. A consulting firm submitted a bid for a large research project. The firm's management initially felt they had a 50/50 chance of getting the project. However, the agency to which the bid was submitted subsequently requested additional information on the bid. Past experience indicates that for 75% of the successful bids and 40% of the unsuccessful bids the agency requested additional information.
    a. What is the prior probability of the bid being successful (that is, prior to the request for additional information)?
    b. What is the conditional probability of a request for additional information given that the bid will ultimately be successful?

c. Compute the posterior probability that the bid will be successful given a request for additional information.

42. A local bank reviewed its credit card policy with the intention of recalling some of its credit cards. In the past approximately 5% of cardholders defaulted, leaving the bank unable to collect the outstanding balance. Hence, management established a prior probability of .05 that any particular cardholder will default. The bank also found that the probability of missing a monthly payment is .20 for customers who do not default. Of course, the probability of missing a monthly payment for those who default is 1.

a. Given that a customer missed one or more monthly payments, compute the posterior probability that the customer will default.

b. The bank would like to recall its card if the probability that a customer will default is greater than .20. Should the bank recall its card if the customer misses a monthly payment? Why or why not?

43. Small cars get better gas mileage, but they are not as safe as bigger cars. Small cars accounted for 18% of the vehicles on the road, but accidents involving small cars led to 11,898 fatalities during a recent year (*Reader's Digest,* May 2000). Assume the probability a small car is involved in an accident is .18. The probability of an accident involving a small car leading to a fatality is .128 and the probability of an accident not involving a small car leading to a fatality is .05. Suppose you learn of an accident involving a fatality. What is the probability a small car was involved? Assume that the likelihood of getting into an accident is independent of car size.

44. The American Council of Education reported that 47% of college freshmen earn a degree and graduate within five years (Associated Press, May 6, 2002). Assume that graduation records show women make up 50% of the students who graduate within five years, but only 45% of the students who do not graduate within five years. The students who do not graduate within five years either drop out or are still working on their degrees.

a. Let A_1 = a student graduated within five years
A_2 = a student did not graduate within five years
W = a student is a female student
Using the given information, what are the values for $P(A_1)$, $P(A_2)$, $P(W \mid A_1)$, and $P(W \mid A_2)$?

b. What is the probability that a female student will graduate within five years?

c. What is the probability that a male student will graduate within five years?

d. Given the preceding results, what are the percentage of women and the percentage of men in the entering freshman class?

45. In an article about investment growth, *Money* magazine reported that drug stocks show powerful long-term trends and offer investors unparalleled potential for strong and steady gains. The federal Health Care Financing Administration supports this conclusion through its forecast that annual prescription drug expenditures will reach $366 billion by 2010, up from $117 billion in 2000. Many individuals age 65 and older rely heavily on prescription drugs. For this group, 82% take prescription drugs regularly, 55% take three or more prescriptions regularly, and 40% currently use five or more prescriptions. In contrast, 49% of people under age 65 take prescriptions regularly, with 37% taking three or more prescriptions regularly and 28% using five or more prescriptions (*Money,* September 2001). The U.S. Census Bureau reports that of the 281,421,906 people in the United States, 34,991,753 are age 65 years and older (U.S. Census Bureau, *Census 2000*).

a. Compute the probability that a person in the United States is age 65 or older.

b. Given a person uses five or more prescriptions, compute the probability that the person is age 65 or older.

Summary

In this chapter we introduced basic probability concepts and illustrated how probability analysis can be used to provide helpful information for decision making. We described how probability can be interpreted as a numerical measure of the likelihood that an event will occur. In addition, we saw that the probability of an event can be computed either by summing the probabilities of the experimental outcomes (sample points) comprising the event or by using the relationships established by the addition, conditional probability, and multiplication laws of probability. For cases in which additional information is available, we showed how Bayes' theorem can be used to obtain revised or posterior probabilities.

Glossary

Probability A numerical measure of the likelihood that an event will occur.

Experiment A process that generates well-defined outcomes.

Sample space The set of all experimental outcomes.

Sample point An element of the sample space. A sample point represents an experimental outcome.

Tree diagram A graphical representation that helps in visualizing a multiple-step experiment.

Basic requirements for assigning probabilities Two requirements that restrict the manner in which probability assignments can be made: (1) for each experimental outcome E_i we must have $0 \leq P(E_i) \leq 1$; (2) considering all experimental outcomes, we must have $P(E_1) + P(E_2) + \cdots + P(E_n) = 1.0$.

Classical method A method of assigning probabilities that is appropriate when all the experimental outcomes are equally likely.

Relative frequency method A method of assigning probabilities that is appropriate when data are available to estimate the proportion of the time the experimental outcome will occur if the experiment is repeated a large number of times.

Subjective method A method of assigning probabilities on the basis of judgment.

Event A collection of sample points.

Complement of A The event consisting of all sample points that are not in A.

Venn diagram A graphical representation for showing symbolically the sample space and operations involving events in which the sample space is represented by a rectangle and events are represented as circles within the sample space.

Union of A and B The event containing all sample points belonging to A or B or both. The union is denoted $A \cup B$.

Intersection of A and B The event containing the sample points belonging to both A and B. The intersection is denoted $A \cap B$.

Addition law A probability law used to compute the probability of the union of two events. It is $P(A \cup B) = P(A) + P(B) - P(A \cap B)$. For mutually exclusive events, $P(A \cap B) = 0$; in this case the addition law reduces to $P(A \cup B) = P(A) + P(B)$.

Mutually exclusive events Events that have no sample points in common; that is, $A \cap B$ is empty and $P(A \cap B) = 0$.

Conditional probability The probability of an event given that another event already occurred. The conditional probability of A given B is $P(A \mid B) = P(A \cap B)/P(B)$.

Joint probability The probability of two events both occurring; that is, the probability of the intersection of two events.

Marginal probability The values in the margins of a joint probability table that provide the probabilities of each event separately.

Independent events Two events A and B where $P(A \mid B) = P(A)$ or $P(B \mid A) = P(B)$; that is, the events have no influence on each other.

Multiplication law A probability law used to compute the probability of the intersection of two events. It is $P(A \cap B) = P(B)P(A \mid B)$ or $P(A \cap B) = P(A)P(B \mid A)$. For independent events it reduces to $P(A \cap B) = P(A)P(B)$.

Prior probabilities Initial estimates of the probabilities of events.

Posterior probabilities Revised probabilities of events based on additional information.

Bayes' theorem A method used to compute posterior probabilities.

Key Formulas

Counting Rule for Combinations

$$C_n^N = \binom{N}{n} = \frac{N!}{n!(N-n)!} \tag{4.1}$$

Counting Rule for Permutations

$$P_n^N = n!\binom{N}{n} = \frac{N!}{(N-n)!} \tag{4.2}$$

Computing Probability Using the Complement

$$P(A) = 1 - P(A^c) \tag{4.5}$$

Addition Law

$$P(A \cup B) = P(A) + P(B) - P(A \cap B) \tag{4.6}$$

Conditional Probability

$$P(A \mid B) = \frac{P(A \cap B)}{P(B)} \tag{4.7}$$

$$P(B \mid A) = \frac{P(A \cap B)}{P(A)} \tag{4.8}$$

Multiplication Law

$$P(A \cap B) = P(B)P(A \mid B) \tag{4.11}$$

$$P(A \cap B) = P(A)P(B \mid A) \tag{4.12}$$

Multiplication Law for Independent Events

$$P(A \cap B) = P(A)P(B) \tag{4.13}$$

Bayes' Theorem

$$P(A_i \mid B) = \frac{P(A_i)P(B \mid A_i)}{P(A_1)P(B \mid A_1) + P(A_2)P(B \mid A_2) + \cdots + P(A_n)P(B \mid A_n)} \tag{4.19}$$

Supplementary Exercises

46. In a *Wall Street Journal*/Harris Interactive Personal Finance Poll, 2082 adults were asked if they owned their own home (*http://www.allbusiness.com,* January 23, 2008). Sixty percent of the respondents said yes. The percentages saying yes by age group were 26% for the 18–34 age group, 50% for the 35–44 age group, 71% for the 45–54 age group, and 88% for the 55 and over age group.
    a. What is the probability that a respondent in the 18–34 age group owns his or her own home?
    b. What is the probability that a respondent indicates he or she does not own a home?
    c. How many of the survey respondents own a home?

47. A financial manager made two new investments—one in the oil industry and one in municipal bonds. After a one-year period, each of the investments will be classified as either successful or unsuccessful. Consider the making of the two investments as an experiment.
    a. How many sample points exist for this experiment?
    b. Show a tree diagram and list the sample points.
    c. Let $O =$ the event that the oil industry investment is successful and $M =$ the event that the municipal bond investment is successful. List the sample points in O and in M.

    d.   List the sample points in the union of the events ($O \cup M$).

    e.   List the sample points in the intersection of the events ($O \cap M$).

    f.   Are events O and M mutually exclusive? Explain.

48. In early 2003, President Bush proposed eliminating the taxation of dividends to shareholders on the grounds that it was double taxation. Corporations pay taxes on the earnings that are later paid out in dividends. In a poll of 671 Americans, TechnoMetrica Market Intelligence found that 47% favored the proposal, 44% opposed it, and 9% were not sure (*Investor's Business Daily,* January 13, 2003). In looking at the responses across party lines the poll showed that 29% of Democrats were in favor, 64% of Republicans were in favor, and 48% of Independents were in favor.

    a.   How many of those polled favored elimination of the tax on dividends?

    b.   What is the conditional probability in favor of the proposal given the person polled is a Democrat?

    c.   Is party affiliation independent of whether one is in favor of the proposal?

    d.   If we assume people's responses were consistent with their own self-interest, which group do you believe will benefit most from passage of the proposal?

49. A study of 31,000 hospital admissions in New York State found that 4% of the admissions led to treatment-caused injuries. One-seventh of these treatment-caused injuries resulted in death, and one-fourth were caused by negligence. Malpractice claims were filed in one out of 7.5 cases involving negligence, and payments were made in one out of every two claims.

    a.   What is the probability a person admitted to the hospital will suffer a treatment-caused injury due to negligence?

    b.   What is the probability a person admitted to the hospital will die from a treatment-caused injury?

    c.   In the case of a negligent treatment-caused injury, what is the probability a malpractice claim will be paid?

50. A telephone survey to determine viewer response to a new television show obtained the following data.

Rating	Frequency
Poor	4
Below average	8
Average	11
Above average	14
Excellent	13

    a.   What is the probability that a randomly selected viewer will rate the new show as average or better?

    b.   What is the probability that a randomly selected viewer will rate the new show below average or worse?

51. The following crosstabulation shows household income by educational level of the head of household (*Statistical Abstract of the United States: 2002*).

Education Level	Household Income ($1000s)					Total
	Under 25	25.0– 49.9	50.0– 74.9	75.0– 99.9	100 or more	
Not H.S. Graduate	9,285	4,093	1,589	541	354	15,862
H.S. Graduate	10,150	9,821	6,050	2,737	2,028	30,786
Some College	6,011	8,221	5,813	3,215	3,120	26,380
Bachelor's Degree	2,138	3,985	3,952	2,698	4,748	17,521
Beyond Bach. Deg.	813	1,497	1,815	1,589	3,765	9,479
Total	28,397	27,617	19,219	10,780	14,015	100,028

a. Develop a joint probability table.
b. What is the probability of a head of household not being a high school graduate?
c. What is the probability of a head of household having a bachelor's degree or more education?
d. What is the probability of a household headed by someone with a bachelor's degree earning $100,000 or more?
e. What is the probability of a household having income below $25,000?
f. What is the probability of a household headed by someone with a bachelor's degree earning less than $25,000?
g. Is household income independent of educational level?

52. A GMAC MBA new-matriculants survey provided the following data for 2018 students.

		Applied to More Than One School	
		Yes	No
	23 and under	207	201
	24–26	299	379
Age	**27–30**	185	268
Group	**31–35**	66	193
	36 and over	51	169

a. For a randomly selected MBA student, prepare a joint probability table for the experiment consisting of obtaining the student's age and whether the student applied to one or more schools.
b. What is the probability that a randomly selected applicant is 23 or under?
c. What is the probability that a randomly selected applicant is older than 26?
d. What is the probability that a randomly selected applicant applied to more than one school?

53. Refer again to the data from the GMAC new-matriculants survey in exercise 52.
a. Given that a person applied to more than one school, what is the probability that the person is 24–26 years old?
b. Given that a person is in the 36-and-over age group, what is the probability that the person applied to more than one school?
c. What is the probability that a person is 24–26 years old or applied to more than one school?
d. Suppose a person is known to have applied to only one school. What is the probability that the person is 31 or more years old?
e. Is the number of schools applied to independent of age? Explain.

54. An IBD/TIPP poll conducted to learn about attitudes toward investment and retirement (*Investor's Business Daily,* May 5, 2000) asked male and female respondents how important they felt level of risk was in choosing a retirement investment. The following joint probability table was constructed from the data provided. "Important" means the respondent said level of risk was either important or very important.

	Male	Female	Total
Important	.22	.27	.49
Not Important	.28	.23	.51
Total	.50	.50	1.00

a. What is the probability a survey respondent will say level of risk is important?
b. What is the probability a male respondent will say level of risk is important?

c. What is the probability a female respondent will say level of risk is important?
d. Is the level of risk independent of the gender of the respondent? Why or why not?
e. Do male and female attitudes toward risk differ?

55. A large consumer goods company ran a television advertisement for one of its soap products. On the basis of a survey that was conducted, probabilities were assigned to the
following events.

$$B = \text{individual purchased the product}$$
$$S = \text{individual recalls seeing the advertisement}$$
$$B \cap S = \text{individual purchased the product and recalls seeing the advertisement}$$

The probabilities assigned were $P(B) = .20$, $P(S) = .40$, and $P(B \cap S) = .12$.

a. What is the probability of an individual's purchasing the product given that the individual recalls seeing the advertisement? Does seeing the advertisement increase
the probability that the individual will purchase the product? As a decision maker,
would you recommend continuing the advertisement (assuming that the cost is
reasonable)?
b. Assume that individuals who do not purchase the company's soap product buy from
its competitors. What would be your estimate of the company's market share? Would
you expect that continuing the advertisement will increase the company's market
share? Why or why not?
c. The company also tested another advertisement and assigned it values of $P(S) = .30$
and $P(B \cap S) = .10$. What is $P(B \mid S)$ for this other advertisement? Which advertisement seems to have had the bigger effect on customer purchases?

56. Cooper Realty is a small real estate company located in Albany, New York, specializing
primarily in residential listings. They recently became interested in determining the likelihood of one of their listings being sold within a certain number of days. An analysis of
company sales of 800 homes in previous years produced the following data.

		Days Listed Until Sold			
		Under 30	31–90	Over 90	Total
	Under $150,000	50	40	10	100
Initial Asking Price	$150,000–$199,999	20	150	80	250
	$200,000–$250,000	20	280	100	400
	Over $250,000	10	30	10	50
	Total	100	500	200	800

a. If A is defined as the event that a home is listed for more than 90 days before being
sold, estimate the probability of A.
b. If B is defined as the event that the initial asking price is under $150,000, estimate the
probability of B.
c. What is the probability of $A \cap B$?
d. Assuming that a contract was just signed to list a home with an initial asking price of
less than $150,000, what is the probability that the home will take Cooper Realty more
than 90 days to sell?
e. Are events A and B independent?

57. A company studied the number of lost-time accidents occurring at its Brownsville, Texas,
plant. Historical records show that 6% of the employees suffered lost-time accidents last
year. Management believes that a special safety program will reduce such accidents to 5%

during the current year. In addition, it estimates that 15% of employees who had lost-time accidents last year will experience a lost-time accident during the current year.

    a.   What percentage of the employees will experience lost-time accidents in both years?

    b.   What percentage of the employees will suffer at least one lost-time accident over the two-year period?

58.   A survey conducted by the Pew Internet & American Life Project showed that 8% of Internet users age 18 and older report keeping a blog. Referring to the 18–29 age group as young adults, the survey results showed that for bloggers 54% are young adults and for nonbloggers 24% are young adults (Pew Internet & American Life Project, July 19, 2006).

    a.   Develop a joint probability table for these data with two rows (bloggers vs. non-bloggers) and two columns (young adults vs. older adults).

    b.   What is the probability that an Internet user is a young adult?

    c.   What is the probability that an Internet user keeps a blog and is a young adult?

    d.   Suppose that in a follow-up phone survey we contact a respondent who is 24 years old. What is the probability that this respondent keeps a blog?

59.   An oil company purchased an option on land in Alaska. Preliminary geologic studies assigned the following prior probabilities.

$$P(\text{high-quality oil}) = .50$$
$$P(\text{medium-quality oil}) = .20$$
$$P(\text{no oil}) = .30$$

    a.   What is the probability of finding oil?

    b.   After 200 feet of drilling on the first well, a soil test is taken. The probabilities of finding the particular type of soil identified by the test follow.

$$P(\text{soil} \mid \text{high-quality oil}) = .20$$
$$P(\text{soil} \mid \text{medium-quality oil}) = .80$$
$$P(\text{soil} \mid \text{no oil}) = .20$$

How should the firm interpret the soil test? What are the revised probabilities, and what is the new probability of finding oil?

60.   Companies that do business over the Internet can often obtain probability information about website visitors from previous websites visited. The article "Internet Marketing" (*Interfaces*, March/April 2001) described how clickstream data on websites visited could be used in conjunction with a Bayesian updating scheme to determine the gender of a website visitor. Par Fore created a website to market golf equipment and apparel. Management would like a certain offer to appear for female visitors and a different offer to appear for male visitors. From a sample of past website visits, management learned that 60% of the visitors to ParFore.com are male and 40% are female.

    a.   What is the prior probability that the next visitor to the website will be female?

    b.   Suppose you know that the current visitor to ParFore.com previously visited the Dillard's website, and that women are three times as likely to visit the Dillard's website as men. What is the revised probability that the current visitor to ParFore.com is female? Should you display the offer that appeals more to female visitors or the one that appeals more to male visitors?

Case Problem   Hamilton County Judges

Hamilton County judges try thousands of cases per year. In an overwhelming majority of the cases disposed, the verdict stands as rendered. However, some cases are appealed, and of those appealed, some of the cases are reversed. Kristen DelGuzzi of the *Cincinnati Enquirer* conducted a study of cases handled by Hamilton County judges over a three-year period. Shown in Table 4.8 are the results for 182,908 cases handled (disposed)

TABLE 4.8 TOTAL CASES DISPOSED, APPEALED, AND REVERSED IN HAMILTON COUNTY COURTS

Judge

Common Pleas Court

Judge	Total Cases Disposed	Appealed Cases	Reversed Cases
Fred Cartolano	3,037	137	12
Thomas Crush	3,372	119	10
Patrick Dinkelacker	1,258	44	8
Timothy Hogan	1,954	60	7
Robert Kraft	3,138	127	7
William Mathews	2,264	91	18
William Morrissey	3,032	121	22
Norbert Nadel	2,959	131	20
Arthur Ney, Jr.	3,219	125	14
Richard Niehaus	3,353	137	16
Thomas Nurre	3,000	121	6
John O'Connor	2,969	129	12
Robert Ruehlman	3,205	145	18
J. Howard Sundermann	955	60	10
Ann Marie Tracey	3,141	127	13
Ralph Winkler	3,089	88	6
Total	43,945	1762	199

Domestic Relations Court

Judge	Total Cases Disposed	Appealed Cases	Reversed Cases
Penelope Cunningham	2,729	7	1
Patrick Dinkelacker	6,001	19	4
Deborah Gaines	8,799	48	9
Ronald Panioto	12,970	32	3
Total	30,499	106	17

Municipal Court

Judge	Total Cases Disposed	Appealed Cases	Reversed Cases
Mike Allen	6,149	43	4
Nadine Allen	7,812	34	6
Timothy Black	7,954	41	6
David Davis	7,736	43	5
Leslie Isaiah Gaines	5,282	35	13
Karla Grady	5,253	6	0
Deidra Hair	2,532	5	0
Dennis Helmick	7,900	29	5
Timothy Hogan	2,308	13	2
James Patrick Kenney	2,798	6	1
Joseph Luebbers	4,698	25	8
William Mallory	8,277	38	9
Melba Marsh	8,219	34	7
Beth Mattingly	2,971	13	1
Albert Mestemaker	4,975	28	9
Mark Painter	2,239	7	3
Jack Rosen	7,790	41	13
Mark Schweikert	5,403	33	6
David Stockdale	5,371	22	4
John A. West	2,797	4	2
Total	108,464	500	104

by 38 judges in Common Pleas Court, Domestic Relations Court, and Municipal Court. Two of the judges (Dinkelacker and Hogan) did not serve in the same court for the entire three-year period.

The purpose of the newspaper's study was to evaluate the performance of the judges. Appeals are often the result of mistakes made by judges, and the newspaper wanted to know which judges were doing a good job and which were making too many mistakes. You are called in to assist in the data analysis. Use your knowledge of probability and conditional probability to help with the ranking of the judges. You also may be able to analyze the likelihood of appeal and reversal for cases handled by different courts.

Managerial Report

Prepare a report with your rankings of the judges. Also, include an analysis of the likelihood of appeal and case reversal in the three courts. At a minimum, your report should include the following:

1. The probability of cases being appealed and reversed in the three different courts.
2. The probability of a case being appealed for each judge.
3. The probability of a case being reversed for each judge.
4. The probability of reversal given an appeal for each judge.
5. Rank the judges within each court. State the criteria you used and provide a rationale for your choice.

CHAPTER 5

Discrete Probability Distributions

CONTENTS

STATISTICS *in* PRACTICE

CITIBANK*
LONG ISLAND CITY, NEW YORK

Citibank, a division of Citigroup, makes available a wide range of financial services, including checking and savings accounts, loans and mortgages, insurance, and investment services, within the framework of a unique strategy for delivering those services called Citibanking. Citibanking entails a consistent brand identity all over the world, consistent product offerings, and high-level customer service. Citibanking lets you manage your money anytime, any where, any way you choose. Whether you need to save for the future or borrow for today, you can do it all at Citibank.

Citibank's state-of-the-art automatic teller machines (ATMs) located in Citicard Banking Centers (CBCs) let customers do all their banking in one place with the touch of a finger, 24 hours a day, 7 days a week. More than 150 different banking functions from deposits to managing investments can be performed with ease. Citibanking ATMs are so much more than just cash machines that customers today use them for 80% of their transactions.

Each Citibank CBC operates as a waiting line system with randomly arriving customers seeking service at one of the ATMs. If all ATMs are busy, the arriving customers wait in line. Periodic CBC capacity studies are used to analyze customer waiting times and to determine whether additional ATMs are needed.

Data collected by Citibank showed that the random customer arrivals followed a probability distribution known as the Poisson distribution. Using the Poisson distribution, Citibank can compute probabilities for the number of customers arriving at a CBC during any time period and make decisions concerning the number of ATMs needed. For example, let x = the number of customers arriving during a one-minute period. Assuming that a particular CBC has a mean arrival rate of two customers per minute, the following table shows the

*The authors are indebted to Ms. Stacey Karter, Citibank, for providing this Statistics in Practice.

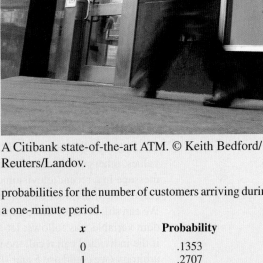

A Citibank state-of-the-art ATM. © Keith Bedford/ Reuters/Landov.

probabilities for the number of customers arriving during a one-minute period.

x	Probability
0	.1353
1	.2707
2	.2707
3	.1804
4	.0902
5 or more	.0527

Discrete probability distributions, such as the one used by Citibank, are the topic of this chapter. In addition to the Poisson distribution, you will learn about the binomial and hypergeometric distributions and how they can be used to provide helpful probability information.

In this chapter we continue the study of probability by introducing the concepts of random variables and probability distributions. The focus of this chapter is discrete probability distributions. Three special discrete probability distributions—the binomial, Poisson, and hypergeometric—are covered.

5.1 Random Variables

In Chapter 4 we defined the concept of an experiment and its associated experimental outcomes. A random variable provides a means for describing experimental outcomes using numerical values. Random variables must assume numerical values.

> **RANDOM VARIABLE**
>
> A **random variable** is a numerical description of the outcome of an experiment.

Random variables must assume numerical values.

In effect, a random variable associates a numerical value with each possible experimental outcome. The particular numerical value of the random variable depends on the outcome of the experiment. A random variable can be classified as being either *discrete* or *continuous* depending on the numerical values it assumes.

Discrete Random Variables

A random variable that may assume either a finite number of values or an infinite sequence of values such as 0, 1, 2, . . . is referred to as a **discrete random variable**. For example, consider the experiment of an accountant taking the certified public accountant (CPA) examination. The examination has four parts. We can define a random variable as x = the number of parts of the CPA examination passed. It is a discrete random variable because it may assume the finite number of values 0, 1, 2, 3, or 4.

As another example of a discrete random variable, consider the experiment of cars arriving at a tollbooth. The random variable of interest is x = the number of cars arriving during a one-day period. The possible values for x come from the sequence of integers 0, 1, 2, and so on. Hence, x is a discrete random variable assuming one of the values in this infinite sequence.

Although the outcomes of many experiments can naturally be described by numerical values, others cannot. For example, a survey question might ask an individual to recall the message in a recent television commercial. This experiment would have two possible outcomes: the individual cannot recall the message and the individual can recall the message. We can still describe these experimental outcomes numerically by defining the discrete random variable x as follows: let x = 0 if the individual cannot recall the message and x = 1 if the individual can recall the message. The numerical values for this random variable are arbitrary (we could use 5 and 10), but they are acceptable in terms of the definition of a random variable—namely, x is a random variable because it provides a numerical description of the outcome of the experiment.

Table 5.1 provides some additional examples of discrete random variables. Note that in each example the discrete random variable assumes a finite number of values or an infinite

TABLE 5.1   EXAMPLES OF DISCRETE RANDOM VARIABLES

Experiment	Random Variable (x)	Possible Values for the Random Variable
Contact five customers	Number of customers who place an order	0, 1, 2, 3, 4, 5
Inspect a shipment of 50 radios	Number of defective radios	0, 1, 2, . . . , 49, 50
Operate a restaurant for one day	Number of customers	0, 1, 2, 3, . . .
Sell an automobile	Gender of the customer	0 if male; 1 if female

sequence of values such as 0, 1, 2, ... These types of discrete random variables are discussed in detail in this chapter.

Continuous Random Variables

A random variable that may assume any numerical value in an interval or collection of intervals is called a **continuous random variable**. Experimental outcomes based on measurement scales such as time, weight, distance, and temperature can be described by continuous random variables. For example, consider an experiment of monitoring incoming telephone calls to the claims office of a major insurance company. Suppose the random variable of interest is x = the time between consecutive incoming calls in minutes. This random variable may assume any value in the interval $x \geq 0$. Actually, an infinite number of values are possible for x, including values such as 1.26 minutes, 2.751 minutes, 4.3333 minutes, and so on. As another example, consider a 90-mile section of interstate highway I-75 north of Atlanta, Georgia. For an emergency ambulance service located in Atlanta, we might define the random variable as x = number of miles to the location of the next traffic accident along this section of I-75. In this case, x would be a continuous random variable assuming any value in the interval $0 \leq x \leq 90$. Additional examples of continuous random variables are listed in Table 5.2. Note that each example describes a random variable that may assume any value in an interval of values. Continuous random variables and their probability distributions will be the topic of Chapter 6.

TABLE 5.2   EXAMPLES OF CONTINUOUS RANDOM VARIABLES

Experiment	Random Variable (x)	Possible Values for the Random Variable
Operate a bank	Time between customer arrivals in minutes	$x \geq 0$
Fill a soft drink can (max = 12.1 ounces)	Number of ounces	$0 \leq x \leq 12.1$
Construct a new library	Percentage of project complete after six months	$0 \leq x \leq 100$
Test a new chemical process	Temperature when the desired reaction takes place (min 150° F; max 212° F)	$150 \leq x \leq 212$

NOTES AND COMMENTS

One way to determine whether a random variable is discrete or continuous is to think of the values of the random variable as points on a line segment. Choose two points representing values of the random variable. If the entire line segment between the two points also represents possible values for the random variable, then the random variable is continuous.

Exercises

Methods

1. Consider the experiment of tossing a coin twice.
   a. List the experimental outcomes.
   b. Define a random variable that represents the number of heads occurring on the two tosses.
   c. Show what value the random variable would assume for each of the experimental outcomes.
   d. Is this random variable discrete or continuous?

2. Consider the experiment of a worker assembling a product.
   a. Define a random variable that represents the time in minutes required to assemble the product.
   b. What values may the random variable assume?
   c. Is the random variable discrete or continuous?

Applications

3. Three students scheduled interviews for summer employment at the Brookwood Institute. In each case the interview results in either an offer for a position or no offer. Experimental outcomes are defined in terms of the results of the three interviews.
   a. List the experimental outcomes.
   b. Define a random variable that represents the number of offers made. Is the random variable continuous?
   c. Show the value of the random variable for each of the experimental outcomes.

4. In November the U.S. unemployment rate was 4.5% (*USA Today,* January 4, 2007). The Census Bureau includes nine states in the Northeast region. Assume that the random variable of interest is the number of Northeastern states with an unemployment rate in November that was less than 4.5%. What values may this random variable assume?

5. To perform a certain type of blood analysis, lab technicians must perform two procedures. The first procedure requires either one or two separate steps, and the second procedure requires either one, two, or three steps.
   a. List the experimental outcomes associated with performing the blood analysis.
   b. If the random variable of interest is the total number of steps required to do the complete analysis (both procedures), show what value the random variable will assume for each of the experimental outcomes.

6. Listed is a series of experiments and associated random variables. In each case, identify the values that the random variable can assume and state whether the random variable is discrete or continuous.

Experiment	Random Variable (x)
a. Take a 20-question examination	Number of questions answered correctly
b. Observe cars arriving at a tollbooth for 1 hour	Number of cars arriving at tollbooth
c. Audit 50 tax returns	Number of returns containing errors
d. Observe an employee's work	Number of nonproductive hours in an eight-hour workday
e. Weigh a shipment of goods	Number of pounds

5.2 Discrete Probability Distributions

The **probability distribution** for a random variable describes how probabilities are distributed over the values of the random variable. For a discrete random variable x, the probability distribution is defined by a **probability function**, denoted by $f(x)$. The probability function provides the probability for each value of the random variable.

As an illustration of a discrete random variable and its probability distribution, consider the sales of automobiles at DiCarlo Motors in Saratoga, New York. Over the past 300 days of operation, sales data show 54 days with no automobiles sold, 117 days with 1 automobile sold, 72 days with 2 automobiles sold, 42 days with 3 automobiles sold, 12 days with 4 automobiles sold, and 3 days with 5 automobiles sold. Suppose we consider the experiment of selecting a day of operation at DiCarlo Motors and define the random variable of interest as $x =$ the number of automobiles sold during a day. From historic data, we know

x is a discrete random variable that can assume the values 0, 1, 2, 3, 4, or 5. In probability function notation, $f(0)$ provides the probability of 0 automobiles sold, $f(1)$ provides the probability of 1 automobile sold, and so on. Because historic data show 54 of 300 days with 0 automobiles sold, we assign the value $54/300 = .18$ to $f(0)$, indicating that the probability of 0 automobiles being sold during a day is .18. Similarly, because 117 of 300 days had 1 automobile sold, we assign the value $117/300 = .39$ to $f(1)$, indicating that the probability of exactly 1 automobile being sold during a day is .39. Continuing in this way for the other values of the random variable, we compute the values for $f(2), f(3), f(4)$, and $f(5)$ as shown in Table 5.3, the probability distribution for the number of automobiles sold during a day at DiCarlo Motors.

A primary advantage of defining a random variable and its probability distribution is that once the probability distribution is known, it is relatively easy to determine the probability of a variety of events that may be of interest to a decision maker. For example, using the probability distribution for DiCarlo Motors as shown in Table 5.3, we see that the most probable number of automobiles sold during a day is 1 with a probability of $f(1) = .39$. In addition, there is an $f(3) + f(4) + f(5) = .14 + .04 + .01 = .19$ probability of selling three or more automobiles during a day. These probabilities, plus others the decision maker may ask about, provide information that can help the decision maker understand the process of selling automobiles at DiCarlo Motors.

In the development of a probability function for any discrete random variable, the following two conditions must be satisfied.

These conditions are the analogs to the two basic requirements for assigning probabilities to experimental outcomes presented in Chapter 4.

REQUIRED CONDITIONS FOR A DISCRETE PROBABILITY FUNCTION

$$f(x) \geq 0 \tag{5.1}$$

$$\Sigma f(x) = 1 \tag{5.2}$$

Table 5.3 shows that the probabilities for the random variable x satisfy equation (5.1); $f(x)$ is greater than or equal to 0 for all values of x. In addition, because the probabilities sum to 1, equation (5.2) is satisfied. Thus, the DiCarlo Motors probability function is a valid discrete probability function.

We can also present probability distributions graphically. In Figure 5.1 the values of the random variable x for DiCarlo Motors are shown on the horizontal axis and the probability associated with these values is shown on the vertical axis.

In addition to tables and graphs, a formula that gives the probability function, $f(x)$, for every value of x is often used to describe probability distributions. The simplest example of

TABLE 5.3 PROBABILITY DISTRIBUTION FOR THE NUMBER OF AUTOMOBILES SOLD DURING A DAY AT DICARLO MOTORS

x	$f(x)$
0	.18
1	.39
2	.24
3	.14
4	.04
5	.01
Total	1.00

FIGURE 5.1   GRAPHICAL REPRESENTATION OF THE PROBABILITY DISTRIBUTION FOR THE NUMBER OF AUTOMOBILES SOLD DURING A DAY AT DICARLO MOTORS

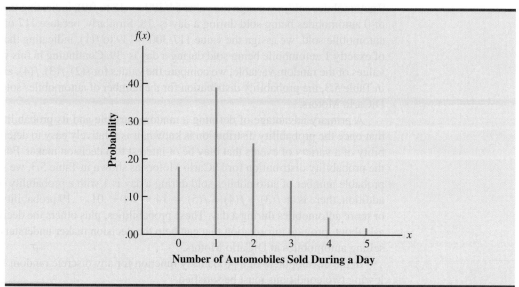

a discrete probability distribution given by a formula is the **discrete uniform probability distribution**. Its probability function is defined by equation (5.3).

DISCRETE UNIFORM PROBABILITY FUNCTION

$$f(x) = 1/n \qquad (5.3)$$

where

$$n = \text{the number of values the random variable may assume}$$

For example, suppose that for the experiment of rolling a die we define the random variable x to be the number of dots on the upward face. For this experiment, $n = 6$ values are possible for the random variable; $x = 1, 2, 3, 4, 5, 6$. Thus, the probability function for this discrete uniform random variable is

$$f(x) = 1/6 \qquad x = 1, 2, 3, 4, 5, 6$$

The possible values of the random variable and the associated probabilities are shown.

x	$f(x)$
1	1/6
2	1/6
3	1/6
4	1/6
5	1/6
6	1/6

As another example, consider the random variable x with the following discrete probability distribution.

x	$f(x)$
1	1/10
2	2/10
3	3/10
4	4/10

This probability distribution can be defined by the formula

$$f(x) = \frac{x}{10} \qquad \text{for } x = 1, 2, 3, \text{ or } 4$$

Evaluating $f(x)$ for a given value of the random variable will provide the associated probability. For example, using the preceding probability function, we see that $f(2) = 2/10$ provides the probability that the random variable assumes a value of 2.

The more widely used discrete probability distributions generally are specified by formulas. Three important cases are the binomial, Poisson, and hypergeometric distributions; these distributions are discussed later in the chapter.

Exercises

Methods

7. The probability distribution for the random variable x follows.

x	$f(x)$
20	.20
25	.15
30	.25
35	.40

a. Is this probability distribution valid? Explain. yes
b. What is the probability that $x = 30$?
c. What is the probability that x is less than or equal to 25?
d. What is the probability that x is greater than 30?

Applications

8. The following data were collected by counting the number of operating rooms in use at Tampa General Hospital over a 20-day period: On 3 of the days only one operating room was used, on 5 of the days two were used, on 8 of the days three were used, and on 4 days all four of the hospital's operating rooms were used.
    a. Use the relative frequency approach to construct a probability distribution for the number of operating rooms in use on any given day.
    b. Draw a graph of the probability distribution.
    c. Show that your probability distribution satisfies the required conditions for a valid discrete probability distribution.

9. Nationally, 38% of fourth-graders cannot read an age-appropriate book. The following data show the number of children, by age, identified as learning disabled under special education. Most of these children have reading problems that should be identified and corrected before third grade. Current federal law prohibits most children from receiving extra help from special education programs until they fall behind by approximately two years' worth of learning, and that typically means third grade or later (*USA Today*, September 6, 2001).

Age	Number of Children
6	37,369
7	87,436
8	160,840
9	239,719
10	286,719
11	306,533
12	310,787
13	302,604
14	289,168

Suppose that we want to select a sample of children identified as learning disabled under special education for a program designed to improve reading ability. Let x be a random variable indicating the age of one randomly selected child.
   a. Use the data to develop a probability distribution for x. Specify the values for the random variable and the corresponding values for the probability function $f(x)$.
   b. Draw a graph of the probability distribution.
   c. Show that the probability distribution satisfies equations (5.1) and (5.2).

10. Table 5.4 shows the percent frequency distributions of job satisfaction scores for a sample of information systems (IS) senior executives and IS middle managers. The scores range from a low of 1 (very dissatisfied) to a high of 5 (very satisfied).

TABLE 5.4   PERCENT FREQUENCY DISTRIBUTION OF JOB SATISFACTION SCORES FOR INFORMATION SYSTEMS EXECUTIVES AND MIDDLE MANAGERS

Job Satisfaction Score	IS Senior Executives (%)	IS Middle Managers (%)
1	5	4
2	9	10
3	3	12
4	42	46
5	41	28

   a. Develop a probability distribution for the job satisfaction score of a senior executive.
   b. Develop a probability distribution for the job satisfaction score of a middle manager.
   c. What is the probability a senior executive will report a job satisfaction score of 4 or 5?
   d. What is the probability a middle manager is very satisfied?
   e. Compare the overall job satisfaction of senior executives and middle managers.

11. A technician services mailing machines at companies in the Phoenix area. Depending on the type of malfunction, the service call can take 1, 2, 3, or 4 hours. The different types of malfunctions occur at about the same frequency.

    a. Develop a probability distribution for the duration of a service call.

    b. Draw a graph of the probability distribution.

    c. Show that your probability distribution satisfies the conditions required for a discrete probability function.

    d. What is the probability a service call will take three hours?

    e. A service call has just come in, but the type of malfunction is unknown. It is 3:00 P.M. and service technicians usually get off at 5:00 P.M. What is the probability the service technician will have to work overtime to fix the machine today?

12. The nation's two biggest cable providers are Comcast Cable Communications, with 21.5 million subscribers, and Time Warner Cable, with 11.0 million subscribers (*The New York Times 2007 Almanac*). Suppose that the management of Time Warner Cable subjectively assessed a probability distribution for x, the number of new subscribers they will obtain over the next year in the state of New York, as follows:

x	$f(x)$
100,000	.10
200,000	.20
300,000	.25
400,000	.30
500,000	.10
600,000	.05

    a. Is this probability distribution valid? Explain.

    b. What is the probability Time Warner will obtain more than 400,000 new subscribers?

    c. What is the probability Time Warner will obtain fewer than 200,000 new subscribers?

13. A psychologist determined that the number of sessions required to obtain the trust of a new patient is either 1, 2, or 3. Let x be a random variable indicating the number of sessions required to gain the patient's trust. The following probability function has been proposed.

$$f(x) = \frac{x}{6} \qquad \text{for } x = 1, 2, \text{ or } 3$$

    a. Is this probability function valid? Explain.

    b. What is the probability that it takes exactly 2 sessions to gain the patient's trust?

    c. What is the probability that it takes at least 2 sessions to gain the patient's trust?

14. The following table is a partial probability distribution for the MRA Company's projected profits (x = profit in \$1000s) for the first year of operation (the negative value denotes a loss).

x	$f(x)$
−100	.10
0	.20
50	.30
100	.25
150	.10
200	

    a. What is the proper value for $f(200)$? What is your interpretation of this value?

    b. What is the probability that MRA will be profitable?

    c. What is the probability that MRA will make at least \$100,000?

5.3 Expected Value and Variance

Expected Value

The **expected value**, or mean, of a random variable is a measure of the central location for the random variable. The formula for the expected value of a discrete random variable x follows.

The expected value is a weighted average of the values the random variable may assume. The weights are the probabilities.

> **EXPECTED VALUE OF A DISCRETE RANDOM VARIABLE**
>
> $$E(x) = \mu = \Sigma x f(x) \tag{5.4}$$

Both the notations $E(x)$ and μ are used to denote the expected value of a random variable.

Equation (5.4) shows that to compute the expected value of a discrete random variable, we must multiply each value of the random variable by the corresponding probability $f(x)$ and then add the resulting products. Using the DiCarlo Motors automobile sales example from Section 5.2, we show the calculation of the expected value for the number of automobiles sold during a day in Table 5.5. The sum of the entries in the $xf(x)$ column shows that the expected value is 1.50 automobiles per day. We therefore know that although sales of 0, 1, 2, 3, 4, or 5 automobiles are possible on any one day, over time DiCarlo can anticipate selling an average of 1.50 automobiles per day. Assuming 30 days of operation during a month, we can use the expected value of 1.50 to forecast average monthly sales of $30(1.50) = 45$ automobiles.

The expected value does not have to be a value the random variable can assume.

Variance

Even though the expected value provides the mean value for the random variable, we often need a measure of variability, or dispersion. Just as we used the variance in Chapter 3 to summarize the variability in data, we now use **variance** to summarize the variability in the values of a random variable. The formula for the variance of a discrete random variable follows.

The variance is a weighted average of the squared deviations of a random variable from its mean. The weights are the probabilities.

> **VARIANCE OF A DISCRETE RANDOM VARIABLE**
>
> $$\text{Var}(x) = \sigma^2 = \Sigma(x - \mu)^2 f(x) \tag{5.5}$$

TABLE 5.5   CALCULATION OF THE EXPECTED VALUE FOR THE NUMBER OF AUTOMOBILES SOLD DURING A DAY AT DICARLO MOTORS

x	$f(x)$	$xf(x)$
0	.18	$0(.18) =$ .00
1	.39	$1(.39) =$ .39
2	.24	$2(.24) =$ .48
3	.14	$3(.14) =$ .42
4	.04	$4(.04) =$ .16
5	.01	$5(.01) =$ .05
		1.50

$$E(x) = \mu = \Sigma x f(x)$$

TABLE 5.6   CALCULATION OF THE VARIANCE FOR THE NUMBER OF AUTOMOBILES
             SOLD DURING A DAY AT DICARLO MOTORS

x _values_	$x - \mu$	$(x - \mu)^2$	_expected frequency_ $f(x)$	$(x - \mu)^2 f(x)$
0	$0 - 1.50 = -1.50$	2.25	.18	$2.25(.18) = .4050$
1	$1 - 1.50 = -.50$	.25	.39	$.25(.39) = .0975$
2	$2 - 1.50 = .50$	.25	.24	$.25(.24) = .0600$
3	$3 - 1.50 = 1.50$	2.25	.14	$2.25(.14) = .3150$
4	$4 - 1.50 = 2.50$	6.25	.04	$6.25(.04) = .2500$
5	$5 - 1.50 = 3.50$	12.25	.01	$12.25(.01) = .1225$
				$\overline{1.2500}$

$$\sigma^2 = \Sigma(x - \mu)^2 f(x)$$

As equation (5.5) shows, an essential part of the variance formula is the deviation, $x - \mu$, which measures how far a particular value of the random variable is from the expected value, or mean, μ. In computing the variance of a random variable, the deviations are squared and then weighted by the corresponding value of the probability function. The sum of these weighted squared deviations for all values of the random variable is referred to as the *variance*. The notations Var(x) and σ^2 are both used to denote the variance of a random variable.

The calculation of the variance for the probability distribution of the number of automobiles sold during a day at DiCarlo Motors is summarized in Table 5.6. We see that the variance is 1.25. The **standard deviation**, σ, is defined as the positive square root of the variance. Thus, the standard deviation for the number of automobiles sold during a day is

$$\sigma = \sqrt{1.25} = 1.118$$

The standard deviation is measured in the same units as the random variable ($\sigma = 1.118$ automobiles) and therefore is often preferred in describing the variability of a random variable. The variance σ^2 is measured in squared units and is thus more difficult to interpret.

Using Excel to Compute the Expected Value, Variance, and Standard Deviation

The calculations involved in computing the expected value and variance for a discrete random variable can easily be made in an Excel worksheet. One approach is to enter the formulas necessary to make the calculations in Tables 5.5 and 5.6. An easier way, however, is to make use of Excel's SUMPRODUCT function. In this subsection we show how to use the SUMPRODUCT function to compute the expected value and variance for daily automobile sales at DiCarlo Motors. Refer to Figure 5.2 as we describe the tasks involved. The formula worksheet is in the background; the value worksheet is in the foreground.

Enter Data: The data needed are the values for the random variable and the corresponding probabilities. Labels, values for the random variable, and the corresponding probabilities are entered in cells A1:B7.

Enter Functions and Formulas: The SUMPRODUCT function multiplies each value in one range by the corresponding value in another range and sums the products. To use the SUMPRODUCT function to compute the expected value of daily automobile sales at DiCarlo Motors, we entered the following formula into cell B9:

$$=\text{SUMPRODUCT(A2:A7,B2:B7)}$$

FIGURE 5.2 EXCEL WORKSHEET FOR EXPECTED VALUE, VARIANCE, AND STANDARD DEVIATION

	A	B	C	D
1	Sales	Probability	Sq Dev from Mean	
2	0	0.18	=(A2-$B$9)^2	
3	1	0.39	=(A3-$B$9)^2	
4	2	0.24	=(A4-$B$9)^2	
5	3	0.14	=(A5-$B$9)^2	
6	4	0.04	=(A6-$B$9)^2	
7	5	0.01	=(A7-$B$9)^2	
8				
9	Expected Value	=SUMPRODUCT(A2:A7,B2:B7)		
10				
11	Variance	=SUMPRODUCT(C2:C7,B2:B7)		
12				
13	Std Deviation	=SQRT(B11)		
14				

	A	B	C	D
1	Sales	Probability	Sq Dev from Mean	
2	0	0.18	2.25	
3	1	0.39	0.25	
4	2	0.24	0.25	
5	3	0.14	2.25	
6	4	0.04	6.25	
7	5	0.01	12.25	
8				
9	Expected Value	1.5		
10				
11	Variance	1.25		
12				
13	Std Deviation	1.118034		
14				

Note that the first range, A2:A7, contains the values for the random variable, daily automobile sales. The second range, B2:B7, contains the corresponding probabilities. Thus, the SUMPRODUCT function in cell B9 is computing A2*B2 + A3*B3 + A4*B4 + A5*B5 + A6*B6 + A7*B7; hence, it is applying the formula in equation (5.4) to compute the expected value. The result, shown in cell B9 of the value worksheet, is 1.5.

The formulas in cells C2:C7 are used to compute the squared deviations from the expected value or mean of 1.5 (the mean is in cell B9). The results, shown in the value worksheet, are the same as the results shown in Table 5.6. The formula necessary to compute the variance for daily automobile sales was entered into cell B11. It uses the SUMPRODUCT function to multiply each value in the range C2:C7 by each corresponding value in the range B2:B7 and sums the products. The result, shown in the value worksheet, is 1.25. Because the standard deviation is the square root of the variance, we entered the formula =SQRT(B11) into cell B13 to compute the standard deviation for daily automobile sales. The result, shown in the value worksheet, is 1.118034.

Exercises

Methods

15. The following table provides a probability distribution for the random variable x.

x	$f(x)$
3	.25
6	.50
9	.25

a. Compute $E(x)$, the expected value of x.
b. Compute σ^2, the variance of x.
c. Compute σ, the standard deviation of x.

16. The following table provides a probability distribution for the random variable *y*.

y	$f(y)$
2	.20
4	.30
7	.40
8	.10

   a. Compute $E(y)$.
   b. Compute $\text{Var}(y)$ and σ.

Applications

17. A volunteer ambulance service handles 0 to 5 service calls on any given day. The probability distribution for the number of service calls is as follows.

Number of Service Calls	Probability	Number of Service Calls	Probability
0	.10	3	.20
1	.15	4	.15
2	.30	5	.10

   a. What is the expected number of service calls?
   b. What is the variance in the number of service calls? What is the standard deviation?

18. The American Housing Survey reported the following data on the number of bedrooms in owner-occupied and renter-occupied houses in central cities (*http://www.census.gov*, March 31, 2003).

	Number of Houses (1000s)	
Bedrooms	**Renter-Occupied**	**Owner-Occupied**
0	547	23
1	5012	541
2	6100	3832
3	2644	8690
4 or more	557	3783

   a. Define a random variable x = number of bedrooms in renter-occupied houses and develop a probability distribution for the random variable. (Let $x = 4$ represent 4 or more bedrooms.)
   b. Compute the expected value and variance for the number of bedrooms in renter-occupied houses.
   c. Define a random variable y = number of bedrooms in owner-occupied houses and develop a probability distribution for the random variable. (Let $y = 4$ represent 4 or more bedrooms.)
   d. Compute the expected value and variance for the number of bedrooms in owner-occupied houses.
   e. What observations can you make from a comparison of the number of bedrooms in renter-occupied versus owner-occupied homes?

19. The National Basketball Association (NBA) records a variety of statistics for each team. Two of these statistics are the percentage of field goals made by the team and the percentage of three-point shots made by the team. For a portion of the 2004 season, the shooting records of the 29 teams in the NBA showed the probability of scoring two points by making

a field goal was .44, and the probability of scoring three points by making a three-point shot was .34 (*http://www.nba.com,* January 3, 2004).

a. What is the expected value of a two-point shot for these teams?

b. What is the expected value of a three-point shot for these teams?

c. If the probability of making a two-point shot is greater than the probability of making a three-point shot, why do coaches allow some players to shoot the three-point shot if they have the opportunity? Use expected value to explain your answer.

20. The probability distribution for damage claims paid by the Newton Automobile Insurance Company on collision insurance follows.

Payment ($)	Probability
0	.85
500	.04
1000	.04
3000	.03
5000	.02
8000	.01
10000	.01

a. Use the expected collision payment to determine the collision insurance premium that would enable the company to break even.

b. The insurance company charges an annual rate of $520 for the collision coverage. What is the expected value of the collision policy for a policyholder? (*Hint:* It is the expected payments from the company minus the cost of coverage.) Why does the policyholder purchase a collision policy with this expected value?

21. The following probability distributions of job satisfaction scores for a sample of information systems (IS) senior executives and IS middle managers range from a low of 1 (very dissatisfied) to a high of 5 (very satisfied).

	Probability	
Job Satisfaction Score	IS Senior Executives	IS Middle Managers
1	.05	.04
2	.09	.10
3	.03	.12
4	.42	.46
5	.41	.28

a. What is the expected value of the job satisfaction score for senior executives?

b. What is the expected value of the job satisfaction score for middle managers?

c. Compute the variance of job satisfaction scores for executives and middle managers.

d. Compute the standard deviation of job satisfaction scores for both probability distributions.

e. Compare the overall job satisfaction of senior executives and middle managers.

22. The demand for a product of Carolina Industries varies greatly from month to month. The probability distribution in the following table, based on the past two years of data, shows the company's monthly demand.

Unit Demand	Probability
300	.20
400	.30
500	.35
600	.15

a. If the company bases monthly orders on the expected value of the monthly demand, what should Carolina's monthly order quantity be for this product?

b. Assume that each unit demanded generates $70 in revenue and that each unit ordered costs $50. How much will the company gain or lose in a month if it places an order based on your answer to part (a) and the actual demand for the item is 300 units?

23. The 2002 New York City Housing and Vacancy Survey showed a total of 59,324 rent-controlled housing units and 236,263 rent-stabilized units built in 1947 or later. For these rental units, the probability distributions for the number of persons living in the unit are given (*http://www.census.gov*, January 12, 2004).

Number of Persons	Rent-Controlled	Rent-Stabilized
1	.61	.41
2	.27	.30
3	.07	.14
4	.04	.11
5	.01	.03
6	.00	.01

a. What is the expected value of the number of persons living in each type of unit?

b. What is the variance of the number of persons living in each type of unit?

c. Make some comparisons between the number of persons living in rent-controlled units and the number of persons living in rent-stabilized units.

24. The J. R. Ryland Computer Company is considering a plant expansion to enable the company to begin production of a new computer product. The company's president must determine whether to make the expansion a medium- or large-scale project. Demand for the new product is uncertain, which for planning purposes may be low demand, medium demand, or high demand. The probability estimates for demand are .20, .50, and .30, respectively. Letting x and y indicate the annual profit in thousands of dollars, the firm's planners developed the following profit forecasts for the medium- and large-scale expansion projects.

		Medium-Scale Expansion Profit		Large-Scale Expansion Profit	
		x	$f(x)$	y	$f(y)$
	Low	50	.20	0	.20
Demand	Medium	150	.50	100	.50
	High	200	.30	300	.30

a. Compute the expected value for the profit associated with the two expansion alternatives. Which decision is preferred for the objective of maximizing the expected profit?

b. Compute the variance for the profit associated with the two expansion alternatives. Which decision is preferred for the objective of minimizing the risk or uncertainty?

5.4 Binomial Probability Distribution

The binomial probability distribution is a discrete probability distribution that has many applications. It is associated with a multiple-step experiment that we call the binomial experiment.

A Binomial Experiment

A **binomial experiment** exhibits the following four properties.

> **PROPERTIES OF A BINOMIAL EXPERIMENT**
>
> 1. The experiment consists of a sequence of n identical trials.
> 2. Two outcomes are possible on each trial. We refer to one outcome as a *success* and the other outcome as a *failure*.
> 3. The probability of a success, denoted by p, does not change from trial to trial. Consequently, the probability of a failure, denoted by $1 - p$, does not change from trial to trial.
> 4. The trials are independent.

Jakob Bernoulli (1654–1705), the first of the Bernoulli family of Swiss mathematicians, published a treatise on probability that contained the theory of permutations and combinations, as well as the binomial theorem.

If properties 2, 3, and 4 are present, we say the trials are generated by a Bernoulli process. If, in addition, property 1 is present, we say we have a binomial experiment. Figure 5.3 depicts one possible sequence of successes and failures for a binomial experiment involving eight trials.

In a binomial experiment, our interest is in the *number of successes occurring in the n trials*. If we let x denote the number of successes occurring in the n trials, we see that x can assume the values of 0, 1, 2, 3, . . . , n. Because the number of values is finite, x is a *discrete* random variable. The probability distribution associated with this random variable is called the **binomial probability distribution**. For example, consider the experiment of tossing a coin five times and on each toss observing whether the coin lands with a head or a tail on its upward face. Suppose we want to count the number of heads appearing over the five tosses. Does this experiment show the properties of a binomial experiment? What is the random variable of interest? Note that

1. The experiment consists of five identical trials; each trial involves the tossing of one coin.
2. Two outcomes are possible for each trial: a head or a tail. We can designate head a success and tail a failure.
3. The probability of a head and the probability of a tail are the same for each trial, with $p = .5$ and $1 - p = .5$.
4. The trials or tosses are independent because the outcome on any one trial is not affected by what happens on other trials or tosses.

FIGURE 5.3   ONE POSSIBLE SEQUENCE OF SUCCESSES AND FAILURES FOR AN EIGHT-TRIAL BINOMIAL EXPERIMENT

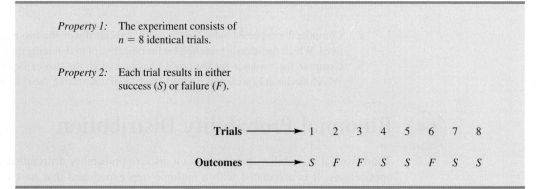

Property 1:   The experiment consists of $n = 8$ identical trials.

Property 2:   Each trial results in either success (S) or failure (F).

Trials ⟶ 1   2   3   4   5   6   7   8

Outcomes ⟶ S F F S S F S S

Checking the properties PS. 222

Thus, the properties of a binomial experiment are satisfied. The random variable of interest is $x =$ the number of heads appearing in the five trials. In this case, x can assume the values of 0, 1, 2, 3, 4, or 5.

As another example, consider an insurance salesperson who visits 10 randomly selected families. The outcome associated with each visit is classified as a success if the family purchases an insurance policy and a failure if the family does not. From past experience, the salesperson knows the probability that a randomly selected family will purchase an insurance policy is .10. Checking the properties of a binomial experiment, we observe that

1. The experiment consists of 10 identical trials; each trial involves contacting one family.
2. Two outcomes are possible on each trial: the family purchases a policy (success) or the family does not purchase a policy (failure).
3. The probabilities of a purchase and a nonpurchase are assumed to be the same for each sales call, with $p = .10$ and $1 - p = .90$.
4. The trials are independent because the families are randomly selected.

Because the four assumptions are satisfied, this example is a binomial experiment. The random variable of interest is the number of sales obtained in contacting the 10 families. In this case, x can assume the values of 0, 1, 2, 3, 4, 5, 6, 7, 8, 9, and 10.

Property 3 of the binomial experiment is called the *stationarity assumption* and is sometimes confused with property 4, independence of trials. To see how they differ, consider again the case of the salesperson calling on families to sell insurance policies. If, as the day wore on, the salesperson got tired and lost enthusiasm, the probability of success (selling a policy) might drop to .05, for example, by the tenth call. In such a case, property 3 (stationarity) would not be satisfied, and we would not have a binomial experiment. Even if property 4 held—that is, the purchase decisions of each family were made independently—it would not be a binomial experiment if property 3 was not satisfied.

In applications involving binomial experiments, a special mathematical formula, called the *binomial probability function,* can be used to compute the probability of x successes in the n trials. Using probability concepts introduced in Chapter 4, we will show in the context of an illustrative problem how the formula can be developed.

Martin Clothing Store Problem

Let us consider the purchase decisions of the next three customers who enter the Martin Clothing Store. On the basis of past experience, the store manager estimates the probability that any one customer will make a purchase is .30. What is the probability that two of the next three customers will make a purchase?

Using a tree diagram (Figure 5.4), we can see that the experiment of observing the three customers each making a purchase decision has eight possible outcomes. Using S to denote success (a purchase) and F to denote failure (no purchase), we are interested in experimental outcomes involving two successes in the three trials (purchase decisions). Next, let us verify that the experiment involving the sequence of three purchase decisions can be viewed as a binomial experiment. Checking the four requirements for a binomial experiment, we note that

1. The experiment can be described as a sequence of three identical trials, one trial for each of the three customers who will enter the store.
2. Two outcomes—the customer makes a purchase (success) or the customer does not make a purchase (failure)—are possible for each trial.
3. The probability that the customer will make a purchase (.30) or will not make a purchase (.70) is assumed to be the same for all customers.
4. The purchase decision of each customer is independent of the decisions of the other customers.

FIGURE 5.4   TREE DIAGRAM FOR THE MARTIN CLOTHING STORE PROBLEM

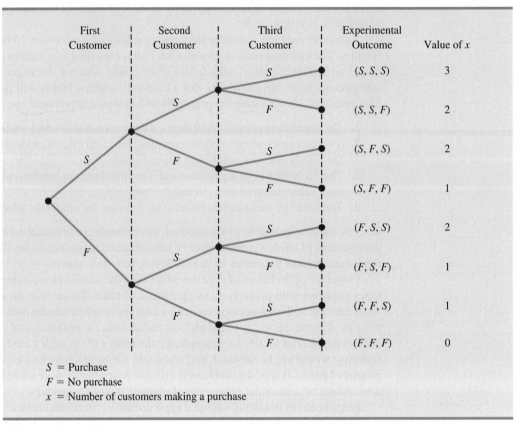

S = Purchase
F = No purchase
x = Number of customers making a purchase

Hence, the properties of a binomial experiment are present.

The number of experimental outcomes resulting in exactly x successes in n trials can be computed using the following formula.[1]

NUMBER OF EXPERIMENTAL OUTCOMES PROVIDING EXACTLY x
SUCCESSES IN n TRIALS

$$\binom{n}{x} = \frac{n!}{x!(n-x)!} \tag{5.6}$$

where

$$n! = n(n-1)(n-2) \cdots (2)(1)$$

and, by definition,

$$0! = 1$$

Now let us return to the Martin Clothing Store experiment involving three customer purchase decisions. Equation (5.6) can be used to determine the number of experimental

---

[1]This formula, introduced in Chapter 4, determines the number of combinations of n objects selected x at a time. For the binomial experiment, this combinatorial formula provides the number of experimental outcomes (sequences of n trials) resulting in x successes.

outcomes involving two purchases; that is, the number of ways of obtaining $x = 2$ successes in the $n = 3$ trials. From equation (5.6) we have

$$\binom{n}{x} = \binom{3}{2} = \frac{3!}{2!(3-2)!} = \frac{(3)(2)(1)}{(2)(1)(1)} = \frac{6}{2} = 3$$

Equation (5.6) shows that three of the experimental outcomes yield two successes. From Figure 5.4 we see these three outcomes are denoted by (S, S, F), (S, F, S), and (F, S, S).

Using equation (5.6) to determine how many experimental outcomes have three successes (purchases) in the three trials, we obtain

$$\binom{n}{x} = \binom{3}{3} = \frac{3!}{3!(3-3)!} = \frac{3!}{3!0!} = \frac{(3)(2)(1)}{3(2)(1)(1)} = \frac{6}{6} = 1$$

From Figure 5.4 we see that the one experimental outcome with three successes is identified by (S, S, S).

We know that equation (5.6) can be used to determine the number of experimental outcomes that result in x successes. If we are to determine the probability of x successes in n trials, however, we must also know the probability associated with each of these experimental outcomes. Because the trials of a binomial experiment are independent, we can simply multiply the probabilities associated with each trial outcome to find the probability of a particular sequence of successes and failures.

The probability of purchases by the first two customers and no purchase by the third customer, denoted (S, S, F), is given by

$$pp(1-p)$$

With a .30 probability of a purchase on any one trial, the probability of a purchase on the first two trials and no purchase on the third is given by

$$(.30)(.30)(.70) = (.30)^2(.70) = .063$$

Two other experimental outcomes also result in two successes and one failure. The probabilities for all three experimental outcomes involving two successes follow.

	Trial Outcomes			Probability of
1st Customer	**2nd Customer**	**3rd Customer**	**Experimental Outcome**	**Experimental Outcome**
Purchase	Purchase	No purchase	(S, S, F)	$pp(1-p) = p^2(1-p)$ $= (.30)^2(.70) = .063$
Purchase	No purchase	Purchase	(S, F, S)	$p(1-p)p = p^2(1-p)$ $= (.30)^2(.70) = .063$
No purchase	Purchase	Purchase	(F, S, S)	$(1-p)pp = p^2(1-p)$ $= (.30)^2(.70) = .063$

Observe that all three experimental outcomes with two successes have exactly the same probability. This observation holds in general. In any binomial experiment, all sequences of trial outcomes yielding x successes in n trials have the *same probability* of occurrence. The probability of each sequence of trials yielding x successes in n trials follows.

Probability of a particular
sequence of trial outcomes $= p^x(1 - p)^{(n-x)}$ **(5.7)**
with x successes in n trials

For the Martin Clothing Store, this formula shows that any experimental outcome with two successes has a probability of $p^2(1 - p)^{(3-2)} = p^2(1 - p)^1 = (.30)^2(.70)^1 = .063$.

Because equation (5.6) shows the number of outcomes in a binomial experiment with x successes and equation (5.7) gives the probability for each sequence involving x successes, we combine equations (5.6) and (5.7) to obtain the following **binomial probability function**.

BINOMIAL PROBABILITY FUNCTION

$$f(x) = \binom{n}{x} p^x(1 - p)^{(n-x)} \qquad \textbf{(5.8)}$$

where

$f(x)$ = the probability of x successes in n trials

n = the number of trials

$\binom{n}{x} = \dfrac{n!}{x!(n - x)!}$

p = the probability of a success on any one trial

$1 - p$ = the probability of a failure on any one trial

In the Martin Clothing Store example, let us compute the probability that no customer makes a purchase, exactly one customer makes a purchase, exactly two customers make a purchase, and all three customers make a purchase. The calculations are summarized in Table 5.7, which gives the probability distribution of the number of customers making a purchase. Figure 5.5 is a graph of this probability distribution.

The binomial probability function can be applied to *any* binomial experiment. If we are satisfied that a situation demonstrates the properties of a binomial experiment and if we know the values of n and p, we can use equation (5.8) to compute the probability of x successes in the n trials.

TABLE 5.7   PROBABILITY DISTRIBUTION FOR THE NUMBER OF CUSTOMERS MAKING A PURCHASE

x	$f(x)$
0	$\dfrac{3!}{0!3!}(.30)^0(.70)^3 = .343$
1	$\dfrac{3!}{1!2!}(.30)^1(.70)^2 = .441$
2	$\dfrac{3!}{2!1!}(.30)^2(.70)^1 = .189$
3	$\dfrac{3!}{3!0!}(.30)^3(.70)^0 = \underline{.027}$
	1.000

FIGURE 5.5   GRAPHICAL REPRESENTATION OF THE PROBABILITY DISTRIBUTION
FOR THE NUMBER OF CUSTOMERS MAKING A PURCHASE

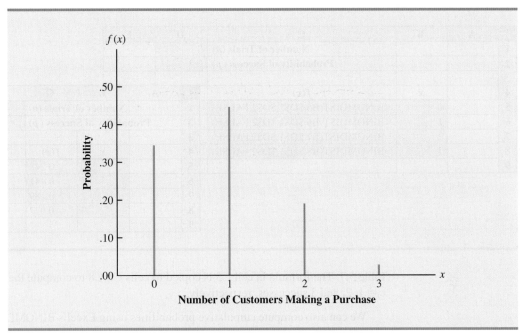

If we consider variations of the Martin experiment, such as 10 customers rather than 3 entering the store, the binomial probability function given by equation (5.8) is still applicable. Suppose we have a binomial experiment with $n = 10$, $x = 4$, and $p = .30$. The probability of making exactly four sales to 10 customers entering the store is

$$f(4) = \frac{10!}{4!6!}\,(.30)^4(.70)^6 = .2001$$

Using Excel to Compute Binomial Probabilities

For many probability functions that can be specified as formulas, Excel provides functions for computing probabilities and cumulative probabilities. In this section, we show how Excel's BINOMDIST function can be used to compute binomial probabilities and cumulative binomial probabilities. We begin by showing how to compute the binomial probabilities for the Martin Clothing Store example shown in Table 5.7. Refer to Figure 5.6 as we describe the tasks involved. The formula worksheet is in the background; the value worksheet is in the foreground.

Enter Data: In order to compute a binomial probability we must know the number of trials (n), the probability of success (p), and the value of the random variable (x). For the Martin Clothing Store example, the number of trials is 3; this value has been entered into cell D1. The probability of success is .3; this value has been entered into cell D2. Because we want to compute the probability for $x = 0$, 1, 2, and 3, these values were entered into cells B5:B8.

Enter Functions and Formulas: The BINOMDIST function has four inputs: the first is the value of x, the second is the value of n, the third is the value of p, and the fourth is FALSE or TRUE. We choose FALSE for the fourth input if a probability is desired and TRUE if a cumulative probability is desired. The formula =BINOMDIST(B5,$D$1,$D$2,FALSE) has been entered into cell C5 to compute the probability of 0 successes in 3 trials. Note in the value worksheet that the probability computed for $f(0)$, .343, is the same as that shown in

FIGURE 5.6 EXCEL WORKSHEET FOR COMPUTING BINOMIAL PROBABILITIES OF NUMBER OF CUSTOMERS MAKING A PURCHASE

	A	B	C	D	E
1			Number of Trials (*n*)	3	
2			Probability of Success (*p*)	0.3	
3					
4		*x*	*f(x)*		
5		0	=BINOMDIST(B5,$D$1,$D$2,FALSE)		
6		1	=BINOMDIST(B6,$D$1,$D$2,FALSE)		
7		2	=BINOMDIST(B7,$D$1,$D$2,FALSE)		
8		3	=BINOMDIST(B8,$D$1,$D$2,FALSE)		
9					

	A	B	C	D	E
1		Number of Trials (*n*)		3	
2		Probability of Success (*p*)		0.3	
3					
4		*x*	*f(x)*		
5		0	0.343		
6		1	0.441		
7		2	0.189		
8		3	0.027		
9					

Table 5.7. The formula in cell C5 is copied to cells C6:C8 to compute the probabilities for *x* = 1, 2, and 3 successes, respectively.

We can also compute cumulative probabilities using Excel's BINOMDIST function. To illustrate, let us consider the case of 10 customers entering the Martin Clothing Store and compute the probabilities and cumulative probabilities for the number of customers making a purchase. Recall that the cumulative probability for *x* = 1 is the probability of 1 or fewer purchases, the cumulative probability for *x* = 2 is the probability of 2 or fewer purchases, and so on. So, the cumulative probability for *x* = 10 is 1. Refer to Figure 5.7 as we describe the tasks involved in computing these cumulative probabilities. The formula worksheet is in the background; the value worksheet is in the foreground.

Enter Data: We entered the number of trials (10) into cell D1, the probability of success (.3) into cell D2, and the values for the random variable into cells B5:B15.

FIGURE 5.7 EXCEL WORKSHEET FOR COMPUTING PROBABILITIES AND CUMULATIVE PROBABILITIES FOR NUMBER OF PURCHASES WITH 10 CUSTOMERS

	A	B	C	D	E
1			Number of Trials (*n*)	10	
2			Probability of Success (*p*)	0.3	
3					
4		*x*	*f(x)*	Cum Prob	
5		0	=BINOMDIST(B5,$D$1,$D$2,FALSE)	=BINOMDIST(B5,$D$1,$D$2,TRUE)	
6		1	=BINOMDIST(B6,$D$1,$D$2,FALSE)	=BINOMDIST(B6,$D$1,$D$2,TRUE)	
7		2	=BINOMDIST(B7,$D$1,$D$2,FALSE)	=BINOMDIST(B7,$D$1,$D$2,TRUE)	
8		3	=BINOMDIST(B8,$D$1,$D$2,FALSE)	=BINOMDIST(B8,$D$1,$D$2,TRUE)	
9		4	=BINOMDIST(B9,$D$1,$D$2,FALSE)	=BINOMDIST(B9,$D$1,$D$2,TRUE)	
10		5	=BINOMDIST(B10,$D$1,$D$2,FALSE)	=BINOMDIST(B10,$D$1,$D$2,TRUE)	
11		6	=BINOMDIST(B11,$D$1,$D$2,FALSE)	=BINOMDIST(B11,$D$1,$D$2,TRUE)	
12		7	=BINOMDIST(B12,$D$1,$D$2,FALSE)	=BINOMDIST(B12,$D$1,$D$2,TRUE)	
13		8	=BINOMDIST(B13,$D$1,$D$2,FALSE)	=BINOMDIST(B13,$D$1,$D$2,TRUE)	
14		9	=BINOMDIST(B14,$D$1,$D$2,FALSE)	=BINOMDIST(B14,$D$1,$D$2,TRUE)	
15		10	=BINOMDIST(B15,$D$1,$D$2,FALSE)	=BINOMDIST(B15,$D$1,$D$2,TRUE)	
16					

	A	B	C	D	E
1		Number of Trials (*n*)		10	
2		Probability of Success (*p*)		0.3	
3					
4		*x*	*f(x)*	Cum Prob	
5		0	0.0282	0.0282	
6		1	0.1211	0.1493	
7		2	0.2335	0.3828	
8		3	0.2668	0.6496	
9		4	0.2001	0.8497	
10		5	0.1029	0.9527	
11		6	0.0368	0.9894	
12		7	0.0090	0.9984	
13		8	0.0014	0.9999	
14		9	0.0001	1.0000	
15		10	0.0000	1.0000	
16					

Enter Functions and Formulas: The binomial probabilities for each value of the random variable are computed in column C and the cumulative probabilities are computed in column D. We entered the formula =BINOMDIST(B5,$D$1,$D$2,FALSE) into cell C5 to compute the probability of 0 successes in 10 trials. Note that we used FALSE as the fourth input in the BINOMDIST function. The probability (.0282) is shown in cell C5 of the value worksheet. The formula in cell C5 is simply copied to cells C6:C15 to compute the remaining probabilities.

To compute the cumulative probabilities we start by entering the formula =BINOMDIST(B5,$D$1,$D$2,TRUE) into cell D5. Note that we used TRUE as the fourth input in the BINOMDIST function. The formula in cell D5 is then copied to cells D6:D15 to compute the remaining cumulative probabilities. In cell D5 of the value worksheet we see that the cumulative probability for $x = 0$ is the same as the probability for $x = 0$. Each of the remaining cumulative probabilities is the sum of the previous cumulative probability and the individual probability in column C. For instance, the cumulative probability for $x = 4$ is given by .6496 + .2001 = .8497. Note also that the cumulative probability for $x = 10$ is 1. The cumulative probability of $x = 9$ is also 1 because the probability of $x = 10$ is zero (to four decimal places of accuracy).

Expected Value and Variance for the Binomial Distribution

In Section 5.3 we provided formulas for computing the expected value and variance of a discrete random variable. In the special case where the random variable has a binomial distribution with a known number of trials n and a known probability of success p, the general formulas for the expected value and variance can be simplified. The results follow.

EXPECTED VALUE AND VARIANCE FOR THE BINOMIAL DISTRIBUTION

$$E(x) = \mu = np \tag{5.9}$$
$$\mathrm{Var}(x) = \sigma^2 = np(1 - p) \tag{5.10}$$

For the Martin Clothing Store problem with three customers, we can use equation (5.9) to compute the expected number of customers who will make a purchase.

$$E(x) = np = 3(.30) = .9$$

Suppose that for the next month the Martin Clothing Store forecasts 1000 customers will enter the store. What is the expected number of customers who will make a purchase? The answer is $\mu = np = (1000)(.3) = 300$. Thus, to increase the expected number of purchases, Martin's must induce more customers to enter the store and/or somehow increase the probability that any individual customer will make a purchase after entering.

For the Martin Clothing Store problem with three customers, we see that the variance and standard deviation for the number of customers who will make a purchase are

$$\sigma^2 = np(1 - p) = 3(.3)(.7) = .63$$
$$\sigma = \sqrt{.63} = .79$$

For the next 1000 customers entering the store, the variance and standard deviation for the number of customers who will make a purchase are

$$\sigma^2 = np(1 - p) = 1000(.3)(.7) = 210$$
$$\sigma = \sqrt{210} = 14.49$$

NOTES AND COMMENTS

Statisticians have developed tables that give probabilities and cumulative probabilities for a binomial random variable. These tables can be found in some statistics textbooks. With modern calculators and the capability of the BINOMDIST function in Excel, such tables are unnecessary.

Exercises

Methods

25. Consider a binomial experiment with two trials and $p = .4$.
    a. Draw a tree diagram for this experiment (see Figure 5.4).
    b. Compute the probability of one success, $f(1)$.
    c. Compute $f(0)$.
    d. Compute $f(2)$.
    e. Compute the probability of at least one success.
    f. Compute the expected value, variance, and standard deviation.

26. Consider a binomial experiment with $n = 10$ and $p = .10$.
    a. Compute $f(0)$.
    b. Compute $f(2)$.
    c. Compute $P(x \leq 2)$.
    d. Compute $P(x \geq 1)$.
    e. Compute $E(x)$.
    f. Compute $\text{Var}(x)$ and σ.

27. Consider a binomial experiment with $n = 20$ and $p = .70$.
    a. Compute $f(12)$.
    b. Compute $f(16)$.
    c. Compute $P(x \geq 16)$.
    d. Compute $P(x \leq 15)$.
    e. Compute $E(x)$.
    f. Compute $\text{Var}(x)$ and σ.

Applications

28. A Harris Interactive survey for InterContinental Hotels & Resorts asked respondents, "When traveling internationally, do you generally venture out on your own to experience culture, or stick with your tour group and itineraries?" The survey found that 23% of the respondents stick with their tour group (*USA Today,* January 21, 2004).
    a. In a sample of 6 international travelers, what is the probability that 2 will stick with their tour group?
    b. In a sample of 6 international travelers, what is the probability that at least 2 will stick with their tour group?
    c. In a sample of 10 international travelers, what is the probability that none will stick with the tour group?

29. In San Francisco, 30% of workers take public transportation daily (*USA Today,* December 21, 2005).
    a. In a sample of 10 workers, what is the probability that exactly 3 workers take public transportation daily?
    b. In a sample of 10 workers, what is the probability that at least 3 workers take public transportation daily?

30. When a new machine is functioning properly, only 3% of the items produced are defective. Assume that we will randomly select two parts produced on the machine and that we are interested in the number of defective parts found.
    a. Describe the conditions under which this situation would be a binomial experiment.
    b. Draw a tree diagram similar to Figure 5.4 showing this problem as a two-trial experiment.
    c. How many experimental outcomes result in exactly one defect being found?
    d. Compute the probabilities associated with finding no defects, exactly one defect, and two defects.

31. Nine percent of undergraduate students carry credit card balances greater than $7000 (*Reader's Digest,* July 2002). Suppose 10 undergraduate students are selected randomly to be interviewed about credit card usage.
    a. Is the selection of 10 students a binomial experiment? Explain.
    b. What is the probability that 2 of the students will have a credit card balance greater than $7000?
    c. What is the probability that none will have a credit card balance greater than $7000?
    d. What is the probability that at least 3 will have a credit card balance greater than $7000?

32. Military radar and missile detection systems are designed to warn a country of an enemy attack. A reliability question is whether a detection system will be able to identify an attack and issue a warning. Assume that a particular detection system has a .90 probability of detecting a missile attack. Use the binomial probability distribution to answer the following questions.
    a. What is the probability that a single detection system will detect an attack?
    b. If two detection systems are installed in the same area and operate independently, what is the probability that at least one of the systems will detect the attack?
    c. If three systems are installed, what is the probability that at least one of the systems will detect the attack?
    d. Would you recommend that multiple detection systems be used? Explain.

33. Fifty percent of Americans believed the country was in a recession, even though technically the economy had not shown two straight quarters of negative growth (*BusinessWeek,* July 30, 2001). For a sample of 20 Americans, make the following calculations.
    a. Compute the probability that exactly 12 people believed the country was in a recession.
    b. Compute the probability that no more than 5 people believed the country was in a recession.
    c. How many people would you expect to say the country was in a recession?
    d. Compute the variance and standard deviation of the number of people who believed the country was in a recession.

34. The Census Bureau's Current Population Survey shows 28% of individuals, ages 25 and older, have completed four years of college (*The New York Times Almanac,* 2006). For a sample of 15 individuals, ages 25 and older, answer the following questions:
    a. What is the probability 4 will have completed four years of college?
    b. What is the probability 3 or more will have completed four years of college?

35. A university found that 20% of its students withdraw without completing the introductory statistics course. Assume that 20 students registered for the course.
    a. Compute the probability that 2 or fewer will withdraw.
    b. Compute the probability that exactly 4 will withdraw.
    c. Compute the probability that more than 3 will withdraw.
    d. Compute the expected number of withdrawals.

36. According to a survey conducted by TD Ameritrade, one out of four investors have exchange-traded funds in their portfolios (*USA Today,* January 11, 2007). For a sample of 20 investors, answer the following questions.
    a. Compute the probability that exactly 4 investors have exchange-traded funds in their portfolios.
    b. Compute the probability that at least 2 of the investors have exchange-traded funds in their portfolios.

c.   If you found that exactly 12 of the investors have exchange-traded funds in their portfolios, would you doubt the accuracy of the survey results?

d.   Compute the expected number of investors who have exchange-traded funds in their portfolios.

37. Twenty-three percent of automobiles are not covered by insurance (CNN, February 23, 2006). On a particular weekend, 35 automobiles are involved in traffic accidents.

a.   What is the expected number of these automobiles that are not covered by insurance?

b.   What is the variance and standard deviation?

5.5 Poisson Probability Distribution

The Poisson probability distribution is often used to model random arrivals in waiting line situations.

In this section we consider a discrete random variable that is often useful in estimating the number of occurrences over a specified interval of time or space. For example, the random variable of interest might be the number of arrivals at a car wash in one hour, the number of repairs needed in 10 miles of highway, or the number of leaks in 100 miles of pipeline. If the following two properties are satisfied, the number of occurrences is a random variable described by the **Poisson probability distribution**.

PROPERTIES OF A POISSON EXPERIMENT

1. The probability of an occurrence is the same for any two intervals of equal length.
2. The occurrence or nonoccurrence in any interval is independent of the occurrence or nonoccurrence in any other interval.

The **Poisson probability function** is defined by equation (5.11).

POISSON PROBABILITY FUNCTION

Siméon Poisson taught mathematics at the Ecole Polytechnique in Paris from 1802 to 1808. In 1837, he published a work entitled, "Researches on the Probability of Criminal and Civil Verdicts," which includes a discussion of what later became known as the Poisson distribution.

$$f(x) = \frac{\mu^x e^{-\mu}}{x!}$$ (5.11)

where

$f(x)$ = the probability of x occurrences in an interval

μ = expected value or mean number of occurrences in an interval

e = 2.71828

Before we consider a specific example to see how the Poisson distribution can be applied, note that the number of occurrences, x, has no upper limit. It is a discrete random variable that may assume an infinite sequence of values ($x = 0, 1, 2, \ldots$).

An Example Involving Time Intervals

Bell Labs used the Poisson distribution to model the arrival of phone calls.

Suppose that we are interested in the number of arrivals at the drive-up teller window of a bank during a 15-minute period on weekday mornings. If we can assume that the probability of a car arriving is the same for any two time periods of equal length and that the arrival or nonarrival of a car in any time period is independent of the arrival or nonarrival in any other time period, the Poisson probability function is applicable. Suppose these assumptions are satisfied and an analysis of historic data shows that the average number of cars arriving in a 15-minute period of time is 10; in this case, the following probability function applies.

$$f(x) = \frac{10^x e^{-10}}{x!}$$

The random variable here is x = number of cars arriving in any 15-minute period.

If management wanted to know the probability of exactly 5 arrivals in 15 minutes, we would set $x = 5$ and thus obtain

$$\text{Probability of exactly} \atop \text{5 arrivals in 15 minutes} = f(5) = \frac{10^5 e^{-10}}{5!} = .0378$$

The probability of 5 arrivals in 15 minutes was obtained by using a calculator to evaluate the probability function. Excel also provides a function called POISSON for computing Poisson probabilities and cumulative probabilities. This function is easier to use when numerous probabilities and cumulative probabilities are desired. We show how to compute these probabilities with Excel at the end of this section.

A property of the Poisson distribution is that the mean and variance are equal.

In the preceding example, the mean of the Poisson distribution is $\mu = 10$ arrivals per 15-minute period. A property of the Poisson distribution is that the mean of the distribution and the variance of the distribution are *equal*. Thus, the variance for the number of arrivals during 15-minute periods is $\sigma^2 = 10$. The standard deviation is $\sigma = \sqrt{10} = 3.16$.

Our illustration involves a 15-minute period, but other time periods can be used. Suppose we want to compute the probability of 1 arrival in a 3-minute period. Because 10 is the expected number of arrivals in a 15-minute period, we see that $10/15 = 2/3$ is the expected number of arrivals in a 1-minute period and that $(2/3)(3 \text{ minutes}) = 2$ is the expected number of arrivals in a 3-minute period. Thus, the probability of x arrivals in a 3-minute time period with $\mu = 2$ is given by the following Poisson probability function:

$$f(x) = \frac{2^x e^{-2}}{x!}$$

The probability of 1 arrival in a 3-minute period is calculated as follows:

$$\text{Probability of exactly} \atop \text{1 arrival in 3 minutes} = f(1) = \frac{2^1 e^{-2}}{1!} = .2707$$

Earlier we computed the probability of 5 arrivals in a 15-minute period; it was .0378. Note that the probability of 1 arrival in a 3-minute period (.2707) is not the same. When computing a Poisson probability for a different time interval, we must first convert the mean arrival rate to the time period of interest and then compute the probability.

An Example Involving Length or Distance Intervals

Let us illustrate an application not involving time intervals in which the Poisson distribution is useful. Suppose we are concerned with the occurrence of major defects in a highway one month after resurfacing. We will assume that the probability of a defect is the same for any two highway intervals of equal length and that the occurrence or nonoccurrence of a defect in any one interval is independent of the occurrence or nonoccurrence of a defect in any other interval. Hence, the Poisson distribution can be applied.

Suppose we learn that major defects one month after resurfacing occur at the average rate of two per mile. Let us find the probability of no major defects in a particular 3-mile section of the highway. Because we are interested in an interval with a length of 3 miles, $\mu = (2 \text{ defects/mile})(3 \text{ miles}) = 6$ represents the expected number of major defects over the 3-mile section of highway. Using equation (5.11), the probability of no major defects is $f(0) = 6^0 e^{-6}/0! = .0025$. Thus, it is unlikely that no major defects will occur in the 3-mile section. In fact, this example indicates a $1 - .0025 = .9975$ probability of at least one major defect in the 3-mile highway section.

Using Excel to Compute Poisson Probabilities

The Excel function for computing Poisson probabilities and cumulative probabilities is called POISSON. It works in much the same way as the Excel function for computing binomial probabilities. Here we show how to use it to compute Poisson probabilities and cumulative probabilities. To illustrate, we use the example introduced earlier in this section; cars arrive at a bank drive-up teller window at the mean rate of 10 per 15-minute time interval. Refer to Figure 5.8 as we describe the tasks involved.

Enter Data: In order to compute a Poisson probability we must know the mean number of occurrences (μ) per time period and the number of occurrences for which we want to compute the probability (x). For the drive-up teller window example, the occurrences of interest are the arrivals of cars. The mean arrival rate is 10, which has been entered into cell D1. Earlier in this section, we computed the probability of 5 arrivals. But suppose we now want to compute the probability of 0 up through 20 arrivals. To do so, we enter the values 0, 1, 2, . . . , 20 into cells A4:A24.

Enter Functions and Formulas: The POISSON function has three inputs: the first is the value of x, the second is the value of μ, and the third is FALSE or TRUE. We choose FALSE for the third input if a probability is desired. The formula =POISSON(A4,$D$1,FALSE) has been entered into cell B4 to compute the probability of 0 arrivals in a 15-minute period. The value worksheet in the foreground shows that the probability of 0 arrivals is 0.0000. The formula in cell B4 is copied to cells B5:B24 to compute the probabilities for 1 through 20

FIGURE 5.8   EXCEL WORKSHEET FOR COMPUTING POISSON PROBABILITIES

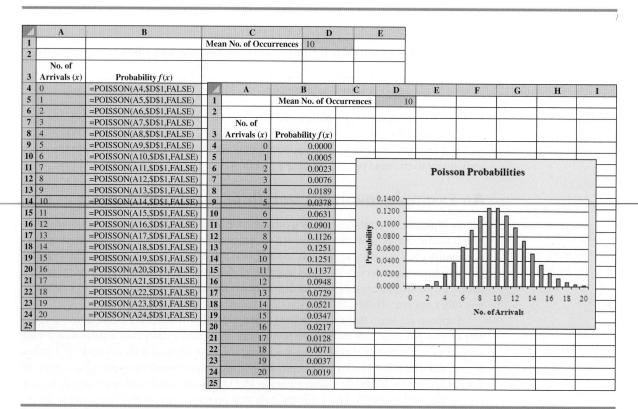

arrivals. Note, in cell B9 of the value worksheet, that the probability of 5 arrivals is .0378. This result is the same as we calculated earlier in the text.

Notice how easy it was to compute all the probabilities for 0 through 20 arrivals using the POISSON function. These calculations would take quite a bit of work using a calculator. We have also used Excel's chart tool to develop a graph of the Poisson probability distribution of arrivals. See the value worksheet in Figure 5.8. This chart gives a nice graphical presentation of the probabilities for the various number of arrival possibilities in a 15-minute interval. We can quickly see that the most likely number of arrivals is 9 or 10 and that the probabilities fall off rather smoothly for smaller and larger values.

Let us now see how cumulative probabilities are generated using Excel's POISSON function. It is really a simple extension of what we have already done. We again use the example of arrivals at a drive-up teller window. Refer to Figure 5.9 as we describe the tasks involved.

Enter Data: To compute cumulative Poisson probabilities we must provide the mean number of occurrences (μ) per time period and the values of x that we are interested in. The mean arrival rate (10) has been entered into cell D1. Suppose we want to compute the

FIGURE 5.9   EXCEL WORKSHEET FOR COMPUTING CUMULATIVE POISSON PROBABILITIES

	A	B	C	D	E
1			Mean No. of Occurrences	10	
2					
3	No. of Arrivals (x)	Probability f(x)			
4	0	=POISSON(A4,$D$1,TRUE)			
5	1	=POISSON(A5,$D$1,TRUE)			
6	2	=POISSON(A6,$D$1,TRUE)			
7	3	=POISSON(A7,$D$1,TRUE)			
8	4	=POISSON(A8,$D$1,TRUE)			
9	5	=POISSON(A9,$D$1,TRUE)			
10	6	=POISSON(A10,$D$1,TRUE)			
11	7	=POISSON(A11,$D$1,TRUE)			
12	8	=POISSON(A12,$D$1,TRUE)			
13	9	=POISSON(A13,$D$1,TRUE)			
14	10	=POISSON(A14,$D$1,TRUE)			
15	11	=POISSON(A15,$D$1,TRUE)			
16	12	=POISSON(A16,$D$1,TRUE)			
17	13	=POISSON(A17,$D$1,TRUE)			
18	14	=POISSON(A18,$D$1,TRUE)			
19	15	=POISSON(A19,$D$1,TRUE)			
20	16	=POISSON(A20,$D$1,TRUE)			
21	17	=POISSON(A21,$D$1,TRUE)			
22	18	=POISSON(A22,$D$1,TRUE)			
23	19	=POISSON(A23,$D$1,TRUE)			
24	20	=POISSON(A24,$D$1,TRUE)			
25					

	A	B	C	D	E
1		Mean No. of Occurrences		10	
2					
3	No. of Arrivals (x)	Probability f(x)			
4	0	0.0000			
5	1	0.0005			
6	2	0.0028			
7	3	0.0103			
8	4	0.0293			
9	5	0.0671			
10	6	0.1301			
11	7	0.2202			
12	8	0.3328			
13	9	0.4579			
14	10	0.5830			
15	11	0.6968			
16	12	0.7916			
17	13	0.8645			
18	14	0.9165			
19	15	0.9513			
20	16	0.9730			
21	17	0.9857			
22	18	0.9928			
23	19	0.9965			
24	20	0.9984			
25					

cumulative probabilities for a number of arrivals ranging from zero up through 20. To do so, we enter the values 0, 1, 2, . . . , 20 into cells A4:A24.

Enter Functions and Formulas: Refer to the formula worksheet in the background of Figure 5.8. The formulas we enter into cells B4:B24 of Figure 5.9 are the same as in Figure 5.8 with one exception. Instead of FALSE for the third input we enter the word TRUE to obtain cumulative probabilities. After entering these formulas into cells B4:B24 of the worksheet in Figure 5.9 the cumulative probabilities shown were obtained.

Note, in Figure 5.9, that the probability of 5 or fewer arrivals is .0671 and that the probability of 4 or fewer arrivals is .0293. Thus, the probability of exactly 5 arrivals is the difference in these two numbers: $f(5) = .0671 - .0293 = .0378$. We computed this probability earlier in this section and in Figure 5.8. Using these cumulative probabilities it is easy to compute the probability that a random variable lies within a certain interval. For instance, suppose we wanted to know the probability of more than 5 and fewer than 16 arrivals. We would just find the cumulative probability of 15 arrivals and subtract from that the cumulative probability for 5 arrivals. Referring to Figure 5.9 to obtain the appropriate probabilities, we obtain $.9513 - .0671 = .8842$. With such a high probability, we could conclude that 6 to 15 cars will arrive in most 15-minute intervals. Using the cumulative probability for 20 arrivals, we can also conclude that the probability of more than 20 arrivals in a 15-minute period is $1 - .9984 = .0016$; thus, there is almost no chance of more than 20 cars arriving.

Exercises

Methods

38.   Consider a Poisson distribution with $\mu = 3$.
   a.   Write the appropriate Poisson probability function.
   b.   Compute $f(2)$.
   c.   Compute $f(1)$.
   d.   Compute $P(x \geq 2)$.

39.   Consider a Poisson distribution with a mean of two occurrences per time period.
   a.   Write the appropriate Poisson probability function.
   b.   What is the expected number of occurrences in three time periods?
   c.   Write the appropriate Poisson probability function to determine the probability of x occurrences in three time periods.
   d.   Compute the probability of two occurrences in one time period.
   e.   Compute the probability of six occurrences in three time periods.
   f.   Compute the probability of five occurrences in two time periods.

Applications

40.   Phone calls arrive at the rate of 48 per hour at the reservation desk for Regional Airways.
   a.   Compute the probability of receiving 3 calls in a 5-minute interval of time.
   b.   Compute the probability of receiving exactly 10 calls in 15 minutes.
   c.   Suppose no calls are currently on hold. If the agent takes 5 minutes to complete the current call, how many callers do you expect to be waiting by that time? What is the probability that none will be waiting?
   d.   If no calls are currently being processed, what is the probability that the agent can take 3 minutes for personal time without being interrupted by a call?

41. During the period of time that a local university takes phone-in registrations, calls come in at the rate of 1 every 2 minutes.
    a. What is the expected number of calls in 1 hour?
    b. What is the probability of 3 calls in 5 minutes?
    c. What is the probability of no calls in a 5-minute period?

42. More than 50 million guests stay at bed and breakfasts (B&Bs) each year. The website for the Bed and Breakfast Inns of North America (*http://www.bestinns.net*), which averages approximately 7 visitors per minute, enables many B&Bs to attract guests (*Time, September 2001*).
    a. Compute the probability of no website visitors in a 1-minute period.
    b. Compute the probability of 2 or more website visitors in a 1-minute period.
    c. Compute the probability of 1 or more website visitors in a 30-second period.
    d. Compute the probability of 5 or more website visitors in a 1-minute period.

43. Airline passengers arrive randomly and independently at the passenger-screening facility at a major international airport. The mean arrival rate is 10 passengers per minute.
    a. Compute the probability of no arrivals in a 1-minute period.
    b. Compute the probability that 3 or fewer passengers arrive in a 1-minute period.
    c. Compute the probability of no arrivals in a 15-second period.
    d. Compute the probability of at least 1 arrival in a 15-second period.

44. An average of 15 aircraft accidents occur each year (*The World Almanac and Book of Facts,* 2004).
    a. Compute the mean number of aircraft accidents per month.
    b. Compute the probability of no accidents during a month.
    c. Compute the probability of exactly 1 accident during a month.
    d. Compute the probability of more than 1 accident during a month.

45. The National Safety Council (NSC) estimates that off-the-job accidents cost U.S. businesses almost $200 billion annually in lost productivity (National Safety Council, March 2006). Based on NSC estimates, companies with 50 employees are expected to average 3 employee off-the-job accidents per year. Answer the following questions for companies with 50 employees.
    a. What is the probability of no off-the-job accidents during a one-year period?
    b. What is the probability of at least 2 off-the-job accidents during a one-year period?
    c. What is the expected number of off-the-job accidents during six months?
    d. What is the probability of no off-the-job accidents during the next six months?

5.6 Hypergeometric Probability Distribution

The **hypergeometric probability distribution** is closely related to the binomial distribution. The two probability distributions differ in two key ways. With the hypergeometric distribution, the trials are not independent; and the probability of success changes from trial to trial.

In the usual notation for the hypergeometric distribution, r denotes the number of elements in the population of size N labeled success, and $N - r$ denotes the number of elements in the population labeled failure. The **hypergeometric probability function** is used to compute the probability that in a random selection of n elements, selected without replacement, we obtain x elements labeled success and $n - x$ elements labeled failure. For this outcome to occur, we must obtain x successes from the r successes in the population and $n - x$ failures from the $N - r$ failures. The following hypergeometric probability function provides $f(x)$, the probability of obtaining x successes in a sample of size n.

HYPERGEOMETRIC PROBABILITY FUNCTION

$$f(x) = \frac{\binom{r}{x}\binom{N-r}{n-x}}{\binom{N}{n}} \quad \text{for } 0 \le x \le r \quad (5.12)$$

where

$f(x) =$ probability of x successes in n trials
$n =$ number of trials
$N =$ number of elements in the population
$r =$ number of elements in the population labeled success

Note that $\binom{N}{n}$ represents the number of ways a sample of size n can be selected from a population of size N; $\binom{r}{x}$ represents the number of ways that x successes can be selected from a total of r successes in the population; and $\binom{N-r}{n-x}$ represents the number of ways that $n - x$ failures can be selected from a total of $N - r$ failures in the population.

To illustrate the computations involved in using equation (5.12), let us consider the following quality control application. Electric fuses produced by Ontario Electric are packaged in boxes of 12 units each. Suppose an inspector randomly selects 3 of the 12 fuses in a box for testing. If the box contains exactly 5 defective fuses, what is the probability that the inspector will find exactly 1 of the 3 fuses defective? In this application, $n = 3$ and $N = 12$. With $r = 5$ defective fuses in the box the probability of finding $x = 1$ defective fuse is

$$f(1) = \frac{\binom{5}{1}\binom{7}{2}}{\binom{12}{3}} = \frac{\left(\frac{5!}{1!4!}\right)\left(\frac{7!}{2!5!}\right)}{\left(\frac{12!}{3!9!}\right)} = \frac{(5)(21)}{220} = .4773$$

Now suppose that we wanted to know the probability of finding *at least* 1 defective fuse. The easiest way to answer this question is to first compute the probability that the inspector does not find any defective fuses. The probability of $x = 0$ is

$$f(0) = \frac{\binom{5}{0}\binom{7}{3}}{\binom{12}{3}} = \frac{\left(\frac{5!}{0!5!}\right)\left(\frac{7!}{3!4!}\right)}{\left(\frac{12!}{3!9!}\right)} = \frac{(1)(35)}{220} = .1591$$

With a probability of zero defective fuses $f(0) = .1591$, we conclude that the probability of finding at least one defective fuse must be $1 - .1591 = .8409$. Thus, there is a reasonably high probability that the inspector will find at least 1 defective fuse.

The mean and variance of a hypergeometric distribution are as follows:

$$E(x) = \mu = n\left(\frac{r}{N}\right) \quad (5.13)$$

$$\text{Var}(x) = \sigma^2 = n\left(\frac{r}{N}\right)\left(1 - \frac{r}{N}\right)\left(\frac{N-n}{N-1}\right) \qquad (5.14)$$

In the preceding example $n = 3$, $r = 5$, and $N = 12$. Thus, the mean and variance for the number of defective fuses is

$$\mu = n\left(\frac{r}{N}\right) = 3\left(\frac{5}{12}\right) = 1.25$$

$$\sigma^2 = n\left(\frac{r}{N}\right)\left(1 - \frac{r}{N}\right)\left(\frac{N-n}{N-1}\right) = 3\left(\frac{5}{12}\right)\left(1 - \frac{5}{12}\right)\left(\frac{12-3}{12-1}\right) = .60$$

The standard deviation is $\sigma = \sqrt{.60} = .77$.

Using Excel to Compute Hypergeometric Probabilities

The Excel function for computing hypergeometric probabilities is called HYPGEOMDIST. It only computes probabilities, not cumulative probabilities. The HYPGEOMDIST function has four inputs: x, n, r, N. Its usage is similar to that of BINOMDIST for the binomial distribution and POISSON for the Poisson distribution, so we dispense with showing a worksheet figure and just explain how to use the function. Let us reconsider the example of selecting 3 fuses for inspection from a fuse box containing 12 fuses, 5 of which are defective. We want to compute the probability that 1 of the 3 fuses selected is defective. In this case $x = 1$, $n = 3$, $r = 5$, and $N = 12$. So the appropriate formula to place in a cell of an Excel worksheet would be =HYPGEOMDIST(1,3,5,12). Placing this formula in a cell of an Excel worksheet provides a hypergeometric probability of .4773.

If we want to know the probability that none of the 3 fuses selected is defective, we have $x = 0$, $n = 3$, $r = 5$, and $N = 12$. So, using the HYPGEOMDIST function to compute the probability of randomly selecting 3 fuses without any being defective, we would enter the following formula into an Excel worksheet: =HYPGEOMDIST(0,3,5,12). The probability computed is .1591.

NOTES AND COMMENTS

Consider a hypergeometric distribution with n trials. Let $p = (r/N)$ denote the probability of a success on the first trial. If the population size is large, the term $(N-n)/(N-1)$ in equation (5.14) approaches 1. As a result, the expected value and variance can be written $E(x) = np$ and $\text{Var}(x) = np(1-p)$. Note that these expressions are the same as the expressions used to compute the expected value and variance of a binomial distribution, as in equations (5.9) and (5.10). When the population size is large, a hypergeometric distribution can be approximated by a binomial distribution with n trials and a probability of success $p = (r/N)$.

Exercises

Methods

46. Suppose $N = 10$ and $r = 3$. Compute the hypergeometric probabilities for the following values of n and x.
    a. $n = 4$, $x = 1$
    b. $n = 2$, $x = 2$
    c. $n = 2$, $x = 0$
    d. $n = 4$, $x = 2$

47. Suppose $N = 15$ and $r = 4$. What is the probability of $x = 3$ for $n = 10$?

Applications

48. In a survey conducted by the Gallup Organization, respondents were asked, "What is your favorite sport to watch?" Football and basketball ranked number one and two in terms of preference (*http://www.gallup.com,* January 3, 2004). Assume that in a group of 10 individuals, 7 preferred football and 3 preferred basketball. A random sample of 3 of these individuals is selected.
    a. What is the probability that exactly 2 preferred football?
    b. What is the probability that the majority (either 2 or 3) preferred football?

49. Blackjack, or twenty-one as it is frequently called, is a popular gambling game played in Las Vegas casinos. A player is dealt two cards. Face cards (jacks, queens, and kings) and tens have a point value of 10. Aces have a point value of 1 or 11. A 52-card deck contains 16 cards with a point value of 10 (jacks, queens, kings, and tens) and 4 aces.
    a. What is the probability that both cards dealt are aces or 10-point cards?
    b. What is the probability that both of the cards are aces?
    c. What is the probability that both of the cards have a point value of 10?
    d. A blackjack is a 10-point card and an ace for a value of 21. Use your answers to parts (a), (b), and (c) to determine the probability that a player is dealt blackjack. (*Hint:* Part (d) is not a hypergeometric problem. Develop your own logical relationship as to how the hypergeometric probabilities from parts (a), (b), and (c) can be combined to answer this question.)

SELF test

50. Axline Computers manufactures personal computers at two plants, one in Texas and the other in Hawaii. The Texas plant has 40 employees; the Hawaii plant has 20. A random sample of 10 employees is to be asked to fill out a benefits questionnaire.
    a. What is the probability that none of the employees in the sample work at the plant in Hawaii?
    b. What is the probability that 1 of the employees in the sample works at the plant in Hawaii?
    c. What is the probability that 2 or more of the employees in the sample work at the plant in Hawaii?
    d. What is the probability that 9 of the employees in the sample work at the plant in Texas?

51. The *2003 Zagat Restaurant Survey* provides food, decor, and service ratings for some of the top restaurants across the United States. For 15 top-ranking restaurants located in Boston, the average price of a dinner, including one drink and tip, was $48.60. You are leaving for a business trip to Boston and will eat dinner at 3 of these restaurants. Your company will reimburse you for a maximum of $50 per dinner. Business associates familiar with these restaurants have told you that the meal cost at one-third of these restaurants will exceed $50. Suppose that you randomly select 3 of these restaurants for dinner.
    a. What is the probability that none of the meals will exceed the cost covered by your company?
    b. What is the probability that 1 of the meals will exceed the cost covered by your company?
    c. What is the probability that 2 of the meals will exceed the cost covered by your company?
    d. What is the probability that all 3 of the meals will exceed the cost covered by your company?

52. A shipment of 10 items has 2 defective and 8 nondefective items. In the inspection of the shipment, a sample of items will be selected and tested. If a defective item is found, the shipment of 10 items will be rejected.
    a. If a sample of 3 items is selected, what is the probability that the shipment will be rejected?
    b. If a sample of 4 items is selected, what is the probability that the shipment will be rejected?
    c. If a sample of 5 items is selected, what is the probability that the shipment will be rejected?
    d. If management would like a .90 probability of rejecting a shipment with 2 defective and 8 nondefective items, how large a sample would you recommend?

Summary

A random variable provides a numerical description of the outcome of an experiment. The probability distribution for a random variable describes how the probabilities are distributed over the values the random variable can assume. For any discrete random variable x, the probability distribution is defined by a probability function, denoted by $f(x)$, which provides the probability associated with each value of the random variable. Once the probability function is defined, we can compute the expected value, variance, and standard deviation for the random variable.

The binomial distribution can be used to determine the probability of x successes in n trials whenever the experiment has the following properties:

1. The experiment consists of a sequence of n identical trials.
2. Two outcomes are possible on each trial, one called success and the other failure.
3. The probability of a success p does not change from trial to trial. Consequently, the probability of failure, $1 - p$, does not change from trial to trial.
4. The trials are independent.

When the four properties hold, the binomial probability function can be used to determine the probability of obtaining x successes in n trials. Formulas were also presented for the mean and variance of the binomial distribution.

The Poisson distribution is used when it is desirable to determine the probability of obtaining x occurrences over an interval of time or space. The following assumptions are necessary for the Poisson distribution to be applicable.

1. The probability of an occurrence of the event is the same for any two intervals of equal length.
2. The occurrence or nonoccurrence of the event in any interval is independent of the occurrence or nonoccurrence of the event in any other interval.

A third discrete probability distribution, the hypergeometric, was introduced in Section 5.6. Like the binomial, it is used to compute the probability of x successes in n trials. But, in contrast to the binomial, the probability of success changes from trial to trial.

Glossary

Random variable A numerical description of the outcome of an experiment.

Discrete random variable A random variable that may assume either a finite number of values or an infinite sequence of values.

Continuous random variable A random variable that may assume any numerical value in an interval or collection of intervals.

Probability distribution A description of how the probabilities are distributed over the values of the random variable.

Probability function A function, denoted by $f(x)$, that provides the probability that x assumes a particular value for a discrete random variable.

Discrete uniform probability distribution A probability distribution for which each possible value of the random variable has the same probability.

Expected value A measure of the central location of a random variable.

Variance A measure of the variability, or dispersion, of a random variable.

Standard deviation The positive square root of the variance.

Binomial experiment An experiment having the four properties stated at the beginning of Section 5.4.

Binomial probability distribution A probability distribution showing the probability of x successes in n trials of a binomial experiment.

Binomial probability function The function used to compute binomial probabilities.
Poisson probability distribution A probability distribution showing the probability of x occurrences of an event over a specified interval of time or space.
Poisson probability function The function used to compute Poisson probabilities.
Hypergeometric probability distribution A probability distribution showing the probability of x successes in n trials from a population with r successes and $N - r$ failures.
Hypergeometric probability function The function used to compute hypergeometric probabilities.

Key Formulas

Discrete Uniform Probability Function

$$f(x) = 1/n \tag{5.3}$$

Expected Value of a Discrete Random Variable

$$E(x) = \mu = \Sigma x f(x) \tag{5.4}$$

Variance of a Discrete Random Variable

$$\text{Var}(x) = \sigma^2 = \Sigma(x - \mu)^2 f(x) \tag{5.5}$$

Number of Experimental Outcomes Providing Exactly x Successes in n Trials

$$\binom{n}{x} = \frac{n!}{x!(n-x)!} \tag{5.6}$$

Binomial Probability Function

$$f(x) = \binom{n}{x} p^x (1-p)^{(n-x)} \tag{5.8}$$

Expected Value for the Binomial Distribution

$$E(x) = \mu = np \tag{5.9}$$

Variance for the Binomial Distribution

$$\text{Var}(x) = \sigma^2 = np(1-p) \tag{5.10}$$

Poisson Probability Function

$$f(x) = \frac{\mu^x e^{-\mu}}{x!} \tag{5.11}$$

Hypergeometric Probability Function

$$f(x) = \frac{\binom{r}{x}\binom{N-r}{n-x}}{\binom{N}{n}} \quad \text{for } 0 \le x \le r \tag{5.12}$$

Expected Value for the Hypergeometric Distribution

$$E(x) = \mu = n\left(\frac{r}{N}\right) \tag{5.13}$$

Variance for the Hypergeometric Distribution

$$\text{Var}(x) = \sigma^2 = n\left(\frac{r}{N}\right)\left(1 - \frac{r}{N}\right)\left(\frac{N-n}{N-1}\right) \tag{5.14}$$

Supplementary Exercises

53. The *Barron's* Big Money Poll asked 131 investment managers across the United States about their short-term investment outlook (*Barron's,* October 28, 2002). Their responses showed 4% were very bullish, 39% were bullish, 29% were neutral, 21% were bearish, and 7% were very bearish. Let x be the random variable reflecting the level of optimism about the market. Set $x = 5$ for very bullish down through $x = 1$ for very bearish.
    a. Develop a probability distribution for the level of optimism of investment managers.
    b. Compute the expected value for the level of optimism.
    c. Compute the variance and standard deviation for the level of optimism.
    d. Comment on what your results imply about the level of optimism and its variability.

54. The American Association of Individual Investors publishes an annual guide to the top mutual funds (*The Individual Investor's Guide to the Top Mutual Funds,* 22e, American Association of Individual Investors, 2003). Table 5.8 contains their ratings of the total risk for 29 categories of mutual funds.
    a. Let $x = 1$ for low risk up through $x = 5$ for high risk, and develop a probability distribution for level of risk.
    b. What are the expected value and variance for total risk?
    c. It turns out that 11 of the fund categories were bond funds. For the bond funds, 7 categories were rated low and 4 were rated below average. Compare the total risk of the bond funds with the 18 categories of stock funds.

TABLE 5.8   RISK RATING FOR 29 CATEGORIES OF MUTUAL FUNDS

Total Risk	Number of Fund Categories
Low	7
Below Average	6
Average	3
Above Average	6
High	7

55. The budgeting process for a midwestern college resulted in expense forecasts for the coming year (in $ millions) of $9, $10, $11, $12, and $13. Because the actual expenses are unknown, the following respective probabilities are assigned: .3, .2, .25, .05, and .2.
    a. Show the probability distribution for the expense forecast.
    b. What is the expected value of the expense forecast for the coming year?
    c. What is the variance of the expense forecast for the coming year?
    d. If income projections for the year are estimated at $12 million, comment on the financial position of the college.

56. A survey conducted by the Bureau of Transportation Statistics (BTS) showed that the average commuter spends about 26 minutes on a one-way door-to-door trip from home to work. In addition, 5% of commuters reported a one-way commute of more than 1 hour (*http://www.bts.gov,* January 12, 2004).
    a. If 20 commuters are surveyed on a particular day, what is the probability that 3 will report a one-way commute of more than 1 hour?
    b. If 20 commuters are surveyed on a particular day, what is the probability that none will report a one-way commute of more than 1 hour?
    c. If a company has 2000 employees, what is the expected number of employees that have a one-way commute of more than 1 hour?
    d. If a company has 2000 employees, what is the variance and standard deviation of the number of employees that have a one-way commute of more than 1 hour?

57. A political action group is planning to interview home owners to assess the impact on their spending caused by the recent slump in housing prices. According to a *Wall Street Journal*/Harris Interactive Personal Finance poll, 26% of individuals aged 18–34, 50% of individuals aged 35–44, and 88% of individuals aged 55 and over own their own homes (*http://www.allbusiness.com,* January 23, 2008).
    a. How many people from the 18–34 age group must be sampled to find an expected number of at least 20 home owners?
    b. How many people from the 35–44 age group must be sampled to find an expected number of at least 20 home owners?
    c. How many people from the 55 and over age group must be sampled to find an expected number of at least 20 home owners?
    d. If the number of 18–34 year olds sampled is equal to the value identified in part (a), what is the standard deviation of the number who will be home owners?
    e. If the number of 35–44 year olds sampled is equal to the value identified in part (b), what is the standard deviation of the number who will be home owners?

58. Many companies use a quality control technique called acceptance sampling to monitor incoming shipments of parts, raw materials, and so on. In the electronics industry, component parts are commonly shipped from suppliers in large lots. Inspection of a sample of n components can be viewed as the n trials of a binomial experiment. The outcome for each component tested (trial) will be that the component is classified as good or defective. Reynolds Electronics accepts a lot from a particular supplier if the defective components in the lot do not exceed 1%. Suppose a random sample of five items from a recent shipment is tested.
    a. Assume that 1% of the shipment is defective. Compute the probability that no items in the sample are defective.
    b. Assume that 1% of the shipment is defective. Compute the probability that exactly one item in the sample is defective.
    c. What is the probability of observing one or more defective items in the sample if 1% of the shipment is defective?
    d. Would you feel comfortable accepting the shipment if one item was found to be defective? Why or why not?

59. The unemployment rate in the state of Arizona is 4.1% (*http://money.cnn.com,* May 2, 2007). Assume that 100 employable people in Arizona are selected randomly.
    a. What is the expected number of people who are unemployed?
    b. What are the variance and standard deviation of the number of people who are unemployed?

60. A poll conducted by Zogby International showed that of those Americans who said music plays a "very important" role in their lives, 30% said their local radio stations "always" play the kind of music they like (*http://www.zogby.com,* January 12, 2004). Suppose a sample of 800 people who say music plays an important role in their lives is taken.

a. How many would you expect to say that their local radio stations always play the kind of music they like?

b. What is the standard deviation of the number of respondents who think their local radio stations always play the kind of music they like?

c. What is the standard deviation of the number of respondents who do not think their local radio stations always play the kind of music they like?

61. Cars arrive at a car wash randomly and independently; the probability of an arrival is the same for any two time intervals of equal length. The mean arrival rate is 15 cars per hour. What is the probability that 20 or more cars will arrive during any given hour of operation?

62. A new automated production process averages 1.5 breakdowns per day. Because of the cost associated with a breakdown, management is concerned about the possibility of having three or more breakdowns during a day. Assume that breakdowns occur randomly, that the probability of a breakdown is the same for any two time intervals of equal length, and that breakdowns in one period are independent of breakdowns in other periods. What is the probability of having three or more breakdowns during a day?

63. A regional director responsible for business development in the state of Pennsylvania is concerned about the number of small business failures. If the mean number of small business failures per month is 10, what is the probability that exactly 4 small businesses will fail during a given month? Assume that the probability of a failure is the same for any two months and that the occurrence or nonoccurrence of a failure in any month is independent of failures in any other month.

64. Customer arrivals at a bank are random and independent; the probability of an arrival in any one-minute period is the same as the probability of an arrival in any other one-minute period. Answer the following questions, assuming a mean arrival rate of three customers per minute.

a. What is the probability of exactly three arrivals in a one-minute period?

b. What is the probability of at least three arrivals in a one-minute period?

65. A deck of playing cards contains 52 cards, four of which are aces. What is the probability that the deal of a five-card hand provides:

a. A pair of aces?

b. Exactly one ace?

c. No aces?

d. At least one ace?

66. Through the week ending September 16, 2001, Tiger Woods was the leading money winner on the PGA Tour, with total earnings of $5,517,777. Of the top 10 money winners, 7 players used a Titleist brand golf ball (*http://www.pgatour.com*). Suppose that we randomly select 2 of the top 10 money winners.

a. What is the probability that exactly 1 uses a Titleist golf ball?

b. What is the probability that both use Titleist golf balls?

c. What is the probability that neither uses a Titleist golf ball?

Continuous Probability Distributions

CONTENTS

STATISTICS IN PRACTICE:
PROCTER & GAMBLE

6.1 UNIFORM PROBABILITY DISTRIBUTION
Area as a Measure of Probability

6.2 NORMAL PROBABILITY DISTRIBUTION
Normal Curve
Standard Normal Probability Distribution
Computing Probabilities for Any Normal Probability Distribution
Grear Tire Company Problem
Using Excel to Compute Normal Probabilities

6.3 EXPONENTIAL PROBABILITY DISTRIBUTION
Computing Probabilities for the Exponential Distribution
Relationship Between the Poisson and Exponential Distributions
Using Excel to Compute Exponential Probabilities

PROCTER & GAMBLE*
CINCINNATI, OHIO

Procter & Gamble (P&G) produces and markets such products as detergents, disposable diapers, over-the-counter pharmaceuticals, dentifrices, bar soaps, mouthwashes, and paper towels. Worldwide, it has the leading brand in more categories than any other consumer products company. Since its merger with Gillette, P&G also produces and markets razors, blades, and many other personal care products.

As a leader in the application of statistical methods in decision making, P&G employs people with diverse academic backgrounds: engineering, statistics, operations research, and business. The major quantitative technologies for which these people provide support are probabilistic decision and risk analysis, advanced simulation, quality improvement, and quantitative methods (e.g., linear programming, regression analysis, probability analysis).

The Industrial Chemicals Division of P&G is a major supplier of fatty alcohols derived from natural substances such as coconut oil and from petroleum-based derivatives. The division wanted to know the economic risks and opportunities of expanding its fatty-alcohol production facilities, so it called in P&G's experts in probabilistic decision and risk analysis to help. After structuring and modeling the problem, they determined that the key to profitability was the cost difference between the petroleum- and coconut-based raw materials. Future costs were unknown, but the analysts were able to approximate them with the following continuous random variables.

x = the coconut oil price per pound of fatty alcohol

and

y = the petroleum raw material price per pound
of fatty alcohol

Because the key to profitability was the difference between these two random variables, a third random variable, $d = x - y$, was used in the analysis. Experts were interviewed to determine the probability distributions for x and y. In turn, this information was used to develop a probability distribution for the difference in prices d. This continuous probability distribution showed a .90 probability that the price difference would be $.0655 or less and

The Procter & Gamble headquarters in Cincinnati, Ohio. © Mike Simons/Getty Images.

a .50 probability that the price difference would be $.035 or less. In addition, there was only a .10 probability that the price difference would be $.0045 or less.[†]

The Industrial Chemicals Division thought that being able to quantify the impact of raw material price differences was key to reaching a consensus. The probabilities obtained were used in a sensitivity analysis of the raw material price difference. The analysis yielded sufficient insight to form the basis for a recommendation to management.

The use of continuous random variables and their probability distributions was helpful to P&G in analyzing the economic risks associated with its fatty-alcohol production. In this chapter, you will gain an understanding of continuous random variables and their probability distributions, including one of the most important probability distributions in statistics, the normal distribution.

*The authors are indebted to Joel Kahn of Procter & Gamble for providing this Statistics in Practice.

[†]The price differences stated here have been modified to protect proprietary data.

In the preceding chapter we discussed discrete random variables and their probability distributions. In this chapter we turn to the study of continuous random variables. Specifically, we discuss three continuous probability distributions: the uniform, the normal, and the exponential.

A fundamental difference separates discrete and continuous random variables in terms of how probabilities are computed. For a discrete random variable, the probability function $f(x)$ provides the probability that the random variable assumes a particular value. With continuous random variables, the counterpart of the probability function is the **probability density function**, also denoted by $f(x)$. The difference is that the probability density function does not directly provide probabilities. However, the area under the graph of $f(x)$ corresponding to a given interval does provide the probability that the continuous random variable x assumes a value in that interval. So when we compute probabilities for continuous random variables we are computing the probability that the random variable assumes any value in an interval.

Because the area under the graph of $f(x)$ at any particular point is zero, one of the implications of the definition of probability for continuous random variables is that the probability of any particular value of the random variable is zero. In Section 6.1 we demonstrate these concepts for a continuous random variable that has a uniform distribution.

Much of the chapter is devoted to describing and showing applications of the normal distribution. The normal distribution is of major importance because of its wide applicability and its extensive use in statistical inference. The chapter closes with a discussion of the exponential distribution. The exponential distribution is useful in applications involving such factors as waiting times and service times.

6.1 Uniform Probability Distribution

Consider the random variable x representing the flight time of an airplane traveling from Chicago to New York. Suppose the flight time can be any value in the interval from 120 minutes to 140 minutes. Because the random variable x can assume any value in that interval, x is a continuous rather than a discrete random variable. Let us assume that sufficient actual flight data are available to conclude that the probability of a flight time within any 1-minute interval is the same as the probability of a flight time within any other 1-minute interval contained in the larger interval from 120 to 140 minutes. With every 1-minute interval being equally likely, the random variable x is said to have a **uniform probability distribution**. The probability density function, which defines the uniform distribution for the flight-time random variable, is

Whenever the probability is proportional to the length of the interval, the random variable is uniformly distributed.

$$f(x) = \begin{cases} 1/20 & \text{for } 120 \leq x \leq 140 \\ 0 & \text{elsewhere} \end{cases}$$

Figure 6.1 is a graph of this probability density function. In general, the uniform probability density function for a random variable x is defined by the following formula.

UNIFORM PROBABILITY DENSITY FUNCTION

$$f(x) = \begin{cases} \dfrac{1}{b - a} & \text{for } a \leq x \leq b \\ 0 & \text{elsewhere} \end{cases} \tag{6.1}$$

For the flight-time random variable, $a = 120$ and $b = 140$.

FIGURE 6.1 UNIFORM PROBABILITY DISTRIBUTION FOR FLIGHT TIME

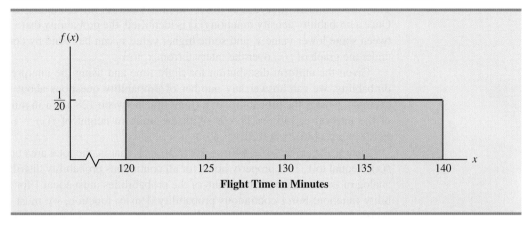

As noted in the introduction, for a continuous random variable, we consider probability only in terms of the likelihood that a random variable assumes a value within a specified interval. In the flight time example, an acceptable probability question is: What is the probability that the flight time is between 120 and 130 minutes? That is, what is $P(120 \le x \le 130)$? Because the flight time must be between 120 and 140 minutes and because the probability is described as being uniform over this interval, we feel comfortable saying $P(120 \le x \le 130) = .50$. In the following subsection we show that this probability can be computed as the area under the graph of $f(x)$ from 120 to 130 (see Figure 6.2).

Area as a Measure of Probability

Let us make an observation about the graph in Figure 6.2. Consider the area under the graph of $f(x)$ in the interval from 120 to 130. The area is rectangular, and the area of a rectangle is simply the width multiplied by the height. With the width of the interval equal to $130 - 120 = 10$ and the height equal to the value of the probability density function $f(x) = 1/20$, we have area = width $\times$ height = $10(1/20) = 10/20 = .50$.

FIGURE 6.2 AREA PROVIDES PROBABILITY OF A FLIGHT TIME BETWEEN 120 AND 130 MINUTES

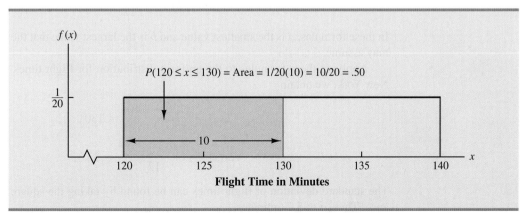

What observation can you make about the area under the graph of $f(x)$ and probability? They are identical! Indeed, this observation is valid for all continuous random variables. Once a probability density function $f(x)$ is identified, the probability that x takes a value between some lower value x_1 and some higher value x_2 can be found by computing the area under the graph of $f(x)$ over the interval from x_1 to x_2.

Given the uniform distribution for flight time and using the interpretation of area as probability, we can answer any number of probability questions about flight times. For example, what is the probability of a flight time between 128 and 136 minutes? The width of the interval is $136 - 128 = 8$. With the uniform height of $f(x) = 1/20$, we see that $P(128 \leq x \leq 136) = 8(1/20) = .40$.

Note that $P(120 \leq x \leq 140) = 20(1/20) = 1$; that is, the total area under the graph of $f(x)$ is equal to 1. This property holds for all continuous probability distributions and is the analog of the condition that the sum of the probabilities must equal 1 for a discrete probability function. For a continuous probability density function, we must also require that $f(x) \geq 0$ for all values of x. This requirement is the analog of the requirement that $f(x) \geq 0$ for discrete probability functions.

Two major differences stand out between the treatment of continuous random variables and the treatment of their discrete counterparts.

1. We no longer talk about the probability of the random variable assuming a particular value. Instead, we talk about the probability of the random variable assuming a value within some given interval.

To see that the probability of any single point is 0, refer to Figure 6.2 and compute the probability of a single point, say, $x = 125$. $P(x = 125) = P(125 \leq x \leq 125) = 0(1/20) = 0$.

2. The probability of a continuous random variable assuming a value within some given interval from x_1 to x_2 is defined to be the area under the graph of the probability density function between x_1 and x_2. Because a single point is an interval of zero width, this implies that the probability of a continuous random variable assuming any particular value exactly is zero. It also means that the probability of a continuous random variable assuming a value in any interval is the same whether or not the endpoints are included.

The calculation of the expected value and variance for a continuous random variable is analogous to that for a discrete random variable. However, because the computational procedure involves integral calculus, we leave the derivation of the appropriate formulas to more advanced texts.

For the uniform continuous probability distribution introduced in this section, the formulas for the expected value and variance are

$$E(x) = \frac{a + b}{2}$$

$$\text{Var}(x) = \frac{(b - a)^2}{12}$$

In these formulas, a is the smallest value and b is the largest value that the random variable may assume.

Applying these formulas to the uniform distribution for flight times from Chicago to New York, we obtain

$$E(x) = \frac{(120 + 140)}{2} = 130$$

$$\text{Var}(x) = \frac{(140 - 120)^2}{12} = 33.33$$

The standard deviation of flight times can be found by taking the square root of the variance. Thus, $\sigma = 5.77$ minutes.

NOTES AND COMMENTS

To see more clearly why the height of a probability density function is not a probability, think about a random variable with the following uniform probability distribution.

$$f(x) = \begin{cases} 2 & \text{for } 0 \leq x \leq .5 \\ 0 & \text{elsewhere} \end{cases}$$

The height of the probability density function, $f(x)$, is 2 for values of x between 0 and .5. However, we know probabilities can never be greater than 1. Thus, we see that $f(x)$ cannot be interpreted as the probability of x.

Exercises

Methods

1. The random variable x is known to be uniformly distributed between 1.0 and 1.5.
   a. Show the graph of the probability density function.
   b. Compute $P(x = 1.25)$.
   c. Compute $P(1.0 \leq x \leq 1.25)$.
   d. Compute $P(1.20 < x < 1.5)$.

2. The random variable x is known to be uniformly distributed between 10 and 20.
   a. Show the graph of the probability density function.
   b. Compute $P(x < 15)$.
   c. Compute $P(12 \leq x \leq 18)$.
   d. Compute $E(x)$.
   e. Compute $Var(x)$.

Applications

3. Delta Airlines quotes a flight time of 2 hours, 5 minutes for its flights from Cincinnati to Tampa. Suppose we believe that actual flight times are uniformly distributed between 2 hours and 2 hours, 20 minutes.
   a. Show the graph of the probability density function for flight time.
   b. What is the probability that the flight will be no more than 5 minutes late?
   c. What is the probability that the flight will be more than 10 minutes late?
   d. What is the expected flight time?

4. Most computer languages include a function that can be used to generate random numbers. In Excel, the RAND function can be used to generate random numbers between 0 and 1. If we let x denote a random number generated using RAND, then x is a continuous random variable with the following probability density function.

$$f(x) = \begin{cases} 1 & \text{for } 0 \leq x \leq 1 \\ 0 & \text{elsewhere} \end{cases}$$

   a. Graph the probability density function.
   b. What is the probability of generating a random number between .25 and .75?
   c. What is the probability of generating a random number with a value less than or equal to .30?
   d. What is the probability of generating a random number with a value greater than .60?

e.   Generate 50 random numbers by entering =RAND() into 50 cells of an Excel worksheet.

f.   Compute the mean and standard deviation for the random numbers in part (e).

5.   The driving distance for the top 100 golfers on the PGA tour is between 284.7 and 310.6 yards (*Golfweek,* March 29, 2003). Assume that the driving distance for these golfers is uniformly distributed over this interval.

a.   Give a mathematical expression for the probability density function of driving distance.

b.   What is the probability the driving distance for one of these golfers is less than 290 yards?

c.   What is the probability the driving distance for one of these golfers is at least 300 yards?

d.   What is the probability the driving distance for one of these golfers is between 290 and 305 yards?

e.   How many of these golfers drive the ball at least 290 yards?

6.   On average, 30-minute television sitcoms have 22 minutes of programming (CNBC, February 23, 2006). Assume that the probability distribution for minutes of programming can be approximated by a uniform distribution from 18 minutes to 26 minutes.

a.   What is the probability a sitcom will have 25 or more minutes of programming?

b.   What is the probability a sitcom will have between 21 and 25 minutes of programming?

c.   What is the probability a sitcom will have more than 10 minutes of commercials or other nonprogramming interruptions?

7.   Suppose we are interested in bidding on a piece of land and we know one other bidder is interested.[1] The seller announced that the highest bid in excess of $10,000 will be accepted. Assume that the competitor's bid x is a random variable that is uniformly distributed between $10,000 and $15,000.

a.   Suppose you bid $12,000. What is the probability that your bid will be accepted?

b.   Suppose you bid $14,000. What is the probability that your bid will be accepted?

c.   What amount should you bid to maximize the probability that you get the property?

d.   Suppose you know someone who is willing to pay you $16,000 for the property. Would you consider bidding less than the amount in part (c)? Why or why not?

6.2   Normal Probability Distribution

Abraham de Moivre, a French mathematician, published The Doctrine of Chances *in 1733. He derived the normal distribution.*

The most important probability distribution for describing a continuous random variable is the **normal probability distribution**. The normal distribution has been used in a wide variety of practical applications in which the random variables are heights and weights of people, test scores, scientific measurements, amounts of rainfall, and other similar values. It is also widely used in statistical inference, which is the major topic of the remainder of this book. In such applications, the normal distribution provides a description of the likely results obtained through sampling.

Normal Curve

The form, or shape, of the normal distribution is illustrated by the bell-shaped normal curve in Figure 6.3. The probability density function that defines the bell-shaped curve of the normal distribution follows.

---

[1]This exercise is based on a problem suggested to us by Professor Roger Myerson of Northwestern University.

FIGURE 6.3   BELL-SHAPED CURVE FOR THE NORMAL DISTRIBUTION

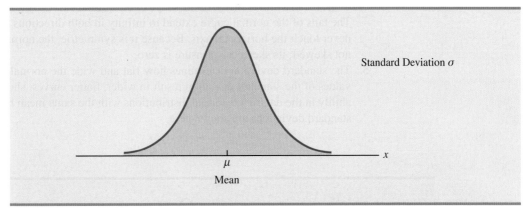

Standard Deviation σ

μ
Mean

x

NORMAL PROBABILITY DENSITY FUNCTION

$$f(x) = \frac{1}{\sigma\sqrt{2\pi}} e^{-(x-\mu)^2/2\sigma^2} \tag{6.2}$$

where

μ = mean
σ = standard deviation
π = 3.14159
e = 2.71828

We make several observations about the characteristics of the normal distribution.

The normal curve has two parameters, μ and σ. They determine the location and shape of the normal distribution.

1. The entire family of normal distributions is differentiated by two parameters: the mean μ and the standard deviation σ.
2. The highest point on the normal curve is at the mean, which is also the median and mode of the distribution.
3. The mean of the distribution can be any numerical value: negative, zero, or positive. Three normal distributions with the same standard deviation but three different means (-10, 0, and 20) are shown here.

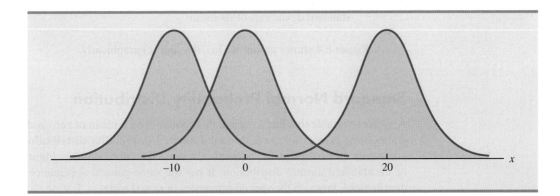

-10 0 20 x

4. The normal distribution is symmetric, with the shape of the normal curve to the left of the mean a mirror image of the shape of the normal curve to the right of the mean. The tails of the normal curve extend to infinity in both directions and theoretically never touch the horizontal axis. Because it is symmetric, the normal distribution is not skewed; its skewness measure is zero.

5. The standard deviation determines how flat and wide the normal curve is. Larger values of the standard deviation result in wider, flatter curves, showing more variability in the data. Two normal distributions with the same mean but with different standard deviations are shown here.

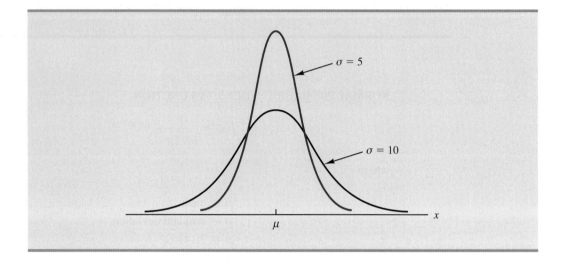

6. Probabilities for the normal random variable are given by areas under the normal curve. The total area under the curve for the normal distribution is 1. Because the distribution is symmetric, the area under the curve to the left of the mean is .50 and the area under the curve to the right of the mean is .50.

7. The percentage of values in some commonly used intervals are

   a. 68.3% of the values of a normal random variable are within plus or minus one standard deviation of its mean.

   These percentages are the basis for the empirical rule introduced in Section 3.3.

   b. 95.4% of the values of a normal random variable are within plus or minus two standard deviations of its mean.

   c. 99.7% of the values of a normal random variable are within plus or minus three standard deviations of its mean.

   Figure 6.4 shows properties (a), (b), and (c) graphically.

Standard Normal Probability Distribution

A random variable that has a normal distribution with a mean of zero and a standard deviation of one is said to have a **standard normal probability distribution**. The letter z is commonly used to designate this particular normal random variable. Figure 6.5 is the graph of the standard normal distribution. It has the same general appearance as other normal distributions, but with the special properties of $\mu = 0$ and $\sigma = 1$.

FIGURE 6.4   AREAS UNDER THE CURVE FOR ANY NORMAL DISTRIBUTION

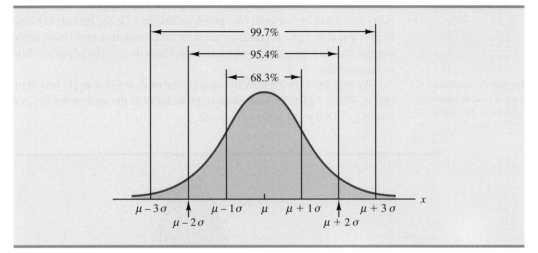

FIGURE 6.5   THE STANDARD NORMAL DISTRIBUTION

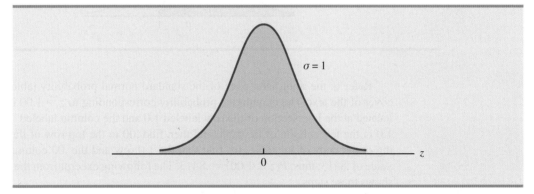

Because $\mu = 0$ and $\sigma = 1$, the formula for the standard normal probability density function is a simpler version of equation (6.2).

> **STANDARD NORMAL DENSITY FUNCTION**
>
> $$f(z) = \frac{1}{\sqrt{2\pi}}\, e^{-z^2/2}$$

As with other continuous random variables, probability calculations with any normal distribution are made by computing areas under the graph of the probability density function. Thus, to find the probability that a normal random variable is within any specific interval, we must compute the area under the normal curve over that interval.

For the normal probability density function, the height of the normal curve varies and more advanced mathematics is required to compute the areas that represent probability.

For the standard normal distribution, areas under the normal curve have been computed and are available in tables that can be used to compute probabilities. Such a table appears on the two pages inside the front cover of the text. The table on the left-hand page contains areas, or cumulative probabilities, for z values less than or equal to the mean of zero. The table on the right-hand page contains areas, or cumulative probabilities, for z values greater than or equal to the mean of zero.

The three types of probabilities we need to compute include (1) the probability that the standard normal random variable z will be less than or equal to a given value; (2) the probability that z will be between two given values; and (3) the probability that z will be greater than or equal to a given value. To see how the cumulative probability table for the standard normal distribution can be used to compute these three types of probabilities, let us consider some examples.

Because the standard normal random variable is continuous, $P(z \le 1.00) = P(z < 1.00)$.

We start by showing how to compute the probability that z is less than or equal to 1.00; that is, $P(z \le 1.00)$. This cumulative probability is the area under the normal curve to the left of $z = 1.00$ in the following graph.

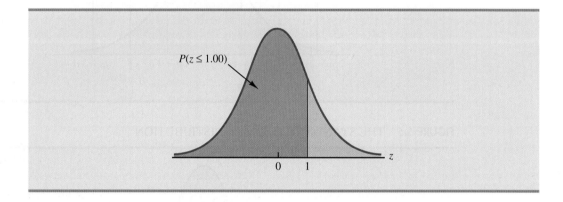

Refer to the right-hand page of the standard normal probability table inside the front cover of the text. The cumulative probability corresponding to $z = 1.00$ is the table value located at the intersection of the row labeled 1.0 and the column labeled .00. First we find 1.0 in the left column of the table and then find .00 in the top row of the table. By looking in the body of the table, we find that the 1.0 row and the .00 column intersect at the value of .8413; thus, $P(z \le 1.00) = .8413$. The following excerpt from the probability table shows these steps.

z	.00	.01	.02
.			
.			
.			
.9	.8159	.8186	.8212
1.0	**.8413**	.8438	.8461
1.1	.8643	.8665	.8686
1.2	.8849	.8869	.8888
.			
.			

$P(z \le 1.00)$

To illustrate the second type of probability calculation we show how to compute the probability that z is in the interval between $-.50$ and 1.25; that is, $P(-.50 \le z \le 1.25)$. The following graph shows this area, or probability.

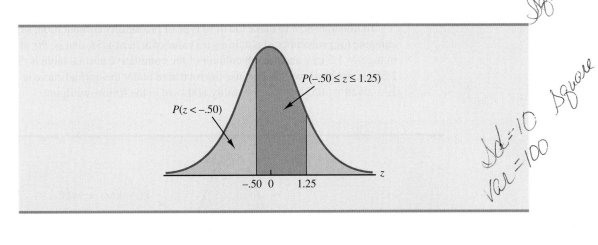

Three steps are required to compute this probability. First, we find the area under the normal curve to the left of $z = 1.25$. Second, we find the area under the normal curve to the left of $z = -.50$. Finally, we subtract the area to the left of $z = -.50$ from the area to the left of $z = 1.25$ to find $P(-.50 \leq z \leq 1.25)$.

To find the area under the normal curve to the left of $z = 1.25$, we first locate the 1.2 row in the standard normal probability table and then move across to the .05 column. Because the table value in the 1.2 row and the .05 column is .8944, $P(z \leq 1.25) = .8944$. Similarly, to find the area under the curve to the left of $z = -.50$ we use the left-hand page of the table to locate the table value in the $-.5$ row and the .00 column; with a table value of .3085, $P(z \leq -.50) = .3085$. Thus, $P(-.50 \leq z \leq 1.25) = P(z \leq 1.25) - P(z \leq -.50) = .8944 - .3085 = .5859$.

Let us consider another example of computing the probability that z is in the interval between two given values. Often it is of interest to compute the probability that a normal random variable assumes a value within a certain number of standard deviations of the mean. Suppose we want to compute the probability that the standard normal random variable is within one standard deviation of the mean; that is, $P(-1.00 \leq z \leq 1.00)$. To compute this probability we must find the area under the curve between -1.00 and 1.00. Earlier we found that $P(z \leq 1.00) = .8413$. Referring again to the table inside the front cover of the book, we find that the area under the curve to the left of $z = -1.00$ is .1587, so $P(z \leq -1.00) = .1587$. Therefore, $P(-1.00 \leq z \leq 1.00) = P(z \leq 1.00) - P(z \leq -1.00) = .8413 - .1587 = .6826$. This probability is shown graphically in the following figure.

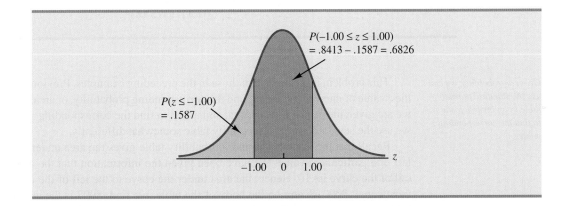

To illustrate how to make the third type of probability computation, suppose we want to compute the probability of obtaining a z value of at least 1.58; that is, $P(z \geq 1.58)$. The value in the $z = 1.5$ row and the .08 column of the cumulative normal table is .9429; thus, $P(z < 1.58) = .9429$. However, because the total area under the normal curve is 1, $P(z \geq 1.58) = 1 - .9429 = .0571$. This probability is shown in the following figure.

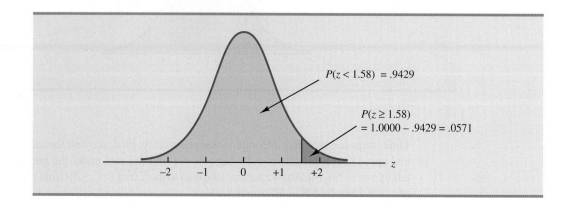

In the preceding illustrations, we showed how to compute probabilities given specified z values. In some situations, we are given a probability and are interested in working backward to find the corresponding z value. Suppose we want to find a z value such that the probability of obtaining a larger z value is .10. The following figure shows this situation graphically.

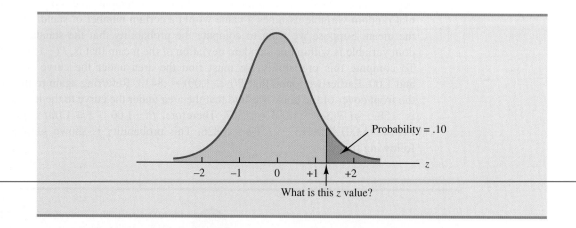

Given a probability, we can use the standard normal table in an inverse fashion to find the corresponding z value.

This problem is the inverse of those in the preceding examples. Previously, we specified the z value of interest and then found the corresponding probability, or area. In this example, we are given the probability, or area, and asked to find the corresponding z value. To do so, we use the standard normal probability table somewhat differently.

Recall that the standard normal probability table gives the area under the curve to the left of a particular z value. We have been given the information that the area in the upper tail of the curve is .10. Hence, the area under the curve to the left of the unknown z value must equal .9000. Scanning the body of the table, we find .8997 is the cumulative probability value closest to .9000. The section of the table providing this result follows.

z	.06	.07	.08	.09
.				
.				
.				
1.0	.8554	.8577	.8599	.8621
1.1	.8770	.8790	.8810	.8830
1.2	.8962	.8980	.8997	.9015
1.3	.9131	.9147	.9162	.9177
1.4	.9279	.9292	.9306	.9319
.				
.			Cumulative probability value	
.			closest to .9000	

Reading the z value from the leftmost column and the top row of the table, we find that the corresponding z value is 1.28. Thus, an area of approximately .9000 (actually .8997) will be to the left of $z = 1.28$.[2] In terms of the question originally asked, there is an approximately .10 probability of a z value larger than 1.28.

The examples illustrate that the table of cumulative probabilities for the standard normal probability distribution can be used to find probabilities associated with values of the standard normal random variable z. Two types of questions can be asked. The first type of question specifies a value, or values, for z and asks us to use the table to determine the corresponding areas or probabilities. The second type of question provides an area, or probability, and asks us to use the table to determine the corresponding z value. Thus, we need to be flexible in using the standard normal probability table to answer the desired probability question. In most cases, sketching a graph of the standard normal probability distribution and shading the appropriate area will help to visualize the situation and aid in determining the correct answer.

Computing Probabilities for Any Normal Probability Distribution

The reason for discussing the standard normal distribution so extensively is that probabilities for all normal distributions are computed by using the standard normal distribution. That is, when we have a normal distribution with any mean μ and any standard deviation σ, we answer probability questions about the distribution by first converting to the standard normal distribution. Then we can use the standard normal probability table and the appropriate z values to find the desired probabilities. The formula used to convert any normal random variable x with mean μ and standard deviation σ to the standard normal random variable z follows.

The formula for the standard normal random variable is similar to the formula we introduced in Chapter 3 for computing z-scores for a data set.

CONVERTING TO THE STANDARD NORMAL RANDOM VARIABLE

$$z = \frac{x - \mu}{\sigma} \qquad (6.3)$$

---

[2]We could use interpolation in the body of the table to get a better approximation of the z value that corresponds to an area of .9000. Doing so to provide one more decimal place of accuracy would yield a z value of 1.282. However, in most practical situations, sufficient accuracy is obtained by simply using the table value closest to the desired probability.

A value of x equal to its mean μ results in $z = (\mu - \mu)/\sigma = 0$. Thus, we see that a value of x equal to its mean μ corresponds to $z = 0$. Now suppose that x is one standard deviation above its mean; that is, $x = \mu + \sigma$. Applying equation (6.3), we see that the corresponding z value is $z = [(\mu + \sigma) - \mu]/\sigma = \sigma/\sigma = 1$. Thus, an x value that is one standard deviation above its mean corresponds to $z = 1$. In other words, *we can interpret z as the number of standard deviations that the normal random variable x is from its mean μ.*

To see how this conversion enables us to compute probabilities for any normal distribution, suppose we have a normal distribution with $\mu = 10$ and $\sigma = 2$. What is the probability that the random variable x is between 10 and 14? Using equation (6.3), we see that at $x = 10$, $z = (x - \mu)/\sigma = (10 - 10)/2 = 0$ and that at $x = 14$, $z = (14 - 10)/2 = 4/2 = 2$. Thus, the answer to our question about the probability of x being between 10 and 14 is given by the equivalent probability that z is between 0 and 2 for the standard normal distribution. In other words, the probability that we are seeking is the probability that the random variable x is between its mean and two standard deviations above the mean. Using $z = 2.00$ and the standard normal probability table inside the front cover of the text, we see that $P(z \le 2) = .9772$. Because $P(z \le 0) = .5000$, we can compute $P(.00 \le z \le 2.00) = P(z \le 2) - P(z \le 0) = .9772 - .5000 = .4772$. Hence the probability that x is between 10 and 14 is .4772.

Grear Tire Company Problem

We turn now to an application of the normal probability distribution. Suppose the Grear Tire Company developed a new steel-belted radial tire to be sold through a national chain of discount stores. Because the tire is a new product, Grear's managers believe that the mileage guarantee offered with the tire will be an important factor in the acceptance of the product. Before finalizing the tire mileage guarantee policy, Grear's managers want probability information about $x =$ number of miles the tires will last.

From actual road tests with the tires, Grear's engineering group estimated that the mean tire mileage is $\mu = 36{,}500$ miles and that the standard deviation is $\sigma = 5000$. In addition, the data collected indicate that a normal distribution is a reasonable assumption. What percentage of the tires can be expected to last more than 40,000 miles? In other words, what is the probability that the tire mileage, x, will exceed 40,000? This question can be answered by finding the area of the darkly shaded region in Figure 6.6.

FIGURE 6.6   GREAR TIRE COMPANY MILEAGE DISTRIBUTION

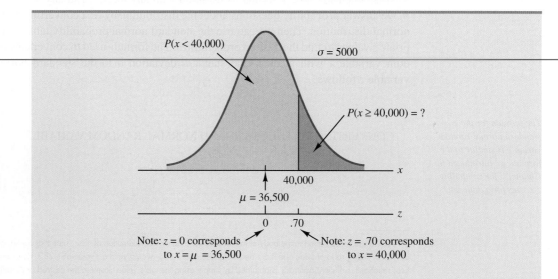

At $x = 40,000$, we have

$$z = \frac{x - \mu}{\sigma} = \frac{40,000 - 36,500}{5000} = \frac{3500}{5000} = .70$$

Refer now to the bottom of Figure 6.6. We see that a value of $x = 40,000$ on the Grear Tire normal distribution corresponds to a value of $z = .70$ on the standard normal distribution. Using the standard normal probability table, we see that the area under the standard normal curve to the left of $z = .70$ is .7580. Thus, $1.000 - .7580 = .2420$ is the probability that z will exceed .70 and hence x will exceed 40,000. We can conclude that about 24.2% of the tires will exceed 40,000 in mileage.

Let us now assume that Grear is considering a guarantee that will provide a discount on replacement tires if the original tires do not provide the guaranteed mileage. What should the guarantee mileage be if Grear wants no more than 10% of the tires to be eligible for the discount guarantee? This question is interpreted graphically in Figure 6.7.

According to Figure 6.7, the area under the curve to the left of the unknown guarantee mileage must be .10. So, we must first find the z value that cuts off an area of .10 in the left tail of a standard normal distribution. Using the standard normal probability table, we see that $z = -1.28$ cuts off an area of .10 in the lower tail. Hence, $z = -1.28$ is the value of the standard normal random variable corresponding to the desired mileage guarantee on the Grear Tire normal distribution. To find the value of x corresponding to $z = -1.28$, we have

The guarantee mileage we need to find is 1.28 standard deviations below the mean. Thus, $x = \mu - 1.28\sigma$.

$$z = \frac{x - \mu}{\sigma} = -1.28$$
$$x - \mu = -1.28\sigma$$
$$x = \mu - 1.28\sigma$$

With $\mu = 36,500$ and $\sigma = 5000$,

$$x = 36,500 - 1.28(5000) = 30,100$$

With the guarantee set at 30,000 miles, the actual percentage eligible for the guarantee will be 9.68%.

Thus, a guarantee of 30,100 miles will meet the requirement that approximately 10% of the tires will be eligible for the guarantee. Perhaps, with this information, the firm will set its tire mileage guarantee at 30,000 miles.

FIGURE 6.7   GREAR'S DISCOUNT GUARANTEE

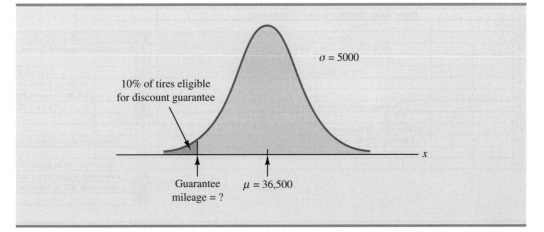

Again, we see the important role that probability distributions play in providing decision-making information. Namely, once a probability distribution is established for a particular application, it can be used to obtain probability information about the problem. Probability does not make a decision recommendation directly, but it provides information that helps the decision maker better understand the risks and uncertainties associated with the problem. Ultimately, this information may assist the decision maker in reaching a good decision.

Using Excel to Compute Normal Probabilities

Excel provides two functions for computing probabilities and z values for a standard normal probability distribution: NORMSDIST and NORMSINV. The NORMSDIST function computes the cumulative probability given a z value, and the NORMSINV function computes the z value given a cumulative probability. Two similar functions, NORMDIST and NORMINV, are available for computing the cumulative probability and the x value for any normal distribution. We begin by showing how to use the NORMSDIST and NORMSINV functions.

The letter S that appears in the name of the NORMSDIST and NORMSINV functions reminds us that these functions relate to the standard normal probability distribution.

The NORMSDIST function provides the area under the standard normal curve to the left of a given z value; thus, it provides the same cumulative probability we would obtain if we used the standard normal probability table inside the front cover of the text. Using the NORMSDIST function is just like having Excel look up cumulative normal probabilities for you. The NORMSINV function is the inverse of the NORMSDIST function; it takes a cumulative probability as input and provides the z value corresponding to that cumulative probability.

Let's see how both of these functions work by computing the probabilities and z values obtained earlier in this section using the standard normal probability table. Refer to Figure 6.8 as we describe the tasks involved. The formula worksheet is in the background; the value worksheet is in the foreground.

Enter Data: No data are entered in the worksheet. We will simply enter the appropriate z values and probabilities directly into the formulas as needed.

Enter Functions and Formulas: The NORMSDIST function has one input: the z value for which we want to obtain the cumulative probability. To illustrate the use of the NORMSDIST function we compute the four probabilities shown in cells D3:D6 of Figure 6.8.

FIGURE 6.8   EXCEL WORKSHEET FOR COMPUTING PROBABILITIES AND z VALUES
FOR THE STANDARD NORMAL DISTRIBUTION

	A	B	C	D	E
1			Probabilities: Standard Normal Distribution		
2					
3			$P(z <= 1)$	=NORMSDIST(1)	
4			$P(-.50 <= z <= 1.25)$	=NORMSDIST(1.25)-NORMSDIST(-0.5)	
5			$P(-1.00 <= z <= 1.00)$	=NORMSDIST(1)-NORMSDIST(-1)	
6			$P(z >= 1.58)$	=1-NORMSDIST(1.58)	
7					
8					
9			Finding z-values Given Probabilities		
10					
11			z value with .10 in upper tail	=NORMSINV(0.9)	
12			z value with .025 in upper tail	=NORMSINV(0.975)	
13			z value with .025 in lower tail	=NORMSINV(0.025)	
14					

	A	B	C	D	E
1	Probabilities: Standard Normal Distribution				
2					
3			$P(z <= 1)$	0.8413	
4			$P(-.50 <= z <= 1.25)$	0.5858	
5			$P(-1.00 <= z <= 1.00)$	0.6827	
6			$P(z >= 1.58)$	0.0571	
7					
8					
9		Finding z-values Given Probabilities			
10					
11		z value with .10 in upper tail		1.28	
12		z value with .025 in upper tail		1.96	
13		z value with .025 in lower tail		-1.96	
14					

To compute the cumulative probability to the left of a given z value (area in lower tail), we simply evaluate NORMSDIST at the z value. For instance, to compute $P(z \leq 1)$ we entered the formula =NORMSDIST(1) into cell D3. The result, .8413, is the same as obtained using the standard normal probability table.

To compute the probability of z being in an interval we compute the value of NORMSDIST at the upper endpoint of the interval and subtract the value of NORMSDIST at the lower endpoint of the interval. For instance, to find $P(-.50 \leq z \leq 1.25)$, we enter the formula =NORMSDIST(1.25)-NORMSDIST(-.50) into cell D4. The interval probability in cell D5 is computed in a similar fashion.

The probabilities in cells D4, 0.5858, and D5, 0.6827, differ from what we computed earlier due to rounding.

To compute the probability to the right of a given z value (upper tail area), we must subtract the cumulative probability represented by the area under the curve below the z value (lower tail area) from 1. For example, to compute $P(z \geq 1.58)$ we entered the formula =1-NORMSDIST(1.58) into cell D6.

To compute the z value for a given cumulative probability (lower tail area), we use the NORMSINV function. To find the z value corresponding to an upper tail probability of .10, we note that the corresponding lower tail area is .90 and enter the formula =NORMSINV(0.9) into cell D11. Actually, NORMSINV(0.9) gives us the z value providing a cumulative probability (lower tail area) of .9. But it is also the z value associated with an upper tail area of .10.

Two other z values are computed in Figure 6.8. These z values will be used extensively in succeeding chapters. To compute the z value corresponding to an upper tail probability of .025, we entered the formula =NORMSINV(0.975) into cell D12. To compute the z value corresponding to a lower tail probability of .025, we entered the formula =NORMSINV(0.025) into cell D13. We see that $z = 1.96$ corresponds to an upper tail probability of .025, and $z = -1.96$ corresponds to a lower tail probability of .025.

Let us now turn to the Excel functions for computing cumulative probabilities and x values for any normal distribution. The NORMDIST function provides the area under the normal curve to the left of a given value of the random variable x; thus it provides cumulative probabilities. The NORMINV function is the inverse of the NORMDIST function; it takes a cumulative probability as input and provides the value of x corresponding to that cumulative probability. The NORMDIST and NORMINV functions do the same thing for any normal distribution that the NORMSDIST and NORMSINV functions do for the standard normal distribution.

Let's see how both of these functions work by computing probabilities and x values for the Grear Tire Company example introduced earlier in this section. Recall that the lifetime of a Grear tire has a mean of 36,500 miles and a standard deviation of 5000 miles. Refer to Figure 6.9 as we describe the tasks involved. The formula worksheet is in the background; the value worksheet is in the foreground.

Enter Data: No data are entered in the worksheet. We simply enter the appropriate x values and probabilities directly into the formulas as needed.

Enter Functions and Formulas: The NORMDIST function has four inputs: (1) the x value we want to compute the cumulative probability for, (2) the mean, (3) the standard deviation, and (4) a value of TRUE or FALSE. For the fourth input, we enter TRUE if a cumulative probability is desired, and we enter FALSE if the height of the curve is desired. Because we will always be using NORMDIST to compute cumulative probabilities, we will always choose TRUE for the fourth input.

To compute the cumulative probability to the left of a given x value (lower tail area), we simply evaluate NORMDIST at the x value. For instance, to compute the probability that a Grear tire will last 20,000 miles or less, we entered the formula =NORMDIST(20000,36500,5000,TRUE) into cell D3. The value worksheet shows that this cumulative probability is .0005. So, we can conclude that almost all Grear tires will last at least 20,000 miles.

FIGURE 6.9   EXCEL WORKSHEET FOR COMPUTING PROBABILITIES AND x VALUES FOR THE NORMAL DISTRIBUTION

	A	B	C	D	E	F
1			Probabilities: Normal Distribution			
2						
3			$P(x <= 20000)$	=NORMDIST(20000,36500,5000,TRUE)		
4			$P(20000 <= x <= 40000)$	=NORMDIST(40000,36500,5000,TRUE)-NORMDIST(20000,36500,5000,TRUE)		
5			$P(x >= 40000)$	=1-NORMDIST(40000,36500,5000,TRUE)		
6						
7			Finding x values Given Probabilities			
8						
9			x value with .10 in lower tail	=NORMINV(0.1,36500,5000)		
10			x value with .025 in upper tail	=NORMINV(0.975,36500,5000)		
11						

	A	B	C	D	E	F
1		Probabilities: Normal Distribution				
2						
3			$P(x <= 20000)$	0.0005		
4			$P(20000 <= x <= 40000)$	0.7576		
5			$P(x >= 40000)$	0.2420		
6						
7		Finding x values Given Probabilities				
8						
9		x value with .10 in lower tail		30092.24		
10		x value with .025 in upper tail		46299.82		
11						

w/out the "S"

To compute the probability of x being in an interval we compute the value of NORMDIST at the upper endpoint of the interval and subtract the value of NORMDIST at the lower endpoint of the interval. The formula in cell D4 provides the probability that a tire's lifetime is between 20,000 and 40,000 miles, $P(20,000 \leq x \leq 40,000)$. In the value worksheet, we see that this probability is .7576.

To compute the probability to the right of a given x value (upper tail area), we must subtract the cumulative probability represented by the area under the curve below the x value (lower tail area) from 1. The formula in cell D5 computes the probability that a Grear tire will last for at least 40,000 miles. We see that this probability is .2420.

To compute the x value for a given cumulative probability, we use the NORMINV function. The NORMINV function has only three inputs. The first input is the cumulative probability; the second and third inputs are the mean and standard deviation. For instance, to compute the tire mileage corresponding to a lower tail area of .1 for Grear Tire, we enter the formula =NORMINV(0.1,36500,5000) into cell D9. From the value worksheet, we see that 10% of the Grear tires will last for 30,092.24 miles or less.

To compute the minimum tire mileage for the top 2.5% of Grear tires, we want to find the value of x corresponding to an area of .025 in the upper tail. This calculation is the same as finding the x value that provides a cumulative probability of .975. Thus we entered the formula =NORMINV(0.975,36500,5000) into cell D10 to compute this tire mileage. From the value worksheet, we see that 2.5% of the Grear tires will last at least 46,299.82 miles.

EXERCISES

Methods

8. Using Figure 6.4 as a guide, sketch a normal curve for a random variable x that has a mean of $\mu = 100$ and a standard deviation of $\sigma = 10$. Label the horizontal axis with values of 70, 80, 90, 100, 110, 120, and 130.

9. A random variable is normally distributed with a mean of $\mu = 50$ and a standard deviation of $\sigma = 5$.
   a. Sketch a normal curve for the probability density function. Label the horizontal axis with values of 35, 40, 45, 50, 55, 60, and 65. Figure 6.4 shows that the normal curve almost touches the horizontal axis at three standard deviations below and at three standard deviations above the mean (in this case at 35 and 65).
   b. What is the probability the random variable will assume a value between 45 and 55?
   c. What is the probability the random variable will assume a value between 40 and 60?

10. Draw a graph for the standard normal distribution. Label the horizontal axis at values of $-3, -2, -1, 0, 1, 2,$ and 3. Then use the table of probabilities for the standard normal distribution inside the front cover of the text to compute the following probabilities.
   a. $P(z \leq 1.5)$
   b. $P(z \leq 1)$
   c. $P(1 \leq z \leq 1.5)$
   d. $P(0 < z < 2.5)$

11. Given that z is a standard normal random variable, compute the following probabilities.
   a. $P(z \leq -1.0)$
   b. $P(z \geq -1)$
   c. $P(z \geq -1.5)$
   d. $P(-2.5 \leq z)$
   e. $P(-3 < z \leq 0)$

12. Given that z is a standard normal random variable, compute the following probabilities.
   a. $P(0 \leq z \leq .83)$
   b. $P(-1.57 \leq z \leq 0)$
   c. $P(z > .44)$
   d. $P(z \geq -.23)$
   e. $P(z < 1.20)$
   f. $P(z \leq -.71)$

13. Given that z is a standard normal random variable, compute the following probabilities.
   a. $P(-1.98 \leq z \leq .49)$
   b. $P(.52 \leq z \leq 1.22)$
   c. $P(-1.75 \leq z \leq -1.04)$

14. Given that z is a standard normal random variable, find z for each situation.
   a. The area to the left of z is .9750.
   b. The area between 0 and z is .4750.
   c. The area to the left of z is .7291.
   d. The area to the right of z is .1314.
   e. The area to the left of z is .6700.
   f. The area to the right of z is .3300.

15. Given that z is a standard normal random variable, find z for each situation.
   a. The area to the left of z is .2119.
   b. The area between $-z$ and z is .9030.
   c. The area between $-z$ and z is .2052.
   d. The area to the left of z is .9948.
   e. The area to the right of z is .6915.

16. Given that z is a standard normal random variable, find z for each situation.
   a. The area to the right of z is .01.
   b. The area to the right of z is .025.
   c. The area to the right of z is .05.
   d. The area to the right of z is .10.

Applications

17. For borrowers with good credit scores, the mean debt for revolving and installment accounts is $15,015 (*BusinessWeek,* March 20, 2006). Assume the standard deviation is $3540 and that debt amounts are normally distributed.
    a. What is the probability that the debt for a randomly selected borrower with good credit is more than $18,000?
    b. What is the probability that the debt for a randomly selected borrower with good credit is less than $10,000?
    c. What is the probability that the debt for a randomly selected borrower with good credit is between $12,000 and $18,000?
    d. What is the probability that the debt for a randomly selected borrower with good credit is no more than $14,000?

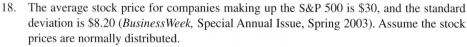

18. The average stock price for companies making up the S&P 500 is $30, and the standard deviation is $8.20 (*BusinessWeek,* Special Annual Issue, Spring 2003). Assume the stock prices are normally distributed.
    a. What is the probability a company will have a stock price of at least $40?
    b. What is the probability a company will have a stock price no higher than $20?
    c. How high does a stock price have to be to put a company in the top 10%?

19. The average amount of precipitation in Dallas, Texas, during the month of April is 3.5 inches (*The World Almanac,* 2000). Assume that a normal distribution applies and that the standard deviation is .8 inches.
    a. What percentage of the time does the amount of rainfall in April exceed 5 inches?
    b. What percentage of the time is the amount of rainfall in April less than 3 inches?
    c. A month is classified as extremely wet if the amount of rainfall is in the upper 10% for that month. How much precipitation must fall in April for it to be classified as extremely wet?

20. In January 2003, the American worker spent an average of 77 hours logged on to the Internet while at work (CNBC, March 15, 2003). Assume the population mean is 77 hours, the times are normally distributed, and that the standard deviation is 20 hours.
    a. What is the probability that in January 2003 a randomly selected worker spent fewer than 50 hours logged on to the Internet?
    b. What percentage of workers spent more than 100 hours in January 2003 logged on to the Internet?
    c. A person is classified as a heavy user if he or she is in the upper 20% of usage. In January 2003, how many hours did a worker have to be logged on to the Internet to be considered a heavy user?

21. A person must score in the upper 2% of the population on an IQ test to qualify for membership in Mensa, the international high-IQ society (*U.S. Airways Attaché,* September 2000). If IQ scores are normally distributed with a mean of 100 and a standard deviation of 15, what score must a person have to qualify for Mensa?

22. The mean hourly pay rate for financial managers in the East North Central region is $32.62, and the standard deviation is $2.32 (Bureau of Labor Statistics, September 2005). Assume that pay rates are normally distributed.
    a. What is the probability a financial manager earns between $30 and $35 per hour?
    b. How high must the hourly rate be to put a financial manager in the top 10% with respect to pay?
    c. For a randomly selected financial manager, what is the probability the manager earned less than $28 per hour?

23. The time needed to complete a final examination in a particular college course is normally distributed with a mean of 80 minutes and a standard deviation of 10 minutes. Answer the following questions.
    a. What is the probability of completing the exam in one hour or less?
    b. What is the probability that a student will complete the exam in more than 60 minutes but less than 75 minutes?

c.   Assume that the class has 60 students and that the examination period is 90 minutes in length. How many students do you expect will be unable to complete the exam in the allotted time?

Volume

24.   Trading volume on the New York Stock Exchange is heaviest during the first half hour (early morning) and last half hour (late afternoon) of the trading day. The early morning trading volumes (millions of shares) for 13 days in January and February are shown here (*Barron's,* January 23, 2006; February 13, 2006; and February 27, 2006).

214	163	265	194	180
202	198	212	201	
174	171	211	211	

The probability distribution of trading volume is approximately normal.
a.   Compute the mean and standard deviation to use as estimates of the population mean and standard deviation.
b.   What is the probability that, on a randomly selected day, the early morning trading volume will be less than 180 million shares?
c.   What is the probability that, on a randomly selected day, the early morning trading volume will exceed 230 million shares?
d.   How many shares would have to be traded for the early morning trading volume on a particular day to be among the busiest 5% of days?

25.   According to the Sleep Foundation, the average night's sleep is 6.8 hours (*Fortune,* March 20, 2006). Assume the standard deviation is .6 hours and that the probability distribution is normal.
a.   What is the probability that a randomly selected person sleeps more than 8 hours?
b.   What is the probability that a randomly selected person sleeps 6 hours or less?
c.   Doctors suggest getting between 7 and 9 hours of sleep each night. What percentage of the population gets this much sleep?

6.3 Exponential Probability Distribution

The **exponential probability distribution** may be used for random variables such as the time between arrivals at a car wash, the time required to load a truck, the distance between major defects in a highway, and so on. The exponential probability density function follows.

EXPONENTIAL PROBABILITY DENSITY FUNCTION

$$f(x) = \frac{1}{\mu} e^{-x/\mu} \qquad \text{for } x \geq 0, \mu > 0 \tag{6.4}$$

where μ = expected value or mean

As an example of the exponential distribution, suppose that x represents the loading time for a truck at the Schips loading dock and follows such a distribution. If the mean, or average, loading time is 15 minutes ($\mu = 15$), the appropriate probability density function for x is

$$f(x) = \frac{1}{15} e^{-x/15}$$

Figure 6.10 is the graph of this probability density function.

FIGURE 6.10   EXPONENTIAL DISTRIBUTION FOR THE SCHIPS LOADING
DOCK EXAMPLE

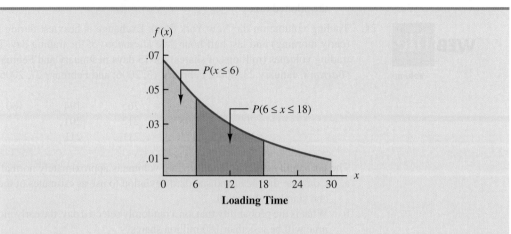

Computing Probabilities for the Exponential Distribution

As with any continuous probability distribution, the area under the curve corresponding to an interval provides the probability that the random variable assumes a value in that interval. In the Schips loading dock example, the probability that loading a truck will take 6 minutes or less $P(x \leq 6)$ is defined to be the area under the curve in Figure 6.10 from $x = 0$ to $x = 6$. Similarly, the probability that the loading time will be 18 minutes or less $P(x \leq 18)$ is the area under the curve from $x = 0$ to $x = 18$. Note also that the probability that the loading time will be between 6 minutes and 18 minutes $P(6 \leq x \leq 18)$ is given by the area under the curve from $x = 6$ to $x = 18$.

In waiting line applications, the exponential distribution is often used for service time.

To compute exponential probabilities such as those just described, we use the following formula. It provides the cumulative probability of obtaining a value for the exponential random variable of less than or equal to some specific value denoted by x_0.

EXPONENTIAL DISTRIBUTION: CUMULATIVE PROBABILITIES

$$P(x \leq x_0) = 1 - e^{-x_0/\mu} \tag{6.5}$$

For the Schips loading dock example, $x =$ loading time in minutes and $\mu = 15$ minutes. Using equation (6.5)

$$P(x \leq x_0) = 1 - e^{-x_0/15}$$

Hence, the probability that loading a truck will take 6 minutes or less is

$$P(x \leq 6) = 1 - e^{-6/15} = .3297$$

Using equation (6.5), we calculate the probability of loading a truck in 18 minutes or less.

$$P(x \leq 18) = 1 - e^{-18/15} = .6988$$

Thus, the probability that loading a truck will take between 6 minutes and 18 minutes is equal to $.6988 - .3297 = .3691$. Probabilities for any other interval can be computed similarly.

A property of the exponential distribution is that the mean and standard deviation are equal.

In the preceding example, the mean time it takes to load a truck is $\mu = 15$ minutes. A property of the exponential distribution is that the mean of the distribution and the standard deviation of the distribution are *equal*. Thus, the standard deviation for the time it takes to load a truck is $\sigma = 15$ minutes. The variance is $\sigma^2 = (15)^2 = 225$.

Relationship Between the Poisson and Exponential Distributions

In Section 5.5 we introduced the Poisson distribution as a discrete probability distribution that is often useful in examining the number of occurrences of an event over a specified interval of time or space. Recall that the Poisson probability function is

$$f(x) = \frac{\mu^x e^{-\mu}}{x!}$$

where

$$\mu = \text{expected value or mean number of}$$
$$\text{occurrences over a specified interval}$$

If arrivals follow a Poisson distribution, the time between arrivals must follow an exponential distribution.

The continuous exponential probability distribution is related to the discrete Poisson distribution. If the Poisson distribution provides an appropriate description of the number of occurrences per interval, the exponential distribution provides a description of the length of the interval between occurrences.

To illustrate this relationship, suppose the number of cars that arrive at a car wash during one hour is described by a Poisson probability distribution with a mean of 10 cars per hour. The Poisson probability function that gives the probability of x arrivals per hour is

$$f(x) = \frac{10^x e^{-10}}{x!}$$

Because the average number of arrivals is 10 cars per hour, the average time between cars arriving is

$$\frac{1 \text{ hour}}{10 \text{ cars}} = .1 \text{ hour/car}$$

Thus, the corresponding exponential distribution that describes the time between the arrivals has a mean of $\mu = .1$ hour per car; as a result, the appropriate exponential probability density function is

$$f(x) = \frac{1}{.1} e^{-x/.1} = 10e^{-10x}$$

Using Excel to Compute Exponential Probabilities

Excel's EXPONDIST function can be used to compute exponential probabilities. We will illustrate by computing probabilities associated with the time it takes to load a truck at the Schips loading dock. This example was introduced at the beginning of the section. Refer to Figure 6.11 as we describe the tasks involved. The formula worksheet is in the background; the value worksheet is in the foreground.

Enter Data: No data are entered in the worksheet. We simply enter the appropriate values for the exponential random variable into the formulas as needed. The random variable is $x = $ loading time.

FIGURE 6.11   EXCEL WORKSHEET FOR COMPUTING PROBABILITIES FOR THE EXPONENTIAL PROBABILITY DISTRIBUTION

	A	B	C	D	E	F	G
1			Probabilities: Exponential Distribution				
2							
3			P(x <= 18)	=EXPONDIST(18,1/15,TRUE)			
4			P(6 <= x <= 18)	=EXPONDIST(18,1/15,TRUE)-EXPONDIST(6,1/15,TRUE)			
5			P(x >= 8)	=1-EXPONDIST(8,1/15,TRUE)			
6							

	A	B	C	D	E
1		Probabilities: Exponential Distribution			
2					
3			P(x <= 18)	0.6988	
4			P(6 <= x <= 18)	0.3691	
5			P(x >= 8)	0.5866	
6					

Enter Functions and Formulas: The EXPONDIST function has three inputs: the first is the value of x, the second is $1/\mu$, and the third is TRUE or FALSE. We choose TRUE for the third input if a cumulative probability is desired and FALSE if the height of the probability density function is desired. We will always use TRUE because we will be computing cumulative probabilities.

The first probability we compute is the probability that the loading time is 18 minutes or less. For the Schips problem, $1/\mu = 1/15$, so we enter the formula =EXPONDIST (18,1/15,TRUE) into cell D3 to compute the desired cumulative probability. From the value worksheet, we see that the probability of loading a truck in 18 minutes or less is .6988.

The second probability we compute is the probability that the loading time is between 6 and 18 minutes. To find this probability we first compute the cumulative probability for the upper endpoint of the time interval and subtract the cumulative probability for the lower endpoint of the interval. The formula we have entered into cell D4 calculates this probability. The value worksheet shows that this probability is .3691.

The last probability we calculate is the probability that the loading time is at least 8 minutes. Because the EXPONDIST function only computes cumulative (lower tail) probabilities, we compute this probability by entering the formula =1-EXPONDIST(8,1/15,TRUE) into cell D5. The value worksheet shows that the probability of a loading time of 8 minutes or more is .5866.

NOTES AND COMMENTS

As we can see in Figure 6.10, the exponential distribution is skewed to the right. Indeed, the skewness measure for exponential distributions is 2. The exponential distribution gives us a good idea what a skewed distribution looks like.

Exercises

Methods

26.   Consider the following exponential probability density function.

$$f(x) = \frac{1}{8} e^{-x/8} \qquad \text{for } x \geq 0$$

    a.   Find $P(x \leq 6)$.
    b.   Find $P(x \leq 4)$.
    c.   Find $P(x \geq 6)$.
    d.   Find $P(4 \leq x \leq 6)$.

27. Consider the following exponential probability density function.

$$f(x) = \frac{1}{3}\, e^{-x/3} \qquad \text{for } x \geq 0$$

   a.   Write the formula for $P(x \leq x_0)$.
   b.   Find $P(x \leq 2)$.
   c.   Find $P(x \geq 3)$.
   d.   Find $P(x \leq 5)$.
   e.   Find $P(2 \leq x \leq 5)$.

Applications

28. The time required to pass through security screening at the airport can be annoying to travelers. The mean wait time during peak periods at Cincinnati/Northern Kentucky International Airport is 12.1 minutes (*The Cincinnati Enquirer,* February 2, 2006). Assume the time to pass through security screening follows an exponential distribution.
   a.   What is the probability it will take less than 10 minutes to pass through security screening during a peak period?
   b.   What is the probability it will take more than 20 minutes to pass through security screening during a peak period?
   c.   What is the probability it will take between 10 and 20 minutes to pass through security screening during a peak period?
   d.   It is 8:00 A.M. (a peak period) and you just entered the security line. To catch your plane you must be at the gate within 30 minutes. If it takes 12 minutes from the time you clear security until you reach your gate, what is the probability you will miss your flight?

29. The time between arrivals of vehicles at a particular intersection follows an exponential probability distribution with a mean of 12 seconds.
   a.   Sketch this exponential probability distribution.
   b.   What is the probability that the arrival time between vehicles is 12 seconds or less?
   c.   What is the probability that the arrival time between vehicles is 6 seconds or less?
   d.   What is the probability of 30 or more seconds between vehicle arrivals?

30. The lifetime (hours) of an electronic device is a random variable with the following exponential probability density function.

$$f(x) = \frac{1}{50}\, e^{-x/50} \qquad \text{for } x \geq 0$$

   a.   What is the mean lifetime of the device?
   b.   What is the probability that the device will fail in the first 25 hours of operation?
   c.   What is the probability that the device will operate 100 or more hours before failure?

31. Collina's Italian Café in Houston, Texas, advertises that carryout orders take about 25 minutes (*http://www.collinas.com,* February 27, 2008). Service times such as these frequently follow the exponential distribution. Using 25 minutes as the average time needed for an order to be ready for pickup, answer the following questions.
   a.   What is the probability your order will be ready within 20 minutes of when it was placed?
   b.   If you arrive to pick up your order 30 minutes after placing it, what is the probability your order will not be ready?
   c.   Once your order is ready, it takes you about 15 minutes to pay for it and drive home. It is now 5:20 P.M. and you have just placed your order at Colina's. What is the probability that you can make it home with your order by 6:00 P.M.?

32. Do interruptions while you are working reduce your productivity? According to a University of California–Irvine study, businesspeople are interrupted at the rate of approximately 5½ times per hour (*Fortune,* March 20, 2006). Suppose the number of interruptions follows a Poisson probability distribution.
   a.   Show the probability distribution for the time between interruptions.

b. What is the probability a businessperson will have no interruptions during a 15-minute period?
c. What is the probability that the next interruption will occur within 10 minutes for a particular businessperson?

Summary

This chapter extended the discussion of probability distributions to the case of continuous random variables. The major conceptual difference between discrete and continuous probability distributions involves the method of computing probabilities. With discrete distributions, the probability function $f(x)$ provides the probability that the random variable x assumes various values. With continuous distributions, the probability density function $f(x)$ does not provide probability values directly. Instead, probabilities are given by areas under the curve or graph of the probability density function $f(x)$. Because the area under the curve above a single point is zero, we observe that the probability of any particular value is zero for a continuous random variable.

Three continuous probability distributions—the uniform, normal, and exponential distributions—were treated in detail. The normal distribution is used widely in statistical inference and will be used extensively throughout the remainder of the text.

Glossary

Probability density function A function used to compute probabilities for a continuous random variable. The area under the graph of a probability density function over an interval represents probability.

Uniform probability distribution A continuous probability distribution for which the probability that the random variable will assume a value in any interval is the same for each interval of equal length.

Normal probability distribution A continuous probability distribution. Its probability density function is bell-shaped and determined by its mean μ and standard deviation σ.

Standard normal probability distribution A normal distribution with a mean of zero and a standard deviation of one.

Exponential probability distribution A continuous probability distribution that is useful in computing probabilities for the time it takes to complete a task.

Key Formulas

Uniform Probability Density Function

$$f(x) = \begin{cases} \dfrac{1}{b-a} & \text{for } a \leq x \leq b \\ 0 & \text{elsewhere} \end{cases} \tag{6.1}$$

Normal Probability Density Function

$$f(x) = \frac{1}{\sigma\sqrt{2\pi}}\, e^{-(x-\mu)^2/2\sigma^2} \tag{6.2}$$

Converting to the Standard Normal Random Variable

$$z = \frac{x - \mu}{\sigma} \qquad\qquad (6.3)$$

Exponential Probability Density Function

$$f(x) = \frac{1}{\mu} e^{-x/\mu} \qquad \text{for } x \geq 0, \mu > 0 \qquad\qquad (6.4)$$

Exponential Distribution: Cumulative Probabilities

$$P(x \leq x_0) = 1 - e^{-x_0/\mu} \qquad\qquad (6.5)$$

Supplementary Exercises

33. A business executive, transferred from Chicago to Atlanta, needs to sell her house in Chicago quickly. The executive's employer has offered to buy the house for $210,000, but the offer expires at the end of the week. The executive does not currently have a better offer but can afford to leave the house on the market for another month. From conversations with her realtor, the executive believes the price she will get by leaving the house on the market for another month is uniformly distributed between $200,000 and $225,000.
    a. If she leaves the house on the market for another month, what is the mathematical expression for the probability density function of the sales price?
    b. If she leaves it on the market for another month, what is the probability she will get at least $215,000 for the house?
    c. If she leaves it on the market for another month, what is the probability she will get less than $210,000?
    d. Should the executive leave the house on the market for another month? Why or why not?

34. The U.S. Bureau of Labor Statistics reports that the average annual expenditure on food and drink for all families is $5700 (*Money,* December 2003). Assume that annual expenditure on food and drink is normally distributed and that the standard deviation is $1500.
    a. What is the range of expenditures of the 10% of families with the lowest annual spending on food and drink?
    b. What percentage of families spend more than $7000 annually on food and drink?
    c. What is the range of expenditures for the 5% of families with the highest annual spending on food and drink?

35. Motorola used the normal distribution to determine the probability of defects and the number of defects expected in a production process. Assume a production process produces items with a mean weight of 10 ounces. Calculate the probability of a defect and the expected number of defects for a 1000-unit production run in the following situations.
    a. The process standard deviation is .15, and the process control is set at plus or minus one standard deviation. Units with weights less than 9.85 or greater than 10.15 ounces will be classified as defects.
    b. Through process design improvements, the process standard deviation can be reduced to .05. Assume the process control remains the same, with weights less than 9.85 or greater than 10.15 ounces being classified as defects.
    c. What is the advantage of reducing process variation, thereby causing process control limits to be at a greater number of standard deviations from the mean?

36. The average annual amount American households spend for daily transportation is $6312 (*Money,* August 2001). Assume that the amount spent is normally distributed.
    a. Suppose you learn that 5% of American households spend less than $1000 for daily transportation. What is the standard deviation of the amount spent?

b.   What is the probability that a household spends between $4000 and $6000?
c.   What is the range of spending for the 3% of households with the highest daily transportation cost?

37. *Condé Nast Traveler* publishes a Gold List of the top hotels all over the world. The Broadmoor Hotel in Colorado Springs contains 700 rooms and is on the 2004 Gold List (*Condé Nast Traveler,* January 2004). Suppose Broadmoor's marketing group forecasts a mean demand of 670 rooms for the coming weekend. Assume that demand for the upcoming weekend is normally distributed with a standard deviation of 30.
a.   What is the probability all the hotel's rooms will be rented?
b.   What is the probability 50 or more rooms will not be rented?
c.   Would you recommend the hotel consider offering a promotion to increase demand? What considerations would be important?

38. Ward Doering Auto Sales is considering offering a special service contract that will cover the total cost of any service work required on leased vehicles. From experience, the company manager estimates that yearly service costs are approximately normally distributed, with a mean of $150 and a standard deviation of $25.
a.   If the company offers the service contract to customers for a yearly charge of $200, what is the probability that any one customer's service costs will exceed the contract price of $200?
b.   What is Ward's expected profit per service contract?

39. Is lack of sleep causing traffic fatalities? A study conducted under the auspices of the National Highway Traffic Safety Administration found that the average number of fatal crashes caused by drowsy drivers each year was 1550 (*BusinessWeek,* January 26, 2004). Assume the annual number of fatal crashes per year is normally distributed with a standard deviation of 300.
a.   What is the probability of fewer than 1000 fatal crashes in a year?
b.   What is the probability the number of fatal crashes will be between 1000 and 2000 for a year?
c.   For a year to be in the upper 5% with respect to the number of fatal crashes, how many fatal crashes would have to occur?

40. Assume that the test scores from a college admissions test are normally distributed, with a mean of 450 and a standard deviation of 100.
a.   What percentage of the people taking the test score between 400 and 500?
b.   Suppose someone receives a score of 630. What percentage of the people taking the test score better? What percentage score worse?
c.   If a particular university will not admit anyone scoring below 480, what percentage of the persons taking the test would be acceptable to the university?

41. According to Salary Wizard, the average base salary for a brand manager in Houston, Texas, is $88,592 and the average base salary for a brand manager in Los Angeles, California, is $97,417 (*http://swz.salary.com,* February 27, 2008). Assume salaries are approximately normally distributed, that the standard deviation for brand managers in Houston is $19,900, and that the standard deviation for brand managers in Los Angeles is $21,800.
a.   What is the probability that a brand manager in Houston has a base salary in excess of $100,000?
b.   What is the probability that a brand manager in Los Angeles has a base salary in excess of $100,000?
c.   What is the probability that a brand manager in Los Angeles has a base salary of less than $75,000?
d.   How much would a brand manager in Los Angeles have to make in order to have a higher salary than 99% of the brand managers in Houston?

42. A machine fills containers with a particular product. The standard deviation of filling weights is known from past data to be .6 ounce. If only 2% of the containers hold less than 18 ounces, what is the mean filling weight for the machine? That is, what must μ equal? Assume the filling weights have a normal distribution.

43. The time in minutes for which a student uses a computer terminal at the computer center of a major university follows an exponential probability distribution with a mean of 36 minutes. Assume a student arrives at the terminal just as another student is beginning to work on the terminal.
    a. What is the probability that the wait for the second student will be 15 minutes or less?
    b. What is the probability that the wait for the second student will be between 15 and 45 minutes?
    c. What is the probability that the second student will have to wait an hour or more?

44. The website for the Bed and Breakfast Inns of North America (*http://www.cimarron.net*) gets approximately seven visitors per minute (*Time,* September 2001). Suppose the number of website visitors per minute follows a Poisson probability distribution.
    a. What is the mean time between visits to the website?
    b. Show the exponential probability density function for the time between website visits.
    c. What is the probability no one will access the website in a 1-minute period?
    d. What is the probability no one will access the website in a 12-second period?

45. The average travel time to work for New York City residents is 36.5 minutes (*Time Almanac,* 2001).
    a. Assume the exponential probability distribution is applicable and show the probability density function for the travel time to work for a typical New Yorker.
    b. What is the probability it will take a typical New Yorker between 20 and 40 minutes to travel to work?
    c. What is the probability it will take a typical New Yorker more than 40 minutes to travel to work?

46. The time (in minutes) between telephone calls at an insurance claims office has the following exponential probability distribution.

$$f(x) = .50e^{-.50x} \qquad \text{for } x \geq 0$$

    a. What is the mean time between telephone calls?
    b. What is the probability of having 30 seconds or less between telephone calls?
    c. What is the probability of having 1 minute or less between telephone calls?
    d. What is the probability of having 5 or more minutes without a telephone call?

Case Problem   Specialty Toys

Specialty Toys, Inc., sells a variety of new and innovative children's toys. Management learned that the preholiday season is the best time to introduce a new toy, because many families use this time to look for new ideas for December holiday gifts. When Specialty discovers a new toy with good market potential, it chooses an October market entry date.

In order to get toys in its stores by October, Specialty places one-time orders with its manufacturers in June or July of each year. Demand for children's toys can be highly volatile. If a new toy catches on, a sense of shortage in the marketplace often increases the demand to high levels and large profits can be realized. However, new toys can also flop, leaving Specialty stuck with high levels of inventory that must be sold at reduced prices. The most important question the company faces is deciding how many units of a new toy should be purchased to meet anticipated sales demand. If too few are purchased, sales will be lost; if too many are purchased, profits will be reduced because of low prices realized in clearance sales.

For the coming season, Specialty plans to introduce a new product called Weather Teddy. This variation of a talking teddy bear is made by a company in Taiwan. When a child presses Teddy's hand, the bear begins to talk. A built-in barometer selects one of five responses that predict the weather conditions. The responses range from "It looks to be a very nice day! Have fun" to "I think it may rain today. Don't forget your umbrella." Tests with the product show that, even though it is not a perfect weather predictor, its predictions are surprisingly good. Several of Specialty's managers claimed Teddy gave predictions of the weather that were as good as many local television weather forecasters.

As with other products, Specialty faces the decision of how many Weather Teddy units to order for the coming holiday season. Different members of the management team suggested order quantities of 15,000, 18,000, 24,000, or 28,000 units. The wide range of order quantities suggested indicates considerable disagreement concerning the market potential. The product management team asks you for an analysis of the stock-out probabilities for various order quantities, an estimate of the profit potential, and to help make an order quantity recommendation. Specialty expects to sell Weather Teddy for $24 based on a cost of $16 per unit. If inventory remains after the holiday season, Specialty will sell all surplus inventory for $5 per unit. After reviewing the sales history of similar products, Specialty's senior sales forecaster predicted an expected demand of 20,000 units with a .95 probability that demand would be between 10,000 units and 30,000 units.

Managerial Report

Prepare a managerial report that addresses the following issues and recommends an order quantity for the Weather Teddy product.

1. Use the sales forecaster's prediction to describe a normal probability distribution that can be used to approximate the demand distribution. Sketch the distribution and show its mean and standard deviation.
2. Compute the probability of a stock-out for the order quantities suggested by members of the management team.
3. Compute the projected profit for the order quantities suggested by the management team under three scenarios: worst case in which sales = 10,000 units, most likely case in which sales = 20,000 units, and best case in which sales = 30,000 units.
4. One of Specialty's managers felt that the profit potential was so great that the order quantity should have a 70% chance of meeting demand and only a 30% chance of any stock-outs. What quantity would be ordered under this policy, and what is the projected profit under the three sales scenarios?
5. Provide your own recommendation for an order quantity and note the associated profit projections. Provide a rationale for your recommendation.

Sampling and Sampling Distributions

CONTENTS

MEADWESTVACO CORPORATION*
STAMFORD, CONNECTICUT

MeadWestvaco Corporation, a leading producer of packaging, coated and specialty papers, consumer and office products, and specialty chemicals, employs more than 30,000 people. It operates worldwide in 29 countries and serves customers located in approximately 100 countries. MeadWestvaco holds a leading position in paper production, with an annual capacity of 1.8 million tons. The company's products include textbook paper, glossy magazine paper, beverage packaging systems, and office products. MeadWestvaco's internal consulting group uses sampling to provide a variety of information that enables the company to obtain significant productivity benefits and remain competitive.

For example, MeadWestvaco maintains large woodland holdings, which supply the trees, or raw material, for many of the company's products. Managers need reliable and accurate information about the timberlands and forests to evaluate the company's ability to meet its future raw material needs. What is the present volume in the forests? What is the past growth of the forests? What is the projected future growth of the forests? With answers to these important questions MeadWestvaco's managers can develop plans for the future, including long-term planting and harvesting schedules for the trees.

How does MeadWestvaco obtain the information it needs about its vast forest holdings? Data collected from sample plots throughout the forests are the basis for learning about the population of trees owned by the company. To identify the sample plots, the timberland holdings are first divided into three sections based on location and types of trees. Using maps and random numbers, MeadWestvaco analysts identify random samples of 1/5- to 1/7-acre plots in each section of the forest. MeadWestvaco foresters collect data from these sample plots to learn about the forest population.

Foresters throughout the organization participate in the field data collection process. Periodically, two-person teams gather information on each tree in every sample plot. The sample data are entered into the company's continuous forest inventory (CFI) computer system. Reports

Random sampling of its forest holdings enables MeadWestvaco Corporation to meet future raw material needs. © Lester Lefkowitz/The Image Bank/Getty Images

from the CFI system include a number of frequency distribution summaries containing statistics on types of trees, present forest volume, past forest growth rates, and projected future forest growth and volume. Sampling and the associated statistical summaries of the sample data provide the reports essential for the effective management of MeadWestvaco's forests and timberlands.

In this chapter you will learn about simple random sampling and the sample selection process. In addition, you will learn how statistics such as the sample mean and sample proportion are used to estimate the population mean and population proportion. The important concept of a sampling distribution is also introduced.

*The authors are indebted to Dr. Edward P. Winkofsky for providing this Statistics in Practice.

In Chapter 1, we presented the following definitions of an element, a population, and a sample.

- An *element* is the entity on which data are collected.
- A *population* is the collection of all the elements of interest.
- A *sample* is a subset of the population.

The reason we select a sample is to collect data to answer a research question about a population.

Let us begin by citing two examples in which samples were used to answer a research question about a population.

1. Members of a political party in Texas were considering supporting a particular candidate for election to the U.S. Senate, and party leaders wanted an estimate of the proportion of registered voters favoring the candidate. A sample of 400 registered voters was selected and 160 of the 400 voters indicated a preference for the candidate. Thus, an estimate of the proportion of the population of registered voters favoring the candidate is 160/400 = .40.
2. A tire manufacturer is considering producing a new tire designed to provide an increase in mileage over the firm's current line of tires. To estimate the mean useful life of the new tires, the manufacturer produced a sample of 120 tires for testing. The test results provided a sample mean of 36,500 miles. Hence, an estimate of the mean useful life for the population of new tires was 36,500 miles.

A sample mean provides an estimate of a population mean, and a sample proportion provides an estimate of a population proportion. With estimates such as these, some estimation error can be expected. This chapter provides the basis for determining how large that error might be.

It is important to realize that sample results provide only *estimates* of the values of the corresponding population characteristics. We do not expect exactly .40, or 40%, of the population of registered voters to favor the candidate, nor do we expect the sample mean of 36,500 miles to exactly equal the mean mileage for the population of all new tires produced. The reason is simply that the sample contains only a portion of the population. Some sampling error is to be expected. With proper sampling methods, the sample results will provide "good" estimates of the population **parameters**. But how good can we expect the sample results to be? Fortunately, statistical procedures are available for answering this question.

Let us define some of the terms used in sampling. The **sampled population** is the population from which the sample is drawn, and a **frame** is a list of the elements that the sample will be selected from. In the first example, the sampled population is all registered voters in Texas, and the frame is a list of all the registered voters. Because the number of registered voters in Texas is a finite number, the first example is an illustration of sampling from a finite population. In Section 7.2, we discuss how a simple random sample can be selected when sampling from a finite population.

The sampled population for the tire mileage example is more difficult to define because the sample of 120 tires was obtained from a production process at a particular point in time. We can think of the sampled population as the conceptual population of all the tires that could have been made by the production process at that particular point in time. In this sense the sampled population is considered infinite, making it impossible to construct a frame to draw the sample from. In Section 7.2, we discuss how to select a random sample from such a process.

In this chapter, we show how simple random sampling can be used to select a sample from a finite population and describe how a random sample can be taken from a process. We then show how data obtained from a sample can be used to compute estimates of a population mean, a population standard deviation, and a population proportion. In addition, we introduce the important concept of a sampling distribution. As we will show, knowledge of the appropriate sampling distribution enables us to make statements about how close the sample estimates are to the corresponding population parameters. The last section discusses some alternatives to simple random sampling that are often employed in practice.

7.1 The Electronics Associates Sampling Problem

WEB file

EAI

The director of personnel for Electronics Associates, Inc. (EAI), has been assigned the task of developing a profile of the company's 2500 managers. The characteristics to be identified include the mean annual salary for the managers and the proportion of managers having completed the company's management training program.

Using the 2500 managers as the population for this study, we can find the annual salary and the training program status for each individual by referring to the firm's personnel records. The data file containing this information for all 2500 managers in the population is on the website that accompanies the text.

Using the EAI data and the formulas presented in Chapter 3, we compute the population mean and the population standard deviation for the annual salary data.

$$\text{Population mean:} \quad \mu = \$51{,}800$$
$$\text{Population standard deviation:} \quad \sigma = \$4000$$

The data for the training program status show that 1500 of the 2500 managers completed the training program. Letting p denote the proportion of the population that completed the training program, we see that $p = 1500/2500 = .60$. The population mean annual salary ($\mu = \$51{,}800$), the population standard deviation of annual salary ($\sigma = \$4000$), and the population proportion that completed the training program ($p = .60$) are parameters of the population of EAI managers.

Now, suppose that the necessary information on all the EAI managers was not readily available in the company's database. The question we now consider is how the firm's director of personnel can obtain estimates of the population parameters by using a sample of managers rather than all 2500 managers in the population. Suppose that a sample of 30 managers will be used. Clearly, the time and the cost of developing a profile would be substantially less for 30 managers than for the entire population. If the personnel director could be assured that a sample of 30 managers would provide adequate information about the population of 2500 managers, working with a sample would be preferable to working with the entire population. Let us explore the possibility of using a sample for the EAI study by first considering how we can identify a sample of 30 managers.

Often the cost of collecting information from a sample is substantially less than from a population, especially when personal interviews must be conducted to collect the information.

7.2 Selecting a Sample

In this section we describe how to select a sample. We first consider the case of sampling from a finite population and describe the simple random sampling procedure. We then describe how to select a random sample from a process where the population we sample from is the conceptual population of all units that could be generated by the process.

Sampling from a Finite Population

A simple random sample of size n from a finite population of size N is defined as follows.

SIMPLE RANDOM SAMPLE (FINITE POPULATION)

A **simple random sample** of size n from a finite population of size N is a sample selected such that each possible sample of size n has the same probability of being selected.

The random numbers generated using Excel's RAND function follow a uniform probability distribution between 0 and 1.

The procedures used to select a simple random sample from a finite population are based upon the use of random numbers. We can use Excel's RAND function to generate a random number between 0 and 1 by entering the formula =RAND() into any cell in a worksheet.

The number generated is called a random number because the mathematical procedure used by the RAND function guarantees that every number between 0 and 1 has the same probability of being selected. Let us see how these random numbers can be used to select a simple random sample.

Our procedure for selecting a simple random sample of size n from a population of size N involves two steps.

Step 1. Assign a random number to each element of the population.
Step 2. Select the n elements corresponding to the n smallest random numbers.

Because each set of n elements in the population has the same probability of being assigned the n smallest random numbers, each set of n elements has the same probability of being selected for the sample. If we select the sample using this two-step procedure, every sample of size n has the same probability of being selected; thus, the sample selected satisfies the definition of a simple random sample.

Let us consider an example involving selecting a simple random sample of size $n = 5$ from a population of size $N = 16$. Table 7.1 contains a list of the 16 teams in the National Baseball League. Suppose we want to select a simple random sample of 5 teams to conduct in-depth interviews about how they manage their minor league franchises.

Step 1 of our simple random sampling procedure requires that we assign a random number to each of the 16 teams in the population. Figure 7.1 shows a worksheet used to generate a random number corresponding to each of the 16 teams in the population. The names of the baseball teams are in column A, and the random numbers generated are in column B. From the formula worksheet in the background we see that the formula =RAND() has been entered into cells B2:B17 to generate the random numbers between 0 and 1. From the value worksheet in the foreground we see that Arizona is assigned the random number .850862, Atlanta has been assigned the random number .706245, and so on.

The second step is to select the 5 teams corresponding to the five smallest random numbers as our sample. Looking through the random numbers in Figure 7.1, we see that the team corresponding to the smallest random number (.066942) is St. Louis, and that the 4 teams corresponding to the next four smallest random numbers are Washington, Houston, San Diego, and San Francisco. Thus, these 5 teams make up the simple random sample.

Searching through the list of random numbers in Figure 7.1 to find the five smallest random numbers is tedious, and it is easy to make mistakes. Excel's Sort procedure simplifies this step. We illustrate by sorting the list of baseball teams in Figure 7.1 to find the 5 teams corresponding to the five smallest random numbers. Refer to the foreground worksheet in Figure 7.1 as we describe the steps involved.

Step 1. Select any cell in the range B2:B17
Step 2. Click the **Home** tab on the Ribbon
Step 3. In the **Editing** group, click **Sort & Filter**
Step 4. Choose **Sort Smallest to Largest**

TABLE 7.1   NATIONAL BASEBALL LEAGUE TEAMS

Arizona	Milwaukee
Atlanta	New York
Chicago	Philadelphia
Cincinnati	Pittsburgh
Colorado	San Diego
Florida	San Francisco
Houston	St. Louis
Los Angeles	Washington

FIGURE 7.1 WORKSHEET USED TO GENERATE A RANDOM NUMBER CORRESPONDING TO EACH TEAM

WEB file

National League

	A	B	C
1	Team	Random Numbers	
2	Arizona	=RAND()	
3	Atlanta	=RAND()	
4	Chicago	=RAND()	
5	Cincinnati	=RAND()	
6	Colorado	=RAND()	
7	Florida	=RAND()	
8	Houston	=RAND()	
9	Los Angeles	=RAND()	
10	Milwaukee	=RAND()	
11	New York	=RAND()	
12	Philadelphia	=RAND()	
13	Pittsburgh	=RAND()	
14	San Diego	=RAND()	
15	San Francisco	=RAND()	
16	St. Louis	=RAND()	
17	Washington	=RAND()	
18			

	A	B	C
1	Team	Random Numbers	
2	Arizona	0.850862	
3	Atlanta	0.706245	
4	Chicago	0.724789	
5	Cincinnati	0.614784	
6	Colorado	0.553815	
7	Florida	0.857324	
8	Houston	0.179123	
9	Los Angeles	0.525636	
10	Milwaukee	0.471490	
11	New York	0.523103	
12	Philadelphia	0.851552	
13	Pittsburgh	0.806185	
14	San Diego	0.327713	
15	San Francisco	0.374168	
16	St. Louis	0.066942	
17	Washington	0.158452	
18			

After completing these steps we obtain the worksheet shown in Figure 7.2.[1] The teams listed in rows 2–6 are the ones corresponding to the smallest five random numbers; they are our simple random sample. Note that the random numbers shown in Figure 7.2 are in ascending order, and that the teams are not in their original order. For instance, St. Louis is the next to last team listed in Figure 7.1, but it is the first team selected in the simple random sample. Washington, the second team in our sample, is the sixteenth team in the original list, and so on.

We now use this simple random sampling procedure to select a simple random sample of 30 EAI managers from the population of 2500 EAI managers. We begin by generating 2500 random numbers, one for each manager in the population. Then we select 30 managers corresponding to the 30 smallest random numbers as our sample. Refer to Figure 7.3 as we describe the steps involved.

The Excel Sort procedure for identifying the managers associated with the 30 smallest random numbers is especially valuable with such a large population.

Enter Data: The first three columns of the worksheet in the background show the annual salary data and training program status for the first 30 managers in the population of 2500 EAI managers. (The complete worksheet contains all 2500 managers.)

Enter Functions and Formulas: In the background worksheet, the label **Random Numbers** has been entered into cell D1 and the formula =RAND() has been entered into cells D2:D2501 to generate a random number between 0 and 1 for each of the 2500 EAI managers. The random number generated for the first manager is 0.613872, the random number generated for the second manager is 0.473204, and so on.

---

[1]In order to show the random numbers from Figure 7.1 in ascending order in this worksheet, we turned off the automatic recalculation option prior to sorting for illustrative purposes. If the recalculation option were not turned off, a new set of random numbers would have been generated when the sort was completed. But the same five teams would be selected.

FIGURE 7.2 USING EXCEL'S SORT PROCEDURE TO SELECT THE SIMPLE RANDOM SAMPLE OF FIVE TEAMS

	A	B	C
1	**Team**	**Random Numbers**	
2	St. Louis	0.066942	
3	Washington	0.158452	
4	Houston	0.179123	
5	San Diego	0.327713	
6	San Francisco	0.374168	
7	Milwaukee	0.471490	
8	New York	0.523103	
9	Los Angeles	0.525636	
10	Colorado	0.553815	
11	Cincinnati	0.614784	
12	Atlanta	0.706245	
13	Chicago	0.724789	
14	Pittsburgh	0.806185	
15	Arizona	0.850862	
16	Philadelphia	0.851552	
17	Florida	0.857324	
18			

Apply Tools: All that remains is to find the managers associated with the 30 smallest random numbers. To do so, we sort the data in columns A through D into ascending order by the random numbers in column D.

Step 1. Select any cell in the range D2:D2501
Step 2. Click the **Home** tab on the Ribbon
Step 3. In the **Editing** group, click **Sort & Filter**
Step 4. Choose **Sort Smallest to Largest**

After completing these steps we obtain the worksheet shown in the foreground of Figure 7.3. The managers listed in rows 2–31 are the ones corresponding to the smallest 30 random numbers that were generated. Hence, this group of 30 managers is a simple random sample. Note that the random numbers shown in the foreground of Figure 7.3 are in ascending order, and that the managers are not in their original order. For instance, manager 812 in the population is associated with the smallest random number and is the first element in the sample, and manager 13 in the population (see row 14 of the background worksheet) has been included as the 22nd observation in the sample (row 23 of the foreground worksheet).

Sampling from a Process

Sometimes we want to take a sample to make an inference about a population, but the sampled population is such that a frame cannot be constructed. In such a case, we cannot use simple random sampling. One such situation is sampling from an ongoing process in which the sampled population is conceptually infinite. Another situation is sampling from a very large population or any other situation where it is not possible or, perhaps, not feasible to identify all the elements.

FIGURE 7.3   USING EXCEL TO SELECT A SIMPLE RANDOM SAMPLE WITHOUT REPLACEMENT

	A	B	C	D
1	**Manager**	**Annual Salary**	**Training Program**	**Random Numbers**
2	1	55769.50	No	0.613872
3	2	50823.00	Yes	0.473204
4	3	48408.20	No	0.549011
5	4	49787.50	No	0.047482
6	5	52801.60	Yes	0.531085
7	6	51767.70	No	0.994296
8	7	58346.60	Yes	0.189065
9	8	46670.20	No	0.020714
10	9	50246.80	Yes	0.647318
11	10	51255.00	No	0.524341
12	11	52546.60	No	0.764998
13	12	49512.50	Yes	0.255244
14	13	51753.00	Yes	0.010923
15	14	53547.10	No	0.238003
16	15	48052.20	No	0.635675
17	16	44652.50	Yes	0.177294
18	17	51764.90	Yes	0.415097
19	18	45187.80	Yes	0.883440
20	19	49867.50	Yes	0.476824
21	20	53706.30	Yes	0.101065
22	21	52039.50	Yes	0.775323
23	22	52973.60	No	0.011729
24	23	53372.50	No	0.762026
25	24	54592.00	Yes	0.066344
26	25	55738.10	Yes	0.776766
27	26	52975.10	Yes	0.828493
28	27	52386.20	Yes	0.841532
29	28	51051.60	Yes	0.899427
30	29	52095.60	Yes	0.486284
31	30	44956.50	No	0.264628

The formula in cells D2:D2501 is =RAND().

Note: Rows 32–2501 are not shown.

	A	B	C	D	E
1	**Manager**	**Annual Salary**	**Training Program**	**Random Numbers**	
2	812	49094.30	Yes	0.000193	
3	1411	53263.90	Yes	0.000484	
4	1795	49643.50	Yes	0.002641	
5	2095	49894.90	Yes	0.002763	
6	1235	47621.60	No	0.002940	
7	744	55924.00	Yes	0.002977	
8	470	49092.30	Yes	0.003182	
9	1606	51404.40	Yes	0.003448	
10	1744	50957.70	Yes	0.004203	
11	179	55109.70	Yes	0.005293	
12	1387	45922.60	Yes	0.005709	
13	1782	57268.40	No	0.005729	
14	1006	55688.80	Yes	0.005796	
15	278	51564.70	No	0.005966	
16	1850	56188.20	No	0.006250	
17	844	51766.00	Yes	0.006708	
18	2028	52541.30	No	0.007767	
19	1654	44980.00	Yes	0.008095	
20	444	51932.60	Yes	0.009686	
21	556	52973.00	Yes	0.009711	
22	2449	45120.90	Yes	0.010595	
23	13	51753.00	Yes	0.010923	
24	2187	54391.80	No	0.011364	
25	1633	50164.20	No	0.011603	
26	22	52973.60	No	0.011729	
27	1530	50241.30	No	0.013570	
28	820	52793.90	No	0.013669	
29	1258	50979.40	Yes	0.014042	
30	2349	55860.90	Yes	0.014532	
31	1698	57309.10	No	0.014539	

Suppose we want to take a sample of the elements generated by a production process. For instance, consider the example given in the chapter introduction. In this example the manufacturer produced a sample of 120 new tires in order to estimate the mean useful life for the population of new tires. In this type of situation we consider the sampled population to be all the tires that could have been produced by the production process at that particular point in time. This conceptual population is considered to be infinitely large. When sampling from a conceptual population such as this or any other population where it is not feasible to construct a frame, we cannot select a simple random sample. But we can, by exercising care and judgment, select what statisticians call a random sample.

A random sample is one in which each of the sampled elements is independent and follows the same probability distribution as the elements in the population. If a production process, such as our tire production example, is operating properly, then each unit produced is independent of each other unit and the differences in the units are only attributable to chance variation. In such a situation we can select a random sample by selecting any *n* units produced while the process is operating properly. A sample taken when the process is not working properly due to a machine out of adjustment, for example, will not provide a sample that is representative of typical production.

Situations involving sampling from a process are often associated with an ongoing process that operates continuously over time. For example, parts being manufactured on a production line, transactions occurring at a bank, telephone calls arriving at a technical support center, and customers entering stores may all be viewed as coming from a process generating elements from a conceptually infinite population. When faced with this type of sampling situation, it is usually not possible to develop a frame consisting of all the elements in the population and the statistician needs to use a creative approach to choose a random sample. Whatever approach is used, the goal is to obtain a random sample; that is, all the units selected must be independent and follow the same probability distribution as the population.

NOTES AND COMMENTS

The number of different simple random samples of size *n* that can be selected from a finite population of size *N* is

$$\frac{N!}{n!(N-n)!}$$

In this formula, *N*! and *n*! are the factorial computations discussed in Chapter 4. For the EAI problem with $N = 2500$ and $n = 30$, this expression can be used to show that approximately 2.75×10^{69} different simple random samples of 30 EAI managers are possible.

Exercises

Methods

SELF test

1. Consider a finite population with five elements labeled A, B, C, D, and E. Ten possible simple random samples of size 2 can be selected.
   a. List the 10 samples beginning with AB, AC, and so on.
   b. Using simple random sampling, what is the probability that each sample of size 2 is selected?
   c. Suppose we use Excel's RAND function to assign random numbers to the five elements: A (.7266), B (.0476), C (.2459), D (.0957), E (.9408). List the simple random sample of size 2 that will be selected by using these random numbers.

2. Assume a finite population has 10 elements. Number the elements from 1 to 10 and use the following 10 random numbers to select a sample of size 4.

   .7545   .0936   .0341   .3242   .1449   .9060   .2420   .9773   .5428   .0729

SELF test

3. The American League consists of 14 baseball teams. Suppose a sample of 5 teams is to be selected to conduct player interviews. The following table lists the 14 teams and the random numbers assigned by Excel's RAND function. Use these random numbers to select a sample of size 5.

American
League

Team	Random Number	Team	Random Number
New York	0.178624 \	Boston	0.290197 Ꮞ
Baltimore	0.578370	Tampa Bay	0.867778
Toronto	0.965807	Minnesota	0.811810
Chicago	0.562178	Cleveland	0.960271
Detroit	0.253574 ᴤ	Kansas City	0.326836 ⑤
Oakland	0.288287 ⑦	Anaheim	0.895267
Texas	0.500879	Seattle	0.839071

4. The 10 most active issues on the New York Stock Exchange on September 17, 2004, are listed here (*The Sun News,* September 18, 2004).

Nortel	General Electric	Lucent	Pfizer	Texas Instruments
Exxon/Mobil	Citigroup	Wal-Mart	EMC	Motorola

Exchange authorities decided to sample three of these companies to investigate trading practices. Select a simple random sample of three companies for this investigation.

5. In this section we used a two-step procedure to select a simple random sample of 30 EAI managers. Use this procedure to select a simple random sample of 50 EAI managers.

EAI

6. Indicate which of the following situations involve sampling from a finite population and which involve sampling from a process. In cases where the sampled population is finite, describe how you would construct a frame.
   a. Select a sample of licensed drivers in the state of New York.
   b. Select a sample of boxes of cereal produced by the Breakfast Choice Company.
   c. Select a sample of cars crossing the Golden Gate Bridge on a typical weekday.
   d. Select a sample of students in a statistics course at Indiana University.
   e. Select a sample of the orders that could be processed by a mail-order firm.

7.3   Point Estimation

Now that we have described how to select a simple random sample, let us return to the EAI problem. A simple random sample of 30 managers and the corresponding data on annual salary and management training program participation are as shown in Table 7.2. The notation x_1, x_2, and so on is used to denote the annual salary of the first manager in the sample, the annual salary of the second manager in the sample, and so on. Participation in the management training program is indicated by Yes in the management training program column.

To estimate the value of a population parameter, we compute a corresponding characteristic of the sample, referred to as a **sample statistic**. For example, to estimate the population mean μ and the population standard deviation σ for the annual salary of EAI managers, we use the data in Table 7.2 to calculate the corresponding sample statistics: the sample mean $\bar{x}$ and the sample standard deviation s. Using the formulas for a sample mean and a sample standard deviation presented in Chapter 3, the sample mean is

$$\bar{x} = \frac{\Sigma x_i}{n} = \frac{1{,}554{,}420}{30} = \$51{,}814$$

and the sample standard deviation is

$$s = \sqrt{\frac{\Sigma(x_i - \bar{x})^2}{n-1}} = \sqrt{\frac{325{,}009{,}260}{29}} = \$3348$$

To estimate p, the proportion of managers in the population who completed the management training program, we use the corresponding sample proportion $\bar{p}$. Let x denote the

TABLE 7.2   ANNUAL SALARY AND TRAINING PROGRAM STATUS FOR A SIMPLE RANDOM SAMPLE OF 30 EAI MANAGERS

Annual Salary ($)	Management Training Program	Annual Salary ($)	Management Training Program
$x_1 = 49{,}094.30$	Yes	$x_{16} = 51{,}766.00$	Yes
$x_2 = 53{,}263.90$	Yes	$x_{17} = 52{,}541.30$	No
$x_3 = 49{,}643.50$	Yes	$x_{18} = 44{,}980.00$	Yes
$x_4 = 49{,}894.90$	Yes	$x_{19} = 51{,}932.60$	Yes
$x_5 = 47{,}621.60$	No	$x_{20} = 52{,}973.00$	Yes
$x_6 = 55{,}924.00$	Yes	$x_{21} = 45{,}120.90$	Yes
$x_7 = 49{,}092.30$	Yes	$x_{22} = 51{,}753.00$	Yes
$x_8 = 51{,}404.40$	Yes	$x_{23} = 54{,}391.80$	No
$x_9 = 50{,}957.70$	Yes	$x_{24} = 50{,}164.20$	No
$x_{10} = 55{,}109.70$	Yes	$x_{25} = 52{,}973.60$	No
$x_{11} = 45{,}922.60$	Yes	$x_{26} = 50{,}241.30$	No
$x_{12} = 57{,}268.40$	No	$x_{27} = 52{,}793.90$	No
$x_{13} = 55{,}688.80$	Yes	$x_{28} = 50{,}979.40$	Yes
$x_{14} = 51{,}564.70$	No	$x_{29} = 55{,}860.90$	Yes
$x_{15} = 56{,}188.20$	No	$x_{30} = 57{,}309.10$	No

number of managers in the sample who completed the management training program. The data in Table 7.2 show that $x = 19$. Thus, with a sample size of $n = 30$, the sample proportion is

$$\bar{p} = \frac{x}{n} = \frac{19}{30} = .63$$

By making the preceding computations, we perform the statistical procedure called *point estimation.* We refer to the sample mean $\bar{x}$ as the **point estimator** of the population mean μ, the sample standard deviation s as the point estimator of the population standard deviation σ, and the sample proportion $\bar{p}$ as the point estimator of the population proportion p. The numerical value obtained for $\bar{x}$, s, or $\bar{p}$ is called the **point estimate**. Thus, for the simple random sample of 30 EAI managers shown in Table 7.2, $\$51{,}814$ is the point estimate of μ, $\$3348$ is the point estimate of σ, and .63 is the point estimate of p. Table 7.3 summarizes the sample results and compares the point estimates to the actual values of the population parameters.

As evident from Table 7.3, the point estimates differ somewhat from the corresponding population parameters. This difference is to be expected because a sample, and not a census of the entire population, is being used to develop the point estimates. In the next chapter, we will show how to construct an interval estimate in order to provide information about how close the point estimate is to the population parameter.

TABLE 7.3   SUMMARY OF POINT ESTIMATES OBTAINED FROM A SIMPLE RANDOM SAMPLE OF 30 EAI MANAGERS

Population Parameter	Parameter Value	Point Estimator	Point Estimate
μ = Population mean annual salary	$51,800	$\bar{x}$ = Sample mean annual salary	$51,814
σ = Population standard deviation for annual salary	$4000	s = Sample standard deviation for annual salary	$3348
p = Population proportion having completed the management training program	.60	$\bar{p}$ = Sample proportion having completed the management training program	.63

Practical Advice

The subject matter of most of the rest of the book is concerned with statistical inference. Point estimation is a form of statistical inference. We use a sample statistic to make an inference about a population parameter. When making inferences about a population based on a sample, it is important to have a close correspondence between the sampled population and the target population. The **target population** is the population we want to make inferences about, while the sampled population is the population from which the sample is actually taken. In this section, we have described the process of drawing a simple random sample from the population of EAI managers and making point estimates of characteristics of that same population. So the sampled population and the target population are identical, which is the desired situation. But in other cases care must be exercised to obtain a close correspondence between the sampled and target population.

Consider the case of an amusement park selecting a sample of its customers to learn about characteristics such as age and time spent at the park. Suppose all the sample elements were selected on a day when park attendance was restricted to employees of a large company. Then the sampled population would be composed of employees of that company and members of their families. If the target population we wanted to make inferences about were typical park customers over a typical summer day, then we might encounter a significant difference between the sampled population and the target population. In such a case, we would question the validity of the point estimates being made. Park management would be in the best position to know whether a sample taken on a particular day was likely to be representative of the target population.

In summary, whenever a sample is used to make inferences about a population we should make sure that the study is designed so that the sampled population and the target population are in close agreement. This issue is not mathematical, but it requires good judgment.

Exercises

Methods

7. The following data are from a simple random sample.

$$5 \quad 8 \quad 10 \quad 7 \quad 10 \quad 14$$

   a. What is the point estimate of the population mean?
   b. What is the point estimate of the population standard deviation?

8. A survey question for a sample of 150 individuals yielded 75 Yes responses, 55 No responses, and 20 No Opinions.
   a. What is the point estimate of the proportion in the population who respond Yes?
   b. What is the point estimate of the proportion in the population who respond No?

Applications

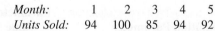

9. A simple random sample of 5 months of sales data provided the following information:

Month:	1	2	3	4	5
Units Sold:	94	100	85	94	92

   a. Develop a point estimate of the population mean number of units sold per month.
   b. Develop a point estimate of the population standard deviation.

MutualFund

10. *BusinessWeek* published information on 283 equity mutual funds (*BusinessWeek*, January 26, 2004). A sample of 40 of those funds is contained in the data set MutualFund. Use the data set to answer the following questions.
    a. Develop a point estimate of the proportion of the *BusinessWeek* equity funds that are load funds.

b.   Develop a point estimate of the proportion of funds that are classified as high risk.

c.   Develop a point estimate of the proportion of funds that have a below-average risk rating.

11.   Many drugs used to treat cancer are expensive. *BusinessWeek* reported on the cost per treatment of Herceptin, a drug used to treat breast cancer (*BusinessWeek,* January 30, 2006). Typical treatment costs (in dollars) for Herceptin are provided by a simple random sample of 10 patients.

4376	5578	2717	4920	4495
4798	6446	4119	4237	3814

a.   Develop a point estimate of the mean cost per treatment with Herceptin.

b.   Develop a point estimate of the standard deviation of the cost per treatment with Herceptin.

12.   A sample of 50 *Fortune* 500 companies (*Fortune,* April 14, 2003) showed 5 were based in New York, 6 in California, 2 in Minnesota, and 1 in Wisconsin.

a.   Develop an estimate of the proportion of *Fortune* 500 companies based in New York.

b.   Develop an estimate of the number of *Fortune* 500 companies based in Minnesota.

c.   Develop an estimate of the proportion of *Fortune* 500 companies that are not based in these four states.

13.   The American Association of Individual Investors (AAII) polls its subscribers on a weekly basis to determine the number who are bullish, bearish, or neutral on the short-term prospects for the stock market. Their findings for the week ending March 2, 2006, are consistent with the following sample results (*http://www.aaii.com*).

Bullish   409   Neutral   299   Bearish   291

Develop a point estimate of the following population parameters.

a.   The proportion of all AAII subscribers who are bullish on the stock market.

b.   The proportion of all AAII subscribers who are neutral on the stock market.

c.   The proportion of all AAII subscribers who are bearish on the stock market.

14.   In this section we showed how a simple random sample of 30 EAI managers can be used to develop point estimates of the population mean annual salary, the population standard deviation for annual salary, and the population proportion having completed the management training program.

EAI

a.   Use Excel to select a simple random sample of 50 EAI managers.

b.   Develop a point estimate of the mean annual salary.

c.   Develop a point estimate of the population standard deviation for annual salary.

d.   Develop a point estimate of the population proportion having completed the management training program.

(7.4) Introduction to Sampling Distributions

In the preceding section we said that the sample mean $\bar{x}$ is the point estimator of the population mean μ, and the sample proportion $\bar{p}$ is the point estimator of the population proportion p. For the simple random sample of 30 EAI managers shown in Table 7.2, the point estimate of μ is $\bar{x} = \$51,814$ and the point estimate of p is $\bar{p} = .63$. Suppose we select another simple random sample of 30 EAI managers and obtain the following point estimates:

Sample mean: $\bar{x} = \$52,670$

Sample proportion: $\bar{p} = .70$

Note that different values of $\bar{x}$ and $\bar{p}$ were obtained. Indeed, a second simple random sample of 30 EAI managers cannot be expected to provide the same point estimates as the first sample.

Now, suppose we repeat the process of selecting a simple random sample of 30 EAI managers over and over again, each time computing the values of $\bar{x}$ and $\bar{p}$. Table 7.4 contains a portion of the results obtained for 500 simple random samples, and Table 7.5 shows

TABLE 7.4   VALUES OF $\bar{x}$ AND $\bar{p}$ FROM 500 SIMPLE RANDOM SAMPLES OF 30 EAI MANAGERS

Sample Number	Sample Mean ($\bar{x}$)	Sample Proportion ($\bar{p}$)
1	51,814	.63
2	52,670	.70
3	51,780	.67
4	51,588	.53
.	.	.
.	.	.
.	.	.
500	51,752	.50

the frequency and relative frequency distributions for the 500 $\bar{x}$ values. Figure 7.4 shows the relative frequency histogram for the $\bar{x}$ values.

The ability to understand the material in subsequent chapters depends heavily on the ability to understand and use the sampling distributions presented in this chapter.

In Chapter 5 we defined a random variable as a numerical description of the outcome of an experiment. If we consider the process of selecting a simple random sample as an experiment, the sample mean $\bar{x}$ is the numerical description of the outcome of the experiment. Thus, the sample mean $\bar{x}$ is a random variable. As a result, just like other random variables, $\bar{x}$ has a mean or expected value, a standard deviation, and a probability distribution. Because the various possible values of $\bar{x}$ are the result of different simple random samples, the probability distribution of $\bar{x}$ is called the **sampling distribution** of $\bar{x}$. Knowledge of this sampling distribution and its properties will enable us to make probability statements about how close the sample mean $\bar{x}$ is to the population mean μ.

Let us return to Figure 7.4. We would need to enumerate every possible sample of 30 managers and compute each sample mean to completely determine the sampling distribution of $\bar{x}$. However, the histogram of 500 $\bar{x}$ values gives an approximation of this sampling distribution. From the approximation we observe the bell-shaped appearance of the distribution. We note that the largest concentration of the $\bar{x}$ values and the mean of the 500 $\bar{x}$ values is near the population mean $\mu = \$51,800$. We will describe the properties of the sampling distribution of $\bar{x}$ more fully in the next section.

The 500 values of the sample proportion $\bar{p}$ are summarized by the relative frequency histogram in Figure 7.5. As in the case of $\bar{x}$, $\bar{p}$ is a random variable. If every possible sample of size 30 were selected from the population and if a value of $\bar{p}$ were computed for each sample, the resulting probability distribution would be the sampling distribution of $\bar{p}$. The

TABLE 7.5   FREQUENCY DISTRIBUTION OF $\bar{x}$ FROM 500 SIMPLE RANDOM SAMPLES OF 30 EAI MANAGERS

Mean Annual Salary ($)	Frequency	Relative Frequency
49,500.00–49,999.99	2	.004
50,000.00–50,499.99	16	.032
50,500.00–50,999.99	52	.104
51,000.00–51,499.99	101	.202
51,500.00–51,999.99	133	.266
52,000.00–52,499.99	110	.220
52,500.00–52,999.99	54	.108
53,000.00–53,499.99	26	.052
53,500.00–53,999.99	6	.012
Totals	500	1.000

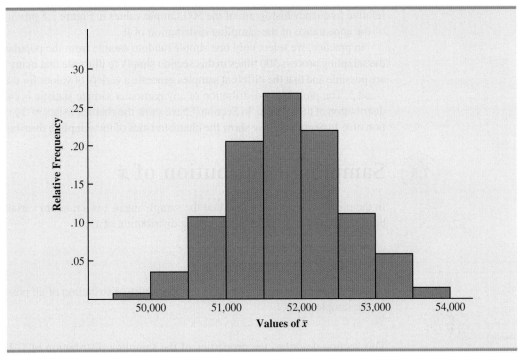

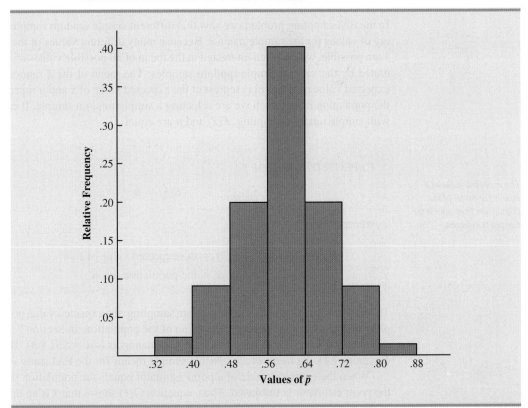

relative frequency histogram of the 500 sample values in Figure 7.5 provides a general idea of the appearance of the sampling distribution of $\bar{p}$.

In practice, we select only one simple random sample from the population. We repeated the sampling process 500 times in this section simply to illustrate that many different samples are possible and that the different samples generate a variety of values for the sample statistics $\bar{x}$ and $\bar{p}$. The probability distribution of any particular sample statistic is called the sampling distribution of the statistic. In Section 7.5 we show the characteristics of the sampling distribution of $\bar{x}$. In Section 7.6 we show the characteristics of the sampling distribution of $\bar{p}$.

7.5 Sampling Distribution of $\bar{x}$

In the previous section we said that the sample mean $\bar{x}$ is a random variable and its probability distribution is called the sampling distribution of $\bar{x}$.

> **SAMPLING DISTRIBUTION OF $\bar{x}$**
>
> The sampling distribution of $\bar{x}$ is the probability distribution of all possible values of the sample mean $\bar{x}$.

This section describes the properties of the sampling distribution of $\bar{x}$. Just as with other probability distributions we studied, the sampling distribution of $\bar{x}$ has an expected value or mean, a standard deviation, and a characteristic shape or form. Let us begin by considering the mean of all possible $\bar{x}$ values, which is referred to as the expected value of $\bar{x}$.

Expected Value of $\bar{x}$

In the EAI sampling problem we saw that different simple random samples result in a variety of values for the sample mean $\bar{x}$. Because many different values of the random variable $\bar{x}$ are possible, we are often interested in the mean of all possible values of $\bar{x}$ that can be generated by the various simple random samples. The mean of the $\bar{x}$ random variable is the expected value of $\bar{x}$. Let $E(\bar{x})$ represent the expected value of $\bar{x}$ and μ represent the mean of the population from which we are selecting a simple random sample. It can be shown that with simple random sampling, $E(\bar{x})$ and μ are equal.

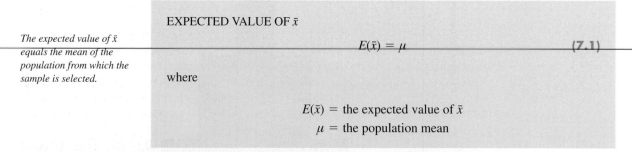

The expected value of $\bar{x}$ equals the mean of the population from which the sample is selected.

EXPECTED VALUE OF $\bar{x}$

$$E(\bar{x}) = \mu \qquad (7.1)$$

where

$$E(\bar{x}) = \text{the expected value of } \bar{x}$$
$$\mu = \text{the population mean}$$

This result shows that with simple random sampling, the expected value or mean of the sampling distribution of $\bar{x}$ is equal to the mean of the population. In Section 7.1 we saw that the mean annual salary for the population of EAI managers is $\mu = \$51,800$. Thus, according to equation (7.1), the mean of all possible sample means for the EAI study is also \$51,800.

When the expected value of a point estimator equals the population parameter, we say the point estimator is **unbiased**. Thus, equation (7.1) shows that $\bar{x}$ is an unbiased estimator of the population mean μ.

Standard Deviation of $\bar{x}$

Let us define the standard deviation of the sampling distribution of $\bar{x}$. We will use the following notation.

$$\sigma_{\bar{x}} = \text{the standard deviation of } \bar{x}$$
$$\sigma = \text{the standard deviation of the population}$$
$$n = \text{the sample size}$$
$$N = \text{the population size}$$

It can be shown that when sampling from a finite population, the standard deviation of $\bar{x}$ is as follows:

STANDARD DEVIATION OF $\bar{x}$: FINITE POPULATION

$$\sigma_{\bar{x}} = \sqrt{\frac{N-n}{N-1}}\left(\frac{\sigma}{\sqrt{n}}\right) \qquad (7.2)$$

Exercise 17 shows that when n/N ≤ .05, the finite population correction factor has little effect on the value of $\sigma_{\bar{x}}$.

In equation (7.2) the factor $\sqrt{(N-n)/(N-1)}$ is commonly referred to as the **finite population correction factor**. In most practical sampling situations, we find that the population involved, although finite, is "large," whereas the sample size is relatively "small." In such situations the finite population factor $\sqrt{(N-n)/(N-1)}$ is close to 1 and $\sigma_{\bar{x}} = \sigma/\sqrt{n}$ becomes a good approximation to the standard deviation of $\bar{x}$. We recommend using $\sigma_{\bar{x}} = \sigma/\sqrt{n}$ to compute the standard deviation of $\bar{x}$ if the sample size is less than or equal to 5% of the population size; that is, $n/N \leq .05$. In cases where the sample is selected from a process and the conceptual population is infinite, the standard deviation of $\bar{x}$ is also computed using $\sigma_{\bar{x}} = \sigma/\sqrt{n}$. Unless otherwise noted, throughout the text we will compute the standard deviation of $\bar{x}$ as follows:

STANDARD DEVIATION OF $\bar{x}$

$$\sigma_{\bar{x}} = \frac{\sigma}{\sqrt{n}} \qquad (7.3)$$

The term standard error is used throughout statistical inference to refer to the standard deviation of a point estimator.

To compute $\sigma_{\bar{x}}$, we need to know σ, the standard deviation of the population. To further emphasize the difference between $\sigma_{\bar{x}}$ and σ, we refer to the standard deviation of $\bar{x}$, $\sigma_{\bar{x}}$, as the **standard error** of the mean. In general, the term *standard error* refers to the standard deviation of a point estimator. Later we will see that the value of the standard error of the mean is helpful in determining how far the sample mean may be from the population mean. Let us now return to the EAI example and compute the standard error of the mean associated with simple random samples of 30 EAI managers.

In Section 7.1 we saw that the standard deviation of annual salary for the population of 2500 EAI managers is $\sigma = 4000$. In this case, the population is finite, with $N = 2500$. However, with a sample size of 30, we have $n/N = 30/2500 = .012$. Because the sample size is less than 5% of the population size, we can ignore the finite population correction factor and use equation (7.3) to compute the standard error.

$$\sigma_{\bar{x}} = \frac{\sigma}{\sqrt{n}} = \frac{4000}{\sqrt{30}} = 730.3$$

Form of the Sampling Distribution of $\bar{x}$

The preceding results concerning the expected value and standard deviation for the sampling distribution of $\bar{x}$ are applicable for any population. The final step in identifying the characteristics of the sampling distribution of $\bar{x}$ is to determine the form or shape of the sampling distribution. We will consider two cases: (1) the population has a normal distribution; and (2) the population does not have a normal distribution.

Population has a normal distribution In many situations it is reasonable to assume that the population from which we are selecting a simple random sample has a normal, or nearly normal, distribution. When the population has a normal distribution, the sampling distribution of $\bar{x}$ is normally distributed for any sample size.

Population does not have a normal distribution When the population from which we are selecting a simple random sample does not have a normal distribution, the **central limit theorem** is helpful in identifying the shape of the sampling distribution of $\bar{x}$. A statement of the central limit theorem as it applies to the sampling distribution of $\bar{x}$ follows.

CENTRAL LIMIT THEOREM

In selecting simple random samples of size n from a population, the sampling distribution of the sample mean $\bar{x}$ can be approximated by a *normal distribution* as the sample size becomes large.

Figure 7.6 shows how the central limit theorem works for three different populations; each column refers to one of the populations. The top panel of the figure shows that none of the populations are normally distributed. Population I follows a uniform distribution. Population II is often called the rabbit-eared distribution. It is symmetric, but the more likely values fall in the tails of the distribution. Population III is shaped like the exponential distribution; it is skewed to the right.

The bottom three panels of Figure 7.6 show the shape of the sampling distribution for samples of size $n = 2$, $n = 5$, and $n = 30$. When the sample size is 2, we see that the shape of each sampling distribution is different from the shape of the corresponding population distribution. For samples of size 5, we see that the shapes of the sampling distributions for populations I and II begin to look similar to the shape of a normal distribution. Even though the shape of the sampling distribution for population III begins to look similar to the shape of a normal distribution, some skewness to the right is still present. Finally, for samples of size 30, the shapes of each of the three sampling distributions are approximately normal.

From a practitioner standpoint, we often want to know how large the sample size needs to be before the central limit theorem applies and we can assume that the shape of the sampling distribution is approximately normal. Statistical researchers have investigated this question by studying the sampling distribution of $\bar{x}$ for a variety of populations and a variety of sample sizes. General statistical practice is to assume that, for most applications, the sampling distribution of $\bar{x}$ can be approximated by a normal distribution whenever the sample is size 30 or more. In cases where the population is highly skewed or outliers are present, samples of size 50 may be needed. Finally, if the population is discrete, the sample size needed for a normal approximation often depends on the population proportion. We say more about this issue when we discuss the sampling distribution of $\bar{p}$ in Section 7.6.

FIGURE 7.6   ILLUSTRATION OF THE CENTRAL LIMIT THEOREM FOR THREE POPULATIONS

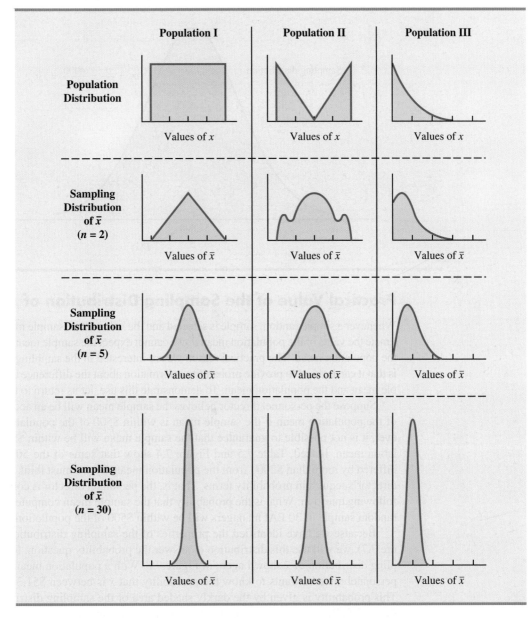

Sampling Distribution of $\bar{x}$ for the EAI Problem

Let us return to the EAI problem where we previously showed that $E(\bar{x}) = \$51,800$ and $\sigma_{\bar{x}} = 730.3$. At this point, we do not have any information about the population distribution; it may or may not be normally distributed. If the population has a normal distribution, the sampling distribution of $\bar{x}$ is normally distributed. If the population does not have a normal distribution, the simple random sample of 30 managers and the central limit theorem enable us to conclude that the sampling distribution of $\bar{x}$ can be approximated by a normal distribution. In either case, we are comfortable proceeding with the conclusion that the sampling distribution of $\bar{x}$ can be described by the normal distribution shown in Figure 7.7.

FIGURE 7.7 SAMPLING DISTRIBUTION OF $\bar{x}$ FOR THE MEAN ANNUAL SALARY OF A SIMPLE RANDOM SAMPLE OF 30 EAI MANAGERS

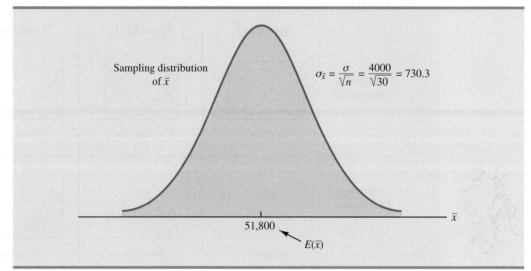

Practical Value of the Sampling Distribution of $\bar{x}$

Whenever a simple random sample is selected and the value of the sample mean is used to estimate the value of the population mean μ, we cannot expect the sample mean to exactly equal the population mean. The practical reason we are interested in the sampling distribution of $\bar{x}$ is that it can be used to provide probability information about the difference between the sample mean and the population mean. To demonstrate this use, let us return to the EAI problem.

Suppose the personnel director believes the sample mean will be an acceptable estimate of the population mean if the sample mean is within $500 of the population mean. However, it is not possible to guarantee that the sample mean will be within $500 of the population mean. Indeed, Table 7.5 and Figure 7.4 show that some of the 500 sample means differed by more than $2000 from the population mean. So we must think of the personnel director's request in probability terms. That is, the personnel director is concerned with the following question: What is the probability that the sample mean computed using a simple random sample of 30 EAI managers will be within $500 of the population mean?

Because we have identified the properties of the sampling distribution of $\bar{x}$ (see Figure 7.7), we will use this distribution to answer the probability question. Refer to the sampling distribution of $\bar{x}$ shown again in Figure 7.8. With a population mean of $51,800, the personnel director wants to know the probability that $\bar{x}$ is between $51,300 and $52,300. This probability is given by the darkly shaded area of the sampling distribution shown in Figure 7.8. Because the sampling distribution is normally distributed, with mean 51,800 and standard error of the mean 730.3, we can use the standard normal probability table to find the area or probability.

We first calculate the z value at the upper endpoint of the interval (52,300) and use the table to find the area under the curve to the left of that point (left tail area). Then we compute the z value at the lower endpoint of the interval (51,300) and use the table to find the area under the curve to the left of that point (another left tail area). Subtracting the second tail area from the first gives us the desired probability.

At $\bar{x} = 52,300$, we have

$$z = \frac{52,300 - 51,800}{730.30} = .68$$

FIGURE 7.8 PROBABILITY OF A SAMPLE MEAN BEING WITHIN $500
OF THE POPULATION MEAN FOR A SIMPLE RANDOM
SAMPLE OF 30 EAI MANAGERS

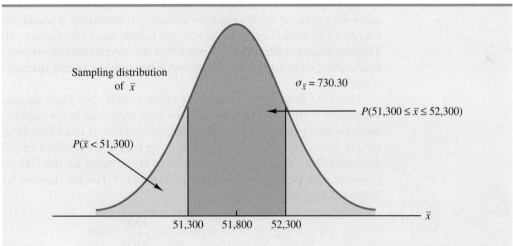

Referring to the standard normal probability table, we find a cumulative probability (area to the left of $z = .68$) of .7517.

At $\bar{x} = 51,300$, we have

$$z = \frac{51,300 - 51,800}{730.30} = -.68$$

The area under the curve to the left of $z = -.68$ is .2483. Therefore, $P(51,300 \leq \bar{x} \leq 52,300) = P(z \leq .68) - P(z < -.68) = .7517 - .2483 = .5034$.

Using Excel's NORMDIST function is easier and provides more accurate results than using the tables with rounded values for z.

The desired probability can also be computed using Excel's NORMDIST function. The advantage of using the NORMDIST function is that we do not have to make a separate computation of the z value. Evaluating the NORMDIST function at the upper endpoint of the interval provides the area under the curve to the left of 52,300. Entering the formula =NORMDIST(52300,51800,730.30,TRUE) into a cell of an Excel worksheet provides .7532 for this cumulative probability. Evaluating the NORMDIST function at the lower endpoint of the interval provides the area under the curve to the left of 51,300. Entering the formula =NORMDIST(51300,51800,730.30,TRUE) into a cell of an Excel worksheet provides .2468 for this cumulative probability. The probability of $\bar{x}$ being in the interval from 51,300 to 52,300 is then given by .7532 − .2468 = .5064. We note that this result is slightly different from the probability obtained using the table, because in using the normal table we rounded to two decimal places of accuracy when computing the z value. The result obtained using NORMDIST is thus more accurate.

The sampling distribution of $\bar{x}$ can be used to provide probability information about how close the sample mean $\bar{x}$ is to the population mean μ.

The preceding computations show that a simple random sample of 30 EAI managers has a .5064 probability of providing a sample mean $\bar{x}$ that is within $500 of the population mean. Thus, there is a $1 - .5064 = .4936$ probability that the sampling error will be more than $500. In other words, a simple random sample of 30 EAI managers has roughly a 50/50 chance of providing a sample mean within the allowable $500. Perhaps a larger sample size should be considered. Let us explore this possibility by considering the relationship between the sample size and the sampling distribution of $\bar{x}$.

Relationship Between Sample Size and the Sampling Distribution of $\bar{x}$

Suppose that in the EAI sampling problem we select a simple random sample of 100 EAI managers instead of the 30 originally considered. Intuitively, it would seem that with more data provided by the larger sample size, the sample mean based on $n = 100$ should provide a better estimate of the population mean than the sample mean based on $n = 30$. To see how much better, let us consider the relationship between the sample size and the sampling distribution of $\bar{x}$.

First note that $E(\bar{x}) = \mu$ regardless of the sample size. Thus, the mean of all possible values of $\bar{x}$ is equal to the population mean μ regardless of the sample size n. However, note that the standard error of the mean, $\sigma_{\bar{x}} = \sigma / \sqrt{n}$, is related to the square root of the sample size. Whenever the sample size is increased, the standard error of the mean $\sigma_{\bar{x}}$ is decreased. With $n = 30$, the standard error of the mean for the EAI problem is 730.30. However, with the increase in the sample size to $n = 100$, the standard error of the mean is decreased to

$$\sigma_{\bar{x}} = \frac{\sigma}{\sqrt{n}} = \frac{4000}{\sqrt{100}} = 400$$

The sampling distributions of $\bar{x}$ with $n = 30$ and $n = 100$ are shown in Figure 7.9. Because the sampling distribution with $n = 100$ provides a smaller standard error, the values of $\bar{x}$ vary less and tend to be grouped closer around the population mean than the values of $\bar{x}$ with $n = 30$.

We can use the sampling distribution of $\bar{x}$ for the case with $n = 100$ to compute the probability that a simple random sample of 100 EAI managers will provide a sample mean that is within \$500 of the population mean. In this case the sampling distribution is normal with a mean of 51,800 and a standard deviation of 400 (see Figure 7.10). Again, we could compute the appropriate z values and use the standard normal probability distribution table to make this probability calculation. However, Excel's NORMDIST function is easier to use and provides more accurate results. Entering the formula =NORMDIST(52300,51800,400,TRUE) into a cell of an Excel worksheet provides the cumulative probability corresponding to $\bar{x} = 52,300$. The value provided by Excel is .8944. Entering the formula =NORMDIST (51300,51800,400,TRUE) into a cell of an Excel worksheet provides the cumulative

FIGURE 7.9   COMPARISON OF THE SAMPLING DISTRIBUTIONS OF $\bar{x}$ FOR SIMPLE RANDOM SAMPLES OF $n = 30$ AND $n = 100$ EAI MANAGERS

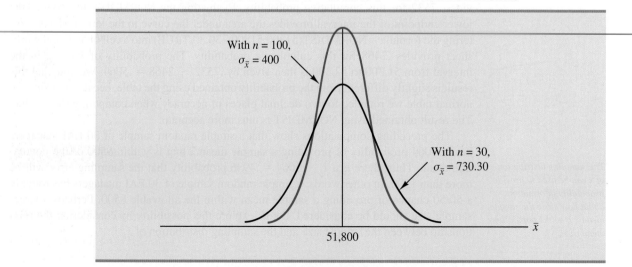

FIGURE 7.10   PROBABILITY OF A SAMPLE MEAN BEING WITHIN $500
OF THE POPULATION MEAN FOR A SIMPLE RANDOM SAMPLE
OF 100 EAI MANAGERS

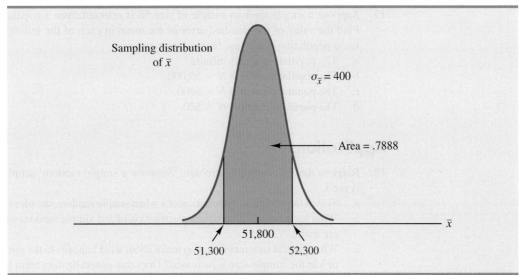

probability corresponding to $\bar{x} = 51,300$. The value provided by Excel is .1056. Thus, the probability of $\bar{x}$ being in the interval from 51,300 to 52,300 is given by .8944 − .1056 = .7888. By increasing the sample size from 30 to 100 EAI managers, we increase the probability that the sampling error will be $500 or less; that is, the probability of obtaining a sample mean within $500 of the population mean increases from .5064 to .7888.

The important point in this discussion is that as the sample size increases, the standard error of the mean decreases. As a result, a larger sample size will provide a higher probability that the sample mean falls within a specified distance of the population mean.

NOTES AND COMMENTS

1. In presenting the sampling distribution of $\bar{x}$ for the EAI problem, we took advantage of the fact that the population mean $\mu = 51,800$ and the population standard deviation $\sigma = 4000$ were known. However, usually the values of the population mean μ and the population standard deviation σ that are needed to determine the sampling distribution of $\bar{x}$ will be unknown. In Chapter 8 we show how the sample mean $\bar{x}$ and the sample standard deviation s are used when μ and σ are unknown.

2. The theoretical proof of the central limit theorem requires independent observations in the sample. This condition is met for infinite populations and for finite populations where sampling is done with replacement. Although the central limit theorem does not directly address sampling without replacement from finite populations, general statistical practice applies the findings of the central limit theorem when the population size is large.

Exercises

Methods

SELF test

15. A population has a mean of 200 and a standard deviation of 50. Suppose a simple random sample of size 100 is selected and $\bar{x}$ is used to estimate μ.
    a. What is the probability that the sample mean will be within ±5 of the population mean?
    b. What is the probability that the sample mean will be within ±10 of the population mean?

16. Assume the population standard deviation is $\sigma = 25$. Compute the standard error of the mean, $\sigma_{\bar{x}}$, for sample sizes of 50, 100, 150, and 200. What can you say about the size of the standard error of the mean as the sample size is increased?

17. Suppose a simple random sample of size 50 is selected from a population with $\sigma = 10$. Find the value of the standard error of the mean in each of the following cases (use the finite population correction factor if appropriate).
    a. The population size is infinite.
    b. The population size is $N = 50,000$.
    c. The population size is $N = 5000$.
    d. The population size is $N = 500$.

Applications

18. Refer to the EAI sampling problem. Suppose a simple random sample of 60 managers is used.
    a. Sketch the sampling distribution of $\bar{x}$ when simple random samples of size 60 are used.
    b. What happens to the sampling distribution of $\bar{x}$ if simple random samples of size 120 are used?
    c. What general statement can you make about what happens to the sampling distribution of $\bar{x}$ as the sample size is increased? Does this generalization seem logical? Explain.

19. In the EAI sampling problem (see Figure 7.8), we showed that for $n = 30$, there was .5064 probability of obtaining a sample mean within $\pm\$500$ of the population mean.
    a. What is the probability that $\bar{x}$ is within $500 of the population mean if a sample of size 60 is used?
    b. Answer part (a) for a sample of size 120.

20. For unemployed individuals, *Barron's* reported that the average number of weeks of unemployment in January 2008 was 17.5 (*Barron's*, February 18, 2008). Use this value as the population mean and assume that the population standard deviation is 4 weeks. Suppose that a random sample of 50 unemployed individuals will be selected.
    a. Show the sampling distribution of $\bar{x}$, the sample mean average for the sample of 50 unemployed individuals.
    b. What is the probability that a simple random sample will provide a sample mean within 3 weeks of the population mean?
    c. What is the probability that a simple random sample will provide a sample mean within 1 week of the population mean?

21. The College Board American College Testing Program reported a population mean SAT score of $\mu = 1020$ (*The World Almanac*, 2003). Assume that the population standard deviation is $\sigma = 100$.
    a. What is the probability that a random sample of 75 students will provide a sample mean SAT score within 10 of the population mean?
    b. What is the probability a random sample of 75 students will provide a sample mean SAT score within 20 of the population mean?

22. The mean annual cost of automobile insurance is $939 (CNBC, February 23, 2006). Assume that the standard deviation is $\sigma = \$245$.
    a. What is the probability that a simple random sample of automobile insurance policies will have a sample mean within $25 of the population mean for each of the following sample sizes: 30, 50, 100, and 400?
    b. What is the advantage of a larger sample size when attempting to estimate the population mean?

23. *BusinessWeek* conducted a survey of graduates from 30 top MBA programs (*BusinessWeek*, September 22, 2003). On the basis of the survey, assume that the mean annual salary

for male and female graduates 10 years after graduation is $168,000 and $117,000, respectively. Assume the standard deviation for the male graduates is $40,000, and for the female graduates it is $25,000.

a.   What is the probability that a simple random sample of 40 male graduates will provide a sample mean within $10,000 of the population mean, $168,000?

b.   What is the probability that a simple random sample of 40 female graduates will provide a sample mean within $10,000 of the population mean, $117,000?

c.   In which of the preceding two cases, part (a) or part (b), do we have a higher probability of obtaining a sample estimate within $10,000 of the population mean? Why?

d.   What is the probability that a simple random sample of 100 male graduates will provide a sample mean more than $4000 below the population mean?

24.   The average score for male golfers is 95 and the average score for female golfers is 106 (*Golf Digest,* April 2006). Use these values as the population means for men and women and assume that the population standard deviation is $\sigma = 14$ strokes for both. A simple random sample of 30 male golfers and another simple random sample of 45 female golfers will be taken.

a.   Show the sampling distribution of $\bar{x}$ for male golfers.

b.   What is the probability that the sample mean is within 3 strokes of the population mean for the sample of male golfers?

c.   What is the probability that the sample mean is within 3 strokes of the population mean for the sample of female golfers?

d.   In which case, part (b) or part (c), is the probability of obtaining a sample mean within 3 strokes of the population mean higher? Why?

25.   The average price of a gallon of unleaded regular gasoline was reported to be $3.13 in Illinois (*http://www.cincygasprices.com*). Use this price as the population mean, and assume the population standard deviation is $.20.

a.   What is the probability that the mean price for a sample of 30 service stations is within $.03 of the population mean?

b.   What is the probability that the mean price for a sample of 50 service stations is within $.03 of the population mean?

c.   What is the probability that the mean price for a sample of 100 service stations is within $.03 of the population mean?

d.   Which, if any, of the sample sizes in parts (a), (b), and (c) would you recommend to have at least a .95 probability that the sample mean is within $.03 of the population mean?

26.   To estimate the mean age for a population of 4000 employees, a simple random sample of 40 employees is selected.

a.   Would you use the finite population correction factor in calculating the standard error of the mean? Explain.

b.   If the population standard deviation is $\sigma = 8.2$ years, compute the standard error both with and without the finite population correction factor. What is the rationale for ignoring the finite population correction factor whenever $n/N \leq .05$?

c.   What is the probability that the sample mean age of the employees will be within ± 2 years of the population mean age?

7.6   Sampling Distribution of $\bar{p}$

The sample proportion $\bar{p}$ is the point estimator of the population proportion p. The formula for computing the sample proportion is

$$\bar{p} = \frac{x}{n}$$

where

> x = the number of elements in the sample that possess the characteristic of interest
> n = sample size

As noted in Section 7.4, the sample proportion $\bar{p}$ is a random variable and its probability distribution is called the sampling distribution of $\bar{p}$.

SAMPLING DISTRIBUTION OF $\bar{p}$

The sampling distribution of $\bar{p}$ is the probability distribution of all possible values of the sample proportion $\bar{p}$.

To determine how close the sample proportion $\bar{p}$ is to the population proportion p, we need to understand the properties of the sampling distribution of $\bar{p}$: the expected value of $\bar{p}$, the standard deviation of $\bar{p}$, and the shape or form of the sampling distribution of $\bar{p}$.

Expected Value of $\bar{p}$

The expected value of $\bar{p}$, the mean of all possible values of $\bar{p}$, is equal to the population proportion p.

EXPECTED VALUE OF $\bar{p}$

$$E(\bar{p}) = p \tag{7.4}$$

where

$$E(\bar{p}) = \text{the expected value of } \bar{p}$$
$$p = \text{the population proportion}$$

Because $E(\bar{p}) = p$, $\bar{p}$ is an unbiased estimator of p. Recall from Section 7.1 we noted that $p = .60$ for the EAI population, where p is the proportion of the population of managers who participated in the company's management training program. Thus, the expected value of $\bar{p}$ for the EAI sampling problem is .60.

Standard Deviation of $\bar{p}$

It can be shown that when sampling from a finite population, the standard deviation of $\bar{p}$ is as follows:

STANDARD DEVIATION OF $\bar{p}$: FINITE POPULATION

$$\sigma_{\bar{p}} = \sqrt{\frac{N-n}{N-1}} \sqrt{\frac{p(1-p)}{n}} \tag{7.5}$$

As was the case for the sample mean $\bar{x}$, $\sqrt{(N-n)/(N-1)}$ is referred to as the finite population correction factor. We follow the same rule of thumb that we recommended for the sample mean: if the population is "large" relative to the sample size ($n/N \leq .05$), we will use $\sigma_{\bar{p}} = \sqrt{p(1-p)/n}$ to compute the standard deviation of $\bar{p}$. In cases where the sample is selected from a process and the conceptual population is infinite, the standard deviation of $\bar{p}$ is also computed using $\sigma_{\bar{p}} = \sqrt{p(1-p)/n}$. Unless otherwise noted, throughout the text we will compute the standard deviation of $\bar{p}$ as follows:

STANDARD DEVIATION OF $\bar{p}$

$$\sigma_{\bar{p}} = \sqrt{\frac{p(1-p)}{n}} \tag{7.6}$$

In Section 7.5 we used standard error of the mean to refer to the standard deviation of $\bar{x}$. We stated that in general the term standard error refers to the standard deviation of a point estimator. Thus, for proportions we use *standard error of the proportion* to refer to the standard deviation of $\bar{p}$. Let us now return to the EAI example and compute the standard error of the proportion associated with simple random samples of 30 EAI managers.

For the EAI study we know that the population proportion of managers who participated in the management training program is $p = .60$. With $n/N = 30/2500 = .012$, we can ignore the finite population correction factor when we compute the standard error of the proportion. For the simple random sample of 30 managers, $\sigma_{\bar{p}}$ is

$$\sigma_{\bar{p}} = \sqrt{\frac{p(1-p)}{n}} = \sqrt{\frac{.60(1-.60)}{30}} = .0894$$

Form of the Sampling Distribution of $\bar{p}$

Now that we know the mean and standard deviation of the sampling distribution of $\bar{p}$, the final step is to determine the form or shape of the sampling distribution. The sample proportion is $\bar{p} = x/n$. For a simple random sample from a large population, the value of x is a binomial random variable indicating the number of elements in the sample with the characteristic of interest. Because n is a constant, the probability of x/n is the same as the binomial probability of x, which means that the sampling distribution of $\bar{p}$ is also a discrete probability distribution and that the probability for each value of x/n is the same as the probability of x.

Statisticians have shown that a binomial distribution can be approximated by a normal distribution whenever the sample size is large enough to satisfy the following two conditions:

$$np \geq 5 \quad \text{and} \quad n(1-p) \geq 5$$

Assuming these two conditions are satisfied, the probability distribution of x in the sample proportion, $\bar{p} = x/n$, can be approximated by a normal distribution. And because n is a constant, the sampling distribution of $\bar{p}$ can also be approximated by a normal distribution. This approximation is stated as follows:

The sampling distribution of $\bar{p}$ can be approximated by a normal distribution whenever $np \geq 5$ and $n(1-p) \geq 5$.

In practical applications, when an estimate of a population proportion is desired, we find that sample sizes are almost always large enough to permit the use of a normal approximation for the sampling distribution of $\bar{p}$.

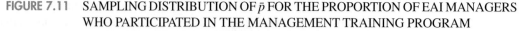

FIGURE 7.11   SAMPLING DISTRIBUTION OF $\bar{p}$ FOR THE PROPORTION OF EAI MANAGERS WHO PARTICIPATED IN THE MANAGEMENT TRAINING PROGRAM

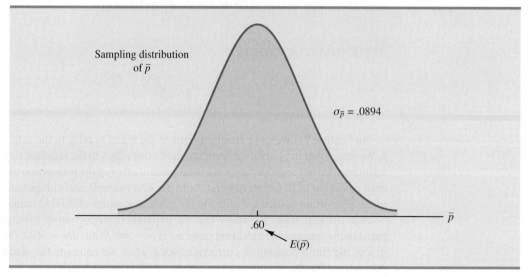

Recall that for the EAI sampling problem we know that the population proportion of managers who participated in the training program is $p = .60$. With a simple random sample of size 30, we have $np = 30(.60) = 18$ and $n(1 - p) = 30(.40) = 12$. Thus, the sampling distribution of $\bar{p}$ can be approximated by the normal distribution shown in Figure 7.11.

Practical Value of the Sampling Distribution of $\bar{p}$

The practical value of the sampling distribution of $\bar{p}$ is that it can be used to provide probability information about the difference between the sample proportion and the population proportion. For instance, suppose that in the EAI problem the personnel director wants to know the probability of obtaining a value of $\bar{p}$ that is within .05 of the population proportion of EAI managers who participated in the training program. That is, what is the probability of obtaining a sample with a sample proportion $\bar{p}$ between .55 and .65? The darkly shaded area in Figure 7.12 shows this probability. Using the fact that the sampling distribution of $\bar{p}$ can be approximated by a normal probability distribution with a mean of .60 and a standard error of $\sigma_{\bar{p}} = .0894$, we can use Excel's NORMDIST function to make this calculation. Entering the formula =NORMDIST(.65,.60,.0894,TRUE) into a cell of an Excel worksheet provides the cumulative probability corresponding to $\bar{p} = .65$. The value calculated by Excel is .7120. Entering the formula =NORMDIST(.55,.60,.0894,TRUE) into a cell of an Excel worksheet provides the cumulative probability corresponding to $\bar{p} = .55$. The value calculated by Excel is .2880. Thus, the probability of $\bar{p}$ being in the interval from .55 to .65 is given by $.7120 - .2880 = .4240$.

If we consider increasing the sample size to $n = 100$, the standard error of the proportion becomes

$$\sigma_{\bar{p}} = \sqrt{\frac{.60(1 - .60)}{100}} = .0490$$

With a sample size of 100 EAI managers, the probability of the sample proportion having a value within .05 of the population proportion can now be computed. Because the sampling distribution is approximately normal, with mean .60 and standard deviation .0490, we can use Excel's NORMDIST function to make this calculation. Entering the formula

FIGURE 7.12 PROBABILITY OF OBTAINING $\bar{p}$ BETWEEN .55 AND .65

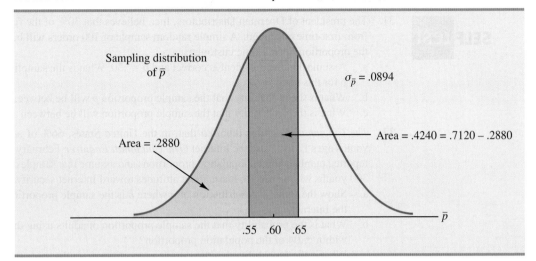

=NORMDIST(.65,.60,.0490,TRUE) into a cell of an Excel worksheet provides the cumulative probability corresponding to $\bar{p}$ = .65. The value calculated by Excel is .8462. Entering the formula =NORMDIST(.55,.60,.0490,TRUE) into a cell of an Excel worksheet provides the cumulative probability corresponding to $\bar{p}$ = .55. The value calculated by Excel is .1538. Thus, the probability of $\bar{p}$ being in the interval from .55 to .65 is given by .8462 − .1538 = .6924. Increasing the sample size increases the probability that the sampling error will be less than or equal to .05 by .2684 (from .4240 to .6924).

Exercises

Methods

27. A simple random sample of size 100 is selected from a population with p = .40.
    a. What is the expected value of $\bar{p}$?
    b. What is the standard error of $\bar{p}$?
    c. Show the sampling distribution of $\bar{p}$.
    d. What does the sampling distribution of $\bar{p}$ show?

28. A population proportion is .40. A simple random sample of size 200 will be taken and the sample proportion $\bar{p}$ will be used to estimate the population proportion.
    a. What is the probability that the sample proportion will be within ±.03 of the population proportion?
    b. What is the probability that the sample proportion will be within ±.05 of the population proportion?

29. Assume that the population proportion is .55. Compute the standard error of the proportion, $\sigma_{\bar{p}}$, for sample sizes of 100, 200, 500, and 1000. What can you say about the size of the standard error of the proportion as the sample size is increased?

30. The population proportion is .30. What is the probability that a sample proportion will be within ±.04 of the population proportion for each of the following sample sizes?
    a. n = 100
    b. n = 200
    c. n = 500
    d. n = 1000
    e. What is the advantage of a larger sample size?

Applications

31. The president of Doerman Distributors, Inc., believes that 30% of the firm's orders come from first-time customers. A simple random sample of 100 orders will be used to estimate the proportion of first-time customers.
    a.   Assume that the president is correct and $p = .30$. What is the sampling distribution of $\bar{p}$ for this study?
    b.   What is the probability that the sample proportion $\bar{p}$ will be between .20 and .40?
    c.   What is the probability that the sample proportion will be between .25 and .35?

32. *The Cincinnati Enquirer* reported that, in the United States, 66% of adults and 87% of youths ages 12 to 17 use the Internet (*The Cincinnati Enquirer,* February 7, 2006). Use the reported numbers as the population proportions and assume that samples of 300 adults and 300 youths will be used to learn about attitudes toward Internet security.
    a.   Show the sampling distribution of $\bar{p}$ where $\bar{p}$ is the sample proportion of adults using the Internet.
    b.   What is the probability that the sample proportion of adults using the Internet will be within $\pm.04$ of the population proportion?
    c.   What is the probability that the sample proportion of youths using the Internet will be within $\pm.04$ of the population proportion?
    d.   Is the probability different in parts (b) and (c)? If so, why?
    e.   Answer part (b) for a sample of size 600. Is the probability smaller? Why?

33. *Time*/CNN voter polls monitored public opinion for the presidential candidates during the 2000 presidential election campaign. One *Time*/CNN poll conducted by Yankelovich Partners, Inc., used a sample of 589 likely voters (*Time,* June 26, 2000). Assume the population proportion for a presidential candidate is $p = .50$. Let $\bar{p}$ be the sample proportion of likely voters favoring the presidential candidate.
    a.   Show the sampling distribution of $\bar{p}$.
    b.   What is the probability the *Time*/CNN poll will provide a sample proportion within $\pm.04$ of the population proportion?
    c.   What is the probability the *Time*/CNN poll will provide a sample proportion within $\pm.03$ of the population proportion?
    d.   What is the probability the *Time*/CNN poll will provide a sample proportion within $\pm.02$ of the population proportion?

34. Roper ASW conducted a survey to learn about American adults' attitudes toward money and happiness (*Money,* October 2003). Fifty-six percent of the respondents said they balance their checkbook at least once a month.
    a.   Suppose a sample of 400 American adults were taken. Show the sampling distribution of the proportion of adults who balance their checkbook at least once a month.
    b.   What is the probability that the sample proportion will be within $\pm.02$ of the population proportion?
    c.   What is the probability that the sample proportion will be within $\pm.04$ of the population proportion?

35. The *Rochester Democrat and Chronicle* reported that 25% of the flights arriving at the San Diego airport during the first five months of 2001 were late (*Rochester Democrat and Chronicle,* July 23, 2001). Assume the population proportion is $p = .25$.
    a.   Show the sampling distribution of $\bar{p}$, the proportion of late flights in a sample of 1000 flights.
    b.   What is the probability that the sample proportion will be within $\pm.03$ of the population proportion if a sample of size 1000 is selected?
    c.   Answer part (b) for a sample of 500 flights.

36. The Grocery Manufacturers of America reported that 76% of consumers read the ingredients listed on a product's label. Assume the population proportion is $p = .76$ and a sample of 400 consumers is selected from the population.

a. Show the sampling distribution of the sample proportion $\bar{p}$ where $\bar{p}$ is the proportion of the sampled consumers who read the ingredients listed on a product's label.
b. What is the probability that the sample proportion will be within $\pm.03$ of the population proportion?
c. Answer part (b) for a sample of 750 consumers.

37. The Food Marketing Institute shows that 17% of households spend more than $100 per week on groceries. Assume the population proportion is $p = .17$ and a simple random sample of 800 households will be selected from the population.
a. Show the sampling distribution of $\bar{p}$, the sample proportion of households spending more than $100 per week on groceries.
b. What is the probability that the sample proportion will be within $\pm.02$ of the population proportion?
c. Answer part (b) for a sample of 1600 households.

(7.7)

Other Sampling Methods

We described the simple random sampling procedure and discussed the properties of the sampling distributions of $\bar{x}$ and $\bar{p}$ when simple random sampling is used. However, simple random sampling is not the only sampling method available. Such methods as stratified random sampling, cluster sampling, and systematic sampling provide advantages over simple random sampling in some situations. In this section we briefly introduce these alternative sampling methods. A more in-depth treatment is provided in Chapter 20, which is located on the website that accompanies the text.

This section provides a brief introduction to sampling methods other than simple random sampling.

Stratified Random Sampling

In **stratified random sampling**, the elements in the population are first divided into groups called *strata,* such that each element in the population belongs to one and only one stratum. The basis for forming the strata, such as department, location, age, industry type, and so on, is at the discretion of the designer of the sample. However, the best results are obtained when the elements within each stratum are as much alike as possible. Figure 7.13 is a diagram of a population divided into H strata.

Stratified random sampling works best when the variance among elements in each stratum is relatively small.

After the strata are formed, a simple random sample is taken from each stratum. Formulas are available for combining the results for the individual stratum samples into one estimate of the population parameter of interest. The value of stratified random sampling depends on how homogeneous the elements are within the strata. If elements within strata are alike, the strata will have low variances. Thus relatively small sample sizes can be

FIGURE 7.13   DIAGRAM FOR STRATIFIED RANDOM SAMPLING

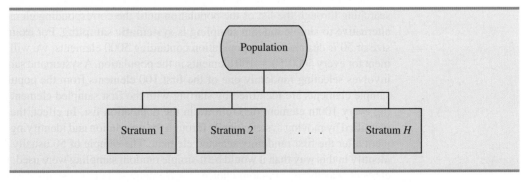

FIGURE 7.14   DIAGRAM FOR CLUSTER SAMPLING

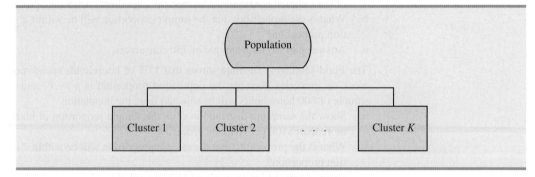

used to obtain good estimates of the strata characteristics. If strata are homogeneous, the stratified random sampling procedure provides results just as precise as those of simple random sampling by using a smaller total sample size.

Cluster Sampling

Cluster sampling works best when each cluster provides a small-scale representation of the population.

In **cluster sampling**, the elements in the population are first divided into separate groups called *clusters*. Each element of the population belongs to one and only one cluster (see Figure 7.14). A simple random sample of the clusters is then taken. All elements within each sampled cluster form the sample. Cluster sampling tends to provide the best results when the elements within the clusters are not alike. In the ideal case, each cluster is a representative small-scale version of the entire population. The value of cluster sampling depends on how representative each cluster is of the entire population. If all clusters are alike in this regard, sampling a small number of clusters will provide good estimates of the population parameters.

One of the primary applications of cluster sampling is area sampling, where clusters are city blocks or other well-defined areas. Cluster sampling generally requires a larger total sample size than either simple random sampling or stratified random sampling. However, it can result in cost savings because of the fact that when an interviewer is sent to a sampled cluster (e.g., a city-block location), many sample observations can be obtained in a relatively short time. Hence, a larger sample size may be obtainable with a significantly lower total cost.

Systematic Sampling

In some sampling situations, especially those with large populations, it is time-consuming to select a simple random sample by first finding a random number and then counting or searching through the list of the population until the corresponding element is found. An alternative to simple random sampling is **systematic sampling**. For example, if a sample size of 50 is desired from a population containing 5000 elements, we will sample one element for every 5000/50 = 100 elements in the population. A systematic sample for this case involves selecting randomly one of the first 100 elements from the population list. Other sample elements are identified by starting with the first sampled element and then selecting every 100th element that follows in the population list. In effect, the sample of 50 is identified by moving systematically through the population and identifying every 100th element after the first randomly selected element. The sample of 50 usually will be easier to identify in this way than it would be if simple random sampling were used. Because the first element selected is a random choice, a systematic sample is usually assumed to have the properties of a simple random sample. This assumption is especially applicable when the list of elements in the population is a random ordering of the elements.

Convenience Sampling

The sampling methods discussed thus far are referred to as *probability sampling* techniques. Elements selected from the population have a known probability of being included in the sample. The advantage of probability sampling is that the sampling distribution of the appropriate sample statistic generally can be identified. Formulas such as the ones for simple random sampling presented in this chapter can be used to determine the properties of the sampling distribution. Then the sampling distribution can be used to make probability statements about the error associated with using the sample results to make inferences about the population.

Convenience sampling is a *nonprobability sampling* technique. As the name implies, the sample is identified primarily by convenience. Elements are included in the sample without prespecified or known probabilities of being selected. For example, a professor conducting research at a university may use student volunteers to constitute a sample simply because they are readily available and will participate as subjects for little or no cost. Similarly, an inspector may sample a shipment of oranges by selecting oranges haphazardly from among several crates. Labeling each orange and using a probability method of sampling would be impractical. Samples such as wildlife captures and volunteer panels for consumer research are also convenience samples.

Convenience samples have the advantage of relatively easy sample selection and data collection; however, it is impossible to evaluate the "goodness" of the sample in terms of its representativeness of the population. A convenience sample may provide good results or it may not; no statistically justified procedure allows a probability analysis and inference about the quality of the sample results. Sometimes researchers apply statistical methods designed for probability samples to a convenience sample, arguing that the convenience sample can be treated as though it were a probability sample. However, this argument cannot be supported, and we should be cautious in interpreting the results of convenience samples that are used to make inferences about populations.

Judgment Sampling

One additional nonprobability sampling technique is **judgment sampling**. In this approach, the person most knowledgeable on the subject of the study selects elements of the population that he or she feels are most representative of the population. Often this method is a relatively easy way of selecting a sample. For example, a reporter may sample two or three senators, judging that those senators reflect the general opinion of all senators. However, the quality of the sample results depends on the judgment of the person selecting the sample. Again, great caution is warranted in drawing conclusions based on judgment samples used to make inferences about populations.

NOTES AND COMMENTS

We recommend using probability sampling methods: simple random sampling, stratified random sampling, cluster sampling, or systematic sampling. For these methods, formulas are available for evaluating the "goodness" of the sample results in terms of the closeness of the results to the population parameters being estimated. An evaluation of the goodness cannot be made with convenience or judgment sampling. Thus, great care should be used in interpreting the results based on nonprobability sampling methods.

Summary

In this chapter we presented the concepts of simple random sampling and sampling distributions. We demonstrated how a simple random sample can be selected and how the data collected for the sample can be used to develop point estimates of population parameters. Because different simple random samples provide different values for the point estimators, point estimators such as $\bar{x}$ and $\bar{p}$ are random variables. The probability distribution of such a random variable is called a sampling distribution. In particular, we described the sampling distributions of the sample mean $\bar{x}$ and the sample proportion $\bar{p}$.

In considering the characteristics of the sampling distributions of $\bar{x}$ and $\bar{p}$, we stated that $E(\bar{x}) = \mu$ and $E(\bar{p}) = p$. After developing the standard deviation or standard error formulas for these estimators, we described the conditions necessary for the sampling distributions of $\bar{x}$ and $\bar{p}$ to follow a normal distribution. Other sampling methods including stratified random sampling, cluster sampling, systematic sampling, convenience sampling, and judgment sampling were discussed.

Glossary

Parameter A numerical characteristic of a population, such as a population mean μ, a population standard deviation σ, a population proportion p, and so on.

Sampled population The population from which the sample is taken.

Frame A listing of the elements that the sample will be selected from.

Simple random sample (Finite population) A sample selected such that each possible sample of size n has the same probability of being selected.

Sample statistic A sample characteristic, such as a sample mean $\bar{x}$, a sample standard deviation s, a sample proportion $\bar{p}$, and so on. The value of the sample statistic is used to estimate the value of the corresponding population parameter.

Point estimator The sample statistic, such as $\bar{x}$, s, or $\bar{p}$, that provides the point estimate of the population parameter.

Point estimate The value of a point estimator used in a particular instance as an estimate of a population parameter.

Target population The population for which statistical inferences such as point estimates are made. It is important for the target population to correspond as closely as possible to the sampled population.

Sampling distribution A probability distribution consisting of all possible values of a sample statistic.

Unbiased A property of a point estimator that is present when the expected value of the point estimator is equal to the population parameter it estimates.

Finite population correction factor The term $\sqrt{(N - n)/(N - 1)}$ that is used in the formulas for $\sigma_{\bar{x}}$ and $\sigma_{\bar{p}}$ whenever a finite population, rather than an infinite population, is being sampled. The generally accepted rule of thumb is to ignore the finite population correction factor whenever $n/N \leq .05$.

Standard error The standard deviation of a point estimator.

Central limit theorem A theorem that enables one to use the normal probability distribution to approximate the sampling distribution of $\bar{x}$ whenever the sample size is large.

Stratified random sampling A probability sampling method in which the population is first divided into strata and a simple random sample is then taken from each stratum.

Cluster sampling A probability sampling method in which the population is first divided into clusters and then a simple random sample of the clusters is taken.

Systematic sampling A probability sampling method in which we randomly select one of the first k elements and then select every kth element thereafter.

Convenience sampling A nonprobability method of sampling whereby elements are selected for the sample on the basis of convenience.

Judgment sampling A nonprobability method of sampling whereby elements are selected for the sample based on the judgment of the person doing the study.

Key Formulas

Expected Value of $\bar{x}$

$$E(\bar{x}) = \mu \tag{7.1}$$

Standard Deviation of $\bar{x}$: Finite Population

$$\sigma_{\bar{x}} = \sqrt{\frac{N-n}{N-1}} \left(\frac{\sigma}{\sqrt{n}} \right) \tag{7.2}$$

Standard Deviation of $\bar{x}$

$$\sigma_{\bar{x}} = \frac{\sigma}{\sqrt{n}} \tag{7.3}$$

Expected Value of $\bar{p}$

$$E(\bar{p}) = p \tag{7.4}$$

Standard Deviation of $\bar{p}$: Finite Population

$$\sigma_{\bar{p}} = \sqrt{\frac{N-n}{N-1}} \sqrt{\frac{p(1-p)}{n}} \tag{7.5}$$

Standard Deviation of $\bar{p}$

$$\sigma_{\bar{p}} = \sqrt{\frac{p(1-p)}{n}} \tag{7.6}$$

Supplementary Exercises

Dining

38. Bob Miller, a food critic, wants to prepare an article on the quality of food at locally owned restaurants in Myrtle Beach, South Carolina. A list of 44 locally owned restaurants is contained in the data file named Dining that is on the website that accompanies this text (*Coastal Carolina Dining,* Fall 2004). Bob only has time to sample the food at 5 of these restaurants.
    a. In the data file the restaurants are listed in column A of an Excel worksheet. In column B we generated a random number for each of the restaurants in column A. Use these random numbers to select a simple random sample of five restaurants for Bob.
    b. Generate a new set of random numbers and use them to select a new simple random sample. Did you select the same restaurants?

39. Americans have become increasingly concerned about the rising cost of Medicare. In 1990, the average annual Medicare spending per enrollee was $3267; in 2003, the average annual Medicare spending per enrollee was $6883 (*Money,* Fall 2003). Suppose you hired a consulting firm to take a sample of 50 2003 Medicare enrollees to further

investigate the nature of expenditures. Assume the population standard deviation for 2003 was $2000.

a. Show the sampling distribution of the mean amount of Medicare spending for a sample of 50 2003 enrollees.

b. What is the probability the sample mean will be within ±$300 of the population mean?

c. What is the probability the sample mean will be greater than $7500? If the consulting firm tells you the sample mean for the Medicare enrollees they interviewed was $7500, would you question whether they followed correct simple random sampling procedures? Why or why not?

40. *BusinessWeek* surveyed MBA alumni 10 years after graduation (*BusinessWeek,* September 22, 2003). One finding was that alumni spend an average of $115.50 per week eating out socially. You have been asked to conduct a follow-up study by taking a sample of 40 of these MBA alumni. Assume the population standard deviation is $35.

a. Show the sampling distribution of $\bar{x}$, the sample mean weekly expenditure for the 40 MBA alumni.

b. What is the probability the sample mean will be within $10 of the population mean?

c. Suppose you find a sample mean of $100. What is the probability of finding a sample mean of $100 or less? Would you consider this sample to be an unusually low spending group of alumni? Why or why not?

41. The mean television viewing time for Americans is 15 hours per week (*Money,* November 2003). Suppose a sample of 60 Americans is taken to further investigate viewing habits. Assume the population standard deviation for weekly viewing time is $\sigma = 4$ hours.

a. What is the probability the sample mean will be within 1 hour of the population mean?

b. What is the probability the sample mean will be within 45 minutes of the population mean?

42. The average annual salary for federal government employees in Indiana is $41,979 (*The World Almanac,* 2001). Use this figure as the population mean and assume the population standard deviation is $\sigma = \$5000$. Suppose that a random sample of 50 federal government employees will be selected from the population.

a. What is the value of the standard error of the mean?

b. What is the probability that the sample mean will be more than $41,979?

c. What is the probability the sample mean will be within $1000 of the population mean?

d. How would the probability in part (c) change if the sample size were increased to 100?

43. Three firms carry inventories that differ in size. Firm A's inventory contains 2000 items, firm B's inventory contains 5000 items, and firm C's inventory contains 10,000 items. The population standard deviation for the cost of the items in each firm's inventory is $\sigma = 144$. A statistical consultant recommends that each firm take a sample of 50 items from its inventory to provide statistically valid estimates of the average cost per item. Managers of the small firm state that because it has the smallest population, it should be able to make the estimate from a much smaller sample than that required by the larger firms. However, the consultant states that to obtain the same standard error and thus the same precision in the sample results, all firms should use the same sample size regardless of population size.

a. Using the finite population correction factor, compute the standard error for each of the three firms given a sample of size 50.

b. What is the probability that for each firm the sample mean $\bar{x}$ will be within ±25 of the population mean μ?

44. A researcher reports survey results by stating that the standard error of the mean is 20. The population standard deviation is 500.

a. How large was the sample used in this survey?

b. What is the probability that the point estimate was within ±25 of the population mean?

45. A production process is checked periodically by a quality control inspector. The inspector selects simple random samples of 30 finished products and computes the sample mean product weights $\bar{x}$. If test results over a long period of time show that 5% of the $\bar{x}$ values are over 2.1 pounds and 5% are under 1.9 pounds, what are the mean and the standard deviation for the population of products produced with this process?

46. About 28% of private companies are owned by women (*The Cincinnati Enquirer,* January 26, 2006). Answer the following questions based on a sample of 240 private companies.
    a. Show the sampling distribution of $\bar{p}$, the sample proportion of companies that are owned by women.
    b. What is the probability the sample proportion will be within $\pm.04$ of the population proportion?
    c. What is the probability the sample proportion will be within $\pm.02$ of the population proportion?

47. A market research firm conducts telephone surveys with a 40% historic response rate. What is the probability that in a new sample of 400 telephone numbers, at least 150 individuals will cooperate and respond to the questions? In other words, what is the probability that the sample proportion will be at least 150/400 = .375?

48. Advertisers contract with Internet service providers and search engines to place ads on websites. They pay a fee based on the number of potential customers who click on their ad. Unfortunately, click fraud—the practice of someone clicking on an ad solely for the purpose of driving up advertising revenue—has become a problem. Forty percent of advertisers claim they have been a victim of click fraud (*BusinessWeek,* March 13, 2006). Suppose a simple random sample of 380 advertisers will be taken to learn more about how they are affected by this practice.
    a. What is the probability that the sample proportion will be within $\pm.04$ of the population proportion experiencing click fraud?
    b. What is the probability that the sample proportion will be greater than .45?

49. The proportion of individuals insured by the All-Driver Automobile Insurance Company who received at least one traffic ticket during a five-year period is .15.
    a. Show the sampling distribution of $\bar{p}$ if a random sample of 150 insured individuals is used to estimate the proportion having received at least one ticket.
    b. What is the probability that the sample proportion will be within $\pm.03$ of the population proportion?

50. Lori Jeffrey is a successful sales representative for a major publisher of college textbooks. Historically, Lori obtains a book adoption on 25% of her sales calls. Viewing her sales calls for one month as a sample of all possible sales calls, assume that a statistical analysis of the data yields a standard error of the proportion of .0625.
    a. How large was the sample used in this analysis? That is, how many sales calls did Lori make during the month?
    b. Let $\bar{p}$ indicate the sample proportion of book adoptions obtained during the month. Show the sampling distribution of $\bar{p}$.
    c. Using the sampling distribution of $\bar{p}$, compute the probability that Lori will obtain book adoptions on 30% or more of her sales calls during a one-month period.

Appendix   Random Sampling with StatTools

MetAreas

If a list of all the elements in a population is available in an Excel file, StatTools Random Sample Utility can be used to select a simple random sample. For example, a list of the top 100 metropolitan areas in the United States and Canada is provided in column A of the data set MetAreas (*Places Rated Almanac—The Millennium Edition 2000*). Column B contains the overall rating of each metropolitan area. Assume that you would like to select a simple random sample of 30 metropolitan areas in order to do an in-depth study of the cost of living in the United States and Canada.

Begin by using the Data Set Manager to create a StatTools data set for these data using the procedure described in the appendix to Chapter 1. The following steps will generate a simple random sample of 30 metropolitan areas.

Step 1. Click the **StatTools** tab on the Ribbon
Step 2. In the **Data Group** click **Data Utilities**
Step 3. Choose the **Random Sample** option
Step 4. When the StatTools—Random Sample Utility dialog box appears,
In the **Variables** section,
    Select **Metropolitan Area**
    Select **Rating**
In the **Options** section,
    Enter 1 in the **Number of Samples** box
    Enter 30 in the **Sample Size** box
Click **OK**

The random sample of 30 metropolitan areas will appear in columns A and B of the worksheet entitled Random Sample.

CHAPTER 8

Interval Estimation

CONTENTS

FOOD LION*
SALISBURY, NORTH CAROLINA

Founded in 1957 as Food Town, Food Lion is one of the largest supermarket chains in the United States with 1200 stores in 11 Southeastern and Mid-Atlantic states. The company sells more than 24,000 different products and offers nationally and regionally advertised brand-name merchandise, as well as a growing number of high-quality private label products manufactured especially for Food Lion. The company maintains its low price leadership and quality assurance through operating efficiencies such as standard store formats, innovative warehouse design, energy-efficient facilities, and data synchronization with suppliers. Food Lion looks to a future of continued innovation, growth, price leadership, and service to its customers.

Being in an inventory-intense business, Food Lion made the decision to adopt the LIFO (last-in, first-out) method of inventory valuation. This method matches current costs against current revenues, which minimizes the effect of radical price changes on profit and loss results. In addition, the LIFO method reduces net income, thereby reducing income taxes during periods of inflation.

Food Lion establishes a LIFO index for each of seven inventory pools: Grocery, Paper/Household, Pet Supplies, Health & Beauty Aids, Dairy, Cigarette/Tobacco, and Beer/Wine. For example, a LIFO index of 1.008 for the Grocery pool would indicate that the company's grocery inventory value at current costs reflects a 0.8% increase due to inflation over the most recent one-year period.

A LIFO index for each inventory pool requires that the year-end inventory count for each product be valued at the current year-end cost and at the preceding year-end cost. To avoid excessive time and expense associated

The Food Lion store in the Cambridge Shopping Center, Charlotte, North Carolina. © Courtesy of Food Lion.

with counting the inventory in all 1200 store locations, Food Lion selects a random sample of 50 stores. Year-end physical inventories are taken in each of the sample stores. The current-year and preceding-year costs for each item are then used to construct the required LIFO indexes for each inventory pool.

For a recent year, the sample estimate of the LIFO index for the Health & Beauty Aids inventory pool was 1.015. Using a 95% confidence level, Food Lion computed a margin of error of .006 for the sample estimate. Thus, the interval from 1.009 to 1.021 provided a 95% confidence interval estimate of the population LIFO index. This level of precision was judged to be very good.

In this chapter you will learn how to compute the margin of error associated with sample estimates. You will also learn how to use this information to construct and interpret interval estimates of a population mean and a population proportion.

*The authors are indebted to Keith Cunningham, Tax Director, and Bobby Harkey, Staff Tax Accountant, at Food Lion for providing this Statistics in Practice.

In Chapter 7, we stated that a point estimator is a sample statistic used to estimate a population parameter. For instance, the sample mean $\bar{x}$ is a point estimator of the population mean μ and the sample proportion $\bar{p}$ is a point estimator of the population proportion p. Because a point estimator cannot be expected to provide the exact value of the population parameter, an **interval estimate** is often computed by adding and subtracting a value, called the **margin of error**, to the point estimate. The general form of an interval estimate is as follows:

$$\text{Point estimate} \pm \text{Margin of error}$$

The purpose of an interval estimate is to provide information about how close the point estimate, provided by the sample, is to the value of the population parameter.

In this chapter we show how to compute interval estimates of a population mean μ and a population proportion p. The general form of an interval estimate of a population mean is

$$\bar{x} \pm \text{Margin of error}$$

Similarly, the general form of an interval estimate of a population proportion is

$$\bar{p} \pm \text{Margin of error}$$

The sampling distributions of $\bar{x}$ and $\bar{p}$ play key roles in computing these interval estimates.

8.1   Population Mean: σ Known

In order to develop an interval estimate of a population mean, either the population standard deviation σ or the sample standard deviation s must be used to compute the margin of error. In most applications σ is not known, and s is used to compute the margin of error. In some applications, however, large amounts of relevant historic data are available and can be used to estimate the population standard deviation prior to sampling. Also, in quality control applications where a process is assumed to be operating correctly, or "in control," it is appropriate to treat the population standard deviation as known. We refer to such cases as the **σ known** case. In this section we introduce an example in which it is reasonable to treat σ as known and show how to construct an interval estimate for this case.

Each week Lloyd's Department Store selects a simple random sample of 100 customers in order to learn about the amount spent per shopping trip. With x representing the amount spent per shopping trip, the sample mean $\bar{x}$ provides a point estimate of μ, the mean amount spent per shopping trip for the population of all Lloyd's customers. Lloyd's has been using the weekly survey for several years. Based on the historic data, Lloyd's now assumes a known value of $\sigma = \$20$ for the population standard deviation. The historic data also indicate that the population follows a normal distribution.

WEB file

Lloyd's

During the most recent week, Lloyd's surveyed 100 customers ($n = 100$) and obtained a sample mean of $\bar{x} = \$82$. The sample mean amount spent provides a point estimate of the population mean amount spent per shopping trip, μ. In the discussion that follows, we show how to compute the margin of error for this estimate and develop an interval estimate of the population mean.

Margin of Error and the Interval Estimate

In Chapter 7 we showed that the sampling distribution of $\bar{x}$ can be used to compute the probability that $\bar{x}$ will be within a given distance of μ. In the Lloyd's example, the historic data show that the population of amounts spent is normally distributed with a standard deviation of $\sigma = 20$. So, using what we learned in Chapter 7, we can conclude that the sampling distribution of $\bar{x}$ follows a normal distribution with an unknown mean μ and a known standard error of $\sigma_{\bar{x}} = \sigma/\sqrt{n} = 20/\sqrt{100} = 2$. This sampling distribution is shown in Figure 8.1.[1]

---

[1]We use the fact that the population of amounts spent has a normal distribution to conclude that the sampling distribution of $\bar{x}$ has a normal distribution. If the population did not have a normal distribution, we could rely on the central limit theorem and the large sample size of $n = 100$ to conclude that the sampling distribution of $\bar{x}$ is approximately normal. In either case, the sampling distribution of $\bar{x}$ would appear as shown in Figure 8.1.

FIGURE 8.1 SAMPLING DISTRIBUTION OF THE SAMPLE MEAN AMOUNT SPENT FROM SIMPLE RANDOM SAMPLES OF 100 CUSTOMERS

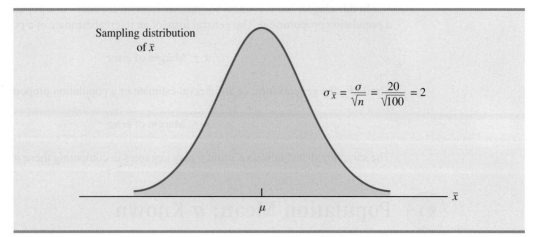

Because the sampling distribution shows how values of $\bar{x}$ are distributed around the population mean μ, the sampling distribution of $\bar{x}$ provides information about the possible differences between $\bar{x}$ and μ.

Using the standard normal probability table, we find that 95% of the values of any normally distributed random variable are within ± 1.96 standard deviations of the mean. Thus, when the sampling distribution of $\bar{x}$ is normally distributed, 95% of the $\bar{x}$ values must be within $\pm 1.96\sigma_{\bar{x}}$ of the mean μ. In the Lloyd's example we know that the sampling distribution of $\bar{x}$ is normally distributed with a standard error of $\sigma_{\bar{x}} = 2$. Because $\pm 1.96\sigma_{\bar{x}} = 1.96(2) = 3.92$, we can conclude that 95% of all $\bar{x}$ values obtained using a sample size of $n = 100$ will be within ± 3.92 of the population mean μ. See Figure 8.2.

FIGURE 8.2 SAMPLING DISTRIBUTION OF $\bar{x}$ SHOWING THE LOCATION OF SAMPLE MEANS THAT ARE WITHIN 3.92 OF μ

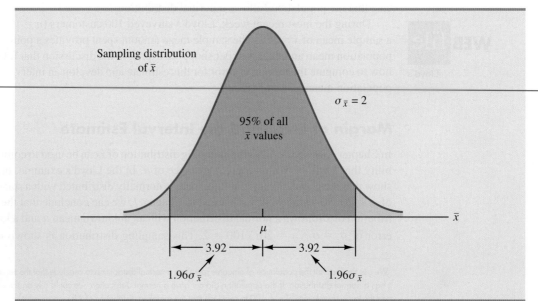

In the introduction to this chapter we said that the general form of an interval estimate of the population mean μ is $\bar{x} \pm$ margin of error. For the Lloyd's example, suppose we set the margin of error equal to 3.92 and compute the interval estimate of μ using $\bar{x} \pm 3.92$. To provide an interpretation for this interval estimate, let us consider the values of $\bar{x}$ that could be obtained if we took three *different* simple random samples, each consisting of 100 Lloyd's customers. The first sample mean might turn out to have the value shown as $\bar{x}_1$ in Figure 8.3. In this case, Figure 8.3 shows that the interval formed by subtracting 3.92 from $\bar{x}_1$ and adding 3.92 to $\bar{x}_1$ includes the population mean μ. Now consider what happens if the second sample mean turns out to have the value shown as $\bar{x}_2$ in Figure 8.3. Although this sample mean differs from the first sample mean, we see that the interval formed by subtracting 3.92 from $\bar{x}_2$ and adding 3.92 to $\bar{x}_2$ also includes the population mean μ. However, consider what happens if the third sample mean turns out to have the value shown as $\bar{x}_3$ in Figure 8.3. In this case, the interval formed by subtracting 3.92 from $\bar{x}_3$ and adding 3.92 to $\bar{x}_3$ does not include the population mean μ. Because $\bar{x}_3$ falls in the upper tail of the sampling distribution and is farther than 3.92 from μ, subtracting and adding 3.92 to $\bar{x}_3$ forms an interval that does not include μ.

Any sample mean $\bar{x}$ that is within the darkly shaded region of Figure 8.3 will provide an interval that contains the population mean μ. Because 95% of all possible sample means are in the darkly shaded region, 95% of all intervals formed by subtracting 3.92 from $\bar{x}$ and adding 3.92 to $\bar{x}$ will include the population mean μ.

Recall that during the most recent week, the quality assurance team at Lloyd's surveyed 100 customers and obtained a sample mean amount spent of $\bar{x} = 82$. Using $\bar{x} \pm 3.92$ to construct the interval estimate, we obtain 82 ± 3.92. Thus, the specific interval estimate of

FIGURE 8.3   INTERVALS FORMED FROM SELECTED SAMPLE MEANS AT LOCATIONS $\bar{x}_1$, $\bar{x}_2$, AND $\bar{x}_3$

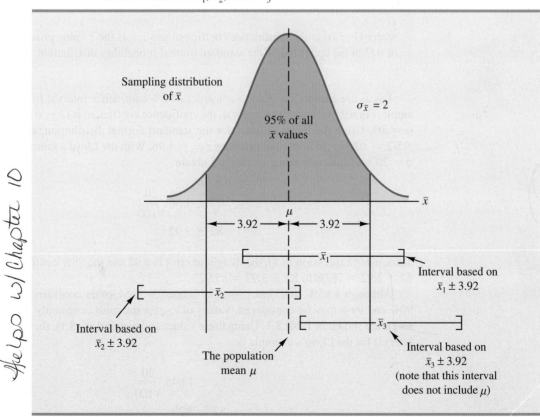

This discussion provides insight as to why the interval is called a 95% confidence interval.

μ based on the data from the most recent week is $82 - 3.92 = 78.08$ to $82 + 3.92 = 85.92$. Because 95% of all the intervals constructed using $\bar{x} \pm 3.92$ will contain the population mean, we say that we are 95% confident that the interval 78.08 to 85.92 includes the population mean μ. We say that this interval has been established at the 95% **confidence level**. The value .95 is referred to as the **confidence coefficient**, and the interval 78.08 to 85.92 is called the 95% **confidence interval**.

Another term sometimes associated with an interval estimate is the **level of significance**. The level of significance associated with an interval estimate is denoted by the Greek letter α. The level of significance and the confidence coefficient are related as follows:

$$\alpha = \text{Level of Significance} = 1 - \text{Confidence Coefficient}$$

The level of significance is also referred to as the significance level.

The level of significance is the probability that the interval estimation procedure will generate an interval that does not contain μ. For example, the level of significance corresponding to a .95 confidence coefficient is $\alpha = 1 - .95 = .05$. In Lloyd's case, the level of significance ($\alpha = .05$) is the probability of drawing a sample, computing the sample mean, and finding that $\bar{x}$ lies in one of the tails of the sampling distribution (see $\bar{x}_3$ in Figure 8.3). When the sample mean happens to fall in the tail of the sampling distribution (and it will 5% of the time), the confidence interval generated will not contain μ.

With the margin of error given by $z_{\alpha/2}(\sigma/\sqrt{n})$, the general form of an interval estimate of a population mean for the σ known case follows.

INTERVAL ESTIMATE OF A POPULATION MEAN: σ KNOWN

$$\bar{x} \pm z_{\alpha/2}\frac{\sigma}{\sqrt{n}} \tag{8.1}$$

where $(1 - \alpha)$ is the confidence coefficient and $z_{\alpha/2}$ is the z value providing an area of $\alpha/2$ in the upper tail of the standard normal probability distribution.

Let us use expression (8.1) to construct a 95% confidence interval for the Lloyd's example. For a 95% confidence interval, the confidence coefficient is $(1 - \alpha) = .95$ and thus, $\alpha = .05$. Using the tables of areas for the standard normal distribution, an area of $\alpha/2 = .05/2 = .025$ in the upper tail provides $z_{.025} = 1.96$. With the Lloyd's sample mean $\bar{x} = 82$, $\sigma = 20$, and a sample size $n = 100$, we obtain

$$82 \pm 1.96\frac{20}{\sqrt{100}}$$

$$82 \pm 3.92$$

Thus, using expression (8.1), the margin of error is 3.92 and the 95% confidence interval is $82 - 3.92 = 78.08$ to $82 + 3.92 = 85.92$.

Although a 95% confidence level is frequently used, other confidence levels such as 90% and 99% may be considered. Values of $z_{\alpha/2}$ for the most commonly used confidence levels are shown in Table 8.1. Using these values and expression (8.1), the 90% confidence interval for the Lloyd's example is

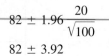

$$82 \pm 1.645\frac{20}{\sqrt{100}}$$

$$82 \pm 3.29$$

TABLE 8.1 VALUES OF $z_{\alpha/2}$ FOR THE MOST COMMONLY USED CONFIDENCE LEVELS

Confidence Level	α	$\alpha/2$	$z_{\alpha/2}$
90%	.10	.05	1.645
95%	.05	.025	1.960
99%	.01	.005	2.576

Thus, at 90% confidence, the margin of error is 3.29 and the confidence interval is $82 - 3.29 = 78.71$ to $82 + 3.29 = 85.29$. Similarly, the 99% confidence interval is

$$82 \pm 2.576 \frac{20}{\sqrt{100}}$$

$$82 \pm 5.15$$

Thus, at 99% confidence, the margin of error is 5.15 and the confidence interval is $82 - 5.15 = 76.85$ to $82 + 5.15 = 87.15$.

Comparing the results for the 90%, 95%, and 99% confidence levels, we see that in order to have a higher degree of confidence, the margin of error and thus the width of the confidence interval must be larger.

Using Excel

We will use the Lloyd's Department Store data to illustrate how Excel can be used to construct an interval estimate of the population mean for the σ known case. Refer to Figure 8.4 as we describe the tasks involved. The formula worksheeet is in the background; the value worksheet appears in the foreground.

Enter Data: A label and the sales data are entered into cells A1:A101.

Enter Functions and Formulas: The sample size and sample mean are computed in cells D4:D5 using Excel's COUNT and AVERAGE functions, respectively. The value worksheet shows that the sample size is 100 and the sample mean is 82. The value of the known population standard deviation (20) is entered into cell D7 and the desired confidence coefficient (.95) is entered into cell D8. The level of significance is computed in cell D9 by entering the formula =1−D8; the value worksheet shows that the level of significance associated with a confidence coefficient of .95 is .05. The margin of error is computed in cell D11 using Excel's CONFIDENCE function. The CONFIDENCE function has three inputs: the level of significance (cell D9); the population standard deviation (cell D7); and the sample size (cell D4). Thus, to compute the margin of error associated with a 95% confidence interval, the following formula is entered into cell D11:

$$=\text{CONFIDENCE(D9,D7,D4)}$$

The resulting value of 3.92 is the margin of error associated with the interval estimate of the population mean amount spent per week.

Cells D13:D15 provide the point estimate and the lower and upper limits for the confidence interval. Because the point estimate is just the sample mean, the formula =D5 is entered into cell D13. To compute the lower limit of the 95% confidence interval, $\bar{x}$ − (margin of error), we enter the formula =D13-D11 into cell D14. To compute the upper limit of the 95% confidence interval, $\bar{x}$ + (margin of error), we enter the formula =D13+D11 into cell D15. The value worksheet shows a lower limit of 78.08 and an upper limit of 85.92. In other words, the 95% confidence interval for the population mean is from 78.08 to 85.92.

FIGURE 8.4   EXCEL WORKSHEET: CONSTRUCTING A 95% CONFIDENCE INTERVAL FOR LLOYD'S DEPARTMENT STORE

	A	B	C	D	E
1	Amount		Interval Estimate of a Population Mean:		
2	72		σ Known Case		
3	91				
4	74		Sample Size	=COUNT(A1:A101)	
5	115		Sample Mean	=AVERAGE(A1:A101)	
6	71				
7	120		Population Standard Deviation	20	
8	37		Confidence Coefficient	0.95	
9	96		Level of Significance	=1-D8	
10	91				
11	105		Margin of Error	=CONFIDENCE(D9,D7,D4)	
12	104				
13	89		Point Estimate	=D5	
14	70		Lower Limit	=D13-D11	
15	125		Upper Limit	=D13+D11	
16	43				
17	61				
100	71				
101	84				
102					

If you know the population mean

	A	B	C	D	E
1	Amount		Interval Estimate of a Population Mean:		
2	72		σ Known Case		
3	91				
4	74		Sample Size	100	
5	115		Sample Mean	82	
6	71				
7	120		Population Standard Deviation	20	
8	37		Confidence Coefficient	0.95	
9	96		Level of Significance	0.05	
10	91				
11	105		Margin of Error	3.92	
12	104				
13	89		Point Estimate	82	
14	70		Lower Limit	78.08	
15	125		Upper Limit	85.92	
16	43				
17	61				
100	71				
101	84				
102					

We are 95% confident the interval contains the population mean.

Note: Rows 18–99 are hidden.

A template for other problems To use this worksheet as a template for another problem of this type, we must first enter the new problem data in column A. Then, the cell formulas in cells D4 and D5 must be updated with the new data range and the known population standard deviation must be entered into cell D7. After doing so, the point estimate and a 95% confidence interval will be displayed in cells D13:D15. If a confidence interval with a different confidence coefficient is desired, we simply change the value in cell D8.

We can further simplify the use of Figure 8.4 as a template for other problems by eliminating the need to enter new data ranges in cells D4 and D5. To do so we rewrite the cell formulas as follows:

Cell D4: =COUNT(A:A)

Cell D5: =AVERAGE(A:A)

With the A:A method of specifying data ranges, Excel's COUNT function will count the number of numeric values in column A and Excel's AVERAGE function will compute the

The Lloyd's data set includes a worksheet entitled Template that uses the A:A method for entering the data ranges.

average of the numeric values in column A. Thus, to solve a new problem it is only necessary to enter the new data into column A and enter the value of the known population standard deviation in cell D7.

This worksheet can also be used as a template for text exercises in which the sample size, sample mean, and the population standard deviation are given. In this type of situation we simply replace the values in cells D4, D5, and D7 with the given values of the sample size, sample mean, and the population standard deviation.

Practical Advice

If the population follows a normal distribution, the confidence interval provided by expression (8.1) is exact. In other words, if expression (8.1) were used repeatedly to generate 95% confidence intervals, exactly 95% of the intervals generated would contain the population mean. If the population does not follow a normal distribution, the confidence interval provided by expression (8.1) will be approximate. In this case, the quality of the approximation depends on both the distribution of the population and the sample size.

In most applications, a sample size of $n \geq 30$ is adequate when using expression (8.1) to develop an interval estimate of a population mean. If the population is not normally distributed, but is roughly symmetric, sample sizes as small as 15 can be expected to provide good approximate confidence intervals. With smaller sample sizes, expression (8.1) should only be used if the analyst believes, or is willing to assume, that the population distribution is at least approximately normal.

NOTES AND COMMENTS

1. The interval estimation procedure discussed in this section is based on the assumption that the population standard deviation σ is known. By σ known we mean that historic data or other information are available that permit us to obtain a good estimate of the population standard deviation prior to taking the sample that will be used to develop an estimate of the population mean. So technically we don't mean that σ is actually known with certainty. We just mean that we obtained a good estimate of the standard deviation prior to sampling and thus we won't be using the same sample to estimate both the population mean and the population standard deviation.

2. The sample size n appears in the denominator of the interval estimation expression (8.1). Thus, if a particular sample size provides too wide an interval to be of any practical use, we may want to consider increasing the sample size. With n in the denominator, a larger sample size will provide a smaller margin of error, a narrower interval, and greater precision. The procedure for determining the size of a simple random sample necessary to obtain a desired precision is discussed in Section 8.3.

Exercises

Methods

1. A simple random sample of 40 items resulted in a sample mean of 25. The population standard deviation is $\sigma = 5$.
   a. What is the standard error of the mean, $\sigma_{\bar{x}}$?
   b. At 95% confidence, what is the margin of error?

2. A simple random sample of 50 items from a population with $\sigma = 6$ resulted in a sample mean of 32.
   a. Provide a 90% confidence interval for the population mean.
   b. Provide a 95% confidence interval for the population mean.
   c. Provide a 99% confidence interval for the population mean.

3. A simple random sample of 60 items resulted in a sample mean of 80. The population standard deviation is $\sigma = 15$.
   a. Compute the 95% confidence interval for the population mean.
   b. Assume that the same sample mean was obtained from a sample of 120 items. Provide a 95% confidence interval for the population mean.
   c. What is the effect of a larger sample size on the interval estimate?

4. A 95% confidence interval for a population mean was reported to be 152 to 160. If $\sigma = 15$, what sample size was used in this study?

Applications

Restaurant

5. In an effort to estimate the mean amount spent per customer for dinner at an Atlanta restaurant, data were collected for a sample of 49 customers. The data collected are shown in the website file named Restaurant. Based upon past studies the population standard deviation is assumed known with $\sigma = \$5$.
   a. At 95% confidence, what is the margin of error?
   b. Develop a 95% confidence interval estimate of the mean amount spent for dinner.

Nielsen

6. Nielsen Media Research conducted a study of household television viewing times during the 8 P.M. to 11 P.M. time period. The data contained in the website file named Nielsen are consistent with the findings reported (*The World Almanac,* 2003). Based upon past studies the population standard deviation is assumed known with $\sigma = 3.5$ hours. Develop a 95% confidence interval estimate of the mean television viewing time per week during the 8 P.M. to 11 P.M. time period.

7. *The Wall Street Journal* reported that automobile crashes cost the United States $162 billion annually (*The Wall Street Journal,* March 5, 2008). The average cost per person for crashes in the Tampa, Florida, area was reported to be $1599. Suppose this average cost was based on a sample of 50 persons who had been involved in car crashes and that the population standard deviation is $\sigma = \$600$. What is the margin of error for a 95% confidence interval? What would you recommend if the study required a margin of error of $150 or less?

8. The National Quality Research Center at the University of Michigan provides a quarterly measure of consumer opinions about products and services (*The Wall Street Journal,* February 18, 2003). A survey of 10 restaurants in the Fast Food/Pizza group showed a sample mean customer satisfaction index of 71. Past data indicate that the population standard deviation of the index has been relatively stable with $\sigma = 5$.
   a. What assumption should the researcher be willing to make if a margin of error is desired?
   b. Using 95% confidence, what is the margin of error?
   c. What is the margin of error if 99% confidence is desired?

TaxReturn

9. AARP reported on a study conducted to learn how long it takes individuals to prepare their federal income tax return (*AARP Bulletin,* April 2008). The data contained in the file named TaxReturn are consistent with the study results. These data provide the time in hours required for 40 individuals to complete their federal income tax returns. Using past years' data, the population standard deviation can be assumed known with $\sigma = 9$ hours. What is the 95% confidence interval estimate of the mean time it takes an individual to complete a federal income tax return?

10. *Playbill* magazine reported that the mean annual household income of its readers is $119,155 (*Playbill,* January 2006). Assume this estimate of the mean annual household income is based on a sample of 80 households and, based on past studies, the population standard deviation is known to be $\sigma = \$30,000$.
    a. Develop a 90% confidence interval estimate of the population mean.
    b. Develop a 95% confidence interval estimate of the population mean.
    c. Develop a 99% confidence interval estimate of the population mean.
    d. Discuss what happens to the width of the confidence interval as the confidence level is increased. Does this result seem reasonable? Explain.

8.2 Population Mean: σ Unknown

When developing an interval estimate of a population mean we usually do not have a good estimate of the population standard deviation either. In these cases, we must use the same sample to estimate μ and σ. This situation represents the **σ unknown** case. When s is used to estimate σ, the margin of error and the interval estimate for the population mean are based on a probability distribution known as the **t distribution**. Although the mathematical development of the t distribution is based on the assumption of a normal distribution for the population we are sampling from, research shows that the t distribution can be successfully applied in many situations where the population deviates significantly from normal. Later in this section we provide guidelines for using the t distribution if the population is not normally distributed.

William Sealy Gosset, writing under the name "Student," is the founder of the t distribution. Gosset, an Oxford graduate in mathematics, worked for the Guinness Brewery in Dublin, Ireland. He developed the t distribution while working on small-scale materials and temperature experiments.

The t distribution is a family of similar probability distributions, with a specific t distribution depending on a parameter known as the **degrees of freedom**. The t distribution with 1 degree of freedom is unique, as is the t distribution with 2 degrees of freedom, with 3 degrees of freedom, and so on. As the number of degrees of freedom increases, the difference between the t distribution and the standard normal distribution becomes smaller and smaller. Figure 8.5 shows t distributions with 10 and 20 degrees of freedom and their relationship to the standard normal probability distribution. Note that a t distribution with more degrees of freedom exhibits less variability and more closely resembles the standard normal distribution. Note also that the mean of the t distribution is zero.

We place a subscript on t to indicate an area in the upper tail of the t distribution. For example, just as we used $z_{.025}$ to indicate the z value providing a .025 area in the upper tail of a standard normal distribution, we will use $t_{.025}$ to indicate the t value providing a .025 area in the upper tail of a t distribution. In general, we will use the notation $t_{\alpha/2}$ to represent a t value with an area of $\alpha/2$ in the upper tail of the t distribution. See Figure 8.6.

FIGURE 8.5 COMPARISON OF THE STANDARD NORMAL DISTRIBUTION WITH t DISTRIBUTIONS HAVING 10 AND 20 DEGREES OF FREEDOM

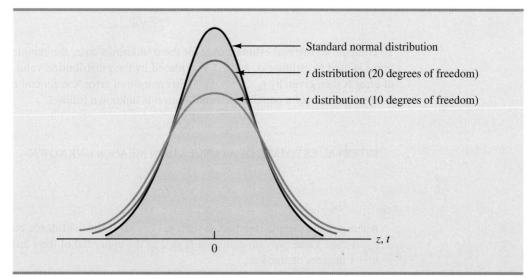

FIGURE 8.6 *t* DISTRIBUTION WITH $\alpha/2$ AREA OR PROBABILITY IN THE UPPER TAIL

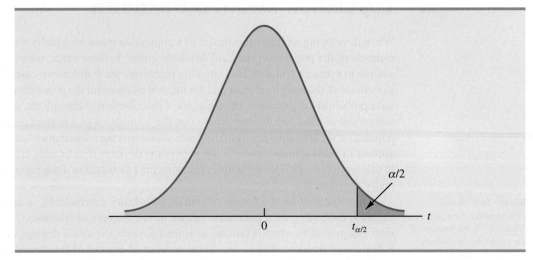

Table 2 in Appendix B contains a table for the *t* distribution. A portion of this table is shown in Table 8.2. Each row in the table corresponds to a separate *t* distribution with the degrees of freedom shown. For example, for a *t* distribution with 9 degrees of freedom, $t_{.025} = 2.262$. Similarly, for a *t* distribution with 60 degrees of freedom, $t_{.025} = 2.000$. As the degrees of freedom continue to increase, $t_{.025}$ approaches $z_{.025} = 1.96$. In fact, the standard normal distribution *z* values can be found in the infinite degrees of freedom row (labeled ∞) of the *t* distribution table. If the degrees of freedom exceed 100, the infinite degrees of freedom row can be used to approximate the actual *t* value; in other words, for more than 100 degrees of freedom, the standard normal *z* value provides a good approximation to the *t* value.

As the degrees of freedom increase, the t distribution approaches the standard normal distribution.

Margin of Error and the Interval Estimate

In Section 8.1 we showed that an interval estimate of a population mean for the σ known case is

$$\bar{x} \pm z_{\alpha/2}\frac{\sigma}{\sqrt{n}}$$

To compute an interval estimate of μ for the σ unknown case, the sample standard deviation s is used to estimate σ, and $z_{\alpha/2}$ is replaced by the *t* distribution value $t_{\alpha/2}$. The margin of error is then given by $t_{\alpha/2} s/\sqrt{n}$. With this margin of error, the general expression for an interval estimate of a population mean when σ is unknown follows.

INTERVAL ESTIMATE OF A POPULATION MEAN: σ UNKNOWN

$$\bar{x} \pm t_{\alpha/2}\frac{s}{\sqrt{n}} \tag{8.2}$$

where s is the sample standard deviation, $(1 - \alpha)$ is the confidence coefficient, and $t_{\alpha/2}$ is the *t* value providing an area of $\alpha/2$ in the upper tail of the *t* distribution with $n - 1$ degrees of freedom.

TABLE 8.2 SELECTED VALUES FROM THE t DISTRIBUTION TABLE*

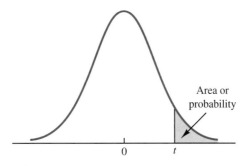

Degrees of Freedom	Area in Upper Tail					
	.20	**.10**	**.05**	**.025**	**.01**	**.005**
1	1.376	3.078	6.314	12.706	31.821	63.656
2	1.061	1.886	2.920	4.303	6.965	9.925
3	.978	1.638	2.353	3.182	4.541	5.841
4	.941	1.533	2.132	2.776	3.747	4.604
5	.920	1.476	2.015	2.571	3.365	4.032
6	.906	1.440	1.943	2.447	3.143	3.707
7	.896	1.415	1.895	2.365	2.998	3.499
8	.889	1.397	1.860	2.306	2.896	3.355
9	.883	1.383	1.833	2.262	2.821	3.250
⋮	⋮	⋮	⋮	⋮	⋮	⋮
60	.848	1.296	1.671	2.000	2.390	2.660
61	.848	1.296	1.670	2.000	2.389	2.659
62	.847	1.295	1.670	1.999	2.388	2.657
63	.847	1.295	1.669	1.998	2.387	2.656
64	.847	1.295	1.669	1.998	2.386	2.655
65	.847	1.295	1.669	1.997	2.385	2.654
66	.847	1.295	1.668	1.997	2.384	2.652
67	.847	1.294	1.668	1.996	2.383	2.651
68	.847	1.294	1.668	1.995	2.382	2.650
69	.847	1.294	1.667	1.995	2.382	2.649
⋮	⋮	⋮	⋮	⋮	⋮	⋮
90	.846	1.291	1.662	1.987	2.368	2.632
91	.846	1.291	1.662	1.986	2.368	2.631
92	.846	1.291	1.662	1.986	2.368	2.630
93	.846	1.291	1.661	1.986	2.367	2.630
94	.845	1.291	1.661	1.986	2.367	2.629
95	.845	1.291	1.661	1.985	2.366	2.629
96	.845	1.290	1.661	1.985	2.366	2.628
97	.845	1.290	1.661	1.985	2.365	2.627
98	.845	1.290	1.661	1.984	2.365	2.627
99	.845	1.290	1.660	1.984	2.364	2.626
100	.845	1.290	1.660	1.984	2.364	2.626
∞	.842	1.282	1.645	1.960	2.326	2.576

Note: The complete table is provided as Table 2 of Appendix B.

The reason the number of degrees of freedom associated with the t value in expression (8.2) is $n - 1$ concerns the use of s as an estimate of the population standard deviation σ. The expression for the sample standard deviation is

$$s = \sqrt{\frac{\Sigma(x_i - \bar{x})^2}{n - 1}}$$

Degrees of freedom refer to the number of independent pieces of information that go into the computation of $\Sigma(x_i - \bar{x})^2$. The n pieces of information involved in computing $\Sigma(x_i - \bar{x})^2$ are as follows: $x_1 - \bar{x}, x_2 - \bar{x}, \ldots, x_n - \bar{x}$. In Section 3.2 we indicated that $\Sigma(x_i - \bar{x}) = 0$ for any data set. Thus, only $n - 1$ of the $x_i - \bar{x}$ values are independent; that is, if we know $n - 1$ of the values, the remaining value can be determined exactly by using the condition that the sum of the $x_i - \bar{x}$ values must be 0. Thus, $n - 1$ is the number of degrees of freedom associated with $\Sigma(x_i - \bar{x})^2$ and hence the number of degrees of freedom for the t distribution in expression (8.2).

To illustrate the interval estimation procedure for the σ unknown case, we will consider a study designed to estimate the mean credit card debt for the population of U.S. households. A sample of $n = 70$ households provided the credit card balances shown in Table 8.3. For this situation, no previous estimate of the population standard deviation σ is available. Thus, the sample data must be used to estimate both the population mean and the population standard deviation. Using the data in Table 8.3, we compute the sample mean $\bar{x} = \$9312$ and the sample standard deviation $s = \$4007$. With 95% confidence and $n - 1 = 69$ degrees of freedom, Table 8.2 can be used to obtain the appropriate value for $t_{.025}$. We want the t value in the row with 69 degrees of freedom, and the column corresponding to .025 in the upper tail. The value shown is $t_{.025} = 1.995$.

We use expression (8.2) to compute an interval estimate of the population mean credit card balance.

$$9312 \pm 1.995 \frac{4007}{\sqrt{70}}$$

$$9312 \pm 955$$

The point estimate of the population mean is \$9312, the margin of error is \$955, and the 95% confidence interval is $9312 - 955 = \$8357$ to $9312 + 955 = \$10{,}267$. Thus, we are 95% confident that the mean credit card balance for the population of all households is between \$8357 and \$10,267.

TABLE 8.3   CREDIT CARD BALANCES FOR A SAMPLE OF 70 HOUSEHOLDS

WEB file

NewBalance

9430	14661	7159	9071	9691	11032
7535	12195	8137	3603	11448	6525
4078	10544	9467	16804	8279	5239
5604	13659	12595	13479	5649	6195
5179	7061	7917	14044	11298	12584
4416	6245	11346	6817	4353	15415
10676	13021	12806	6845	3467	15917
1627	9719	4972	10493	6191	12591
10112	2200	11356	615	12851	9743
6567	10746	7117	13627	5337	10324
13627	12744	9465	12557	8372	
18719	5742	19263	6232	7445	

Using Excel

We will use the credit card balances in Table 8.3 to illustrate how Excel can be used to construct an interval estimate of the population mean for the σ unknown case. We start by summarizing the data using Excel's Descriptive Statistics tool described in Chapter 3. Refer to Figure 8.7 as we describe the tasks involved. The formula worksheet is in the background; the value worksheet is in the foreground.

Enter Data: A label and the credit card balances are entered into cells A1:A71.

Apply Analysis Tools: The following steps describe how to use Excel's Descriptive Statistics tool for these data:

> **Step 1.** Click the **Data** tab on the Ribbon
> **Step 2.** In the **Analysis** group, click **Data Analysis**
> **Step 3.** Choose **Descriptive Statistics** from the list of Analysis Tools
> **Step 4.** When the Descriptive Statistics dialog box appears,
> > Enter A1:A71 in the **Input Range** box
> > Select **Grouped By Columns**
> > Select **Labels in First Row**
> > Select **Output Range**
> > > Enter C1 in the **Output Range** box
> > Select **Summary Statistics**
> > Select **Confidence Level for Mean**
> > > Enter 95 in the **Confidence Level for Mean** box
> > Click **OK**

FIGURE 8.7   EXCEL WORKSHEET: 95% CONFIDENCE INTERVAL FOR CREDIT CARD BALANCES

	A	B	C	D	E
1	NewBalance		*NewBalance*		
2	9430				
3	7535		Mean	9312	
4	4078		Standard Error	478.9281	
5	5604		Median	9466	
6	5179		Mode	13627	
7	4416		Standard Deviation	4007	
8	10676		Sample Variance	16056048	
9	1627		Kurtosis	−0.2960	
10	10112		Skewness	0.1879	
11	6567		Range	18648	
12	13627		Minimum	615	
13	18719		Maximum	19263	
14	14661		Sum	651840	
15	12195		Count	70	
16	10544		Confidence Level(95.0%)	955	
17	13659				
18	7061		Point Estimate	=D3	
19	6245		Lower Limit	=D18-D16	
20	13021		Upper Limit	=D18+D16	
70	9743				
71	10324				
72					

Note: Rows 21–69 are hidden.

	A	B	C	D	E	F
1	NewBalance		*NewBalance*			
2	9430					Point Estimate
3	7535		Mean	9312		
4	4078		Standard Error	478.9281		
5	5604		Median	9466		
6	5179		Mode	13627		
7	4416		Standard Deviation	4006.9998		
8	10676		Sample Variance	16056048		
9	1627		Kurtosis	−0.2960		
10	10112		Skewness	0.1879		
11	6567		Range	18648		
12	13627		Minimum	615		
13	18719		Maximum	19263		
14	14661		Sum	651840		
15	12195		Count	70		
16	10544		Confidence Level(95.0%)	955		Margin of Error
17	13659					
18	7061		Point Estimate	9312		
19	6245		Lower Limit	8357		
20	13021		Upper Limit	10267		
70	9743					
71	10324					
72						

The sample mean ($\bar{x}$) is in cell D3. The margin of error, labeled "Confidence Level(95%)," appears in cell D16. The value worksheet shows $\bar{x} = 9312$ and a margin of error equal to 955.

Enter Functions and Formulas: Cells D18:D20 provide the point estimate and the lower and upper limits for the confidence interval. Because the point estimate is just the sample mean, the formula =D3 is entered into cell D18. To compute the lower limit of the 95% confidence interval, $\bar{x}$ − (margin of error), we enter the formula =D18-D16 into cell D19. To compute the upper limit of the 95% confidence interval, $\bar{x}$ + (margin of error), we enter the formula =D18+D16 into cell D20. The value worksheet shows a lower limit of 8357 and an upper limit of 10267. In other words, the 95% confidence interval for the population mean is from 8357 to 10,267.

Practical Advice

If the population follows a normal distribution, the confidence interval provided by expression (8.2) is exact and can be used for any sample size. If the population does not follow a normal distribution, the confidence interval provided by expression (8.2) will be approximate. In this case, the quality of the approximation depends on both the distribution of the population and the sample size.

Larger sample sizes are needed if the distribution of the population is highly skewed or includes outliers.

In most applications, a sample size of $n \geq 30$ is adequate when using expression (8.2) to develop an interval estimate of a population mean. However, if the population distribution is highly skewed or contains outliers, most statisticians would recommend increasing the sample size to 50 or more. If the population is not normally distributed but is roughly symmetric, sample sizes as small as 15 can be expected to provide good approximate confidence intervals. With smaller sample sizes, expression (8.2) should only be used if the analyst believes, or is willing to assume, that the population distribution is at least approximately normal.

Using a Small Sample

In the following example we develop an interval estimate for a population mean when the sample size is small. As we already noted, an understanding of the distribution of the population becomes a factor in deciding whether the interval estimation procedure provides acceptable results.

Scheer Industries is considering a new computer-assisted program to train maintenance employees to do machine repairs. In order to fully evaluate the program, the director of manufacturing requested an estimate of the population mean time required for maintenance employees to complete the computer-assisted training.

A sample of 20 employees is selected, with each employee in the sample completing the training program. Data on the training time in days for the 20 employees are shown in Table 8.4. A histogram of the sample data appears in Figure 8.8. What can we say about the distribution of the population based on this histogram? First, the sample data do not support

TABLE 8.4 TRAINING TIME IN DAYS FOR A SAMPLE OF 20 SCHEER INDUSTRIES EMPLOYEES

WEB file

Scheer

52	59	54	42
44	50	42	48
55	54	60	55
44	62	62	57
45	46	43	56

FIGURE 8.8 HISTOGRAM OF TRAINING TIMES FOR THE SCHEER INDUSTRIES SAMPLE

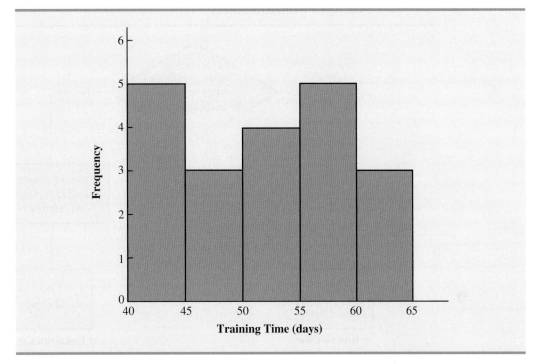

the conclusion that the distribution of the population is normal, yet we do not see any evidence of skewness or outliers. Therefore, using the practical advice in the previous subsection, we conclude that an interval estimate based on the t distribution appears acceptable for the sample of 20 employees.

We continue by computing the sample mean and sample standard deviation as follows.

$$\bar{x} = \frac{\Sigma x_i}{n} = \frac{1030}{20} = 51.5 \text{ days}$$

$$s = \sqrt{\frac{\Sigma (x_i - \bar{x})^2}{n - 1}} = \sqrt{\frac{889}{20 - 1}} = 6.84 \text{ days}$$

For a 95% confidence interval, we use Table 8.2 and $n - 1 = 19$ degrees of freedom to obtain $t_{.025} = 2.093$. Expression (8.2) provides the interval estimate of the population mean.

$$51.5 \pm 2.093 \left(\frac{6.84}{\sqrt{20}} \right)$$

$$51.5 \pm 3.2$$

The point estimate of the population mean is 51.5 days. The margin of error is 3.2 days and the 95% confidence interval is $51.5 - 3.2 = 48.3$ days to $51.5 + 3.2 = 54.7$ days.

Using a histogram of the sample data to learn about the distribution of a population is not always conclusive, but in many cases it provides the only information available. The histogram, along with judgment on the part of the analyst, can often be used to decide whether expression (8.2) can be used to develop the interval estimate.

FIGURE 8.9 SUMMARY OF INTERVAL ESTIMATION PROCEDURES
FOR A POPULATION MEAN

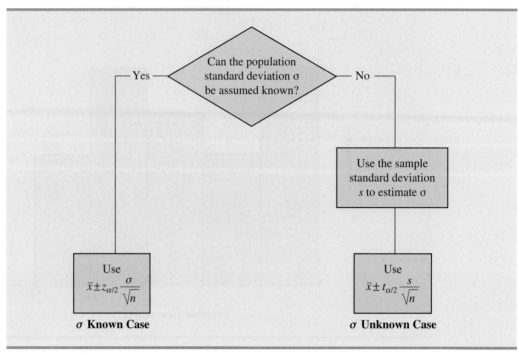

Summary of Interval Estimation Procedures

We provided two approaches to developing an interval estimate of a population mean. For the σ known case, σ and the standard normal distribution are used in expression (8.1) to compute the margin of error and to develop the interval estimate. For the σ unknown case, the sample standard deviation s and the t distribution are used in expression (8.2) to compute the margin of error and to develop the interval estimate.

A summary of the interval estimation procedures for the two cases is shown in Figure 8.9. In most applications, a sample size of $n \geq 30$ is adequate. If the population has a normal or approximately normal distribution, however, smaller sample sizes may be used. For the σ unknown case a sample size of $n \geq 50$ is recommended if the population distribution is believed to be highly skewed or has outliers.

NOTES AND COMMENTS

1. When σ is known, the margin of error, $z_{\alpha/2}(\sigma/\sqrt{n})$, is fixed and is the same for all samples of size n. When σ is unknown, the margin of error, $t_{\alpha/2}(s/\sqrt{n})$, varies from sample to sample. This variation occurs because the sample standard deviation s varies depending upon the sample selected. A large value for s provides a larger margin of error, while a small value for s provides a smaller margin of error.

2. What happens to confidence interval estimates when the population is skewed? Consider a population that is skewed to the right with large data values stretching the distribution to the right. When such skewness exists, the sample mean $\bar{x}$ and the sample standard deviation s are positively correlated. Larger values of s tend to be associated with larger values of $\bar{x}$. Thus, when $\bar{x}$ is larger than the population mean, s tends to be larger than σ. This skewness causes the margin of error, $t_{\alpha/2}(s/\sqrt{n})$, to be larger than it would be with σ known. The confidence interval with the

larger margin of error tends to include the population mean μ more often than it would if the true value of σ were used. But when $\bar{x}$ is smaller than the population mean, the correlation between $\bar{x}$ and s causes the margin of error to be small. In this case, the confidence interval with the smaller margin of error tends to miss the population mean more than it would if we knew σ and used it. For this reason, we recommend using larger sample sizes with highly skewed population distributions.

Exercises

Methods

11. For a t distribution with 16 degrees of freedom, find the area, or probability, in each region.
    a. To the right of 2.120
    b. To the left of 1.337
    c. To the left of -1.746
    d. To the right of 2.583
    e. Between -2.120 and 2.120
    f. Between -1.746 and 1.746

12. Find the t value(s) for each of the following cases.
    a. Upper tail area of .025 with 12 degrees of freedom
    b. Lower tail area of .05 with 50 degrees of freedom
    c. Upper tail area of .01 with 30 degrees of freedom
    d. Where 90% of the area falls between these two t values with 25 degrees of freedom
    e. Where 95% of the area falls between these two t values with 45 degrees of freedom
       (See Table 2 of Appendix B for a complete t table.)

13. The following sample data are from a normal population: 10, 8, 12, 15, 13, 11, 6, 5.
    a. What is the point estimate of the population mean?
    b. What is the point estimate of the population standard deviation?
    c. With 95% confidence, what is the margin of error for the estimation of the population mean?
    d. What is the 95% confidence interval for the population mean?

14. A simple random sample with $n = 54$ provided a sample mean of 22.5 and a sample standard deviation of 4.4. (See Table 2 of Appendix B for the complete t table.)
    a. Develop a 90% confidence interval for the population mean.
    b. Develop a 95% confidence interval for the population mean.
    c. Develop a 99% confidence interval for the population mean.
    d. What happens to the margin of error and the confidence interval as the confidence level is increased?

Applications

15. Sales personnel for Skillings Distributors submit weekly reports listing the customer contacts made during the week. A sample of 65 weekly reports showed a sample mean of 19.5 customer contacts per week. The sample standard deviation was 5.2. Provide 90% and 95% confidence intervals for the population mean number of weekly customer contacts for the sales personnel.

16. The mean number of hours of flying time for pilots at Continental Airlines is 49 hours per month (*The Wall Street Journal,* February 25, 2003). Assume that this mean was based on actual flying times for a sample of 100 Continental pilots and that the sample standard deviation was 8.5 hours.

a. At 95% confidence, what is the margin of error?

b. What is the 95% confidence interval estimate of the population mean flying time for the pilots?

c. The mean number of hours of flying time for pilots at United Airlines is 36 hours per month. Use your results from part (b) to discuss differences between the flying times for the pilots at the two airlines. *The Wall Street Journal* reported United Airlines as having the highest labor cost among all airlines. Does the information in this exercise provide insight as to why United Airlines might expect higher labor costs?

17. The International Air Transport Association surveys business travelers to develop quality ratings for transatlantic gateway airports. The maximum possible rating is 10. Suppose a simple random sample of 50 business travelers is selected and each traveler is asked to provide a rating for the Miami International Airport. The ratings obtained from the sample of 50 business travelers follow.

WEB file

Miami

6	4	6	8	7	7	6	3	3	8	10	4	8
7	8	7	5	9	5	8	4	3	8	5	5	4
4	4	8	4	5	6	2	5	9	9	8	4	8
9	9	5	9	7	8	3	10	8	9	6		

Develop a 95% confidence interval estimate of the population mean rating for Miami.

WEB file

JobSearch

18. Older people often have a hard time finding work. AARP reported on the number of weeks it takes a worker aged 55 plus to find a job. The data on number of weeks spent searching for a job contained in the file JobSearch are consistent with the AARP findings (*AARP Bulletin*, April 2008).

a. Provide a point estimate of the population mean number of weeks it takes a worker aged 55 plus to find a job.

b. At 95% confidence, what is the margin of error?

c. What is the 95% confidence interval estimate of the mean?

d. Discuss the degree of skewness found in the sample data. What suggestion would you make for a repeat of this study?

19. A National Retail Foundation survey found households intended to spend an average of $649 during the December holiday season (*The Wall Street Journal*, December 2, 2002). Assume that the survey included 600 households and that the sample standard deviation was $175.

a. With 95% confidence, what is the margin of error?

b. What is the 95% confidence interval estimate of the population mean?

c. The prior year, the population mean expenditure per household was $632. Discuss the change in holiday season expenditures over the one-year period.

WEB file

Program

20. Is your favorite TV program often interrupted by advertising? CNBC presented statistics on the average number of programming minutes in a half-hour sitcom (CNBC, February 23, 2006). The following data (in minutes) are representative of their findings.

21.06	22.24	20.62
21.66	21.23	23.86
23.82	20.30	21.52
21.52	21.91	23.14
20.02	22.20	21.20
22.37	22.19	22.34
23.36	23.44	

Assume the population is approximately normal. Provide a point estimate and a 95% confidence interval for the mean number of programming minutes during a half-hour television sitcom.

21. Consumption of alcoholic beverages by young women of drinking age has been increasing in the United Kingdom, the United States, and Europe (*The Wall Street Journal*, February 15, 2006). Data (annual consumption in liters) consistent with the findings

WEB file

Alcohol

reported in *The Wall Street Journal* article are shown for a sample of 20 European young women.

266	82	199	174	97
170	222	115	130	169
164	102	113	171	0
93	0	93	110	130

Assuming the population is roughly symmetric, construct a 95% confidence interval for the mean annual consumption of alcoholic beverages by European young women.

22. The first few weeks of 2004 were good for the stock market. A sample of 25 large open-end funds showed the following year-to-date returns through January 16, 2004 (*Barron's*, January 19, 2004).

WEB file

OpenEndFunds

7.0	3.2	1.4	5.4	8.5
2.5	2.5	1.9	5.4	1.6
1.0	2.1	8.5	4.3	6.2
1.5	1.2	2.7	3.8	2.0
1.2	2.6	4.0	2.6	0.6

a. What is the point estimate of the population mean year-to-date return for large open-end funds?
b. Given that the population has a normal distribution, develop a 95% confidence interval for the population mean year-to-date return for open-end funds.

8.3

Determining the Sample Size

In providing practical advice in the two preceding sections, we commented on the role of the sample size in providing approximate confidence intervals when the population is not normally distributed. In this section, we focus on another aspect of the sample size issue. We describe how to choose a sample size large enough to provide a desired margin of error. To see how this is done, we return to the σ known case presented in Section 8.1. Using expression (8.1), the interval estimate is

If a desired margin of error is selected prior to sampling, the procedures in this section can be used to determine the sample size necessary to satisfy the margin of error requirement.

$$\bar{x} \pm z_{\alpha/2} \frac{\sigma}{\sqrt{n}}$$

The quantity $z_{\alpha/2}(\sigma/\sqrt{n})$ is the margin of error. Thus, we see that $z_{\alpha/2}$, the population standard deviation σ, and the sample size n combine to determine the margin of error. Once we select a confidence coefficient $1 - \alpha$, $z_{\alpha/2}$ can be determined. Then, if we have a value for σ, we can determine the sample size n needed to provide any desired margin of error. Development of the formula used to compute the required sample size n follows.

Let E = the desired margin of error:

$$E = z_{\alpha/2} \frac{\sigma}{\sqrt{n}}$$

Solving for $\sqrt{n}$, we have

$$\sqrt{n} = \frac{z_{\alpha/2}\sigma}{E}$$

Squaring both sides of this equation, we obtain the following expression for the sample size.

Equation (8.3) can be used to provide a sample size recommendation. However, judgment on the part of the analyst should be used to determine whether the final sample size should be adjusted upward.

SAMPLE SIZE FOR AN INTERVAL ESTIMATE OF A POPULATION MEAN

$$n = \frac{(z_{\alpha/2})^2 \sigma^2}{E^2} \qquad (8.3)$$

This sample size provides the desired margin of error at the chosen confidence level.

In equation (8.3) E is the margin of error that the user is willing to accept, and the value of $z_{\alpha/2}$ follows directly from the confidence level to be used in developing the interval estimate. Although user preference must be considered, 95% confidence is the most frequently chosen value ($z_{.025} = 1.96$).

Finally, use of equation (8.3) requires a value for the population standard deviation σ. However, even if σ is unknown, we can use equation (8.3) provided we have a preliminary or *planning value* for σ. In practice, one of the following procedures can be chosen.

A planning value for the population standard deviation σ must be specified before the sample size can be determined. Three methods of obtaining a planning value for σ are discussed here.

1. Use the estimate of the population standard deviation computed from data of previous studies as the planning value for σ.
2. Use a pilot study to select a preliminary sample. The sample standard deviation from the preliminary sample can be used as the planning value for σ.
3. Use judgment or a "best guess" for the value of σ. For example, we might begin by estimating the largest and smallest data values in the population. The difference between the largest and smallest values provides an estimate of the range for the data. Finally, the range divided by 4 is often suggested as a rough approximation of the standard deviation and thus an acceptable planning value for σ.

Let us demonstrate the use of equation (8.3) to determine the sample size by considering the following example. A previous study that investigated the cost of renting automobiles in the United States found a mean cost of approximately $55 per day for renting a midsize automobile. Suppose that the organization that conducted this study would like to conduct a new study in order to estimate the population mean daily rental cost for a midsize automobile in the United States. In designing the new study, the project director specifies that the population mean daily rental cost be estimated with a margin of error of $2 and a 95% level of confidence.

The project director specified a desired margin of error of $E = 2$, and the 95% level of confidence indicates $z_{.025} = 1.96$. Thus, we only need a planning value for the population standard deviation σ in order to compute the required sample size. At this point, an analyst reviewed the sample data from the previous study and found that the sample standard deviation for the daily rental cost was $9.65. Using 9.65 as the planning value for σ, we obtain

Equation (8.3) provides the minimum sample size needed to satisfy the desired margin of error requirement. If the computed sample size is not an integer, rounding up to the next integer value will provide a margin of error slightly smaller than required.

$$n = \frac{(z_{\alpha/2})^2 \sigma^2}{E^2} = \frac{(1.96)^2 (9.65)^2}{2^2} = 89.43$$

Thus, the sample size for the new study needs to be at least 89.43 midsize automobile rentals in order to satisfy the project director's $2 margin-of-error requirement. In cases where the computed n is not an integer, we round up to the next integer value; hence, the recommended sample size is 90 midsize automobile rentals.

Exercises

Methods

23. How large a sample should be selected to provide a 95% confidence interval with a margin of error of 10? Assume that the population standard deviation is 40.

24. The range for a set of data is estimated to be 36.
    a. What is the planning value for the population standard deviation?
    b. At 95% confidence, how large a sample would provide a margin of error of 3?
    c. At 95% confidence, how large a sample would provide a margin of error of 2?

Applications

25. Refer to the Scheer Industries example in Section 8.2. Use 6.84 days as a planning value for the population standard deviation.
    a. Assuming 95% confidence, what sample size would be required to obtain a margin of error of 1.5 days?
    b. If the precision statement was made with 90% confidence, what sample size would be required to obtain a margin of error of 2 days?

26. The average cost of a gallon of unleaded gasoline in Greater Cincinnati was reported to be $2.41 (*The Cincinnati Enquirer*, February 3, 2006). During periods of rapidly changing prices, the newspaper samples service stations and prepares reports on gasoline prices frequently. Assume the standard deviation is $.15 for the price of a gallon of unleaded regular gasoline, and recommend the appropriate sample size for the newspaper to use if they wish to report a margin of error at 95% confidence.
    a. Suppose the desired margin of error is $.07.
    b. Suppose the desired margin of error is $.05.
    c. Suppose the desired margin of error is $.03.

27. Annual starting salaries for college graduates with degrees in business administration are generally expected to be between $30,000 and $45,000. Assume that a 95% confidence interval estimate of the population mean annual starting salary is desired. What is the planning value for the population standard deviation? How large a sample should be taken if the desired margin of error is
    a. $500?
    b. $200?
    c. $100?
    d. Would you recommend trying to obtain the $100 margin of error? Explain.

28. An online survey by ShareBuilder, a retirement plan provider, and Harris Interactive reported that 60% of female business owners are not confident they are saving enough for retirement (*SmallBiz*, Winter 2006). Suppose we would like to do a follow-up study to determine how much female business owners are saving each year toward retirement and want to use $100 as the desired margin of error for an interval estimate of the population mean. Use $1100 as a planning value for the standard deviation and recommend a sample size for each of the following situations.
    a. A 90% confidence interval is desired for the mean amount saved.
    b. A 95% confidence interval is desired for the mean amount saved.
    c. A 99% confidence interval is desired for the mean amount saved.
    d. When the desired margin of error is set, what happens to the sample size as the confidence level is increased? Would you recommend using a 99% confidence interval in this case? Discuss.

29. The travel-to-work time for residents of the 15 largest cities in the United States is reported in the *2003 Information Please Almanac*. Suppose that a preliminary simple random sample of residents of San Francisco is used to develop a planning value of 6.25 minutes for the population standard deviation.

a. If we want to estimate the population mean travel-to-work time for San Francisco residents with a margin of error of 2 minutes, what sample size should be used? Assume 95% confidence.

b. If we want to estimate the population mean travel-to-work time for San Francisco residents with a margin of error of 1 minute, what sample size should be used? Assume 95% confidence.

30. During the first quarter of 2003, the price/earnings (P/E) ratio for stocks listed on the New York Stock Exchange generally ranged from 5 to 60 (*The Wall Street Journal*, March 7, 2003). Assume that we want to estimate the population mean P/E ratio for all stocks listed on the exchange. How many stocks should be included in the sample if we want a margin of error of 3? Use 95% confidence.

8.4 Population Proportion

In the introduction to this chapter we said that the general form of an interval estimate of a population proportion p is

$$\bar{p} \pm \text{Margin of error}$$

The sampling distribution of $\bar{p}$ plays a key role in computing the margin of error for this interval estimate.

In Chapter 7 we said that the sampling distribution of $\bar{p}$ can be approximated by a normal distribution whenever $np \geq 5$ and $n(1 - p) \geq 5$. Figure 8.10 shows the normal approximation of the sampling distribution of $\bar{p}$. The mean of the sampling distribution of $\bar{p}$ is the population proportion p, and the standard error of $\bar{p}$ is

$$\sigma_{\bar{p}} = \sqrt{\frac{p(1 - p)}{n}} \tag{8.4}$$

Because the sampling distribution of $\bar{p}$ is normally distributed, if we choose $z_{\alpha/2}\sigma_{\bar{p}}$ as the margin of error in an interval estimate of a population proportion, we know that $100(1 - \alpha)\%$ of the intervals generated will contain the true population proportion. Unfortunately, $\sigma_{\bar{p}}$ cannot be used directly in the computation of the margin of error because p

FIGURE 8.10   NORMAL APPROXIMATION OF THE SAMPLING DISTRIBUTION OF $\bar{p}$

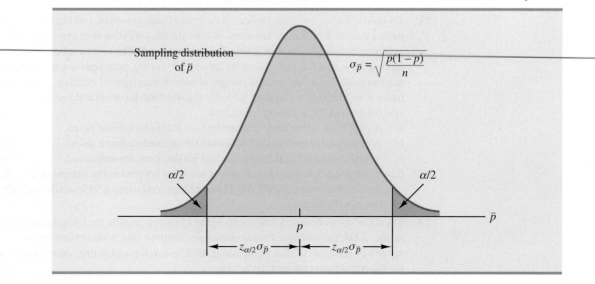

will not be known; p is what we are trying to estimate. So, $\bar{p}$ is substituted for p and the margin of error for an interval estimate of a population proportion is given by

$$\text{Margin of error} = z_{\alpha/2} \sqrt{\frac{\bar{p}(1 - \bar{p})}{n}} \tag{8.5}$$

With this margin of error, the general expression for an interval estimate of a population proportion is as follows.

INTERVAL ESTIMATE OF A POPULATION PROPORTION

$$\bar{p} \pm z_{\alpha/2} \sqrt{\frac{\bar{p}(1 - \bar{p})}{n}} \tag{8.6}$$

where $1 - \alpha$ is the confidence coefficient and $z_{\alpha/2}$ is the z value providing an area of $\alpha/2$ in the upper tail of the standard normal distribution.

When developing confidence intervals for proportions, the quantity $z_{\alpha/2}\sqrt{\bar{p}(1 - \bar{p})/n}$ provides the margin of error.

TeeTimes

The following example illustrates the computation of the margin of error and interval estimate for a population proportion. A national survey of 900 women golfers was conducted to learn how women golfers view their treatment at golf courses in the United States. The survey found that 396 of the women golfers were satisfied with the availability of tee times. Thus, the point estimate of the proportion of the population of women golfers who are satisfied with the availability of tee times is $396/900 = .44$. Using expression (8.6) and a 95% confidence level,

$$\bar{p} \pm z_{\alpha/2} \sqrt{\frac{\bar{p}(1 - \bar{p})}{n}}$$

$$.44 \pm 1.96 \sqrt{\frac{.44(1 - .44)}{900}}$$

$$.44 \pm .0324$$

Thus, the margin of error is .0324 and the 95% confidence interval estimate of the population proportion is .4076 to .4724. Using percentages, the survey results enable us to state with 95% confidence that between 40.76% and 47.24% of all women golfers are satisfied with the availability of tee times.

Using Excel

Excel can be used to construct an interval estimate of the population proportion of women golfers who are satisfied with the availability of tee times. The responses in the survey were recorded as a Yes or No for each woman surveyed. Refer to Figure 8.11 as we describe the tasks involved in constructing a 95% confidence interval. The formula worksheet is in the background; the value worksheet appears in the foreground.

Enter Data: The Yes/No data for the 900 women golfers are entered into cells A2:A901.

Enter Functions and Formulas: The descriptive statistics we need and the response of interest are provided in cells D3:D6. Because Excel's COUNT function only works with numerical data, we used the COUNTA function in cell D3 to compute the sample size. The response for which we want to develop an interval estimate, Yes or No, is entered into cell D4. Figure 8.11 shows that Yes has been entered into cell D4, indicating that we want to develop an interval estimate of the population proportion of women golfers who are satisfied with the availability of tee times. If we had wanted to develop an interval estimate of the population proportion of women golfers who are not satisfied with the availability of tee times, we would have entered No in cell D4. With Yes entered in cell D4, the COUNTIF function in cell D5

FIGURE 8.11   EXCEL WORKSHEET: 95% CONFIDENCE INTERVAL FOR SURVEY OF WOMEN GOLFERS

	A	B	C	D	E
1	Response		**Interval Estimate of a Population Proportion**		
2	Yes				
3	No		Sample Size	=COUNTA(A2:A901)	
4	Yes		Response of Interest	Yes	
5	Yes		Count for Response	=COUNTIF(A2:A901,D4)	
6	No		Sample Proportion	=D5/D3	
7	No				
8	No		Confidence Coefficient	0.95	
9	Yes		Level of Significance (alpha)	=1-D8	
10	Yes		z Value	=NORMSINV(1-D9/2)	
11	Yes				
12	No		Standard Error	=SQRT(D6*(1-D6)/D3)	
13	No		Margin of Error	=D10*D12	
14	Yes				
15	No		Point Estimate	=D6	
16	No		Lower Limit	=D15-D13	
17	Yes		Upper Limit	=D15+D13	
18	No				
900	Yes				
901	Yes				
902					

WEB file

TeeTimes

Note: Rows 19 to 899 are hidden.

	A	B	C	D	E	F	G
1	Response		**Interval Estimate of a Population Proportion**				
2	Yes						
3	No		Sample Size	900		Enter Yes as the	
4	Yes		Response of Interest	Yes		Response of Interest	
5	Yes		Count for Response	396			
6	No		Sample Proportion	0.44			
7	No						
8	No		Confidence Coefficient	0.95			
9	Yes		Level of Significance	0.05			
10	Yes		z Value	1.96			
11	Yes						
12	No		Standard Error	0.0165			
13	No		Margin of Error	0.0324			
14	Yes						
15	No		Point Estimate	0.44			
16	No		Lower Limit	0.4076			
17	Yes		Upper Limit	0.4724			
18	No						
900	Yes						
901	Yes						
902							

counts the number of Yes responses in the sample. The sample proportion is then computed in cell D6 by dividing the number of Yes responses in cell D5 by the sample size in cell D3.

Cells D8:D10 are used to compute the appropriate z value. The confidence coefficient (0.95) is entered into cell D8 and the level of significance (α) is computed in cell D9 by entering the formula =1-D8. The z value corresponding to an upper tail area of $\alpha/2$ is computed by entering the formula =NORMSINV(1-D9/2) into cell D10. The value worksheet shows that $z_{.025} = 1.960$.

Cells D12:D13 provide the estimate of the standard error and the margin of error. In cell D12, we entered the formula =SQRT(D6*(1-D6)/D3) to compute the standard error using the sample proportion and the sample size as inputs. The formula =D10*D12 is entered into cell D13 to compute the margin of error.

Cells D15:D17 provide the point estimate and the lower and upper limits for a confidence interval. The point estimate in cell D15 is the sample proportion. The lower and upper limits in cells D16 and D17 are obtained by subtracting and adding the margin of error to the point estimate. We note that the 95% confidence interval for the proportion of women golfers who are satisfied with the availability of tee times is .4076 to .4724.

A template for other problems The worksheet in Figure 8.11 can be used as a template for developing confidence intervals about a population proportion p. To use this worksheet for another problem of this type, we must first enter the new problem data in column A. The response of interest would then be typed in cell D4 and the ranges for the formulas in cells D3 and D5 would be revised to correspond to the new data. After doing so, the point estimate and a 95% confidence interval will be displayed in cells D15:D17. If a confidence interval with a different confidence coefficient is desired, we simply change the value in cell D8.

Determining the Sample Size

Let us consider the question of how large the sample size should be to obtain an estimate of a population proportion at a specified level of precision. The rationale for the sample size determination in developing interval estimates of p is similar to the rationale used in Section 8.3 to determine the sample size for estimating a population mean.

Previously in this section we said that the margin of error associated with an interval estimate of a population proportion is $z_{\alpha/2}\sqrt{\bar{p}(1-\bar{p})/n}$. The margin of error is based on the value of $z_{\alpha/2}$, the sample proportion $\bar{p}$, and the sample size n. Larger sample sizes provide a smaller margin of error and better precision.

Let E denote the desired margin of error.

$$E = z_{\alpha/2}\sqrt{\frac{\bar{p}(1-\bar{p})}{n}}$$

Solving this equation for n provides a formula for the sample size that will provide a margin of error of size E.

$$n = \frac{(z_{\alpha/2})^2\bar{p}(1-\bar{p})}{E^2}$$

Note, however, that we cannot use this formula to compute the sample size that will provide the desired margin of error because $\bar{p}$ will not be known until after we select the sample. What we need, then, is a planning value for $\bar{p}$ that can be used to make the computation. Using p^* to denote the planning value for $\bar{p}$, the following formula can be used to compute the sample size that will provide a margin of error of size E.

SAMPLE SIZE FOR AN INTERVAL ESTIMATE OF A POPULATION PROPORTION

$$n = \frac{(z_{\alpha/2})^2 p^*(1-p^*)}{E^2} \tag{8.7}$$

In practice, the planning value p^* can be chosen by one of the following procedures.

1. Use the sample proportion from a previous sample of the same or similar units.
2. Use a pilot study to select a preliminary sample. The sample proportion from this sample can be used as the planning value, p^*.
3. Use judgment or a "best guess" for the value of p^*.
4. If none of the preceding alternatives apply, use a planning value of $p^* = .50$.

Let us return to the survey of women golfers and assume that the company is interested in conducting a new survey to estimate the current proportion of the population of women golfers who are satisfied with the availability of tee times. How large should the sample be if the survey director wants to estimate the population proportion with a margin of error of .025 at 95% confidence? With $E = .025$ and $z_{\alpha/2} = 1.96$, we need a planning value p^* to answer the sample size question. Using the previous survey result of $\bar{p} = .44$ as the planning value p^*, equation (8.7) shows that

$$n = \frac{(z_{\alpha/2})^2 p^*(1 - p^*)}{E^2} = \frac{(1.96)^2(.44)(1 - .44)}{(.025)^2} = 1514.5$$

Thus, the sample size must be at least 1514.5 women golfers to satisfy the margin of error requirement. Rounding up to the next integer value indicates that a sample of 1515 women golfers is recommended to satisfy the margin of error requirement.

The fourth alternative suggested for selecting a planning value p^* is to use $p^* = .50$. This value of p^* is frequently used when no other information is available. To understand why, note that the numerator of equation (8.7) shows that the sample size is proportional to the quantity $p^*(1 - p^*)$. A larger value for the quantity $p^*(1 - p^*)$ will result in a larger sample size. Table 8.5 gives some possible values of $p^*(1 - p^*)$. Note that the largest value of $p^*(1 - p^*)$ occurs when $p^* = .50$. Thus, in case of any uncertainty about an appropriate planning value, we know that $p^* = .50$ will provide the largest sample size recommendation. In effect, we play it safe by recommending the largest necessary sample size. If the sample proportion turns out to be different from the .50 planning value, the margin of error will be smaller than anticipated. Thus, in using $p^* = .50$, we guarantee that the sample size will be sufficient to obtain the desired margin of error.

In the survey of women golfers example, a planning value of $p^* = .50$ would have provided the sample size

$$n = \frac{(z_{\alpha/2})^2 p^*(1 - p^*)}{E^2} = \frac{(1.96)^2(.50)(1 - .50)}{(.025)^2} = 1536.6$$

Thus, a slightly larger sample size of 1537 women golfers would be recommended.

TABLE 8.5 SOME POSSIBLE VALUES FOR $p^*(1 - p^*)$

p^*	$p^*(1 - p^*)$	
.10	(.10)(.90) = .09	
.30	(.30)(.70) = .21	
.40	(.40)(.60) = .24	
.50	(.50)(.50) = .25	← Largest value for $p^*(1 - p^*)$
.60	(.60)(.40) = .24	
.70	(.70)(.30) = .21	
.90	(.90)(.10) = .09	

NOTES AND COMMENTS

The desired margin of error for estimating a population proportion is almost always .10 or less. In national public opinion polls conducted by organizations such as Gallup and Harris, a .03 or .04 margin of error is common. With such margins of error, equation (8.7) will almost always provide a sample size that is large enough to satisfy the requirements of $np \geq 5$ and $n(1 - p) \geq 5$ for using a normal distribution as an approximation for the sampling distribution of $\bar{p}$.

Exercises

Methods

31. A simple random sample of 400 individuals provides 100 Yes responses.
    a. What is the point estimate of the proportion of the population that would provide Yes responses?
    b. What is your estimate of the standard error of $\bar{p}$, $\sigma_{\bar{p}}$?
    c. Compute the 95% confidence interval for the population proportion.

32. A simple random sample of 800 elements generates a sample proportion $\bar{p} = .70$.
    a. Provide a 90% confidence interval for the population proportion.
    b. Provide a 95% confidence interval for the population proportion.

33. In a survey, the planning value for the population proportion is $p^* = .35$. How large a sample should be taken to provide a 95% confidence interval with a margin of error of .05?

34. At 95% confidence, how large a sample should be taken to obtain a margin of error of .03 for the estimation of a population proportion? Assume that past data are not available for developing a planning value for p^*.

Applications

35. A survey of 611 office workers investigated telephone answering practices, including how often each office worker was able to answer incoming telephone calls and how often incoming telephone calls went directly to voice mail (*USA Today,* April 21, 2002). A total of 281 office workers indicated that they never need voice mail and are able to take every telephone call.
    a. What is the point estimate of the proportion of the population of office workers who are able to take every telephone call?
    b. At 90% confidence, what is the margin of error?
    c. What is the 90% confidence interval for the proportion of the population of office workers who are able to take every telephone call?

36. According to statistics reported on CNBC, a surprising number of motor vehicles are not covered by insurance (CNBC, February 23, 2006). Sample results, consistent with the CNBC report, showed 46 of 200 vehicles were not covered by insurance.
    a. What is the point estimate of the proportion of vehicles not covered by insurance?
    b. Develop a 95% confidence interval for the population proportion.

JobSatisfaction

37. Towers Perrin, a New York human resources consulting firm, conducted a survey of 1100 employees at medium-sized and large companies to determine how dissatisfied employees were with their jobs (*The Wall Street Journal,* January 29, 2003). The data are shown in the file named JobSatisfaction. A response of Yes indicates that the employee strongly dislikes the current work experience.
    a. What is the point estimate of the proportion of the population of employees who strongly dislike the current work experience?
    b. At 95% confidence, what is the margin of error?

    c.   What is the 95% confidence interval for the proportion of the population of employees who strongly dislike the current work experience?

    d.   Towers Perrin estimates that it costs employers one-third of an hourly employee's annual salary to find a successor and as much as 1.5 times the annual salary to find a successor for a highly compensated employee. What message did this survey send to employers?

38.   According to Thomson Financial, through January 25, 2006, the majority of companies reporting profits had beaten estimates (*BusinessWeek,* February 6, 2006). A sample of 162 companies showed 104 beat estimates, 29 matched estimates, and 29 fell short.

    a.   What is the point estimate of the proportion that fell short of estimates?

    b.   Determine the margin of error and provide a 95% confidence interval for the proportion that beat estimates.

    c.   How large a sample is needed if the desired margin of error is .05?

39.   The percentage of people not covered by health care insurance in 2003 was 15.6% (*Statistical Abstract of the United States*, 2006). A congressional committee has been charged with conducting a sample survey to obtain more current information.

    a.   What sample size would you recommend if the committee's goal is to estimate the current proportion of individuals without health care insurance with a margin of error of .03? Use a 95% confidence level.

    b.   Repeat part (a) using a 99% confidence level.

40.   The professional baseball home run record of 61 home runs in a season was held for 37 years by Roger Maris of the New York Yankees. However, between 1998 and 2001, three players—Mark McGwire, Sammy Sosa, and Barry Bonds—broke the standard set by Maris, with Bonds holding the current record of 73 home runs in a single season. With the long-standing home run record being broken and with many other new offensive records being set, suspicion arose that baseball players might be using illegal muscle-building drugs called steroids. A *USA Today*/CNN/Gallup poll found that 86% of baseball fans think professional baseball players should be tested for steroids (*USA Today,* July 8, 2002). If 650 baseball fans were included in the sample, compute the margin of error and the 95% confidence interval for the population proportion of baseball fans who think professional baseball players should be tested for steroids.

41.   America's young people are heavy Internet users; 87% of Americans ages 12 to 17 are Internet users (*The Cincinnati Enquirer,* February 7, 2006). MySpace was voted the most popular website by 9% in a sample survey of Internet users in this age group. Suppose 1400 youths participated in the survey. What is the margin of error, and what is the interval estimate of the population proportion for which MySpace is the most popular website? Use a 95% confidence level.

42.   A poll for the presidential campaign sampled 491 potential voters in June. A primary purpose of the poll was to obtain an estimate of the proportion of potential voters who favor each candidate. Assume a planning value of $p^* = .50$ and a 95% confidence level.

    a.   For $p^* = .50$, what was the planned margin of error for the June poll?

    b.   Closer to the November election, better precision and smaller margins of error are desired. Assume the following margins of error are requested for surveys to be conducted during the presidential campaign. Compute the recommended sample size for each survey.

Survey	Margin of Error
September	.04
October	.03
Early November	.02
Pre-Election Day	.01

43. A Phoenix Wealth Management/Harris Interactive survey of 1500 individuals with net worth of $1 million or more provided a variety of statistics on wealthy people (*Business-Week*, September 22, 2003). The previous three-year period had been bad for the stock market, which motivated some of the questions asked.

    a. The survey reported that 53% of the respondents lost 25% or more of their portfolio value over the past three years. Develop a 95% confidence interval for the proportion of wealthy people who lost 25% or more of their portfolio value over the past three years.

    b. The survey reported that 31% of the respondents feel they have to save more for retirement to make up for what they lost. Develop a 95% confidence interval for the population proportion.

    c. Five percent of the respondents gave $25,000 or more to charity over the previous year. Develop a 95% confidence interval for the proportion who gave $25,000 or more to charity.

    d. Compare the margin of error for the interval estimates in parts (a), (b), and (c). How is the margin of error related to $\bar{p}$? When the same sample is being used to estimate a variety of proportions, which of the proportions should be used to choose the planning value p^*? Why do you think $p^* = .50$ is often used in these cases?

Summary

In this chapter we presented methods for developing interval estimates of a population mean and a population proportion. A point estimator may or may not provide a good estimate of a population parameter. The use of an interval estimate provides a measure of the precision of an estimate. Both the interval estimate of the population mean and the population proportion are of the form: point estimate $\pm$ margin of error.

We presented interval estimates for a population mean for two cases. In the σ known case, historical data or other information is used to develop an estimate of σ prior to taking a sample. Analysis of new sample data then proceeds based on the assumption that σ is known. In the σ unknown case, the sample data are used to estimate both the population mean and the population standard deviation. The final choice of which interval estimation procedure to use depends upon the analyst's understanding of which method provides the best estimate of σ.

In the σ known case, the interval estimation procedure is based on the assumed value of σ and the use of the standard normal distribution. In the σ unknown case, the interval estimation procedure uses the sample standard deviation s and the t distribution. In both cases the quality of the interval estimates obtained depends on the distribution of the population and the sample size. If the population is normally distributed, the interval estimates will be exact in both cases, even for small sample sizes. If the population is not normally distributed, the interval estimates obtained will be approximate. Larger sample sizes will provide better approximations, but the more highly skewed the population is, the larger the sample size needs to be to obtain a good approximation. Practical advice about the sample size necessary to obtain good approximations was included in Sections 8.1 and 8.2. In most cases a sample of size 30 or more will provide good approximate confidence intervals.

The general form of the interval estimate for a population proportion is $\bar{p} \pm$ margin of error. In practice the sample sizes used for interval estimates of a population proportion are generally large. Thus, the interval estimation procedure is based on the standard normal distribution.

Often a desired margin of error is specified prior to developing a sampling plan. We showed how to choose a sample size large enough to provide the desired precision.

Glossary

Interval estimate An estimate of a population parameter that provides an interval believed to contain the value of the parameter. For the interval estimates in this chapter, it has the form: point estimate ± margin of error.

Margin of error The ± value added to and subtracted from a point estimate in order to develop an interval estimate of a population parameter.

σ known The case when historical data or other information provides a good value for the population standard deviation prior to taking a sample. The interval estimation procedure uses this known value of σ in computing the margin of error.

Confidence level The confidence associated with an interval estimate. For example, if an interval estimation procedure provides intervals such that 95% of the intervals formed using the procedure will include the population parameter, the interval estimate is said to be constructed at the 95% confidence level.

Confidence coefficient The confidence level expressed as a decimal value. For example, .95 is the confidence coefficient for a 95% confidence level.

Confidence interval Another name for an interval estimate.

Level of significance The probability that the interval estimation procedure will generate an interval that does not contain μ.

σ unknown The more common case when no good basis exists for estimating the population standard deviation prior to taking the sample. The interval estimation procedure uses the sample standard deviation s in computing the margin of error.

t distribution A family of probability distributions that can be used to develop an interval estimate of a population mean whenever the population standard deviation σ is unknown and is estimated by the sample standard deviation s.

Degrees of freedom A parameter of the t distribution. When the t distribution is used in the computation of an interval estimate of a population mean, the appropriate t distribution has $n - 1$ degrees of freedom, where n is the size of the simple random sample.

Key Formulas

Interval Estimate of a Population Mean: σ Known

$$\bar{x} \pm z_{\alpha/2} \frac{\sigma}{\sqrt{n}} \tag{8.1}$$

Interval Estimate of a Population Mean: σ Unknown

$$\bar{x} \pm t_{\alpha/2} \frac{s}{\sqrt{n}} \tag{8.2}$$

Sample Size for an Interval Estimate of a Population Mean

$$n = \frac{(z_{\alpha/2})^2 \sigma^2}{E^2} \tag{8.3}$$

Interval Estimate of a Population Proportion

$$\bar{p} \pm z_{\alpha/2} \sqrt{\frac{\bar{p}(1 - \bar{p})}{n}} \tag{8.6}$$

Sample Size for an Interval Estimate of a Population Proportion

$$n = \frac{(z_{\alpha/2})^2 p^*(1 - p^*)}{E^2} \tag{8.7}$$

Supplementary Exercises

44. A sample survey of 54 discount brokers showed that the mean price charged for a trade of 100 shares at $50 per share was $33.77 (*AAII Journal,* February 2006). The survey is conducted annually. With the historical data available, assume a known population standard deviation of $15.
    a. Using the sample data, what is the margin of error associated with a 95% confidence interval?
    b. Develop a 95% confidence interval for the mean price charged by discount brokers for a trade of 100 shares at $50 per share.

45. A survey conducted by the American Automobile Association showed that a family of four spends an average of $215.60 per day while on vacation. Suppose a sample of 64 families of four vacationing at Niagara Falls resulted in a sample mean of $252.45 per day and a sample standard deviation of $74.50.
    a. Develop a 95% confidence interval estimate of the mean amount spent per day by a family of four visiting Niagara Falls.
    b. Based on the confidence interval from part (a), does it appear that the population mean amount spent per day by families visiting Niagara Falls differs from the mean reported by the American Automobile Association? Explain.

46. The 92 million Americans of age 50 and over control 50 percent of all discretionary income (*AARP Bulletin,* March 2008). AARP estimated that the average annual expenditure on restaurants and carryout food was $1873 for individuals in this age group. Suppose this estimate is based on a sample of 80 persons and that the sample standard deviation is $550.
    a. At 95% confidence, what is the margin of error?
    b. What is the 95% confidence interval for the population mean amount spent on restaurants and carryout food?
    c. What is your estimate of the total amount spent by Americans of age 50 and over on restaurants and carryout food?
    d. If the amount spent on restaurants and carryout food is skewed to the right, would you expect the median amount spent to be greater or less than $1873?

47. Many stock market observers say that when the P/E ratio for stocks gets over 20 the market is overvalued. The P/E ratio is the stock price divided by the most recent 12 months of earnings. Suppose you are interested in seeing whether the current market is overvalued and would also like to know the proportion of companies that pay dividends. A random sample of 30 companies listed on the New York Stock Exchange (NYSE) is provided (*Barron's,* January 19, 2004).

NYSEStocks

Company	Dividend	P/E Ratio	Company	Dividend	P/E Ratio
Albertsons	Yes	14	NY Times A	Yes	25
BRE Prop	Yes	18	Omnicare	Yes	25
CityNtl	Yes	16	PallCp	Yes	23
DelMonte	No	21	PubSvcEnt	Yes	11
EnrgzHldg	No	20	SensientTch	Yes	11
Ford Motor	Yes	22	SmtProp	Yes	12
Gildan A	No	12	TJX Cos	Yes	21
HudsnUtdBcp	Yes	13	Thomson	Yes	30
IBM	Yes	22	USB Hldg	Yes	12
JeffPilot	Yes	16	US Restr	Yes	26
KingswayFin	No	6	Varian Med	No	41
Libbey	Yes	13	Visx	No	72
MasoniteIntl	No	15	Waste Mgt	No	23
Motorola	Yes	68	Wiley A	Yes	21
Ntl City	Yes	10	Yum Brands	No	18

a. What is a point estimate of the P/E ratio for the population of stocks listed on the New York Stock Exchange? Develop a 95% confidence interval.

b. Based on your answer to part (a), do you believe that the market is overvalued?

c. What is a point estimate of the proportion of companies on the NYSE that pay dividends? Is the sample size large enough to justify using the normal distribution to construct a confidence interval for this proportion? Why or why not?

Flights

48. US Airways conducted a number of studies that indicated a substantial savings could be obtained by encouraging Dividend Miles frequent flyer customers to redeem miles and schedule award flights online (*US Airways Attaché,* February 2003). One study collected data on the amount of time required to redeem miles and schedule an award flight over the telephone. A sample showing the time in minutes required for each of 150 award flights scheduled by telephone is contained in the data set Flights. Use Excel to help answer the following questions.

a. What is the sample mean number of minutes required to schedule an award flight by telephone?

b. What is the 95% confidence interval for the population mean time to schedule an award flight by telephone?

c. Assume a telephone ticket agent works 7.5 hours per day. How many award flights can one ticket agent be expected to handle a day?

d. Discuss why this information supported US Airways's plans to use an online system to reduce costs.

WEB file

ActTemps

49. A survey by Accountemps asked a sample of 200 executives to provide data on the number of minutes per day office workers waste trying to locate mislabeled, misfiled, or misplaced items. Data consistent with this survey are contained in the data set ActTemps.

a. Use ActTemps to develop a point estimate of the number of minutes per day office workers waste trying to locate mislabeled, misfiled, or misplaced items.

b. What is the sample standard deviation?

c. What is the 95% confidence interval for the mean number of minutes wasted per day?

50. Mileage tests are conducted for a particular model of automobile. If a 98% confidence interval with a margin of error of 1 mile per gallon is desired, how many automobiles should be used in the test? Assume that preliminary mileage tests indicate the standard deviation is 2.6 miles per gallon.

51. In developing patient appointment schedules, a medical center wants to estimate the mean time that a staff member spends with each patient. How large a sample should be taken if the desired margin of error is two minutes at a 95% level of confidence? How large a sample should be taken for a 99% level of confidence? Use a planning value for the population standard deviation of eight minutes.

52. Annual salary plus bonus data for chief executive officers are presented in the *Business-Week* Annual Pay Survey. A preliminary sample showed that the standard deviation is $675 with data provided in thousands of dollars. How many chief executive officers should be in a sample if we want to estimate the population mean annual salary plus bonus with a margin of error of $100,000? (*Note:* The desired margin of error would be $E = 100$ if the data are in thousands of dollars.) Use 95% confidence.

53. The National Center for Education Statistics reported that 47% of college students work to pay for tuition and living expenses. Assume that a sample of 450 college students was used in the study.

a. Provide a 95% confidence interval for the population proportion of college students who work to pay for tuition and living expenses.

b. Provide a 99% confidence interval for the population proportion of college students who work to pay for tuition and living expenses.

c. What happens to the margin of error as the confidence is increased from 95% to 99%?

54. An Employee Benefits Research Institute survey of 1250 workers over the age of 25 collected opinions on the health care system in America and on retirement planning (*AARP Bulletin*, January 2007).
    a. The American health care system was rated as poor by 388 of the respondents. Construct a 95% confidence interval for the proportion of workers over 25 who rate the American health care system as poor.
    b. Eighty-two percent of the respondents reported being confident of having enough money to meet basic retirement expenses. Construct a 95% confidence interval for the proportion of workers who are confident of having enough money to meet basic retirement expenses.
    c. Compare the margin of error in part (a) to the margin of error in part (b). The sample size is 1250 in both cases, but the margin of error is different. Explain why.

55. Which would be hardest for you to give up: your computer or your television? In a recent survey of 1677 U.S. Internet users, 74% of the young tech elite (average age of 22) say their computer would be very hard to give up (*PC Magazine,* February 3, 2004). Only 48% say their television would be very hard to give up.
    a. Develop a 95% confidence interval for the proportion of the young tech elite that would find it very hard to give up their computer.
    b. Develop a 99% confidence interval for the proportion of the young tech elite that would find it very hard to give up their television.
    c. In which case, part (a) or part (b), is the margin of error larger? Explain why.

56. Cincinnati/Northern Kentucky International Airport had the second highest on-time arrival rate for 2005 among the nation's busiest airports (*The Cincinnati Enquirer,* February 3, 2006). Assume the findings were based on 455 on-time arrivals out of a sample of 550 flights.
    a. Develop a point estimate of the on-time arrival rate (proportion of flights arriving on time) for the airport.
    b. Construct a 95% confidence interval for the on-time arrival rate of the population of all flights at the airport during 2005.

57. The *2003 Statistical Abstract of the United States* reported the percentage of people 18 years of age and older who smoke. Suppose that a study designed to collect new data on smokers and nonsmokers uses a preliminary estimate of the proportion who smoke of .30.
    a. How large a sample should be taken to estimate the proportion of smokers in the population with a margin of error of .02? Use 95% confidence.
    b. Assume that the study uses your sample size recommendation in part (a) and finds 520 smokers. What is the point estimate of the proportion of smokers in the population?
    c. What is the 95% confidence interval for the proportion of smokers in the population?

58. A well-known bank credit card firm wishes to estimate the proportion of credit card holders who carry a nonzero balance at the end of the month and incur an interest charge. Assume that the desired margin of error is .03 at 98% confidence.
    a. How large a sample should be selected if it is anticipated that roughly 70% of the firm's card holders carry a nonzero balance at the end of the month?
    b. How large a sample should be selected if no planning value for the proportion could be specified?

59. In a survey, 200 people were asked to identify their major source of news information; 110 stated that their major source was television news.
    a. Construct a 95% confidence interval for the proportion of people in the population who consider television their major source of news information.
    b. How large a sample would be necessary to estimate the population proportion with a margin of error of .05 at 95% confidence?

60. Although airline schedules and cost are important factors for business travelers when choosing an airline carrier, a *USA Today* survey found that business travelers list an airline's frequent flyer program as the most important factor. From a sample of $n = 1993$

business travelers who responded to the survey, 618 listed a frequent flyer program as the most important factor.

a. What is the point estimate of the proportion of the population of business travelers who believe a frequent flyer program is the most important factor when choosing an airline carrier?

b. Develop a 95% confidence interval estimate of the population proportion.

c. How large a sample would be required to report the margin of error of .01 at 95% confidence? Would you recommend that *USA Today* attempt to provide this degree of precision? Why or why not?

Case Problem 1   *Young Professional* Magazine

Young Professional magazine was developed for a target audience of recent college graduates who are in their first 10 years in a business/professional career. In its two years of publication, the magazine has been fairly successful. Now the publisher is interested in expanding the magazine's advertising base. Potential advertisers continually ask about the demographics and interests of subscribers to *Young Professional*. To collect this information, the magazine commissioned a survey to develop a profile of its subscribers. The survey results will be used to help the magazine choose articles of interest and provide advertisers with a profile of subscribers. As a new employee of the magazine, you have been asked to help analyze the survey results.

Some of the survey questions follow:

Professional

1. What is your age?
2. Are you: Male_____   Female_____
3. Do you plan to make any real estate purchases in the next two years? Yes_____ No_____
4. What is the approximate total value of financial investments, exclusive of your home, owned by you or members of your household?
5. How many stock/bond/mutual fund transactions have you made in the past year?
6. Do you have broadband access to the Internet at home? Yes_____   No_____
7. Please indicate your total household income last year.
8. Do you have children? Yes_____   No_____

The file entitled Professional contains the responses to these questions. Table 8.6 shows the portion of the file pertaining to the first five survey respondents. The entire file is on the website that accompanies this text.

Managerial Report

Prepare a managerial report summarizing the results of the survey. In addition to statistical summaries, discuss how the magazine might use these results to attract advertisers. You

TABLE 8.6   PARTIAL SURVEY RESULTS FOR *YOUNG PROFESSIONAL* MAGAZINE

Age	Gender	Real Estate Purchases	Value of Investments($)	Number of Transactions	Broadband Access	Household Income($)	Children
38	Female	No	12200	4	Yes	75200	Yes
30	Male	No	12400	4	Yes	70300	Yes
41	Female	No	26800	5	Yes	48200	No
28	Female	Yes	19600	6	No	95300	No
31	Female	Yes	15100	5	No	73300	Yes
⋮	⋮	⋮	⋮	⋮	⋮	⋮	⋮

might also comment on how the survey results could be used by the magaz
identify topics that would be of interest to readers. Your report should ad
ing issues, but do not limit your analysis to just these areas.

1. Develop appropriate descriptive statistics to summarize the data.
2. Develop 95% confidence intervals for the mean age and household income of subscribers.
3. Develop 95% confidence intervals for the proportion of subscribers who have broadband access at home and the proportion of subscribers who have children.
4. Would *Young Professional* be a good advertising outlet for online brokers? Justify your conclusion with statistical data.
5. Would this magazine be a good place to advertise for companies selling educational software and computer games for young children?
6. Comment on the types of articles you believe would be of interest to readers of *Young Professional*.

Case Problem 2   Gulf Real Estate Properties

Gulf Real Estate Properties, Inc., is a real estate firm located in southwestern Florida. The company, which advertises itself as "expert in the real estate market," monitors condominium sales by collecting data on location, list price, sale price, and number of days it takes to sell each unit. Each condominium is classified as *Gulf View* if it is located directly on the Gulf of Mexico or *No Gulf View* if it is located on the bay or a golf course, near but not on the Gulf. Sample data from the Multiple Listing Service in Naples, Florida, provided recent sales data for 40 Gulf View condominiums and 18 No Gulf View condominiums.* Prices are in thousands of dollars. The data are shown in Table 8.7.

Managerial Report

1. Use appropriate descriptive statistics to summarize each of the three variables for the 40 Gulf View condominiums.
2. Use appropriate descriptive statistics to summarize each of the three variables for the 18 No Gulf View condominiums.
3. Compare your summary results. Discuss any specific statistical results that would help a real estate agent understand the condominium market.
4. Develop a 95% confidence interval estimate of the population mean sales price and population mean number of days to sell for Gulf View condominiums. Interpret your results.
5. Develop a 95% confidence interval estimate of the population mean sales price and population mean number of days to sell for No Gulf View condominiums. Interpret your results.
6. Assume the branch manager requested estimates of the mean selling price of Gulf View condominiums with a margin of error of $40,000 and the mean selling price of No Gulf View condominiums with a margin of error of $15,000. Using 95% confidence, how large should the sample sizes be?
7. Gulf Real Estate Properties just signed contracts for two new listings: a Gulf View condominium with a list price of $589,000 and a No Gulf View condominium with a list price of $285,000. What is your estimate of the final selling price and number of days required to sell each of these units?

---

*Data based on condominium sales reported in the Naples MLS (Coldwell Banker, June 2000).

TABLE 8.7   SALES DATA FOR GULF REAL ESTATE PROPERTIES

Gulf View Condominiums			No Gulf View Condominiums		
List Price	Sale Price	Days to Sell	List Price	Sale Price	Days to Sell
495.0	475.0	130	217.0	217.0	182
379.0	350.0	71	148.0	135.5	338
529.0	519.0	85	186.5	179.0	122
552.5	534.5	95	239.0	230.0	150
334.9	334.9	119	279.0	267.5	169
550.0	505.0	92	215.0	214.0	58
169.9	165.0	197	279.0	259.0	110
210.0	210.0	56	179.9	176.5	130
975.0	945.0	73	149.9	144.9	149
314.0	314.0	126	235.0	230.0	114
315.0	305.0	88	199.8	192.0	120
885.0	800.0	282	210.0	195.0	61
975.0	975.0	100	226.0	212.0	146
469.0	445.0	56	149.9	146.5	137
329.0	305.0	49	160.0	160.0	281
365.0	330.0	48	322.0	292.5	63
332.0	312.0	88	187.5	179.0	48
520.0	495.0	161	247.0	227.0	52
425.0	405.0	149			
675.0	669.0	142			
409.0	400.0	28			
649.0	649.0	29			
319.0	305.0	140			
425.0	410.0	85			
359.0	340.0	107			
469.0	449.0	72			
895.0	875.0	129			
439.0	430.0	160			
435.0	400.0	206			
235.0	227.0	91			
638.0	618.0	100			
629.0	600.0	97			
329.0	309.0	114			
595.0	555.0	45			
339.0	315.0	150			
215.0	200.0	48			
395.0	375.0	135			
449.0	425.0	53			
499.0	465.0	86			
439.0	428.5	158			

WEB file

GulfProp

Case Problem 3   Metropolitan Research, Inc.

Metropolitan Research, Inc., a consumer research organization, conducts surveys designed to evaluate a wide variety of products and services available to consumers. In one particular study, Metropolitan looked at consumer satisfaction with the performance of automobiles produced by a major Detroit manufacturer. A questionnaire sent to owners of one of the manufacturer's full-sized cars revealed several complaints about early transmission problems. To learn more about the transmission failures, Metropolitan used a sample of actual transmission repairs provided by a transmission repair firm in the Detroit area. The following data show the actual number of miles driven for 50 vehicles at the time of transmission failure.

WEB file

Auto

85,092	32,609	59,465	77,437	32,534	64,090	32,464	59,902
39,323	89,641	94,219	116,803	92,857	63,436	65,605	85,861
64,342	61,978	67,998	59,817	101,769	95,774	121,352	69,568
74,276	66,998	40,001	72,069	25,066	77,098	69,922	35,662
74,425	67,202	118,444	53,500	79,294	64,544	86,813	116,269
37,831	89,341	73,341	85,288	138,114	53,402	85,586	82,256
77,539	88,798						

Managerial Report

1. Use appropriate descriptive statistics to summarize the transmission failure data.
2. Develop a 95% confidence interval for the mean number of miles driven until transmission failure for the population of automobiles with transmission failure. Provide a managerial interpretation of the interval estimate.
3. Discuss the implication of your statistical finding in terms of the belief that some owners of the automobiles experienced early transmission failures.
4. How many repair records should be sampled if the research firm wants the population mean number of miles driven until transmission failure to be estimated with a margin of error of 5000 miles? Use 95% confidence.
5. What other information would you like to gather to evaluate the transmission failure problem more fully?

Appendix Interval Estimation with StatTools

In this appendix we show how StatTools can be used to develop an interval estimate of a population mean for the σ unknown case and determine the sample size needed to provide a desired margin of error.

Interval Estimation of Population Mean: σ Unknown Case

In this case the population standard deviation σ will be estimated by the sample standard deviation s. We use the credit card balance data in Table 8.3 to illustrate. Begin by using the Data Set Manager to create a StatTools data set for these data using the procedure described in the appendix to Chapter 1. The following steps can be used to compute a 95% confidence interval estimate of the population mean.

WEB file

NewBalance

Step 1. Click the **StatTools** tab on the Ribbon
Step 2. In the **Analyses** group, click **Statistical Inference**
Step 3. Choose the **Confidence Interval** option
Step 4. When the StatTools—Confidence Interval dialog box appears,
For **Analysis Type** choose **One-Sample Analysis**
In the **Variables** section, select **NewBalance**
In the **Confidence Intervals to Calculate** section,
Select the **For the Mean** option
Select 95% for the **Confidence Level**
Click **OK**

Some descriptive statistics and the confidence interval will appear.

Determining the Sample Size

In Section 8.3 we showed how to determine the sample size needed to provide a desired margin of error. The example used involved a study designed to estimate the population mean daily rental cost for a midsize automobile in the United States. The project director specified that the population mean daily rental cost be estimated with a margin of error of $2 and a 95% level of confidence. Sample data from a previous study provided a sample standard deviation of $9.65; this value was used as the planning value for the population standard deviation. The following steps can be used to compute the recommended sample size required to provide a 95% confidence interval estimate of the population mean with a margin of error of $2.

The half-length of interval is the margin of error.

Step 1. Click the **StatTools** tab on the Ribbon
Step 2. In the **Analyses** group, click **Statistical Inference**
Step 3. Choose the **Sample Size Selection** option
Step 4. When the StatTools—Sample Size Selection dialog box appears,
In the **Parameter to Estimate** section, select **Mean**
In the **Confidence Interval Specification** section,
Select **95%** for the **Confidence Level**
Enter **2** in the **Half-Length of Interval** box
Enter **9.65** in the **Estimated Std Dev** box
Click **OK**

The output showing a recommended sample size of 90 will appear.

CHAPTER 9

Hypothesis Tests

CONTENTS

JOHN MORRELL & COMPANY*
CINCINNATI, OHIO

John Morrell & Company, which began in England in 1827, is considered the oldest continuously operating meat manufacturer in the United States. It is a wholly owned and independently managed subsidiary of Smithfield Foods, Smithfield, Virginia. John Morrell & Company offers an extensive product line of processed meats and fresh pork to consumers under 13 regional brands including John Morrell, E-Z-Cut, Tobin's First Prize, Dinner Bell, Hunter, Kretschmar, Rath, Rodeo, Shenson, Farmers Hickory Brand, Iowa Quality, and Peyton's. Each regional brand enjoys high brand recognition and loyalty among consumers.

Market research at Morrell provides management with up-to-date information on the company's various products and how the products compare with competing brands of similar products. A recent study compared a Beef Pot Roast made by Morrell to similar beef products from two major competitors. In the three-product comparison test, a sample of consumers was used to indicate how the products rated in terms of taste, appearance, aroma, and overall preference.

One research question concerned whether the Beef Pot Roast made by Morrell was the preferred choice of more than 50% of the consumer population. Letting p indicate the population proportion preferring Morrell's product, the hypothesis test for the research question is as follows:

$$H_0: p \leq .50$$
$$H_a: p > .50$$

The null hypothesis H_0 indicates the preference for Morrell's product is less than or equal to 50%. If the sample data support rejecting H_0 in favor of the alternative hypothesis H_a, Morrell will draw the research conclusion that in a three-product comparison, their Beef Pot Roast is preferred by more than 50% of the consumer population.

In an independent taste test study using a sample of 224 consumers in Cincinnati, Milwaukee, and Los Angeles, 150 consumers selected the Beef Pot Roast

Fully-cooked entrees allow consumers to heat and serve in the same microwaveable tray. © Brian Leatart/FoodPix/Jupiter Images.

made by Morrell as the preferred product. Using statistical hypothesis testing procedures, the null hypothesis H_0 was rejected. The study provided statistical evidence supporting H_a and the conclusion that the Morrell product is preferred by more than 50% of the consumer population.

The point estimate of the population proportion was $\bar{p} = 150/224 = .67$. Thus, the sample data provided support for a food magazine advertisement showing that in a three-product taste comparison, Beef Pot Roast made by Morrell was "preferred 2 to 1 over the competition."

In this chapter we will discuss how to formulate hypotheses and how to conduct tests like the one used by Morrell. Through the analysis of sample data, we will be able to determine whether a hypothesis should or should not be rejected.

---

*The authors are indebted to Marty Butler, vice president of Marketing, John Morrell, for providing this Statistics in Practice.

In Chapters 7 and 8 we showed how a sample could be used to develop point and interval estimates of population parameters. In this chapter we continue the discussion of statistical inference by showing how hypothesis tests can be used to determine whether a statement about the value of a population parameter should or should not be rejected.

In hypothesis testing we begin by making a tentative assumption about a population parameter. This tentative assumption is called the **null hypothesis** and is denoted by H_0. We then define another hypothesis, called the **alternative hypothesis**, which is the opposite of what is stated in the null hypothesis. The alternative hypothesis is denoted by H_a. The hypothesis testing procedure uses data from a sample to test the two competing statements indicated by H_0 and H_a.

This chapter shows how hypothesis tests can be conducted about a population mean and a population proportion. We begin by providing examples that illustrate approaches to developing null and alternative hypotheses.

9.1 Developing Null and Alternative Hypotheses

Learning to formulate hypotheses correctly will take practice. Expect some initial confusion over the proper choice for H_0 and H_a. The examples in this section show a variety of forms for H_0 and H_a depending upon the application.

In some applications it may not be obvious how the null and alternative hypotheses should be formulated. Care must be taken to structure the hypotheses appropriately so that the hypothesis testing conclusion provides the information the researcher or decision maker wants. Guidelines for establishing the null and alternative hypotheses will be given for three types of situations in which hypothesis testing procedures are commonly employed.

Testing Research Hypotheses

Consider a particular automobile model that currently attains an average fuel efficiency of 24 miles per gallon. A product research group developed a new fuel injection system specifically designed to increase the miles-per-gallon rating. To evaluate the new system, several will be manufactured, installed in automobiles, and subjected to research-controlled driving tests. Here the product research group is looking for evidence to conclude that the new system *increases* the mean miles-per-gallon rating. In this case, the research hypothesis is that the new fuel injection system will provide a mean miles-per-gallon rating exceeding 24; that is, $\mu > 24$. As a general guideline, a research hypothesis should be stated as the *alternative hypothesis*. Hence, the appropriate null and alternative hypotheses for the study are

$$H_0: \mu \leq 24$$
$$H_a: \mu > 24$$

The conclusion that the research hypothesis is true is made if the sample data contradict the null hypothesis.

If the sample results indicate that H_0 cannot be rejected, researchers cannot conclude that the new fuel injection system is better. Perhaps more research and subsequent testing should be conducted. However, if the sample results indicate that H_0 can be rejected, researchers can make the inference that $H_a: \mu > 24$ is true. With this conclusion, the researchers gain the statistical support necessary to state that the new system increases the mean number of miles per gallon. Production with the new system should be considered.

In research studies such as these, the null and alternative hypotheses should be formulated so that the rejection of H_0 supports the research conclusion. The research hypothesis therefore should be expressed as the alternative hypothesis.

Testing the Validity of a Claim

As an illustration of testing the validity of a claim, consider the situation of a manufacturer of soft drinks who states that 2-liter soft drink containers are filled with an average of at least 67.6 fluid ounces. A sample of 2-liter containers will be selected, and the contents will be measured to test the manufacturer's claim. In this type of hypothesis testing situation, we generally assume that the manufacturer's claim is true unless the sample evidence is contradictory. Using this approach for the soft-drink example, we would state the null and alternative hypotheses as follows:

$$H_0: \mu \geq 67.6$$
$$H_a: \mu < 67.6$$

A manufacturer's claim is usually given the benefit of the doubt and stated as the null hypothesis. The conclusion that the claim is false can be made if the null hypothesis is rejected.

If the sample results indicate H_0 cannot be rejected, the manufacturer's claim will not be challenged. However, if the sample results indicate H_0 can be rejected, the inference will be made that $H_a: \mu < 67.6$ is true. With this conclusion, statistical evidence indicates that the manufacturer's claim is incorrect and that the soft-drink containers are being filled with a mean less than the claimed 67.6 ounces. Appropriate action against the manufacturer may be considered.

In any situation that involves testing the validity of a claim, the null hypothesis is generally based on the assumption that the claim is true. The alternative hypothesis is then formulated so that rejection of H_0 will provide statistical evidence that the stated assumption is incorrect. Action to correct the claim should be considered whenever H_0 is rejected.

Testing in Decision-Making Situations

In testing research hypotheses or testing the validity of a claim, action is taken if H_0 is rejected. In some instances, however, action must be taken both when H_0 cannot be rejected and when H_0 can be rejected. In general, this type of situation occurs when a decision maker must choose between two courses of action, one associated with the null hypothesis and another associated with the alternative hypothesis. For example, on the basis of a sample of parts from a shipment just received, a quality control inspector must decide whether to accept the shipment or to return the shipment to the supplier because it does not meet specifications. Assume that specifications for a particular part require a mean length of 2 inches per part. If the mean length is greater or less than the 2-inch standard, the parts will cause quality problems in the assembly operation. In this case, the null and alternative hypotheses would be formulated as follows.

This type of hypothesis test is employed in the quality control procedure called lot-acceptance sampling.

$$H_0: \mu = 2$$
$$H_a: \mu \neq 2$$

If the sample results indicate H_0 cannot be rejected, the quality control inspector will have no reason to doubt that the shipment meets specifications, and the shipment will be accepted. However, if the sample results indicate H_0 should be rejected, the conclusion will be that the parts do not meet specifications. In this case, the quality control inspector will have sufficient evidence to return the shipment to the supplier. Thus, we see that for these types of situations, action is taken both when H_0 cannot be rejected and when H_0 can be rejected.

Summary of Forms for Null and Alternative Hypotheses

The hypothesis tests in this chapter involve two population parameters: the population mean and the population proportion. Depending on the situation, hypothesis tests about a population parameter may take one of three forms: two use inequalities in the null hypothesis; the third uses an equality in the null hypothesis. For hypothesis tests involving a population mean, we let μ_0 denote the hypothesized value and we must choose one of the following three forms for the hypothesis test.

The three possible forms of hypotheses H_0 and H_a are shown here. Note that the equality always appears in the null hypothesis H_0.

$$H_0: \mu \geq \mu_0 \qquad H_0: \mu \leq \mu_0 \qquad H_0: \mu = \mu_0$$
$$H_a: \mu < \mu_0 \qquad H_a: \mu > \mu_0 \qquad H_a: \mu \neq \mu_0$$

For reasons that will be clear later, the first two forms are called one-tailed tests. The third form is called a two-tailed test.

In many situations, the choice of H_0 and H_a is not obvious and judgment is necessary to select the proper form. However, as the preceding forms show, the equality part of the expression (either $\geq$, $\leq$, or $=$) *always* appears in the null hypothesis. In selecting the proper form of H_0 and H_a, keep in mind that the alternative hypothesis is often what the test is attempting to establish. Hence, asking whether the user is looking for evidence to support $\mu < \mu_0, \mu > \mu_0$, or $\mu \neq \mu_0$ will help determine H_a. The following exercises are designed to provide practice in choosing the proper form for a hypothesis test involving a population mean.

Exercises

1. The manager of the Danvers-Hilton Resort Hotel stated that the mean guest bill for a weekend is $600 or less. A member of the hotel's accounting staff noticed that the total charges for guest bills have been increasing in recent months. The accountant will use a sample of weekend guest bills to test the manager's claim.

    a.   Which form of the hypotheses should be used to test the manager's claim? Explain.

H_0: $\mu \geq 600$	H_0: $\mu \leq 600$	H_0: $\mu = 600$
H_a: $\mu < 600$	H_a: $\mu > 600$	H_a: $\mu \neq 600$

    b.   What conclusion is appropriate when H_0 cannot be rejected?
    c.   What conclusion is appropriate when H_0 can be rejected?

2. The manager of an automobile dealership is considering a new bonus plan designed to increase sales volume. Currently, the mean sales volume is 14 automobiles per month. The manager wants to conduct a research study to see whether the new bonus plan increases sales volume. To collect data on the plan, a sample of sales personnel will be allowed to sell under the new bonus plan for a one-month period.

    a.   Develop the null and alternative hypotheses most appropriate for this research situation.
    b.   Comment on the conclusion when H_0 cannot be rejected.
    c.   Comment on the conclusion when H_0 can be rejected.

3. A production line operation is designed to fill cartons with laundry detergent to a mean weight of 32 ounces. A sample of cartons is periodically selected and weighed to determine whether underfilling or overfilling is occurring. If the sample data lead to a conclusion of underfilling or overfilling, the production line will be shut down and adjusted to obtain proper filling.

    a.   Formulate the null and alternative hypotheses that will help in deciding whether to shut down and adjust the production line.
    b.   Comment on the conclusion and the decision when H_0 cannot be rejected.
    c.   Comment on the conclusion and the decision when H_0 can be rejected.

4. Because of high production-changeover time and costs, a director of manufacturing must convince management that a proposed manufacturing method reduces costs before the new method can be implemented. The current production method operates with a mean cost of $220 per hour. A research study will measure the cost of the new method over a sample production period.

    a.   Develop the null and alternative hypotheses most appropriate for this study.
    b.   Comment on the conclusion when H_0 cannot be rejected.
    c.   Comment on the conclusion when H_0 can be rejected.

9.2   Type I and Type II Errors

The null and alternative hypotheses are competing statements about the population. Either the null hypothesis H_0 is true or the alternative hypothesis H_a is true, but not both. Ideally the hypothesis testing procedure should lead to the acceptance of H_0 when H_0 is true and the

TABLE 9.1   ERRORS AND CORRECT CONCLUSIONS IN HYPOTHESIS TESTING

		Population Condition	
		H_0 **True**	H_a **True**
Conclusion	**Accept H_0**	Correct Conclusion	Type II Error
	Reject H_0	Type I Error	Correct Conclusion

rejection of H_0 when H_a is true. Unfortunately, the correct conclusions are not always possible. Because hypothesis tests are based on sample information, we must allow for the possibility of errors. Table 9.1 illustrates the two kinds of errors that can be made in hypothesis testing.

The first row of Table 9.1 shows what can happen if the conclusion is to accept H_0. If H_0 is true, this conclusion is correct. However, if H_a is true, we make a **Type II error**; that is, we accept H_0 when it is false. The second row of Table 9.1 shows what can happen if the conclusion is to reject H_0. If H_0 is true, we make a **Type I error**; that is, we reject H_0 when it is true. However, if H_a is true, rejecting H_0 is correct.

Recall the hypothesis testing illustration discussed in Section 9.1 in which an automobile product research group developed a new fuel injection system designed to increase the miles-per-gallon rating of a particular automobile. With the current model obtaining an average of 24 miles per gallon, the hypothesis test was formulated as follows.

$$H_0: \mu \leq 24$$
$$H_a: \mu > 24$$

The alternative hypothesis, $H_a: \mu > 24$, indicates that the researchers are looking for sample evidence to support the conclusion that the population mean miles per gallon with the new fuel injection system is greater than 24.

In this application, the Type I error of rejecting H_0 when it is true corresponds to the researchers claiming that the new system improves the miles-per-gallon rating ($\mu > 24$) when in fact the new system is not any better than the current system. In contrast, the Type II error of accepting H_0 when it is false corresponds to the researchers concluding that the new system is not any better than the current system ($\mu \leq 24$) when in fact the new system improves miles-per-gallon performance.

For the miles-per-gallon rating hypothesis test, the null hypothesis is $H_0: \mu \leq 24$. Suppose the null hypothesis is true as an equality; that is, $\mu = 24$. The probability of making a Type I error when the null hypothesis is true as an equality is called the **level of significance**. Thus, for the miles-per-gallon rating hypothesis test, the level of significance is the probability of rejecting $H_0: \mu \leq 24$ when $\mu = 24$. Because of the importance of this concept, we now restate the definition of level of significance.

LEVEL OF SIGNIFICANCE

The level of significance is the probability of making a Type I error when the null hypothesis is true as an equality.

The Greek symbol α (alpha) is used to denote the level of significance, and common choices for α are .05 and .01.

In practice, the person responsible for the hypothesis test specifies the level of significance. By selecting α, that person is controlling the probability of making a Type I error. If the cost of making a Type I error is high, small values of α are preferred. If the cost of making a Type I error is not too high, larger values of α are typically used. Applications of hypothesis testing that only control for the Type I error are called *significance tests*. Many applications of hypothesis testing are of this type.

Although most applications of hypothesis testing control for the probability of making a Type I error, they do not always control for the probability of making a Type II error. Hence, if we decide to accept H_0, we cannot determine how confident we can be with that decision. Because of the uncertainty associated with making a Type II error when conducting significance tests, statisticians usually recommend that we use the statement "do not reject H_0" instead of "accept H_0." Using the statement "do not reject H_0" carries the recommendation to withhold both judgment and action. In effect, by not directly accepting H_0, the statistician avoids the risk of making a Type II error. Whenever the probability of making a Type II error has not been determined and controlled, we will not make the statement "accept H_0." In such cases, only two conclusions are possible: *do not reject H_0* or *reject H_0*.

Although controlling for a Type II error in hypothesis testing is not common, it can be done. More advanced texts describe procedures for determining and controlling the probability of making a Type II error.[1] If proper controls have been established for this error, action based on the "accept H_0" conclusion can be appropriate.

If the sample data are consistent with the null hypothesis H_0, we will follow the practice of concluding "do not reject H_0." This conclusion is preferred over "accept H_0," unless we have specifically controlled for the Type II error.

NOTES AND COMMENTS

Walter Williams, syndicated columnist and professor of economics at George Mason University, points out that the possibility of making a Type I or a Type II error is always present in decision making (*The Cincinnati Enquirer*, August 14, 2005). He notes that the Food and Drug Administration runs the risk of making these errors in their drug approval process. With a Type I error, the FDA fails to approve a drug that is safe and effective. A Type II error means the FDA approves a drug that is not safe and effective. Regardless of the decision made, the possibility of making a costly error cannot be eliminated. But, with proper hypothesis testing, it can be minimized.

Exercises

SELF test

5. Nielsen reported that young men in the United States watch 56.2 minutes of prime-time TV daily (*The Wall Street Journal Europe*, November 18, 2003). A researcher believes that young men in Germany spend more time watching prime-time TV. A sample of German young men will be selected by the researcher and the time they spend watching TV in one day will be recorded. The sample results will be used to test the following null and alternative hypotheses.

$$H_0: \mu \leq 56.2$$
$$H_a: \mu > 56.2$$

a. What is the Type I error in this situation? What are the consequences of making this error?
b. What is the Type II error in this situation? What are the consequences of making this error?

6. The label on a 3-quart container of orange juice claims that the orange juice contains an average of 1 gram of fat or less. Answer the following questions for a hypothesis test that could be used to test the claim on the label.

a. Develop the appropriate null and alternative hypotheses.

---

[1]See, for example, D. R. Anderson, D. J. Sweeney, and T. A. Williams, *Statistics for Business and Economics*, 10th ed. (Cincinnati: South-Western, 2008).

b.   What is the Type I error in this situation? What are the consequences of making this error?
c.   What is the Type II error in this situation? What are the consequences of making this error?

7.   Carpetland salespersons average $8000 per week in sales. Steve Contois, the firm's vice president, proposes a compensation plan with new selling incentives. Steve hopes that the results of a trial selling period will enable him to conclude that the compensation plan increases the average sales per salesperson.
a.   Develop the appropriate null and alternative hypotheses.
b.   What is the Type I error in this situation? What are the consequences of making this error?
c.   What is the Type II error in this situation? What are the consequences of making this error?

8.   Suppose a new production method will be implemented if a hypothesis test supports the conclusion that the new method reduces the mean operating cost per hour.
a.   State the appropriate null and alternative hypotheses if the mean cost for the current production method is $220 per hour.
b.   What is the Type I error in this situation? What are the consequences of making this error?
c.   What is the Type II error in this situation? What are the consequences of making this error?

(9.3) Population Mean: σ Known

In Chapter 8 we said that the σ known case corresponds to applications in which historical data and/or other information is available that enable us to obtain a good estimate of the population standard deviation prior to sampling. In such cases the population standard deviation can, for all practical purposes, be considered known. In this section we show how to conduct a hypothesis test about a population mean for the σ known case.

The methods presented in this section are exact if the sample is selected from a population that is normally distributed. In cases where it is not reasonable to assume the population is normally distributed, these methods are still applicable if the sample size is large enough. We provide some practical advice concerning the population distribution and the sample size at the end of this section.

One-Tailed Tests

One-tailed tests about a population mean take one of the following two forms.

Lower Tail Test	Upper Tail Test
$H_0: \mu \geq \mu_0$	$H_0: \mu \leq \mu_0$
$H_a: \mu < \mu_0$	$H_a: \mu > \mu_0$

Let us consider an example involving a lower tail test.

The Federal Trade Commission (FTC) periodically conducts statistical studies designed to test the claims that manufacturers make about their products. For example, the label on a large can of Hilltop Coffee states that the can contains 3 pounds of coffee. The FTC knows that Hilltop's production process cannot place exactly 3 pounds of coffee in each can, even if the mean filling weight for the population of all cans filled is 3 pounds per can. However, as long as the population mean filling weight is at least 3 pounds per can, the rights of consumers will be protected. Thus, the FTC interprets the label information on a large can of coffee as a claim by Hilltop that the population mean filling weight is at least 3 pounds per can. We will show how the FTC can check Hilltop's claim by conducting a lower tail hypothesis test.

The first step is to develop the null and alternative hypotheses for the test. If the population mean filling weight is at least 3 pounds per can, Hilltop's claim is correct. This outcome establishes the null hypothesis for the test. However, if the population mean weight is less than 3 pounds per can, Hilltop's claim is incorrect. This outcome establishes the alternative hypothesis. With μ denoting the population mean filling weight, the null and alternative hypotheses are as follows:

$$H_0: \mu \geq 3$$
$$H_a: \mu < 3$$

Note that the hypothesized value of the population mean is $\mu_0 = 3$.

If the sample data indicate that H_0 cannot be rejected, the statistical evidence does not support the conclusion that a label violation has occurred. Hence, no action should be taken against Hilltop. However, if the sample data indicate H_0 can be rejected, we will conclude that the alternative hypothesis, $H_a: \mu < 3$, is true. In this case a conclusion of underfilling and a charge of a label violation against Hilltop would be justified.

Suppose a sample of 36 cans of coffee is selected and the sample mean $\bar{x}$ is computed as an estimate of the population mean μ. If the value of the sample mean $\bar{x}$ is less than 3 pounds, the sample results will cast doubt on the null hypothesis. What we want to know is how much less than 3 pounds must $\bar{x}$ be before we would be willing to declare the difference significant and risk making a Type I error by falsely accusing Hilltop of a label violation. A key factor in addressing this issue is the value the decision maker selects for the level of significance.

As noted in the preceding section, the level of significance, denoted by α, is the probability of making a Type I error by rejecting H_0 when the null hypothesis is true as an equality. The decision maker must specify the level of significance. If the cost of making a Type I error is high, a small value should be chosen for the level of significance. If the cost is not high, a larger value is more appropriate. In the Hilltop Coffee study, the director of the FTC's testing program made the following statement: "If the company is meeting its weight specifications at $\mu = 3$, I do not want to take action against them. But I am willing to risk a 1% chance of making such an error." From the director's statement, we set the level of significance for the hypothesis test at $\alpha = .01$. Thus, we must design the hypothesis test so that the probability of making a Type I error when $\mu = 3$ is .01.

For the Hilltop Coffee study, by developing the null and alternative hypotheses and specifying the level of significance for the test, we carry out the first two steps required in conducting every hypothesis test. We are now ready to perform the third step of hypothesis testing: collect the sample data and compute the value of what is called a test statistic.

Test statistic For the Hilltop Coffee study, previous FTC tests show that the population standard deviation can be assumed known with a value of $\sigma = .18$. In addition, these tests also show that the population of filling weights can be assumed to have a normal distribution. From the study of sampling distributions in Chapter 7 we know that if the population from which we are sampling is normally distributed, the sampling distribution of $\bar{x}$ will also be normally distributed. Thus, for the Hilltop Coffee study, the sampling distribution of $\bar{x}$ is normally distributed. With a known value of $\sigma = .18$ and a sample size of $n = 36$, Figure 9.1 shows the sampling distribution of $\bar{x}$ when the null hypothesis is true as an equality; that is, when $\mu = \mu_0 = 3$.[2] Note that the standard error of $\bar{x}$ is given by

The standard error of $\bar{x}$ is the standard deviation of the sampling distribution of $\bar{x}$.

$\sigma_{\bar{x}} = \sigma/\sqrt{n} = .18/\sqrt{36} = .03$.

Because the sampling distribution of $\bar{x}$ is normally distributed, the sampling distribution of

$$z = \frac{\bar{x} - \mu_0}{\sigma_{\bar{x}}} = \frac{\bar{x} - 3}{.03}$$

---

[2]In constructing sampling distributions for hypothesis tests, it is assumed that H_0 is satisfied as an equality.

FIGURE 9.1   SAMPLING DISTRIBUTION OF $\bar{x}$ FOR THE HILLTOP COFFEE STUDY
WHEN THE NULL HYPOTHESIS IS TRUE AS AN EQUALITY ($\mu = 3$)

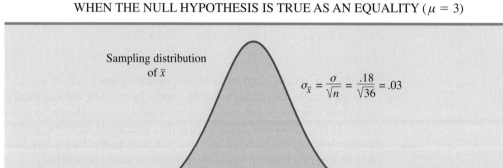

is a standard normal distribution. A value of $z = -1$ means that the value of $\bar{x}$ is one standard error below the hypothesized value of the mean, a value of $z = -2$ means that the value of $\bar{x}$ is two standard errors below the hypothesized value of the mean, and so on. We can use the standard normal probability table to find the lower tail probability corresponding to any z value. For instance, the lower tail area at $z = -3.00$ is .0013. Hence, the probability of obtaining a value of z that is three or more standard errors below the mean is .0013. As a result, the probability of obtaining a value of $\bar{x}$ that is three or more standard errors below the hypothesized population mean $\mu_0 = 3$ is also .0013. Such a result is unlikely if the null hypothesis is true.

For hypothesis tests about a population mean in the σ known case, we use the standard normal random variable z as a **test statistic** to determine whether $\bar{x}$ deviates from the hypothesized value of μ enough to justify rejecting the null hypothesis. With $\sigma_{\bar{x}} = \sigma/\sqrt{n}$, the test statistic is as follows.

**TEST STATISTIC FOR HYPOTHESIS TESTS ABOUT A POPULATION MEAN:
σ KNOWN**

$$z = \frac{\bar{x} - \mu_0}{\sigma/\sqrt{n}} \tag{9.1}$$

The key question for a lower tail test is: How small must the test statistic z be before we choose to reject the null hypothesis? Two approaches can be used to answer this question: the p-value approach and the critical value approach.

***p*-value approach**   The p-value approach uses the value of the test statistic z to compute a probability called a *p*-value.

A small p-value indicates the value of the test statistic is unusual given the assumption that H_0 is true.

***p*-VALUE**

A *p*-value is a probability that provides a measure of the evidence against the null hypothesis provided by the sample. Smaller *p*-values indicate more evidence against H_0.

The *p*-value is used to determine whether the null hypothesis should be rejected.

Let us see how the *p*-value is computed and used. The value of the test statistic is used to compute the *p*-value. The method used depends on whether the test is a lower tail, an upper tail, or a two-tailed test. For a lower tail test, the *p*-value is the probability of obtaining a value for the test statistic as small as or smaller than that provided by the sample. Thus, to compute the *p*-value for the lower tail test in the σ known case, we must find the area under the standard normal curve to the left of the test statistic. After computing the *p*-value, we must then decide whether it is small enough to reject the null hypothesis; as we will show, this decision involves comparing the *p*-value to the level of significance.

Coffee

Let us now compute the *p*-value for the Hilltop Coffee lower tail test. Suppose the sample of 36 Hilltop coffee cans provides a sample mean of $\bar{x} = 2.92$ pounds. Is $\bar{x} = 2.92$ small enough to cause us to reject H_0? Because this is a lower tail test, the *p*-value is the area under the standard normal curve to the left of the test statistic. Using $\bar{x} = 2.92$, $\sigma = .18$, and $n = 36$, we compute the value of the test statistic *z*:

$$ z = \frac{\bar{x} - \mu_0}{\sigma/\sqrt{n}} = \frac{2.92 - 3}{.18/\sqrt{36}} = -2.67 $$

Thus, the *p*-value is the probability that the test statistic *z* is less than or equal to -2.67 (the area under the standard normal curve to the left of the test statistic).

Using the standard normal probability table, we find that the lower tail area at $z = -2.67$ is .0038. Figure 9.2 shows that $\bar{x} = 2.92$ corresponds to $z = -2.67$ and a *p*-value = .0038. This *p*-value indicates a small probability of obtaining a sample mean of $\bar{x} = 2.92$ (and a test statistic of -2.67) or smaller when sampling from a population with $\mu = 3$. This

FIGURE 9.2   *p*-VALUE FOR THE HILLTOP COFFEE STUDY WHEN $\bar{x} = 2.92$ AND $z = -2.67$

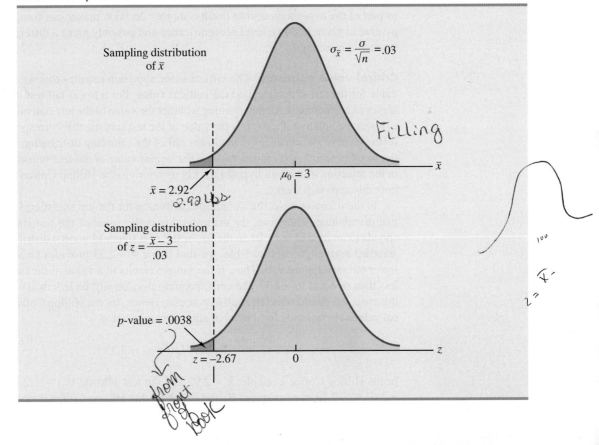

p-value does not provide much support for the null hypothesis, but is it small enough to cause us to reject H_0? The answer depends upon the level of significance for the test.

As noted previously, the director of the FTC's testing program selected a value of .01 for the level of significance. The selection of $\alpha = .01$ means that the director is willing to tolerate a probability of .01 of rejecting the null hypothesis when it is true as an equality ($\mu_0 = 3$). The sample of 36 coffee cans in the Hilltop Coffee study resulted in a p-value $= .0038$, which means that the probability of obtaining a value of $\bar{x} = 2.92$ or less when the null hypothesis is true as an equality is .0038. Because .0038 is less than or equal to $\alpha = .01$, we reject H_0. Therefore, we find sufficient statistical evidence to reject the null hypothesis at the .01 level of significance.

We can now state the general rule for determining whether the null hypothesis can be rejected when using the p-value approach. For a level of significance α, the rejection rule using the p-value approach is as follows:

REJECTION RULE USING p-VALUE

$$\text{Reject } H_0 \text{ if } p\text{-value} \leq \alpha$$

In the Hilltop Coffee test, the p-value of .0038 resulted in the rejection of the null hypothesis. Although the basis for making the rejection decision involves a comparison of the p-value to the level of significance specified by the FTC director, the observed p-value of .0038 means that we would reject H_0 for any value of $\alpha \geq .0038$. For this reason, the p-value is also called the *observed level of significance*.

Different decision makers may express different opinions concerning the cost of making a Type I error and may choose a different level of significance. By providing the p-value as part of the hypothesis testing results, another decision maker can compare the reported p-value to his or her own level of significance and possibly make a different decision with respect to rejecting H_0.

Critical value approach The critical value approach requires that we first determine a value for the test statistic called the **critical value**. For a lower tail test, the critical value serves as a benchmark for determining whether the value of the test statistic is small enough to reject the null hypothesis. It is the value of the test statistic that corresponds to an area of α (the level of significance) in the lower tail of the sampling distribution of the test statistic. In other words, the critical value is the largest value of the test statistic that will result in the rejection of the null hypothesis. Let us return to the Hilltop Coffee example and see how this approach works.

In the σ known case, the sampling distribution for the test statistic z is a standard normal distribution. Therefore, the critical value is the value of the test statistic that corresponds to an area of $\alpha = .01$ in the lower tail of a standard normal distribution. Using the standard normal probability table, we find that $z = -2.33$ provides an area of .01 in the lower tail (see Figure 9.3). Thus, if the sample results in a value of the test statistic that is less than or equal to -2.33, the corresponding p-value will be less than or equal to .01; in this case, we should reject the null hypothesis. Hence, for the Hilltop Coffee study the critical value rejection rule for a level of significance of .01 is

$$\text{Reject } H_0 \text{ if } z \leq -2.33$$

In the Hilltop Coffee example, $\bar{x} = 2.92$ and the test statistic is $z = -2.67$. Because $z = -2.67 < -2.33$, we can reject H_0 and conclude that Hilltop Coffee is underfilling cans.

FIGURE 9.3 CRITICAL VALUE = −2.33 FOR THE HILLTOP COFFEE HYPOTHESIS TEST

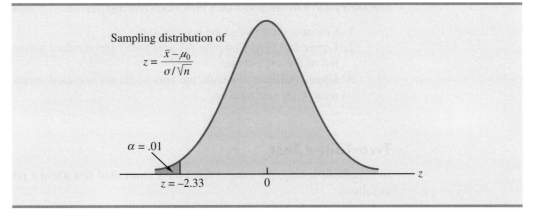

We can generalize the rejection rule for the critical value approach to handle any level of significance. The rejection rule for a lower tail test follows.

REJECTION RULE FOR A LOWER TAIL TEST: CRITICAL VALUE APPROACH

$$\text{Reject } H_0 \text{ if } z \leq -z_\alpha$$

where $-z_\alpha$ is the critical value; that is, the z value that provides an area of α in the lower tail of the standard normal distribution.

Summary The p-value approach to hypothesis testing and the critical value approach will always lead to the same rejection decision; that is, whenever the p-value is less than or equal to α, the value of the test statistic will be less than or equal to the critical value. The advantage of the p-value approach is that the p-value tells us *how* significant the results are (the observed level of significance). If we use the critical value approach, we only know that the results are significant at the stated level of significance.

At the beginning of this section, we said that one-tailed tests about a population mean take one of the following two forms:

Lower Tail Test	Upper Tail Test
$H_0: \mu \geq \mu_0$	$H_0: \mu \leq \mu_0$
$H_a: \mu < \mu_0$	$H_a: \mu > \mu_0$

We used the Hilltop Coffee study to illustrate how to conduct a lower tail test. We can use the same general approach to conduct an upper tail test. The test statistic z is still computed using equation (9.1). But, for an upper tail test, the p-value is the probability of obtaining a value for the test statistic as large as or larger than that provided by the sample. Thus, to compute the p-value for the upper tail test in the σ known case, we must find the area under the standard normal curve to the right of the test statistic. Using the critical value approach causes us to reject the null hypothesis if the value of the test statistic is greater than or equal to the critical value z_α; in other words, we reject H_0 if $z \geq z_\alpha$.

The computation of p-values can be confusing. Let us summarize the steps involved in computing p-values for one-tailed hypothesis tests.

COMPUTATION OF p-VALUES FOR ONE-TAILED TESTS

1. Compute the value of the test statistic z.
2. **Lower tail test:** Compute the area under the standard normal curve to the left of the test statistic.
3. **Upper tail test:** Compute the area under the standard normal curve to the right of the test statistic.

Two-Tailed Test

In hypothesis testing, the general form for a **two-tailed test** about a population mean is as follows:

$$H_0: \mu = \mu_0$$
$$H_a: \mu \neq \mu_0$$

In this subsection we show how to conduct a two-tailed test about a population mean for the σ known case. As an illustration, we consider the hypothesis testing situation facing MaxFlight, Inc.

The U.S. Golf Association (USGA) establishes rules that manufacturers of golf equipment must meet if their products are to be acceptable for use in USGA events. MaxFlight uses a high-technology manufacturing process to produce golf balls with a mean driving distance of 295 yards. Sometimes, however, the process gets out of adjustment and produces golf balls with a mean driving distance different from 295 yards. When the mean distance falls below 295 yards, the company worries about losing sales because the golf balls do not provide as much distance as advertised. When the mean distance passes 295 yards, MaxFlight's golf balls may be rejected by the USGA for exceeding the overall distance standard concerning carry and roll.

MaxFlight's quality control program involves taking periodic samples of 50 golf balls to monitor the manufacturing process. For each sample, a hypothesis test is conducted to determine whether the process has fallen out of adjustment. Let us develop the null and alternative hypotheses. We begin by assuming that the process is functioning correctly; that is, the golf balls being produced have a mean distance of 295 yards. This assumption establishes the null hypothesis. The alternative hypothesis is that the mean distance is not equal to 295 yards. With a hypothesized value of $\mu_0 = 295$, the null and alternative hypotheses for the MaxFlight hypothesis test are as follows:

$$H_0: \mu = 295$$
$$H_a: \mu \neq 295$$

If the sample mean $\bar{x}$ is significantly less than 295 yards or significantly greater than 295 yards, we will reject H_0. In this case, corrective action will be taken to adjust the manufacturing process. On the other hand, if $\bar{x}$ does not deviate from the hypothesized mean $\mu_0 = 295$ by a significant amount, H_0 will not be rejected and no action will be taken to adjust the manufacturing process.

The quality control team selected $\alpha = .05$ as the level of significance for the test. Data from previous tests conducted when the process was known to be in adjustment show that the population standard deviation can be assumed known with a value of $\sigma = 12$. Thus, with a sample size of $n = 50$, the standard error of $\bar{x}$ is

$$\sigma_{\bar{x}} = \frac{\sigma}{\sqrt{n}} = \frac{12}{\sqrt{50}} = 1.7$$

Because the sample size is large, the central limit theorem (see Chapter 7) allows us to conclude that the sampling distribution of $\bar{x}$ can be approximated by a normal distribution.

FIGURE 9.4 SAMPLING DISTRIBUTION OF $\bar{x}$ FOR THE MAXFLIGHT HYPOTHESIS TEST

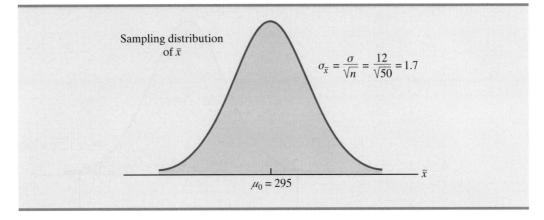

Figure 9.4 shows the sampling distribution of $\bar{x}$ for the MaxFlight hypothesis test with a hypothesized population mean of $\mu_0 = 295$.

Suppose that a sample of 50 golf balls is selected and that the sample mean is $\bar{x} = 297.6$ yards. This sample mean provides support for the conclusion that the population mean is larger than 295 yards. Is this value of $\bar{x}$ enough larger than 295 to cause us to reject H_0 at the .05 level of significance? In the previous section we described two approaches that can be used to answer this question: the p-value approach and the critical value approach.

GolfTest

p-**value approach** Recall that the p-value is a probability used to determine whether the null hypothesis should be rejected. For a two-tailed test, values of the test statistic in *either* tail provide evidence against the null hypothesis. For a two-tailed test, the p-value is the probability of obtaining a value for the test statistic *as unlikely as or more unlikely than* that provided by the sample. Let us see how the p-value is computed for the MaxFlight hypothesis test.

First we compute the value of the test statistic. For the σ known case, the test statistic z is a standard normal random variable. Using equation (9.1) with $\bar{x} = 297.6$, the value of the test statistic is

$$z = \frac{\bar{x} - \mu_0}{\sigma/\sqrt{n}} = \frac{297.6 - 295}{12/\sqrt{50}} = 1.53$$

Now to compute the p-value we must find the probability of obtaining a value for the test statistic *at least as unlikely as* $z = 1.53$. Clearly values of $z \geq 1.53$ are *at least as unlikely*. But, because this is a two-tailed test, values of $z \leq -1.53$ are also *at least as unlikely as* the value of the test statistic provided by the sample. In Figure 9.5, we see that the two-tailed p-value in this case is given by $P(z \leq -1.53) + P(z \geq 1.53)$. Because the normal curve is symmetric, we can compute this probability by finding the area under the standard normal curve to the right of $z = 1.53$ and doubling it. The table for the standard normal distribution shows that the area to the left of $z = 1.53$ is .9370. Thus, the area under the standard normal curve to the right of the test statistic $z = 1.53$ is $1.0000 - .9370 = .0630$. Doubling this probability, we find the p-value for the MaxFlight two-tailed hypothesis test is p-value $= 2(.0630) = .1260$.

Next we compare the p-value to the level of significance to see whether the null hypothesis should be rejected. With a level of significance of $\alpha = .05$, we do not reject H_0 because the p-value $= .1260 > .05$. Because the null hypothesis is not rejected, no action will be taken to adjust the MaxFlight manufacturing process.

FIGURE 9.5 *p*-VALUE FOR THE MAXFLIGHT HYPOTHESIS TEST

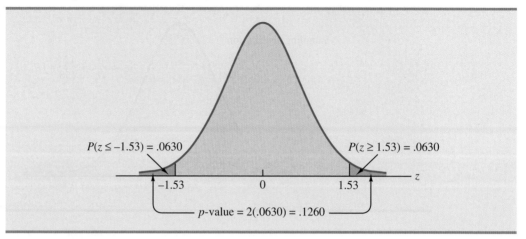

The computation of the *p*-value for a two-tailed test may seem a bit confusing as compared to the computation of the *p*-value for a one-tailed test. But it can be simplified by following three steps.

COMPUTATION OF *p*-VALUE FOR A TWO-TAILED TEST

1. Compute the value of the test statistic z.
2. If the value of the test statistic is in the upper tail ($z > 0$), find the area under the standard normal curve to the right of z. If the value of the test statistic is in the lower tail ($z < 0$), find the area under the standard normal curve to the left of z.
3. Double the tail area, or probability, obtained in step 2 to obtain the *p*-value.

Critical value approach Before leaving this section, let us see how the test statistic z can be compared to a critical value to make the hypothesis testing decision for a two-tailed test. Figure 9.6 shows that the critical values for the test will occur in both the lower and upper tails of the standard normal distribution. With a level of significance of $\alpha = .05$, the area in each tail beyond the critical values is $\alpha/2 = .05/2 = .025$. Using the standard

FIGURE 9.6 CRITICAL VALUES FOR THE MAXFLIGHT HYPOTHESIS TEST

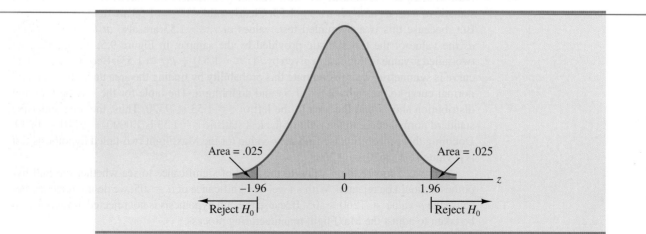

normal probability table, we find the critical values for the test statistic are $-z_{.025} = -1.96$ and $z_{.025} = 1.96$. Thus, using the critical value approach, the two-tailed rejection rule is

$$\text{Reject } H_0 \text{ if } z \leq -1.96 \text{ or if } z \geq 1.96$$

Because the value of the test statistic for the MaxFlight study is $z = 1.53$, the statistical evidence will not permit us to reject the null hypothesis at the .05 level of significance.

Using Excel

Excel can be used to conduct one-tailed and two-tailed hypothesis tests about a population mean for the σ known case using the p-value approach. Recall that the method used to compute a p-value depends upon whether the test is lower tail, upper tail, or two-tailed. Therefore, in the Excel procedure we describe we will use the sample results to compute three p-values: p-value (Lower Tail); p-value (Upper Tail); and p-value (Two Tail). The user can then choose α and draw a conclusion using whichever p-value is appropriate for the type of hypothesis test being conducted. We will illustrate using the MaxFlight two-tailed hypothesis test. Refer to Figure 9.7 as we describe the tasks involved. The formula worksheet is in the background; the value worksheet is in the foreground.

Enter Data: A label and the distance data for the sample of 50 golf balls are entered into cells A1:A51.

Enter Functions and Formulas: The descriptive statistics needed are provided in cells D4 and D5. Excel's COUNT and AVERAGE functions compute the sample size and the sample mean, respectively. The value of the known population standard deviation (12) is entered into cell D7, and the hypothesized value of the population mean (295) is entered into cell D8.

The standard error is obtained in cell D10 by entering the formula =D7/SQRT(D4). The formula =(D5-D8)/D10 entered into cell D11 computes the test statistic $z(1.5321)$. To compute the p-value for a lower tail test, we enter the formula =NORMSDIST(D11) into cell D13. The p-value for an upper tail test is then computed in cell D14 as 1 minus the p-value for the lower tail test. Finally, the p-value for a two-tailed test is computed in cell D15 as two times the minimum of the two one-tailed p-values. The value worksheet shows that p-value (Lower Tail) = 0.9372, p-value (Upper Tail) = 0.0628, and p-value (Two Tail) = 0.1255.

The development of the worksheet is now complete. For the two-tailed MaxFlight problem we cannot reject H_0: $\mu = 295$ using $\alpha = .05$ because the p-value (Two Tail) = 0.1255 is greater than α. Thus, the quality control manager has no reason to doubt that the manufacturing process is producing golf balls with a population mean distance of 295 yards.

A template for other problems The worksheet in Figure 9.7 can be used as a template for conducting any one-tailed and two-tailed hypothesis tests for the σ known case. Just enter the appropriate data in column A, adjust the ranges for the formulas in cells D4 and D5, enter the population standard deviation in cell D7, and enter the hypothesized value in cell D8. The standard error, the test statistic, and the three p-values will then appear. Depending on the form of the hypothesis test (lower tail, upper tail, or two-tailed), we can then choose the appropriate p-value to make the rejection decision.

We can further simplify the use of Figure 9.7 as a template for other problems by eliminating the need to enter new data ranges in cells D4 and D5. To do so we rewrite the cell formulas as follows:

Cell D4: =COUNT(A:A)
Cell D5: =AVERAGE(A:A)

FIGURE 9.7   EXCEL WORKSHEET: HYPOTHESIS TEST FOR THE σ KNOWN CASE

	A	B	C	D	E
1	Yards		**Hypothesis Test about a Population Mean:**		
2	303		σ **Known Case**		
3	282				
4	289		**Sample Size**	=COUNT(A2:A51)	
5	298		**Sample Mean**	=AVERAGE(A2:A51)	
6	283				
7	317		**Population Standard Deviation**	12	
8	297		**Hypothesized Value**	295	
9	308				
10	317		**Standard Error**	=D7/SQRT(D4)	
11	293		**Test Statistic** z	=(D5-D8)/D10	
12	284				
13	290		p-**value (Lower Tail)**	=NORMSDIST(D11)	
14	304		p-**value (Upper Tail)**	=1-D13	
15	290		p-**value (Two Tail)**	=2*(MIN(D13,D14))	
16	311				
50	301				
51	292				
52					

WEB file

GolfTest

	A	B	C	D	E
1	Yards		**Hypothesis Test about a Population Mean:**		
2	303		σ **Known Case**		
3	282				
4	289		**Sample Size**	50	
5	298		**Sample Mean**	297.6	
6	283				
7	317		**Population Standard Deviation**	12	
8	297		**Hypothesized Value**	295	
9	308				
10	317		**Standard Error**	1.6971	
11	293		**Test Statistic** z	1.5321	
12	284				
13	290		p-**value (Lower Tail)**	0.9372	
14	304		p-**value (Upper Tail)**	0.0628	
15	290		p-**value (Two Tail)**	0.1255	
16	311				
50	301				
51	292				
52					

Note: Rows 17–49 are hidden.

The GolfTest data set includes a worksheet entitled Template that uses the A:A method for entering the data ranges.

With the A:A method of specifying data ranges, Excel's COUNT function will count the number of numeric values in column A and Excel's AVERAGE function will compute the average of the numeric values in column A. Thus, to solve a new problem it is only necessary to enter the new data in column A, enter the value of the known population standard deviation in cell D7, and enter the hypothesized value of the population mean in cell D8.

The worksheet can also be used as a template for text exercises in which n, $\bar{x}$, and σ are given. Just ignore the data in column A and enter the values for n, $\bar{x}$, and σ into cells D4, D5, and D7, respectively. Then enter the appropriate hypothesized value for the population mean into cell D8. The p-values corresponding to lower tail, upper tail, and two-tailed hypothesis tests will then appear in cells D13:D15.

TABLE 9.2 SUMMARY OF HYPOTHESIS TESTS ABOUT A POPULATION MEAN: σ KNOWN CASE

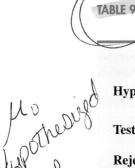

(handwritten margin note: μ_0 Hypothesized Value)

	Lower Tail Test	**Upper Tail Test**	**Two-Tailed Test**
Hypotheses	$H_0: \mu \geq \mu_0$ $H_a: \mu < \mu_0$	$H_0: \mu \leq \mu_0$ $H_a: \mu > \mu_0$	$H_0: \mu = \mu_0$ $H_a: \mu \neq \mu_0$
Test Statistic	$z = \dfrac{\bar{x} - \mu_0}{\sigma/\sqrt{n}}$	$z = \dfrac{\bar{x} - \mu_0}{\sigma/\sqrt{n}}$	$z = \dfrac{\bar{x} - \mu_0}{\sigma/\sqrt{n}}$
Rejection Rule: *p*-**Value Approach**	Reject H_0 if p-value $\leq \alpha$	Reject H_0 if p-value $\leq \alpha$	Reject H_0 if p-value $\leq \alpha$
Rejection Rule: Critical Value Approach	Reject H_0 if $z \leq -z_\alpha$	Reject H_0 if $z \geq z_\alpha$	Reject H_0 if $z \leq -z_{\alpha/2}$ or if $z \geq z_{\alpha/2}$

Summary and Practical Advice

We presented examples of a lower tail test and a two-tailed test about a population mean. Based upon these examples, we can now summarize the hypothesis testing procedures about a population mean for the σ known case as shown in Table 9.2. Note that μ_0 is the hypothesized value of the population mean.

The hypothesis testing steps followed in the two examples presented in this section are common to every hypothesis test.

STEPS OF HYPOTHESIS TESTING

Step 1. Develop the null and alternative hypotheses.
Step 2. Specify the level of significance.
Step 3. Collect the sample data and compute the value of the test statistic.

p-Value Approach

Step 4. Use the value of the test statistic to compute the *p*-value.
Step 5. Reject H_0 if the *p*-value $\leq \alpha$.

Critical Value Approach

Step 4. Use the level of significance to determine the critical value and the rejection rule.
Step 5. Use the value of the test statistic and the rejection rule to determine whether to reject H_0.

Practical advice about the sample size for hypothesis tests is similar to the advice we provided about the sample size for interval estimation in Chapter 8. In most applications, a sample size of $n \geq 30$ is adequate when using the hypothesis testing procedure described in this section. In cases where the sample size is less than 30, the distribution of the population from which we are sampling becomes an important consideration. If the population is normally distributed, the hypothesis testing procedure that we described is exact and can be used for any sample size. If the population is not normally distributed but is at least roughly symmetric, sample sizes as small as 15 can be expected to provide acceptable results.

(handwritten margin note: Number to closest to 0 shows less skewness)

Relationship Between Interval Estimation and Hypothesis Testing

In Chapter 8 we showed how to develop a confidence interval estimate of a population mean. For the σ known case, the $(1 - \alpha)\%$ confidence interval estimate of a population mean is given by

$$\bar{x} \pm z_{\alpha/2} \frac{\sigma}{\sqrt{n}}$$

In this chapter, we showed that a two-tailed hypothesis test about a population mean takes the following form:

$$H_0: \mu = \mu_0$$
$$H_a: \mu \neq \mu_0$$

where μ_0 is the hypothesized value for the population mean.

Suppose that we follow the procedure described in Chapter 8 for constructing a $(1 - \alpha)\%$ confidence interval for the population mean. We know that $(1 - \alpha)\%$ of the confidence intervals generated will contain the population mean and $\alpha\%$ of the confidence intervals generated will not contain the population mean. Thus, if we reject H_0 whenever the confidence interval does not contain μ_0, we will be rejecting the null hypothesis when it is true $(\mu = \mu_0)$ with probability α. Recall that the level of significance is the probability of rejecting the null hypothesis when it is true. So constructing a $(1 - \alpha)\%$ confidence interval and rejecting H_0 whenever the interval does not contain μ_0 is equivalent to conducting a two-tailed hypothesis test with α as the level of significance. The procedure for using a confidence interval to conduct a two-tailed hypothesis test can now be summarized.

A CONFIDENCE INTERVAL APPROACH TO TESTING A HYPOTHESIS
OF THE FORM

$$H_0: \mu = \mu_0$$
$$H_a: \mu \neq \mu_0$$

1. Select a simple random sample from the population and use the value of the sample mean $\bar{x}$ to develop the confidence interval for the population mean μ.

$$\bar{x} \pm z_{\alpha/2} \frac{\sigma}{\sqrt{n}}$$

For a two-tailed hypothesis test, the null hypothesis can be rejected if the confidence interval does not include μ_0.

2. If the confidence interval contains the hypothesized value μ_0, do not reject H_0. Otherwise, reject[3] H_0.

Let us illustrate by conducting the MaxFlight hypothesis test using the confidence interval approach. The MaxFlight hypothesis test takes the following form:

$$H_0: \mu = 295$$
$$H_a: \mu \neq 295$$

---

[3]To be consistent with the rule for rejecting H_0 when the p-value $\leq \alpha$, we would also reject H_0 if μ_0 happens to be equal to one of the endpoints of the $(1 - \alpha)\%$ confidence interval.

To test these hypotheses with a level of significance of $\alpha = .05$, we sampled 50 golf balls and found a sample mean distance of $\bar{x} = 297.6$ yards. Recall that the population standard deviation is $\sigma = 12$. Using these results with $z_{.025} = 1.96$, we find that the 95% confidence interval estimate of the population mean is

$$\bar{x} \pm z_{.025} \frac{\sigma}{\sqrt{n}}$$

$$297.6 \pm 1.96 \frac{12}{\sqrt{50}}$$

$$297.6 \pm 3.3$$

or

$$294.3 \text{ to } 300.9$$

This finding enables the quality control manager to conclude with 95% confidence that the mean distance for the population of golf balls is between 294.3 and 300.9 yards. Because the hypothesized value for the population mean, $\mu_0 = 295$, is in this interval, the hypothesis testing conclusion is that the null hypothesis, $H_0: \mu = 295$, cannot be rejected.

Note that this discussion and example pertain to two-tailed hypothesis tests about a population mean. However, the same confidence interval and two-tailed hypothesis testing relationship exists for other population parameters. The relationship can also be extended to one-tailed tests about population parameters. Doing so, however, requires the development of one-sided confidence intervals, which are rarely used in practice.

NOTES AND COMMENTS

We have shown how to use p-values. The smaller the p-value the greater the evidence against H_0 and the more the evidence in favor of H_a. Here are some guidelines statisticians suggest for interpreting small p-values.

- Less than .01—Overwhelming evidence to conclude H_a is true.

- Between .01 and .05—Strong evidence to conclude H_a is true.
- Between .05 and .10—Weak evidence to conclude H_a is true.
- Greater than .10—Insufficient evidence to conclude H_a is true.

Exercises

Note to Student: Some of the exercises that follow ask you to use the p-value approach and others ask you to use the critical value approach. Both methods will provide the same hypothesis testing conclusion. We provide exercises with both methods to give you practice using both. In later sections and in following chapters, we will generally emphasize the p-value approach as the preferred method, but you may select either based on personal preference.

Methods

9. Consider the following hypothesis test:

$$H_0: \mu \geq 20$$
$$H_a: \mu < 20$$

A sample of 50 provided a sample mean of 19.4. The population standard deviation is 2.
a. Compute the value of the test statistic.
b. What is the p-value?
c. Using $\alpha = .05$, what is your conclusion?
d. What is the rejection rule using the critical value? What is your conclusion?

10. Consider the following hypothesis test:

$$H_0: \mu \leq 25$$
$$H_a: \mu > 25$$

A sample of 40 provided a sample mean of 26.4. The population standard deviation is 6.
a. Compute the value of the test statistic.
b. What is the p-value?
c. At $\alpha = .01$, what is your conclusion?
d. What is the rejection rule using the critical value? What is your conclusion?

11. Consider the following hypothesis test:

$$H_0: \mu = 15$$
$$H_a: \mu \neq 15$$

A sample of 50 provided a sample mean of 14.15. The population standard deviation is 3.
a. Compute the value of the test statistic.
b. What is the p-value?
c. At $\alpha = .05$, what is your conclusion?
d. What is the rejection rule using the critical value? What is your conclusion?

12. Consider the following hypothesis test:

$$H_0: \mu \geq 80$$
$$H_a: \mu < 80$$

A sample of 100 is used and the population standard deviation is 12. Compute the p-value and state your conclusion for each of the following sample results. Use $\alpha = .01$.
a. $\bar{x} = 78.5$
b. $\bar{x} = 77$
c. $\bar{x} = 75.5$
d. $\bar{x} = 81$

13. Consider the following hypothesis test:

$$H_0: \mu \leq 50$$
$$H_a: \mu > 50$$

A sample of 60 is used and the population standard deviation is 8. Use the critical value approach to state your conclusion for each of the following sample results. Use $\alpha = .05$.
a. $\bar{x} = 52.5$
b. $\bar{x} = 51$
c. $\bar{x} = 51.8$

14. Consider the following hypothesis test:

$$H_0: \mu = 22$$
$$H_a: \mu \neq 22$$

A sample of 75 is used and the population standard deviation is 10. Compute the *p*-value and state your conclusion for each of the following sample results. Use $\alpha = .01$.

a. $\bar{x} = 23$

b. $\bar{x} = 25.1$

c. $\bar{x} = 20$

Applications

15. Individuals filing federal income tax returns prior to March 31 received an average refund of $1056. Consider the population of "last-minute" filers who mail their tax return during the last five days of the income tax period (typically April 10 to April 15).

a. A researcher suggests that a reason individuals wait until the last five days is that on average these individuals receive lower refunds than do early filers. Develop appropriate hypotheses such that rejection of H_0 will support the researcher's contention.

b. For a sample of 400 individuals who filed a tax return between April 10 and 15, the sample mean refund was $910. Based on prior experience a population standard deviation of $\sigma = \$1600$ may be assumed. What is the *p*-value?

c. At $\alpha = .05$, what is your conclusion?

d. Repeat the preceding hypothesis test using the critical value approach.

RentalRates

16. Reis, Inc., a New York real estate research firm, tracks the cost of apartment rentals in the United States. In mid-2002, the nationwide mean apartment rental rate was $895 per month (*The Wall Street Journal,* July 8, 2002). Assume that, based on the historical quarterly surveys, a population standard deviation of $\sigma = \$225$ is reasonable. In a current study of apartment rental rates, a sample of 180 apartments nationwide provided the apartment rental rates shown in the website file named RentalRates. Do the sample data enable Reis to conclude that the population mean apartment rental rate now exceeds the level reported in 2002?

a. State the null and alternative hypotheses.

b. What is the *p*-value?

c. At $\alpha = .01$, what is your conclusion?

d. What would you recommend Reis consider doing at this time?

17. Wall Street securities firms paid out record year-end bonuses of $125,500 per employee for 2005 (*Fortune,* February 6, 2006). Suppose we would like to take a sample of employees at the Jones & Ryan securities firm to see whether the mean year-end bonus is different from the reported mean of $125,500 for the population.

a. State the null and alternative hypotheses you would use to test whether the year-end bonuses paid by Jones & Ryan were different from the population mean.

b. Suppose a sample of 40 Jones & Ryan employees showed a sample mean year-end bonus of $118,000. Assume a population standard deviation of $\sigma = \$30,000$ and compute the *p*-value.

c. With $\alpha = .05$ as the level of significance, what is your conclusion?

d. Repeat the preceding hypothesis test using the critical value approach.

18. The average annual total return for U.S. Diversified Equity mutual funds from 1999 to 2003 was 4.1% (*BusinessWeek,* January 26, 2004). A researcher would like to conduct a hypothesis test to see whether the returns for mid-cap growth funds over the same period are significantly different from the average for U.S. Diversified Equity funds.

a. Formulate the hypotheses that can be used to determine whether the mean annual return for mid-cap growth funds differ from the mean for U.S. Diversified Equity funds.

b. A sample of 40 mid-cap growth funds provides a mean return of $\bar{x} = 3.4\%$. Assume the population standard deviation for mid-cap growth funds is known from previous studies to be $\sigma = 2\%$. Use the sample results to compute the test statistic and *p*-value for the hypothesis test.

c. At $\alpha = .05$, what is your conclusion?

19. In 2001, the U.S. Department of Labor reported the average hourly earnings for U.S. pro-
     duction workers to be $14.32 per hour (*The World Almanac,* 2003). A sample of 75 pro-
     duction workers during 2003 showed a sample mean of $14.68 per hour. Assuming the
     population standard deviation $\sigma = \$1.45$, can we conclude that an increase occurred in the
     mean hourly earnings since 2001? Use $\alpha = .05$.

20. For the United States, the mean monthly Internet bill is $32.79 per household (CNBC,
     January 18, 2006). A sample of 50 households in a southern state showed a sample mean
     of $30.63. Use a population standard deviation of $\sigma = \$5.60$.
     a. Formulate hypotheses for a test to determine whether the sample data support the con-
         clusion that the mean monthly Internet bill in the southern state is less than the national
         mean of $32.79.
     b. What is the value of the test statistic?
     c. What is the *p*-value?
     d. At $\alpha = .01$, what is your conclusion?

21. Fowle Marketing Research, Inc., bases charges to a client on the assumption that telephone
     surveys can be completed in a mean time of 15 minutes or less. If a longer mean survey
     time is necessary, a premium rate is charged. A sample of 35 surveys provided the survey
     times shown in the website file named Fowle. Based upon past studies, the population stan-
     dard deviation is assumed known with $\sigma = 4$ minutes. Is the premium rate justified?
     a. Formulate the null and alternative hypotheses for this application.
     b. Compute the value of the test statistic.
     c. What is the *p*-value?
     d. At $\alpha = .01$, what is your conclusion?

22. CCN and ActMedia provided a television channel targeted to individuals waiting in super-
     market checkout lines. The channel showed news, short features, and advertisements. The
     length of the program was based on the assumption that the population mean time a shop-
     per stands in a supermarket checkout line is 8 minutes. A sample of actual waiting times
     will be used to test this assumption and determine whether actual mean waiting time dif-
     fers from this standard.
     a. Formulate the hypotheses for this application.
     b. A sample of 120 shoppers showed a sample mean waiting time of 8.5 minutes. As-
         sume a population standard deviation $\sigma = 3.2$ minutes. What is the *p*-value?
     c. At $\alpha = .05$, what is your conclusion?
     d. Compute a 95% confidence interval for the population mean. Does it support your
         conclusion?

9.4   Population Mean: σ Unknown

In this section we describe how to conduct hypothesis tests about a population mean for
the σ unknown case. Because the σ unknown case corresponds to situations in which an
estimate of the population standard deviation cannot be developed prior to sampling, the
sample must be used to develop an estimate of both μ and σ. Thus, to conduct a hypothesis
test about a population mean for the σ unknown case, the sample mean $\bar{x}$ is used as an estimate of μ and the sample standard deviation s is used as an estimate of σ.

The steps of the hypothesis testing procedure for the σ unknown case are the same as
those for the σ known case described in Section 9.3. But, with σ unknown, the computation
of the test statistic and *p*-value is a bit different. Recall that for the σ known case, the sampling distribution of the test statistic has a standard normal distribution. For the σ unknown
case, however, the sampling distribution of the test statistic follows the *t* distribution; it has
slightly more variability because the sample is used to develop estimates of both μ and σ.

In Section 8.2 we showed that an interval estimate of a population mean for the σ
unknown case is based on a probability distribution known as the *t* distribution. Hypothesis

tests about a population mean for the σ unknown case are also based on the t distribution. For the σ unknown case, the test statistic has a t distribution with $n - 1$ degrees of freedom.

TEST STATISTIC FOR HYPOTHESIS TESTS ABOUT A POPULATION MEAN: σ UNKNOWN

$$t = \frac{\bar{x} - \mu_0}{s/\sqrt{n}} \qquad (9.2)$$

In Chapter 8 we said that the t distribution is based on an assumption that the population from which we are sampling has a normal distribution. However, research shows that this assumption can be relaxed considerably when the sample size is large enough. We provide some practical advice concerning the population distribution and sample size at the end of the section.

One-Tailed Tests

WEB file

AirRating

Let us consider an example of a one-tailed test about a population mean for the σ unknown case. A business travel magazine wants to classify transatlantic gateway airports according to the mean rating for the population of business travelers. A rating scale with a low score of 0 and a high score of 10 will be used, and airports with a population mean rating greater than 7 will be designated as superior service airports. The magazine staff surveyed a sample of 60 business travelers at each airport to obtain the ratings data. The sample for London's Heathrow Airport provided a sample mean rating of $\bar{x} = 7.25$ and a sample standard deviation of $s = 1.052$. Do the data indicate that Heathrow should be designated as a superior service airport?

We want to develop a hypothesis test for which the decision to reject H_0 will lead to the conclusion that the population mean rating for the Heathrow Airport is *greater* than 7. Thus, an upper tail test with H_a: $\mu > 7$ is required. The null and alternative hypotheses for this upper tail test are as follows:

$$H_0: \mu \leq 7$$
$$H_a: \mu > 7$$

We will use $\alpha = .05$ as the level of significance for the test.

Using equation (9.2) with $\bar{x} = 7.25, \mu_0 = 7, s = 1.052$, and $n = 60$, the value of the test statistic is

$$t = \frac{\bar{x} - \mu_0}{s/\sqrt{n}} = \frac{7.25 - 7}{1.052/\sqrt{60}} = 1.84$$

The sampling distribution of t has $n - 1 = 60 - 1 = 59$ degrees of freedom. Because the test is an upper tail test, the p-value is the area under the curve of the t distribution to the right of $t = 1.84$.

The t distribution table provided in most textbooks will not contain sufficient detail to determine the exact p-value, such as the p-value corresponding to $t = 1.84$. For instance, using Table 2 in Appendix B, the t distribution with 59 degrees of freedom provides the following information.

Area in Upper Tail	.20	.10	.05	.025	.01	.005
t Value (59 *df*)	.848	1.296	1.671	2.001	2.391	2.662

$t = 1.84$

We see that $t = 1.84$ is between 1.671 and 2.001. Although the table does not provide the exact p-value, the values in the "Area in Upper Tail" row show that the p-value must be less than .05 and greater than .025. With a level of significance of $\alpha = .05$, this placement is all we need to know to make the decision to reject the null hypothesis and conclude that Heathrow should be classified as a superior service airport.

Excel's TDIST function can be used to determine the exact p-value associated with the test statistic $t = 1.84$. The general form of the TDIST function is as follows:

$$\text{TDIST(test statistic,degrees of freedom,tails)}$$

In the upcoming "Using Excel" section, we illustrate how to use the TDIST function to compute the area in the lower tail of the t distribution when the value of the test statistic is negative.

Only nonnegative values are allowed for *test statistic*. If the value of *tails* is 1, the function returns the area in the upper tail of the t distribution corresponding to the value of the test statistic. In the Heathrow Airport study we found a value for the test statistic of $t = 1.84$. If we enter the function =TDIST(1.84,59,1) into an Excel worksheet, the value obtained is .0354. A p-value $= .0354 < .05$ leads to the rejection of the null hypothesis and to the conclusion that Heathrow should be classified as a superior service airport.

The critical value approach can also be used to make the rejection decision. With $\alpha = .05$ and the t distribution with 59 degrees of freedom, $t_{.05} = 1.671$ is the critical value for the test. The rejection rule is thus

$$\text{Reject } H_0 \text{ if } t \geq 1.671$$

With the test statistic $t = 1.84 \geq 1.671$, H_0 is rejected and we can conclude that Heathrow can be classified as a superior service airport.

Two-Tailed Test

To illustrate how to conduct a two-tailed test about a population mean for the σ unknown case, let us consider the hypothesis testing situation facing Holiday Toys. The company manufactures and distributes its products through more than 1000 retail outlets. In planning production levels for the coming winter season, Holiday must decide how many units of each product to produce prior to knowing the actual demand at the retail level. For this year's most important new toy, Holiday's marketing director is expecting demand to average 40 units per retail outlet. Prior to making the final production decision based upon this estimate, Holiday decided to survey a sample of 25 retailers in order to develop more information about the demand for the new product. Each retailer was provided with information about the features of the new toy along with the cost and the suggested selling price. Then each retailer was asked to specify an anticipated order quantity.

With μ denoting the population mean order quantity per retail outlet, the sample data will be used to conduct the following two-tailed hypothesis test:

$$H_0: \mu = 40$$
$$H_a: \mu \neq 40$$

If H_0 cannot be rejected, Holiday will continue its production planning based on the marketing director's estimate that the population mean order quantity per retail outlet will be $\mu = 40$ units. However, if H_0 is rejected, Holiday will immediately reevaluate its production plan for the product. A two-tailed hypothesis test is used because Holiday wants to reevaluate the production plan if the population mean quantity per retail outlet is less than anticipated or greater than anticipated. Because no historical data are available (it's a new product), the population mean μ and the population standard deviation must both be estimated using $\bar{x}$ and s from the sample data.

The sample of 25 retailers provided a mean of $\bar{x} = 37.4$ and a standard deviation of $s = 11.79$ units. Before going ahead with the use of the t distribution, the analyst constructed a histogram of the sample data in order to check on the form of the population distribution. The histogram of the sample data showed no evidence of skewness or any extreme

outliers, so the analyst concluded that the use of the t distribution with $n - 1 = 24$ degrees of freedom was appropriate. Using equation (9.2) with $\bar{x} = 37.4$, $\mu_0 = 40$, $s = 11.79$, and $n = 25$, the value of the test statistic is

$$t = \frac{\bar{x} - \mu_0}{s/\sqrt{n}} = \frac{37.4 - 40}{11.79/\sqrt{25}} = -1.10$$

Because we have a two-tailed test, the p-value is two times the area under the curve for the t distribution to the left of $t = -1.10$. Using Table 2 in Appendix B, the t distribution table for 24 degrees of freedom provides the following information.

Area in Upper Tail	.20	.10	.05	.025	.01	.005
t Value (24 *df*)	.857	1.318	1.711	2.064	2.492	2.797

$t = 1.10$

The t distribution table only contains positive t values. Because the t distribution is symmetric, however, the area under the curve to the right of $t = 1.10$ is the same as the area under the curve to the left of $t = -1.10$. We see that $t = 1.10$ is between 0.857 and 1.318. From the "Area in Upper Tail" row, we see that the area in the tail to the right of $t = 1.10$ is between .20 and .10. When we double these amounts, we see that the p-value must be between .40 and .20. With a level of significance of $\alpha = .05$, we now know that the p-value is greater than α. Therefore, H_0 cannot be rejected. Sufficient evidence is not available to conclude that Holiday should change its production plan for the coming season.

Excel's TDIST function can be used to determine the p-value for a two-tailed hypothesis test. Recall that the general form of the TDIST function is as follows:

TDIST(test statistic,degrees of freedom,tails)

Excel's TDIST function makes it easy to compute p-values.

Only nonnegative values are allowed for the test statistic and the value of tails is 1 or 2, depending upon whether the test is one- or two-tailed. For the two-tailed Holiday Toys hypothesis test, the value of the test statistic is -1.10, with 24 degrees of freedom. With 2 for the value of tails, entering the function =TDIST(1.10,24,2) into a cell of an Excel worksheet provides the area under the curve of the t distribution to the right of the value of 1.10 plus the area under the curve of the t distribution to the left of -1.10; it provides the p-value for the two-tailed Holiday Toys hypothesis test. The value obtained is .2822. With a level of significance of $\alpha = .05$, we cannot reject H_0 because the p-value is greater than α.

The test statistic can also be compared to the critical value to make the two-tailed hypothesis testing decision. With $\alpha = .05$ and the t distribution with 24 degrees of freedom, $-t_{.025} = -2.064$ and $t_{.025} = 2.064$ are the critical values for the two-tailed test. The rejection rule using the test statistic is

Reject H_0 if $t \leq -2.064$ or if $t \geq 2.064$

Based on the test statistic $t = -1.10$, H_0 cannot be rejected. This result indicates that Holiday should continue its production planning for the coming season based on the expectation that $\mu = 40$.

Using Excel

Excel can be used to conduct one-tailed and two-tailed hypothesis tests about a population mean for the σ unknown case. The approach is similar to the procedure used in the σ known case. The sample data and the test statistic (t) are used to compute three p-values: p-value

(Lower Tail), p-value (Upper Tail), and p-value (Two Tail). The user can then choose α and draw a conclusion using whichever p-value is appropriate for the type of hypothesis test being conducted.

Let's start by showing how to use Excel's TDIST function to compute a lower tail p-value. Previously, we showed that the general form of the TDIST function is as follows:

TDIST(test statistic,degrees of freedom,tails)

Recall that only nonnegative values are allowed for the test statistic and a tails value of 1 provides the area under the curve of the t distribution to the right of the value of the test statistic. For a lower tail hypothesis test the value of the test statistic is usually negative and the p-value is the area under the curve for the t distribution to the left of the test statistic. Because the t distribution is symmetric, the area under the curve to the left of the test statistic (the lower tail p-value) is the same as the area under the curve to the right of the negative of the test statistic. Thus, when the test statistic is *negative,* the TDIST function is used to compute the lower tail p-value in the following manner:

TDIST(-test statistic,degrees of freedom,1)

To compute the p-value (Lower Tail) when the test statistic is *nonnegative,* we subtract the upper tail area provided by the TDIST function from 1 as follows:

1-TDIST(test statistic,degrees of freedom,1)

We can use Excel's IF function to determine whether the value of the test statistic is negative or nonnegative and to specify how the TDIST function is used to compute the lower tail p-value.

IF(test statistic<0,negative t,nonnegative t)

where

negative t: TDIST(-test statistic,degrees of freedom,1)
nonnegative t: 1-TDIST(test statistic,degrees of freedom,1)

Thus, if the value of the test statistic is negative, the first form of the TDIST function is used to compute the lower tail p-value; if the value of the test statistic is nonnegative, the second form is used.

Once the lower tail p-value has been computed, it is easy to compute the upper tail and the two-tailed p-values. The upper tail p-value is just 1 minus the lower tail p-value. And the two-tailed p-value is given by two times the smaller of the lower and upper tail p-values.

Let us now construct an Excel worksheet to conduct the two-tailed hypothesis test for the Holiday Toys study. Refer to Figure 9.8 as we describe the tasks involved. The formula worksheet is in the background; the value worksheet is in the foreground.

Enter Data: A label and the order quantity data for the sample of 25 retailers are entered into cells A1:A26.

Enter Functions and Formulas: The descriptive statistics needed are provided in cells D4:D6. Excel's COUNT, AVERAGE, and STDEV functions compute the sample size, the sample mean, and the sample standard deviation, respectively. The hypothesized value of the population mean (40) is entered into cell D8.

Using the sample standard deviation as an estimate of the population standard deviation, an estimate of the standard error is obtained in cell D10 by dividing the sample standard deviation in cell D6 by the square root of the sample size in cell D4. The formula =(D5-D8)/D10 entered into cell D11 computes the test statistic t(-1.1026). The degrees of freedom are computed in cell D12 as the sample size in cell D4 minus 1.

FIGURE 9.8   EXCEL WORKSHEET: HYPOTHESIS TEST FOR THE σ UNKNOWN CASE

	A	B	C	D	E
1	Units		Hypothesis Test about a Population Mean:		
2	26		σ Unknown Case		
3	23				
4	32		Sample Size	=COUNT(A2:A26)	
5	47		Sample Mean	=AVERAGE(A2:A26)	
6	45		Sample Standard Deviation	=STDEV(A2:A26)	
7	31				
8	47		Hypothesized Value	40	
9	59				
10	21		Standard Error	=D6/SQRT(D4)	
11	52		Test Statistic *t*	=(D5-D8)/D10	
12	45		Degrees of Freedom	=D4-1	
13	53				
14	34		*p*-value (Lower Tail)	=IF(D11<0,TDIST(-D11,D12,1),1-TDIST(D11,D12,1))	
15	45		*p*-value (Upper Tail)	=1-D14	
16	39		*p*-value (Two Tail)	=2*MIN(D14,D15)	
17	52				
25	30				
26	28				
27					

WEB file

Orders

	A	B	C	D	E	F
1	Units		Hypothesis Test about a Population Mean:			
2	26		σ Unknown Case			
3	23					
4	32		Sample Size	25		
5	47		Sample Mean	37.4		
6	45		Sample Standard Deviation	11.79		
7	31					
8	47		Hypothesized Value	40		
9	59					
10	21		Standard Error	2.3580		
11	52		Test Statistic *t*	-1.1026		
12	45		Degrees of Freedom	24		
13	53					
14	34		*p*-value (Lower Tail)	0.1406		
15	45		*p*-value (Upper Tail)	0.8594		
16	39		*p*-value (Two Tail)	0.2811		
17	52					
25	30					
26	28					
27						

Note: Rows 18–24 are hidden.

To compute the *p*-value for a lower tail test, we enter the following formula into cell D14:

$$=IF(D11<0,TDIST(-D11,D12,1),1-TDIST(D11,D12,1))$$

The *p*-value for an upper tail test is then computed in cell D15 as 1 minus the *p*-value for the lower tail test. Finally, the *p*-value for a two-tailed test is computed in cell D16 as two times the minimum of the two one-tailed *p*-values. The value worksheet shows that the three *p*-values are *p*-value (Lower Tail) = 0.1406, *p*-value (Upper Tail) = 0.8594, and *p*-value (Two Tail) = 0.2811.

The development of the worksheet is now complete. For the two-tailed Holiday Toys problem we cannot reject H_0: $\mu = 40$ using $\alpha = .05$ because the *p*-value (Two Tail) = 0.2811 is greater than α. This result indicates that Holiday should continue its production planning for the coming season based on the expectation that $\mu = 40$. The worksheet in Figure 9.8 can also be used for any one-tailed hypothesis test involving the t distribution. If a lower tail test is required, compare the p-value (Lower Tail) with α to make the rejection decision. If an upper tail test is required, compare the p-value (Upper Tail) with α to make the rejection decision.

A template for other problems   The worksheet in Figure 9.8 can be used as a template for any hypothesis tests about a population mean for the σ unknown case. Just enter the appropriate data in column A, adjust the ranges for the formulas in cells D4:D6, and enter the hypothesized value in cell D8. The standard error, the test statistic, and the three p-values will then appear. Depending on the form of the hypothesis test (lower tail, upper tail, or two-tailed), we can then choose the appropriate p-value to make the rejection decision.

We can further simplify the use of Figure 9.8 as a template for other problems by eliminating the need to enter new data ranges in cells D4:D6. To do so we rewrite the cell formulas as follows:

Cell D4: =COUNT(A:A)

Cell D5: =AVERAGE(A:A)

Cell D6: =STDEV(A:A)

The Orders data set includes a worksheet entitled Template that uses the A:A method for entering the data ranges.

With the A:A method of specifying data ranges, Excel's COUNT function will count the number of numeric values in column A, Excel's AVERAGE function will compute the average of the numeric values in column A, and Excel's STDEV function will compute the standard deviation of the numeric values in Column A. Thus, to solve a new problem it is only necessary to enter the new data in column A and enter the hypothesized value of the population mean in cell D8.

Summary and Practical Advice

Table 9.3 provides a summary of the hypothesis testing procedures about a population mean for the σ unknown case. The key difference between these procedures and the ones for the σ known case is that s is used, instead of σ, in the computation of the test statistic. For this reason, the test statistic follows the t distribution.

The applicability of the hypothesis testing procedures of this section is dependent on the distribution of the population being sampled from and the sample size. When the population is normally distributed, the hypothesis tests described in this section provide exact

TABLE 9.3   SUMMARY OF HYPOTHESIS TESTS ABOUT A POPULATION MEAN: σ UNKNOWN CASE

	Lower Tail Test	**Upper Tail Test**	**Two-Tailed Test**
Hypotheses	$H_0: \mu \geq \mu_0$ $H_a: \mu < \mu_0$	$H_0: \mu \leq \mu_0$ $H_a: \mu > \mu_0$	$H_0: \mu = \mu_0$ $H_a: \mu \neq \mu_0$
Test Statistic	$t = \dfrac{\bar{x} - \mu_0}{s/\sqrt{n}}$	$t = \dfrac{\bar{x} - \mu_0}{s/\sqrt{n}}$	$t = \dfrac{\bar{x} - \mu_0}{s/\sqrt{n}}$
Rejection Rule: *p*-**Value Approach**	Reject H_0 if p-value $\leq \alpha$	Reject H_0 if p-value $\leq \alpha$	Reject H_0 if p-value $\leq \alpha$
Rejection Rule: **Critical Value** **Approach**	Reject H_0 if $t \leq -t_\alpha$	Reject H_0 if $t \geq t_\alpha$	Reject H_0 if $t \leq -t_{\alpha/2}$ or if $t \geq t_{\alpha/2}$

results for any sample size. When the population is not normally distributed, the procedures are approximations. Nonetheless, we find that sample sizes of 30 or greater will provide good results in most cases. If the population is approximately normal, small sample sizes (e.g., $n < 15$) can provide acceptable results. If the population is highly skewed or contains outliers, sample sizes approaching 50 are recommended.

Exercises

Methods

23. Consider the following hypothesis test:

$$H_0: \mu \le 12$$
$$H_a: \mu > 12$$

A sample of 25 provided a sample mean $\bar{x} = 14$ and a sample standard deviation $s = 4.32$.
  a. Compute the value of the test statistic.
  b. Use the t distribution table (Table 2 in Appendix B) to compute a range for the p-value.
  c. At $\alpha = .05$, what is your conclusion?
  d. What is the rejection rule using the critical value? What is your conclusion?

24. Consider the following hypothesis test:

$$H_0: \mu = 18$$
$$H_a: \mu \ne 18$$

A sample of 48 provided a sample mean $\bar{x} = 17$ and a sample standard deviation $s = 4.5$.
  a. Compute the value of the test statistic.
  b. Use the t distribution table (Table 2 in Appendix B) to compute a range for the p-value.
  c. At $\alpha = .05$, what is your conclusion?
  d. What is the rejection rule using the critical value? What is your conclusion?

25. Consider the following hypothesis test:

$$H_0: \mu \ge 45$$
$$H_a: \mu < 45$$

A sample of 36 is used. Identify the p-value and state your conclusion for each of the following sample results. Use $\alpha = .01$.
  a. $\bar{x} = 44$ and $s = 5.2$
  b. $\bar{x} = 43$ and $s = 4.6$
  c. $\bar{x} = 46$ and $s = 5.0$

26. Consider the following hypothesis test:

$$H_0: \mu = 100$$
$$H_a: \mu \ne 100$$

A sample of 65 is used. Identify the p-value and state your conclusion for each of the following sample results. Use $\alpha = .05$.
  a. $\bar{x} = 103$ and $s = 11.5$
  b. $\bar{x} = 96.5$ and $s = 11.0$
  c. $\bar{x} = 102$ and $s = 10.5$

Applications

27. The Employment and Training Administration reported the U.S. mean unemployment insurance benefit of $238 per week (*The World Almanac,* 2003). A researcher in the state of Virginia anticipated that sample data would show evidence that the mean weekly unemployment insurance benefit in Virginia was below the national level.
    a. Develop appropriate hypotheses such that rejection of H_0 will support the researcher's contention.
    b. For a sample of 100 individuals, the sample mean weekly unemployment insurance benefit was $231 with a sample standard deviation of $80. What is the *p*-value?
    c. At $\alpha = .05$, what is your conclusion?
    d. Repeat the preceding hypothesis test using the critical value approach.

28. A shareholders' group, in lodging a protest, claimed that the mean tenure for a chief executive officer (CEO) was at least nine years. A survey of companies reported in *The Wall Street Journal* found a sample mean tenure of $\bar{x} = 7.27$ years for CEOs with a standard deviation of $s = 6.38$ years (*The Wall Street Journal,* January 2, 2007).
    a. Formulate hypotheses that can be used to test the validity of the claim made by the shareholders' group.
    b. Assume 85 companies were included in the sample. What is the *p*-value for your hypothesis test?
    c. At $\alpha = .01$, what is your conclusion?

Diamonds

29. The cost of a one-carat VS2 clarity, H color diamond from Diamond Source USA is $5600 (*http://www.diasource.com,* March 2003). A midwestern jeweler makes calls to contacts in the diamond district of New York City to see whether the mean price of diamonds there differs from $5600.
    a. Formulate hypotheses that can be used to determine whether the mean price in New York City differs from $5600.
    b. A sample of 25 New York City contacts provided the prices shown in the website file named Diamonds. What is the *p*-value?
    c. At $\alpha = .05$, can the null hypothesis be rejected? What is your conclusion?
    d. Repeat the preceding hypothesis test using the critical value approach.

30. AOL Time Warner Inc.'s CNN has been the longtime ratings leader of cable television news. Nielsen Media Research indicated that the mean CNN viewing audience was 600,000 viewers per day during 2002 (*The Wall Street Journal,* March 10, 2003). Assume that for a sample of 40 days during the first half of 2003, the daily audience was 612,000 viewers with a sample standard deviation of 65,000 viewers.
    a. What are the hypotheses if CNN management would like information on any change in the CNN viewing audience?
    b. What is the *p*-value?
    c. Select your own level of significance. What is your conclusion?
    d. What recommendation would you make to CNN management in this application?

31. Raftelis Financial Consulting reported that the mean quarterly water bill in the United States is $47.50 (*U.S. News & World Report,* August 12, 2002). Some water systems are operated by public utilities, whereas other water systems are operated by private companies. An economist pointed out that privatization does not equal competition and that monopoly powers provided to public utilities are now being transferred to private companies. The concern is that consumers end up paying higher-than-average rates for water provided by private companies. The water system for Atlanta, Georgia, is provided by a private company. A sample of 64 Atlanta consumers showed a mean quarterly water bill of $51 with a sample standard deviation of $12. At $\alpha = .05$, does the Atlanta sample support the conclusion that above-average rates exist for this private water system? What is your conclusion?

UsedCars

32. According to the National Automobile Dealers Association, the mean price for used cars is $10,192. A manager of a Kansas City used car dealership reviewed a sample of 50 recent used car sales at the dealership in an attempt to determine whether the population

mean price for used cars at this particular dealership differed from the national mean. The prices for the sample of 50 cars are shown in the website file named UsedCars.

    a. Formulate the hypotheses that can be used to determine whether a difference exists in the mean price for used cars at the dealership.

    b. What is the p-value?

    c. At $\alpha = .05$, what is your conclusion?

33. Annual per capita consumption of milk is 21.6 gallons (*Statistical Abstract of the United States: 2006*). Being from the Midwest, you believe milk consumption is higher there and wish to support your opinion. A sample of 16 individuals from the midwestern town of Webster City showed a sample mean annual consumption of 24.1 gallons with a standard deviation of $s = 4.8$.

    a. Develop a hypothesis test that can be used to determine whether the mean annual consumption in Webster City is higher than the national mean.

    b. What is a point estimate of the difference between mean annual consumption in Webster City and the national mean?

    c. At $\alpha = .05$, test for a significant difference. What is your conclusion?

34. Joan's Nursery specializes in custom-designed landscaping for residential areas. The estimated labor cost associated with a particular landscaping proposal is based on the number of plantings of trees, shrubs, and so on to be used for the project. For cost-estimating purposes, managers use two hours of labor time for the planting of a medium-sized tree. Actual times from a sample of 10 plantings during the past month follow (times in hours).

1.7	1.5	2.6	2.2	2.4	2.3	2.6	3.0	1.4	2.3

With a .05 level of significance, test to see whether the mean tree-planting time differs from two hours.

    a. State the null and alternative hypotheses.

    b. Compute the sample mean.

    c. Compute the sample standard deviation.

    d. What is the p-value?

    e. What is your conclusion?

9.5 Population Proportion

In this section we show how to conduct a hypothesis test about a population proportion p. Using p_0 to denote the hypothesized value for the population proportion, the three forms for a hypothesis test about a population proportion are as follows.

$$H_0: p \geq p_0 \qquad H_0: p \leq p_0 \qquad H_0: p = p_0$$
$$H_a: p < p_0 \qquad H_a: p > p_0 \qquad H_a: p \neq p_0$$

The first form is called a lower tail test, the second form is called an upper tail test, and the third form is called a two-tailed test.

    Hypothesis tests about a population proportion are based on the difference between the sample proportion $\bar{p}$ and the hypothesized population proportion p_0. The methods used to conduct the hypothesis test are similar to those used for hypothesis tests about a population mean. The only difference is that we use the sample proportion and its standard error to compute the test statistic. The p-value approach or the critical value approach is then used to determine whether the null hypothesis should be rejected.

    Let us consider an example involving a situation faced by Pine Creek golf course. Over the past year, 20% of the players at Pine Creek were women. In an effort to increase the proportion of women players, Pine Creek implemented a special promotion designed to attract women golfers. One month after the promotion was implemented, the course manager requested a statistical study to determine whether the proportion of women players at Pine Creek had increased. Because the objective of the study is to determine whether the proportion of women golfers increased, an upper tail test with H_a: $p > .20$ is appropriate. The null and alternative hypotheses for the Pine Creek hypothesis test are as follows:

$$H_0: p \leq .20$$
$$H_a: p > .20$$

If H_0 can be rejected, the test results will give statistical support for the conclusion that the proportion of women golfers increased and the promotion was beneficial. The course manager specified that a level of significance of $\alpha = .05$ be used in carrying out this hypothesis test.

The next step of the hypothesis testing procedure is to select a sample and compute the value of an appropriate test statistic. To show how this step is done for the Pine Creek upper tail test, we begin with a general discussion of how to compute the value of the test statistic for any form of a hypothesis test about a population proportion. The sampling distribution of $\bar{p}$, the point estimator of the population parameter p, is the basis for developing the test statistic.

When the null hypothesis is true as an equality, the expected value of $\bar{p}$ equals the hypothesized value p_0; that is, $E(\bar{p}) = p_0$. The standard error of $\bar{p}$ is given by

$$\sigma_{\bar{p}} = \sqrt{\frac{p_0(1 - p_0)}{n}}$$

In Chapter 7 we said that if $np \geq 5$ and $n(1 - p) \geq 5$, the sampling distribution of $\bar{p}$ can be approximated by a normal distribution.[4] Under these conditions, which usually apply in practice, the quantity

$$z = \frac{\bar{p} - p_0}{\sigma_{\bar{p}}} \tag{9.3}$$

has a standard normal probability distribution. With $\sigma_{\bar{p}} = \sqrt{p_0(1 - p_0)/n}$, the standard normal random variable z is the test statistic used to conduct hypothesis tests about a population proportion.

TEST STATISTIC FOR HYPOTHESIS TESTS ABOUT A POPULATION PROPORTION

$$z = \frac{\bar{p} - p_0}{\sqrt{\dfrac{p_0(1 - p_0)}{n}}} \tag{9.4}$$

WEB file
WomenGolf

We can now compute the test statistic for the Pine Creek hypothesis test. Suppose a random sample of 400 players was selected, and that 100 of the players were women. The proportion of women golfers in the sample is

$$\bar{p} = \frac{100}{400} = .25$$

Using equation (9.4), the value of the test statistic is

$$z = \frac{\bar{p} - p_0}{\sqrt{\dfrac{p_0(1 - p_0)}{n}}} = \frac{.25 - .20}{\sqrt{\dfrac{.20(1 - .20)}{400}}} = \frac{.05}{.02} = 2.50$$

---

[4]In most applications involving hypothesis tests of a population proportion, sample sizes are large enough to use the normal approximation. The exact sampling distribution of $\bar{p}$ is discrete with the probability for each value of $\bar{p}$ given by the binomial distribution. So hypothesis testing is a bit more complicated for small samples when the normal approximation cannot be used.

FIGURE 9.9   CALCULATION OF THE *p*-VALUE FOR THE PINE CREEK HYPOTHESIS TEST

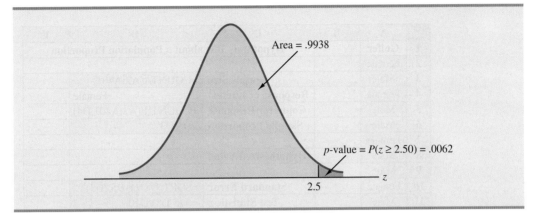

Because the Pine Creek hypothesis test is an upper tail test, the *p*-value is the probability that *z* is greater than or equal to *z* = 2.50; that is, it is the area under the standard normal curve to the right of *z* = 2.50. Using the standard normal probability table, we find that the area to the left of *z* = 2.50 is .9938. Thus, the *p*-value for the Pine Creek test is 1.0000 − .9938 = .0062. Figure 9.9 shows this *p*-value calculation.

Recall that the course manager specified a level of significance of α = .05. A *p*-value = .0062 < .05 gives sufficient statistical evidence to reject H_0 at the .05 level of significance. Thus, the test provides statistical support for the conclusion that the special promotion increased the proportion of women players at the Pine Creek golf course.

The decision whether to reject the null hypothesis can also be made using the critical value approach. The critical value corresponding to an area of .05 in the upper tail of a normal probability distribution is $z_{.05}$ = 1.645. Thus, the rejection rule using the critical value approach is to reject H_0 if *z* ≥ 1.645. Because *z* = 2.50 > 1.645, H_0 is rejected.

Again, we see that the *p*-value approach and the critical value approach lead to the same hypothesis testing conclusion, but the *p*-value approach provides more information. With a *p*-value = .0062, the null hypothesis would be rejected for any level of significance greater than or equal to .0062.

Using Excel

Excel can be used to conduct one-tailed and two-tailed hypothesis tests about a population proportion using the *p*-value approach. The procedure is similar to the approach used with Excel in conducting hypothesis tests about a population mean. The primary difference is that the test statistic is based on the sampling distribution of $\bar{x}$ for hypothesis tests about a population mean and on the sampling distribution of $\bar{p}$ for hypothesis tests about a population proportion. Thus, although different formulas are used to compute the test statistic needed to make the hypothesis testing decision, the computations of the critical value and the *p*-value for the tests are identical.

We will illustrate the procedure by showing how Excel can be used to conduct the upper tail hypothesis test for the Pine Creek golf course study. Refer to Figure 9.10 as we describe the tasks involved. The formula worksheet is in the background; the value worksheet is in the foreground.

Enter Data: A label and the gender of each golfer in the study are entered into cells A1:A401.

Enter Functions and Formulas: The descriptive statistics needed are provided in cells D3, D5, and D6. Because the data are not numeric, Excel's COUNTA function, not the COUNT function, is used in cell D3 to determine the sample size. We entered Female in cell D4 to identify the response for which we wish to compute a proportion. The COUNTIF

FIGURE 9.10 EXCEL WORKSHEET: HYPOTHESIS TEST FOR PINE CREEK GOLF COURSE

	A	B	C	D	E
1	Golfer		**Hypothesis Test about a Population Proportion**		
2	Female				
3	Male		Sample Size	=COUNTA(A2:A401)	
4	Female		Response of Interest	Female	
5	Male		Count for Response	=COUNTIF(A2:A401,D4)	
6	Male		Sample Proportion	=D5/D3	
7	Female				
8	Male		Hypothesized Value	0.2	
9	Male				
10	Female		Standard Error	=SQRT(D8*(1-D8)/D3)	
11	Male		Test Statistic z	=(D6-D8)/D10	
12	Male				
13	Male		*p*-value (Lower Tail)	=NORMSDIST(D11)	
14	Male		*p*-value (Upper Tail)	=1-D13	
15	Male		*p*-value (Two Tail)	=2*MIN(D13,D14)	
16	Female				
400	Male				
401	Male				
402					

WEB file

WomenGolf

	A	B	C	D	E	F
1	Golfer		**Hypothesis Test about a Population Proportion**			
2	Female					
3	Male		Sample Size	400		
4	Female		Response of Interest	Female		
5	Male		Count for Response	100		
6	Male		Sample Proportion	0.25		
7	Female					
8	Male		Hypothesized Value	0.20		
9	Male					
10	Female		Standard Error	0.02		
11	Male		Test Statistic z	2.5000		
12	Male					
13	Male		*p*-value (Lower Tail)	0.9938		
14	Male		*p*-value (Upper Tail)	0.0062		
15	Male		*p*-value (Two Tail)	0.0124		
16	Female					
400	Male					
401	Male					
402						

Note: Rows 17–399 are hidden.

function is then used in cell D5 to determine the number of responses of the type identified in cell D4. The sample proportion is then computed in cell D6 by dividing the response count by the sample size.

The hypothesized value of the population proportion (.20) is entered into cell D8. The standard error is obtained in cell D10 by entering the formula =SQRT(D8*(1-D8)/D3). The formula =(D6-D8)/D10 entered into cell D11 computes the test statistic z (2.50). To compute the *p*-value for a lower tail test, we enter the formula =NORMSDIST(D11) into cell D13. The *p*-value for an upper tail test is then computed in cell D14 as 1 minus the *p*-value for the lower tail test. Finally, the *p*-value for a two-tailed test is computed in cell D15 as two times the minimum of the two one-tailed *p*-values. The value worksheet shows that the three *p*-values are as follows: *p*-value (Lower Tail) = 0.9938; *p*-value (Upper Tail) = 0.0062; and *p*-value (Two Tail) = 0.0124.

TABLE 9.4   SUMMARY OF HYPOTHESIS TESTS ABOUT A POPULATION PROPORTION

	Lower Tail Test	**Upper Tail Test**	**Two-Tailed Test**
Hypotheses	$H_0\colon p \geq p_0$ $H_a\colon p < p_0$	$H_0\colon p \leq p_0$ $H_a\colon p > p_0$	$H_0\colon p = p_0$ $H_a\colon p \neq p_0$
Test Statistic	$z = \dfrac{\bar{p} - p_0}{\sqrt{\dfrac{p_0(1 - p_0)}{n}}}$	$z = \dfrac{\bar{p} - p_0}{\sqrt{\dfrac{p_0(1 - p_0)}{n}}}$	$z = \dfrac{\bar{p} - p_0}{\sqrt{\dfrac{p_0(1 - p_0)}{n}}}$
Rejection Rule: **p-Value Approach**	Reject H_0 if p-value $\leq \alpha$	Reject H_0 if p-value $\leq \alpha$	Reject H_0 if p-value $\leq \alpha$
Rejection Rule: **Critical Value** **Approach**	Reject H_0 if $z \leq -z_\alpha$	Reject H_0 if $z \geq z_\alpha$	Reject H_0 if $z \leq -z_{\alpha/2}$ or if $z \geq z_{\alpha/2}$

The development of the worksheet is now complete. For the Pine Creek upper tail hypothesis test we reject the null hypothesis that the population proportion is .20 or less because the p-value (Upper Tail) = 0.0062 is less than $\alpha = .05$. Indeed, with this p-value we would reject the hull hypothesis for any level of significance of .0062 or greater.

A template for other problems   The worksheet in Figure 9.10 can be used as a template for hypothesis tests about a population proportion whenever $np \geq 5$ and $n(1 - p) \geq 5$. Just enter the appropriate data in column A, adjust the ranges for the formulas in cells D3 and D5, enter the appropriate response in cell D4, and enter the hypothesized value in cell D8. The standard error, the test statistic, and the three p-values will then appear. Depending on the form of the hypothesis test (lower tail, upper tail, or two-tailed), we can then choose the appropriate p-value to make the rejection decision.

Summary

The procedure used to conduct a hypothesis test about a population proportion is similar to the procedure used to conduct a hypothesis test about a population mean. Although we only illustrated how to conduct a hypothesis test about a population proportion for an upper tail test, similar procedures can be used for lower tail and two-tailed tests. Table 9.4 provides a summary of the hypothesis tests about a population proportion. We assume that $np \geq 5$ and $n(1 - p) \geq 5$; thus the normal probability distribution can be used to approximate the sampling distribution of $\bar{p}$.

Exercises

Methods

35. Consider the following hypothesis test:

$$H_0\colon p = .20$$
$$H_a\colon p \neq .20$$

A sample of 400 provided a sample proportion $\bar{p} = .175$.
a. Compute the value of the test statistic.
b. What is the p-value?
c. At $\alpha = .05$, what is your conclusion?
d. What is the rejection rule using the critical value? What is your conclusion?

36. Consider the following hypothesis test:

$$H_0: p \geq .75$$
$$H_a: p < .75$$

A sample of 300 items was selected. Compute the p-value and state your conclusion for each of the following sample results. Use $\alpha = .05$.

a. $\bar{p} = .68$ c. $\bar{p} = .70$

b. $\bar{p} = .72$ d. $\bar{p} = .77$

Applications

37. A study found that, in 2005, 12.5% of U.S. workers belonged to unions (*The Wall Street Journal,* January 21, 2006). Suppose a sample of 400 U.S. workers is collected in 2006 to determine whether union efforts to organize have increased union membership.
    a. Formulate the hypotheses that can be used to determine whether union membership increased in 2006.
    b. If the sample results show that 52 of the workers belonged to unions, what is the p-value for your hypothesis test?
    c. At $\alpha = .05$, what is your conclusion?

38. A study by *Consumer Reports* showed that 64% of supermarket shoppers believe supermarket brands to be as good as national name brands. To investigate whether this result applies to its own product, the manufacturer of a national name-brand ketchup asked a sample of shoppers whether they believed that supermarket ketchup was as good as the national brand ketchup.
    a. Formulate the hypotheses that could be used to determine whether the percentage of supermarket shoppers who believe that the supermarket ketchup was as good as the national brand ketchup differed from 64%.
    b. If a sample of 100 shoppers showed 52 stating that the supermarket brand was as good as the national brand, what is the p-value?
    c. At $\alpha = .05$, what is your conclusion?
    d. Should the national brand ketchup manufacturer be pleased with this conclusion? Explain.

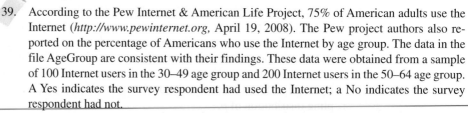

39. According to the Pew Internet & American Life Project, 75% of American adults use the Internet (*http://www.pewinternet.org,* April 19, 2008). The Pew project authors also reported on the percentage of Americans who use the Internet by age group. The data in the file AgeGroup are consistent with their findings. These data were obtained from a sample of 100 Internet users in the 30–49 age group and 200 Internet users in the 50–64 age group. A Yes indicates the survey respondent had used the Internet; a No indicates the survey respondent had not.
    a. Formulate hypotheses that could be used to determine whether the percentage of Internet users in the two age groups differs from the overall average of 75%.
    b. Estimate the proportion of Internet users in the 30–49 age group. Does this proportion differ significantly from the overall proportion of .75? Use $\alpha = .05$.
    c. Estimate the proportion of Internet users in the 50–64 age group. Does this proportion differ significantly from the overall proportion of .75? Use $\alpha = .05$.
    d. Would you expect the proportion of users in the 18–29 age group to be larger or smaller than the proportion for the 30–49 age group? Support your conclusion with the results obtained in parts (b) and (c).

40. Before the 2003 Super Bowl, ABC predicted that 22% of the Super Bowl audience would express an interest in seeing one of its forthcoming new television shows, including *8 Simple Rules, Are You Hot?,* and *Dragnet.* ABC ran commercials for these television shows during the Super Bowl. The day after the Super Bowl, Intermediate Advertising Group of New York sampled 1532 viewers who saw the commercials and found that 414 said that they

would watch one of the ABC advertised television shows (*The Wall Street Journal,* January 30, 2003).

   a.   What is the point estimate of the proportion of the audience that said they would watch the television shows after seeing the television commercials?

   b.   At $\alpha = .05$, determine whether the intent to watch the ABC television shows significantly increased after seeing the television commercials. Formulate the appropriate hypotheses, compute the *p*-value, and state your conclusion.

   c.   Why are such studies valuable to companies and advertising firms?

41.   Speaking to a group of analysts in January 2006, a brokerage firm executive claimed that at least 70% of investors are currently confident of meeting their investment objectives. A UBS Investor Optimism Survey, conducted over the period January 2 to January 15, found that 67% of investors were confident of meeting their investment objectives (CNBC, January 20, 2006).

   a.   Formulate the hypotheses that can be used to test the validity of the brokerage firm executive's claim.

   b.   Assume the UBS Investor Optimism Survey collected information from 300 investors. What is the *p*-value for the hypothesis test?

   c.   At $\alpha = .05$, should the executive's claim be rejected?

42.   According to the University of Nevada Center for Logistics Management, 6% of all merchandise sold in the United States gets returned (*BusinessWeek,* January 15, 2007). A Houston department store sampled 80 items sold in January and found that 12 of the items were returned.

   a.   Construct a point estimate of the proportion of items returned for the population of sales transactions at the Houston store.

   b.   Construct a 95% confidence interval for the proportion of returns at the Houston store.

   c.   Is the proportion of returns at the Houston store significantly different from the returns for the nation as a whole? Provide statistical support for your answer.

WEB file

Eagle

43.   Eagle Outfitters is a chain of stores specializing in outdoor apparel and camping gear. They are considering a promotion that involves mailing discount coupons to all their credit card customers. This promotion will be considered a success if more than 10% of those receiving the coupons use them. Before going national with the promotion, coupons were sent to a sample of 100 credit card customers.

   a.   Develop hypotheses that can be used to test whether the population proportion of those who will use the coupons is sufficient to go national.

   b.   The file Eagle contains the sample data. Develop a point estimate of the population proportion.

   c.   Use $\alpha = .05$ to conduct your hypothesis test. Should Eagle go national with the promotion?

WEB file

Drowsy

44.   In a cover story, *BusinessWeek* published information about sleep habits of Americans (*BusinessWeek,* January 26, 2004). The article noted that sleep deprivation causes a number of problems, including highway deaths. Fifty-one percent of adult drivers admit to driving while drowsy. A researcher hypothesized that this issue was an even bigger problem for night-shift workers.

   a.   Formulate the hypotheses that can be used to help determine whether more than 51% of the population of night-shift workers admit to driving while drowsy.

   b.   A sample of 500 night-shift workers identified those who admitted to driving while drowsy. What is the sample proportion? What is the *p*-value?

   c.   At $\alpha = .01$, what is your conclusion?

45.   Many investors and financial analysts believe the Dow Jones Industrial Average (DJIA) provides a good barometer of the overall stock market. On January 31, 2006, 9 of the 30 stocks making up the DJIA increased in price (*The Wall Street Journal,* February 1, 2006). On the basis of this fact, a financial analyst claims we can assume that 30% of the stocks traded on the New York Stock Exchange (NYSE) went up the same day.

   a.   Formulate null and alternative hypotheses to test the analyst's claim.

b. A sample of 50 stocks traded on the NYSE that day showed that 24 went up. What is your point estimate of the population proportion of stocks that went up?
c. Conduct your hypothesis test using $\alpha = .01$ as the level of significance. What is your conclusion?

Summary

Hypothesis testing is a statistical procedure that uses sample data to determine whether a statement about the value of a population parameter should or should not be rejected. The hypotheses are two competing statements about a population parameter. One statement is called the null hypothesis (H_0), and the other statement is called the alternative hypothesis (H_a). In Section 9.1 we provided guidelines for developing hypotheses for three situations frequently encountered in practice.

Whenever historical data or other information provides a basis for assuming that the population standard deviation is known, the hypothesis testing procedure for the population mean is based on the standard normal distribution. Whenever σ is unknown, the sample standard deviation s is used to estimate σ and the hypothesis testing procedure is based on the t distribution. In both cases, the quality of results depends on both the form of the population distribution and the sample size. If the population has a normal distribution, both hypothesis testing procedures are applicable, even with small sample sizes. If the population is not normally distributed, larger sample sizes are needed. General guidelines about the sample size were provided in Sections 9.3 and 9.4. In the case of hypothesis tests about a population proportion, the hypothesis testing procedure uses a test statistic based on the standard normal distribution.

In all cases, the value of the test statistic can be used to compute a p-value for the test. A p-value is a probability used to determine whether the null hypothesis should be rejected. If the p-value is less than or equal to the level of significance α, the null hypothesis can be rejected.

Hypothesis testing conclusions can also be made by comparing the value of the test statistic to a critical value. For lower tail tests, the null hypothesis is rejected if the value of the test statistic is less than or equal to the critical value. For upper tail tests, the null hypothesis is rejected if the value of the test statistic is greater than or equal to the critical value. Two-tailed tests consist of two critical values: one in the lower tail of the sampling distribution and one in the upper tail. In this case, the null hypothesis is rejected if the value of the test statistic is less than or equal to the critical value in the lower tail or greater than or equal to the critical value in the upper tail.

Glossary

Null hypothesis The hypothesis tentatively assumed true in the hypothesis testing procedure.
Alternative hypothesis The hypothesis concluded to be true if the null hypothesis is rejected.
Type II error The error of accepting H_0 when it is false.
Type I error The error of rejecting H_0 when it is true.
Level of significance The probability of making a Type I error when the null hypothesis is true as an equality.
One-tailed test A hypothesis test in which rejection of the null hypothesis occurs for values of the test statistic in one tail of its sampling distribution.
Test statistic A statistic whose value helps determine whether a null hypothesis should be rejected.
p-value A probability that provides a measure of the evidence against the null hypothesis provided by the sample. Smaller p-values indicate more evidence against H_0. For a lower tail test, the p-value is the probability of obtaining a value for the test statistic as small as

or smaller than that provided by the sample. For an upper tail test, the *p*-value is the probability of obtaining a value for the test statistic as large as or larger than that provided by the sample. For a two-tailed test, the *p*-value is the probability of obtaining a value for the test statistic at least as unlikely as or more unlikely than that provided by the sample.

Critical value A value that is compared with the test statistic to determine whether H_0 should be rejected.

Two-tailed test A hypothesis test in which rejection of the null hypothesis occurs for values of the test statistic in either tail of its sampling distribution.

Key Formulas

Test Statistic for Hypothesis Tests About a Population Mean: σ Known

$$z = \frac{\bar{x} - \mu_0}{\sigma/\sqrt{n}} \tag{9.1}$$

Test Statistic for Hypothesis Tests About a Population Mean: σ Unknown

$$t = \frac{\bar{x} - \mu_0}{s/\sqrt{n}} \tag{9.2}$$

Test Statistic for Hypothesis Tests About a Population Proportion

$$z = \frac{\bar{p} - p_0}{\sqrt{\dfrac{p_0(1 - p_0)}{n}}} \tag{9.4}$$

Supplementary Exercises

46. A production line operates with a mean filling weight of 16 ounces per container. Overfilling or underfilling presents a serious problem and when detected requires the operator to shut down the production line to readjust the filling mechanism. From past data, a population standard deviation $\sigma = .8$ ounces is assumed. A quality control inspector selects a sample of 30 items every hour and at that time makes the decision of whether to shut down the line for readjustment. The level of significance is $\alpha = .05$.
    a. State the hypothesis test for this quality control application.
    b. If a sample mean of $\bar{x} = 16.32$ ounces were found, what is the *p*-value? What action would you recommend?
    c. If a sample mean of $\bar{x} = 15.82$ ounces were found, what is the *p*-value? What action would you recommend?
    d. Use the critical value approach. What is the rejection rule for the preceding hypothesis testing procedure? Repeat parts (b) and (c). Do you reach the same conclusion?

47. At Western University the historical mean of scholarship examination scores for freshman applications is 900. A historical population standard deviation $\sigma = 180$ is assumed known. Each year, the assistant dean uses a sample of applications to determine whether the mean examination score for the new freshman applications has changed.
    a. State the hypotheses.
    b. What is the 95% confidence interval estimate of the population mean examination score if a sample of 200 applications provided a sample mean of $\bar{x} = 935$?
    c. Use the confidence interval to conduct a hypothesis test. Using $\alpha = .05$, what is your conclusion?
    d. What is the *p*-value?

48. *Playbill* is a magazine distributed around the country to people attending musicals and other theatrical productions. The mean annual household income for the population of *Playbill* readers is $119,155 (*Playbill*, January 2006). Assume the standard deviation is $\sigma = \$20,700$. A San Francisco civic group has asserted that the mean for theater goers in

the Bay Area is higher. A sample of 60 theater attendees in the Bay Area showed a sample mean household income of $126,100.

a. Develop hypotheses that can be used to determine whether the sample data support the conclusion that theater attendees in the Bay Area have a higher mean household income than that for all *Playbill* readers.

b. What is the *p*-value based on the sample of 60 theater attendees in the Bay Area?

c. Use $\alpha = .01$ as the level of significance. What is your conclusion?

49. On Friday, Wall Street traders were anxiously awaiting the federal government's release of numbers on the January increase in nonfarm payrolls. The early consensus estimate among economists was for a growth of 250,000 new jobs (CNBC, February 3, 2006). However, a sample of 20 economists taken Thursday afternoon provided a sample mean of 266,000 with a sample standard deviation of 24,000. Financial analysts often call such a sample mean, based on late-breaking news, the *whisper number.* Treat the "consensus estimate" as the population mean. Conduct a hypothesis test to determine whether the whisper number justifies a conclusion of a statistically significant increase in the consensus estimate of economists. Use $\alpha = .01$ as the level of significance.

50. The College Board reported that the average number of freshman class applications to public colleges and universities is 6000 (*USA Today,* December 26, 2002). During a recent application/enrollment period, a sample of 32 colleges and universities showed that the sample mean number of freshman class applications was 5812 with a sample standard deviation of 1140. Do the data indicate a change in the mean number of applications? Use $\alpha = .05$.

51. An extensive study of the cost of health care in the United States presented data showing that the mean spending per Medicare enrollee in 2003 was $6883 (*Money,* Fall 2003). To investigate differences across the country, a researcher took a sample of 40 Medicare enrollees in Indianapolis. For the Indianapolis sample, the mean 2003 Medicare spending was $5980 and the standard deviation was $2518.

a. State the hypotheses that should be used if we would like to determine whether the mean annual Medicare spending in Indianapolis is lower than the national mean.

b. Use the preceding sample results to compute the test statistic and the *p*-value.

c. Use $\alpha = .05$. What is your conclusion?

d. Repeat the hypothesis test using the critical value approach.

52. The chamber of commerce of a Florida Gulf Coast community advertises that area residential property is available at a mean cost of $125,000 or less per lot. Suppose a sample of 32 properties provided a sample mean of $130,000 per lot and a sample standard deviation of $12,500. Use a .05 level of significance to test the validity of the advertising claim.

53. The U.S. Energy Administration reported that the mean price for a gallon of regular gasoline in the United States was $2.357 (U.S. Energy Administration, January 30, 2006). Data for a sample of regular gasoline prices at 50 service stations in the Lower Atlantic states are contained in the data file named Gasoline. Conduct a hypothesis test to determine whether the mean price for a gallon of gasoline in the Lower Atlantic states is different from the national mean. Use $\alpha = .05$ for the level of significance, and state your conclusion.

54. A study by the Centers for Disease Control (CDC) found that 23.3% of adults are smokers and that roughly 70% of those who do smoke indicate that they want to quit (Associated Press, July 26, 2002). CDC reported that, of people who smoked at some point in their lives, 50% have been able to kick the habit. Part of the study suggested that the success rate for quitting rose by education level. Assume that a sample of 100 college graduates who smoked at some point in their lives showed that 64 had been able to successfully stop smoking.

a. State the hypotheses that can be used to determine whether the population of college graduates has a success rate higher than the overall population when it comes to breaking the smoking habit.

b. Given the sample data, what is the proportion of college graduates who, having smoked at some point in their lives, were able to stop smoking?

c. What is the *p*-value? At $\alpha = .01$, what is your hypothesis testing conclusion?

55. An airline promotion to business travelers is based on the assumption that two-thirds of business travelers use a laptop computer on overnight business trips.
    a. State the hypotheses that can be used to test the assumption.
    b. What is the sample proportion from an American Express sponsored survey that found 355 of 546 business travelers use a laptop computer on overnight business trips?
    c. What is the p-value?
    d. Use $\alpha = .05$. What is your conclusion?

56. Virtual call centers are staffed by individuals working out of their homes. Most home agents earn $10 to $15 per hour without benefits versus $7 to $9 per hour with benefits at a traditional call center (*BusinessWeek,* January 23, 2006). Regional Airways is considering employing home agents, but only if a level of customer satisfaction greater than 80% can be maintained. A test was conducted with home service agents. In a sample of 300 customers, 252 reported that they were satisfied with service.
    a. Develop hypotheses for a test to determine whether the sample data support the conclusion that customer service with home agents meets the Regional Airways criterion.
    b. What is your point estimate of the percentage of satisfied customers?
    c. What is the p-value provided by the sample data?
    d. What is your hypothesis testing conclusion? Use $\alpha = .05$ as the level of significance.

57. During the 2004 election year, new polling results were reported daily. In an IBD/TIPP poll of 910 adults, 503 respondents reported that they were optimistic about the national outlook, and President Bush's leadership index jumped 4.7 points to 55.3 (*Investor's Business Daily,* January 14, 2004).
    a. What is the sample proportion of respondents who are optimistic about the national outlook?
    b. A campaign manager wants to claim that this poll indicates that the majority of adults are optimistic about the national outlook. Construct a hypothesis test so that rejection of the null hypothesis will permit the conclusion that the proportion optimistic is greater than 50%.
    c. Use the polling data to compute the p-value for the hypothesis test in part (b). Explain to the manager what this p-value means about the level of significance of the results.

58. A radio station in Myrtle Beach announced that at least 90% of the hotels and motels would be full for the Memorial Day weekend. The station advised listeners to make reservations in advance if they planned to be in the resort over the weekend. On Saturday night a sample of 58 hotels and motels showed 49 with a no-vacancy sign and 9 with vacancies. What is your reaction to the radio station's claim after seeing the sample evidence? Use $\alpha = .05$ in making the statistical test. What is the p-value?

59. According to the federal government, 24% of workers covered by their company's health care plan were not required to contribute to the premium (*Statistical Abstract of the United States: 2006*). A recent study found that 81 out of 400 workers sampled were not required to contribute to their company's health care plan.
    a. Develop hypotheses that can be used to test whether the percent of workers not required to contribute to their company's health care plan has declined.
    b. What is a point estimate of the proportion receiving free company-sponsored health care insurance?
    c. Has a statistically significant decline occurred in the proportion of workers receiving free company-sponsored health care insurance? Use $\alpha = .05$.

Case Problem 1   Quality Associates, Inc.

Quality Associates, Inc., a consulting firm, advises its clients about sampling and statistical procedures that can be used to control their manufacturing processes. In one particular application, a client gave Quality Associates a sample of 800 observations taken during a

time in which that client's process was operating satisfactorily. The sample standard deviation for these data was .21; hence, with so much data, the population standard deviation was assumed to be .21. Quality Associates then suggested that random samples of size 30 be taken periodically to monitor the process on an ongoing basis. By analyzing the new samples, the client could quickly learn whether the process was operating satisfactorily. When the process was not operating satisfactorily, corrective action could be taken to eliminate the problem. The design specification indicated the mean for the process should be 12. The hypothesis test suggested by Quality Associates follows.

$$H_0: \mu = 12$$
$$H_a: \mu \neq 12$$

Corrective action will be taken any time H_0 is rejected.

The samples below were collected at hourly intervals during the first day of operation of the new statistical process control procedure. These data are available in the data set Quality.

Managerial Report

1. Conduct a hypothesis test for each sample at the .01 level of significance and determine what action, if any, should be taken. Provide the test statistic and p-value for each test.

Quality

Sample 1	Sample 2	Sample 3	Sample 4
11.55	11.62	11.91	12.02
11.62	11.69	11.36	12.02
11.52	11.59	11.75	12.05
11.75	11.82	11.95	12.18
11.90	11.97	12.14	12.11
11.64	11.71	11.72	12.07
11.80	11.87	11.61	12.05
12.03	12.10	11.85	11.64
11.94	12.01	12.16	12.39
11.92	11.99	11.91	11.65
12.13	12.20	12.12	12.11
12.09	12.16	11.61	11.90
11.93	12.00	12.21	12.22
12.21	12.28	11.56	11.88
12.32	12.39	11.95	12.03
11.93	12.00	12.01	12.35
11.85	11.92	12.06	12.09
11.76	11.83	11.76	11.77
12.16	12.23	11.82	12.20
11.77	11.84	12.12	11.79
12.00	12.07	11.60	12.30
12.04	12.11	11.95	12.27
11.98	12.05	11.96	12.29
12.30	12.37	12.22	12.47
12.18	12.25	11.75	12.03
11.97	12.04	11.96	12.17
12.17	12.24	11.95	11.94
11.85	11.92	11.89	11.97
12.30	12.37	11.88	12.23
12.15	12.22	11.93	12.25

2. Compute the standard deviation for each of the four samples. Does the assumption of .21 for the population standard deviation appear reasonable?
3. Compute limits for the sample mean $\bar{x}$ around $\mu = 12$ such that, as long as a new sample mean is within those limits, the process will be considered to be operating satisfactorily. If $\bar{x}$ exceeds the upper limit or if $\bar{x}$ is below the lower limit, corrective action will be taken. These limits are referred to as upper and lower control limits for quality control purposes.
4. Discuss the implications of changing the level of significance to a larger value. What mistake or error could increase if the level of significance is increased?

Case Problem 2   Unemployment Study

Each month the U.S. Bureau of Labor Statistics publishes a variety of unemployment statistics, including the number of individuals who are unemployed and the mean length of time the individuals have been unemployed. For November 1998, the Bureau of Labor Statistics reported that the national mean length of time of unemployment was 14.6 weeks.

The mayor of Philadelphia requested a study on the status of unemployment in the Philadelphia area. A sample of 50 unemployed residents of Philadelphia included data on their age and the number of weeks without a job. A portion of the data collected in November 1998 follows. The complete data set is available in the data file BLS.

WEB file

BLS

Age	Weeks	Age	Weeks	Age	Weeks
56	22	22	11	25	12
35	19	48	6	25	1
22	7	48	22	59	33
57	37	25	5	49	26
40	18	40	20	33	13

Managerial Report

1. Use descriptive statistics to summarize the data.
2. Develop a 95% confidence interval estimate of the mean age of unemployed individuals in Philadelphia.
3. Conduct a hypothesis test to determine whether the mean duration of unemployment in Philadelphia is greater than the national mean duration of 14.6 weeks. Use a .01 level of significance. What is your conclusion?
4. Is there a relationship between the age of an unemployed individual and the number of weeks of unemployment? Explain.

Appendix   Hypothesis Testing with StatTools

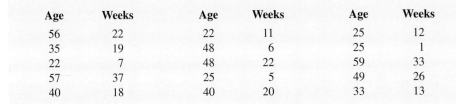

In this appendix we show how StatTools can be used to conduct hypothesis tests about a population mean for the σ unknown case

Population Mean: σ Unknown Case

WEB file

AirRating

In this case the population standard deviation σ will be estimated by the sample standard deviation s. We use the example discussed in Section 9.4 involving ratings that 60 business travelers gave for Heathrow Airport.

Begin by using the Data Set Manager to create a StatTools data set for these data using the procedure described in the appendix in Chapter 1. The following steps can be used to test the hypothesis $H_0: \mu \leq 7$ against $H_a: \mu > 7$.

Step 1. Click the **StatTools** tab on the Ribbon

Step 2. In the **Analyses** group, click **Statistical Inference**

Step 3. Choose the **Hypothesis Test** option

Step 4. When the StatTools—Hypothesis Test dialog box appears,

        For **Analysis Type,** choose **One-Sample Analysis**

        In the **Variables** section, select **Rating**

        In the **Hypothesis Tests to Perform** section,

          Select the **Mean** option

          Enter 7 in the **Null Hypothesis Value** box

          Select **Greater Than Null Value (One-Tailed Test)** in the **Alternative Hypothesis** box

        If selected, remove the check in the **Standard Deviation** box

        Click **OK**

The results from the hypothesis test will appear. They include the *p*-value and the value of the test statistic.

Comparisons Involving Means, Experimental Design, and Analysis of Variance

CONTENTS

U.S. FOOD AND DRUG ADMINISTRATION
WASHINGTON, D.C.

It is the responsibility of the U.S. Food and Drug Administration (FDA), through its Center for Drug Evaluation and Research (CDER), to ensure that drugs are safe and effective. But CDER does not do the actual testing of new drugs itself. It is the responsibility of the company seeking to market a new drug to test it and submit evidence that it is safe and effective. CDER statisticians and scientists then review the evidence submitted.

Companies seeking approval of a new drug conduct extensive statistical studies to support their application. The testing process in the pharmaceutical industry usually consists of three stages: (1) preclinical testing, (2) testing for long-term usage and safety, and (3) clinical efficacy testing. At each successive stage, the chance that a drug will pass the rigorous tests decreases; however, the cost of further testing increases dramatically. Industry surveys indicate that on average the research and development for one new drug costs $250 million and takes 12 years. Hence, it is important to eliminate unsuccessful new drugs in the early stages of the testing process, as well as to identify promising ones for further testing.

Statistics plays a major role in pharmaceutical research, where government regulations are stringent and rigorously enforced. In preclinical testing, a two- or three-population statistical study typically is used to determine whether a new drug should continue to be studied in the long-term usage and safety program. The populations may consist of the new drug, a control, and a standard drug. The preclinical testing process begins when a new drug is sent to the pharmacology group for evaluation of efficacy—the capacity of the drug to produce the desired effects. As part of the process, a statistician is asked to design an experiment that can be used to test the new drug. The design must specify the sample size and the statistical methods of analysis. In a two-population study, one sample is used to obtain data on the efficacy of the new drug (population 1) and a second sample is used to obtain data on the efficacy of a standard drug (population 2). Depending on the intended use, the new and standard drugs are tested in such disciplines as neurology, cardiology, and immunology. In most studies, the statistical method involves hypothesis testing for the difference between the means of the new drug population

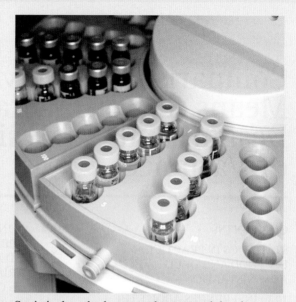

Statistical methods are used to test and develop new drugs. © Paxton/Workbook Stock/Jupiter Images.

and the standard drug population. If a new drug lacks efficacy or produces undesirable effects in comparison with the standard drug, the new drug is rejected and withdrawn from further testing. Only new drugs that show promising comparisons with the standard drugs are forwarded to the long-term usage and safety testing program.

Further data collection and multipopulation studies are conducted in the long-term usage and safety testing program and in the clinical testing programs. The FDA requires that statistical methods be defined prior to such testing to avoid data-related biases. In addition, to avoid human biases, some of the clinical trials are double or triple blind. That is, neither the subject nor the investigator knows what drug is administered to whom. If the new drug meets all requirements in relation to the standard drug, a new drug application (NDA) is filed with the FDA. The application is rigorously scrutinized by statisticians and scientists at the agency.

In this chapter you will learn how to construct interval estimates and make hypothesis tests about means with two or more populations. Techniques will be presented for analyzing independent random samples as well as matched samples.

In Chapters 8 and 9 we showed how to develop interval estimates and conduct hypothesis tests for situations involving a single population mean and a single population proportion. In Sections 10.1–10.3 we continue our discussion of statistical inference by showing how interval estimates and hypothesis tests can be developed for situations involving two populations, when the difference between the two population means is of prime importance. For example, we may want to develop an interval estimate of the difference between the mean starting salary for a population of men and the mean starting salary for a population of women or conduct a hypothesis test to determine whether any difference is present between the two population means.

In Section 10.4 we introduce the basic principles of an experimental study and show how they are used in a completely randomized design. We also provide a conceptual overview of the statistical procedure called analysis of variance (ANOVA). In Section 10.5 we show how ANOVA can be used to test for the equality of k population means using data obtained from a completely randomized design as well as data obtained from an observational study. So, in this sense, ANOVA extends the statistical material in Sections 10.1–10.3 from two population means to three or more population means.

We begin our discussion of statistical inference about two populations by showing how to develop interval estimates and conduct hypothesis tests about the difference between the means of two populations when the standard deviations of the two populations are assumed known.

(10.1) Inferences About the Difference Between Two Population Means: σ_1 and σ_2 Known

Letting μ_1 denote the mean of population 1 and μ_2 denote the mean of population 2, we will focus on inferences about the difference between the means: $\mu_1 - \mu_2$. To make an inference about this difference, we select a simple random sample of n_1 elements from population 1 and a second simple random sample of n_2 elements from population 2. The two samples, taken separately and independently, are referred to as **independent simple random samples**. In this section, we assume that information is available such that the two population standard deviations, σ_1 and σ_2, can be assumed known prior to collecting the samples. We refer to this situation as the σ_1 and σ_2 known case. In the following example we show how to compute a margin of error and develop an interval estimate of the difference between the two population means when σ_1 and σ_2 are known.

Interval Estimation of $\mu_1 - \mu_2$

HomeStyle sells furniture at two stores: one is located in the inner city and the other is located in a suburban shopping center. The regional manager noticed that products that sell well in one store do not always sell well in the other. The manager believes this situation may be attributable to differences in customer demographics at the two locations. Customers may differ in age, education, income, and so on. Suppose the manager asks us to investigate the difference between the mean ages of the customers who shop at the two stores.

Let us define population 1 as all customers who shop at the inner-city store and population 2 as all customers who shop at the suburban store.

μ_1 = mean of population 1 (i.e., the mean age of all customers who shop at the inner-city store)

μ_2 = mean of population 2 (i.e., the mean age of all customers who shop at the suburban store)

The difference between the two population means is $\mu_1 - \mu_2$.

FIGURE 10.1   ESTIMATING THE DIFFERENCE BETWEEN TWO POPULATION MEANS

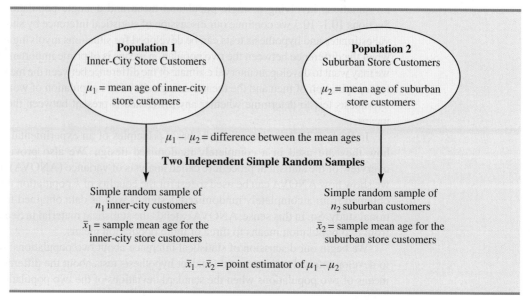

To estimate $\mu_1 - \mu_2$, we will select a simple random sample of n_1 customers from population 1 and a simple random sample of n_2 customers from population 2. We then compute the two sample means.

$\bar{x}_1$ = sample mean age for the simple random sample of n_1 inner-city customers

$\bar{x}_2$ = sample mean age for the simple random sample of n_2 suburban customers

The point estimator of the difference between the two population means is the difference between the two sample means.

POINT ESTIMATOR OF THE DIFFERENCE BETWEEN TWO POPULATION MEANS

$$\bar{x}_1 - \bar{x}_2 \qquad \textbf{(10.1)}$$

Figure 10.1 provides an overview of the process used to estimate the difference between two population means based on two independent simple random samples.

As with other point estimators, the point estimator $\bar{x}_1 - \bar{x}_2$ has a standard error that describes the variation in the sampling distribution of the estimator. With two independent simple random samples, the standard error of $\bar{x}_1 - \bar{x}_2$ is as follows:

The standard error of $\bar{x}_1 - \bar{x}_2$ is the standard deviation of the sampling distribution of $\bar{x}_1 - \bar{x}_2$.

STANDARD ERROR OF $\bar{x}_1 - \bar{x}_2$

$$\sigma_{\bar{x}_1 - \bar{x}_2} = \sqrt{\frac{\sigma_1^2}{n_1} + \frac{\sigma_2^2}{n_2}} \qquad \textbf{(10.2)}$$

If both populations have a normal distribution, or if the sample sizes are large enough that the central limit theorem enables us to conclude that the sampling distributions of $\bar{x}_1$ and $\bar{x}_2$ can be approximated by a normal distribution, the sampling distribution of $\bar{x}_1 - \bar{x}_2$ will have a normal distribution with mean given by $\mu_1 - \mu_2$.

As we showed in Chapter 8, an interval estimate is given by a point estimate $\pm$ a margin of error. When estimating the difference between two population means, the interval estimate takes the following form:

$$\bar{x}_1 - \bar{x}_2 \pm \text{Margin of error}$$

With the sampling distribution of $\bar{x}_1 - \bar{x}_2$ having a normal distribution, we can write the margin of error as follows:

The margin of error is given by multiplying the standard error by $z_{\alpha/2}$.

$$\text{Margin of error} = z_{\alpha/2}\sigma_{\bar{x}_1 - \bar{x}_2} = z_{\alpha/2}\sqrt{\frac{\sigma_1^2}{n_1} + \frac{\sigma_2^2}{n_2}} \tag{10.3}$$

Thus, the interval estimate of the difference between two population means is as follows:

> **INTERVAL ESTIMATE OF THE DIFFERENCE BETWEEN TWO POPULATION MEANS: σ_1 AND σ_2 KNOWN**
>
> $$\bar{x}_1 - \bar{x}_2 \pm z_{\alpha/2}\sqrt{\frac{\sigma_1^2}{n_1} + \frac{\sigma_2^2}{n_2}} \tag{10.4}$$
>
> where $1 - \alpha$ is the confidence coefficient.

Let us return to the HomeStyle example. Based on data from previous customer demographic studies, the two population standard deviations are assumed known with $\sigma_1 = 9$ years and $\sigma_2 = 10$ years. The data collected from the two independent simple random samples of HomeStyle customers provided the following results.

WEB file

HomeStyle

	Inner-City Store	**Suburban Store**
Sample Size	$n_1 = 36$	$n_2 = 49$
Sample Mean	$\bar{x}_1 = 40$ years	$\bar{x}_2 = 35$ years

Using expression (10.1), we find that the point estimate of the difference between the mean ages of the two populations is $\bar{x}_1 - \bar{x}_2 = 40 - 35 = 5$ years. Thus, we estimate that the customers at the inner-city store have a mean age 5 years greater than the mean age of the suburban store customers. We can now use expression (10.4) to compute the margin of error and provide the interval estimate of $\mu_1 - \mu_2$. Using 95% confidence and $z_{\alpha/2} = z_{.025} = 1.96$, we have

$$\bar{x}_1 - \bar{x}_2 \pm z_{\alpha/2}\sqrt{\frac{\sigma_1^2}{n_1} + \frac{\sigma_2^2}{n_2}}$$

$$40 - 35 \pm 1.96\sqrt{\frac{9^2}{36} + \frac{10^2}{49}}$$

$$5 \pm 4.06$$

Thus, the margin of error is 4.06 years and the 95% confidence interval estimate of the difference between the two population means is $5 - 4.06 = .94$ years to $5 + 4.06 = 9.06$ years.

Using Excel to Construct a Confidence Interval

Excel's data analysis tools do not provide a procedure for developing interval estimates involving two population means. However, we can develop an Excel worksheet that can be used as a template to construct interval estimates. We will illustrate by constructing an interval estimate of the difference between the population means in the HomeStyle Furniture Stores study. Refer to Figure 10.2 as we describe the tasks involved. The formula worksheet is in the background; the value worksheet is in the foreground.

Enter Data: Column A contains the age data for the simple random sample of 36 inner-city customers, and column B contains the age data for the simple random sample of 49 suburban customers.

FIGURE 10.2   EXCEL WORKSHEET: CONSTRUCTING A 95% CONFIDENCE INTERVAL FOR HOMESTYLE FURNITURE STORES

	A	B	C	D	E	F	G
1	Inner City	Suburban		Interval Estimate of Difference in Population Means:			
2	38	29		σ_1 and σ_2 Known Case			
3	46	35					
4	32	39			Inner City	Suburban	
5	23	10		Sample Size	=COUNT(A2:A37)	=COUNT(B2:B50)	
6	39	37		Sample Mean	=AVERAGE(A2:A37)	=AVERAGE(B2:B50)	
7	40	52					
8	35	40		Population Standard Deviation	9	10	
9	35	37		Standard Error	=SQRT(E8^2/E5+F8^2/F5)		
10	36	43					
11	41	38		Confidence Coefficient	0.95		
12	32	28		Level of Significance	=1-E11		
13	38	37		z Value	=NORMSINV(1-E12/2)		
14	44	51		Margin of Error	=E13*E9		
15	50	23					
16	47	25		Point Estimate of Difference	=E6-F6		
17	59	37		Lower Limit	=E16-E14		
18	38	38		Upper Limit	=E16+E14		
36	44	19					
37	62	40					
49		22					
50		47					
51							

	A	B	C	D	E	F	G
1	Inner City	Suburban		Interval Estimate of Difference in Population Means:			
2	38	29		σ_1 and σ_2 Known Case			
3	46	35					
4	32	39			Inner City	Suburban	
5	23	10		Sample Size	36	49	
6	39	37		Sample Mean	40	35	
7	40	52					
8	35	40		Population Standard Deviation	9	10	
9	35	37		Standard Error	2.07		
10	36	43					
11	41	38		Confidence Coefficient	0.95		
12	32	28		Level of Significance	0.05		
13	38	37		z Value	1.960		
14	44	51		Margin of Error	4.06		
15	50	23					
16	47	25		Point Estimate of Difference	5		
17	59	37		Lower Limit	0.94		
18	38	38		Upper Limit	9.06		
36	44	19					
37	62	40					
49		22					
50		47					
51							

Note: Rows 19–35 and 38–48 are hidden.

Enter Functions and Formulas: The descriptive statistics needed are provided in cells E5:F6. The known population standard deviations are entered into cells E8 and F8. Using the two population standard deviations and the sample sizes, the standard error of the point estimator, $\bar{x}_1 - \bar{x}_2$, is computed using equation (10.2) by entering the following formula into cell E9:

$$=\text{SQRT}(\text{E8}^2/\text{E5}+\text{F8}^2/\text{F5})$$

Cells E11:E14 are used to compute the appropriate z value and the margin of error. The confidence coefficient is entered into cell E11 (.95) and the corresponding level of significance ($\alpha = 1 - $ confidence coefficient) is computed in cell E12. In cell E13, we used the NORMSINV function to compute the z value needed for the interval estimate. The margin of error is computed in cell E14 by multiplying the z value by the standard error.

In cell E16 the difference in the sample means is used to compute the point estimate of the difference in the two population means. The lower limit of the confidence interval is computed in cell E17 (.94) and the upper limit is computed in cell E18 (9.06); thus, the 95% confidence interval estimate of the difference in the two population means is .94 to 9.06.

A template for other problems   This worksheet can be used as a template for developing interval estimates of the difference in population means when the population standard deviations are assumed known. For another problem of this type, we must first enter the new problem data in columns A and B. The data ranges in cells E5:F6 must be modified in order to compute the sample means and sample sizes for the new data. Also, the assumed known population standard deviations must be entered into cells E8 and F8. After doing so, the point estimate and a 95% confidence interval will be displayed in cells E16:E18. If a confidence interval with a different confidence coefficient is desired, we simply change the value in cell E11.

We can further simplify the use of Figure 10.2 as a template for other problems by eliminating the need to enter new data ranges in cells E5:F6. We rewrite the cell formulas as follows:

Cell E5:   =COUNT(A:A)

Cell F5:   =COUNT(B:B)

Cell E6:   =AVERAGE(A:A)

Cell F6:   =AVERAGE(B:B)

The HomeStyle data set includes a worksheet entitled Template that uses the A:A and B:B methods for entering the data ranges.

Using the A:A method of specifying data ranges in cells E5 and E6, Excel's COUNT function will count the number of numeric values in column A and Excel's AVERAGE function will compute the average of the numeric values in column A. Similarly, using the B:B method of specifying data ranges in cells F5 and F6, Excel's COUNT function will count the number of numeric values in column B and Excel's AVERAGE function will compute the average of the numeric values in column B. Thus, to solve a new problem it is only necessary to enter the new data into columns A and B and enter the known population standard deviations in cells E8 and F8.

This worksheet can also be used as a template for text exercises in which the sample sizes, sample means, and population standard deviations are given. In this type of situation, no change in the data is necessary. We simply replace the values in cells E5:F6 and E8:F8 with the given values of the sample sizes, sample means, and population standard deviations. If something other than a 95% confidence interval is desired, the confidence coefficient in cell E11 must also be changed.

Hypothesis Tests About $\mu_1 - \mu_2$

Let us consider hypothesis tests about the difference between two population means. Using D_0 to denote the hypothesized difference between μ_1 and μ_2, the three forms for a hypothesis test are as follows:

$$H_0: \mu_1 - \mu_2 \geq D_0 \qquad H_0: \mu_1 - \mu_2 \leq D_0 \qquad H_0: \mu_1 - \mu_2 = D_0$$
$$H_a: \mu_1 - \mu_2 < D_0 \qquad H_a: \mu_1 - \mu_2 > D_0 \qquad H_a: \mu_1 - \mu_2 \neq D_0$$

In most applications, $D_0 = 0$. Using the two-tailed test as an example, when $D_0 = 0$ the null hypothesis is $H_0: \mu_1 - \mu_2 = 0$. In this case, the null hypothesis is that μ_1 and μ_2 are equal. Rejection of H_0 leads to the conclusion that $H_a: \mu_1 - \mu_2 \neq 0$ is true; that is, μ_1 and μ_2 are not equal.

The steps for conducting hypothesis tests presented in Chapter 9 are applicable here. We must choose a level of significance, compute the value of the test statistic, and find the p-value to determine whether the null hypothesis should be rejected. With two independent simple random samples, we showed that the point estimator $\bar{x}_1 - \bar{x}_2$ has a standard error $\sigma_{\bar{x}_1 - \bar{x}_2}$ given by expression (10.2) and the sampling distribution of $\bar{x}_1 - \bar{x}_2$ can be described by a normal distribution. In this case, the test statistic for the difference between two population means when σ_1 and σ_2 are known is as follows.

TEST STATISTIC FOR HYPOTHESIS TESTS ABOUT $\mu_1 - \mu_2$: σ_1 AND σ_2 KNOWN

$$z = \frac{(\bar{x}_1 - \bar{x}_2) - D_0}{\sqrt{\dfrac{\sigma_1^2}{n_1} + \dfrac{\sigma_2^2}{n_2}}} \qquad (10.5)$$

Let us demonstrate the use of this test statistic in the following hypothesis testing example.

As part of a study to evaluate differences in education quality between two training centers, a standardized examination is given to individuals who are trained at the centers. The difference between the mean examination scores is used to assess quality differences between the centers. The population means for the two centers are as follows.

$\mu_1 = $ the mean examination score for the population
of individuals trained at center A

$\mu_2 = $ the mean examination score for the population
of individuals trained at center B

We begin with the tentative assumption that no difference exists between the training quality provided at the two centers. Hence, in terms of the mean examination scores, the null hypothesis is that $\mu_1 - \mu_2 = 0$. If sample evidence leads to the rejection of this hypothesis, we will conclude that the mean examination scores differ for the two populations. This conclusion indicates a quality differential between the two centers and suggests that a follow-up study investigating the reason for the differential may be warranted. The null and alternative hypotheses for this two-tailed test are written as follows.

$$H_0: \mu_1 - \mu_2 = 0$$
$$H_a: \mu_1 - \mu_2 \neq 0$$

WEB file

ExamScores

The standardized examination given previously in a variety of settings always resulted in an examination score standard deviation near 10 points. Thus, we will use this information to assume that the population standard deviations are known with $\sigma_1 = 10$ and $\sigma_2 = 10$. An $\alpha = .05$ level of significance is specified for the study.

Independent simple random samples of $n_1 = 30$ individuals from training center A and $n_2 = 40$ individuals from training center B are taken. The respective sample means are $\bar{x}_1 = 82$ and $\bar{x}_2 = 78$. Do these data suggest a significant difference between the population means at the two training centers? To help answer this question, we compute the test statistic using equation (10.5).

$$z = \frac{(\bar{x}_1 - \bar{x}_2) - D_0}{\sqrt{\dfrac{\sigma_1^2}{n_1} + \dfrac{\sigma_2^2}{n_2}}} = \frac{(82 - 78) - 0}{\sqrt{\dfrac{10^2}{30} + \dfrac{10^2}{40}}} = 1.66$$

Next let us compute the p-value for this two-tailed test. Because the test statistic z is in the upper tail, we first compute the area under the curve to the right of $z = 1.66$. Using the standard normal distribution table, the area to the left of $z = 1.66$ is .9515. Thus, the area in the upper tail of the distribution is $1.0000 - .9515 = .0485$. Because this test is a two-tailed test, we must double the tail area: p-value $= 2(.0485) = .0970$. Following the usual rule to reject H_0 if p-value $\le \alpha$, we see that the p-value of .0970 does not allow us to reject H_0 at the .05 level of significance. The sample results do not provide sufficient evidence to conclude that the training centers differ in quality.

In this chapter we will use the p-value approach to hypothesis testing as described in Chapter 9. However, if you prefer, the test statistic and the critical value rejection rule may be used. With $\alpha = .05$ and $z_{\alpha/2} = z_{.025} = 1.96$, the rejection rule employing the critical value approach would be reject H_0 if $z \le -1.96$ or if $z \ge 1.96$. With $z = 1.66$, we reach the same do not reject H_0 conclusion.

In the preceding example, we demonstrated a two-tailed hypothesis test about the difference between two population means. Lower tail and upper tail tests can also be considered. These tests use the same test statistic as given in equation (10.5). The procedure for computing the p-value and the rejection rules for these one-tailed tests are the same as those presented in Chapter 9.

Using Excel to Conduct a Hypothesis Test

The Excel tool used to conduct the hypothesis test to determine whether there is a significant difference in population means when σ_1 and σ_2 are assumed known is called *z-Test: Two Sample for Means*. We illustrate using the sample data for exam scores at center A and at center B. With an assumed known standard deviation of 10 points at each center, the known variance of exam scores for each of the two populations is equal to $10^2 = 100$. Refer to the Excel worksheet shown in Figure 10.3 and the dialog box in Figure 10.4 as we describe the tasks involved.

Enter Data: Column A contains the examination score data for the simple random sample of 30 individuals trained at center A, and column B contains the examination score data for the simple random sample of 40 individuals trained at center B.

Apply Tools: The following steps will provide the information needed to conduct the hypothesis test to see whether there is a significant difference in test scores at the two centers.

Step 1. Click the **Data** tab on the Ribbon
Step 2. In the **Analysis** group, click **Data Analysis**
Step 3. Choose **z-Test: Two Sample for Means** from the list of Analysis Tools
Step 4. When the z-Test: Two Sample for Means dialog box appears (Figure 10.4),
      Enter A1:A31 in the **Variable 1 Range** box
      Enter B1:B41 in the **Variable 2 Range** box
      Enter 0 in the **Hypothesized Mean Difference** box
      Enter 100 in the **Variable 1 Variance (known)** box

FIGURE 10.3   USING EXCEL TO CONDUCT A HYPOTHESIS TEST ABOUT EQUALITY OF MEAN EXAM SCORES AT TWO CENTERS

	A	B	C	D	E	F	G
1	Center A	Center B					
2	97	64					
3	95	85					
4	89	72		z-Test: Two Sample for Means			
5	79	64					
6	78	74			*Center A*	*Center B*	
7	87	93		**Mean**	82	78	
8	83	70		**Known Variance**	100	100	
9	94	79		**Observations**	30	40	
10	76	79		**Hypothesized Mean Difference**	0		
11	79	75		z	1.6562		
12	83	66		P(Z<=z) one-tail	0.0488		
13	84	83		z Critical one-tail	1.6449		
14	76	74		P(Z<=z) two-tail	0.0977		
15	82	70		z Critical two-tail	1.9600		
16	85	82					
17	85	82					
29	88	65					
30	60	78					
31	73	66					
32		84					
40		80					
41		76					
42							

Note: Rows 18–28 and 33–39 are hidden.

Enter 100 in the **Variable 2 Variance (known)** box
Select **Labels**
Enter .05 in the **Alpha** box
Select **Output Range** and enter D4 in the box
Click **OK**

The value of the test statistic shown here (1.6562) and the p-value (.0977) differ slightly from those shown previously, because we rounded the test statistic to two places (1.66) in the text.

    Descriptive statistics for the two samples are shown in cells E7:F9. The value of the test statistic, 1.6562, is shown in cell E11. The *p*-value for the test, labeled P(Z<=z) two-tail, is shown in cell E14. Because the *p*-value, .0977, is greater than the level of significance, $\alpha = .05$, we cannot conclude that the means for the two populations are different.

    The z-Test: Two Sample for Means tool can also be used to conduct one-tailed hypothesis tests. The only change required to make the hypothesis testing decision is that we need to use the *p*-value for a one-tailed test, labeled P(Z<=z) one-tail (see cell E12).

Practical Advice

In most applications of the interval estimation and hypothesis testing procedures presented in this section, random samples with $n_1 \geq 30$ and $n_2 \geq 30$ are adequate. In cases where either or both sample sizes are less than 30, the distributions of the populations become important considerations. In general, with smaller sample sizes, it is more important for the analyst to be satisfied that it is reasonable to assume that the distributions of the two populations are at least approximately normal.

FIGURE 10.4   DIALOG BOX FOR EXCEL'S z-TEST: TWO SAMPLE FOR MEANS TOOL

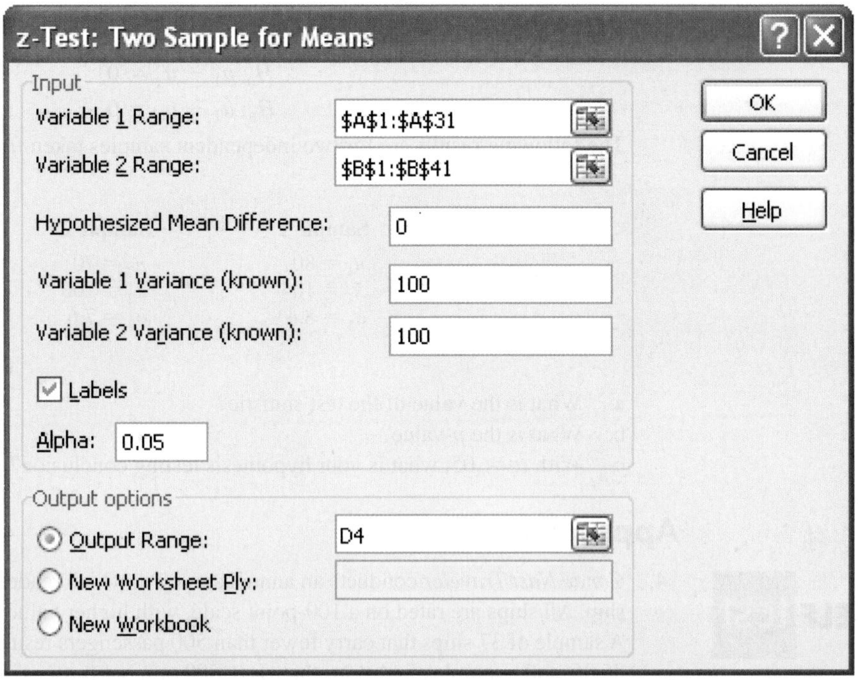

z-Test: Two Sample for Means   [?][X]

Input
Variable 1 Range: | $A$1:$A$31
Variable 2 Range: | $B$1:$B$41
Hypothesized Mean Difference: | 0
Variable 1 Variance (known): | 100
Variable 2 Variance (known): | 100
☑ Labels
Alpha: 0.05

OK
Cancel
Help

Output options
◉ Output Range: | D4
○ New Worksheet Ply:
○ New Workbook

Exercises

Methods

1. The following results are for two independent random samples taken from two populations.

Sample 1	Sample 2
$n_1 = 50$	$n_2 = 35$
$\bar{x}_1 = 13.6$	$\bar{x}_2 = 11.6$
$\sigma_1 = 2.2$	$\sigma_2 = 3.0$

   a. What is the point estimate of the difference between the two population means?
   b. Provide a 90% confidence interval for the difference between the two population means.
   c. Provide a 95% confidence interval for the difference between the two population means.

2. Consider the following hypothesis test.

$$H_0: \mu_1 - \mu_2 \leq 0$$
$$H_a: \mu_1 - \mu_2 > 0$$

The following results are for two independent samples taken from the two populations.

Sample 1	Sample 2
$n_1 = 40$	$n_2 = 50$
$\bar{x}_1 = 25.2$	$\bar{x}_2 = 22.8$
$\sigma_1 = 5.2$	$\sigma_2 = 6.0$

    a.   What is the value of the test statistic?

    b.   What is the *p*-value?

    c.   With $\alpha = .05$, what is your hypothesis testing conclusion?

3.   Consider the following hypothesis test.

$$H_0: \mu_1 - \mu_2 = 0$$
$$H_a: \mu_1 - \mu_2 \neq 0$$

The following results are for two independent samples taken from the two populations.

Sample 1	Sample 2
$n_1 = 80$	$n_2 = 70$
$\bar{x}_1 = 104$	$\bar{x}_2 = 106$
$\sigma_1 = 8.4$	$\sigma_2 = 7.6$

    a.   What is the value of the test statistic?

    b.   What is the *p*-value?

    c.   With $\alpha = .05$, what is your hypothesis testing conclusion?

Applications

4.   *Condé Nast Traveler* conducts an annual survey in which readers rate their favorite cruise ship. All ships are rated on a 100-point scale, with higher values indicating better service. A sample of 37 ships that carry fewer than 500 passengers resulted in an average rating of 85.36, and a sample of 44 ships that carry 500 or more passengers provided an average rating of 81.40 (*Condé Nast Traveler,* February 2008). Assume that the population standard deviation is 4.55 for ships that carry fewer than 500 passengers and 3.97 for ships that carry 500 or more passengers.

    a.   What is the point estimate of the difference between the population mean rating for ships that carry fewer than 500 passengers and the population mean rating for ships that carry 500 or more passengers?

    b.   At 95% confidence, what is the margin of error?

    c.   What is a 95% confidence interval estimate of the difference between the population mean ratings for the two sizes of ships?

5.   The average expenditure on Valentine's Day was expected to be $100.89 (*USA Today,* February 13, 2006). Do male and female consumers differ in the amounts they spend? The average expenditure in a sample survey of 40 male consumers was $135.67, and the average expenditure in a sample survey of 30 female consumers was $68.64. Based on past surveys, the standard deviation for male consumers is assumed to be $35, and the standard deviation for female consumers is assumed to be $20.

    a.   What is the point estimate of the difference between the population mean expenditure for males and the population mean expenditure for females?

    b.   At 99% confidence, what is the margin of error?

    c.   Develop a 99% confidence interval for the difference between the two population means.

Mortgage

6.   The nation's 40,000 mortgage brokers are some of the most profitable small businesses in the United States. These low-profile companies find loans for companies in exchange for commissions. Mortgage Bankers Association of America provides data on the average size of loans handled by mortgage brokers (*The Wall Street Journal,* February 24, 2003). The website file named Mortgage contains data from a sample of 250 loans made in 2001 and a sample of 270 loans made in 2002 that are consistent with these data. Based on historical loan data, the population standard deviations for loan amounts can be assumed known at $50,000 in 2001 and $55,000 in 2002. Do the sample data indicate an increase in the mean loan amount between 2001 and 2002? Use $\alpha = .05$.

7. During the 2003 season, Major League Baseball took steps to speed up the play of baseball games in order to maintain fan interest (*CNN Headline News,* September 30, 2003). The following results come from a sample of 60 games played during the summer of 2002 and a sample of 50 games played during the summer of 2003. The sample mean shows the mean duration of the games included in each sample.

2002 Season	2003 Season
$n_1 = 60$	$n_2 = 50$
$\bar{x}_1 = 2$ hours, 52 minutes	$\bar{x}_2 = 2$ hours, 46 minutes

   a. A research hypothesis was that the steps taken during the 2003 season would reduce the population mean duration of baseball games. Formulate the null and alternative hypotheses.
   b. What is the point estimate of the reduction in the mean duration of games during the 2003 season?
   c. Historical data indicate a population standard deviation of 12 minutes is a reasonable assumption for both years. Conduct the hypothesis test and report the *p*-value. At a .05 level of significance, what is your conclusion?
   d. Provide a 95% confidence interval estimate of the reduction in the mean duration of games during the 2003 season.
   e. What was the percentage reduction in the mean time of baseball games during the 2003 season? Should management be pleased with the results of the statistical analysis? Discuss. Should the length of baseball games continue to be an issue in future years? Explain.

8. Arnold Palmer and Tiger Woods are two of the best golfers to ever play the game. To show how these two golfers would compare if both were playing at the top of their game, the following sample data provide the results of 18-hole scores during a PGA tournament competition. Palmer's scores are from his 1960 season, while Woods's scores are from his 1999 season (*Golf Magazine,* February 2000).

Arnold Palmer	Tiger Woods
$n_1 = 112$	$n_2 = 84$
$\bar{x}_1 = 69.95$	$\bar{x}_2 = 69.56$

   Use the sample results to test the hypothesis of no difference between the population mean 18-hole scores for the two golfers.
   a. Assume a population standard deviation of 2.5 for both golfers. What is the value of the test statistic?
   b. What is the *p*-value?
   c. At $\alpha = .01$, what is your conclusion?

10.2 Inferences About the Difference Between Two Population Means: $\boldsymbol{\sigma}_1$ and $\boldsymbol{\sigma}_2$ Unknown

In this section we extend the discussion of inferences about the difference between two population means to the case when the two population standard deviations, σ_1 and σ_2, are unknown. In this case, we will use the sample standard deviations, s_1 and s_2, to estimate the unknown population standard deviations. When we use the sample standard deviations, the interval estimation and hypothesis testing procedures will be based on the *t* distribution rather than the standard normal distribution.

Interval Estimation of $\mu_1 - \mu_2$

In the following example we show how to compute a margin of error and develop an interval estimate of the difference between two population means when σ_1 and σ_2 are unknown. Clearwater National Bank is conducting a study designed to identify differences between checking account practices by customers at two of its branch banks. A simple random sample of 28 checking accounts is selected from the Cherry Grove Branch and an independent simple random sample of 22 checking accounts is selected from the Beechmont Branch. The current checking account balance is recorded for each of the checking accounts. A summary of the account balances follows:

WEB file

CheckAcct

	Cherry Grove	**Beechmont**
Sample Size	$n_1 = 28$	$n_2 = 22$
Sample Mean	$\bar{x}_1 = \$1025$	$\bar{x}_2 = \$910$
Sample Standard Deviation	$s_1 = \$150$	$s_2 = \$125$

Clearwater National Bank would like to estimate the difference between the mean checking account balance maintained by the population of Cherry Grove customers and the population of Beechmont customers. Let us develop the margin of error and an interval estimate of the difference between these two population means.

In Section 10.1, we provided the following interval estimate for the case when the population standard deviations, σ_1 and σ_2, are known.

$$\bar{x}_1 - \bar{x}_2 \pm z_{\alpha/2} \sqrt{\frac{\sigma_1^2}{n_1} + \frac{\sigma_2^2}{n_2}}$$

When σ_1 and σ_2 are estimated by s_1 and s_2, the t distribution is used to make inferences about the difference between two population means.

With σ_1 and σ_2 unknown, we will use the sample standard deviations s_1 and s_2 to estimate σ_1 and σ_2 and replace $z_{\alpha/2}$ with $t_{\alpha/2}$. As a result, the interval estimate of the difference between two population means is given by the following expression:

INTERVAL ESTIMATE OF THE DIFFERENCE BETWEEN TWO POPULATION MEANS: σ_1 AND σ_2 UNKNOWN

$$\bar{x}_1 - \bar{x}_2 \pm t_{\alpha/2} \sqrt{\frac{s_1^2}{n_1} + \frac{s_2^2}{n_2}} \qquad (10.6)$$

where $1 - \alpha$ is the confidence coefficient.

In this expression, the use of the t distribution is an approximation, but it provides excellent results and is relatively easy to use. The only difficulty that we encounter in using expression (10.6) is determining the appropriate degrees of freedom for $t_{\alpha/2}$. The formula used is as follows:

DEGREES OF FREEDOM: t DISTRIBUTION WITH TWO INDEPENDENT RANDOM SAMPLES

The Excel worksheet in Figure 10.5 makes this computation easy.

$$df = \frac{\left(\dfrac{s_1^2}{n_1} + \dfrac{s_2^2}{n_2}\right)^2}{\dfrac{1}{n_1 - 1}\left(\dfrac{s_1^2}{n_1}\right)^2 + \dfrac{1}{n_2 - 1}\left(\dfrac{s_2^2}{n_2}\right)^2} \qquad (10.7)$$

Let us return to the Clearwater National Bank example and show how to use expression (10.6) to provide a 95% confidence interval estimate of the difference between the population mean checking account balances at the two branch banks. The sample data show $n_1 = 28$, $\bar{x}_1 = \$1025$, and $s_1 = \$150$ for the Cherry Grove Branch, and $n_2 = 22$, $\bar{x}_2 = \$910$, and $s_2 = \$125$ for the Beechmont Branch. The calculation for degrees of freedom for $t_{\alpha/2}$ is as follows:

$$df = \frac{\left(\dfrac{s_1^2}{n_1} + \dfrac{s_2^2}{n_2}\right)^2}{\dfrac{1}{n_1 - 1}\left(\dfrac{s_1^2}{n_1}\right)^2 + \dfrac{1}{n_2 - 1}\left(\dfrac{s_2^2}{n_2}\right)^2} = \frac{\left(\dfrac{150^2}{28} + \dfrac{125^2}{22}\right)^2}{\dfrac{1}{28 - 1}\left(\dfrac{150^2}{28}\right)^2 + \dfrac{1}{22 - 1}\left(\dfrac{125^2}{22}\right)^2} = 47.8$$

We round the noninteger degrees of freedom *down* to 47 to provide a larger t value and a more conservative (wider) interval estimate. Using the t distribution table with 47 degrees of freedom, we find $t_{.025} = 2.012$. Using expression (10.6), we develop the 95% confidence interval estimate of the difference between the two population means as follows.

$$\bar{x}_1 - \bar{x}_2 \pm t_{.025}\sqrt{\frac{s_1^2}{n_1} + \frac{s_2^2}{n_2}}$$

$$1025 - 910 \pm 2.012\sqrt{\frac{150^2}{28} + \frac{125^2}{22}}$$

$$115 \pm 78$$

The point estimate of the difference between the population mean checking account balances at the two branches is $115 and the margin of error is $78. Thus the 95% confidence interval estimate of the difference between the two population means is $115 - 78 = \$37$ to $115 + 78 = \$193$.

This suggestion should help if you are using equation (10.7) to calculate the degrees of freedom by hand.

The computation of the degrees of freedom in equation (10.7) is cumbersome if you are doing the calculation by hand. However, note that the expressions s_1^2/n_1 and s_2^2/n_2 appear in both expression (10.6) and equation (10.7). These values only need to be computed once in order to evaluate both (10.6) and (10.7).

Using Excel to Construct a Confidence Interval

Excel's data analysis tools do not provide a procedure for developing interval estimates involving two population means. However, we can develop an Excel worksheet that can be used as a template to construct interval estimates. We will illustrate by constructing an interval estimate of the difference between the population means in the Clearwater National Bank study. Refer to Figure 10.5 as we describe the tasks involved. The formula worksheet is in the background; the value worksheet is in the foreground.

Enter Data: Column A contains the account balances for the simple random sample of 28 customers at the Cherry Grove Branch, and column B contains the account balances for the simple random sample of 22 customers at the Beechmont Branch.

Enter Functions and Formulas: The descriptive statistics needed are provided in cells E5:F7. Using the two sample standard deviations and the sample sizes, an estimate of the variance of the point estimator $\bar{x}_1 - \bar{x}_2$ is computed by entering the following formula into cell E9:

$$=E7^2/E5 + F7^2/F5$$

An estimate of the standard error is then computed in cell E10 by taking the square root of the variance.

FIGURE 10.5 EXCEL WORKSHEET: CONSTRUCTING A 95% CONFIDENCE INTERVAL FOR CLEARWATER NATIONAL BANK

	A	B	C	D	E	F	G
1	Cherry Grove	Beechmont		Interval Estimate of Difference in Population Means:			
2	1263	997		σ_1 and σ_2 Unknown Case			
3	897	897					
4	849	912			Cherry Grove	Beechmont	
5	891	895		Sample Size	=COUNT(A2:A29)	=COUNT(B2:B23)	
6	964	785		Sample Mean	=AVERAGE(A2:A29)	=AVERAGE(B2:B23)	
7	810	751		Sample Standard Deviation	=STDEV(A2:A29)	=STDEV(B2:B23)	
8	877	882					
9	899	1110		Estimate of Variance	=E7^2/E5+F7^2/F5		
10	847	907		Standard Error	=SQRT(E9)		
11	1070	1226					
12	1252	762		Confidence Coefficient	0.95		
13	920	836		Level of Significance	=1-E12		
14	1256	1048		Degrees of Freedom	=E9^2/((1/(E5-1))*(E7^2/E5)^2+(1/(F5-1)*(F7^2/F5)^2))		
15	1196	774		t Value	=TINV(E13,E14)		
16	1150	807		Margin of Error	=E15*E10		
17	1024	972					
18	1016	980		Point Estimate of Difference	=E6-F6		
19	1126	877		Lower Limit	=E18-E16		
20	1289	943		Upper Limit	=E18+E16		
21	1220	993					
22	912	704					
23	1026	963					
24	786						
25	989						
26	1133						
27	990						
28	999						
29	1049						
30							

	A	B	C	D	E	F	G
1	Cherry Grove	Beechmont		Interval Estimate of Difference in Population Means:			
2	1263	997		σ_1 and σ_2 Unknown Case			
3	897	897					
4	849	912			Cherry Grove	Beechmont	
5	891	895		Sample Size	28	22	
6	964	785		Sample Mean	1025	910	
7	810	751		Sample Standard Deviation	150	125	
8	877	882					
9	899	1110		Estimate of Variance	1513.8550		
10	847	907		Standard Error	38.9083		
11	1070	1226					
12	1252	762		Confidence Coefficient	0.95		
13	920	836		Level of Significance	0.05		
14	1256	1048		Degrees of Freedom	47.8		
15	1196	774		t Value	2.012		
16	1150	807		Margin of Error	78		
17	1024	972					
18	1016	980		Point Estimate of Difference	115		
19	1126	877		Lower Limit	37		
20	1289	943		Upper Limit	193		
21	1220	993					
22	912	704					
23	1026	963					
24	786						
25	989						
26	1133						
27	990						
28	999						
29	1049						
30							

Cells E12:E16 are used to compute the appropriate *t* value and the margin of error. The confidence coefficient is entered into cell E12 (.95) and the corresponding level of significance is computed in cell E13 ($\alpha = .05$). In cell E14, we used formula (10.7) to compute the degrees of freedom (47.8). In cell E15, we used the TINV function to compute the *t* value needed for the interval estimate. The margin of error is computed in cell E16 by multiplying the *t* value by the standard error.

In cell E18 the difference in the sample means is used to compute the point estimate of the difference in the two population means (115). The lower limit of the confidence interval is computed in cell E19 (37) and the upper limit is computed in cell E20 (193);

thus, the 95% confidence interval estimate of the difference in the two population means is 37 to 193.

A template for other problems   This worksheet can be used as a template for developing interval estimates of the difference in population means when the population standard deviations are unknown. For another problem of this type, we must first enter the new problem data in columns A and B. The data ranges in cells E5:F7 must be modified in order to compute the sample means, sample sizes, and sample standard deviations for the new data. After doing so the point estimate and a 95% confidence interval will be displayed in cells E18:E20. If a confidence interval with a different confidence coefficient is desired, we simply change the value in cell E12.

We can further simplify the use of Figure 10.5 as a template for other problems by eliminating the need to enter new data ranges in cells E5:F7. We rewrite the cell formulas as follows:

> Cell E5: =COUNT(A:A)
>
> Cell F5: =COUNT(B:B)
>
> Cell E6: =AVERAGE(A:A)
>
> Cell F6: =AVERAGE(B:B)
>
> Cell E7: =STDEV(A:A)
>
> Cell F7: =STDEV(B:B)

The CheckAcct data set includes a worksheet entitled Template that uses the A:A and B:B methods for entering the data ranges.

Using the A:A method of specifying data ranges in cells E5:F7, Excel's COUNT function will count the number of numeric values in column A, Excel's AVERAGE function will compute the average of the numeric values in column A, and Excel's STDEV function will compute the standard deviation of the numeric values in column A. Similarly, using the B:B method of specifying data ranges in cells F5:F7, Excel's COUNT function will count the number of numeric values in column B, Excel's AVERAGE function will compute the average of the numeric values in column B, and Excel's STDEV function will compute the standard deviation of the numeric values in column B. Thus, to solve a new problem it is only necessary to enter the new data into columns A and B.

This worksheet can also be used as a template for text exercises in which the sample sizes, sample means, and sample standard deviations are given. In this type of situation, no change in the data is necessary. We simply replace the values in cells E5:F7 with the given values of the sample sizes, sample means, and sample standard deviations. If something other than a 95% confidence interval is desired, the confidence coefficient in cell E12 must also be changed.

Hypothesis Tests About $\mu_1 - \mu_2$

Let us now consider hypothesis tests about the difference between the means of two populations when the population standard deviations σ_1 and σ_2 are unknown. Letting D_0 denote the hypothesized difference between μ_1 and μ_2, Section 10.1 showed that the test statistic used for the case where σ_1 and σ_2 are known is as follows.

$$z = \frac{(\bar{x}_1 - \bar{x}_2) - D_0}{\sqrt{\dfrac{\sigma_1^2}{n_1} + \dfrac{\sigma_2^2}{n_2}}}$$

The test statistic, z, follows the standard normal distribution.

When σ_1 and σ_2 are unknown, we use s_1 as an estimator of σ_1 and s_2 as an estimator of σ_2. Substituting these sample standard deviations for σ_1 and σ_2 provides the following test statistic when σ_1 and σ_2 are unknown.

TEST STATISTIC FOR HYPOTHESIS TESTS ABOUT $\mu_1 - \mu_2$: σ_1 AND σ_2 UNKNOWN

$$t = \frac{(\bar{x}_1 - \bar{x}_2) - D_0}{\sqrt{\dfrac{s_1^2}{n_1} + \dfrac{s_2^2}{n_2}}} \tag{10.8}$$

The degrees of freedom for t are given by equation (10.7).

Let us demonstrate the use of this test statistic in the following hypothesis testing example.

Consider a new computer software package developed to help systems analysts reduce the time required to design, develop, and implement an information system. To evaluate the benefits of the new software package, a random sample of 24 systems analysts is selected. Each analyst is given specifications for a hypothetical information system. Then 12 of the analysts are instructed to produce the information system by using current technology. The other 12 analysts are trained in the use of the new software package and then instructed to use it to produce the information system.

This study involves two populations: a population of systems analysts using the current technology and a population of systems analysts using the new software package. In terms of the time required to complete the information system design project, the population means are as follow.

μ_1 = the mean project completion time for systems analysts using the current technology

μ_2 = the mean project completion time for systems analysts using the new software package

The researcher in charge of the new software evaluation project hopes to show that the new software package will provide a shorter mean project completion time. Thus, the researcher is looking for evidence to conclude that μ_2 is less than μ_1; in this case, the difference between the two population means, $\mu_1 - \mu_2$, will be greater than zero. The research hypothesis $\mu_1 - \mu_2 > 0$ is stated as the alternative hypothesis. Thus, the hypothesis test becomes

$$H_0: \mu_1 - \mu_2 \leq 0$$
$$H_a: \mu_1 - \mu_2 > 0$$

We will use $\alpha = .05$ as the level of significance.

Suppose that the 24 analysts complete the study with the results shown in Table 10.1. Using the test statistic in equation (10.8), we have

$$t = \frac{(\bar{x}_1 - \bar{x}_2) - D_0}{\sqrt{\dfrac{s_1^2}{n_1} + \dfrac{s_2^2}{n_2}}} = \frac{(325 - 286) - 0}{\sqrt{\dfrac{40^2}{12} + \dfrac{44^2}{12}}} = 2.27$$

TABLE 10.1   COMPLETION TIME DATA AND SUMMARY STATISTICS
FOR THE SOFTWARE TESTING STUDY

	Current Technology	New Software
	300	274
	280	220
	344	308
	385	336
	372	198
	360	300
	288	315
	321	258
	376	318
	290	310
	301	332
	283	263
Summary Statistics		
Sample size	$n_1 = 12$	$n_2 = 12$
Sample mean	$\bar{x}_1 = 325$ hours	$\bar{x}_2 = 286$ hours
Sample standard deviation	$s_1 = 40$	$s_2 = 44$

WEB file

SoftwareTest

Computing the degrees of freedom using equation (10.7), we have

$$ df = \frac{\left(\dfrac{s_1^2}{n_1} + \dfrac{s_2^2}{n_2}\right)^2}{\dfrac{1}{n_1 - 1}\left(\dfrac{s_1^2}{n_1}\right)^2 + \dfrac{1}{n_2 - 1}\left(\dfrac{s_2^2}{n_2}\right)^2} = \frac{\left(\dfrac{40^2}{12} + \dfrac{44^2}{12}\right)^2}{\dfrac{1}{12 - 1}\left(\dfrac{40^2}{12}\right)^2 + \dfrac{1}{12 - 1}\left(\dfrac{44^2}{12}\right)^2} = 21.8 $$

Rounding down, we will use a t distribution with 21 degrees of freedom. This row of the
t distribution table is as follows:

Area in Upper Tail	.20	.10	.05	.025	.01	.005
t Value (21 df)	.859	1.323	1.721	2.080	2.518	2.831

$t = 2.27$

Using the t distribution table, we can only determine a range for the p-value. Use of Excel (see Figure 10.6) shows the p-value = .0166.

With an upper tail test, the p-value is the area in the upper tail to the right of $t = 2.27$. From
the preceding results, we see that the p-value is between .025 and .01. Thus, the p-value is
less than $\alpha = .05$ and H_0 is rejected. The sample results enable the researcher to conclude
that $\mu_1 - \mu_2 > 0$, or $\mu_2 < \mu_1$. Thus, the research study supports the conclusion that the new
software package provides a smaller population mean completion time.

Using Excel to Conduct a Hypothesis Test

The Excel tool used to conduct a hypothesis test to determine whether there is a significant
difference in population means when the population standard deviations are unknown is
called *t-Test: Two-Sample Assuming Unequal Variances*. We illustrate using the sample
data for the software evaluation study. Twelve systems analysts developed an information
system using current technology, and 12 systems analysts developed an information system
using a new software package. A one-tailed hypothesis test is to be conducted to see
whether the mean completion time is shorter using the new software package. Refer to the

Excel worksheet shown in Figure 10.6 and the dialog box in Figure 10.7 as we describe the tasks involved.

Enter Data: Column A contains the completion time data for the simple random sample of 12 individuals using the current technology, and column B contains the completion time data for the simple random sample of 12 individuals using the new software.

Apply Tools: The following steps will provide the information needed to conduct the hypothesis test to see whether there is a significant difference in favor of the new software.

> **Step 1.** Click the **Data** tab on the Ribbon
> **Step 2.** In the **Analysis** group, click **Data Analysis**
> **Step 3.** Choose **t-Test: Two-Sample Assuming Unequal Variances** from the list of Analysis Tools
> **Step 4.** When the t-Test: Two-Sample Assuming Unequal Variances dialog box appears,
> > Enter A1:A13 in the **Variable 1 Range** box
> > Enter B1:B13 in the **Variable 2 Range** box
> > Enter 0 in the **Hypothesized Means Difference** box
> > Select **Labels**
> > Enter .05 in the **Alpha** box
> > Select **Output Range** and enter D1 in the box
> > Click **OK**

Descriptive statistics for the two samples are shown in cells E4:F6. The value of the test statistic, 2.2721, is shown in cell E9. The p-value for the test, labeled P(T<=t) one-tail, is shown in cell E10. Because the p-value, .0166, is less than the level of significance $\alpha = .05$, we can conclude that the mean completion time for the population using the new software package is smaller.

The t-Test: Two-Sample Assuming Unequal Variances tool can also be used to conduct two-tailed hypothesis tests. The only change required to make the hypothesis testing decision is that we need to use the p-value for a two-tailed test, labeled P(T<=t) two-tail (see cell E12).

FIGURE 10.6   USING EXCEL TO CONDUCT A HYPOTHESIS TEST ABOUT EQUALITY OF MEAN PROJECT COMPLETION TIMES

	A	B	C	D	E	F	G
1	Current	New		t-Test: Two-Sample Assuming Unequal Variances			
2	300	274					
3	280	220			Current	New	
4	344	308		Mean	325	286	
5	385	336		Variance	1599.6364	1935.8182	
6	372	198		Observations	12	12	
7	360	300		Hypothesized Mean Difference	0		
8	288	315		df	22		
9	321	258		t Stat	2.2721		
10	376	318		P(T<=t) one-tail	0.0166		
11	290	310		t Critical one-tail	1.7171		
12	301	332		P(T<=t) two-tail	0.0332		
13	283	263		t Critical two-tail	2.0739		
14							

FIGURE 10.7 DIALOG BOX FOR EXCEL'S t-TEST: TWO-SAMPLE ASSUMING UNEQUAL VARIANCES TOOL

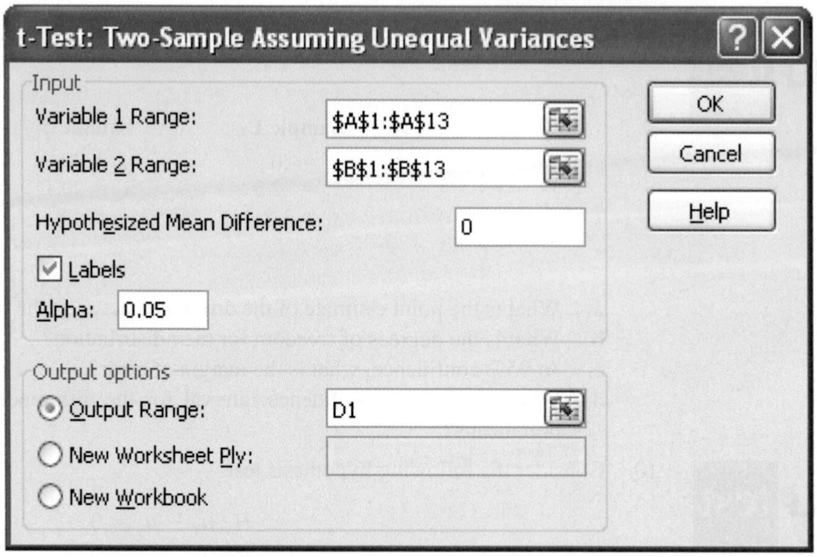

Practical Advice

The interval estimation and hypothesis testing procedures presented in this section are robust and can be used with relatively small sample sizes. In most applications, sample sizes that are equal or nearly equal and result in a total sample size of $n_1 + n_2 \geq 20$ will provide very good results even if the populations are not normal. However, larger sample sizes are recommended if the distributions of the populations are highly skewed or contain outliers. Smaller sample sizes should only be used if the analyst is satisfied that the distributions of the populations are at least approximately normal.

NOTES AND COMMENTS

Another approach used to make inferences about the difference between two population means when σ_1 and σ_2 are unknown is based on the assumption that the two population standard deviations are *equal* ($\sigma_1 = \sigma_2 = \sigma$). Under this assumption, the two sample standard deviations are combined to provide the following *pooled sample variance*:

$$s_p^2 = \frac{(n_1 - 1)s_1^2 + (n_2 - 1)s_2^2}{n_1 + n_2 - 2}$$

The t test statistic becomes

$$t = \frac{(\bar{x}_1 - \bar{x}_2) - D_0}{s_p\sqrt{\dfrac{1}{n_1} + \dfrac{1}{n_2}}}$$

and has $n_1 + n_2 - 2$ degrees of freedom. At this point, the computation of the p-value and the interpretation of the sample results are identical to the procedures discussed earlier in this section.

A difficulty with this procedure is that the assumption that the two population standard deviations are equal is usually difficult to verify. Unequal population standard deviations are frequently encountered. Using the pooled procedure may not provide satisfactory results, especially if the sample sizes n_1 and n_2 are quite different.

The t procedure that we presented in this section does not require the assumption of equal population standard deviations and can be applied whether the population standard deviations are equal or not. It is a more general procedure and is recommended for most applications.

Exercises

Methods

9. The following results are for independent random samples taken from two populations.

Sample 1	Sample 2
$n_1 = 20$	$n_2 = 30$
$\bar{x}_1 = 22.5$	$\bar{x}_2 = 20.1$
$s_1 = 2.5$	$s_2 = 4.8$

a. What is the point estimate of the difference between the two population means?
b. What is the degrees of freedom for the t distribution?
c. At 95% confidence, what is the margin of error?
d. What is the 95% confidence interval for the difference between the two population means?

10. Consider the following hypothesis test.

$$H_0: \mu_1 - \mu_2 = 0$$
$$H_a: \mu_1 - \mu_2 \neq 0$$

The following results are from independent samples taken from two populations.

Sample 1	Sample 2
$n_1 = 35$	$n_2 = 40$
$\bar{x}_1 = 13.6$	$\bar{x}_2 = 10.1$
$s_1 = 5.2$	$s_2 = 8.5$

a. What is the value of the test statistic?
b. What is the value of the degrees of freedom for the t distribution?
c. What is the p-value?
d. At $\alpha = .05$, what is your conclusion?

11. Consider the following data for two independent random samples taken from two normal populations.

Sample 1	10	7	13	7	9	8
Sample 2	8	7	8	4	6	9

a. Compute the two sample means.
b. Compute the two sample standard deviations.
c. What is the point estimate of the difference between the two population means?
d. What is the 90% confidence interval estimate of the difference between the two population means?

Applications

12. The U.S. Department of Transportation provides the number of miles that residents of the 75 largest metropolitan areas travel per day in a car. Suppose that for a simple random sample of 50 Buffalo residents the mean is 22.5 miles a day and the standard deviation is 8.4 miles a day, and for an independent simple random sample of 40 Boston residents the mean is 18.6 miles a day and the standard deviation is 7.4 miles a day.

a. What is the point estimate of the difference between the mean number of miles that Buffalo residents travel per day and the mean number of miles that Boston residents travel per day?
b. What is the 95% confidence interval for the difference between the two population means?

13. FedEx and United Parcel Service (UPS) are the world's two leading cargo carriers by volume and revenue (*The Wall Street Journal,* January 27, 2004). According to the Airports Council International, the Memphis International Airport (FedEx) and the Louisville International Airport (UPS) are 2 of the 10 largest cargo airports in the world. The following random samples show the tons of cargo per day handled by these airports. Data are in thousands of tons.

Cargo

Memphis					
9.1	15.1	8.8	10.0	7.5	10.5
8.3	9.1	6.0	5.8	12.1	9.3

Louisville				
4.7	5.0	4.2	3.3	5.5
2.2	4.1	2.6	3.4	7.0

a. Compute the sample mean and sample standard deviation for each airport.
b. What is the point estimate of the difference between the two population means? Interpret this value in terms of the higher-volume airport and a comparison of the volume difference between the two airports.
c. Develop a 95% confidence interval of the difference between the daily population means for the two airports.

14. Are nursing salaries in Tampa, Florida, lower than those in Dallas, Texas? Salary data provided by *http://www.salary.com* shows staff nurses in Tampa earn less than staff nurses in Dallas (*The Tampa Tribune,* January 15, 2007). Suppose that in a follow-up study of 40 staff nurses in Tampa and 50 staff nurses in Dallas you obtain the following results.

Tampa Bay	**Dallas**
$n_1 = 40$	$n_2 = 50$
$\bar{x}_1 = \$56{,}100$	$\bar{x}_2 = \$59{,}400$
$s_1 = \$6000$	$s_2 = \$7000$

a. Formulate hypotheses so that, if the null hypothesis is rejected, we can conclude that salaries for staff nurses in Tampa Bay are significantly lower than for those in Dallas. Use $\alpha = .05$.
b. What is the value of the test statistic?
c. What is the *p*-value?
d. What is your conclusion?

15. Injuries to Major League Baseball players have been increasing in recent years. For the period 1992 to 2001, league expansion caused Major League Baseball rosters to increase 15%. However, the number of players being put on the disabled list due to injury increased 32% over the same period (*USA Today,* July 8, 2002). A research question addressed whether Major League Baseball players being put on the disabled list are on the list longer in 2001 than players put on the disabled list a decade earlier.

a. Using the population mean number of days a player is on the disabled list, formulate null and alternative hypotheses that can be used to test the research question.

b. Assume that the following data apply:

	2001 Season	1992 Season
Sample size	$n_1 = 45$	$n_2 = 38$
Sample mean	$\bar{x}_1 = 60$ days	$\bar{x}_2 = 51$ days
Sample standard deviation	$s_1 = 18$ days	$s_2 = 15$ days

What is the point estimate of the difference between population mean number of days on the disabled list for 2001 compared to 1992? What is the percentage increase in the number of days on the disabled list?

c. Use $\alpha = .01$. What is your conclusion about the number of days on the disabled list? What is the p-value?

d. Do these data suggest that Major League Baseball should be concerned about the situation?

16. *Consumer Reports* rated 15 midpriced family sedans and 15 affordable family sedans. The following data show the road-test scores for the 30 cars (*Consumer Reports*, February 2008).

Midpriced Family Sedans	Affordable Family Sedans
89	85
88	79
87	78
86	77
84	76
77	75
77	74
75	69
70	69
69	69
64	64
58	62
56	59
48	49
46	44

a. Formulate hypotheses so that if the null hypothesis is rejected, we can conclude that the mean road-test score for midpriced family sedans is significantly greater than the mean road-test score for affordable family sedans. Use $\alpha = .05$.

b. What is the point estimate of the difference between the mean road-test score for midpriced family sedans and the mean road-test score for affordable family sedans?

c. Compute the p-value for the hypotheses formulated in part (c).

d. Using the p-value computed in part (d) and $\alpha = .05$, what is your conclusion.

17. Periodically, Merrill Lynch customers are asked to evaluate Merrill Lynch financial consultants and services (2000 Merrill Lynch Client Satisfaction Survey). Higher ratings on the client satisfaction survey indicate better service with 7 the maximum service rating. Independent samples of service ratings for two financial consultants are summarized here. Consultant A has 10 years of experience, whereas consultant B has 1 year of experience. Use $\alpha = .05$ and test to see whether the consultant with more experience has the higher population mean service rating.

Consultant A	Consultant B
$n_1 = 16$	$n_2 = 10$
$\bar{x}_1 = 6.82$	$\bar{x}_2 = 6.25$
$s_1 = .64$	$s_2 = .75$

    a.   State the null and alternative hypotheses.
    b.   Compute the value of the test statistic.
    c.   What is the p-value?
    d.   What is your conclusion?

18.   The Tire Rack, America's leading online distributor of tires and wheels, conducts extensive testing to provide customers with products that are right for their vehicle, driving style, and conditions in which they drive. In addition, they have maintained an independent consumer survey to help drivers help each other by sharing their long-term tire experiences. The data shown below show survey ratings (1 to 10 scale with 10 the highest rating) for two all-season passenger tires, the Dunlop SP60 and the Michelin MX4 (*http://www.tirerack.com,* April 18, 2008).

Dunlop

7.7	8.1	9.1	8.6	7.4	8.3	9.7	9.5	9.0	8.2
9.8	8.0	10.0	8.5	9.3	7.7	8.9	9.6	7.9	10.0
8.3	8.1	5.1	7.3	8.0	8.5	9.4	7.6	8.4	4.2
7.6	5.9								

WEB file

TireRack

Michelin

8.0	7.2	7.1	4.4	8.5	6.6	7.4	9.5	6.6	8.0
7.3	6.4	8.9	8.6	5.9	7.2	6.6	2.3	7.7	5.5
7.6	7.3	8.6	8.1	8.9	9.0	8.0	8.6	6.6	6.9
8.1	3.9	5.2	6.6	6.0	6.4	8.3	6.6	3.4	8.4

    a.   Formulate the hypotheses that can be used to determine whether the sample data support the hypothesis that the mean rating for Dunlop SP60 tires is greater than the mean rating for Michelin MX4 tires.
    b.   What is the point estimate of the difference between the means for the two populations?
    c.   Compute the p-value for the hypothesis test.
    d.   At $\alpha = .05$, what is your conclusion?

(10.3) Inferences About the Difference Between Two Population Means: Matched Samples

Suppose employees at a manufacturing company can use two different methods to perform a production task. To maximize production output, the company wants to identify the method with the shorter population mean completion time. Let μ_1 denote the population mean completion time for production method 1 and μ_2 denote the population mean completion time for production method 2. With no preliminary indication of the preferred production method, we begin by tentatively assuming that the two production methods have the same population mean completion time. Thus, the null hypothesis is $H_0: \mu_1 - \mu_2 = 0$. If this hypothesis is rejected, we can conclude that the population mean completion times differ. In this case, the method providing the shorter mean completion time would be recommended. The null and alternative hypotheses are written as follows:

$$H_0: \mu_1 - \mu_2 = 0$$
$$H_a: \mu_1 - \mu_2 \neq 0$$

In choosing the sampling procedure that will be used to collect production time data and test the hypotheses, we consider two alternative designs. One is based on **independent simple random samples** and the other is based on **matched samples**.

1. *Independent sample design:* A simple random sample of workers is selected and each worker in the sample uses method 1. A second independent simple random sample of workers is selected and each worker in this sample uses method 2. The test of the difference between population means is based on the procedures in Section 10.2.
2. *Matched sample design:* One simple random sample of workers is selected. Each worker first uses one method and then uses the other method. The order of the two methods is assigned randomly to the workers, with some workers performing method 1 first and others performing method 2 first. Each worker provides a pair of data values, one value for method 1 and another value for method 2.

In the matched sample design the two production methods are tested under similar conditions (i.e., with the same workers); hence this design often leads to a smaller sampling error than the independent sample design. The primary reason is that in a matched sample design, variation between workers is eliminated because the same workers are used for both production methods.

Let us demonstrate the analysis of a matched sample design by assuming it is the method used to test the difference between population means for the two production methods. A random sample of six workers is used. The data on completion times for the six workers are given in Table 10.2. Note that each worker provides a pair of data values, one for each production method. Also note that the last column contains the difference in completion times d_i for each worker in the sample.

The key to the analysis of the matched sample design is to realize that we consider only the column of differences. Therefore, we have six data values (.6, −.2, .5, .3, .0, and .6) that will be used to analyze the difference between population means of the two production methods.

Let μ_d = the mean of the *difference* values for the population of workers. With this notation, the null and alternative hypotheses are rewritten as follows:

$$H_0: \mu_d = 0$$
$$H_a: \mu_d \neq 0$$

If H_0 is rejected, we can conclude that the population mean completion times differ.

TABLE 10.2   TASK COMPLETION TIMES FOR A MATCHED SAMPLE DESIGN

Worker	Completion Time for Method 1 (minutes)	Completion Time for Method 2 (minutes)	Difference in Completion Times (d_i)
1	6.0	5.4	.6
2	5.0	5.2	−.2
3	7.0	6.5	.5
4	6.2	5.9	.3
5	6.0	6.0	.0
6	6.4	5.8	.6

WEB file

Matched

Other than the use of the d notation, the formulas for the sample mean and sample standard deviation are the same ones used previously in the text.

The d notation is a reminder that the matched sample provides *difference* data. The sample mean and sample standard deviation for the six difference values in Table 10.2 follow.

$$\bar{d} = \frac{\Sigma d_i}{n} = \frac{1.8}{6} = .30$$

$$s_d = \sqrt{\frac{\Sigma(d_i - \bar{d})^2}{n - 1}} = \sqrt{\frac{.56}{5}} = .3347$$

With the small sample of $n = 6$ workers, we need to make the assumption that the population of differences has a normal distribution. This assumption is necessary so that we may use the t distribution for hypothesis testing and interval estimation procedures. Based on this assumption, the following test statistic has a t distribution with $n - 1$ degrees of freedom.

It is not necessary to make the assumption that the population has a normal distribution if the sample size is large. Sample size guidelines for using the t distribution were presented in Chapters 8 and 9.

TEST STATISTIC FOR HYPOTHESIS TESTS INVOLVING MATCHED SAMPLES

$$t = \frac{\bar{d} - \mu_d}{s_d/\sqrt{n}} \qquad (10.9)$$

Once the difference data are computed, the t distribution procedure for matched samples is the same as the one-population estimation and hypothesis testing procedures described in Chapters 8 and 9.

Let us use equation (10.9) to test the hypotheses H_0: $\mu_d = 0$ and H_a: $\mu_d \neq 0$, using $\alpha = .05$. Substituting the sample results $\bar{d} = .30$, $s_d = .3347$, and $n = 6$ into equation (10.9), we compute the value of the test statistic.

$$t = \frac{\bar{d} - \mu_d}{s_d/\sqrt{n}} = \frac{.30 - 0}{.3347/\sqrt{6}} = 2.20$$

Now let us compute the p-value for this two-tailed test. Because $t = 2.20 > 0$, the test statistic is in the upper tail of the t distribution. With $t = 2.20$, the area in the upper tail to the right of the test statistic can be found by using the t distribution table with degrees of freedom $= n - 1 = 6 - 1 = 5$. Information from the 5 degrees of freedom row of the t distribution table is as follows:

Area in Upper Tail	.20	.10	.05	.025	.01	.005
t Value (5 *df*)	0.920	1.476	2.015	2.571	3.365	4.032

$t = 2.20$

Thus, we see that the area in the upper tail is between .05 and .025. Because this test is a two-tailed test, we double these values to conclude that the p-value is between .10 and .05. This p-value is greater than $\alpha = .05$. Thus, the null hypothesis H_0: $\mu_d = 0$ is not rejected. Using Excel and the data in Table 10.2, we find the p-value $= .0795$.

We can also obtain an interval estimate of the difference between the two population means by using the single population methodology of Chapter 8. At 95% confidence, the calculation follows.

$$\bar{d} \pm t_{.025}\frac{s_d}{\sqrt{n}}$$

$$.3 \pm 2.571\left(\frac{.3347}{\sqrt{6}}\right)$$

$$.3 \pm .35$$

FIGURE 10.8   USING EXCEL FOR A HYPOTHESIS TEST IN THE MATCHED SAMPLES STUDY

	A	B	C	D	E	F	G	H
1	Worker	Method 1	Method 2		t-Test: Paired Two Sample for Means			
2	1	6	5.4					
3	2	5	5.2			*Method 1*	*Method 2*	
4	3	7	6.5		**Mean**	6.1	5.8	
5	4	6.2	5.9		**Variance**	0.428	0.212	
6	5	6	6		**Observations**	6	6	
7	6	6.4	5.8		**Pearson Correlation**	0.8764		
8					**Hypothesized Mean Difference**	0		
9					**df**	5		
10					**t Stat**	2.196		
11					**P(T<=t) one-tail**	0.0398		
12					**t Critical one-tail**	2.015		
13					**P(T<=t) two-tail**	0.0795		
14					**t Critical two-tail**	2.571		
15								

Thus, the margin of error is .35 and the 95% confidence interval for the difference between the population means of the two production methods is $-.05$ minutes to .65 minutes.

Using Excel to Conduct a Hypothesis Test

Excel's t-Test: Paired Two Sample for Means tool can be used to conduct a hypothesis test about the difference between the population means when a matched sample design is used. We illustrate by conducting the hypothesis test involving the two production methods. Refer to the Excel worksheet shown in Figure 10.8 and the dialog box in Figure 10.9 as we describe the tasks involved.

FIGURE 10.9   DIALOG BOX FOR EXCEL'S t-TEST: PAIRED TWO SAMPLE FOR MEANS TOOL

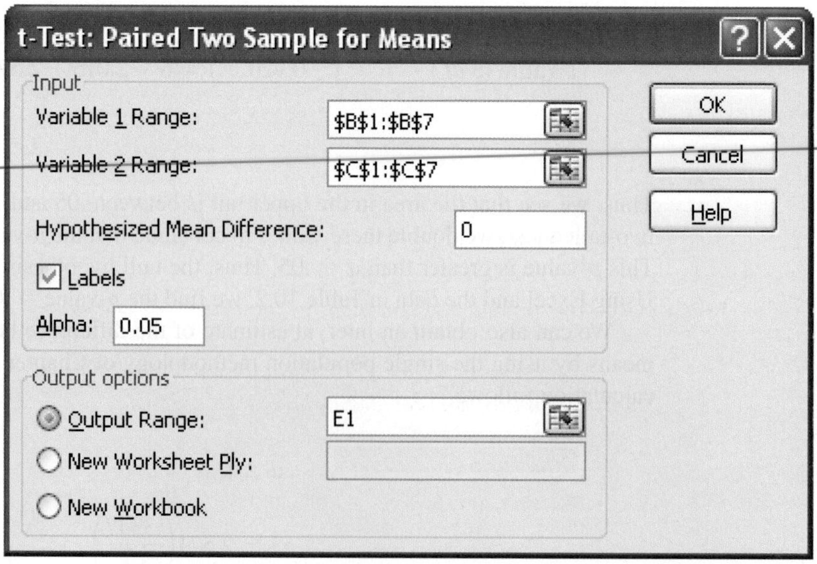

Enter Data: Column A is used to identify each of the six workers who participated in the study. Column B contains the completion time data for each worker using method 1, and column C contains the completion time data for each worker using method 2.

Apply Tools: The following steps describe how to use Excel's t-Test: Paired Two Sample for Means tool to conduct the hypothesis test about the difference between the means of the two production methods

Step 1. Click the **Data** tab on the Ribbon
Step 2. In the **Analysis** group, click **Data Analysis**
Step 3. Choose **t-Test: Paired Two Sample for Means** from the list of Analysis Tools
Step 4. When the t-Test: Paired Two Sample for Means dialog box appears (see Figure 10.9),

Enter B1:B7 in the **Variable 1 Range** box
Enter C1:C7 in the **Variable 2 Range** box
Enter 0 in the **Hypothesized Mean Difference** box
Select **Labels**
Enter .05 in the **Alpha** box
Select **Output Range**
Enter E1 in the **Output Range** box (to identify the upper left corner of the section of the worksheet where the output will appear)
Click **OK**

The results are shown in cells E1:G14 of the worksheet shown in Figure 10.8. The *p*-value for the test, labeled P(T<= t) two-tail, is shown in cell F13. Because the *p*-value, .0795, is greater than the level of significance $\alpha = .05$, we cannot reject the null hypothesis that the mean completion times are equal.

The same procedure can also be used to conduct one-tailed hypothesis tests. The only change required to make the hypothesis testing decision is that we need to use the *p*-value for a one-tailed test, labeled P(T<= t) one-tail (see cell F11).

NOTES AND COMMENTS

1. In the example presented in this section, workers performed the production task with first one method and then the other method. This example illustrates a matched sample design in which each sampled element (worker) provides a pair of data values. It is also possible to use different but "similar" elements to provide the pair of data values. For example, a worker at one location could be matched with a similar worker at another location (similarity based on age, education, gender, experience, etc.). The pairs of workers would provide the difference data that could be used in the matched sample analysis.

2. A matched sample procedure for inferences about two population means generally provides better precision than the independent sample approach; therefore, it is the recommended design. However, in some applications the matching cannot be achieved, or perhaps the time and cost associated with matching are excessive. In such cases, the independent sample design should be used.

Exercises

Methods

19. Consider the following hypothesis test.

$$H_0: \mu_d \leq 0$$
$$H_a: \mu_d > 0$$

The following data are from matched samples taken from two populations.

| | Population | |
Element	1	2
1	21	20
2	28	26
3	18	18
4	20	20
5	26	24

a. Compute the difference value for each element.
b. Compute $\bar{d}$.
c. Compute the standard deviation s_d.
d. Conduct a hypothesis test using $\alpha = .05$. What is your conclusion?

20. The following data are from matched samples taken from two populations.

| | Population | |
Element	1	2
1	11	8
2	7	8
3	9	6
4	12	7
5	13	10
6	15	15
7	15	14

a. Compute the difference value for each element.
b. Compute $\bar{d}$.
c. Compute the standard deviation s_d.
d. What is the point estimate of the difference between the two population means?
e. Provide a 95% confidence interval for the difference between the two population means.

Applications

21. A market research firm used a sample of individuals to rate the purchase potential of a particular product before and after the individuals saw a new television commercial about the product. The purchase potential ratings were based on a 0 to 10 scale, with higher values indicating a higher purchase potential. The null hypothesis stated that the mean rating "after" would be less than or equal to the mean rating "before." Rejection of this hypothesis would show that the commercial improved the mean purchase potential rating. Use $\alpha = .05$ and the following data to test the hypothesis and comment on the value of the commercial.

| | Purchase Rating | | | Purchase Rating | |
Individual	After	Before	Individual	After	Before
1	6	5	5	3	5
2	6	4	6	9	8
3	7	7	7	7	5
4	4	3	8	6	6

Earnings2005

22. Per-share earnings data comparing the current quarter's earnings with the previous quarter are in the file named Earnings2005 (*The Wall Street Journal,* January 27, 2006). Provide a 95% confidence interval estimate of the difference between the population mean for the current quarter versus the previous quarter. Have earnings increased?

23. Bank of America's Consumer Spending Survey collected data on annual credit card charges in seven different categories of expenditures: transportation, groceries, dining out, household expenses, home furnishings, apparel, and entertainment (*US Airways Attaché,* December 2003). Using data from a sample of 42 credit card accounts, assume that each account was used to identify the annual credit card charges for groceries (population 1) and the annual credit card charges for dining out (population 2). Using the difference data, the sample mean difference was $\bar{d} = \$850$, and the sample standard deviation was $s_d = \$1123$.

    a. Formulate the null and alternative hypotheses to test for no difference between the population mean credit card charges for groceries and the population mean credit card charges for dining out.

    b. Use a .05 level of significance. Can you conclude that the population means differ? What is the *p*-value?

    c. Which category, groceries or dining out, has a higher population mean annual credit card charge? What is the point estimate of the difference between the population means? What is the 95% confidence interval estimate of the difference between the population means?

24. Airline travelers often choose which airport to fly from based on flight cost. Cost data (in dollars) for a sample of flights to eight cities from Dayton, Ohio, and Louisville, Kentucky, were collected to help determine which of the two airports was more costly to fly from (*The Cincinnati Enquirer,* February 19, 2006). A researcher argued that it is significantly more costly to fly out of Dayton than Louisville. Use the sample data to see whether they support the researcher's argument. Use $\alpha = .05$ as the level of significance.

AirFare

Destination	Dayton	Louisville
Chicago-O'Hare	$319	$142
Grand Rapids, Michigan	192	213
Portland, Oregon	503	317
Atlanta	256	387
Seattle	339	317
South Bend, Indiana	379	167
Miami	268	273
Dallas–Ft. Worth	288	274

25. In recent years, a growing array of entertainment options competes for consumer time. By 2004, cable television and radio surpassed broadcast television, recorded music, and the daily newspaper to become the two entertainment media with the greatest usage (*The Wall Street Journal,* January 26, 2004). Researchers used a sample of 15 individuals and collected data on the hours per week spent watching cable television and hours per week spent listening to the radio.

TVRadio

Individual	Television	Radio	Individual	Television	Radio
1	22	25	9	21	21
2	8	10	10	23	23
3	25	29	11	14	15
4	22	19	12	14	18
5	12	13	13	14	17
6	26	28	14	16	15
7	22	23	15	24	23
8	19	21			

    a. Use a .05 level of significance and test for a difference between the population mean usage for cable television and radio. What is the *p*-value?

    b. What is the sample mean number of hours per week spent watching cable television? What is the sample mean number of hours per week spent listening to radio? Which medium has the greater usage?

26. StreetInsider.com reported 2002 earnings per share data for a sample of major companies (February 12, 2003). Prior to 2002, financial analysts predicted the 2002 earnings per share for these same companies (*Barron's,* September 10, 2001). Use the following data to comment on differences between actual and estimated earnings per share.

Earnings

Company	Actual	Predicted
AT&T	1.29	0.38
American Express	2.01	2.31
Citigroup	2.59	3.43
Coca-Cola	1.60	1.78
DuPont	1.84	2.18
ExxonMobil	2.72	2.19
General Electric	1.51	1.71
Johnson & Johnson	2.28	2.18
McDonald's	0.77	1.55
Wal-Mart	1.81	1.74

    a. Use $\alpha = .05$ and test for any difference between the population mean actual and population mean predicted earnings per share. What is the *p*-value? What is your conclusion?

    b. What is the point estimate of the difference between the two means? Did the analysts tend to underestimate or overestimate the earnings?

    c. At 95% confidence, what is the margin of error for the estimate in part (b)? What would you recommend based on this information?

27. A manufacturer produces both a deluxe and a standard model of an automatic sander designed for home use. Selling prices obtained from a sample of retail outlets follow.

	Model Price ($)				Model Price ($)	
Retail Outlet	Deluxe	Standard		Retail Outlet	Deluxe	Standard
1	39	27		5	40	30
2	39	28		6	39	34
3	45	35		7	35	29
4	38	30				

    a. The manufacturer's suggested retail prices for the two models show a $10 price differential. Use a .05 level of significance and test that the mean difference between the prices of the two models is $10.

    b. What is the 95% confidence interval for the difference between the mean prices of the two models?

10.4   An Introduction to Experimental Design and Analysis of Variance

In Chapter 1 we stated that statistical studies can be classified as either experimental or observational. In an experimental statistical study, an experiment is conducted to generate the data. An experiment begins with identifying a variable of interest. Then one or more other variables, thought to be related, are identified and controlled, and data are collected about how those variables influence the variable of interest.

In an observational study, data are usually obtained through sample surveys and not a controlled experiment. Good design principles are still employed, but the rigorous controls associated with an experimental statistical study are often not possible. For instance, in a study of the relationship between smoking and lung cancer the researcher cannot assign a smoking habit to subjects. The researcher is restricted to simply observing the effects of smoking on people who already smoke and the effects of not smoking on people who already do not smoke.

Sir Ronald Alymer Fisher (1890–1962) invented the branch of statistics known as experimental design. In addition to being accomplished in statistics, he was a noted scientist in the field of genetics.

In this section we introduce the basic principles of an experimental study and show how they are used in a completely randomized design. We also provide a conceptual overview of the statistical procedure called analysis of variance (ANOVA). In the following section we show how ANOVA can be used to test for the equality of k population means using data obtained from a completely randomized design as well as data obtained from an observational study. So, in this sense, ANOVA extends the statistical material in the preceding sections from two population means to three or more population means. In later chapters, we will see that ANOVA plays a key role in analyzing the results of regression studies involving both experimental and observational data.

Cause-and-effect relationships can be difficult to establish in observational studies; such relationships are easier to establish in experimental studies.

As an example of an experimental statistical study, let us consider the problem facing Chemitech, Inc. Chemitech developed a new filtration system for municipal water supplies. The components for the new filtration system will be purchased from several suppliers, and Chemitech will assemble the components at its plant in Columbia, South Carolina. The industrial engineering group is responsible for determining the best assembly method for the new filtration system. After considering a variety of possible approaches, the group narrows the alternatives to three: method A, method B, and method C. These methods differ in the sequence of steps used to assemble the system. Managers at Chemitech want to determine which assembly method can produce the greatest number of filtration systems per week.

In the Chemitech experiment, assembly method is the independent variable or **factor**. Because three assembly methods correspond to this factor, we say that three treatments are associated with this experiment; each **treatment** corresponds to one of the three assembly methods. The Chemitech problem is an example of a **single-factor experiment**; it involves one categorical factor (method of assembly). More complex experiments may consist of multiple factors; some factors may be categorical and others may be quantitative.

The three assembly methods or treatments define the three populations of interest for the Chemitech experiment. One population is all Chemitech employees who use assembly method A, another is those who use method B, and the third is those who use method C. Note that for each population the dependent or **response variable** is the number of filtration systems produced per week, and the primary statistical objective of the experiment is to determine whether the mean number of units produced per week is the same for all three populations (methods).

Randomization is the process of assigning the treatments to the experimental units at random. Prior to the work of Sir R. A. Fisher, treatments were assigned on a systematic or subjective basis.

Suppose a random sample of three employees is selected from all assembly workers at the Chemitech production facility. In experimental design terminology, the three randomly selected workers are the **experimental units**. The experimental design that we will use for the Chemitech problem is called a **completely randomized design**. This type of design requires that each of the three assembly methods or treatments be assigned randomly to one of the experimental units or workers. For example, method A might be randomly assigned to the second worker, method B to the first worker, and method C to the third worker. The concept of *randomization,* as illustrated in this example, is an important principle of all experimental designs.

To obtain additional data for each assembly method, we must repeat or replicate the basic experimental process. Suppose, for example, that instead of selecting just 3 workers at random we selected 15 workers and then randomly assigned each of the three treatments to

FIGURE 10.10   COMPLETELY RANDOMIZED DESIGN FOR EVALUATING
THE CHEMITECH ASSEMBLY METHOD EXPERIMENT

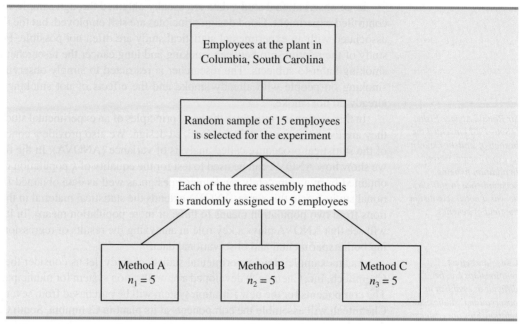

5 of the workers. Because each method of assembly is assigned to 5 workers, we say that five replicates have been obtained. The process of *replication* is another important principle of experimental design. Figure 10.10 shows the completely randomized design for the Chemitech experiment.

Data Collection

Once we are satisfied with the experimental design, we proceed by collecting and analyzing the data. In the Chemitech case, the employees would be instructed in how to perform the assembly method assigned to them and then would begin producing the new filtration systems using that method. After this assignment and training, the number of units produced by each employee during one week is as shown in Table 10.3. The sample means, sample variances, and sample standard deviations for each assembly method are also provided. Thus, the sample mean number of units produced using method A is 62; the sample mean using method B is 66; and the sample mean using method C is 52. From these data, method B appears to result in higher production rates than either of the other methods.

The real issue is whether the three sample means observed are different enough for us to conclude that the means of the populations corresponding to the three methods of assembly are different. To write this question in statistical terms, we introduce the following notation:

$$\mu_1 = \text{mean number of units produced per week using method A}$$
$$\mu_2 = \text{mean number of units produced per week using method B}$$
$$\mu_3 = \text{mean number of units produced per week using method C}$$

If H_0 is rejected, we cannot conclude that all population means are different. Rejecting H_0 means that at least two population means have different values.

Although we will never know the actual values of μ_1, μ_2, and μ_3, we want to use the sample means to test the following hypotheses.

$$H_0: \mu_1 = \mu_2 = \mu_3$$
$$H_a: \text{Not all population means are equal}$$

TABLE 10.3   NUMBER OF UNITS PRODUCED BY 15 WORKERS

WEB file

Chemitech

	Method		
	A	**B**	**C**
	58	58	48
	64	69	57
	55	71	59
	66	64	47
	67	68	49
Sample mean	62	66	52
Sample variance	27.5	26.5	31.0
Sample standard deviation	5.244	5.148	5.568

As we will demonstrate shortly, analysis of variance (ANOVA) is the statistical procedure used to determine whether the observed differences in the three sample means are large enough to reject H_0.

Assumptions for Analysis of Variance

Three assumptions are required to use analysis of variance.

If the sample sizes are equal, analysis of variance is not sensitive to departures from the assumption of normally distributed populations.

1. **For each population, the response variable is normally distributed.** Implication: In the Chemitech experiment the number of units produced per week (response variable) must be normally distributed for each assembly method.
2. **The variance of the response variable, denoted σ^2, is the same for all the populations.** Implication: In the Chemitech experiment, the variance of the number of units produced per week must be the same for each assembly method.
3. **The observations must be independent.** Implication: In the Chemitech experiment, the number of units produced per week for each employee must be independent of the number of units produced per week for any other employee.

Analysis of Variance: A Conceptual Overview

If the means for the three populations are equal, we would expect the three sample means to be close together. In fact, the closer the three sample means are to one another, the more evidence we have for the conclusion that the population means are equal. Alternatively, the more the sample means differ, the more evidence we have for the conclusion that the population means are not equal. In other words, if the variability among the sample means is "small," it supports H_0; if the variability among the sample means is "large," it supports H_a.

If the null hypothesis, $H_0: \mu_1 = \mu_2 = \mu_3$, is true, we can use the variability among the sample means to develop an estimate of σ^2. First, note that if the assumptions for analysis of variance are satisfied, each sample will have come from the same normal distribution with mean μ and variance σ^2. Recall from Chapter 7 that the sampling distribution of the sample mean $\bar{x}$ for a simple random sample of size n from a normal population will be normally distributed with mean μ and variance σ^2/n. Figure 10.11 illustrates such a sampling distribution.

Thus, if the null hypothesis is true, we can think of each of the three sample means, $\bar{x}_1 = 62$, $\bar{x}_2 = 66$, and $\bar{x}_3 = 52$ from Table 10.3, as values drawn at random from the sampling distribution shown in Figure 10.11. In this case, the mean and variance of the three $\bar{x}$ values can be used to estimate the mean and variance of the sampling distribution. When

FIGURE 10.11   SAMPLING DISTRIBUTION OF $\bar{x}$ GIVEN H_0 IS TRUE

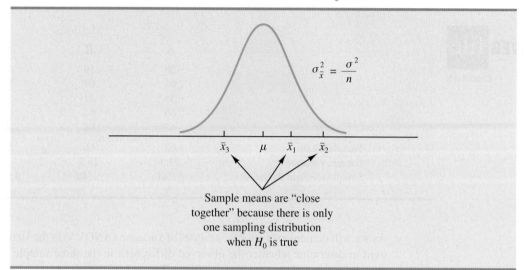

the sample sizes are equal, as in the Chemitech experiment, the best estimate of the mean of the sampling distribution of $\bar{x}$ is the mean or average of the sample means. Thus, in the Chemitech experiment, an estimate of the mean of the sampling distribution of $\bar{x}$ is $(62 + 66 + 52)/3 = 60$. We refer to this estimate as the *overall sample mean*. An estimate of the variance of the sampling distribution of $\bar{x}$, $\sigma_{\bar{x}}^2$, is provided by the variance of the three sample means.

$$s_{\bar{x}}^2 = \frac{(62 - 60)^2 + (66 - 60)^2 + (52 - 60)^2}{3 - 1} = \frac{104}{2} = 52$$

Because $\sigma_{\bar{x}}^2 = \sigma^2/n$, solving for σ^2 gives

$$\sigma^2 = n\sigma_{\bar{x}}^2$$

Hence,

$$\text{Estimate of } \sigma^2 = n (\text{Estimate of } \sigma_{\bar{x}}^2) = ns_{\bar{x}}^2 = 5(52) = 260$$

The result, $ns_{\bar{x}}^2 = 260$, is referred to as the *between-treatments* estimate of σ^2.

The between-treatments estimate of σ^2 is based on the assumption that the null hypothesis is true. In this case, each sample comes from the same population, and there is only one sampling distribution of $\bar{x}$. To illustrate what happens when H_0 is false, suppose the population means all differ. Note that because the three samples are from normal populations with different means, they will result in three different sampling distributions. Figure 10.12 shows that in this case, the sample means are not as close together as they were when H_0 was true. Thus, $s_{\bar{x}}^2$ will be larger, causing the between-treatments estimate of σ^2 to be larger. In general, when the population means are not equal, the between-treatments estimate will overestimate the population variance σ^2.

The variation within each of the samples also has an effect on the conclusion we reach in analysis of variance. When a simple random sample is selected from each population, each of the sample variances provides an unbiased estimate of σ^2. Hence, we can combine or pool the individual estimates of σ^2 into one overall estimate. The estimate of σ^2 obtained in this

FIGURE 10.12   SAMPLING DISTRIBUTIONS OF $\bar{x}$ GIVEN H_0 IS FALSE

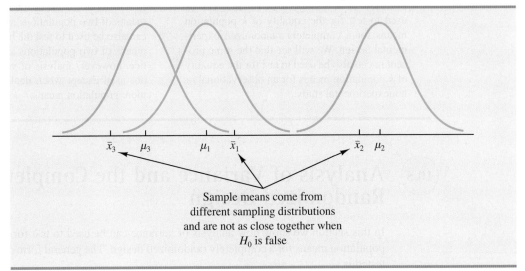

Sample means come from
different sampling distributions
and are not as close together when
H_0 is false

way is called the *pooled* or *within-treatments* estimate of σ^2. Because each sample variance provides an estimate of σ^2 based only on the variation within each sample, the within-treatments estimate of σ^2 is not affected by whether the population means are equal. When the sample sizes are equal, the within-treatments estimate of σ^2 can be obtained by computing the average of the individual sample variances. For the Chemitech experiment we obtain

$$\text{Within-treatments estimate of } \sigma^2 = \frac{27.5 + 26.5 + 31.0}{3} = \frac{85}{3} = 28.33$$

In the Chemitech experiment, the between-treatments estimate of σ^2 (260) is much larger than the within-treatments estimate of σ^2 (28.33). In fact, the ratio of these two estimates is $260/28.33 = 9.18$. Recall, however, that the between-treatments approach provides a good estimate of σ^2 only if the null hypothesis is true; if the null hypothesis is false, the between-treatments approach overestimates σ^2. The within-treatments approach provides a good estimate of σ^2 in either case. Thus, if the null hypothesis is true, the two estimates will be similar and their ratio will be close to 1. If the null hypothesis is false, the between-treatments estimate will be larger than the within-treatments estimate, and their ratio will be large. In the next section we will show how large this ratio must be to reject H_0.

In summary, the logic behind ANOVA is based on the development of two independent estimates of the common population variance σ^2. One estimate of σ^2 is based on the variability among the sample means themselves, and the other estimate of σ^2 is based on the variability of the data within each sample. By comparing these two estimates of σ^2, we will be able to determine whether the population means are equal.

NOTES AND COMMENTS

1. Randomization in experimental design is the analog of probability sampling in an observational study.
2. In many medical experiments, potential bias is eliminated by using a double-blind experi-mental design. With this design, neither the physician applying the treatment nor the subject knows which treatment is being applied. Many other types of experiments could bene-fit from this type of design.

3. In this section we provided a conceptual overview of how analysis of variance can be used to test for the equality of k population means for a completely randomized experimental design. We will see that the same procedure can also be used to test for the equality of k population means for an observational or nonexperimental study.

4. In Sections 10.1 and 10.2 we presented statistical methods for testing the hypothesis that the means of two populations are equal. ANOVA can also be used to test the hypothesis that the means of two populations are equal. In practice, however, analysis of variance is usually not used except when dealing with three or more population means.

10.5   Analysis of Variance and the Completely Randomized Design

In this section we show how analysis of variance can be used to test for the equality of k population means for a completely randomized design. The general form of the hypotheses tested is

$$H_0: \mu_1 = \mu_2 = \cdots = \mu_k$$
$$H_a: \text{Not all population means are equal}$$

where

$$\mu_j = \text{mean of the } j\text{th population}$$

We assume that a simple random sample of size n_j has been selected from each of the k populations or treatments. For the resulting sample data, let

$$x_{ij} = \text{value of observation } i \text{ for treatment } j$$
$$n_j = \text{number of observations for treatment } j$$
$$\bar{x}_j = \text{sample mean for treatment } j$$
$$s_j^2 = \text{sample variance for treatment } j$$
$$s_j = \text{sample standard deviation for treatment } j$$

The formulas for the sample mean and sample variance for treatment j are as follows:

$$\bar{x}_j = \frac{\sum_{i=1}^{n_j} x_{ij}}{n_j} \tag{10.10}$$

$$s_j^2 = \frac{\sum_{i=1}^{n_j} (x_{ij} - \bar{x}_j)^2}{n_j - 1} \tag{10.11}$$

The overall sample mean, denoted $\bar{\bar{x}}$, is the sum of all the observations divided by the total number of observations. That is,

$$\bar{\bar{x}} = \frac{\sum_{j=1}^{k} \sum_{i=1}^{n_j} x_{ij}}{n_T} \tag{10.12}$$

where

$$n_T = n_1 + n_2 + \cdots + n_k \qquad \textbf{(10.13)}$$

If the size of each sample is n, $n_T = kn$; in this case equation (10.12) reduces to

$$\bar{\bar{x}} = \frac{\displaystyle\sum_{j=1}^{k}\sum_{i=1}^{n_j} x_{ij}}{kn} = \frac{\displaystyle\sum_{j=1}^{k}\sum_{i=1}^{n_j} x_{ij}/n}{k} = \frac{\displaystyle\sum_{j=1}^{k} \bar{x}_j}{k} \qquad \textbf{(10.14)}$$

In other words, whenever the sample sizes are the same, the overall sample mean is just the average of the k sample means.

Because each sample in the Chemitech experiment consists of $n = 5$ observations, the overall sample mean can be computed by using equation (10.14). For the data in Table 10.3 we obtained the following result:

$$\bar{\bar{x}} = \frac{62 + 66 + 52}{3} = 60$$

If the null hypothesis is true ($\mu_1 = \mu_2 = \mu_3 = \mu$), the overall sample mean of 60 is the best estimate of the population mean μ.

Between-Treatments Estimate of Population Variance

In the preceding section, we introduced the concept of a between-treatments estimate of σ^2 and showed how to compute it when the sample sizes were equal. This estimate of σ^2 is called the *mean square due to treatments* and is denoted MSTR. The general formula for computing MSTR is

$$\text{MSTR} = \frac{\displaystyle\sum_{j=1}^{k} n_j(\bar{x}_j - \bar{\bar{x}})^2}{k - 1} \qquad \textbf{(10.15)}$$

The numerator in equation (10.15) is called the *sum of squares due to treatments* and is denoted SSTR. The denominator, $k - 1$, represents the degrees of freedom associated with SSTR. Hence, the mean square due to treatments can be computed using the following formula.

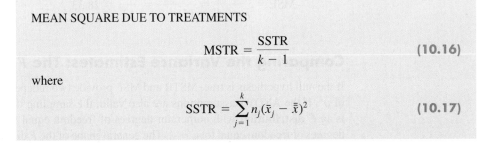

MEAN SQUARE DUE TO TREATMENTS

$$\text{MSTR} = \frac{\text{SSTR}}{k - 1} \qquad \textbf{(10.16)}$$

where

$$\text{SSTR} = \sum_{j=1}^{k} n_j(\bar{x}_j - \bar{\bar{x}})^2 \qquad \textbf{(10.17)}$$

If H_0 is true, MSTR provides an unbiased estimate of σ^2. However, if the means of the k populations are not equal, MSTR is not an unbiased estimate of σ^2; in fact, in that case, MSTR should overestimate σ^2.

For the Chemitech data in Table 10.3, we obtain the following results:

$$\text{SSTR} = \sum_{j=1}^{k} n_j(\bar{x}_j - \bar{\bar{x}})^2 = 5(62 - 60)^2 + 5(66 - 60)^2 + 5(52 - 60)^2 = 520$$

$$\text{MSTR} = \frac{\text{SSTR}}{k-1} = \frac{520}{2} = 260$$

Within-Treatments Estimate of Population Variance

Earlier, we introduced the concept of a within-treatments estimate of σ^2 and showed how to compute it when the sample sizes were equal. This estimate of σ^2 is called the *mean square due to error* and is denoted MSE. The general formula for computing MSE is

$$\text{MSE} = \frac{\sum_{j=1}^{k}(n_j - 1)s_j^2}{n_T - k} \qquad (10.18)$$

The numerator in equation (10.18) is called the *sum of squares due to error* and is denoted SSE. The denominator of MSE is referred to as the degrees of freedom associated with SSE. Hence, the formula for MSE can also be stated as follows.

MEAN SQUARE DUE TO ERROR

$$\text{MSE} = \frac{\text{SSE}}{n_T - k} \qquad (10.19)$$

where

$$\text{SSE} = \sum_{j=1}^{k}(n_j - 1)s_j^2 \qquad (10.20)$$

Note that MSE is based on the variation within each of the treatments; it is not influenced by whether the null hypothesis is true. Thus, MSE always provides an unbiased estimate of σ^2.

For the Chemitech data in Table 10.3 we obtain the following results:

$$\text{SSE} = \sum_{j=1}^{k}(n_j - 1)s_j^2 = (5 - 1)27.5 + (5 - 1)26.5 + (5 - 1)31 = 340$$

$$\text{MSE} = \frac{\text{SSE}}{n_T - k} = \frac{340}{15 - 3} = \frac{340}{12} = 28.33$$

Comparing the Variance Estimates: The F Test

If the null hypothesis is true, MSTR and MSE provide two independent, unbiased estimates of σ^2. If the ANOVA assumptions are also valid, the sampling distribution of MSTR/MSE is an **F distribution** with numerator degrees of freedom equal to $k - 1$ and denominator degrees of freedom equal to $n_T - k$. The general shape of the F distribution is shown in Figure 10.13. If the null hypothesis is true, the value of MSTR/MSE should appear to be from this F distribution.

However, if the null hypothesis is false, the value of MSTR/MSE will be inflated because MSTR overestimates σ^2. Hence, we will reject H_0 if the resulting value of MSTR/MSE appears to be too large to have been selected from an F distribution with $k - 1$ numerator degrees of freedom and $n_T - k$ denominator degrees of freedom. Because the decision to

FIGURE 10.13 COMPUTATION OF p-VALUE USING THE SAMPLING DISTRIBUTION OF MSTR/MSE

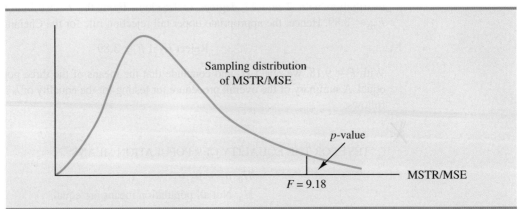

reject H_0 is based on the value of MSTR/MSE, the test statistic used to test for the equality of k population means is as follows.

TEST STATISTIC FOR THE EQUALITY OF k POPULATION MEANS

$$F = \frac{MSTR}{MSE} \qquad (10.21)$$

The test statistic follows an F distribution with $k - 1$ degrees of freedom in the numerator and $n_T - k$ degrees of freedom in the denominator.

Let us return to the Chemitech experiment and use a level of significance $\alpha = .05$ to conduct the hypothesis test. The value of the test statistic is

$$F = \frac{MSTR}{MSE} = \frac{260}{28.33} = 9.18$$

The numerator degrees of freedom is $k - 1 = 3 - 1 = 2$ and the denominator degrees of freedom is $n_T - k = 15 - 3 = 12$. Because we will only reject the null hypothesis for large values of the test statistic, the p-value is the upper tail area of the F distribution to the right of the test statistic $F = 9.18$. Figure 10.13 shows the sampling distribution of $F = $ MSTR/MSE, the value of the test statistic, and the upper tail area that is the p-value for the hypothesis test.

From Table 4 of Appendix B we find the following areas in the upper tail of an F distribution with 2 numerator degrees of freedom and 12 denominator degrees of freedom.

Area in Upper Tail	.10	.05	.025	.01
F Value ($df_1 = 2$, $df_2 = 12$)	2.81	3.89	5.10	6.93

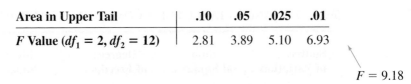

$F = 9.18$

Using Excel, p-value = FDIST(9.18,2,12) = .004.

Because $F = 9.18$ is greater than 6.93, the area in the upper tail at $F = 9.18$ is less than .01. Thus, the p-value is less than .01. Excel can be used to show that the exact p-value is .004. With p-value $\leq \alpha = .05$, H_0 is rejected. The test provides sufficient evidence to conclude that the means of the three populations are not equal. In other words, analysis of variance supports the conclusion that the population mean number of units produced per week for the three assembly methods are not equal.

As with other hypothesis testing procedures, the critical value approach may also be used. With $\alpha = .05$, the critical F value occurs with an area of .05 in the upper tail of an F distribution with 2 and 12 degrees of freedom. From the F distribution table, we find $F_{.05} = 3.89$. Hence, the appropriate upper tail rejection rule for the Chemitech experiment is

$$\text{Reject } H_0 \text{ if } F \geq 3.89$$

With $F = 9.18$, we reject H_0 and conclude that the means of the three populations are not equal. A summary of the overall procedure for testing for the equality of k population means follows.

TEST FOR THE EQUALITY OF k POPULATION MEANS

$$H_0: \mu_1 = \mu_2 = \cdots = \mu_k$$
$$H_a: \text{Not all population means are equal}$$

TEST STATISTIC

$$F = \frac{\text{MSTR}}{\text{MSE}}$$

REJECTION RULE

p-value approach:	Reject H_0 if p-value $\leq \alpha$
Critical value approach:	Reject H_0 if $F \geq F_\alpha$

where the value of F_α is based on an F distribution with $k - 1$ numerator degrees of freedom and $n_T - k$ denominator degrees of freedom.

ANOVA Table

The results of the preceding calculations can be displayed conveniently in a table referred to as the analysis of variance or **ANOVA table**. The general form of the ANOVA table for a completely randomized design is shown in Table 10.4; Table 10.5 is the corresponding ANOVA table for the Chemitech experiment. The sum of squares associated with the source of variation referred to as "Total" is called the total sum of squares (SST). Note that the results for the Chemitech experiment suggest that SST = SSTR + SSE, and that the degrees of freedom associated with this total sum of squares is the sum of the degrees of freedom associated with the sum of squares due to treatments and the sum of squares due to error.

We point out that SST divided by its degrees of freedom $n_T - 1$ is nothing more than the overall sample variance that would be obtained if we treated the entire set of 15 observations

TABLE 10.4 ANOVA TABLE FOR A COMPLETELY RANDOMIZED DESIGN

Source of Variation	Sum of Squares	Degrees of Freedom	Mean Square	F	p-value
Treatments	SSTR	$k - 1$	$\text{MSTR} = \dfrac{\text{SSTR}}{k - 1}$	$\dfrac{\text{MSTR}}{\text{MSE}}$	
Error	SSE	$n_T - k$	$\text{MSE} = \dfrac{\text{SSE}}{n_T - k}$		
Total	SST	$n_T - 1$			

TABLE 10.5   ANOVA TABLE FOR THE CHEMITECH EXPERIMENT

Source of Variation	Sum of Squares	Degrees of Freedom	Mean Square	F	p-value
Treatments	520	2	260.00	9.18	.004
Error	340	12	28.33		
Total	860	14			

as one data set. With the entire data set as one sample, the formula for computing the total sum of squares, SST, is

$$\text{SST} = \sum_{j=1}^{k}\sum_{i=1}^{n_j}(x_{ij} - \bar{\bar{x}})^2 \tag{10.22}$$

It can be shown that the results we observed for the analysis of variance table for the Chemitech experiment also apply to other problems. That is,

$$\text{SST} = \text{SSTR} + \text{SSE} \tag{10.23}$$

Analysis of variance can be thought of as a statistical procedure for partitioning the total sum of squares into separate components.

In other words, SST can be partitioned into two sums of squares: the sum of squares due to treatments and the sum of squares due to error. Note also that the degrees of freedom corresponding to SST, $n_T - 1$, can be partitioned into the degrees of freedom corresponding to SSTR, $k - 1$, and the degrees of freedom corresponding to SSE, $n_T - k$. The analysis of variance can be viewed as the process of **partitioning** the total sum of squares and the degrees of freedom into their corresponding sources: treatments and error. Dividing the sum of squares by the appropriate degrees of freedom provides the variance estimates, the F value, and the p-value used to test the hypothesis of equal population means.

Using Excel

Excel's Anova: Single Factor tool can be used to conduct a hypothesis test about the difference between the population means for the Chemitech experiment. Refer to the Excel worksheet shown in Figure 10.14 as we describe the tasks involved.

Enter Data: Columns A, B, and C contain labels and the number of filtration systems produced per week for each method of assembly.

Apply Tools: The following steps describe how to use Excel's Anova: Single Factor tool to test the hypothesis that the mean number of units produced per week is the same for all three methods of assembly.

> **Step 1.** Click the **Data** tab on the Ribbon
> **Step 2.** In the **Analysis** group, click **Data Analysis**
> **Step 3.** Choose **Anova: Single Factor** from the list of Analysis Tools
> **Step 4.** When the Anova: Single Factor dialog box appears (see Figure 10.15),
> >   Enter A1:C6 in the **Input Range** box
> >   Select **Grouped By: Columns**
> >   Select **Labels in First Row**
> >   Enter .05 in the **Alpha** box
> >   Select **Output Range**
> >   Enter A8 in the **Output Range** box (to identify the upper left corner of the section of the worksheet where the output will appear)
> >   Click **OK**

FIGURE 10.14 EXCEL'S ANOVA: SINGLE FACTOR TOOL OUTPUT FOR THE
CHEMITECH EXPERIMENT

	A	B	C	D	E	F	G	H
1	**Method A**	**Method B**	**Method C**					
2	58	58	48					
3	64	69	57					
4	55	71	59					
5	66	64	47					
6	67	68	49					
7								
8	Anova: Single Factor							
9								
10	SUMMARY							
11	*Groups*	*Count*	*Sum*	*Average*	*Variance*			
12	Method A	5	310	62	27.5			
13	Method B	5	330	66	26.5			
14	Method C	5	260	52	31			
15								
16								
17	ANOVA							
18	*Source of Variation*	*SS*	*df*	*MS*	*F*	*P-value*	*F crit*	
19	Between Groups	520	2	260	9.1765	0.0038	3.8853	
20	Within Groups	340	12	28.3333				
21								
22	Total	860	14					
23								
24								

FIGURE 10.15 DIALOG BOX FOR EXCEL'S ANOVA: SINGLE FACTOR TOOL

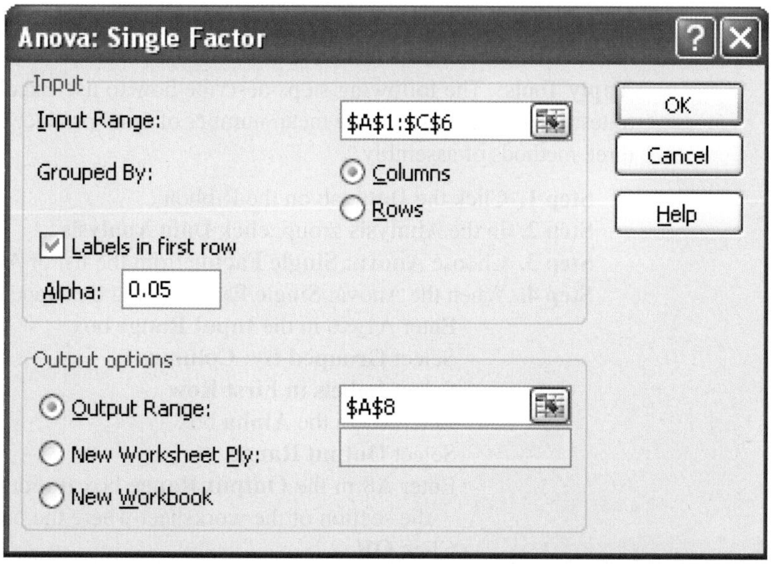

The output, titled *Anova: Single Factor,* appears in cells A8:G22 of the worksheet. Cells A10:E14 provide a summary of the data. Note that the sample mean and sample variance for each method of assembly are the same as shown in Table 10.3. The ANOVA table, shown in cells A17:G22, is basically the same as the ANOVA table shown in Table 10.4. Excel identifies the treatments source of variation using the label *Between Groups* and the error source of variation using the label *Within Groups.* In addition, the Excel output provides the *p*-value associated with the test as well as the critical *F* value.

We can use the *p*-value shown in cell F19, 0.0038, to make the hypothesis testing decision. Thus, at the $\alpha = .05$ level of significance, we reject H_0 because the *p*-value = $0.0038 < \alpha = .05$. Hence, using the *p*-value approach we still conclude that the mean number of units produced per week are not the same for the three assembly methods.

Testing for the Equality of k Population Means: An Observational Study

We have shown how analysis of variance can be used to test for the equality of k population means for a completely randomized experimental design. It is important to understand that ANOVA can also be used to test for the equality of three or more population means using data obtained from an observational study. As an example, let us consider the situation at National Computer Products, Inc. (NCP).

NCP manufactures printers and fax machines at plants located in Atlanta, Dallas, and Seattle. To measure how much employees at these plants know about quality management, a random sample of 6 employees was selected from each plant and the employees selected were given a quality awareness examination. The examination scores for these 18 employees are shown in Table 10.6. The sample means, sample variances, and sample standard deviations for each group are also provided. Managers want to use these data to test the hypothesis that the mean examination score is the same for all three plants.

We define population 1 as all employees at the Atlanta plant, population 2 as all employees at the Dallas plant, and population 3 as all employees at the Seattle plant. Let

μ_1 = mean examination score for population 1

μ_2 = mean examination score for population 2

μ_3 = mean examination score for population 3

Although we will never know the actual values of μ_1, μ_2, and μ_3, we want to use the sample results to test the following hypotheses:

H_0: $\mu_1 = \mu_2 = \mu_3$

H_a: Not all population means are equal

TABLE 10.6   EXAMINATION SCORES FOR 18 EMPLOYEES

WEB file

NCP

	Plant 1 Atlanta	Plant 2 Dallas	Plant 3 Seattle
	85	71	59
	75	75	64
	82	73	62
	76	74	69
	71	69	75
	85	82	67
Sample mean	79	74	66
Sample variance	34	20	32
Sample standard deviation	5.83	4.47	5.66

Exercise 35 will ask you to analyze the NCP data using the analysis of variance procedure.

Note that the hypothesis test for the NCP observational study is exactly the same as the hypothesis test for the Chemitech experiment. Indeed, the same analysis of variance methodology we used to analyze the Chemitech experiment can also be used to analyze the data from the NCP observational study.

Even though the same ANOVA methodology is used for the analysis, it is worth noting how the NCP observational statistical study differs from the Chemitech experimental statistical study. The individuals who conducted the NCP study had no control over how the plants were assigned to individual employees. That is, the plants were already in operation and a particular employee worked at one of the three plants. All that NCP could do was to select a random sample of 6 employees from each plant and administer the quality awareness examination. To be classified as an experimental study, NCP would have had to be able to randomly select 18 employees and then assign the plants to each employee in a random fashion.

NOTES AND COMMENTS

1. The overall sample mean can also be computed as a weighted average of the k sample means.

$$\bar{\bar{x}} = \frac{n_1 \bar{x}_1 + n_2 \bar{x}_2 + \cdots + n_k \bar{x}_k}{n_T}$$

In problems where the sample means are provided, this formula is simpler than equation (10.12) for computing the overall mean.

2. If each sample consists of n observations, equation (10.15) can be written as

$$\text{MSTR} = \frac{n \sum_{j=1}^{k} (\bar{x}_j - \bar{\bar{x}})^2}{k-1} = n \left[\frac{\sum_{j=1}^{k} (\bar{x}_j - \bar{\bar{x}})^2}{k-1} \right]$$

$$= n s_{\bar{x}}^2$$

Note that this result is the same as presented in Section 10.4 when we introduced the concept

of the between-treatments estimate of σ^2. Equation (10.15) is simply a generalization of this result to the unequal sample-size case.

3. If each sample has n observations, $n_T = kn$; thus, $n_T - k = k(n-1)$, and equation (10.18) can be rewritten as

$$\text{MSE} = \frac{\sum_{j=1}^{k} (n-1) s_j^2}{k(n-1)} = \frac{(n-1) \sum_{j=1}^{k} s_j^2}{k(n-1)} = \frac{\sum_{j=1}^{k} s_j^2}{k}$$

In other words, if the sample sizes are the same, MSE is just the average of the k sample variances. Note that it is the same result we used in Section 10.4 when we introduced the concept of the within-treatments estimate of σ^2.

Exercises

Methods

SELF test

28. The following data are from a completely randomized design.

	Treatment		
	A	**B**	**C**
	162	142	126
	142	156	122
	165	124	138
	145	142	140
	148	136	150
	174	152	128
Sample mean	156	142	134
Sample variance	164.4	131.2	110.4

    a. Compute the sum of squares between treatments.
    b. Compute the mean square between treatments.
    c. Compute the sum of squares due to error.
    d. Compute the mean square due to error.
    e. Set up the ANOVA table for this problem.
    f. At the $\alpha = .05$ level of significance, test whether the means for the three treatments are equal.

29. In a completely randomized design, seven experimental units were used for each of the five levels of the factor. Complete the following ANOVA table.

Source of Variation	Sum of Squares	Degrees of Freedom	Mean Square	F	p-value
Treatments	300				
Error					
Total	460				

30. Refer to exercise 29.
    a. What hypotheses are implied in this problem?
    b. At the $\alpha = .05$ level of significance, can we reject the null hypothesis in part (a)? Explain.

31. In an experiment designed to test the output levels of three different treatments, the following results were obtained: SST = 400, SSTR = 150, n_T = 19. Set up the ANOVA table and test for any significant difference between the mean output levels of the three treatments. Use $\alpha = .05$.

32. In a completely randomized design, 12 experimental units were used for the first treatment, 15 for the second treatment, and 20 for the third treatment. Complete the following analysis of variance. At a .05 level of significance, is there a significant difference between the treatments?

Source of Variation	Sum of Squares	Degrees of Freedom	Mean Square	F	p-value
Treatments	1200				
Error					
Total	1800				

33. Develop the analysis of variance computations for the following completely randomized design. At $\alpha = .05$, is there a significant difference between the treatment means?

WEB file

Exer33

	Treatment		
	A	**B**	**C**
	136	107	92
	120	114	82
	113	125	85
	107	104	101
	131	107	89
	114	109	117
	129	97	110
	102	114	120
		104	98
		89	106
$\bar{x}_j$	119	107	100
s_j^2	146.86	96.44	173.78

Applications

34. Three different methods for assembling a product were proposed by an industrial engineer. To investigate the number of units assembled correctly with each method, 30 employees were randomly selected and randomly assigned to the three proposed methods in such a way that each method was used by 10 workers. The number of units assembled correctly was recorded, and the analysis of variance procedure was applied to the resulting data set. The following results were obtained: SST = 10,800; SSTR = 4560.
    a. Set up the ANOVA table for this problem.
    b. Use $\alpha = .05$ to test for any significant difference in the means for the three assembly methods.

35. Refer to the NCP data in Table 10.6. Set up the ANOVA table and test for any significant difference in the mean examination score for the three plants. Use $\alpha = .05$.

36. To study the effect of temperature on yield in a chemical process, five batches were produced at each of three temperature levels. The results follow. Construct an analysis of variance table. Use a .05 level of significance to test whether the temperature level has an effect on the mean yield of the process.

	Temperature	
50°C	**60°C**	**70°C**
34	30	23
24	31	28
36	34	28
39	23	30
32	27	31

37. Auditors must make judgments about various aspects of an audit on the basis of their own direct experience, indirect experience, or a combination of the two. In a study, auditors were asked to make judgments about the frequency of errors to be found in an audit. The judgments by the auditors were then compared to the actual results. Suppose the following data were obtained from a similar study; lower scores indicate better judgments.

WEB file

AudJudg

Direct	**Indirect**	**Combination**
17.0	16.6	25.2
18.5	22.2	24.0
15.8	20.5	21.5
18.2	18.3	26.8
20.2	24.2	27.5
16.0	19.8	25.8
13.3	21.2	24.2

Use $\alpha = .05$ to test to see whether the basis for the judgment affects the quality of the judgment. What is your conclusion?

38. Four different paints are advertised as having the same drying time. To check the manufacturer's claims, five samples were tested for each of the paints. The time in minutes until the paint was dry enough for a second coat to be applied was recorded. The following data were obtained.

	Paint 1	Paint 2	Paint 3	Paint 4
	128	144	133	150
	137	133	143	142
	135	142	137	135
	124	146	136	140
	141	130	131	153

WEB file

Paint

At the $\alpha = .05$ level of significance, test to see whether the mean drying time is the same for each type of paint.

39. A well-known automotive magazine took three top-of-the-line midsize automobiles manufactured in the United States, test-drove them, and compared them on a variety of criteria. In the area of gasoline mileage performance, five automobiles of each brand were each test-driven 500 miles; the miles per gallon data obtained follow. Use $\alpha = .05$ to test whether there is a significant difference in the mean number of miles per gallon for the three types of automobiles.

Automobile		
A	**B**	**C**
19	19	24
21	20	26
20	22	23
19	21	25
21	23	27

Summary

In this chapter we discussed procedures for developing interval estimates and conducting hypothesis tests involving two populations. First, we showed how to make inferences about the difference between two population means when independent simple random samples are selected. We first considered the case where the population standard deviations σ_1 and σ_2 could be assumed known. The standard normal distribution z was used to develop the interval estimate and served as the test statistic for hypothesis tests. We then considered the case where the population standard deviations were unknown and estimated by the sample standard deviations s_1 and s_2. In this case, the t distribution was used to develop the interval estimate and the t value served as the test statistic for hypothesis tests.

Inferences about the difference between two population means were then discussed for the matched sample design. In the matched sample design each element provides a pair of data values, one from each population. The difference between the paired data values is then used in the statistical analysis. The matched sample design is generally preferred to the independent sample design because the matched-sample procedure often improves the precision of the estimate.

In the final two sections we provided an introduction to experimental design and analysis of variance (ANOVA). Experimental studies differ from observational studies in the sense that an experiment is conducted to generate the data. The completely randomized design was described and the analysis of variance was used to test for a treatment effect. The same analysis of variance procedure can be used to test for the difference among k population means in an observational study.

Glossary

Independent simple random samples Samples selected from two populations in such a way that the elements making up one sample are chosen independently of the elements making up the other sample.

Matched samples One simple random sample of elements is selected and two data values are obtained for each element. For example, to compare two production methods, one simple random sample of n workers is selected. Each worker first uses one method and then the other method. The order of the two methods is assigned randomly.

Factor Another word for the independent variable of interest.

Treatments Different levels of a factor.

Single-factor experiment An experiment involving only one factor with k populations or treatments.

Response variable Another word for the dependent variable of interest.

Experimental units The objects of interest in the experiment.

Completely randomized design An experimental design in which the treatments are randomly assigned to the experimental units.

F distribution A probability distribution based on the ratio of two independent estimates of the variance of a normal population. The F distribution is used in hypothesis tests about the equality of k population means.

ANOVA table A table used to summarize the analysis of variance computations and results. It contains columns showing the source of variation, the sum of squares, the degrees of freedom, the mean square, the F value(s), and the p-value(s).

Key Formulas

Point Estimator of the Difference Between Two Population Means

$$\bar{x}_1 - \bar{x}_2 \tag{10.1}$$

Standard Error of $\bar{x}_1 - \bar{x}_2$

$$\sigma_{\bar{x}_1 - \bar{x}_2} = \sqrt{\frac{\sigma_1^2}{n_1} + \frac{\sigma_2^2}{n_2}} \tag{10.2}$$

Interval Estimate of the Difference Between Two Population Means: σ_1 and σ_2 Known

$$\bar{x}_1 - \bar{x}_2 \pm z_{\alpha/2} \sqrt{\frac{\sigma_1^2}{n_1} + \frac{\sigma_2^2}{n_2}} \tag{10.4}$$

Test Statistic for Hypothesis Tests About $\mu_1 - \mu_2$: σ_1 and σ_2 Known

$$z = \frac{(\bar{x}_1 - \bar{x}_2) - D_0}{\sqrt{\dfrac{\sigma_1^2}{n_1} + \dfrac{\sigma_2^2}{n_2}}} \tag{10.5}$$

Interval Estimate of the Difference Between Two Population Means: σ_1 and σ_2 Unknown

$$\bar{x}_1 - \bar{x}_2 \pm t_{\alpha/2} \sqrt{\frac{s_1^2}{n_1} + \frac{s_2^2}{n_2}} \tag{10.6}$$

Degrees of Freedom: t Distribution with Two Independent Random Samples

$$df = \frac{\left(\dfrac{s_1^2}{n_1} + \dfrac{s_2^2}{n_2}\right)^2}{\dfrac{1}{n_1 - 1}\left(\dfrac{s_1^2}{n_1}\right)^2 + \dfrac{1}{n_2 - 1}\left(\dfrac{s_2^2}{n_2}\right)^2} \qquad (10.7)$$

Test Statistic for Hypothesis Tests About $\mu_1 - \mu_2$: σ_1 and σ_2 Unknown

$$t = \frac{(\bar{x}_1 - \bar{x}_2) - D_0}{\sqrt{\dfrac{s_1^2}{n_1} + \dfrac{s_2^2}{n_2}}} \qquad (10.8)$$

Test Statistic for Hypothesis Tests Involving Matched Samples

$$t = \frac{\bar{d} - \mu_d}{s_d/\sqrt{n}} \qquad (10.9)$$

Sample Mean for Treatment j

$$\bar{x}_j = \frac{\sum\limits_{i=1}^{n_j} x_{ij}}{n_j} \qquad (10.10)$$

Sample Variance for Treatment j

$$s_j^2 = \frac{\sum\limits_{i=1}^{n_j} (x_{ij} - \bar{x}_j)^2}{n_j - 1} \qquad (10.11)$$

Overall Sample Mean

$$\bar{\bar{x}} = \frac{\sum\limits_{j=1}^{k} \sum\limits_{i=1}^{n_j} x_{ij}}{n_T} \qquad (10.12)$$

$$n_T = n_1 + n_2 + \cdots + n_k \qquad (10.13)$$

Mean Square Due to Treatments

$$\text{MSTR} = \frac{\text{SSTR}}{k - 1} \qquad (10.16)$$

Sum of Squares Due to Treatments

$$\text{SSTR} = \sum_{j=1}^{k} n_j (\bar{x}_j - \bar{\bar{x}})^2 \qquad (10.17)$$

Mean Square Due to Error

$$\text{MSE} = \frac{\text{SSE}}{n_T - k} \qquad (10.19)$$

Sum of Squares Due to Error

$$\text{SSE} = \sum_{j=1}^{k} (n_j - 1)s_j^2 \qquad (10.20)$$

Test Statistic for the Equality of *k* Population Means

$$F = \frac{\text{MSTR}}{\text{MSE}}$$

(10.21)

Total Sum of Squares

$$\text{SST} = \sum_{j=1}^{k} \sum_{i=1}^{n_j} (x_{ij} - \bar{\bar{x}})^2$$

(10.22)

Partitioning of Sum of Squares

$$\text{SST} = \text{SSTR} + \text{SSE}$$

(10.23)

Supplementary Exercises

40. How much is the cost of a hospital stay increasing? The mean cost of one day in a semiprivate room was reported to be $4848 in 2005 and $5260 in 2006 (*The Wall Street Journal*, January 2, 2007). Assume the estimate for 2005 is a sample mean based on a sample size of 80 and the estimate for 2006 is a sample mean based on a sample size of 60.
    a. Develop a point estimate of the increase in the cost of a semiprivate hospital room from 2005 to 2006.
    b. Historical data indicate that a population standard deviation of $800 is a reasonable assumption for both years. Compute the margin of error for your estimate in part (a). Use 95% confidence.
    c. Develop a 95% confidence interval estimate of the increase in cost for a semiprivate room.

41. The U.S. Department of Energy's Fuel Economy Guide provides fuel efficiency data for cars and trucks (*http://www.fueleconomy.gov*, February 22, 2008). The fuel efficiency rating for city driving in terms of miles per gallon for a random sample of 30 midsize cars and a random sample of 20 large cars provided the following data:

WEB file

CityMPG

Midsize

21	18	21	22	24	19	20	26	19	19
19	24	20	23	18	21	19	28	20	23
21	23	20	21	18	21	24	19	21	24

Large

17	21	16	17	16	18	17	16	17	21
17	19	17	17	17	17	18	17	16	17

    a. What is the point estimate of the difference between the mean fuel efficiency rating for midsize cars and large cars?
    b. Formulate the hypotheses that can be used to determine whether the sample data support the hypothesis that the mean fuel efficiency rating for midsize cars is greater than the mean fuel efficiency rating for large cars.
    c. Compute the *p*-value for the hypothesis test.
    d. At $\alpha = .05$, what is your conclusion?

42. Mutual funds are classified as *load* or *no-load* funds. Load funds require an investor to pay an initial fee based on a percentage of the amount invested in the fund. The no-load funds do not require this initial fee. Some financial advisors argue that the load mutual funds may be worth the extra fee because these funds provide a higher mean rate of return than the no-load mutual funds. A sample of 30 load mutual funds and a sample of 30 no-load mutual

funds were selected. Data were collected on the annual return for the funds over a five-year period. The data are contained in the data set Mutual. The data for the first five load and first five no-load mutual funds are as follows.

Mutual

Mutual Funds—Load	Return	Mutual Funds—No Load	Return
American National Growth	15.51	Amana Income Fund	13.24
Arch Small Cap Equity	14.57	Berger One Hundred	12.13
Bartlett Cap Basic	17.73	Columbia International Stock	12.17
Calvert World International	10.31	Dodge & Cox Balanced	16.06
Colonial Fund A	16.23	Evergreen Fund	17.61

a. Formulate H_0 and H_a such that rejection of H_0 leads to the conclusion that the load mutual funds have a higher mean annual return over the five-year period.
b. Use the 60 mutual funds in the data set Mutual to conduct the hypothesis test. What is the p-value? At $\alpha = .05$, what is your conclusion?

43. The National Association of Home Builders provided data on the cost of the most popular home remodeling projects. Sample data on cost in thousands of dollars for two types of remodeling projects are as follows.

Kitchen	Master Bedroom	Kitchen	Master Bedroom
25.2	18.0	23.0	17.8
17.4	22.9	19.7	24.6
22.8	26.4	16.9	21.0
21.9	24.8	21.8	
19.7	26.9	23.6	

a. Develop a point estimate of the difference between the population mean remodeling costs for the two types of projects.
b. Develop a 90% confidence interval for the difference between the two population means.

44. Typical prices of single-family homes in the state of Florida are shown for a sample of 15 metropolitan areas (*Naples Daily News*, February 23, 2003). Data are in thousands of dollars.

Florida

Metropolitan Area	January 2003	January 2002
Daytona Beach	117	96
Fort Lauderdale	207	169
Fort Myers	143	129
Fort Walton Beach	139	134
Gainesville	131	119
Jacksonville	128	119
Lakeland	91	85
Miami	193	165
Naples	263	233
Ocala	86	90
Orlando	134	121
Pensacola	111	105
Sarasota-Bradenton	168	141
Tallahassee	140	130
Tampa-St. Petersburg	139	129

    a. Use a matched-sample analysis to develop a point estimate of the population mean one-year increase in the price of single-family homes in Florida.

    b. Develop a 90% confidence interval estimate of the population mean one-year increase in the price of single-family homes in Florida.

    c. What was the percentage increase over the one-year period?

45. In a completely randomized experimental design, three brands of paper towels were tested for their ability to absorb water. Equal-size towels were used, with four sections of towels tested per brand. The absorbency rating data follow. At a .05 level of significance, does there appear to be a difference in the ability of the brands to absorb water?

	Brand	
x	*y*	*z*
91	99	83
100	96	88
88	94	89
89	99	76

46. A study reported in the *Journal of Small Business Management* concluded that self-employed individuals do not experience higher job satisfaction than individuals who are not self-employed. In this study, job satisfaction is measured using 18 items, each of which is rated using a Likert-type scale with 1–5 response options ranging from strong agreement to strong disagreement. A higher score on this scale indicates a higher degree of job satisfaction. The sum of the ratings for the 18 items, ranging from 18–90, is used as the measure of job satisfaction. Suppose that this approach was used to measure the job satisfaction for lawyers, physical therapists, cabinetmakers, and systems analysts. The results obtained for a sample of 10 individuals from each profession follow.

WEB file

SatisJob

Lawyer	Physical Therapist	Cabinetmaker	Systems Analyst
44	55	54	44
42	78	65	73
74	80	79	71
42	86	69	60
53	60	79	64
50	59	64	66
45	62	59	41
48	52	78	55
64	55	84	76
38	50	60	62

At the $\alpha = .05$ level of significance, test for any difference in the job satisfaction among the four professions.

47. *Money* magazine reports percentage returns and expense ratios for stock and bond funds. The following data are the expense ratios for 10 midcap stock funds, 10 small-cap stock funds, 10 hybrid stock funds, and 10 specialty stock funds (*Money,* March 2003).

Funds

Midcap	Small-Cap	Hybrid	Specialty
1.2	2.0	2.0	1.6
1.1	1.2	2.7	2.7
1.0	1.7	1.8	2.6
1.2	1.8	1.5	2.5
1.3	1.5	2.5	1.9
1.8	2.3	1.0	1.5
1.4	1.9	0.9	1.6
1.4	1.3	1.9	2.7
1.0	1.2	1.4	2.2
1.4	1.3	0.3	0.7

Use $\alpha = .05$ to test for any significant difference in the mean expense ratio among the four types of stock funds.

48. *Business 2.0*'s first annual employment survey provided data showing the typical annual salary for 97 different jobs. The following data show the annual salary for 30 different jobs in three fields: computer software and hardware, construction, and engineering (*Business 2.0,* March 2003).

JobSalary

Computers		Construction		Engineering	
Job	Salary	Job	Salary	Job	Salary
Data Mgr.	94	Administrator	55	Aeronautical	75
Mfg. Mgr.	90	Architect	53	Agricultural	70
Programmer	63	Architect Mgr.	77	Chemical	88
Project Mgr.	84	Const. Mgr.	60	Civil	77
Software Dev.	73	Foreperson	41	Electrical	89
Sr. Design	75	Interior Design	54	Mechanical	85
Staff Systems	94	Landscape Architect	51	Mining	96
Systems Analyst	77	Sr. Estimator	64	Nuclear	105

Use $\alpha = .05$ to test for any significant difference in the mean annual salary among the three job fields.

49. Three different assembly methods have been proposed for a new product. A completely randomized experimental design was chosen to determine which assembly method results in the greatest number of parts produced per hour, and 30 workers were randomly selected and assigned to use one of the proposed methods. The number of units produced by each worker follows.

Assembly

	Method	
A	B	C
97	93	99
73	100	94
93	93	87
100	55	66
73	77	59
91	91	75
100	85	84
86	73	72
92	90	88
95	83	86

Use these data and test to see whether the mean number of parts produced is the same with each method. Use $\alpha = .05$.

50. In a study conducted to investigate browsing activity by shoppers, each shopper was initially classified as a nonbrowser, light browser, or heavy browser. For each shopper, the study obtained a measure to determine how comfortable the shopper was in a store. Higher scores indicated greater comfort. Suppose the following data were collected.

Browsing

Nonbrowser	Light Browser	Heavy Browser
4	5	5
5	6	7
6	5	5
3	4	7
3	7	4
4	4	6
5	6	5
4	5	7

Use $\alpha = .05$ to test for differences among comfort levels for the three types of browsers.

Case Problem 1   Par, Inc.

Par, Inc., is a major manufacturer of golf equipment. Management believes that Par's market share could be increased with the introduction of a cut-resistant, longer-lasting golf ball. Therefore, the research group at Par has been investigating a new golf ball coating designed to resist cuts and provide a more durable ball. The tests with the coating have been promising.

One of the researchers voiced concern about the effect of the new coating on driving distances. Par would like the new cut-resistant ball to offer driving distances comparable to those of the current-model golf ball. To compare the driving distances for the two balls, 40 balls of both the new and current models were subjected to distance tests. The testing was performed with a mechanical hitting machine so that any difference between the mean distances for the two models could be attributed to a difference in the two models. The results of the tests, with distances measured to the nearest yard, follow. These data are available on the website that accompanies this text in the file named Golf.

WEB file

Golf

Model		Model		Model		Model	
Current	New	Current	New	Current	New	Current	New
264	277	270	272	263	274	281	283
261	269	287	259	264	266	274	250
267	263	289	264	284	262	273	253
272	266	280	280	263	271	263	260
258	262	272	274	260	260	275	270
283	251	275	281	283	281	267	263
258	262	265	276	255	250	279	261
266	289	260	269	272	263	274	255
259	286	278	268	266	278	276	263
270	264	275	262	268	264	262	279

Managerial Report

1. Formulate and present the rationale for a hypothesis test that Par could use to compare the driving distances of the current and new golf balls.
2. Analyze the data to provide the hypothesis testing conclusion. What is the *p*-value for your test? What is your recommendation for Par, Inc.?
3. Provide descriptive statistical summaries of the data for each model.
4. What is the 95% confidence interval for the population mean of each model, and what is the 95% confidence interval for the difference between the means of the two populations?
5. Do you see a need for larger sample sizes and more testing with the golf balls? Discuss.

Case Problem 2   Wentworth Medical Center

As part of a long-term study of individuals 65 years of age or older, sociologists and physicians at the Wentworth Medical Center in upstate New York investigated the relationship between geographic location and depression. A sample of 60 individuals, all in reasonably good health, was selected; 20 individuals were residents of Florida, 20 were residents of New York, and 20 were residents of North Carolina. Each of the individuals sampled was given a standardized test to measure depression. The data collected follow; higher test scores indicate higher levels of depression. These data are available on the website that accompanies this text in the file named Medical1.

A second part of the study considered the relationship between geographic location and depression for individuals 65 years of age or older who had a chronic health condition such as arthritis, hypertension, and/or heart ailment. A sample of 60 individuals with such conditions was identified. Again, 20 were residents of Florida, 20 were residents of New York, and 20 were residents of North Carolina. The levels of depression recorded for this study follow. These data are available on the website that accompanies this text in the file named Medical2.

WEB file
Medical1

WEB file
Medical2

Data from Medical1			Data from Medical2		
Florida	New York	North Carolina	Florida	New York	North Carolina
3	8	10	13	14	10
7	11	7	12	9	12
7	9	3	17	15	15
3	7	5	17	12	18
8	8	11	20	16	12
8	7	8	21	24	14
8	8	4	16	18	17
5	4	3	14	14	8
5	13	7	13	15	14
2	10	8	17	17	16
6	6	8	12	20	18
2	8	7	9	11	17
6	12	3	12	23	19
6	8	9	15	19	15
9	6	8	16	17	13
7	8	12	15	14	14
5	5	6	13	9	11
4	7	3	10	14	12
7	7	8	11	13	13
3	8	11	17	11	11

Managerial Report

1. Use descriptive statistics to summarize the data from the two studies. What are your preliminary observations about the depression scores?
2. Use analysis of variance on both data sets. State the hypotheses being tested in each case. What are your conclusions?
3. Use inferences about individual treatment means where appropriate. What are your conclusions?

Appendix   Comparisons Involving Means Using StatTools

In this appendix we show how StatTools can be used to develop interval estimates and conduct hypothesis tests about the difference between two population means for the σ_1 and σ_2 unknown case. We also show how StatTools can be used to test for the equality of k population means for a completely randomized design.

Interval Estimation of μ_1 and μ_2

CheckAcct

We will use the data for the checking account balances example presented in Section 10.2. Begin by using the Data Set Manager to create a StatTools data set for these data using the procedure described in the appendix in Chapter 1. The following steps can be used to compute a 95% confidence interval estimate of the difference between the two population means.

Step 1. Click the **StatTools** tab on the Ribbon
Step 2. In the **Analyses** group, click **Statistical Inference**
Step 3. Select the **Confidence Interval** option
Step 4. When the StatTools—Confidence Interval dialog box appears,
     For **Analysis Type,** choose **Two-Sample Analysis**
     In the **Variables** section,
        Select **Cherry Grove**
        Select **Beechmont**
     In the **Confidence Intervals to Calculate** section,
        Select the **For the Difference of Means** option
        Select 95% for the **Confidence Level**
     Click **OK**

Because the sample size for Cherry Grove ($n_1 = 28$) differs from the sample size for Beechmont ($n_2 = 22$), StatTools will inform you of this difference after you click OK in step 4. A dialog box will appear saying "The variable Beechmont contains missing data, which the analysis will ignore." Click OK. A Choose Variable Ordering dialog box then appears, indicating that the analysis will compare the difference between the Cherry Grove data set and the Beechmont data set. Click OK and the StatTools interval estimation output will appear.

Hypothesis Tests About μ_1 and μ_2

SoftwareTest

We will use the software evaluation example and the completion time data presented in Table 10.1. Begin by using the Data Set Manager to create a StatTools data set for these data using the procedure described in the appendix in Chapter 1. The following steps can be used to test the hypothesis $H_0: \mu_1 - \mu_2 \leq 0$ against $H_a: \mu_1 - \mu_2 > 0$.

Step 1. Click the **StatTools** tab on the Ribbon
Step 2. In the **Analyses** group, click **Statistical Inference**
Step 3. Choose the **Hypothesis Test** option
Step 4. When the StatTools—Hypothesis Test dialog box appears,
> For **Analysis Type,** choose **Two-Sample Analysis**
> In the **Variables** section,
>> Select **Current**
>> Select **New**
> In the **Hypothesis Tests to Perform** section,
>> Select **Difference of Means**
>> Enter 0 in the **Null Hypothesis Value** box
>> Select **Greater Than Null Value (One-Tailed Test)** in the **Alternative Hypothesis** box
> Click **OK**
> When the Choose Variable Ordering dialog box appears, click **OK**

The results of the hypothesis test will then appear.

Inferences About the Difference Between Two Population Means: Matched Samples

WEB file

Matched

StatTools can be used to develop interval estimates and conduct hypothesis tests for the difference between population means for the matched samples case. We will use the matched-sample completion times in Table 10.2 to illustrate.

Begin by using the Data Set Manager to create a StatTools data set for these data using the procedure described in the appendix in Chapter 1. The following steps can be used to compute a 95% confidence interval estimate of the difference between the population mean completion times.

Step 1. Click the **StatTools** tab on the Ribbon
Step 2. In the **Analyses** group, click **Statistical Inference**
Step 3. Choose the **Confidence Interval** option
Step 4. When the StatTools—Confidence Interval dialog box appears,
> For **Analysis Type,** choose **Paired-Sample Analysis**
> In the **Variables** section,
>> Select **Method 1**
>> Select **Method 2**
> In the **Confidence Intervals to Calculate** section,
>> Select the **For the Difference of Means** option
>> Select 95% for the **Confidence Level**
>> If selected, remove the check in the **For the Standard Deviation** box
> Click **OK**
> When the Choose Variable Ordering dialog box appears, click **OK**

The confidence interval will appear.

Conducting hypothesis tests for the matched samples case is very similar to conducting hypothesis tests for the difference in two means shown above. After selecting the Hypothesis Test option in step 3, select the Paired-Sample Analysis option in step 4.

Analysis of a Completely Randomized Design

StatTools can be used to test for the equality of k population means for a completely randomized design. We use the Chemitech data in Table 10.3 to illustrate. Begin by using the

Data Set Manager to create a StatTools data set for these data using the procedure described in the appendix in Chapter 1. The following steps can be used to test for the equality of the three population means.

Chemitech

Step 1. Click the **StatTools** tab on the Ribbon
Step 2. In the **Analyses** group, click **Statistical Inference**
Step 3. Choose the **One-Way ANOVA** option
Step 4. When the One-Way ANOVA dialog box appears,
    In the **Variables** section,
        Click the **Format button** and select **Unstacked**
        Select **Method A**
        Select **Method B**
        Select **Method C**
    Select 95% in the **Confidence Level** box
    Click **OK**

Note that in step 4 we selected the Unstacked option after clicking the Format button. The Unstacked option means that the data for the three treatments appear in separate columns of the worksheet. In a stacked format, only two columns would be used. For example, the data could have been organized as follows:

	A	B	C
1	**Method**	**Units Produced**	
2	Method A	58	
3	Method A	64	
4	Method A	55	
5	Method A	66	
6	Method A	67	
7	Method B	58	
8	Method B	69	
9	Method B	71	
10	Method B	64	
11	Method B	68	
12	Method C	48	
13	Method C	57	
14	Method C	59	
15	Method C	47	
16	Method C	49	
17			

Data are frequently recorded in a stacked format. For stacked data, simply select the Stacked option after clicking the Format button.

CHAPTER 11

Comparisons Involving Proportions and a Test of Independence

CONTENTS

STATISTICS IN PRACTICE:
UNITED WAY

11.1 INFERENCES ABOUT THE
DIFFERENCE BETWEEN
TWO POPULATION
PROPORTIONS
Interval Estimation of $p_1 - p_2$
Using Excel to Construct a
   Confidence Interval
Hypothesis Tests About $p_1 - p_2$
Using Excel to Conduct a
   Hypothesis Test

11.2 HYPOTHESIS TEST FOR
PROPORTIONS OF A
MULTINOMIAL POPULATION
Using Excel to Conduct a
   Goodness of Fit Test

11.3 TEST OF INDEPENDENCE
Using Excel to Conduct a Test of
   Independence

STATISTICS *in* PRACTICE

UNITED WAY*
ROCHESTER, NEW YORK

United Way of Greater Rochester is a nonprofit organization dedicated to improving the quality of life for all people in the seven counties it serves by meeting the community's most important human care needs.

The annual United Way/Red Cross fund-raising campaign, conducted each spring, funds hundreds of programs offered by more than 200 service providers. These providers meet a wide variety of human needs—physical, mental, and social—and serve people of all ages, backgrounds, and economic means.

Because of enormous volunteer involvement, United Way of Greater Rochester is able to hold its operating costs at just eight cents of every dollar raised.

The United Way of Greater Rochester decided to conduct a survey to learn more about community perceptions of charities. Focus-group interviews were held with professional, service, and general worker groups to get preliminary information on perceptions. The information obtained was then used to help develop the questionnaire for the survey. The questionnaire was pretested, modified, and distributed to 440 individuals; 323 completed questionnaires were obtained.

A variety of descriptive statistics, including frequency distributions and crosstabulations, were provided from the data collected. An important part of the analysis involved the use of contingency tables and chi-square tests of independence. One use of such statistical tests was to determine whether perceptions of administrative expenses were independent of occupation.

The hypotheses for the test of independence were:

H_0: Perception of United Way administrative expenses is independent of the occupation of the respondent.

Statistical surveys help United Way adjust its program to better meet the needs of the people it serves. Ed Bock/Corbis

H_a: Perception of United Way administrative expenses is not independent of the occupation of the respondent.

Two questions in the survey provided the data for the statistical test. One question obtained data on perceptions of the percentage of funds going to administrative expenses (up to 10%, 11–20%, and 21% or more). The other question asked for the occupation of the respondent.

The chi-square test at a .05 level of significance led to rejection of the null hypothesis of independence and to the conclusion that perceptions of United Way's administrative expenses did vary by occupation. Actual administrative expenses were less than 9%, but 35% of the respondents perceived that administrative expenses were 21% or more. Hence, many had inaccurate perceptions of administrative costs. In this group, production-line, clerical, sales, and professional-technical employees had more inaccurate perceptions than other groups.

The community perceptions study helped United Way of Greater Rochester to develop adjustments to its program and fund-raising activities. In this chapter, you will learn how a statistical test of independence, such as that described here, is conducted.

*The authors are indebted to Dr. Philip R. Tyler, Marketing Consultant to the United Way, for providing this Statistics in Practice.

Many statistical applications call for a comparison of population proportions. In Section 11.1, we describe statistical inferences concerning differences in the proportions for two populations. Two samples are required, one from each population, and the statistical inference is based on the two sample proportions. The second section looks at a hypothesis test comparing the proportions of a single multinomial population with the proportions selected in a null hypothesis. One sample from the multinomial population is used, and the hypothesis test is based on comparing the sample proportions with those stated in the null hypothesis. In the last section of the chapter, we show how contingency tables can be used to test for the independence of two variables. One sample is used for the test of independence, but measures on two variables are required for each sampled element. Both Section 11.2 and 11.3 rely on the use of a chi-square statistical test.

(11.1) Inferences About the Difference Between Two Population Proportions

Letting p_1 denote the proportion for population 1 and p_2 denote the proportion for population 2, we consider inferences about the difference between the two population proportions: $p_1 - p_2$. To make an inference about this difference, we will select two independent random samples consisting of n_1 units from population 1 and n_2 units from population 2.

Interval Estimation of $p_1 - p_2$

In the following example, we show how to compute a margin of error and develop an interval estimate of the difference between two population proportions.

A tax preparation firm is interested in comparing the quality of work at two of its regional offices. By randomly selecting samples of tax returns prepared at each office and verifying the sample returns' accuracy, the firm will be able to estimate the proportion of erroneous returns prepared at each office. Of particular interest is the difference between these proportions.

p_1 = proportion of erroneous returns for population 1 (office 1)
p_2 = proportion of erroneous returns for population 2 (office 2)
$\bar{p}_1$ = sample proportion for a simple random sample from population 1
$\bar{p}_2$ = sample proportion for a simple random sample from population 2

The difference between the two population proportions is given by $p_1 - p_2$. The point estimator of $p_1 - p_2$ is as follows.

> **POINT ESTIMATOR OF THE DIFFERENCE BETWEEN TWO POPULATION PROPORTIONS**
>
> $$\bar{p}_1 - \bar{p}_2 \qquad (11.1)$$

Thus, the point estimator of the difference between two population proportions is the difference between the sample proportions of two independent simple random samples.

As with other point estimators, the point estimator $\bar{p}_1 - \bar{p}_2$ has a sampling distribution that reflects the possible values of $\bar{p}_1 - \bar{p}_2$ if we repeatedly took two independent random samples. The mean of this sampling distribution is $p_1 - p_2$ and the standard error is as follows:

$$\sigma_{\bar{p}_1 - \bar{p}_2} = \sqrt{\frac{p_1(1 - p_1)}{n_1} + \frac{p_2(1 - p_2)}{n_2}} \qquad (11.2)$$

Sample sizes involving proportions are usually large enough to use this approximation.

If the sample sizes are large enough that $n_1 p_1, n_1(1 - p_1), n_2 p_2$, and $n_2(1 - p_2)$ are all greater than or equal to 5, the sampling distribution of $\bar{p}_1 - \bar{p}_2$ can be approximated by a normal distribution.

In the estimation of the difference between two population proportions, an interval estimate will take the following form:

$$\bar{p}_1 - \bar{p}_2 \pm \text{Margin of error}$$

With the sampling distribution of $\bar{p}_1 - \bar{p}_2$ approximated by a normal distribution, we would like to use $z_{\alpha/2}\sigma_{\bar{p}_1 - \bar{p}_2}$ as the margin of error. However, $\sigma_{\bar{p}_1 - \bar{p}_2}$ given by equation (11.2) involves the two unknown population proportions, p_1 and p_2. Thus, we use the sample proportion $\bar{p}_1$ to estimate p_1 and the sample proportion $\bar{p}_2$ to estimate p_2. The margin of error is thus:

$$\text{Margin of error} = z_{\alpha/2}\sqrt{\frac{\bar{p}_1(1 - \bar{p}_1)}{n_1} + \frac{\bar{p}_2(1 - \bar{p}_2)}{n_2}} \qquad (11.3)$$

The general form of an interval estimate of the difference between two population proportions is as follows.

INTERVAL ESTIMATE OF THE DIFFERENCE BETWEEN TWO POPULATION
PROPORTIONS

$$\bar{p}_1 - \bar{p}_2 \pm z_{\alpha/2}\sqrt{\frac{\bar{p}_1(1 - \bar{p}_1)}{n_1} + \frac{\bar{p}_2(1 - \bar{p}_2)}{n_2}} \qquad (11.4)$$

where $1 - \alpha$ is the confidence coefficient.

Returning to the tax preparation example, we find that independent simple random samples from the two offices provide the following information.

Office 1	Office 2
$n_1 = 250$	$n_2 = 300$
Number of returns with errors $= 35$	Number of returns with errors $= 27$

TaxPrep

The sample proportions for the two offices follow.

$$\bar{p}_1 = \frac{35}{250} = .14$$

$$\bar{p}_2 = \frac{27}{300} = .09$$

The point estimate of the difference between the proportions of erroneous tax returns for the two populations is $\bar{p}_1 - \bar{p}_2 = .14 - .09 = .05$. Thus, we estimate that office 1 has a .05, or 5%, greater error rate than office 2.

Expression (11.4) can now be used to provide a margin of error and interval estimate of the difference between the two population proportions. Using a 90% confidence interval with $z_{\alpha/2} = z_{.05} = 1.645$, we have

$$\bar{p}_1 - \bar{p}_2 \pm z_{\alpha/2}\sqrt{\frac{\bar{p}_1(1 - \bar{p}_1)}{n_1} + \frac{\bar{p}_2(1 - \bar{p}_2)}{n_2}}$$

$$.14 - .09 \pm 1.645\sqrt{\frac{.14(1 - .14)}{250} + \frac{.09(1 - .09)}{300}}$$

$$.05 \pm .045$$

Thus, the margin of error is .045, and the 90% confidence interval is .005 to .095.

Using Excel to Construct a Confidence Interval

We can create a worksheet for developing an interval estimate of the difference between population proportions. Let us illustrate by developing an interval estimate of the difference between the proportions of erroneous tax returns at the two offices of the tax preparation firm. Refer to Figure 11.1 as we describe the tasks involved. The formula worksheet is in the background; the value worksheet appears in the foreground.

Enter Data: Columns A and B contain Yes or No labels that indicate which of the tax returns from each office contain an error.

FIGURE 11.1 CONSTRUCTING A 90% CONFIDENCE INTERVAL FOR THE DIFFERENCE IN THE PROPORTION OF ERRONEOUS TAX RETURNS PREPARED BY TWO OFFICES

	A	B	C	D	E	F	G
1	Office 1	Office 2		Interval Estimate of Difference			
2	No	No		in Population Proportions			
3	No	No					
4	No	No			Office 1	Office 2	
5	No	No		Sample Size	=COUNTA(A2:A251)	=COUNTA(B2:B301)	
6	No	No		Response of Interest	Yes	Yes	
7	Yes	No		Count for Response	=COUNTIF(A2:A251,E6)	=COUNTIF(B2:B301,F6)	
8	No	No		Sample Proportion	=E7/E5	=F7/F5	
9	No	No					
10	No	No		Confidence Coefficient	0.9		
11	No	No		Level of Significance	=1-E10		
12	No	No		z Value	=NORMSINV(1-E11/2)		
13	No	No					
14	No	No		Standard Error	=SQRT(E8*(1-E8)/E5+F8*(1-F8)/F5)		
15	No	No		Margin of Error	=E12*E14		
16	No	No					
17	No	Yes		Point Estimate of Difference	=E8-F8		
18	Yes	No		Lower Limit	=E17-E15		
19	No	No		Upper Limit	=E17+E15		
250	Yes	No					
251	No	No					
300		No					
301		No					
302							

	A	B	C	D	E	F	G
1	Office 1	Office 2		Interval Estimate of Difference			
2	No	No		in Population Proportions			
3	No	No					
4	No	No			Office 1	Office 2	
5	No	No		Sample Size	250	300	
6	No	No		Response of Interest	Yes	Yes	
7	Yes	No		Count for Response	35	27	
8	No	No		Sample Proportion	0.14	0.09	
9	No	No					
10	No	No		Confidence Coefficient	0.9		
11	No	No		Level of Significance	0.1		
12	No	No		z Value	1.645		
13	No	No					
14	No	No		Standard Error	0.0275		
15	No	No		Margin of Error	0.0452		
16	No	No					
17	No	Yes		Point Estimate of Difference	0.05		
18	Yes	No		Lower Limit	0.0048		
19	No	No		Upper Limit	0.0952		
250	Yes	No					
251	No	No					
300		No					
301		No					
302							

Note: Rows 20–249 and 252–299 are hidden.

Enter Functions and Formulas: The descriptive statistics needed are provided in cells E5:F5 and E7:F8. Note that Excel's COUNTA function is used in cells E5 and F5 to count the number of observations for each of the samples. The value worksheet indicates 250 returns in the sample from office 1 and 300 returns in the sample from office 2. In cells E6 and F6, we type Yes to indicate the response of interest (an erroneous return). Excel's COUNTIF function is used in cells E7 and F7 to count the number of Yes responses from each office. Formulas entered into cells E8 and F8 compute the sample proportions. The confidence coefficient entered into cell E10 (.9) is used to compute the corresponding level of significance ($\alpha = .10$) in cell E11. In cell E12 we use the NORMSINV function to compute the z value needed to compute the margin of error for the interval estimate.

In cell E14, a point estimate of $\sigma_{\bar{p}_1-\bar{p}_2}$, the standard error of the point estimator $\bar{p}_1 - \bar{p}_2$, is computed based on the two sample proportions (E8 and F8) and sample sizes (E5 and F5). The margin of error is then computed in cell E15 by multiplying the z value by the estimate of the standard error.

The point estimate of the difference in the two population proportions is computed in cell E17 as the difference in the sample proportions; the result, shown in the value worksheet, is .05. The lower limit of the confidence interval is computed in cell E18 by subtracting the margin of error from the point estimate. The upper limit is computed in cell E19 by adding the margin of error to the point estimate. The value worksheet shows that the 90% confidence interval estimate of the difference in the two population proportions is .0048 to .0952.

A template for other problems This worksheet can be used as a template for other problems requiring an interval estimate of the difference in population proportions. The new data must be entered in columns A and B. The data ranges in the cells used to compute the sample size (E5:F5) and the cells used to compute a count of the response of interest (E7:F7) must be changed to correctly indicate the location of the new data. The response of interest must be typed into cells E6:F6. The 90% confidence interval for the new data will then appear in cells E17:E19. If an interval estimate with a different confidence coefficient is desired, simply change the entry in cell E10.

This worksheet can also be used as a template for solving text exercises in which the sample data have already been summarized. No change in the data section is necessary. Simply type the values for the given sample sizes in cells E5:F5 and type the given values for the sample proportions in cells E8:F8. The 90% confidence interval will then appear in cells E17:E19. If an interval estimate with a different confidence coefficient is desired, simply change the entry in cell E10.

Hypothesis Tests About $p_1 - p_2$

Let us now consider hypothesis tests about the difference between the proportions of two populations. We focus on tests involving no difference between the two population proportions. In this case, the three forms for a hypothesis test are as follows:

All hypotheses considered use 0 as the difference of interest.

$$H_0: p_1 - p_2 \geq 0 \qquad H_0: p_1 - p_2 \leq 0 \qquad H_0: p_1 - p_2 = 0$$
$$H_a: p_1 - p_2 < 0 \qquad H_a: p_1 - p_2 > 0 \qquad H_a: p_1 - p_2 \neq 0$$

When we assume H_0 is true as an equality, we have $p_1 - p_2 = 0$, which is the same as saying that the population proportions are equal, $p_1 = p_2$.

We will base the test statistic on the sampling distribution of the point estimator $\bar{p}_1 - \bar{p}_2$. In equation (11.2), we showed that the standard error of $\bar{p}_1 - \bar{p}_2$ is given by

$$\sigma_{\bar{p}_1-\bar{p}_2} = \sqrt{\frac{p_1(1-p_1)}{n_1} + \frac{p_2(1-p_2)}{n_2}}$$

Under the assumption H_0 is true as an equality, the population proportions are equal and $p_1 = p_2 = p$. In this case, $\sigma_{\bar{p}_1 - \bar{p}_2}$ becomes as follows:

STANDARD ERROR OF $\bar{p}_1 - \bar{p}_2$ WHEN $p_1 = p_2 = p$

$$\sigma_{\bar{p}_1 - \bar{p}_2} = \sqrt{\frac{p(1-p)}{n_1} + \frac{p(1-p)}{n_2}} = \sqrt{p(1-p)\left(\frac{1}{n_1} + \frac{1}{n_2}\right)} \qquad (11.5)$$

With p unknown, we pool, or combine, the point estimators from the two samples ($\bar{p}_1$ and $\bar{p}_2$) to obtain a single point estimator of p as follows:

POOLED ESTIMATOR OF p WHEN $p_1 = p_2 = p$

$$\bar{p} = \frac{n_1 \bar{p}_1 + n_2 \bar{p}_2}{n_1 + n_2} \qquad (11.6)$$

This **pooled estimator of p** is a weighted average of $\bar{p}_1$ and $\bar{p}_2$.

Substituting $\bar{p}$ for p in equation (11.5), we obtain an estimate of the standard error of $\bar{p}_1 - \bar{p}_2$. This estimate of the standard error is used in the test statistic. The general form of the test statistic for hypothesis tests about the difference between two population proportions is the point estimator divided by the estimate of $\sigma_{\bar{p}_1 - \bar{p}_2}$.

TEST STATISTIC FOR HYPOTHESIS TESTS ABOUT $p_1 - p_2$

$$z = \frac{(\bar{p}_1 - \bar{p}_2)}{\sqrt{\bar{p}(1-\bar{p})\left(\frac{1}{n_1} + \frac{1}{n_2}\right)}} \qquad (11.7)$$

This test statistic applies to large sample situations where $n_1 p_1$, $n_1(1 - p_1)$, $n_2 p_2$, and $n_2(1 - p_2)$ are all greater than or equal to 5.

Let us return to the tax preparation firm example and assume that the firm wants to use a hypothesis test to determine whether the error proportions differ between the two offices. A two-tailed test is required. The null and alternative hypotheses are as follows:

$$H_0: p_1 - p_2 = 0$$
$$H_a: p_1 - p_2 \neq 0$$

If H_0 is rejected, the firm can conclude that the error rates at the two offices differ. We will use $\alpha = .10$ as the level of significance.

The sample data previously collected showed $\bar{p}_1 = .14$ for the $n_1 = 250$ returns sampled at office 1 and $\bar{p}_2 = .09$ for the $n_2 = 300$ returns sampled at office 2. We continue by computing the pooled estimate of p.

$$\bar{p} = \frac{n_1 \bar{p}_1 + n_2 \bar{p}_2}{n_1 + n_2} = \frac{250(.14) + 300(.09)}{250 + 300} = .1127$$

Using this pooled estimate and the difference between the sample proportions, the value of the test statistic is as follows.

$$z = \frac{(\bar{p}_1 - \bar{p}_2)}{\sqrt{\bar{p}(1 - \bar{p})\left(\dfrac{1}{n_1} + \dfrac{1}{n_2}\right)}} = \frac{(.14 - .09)}{\sqrt{.1127(1 - .1127)\left(\dfrac{1}{250} + \dfrac{1}{300}\right)}} = 1.85$$

In computing the p-value for this two-tailed test, we first note that $z = 1.85$ is in the upper tail of the standard normal distribution. Using $z = 1.85$ and the standard normal distribution table, we find the area in the upper tail is $1.0000 - .9678 = .0322$. Doubling this area for a two-tailed test, we find the p-value $= 2(.0322) = .0644$. With the p-value less than $\alpha = .10$, H_0 is rejected at the .10 level of significance. The firm can conclude that the error rates differ between the two offices. This hypothesis testing conclusion is consistent with the earlier 90% confidence interval results that showed the interval estimate of the difference between the population error rates at the two offices to be .005 to .095, with office 1 having the higher error rate.

Using Excel to Conduct a Hypothesis Test

We can create a worksheet for conducting a hypothesis test about the difference between population proportions. Let us illustrate by testing to see whether there is a significant difference between the proportions of erroneous tax returns at the two offices of the tax preparation firm. Refer to Figure 11.2 as we describe the tasks involved. The formula worksheet is in the background; the value worksheet is in the foreground.

Enter Data: Columns A and B contain Yes or No labels that indicate which of the tax returns from each office contain an error.

Enter Functions and Formulas: The descriptive statistics needed to perform the hypothesis test are provided in cells E5:F6 and E7:F8. They are the same as the ones used for an interval estimate (see Figure 11.1). The hypothesized value of the difference between the two populations is zero; it is entered into cell E10. In cell E11, the difference in the sample proportions is used to compute a point estimate of the difference in the two population proportions. Using the two sample proportions and sample sizes, a pooled estimate of the population proportion p is computed in cell E13; its value is .1127. Then, in cell E14, an estimate of $\sigma_{\bar{p}_1 - \bar{p}_2}$ is computed using equation (11.5), with the pooled estimate of p and the sample sizes.

The formula $=$(E11-E10)/E14 entered into cell E15 computes the test statistic z (1.8462). The NORMSDIST function is then used to compute the p-value (Lower Tail) and the p-value (Upper Tail) in cells E17 and E18. The p-value (Two Tail) is computed in cell E19 as twice the minimum of the two one-tailed p-values. The value worksheet shows that p-value (Two Tail) $= .0649$. Because the p-value $= .0649$ is less than the level of significance, $\alpha = .10$, we have sufficient evidence to reject the null hypothesis and conclude that the population proportions are not equal.

The p-value here (.0649) differs from the one we found using the cumulative normal probability tables (.0644) due to rounding.

This worksheet can be used as a template for hypothesis testing problems involving differences between population proportions. The new data can be entered into columns A and B. The ranges for the new data and the response of interest need to be revised in cells E5:F7. The remainder of the worksheet will then be updated as needed to conduct the hypothesis test. If a hypothesized difference other than 0 is to be used, the new value must be entered in cell E10.

To use this worksheet for exercises in which the sample statistics are given, just type in the given values for cells E5:F5 and E7:F8. The remainder of the worksheet will then be updated to conduct the hypothesis test. If a hypothesized difference other than 0 is to be used, the new value must be entered in cell E10.

FIGURE 11.2 HYPOTHESIS TEST CONCERNING DIFFERENCE IN PROPORTION OF ERRONEOUS TAX RETURNS PREPARED BY TWO OFFICES

	A	B	C	D	E	F	G
1	Office 1	Office 2			Hypothesis Test Concerning Difference		
2	No	No			Between Population Proportions		
3	No	No					
4	No	No			Office 1	Office 2	
5	No	No		Sample Size	=COUNTA(A2:A251)	=COUNTA(B2:B301)	
6	No	No		Response of Interest	Yes	Yes	
7	Yes	No		Count for Response	=COUNTIF(A2:A251,E6)	=COUNTIF(B2:B301,F6)	
8	No	No		Sample Proportion	=E7/E5	=F7/F5	
9	No	No					
10	No	No		Hypothesized Value	0		
11	No	No		Point Estimate of Difference	=E8-F8		
12	No	No					
13	No	No		Pooled Estimate of p	=(E5*E8+F5*F8)/(E5+F5)		
14	No	No		Standard Error	=SQRT(E13*(1-E13)*(1/E5+1/F5))		
15	No	No		Test Statistic	=(E11-E10)/E14		
16	No	No					
17	No	Yes		p-value (Lower Tail)	=NORMSDIST(E15)		
18	Yes	No		p-value (Upper Tail)	=1-NORMSDIST(E15)		
19	No	No		p-value (Two Tail)	=2*MIN(E17,E18)		
250	Yes	No					
251	No	No					
300		No					
301		No					
302							

Note: Rows 20–249 and 252–299 are hidden.

	A	B	C	D	E	F	G
1	Office 1	Office 2		Hypothesis Test Concerning Difference			
2	No	No		Between Population Proportions			
3	No	No					
4	No	No			Office 1	Office 2	
5	No	No		Sample Size	250	300	
6	No	No		Response of Interest	Yes	Yes	
7	Yes	No		Count for Response	35	27	
8	No	No		Sample Proportion	0.14	0.09	
9	No	No					
10	No	No		Hypothesized Value	0		
11	No	No		Point Estimate of Difference	0.05		
12	No	No					
13	No	No		Pooled Estimate of p	0.1127		
14	No	No		Standard Error	0.0271		
15	No	No		Test Statistic	1.8462		
16	No	No					
17	No	Yes		p-value (Lower Tail)	0.9676		
18	Yes	No		p-value (Upper Tail)	0.0324		
19	No	No		p-value (Two Tail)	0.0649		
250	Yes	No					
251	No	No					
300		No					
301		No					
302							

Exercises

Methods

1. Consider the following results for independent samples taken from two populations.

Sample 1	Sample 2
$n_1 = 400$	$n_2 = 300$
$\bar{p}_1 = .48$	$\bar{p}_2 = .36$

a.   What is the point estimate of the difference between the two population proportions?
b.   Develop a 90% confidence interval for the difference between the two population proportions.
c.   Develop a 95% confidence interval for the difference between the two population proportions.

2.   Consider the following hypothesis test.

$$H_0: p_1 - p_2 = 0$$
$$H_a: p_1 - p_2 \neq 0$$

The following results are for independent samples taken from the two populations.

Sample 1	Sample 2
$n_1 = 100$	$n_2 = 140$
$\bar{p}_1 = .28$	$\bar{p}_1 = .20$

a.   What is the pooled estimate of p?
b.   What is the p-value?
c.   What is your conclusion?

Applications

3.   The Professional Golf Association (PGA) measured the putting accuracy of professional golfers playing on the PGA Tour and the best amateur golfers playing in the World Amateur Championship (*Golf Magazine,* January 2007). A sample of 1075 6-foot putts by professional golfers found 688 made putts. A sample of 1200 6-foot putts by amateur golfers found 696 made putts.
a.   Estimate the proportion of made 6-foot putts by professional golfers. Estimate the proportion of made 6-foot putts by amateur golfers. Which group had a better putting accuracy?
b.   What is the point estimate of the difference between the proportions of the two populations? What does this estimate tell you about the percentage of putts made by the two groups of golfers?
c.   What is the 95% confidence interval for the difference between the two population proportions? Interpret this confidence interval in terms of the percentage of putts made by the two groups of golfers.

4.   An American Automobile Association (AAA) study investigated the question of whether a man or a woman was more likely to stop and ask for directions (AAA, January 2006). The situation referred to in the study stated the following: "If you and your spouse are driving together and become lost, would you stop and ask for directions?" A sample representative of the data used by AAA showed 300 of 811 women said that they would stop and ask for directions, while 255 of 750 men said that they would stop and ask for directions.
a.   The AAA research hypothesis was that women would be more likely to say that they would stop and ask for directions. Formulate the null and alternative hypotheses for this study.
b.   What is the percentage of women who indicated that they would stop and ask for directions?
c.   What is the percentage of men who indicated that they would stop and ask for directions?
d.   At $\alpha = .05$, test the hypothesis. What is the p-value, and what conclusion would you expect AAA to draw from this study?

5. In recent years, the number of people who use the Internet to obtain political news has grown. Often the political websites ask Internet users to register their opinions by participating in online surveys. Pew Research Center conducted a survey of its own to learn about the participation of Republicans and Democrats in online surveys (Associated Press, January 6, 2003). The following sample data apply.

Political Party	Sample Size	Participate in Online Surveys
Republican	250	115
Democrat	350	98

   a. Compute the point estimate of the proportion of Republicans who indicate they would participate in online surveys. Compute the point estimate for the Democrats.
   b. What is the point estimate of the difference between the two population proportions?
   c. At 95% confidence, what is the margin of error?
   d. Representatives of the scientific polling industry claim that the profusion of online surveys can confuse people about actual public opinion. Do you agree with this statement? Use the 95% confidence interval estimate of the difference between the Republican and Democrat population proportions to help justify your answer.

6. Chicago O'Hare and Atlanta Hartsfield-Jackson are the two busiest airports in the United States. The congestion often leads to delayed flight arrivals as well as delayed flight departures. The Bureau of Transportation tracks the on-time and delayed performance at major airports (*Travel & Leisure,* November 2006). A flight is considered delayed if it is more than 15 minutes behind schedule. The following sample data show the delayed departures at Chicago O'Hare and Atlanta Hartsfield-Jackson airports.

	Chicago O'Hare	Atlanta Hartsfield-Jackson
Flights	900	1200
Delayed Departures	252	312

   a. State the hypothesis that can be used to determine whether the population proportions of delayed departures differ at these two airports.
   b. What is the point estimate of the proportion of flights that have delayed departures at Chicago O'Hare?
   c. What is the point estimate of the proportion of flights that have delayed departures at Atlanta Hartsfield-Jackson?
   d. What is the *p*-value for the hypothesis test? What is your conclusion?

7. *BusinessWeek* reported that there seems to be a difference by age group in how well people like life in Russia (*BusinessWeek,* March 10, 2008). The following sample data are consistent with the *BusinessWeek* findings and show the responses by age group to the question: "Do you like life in Russia?"

	Russian Age Group	
	17–26	40 and over
Sample Size	300	260
Responded Yes	192	117

   a. What is the point estimate of the proportion of Russians aged 17 to 26 who like life in Russia?

    b. What is the point estimate of the proportion of Russians aged 40 and over who like life in Russia?

    c. Provide a 95% confidence interval estimate of the difference between the proportion of young Russians aged 17 to 26 and older Russians aged 40 and over who like life in Russia.

8. During the 2003 Super Bowl, Miller Lite Beer's commercial referred to as "The Miller Lite Girls" ranked among the top three most effective advertisements aired during the Super Bowl (*USA Today,* December 29, 2003). The survey of advertising effectiveness, conducted by *USA Today's* Ad Track poll, reported separate samples by respondent age group to learn about how the Super Bowl advertisement appealed to different age groups. The following sample data apply to the "The Miller Lite Girls" commercial.

Age Group	Sample Size	Liked the Ad a Lot
Under 30	100	49
30 to 49	150	54

    a. Formulate a hypothesis test that can be used to determine whether there is a difference between the population proportions for the two age groups.

    b. What is the point estimate of the difference between the two population proportions?

    c. Conduct the hypothesis test and report the *p*-value. At $\alpha = .05$, what is your conclusion?

    d. Discuss the appeal of the advertisements to the younger and the older age groups. Would the Miller Lite organization find the results of the *USA Today* Ad Track poll encouraging? Explain.

9. In a test of the quality of two television commercials, each commercial was shown in a separate test area six times over a one-week period. The following week a telephone survey was conducted to identify individuals who had seen the commercials. Those individuals were asked to state the primary message in the commercials. The following results were recorded.

	Commercial A	Commercial B
Number Who Saw Commercial	150	200
Number Who Recalled Message	63	60

    a. Use $\alpha = .05$ and test the hypothesis that there is no difference in the recall proportions for the two commercials.

    b. Compute a 95% confidence interval for the difference between the recall proportions for the two populations.

10. A 2003 *New York Times*/CBS News poll sampled 523 adults who were planning a vacation during the next six months and found that 141 were expecting to travel by airplane (*New York Times* News Service, March 2, 2003). A similar survey question in a May 1993 *New York Times*/CBS News poll found that of 477 adults who were planning a vacation in the next six months, 81 were expecting to travel by airplane.

    a. State the hypotheses that can be used to determine whether a significant change occurred in the population proportion planning to travel by airplane over the 10-year period.

    b. What is the sample proportion expecting to travel by airplane in 2003? In 1993?

    c. Use $\alpha = .01$ and test for a significant difference. What is your conclusion?

    d. Discuss reasons that might provide an explanation for this conclusion.

Hypothesis Test for Proportions of a Multinomial Population

In this section we consider the case in which each element of a population is assigned to one and only one of several classes or categories. Such a population is a **multinomial population**. The multinomial distribution can be thought of as an extension of the binomial distribution to the case of three or more categories of outcomes. On each trial of a multinomial experiment, one and only one of the outcomes occurs. Each trial of the experiment is assumed to be independent, and the probabilities of the outcomes remain the same for each trial.

The assumptions for the multinomial experiment parallel those for the binomial experiment with the exception that the multinomial has three or more outcomes per trial.

As an example, consider the market share study being conducted by Scott Marketing Research. Over the past year market shares stabilized at 30% for company A, 50% for company B, and 20% for company C. Recently company C developed a "new and improved" product to replace its current entry in the market. Company C retained Scott Marketing Research to determine whether the new product will alter market shares.

In this case, the population of interest is a multinomial population; each customer is classified as buying from company A, company B, or company C. Thus, we have a multinomial population with three outcomes. Let us use the following notation for the proportions:

$$p_A = \text{market share for company A}$$
$$p_B = \text{market share for company B}$$
$$p_C = \text{market share for company C}$$

Scott Marketing Research will conduct a sample survey and compute the proportion preferring each company's product. A hypothesis test will then be conducted to see whether the new product caused a change in market shares. For the null hypothesis, we assume that company C's new product will not alter the market shares. The null and alternative hypotheses are stated as follows:

$$H_0: p_A = .30, p_B = .50, \text{ and } p_C = .20$$
$$H_a: \text{The population proportions are not}$$
$$p_A = .30, p_B = .50, \text{ and } p_C = .20$$

If the sample results lead to the rejection of H_0, Scott Marketing Research will have evidence that the introduction of the new product affects market shares.

Let us assume that the market research firm has used a consumer panel of 200 customers for the study. Each individual was asked to specify a purchase preference among the three alternatives: company A's product, company B's product, and company C's new product. The 200 responses are summarized here.

The consumer panel of 200 customers in which each individual is asked to select one of three alternatives is equivalent to a multinomial experiment consisting of 200 trials.

Observed Frequency		
Company A's Product	**Company B's Product**	**Company C's New Product**
48	98	54

We now can perform a **goodness of fit test** that will determine whether the sample of 200 customer purchase preferences is consistent with the null hypothesis. The goodness of fit test is based on a comparison of the sample of *observed* results with the *expected* results under the assumption that the null hypothesis is true. Hence, the next step is to compute expected purchase preferences for the 200 customers under the assumption that $p_A = .30$, $p_B = .50$, and $p_C = .20$. Doing so provides the expected results.

	Expected Frequency	
Company A's Product	**Company B's Product**	**Company C's New Product**
200(.30) = 60	200(.50) = 100	200(.20) = 40

Thus, we see that the expected frequency for each category is found by multiplying the sample size of 200 by the hypothesized proportion for the category.

The goodness of fit test now focuses on the differences between the observed frequencies and the expected frequencies. Large differences between observed and expected frequencies cast doubt on the assumption that the hypothesized proportions or market shares are correct. Whether the differences between the observed and expected frequencies are "large" or "small" is a question answered with the aid of the following chi-square test statistic.

TEST STATISTIC FOR GOODNESS OF FIT

$$\chi^2 = \sum_{i=1}^{k} \frac{(f_i - e_i)^2}{e_i} \qquad (11.8)$$

where

f_i = observed frequency for category i

e_i = expected frequency for category i

k = the number of categories

Note: The test statistic has a chi-square distribution with $k - 1$ degrees of freedom provided that the expected frequencies are 5 *or more* for all categories.

Tables of areas or probabilities are readily available for the chi-square distribution. Since the test statistic for goodness of fit is known to have a chi-square distribution whenever the expected frequencies are 5 or more for all categories, we can use the chi-square distribution to conduct the hypothesis test. We will use the notation χ^2_α to denote the value of the chi-square distribution that provides an area or probability of α to the right of the χ^2_α value. For example, refer to Table 11.1 and verify that for a chi-square distribution with 2 degrees of freedom $\chi^2_{.10} = 4.605$, indicating that 10% of the chi-square values are to the right of 4.605.

Let us continue with the Scott Marketing Research example and use the sample data to test the hypothesis that the multinomial population retains the proportions $p_A = .30$, $p_B = .50$, and $p_C = .20$. We will use an $\alpha = .05$ level of significance. Let us proceed by using the observed and expected frequencies to compute the value of the test statistic. With the expected frequencies all 5 or more, the computation of the chi-square test statistic is shown in Table 11.2. At the bottom of the last column, we see that $\chi^2 = 7.34$.

The test for goodness of fit is always a one-tailed test with the rejection occurring in the upper tail of the chi-square distribution.

We will reject the null hypothesis if the differences between the observed and expected frequencies are *large*. Large differences between the observed and expected frequencies will result in a large value for the test statistic. Thus the test of goodness of fit will always be an upper tail test. We can use the upper tail area for the test statistic and the *p*-value approach to determine whether the null hypothesis can be rejected. With $k - 1 = 3 - 1 = 2$ degrees of freedom, the chi-square table provides the following:

Area in Upper Tail	**.10**	**.05**	**.025**	**.01**
χ^2 **Value (2 *df*)**	4.605	5.991	7.378	9.210

$$\chi^2 = 7.34$$

TABLE 11.1 SELECTED VALUES FROM THE CHI-SQUARE DISTRIBUTION TABLE*

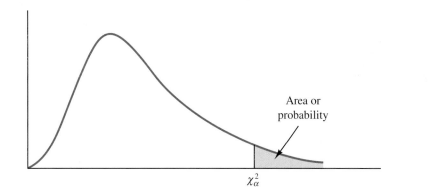

Area or probability

χ_α^2

Degrees of Freedom	Area in Upper Tail							
	.99	.975	.95	.90	.10	.05	.025	.01
1	.000	.001	.004	.016	2.706	3.841	5.024	6.635
2	.020	.051	.103	.211	4.605	5.991	7.378	9.210
3	.115	.216	.352	.584	6.251	7.815	9.348	11.345
4	.297	.484	.711	1.064	7.779	9.488	11.143	13.277
5	.554	.831	1.145	1.610	9.236	11.070	12.832	15.086
6	.872	1.237	1.635	2.204	10.645	12.592	14.449	16.812
7	1.239	1.690	2.167	2.833	12.017	14.067	16.013	18.475
8	1.647	2.180	2.733	3.490	13.362	15.507	17.535	20.090
9	2.088	2.700	3.325	4.168	14.684	16.919	19.023	21.666
10	2.558	3.247	3.940	4.865	15.987	18.307	20.483	23.209
11	3.053	3.816	4.575	5.578	17.275	19.675	21.920	24.725
12	3.571	4.404	5.226	6.304	18.549	21.026	23.337	26.217
13	4.107	5.009	5.892	7.041	19.812	22.362	24.736	27.688
14	4.660	5.629	6.571	7.790	21.064	23.685	26.119	29.141
15	5.229	6.262	7.261	8.547	22.307	24.996	27.488	30.578
16	5.812	6.908	7.962	9.312	23.542	26.296	28.845	32.000
17	6.408	7.564	8.672	10.085	24.769	27.587	30.191	33.409
18	7.015	8.231	9.390	10.865	25.989	28.869	31.526	34.805
19	7.633	8.907	10.117	11.651	27.204	30.144	32.852	36.191
20	8.260	9.591	10.851	12.443	28.412	31.410	34.170	37.566
21	8.897	10.283	11.591	13.240	29.615	32.671	35.479	38.932
22	9.542	10.982	12.338	14.041	30.813	33.924	36.781	40.289
23	10.196	11.689	13.091	14.848	32.007	35.172	38.076	41.638
24	10.856	12.401	13.848	15.659	33.196	36.415	39.364	42.980
25	11.524	13.120	14.611	16.473	34.382	37.652	40.646	44.314
26	12.198	13.844	15.379	17.292	35.563	38.885	41.923	45.642
27	12.878	14.573	16.151	18.114	36.741	40.113	43.195	46.963
28	13.565	15.308	16.928	18.939	37.916	41.337	44.461	48.278
29	14.256	16.047	17.708	19.768	39.087	42.557	45.722	49.588
30	14.953	16.791	18.493	20.599	40.256	43.773	46.979	50.892
40	22.164	24.433	26.509	29.051	51.805	55.758	59.342	63.691
60	37.485	40.482	43.188	46.459	74.397	79.082	83.298	88.379
80	53.540	57.153	60.391	64.278	96.578	101.879	106.629	112.329
100	70.065	74.222	77.929	82.358	118.498	124.342	129.561	135.807

Note: A more extensive table is provided as Table 3 of Appendix B.

TABLE 11.2 COMPUTATION OF THE CHI-SQUARE TEST STATISTIC FOR THE SCOTT MARKETING RESEARCH MARKET SHARE STUDY

Category	Hypothesized Proportion	Observed Frequency (f_i)	Expected Frequency (e_i)	Difference $(f_i - e_i)$	Squared Difference $(f_i - e_i)^2$	Squared Difference Divided by Expected Frequency $(f_i - e_i)^2/e_i$
Company A	.30	48	60	−12	144	2.40
Company B	.50	98	100	−2	4	0.04
Company C	.20	54	40	14	196	4.90
Total		200				$\chi^2 = 7.34$

Using Excel, CHIDIST (7.34,2) = .0255.

The test statistic $\chi^2 = 7.34$ is between 5.991 and 7.378. Thus, the corresponding upper tail area or p-value must be between .05 and .025. Excel can be used to show that $\chi^2 = 7.34$ provides a p-value = .0255. With the p-value $\leq \alpha = .05$, we reject H_0 and conclude that the introduction of the new product by company C will alter the current market share structure.

Instead of using the p-value, we could use the critical value approach to draw the same conclusion. With $\alpha = .05$ and 2 degrees of freedom, the critical value for the test statistic is $\chi^2_{.05} = 5.991$. The upper tail rejection rule becomes

$$\text{Reject } H_0 \text{ if } \chi^2 \geq 5.991$$

With $7.34 > 5.991$, we reject H_0. The p-value approach and critical value approach provide the same hypothesis testing conclusion.

Although no further statistical conclusions can be made as a result of the test, we can compare the observed and expected frequencies informally to obtain an idea of how the market share structure may change. Considering company C, we find that the observed frequency of 54 is larger than the expected frequency of 40. Because the expected frequency was based on current market shares, the larger observed frequency suggests that the new product will have a positive effect on company C's market share. Comparisons of the observed and expected frequencies for the other two companies indicate that company C's gain in market share will hurt company A more than company B.

Let us summarize the general steps that can be used to conduct a goodness of fit test for a hypothesized multinomial population distribution.

MULTINOMIAL DISTRIBUTION GOODNESS OF FIT TEST: A SUMMARY

1. State the null and alternative hypotheses.

   H_0: The population follows a multinomial distribution with specified probabilities for each of the k categories

   H_a: The population does not follow a multinomial distribution with the specified probabilities for each of the k categories

2. Select a random sample and record the observed frequencies f_i for each category.

3. Assume the null hypothesis is true and determine the expected frequency e_i in each category by multiplying the category probability by the sample size.

4. Compute the value of the test statistic.

$$\chi^2 = \sum_{i=1}^{k} \frac{(f_i - e_i)^2}{e_i}$$

5. Rejection rule:

p-value approach: Reject H_0 if p-value $\le \alpha$

Critical value approach: Reject H_0 if $\chi^2 \ge \chi_\alpha^2$

where α is the level of significance for the test and there are $k - 1$ degrees of freedom.

Using Excel to Conduct a Goodness of Fit Test

Excel can be used to conduct a goodness of fit test for the Scott Marketing Research Study. Refer to Figure 11.3 as we describe the tasks involved. The formula worksheet is in the background; the value worksheet is in the foreground.

WEB file

Research

Enter Data: Column A is used to identify each of the 200 customers who made up the consumer panel in the study. Column B shows the purchase preference (A, B, or C) for each customer. The hypothesized proportions, 0.3, 0.5, and 0.2, were entered into cells E4:E6.

FIGURE 11.3   EXCEL WORKSHEET FOR GOODNESS OF FIT TEST CONCERNING MARKET SHARE CHANGE

	A	B	C	D	E	F	G	H	I	J	K
1	Customer	Product								Squared Diff.	
2	1	B			Hyp.	Obs.	Exp.		Squared	Divided by	
3	2	A		Category	Proportion	Freq.	Freq.	Diff.	Diff.	Exp. Freq.	
4	3	C		Company A	0.3	=COUNTIF(B2:B201,"A")	=E4*F7	=F4-G4	=H4^2	=I4/G4	
5	4	C		Company B	0.5	=COUNTIF(B2:B201,"B")	=E5*F7	=F5-G5	=H5^2	=I5/G5	
6	5	C		Company C	0.2	=COUNTIF(B2:B201,"C")	=E6*F7	=F6-G6	=H6^2	=I6/G6	
7	6	A			Total	=SUM(F4:F6)				=SUM(J4:J6)	
8	7	A									
9	8	A		Number of Categories	3						
10	9	C									
11	10	A		Test Statistic	=J7						
12	11	C		Degrees of Freedom	=F9-1						
13	12	B									
14	13	C		p-value	=CHIDIST(F11,F12)						
15	14	A									
200	199	C									
201	200	C									
202											

Note: Rows 16–199 are hidden.

	A	B	C	D	E	F	G	H	I	J	K
1	Customer	Product								Squared Diff.	
2	1	B			Hyp.	Obs.	Exp.		Squared	Divided by	
3	2	A		Category	Proportion	Freq.	Freq.	Diff.	Diff.	Exp. Freq.	
4	3	C		Company A	0.3	48	60	-12	144	2.4	
5	4	C		Company B	0.5	98	100	-2	4	0.04	
6	5	C		Company C	0.2	54	40	14	196	4.9	
7	6	A			Total	200				7.34	
8	7	A									
9	8	A		Number of Categories	3						
10	9	C									
11	10	A		Test Statistic	7.34						
12	11	C		Degrees of Freedom	2						
13	12	B									
14	13	C		p-value	0.0255						
15	14	A									
200	199	C									
201	200	C									
202											

Enter Functions and Formulas: The Excel formulas in cells F4:J7 are used to compute the chi-square test statistic in a fashion parallel to that shown in Table 11.2. The result is the chi-square test statistic shown in cell J7 (7.34). The number of categories, 3, was entered into cell F9 and the two inputs used by Excel's CHIDIST function (test statistic and degrees of freedom) are in cells F11 and F12. The value computed in cell F14 using Excel's CHIDIST function is the area in the upper tail of the chi-square distribution to the right of the test statistic. So, this value is the appropriate p-value for our upper tail hypothesis test.

The value worksheet shows that the resulting p-value is 0.0255. Thus, with $\alpha = .05$, we reject H_0 and conclude that the introduction of the new product by company C will alter the current market share structure.

Exercises

Methods

11. Test the following hypotheses by using the χ^2 goodness of fit test.

$$H_0\colon p_A = .40, p_B = .40, \text{ and } p_C = .20$$
$$H_a\colon \text{The population proportions are not}$$
$$p_A = .40, p_B = .40, \text{ and } p_C = .20$$

A sample of size 200 yielded 60 in category A, 120 in category B, and 20 in category C. Use $\alpha = .01$ and test to see whether the proportions are as stated in H_0.
   a. Use the p-value approach.
   b. Repeat the test using the critical value approach.

12. Suppose we have a multinomial population with four categories: A, B, C, and D. The null hypothesis is that the proportion of items is the same in every category. The null hypothesis is

$$H_0\colon p_A = p_B = p_C = p_D = .25$$

A sample of size 300 yielded the following results.

A: 85   B: 95   C: 50   D: 70

Use $\alpha = .05$ to determine whether H_0 should be rejected. What is the p-value?

Applications

13. During the first 13 weeks of the television season, the Saturday evening 8:00 P.M. to 9:00 P.M. audience proportions were recorded as ABC 29%, CBS 28%, NBC 25%, and independents 18%. A sample of 300 homes two weeks after a Saturday night schedule revision yielded the following viewing audience data: ABC 95 homes, CBS 70 homes, NBC 89 homes, and independents 46 homes. Test with $\alpha = .05$ to determine whether the viewing audience proportions changed.

14. M&M/MARS, makers of M&M® Chocolate Candies, conducted a national poll in which consumers indicated their preference for colors. In the brochure "Colors," made available by M&M/MARS Consumer Affairs, the traditional distribution of colors for the plain candies is as follows:

Brown	Yellow	Red	Orange	Green	Blue
30%	20%	20%	10%	10%	10%

In a follow-up study, 1-pound bags were used to determine whether the reported percentages were valid. The following results were obtained for a sample of 506 plain candies.

Brown	**Yellow**	**Red**	**Orange**	**Green**	**Blue**
177	135	79	41	36	38

Use $\alpha = .05$ to determine whether these data support the percentages reported by the company.

15. Where do women most often buy casual clothing? Data from the U.S. Shopper Database provided the following percentages for women shopping at each of the various outlets (*The Wall Street Journal*, January 28, 2004).

Outlet	**Percentage**	**Outlet**	**Percentage**
Wal-Mart	24	Kohl's	8
Traditional department stores	11	Mail order	12
J.C. Penney	8	Other	37

The other category included outlets such as Target, Kmart, and Sears as well as numerous smaller specialty outlets. No individual outlet in this group accounted for more than 5% of the women shoppers. A recent survey using a sample of 140 women shoppers in Atlanta, Georgia, found 42 Wal-Mart, 20 traditional department store, 8 J.C. Penney, 10 Kohl's, 21 mail order, and 39 other outlet shoppers. Does this sample suggest that women shoppers in Atlanta differ from the shopping preferences expressed in the U.S. Shopper Database? What is the *p*-value? Use $\alpha = .05$. What is your conclusion?

16. The American Bankers Association collects data on the use of credit cards, debit cards, personal checks, and cash when consumers pay for in-store purchases (*The Wall Street Journal*, December 16, 2003). In 1999, the following usages were reported.

In-Store Purchase	**Percentage**
Credit card	22
Debit card	21
Personal check	18
Cash	39

A sample taken in 2003 found that for 220 in-stores purchases, 46 used a credit card, 67 used a debit card, 33 used a personal check, and 74 used cash.

   a. At $\alpha = .01$, can we conclude that a change occurred in how customers paid for in-store purchases over the four-year period from 1999 to 2003? What is the *p*-value?
   b. Compute the percentage of use for each method of payment using the 2003 sample data. What appears to have been the major change or changes over the four-year period?
   c. In 2003, what percentage of payments was made using plastic (credit card or debit card)?

17. *The Wall Street Journal*'s Shareholder Scoreboard tracks the performance of 1000 major U.S. companies (*The Wall Street Journal*, March 10, 2003). The performance of each company is rated based on the annual total return, including stock price changes and the reinvestment of dividends. Ratings are assigned by dividing all 1000 companies into five groups from A (top

20%), B (next 20%), to E (bottom 20%). Shown here are the one-year ratings for a sample of 60 of the largest companies. Do the largest companies differ in performance from the performance of the 1000 companies in the Shareholder Scoreboard? Use $\alpha = .05$.

A	B	C	D	E
5	8	15	20	12

18. How well do airline companies serve their customers? A study showed the following customer ratings: 3% excellent, 28% good, 45% fair, and 24% poor (*BusinessWeek*, September 11, 2000). In a follow-up study of service by telephone companies, assume that a sample of 400 adults found the following customer ratings: 24 excellent, 124 good, 172 fair, and 80 poor. Is the distribution of the customer ratings for telephone companies different from the distribution of customer ratings for airline companies? Test with $\alpha = .01$. What is your conclusion?

(11.3) Test of Independence

Another important application of the chi-square distribution involves using sample data to test for the independence of two variables. Let us illustrate the test of independence by considering the study conducted by the Alber's Brewery of Tucson, Arizona. Alber's manufactures and distributes three types of beer: light, regular, and dark. In an analysis of the market segments for the three beers, the firm's market research group raised the question of whether preferences for the three beers differ among male and female beer drinkers. If beer preference is independent of the gender of the beer drinker, one advertising campaign will be initiated for all of Alber's beers. However, if beer preference depends on the gender of the beer drinker, the firm will tailor its promotions to different target markets.

A test of independence addresses the question of whether the beer preference (light, regular, or dark) is independent of the gender of the beer drinker (male, female). The hypotheses for this test of independence are

H_0: Beer preference is independent of the gender of the beer drinker
H_a: Beer preference is not independent of the gender of the beer drinker

To test whether two variables are independent, one sample is selected and crosstabulation is used to summarize the data for the two variables simultaneously.

Table 11.3 can be used to describe the situation being studied. After identification of the population as all male and female beer drinkers, a sample can be selected and each individual asked to state his or her preference for the three Alber's beers. Every individual in the sample will be classified in one of the six cells in the table. For example, an individual may be a male preferring regular beer [cell (1,2)], a female preferring light beer [cell (2,1)], a female preferring dark beer [cell (2,3)], and so on. Because we have listed all possible

TABLE 11.3 CONTINGENCY TABLE FOR BEER PREFERENCE AND GENDER OF BEER DRINKER

		Beer Preference		
		Light	**Regular**	**Dark**
Gender	**Male**	cell(1,1)	cell(1,2)	cell(1,3)
	Female	cell(2,1)	cell(2,2)	cell(2,3)

TABLE 11.4   SAMPLE RESULTS FOR BEER PREFERENCES OF MALE AND FEMALE
BEER DRINKERS (OBSERVED FREQUENCIES)

| | | Beer Preference | | | |
		Light	Regular	Dark	Total
Gender	Male	20	40	20	80
	Female	30	30	10	70
	Total	50	70	30	150

combinations of beer preference and gender or, in other words, listed all possible contingencies, Table 11.3 is called a **contingency table**. The test of independence uses the contingency table format and for that reason is sometimes referred to as a *contingency table test.*

Suppose a simple random sample of 150 beer drinkers is selected. After tasting each beer, the individuals in the sample are asked to state their preference or first choice. The crosstabulation in Table 11.4 summarizes the responses for the study. As we see, the data for the test of independence are collected in terms of counts or frequencies for each cell or category. Of the 150 individuals in the sample, 20 were men who favored light beer, 40 were men who favored regular beer, 20 were men who favored dark beer, and so on.

The data in Table 11.4 are the observed frequencies for the six classes or categories. If we can determine the expected frequencies under the assumption of independence between beer preference and gender of the beer drinker, we can use the chi-square distribution to determine whether there is a significant difference between observed and expected frequencies.

Expected frequencies for the cells of the contingency table are based on the following rationale. First we assume that the null hypothesis of independence between beer preference and gender of the beer drinker is true. Then we note that in the entire sample of 150 beer drinkers, a total of 50 prefer light beer, 70 prefer regular beer, and 30 prefer dark beer. In terms of fractions we conclude that $^{50}/_{150} = \frac{1}{3}$ of the beer drinkers prefer light beer, $^{70}/_{150} = ^{7}/_{15}$ prefer regular beer, and $^{30}/_{150} = \frac{1}{5}$ prefer dark beer. If the *independence* assumption is valid, we argue that these fractions must be applicable to both male and female beer drinkers. Thus, under the assumption of independence, we would expect the sample of 80 male beer drinkers to show that $(\frac{1}{3})80 = 26.67$ prefer light beer, $(^{7}/_{15})80 = 37.33$ prefer regular beer, and $(\frac{1}{5})80 = 16$ prefer dark beer. Application of the same fractions to the 70 female beer drinkers provides the expected frequencies shown in Table 11.5.

Let e_{ij} denote the expected frequency for the contingency table category in row i and column j. With this notation, let us reconsider the expected frequency calculation for males

TABLE 11.5   EXPECTED FREQUENCIES IF BEER PREFERENCE IS INDEPENDENT
OF THE GENDER OF THE BEER DRINKER

| | | Beer Preference | | | |
		Light	Regular	Dark	Total
Gender	Male	26.67	37.33	16.00	80
	Female	23.33	32.67	14.00	70
	Total	50.00	70.00	30.00	150

(row $i = 1$) who prefer regular beer (column $j = 2$); that is, expected frequency e_{12}. Following the preceding argument for the computation of expected frequencies, we can show that

$$e_{12} = (\tfrac{7}{15})80 = 37.33$$

This expression can be written slightly differently as

$$e_{12} = (\tfrac{7}{15})80 = (\tfrac{70}{150})80 = \frac{(80)(70)}{150} = 37.33$$

Note that 80 in the expression is the total number of males (row 1 total), 70 is the total number of individuals preferring regular beer (column 2 total), and 150 is the total sample size. Hence, we see that

$$e_{12} = \frac{(\text{Row 1 Total})(\text{Column 2 Total})}{\text{Sample Size}}$$

Generalization of the expression shows that the following formula provides the expected frequencies for a contingency table in the test of independence.

EXPECTED FREQUENCIES FOR CONTINGENCY TABLES UNDER THE
ASSUMPTION OF INDEPENDENCE

$$e_{ij} = \frac{(\text{Row } i \text{ Total})(\text{Column } j \text{ Total})}{\text{Sample Size}} \qquad (11.9)$$

Using equation (11.9) for male beer drinkers who prefer dark beer, we find an expected frequency of $e_{13} = (80)(30)/150 = 16.00$, as shown in Table 11.5. Use equation (11.9) to verify the other expected frequencies shown in Table 11.5.

The test procedure for comparing the observed frequencies of Table 11.4 with the expected frequencies of Table 11.5 is similar to the goodness of fit calculations made in Section 11.2. Specifically, the χ^2 value based on the observed and expected frequencies is computed as follows.

TEST STATISTIC FOR INDEPENDENCE

$$\chi^2 = \sum_i \sum_j \frac{(f_{ij} - e_{ij})^2}{e_{ij}} \qquad (11.10)$$

where

f_{ij} = observed frequency for contingency table category in row i and column j
e_{ij} = expected frequency for contingency table category in row i and column j based on the assumption of independence

Note: With n rows and m columns in the contingency table, the test statistic has a chi-square distribution with $(n - 1)(m - 1)$ degrees of freedom provided that the expected frequencies are 5 or more for all categories.

TABLE 11.6 COMPUTATION OF THE CHI-SQUARE TEST STATISTIC FOR DETERMINING WHETHER BEER PREFERENCE IS INDEPENDENT OF THE GENDER OF THE BEER DRINKER

Gender	Beer Preference	Observed Frequency (f_{ij})	Expected Frequency (e_{ij})	Difference $(f_{ij} - e_{ij})$	Squared Difference $(f_{ij} - e_{ij})^2$	Squared Difference Divided by Expected Frequency $(f_{ij} - e_{ij})^2/e_{ij}$
Male	Light	20	26.67	−6.67	44.44	1.67
Male	Regular	40	37.33	2.67	7.11	0.19
Male	Dark	20	16.00	4.00	16.00	1.00
Female	Light	30	23.33	6.67	44.44	1.90
Female	Regular	30	32.67	−2.67	7.11	0.22
Female	Dark	10	14.00	−4.00	16.00	1.14
	Total	150				$\chi^2 = 6.12$

The double summation in equation (11.10) is used to indicate that the calculation must be made for all the cells in the contingency table.

By reviewing the expected frequencies in Table 11.5, we see that the expected frequencies are 5 or more for each category. We therefore proceed with the computation of the chi-square test statistic. The calculations necessary to compute the chi-square test statistic for determining whether beer preference is independent of the gender of the beer drinker are shown in Table 11.6. We see that the value of the test statistic is $\chi^2 = 6.12$.

The number of degrees of freedom for the appropriate chi-square distribution is computed by multiplying the number of rows minus 1 by the number of columns minus 1. With two rows and three columns, we have $(2 - 1)(3 - 1) = 2$ degrees of freedom. Just like the test for goodness of fit, the test for independence rejects H_0 if the differences between observed and expected frequencies provide a large value for the test statistic. Thus the test for independence is also an upper tail test. Using the chi-square table (Table 3 of Appendix B), we conclude that the upper tail area or p-value at $\chi^2 = 6.12$ is between .025 and .05. Excel can be used to show that $\chi^2 = 6.12$ provides a p-value $= .0468$. At the .05 level of significance, p-value $\leq \alpha = .05$. We reject the null hypothesis of independence and conclude that beer preference is not independent of the gender of the beer drinker.

The test for independence is always a one-tailed test with the rejection region in the upper tail of the chi-square distribution.

Although no further statistical conclusions can be made as a result of the test, we can compare the observed and expected frequencies informally to obtain an idea about the dependence between beer preference and gender. Refer to Tables 11.4 and 11.5. We see that male beer drinkers have higher observed than expected frequencies for both regular and dark beers, whereas female beer drinkers have a higher observed than expected frequency only for light beer. These observations give us insight about the beer preference differences between male and female beer drinkers.

Let us summarize the steps in a contingency table test of independence.

TEST OF INDEPENDENCE: A SUMMARY

1. State the null and alternative hypotheses.

   H_0: The column variable is independent of the row variable
   H_a: The column variable is not independent of the row variable

2. Select a random sample and record the observed frequencies for each cell of the contingency table.

3. Use equation (11.9) to compute the expected frequency for each cell.

4. Use equation (11.10) to compute the value of the test statistic.

5. Rejection rule:

p-value approach: Reject H_0 if p-value $\leq \alpha$

Critical value approach: Reject H_0 if $\chi^2 \geq \chi_\alpha^2$

where α is the level of significance, with n rows and m columns providing $(n-1)(m-1)$ degrees of freedom.

Using Excel to Conduct a Test of Independence

Excel can be used to conduct a test of independence for the Alber's Brewery example. Refer to Figure 11.4 as we describe the tasks involved. The formula worksheet is in the background; the value worksheet is in the foreground.

WEB file

Alber's

Enter Data: Column A is used to identify each of the 150 individuals in the study. Column B shows the gender and column C shows the beer preference (Light, Regular, or Dark) for each individual.

Apply Tools: Using Excel's PivotTable tool (see Section 2.4 for details regarding how to use this tool), we developed the crosstabulation shown in cells E3:I7. The values in cells F5:H6 are the observed frequencies for the Alber's Brewery study.

FIGURE 11.4 EXCEL WORKSHEET FOR THE ALBER'S BREWERY TEST OF INDEPENDENCE

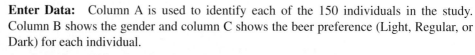

	A	B	C	D	E	F	G	H	I	J
1	Individual	Gender	Preference							
2	1	Female	Light							
3	2	Female	Regular		Count of Individual	Preference ▾				
4	3	Male	Regular		Gender ▾	Light	Regular	Dark	Grand Total	
5	4	Female	Light		Male	20	40	20	80	
6	5	Female	Light		Female	30	30	10	70	
7	6	Female	Regular		Grand Total	50	70	30	150	
8	7	Male	Regular							
9	8	Female	Dark		Expected Frequencies					
10	9	Female	Regular			Light	Regular	Dark		
11	10	Male	Dark		Male	=F7*I5/I7	=G7*I5/I7	=H7*I5/I7		
12	11	Male	Regular		Female	=F7*I6/I7	=G7*I6/I7	=H7*I6/I7		
13	12	Male	Regular							
14	13	Female	Regular				p-value	=CHITEST(F5:H6,F11:H12)		
15	14	Female	Regular							
16	15	Male	Light							
149	148	Male	Regular							
150	149	Female	Light							
151	150	Female	Regular							
152										

Note: Rows 17–148 are hidden.

	A	B	C	D	E	F	G	H	I	J
1	Individual	Gender	Preference							
2	1	Female	Light							
3	2	Female	Regular		Count of Individual	Preference ▾				
4	3	Male	Regular		Gender ▾	Light	Regular	Dark	Grand Total	
5	4	Female	Light		Male	20	40	20	80	
6	5	Female	Light		Female	30	30	10	70	
7	6	Female	Regular		Grand Total	50	70	30	150	
8	7	Male	Regular							
9	8	Female	Dark		Expected Frequencies					
10	9	Female	Regular			Light	Regular	Dark		
11	10	Male	Dark		Male	26.6667	37.3333	16		
12	11	Male	Regular		Female	23.3333	32.6667	14		
13	12	Male	Regular							
14	13	Female	Regular				p-value	0.0468		
15	14	Female	Regular							
16	15	Male	Light							
149	148	Male	Regular							
150	149	Female	Light							
151	150	Female	Regular							
152										

Enter Functions and Formulas: To compute the expected frequencies for the Alber's Brewery contingency table under the assumption of independence, we use equation (11.9). The formulas in cells F11:H12 are used to compute these expected frequencies. Once the observed and expected frequencies have been computed, Excel's CHITEST function can be used to compute the *p*-value for a test of independence. The inputs to the CHITEST function are the range of values for the observed and expected frequencies. To compute the *p*-value for this test of independence, we entered the following function into cell H14:

$$=CHITEST(F5:H6,F11:H12)$$

The value worksheet shows that the resulting *p*-value is .0468. Thus, with $\alpha = .05$ we reject H_0 and conclude that beer preference is not independent of the gender of the beer drinker.

NOTES AND COMMENTS

The test statistic for the chi-square tests in this chapter requires an expected frequency of five for each category. When a category has fewer than five, it is often appropriate to combine two adjacent categories to obtain an expected frequency of five or more in each category.

Exercises

Methods

19.   The following 2×3 contingency table contains observed frequencies for a sample of 200. Test for independence of the row and column variables using the χ^2 test with $\alpha = .05$.

	Column Variable		
Row Variable	A	B	C
P	20	44	50
Q	30	26	30

20.   The following 3×3 contingency table contains observed frequencies for a sample of 240. Test for independence of the row and column variables using the χ^2 test with $\alpha = .05$.

	Column Variable		
Row Variable	A	B	C
P	20	30	20
Q	30	60	25
R	10	15	30

Applications

21.   One of the questions on the *BusinessWeek* Subscriber Study was, "In the past 12 months, when traveling for business, what type of airline ticket did you purchase most often?" The data obtained are shown in the following contingency table.

Type of Ticket	Type of Flight	
	Domestic Flights	**International Flights**
First class	29	22
Business/executive class	95	121
Full fare economy/coach class	518	135

Use $\alpha = .05$ and test for the independence of type of flight and type of ticket. What is your conclusion?

22. Visa Card USA studied how frequently consumers of various age groups use plastic cards (debit and credit cards) when making purchases (Associated Press, January 16, 2006). Sample data for 300 customers shows the use of plastic cards by four age groups.

Payment	Age Group			
	18–24	**25–34**	**35–44**	**45 and over**
Plastic	21	27	27	36
Cash or Check	21	36	42	90

a. Test for the independence between method of payment and age group. What is the p-value? Using $\alpha = .05$, what is your conclusion?
b. If method of payment and age group are not independent, what observation can you make about how different age groups use plastic to make purchases?
c. What implications does this study have for companies such as Visa, MasterCard, and Discover?

23. With double-digit annual percentage increases in the cost of health insurance, more and more workers are likely to lack health insurance coverage (*USA Today,* January 23, 2004). The following sample data provide a comparison of workers with and without health insurance coverage for small, medium, and large companies. For the purposes of this study, small companies are companies that have fewer than 100 employees. Medium companies have 100 to 999 employees, and large companies have 1000 or more employees. Sample data are reported for 50 employees of small companies, 75 employees of medium companies, and 100 employees of large companies.

Size of Company	Health Insurance		
	Yes	**No**	**Total**
Small	36	14	50
Medium	65	10	75
Large	88	12	100

a. Conduct a test of independence to determine whether employee health insurance coverage is independent of the size of the company. Use $\alpha = .05$. What is the p-value, and what is your conclusion?
b. The *USA Today* article indicated employees of small companies are more likely to lack health insurance coverage. Use percentages based on the preceding data to support this conclusion.

24. A State of Washington's Public Interest Research Group (PIRG) study showed that 46% of full-time college students work 25 or more hours per week. The PIRG study provided data on the effects of working on grades (*USA Today,* April 17, 2002). A sample of 200 students

included 90 who worked 1 to 15 hours per week, 60 who worked 16 to 24 hours per week, and 50 who worked 25 to 34 hours per week. The sample number of students indicating their work had a positive effect, no effect, or a negative effect on grades is as follows.

Hours Worked per Week	Effect on Grades			
	Positive	**None**	**Negative**	Total
1–15 hours	26	50	14	90
16–24 hours	16	27	17	60
25–34 hours	11	19	20	50

a. Conduct a test of independence to determine whether the effect on grades is independent of the hours worked per week. Use $\alpha = .05$. What is the p-value, and what is your conclusion?

b. Use row percentages to learn more about how working affects grades. What is your conclusion?

25. FlightStats, Inc., collects data on the number of flights scheduled and the number of flights flown at major airports throughout the United States. FlightStats data showed 56% of flights scheduled at Newark, La Guardia, and Kennedy airports were flown during a three-day snowstorm (*The Wall Street Journal*, February 21, 2006). All airlines say they always operate within set safety parameters—if conditions are too poor, they don't fly. The following data show a sample of 400 scheduled flights during the snowstorm.

Did It Fly?	Airline				
	American	**Continental**	**Delta**	**United**	Total
Yes	48	69	68	25	210
No	52	41	62	35	190

Use the chi-square test of independence with a .05 level of significance to analyze the data. What is your conclusion? Do you have a preference for which airline you would choose to fly during similar snowstorm conditions? Explain.

26. As the price of oil rises, there is increased worldwide interest in alternate sources of energy. A *Financial Times*/Harris Poll surveyed people in six countries to assess attitudes toward a variety of alternate forms of energy (*http://www.harrisinteractive.com*, February 27, 2008). The data in the table below are a portion of the poll's findings concerning whether people favor or oppose the building of new nuclear power plants.

	Great Britain	France	Italy	Spain	Germany	United States
Strongly favor	141	161	298	133	128	204
Favor more than oppose	348	366	309	222	272	326
Oppose more than favor	381	334	219	311	322	316
Strongly oppose	217	215	219	443	389	174

a. How large was the sample in this poll?

b. Conduct a hypothesis test to determine whether people's attitude toward building new nuclear power plants is independent of country.

c. Which country has the most favorable attitude toward building new nuclear power plants?

27. The National Sleep Foundation used a survey to determine whether hours of sleeping per night are independent of age (*Newsweek*, January 19, 2004). The following table shows the

hours of sleep on weeknights for a sample of individuals age 49 and younger and for a sample of individuals age 50 and older.

	Hours of Sleep				
Age	Fewer than 6	6 to 6.9	7 to 7.9	8 or more	Total
49 or younger	38	60	77	65	240
50 or older	36	57	75	92	260

a. Conduct a test of independence to determine whether the hours of sleep on weeknights are independent of age. Use $\alpha = .05$. What is the p-value, and what is your conclusion?

b. What is your estimate of the percentage of people who sleep fewer than 6 hours, 6 to 6.9 hours, 7 to 7.9 hours, and 8 or more hours on weeknights?

28. Samples taken in three cities, Anchorage, Atlanta, and Minneapolis, were used to learn about the percentage of married couples with both the husband and the wife in the workforce (*USA Today,* January 15, 2006). Analyze the following data to see whether both the husband and wife being in the workforce is independent of location. Use a .05 level of significance. What is your conclusion? What is the overall estimate of the percentage of married couples with both the husband and the wife in the workforce?

	Location		
In Workforce	Anchorage	Atlanta	Minneapolis
Both	57	70	63
Only One	33	50	90

Summary

In this chapter, we described statistical procedures for comparisons involving proportions and the contingency table test for independence of two variables. In the first section, we compared a proportion for one population with the same proportion from another population. We described how to construct an interval estimate for the difference between the proportions and how to conduct a hypothesis test to learn whether the difference between the proportions was statistically significant.

In the second section, we focused on a single multinomial population. There we saw how to conduct hypothesis texts to determine whether the sample proportions for the categories of the multinomial population were significantly different than the hypothesized values. The chi-square goodness of fit test was used to make the comparison.

The final section was concerned with test of independence for two variables. A test of independence for two variables is an extension of the methodology employed in the goodness of fit test for a multinomial population. A contingency table is used to determine the observed and expected frequencies. Then a chi-square value is computed. Large chi-square values, caused by large differences between observed and expected frequencies, lead to the rejection of the null hypothesis of independence.

Glossary

Pooled estimator of p An estimator of a population proportion obtained by computing a weighted average of the sample proportions obtained from two independent samples.

Multinomial population A population in which each element is assigned to one and only one of several categories. The multinomial distribution extends the binomial distribution from two to three or more outcomes.

Goodness of fit test A statistical test conducted to determine whether to reject a hypothesized probability distribution for a population.

Contingency table A table used to summarize observed and expected frequencies for a test of independence.

Key Formulas

Point Estimator of the Difference Between Two Population Proportions

$$\bar{p}_1 - \bar{p}_2 \tag{11.1}$$

Standard Error of $\bar{p}_1 - \bar{p}_2$

$$\sigma_{\bar{p}_1 - \bar{p}_2} = \sqrt{\frac{p_1(1 - p_1)}{n_1} + \frac{p_2(1 - p_2)}{n_2}} \tag{11.2}$$

Interval Estimate of the Difference Between Two Population Proportions

$$\bar{p}_1 - \bar{p}_2 \pm z_{\alpha/2}\sqrt{\frac{\bar{p}_1(1 - \bar{p}_1)}{n_1} + \frac{\bar{p}_2(1 - \bar{p}_2)}{n_2}} \tag{11.4}$$

Standard Error of $\bar{p}_1 - \bar{p}_2$ When $p_1 = p_2 = p$

$$\sigma_{\bar{p}_1 - \bar{p}_2} = \sqrt{p(1 - p)\left(\frac{1}{n_1} + \frac{1}{n_2}\right)} \tag{11.5}$$

Pooled Estimator of p When $p_1 = p_2 = p$

$$\bar{p} = \frac{n_1\bar{p}_1 + n_2\bar{p}_2}{n_1 + n_2} \tag{11.6}$$

Test Statistic for Hypothesis Tests About $p_1 - p_2$

$$z = \frac{(\bar{p}_1 - \bar{p}_2)}{\sqrt{\bar{p}(1 - \bar{p})\left(\frac{1}{n_1} + \frac{1}{n_2}\right)}} \tag{11.7}$$

Test Statistic for Goodness of Fit

$$\chi^2 = \sum_{i=1}^{k} \frac{(f_i - e_i)^2}{e_i} \tag{11.8}$$

Expected Frequencies for Contingency Tables Under the Assumption of Independence

$$e_{ij} = \frac{(\text{Row } i \text{ Total})(\text{Column } j \text{ Total})}{\text{Sample Size}} \tag{11.9}$$

Test Statistic for Independence

$$\chi^2 = \sum_i \sum_j \frac{(f_{ij} - e_{ij})^2}{e_{ij}} \tag{11.10}$$

Supplementary Exercises

29. Jupiter Media used a survey to determine how people use their free time. Watching television was the most popular activity selected by both men and women (*The Wall Street Journal*, January 26, 2004). The proportion of men and the proportion of women who selected watching television as their most popular leisure time activity can be estimated from the following sample data.

Gender	Sample Size	Watching Television
Men	800	248
Women	600	156

a. State the hypotheses that can be used to test for a difference between the proportion for the population of men and the proportion for the population of women who selected watching television as their most popular leisure time activity.
b. What is the sample proportion of men who selected watching television as their most popular leisure time activity? What is the sample proportion of women?
c. Conduct the hypothesis test and compute the *p*-value. At a .05 level of significance, what is your conclusion?
d. What is the margin of error and 95% confidence interval estimate of the difference between the population proportions?

30. A large automobile insurance company selected samples of single and married male policyholders and recorded the number who made an insurance claim over the preceding three-year period.

Single Policyholders	Married Policyholders
$n_1 = 400$	$n_2 = 900$
Number making claims = 76	Number making claims = 90

a. Use $\alpha = .05$. Test to determine whether the claim rates differ between single and married male policyholders.
b. Provide a 95% confidence interval for the difference between the proportions for the two populations.

31. Medical tests were conducted to learn about drug-resistant tuberculosis. Of 142 cases tested in New Jersey, 9 were found to be drug-resistant. Of 268 cases tested in Texas, 5 were found to be drug-resistant. Do these data suggest a statistically significant difference between the proportions of drug-resistant cases in the two states? Use a .02 level of significance. What is the *p*-value, and what is your conclusion?

WEB file

Occupancy

32. Vacation occupancy rates were expected to be up during March 2008 in Myrtle Beach, South Carolina (*The Sun News*, February 29, 2008). Data in the file Occupancy will allow you to replicate the findings presented in the newspaper. The data show units rented and not rented for a random sample of vacation properties during the first week of March 2007 and March 2008.
a. Estimate the proportion of units rented during the first week of March 2007 and the first week of March 2008.
b. Provide a 95% confidence interval for the difference in proportions.
c. On the basis of your findings, does it appear March rental rates for 2008 will be up from those a year earlier?

33. In June 2001, 38% of fund managers surveyed believed that the core inflation rate would be higher in one year. One month later a similar survey revealed that 22% of fund managers

expected the core inflation rate to be higher in one year (*Global Research Highlights, Merrill Lynch,* July 20, 2001). Assume that the sample size was 200 in both the June and July surveys.

    a.   Develop a point estimate of the difference between the June and July proportions of fund managers who felt the core inflation rate would be higher in one year.

    b.   Develop hypotheses such that rejection of the null hypothesis allows us to conclude that inflation expectations diminished between June and July.

    c.   Conduct a test of the hypotheses in part (b) using $\alpha = .01$. What is your conclusion?

34.   In setting sales quotas, the marketing manager makes the assumption that order potentials are the same for each of four sales territories. A sample of 200 sales follows. Should the manager's assumption be rejected? Use $\alpha = .05$.

Sales Territories			
I	**II**	**III**	**IV**
60	45	59	36

35.   Seven percent of mutual fund investors rate corporate stocks "very safe," 58% rate them "somewhat safe," 24% rate them "not very safe," 4% rate them "not at all safe," and 7% are "not sure." A *BusinessWeek*/Harris poll asked 529 mutual fund investors how they would rate corporate bonds on safety. The responses are as follows.

Safety Rating	Frequency
Very safe	48
Somewhat safe	323
Not very safe	79
Not at all safe	16
Not sure	63
Total	529

Do mutual fund investors' attitudes toward corporate bonds differ from their attitudes toward corporate stocks? Support your conclusion with a statistical test. Use $\alpha = .01$.

36.   Since 2000, the Toyota Camry, Honda Accord, and Ford Taurus have been the three best selling passenger cars in the United States. Based on the 2003 sales data, the market shares among the top three are as follows: Toyota Camry 37%, Honda Accord 34%, and Ford Taurus 29% (*The World Almanac,* 2004). Assume a sample of 1200 sales of passenger cars during the first quarter of 2004 shows the following.

Passenger Car	Units Sold
Toyota Camry	480
Honda Accord	390
Ford Taurus	330

Can these data be used to conclude that the market shares among the top three passenger cars have changed during the first quarter of 2004? What is the *p*-value? Use a .05 level of significance. What is your conclusion?

37.   A regional transit authority is concerned about the number of riders on one of its bus routes. In setting up the route, the assumption is that the number of riders is the same on every day from Monday through Friday. Using the following data, test with $\alpha = .05$ to determine whether the transit authority's assumption is correct.

Day	Number of Riders
Monday	13
Tuesday	16
Wednesday	28
Thursday	17
Friday	16

38. The results of *Computerworld*'s Annual Job Satisfaction Survey showed that 28% of information systems (IS) managers are very satisfied with their job, 46% are somewhat satisfied, 12% are neither satisfied nor dissatisfied, 10% are somewhat dissatisfied, and 4% are very dissatisfied. Suppose that a sample of 500 computer programmers yielded the following results.

Category	Number of Respondents
Very satisfied	105
Somewhat satisfied	235
Neither	55
Somewhat dissatisfied	90
Very dissatisfied	15

Use $\alpha = .05$ and test to determine whether the job satisfaction for computer programmers is different from the job satisfaction for IS managers.

39. A sample of parts provided the following contingency table data on part quality by production shift.

Shift	Number Good	Number Defective
First	368	32
Second	285	15
Third	176	24

Use $\alpha = .05$ and test the hypothesis that part quality is independent of the production shift. What is your conclusion?

40. *The Wall Street Journal* Subscriber Study showed data on the employment status of subscribers. Sample results corresponding to subscribers of the eastern and western editions are shown here.

	Region	
Employment Status	Eastern Edition	Western Edition
Full-time	1105	574
Part-time	31	15
Self-employed/consultant	229	186
Not employed	485	344

Use $\alpha = .05$ and test the hypothesis that employment status is independent of the region. What is your conclusion?

41. A lending institution supplied the following data on loan approvals by four loan officers. Use $\alpha = .05$ and test to determine whether the loan approval decision is independent of the loan officer reviewing the loan application.

	Loan Approval Decision	
Loan Officer	Approved	Rejected
Miller	24	16
McMahon	17	13
Games	35	15
Runk	11	9

42. Data on the marital status of men and women ages 20 to 29 were obtained as part of a national survey. The results from a sample of 350 men and 400 women follow.

	Marital Status		
Gender	Never Married	Married	Divorced
Men	234	106	10
Women	216	168	16

 a. Use $\alpha = .01$ and test for independence between marital status and gender. What is your conclusion?
 b. Summarize the percentage in each marital status category for men and for women.

43. Barna Research Group collected data showing church attendance by age group (*USA Today,* November 20, 2003). Use the sample data to determine whether attending church is independent of age. Use a .05 level of significance. What is your conclusion? What conclusion can you draw about church attendance as individuals grow older?

	Church Attendance		
Age	Yes	No	Total
20 to 29	31	69	100
30 to 39	63	87	150
40 to 49	94	106	200
50 to 59	72	78	150

44. The office occupancy rates were reported for four California metropolitan areas. Do the following data suggest that the office vacancies were independent of metropolitan area? Use a .05 level of significance. What is your conclusion?

Occupancy Status	Los Angeles	San Diego	San Francisco	San Jose
Occupied	160	116	192	174
Vacant	40	34	33	26

45. A salesperson makes four calls per day. A sample of 100 days gives the following frequencies of sales volumes.

Number of Sales	Observed Frequency (days)
0	30
1	32
2	25
3	10
4	3
Total	100

Records show sales are made to 30% of all sales calls. Assuming independent sales calls, the number of sales per day should follow a binomial distribution. The binomial probability function presented in Chapter 5 is

$$f(x) = \frac{n!}{x!(n-x)!} p^x (1-p)^{n-x}$$

For this exercise, assume that the population has a binomial distribution with $n = 4$, $p = .30$, and $x = 0, 1, 2, 3,$ and 4.

a. Compute the expected frequencies for $x = 0, 1, 2, 3,$ and 4 by using the binomial probability function. Combine categories if necessary to satisfy the requirement that the expected frequency is five or more for all categories.

b. Use the goodness of fit test to determine whether the assumption of a binomial distribution should be rejected. Use $\alpha = .05$. Because no parameters of the binomial distribution were estimated from the sample data, the degrees of freedom are $k - 1$ when k is the number of categories.

Case Problem   A Bipartisan Agenda for Change

A survey of 100 individuals who live in the western region of New York State was conducted in order to obtain their views of how well the state government is functioning. The party affiliation (Democrat, Independent, Republican) of each individual surveyed was recorded, as well as their responses to the following three questions.

1. Should legislative pay be cut for every day the state budget is late?
   Yes _____   No _____
2. Should there be more restrictions on lobbyists?
   Yes _____   No _____
3. Should there be term limits requiring that legislators serve a fixed number of years?
   Yes _____   No _____

NYReform

The responses were coded using 1 for a Yes response and 2 for a No response. The complete data set is available on the website that accompanies the text in the data set named NYReform.

Managerial Report

1. Use descriptive statistics to summarize the data from this study. What are your preliminary conclusions about the independence of the response (Yes or No) and party affiliation for each of the three questions in the survey?
2. With regard to question 1, test for the independence of the response (Yes and No) and party affiliation. Use $\alpha = .05$.
3. With regard to question 2, test for the independence of the response (Yes and No) and party affiliation. Use $\alpha = .05$.
4. With regard to question 3, test for the independence of the response (Yes and No) and party affiliation. Use $\alpha = .05$.
5. Does it appear that there is broad support for change across all political lines? Explain.

Simple Linear Regression

CONTENTS

STATISTICS IN PRACTICE:
ALLIANCE DATA SYSTEMS

ALLIANCE DATA SYSTEMS*
DALLAS, TEXAS

Alliance Data Systems (ADS) provides transaction processing, credit services, and marketing services for clients in the rapidly growing customer relationship management (CRM) industry. ADS clients are concentrated in four industries: retail, petroleum/convenience stores, utilities, and transportation. In 1983, Alliance began offering end-to-end credit processing services to the retail, petroleum, and casual dining industries; today they employ more than 6500 employees who provide services to clients around the world. Operating more than 140,000 point-of-sale terminals in the United States alone, ADS processes in excess of 2.5 billion transactions annually. The company ranks second in the United States in private label credit services by representing 49 private label programs with nearly 72 million cardholders. In 2001, ADS made an initial public offering and is now listed on the New York Stock Exchange.

As one of its marketing services, ADS designs direct mail campaigns and promotions. With its database containing information on the spending habits of more than 100 million consumers, ADS can target those consumers most likely to benefit from a direct mail promotion. The Analytical Development Group uses regression analysis to build models that measure and predict the responsiveness of consumers to direct market campaigns. Some regression models predict the probability of purchase for individuals receiving a promotion, and others predict the amount spent by those consumers making a purchase.

For one particular campaign, a retail store chain wanted to attract new customers. To predict the effect of the campaign, ADS analysts selected a sample from the consumer database, sent the sampled individuals promotional materials, and then collected transaction data on the consumers' response. Sample data were collected on the amount of purchase made by the consumers responding to the campaign, as well as a variety of consumer-specific variables thought to be useful in predicting sales. The consumer-specific variable that contributed most to

Alliance Data analysts discuss use of a regression model to predict sales for a direct marketing campaign. © Courtesy of Alliance Data Systems.

predicting the amount purchased was the total amount of credit purchases at related stores over the past 39 months. ADS analysts developed an estimated regression equation relating the amount of purchase to the amount spent at related stores:

$$\hat{y} = 26.7 + 0.00205x$$

where

$\hat{y}$ = amount of purchase

x = amount spent at related stores

Using this equation, we could predict that someone spending $10,000 over the past 39 months at related stores would spend $47.20 when responding to the direct mail promotion. In this chapter, you will learn how to develop this type of estimated regression equation.

The final model developed by ADS analysts also included several other variables that increased the predictive power of the preceding equation. Some of these variables included the absence/presence of a bank credit card, estimated income, and the average amount spent per trip at a selected store. In the following chapter, we will learn how such additional variables can be incorporated into a multiple regression model.

---

*The authors are indebted to Philip Clemance, Director of Analytical Development at Alliance Data Systems, for providing this Statistics in Practice.

Managerial decisions often are based on the relationship between two or more variables. For example, after considering the relationship between advertising expenditures and sales, a marketing manager might attempt to predict sales for a given level of advertising expenditures. In another case, a public utility might use the relationship between the daily high temperature and the demand for electricity to predict electricity usage on the basis of next month's anticipated daily high temperatures. Sometimes a manager will rely on intuition to judge how two variables are related. However, if data can be obtained, a statistical procedure called *regression analysis* can be used to develop an equation showing how the variables are related.

The statistical methods used in studying the relationship between two variables were first employed by Sir Francis Galton (1822–1911). Galton was interested in studying the relationship between a father's height and the son's height. Galton's disciple, Karl Pearson (1857–1936), analyzed the relationship between the father's height and the son's height for 1078 pairs of subjects.

In regression terminology, the variable being predicted is called the **dependent variable**. The variable or variables being used to predict the value of the dependent variable are called the **independent variables**. For example, in analyzing the effect of advertising expenditures on sales, a marketing manager's desire to predict sales would suggest making sales the dependent variable. Advertising expenditure would be the independent variable used to help predict sales. In statistical notation, y denotes the dependent variable and x denotes the independent variable.

In this chapter we consider the simplest type of regression analysis involving one independent variable and one dependent variable in which the relationship between the variables is approximated by a straight line. It is called **simple linear regression**. Regression analysis involving two or more independent variables is called multiple regression analysis; multiple regression is covered in Chapter 13.

12.1 Simple Linear Regression Model

Armand's Pizza Parlors is a chain of Italian-food restaurants located in a five-state area. Armand's most successful locations are near college campuses. The managers believe that quarterly sales for these restaurants (denoted by y) are related positively to the size of the student population (denoted by x); that is, restaurants near campuses with a large student population tend to generate more sales than those located near campuses with a small student population. Using regression analysis, we can develop an equation showing how the dependent variable y is related to the independent variable x.

Regression Model and Regression Equation

In the Armand's Pizza Parlors example, the population consists of all the Armand's restaurants. For every restaurant in the population, there is a value of x (student population) and a corresponding value of y (quarterly sales). The equation that describes how y is related to x and an error term is called the **regression model**. The regression model used in simple linear regression follows.

SIMPLE LINEAR REGRESSION MODEL

$$y = \beta_0 + \beta_1 x + \epsilon \qquad (12.1)$$

β_0 and β_1 are referred to as the parameters of the model, and ϵ (the Greek letter epsilon) is a random variable referred to as the error term. The error term accounts for the variability in y that cannot be explained by the linear relationship between x and y.

The population of all Armand's restaurants can also be viewed as a collection of sub-populations, one for each distinct value of x. For example, one subpopulation consists of all Armand's restaurants located near college campuses with 8000 students; another subpopulation consists of all Armand's restaurants located near college campuses with 9000 students; and so on. Each subpopulation has a corresponding distribution of y values. Thus, a distribution of y values is associated with restaurants located near campuses with 8000 students; a distribution of y values is associated with restaurants located near campuses with 9000 students; and so on. Each distribution of y values has its own mean or expected value. The equation that describes how the expected value of y, denoted $E(y)$, is related to x is called the **regression equation**. The regression equation for simple linear regression follows.

> SIMPLE LINEAR REGRESSION EQUATION
>
> $$E(y) = \beta_0 + \beta_1 x \tag{12.2}$$

[handwritten annotations: Beta null (y intercept) + slope times X; Expected value of y]

The graph of the simple linear regression equation is a straight line; β_0 is the y-intercept of the regression line, β_1 is the slope, and $E(y)$ is the mean or expected value of y for a given value of x.

Examples of possible regression lines are shown in Figure 12.1. The regression line in Panel A shows that the mean value of y is related positively to x, with larger values of $E(y)$ associated with larger values of x. The regression line in Panel B shows the mean value of y is related negatively to x, with smaller values of $E(y)$ associated with larger values of x. The regression line in Panel C shows the case in which the mean value of y is not related to x; that is, the mean value of y is the same for every value of x.

Estimated Regression Equation

If the values of the population parameters β_0 and β_1 were known, we could use equation (12.2) to compute the mean value of y for a given value of x. In practice, the parameter values are not known and must be estimated using sample data. Sample statistics (denoted b_0 and b_1) are computed as estimates of the population parameters β_0 and β_1. Substituting the values of the sample statistics b_0 and b_1 for β_0 and β_1 in the regression equation, we obtain the

FIGURE 12.1   POSSIBLE REGRESSION LINES IN SIMPLE LINEAR REGRESSION

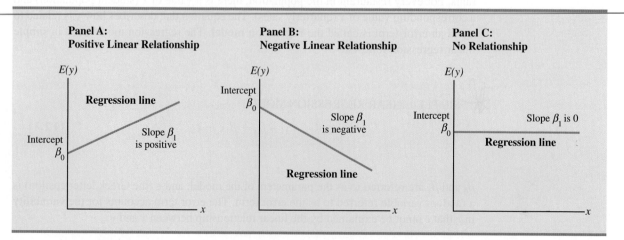

estimated regression equation. The estimated regression equation for simple linear regression follows.

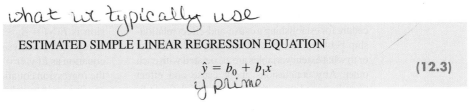

what we typically use

ESTIMATED SIMPLE LINEAR REGRESSION EQUATION

$$\hat{y} = b_0 + b_1 x \qquad (12.3)$$

y prime

The graph of the estimated simple linear regression equation is called the *estimated regression line;* b_0 is the y intercept and b_1 is the slope. In the next section, we show how the least squares method can be used to compute the values of b_0 and b_1 in the estimated regression equation.

In general, $\hat{y}$ is the point estimator of $E(y)$, the mean value of y for a given value of x. Thus, to estimate the mean or expected value of quarterly sales for all restaurants located near campuses with 10,000 students, Armand's would substitute the value of 10,000 for x in equation (12.3). In some cases, however, Armand's may be more interested in predicting sales for one particular restaurant. For example, suppose Armand's would like to predict quarterly sales for the restaurant located near Talbot College, a school with 10,000 students. As it turns out, the best estimate of y for a given value of x is also provided by $\hat{y}$. Thus, to predict quarterly sales for the restaurant located near Talbot College, Armand's would also substitute the value of 10,000 for x in equation (12.3).

Because the value of $\hat{y}$ provides both a point estimate of $E(y)$ for a given value of x and a point estimate of an individual value of y for a given value of x, we will refer to $\hat{y}$ simply as the *estimated value of y*. Figure 12.2 provides a summary of the estimation process for simple linear regression.

FIGURE 12.2   THE ESTIMATION PROCESS IN SIMPLE LINEAR REGRESSION

The estimation of β_0 and β_1 is a statistical process much like the estimation of μ discussed in Chapter 7. β_0 and β_1 are the unknown parameters of interest, and b_0 and b_1 are the sample statistics used to estimate the parameters.

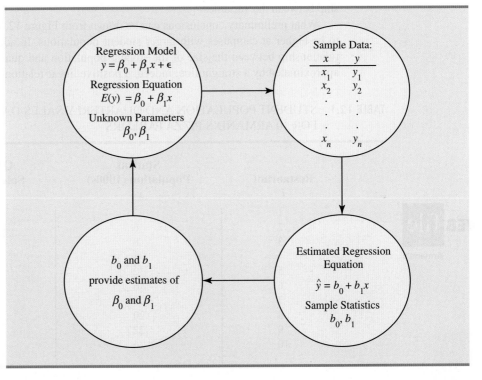

NOTES AND COMMENTS

1. Regression analysis cannot be interpreted as a procedure for establishing a cause-and-effect relationship between variables. It can only indicate how or to what extent variables are associated with each other. Any conclusions about cause and effect must be based upon the judgment of those individuals most knowledgeable about the application.

2. The regression equation in simple linear regression is $E(y) = \beta_0 + \beta_1 x$. More advanced texts in regression analysis often write the regression equation as $E(y|x) = \beta_0 + \beta_1 x$ to emphasize that the regression equation provides the mean value of y for a given value of x.

(12.2) Least Squares Method

In simple linear regression, each observation consists of two values: one for the independent variable and one for the dependent variable.

The **least squares method** is a procedure for using sample data to find the estimated regression equation. To illustrate the least squares method, suppose data were collected from a sample of 10 Armand's Pizza Parlor restaurants located near college campuses. For the *i*th observation or restaurant in the sample, x_i is the size of the student population (in thousands) and y_i is the quarterly sales (in thousands of dollars). The values of x_i and y_i for the 10 restaurants in the sample are summarized in Table 12.1. We see that restaurant 1, with $x_1 = 2$ and $y_1 = 58$, is near a campus with 2000 students and has quarterly sales of $58,000. Restaurant 2, with $x_2 = 6$ and $y_2 = 105$, is near a campus with 6000 students and has quarterly sales of $105,000. The largest sales value is for restaurant 10, which is near a campus with 26,000 students and has quarterly sales of $202,000.

Figure 12.3 is a scatter diagram of the data in Table 12.1. Student population is shown on the horizontal axis and quarterly sales is shown on the vertical axis. **Scatter diagrams** for regression analysis are constructed with the independent variable *x* on the horizontal axis and the dependent variable *y* on the vertical axis. The scatter diagram enables us to observe the data graphically and to draw preliminary conclusions about the possible relationship between the variables.

What preliminary conclusions can be drawn from Figure 12.3? Quarterly sales appear to be higher at campuses with larger student populations. In addition, for these data the relationship between the size of the student population and quarterly sales appears to be approximated by a straight line; indeed, a positive linear relationship is indicated between

TABLE 12.1 STUDENT POPULATION AND QUARTERLY SALES DATA FOR 10 ARMAND'S PIZZA PARLORS

WEB file

Armand's

Restaurant i	Student Population (1000s) x_i	Quarterly Sales ($1000s) y_i
1	2	58
2	6	105
3	8	88
4	8	118
5	12	117
6	16	137
7	20	157
8	20	169
9	22	149
10	26	202

FIGURE 12.3   SCATTER DIAGRAM OF STUDENT POPULATION AND QUARTERLY
                          SALES FOR ARMAND'S PIZZA PARLORS

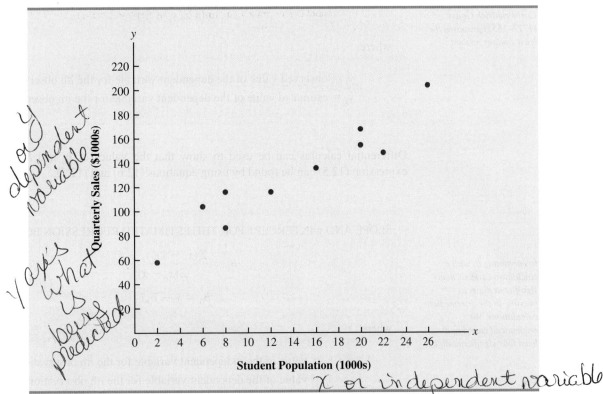

x and *y*. We therefore choose the simple linear regression model to represent the relationship between quarterly sales and student population. Given that choice, our next task is to use the sample data in Table 12.1 to determine the values of b_0 and b_1 in the estimated simple linear regression equation. For the *i*th restaurant, the estimated regression equation provides

$$\hat{y}_i = b_0 + b_1 x_i \qquad\qquad \textbf{(12.4)}$$

where

$\hat{y}_i$ = estimated value of quarterly sales ($1000s) for the *i*th restaurant
b_0 = the *y* intercept of the estimated regression line
b_1 = the slope of the estimated regression line
x_i = size of the student population (1000s) for the *i*th restaurant

With y_i denoting the observed (actual) sales for restaurant *i* and $\hat{y}_i$ in equation (12.4) representing the estimated value of sales for restaurant *i*, every restaurant in the sample will have an observed value of sales y_i and an estimated value of sales $\hat{y}_i$. For the estimated regression line to provide a good fit to the data, we want the differences between the observed sales values and the estimated sales values to be small.

The least squares method uses the sample data to provide the values of b_0 and b_1 that minimize the *sum of the squares of the deviations* between the observed values of the dependent variable y_i and the estimated values of the dependent variable $\hat{y}_i$. The criterion for the least squares method is given by expression (12.5).

Carl Friedrich Gauss
(1777–1855) proposed the
least squares method.

LEAST SQUARES CRITERION

$$\min \Sigma (y_i - \hat{y}_i)^2 \qquad (12.5)$$

where

y_i = observed value of the dependent variable for the ith observation

$\hat{y}_i$ = estimated value of the dependent variable for the ith observation

Differential calculus can be used to show that the values of b_0 and b_1 that minimize expression (12.5) can be found by using equations (12.6) and (12.7).

SLOPE AND y-INTERCEPT FOR THE ESTIMATED REGRESSION EQUATION[1]

In computing b_1 with a calculator, carry as many significant digits as possible in the intermediate calculations. We recommend carrying at least four significant digits.

$$b_1 = \frac{\Sigma(x_i - \bar{x})(y_i - \bar{y})}{\Sigma(x_i - \bar{x})^2} \qquad (12.6)$$

$$b_0 = \bar{y} - b_1\bar{x} \qquad (12.7)$$

where

x_i = value of the independent variable for the ith observation

y_i = value of the dependent variable for the ith observation

$\bar{x}$ = mean value for the independent variable

$\bar{y}$ = mean value for the dependent variable

n = total number of observations

Some of the calculations necessary to develop the least squares estimated regression equation for Armand's Pizza Parlors are shown in Table 12.2. With the sample of 10 restaurants, we have $n = 10$ observations. Because equations (12.6) and (12.7) require $\bar{x}$ and $\bar{y}$ we begin the calculations by computing $\bar{x}$ and $\bar{y}$.

$$\bar{x} = \frac{\Sigma x_i}{n} = \frac{140}{10} = 14$$

$$\bar{y} = \frac{\Sigma y_i}{n} = \frac{1300}{10} = 130$$

Using equations (12.6) and (12.7) and the information in Table 12.2, we can compute the slope and intercept of the estimated regression equation for Armand's Pizza Parlors. The calculation of the slope (b_1) proceeds as follows.

----

[1]An alternate formula for b_1 is

$$b_1 = \frac{\Sigma x_i y_i - (\Sigma x_i \Sigma y_i)/n}{\Sigma x_i^2 - (\Sigma x_i)^2/n}$$

This form of equation (12.6) is often recommended when using a calculator to compute b_1.

TABLE 12.2 CALCULATIONS FOR THE LEAST SQUARES ESTIMATED REGRESSION EQUATION FOR ARMAND'S PIZZA PARLORS

Restaurant i	x_i	y_i	$x_i - \bar{x}$	$y_i - \bar{y}$	$(x_i - \bar{x})(y_i - \bar{y})$	$(x_i - \bar{x})^2$
1	2	58	−12	−72	864	144
2	6	105	−8	−25	200	64
3	8	88	−6	−42	252	36
4	8	118	−6	−12	72	36
5	12	117	−2	−13	26	4
6	16	137	2	7	14	4
7	20	157	6	27	162	36
8	20	169	6	39	234	36
9	22	149	8	19	152	64
10	26	202	12	72	864	144
Totals	140	1300			2840	568
	Σx_i	Σy_i			$\Sigma(x_i - \bar{x})(y_i - \bar{y})$	$\Sigma(x_i - \bar{x})^2$

[handwritten: 2−14, 6−14, 14 is the 140|10]

$$b_1 = \frac{\Sigma(x_i - \bar{x})(y_i - \bar{y})}{\Sigma(x_i - \bar{x})^2}$$

$$= \frac{2840}{568}$$

$$= 5$$

The calculation of the y intercept (b_0) follows.

$$b_0 = \bar{y} - b_1\bar{x}$$
$$= 130 - 5(14)$$
$$= 60$$

Thus, the estimated regression equation is

$$\hat{y} = 60 + 5x$$

Figure 12.4 shows the graph of this equation on the scatter diagram.

The slope of the estimated regression equation ($b_1 = 5$) is positive, implying that as student population increases, sales increase. In fact, we can conclude (based on sales measured in $1000s and student population in 1000s) that an increase in the student population of 1000 is associated with an increase of $5000 in expected sales; that is, quarterly sales are expected to increase by $5 per student.

Using the estimated regression equation to make predictions outside the range of the values of the independent variable should be done with caution because outside that range we cannot be sure that the same relationship is valid.

If we believe the least squares estimated regression equation adequately describes the relationship between x and y, it would seem reasonable to use the estimated regression equation to predict the value of y for a given value of x. For example, if we wanted to predict quarterly sales for a restaurant to be located near a campus with 16,000 students, we would compute

$$\hat{y} = 60 + 5(16) = 140$$

Hence, we would predict quarterly sales of $140,000 for this restaurant. In the following sections we will discuss methods for assessing the appropriateness of using the estimated regression equation for estimation and prediction.

FIGURE 12.4   GRAPH OF THE ESTIMATED REGRESSION EQUATION FOR ARMAND'S PIZZA PARLORS: $\hat{y} = 60 + 5x$

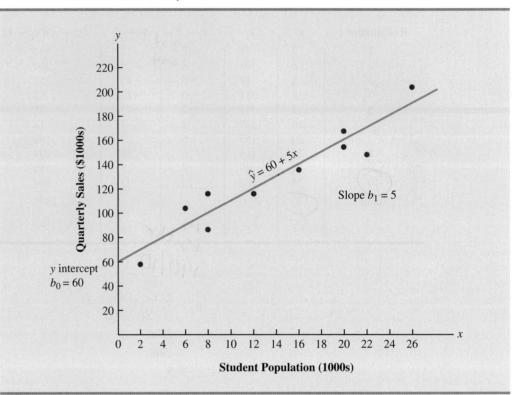

NOTES AND COMMENTS

The least squares method provides an estimated regression equation that minimizes the sum of squared deviations between the observed values of the dependent variable y_i and the estimated values of the dependent variable $\hat{y}_i$. This least squares criterion is used to choose the equation that provides the best fit. If some other criterion were used, such as minimizing the sum of the absolute deviations between y_i and $\hat{y}_i$, a different equation would be obtained. In practice, the least squares method is the most widely used.

Using Excel's Chart Tools to Construct a Scatter Diagram and Compute the Estimated Regression Equation

We can use Excel's chart tools to construct a scatter diagram and compute the estimated regression equation for the Armand's Pizza Parlors data appearing in Table 12.1. Refer to Figure 12.5 as we describe the tasks involved.

Enter Data: Appropriate labels and the sample data have been entered into cells A1:C11 of the worksheet shown in Figure 12.5.

Apply Tools: The following steps describe how to use Excel's chart tools to construct a scatter diagram and compute the estimated regression equation using the data in the worksheet.

    Step 1. Select cells B2:C11
    Step 2. Click the **Insert** tab on the Ribbon
    Step 3. In the **Charts** group, click **Scatter**

FIGURE 12.5 SCATTER DIAGRAM, ESTIMATED REGRESSION EQUATION, AND THE ESTIMATED REGRESSION LINE FOR ARMAND'S PIZZA PARLORS

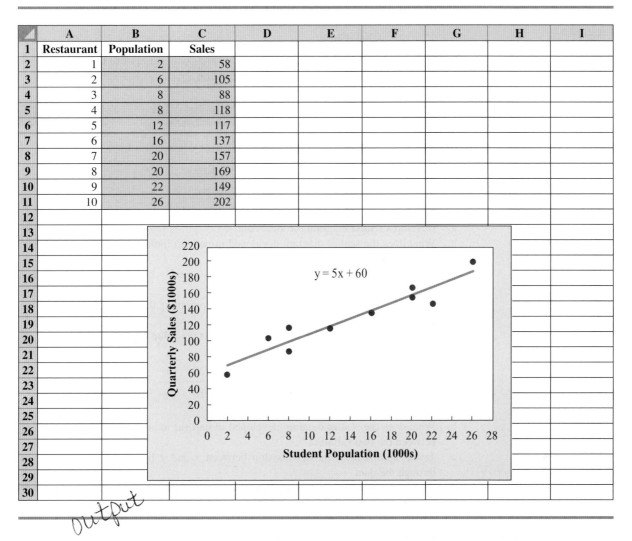

Step 4. When the list of scatter diagram subtypes appears,
　　　　Click **Scatter with only Markers** (the chart in the upper left corner)
Step 5. In the **Chart Layouts** group, click **Layout 1**
Step 6. Right-click on the **Chart Title** to display a list of options; choose **Delete**
Step 7. Select the **Horizontal (Value) Axis Title** and replace it with **Student Population (1000s)**
Step 8. Select the **Vertical (Value) Axis Title** and replace it with **Quarterly Sales ($1000s)**
Step 9. Right-click on the **Series 1 Legend Entry** to display a list of options; choose **Delete**
Step 10. Position the mouse pointer over any **Vertical (Value) Axis Major Gridline** in the scatter diagram and right-click to display a list of options; choose **Delete**
Step 11. Position the mouse pointer over any data point in the scatter diagram and right-click to display a list of options; choose **Add Trendline**

Step 12. When the **Format Trendline** dialog box appears,
Select **Trendline Options** and then
Choose **Linear** from the **Trend/Regression Type** list
Choose **Display Equation on chart**
Click **Close**

The worksheet displayed in Figure 12.5 shows the scatter diagram, the estimated regression line, and the estimated regression equation.

Exercises

Methods

1. Given are five observations for two variables, x and y.

x_i	1	2	3	4	5
y_i	3	7	5	11	14

  a. Develop a scatter diagram for these data.
  b. What does the scatter diagram developed in part (a) indicate about the relationship between the two variables?
  c. Try to approximate the relationship between x and y by drawing a straight line through the data.
  d. Develop the estimated regression equation by computing the values of b_0 and b_1 using equations (12.6) and (12.7).
  e. Use the estimated regression equation to predict the value of y when $x = 4$.

2. Given are five observations for two variables, x and y.

x_i	3	12	6	20	14
y_i	55	40	55	10	15

  a. Develop a scatter diagram for these data.
  b. What does the scatter diagram developed in part (a) indicate about the relationship between the two variables?
  c. Try to approximate the relationship between x and y by drawing a straight line through the data.
  d. Develop the estimated regression equation by computing the values of b_0 and b_1 using equations (12.6) and (12.7).
  e. Use the estimated regression equation to predict the value of y when $x = 10$.

3. Given are five observations collected in a regression study on two variables.

x_i	2	6	9	13	20
y_i	7	18	9	26	23

  a. Develop a scatter diagram for these data.
  b. Develop the estimated regression equation for these data.
  c. Use the estimated regression equation to predict the value of y when $x = 4$.

Applications

4. The following data give the percentage of women working in five companies in the retail and trade industry. The percentage of management jobs held by women in each company is also shown.

% Working	67	45	73	54	61
% Management	49	21	65	47	33

  a. Develop a scatter diagram for these data with the percentage of women working in the company as the independent variable.
  b. What does the scatter diagram developed in part (a) indicate about the relationship between the two variables?

c. Try to approximate the relationship between the percentage of women working in the company and the percentage of management jobs held by women in that company.

d. Develop the estimated regression equation by computing the values of b_0 and b_1.

e. Predict the percentage of management jobs held by women in a company that has 60% women employees.

5. Elliptical trainers are becoming one of the more popular exercise machines. Their smooth and steady low-impact motion makes them a preferred choice for individuals with knee and ankle problems. But selecting the right trainer can be a difficult process. Price and quality are two important factors in any purchase decision. Are higher prices generally associated with higher quality elliptical trainers? *Consumer Reports* conducted extensive tests to develop an overall rating based on ease of use, ergonomics, construction, and exercise range. The following data show the price and rating for eight elliptical trainers tested (*Consumer Reports*, February 2008).

WEB file

Ellipticals

Brand and Model	Price ($)	Rating
Precor 5.31	3700	87
Keys Fitness CG2	2500	84
Octane Fitness Q37e	2800	82
LifeFitness X1 Basic	1900	74
NordicTrack AudioStrider 990	1000	73
Schwinn 430	800	69
Vision Fitness X6100	1700	68
ProForm XP 520 Razor	600	55

a. Develop a scatter diagram with price as the independent variable.

b. An exercise equipment store that sells primarily higher priced equipment has a sign over the display area that says "Quality: You Get What You Pay For." Based upon your analysis of the data for ellipical trainers, do you think this sign fairly reflects the price-quality relationship for elliptical trainers?

c. Use the least squares method to develop the estimated regression equation.

d. Use the estimated regression equation to predict the rating for an ellipitical trainer with a price of $1500.

6. The following data show the annual advertising expenditure in millions of dollars and the market share for six automobile companies (*Advertising Age*, June 23, 2006).

WEB file

MktShare

Company	Advertising ($ millions)	Market Share (%)
DaimlerChrysler	1590	14.9
Ford Motor Co.	1568	18.6
General Motors Corp.	3004	26.2
Honda Motor Co.	854	8.6
Nissan Motor Co.	1023	6.3
Toyota Motor Corp.	1075	13.3

a. Develop a scatter diagram for these data with the advertising expenditure as the independent variable and the market share as the dependent variable.

b. What does the scatter diagram developed in part (a) indicate about the relationship between the two variables?

c. Use the least squares method to develop the estimated regression equation.

d. Provide an interpretation for the slope of the estimated regression equation.

e.   Suppose that Honda Motor Co. believes that the estimated regression equation developed in part (c) is applicable for developing an estimate of market share for next year. Predict Honda's market share if they decide to increase their advertising expenditure to $1200 million next year.

7.   Would you expect more reliable cars to cost more? *Consumer Reports* rated 15 upscale sedans. Reliability was rated on a 5-point scale: poor (1), fair (2), good (3), very good (4), and excellent (5). The price and reliability rating for each of the 15 cars are shown (*Consumer Reports,* February 2004).

Cars

Make and Model	Reliability	Price ($)
Acura TL	4	33,150
BMW 330i	3	40,570
Lexus IS300	5	35,105
Lexus ES330	5	35,174
Mercedes-Benz C320	1	42,230
Lincoln LS Premium (V6)	3	38,225
Audi A4 3.0 Quattro	2	37,605
Cadillac CTS	1	37,695
Nissan Maxima 3.5 SE	4	34,390
Infiniti I35	5	33,845
Saab 9-3 Aero	3	36,910
Infiniti G35	4	34,695
Jaguar X-Type 3.0	1	37,995
Saab 9-5 Arc	3	36,955
Volvo S60 2.5T	3	33,890

a.   Develop a scatter diagram for these data with the reliability rating as the independent variable.
b.   Develop the least squares estimated regression equation.
c.   Based upon your analysis, do you think more reliable cars cost more? Explain.
d.   Estimate the price for an upscale sedan that has a good reliability rating.

8.   According to *Advertising Age*'s annual salary review, Mark Hurd, the 49-year-old chairman, president, and CEO of Hewlett-Packard Co., received an annual salary of $817,000, a bonus of more than $5 million, and other compensation exceeding $17 million. His total compensation was slightly better than the average CEO total pay of $12.4 million. The following table shows the age and annual salary (in thousands of dollars) for Mark Hurd and 14 other executives who led publicly held companies (*Advertising Age,* December 5, 2006).

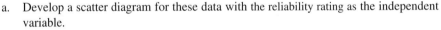

ExecSalary

Executive	Title	Company	Age	Salary ($1000s)
Charles Prince	Chmn/CEO	Citigroup	56	1000
Harold McGraw III	Chmn/Pres/CEO	McGraw-Hill Cos.	57	1172
James Dimon	Pres/CEO	JP Morgan Chase & Co.	50	1000
K. Rupert Murdoch	Chmn/CEO	News Corp.	75	4509
Kenneth D. Lewis	Chmn/Pres/CEO	Bank of America	58	1500
Kenneth I. Chenault	Chmn/CEO	American Express Co.	54	1092
Louis C. Camilleri	Chmn/CEO	Altria Group	51	1663
Mark V. Hurd	Chmn/Pres/CEO	Hewlett-Packard Co.	49	817
Martin S. Sorrell	CEO	WPP Group	61	1562
Robert L. Nardelli	Chmn/Pres/CEO	Home Depot	57	2164
Samuel J. Palmisano	Chmn/Pres/CEO	IBM Corp.	54	1680
David C. Novak	Chmn/Pres/CEO	Yum Brands	53	1173
Henry R. Silverman	Chmn/CEO	Cendant Corp.	65	3300
Robert C. Wright	Chmn/CEO	NBC Universal	62	2500
Sumner Redstone	Exec Chmn/Founder	Viacom	82	5807

a. Develop a scatter diagram for these data with the age of the executive as the independent variable.
b. What does the scatter diagram developed in part (a) indicate about the relationship between the two variables?
c. Develop the least squares estimated regression equation.
d. Suppose Bill Gustin is the 72-year-old chairman, president, and CEO of a major electronics company. Predict the annual salary for Bill Gustin.

9. A sales manager collected the following data on annual sales and years of experience.

Sales

Salesperson	Years of Experience	Annual Sales ($1000s)
1	1	80
2	3	97
3	4	92
4	4	102
5	6	103
6	8	111
7	10	119
8	10	123
9	11	117
10	13	136

a. Develop a scatter diagram for these data with years of experience as the independent variable.
b. Develop an estimated regression equation that can be used to predict annual sales given the years of experience.
c. Use the estimated regression equation to predict annual sales for a salesperson with nine years of experience.

10. Bergans of Norway has been making outdoor gear since 1908. The following data show the temperature rating (F°) and the price ($) for 11 models of sleeping bags produced by Bergans (*Backpacker* 2006 Gear Guide).

SleepingBags

Model	Rating	Price
Ranger 3-Seasons	12	319
Ranger Spring	24	289
Ranger Winter	3	389
Rondane 3-Seasons	13	239
Rondane Summer	38	149
Rondane Winter	4	289
Senja Ice	5	359
Senja Snow	15	259
Senja Zero	25	229
Super Light	45	129
Tight & Light	25	199

a. Develop a scatter diagram for these data with temperature rating (F°) as the independent variable.
b. What does the scatter diagram developed in part (a) indicate about the relationship between temperature rating (F°) and price?
c. Use the least squares method to develop the estimated regression equation.
d. Predict the price for a sleeping bag with a temperature rating (F°) of 20.

11. Although delays at major airports are now less frequent, it helps to know which airports are likely to throw off your schedule. In addition, if your plane is late arriving at a particular

airport where you must make a connection, how likely is it that the departure will be late and thus increase your chances of making the connection? The following data show the percentage of late arrivals and departures during August for 13 airports (*Business 2.0,* February 2002).

Airport

Airport	Late Arrivals (%)	Late Departures (%)
Atlanta	24	22
Charlotte	20	20
Chicago	30	29
Cincinnati	20	19
Dallas	20	22
Denver	23	23
Detroit	18	19
Houston	20	16
Minneapolis	18	18
Phoenix	21	22
Pittsburgh	25	22
Salt Lake City	18	17
St. Louis	16	16

a. Develop a scatter diagram for these data with the percentage of late arrivals as the independent variable.
b. What does the scatter diagram developed in part (a) indicate about the relationship between late arrivals and late departures?
c. Use the least squares method to develop the estimated regression equation.
d. Provide an interpretation for the slope of the estimated regression equation.
e. Suppose the percentage of late arrivals at the Philadelphia airport for August was 22%. What is an estimate of the percentage of late departures?

12. A personal watercraft (PWC) is a vessel propelled by water jets, designed to be operated by a person sitting, standing, or kneeling on the vessel. In the early 1970s, Kawasaki Motors Corp. U.S.A. introduced the JET SKI® watercraft, the first commercially successful PWC. Today, *jet ski* is commonly used as a generic term for personal watercraft. The following data show the weight (rounded to the nearest 10 lbs.) and the price (rounded to the nearest $50) for 10 three-seater personal watercraft (*http://www.jetskinews.com,* 2006).

JetSki

Make and Model	Weight (lbs.)	Price ($)
Honda AquaTrax F-12	750	9500
Honda AquaTrax F-12X	790	10500
Honda AquaTrax F-12X GPScape	800	11200
Kawasaki STX-12F Jetski	740	8500
Yamaha FX Cruiser Waverunner	830	10000
Yamaha FX High Output Waverunner	770	10000
Yamaha FX Waverunner	830	9300
Yamaha VX110 Deluxe Waverunner	720	7700
Yamaha VX110 Sport Waverunner	720	7000
Yamaha XLT1200 Waverunner	780	8500

a. Develop a scatter diagram for these data with weight as the independent variable.
b. What does the scatter diagram developed in part (a) indicate about the relationship between weight and price?
c. Use the least squares method to develop the estimated regression equation.
d. Predict the price for a three-seater PWC with a weight of 750 pounds.

e. The Honda AquaTrax F-12 weighs 750 pounds and has a price of $9500. Shouldn't the predicted price you developed in part (d) for a PWC with a weight of 750 pounds also be $9500?

f. The Kawasaki SX-R 800 Jetski has a seating capacity of one and weighs 350 pounds. Do you think the estimated regression equation developed in part (c) should be used to predict the price for this model?

13. To the Internal Revenue Service, the reasonableness of total itemized deductions depends on the taxpayer's adjusted gross income. Large deductions, which include charity and medical deductions, are more reasonable for taxpayers with large adjusted gross incomes. If a taxpayer claims larger than average itemized deductions for a given level of income, the chances of an IRS audit are increased. Data (in thousands of dollars) on adjusted gross income and the average or reasonable amount of itemized deductions follow.

Adjusted Gross Income ($1000s)	Reasonable Amount of Itemized Deductions ($1000s)
22	9.6
27	9.6
32	10.1
48	11.1
65	13.5
85	17.7
120	25.5

a. Develop a scatter diagram for these data with adjusted gross income as the independent variable.

b. Use the least squares method to develop the estimated regression equation.

c. Estimate a reasonable level of total itemized deductions for a taxpayer with an adjusted gross income of $52,500. If this taxpayer claimed itemized deductions of $20,400, would the IRS agent's request for an audit appear justified? Explain.

14. Starting salaries for accountants and auditors in Rochester, New York, trail those of many other U.S. cities. The following data show the starting salary (in thousands of dollars) and the cost of living index for Rochester and nine other metropolitan areas (*Rochester Democrat and Chronicle,* September 1, 2002). The cost of living index, based on a city's food, housing, taxes, and other costs, ranges from 0 (most expensive) to 100 (least expensive).

Salaries

Metropolitan Area	Index	Salary ($1000s)
Oklahoma City	82.44	23.9
Tampa/St. Petersburg/Clearwater	79.89	24.5
Indianapolis	55.53	27.4
Buffalo/Niagara Falls	41.36	27.7
Atlanta	39.38	27.1
Rochester	28.05	25.6
Sacramento	25.50	28.7
Raleigh/Durham/Chapel Hill	13.32	26.7
San Diego	3.12	27.8
Honolulu	0.57	28.3

a. Develop a scatter diagram for these data with the cost of living index as the independent variable.

b. Develop the estimated regression equation relating the cost of living index to the starting salary.

c. Estimate the starting salary for a metropolitan area with a cost of living index of 50.

12.3 Coefficient of Determination

For the Armand's Pizza Parlors example, we developed the estimated regression equation $\hat{y} = 60 + 5x$ to approximate the linear relationship between the size of the student population x and quarterly sales y. A question now is: How well does the estimated regression equation fit the data? In this section, we show that the **coefficient of determination** provides a measure of the goodness of fit for the estimated regression equation.

For the ith observation, the difference between the observed value of the dependent variable, y_i, and the estimated value of the dependent variable, $\hat{y}_i$, is called the *ith residual*. The ith residual represents the error in using $\hat{y}_i$ to estimate y_i. Thus, for the ith observation, the residual is $y_i - \hat{y}_i$. The sum of squares of these residuals or errors is the quantity that is minimized by the least squares method. This quantity, also known as the *sum of squares due to error*, is denoted by SSE.

> **SUM OF SQUARES DUE TO ERROR**
>
> $$SSE = \Sigma(y_i - \hat{y}_i)^2 \tag{12.8}$$

The value of SSE is a measure of the error in using the estimated regression equation to estimate the values of the dependent variable in the sample.

In Table 12.3 we show the calculations required to compute the sum of squares due to error for the Armand's Pizza Parlors example. For instance, for restaurant 1 the values of the independent and dependent variables are $x_1 = 2$ and $y_1 = 58$. Using the estimated regression equation, we find that the estimated value of quarterly sales for restaurant 1 is $\hat{y}_1 = 60 + 5(2) = 70$. Thus, the error in using $\hat{y}_1$ to estimate y_1 for restaurant 1 is $y_1 - \hat{y}_1 = 58 - 70 = -12$. The squared error, $(-12)^2 = 144$, is shown in the last column of Table 12.3. After computing and squaring the residuals for each restaurant in the sample, we sum them to obtain SSE = 1530. Thus, SSE = 1530 measures the error in using the estimated regression equation $\hat{y} = 60 + 5x$ to predict sales.

Now suppose we are asked to develop an estimate of quarterly sales without knowledge of the size of the student population. Without knowledge of any related variables, we would use the sample mean as an estimate of quarterly sales at any given restaurant. Table 12.2

TABLE 12.3 CALCULATION OF SSE FOR ARMAND'S PIZZA PARLORS

Restaurant i	x_i = Student Population (1000s)	y_i = Quarterly Sales ($1000s)	Predicted Sales $\hat{y}_i = 60 + 5x_i$	Error $y_i - \hat{y}_i$	Squared Error $(y_i - \hat{y}_i)^2$
1	2	58	70	−12	144
2	6	105	90	15	225
3	8	88	100	−12	144
4	8	118	100	18	324
5	12	117	120	−3	9
6	16	137	140	−3	9
7	20	157	160	−3	9
8	20	169	160	9	81
9	22	149	170	−21	441
10	26	202	190	12	144
					SSE = 1530

TABLE 12.4   COMPUTATION OF THE TOTAL SUM OF SQUARES FOR ARMAND'S PIZZA PARLORS

Restaurant i	x_i = Student Population (1000s)	y_i = Quarterly Sales ($1000s)	Deviation $y_i - \bar{y}$	Squared Deviation $(y_i - \bar{y})^2$
1	2	58	−72	5,184
2	6	105	−25	625
3	8	88	−42	1,764
4	8	118	−12	144
5	12	117	−13	169
6	16	137	7	49
7	20	157	27	729
8	20	169	39	1,521
9	22	149	19	361
10	26	202	72	5,184
				SST = 15,730

shows that for the sales data, $\Sigma y_i = 1300$. Hence, the mean value of quarterly sales for the sample of 10 Armand's restaurants is $\bar{y} = \Sigma y_i / n = 1300/10 = 130$. In Table 12.4 we show the sum of squared deviations obtained by using the sample mean $\bar{y} = 130$ to estimate the value of quarterly sales for each restaurant in the sample. For the ith restaurant in the sample, the difference $y_i - \bar{y}$ provides a measure of the error involved in using $\bar{y}$ to estimate y_i. The corresponding sum of squares, called the *total sum of squares,* is denoted SST.

TOTAL SUM OF SQUARES

$$SST = \Sigma(y_i - \bar{y})^2 \qquad (12.9)$$

The sum at the bottom of the last column in Table 12.4 is the total sum of squares for Armand's Pizza Parlors; it is SST = 15,730.

With SST = 15,730 and SSE = 1530, the estimated regression line provides a much better fit to the data than the line y = ȳ.

In Figure 12.6 we show the estimated regression line $\hat{y} = 60 + 5x$ and the line corresponding to $\bar{y} = 130$. Note that the points cluster more closely around the estimated regression line than they do about the line $\bar{y} = 130$. For example, for the 10th restaurant in the sample we see that the error is much larger when $\bar{y} = 130$ is used as an estimate of y_{10} than when $\hat{y}_{10} = 60 + 5(26) = 190$ is used. We can think of SST as a measure of how well the observations cluster about the $\bar{y}$ line and SSE as a measure of how well the observations cluster about the $\hat{y}$ line.

To measure how much the $\hat{y}$ values on the estimated regression line deviate from $\bar{y}$, another sum of squares is computed. This sum of squares, called the *sum of squares due to regression,* is denoted SSR.

SUM OF SQUARES DUE TO REGRESSION

$$SSR = \Sigma(\hat{y}_i - \bar{y})^2 \qquad (12.10)$$

FIGURE 12.6   DEVIATIONS ABOUT THE ESTIMATED REGRESSION LINE AND THE LINE
                  $y = \bar{y}$ **FOR ARMAND'S PIZZA PARLORS**

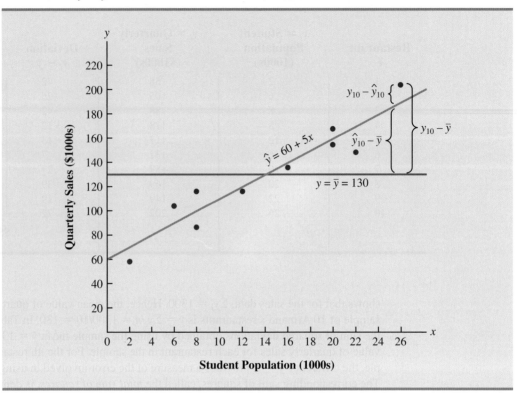

From the preceding discussion, we should expect that SST, SSR, and SSE are related. Indeed, the relationship among these three sums of squares provides one of the most important results in statistics.

<table>
<tr><td colspan="2">RELATIONSHIP AMONG SST, SSR, AND SSE</td></tr>
<tr><td colspan="2" align="center">$$SST = SSR + SSE \qquad\qquad\qquad (12.11)$$</td></tr>
</table>

SSR can be thought of as the explained portion of SST, and SSE can be thought of as the unexplained portion of SST.

where

       SST = total sum of squares
       SSR = sum of squares due to regression
       SSE = sum of squares due to error

Equation (12.11) shows that the total sum of squares can be partitioned into two components, the sum of squares due to regression and the sum of squares due to error. Hence, if the values of any two of these sum of squares are known, the third sum of squares can be computed easily. For instance, in the Armand's Pizza Parlors example, we already know that SSE = 1530 and SST = 15,730; therefore, solving for SSR in equation (12.11), we find that the sum of squares due to regression is

$$SSR = SST - SSE = 15,730 - 1530 = 14,200$$

Now let us see how the three sums of squares, SST, SSR, and SSE, can be used to provide a measure of the goodness of fit for the estimated regression equation. The estimated regression equation would provide a perfect fit if every value of the dependent variable y_i happened to lie on the estimated regression line. In this case, $y_i - \hat{y}_i$ would be zero for each observation, resulting in SSE $= 0$. Because SST $=$ SSR $+$ SSE, we see that for a perfect fit SSR must equal SST, and the ratio (SSR/SST) must equal one. Poorer fits will result in larger values for SSE. Solving for SSE in equation (12.11), we see that SSE $=$ SST $-$ SSR. Hence, the largest value for SSE (and hence the poorest fit) occurs when SSR $= 0$ and SSE $=$ SST.

The ratio SSR/SST, which will take values between zero and one, is used to evaluate the goodness of fit for the estimated regression equation. This ratio is called the *coefficient of determination* and is denoted by r^2.

COEFFICIENT OF DETERMINATION

$$r^2 = \frac{SSR}{SST} \qquad\qquad (12.12)$$

For the Armand's Pizza Parlors example, the value of the coefficient of determination is

$$r^2 = \frac{SSR}{SST} = \frac{14{,}200}{15{,}730} = .9027$$

When we express the coefficient of determination as a percentage, r^2 can be interpreted as the percentage of the total sum of squares that can be explained by using the estimated regression equation. For Armand's Pizza Parlors, we can conclude that 90.27% of the total sum of squares can be explained by using the estimated regression equation $\hat{y} = 60 + 5x$ to predict quarterly sales. In other words, 90.27% of the variability in sales can be explained by the linear relationship between the size of the student population and sales. We should be pleased to find such a good fit for the estimated regression equation.

Using Excel to Compute the Coefficient of Determination

In Section 12.2 we used Excel's chart tools to construct a scatter diagram and compute the estimated regression equation for the Armand's Pizza Parlors data. We will now describe how to compute the coefficient of determination using the scatter diagram in Figure 12.4.

> **Step 1.** Position the mouse pointer over any data point in the scatter diagram and right-click to display a list of options
> **Step 2.** Choose **Add Trendline**
> **Step 3.** When the Format Trendline dialog box appears,
> > Select **Trendline Options** and then
> > > Choose **Display R-squared value on chart**
> > > Click **Close**

Figure 12.7 displays the scatter diagram, the estimated regression equation, the graph of the estimated regression equation, and the coefficient of determination for the Armand's Pizza Parlors data. We see that $r^2 = .9027$.

Correlation Coefficient

In Chapter 3 we introduced the **correlation coefficient** as a descriptive measure of the strength of linear association between two variables, x and y. Values of the correlation coefficient are always between -1 and $+1$. A value of $+1$ indicates that the two variables

FIGURE 12.7   USING EXCEL TO COMPUTE THE COEFFICIENT OF DETERMINATION

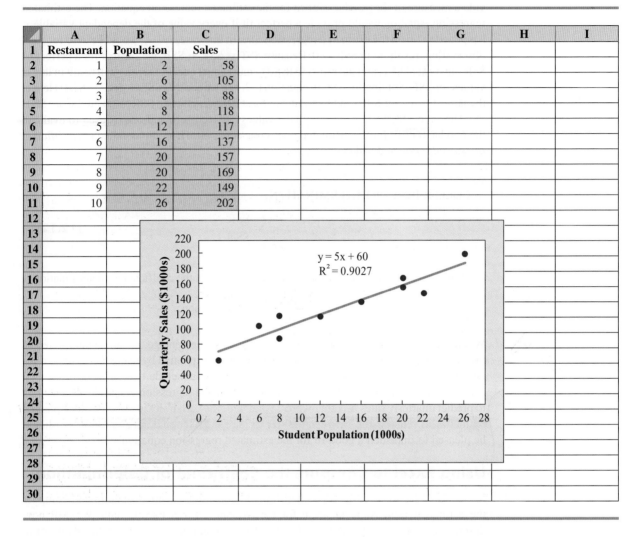

x and y are perfectly related in a positive linear sense. That is, all data points are on a straight line that has a positive slope. A value of -1 indicates that x and y are perfectly related in a negative linear sense, with all data points on a straight line that has a negative slope. Values of the correlation coefficient close to zero indicate that x and y are not linearly related.

In Section 3.5 we presented the equation for computing the sample correlation coefficient. If a regression analysis has already been performed and the coefficient of determination r^2 computed, the sample correlation coefficient can be computed as follows.

SAMPLE CORRELATION COEFFICIENT

$$r_{xy} = (\text{sign of } b_1)\sqrt{\text{Coefficient of determination}}$$
$$= (\text{sign of } b_1)\sqrt{r^2} \qquad\qquad (12.13)$$

where

b_1 = the slope of the estimated regression equation $\hat{y} = b_0 + b_1x$

The sign for the sample correlation coefficient is positive if the estimated regression equation has a positive slope ($b_1 > 0$) and negative if the estimated regression equation has a negative slope ($b_1 < 0$).

For the Armand's Pizza Parlor example, the value of the coefficient of determination corresponding to the estimated regression equation $\hat{y} = 60 + 5x$ is .9027. Because the slope of the estimated regression equation is positive, equation (12.13) shows that the sample correlation coefficient is $+\sqrt{.9027} = +.9501$. With a sample correlation coefficient of $r_{xy} = +.9501$, we would conclude that a strong positive linear association exists between x and y.

In the case of a linear relationship between two variables, both the coefficient of determination and the sample correlation coefficient provide measures of the strength of the relationship. The coefficient of determination provides a measure between zero and one, whereas the sample correlation coefficient provides a measure between -1 and $+1$. Although the sample correlation coefficient is restricted to a linear relationship between two variables, the coefficient of determination can be used for nonlinear relationships and for relationships that have two or more independent variables. Thus, the coefficient of determination provides a wider range of applicability.

NOTES AND COMMENTS

1. In developing the least squares estimated regression equation and computing the coefficient of determination, we made no probabilistic assumptions about the error term ϵ, and no statistical tests for significance of the relationship between x and y were conducted. Larger values of r^2 imply that the least squares line provides a better fit to the data; that is, the observations are more closely grouped about the least squares line. But, using only r^2, we can draw no conclusion about whether the relationship between x and y is statistically significant. Such a conclu-

sion must be based on considerations that involve the sample size and the properties of the appropriate sampling distributions of the least squares estimators.

2. As a practical matter, for typical data found in the social sciences, values of r^2 as low as .25 are often considered useful. For data in the physical and life sciences, r^2 values of .60 or greater are often found; in fact, in some cases, r^2 values greater than .90 can be found. In business applications, r^2 values vary greatly, depending on the unique characteristics of each application.

Exercises

Methods

15. The data from exercise 1 follow.

x_i	1	2	3	4	5
y_i	3	7	5	11	14

The estimated regression equation for these data is $\hat{y} = .20 + 2.60x$.
   a. Compute SSE, SST, and SSR using equations (12.8), (12.9), and (12.10).
   b. Compute the coefficient of determination r^2. Comment on the goodness of fit.
   c. Compute the sample correlation coefficient.

16. The data from exercise 2 follow.

x_i	3	12	6	20	14
y_i	55	40	55	10	15

The estimated regression equation for these data is $\hat{y} = 68 - 3x$.

a.   Compute SSE, SST, and SSR.

b.   Compute the coefficient of determination r^2. Comment on the goodness of fit.

c.   Compute the sample correlation coefficient.

17.   The data from exercise 3 follow.

x_i	2	6	9	13	20
y_i	7	18	9	26	23

The estimated regression equation for these data is $\hat{y} = 7.6 + .9x$. What percentage of the total sum of squares can be accounted for by the estimated regression equation? What is the value of the sample correlation coefficient?

Applications

18.   The following data are the monthly salaries y and the grade point averages x for students who obtained a bachelor's degree in business administration with a major in information systems. The estimated regression equation for these data is $\hat{y} = 1790.5 + 581.1x$.

GPA	Monthly Salary ($)
2.6	3300
3.4	3600
3.6	4000
3.2	3500
3.5	3900
2.9	3600

a.   Compute SST, SSR, and SSE.

b.   Compute the coefficient of determination r^2. Comment on the goodness of fit.

c.   What is the value of the sample correlation coefficient?

19.   The data from exercise 7 follow.

Cars

Make and Model	x = Reliability	y = Price ($)
Acura TL	4	33,150
BMW 330i	3	40,570
Lexus IS300	5	35,105
Lexus ES330	5	35,174
Mercedes-Benz C320	1	42,230
Lincoln LS Premium (V6)	3	38,225
Audi A4 3.0 Quattro	2	37,605
Cadillac CTS	1	37,695
Nissan Maxima 3.5 SE	4	34,390
Infiniti I35	5	33,845
Saab 9-3 Aero	3	36,910
Infiniti G35	4	34,695
Jaguar X-Type 3.0	1	37,995
Saab 9-5 Arc	3	36,955
Volvo S60 2.5T	3	33,890

The estimated regression equation for these data is $\hat{y} = 40{,}639 - 1301.2x$. What percentage of the total sum of squares can be accounted for by the estimated regression equation? Comment on the goodness of fit. What is the sample correlation coefficient?

20. *Consumer Reports* provided extensive testing and ratings for more than 100 HDTVs. An overall score, based primarily on picture quality, was developed for each model. In general, a higher overall score indicates better performance. The following data show the price and overall score for the ten 42-inch plasma televisions (*Consumer Reports,* March 2006).

PlasmaTV

Brand	Price	Score
Dell	2800	62
Hisense	2800	53
Hitachi	2700	44
JVC	3500	50
LG	3300	54
Maxent	2000	39
Panasonic	4000	66
Phillips	3000	55
Proview	2500	34
Samsung	3000	39

a. Use these data to develop an estimated regression equation that could be used to estimate the overall score for a 42-inch plasma television given the price.
b. Compute r^2. Did the estimated regression equation provide a good fit?
c. Estimate the overall score for a 42-inch plasma television with a price of $3200.

21. An important application of regression analysis in accounting is in the estimation of cost. By collecting data on volume and cost and using the least squares method to develop an estimated regression equation relating volume and cost, an accountant can estimate the cost associated with a particular manufacturing volume. Consider the following sample of production volumes and total cost data for a manufacturing operation.

Production Volume (units)	Total Cost ($)
400	4000
450	5000
550	5400
600	5900
700	6400
750	7000

a. Use these data to develop an estimated regression equation that could be used to predict the total cost for a given production volume.
b. What is the variable cost per unit produced?
c. Compute the coefficient of determination. What percentage of the variation in total cost can be explained by production volume?
d. The company's production schedule shows 500 units must be produced next month. What is the estimated total cost for this operation?

22. *PC World* provided ratings for the top five small-office laser printers and five corporate laser printers (*PC World,* February 2003). The highest rated small-office laser printer was the Minolta-QMS PagePro 1250W, with an overall rating of 91. The highest rated corporate

laser printer, the Xerox Phaser 4400/N, had an overall rating of 83. The following data show the speed for plain text printing in pages per minute (ppm) and the price for each printer.

Printers

Name	Type	Speed (ppm)	Price ($)
Minolta-QMS PagePro 1250W	Small Office	12	199
Brother HL-1850	Small Office	10	499
Lexmark E320	Small Office	12.2	299
Minolta-QMS PagePro 1250E	Small Office	10.3	299
HP Laserjet 1200	Small Office	11.7	399
Xerox Phaser 4400/N	Corporate	17.8	1850
Brother HL-2460N	Corporate	16.1	1000
IBM Infoprint 1120n	Corporate	11.8	1387
Lexmark W812	Corporate	19.8	2089
Oki Data B8300n	Corporate	28.2	2200

a. Develop the estimated regression equation with speed as the independent variable.
b. Compute r^2. What percentage of the variation in price can be explained by the printing speed?
c. What is the sample correlation coefficient between speed and price? Does it reflect a strong or weak relationship between printing speed and cost?

12.4 Model Assumptions

In conducting a regression analysis, we begin by making an assumption about the appropriate model for the relationship between the dependent and independent variable(s). For the case of simple linear regression, the assumed regression model is

$$y = \beta_0 + \beta_1 x + \epsilon$$

Then the least squares method is used to develop values for b_0 and b_1, the estimates of the model parameters β_0 and β_1, respectively. The resulting estimated regression equation is

$$\hat{y} = b_0 + b_1 x$$

We saw that the value of the coefficient of determination (r^2) is a measure of the goodness of fit of the estimated regression equation. However, even with a large value of r^2, the estimated regression equation should not be used until further analysis of the appropriateness of the assumed model has been conducted. An important step in determining whether the assumed model is appropriate involves testing for the significance of the relationship. The tests of significance in regression analysis are based on the following assumptions about the error term ϵ.

ASSUMPTIONS ABOUT THE ERROR TERM ϵ IN THE REGRESSION MODEL

$$y = \beta_0 + \beta_1 x + \epsilon$$

1. The error term ϵ is a random variable with a mean or expected value of zero; that is, $E(\epsilon) = 0$.

   Implication: Because β_0 and β_1 are constants, $E(\beta_0) = \beta_0$ and $E(\beta_1) = \beta_1$; thus, for a given value of x, the expected value of y is

   $$E(y) = \beta_0 + \beta_1 x \qquad (12.14)$$

As we indicated previously, equation (14.14) is referred to as the regression equation.

2. The variance of ϵ, denoted by σ^2, is the same for all values of x.

   Implication: The variance of y about the regression line equals σ^2 and is the same for all values of x.

3. The values of ϵ are independent.

   Implication: The value of ϵ for a particular value of x is not related to the value of ϵ for any other value of x; thus, the value of y for a particular value of x is not related to the value of y for any other value of x.

4. The error term ϵ is a normally distributed random variable.

   Implication: Because y is a linear function of ϵ, y is also a normally distributed random variable.

Figure 12.8 illustrates the model assumptions and their implications; note that in this graphical interpretation, the value of $E(y)$ changes according to the specific value of x considered. However, regardless of the x value, the probability distribution of ϵ and hence the probability distributions of y are normally distributed, each with the same variance. The specific value of the error ϵ at any particular point depends on whether the actual value of y is greater than or less than $E(y)$.

At this point, we must keep in mind that we are also making an assumption or hypothesis about the form of the relationship between x and y. That is, we assume that a straight

FIGURE 12.8   ASSUMPTIONS FOR THE REGRESSION MODEL

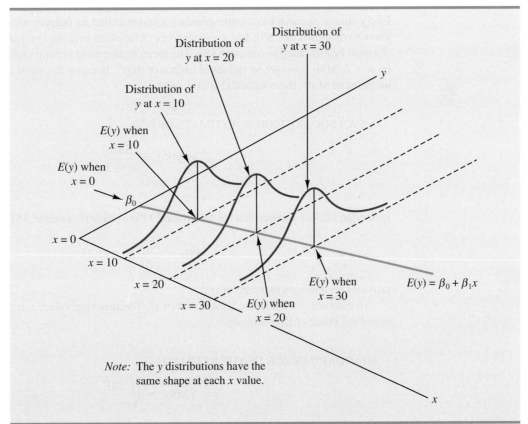

line represented by $\beta_0 + \beta_1 x$ is the basis for the relationship between the variables. We must not lose sight of the fact that some other model, for instance $y = \beta_0 + \beta_1 x^2 + \epsilon$, may turn out to be a better model for the underlying relationship.

12.5 Testing for Significance

In a simple linear regression equation, the mean or expected value of y is a linear function of x: $E(y) = \beta_0 + \beta_1 x$. If the value of β_1 is zero, $E(y) = \beta_0 + (0)x = \beta_0$. In this case, the mean value of y does not depend on the value of x and hence we would conclude that x and y are not linearly related. Alternatively, if the value of β_1 is not equal to zero, we would conclude that the two variables are related. Thus, to test for a significant regression relationship, we must conduct a hypothesis test to determine whether the value of β_1 is zero. Two tests are commonly used. Both require an estimate of σ^2, the variance of ϵ in the regression model.

Estimate of σ^2

From the regression model and its assumptions we can conclude that σ^2, the variance of ϵ, also represents the variance of the y values about the regression line. Recall that the deviations of the y values about the estimated regression line are called residuals. Thus, SSE, the sum of squared residuals, is a measure of the variability of the actual observations about the estimated regression line. The **mean square error** (MSE) provides the estimate of σ^2; it is SSE divided by its degrees of freedom.

With $\hat{y}_i = b_0 + b_1 x_i$, SSE can be written as

$$\text{SSE} = \Sigma(y_i - \hat{y}_i)^2 = \Sigma(y_i - b_0 - b_1 x_i)^2$$

Every sum of squares has a corresponding number called its degrees of freedom. Statisticians have shown that SSE has $n - 2$ degrees of freedom because two parameters (β_0 and β_1) must be estimated to compute SSE. The mean square error is computed by dividing SSE by $n - 2$. MSE provides an unbiased estimator of σ^2. Because the value of MSE provides an estimate of σ^2, the notation s^2 is also used.

MEAN SQUARE ERROR (ESTIMATE OF σ^2)

$$s^2 = \text{MSE} = \frac{\text{SSE}}{n - 2} \qquad (12.15)$$

In Section 12.3 we showed that for the Armand's Pizza Parlors example, SSE $= 1530$; hence,

$$s^2 = \text{MSE} = \frac{1530}{8} = 191.25$$

provides an unbiased estimate of σ^2.

To estimate σ we take the square root of s^2. The resulting value, s, is referred to as the **standard error of the estimate**.

STANDARD ERROR OF THE ESTIMATE

$$s = \sqrt{\text{MSE}} = \sqrt{\frac{\text{SSE}}{n - 2}} \qquad (12.16)$$

For the Armand's Pizza Parlors example, $s = \sqrt{\text{MSE}} = \sqrt{191.25} = 13.829$. In the following discussion, we use the standard error of the estimate in the tests for a significant relationship between x and y.

t Test

The simple linear regression model is $y = \beta_0 + \beta_1 x + \epsilon$. If x and y are linearly related, we must have $\beta_1 \neq 0$. The purpose of the t test is to see whether we can conclude that $\beta_1 \neq 0$. We will use the sample data to test the following hypotheses about the parameter β_1.

$$H_0: \beta_1 = 0$$
$$H_a: \beta_1 \neq 0$$

If H_0 is rejected, we will conclude that $\beta_1 \neq 0$ and that a statistically significant relationship exists between the two variables. However, if H_0 cannot be rejected, we will have insufficient evidence to conclude that a significant relationship exists. The properties of the sampling distribution of b_1, the least squares estimator of β_1, provide the basis for the hypothesis test.

First, let us consider what would happen if we used a different random sample for the same regression study. For example, suppose that Armand's Pizza Parlors used the sales records of a different sample of 10 restaurants. A regression analysis of this new sample might result in an estimated regression equation similar to our previous estimated regression equation $\hat{y} = 60 + 5x$. However, it is doubtful that we would obtain exactly the same equation (with an intercept of exactly 60 and a slope of exactly 5). Indeed, b_0 and b_1, the least squares estimators, are sample statistics with their own sampling distributions. The properties of the sampling distribution of b_1 follow.

SAMPLING DISTRIBUTION OF b_1

Expected Value
$$E(b_1) = \beta_1$$

Standard Deviation
$$\sigma_{b_1} = \frac{\sigma}{\sqrt{\Sigma(x_i - \bar{x})^2}} \tag{12.17}$$

Distribution Form
Normal

Note that the expected value of b_1 is equal to β_1; thus, b_1 is an unbiased estimator of β_1.

Because we do not know the value of σ, we develop an estimate of σ_{b_1}, denoted s_{b_1}, by estimating σ with s in equation (12.17). Thus, we obtain the following estimate of σ_{b_1}.

The standard deviation of b_1 is also referred to as the standard error of b_1. Thus, s_{b_1} provides an estimate of the standard error of b_1.

ESTIMATED STANDARD DEVIATION OF b_1

$$s_{b_1} = \frac{s}{\sqrt{\Sigma(x_i - \bar{x})^2}} \tag{12.18}$$

For Armand's Pizza Parlors, $s = 13.829$. Hence, using $\Sigma(x_i - \bar{x})^2 = 568$ as shown in Table 12.2, we have

$$s_{b_1} = \frac{13.829}{\sqrt{568}} = .5803$$

as the estimated standard deviation of b_1.

The t test for a significant relationship is based on the fact that the test statistic

$$\frac{b_1 - \beta_1}{s_{b_1}}$$

follows a t distribution with $n - 2$ degrees of freedom. If the null hypothesis is true, then $\beta_1 = 0$ and $t = b_1/s_{b_1}$.

Let us conduct this test of significance for Armand's Pizza Parlors at the $\alpha = .01$ level of significance. The test statistic is

$$t = \frac{b_1}{s_{b_1}} = \frac{5}{.5803} = 8.62$$

Using Excel, p-value = TDIST(8.62,8,2) = .000.

The t distribution table shows that with $n - 2 = 10 - 2 = 8$ degrees of freedom, $t = 3.355$ provides an area of .005 in the upper tail. Thus, the area in the upper tail of the t distribution corresponding to the test statistic $t = 8.62$ must be less than .005. Because this test is a two-tailed test, we double this value to conclude that the p-value associated with $t = 8.62$ must be less than $2(.005) = .01$. Excel shows the p-value = .000. Because the p-value is less than $\alpha = .01$, we reject H_0 and conclude that β_1 is not equal to zero. This evidence is sufficient to conclude that a significant relationship exists between student population and quarterly sales. A summary of the t test for significance in simple linear regression follows.

---

t TEST FOR SIGNIFICANCE IN SIMPLE LINEAR REGRESSION

$$H_0: \beta_1 = 0$$
$$H_a: \beta_1 \neq 0$$

TEST STATISTIC

$$t = \frac{b_1}{s_{b_1}} \tag{12.19}$$

REJECTION RULE

p-value approach:　　　Reject H_0 if p-value $\leq \alpha$

Critical value approach:　Reject H_0 if $t \leq -t_{\alpha/2}$ or if $t \geq t_{\alpha/2}$

where $t_{\alpha/2}$ is based on a t distribution with $n - 2$ degrees of freedom.

Confidence Interval for β_1

The form of a confidence interval for β_1 is as follows:

$$b_1 \pm t_{\alpha/2} s_{b_1}$$

The point estimator is b_1 and the margin of error is $t_{\alpha/2}s_{b_1}$. The confidence coefficient associated with this interval is $1 - \alpha$, and $t_{\alpha/2}$ is the t value providing an area of $\alpha/2$ in the upper tail of a t distribution with $n - 2$ degrees of freedom. For example, suppose that we wanted to develop a 99% confidence interval estimate of β_1 for Armand's Pizza Parlors. From Table 2 of Appendix B we find that the t value corresponding to $\alpha = .01$ and $n - 2 = 10 - 2 = 8$ degrees of freedom is $t_{.005} = 3.355$. Thus, the 99% confidence interval estimate of β_1 is

$$b_1 \pm t_{\alpha/2}s_{b_1} = 5 \pm 3.355(.5803) = 5 \pm 1.95$$

or 3.05 to 6.95.

In using the t test for significance, the hypotheses tested were

$$H_0: \beta_1 = 0$$
$$H_a: \beta_1 \neq 0$$

At the $\alpha = .01$ level of significance, we can use the 99% confidence interval as an alternative for drawing the hypothesis testing conclusion for the Armand's data. Because 0, the hypothesized value of β_1, is not included in the confidence interval (3.05 to 6.95), we can reject H_0 and conclude that a significant statistical relationship exists between the size of the student population and quarterly sales. In general, a confidence interval can be used to test any two-sided hypothesis about β_1. If the hypothesized value of β_1 is contained in the confidence interval, do not reject H_0. Otherwise, reject H_0.

F **Test**

The F test and the t test provide identical results for simple linear regression.

An F test, based on the F probability distribution, can also be used to test for significance in regression. With only one independent variable, the F test will provide the same conclusion as the t test; that is, if the t test indicates $\beta_1 \neq 0$ and hence a significant relationship, the F test will also indicate a significant relationship. But with more than one independent variable, only the F test can be used to test for an overall significant relationship.

The logic behind the use of the F test for determining whether the regression relationship is statistically significant is based on the development of two independent estimates of σ^2. We explained how MSE provides an estimate of σ^2. If the null hypothesis $H_0: \beta_1 = 0$ is true, the sum of squares due to regression, SSR, divided by its degrees of freedom provides another independent estimate of σ^2. This estimate is called the *mean square due to regression,* or simply the *mean square regression,* and is denoted MSR. In general,

$$MSR = \frac{SSR}{\text{Regression degrees of freedom}}$$

For the models we consider in this text, the regression degrees of freedom is always equal to the number of independent variables in the model. As a result,

$$MSR = \frac{SSR}{\text{Number of independent variables}} \tag{12.20}$$

Because we consider only regression models with one independent variable in this chapter, we have MSR = SSR/1 = SSR. Hence, for Armand's Pizza Parlors, MSR = SSR = 14,200.

If the null hypothesis ($H_0: \beta_1 = 0$) is true, MSR and MSE are two independent estimates of σ^2 and the sampling distribution of MSR/MSE follows an F distribution with numerator degrees of freedom equal to one and denominator degrees of freedom equal to $n - 2$. Therefore, when $\beta_1 = 0$, the value of MSR/MSE should be close to one. However, if the null hypothesis is false ($\beta_1 \neq 0$), MSR will overestimate σ^2 and the value of MSR/MSE will be inflated; thus, large values of MSR/MSE lead to the rejection of H_0 and the conclusion that the relationship between x and y is statistically significant.

Let us conduct the F test for the Armand's Pizza Parlors example. The test statistic is

$$F = \frac{\text{MSR}}{\text{MSE}} = \frac{14{,}200}{191.25} = 74.25$$

Using Excel, p-value = FDIST(74.25,1,8) = .000.

The F distribution table (Table 4 of Appendix B) shows that with 1 degree of freedom in the numerator and $n - 2 = 10 - 2 = 8$ degrees of freedom in the denominator, $F = 11.26$ provides an area of .01 in the upper tail. Thus, the area in the upper tail of the F distribution corresponding to the test statistic $F = 74.25$ must be less than .01. Thus, we conclude that the p-value must be less than .01. Excel shows the p-value $= .000$. Because the p-value is less than $\alpha = .01$, we reject H_0 and conclude that a significant relationship exists between the size of the student population and quarterly sales. A summary of the F test for significance in simple linear regression follows.

F TEST FOR SIGNIFICANCE IN SIMPLE LINEAR REGRESSION

If H_0 is false, MSE still provides an unbiased estimate of σ^2 and MSR overestimates σ^2. If H_0 is true, both MSE and MSR provide unbiased estimates of σ^2; in this case the value of MSR/MSE should be close to 1.

$$H_0: \beta_1 = 0$$
$$H_a: \beta_1 \neq 0$$

TEST STATISTIC

$$F = \frac{\text{MSR}}{\text{MSE}} \qquad (12.21)$$

REJECTION RULE

p-value approach: Reject H_0 if p-value $\leq \alpha$

Critical value approach: Reject H_0 if $F \geq F_\alpha$

where F_α is based on an F distribution with 1 degree of freedom in the numerator and $n - 2$ degrees of freedom in the denominator.

In Chapter 10 we covered analysis of variance (ANOVA) and showed how an **ANOVA table** could be used to provide a convenient summary of the computational aspects of analysis of variance. A similar ANOVA table can be used to summarize the results of the F test for significance in regression. Table 12.5 is the general form of the ANOVA table for simple linear regression. Table 12.6 is the ANOVA table with the F test computations performed for Armand's Pizza Parlors. Regression, Error, and Total are the labels for the three sources of variation, with SSR, SSE, and SST appearing as the corresponding sum of squares in column 2. The degrees of freedom, 1 for SSR, $n - 2$ for SSE, and $n - 1$ for SST, are shown in column 3. Column 4 contains the values of MSR and MSE, column 5 contains the value of $F = \text{MSR/MSE}$, and column 6 contains the p-value corresponding to the F value in column 5. Almost all computer printouts of regression analysis include an ANOVA table summary of the F test for significance.

TABLE 12.5   GENERAL FORM OF THE ANOVA TABLE FOR SIMPLE
LINEAR REGRESSION

In every analysis of variance table the total sum of squares is the sum of the regression sum of squares and the error sum of squares; in addition, the total degrees of freedom is the sum of the regression degrees of freedom and the error degrees of freedom.

Source of Variation	Sum of Squares	Degrees of Freedom	Mean Square	F	p-value
Regression	SSR	1	$MSR = \dfrac{SSR}{1}$	$F = \dfrac{MSR}{MSE}$	
Error	SSE	$n-2$	$MSE = \dfrac{SSE}{n-2}$		
Total	SST	$n-1$			

Some Cautions About the Interpretation of Significance Tests

Regression analysis, which can be used to identify how variables are associated with one another, cannot be used as evidence of a cause-and-effect relationship.

Rejecting the null hypothesis $H_0: \beta_1 = 0$ and concluding that the relationship between x and y is significant does not enable us to conclude that a cause-and-effect relationship is present between x and y. Concluding a cause-and-effect relationship is warranted only if the analyst can provide some type of theoretical justification that the relationship is in fact causal. In the Armand's Pizza Parlors example, we can conclude that there is a significant relationship between the size of the student population x and quarterly sales y; moreover, the estimated regression equation $\hat{y} = 60 + 5x$ provides the least squares estimate of the relationship. We cannot, however, conclude that changes in student population x *cause* changes in quarterly sales y just because we identified a statistically significant relationship. The appropriateness of such a cause-and-effect conclusion is left to supporting theoretical justification and to good judgment on the part of the analyst. Armand's managers felt that increases in the student population were a likely cause of increased quarterly sales. Thus, the result of the significance test enabled them to conclude that a cause-and-effect relationship is present.

In addition, just because we are able to reject $H_0: \beta_1 = 0$ and demonstrate statistical significance does not enable us to conclude that the relationship between x and y is linear. We can state only that x and y are related and that a linear relationship explains a significant portion of the variability in y over the range of values for x observed in the sample. Figure 12.9 illustrates this situation. The test for significance calls for the rejection of the null hypothesis $H_0: \beta_1 = 0$ and leads to the conclusion that x and y are significantly related, but the figure shows that the actual relationship between x and y is not linear. Although the

TABLE 12.6   ANOVA TABLE FOR THE ARMAND'S PIZZA PARLORS PROBLEM

Source of Variation	Sum of Squares	Degrees of Freedom	Mean Square	F	p-value
Regression	14,200	1	$\dfrac{14{,}200}{1} = 14{,}200$	$\dfrac{14{,}200}{191.25} = 74.25$	.000
Error	1,530	8	$\dfrac{1530}{8} = 191.25$		
Total	15,730	9			

FIGURE 12.9   EXAMPLE OF A LINEAR APPROXIMATION OF A NONLINEAR RELATIONSHIP

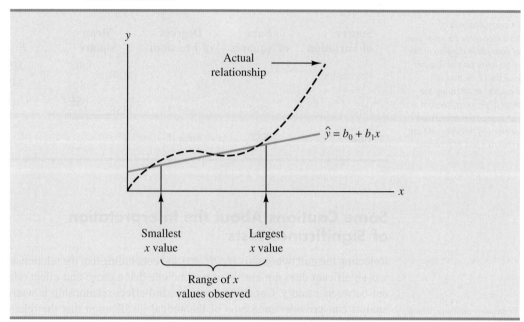

linear approximation provided by $\hat{y} = b_0 + b_1 x$ is good over the range of x values observed in the sample, it becomes poor for x values outside that range.

Given a significant relationship, we should feel confident in using the estimated regression equation for predictions corresponding to x values within the range of the x values observed in the sample. For Armand's Pizza Parlors, this range corresponds to values of x between 2 and 26. Unless other reasons indicate that the model is valid beyond this range, predictions outside the range of the independent variable should be made with caution. For Armand's Pizza Parlors, because the regression relationship has been found significant at the .01 level, we should feel confident using it to predict sales for restaurants where the associated student population is between 2000 and 26,000.

NOTES AND COMMENTS

1. The assumptions made about the error term (Section 12.4) are what allow the tests of statistical significance in this section. The properties of the sampling distribution of b_1 and the subsequent t and F tests follow directly from these assumptions.

2. Do not confuse statistical significance with practical significance. With very large sample sizes, statistically significant results can be obtained for small values of b_1; in such cases, one must exercise care in concluding that the relationship has practical significance.

3. A test of significance for a linear relationship between x and y can also be performed by using the sample correlation coefficient r_{xy}. With ρ_{xy}

denoting the population correlation coefficient, the hypotheses are as follows.

$$H_0: \rho_{xy} = 0$$
$$H_a: \rho_{xy} \neq 0$$

A significant relationship can be concluded if H_0 is rejected. However, the t and F tests presented previously in this section give the same result as the test for significance using the correlation coefficient. Conducting a test for significance using the correlation coefficient therefore is not necessary if a t or F test has already been conducted.

Exercises

Methods

23. The data from exercise 1 follow.

x_i	1	2	3	4	5
y_i	3	7	5	11	14

   a. Compute the mean square error using equation (12.15).
   b. Compute the standard error of the estimate using equation (12.16).
   c. Compute the estimated standard deviation of b_1 using equation (12.18).
   d. Use the t test to test the following hypotheses ($\alpha = .05$):

$$H_0: \beta_1 = 0$$
$$H_a: \beta_1 \neq 0$$

   e. Use the F test to test the hypotheses in part (d) at a .05 level of significance. Present the results in the analysis of variance table format.

24. The data from exercise 2 follow.

x_i	3	12	6	20	14
y_i	55	40	55	10	15

   a. Compute the mean square error using equation (12.15).
   b. Compute the standard error of the estimate using equation (12.16).
   c. Compute the estimated standard deviation of b_1 using equation (12.18).
   d. Use the t test to test the following hypotheses ($\alpha = .05$):

$$H_0: \beta_1 = 0$$
$$H_a: \beta_1 \neq 0$$

   e. Use the F test to test the hypotheses in part (d) at a .05 level of significance. Present the results in the analysis of variance table format.

25. The data from exercise 3 follow.

x_i	2	6	9	13	20
y_i	7	18	9	26	23

   a. What is the value of the standard error of the estimate?
   b. Test for a significant relationship by using the t test. Use $\alpha = .05$.
   c. Use the F test to test for a significant relationship. Use $\alpha = .05$. What is your conclusion?

Applications

26. In exercise 18 the data on grade point average and monthly salary were as follows.

GPA	Monthly Salary ($)	GPA	Monthly Salary ($)
2.6	3300	3.2	3500
3.4	3600	3.5	3900
3.6	4000	2.9	3600

   a. Does the t test indicate a significant relationship between grade point average and monthly salary? What is your conclusion? Use $\alpha = .05$.
   b. Test for a significant relationship using the F test. What is your conclusion? Use $\alpha = .05$.
   c. Show the ANOVA table.

27. *Outside Magazine* tested 10 different models of day hikers and backpacking boots. The following data show the upper support and price for each model tested. Upper support was measured using a rating from 1 to 5, with a rating of 1 denoting average upper support and a rating of 5 denoting excellent upper support (*Outside Magazine Buyer's Guide,* 2001).

WEB file

Boots

Manufacturer and Model	Upper Support	Price ($)
Salomon Super Raid	2	120
Merrell Chameleon Prime	3	125
Teva Challenger	3	130
Vasque Fusion GTX	3	135
Boreal Maigmo	3	150
L.L. Bean GTX Super Guide	5	189
Lowa Kibo	5	190
Asolo AFX 520 GTX	4	195
Raichle Mt. Trail GTX	4	200
Scarpa Delta SL M3	5	220

a. Use these data to develop an estimated regression equation to estimate the price of a day hiker and backpacking boot given the upper support rating.
b. At the .05 level of significance, determine whether upper support and price are related.
c. Would you feel comfortable using the estimated regression equation developed in part (a) to estimate the price for a day hiker or backpacking boot given the upper support rating?
d. Estimate the price for a day hiker with an upper support rating of 4.

28. In exercise 10, data on x = temperature rating (F°) and y = price ($) for 11 sleeping bags manufactured by Bergans of Norway provided the estimated regression equation $\hat{y}$ = 359.2668 − 5.2772x. At the .05 level of significance, test whether temperature rating and price are related. Show the ANOVA table. What is your conclusion?

29. Refer to exercise 21, where data on production volume and cost were used to develop an estimated regression equation relating production volume and cost for a particular manufacturing operation. Use α = .05 to test whether the production volume is significantly related to the total cost. Show the ANOVA table. What is your conclusion?

30. Refer to exercise 22, where the following data were used to determine whether the price of a printer is related to the speed for plain text printing (*PC World,* February 2003).

WEB file

Printers

Name	Type	Speed (ppm)	Price ($)
Minolta-QMS PagePro 1250W	Small Office	12	199
Brother HL-1850	Small Office	10	499
Lexmark E320	Small Office	12.2	299
Minolta-QMS PagePro 1250E	Small Office	10.3	299
HP Laserjet 1200	Small Office	11.7	399
Xerox Phaser 4400/N	Corporate	17.8	1850
Brother HL-2460N	Corporate	16.1	1000
IBM Infoprint 1120n	Corporate	11.8	1387
Lexmark W812	Corporate	19.8	2089
Oki Data B8300n	Corporate	28.2	2200

Does the evidence indicate a significant relationship between printing speed and price? Conduct the appropriate statistical test and state your conclusion. Use α = .05.

31. In exercise 20, data on x = price ($) and y = overall score for ten 42-inch plasma televisions tested by *Consumer Reports* provided the estimated regression equation $\hat{y}$ = 12.0169 + .0127x. For these data SSE = 540.04 and SST = 982.40. Use the F test to determine whether the price for a 42-inch plasma television and the overall score are related at the .05 level of significance.

WEB file

PlasmaTV

(12.6) Excel's Regression Tool

In previous sections of this chapter we have shown how Excel can be used for various tasks in a regression analysis. Excel also has a more comprehensive Regression tool. In this section we will illustrate how Excel's Regression tool can be used to perform a complete regression analysis, including statistical tests of significance for the Armand's Pizza Parlors data in Table 12.1.

Using Excel's Regression Tool for the Armand's Pizza Parlors Example

Refer to Figures 12.10 and 12.11 as we describe the tasks involved to use Excel's Regression tool to perform the regression analysis computations for the Armand's data.

Enter Data: The labels Restaurant, Population, and Sales are entered into cells A1:C1 of the worksheet. To identify each of the 10 observations, we entered the numbers 1 through 10 into cells A2:A11. The sample data are entered into cells B2:C11.

Apply Tools: The following steps describe how to use Excel's Regression tool to perform the regression analysis computations performed in Sections 12.2–12.5.

Step 1. Click the **Data** tab on the Ribbon
Step 2. In the **Analysis** group, click **Data Analysis**

FIGURE 12.10   REGRESSION TOOL OUTPUT FOR ARMAND'S PIZZA PARLORS

	A	B	C	D	E	F	G	H	I	J
1	Restaurant	Population	Sales							
2	1	2	58							
3	2	6	105							
4	3	8	88							
5	4	8	118							
6	5	12	117							
7	6	16	137							
8	7	20	157							
9	8	20	169							
10	9	22	149							
11	10	26	202							
12										
13	SUMMARY OUTPUT									
14										
15	*Regression Statistics*									
16	Multiple R	0.9501								
17	R Square	0.9027								
18	Adjusted R Square	0.8906								
19	Standard Error	13.8293								
20	Observations	10								
21										
22	ANOVA									
23		*df*	*SS*	*MS*	*F*	*Significance F*				
24	Regression	1	14200	14200	74.2484	2.55E-05				
25	Residual	8	1530	191.25						
26	Total	9	15730							
27										
28		*Coefficients*	*Standard Error*	*t Stat*	*P-value*	*Lower 95%*	*Upper 95%*	*Lower 99.0%*	*Upper 99.0%*	
29	Intercept	60	9.2260	6.5033	0.0002	38.7247	81.2753	29.0431	90.9569	
30	Population	5	0.5803	8.6167	2.55E-05	3.6619	6.3381	3.0530	6.9470	
31										

FIGURE 12.11   REGRESSION TOOL DIALOG BOX FOR THE ARMAND'S PIZZA
PARLORS EXAMPLE

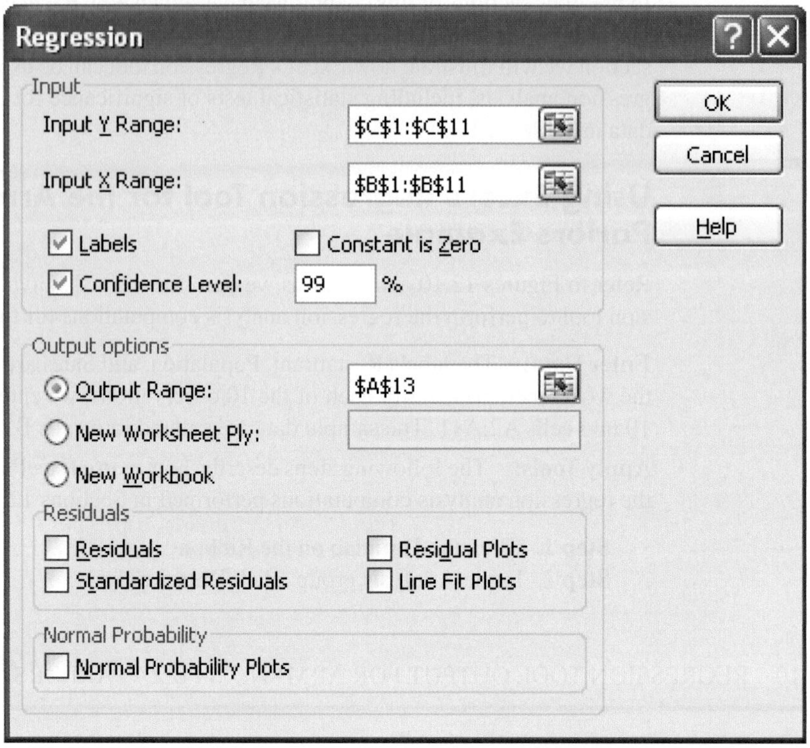

Step 3. Choose **Regression** from the list of Analysis Tools
Step 4. When the Regression dialog box appears (see Figure 12.11),
Enter C1:C11 in the **Input Y Range** box
Enter B1:B11 in the **Input X Range** box
Select **Labels**
Select **Confidence Level**
Enter 99 in the **Confidence Level** box
Select **Output Range**
Enter A13 in the **Output Range** box (to identify the upper left corner of
the section of the worksheet where the output will appear)
Click **OK**

The regression output, titled SUMMARY OUTPUT, begins with row 13 in Figure 12.10.
Because Excel initially displays the output using standard column widths, many of the row
and column labels are unreadable. In several places we have reformatted to improve readability. We have also reformatted cells displaying numerical values to a maximum of four
decimal places. Numbers displayed using scientific notation have not been modified. Regression output in future figures will be similarly reformatted to improve readability.

*The Excel output can be
reformatted to improve
readability.*

The first section of the summary output, titled *Regression Statistics,* contains summary
statistics such as the coefficient of determination (R Square). The second section of the output, titled ANOVA, contains the analysis of variance table. The last section of the output,
which is not titled, contains the estimated regression coefficients and related information.
Let us begin our interpretation of the regression output with the information contained in
rows 29 and 30.

Interpretation of Estimated Regression Equation Output

Row 29 contains information about the y-intercept of the estimated regression line. Row 30 contains information about the slope of the estimated regression line. The y-intercept of the estimated regression line, $b_0 = 60$, is shown in cell B29, and the slope of the estimated regression line, $b_1 = 5$, is shown in cell B30. The label Intercept in cell A29 and the label Population in cell A30 are used to identify these two values.

In Section 12.5 we showed that the estimated standard deviation of b_1 is $s_{b_1} = .5803$. Cell C30 contains the estimated standard deviation of b_1. As we indicated previously, the standard deviation of b_1 is also referred to as the standard error of b_1. Thus, s_{b_1} provides an estimate of the standard error of b_1. The label Standard Error in cell C28 is Excel's way of indicating that the value in cell C30 is the estimate of the standard error, or standard deviation, of b_1.

In Section 12.5 we stated that the form of the null and alternative hypotheses needed to test for a significant relationship between population and sales are as follows:

$$H_0: \beta_1 = 0$$
$$H_a: \beta_1 \neq 0$$

Recall that the t test for a significant relationship required the computation of the t statistic, $t = b_1/s_{b_1}$. For the Armand's data, the value of t that we computed was $t = 5/.5803 = 8.62$. Note that after rounding, the value in cell D30 is 8.62. The label in cell D28, *t Stat,* reminds us that cell D30 contains the value of the t test statistic.

t **Test**   The information in cell E30 provides a means for conducting a test of significance. The value in cell E30 is the p-value associated with the t test for significance. Excel has displayed the p-value using scientific notation. To obtain the decimal equivalent, we move the decimal point 5 places to the left; we obtain a p-value of .0000255. Thus, the p-value associated with the t test for significance is .0000255. Given the level of significance α, the decision of whether to reject H_0 can be made as follows:

$$\text{Reject } H_0 \text{ if } p\text{-value} \leq \alpha$$

Because the p-value $= .0000255 < \alpha = .01$, we can reject H_0 and conclude that we have a significant relationship between student population and sales. Because p-values are provided as part of the computer output for regression analysis, the p-value approach is most often used for hypothesis tests in regression analysis.

The information in cells F28:I30 can be used to develop confidence interval estimates of the y-intercept and slope of the estimated regression equation. Excel always provides the lower and upper limits for a 95% confidence interval. Recall that in the Regression dialog box (see Figure 12.11) we selected Confidence Level and entered 99 in the Confidence Level box. As a result, Excel's Regression tool also provides the lower and upper limits for a 99% confidence interval. For instance, the value in cell H30 is the lower limit for the 99% confidence interval estimate of β_1 and the value in cell I30 is the upper limit. Thus, after rounding, the 99% confidence interval estimate of β_1 is 3.05 to 6.95. The values in cells F30 and G30 provide the lower and upper limits for the 95% confidence interval. Thus, the 95% confidence interval is 3.66 to 6.34.

Interpretation of ANOVA Output

The information in cells A22:F26 summarizes the analysis of variance computations for the Armand's data. The three sources of variation are labeled Regression, Residual, and Total.

Excel refers to the error sum of squares as the residual sum of squares.

The label *df* in cell B23 stands for degrees of freedom, the label *SS* in cell C23 stands for sum of squares, and the label *MS* in cell D23 stands for mean square. Looking at cells C24:C26, we see that the regression sum of squares is 14200, the residual or error sum of squares is 1530, and the total sum of squares is 15730. The values in cells B24:B26 are the degrees of freedom corresponding to each sum of squares. Thus, the regression sum of squares has 1 degree of freedom, the residual or error sum of squares has 8 degrees of freedom, and the total sum of squares has 9 degrees of freedom. As we discussed previously, the regression degrees of freedom plus the residual degrees of freedom are equal to the total degrees of freedom, and the regression sum of squares plus the residual sum of squares are equal to the total sum of squares.

In Section 12.5 we stated that the mean square error, obtained by dividing the error or residual sum of squares by its degrees of freedom, provides an estimate of σ^2. The value in cell D25, 191.25, is the mean square error for the Armand's regression output. We also stated that the mean square regression is the sum of squares due to regression divided by the regression degrees of freedom. The value in cell D24, 14200, is the mean square regression.

F **Test**   In Section 12.5 we showed that an *F* test, based upon the *F* probability distribution, could also be used to test for significance in regression. The value in cell F24, .0000255, is the *p*-value associated with the *F* test for significance. Because the *p*-value = .0000255 < α = .01, we can reject H_0 and conclude that we have a significant relationship between student population and sales. Note that it is the same conclusion that we obtained using the *p*-value approach for the *t* test for significance. In fact, because the *t* test for significance is equivalent to the *F* test for significance in simple linear regression, the *p*-values provided by both approaches are identical. The label Excel uses to identify the *p*-value for the *F* test for significance, shown in cell F23, is *Significance F*. In Chapter 9 we also stated that the *p*-value is often referred to as the observed level of significance. Thus, the label *Significance F* may be more meaningful if you think of the value in cell F24 as the observed level of significance for the *F* test.

Interpretation of Regression Statistics Output

The output in cells A15:B20 summarizes the regression statistics. The number of observations in the data set, 10, is shown in cell B20. The coefficient of determination, .9027, appears in cell B17; the corresponding label, R Square, is shown in cell A17. The square root of the coefficient of determination provides the sample correlation coefficient of 0.9501 shown in cell B16. Note that Excel uses the label Multiple R (cell A16) to identify this value. In cell A19, the label Standard Error is used to identify the value of *s*, the estimate of σ. Cell B19 shows that the value of *s* is 13.8293. We caution the reader to keep in mind that in the Excel output, the label Standard Error appears in two different places. In the Regression Statistics section of the output the label Standard Error refers to *s*, the estimate of σ. In the Estimated Regression Equation section of the output, the label Standard Error refers to s_{b_1}, the estimated standard deviation of the sampling distribution of b_1.

NOTES AND COMMENTS

In the chapter appendix we show how to use Stat-Tools to perform the regression analysis computations for the Armand's Pizza Parlors data. The regression analysis capabilities of StatTools are more comprehensive than those available using Excel's Regression tool.

EXERCISES

Applications

32. Following is a portion of the Excel output for a regression analysis relating maintenance expense (dollars per month) to usage (hours per week) for a particular brand of computer terminal.

ANOVA

	df	SS
Regression	1	1575.76
Residual	8	349.14
Total	9	1924.90

	Coefficients	Standard Error	t Stat
Intercept	6.1092	.9361	
Usage	0.8951	.149	

a. Write the estimated regression equation.
b. Use a t test to determine whether monthly maintenance expense is related to usage at the .05 level of significance.
c. Did the estimated regression equation provide a good fit? Explain.

33. The commercial division of a real estate firm conducted a study to determine the extent of the relationship between annual gross rents ($1000s) and the selling price ($1000s) for apartment buildings. Data were collected on several properties sold, and Excel's Regression tool was used to develop an estimated regression equation. A portion of the Excel output follows.

ANOVA

	df	SS	MS	F
Regression	1	41587.3		
Residual	7			
Total	8	51984.1		

	Coefficients	Standard Error	t Stat
Intercept	20.000	3.2213	6.21
Annual Gross Rents	7.210	1.3626	5.29

a. How many apartment buildings were in the sample?
b. Write the estimated regression equation.
c. Use the t test to determine whether the selling price is related to annual gross rents. Use $\alpha = .05$.
d. Use the F test to determine whether the selling price is related to annual gross rents. Use $\alpha = .05$.
e. Estimate the selling price of an apartment building with gross annual rents of $50,000.

34. A regression model relating the number of salespersons at a branch office to annual sales at the office (in thousands of dollars) provided the following Excel output.

ANOVA

	df	SS	MS	F
Regression		6828.6		
Residual				
Total		9127.4		

	Coefficients	Standard Error	t Stat	P-value
Intercept	80.0	11.333		
Number of Salespersons	50.0	5.482		

a. Write the estimated regression equation.
b. Compute the F statistic and test the significance of the relationship at the .05 level of significance.
c. Compute the t statistic and test the significance of the relationship at the .05 level of significance.
d. Compute the p-value associated with the t test for significance.

35. Health experts recommend that runners drink 4 ounces of water every 15 minutes they run. Although handheld bottles work well for many types of runs, all-day cross-country runs require hip-mounted or over-the-shoulder hydration systems. In addition to carrying more water, hip-mounted or over-the-shoulder hydration systems offer more storage space for food and extra clothing. As the capacity increases, however, the weight and cost of these larger-capacity systems also increase. The following data show the weight (ounces) and the price for 26 hip-mounted or over-the-shoulder hydration systems (*Trail Runner Gear Guide,* 2003).

WEB file

Hydration1

Model	Weight (oz.)	Price ($)	Model	Weight (oz.)	Price ($)
Fastdraw	3	10	Elite	14	60
Fastdraw Plus	4	12	Extender	16	65
Fitness	5	12	Stinger	16	65
Access	7	20	GelFlask Belt	3	20
Access Plus	8	25	GelDraw	1	7
Solo	9	25	GelFlask Clip-on Holster	2	10
Serenade	9	35	GelFlask Holster SS	1	10
Solitaire	11	35	Strider (W)	8	30
Gemini	21	45	Walkabout (W)	14	40
Shadow	15	40	Solitude I.C.E.	9	35
SipStream	18	60	Getaway I.C.E.	19	55
Express	9	30	Profile I.C.E.	14	50
Lightning	12	40	Traverse I.C.E.	13	60

a. Use these data to develop an estimated regression equation that could be used to predict the price of a hydration system given its weight.
b. Test the significance of the relationship at the .05 level of significance.
c. Did the estimated regression equation provide a good fit? Explain.

36. Automobile racing, high-performance driving schools, and driver education programs run by automobile clubs continue to grow in popularity. All these activities require the participant to wear a helmet that is certified by the Snell Memorial Foundation, a not-for-profit organization dedicated to research, education, testing, and development of helmet safety standards. Snell "SA" (Sports Application) rated professional helmets are designed for auto racing and provide extreme impact resistance and high fire protection. One of the key

factors in selecting a helmet is weight, since lower weight helmets tend to place less stress on the neck. The following data show the weight and price for 18 SA helmets (*http://soloracerblog.com*, April 20, 2008).

Helmet	Weight (oz)	Price ($)
Pyrotect Pro Airflow	64	248
Pyrotect Pro Airflow Graphics	64	278
RCi Full Face	64	200
RaceQuip RidgeLine	64	200
HJC AR-10	58	300
HJC Si-12	47	700
HJC HX-10	49	900
Impact Racing Super Sport	59	340
Zamp FSA-1	66	199
Zamp RZ-2	58	299
Zamp RZ-2 Ferrari	58	299
Zamp RZ-3 Sport	52	479
Zamp RZ-3 Sport Painted	52	479
Bell M2	63	369
Bell M4	62	369
Bell M4 Pro	54	559
G Force Pro Force 1	63	250
G Force Pro Force 1 Grafx	63	280

RaceHelmets

a.   Develop a scatter diagram with weight as the independent variable.
b.   Does there appear to be any relationship between these two variables?
c.   Develop the estimated regression equation that could be used to predict the price given the weight.
d.   Test for the significance of the relationship at the .05 level of significance.
e.   Did the estimated regression equation provide a good fit? Explain.

 12.7

Using the Estimated Regression Equation for Estimation and Prediction

When using the simple linear regression model we are making an assumption about the relationship between x and y. We then use the least squares method to obtain the estimated simple linear regression equation. If a significant relationship exists between x and y, and the coefficient of determination shows that the fit is good, the estimated regression equation should be useful for estimation and prediction.

Point Estimation

In the Armand's Pizza Parlors example, the estimated regression equation $\hat{y} = 60 + 5x$ provides an estimate of the relationship between the size of the student population x and quarterly sales y. We can use the estimated regression equation to develop a point estimate of the mean value of y for a particular value of x or to predict an individual value of y corresponding to a given value of x. For instance, suppose Armand's managers want a point estimate of the mean quarterly sales for all restaurants located near college campuses with 10,000 students. Using the estimated regression equation $\hat{y} = 60 + 5x$, we see that for $x = 10$ (or 10,000 students), $\hat{y} = 60 + 5(10) = 110$. Thus, a point estimate of the mean quarterly sales for all restaurants located near campuses with 10,000 students is $110,000.

Now suppose Armand's managers want to predict sales for an individual restaurant located near Talbot College, a school with 10,000 students. In this case we are not interested in the mean value for all restaurants located near campuses with 10,000 students; we are just interested in predicting quarterly sales for one individual restaurant. As it turns out, the point estimate for an individual value of y is the same as the point estimate for the mean value of y. Hence, we would predict quarterly sales of $\hat{y} = 60 + 5(10) = 110$ or \$110,000 for this one restaurant.

Interval Estimation

Confidence intervals and prediction intervals show the precision of the regression results. Narrower intervals provide a higher degree of precision.

Point estimates do not provide any information about the precision associated with an estimate. For that we must develop interval estimates much like those in Chapters 8, 10, and 11. The first type of interval estimate, a **confidence interval**, is an interval estimate of the *mean value of y* for a given value of x. The second type of interval estimate, a **prediction interval**, is used whenever we want an interval estimate of an *individual value of y* for a given value of x. The point estimate of the mean value of y is the same as the point estimate of an individual value of y. But the interval estimates we obtain for the two cases are different. The margin of error is larger for a prediction interval.

Confidence Interval for the Mean Value of y

The estimated regression equation provides a point estimate of the mean value of y for a given value of x. In developing the confidence interval, we will use the following notation.

$$x_p = \text{the particular or given value of the independent variable } x$$

$$y_p = \text{the value of the dependent variable } y \text{ corresponding to the given } x_p$$

$$E(y_p) = \text{the mean or expected value of the dependent variable } y$$
$$\text{corresponding to the given } x_p$$

$$\hat{y}_p = b_0 + b_1 x_p = \text{the point estimate of } E(y_p) \text{ when } x = x_p$$

Using this notation to estimate the mean sales for all Armand's restaurants located near a campus with 10,000 students, we have $x_p = 10$, and $E(y_p)$ denotes the unknown mean value of sales for all restaurants where $x_p = 10$. The point estimate of $E(y_p)$ is provided by $\hat{y}_p = 60 + 5(10) = 110$.

In general, we cannot expect $\hat{y}_p$ to equal $E(y_p)$ exactly. If we want to make an inference about how close $\hat{y}_p$ is to the true mean value $E(y_p)$, we will have to estimate the variance of $\hat{y}_p$. The formula for estimating the variance of $\hat{y}_p$ given x_p, denoted by $s^2_{\hat{y}_p}$, is

$$s^2_{\hat{y}_p} = s^2 \left[\frac{1}{n} + \frac{(x_p - \bar{x})^2}{\Sigma(x_i - \bar{x})^2} \right] \tag{12.22}$$

The estimate of the standard deviation of $\hat{y}_p$ is given by the square root of equation (12.22).

$$s_{\hat{y}_p} = s \sqrt{\frac{1}{n} + \frac{(x_p - \bar{x})^2}{\Sigma(x_i - \bar{x})^2}} \tag{12.23}$$

The computational results for Armand's Pizza Parlors in Section 12.5 provided $s = 13.829$. With $x_p = 10$, $\bar{x} = 14$, and $\Sigma(x_i - \bar{x})^2 = 568$, we can use equation (12.23) to obtain

$$s_{\hat{y}_p} = 13.829 \sqrt{\frac{1}{10} + \frac{(10 - 14)^2}{568}}$$

$$= 13.829 \sqrt{.1282} = 4.95$$

The general expression for a confidence interval follows.

The margin of error associated with this internal estimate is $t_{\alpha/2}s_{\hat{y}_p}$.

> **CONFIDENCE INTERVAL FOR $E(y_p)$**
>
> $$\hat{y}_p \pm t_{\alpha/2}s_{\hat{y}_p} \tag{12.24}$$
>
> where the confidence coefficient is $1 - \alpha$ and $t_{\alpha/2}$ is based on a t distribution with $n - 2$ degrees of freedom.

Using expression (12.24) to develop a 95% confidence interval of the mean quarterly sales for all Armand's restaurants located near campuses with 10,000 students, we need the value of t for $\alpha/2 = .025$ and $n - 2 = 10 - 2 = 8$ degrees of freedom. Using Table 2 of Appendix B, we have $t_{.025} = 2.306$. Thus, with $\hat{y}_p = 110$ and a margin of error of $t_{\alpha/2}s_{\hat{y}_p} = 2.306(4.95) = 11.415$, the 95% confidence interval estimate is

$$110 \pm 11.415$$

In dollars, the 95% confidence interval for the mean quarterly sales of all restaurants near campuses with 10,000 students is $\$110,000 \pm \$11,415$. Therefore, the 95% confidence interval for the mean quarterly sales when the student population is 10,000 is $\$98,585$ to $\$121,415$.

Note that the estimated standard deviation of $\hat{y}_p$ given by equation (12.23) is smallest when $x_p = \bar{x}$ and the quantity $x_p - \bar{x} = 0$. In this case, the estimated standard deviation of $\hat{y}_p$ becomes

$$s_{\hat{y}_p} = s\sqrt{\frac{1}{n} + \frac{(\bar{x} - \bar{x})^2}{\Sigma(x_i - \bar{x})^2}} = s\sqrt{\frac{1}{n}}$$

This result implies that we can make the best or most precise estimate of the mean value of y whenever $x_p = \bar{x}$. In fact, the further x_p is from $\bar{x}$ the larger $x_p - \bar{x}$ becomes. As a result, confidence intervals for the mean value of y will become wider as x_p deviates more from $\bar{x}$. This pattern is shown graphically in Figure 12.12.

Prediction Interval for an Individual Value of y

Suppose that instead of estimating the mean value of sales for all Armand's restaurants located near campuses with 10,000 students, we want to estimate the sales for an individual restaurant located near Talbot College, a school with 10,000 students. As noted previously, the point estimate of y_p, the value of y corresponding to the given x_p, is provided by the estimated regression equation $\hat{y}_p = b_0 + b_1x_p$. For the restaurant at Talbot College, we have $x_p = 10$ and a corresponding predicted quarterly sales of $\hat{y}_p = 60 + 5(10) = 110$, or $\$110,000$. Note that this value is the same as the point estimate of the mean sales for all restaurants located near campuses with 10,000 students.

To develop a prediction interval, we must first determine the variance associated with using $\hat{y}_p$ as an estimate of an individual value of y when $x = x_p$. This variance is made up of the sum of the following two components.

1. The variance of individual y values about the mean $E(y_p)$, an estimate of which is given by s^2
2. The variance associated with using $\hat{y}_p$ to estimate $E(y_p)$, an estimate of which is given by $s_{\hat{y}_p}^2$

FIGURE 12.12 CONFIDENCE INTERVALS FOR THE MEAN SALES *y* AT GIVEN VALUES OF STUDENT POPULATION *x*

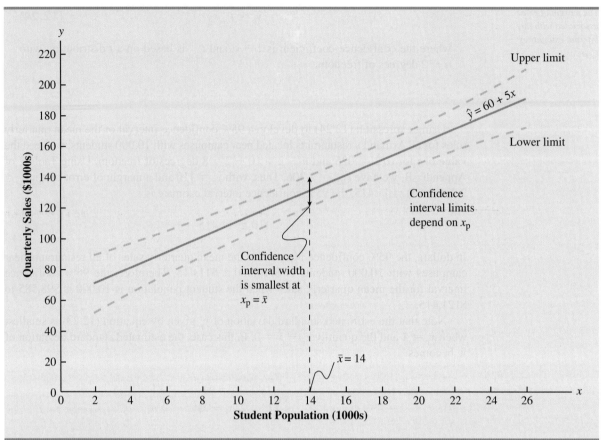

The formula for estimating the variance of an individual value of y_p, denoted by s_{ind}^2, is

$$s_{ind}^2 = s^2 + s_{\hat{y}_p}^2$$

$$= s^2 + s^2\left[\frac{1}{n} + \frac{(x_p - \bar{x})^2}{\Sigma(x_i - \bar{x})^2}\right]$$

$$= s^2\left[1 + \frac{1}{n} + \frac{(x_p - \bar{x})^2}{\Sigma(x_i - \bar{x})^2}\right] \quad \textbf{(12.25)}$$

Hence, an estimate of the standard deviation of an individual value of y_p is given by

$$s_{ind} = s\sqrt{1 + \frac{1}{n} + \frac{(x_p - \bar{x})^2}{\Sigma(x_i - \bar{x})^2}} \quad \textbf{(12.26)}$$

For Armand's Pizza Parlors, the estimated standard deviation corresponding to the prediction of sales for one specific restaurant located near a campus with 10,000 students is computed as follows.

$$s_{ind} = 13.829 \sqrt{1 + \frac{1}{10} + \frac{(10 - 14)^2}{568}}$$

$$= 13.829 \sqrt{1.1282}$$

$$= 14.69$$

The general expression for a prediction interval follows.

PREDICTION INTERVAL FOR y_p

The margin of error associated with this interval estimate is $t_{\alpha/2}s_{ind}$.

$$\hat{y}_p \pm t_{\alpha/2}s_{ind} \tag{12.27}$$

where the confidence coefficient is $1 - \alpha$ and $t_{\alpha/2}$ is based on a t distribution with $n - 2$ degrees of freedom.

The 95% prediction interval for quarterly sales at Armand's Talbot College restaurant can be found by using $t_{.025} = 2.306$ and $s_{ind} = 14.69$. Thus, with $\hat{y}_p = 110$ and a margin of error of $t_{\alpha/2}s_{ind} = 2.306(14.69) = 33.875$, the 95% prediction interval is

$$110 \pm 33.875$$

In dollars, this prediction interval is $110,000 \pm $33,875 or $76,125 to $143,875. Note that the prediction interval for an individual restaurant located near a campus with 10,000 students is wider than the confidence interval for the mean sales of all restaurants located near campuses with 10,000 students. The difference reflects the fact that we are able to estimate the mean value of y more precisely than we can an individual value of y.

In general, the lines for the confidence interval limits and the prediction interval limits both have curvature.

Both confidence interval estimates and prediction interval estimates are most precise when the value of the independent variable is $x_p = \bar{x}$. The general shapes of confidence intervals and the wider prediction intervals are shown together in Figure 12.13.

Using Excel to Develop Confidence and Prediction Interval Estimates

Excel's Regression tool does not have an option for computing confidence and prediction intervals. But, for simple linear regression, formulas can be designed to compute these intervals using equations (12.24) and (12.27) along with the output provided by the Regression tool. The general expression for a confidence or prediction interval is point estimate $\pm$ margin of error. Thus, we must develop formulas for computing a point estimate and the margin of error.

We begin by showing how to develop a 95% confidence interval estimate of the mean quarterly sales for all Armand's restaurants located near a campus with 10,000 students. In Section 12.6, we showed how Excel's Regression tool could be applied to the Armand's problem. The output provided by the Regression tool is shown again in cells A13:I30 of Figure 12.14. Now refer to cells E1:F13 of that figure as we describe the tasks involved in developing a confidence interval. The formula worksheet is in the background; the value worksheet appears in the foreground.

Enter Data: The data (cells B2:C11) and regression output (cells A13:I30) that were initially developed in Figure 12.10 are used as a starting point here.

Enter Functions and Formulas: Because we want to develop a 95% confidence interval estimate of the mean quarterly sales for restaurants near campuses with 10,000 students, $x_p = 10$ and we enter a value of 10 into cell F2. Excel's AVERAGE function is used to compute $\bar{x}$ in cell F3, the formula =F2-F3 is entered into cell F4 to compute the value of $x_p - \bar{x}$, and the formula

FIGURE 12.13 CONFIDENCE AND PREDICTION INTERVALS FOR SALES y AT GIVEN VALUES OF STUDENT POPULATION x

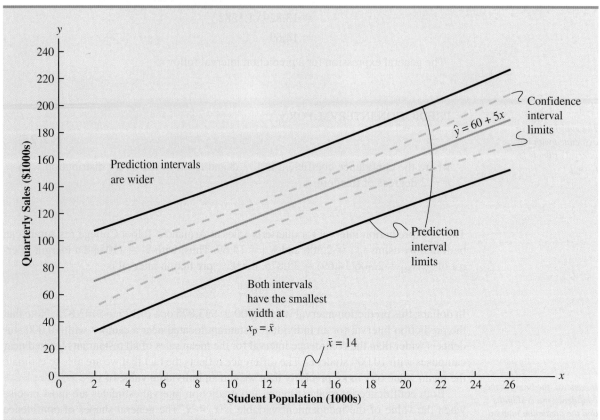

=F4^2 is entered into cell F5 to compute the value of $(x_p - \bar{x})^2$. Excel's DEVSQ function can be used to compute $\Sigma(x_i - \bar{x})^2$ by entering the following formula into cell F6:

$$=\text{DEVSQ(B2:B11)}$$

To identify this sum of squares we entered the label "Sum of (x-xbar)sq" into cell E6.

We can now compute $s_{\hat{y}_p}^2$ using equation (12.22) by entering the formula =D25* (1/B20+F5/F6) into cell F7. We then enter the formula =SQRT(F7) into cell F8 to compute $s_{\hat{y}_p}$, the estimate of the standard deviation of $\hat{y}_p$. To compute the t value required by equation (12.24), we entered the formula =TINV(0.05,8) into cell F9. Finally, the margin of error $t_{\alpha/2}s_{\hat{y}_p}$ is computed by entering the formula =F9*F8 into cell F10. To compute $\hat{y}_p$, the point estimate of $E(y_p)$, we entered the formula =B29+B30*F2 into cell F11. The lower and upper limits of the 95% confidence interval are then computed by entering the formulas =F11-F10 and =F11+F10 into cells F12 and F13, respectively.

The value worksheet shows that the 95% confidence interval estimate is 98.583 to 121.417. In dollars, the 95% confidence interval for the mean quarterly sales of restaurants located near campuses with 10,000 students is $98,583 to $121,417. To develop confidence intervals for other values of x_p we simply use this worksheet as a template and enter another value for student population in cell F2. The new confidence interval will appear in cells F12 and F13. If a confidence interval for another value of α is desired, we can just insert the new value of α for the first argument of the TINV function in cell F9.

The confidence interval formulas developed here cannot be applied directly as a template for other regression problems because the number of observations will likely be

FIGURE 12.14 USING EXCEL TO COMPUTE CONFIDENCE AND PREDICTION INTERVALS

	A	B	C	D	E	F	G	H	I	J
1	Restaurant	Population	Sales		Confidence Interval					
2	1	2	58		Given value of x	10				
3	2	6	105		xbar	=AVERAGE(B2:B11)				
4	3	8	88		x-xbar	=F2-F3				
5	4	8	118		(x-xbar)sq	=F4^2				
6	5	12	117		Sum of (x-xbar)sq	=DEVSQ(B2:B11)				
7	6	16	137		Var of yhat	=D25*(1/B20+F5/F6)				
8	7	20	157		Stdev of yhat	=SQRT(F7)				
9	8	20	169		t value	=TINV(0.05,8)				
10	9	22	149		Margin of Error	=F9*F8				
11	10	26	202		Point Estimate	=B29+B30*F2				
12					Lower Limit	=F11-F10				
13	SUMMARY OUTPUT				Upper Limit	=F11+F10				
14										
15	*Regression Statistics*				Prediction Interval					
16	Multiple R	0.95012295520			Var of yind	=D25+F7				
17	R Square	0.90273363000			Stdev of yind	=SQRT(F16)				
18	Adjusted R Square	0.89057533375			Margin of Error	=F9*F17				
19	Standard Error	13.8293166859			Lower Limit	=F11-F18				
20	Observations	10			Upper Limit	=F11+F18				
21										
22	ANOVA									
23		*df*								
24	Regression	1								
25	Residual	8								
26	Total	9								
27										
28		*Coefficients*								
29	Intercept	60								
30	Population	5								
31										

	A	B	C	D	E	F	G	H	I	J
1	Restaurant	Population	Sales		Confidence Interval					
2	1	2	58		Given value of x	10				
3	2	6	105		xbar	14				
4	3	8	88		x-xbar	-4				
5	4	8	118		(x-xbar)sq	16				
6	5	12	117		Sum of (x-xbar)sq	568				
7	6	16	137		Var of yhat	24.5123				
8	7	20	157		Stdev of yhat	4.9510				
9	8	20	169		t value	2.3060				
10	9	22	149		Margin of Error	11.4170				
11	10	26	202		Point Estimate	110				
12					Lower Limit	98.5830				
13	SUMMARY OUTPUT				Upper Limit	121.4170				
14										
15	*Regression Statistics*				Prediction Interval					
16	Multiple R	0.9501			Var of yind	215.7623				
17	R Square	0.9027			Stdev of yind	14.6889				
18	Adjusted R Square	0.8906			Margin of Error	33.8725				
19	Standard Error	13.8293			Lower Limit	76.1275				
20	Observations	10			Upper Limit	143.8725				
21										
22	ANOVA									
23		*df*	*SS*	*MS*	*F*	*Significance F*				
24	Regression	1	14200	14200	74.2484	2.55E-05				
25	Residual	8	1530	191.25						
26	Total	9	15730							
27										
28		*Coefficients*	*Standard Error*	*t Stat*	*P-value*	*Lower 95%*	*Upper 95%*	*Lower 99.0%*	*Upper 99.0%*	
29	Intercept	60	9.2260	6.5033	0.0002	38.7247	81.2753	29.0431	90.9569	
30	Population	5	0.5803	8.6167	2.55E-05	3.6619	6.3381	3.0530	6.9470	
31										

different and the location of the regression output will not be in the same worksheet cells. The same cells (E1:F13) can be used to develop the confidence interval, but the cell references used in cells F3, F6, F7, and F11 will need to be modified to reflect the location of the data and the regression output. The level of significance and the degrees of freedom used for TINV in cell F9 may also need to be changed.

The design of formulas to compute a prediction interval utilizes some of the same information used to develop a confidence interval. However, equation (12.27) shows that s_{ind}, instead of $s_{\hat{y}_p}$, is used in computing the margin of error. Refer to cells E15:F20 of the worksheet in Figure 12.14 as we describe the tasks involved in computing a 95% prediction interval.

Enter Functions and Formulas: To compute $s_{ind}^2 = s^2 + s_{\hat{y}_p}^2$ we entered the formula =D25+F7 into cell F16. Then, in cell F17 we entered the formula =SQRT(F16) to compute s_{ind}. The labels "Var of yind" and "Stdev of yind" were entered into cells E16 and E17 to identify these values. To compute the margin of error the formula =F9*F17 was entered into cell F18. The formulas =F11-F18 and =F11+F18 were entered into cells F19 and F20, respectively, to compute the lower and upper limits.

The 95% prediction interval is 76.127 to 143.873. In dollars, the 95% prediction interval is $76,127 to $143,873. To develop prediction intervals for other values of x_p we simply enter another value for student population in cell F2 and the new prediction interval will appear in cells F19 and F20. If a prediction interval for another value of α is desired, we can just insert the new value of α for the first argument of the TINV function in cell F9.

NOTES AND COMMENTS

In the chapter appendix we show how to use StatTools to develop prediction interval estimates for the Armand's Pizza Parlors data.

Exercises

Methods

37. The data from exercise 1 follow.

x_i	1	2	3	4	5
y_i	3	7	5	11	14

    a. Use equation (12.23) to estimate the standard deviation of $\hat{y}_p$ when $x = 4$.
    b. Use expression (12.24) to develop a 95% confidence interval for the expected value of y when $x = 4$.
    c. Use equation (12.26) to estimate the standard deviation of an individual value of y when $x = 4$.
    d. Use expression (12.27) to develop a 95% prediction interval for y when $x = 4$.

38. The data from exercise 2 follow.

x_i	3	12	6	20	14
y_i	55	40	55	10	15

    a. Estimate the standard deviation of $\hat{y}_p$ when $x = 8$.
    b. Develop a 95% confidence interval for the expected value of y when $x = 8$.
    c. Estimate the standard deviation of an individual value of y when $x = 8$.
    d. Develop a 95% prediction interval for y when $x = 8$.

39. The data from exercise 3 follow.

x_i	2	6	9	13	20
y_i	7	18	9	26	23

    Develop the 95% confidence and prediction intervals when $x = 12$. Explain why these two intervals are different.

Applications

40. In exercise 18, the data on grade point average x and monthly salary y provided the estimated regression equation $\hat{y} = 1790.5 + 581.1x$.
    a. Develop a 95% confidence interval for the mean starting salary for all students with a 3.0 GPA.
    b. Develop a 95% prediction interval for the starting salary for Joe Heller, a student with a GPA of 3.0.

41. In exercise 10, data on $x =$ temperature rating (F°) and $y =$ price ($) for 11 sleeping bags manufactured by Bergans of Norway provided the estimated regression equation $\hat{y} = 359.2668 - 5.2772x$. For these data $s = 37.9372$.

a.   Develop a point estimate of the price for a sleeping bag with a temperature rating of 30.
b.   Develop a 95% confidence interval for the mean overall temperature rating for all sleeping bags with a temperature rating of 30.
c.   Suppose that Bergans developed a new model with a temperature rating of 30. Develop a 95% prediction interval for the price of this new model.
d.   Discuss the differences in your answers to parts (b) and (c).

42.   In exercise 13, data were given on the adjusted gross income x and the amount of itemized deductions taken by taxpayers. Data were reported in thousands of dollars. With the estimated regression equation $\hat{y} = 4.68 + .16x$, the point estimate of a reasonable level of total itemized deductions for a taxpayer with an adjusted gross income of $52,500 is $13,080.
a.   Develop a 95% confidence interval for the mean amount of total itemized deductions for all taxpayers with an adjusted gross income of $52,500.
b.   Develop a 95% prediction interval estimate for the amount of total itemized deductions for a particular taxpayer with an adjusted gross income of $52,500.
c.   If the particular taxpayer referred to in part (b) claimed total itemized deductions of $20,400, would the IRS agent's request for an audit appear to be justified?
d.   Use your answer to part (b) to give the IRS agent a guideline as to the amount of total itemized deductions a taxpayer with an adjusted gross income of $52,500 should claim before an audit is recommended.

43.   Refer to exercise 21, where data on the production volume x and total cost y for a particular manufacturing operation were used to develop the estimated regression equation $\hat{y} = 1246.67 + 7.6x$.
a.   The company's production schedule shows that 500 units must be produced next month. What is the point estimate of the total cost for next month?
b.   Develop a 99% prediction interval for the total cost for next month.
c.   If an accounting cost report at the end of next month shows that the actual production cost during the month was $6000, should managers be concerned about incurring such a high total cost for the month? Discuss.

44.   Almost all U.S. light-rail systems use electric cars that run on tracks built at street level. The Federal Transit Administration claims light-rail is one of the safest modes of travel, with an accident rate of .99 accidents per million passenger miles as compared to 2.29 for buses. The following data show the miles of track and the weekday ridership in thousands of passengers for six light-rail systems (*USA Today,* January 7, 2003).

City	Miles of Track	Ridership (1000s)
Cleveland	15	15
Denver	17	35
Portland	38	81
Sacramento	21	31
San Diego	47	75
San Jose	31	30
St. Louis	34	42

a.   Use these data to develop an estimated regression equation that could be used to predict the ridership given the miles of track.
b.   Did the estimated regression equation provide a good fit? Explain.
c.   Develop a 95% confidence interval for the mean weekday ridership for all light-rail systems with 30 miles of track.
d.   Suppose that Charlotte is considering construction of a light-rail system with 30 miles of track. Develop a 95% prediction interval for the weekday ridership for the Charlotte system. Do you think that the prediction interval you developed would be of value to Charlotte planners in anticipating the number of weekday riders for their new light-rail system? Explain.

12.8 Residual Analysis: Validating Model Assumptions

Residual analysis is the primary tool for determining whether the assumed regression model is appropriate.

As we noted previously, the *residual* for observation i is the difference between the observed value of the dependent variable (y_i) and the estimated value of the dependent variable ($\hat{y}_i$).

RESIDUAL FOR OBSERVATION i

$$y_i - \hat{y}_i \qquad (12.28)$$

where

y_i is the observed value of the dependent variable

$\hat{y}_i$ is the estimated value of the dependent variable

In other words, the ith residual is the error resulting from using the estimated regression equation to predict the value of the dependent variable. The residuals for the Armand's Pizza Parlors example are computed in Table 12.7. The observed values of the dependent variable are in the second column and the estimated values of the dependent variable, obtained using the estimated regression equation $\hat{y} = 60 + 5x$, are in the third column. An analysis of the corresponding residuals in the fourth column will help determine whether the assumptions made about the regression model are appropriate.

Let us now review the regression assumptions for the Armand's Pizza Parlors example. A simple linear regression model was assumed.

$$y = \beta_0 + \beta_1 x + \epsilon \qquad (12.29)$$

This model indicates that we assumed quarterly sales (y) to be a linear function of the size of the student population (x) plus an error term ϵ. In Section 12.4 we made the following assumptions about the error term ϵ.

1. $E(\epsilon) = 0$.
2. The variance of ϵ, denoted by σ^2, is the same for all values of x.
3. The values of ϵ are independent.
4. The error term ϵ has a normal distribution.

TABLE 12.7   RESIDUALS FOR ARMAND'S PIZZA PARLORS

Student Population x_i	Sales y_i	Estimated Sales $\hat{y}_i = 60 + 5x_i$	Residuals $y_i - \hat{y}_i$
2	58	70	−12
6	105	90	15
8	88	100	−12
8	118	100	18
12	117	120	−3
16	137	140	−3
20	157	160	−3
20	169	160	9
22	149	170	−21
26	202	190	12

These assumptions provide the theoretical basis for the *t* test and the *F* test used to determine whether the relationship between *x* and *y* is significant, and for the confidence and prediction interval estimates presented in Section 12.6. If the assumptions about the error term ϵ appear questionable, the hypothesis tests about the significance of the regression relationship and the interval estimation results may not be valid.

The residuals provide the best information about ϵ; hence an analysis of the residuals is an important step in determining whether the assumptions for ϵ are appropriate. Much of residual analysis is based on an examination of graphical plots. In this section, we discuss the following residual plots: a plot of the residuals against values of the independent variable *x*, and a plot of residuals against the predicted values of the dependent variable $\hat{y}$.

Residual Plot Against *x*

A **residual plot** against the independent variable *x* is a graph in which the values of the independent variable are represented by the horizontal axis and the corresponding residual values are represented by the vertical axis. A point is plotted for each residual. The first coordinate for each point is given by the value of x_i and the second coordinate is given by the corresponding value of the residual $y_i - \hat{y}_i$. For a residual plot against *x* with the Armand's Pizza Parlors data from Table 12.7, the coordinates of the first point are $(2, -12)$, corresponding to $x_1 = 2$ and $y_1 - \hat{y}_1 = -12$; the coordinates of the second point are $(6, 15)$, corresponding to $x_2 = 6$ and $y_2 - \hat{y}_2 = 15$; and so on. Figure 12.15 shows the resulting residual plot.

Before interpreting the results for this residual plot, let us consider some general patterns that might be observed in any residual plot. Three examples appear in Figure 12.16. If the assumption that the variance of ϵ is the same for all values of *x* and the assumed regression model is an adequate representation of the relationship between the variables, the residual plot should give an overall impression of a horizontal band of points such as the one in Panel A of Figure 12.16. However, if the variance of ϵ is not the same for all values

FIGURE 12.15   PLOT OF THE RESIDUALS AGAINST THE INDEPENDENT VARIABLE *x* FOR ARMAND'S PIZZA PARLORS

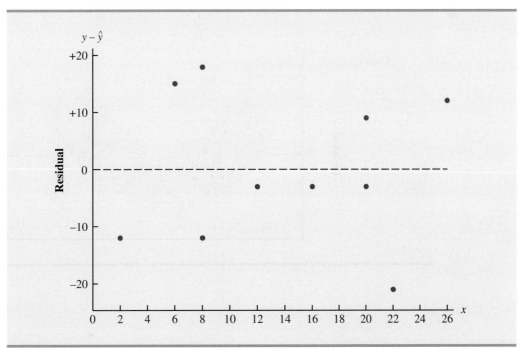

FIGURE 12.16   RESIDUAL PLOTS FROM THREE REGRESSION STUDIES

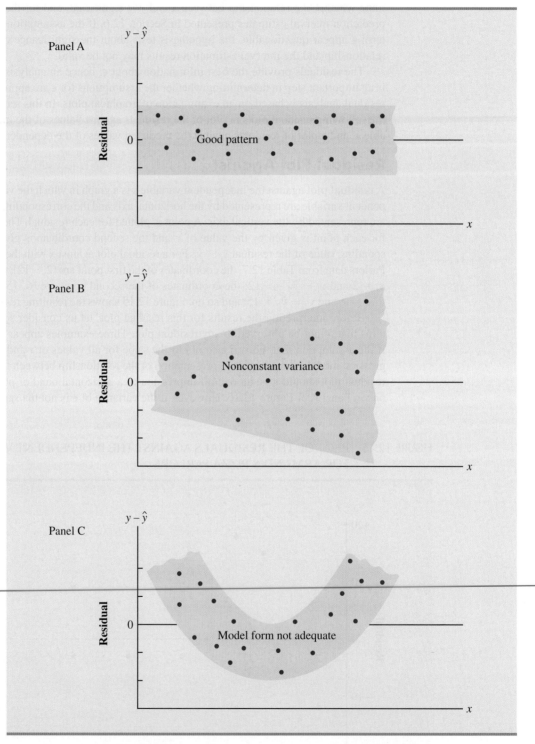

of x—for example, if variability about the regression line is greater for larger values of x— a pattern such as the one in Panel B of Figure 12.16 could be observed. In this case, the assumption of a constant variance of ϵ is violated. Another possible residual plot is shown in Panel C. In this case, we would conclude that the assumed regression model is not an adequate representation of the relationship between the variables. A curvilinear regression model or multiple regression model should be considered.

Now let us return to the residual plot for Armand's Pizza Parlors shown in Figure 12.15. The residuals appear to approximate the horizontal pattern in Panel A of Figure 12.16. Hence, we conclude that the residual plot does not provide evidence that the assumptions made for Armand's regression model should be challenged. At this point, we are confident in the conclusion that Armand's simple linear regression model is valid.

Experience and good judgment are always factors in the effective interpretation of residual plots. Seldom does a residual plot conform precisely to one of the patterns in Figure 12.16. Yet analysts who frequently conduct regression studies and frequently review residual plots become adept at understanding the differences between patterns that are reasonable and patterns that indicate the assumptions of the model should be questioned. A residual plot provides one technique to assess the validity of the assumptions for a regression model.

Residual Plot Against $\hat{y}$

Another residual plot represents the predicted value of the dependent variable $\hat{y}$ on the horizontal axis and the residual values on the vertical axis. A point is plotted for each residual. The first coordinate for each point is given by $\hat{y}_i$ and the second coordinate is given by the corresponding value of the ith residual $y_i - \hat{y}_i$. With the Armand's data from Table 12.7, the coordinates of the first point are $(70, -12)$, corresponding to $\hat{y}_1 = 70$ and $y_1 - \hat{y}_1 = -12$;

FIGURE 12.17   PLOT OF THE RESIDUALS AGAINST THE PREDICTED VALUES $\hat{y}$ FOR ARMAND'S PIZZA PARLORS

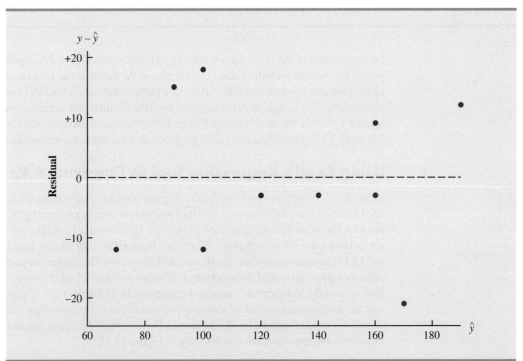

FIGURE 12.18   EXCEL RESIDUAL OUTPUT FOR THE ARMAND'S PIZZA PARLORS PROBLEM

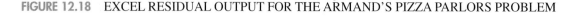

	A	B	C	D	E	F	G	H	I	J
1	Restaurant	Population	Sales							
2	1	2	58							
3	2	6	105							
4	3	8	88							
5	4	8	118							
6	5	12	117							
7	6	16	137							
8	7	20	157							
9	8	20	169							
10	9	22	149							
11	10	26	202							
33										
34	RESIDUAL OUTPUT									
35										
36	*Observation*	*Predicted Sales*	*Residuals*							
37	1	70	-12							
38	2	90	15							
39	3	100	-12							
40	4	100	18							
41	5	120	-3							
42	6	140	-3							
43	7	160	-3							
44	8	160	9							
45	9	170	-21							
46	10	190	12							
47										

Note: Rows 12–32 are hidden.

the coordinates of the second point are (90, 15); and so on. Figure 12.17 provides the residual plot. Note that the pattern of this residual plot is the same as the pattern of the residual plot against the independent variable x. It is not a pattern that would lead us to question the model assumptions. For simple linear regression, both the residual plot against x and the residual plot against $\hat{y}$ provide the same pattern. For multiple regression analysis, the residual plot against $\hat{y}$ is more widely used because of the presence of more than one independent variable.

Using Excel's Regression Tool to Construct a Residual Plot

In Section 12.6 we showed how Excel's Regression tool could be used for regression analysis. The Regression tool also provides the capability to obtain a residual plot. To obtain a residual plot, the steps that we described in Section 12.6 in order to obtain the regression output are performed with one change. When the Regression tool dialog box appears (see Figure 12.11) we must also select the Residual Plots option. The regression output will appear as described previously, and the worksheet will also contain a chart showing a plot of the residuals against the independent variable Population. In addition, a list of predicted values of y and the corresponding residual values is provided below the regression output. Figure 12.18 shows the residual output for the Armand's Pizza Parlors problem. We see that the shape of this plot is the same as shown previously in Figure 12.15.

NOTES AND COMMENTS

1. We use residual plots to validate the assumptions of a regression model. If our review indicates that one or more assumptions are questionable, a different regression model or a transformation of the data should be considered. The appropriate corrective action when the assumptions are violated must be based on good judgment; recommendations from an experienced statistician can be valuable.

2. Analysis of residuals is the primary method statisticians use to verify that the assumptions

associated with a regression model are valid. Even if no violations are found, it does not necessarily follow that the model will yield good predictions. However, if additional statistical tests support the conclusion of significance and the coefficient of determination is large, we should be able to develop good estimates and predictions using the estimated regression equation.

Exercises

Methods

45. Given are data for two variables, x and y.

x_i	6	11	15	18	20
y_i	6	8	12	20	30

a. Develop an estimated regression equation for these data.
b. Compute the residuals.
c. Develop a plot of the residuals against the independent variable x. Do the assumptions about the error terms seem to be satisfied?

46. The following data were used in a regression study.

Observation	x_i	y_i	Observation	x_i	y_i
1	2	4	6	7	6
2	3	5	7	7	9
3	4	4	8	8	5
4	5	6	9	9	11
5	7	4			

a. Develop an estimated regression equation for these data.
b. Construct a plot of the residuals. Do the assumptions about the error term seem to be satisfied?

Applications

47. Data on advertising expenditures and revenue (in thousands of dollars) for the Four Seasons Restaurant follow.

Advertising Expenditures	Revenue
1	19
2	32
4	44
6	40
10	52
14	53
20	54

a. Let x equal advertising expenditures and y equal revenue. Use the method of least squares to develop a straight line approximation of the relationship between the two variables.

b. Test whether revenue and advertising expenditures are related at a .05 level of significance.

c. Prepare a residual plot of $y - \hat{y}$ versus $\hat{y}$. Use the result from part (a) to obtain the values of $\hat{y}$.

d. What conclusions can you draw from residual analysis? Should this model be used, or should we look for a better one?

48. Refer to exercise 9, where an estimated regression equation relating years of experience and annual sales was developed.

a. Compute the residuals and construct a residual plot for this problem.

b. Do the assumptions about the error terms seem reasonable in light of the residual plot?

49. American Depository Receipts (ADRs) are certificates traded on the NYSE representing shares of a foreign company held on deposit in a bank in its home country. The following table shows the price/earnings (P/E) ratio and the percentage return on equity (ROE) for 10 Indian companies that are likely new ADRs (*Bloomberg Personal Finance,* April 2000).

	ROE	P/E
Bharti Televentures	6.43	36.88
Gujarat Ambuja Cements	13.49	27.03
Hindalco Industries	14.04	10.83
ICICI	20.67	5.15
Mahanagar Telephone Nigam	22.74	13.35
NIIT	46.23	95.59
Pentamedia Graphics	28.90	54.85
Satyam Computer Services	54.01	189.21
Silverline Technologies	28.02	75.86
Videsh Sanchar Nigam	27.04	13.17

WEB file

ADRs

a. Use Excel to develop an estimated regression equation relating y = P/E and x = ROE.

b. Construct a residual plot against the independent variable.

c. Do the assumptions about the error terms and model form seem reasonable in light of the residual plot?

Summary

In this chapter we showed how regression analysis can be used to determine how a dependent variable y is related to an independent variable x. In simple linear regression, the regression model is $y = \beta_0 + \beta_1 x + \epsilon$. The simple linear regression equation $E(y) = \beta_0 + \beta_1 x$ describes how the mean or expected value of y is related to x. We used sample data and the least squares method to develop the estimated regression equation $\hat{y} = b_0 + b_1 x$. In effect, b_0 and b_1 are the sample statistics used to estimate the unknown model parameters β_0 and β_1.

The coefficient of determination was presented as a measure of the goodness of fit for the estimated regression equation; it can be interpreted as the proportion of the variation in the dependent variable y that can be explained by the estimated regression equation. We reviewed correlation as a descriptive measure of the strength of a linear relationship between two variables.

The assumptions about the regression model and its associated error term ϵ were discussed, and t and F tests, based on those assumptions, were presented as a means for determining whether the relationship between two variables is statistically significant. We showed how Excel's Regression tool can be used to develop the estimated regression equation. We then discussed how to use the estimated regression equation to develop confidence interval estimates of the mean value of y and prediction interval estimates of individual values of y. The chapter concluded with a section on the use of residual analysis to validate the model assumptions.

Glossary

Dependent variable The variable that is being predicted or explained. It is denoted by y.

Independent variable The variable that is doing the predicting or explaining. It is denoted by x.

Simple linear regression Regression analysis involving one independent variable and one dependent variable in which the relationship between the variables is approximated by a straight line.

Regression model The equation that describes how y is related to x and an error term; in simple linear regression, the regression model is $y = \beta_0 + \beta_1 x + \epsilon$.

Regression equation The equation that describes how the mean or expected value of the dependent variable is related to the independent variable; in simple linear regression, $E(y) = \beta_0 + \beta_1 x$.

Estimated regression equation The estimate of the regression equation developed from sample data by using the least squares method. For simple linear regression, the estimated regression equation is $\hat{y} = b_0 + b_1 x$.

Least squares method A procedure used to develop the estimated regression equation. The objective is to minimize $\Sigma(y_i - \hat{y}_i)^2$.

Scatter diagram A graph of bivariate data in which the independent variable is on the horizontal axis and the dependent variable is on the vertical axis.

Coefficient of determination A measure of the goodness of fit of the estimated regression equation. It can be interpreted as the proportion of the variability in the dependent variable y that is explained by the estimated regression equation.

ith residual The difference between the observed value of the dependent variable and the value predicted using the estimated regression equation; for the ith observation the ith residual is $y_i - \hat{y}_i$.

Correlation coefficient A measure of the strength of the linear relationship between two variables (previously discussed in Chapter 3).

Mean square error The unbiased estimate of the variance of the error term σ^2. It is denoted by MSE or s^2.

Standard error of the estimate The square root of the mean square error, denoted by s. It is the estimate of σ, the standard deviation of the error term ϵ.

ANOVA table The analysis of variance table used to summarize the computations associated with the F test for significance.

Confidence interval The interval estimate of the mean value of y for a given value of x.
Prediction interval The interval estimate of an individual value of y for a given value of x.
Residual analysis The analysis of the residuals used to determine whether the assumptions made about the regression model appear to be valid.
Residual plot Graphical representation of the residuals that can be used to determine whether the assumptions made about the regression model appear to be valid.

Key Formulas

Simple Linear Regression Model

$$y = \beta_0 + \beta_1 x + \epsilon \tag{12.1}$$

Simple Linear Regression Equation

$$E(y) = \beta_0 + \beta_1 x \tag{12.2}$$

Estimated Simple Linear Regression Equation

$$\hat{y} = b_0 + b_1 x \tag{12.3}$$

Least Squares Criterion

$$\min \Sigma(y_i - \hat{y}_i)^2 \tag{12.5}$$

Slope and y-Intercept for the Estimated Regression Equation

$$b_1 = \frac{\Sigma(x_i - \bar{x})(y_i - \bar{y})}{\Sigma(x_i - \bar{x})^2} \tag{12.6}$$

$$b_0 = \bar{y} - b_1\bar{x} \tag{12.7}$$

Sum of Squares Due to Error

$$SSE = \Sigma(y_i - \hat{y}_i)^2 \tag{12.8}$$

Total Sum of Squares

$$SST = \Sigma(y_i - \bar{y})^2 \tag{12.9}$$

Sum of Squares Due to Regression

$$SSR = \Sigma(\hat{y}_i - \bar{y})^2 \tag{12.10}$$

Relationship Among SST, SSR, and SSE

$$SST = SSR + SSE \tag{12.11}$$

Coefficient of Determination

$$r^2 = \frac{SSR}{SST} \tag{12.12}$$

Sample Correlation Coefficient

$$r_{xy} = (\text{sign of } b_1)\sqrt{\text{Coefficient of determination}}$$
$$= (\text{sign of } b_1)\sqrt{r^2} \tag{12.13}$$

Mean Square Error (Estimate of σ^2)

$$s^2 = \text{MSE} = \frac{\text{SSE}}{n-2} \qquad (12.15)$$

Standard Error of the Estimate

$$s = \sqrt{\text{MSE}} = \sqrt{\frac{\text{SSE}}{n-2}} \qquad (12.16)$$

Standard Deviation of b_1

$$\sigma_{b_1} = \frac{\sigma}{\sqrt{\Sigma(x_i - \bar{x})^2}} \qquad (12.17)$$

Estimated Standard Deviation of b_1

$$s_{b_1} = \frac{s}{\sqrt{\Sigma(x_i - \bar{x})^2}} \qquad (12.18)$$

t Test Statistic

$$t = \frac{b_1}{s_{b_1}} \qquad (12.19)$$

Mean Square Regression

$$\text{MSR} = \frac{\text{SSR}}{\text{Number of independent variables}} \qquad (12.20)$$

F Test Statistic

$$F = \frac{\text{MSR}}{\text{MSE}} \qquad (12.21)$$

Estimated Standard Deviation of $\hat{y}_p$

$$s_{\hat{y}_p} = s\sqrt{\frac{1}{n} + \frac{(x_p - \bar{x})^2}{\Sigma(x_i - \bar{x})^2}} \qquad (12.23)$$

Confidence Interval for $E(y_p)$

$$\hat{y}_p \pm t_{\alpha/2}s_{\hat{y}_p} \qquad (12.24)$$

Estimated Standard Deviation for an Individual Value of y

$$s_{\text{ind}} = s\sqrt{1 + \frac{1}{n} + \frac{(x_p - \bar{x})^2}{\Sigma(x_i - \bar{x})^2}} \qquad (12.26)$$

Prediction Interval for y_p

$$\hat{y}_p \pm t_{\alpha/2}s_{\text{ind}} \qquad (12.27)$$

Residual for Observation i

$$y_i - \hat{y}_i \qquad (12.28)$$

Supplementary Exercises

50. Does a high value of r^2 imply that two variables are causally related? Explain.

51. In your own words, explain the difference between an interval estimate of the mean value of y for a given x and an interval estimate for an individual value of y for a given x.

52. What is the purpose of testing whether $\beta_1 = 0$? If we reject $\beta_1 = 0$, does it imply a good fit?

53. The data in the following table show the number of shares selling (millions) and the expected price (average of projected low price and projected high price) for 10 selected initial public stock offerings.

WEB file

IPO

Company	Shares Selling	Expected Price ($)
American Physician	5.0	15
Apex Silver Mines	9.0	14
Dan River	6.7	15
Franchise Mortgage	8.75	17
Gene Logic	3.0	11
International Home Foods	13.6	19
PRT Group	4.6	13
Rayovac	6.7	14
RealNetworks	3.0	10
Software AG Systems	7.7	13

a. Develop an estimated regression equation with the number of shares selling as the independent variable and the expected price as the dependent variable.
b. At the .05 level of significance, is there a significant relationship between the two variables?
c. Did the estimated regression equation provide a good fit? Explain.
d. Use the estimated regression equation to estimate the expected price for a firm considering an initial public offering of 6 million shares.

54. The following data show Morningstar's Fair Value estimate and the Share Price for 28 companies. Fair Value is an estimate of a company's value per share that takes into account estimates of the company's growth, profitability, riskiness, and other factors over the next five years (*Morningstar Stocks 500*, 2008 edition).

WEB file

Stocks500

Company	Fair Value ($)	Share Price ($)
Air Products and Chemicals	80	98.63
Allied Waste Industries	17	11.02
America Mobile	83	61.39
AT&T	35	41.56
Bank of America	70	41.26
Barclays PLC	68	40.37
Citigroup	53	29.44
Costco Wholesale Corp.	75	69.76
Covidien, Ltd.	58	44.29
Darden Restaurants	52	27.71
Dun & Bradstreet	87	88.63
Equifax	42	36.36
Gannett Co.	38	39.00
Genuine Parts	48	46.30

Company	Fair Value ($)	Share Price ($)
GlaxoSmithKline PLC	57	50.39
Iron Mountain	33	37.02
ITT Corporation	83	66.04
Johnson & Johnson	80	66.70
Las Vegas Sands	98	103.05
Macrovision	23	18.33
Marriott International	39	34.18
Nalco Holding Company	29	24.18
National Interstate	25	33.10
Portugal Telecom	15	13.02
Qualcomm	48	39.35
Royal Dutch Shell Ltd.	87	84.20
SanDisk	60	33.17
Time Warner	42	27.60

a. Develop the estimated regression equation that could be used to estimate the Share Price given the Fair Value.

b. At the .05 level of significance, is there a significant relationship between the two variables?

c. Use the estimated regression equation to estimate the Share Price for a company that has a Fair Value of $50.

d. Do you believe the estimated regression equation would provide a good prediction of the share price? Use r^2 to support your answer.

55. The Dow Jones Industrial Average (DJIA) and the Standard & Poor's 500 (S&P) indexes are used as measures of overall movement in the stock market. The DJIA is based on the price movements of 30 large companies; the S&P 500 is an index composed of 500 stocks. Some say the S&P 500 is a better measure of stock market performance because it is broader based. The closing prices for the DJIA and the S&P 500 for 20 weeks, beginning with September 9, 2005, follow (*Barron's,* January 30, 2006).

WEB file

DJIAS&P500

Date	DJIA	S&P 500
September 9	10679	1241
September 16	10642	1238
September 23	10420	1215
September 30	10569	1229
October 7	10292	1196
October 14	10287	1187
October 21	10215	1180
October 28	10403	1198
November 4	10531	1220
November 11	10686	1235
November 18	10766	1248
November 25	10932	1268
December 2	10878	1265
December 9	10779	1259
December 16	10876	1267
December 23	10883	1269
December 30	10718	1248
January 6	10959	1285
January 13	10960	1288
January 20	10667	1261

a.   Develop a scatter diagram for these data with DJIA as the independent variable.
b.   Develop the estimated regression equation.
c.   Test for a significant relationship. Use $\alpha = .05$.
d.   Did the estimated regression equation provide a good fit? Explain.
e.   Suppose that the closing price for the DJIA is 11,000. Estimate the closing price for the S&P 500.
f.   Should we be concerned that the DJIA value of 11,000 used to predict the S&P 500 in part (e) is beyond the range of the data used to develop the estimated regression equation?

56. Jensen Tire & Auto is in the process of deciding whether to purchase a maintenance contract for its new computer wheel alignment and balancing machine. Managers feel that maintenance expense should be related to usage, and they collected the following information on weekly usage (hours) and annual maintenance expense (in hundreds of dollars).

WEB file

Jensen

Weekly Usage (hours)	Annual Maintenance Expense
13	17.0
10	22.0
20	30.0
28	37.0
32	47.0
17	30.5
24	32.5
31	39.0
40	51.5
38	40.0

a.   Develop the estimated regression equation that relates annual maintenance expense to weekly usage.
b.   Test the significance of the relationship in part (a) at a .05 level of significance.
c.   Jensen expects to use the new machine 30 hours per week. Develop a 95% prediction interval for the company's annual maintenance expense.
d.   If the maintenance contract costs $3000 per year, would you recommend purchasing it? Why or why not?

57. In a manufacturing process the assembly line speed (feet per minute) was thought to affect the number of defective parts found during the inspection process. To test this theory, managers devised a situation in which the same batch of parts was inspected visually at a variety of line speeds. They collected the following data.

Line Speed	Number of Defective Parts Found
20	21
20	19
40	15
30	16
60	14
40	17

a.   Develop the estimated regression equation that relates line speed to the number of defective parts found.

b. At a .05 level of significance, determine whether line speed and number of defective parts found are related.
c. Did the estimated regression equation provide a good fit to the data?
d. Develop a 95% confidence interval to predict the mean number of defective parts for a line speed of 50 feet per minute.

58. A sociologist was hired by a large city hospital to investigate the relationship between the number of unauthorized days that employees are absent per year and the distance (miles) between home and work for the employees. A sample of 10 employees was chosen, and the following data were collected.

Absent

Distance to Work	Number of Days Absent
1	8
3	5
4	8
6	7
8	6
10	3
12	5
14	2
14	4
18	2

a. Develop a scatter diagram for these data. Does a linear relationship appear reasonable? Explain.
b. Develop the least squares estimated regression equation.
c. Is there a significant relationship between the two variables? Use $\alpha = .05$.
d. Did the estimated regression equation provide a good fit? Explain.
e. Use the estimated regression equation developed in part (b) to develop a 95% confidence interval for the expected number of days absent for employees living 5 miles from the company.

59. The regional transit authority for a major metropolitan area wants to determine whether there is any relationship between the age of a bus and the annual maintenance cost. A sample of 10 buses resulted in the following data.

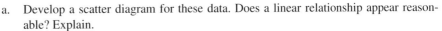

AgeCost

Age of Bus (years)	Maintenance Cost ($)
1	350
2	370
2	480
2	520
2	590
3	550
4	750
4	800
5	790
5	950

a. Develop the least squares estimated regression equation.
b. Test to see whether the two variables are significantly related with $\alpha = .05$.
c. Did the least squares line provide a good fit to the observed data? Explain.
d. Develop a 95% prediction interval for the maintenance cost for a specific bus that is 4 years old.

60. A marketing professor at Givens College is interested in the relationship between hours spent studying and total points earned in a course. Data collected on 10 students who took the course last quarter follow.

Hours Spent Studying	Total Points Earned
45	40
30	35
90	75
60	65
105	90
65	50
90	90
80	80
55	45
75	65

WEB file

HoursPts

a. Develop an estimated regression equation showing how total points earned is related to hours spent studying.
b. Test the significance of the model with $\alpha = .05$.
c. Predict the total points earned by Mark Sweeney. He spent 95 hours studying.
d. Develop a 95% prediction interval for the total points earned by Mark Sweeney.

61. *Bloomberg Personal Finance* (July/August 2001) reported the market beta for Texas Instruments was 1.46. Market betas for individual stocks are determined by simple linear regression. For each stock, the dependent variable is its quarterly percentage return (capital appreciation plus dividends) minus the percentage return that could be obtained from a risk-free investment (the Treasury Bill rate is used as the risk-free rate). The independent variable is the quarterly percentage return (capital appreciation plus dividends) for the stock market (S&P 500) minus the percentage return from a risk-free investment. An estimated regression equation is developed with quarterly data; the market beta for the stock is the slope of the estimated regression equation (b_1). The value of the market beta is often interpreted as a measure of the risk associated with the stock. Market betas greater than 1 indicate that the stock is more volatile than the market average; market betas less than 1 indicate that the stock is less volatile than the market average. Suppose that the following figures are the differences between the percentage return and the risk-free return for 10 quarters for the S&P 500 and Horizon Technology.

WEB file

MktBeta

S&P 500	Horizon
1.2	−0.7
−2.5	−2.0
−3.0	−5.5
2.0	4.7
5.0	1.8
1.2	4.1
3.0	2.6
−1.0	2.0
.5	−1.3
2.5	5.5

a. Develop an estimated regression equation that can be used to dete
beta for Horizon Technology. What is Horizon Technology's market b
b. Test for a significant relationship at the .05 level of significance.
c. Did the estimated regression equation provide a good fit? Explain.
d. Use the market betas of Texas Instruments and Horizon Technology to compa
risk associated with the two stocks.

62. The Transactional Records Access Clearinghouse at Syracuse University reported data
showing the odds of an Internal Revenue Service audit. The following table shows the
average adjusted gross income reported and the percent of the returns that were audited
for 20 selected IRS districts.

IRSAudit

District	Adjusted Gross Income ($)	Percent Audited
Los Angeles	36,664	1.3
Sacramento	38,845	1.1
Atlanta	34,886	1.1
Boise	32,512	1.1
Dallas	34,531	1.0
Providence	35,995	1.0
San Jose	37,799	0.9
Cheyenne	33,876	0.9
Fargo	30,513	0.9
New Orleans	30,174	0.9
Oklahoma City	30,060	0.8
Houston	37,153	0.8
Portland	34,918	0.7
Phoenix	33,291	0.7
Augusta	31,504	0.7
Albuquerque	29,199	0.6
Greensboro	33,072	0.6
Columbia	30,859	0.5
Nashville	32,566	0.5
Buffalo	34,296	0.5

a. Develop the estimated regression equation that could be used to predict the percent
audited given the average adjusted gross income reported.
b. At the .05 level of significance, determine whether the adjusted gross income and the
percent audited are related.
c. Did the estimated regression equation provide a good fit? Explain.
d. Use the estimated regression equation developed in part (a) to calculate a 95% confidence interval for the expected percent audited for districts with an average adjusted
gross income of $35,000.

63. The Australian Public Service Commission's State of the Service Report 2002–2003 reported job satisfaction ratings for employees. One of the survey questions asked employees to choose the five most important workplace factors (from a list of factors) that most
affected how satisfied they were with their job. Respondents were then asked to indicate
their level of satisfaction with their top five factors. The following data show the percentage of employees who nominated the factor in their top five, and a corresponding satisfaction rating measured using the percentage of employees who nominated the factor in
the top five and who were "very satisfied" or "satisfied" with the factor in their current
workplace (*http://www.apsc.gov.au/stateoftheservice*).

rkplace Factor	Top Five (%)	Satisfaction Rating (%)
›ropriate workload	30	49
nce to be creative/innovative	38	64
nce to make a useful contribution to society	40	67
es/expectations made clear	40	69
ible working arrangements	55	86
d working relationships	60	85
esting work provided	48	74
›rtunities for career development	33	43
∪pportunities to develop my skills	46	66
Opportunities to utilize my skills	50	70
Regular feedback/recognition for effort	42	53
Salary	47	62
Seeing tangible results from my work	42	69

a. Develop a scatter diagram with Top Five (%) on the horizontal axis and Satisfaction Rating (%) on the vertical axis.

b. What does the scatter diagram developed in part (a) indicate about the relationship between the two variables?

c. Develop the estimated regression equation that could be used to predict the Satisfaction Rating (%) given the Top Five (%).

d. Test for a significant relationship at the .05 level of significance.

e. Did the estimated regression equation provide a good fit? Explain.

f. What is the value of the sample correlation coefficient?

Case Problem 1   Measuring Stock Market Risk

One measure of the risk or volatility of an individual stock is the standard deviation of the total return (capital appreciation plus dividends) over several periods of time. Although the standard deviation is easy to compute, it does not take into account the extent to which the price of a given stock varies as a function of a standard market index, such as the S&P 500. As a result, many financial analysts prefer to use another measure of risk referred to as *beta*.

Betas for individual stocks are determined by simple linear regression. The dependent variable is the total return for the stock and the independent variable is the total return for the stock market.[2] For this case problem we will use the S&P 500 index as the measure of the total return for the stock market, and an estimated regression equation will be developed using monthly data. The beta for the stock is the slope of the estimated regression equation (b_1). The file named Beta provides the total return (capital appreciation plus dividends) over 36 months for eight widely traded common stocks and the S&P 500.

The value of beta for the stock market will always be 1; thus, stocks that tend to rise and fall with the stock market will also have a beta close to 1. Betas greater than 1 indicate that the stock is more volatile than the market, and betas less than 1 indicate that the stock is less volatile than the market. For instance, if a stock has a beta of 1.4, it is 40% *more* volatile than the market, and if a stock has a beta of .4, it is 60% *less* volatile than the market.

WEB file

Beta

---

[2]Various sources use different approaches for computing betas. For instance, some sources subtract the return that could be obtained from a risk-free investment (e.g., T-bills) from the dependent variable and the independent variable before computing the estimated regression equation. Some also use different indexes for the total return of the stock market; for instance, *Value Line* computes betas using the New York Stock Exchange composite index.

Managerial Report

You have been assigned to analyze the risk characteristics of these stocks. Prepare a report that includes but is not limited to the following items.

    a. Compute descriptive statistics for each stock and the S&P 500. Comment on your results. Which stocks are the most volatile?

    b. Compute the value of beta for each stock. Which of these stocks would you expect to perform best in an up market? Which would you expect to hold their value best in a down market?

    c. Comment on how much of the return for the individual stocks is explained by the market.

Case Problem 2   U.S. Department of Transportation

As part of a study on transportation safety, the U.S. Department of Transportation collected data on the number of fatal accidents per 1000 licenses and the percentage of licensed drivers under the age of 21 in a sample of 42 cities. Data collected over a one-year period follow. These data are available on the website that accompanies this text in the file named Safety.

Safety

Percent Under 21	Fatal Accidents per 1000 Licenses	Percent Under 21	Fatal Accidents per 1000 Licenses
13	2.962	17	4.100
12	0.708	8	2.190
8	0.885	16	3.623
12	1.652	15	2.623
11	2.091	9	0.835
17	2.627	8	0.820
18	3.830	14	2.890
8	0.368	8	1.267
13	1.142	15	3.224
8	0.645	10	1.014
9	1.028	10	0.493
16	2.801	14	1.443
12	1.405	18	3.614
9	1.433	10	1.926
10	0.039	14	1.643
9	0.338	16	2.943
11	1.849	12	1.913
12	2.246	15	2.814
14	2.855	13	2.634
14	2.352	9	0.926
11	1.294	17	3.256

Managerial Report

    1. Develop numerical and graphical summaries of the data.

    2. Use regression analysis to investigate the relationship between the number of fatal accidents and the percentage of drivers under the age of 21. Discuss your findings.

    3. What conclusion and recommendations can you derive from your analysis?

Case Problem 3   Alumni Giving

Alumni donations are an important source of revenue for colleges and universities. If administrators could determine the factors that influence increases in the percentage of alumni who make a donation, they might be able to implement policies that could lead to increased revenues. Research shows that students who are more satisfied with their contact with teachers are more likely to graduate. As a result, one might suspect that smaller class sizes and lower student-faculty ratios might lead to a higher percentage of satisfied graduates, which in turn might lead to increases in the percentage of alumni who make a donation. Table 12.8 shows data for 48 national universities (*America's Best Colleges,* Year 2000 Edition). The column labeled % of Classes Under 20 shows the percentage of classes offered with fewer than 20 students. The column labeled Student/Faculty Ratio is the number of students enrolled divided by the total number of faculty. Finally, the column labeled Alumni Giving Rate is the percentage of alumni that made a donation to the university.

Managerial Report

1. Develop numerical and graphical summaries of the data.
2. Use regression analysis to develop an estimated regression equation that could be used to predict the alumni giving rate given the percentage of classes with fewer than 20 students.
3. Use regression analysis to develop an estimated regression equation that could be used to predict the alumni giving rate given the student-faculty ratio.
4. Which of the two estimated regression equations provides the best fit? For this estimated regression equation, perform an analysis of the residuals and discuss your findings and conclusions.
5. What conclusions and recommendations can you derive from your analysis?

Case Problem 4   Major League Baseball Team Values

A group led by John Henry paid $700 million to purchase the Boston Red Sox in 2002, even though the Red Sox had not won the World Series since 1918 and posted an operating loss of $11.4 million for 2001. Moreover, *Forbes* magazine estimated that the current value of the team was actually $426 million. *Forbes* attributed the difference between the current value for a team and the price investors are willing to pay to the fact that the purchase of a team often includes the acquisition of a grossly undervalued cable network. For instance, in purchasing the Boston Red Sox, the new owners also got an 80% interest in the New England Sports Network. Table 12.9 shows data for the 30 major league teams (*Forbes,* April 15, 2002). The column labeled Value contains the values of the teams based on current stadium deals, without deduction for debt. The column labeled Income indicates the earnings before interest, taxes, and depreciation.

Managerial Report

1. Develop numerical and graphical summaries of the data.
2. Use regression analysis to investigate the relationship between value and income. Discuss your findings.
3. Use regression analysis to investigate the relationship between value and revenue. Discuss your findings.
4. What conclusions and recommendations can you derive from your analysis?

TABLE 12.8   DATA FOR 48 NATIONAL UNIVERSITIES

WEB file

Alumni

	% of Classes Under 20	Student/Faculty Ratio	Alumni Giving Rate
Boston College	39	13	25
Brandeis University	68	8	33
Brown University	60	8	40
California Institute of Technology	65	3	46
Carnegie Mellon University	67	10	28
Case Western Reserve Univ.	52	8	31
College of William and Mary	45	12	27
Columbia University	69	7	31
Cornell University	72	13	35
Dartmouth College	61	10	53
Duke University	68	8	45
Emory University	65	7	37
Georgetown University	54	10	29
Harvard University	73	8	46
Johns Hopkins University	64	9	27
Lehigh University	55	11	40
Massachusetts Inst. of Technology	65	6	44
New York University	63	13	13
Northwestern University	66	8	30
Pennsylvania State Univ.	32	19	21
Princeton University	68	5	67
Rice University	62	8	40
Stanford University	69	7	34
Tufts University	67	9	29
Tulane University	56	12	17
U. of California–Berkeley	58	17	18
U. of California–Davis	32	19	7
U. of California–Irvine	42	20	9
U. of California–Los Angeles	41	18	13
U. of California–San Diego	48	19	8
U. of California–Santa Barbara	45	20	12
U. of Chicago	65	4	36
U. of Florida	31	23	19
U. of Illinois–Urbana Champaign	29	15	23
U. of Michigan–Ann Arbor	51	15	13
U. of North Carolina–Chapel Hill	40	16	26
U. of Notre Dame	53	13	49
U. of Pennsylvania	65	7	41
U. of Rochester	63	10	23
U. of Southern California	53	13	22
U. of Texas–Austin	39	21	13
U. of Virginia	44	13	28
U. of Washington	37	12	12
U. of Wisconsin–Madison	37	13	13
Vanderbilt University	68	9	31
Wake Forest University	59	11	38
Washington University–St. Louis	73	7	33
Yale University	77	7	50

TABLE 12.9   DATA FOR MAJOR LEAGUE BASEBALL TEAMS

MLB

Team	Value	Revenue	Income
New York Yankees	730	215	18.7
New York Mets	482	169	14.3
Los Angeles Dodgers	435	143	−29.6
Boston Red Sox	426	152	−11.4
Atlanta Braves	424	160	9.5
Seattle Mariners	373	166	14.1
Cleveland Indians	360	150	−3.6
Texas Rangers	356	134	−6.5
San Francisco Giants	355	142	16.8
Colorado Rockies	347	129	6.7
Houston Astros	337	125	4.1
Baltimore Orioles	319	133	3.2
Chicago Cubs	287	131	7.9
Arizona Diamondbacks	280	127	−3.9
St. Louis Cardinals	271	123	−5.1
Detroit Tigers	262	114	12.3
Pittsburgh Pirates	242	108	9.5
Milwaukee Brewers	238	108	18.8
Philadelphia Phillies	231	94	2.6
Chicago White Sox	223	101	−3.8
San Diego Padres	207	92	5.7
Cincinnati Reds	204	87	4.3
Anaheim Angels	195	103	5.7
Toronto Blue Jays	182	91	−20.6
Oakland Athletics	157	90	6.8
Kansas City Royals	152	85	2.2
Tampa Bay Devil Rays	142	92	−6.1
Florida Marlins	137	81	1.4
Minnesota Twins	127	75	3.6
Montreal Expos	108	63	−3.4

Appendix   Regression Analysis Using StatTools

Armand's

In this appendix we show how StatTools can be used to perform the regression analysis computations for the Armand's Pizza Parlors problem. Begin by using the Data Set Manager to create a StatTools data set for these data using the procedure described in the appendix in Chapter 1. The following steps describe how StatTools can be used to provide the regression results.

> **Step 1.** Click the **StatTools** tab on the Ribbon
> **Step 2.** In the **Analyses** group, click **Regression and Classification**
> **Step 3.** Choose the **Regression** option

Step 4. When the StatTools—Regression dialog box appears,
Select **Multiple** in the **Regression Type** box
In the **Variables** section,
    Click the **Format button** and select **Unstacked**
    In the column labeled **I** select **Population**
    In the column labeled **D** select **Sales**
Click **OK**

The regression analysis output will appear in a new worksheet.

Note that in step 4 we selected Multiple in the Regression Type box. In StatTools, the Multiple option is used for both simple linear regression and multiple regression. The StatTools—Regression dialog box contains a number of more advanced options for developing prediction interval estimates and producing residual plots. The StatTools Help facility provides information on using all of these options.

Multiple Regression

CONTENTS

STATISTICS *in* PRACTICE

INTERNATIONAL PAPER*
PURCHASE, NEW YORK

International Paper is the world's largest paper and forest products company. The company employs more than 117,000 people in its operations in nearly 50 countries, and exports its products to more than 130 nations. International Paper produces building materials such as lumber and plywood; consumer packaging materials such as disposable cups and containers; industrial packaging materials such as corrugated boxes and shipping containers; and a variety of papers for use in photocopiers, printers, books, and advertising materials.

To make paper products, pulp mills process wood chips and chemicals to produce wood pulp. The wood pulp is then used at a paper mill to produce paper products. In the production of white paper products, the pulp must be bleached to remove any discoloration. A key bleaching agent used in the process is chlorine dioxide, which, because of its combustible nature, is usually produced at a pulp mill facility and then piped in solution form into the bleaching tower of the pulp mill. To improve one of the processes used to produce chlorine dioxide, researchers studied the process's control and efficiency. One aspect of the study looked at the chemical feed rate for chlorine dioxide production.

To produce the chlorine dioxide, four chemicals flow at metered rates into the chlorine dioxide generator. The chlorine dioxide produced in the generator flows to an absorber where chilled water absorbs the chlorine dioxide gas to form a chlorine dioxide solution. The solution is then piped into the paper mill. A key part of controlling the process involves the chemical feed rates. Historically, experienced operators set the chemical feed rates, but this approach led to overcontrol by the operators. Consequently, chemical engineers at the mill requested that a set of control equations, one for each chemical feed, be developed to aid the operators in setting the rates.

Multiple regression analysis assisted in the development of a better bleaching process for making white paper products. © John Zoiner/ Workbook Stock/Jupiter Images.

Using multiple regression analysis, statistical analysts developed an estimated multiple regression equation for each of the four chemicals used in the process. Each equation related the production of chlorine dioxide to the amount of chemical used and the concentration level of the chlorine dioxide solution. The resulting set of four equations was programmed into a microcomputer at each mill. In the new system, operators enter the concentration of the chlorine dioxide solution and the desired production rate; the computer software then calculates the chemical feed needed to achieve the desired production rate. After the operators began using the control equations, the chlorine dioxide generator efficiency increased, and the number of times the concentrations fell within acceptable ranges increased significantly.

This example shows how multiple regression analysis can be used to develop a better bleaching process for producing white paper products. In this chapter we will discuss how computer software packages are used for such purposes. Most of the concepts introduced in Chapter 12 for simple linear regression can be directly extended to the multiple regression case.

---

*The authors are indebted to Marian Williams and Bill Griggs for providing this Statistics in Practice. This application was originally developed at Champion International Corporation, which became part of International Paper in 2000.

In Chapter 12 we presented simple linear regression and demonstrated its use in developing an estimated regression equation that describes the relationship between two variables. Recall that the variable being predicted or explained is called the dependent variable and the variable being used to predict or explain the dependent variable is called the independent variable. In this chapter we continue our study of regression analysis by considering situations involving two or more independent variables. This subject area, called **multiple regression analysis**, enables us to consider more factors and thus obtain better estimates than are possible with simple linear regression.

13.1 Multiple Regression Model

Multiple regression analysis is the study of how a dependent variable y is related to two or more independent variables. In the general case, we will use p to denote the number of independent variables.

Regression Model and Regression Equation

The concepts of a regression model and a regression equation introduced in the preceding chapter are applicable in the multiple regression case. The equation that describes how the dependent variable y is related to the independent variables $x_1, x_2, \ldots, x_p$ and an error term is called the **multiple regression model**. We begin with the assumption that the multiple regression model takes the following form.

MULTIPLE REGRESSION MODEL

$$y = \beta_0 + \beta_1 x_1 + \beta_2 x_2 + \cdots + \beta_p x_p + \epsilon \qquad (13.1)$$

In the multiple regression model, $\beta_0, \beta_1, \beta_2, \ldots, \beta_p$ are the parameters and the error term ϵ (the Greek letter epsilon) is a random variable. A close examination of this model reveals that y is a linear function of $x_1, x_2, \ldots, x_p$ (the $\beta_0 + \beta_1 x_1 + \beta_2 x_2 + \cdots + \beta_p x_p$ part) plus the error term ϵ. The error term accounts for the variability in y that cannot be explained by the linear effect of the p independent variables.

In Section 13.4 we will discuss the assumptions for the multiple regression model and ϵ. One of the assumptions is that the mean or expected value of ϵ is zero. A consequence of this assumption is that the mean or expected value of y, denoted $E(y)$, is equal to $\beta_0 + \beta_1 x_1 + \beta_2 x_2 + \cdots + \beta_p x_p$. The equation that describes how the mean value of y is related to $x_1, x_2, \ldots, x_p$ is called the **multiple regression equation**.

MULTIPLE REGRESSION EQUATION

$$E(y) = \beta_0 + \beta_1 x_1 + \beta_2 x_2 + \cdots + \beta_p x_p \qquad (13.2)$$

Estimated Multiple Regression Equation

If the values of $\beta_0, \beta_1, \beta_2, \ldots, \beta_p$ were known, equation (13.2) could be used to compute the mean value of y at given values of $x_1, x_2, \ldots, x_p$. Unfortunately, these parameter values will not, in general, be known and must be estimated from sample data. A simple random sample is used to compute sample statistics $b_0, b_1, b_2, \ldots, b_p$ that are used as the point

FIGURE 13.1   THE ESTIMATION PROCESS FOR MULTIPLE REGRESSION

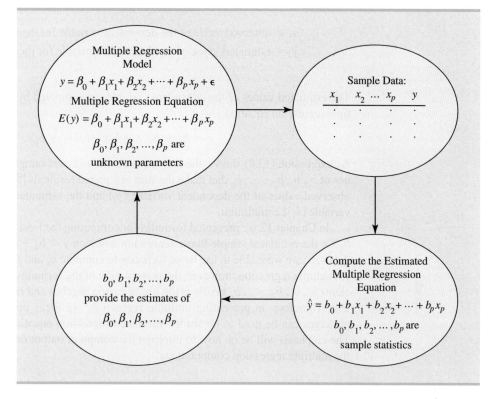

In simple linear regression, b_0 and b_1 were the sample statistics used to estimate the parameters β_0 and β_1. Multiple regression parallels this statistical inference process, with b_0, $b_1, b_2, \ldots, b_p$ denoting the sample statistics used to estimate the parameters $\beta_0, \beta_1, \beta_2, \ldots, \beta_p$.

estimators of the parameters $\beta_0, \beta_1, \beta_2, \ldots, \beta_p$. These sample statistics provide the following **estimated multiple regression equation**.

ESTIMATED MULTIPLE REGRESSION EQUATION

$$\hat{y} = b_0 + b_1x_1 + b_2x_2 + \cdots + b_px_p \qquad (13.3)$$

where

$$b_0, b_1, b_2, \ldots, b_p \text{ are the estimates of } \beta_0, \beta_1, \beta_2, \ldots, \beta_p$$
$$\hat{y} = \text{estimated value of the dependent variable}$$

The estimation process for multiple regression is shown in Figure 13.1.

13.2 Least Squares Method

In Chapter 12, we used the **least squares method** to develop the estimated regression equation that best approximated the straight-line relationship between the dependent and independent variables. This same approach is used to develop the estimated multiple regression equation. The least squares criterion is restated as follows.

LEAST SQUARES CRITERION

$$\min \Sigma(y_i - \hat{y}_i)^2 \qquad (13.4)$$

where

$$y_i = \text{observed value of the dependent variable for the } i\text{th observation}$$
$$\hat{y}_i = \text{estimated value of the dependent variable for the } i\text{th observation}$$

The estimated values of the dependent variable are computed by using the estimated multiple regression equation,

$$\hat{y} = b_0 + b_1 x_1 + b_2 x_2 + \cdots + b_p x_p$$

As expression (13.4) shows, the least squares method uses sample data to provide the values of $b_0, b_1, b_2, \ldots, b_p$ that make the sum of squared residuals [the deviations between the observed values of the dependent variable (y_i) and the estimated values of the dependent variable ($\hat{y}_i$)] a minimum.

In Chapter 12 we presented formulas for computing the least squares estimators b_0 and b_1 for the estimated simple linear regression equation $\hat{y} = b_0 + b_1 x$. With relatively small data sets, we were able to use those formulas to compute b_0 and b_1 by manual calculations. In multiple regression, however, the presentation of the formulas for the regression coefficients $b_0, b_1, b_2, \ldots, b_p$ involves the use of matrix algebra and is beyond the scope of this text. Therefore, in presenting multiple regression, we focus on how computer software packages can be used to obtain the estimated regression equation and other information. The emphasis will be on how to interpret the computer output rather than on how to make the multiple regression computations.

An Example: Butler Trucking Company

As an illustration of multiple regression analysis, we will consider a problem faced by the Butler Trucking Company, an independent trucking company in southern California. A major portion of Butler's business involves deliveries throughout its local area. To develop better work schedules, the managers want to estimate the total daily travel time for their drivers.

Initially the managers believed that the total daily travel time would be closely related to the number of miles traveled in making the daily deliveries. A simple random sample of 10 driving assignments provided the data shown in Table 13.1 and the scatter diagram shown in Figure 13.2. After reviewing this scatter diagram, the managers hypothesized that

TABLE 13.1   PRELIMINARY DATA FOR BUTLER TRUCKING

WEB file

Butler

Driving Assignment	x_1 = Miles Traveled	y = Travel Time (hours)
1	100	9.3
2	50	4.8
3	100	8.9
4	100	6.5
5	50	4.2
6	80	6.2
7	75	7.4
8	65	6.0
9	90	7.6
10	90	6.1

FIGURE 13.2   SCATTER DIAGRAM OF PRELIMINARY DATA FOR BUTLER TRUCKING

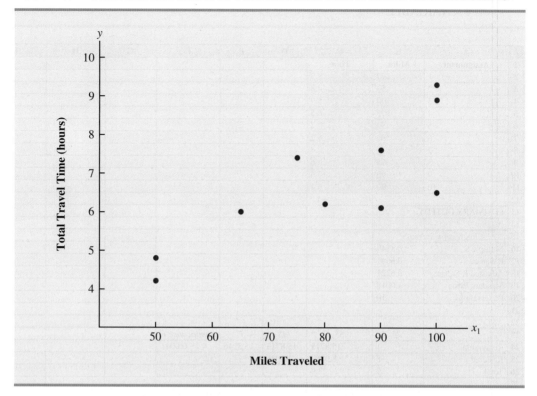

the simple linear regression model $y = \beta_0 + \beta_1 x_1 + \epsilon$ could be used to describe the relationship between the total travel time (y) and the number of miles traveled (x_1). To estimate the parameters β_0 and β_1, the least squares method was used to develop the estimated regression equation.

$$\hat{y} = b_0 + b_1 x_1 \tag{13.5}$$

In Figure 13.3, we show the Excel output[1] from applying simple linear regression to the data in Table 13.1. The estimated regression equation is

$$\hat{y} = 1.2739 + .0678 x_1$$

At the .05 level of significance, the F value of 15.8146 and its corresponding p-value of .0041 indicate that the relationship is significant; that is, we can reject H_0: $\beta_1 = 0$ because the p-value is less than $\alpha = .05$. Note that the same conclusion is obtained from the t value of 3.9768 and its associated p-value of .0041. Thus, we can conclude that the relationship between the total travel time and the number of miles traveled is significant; longer travel times are associated with more miles traveled. With a coefficient of determination of R Square = .6641, we see that 66.41% of the variability in travel time can be explained by the linear effect of the number of miles traveled. This finding is fairly good, but the managers might want to consider adding a second independent variable to explain some of the remaining variability in the dependent variable.

---

[1]Excel's Regression tool was used to obtain the output. Section 12.6 describes how to use Excel's Regression tool for simple linear regression.

FIGURE 13.3 REGRESSION TOOL OUTPUT FOR BUTLER TRUCKING WITH ONE INDEPENDENT VARIABLE

	A	B	C	D	E	F	G	H	I	J
1	Assignment	Miles	Time							
2	1	100	9.3							
3	2	50	4.8							
4	3	100	8.9							
5	4	100	6.5							
6	5	50	4.2							
7	6	80	6.2							
8	7	75	7.4							
9	8	65	6							
10	9	90	7.6							
11	10	90	6.1							
12										
13	SUMMARY OUTPUT									
14										
15	*Regression Statistics*									
16	Multiple R	0.8149								
17	R Square	0.6641								
18	Adjusted R Square	0.6221								
19	Standard Error	1.0018								
20	Observations	10								
21										
22	ANOVA									
23		*df*	*SS*	*MS*	*F*	*Significance F*				
24	Regression	1	15.8713	15.8713	15.8146	0.0041				
25	Residual	8	8.0287	1.0036						
26	Total	9	23.9							
27										
28		*Coefficients*	*Standard Error*	*t Stat*	*P-value*	*Lower 95%*	*Upper 95%*	*Lower 99.0%*	*Upper 99.0%*	
29	Intercept	1.2739	1.4007	0.9095	0.3897	-1.9562	4.5040	-3.4261	5.9739	
30	Miles	0.0678	0.0171	3.9768	0.0041	0.0285	0.1072	0.0106	0.1251	
31										

In attempting to identify another independent variable, the managers felt that the number of deliveries could also contribute to the total travel time. The Butler Trucking data, with the number of deliveries added, are shown in Table 13.2. To develop the estimated multiple-regression equation with both miles traveled (x_1) and number of deliveries (x_2) as independent variables, we will use Excel's Regression tool.

TABLE 13.2 DATA FOR BUTLER TRUCKING WITH MILES TRAVELED (x_1) AND NUMBER OF DELIVERIES (x_2) AS THE INDEPENDENT VARIABLES

WEB file

Butler

Driving Assignment	x_1 = Miles Traveled	x_2 = Number of Deliveries	y = Travel Time (hours)
1	100	4	9.3
2	50	3	4.8
3	100	4	8.9
4	100	2	6.5
5	50	2	4.2
6	80	2	6.2
7	75	3	7.4
8	65	4	6.0
9	90	3	7.6
10	90	2	6.1

Using Excel's Regression Tool to Develop the Estimated Multiple Regression Equation

In Section 12.6 we showed how Excel's Regression tool could be used to determine the estimated regression equation for Armand's Pizza Parlors. We can use the same procedure with minor modifications to develop the estimated multiple regression equation for Butler Trucking. Refer to Figures 13.4 and 13.5 as we describe the tasks involved.

Enter Data: The labels Assignment, Miles, Deliveries, and Time are entered into cells A1:D1 of the worksheet, and the sample data are entered into cells B2:D11. The numbers 1–10 are entered into cells A2:A11 to identify each observation.

Apply Tools: The following steps describe how to use Excel's Regression tool for multiple regression analysis.

Step 1. Select the **Tools** menu
Step 2. Choose the **Data Analysis** option
Step 3. Choose **Regression** from the list of Analysis Tools
Step 4. When the Regression dialog box appears (see Figure 13.5),
    Enter D1:D11 in the **Input Y Range** box
    Enter B1:C11 in the **Input X Range** box

FIGURE 13.4   REGRESSION TOOL OUTPUT FOR BUTLER TRUCKING WITH TWO INDEPENDENT VARIABLES

	A	B	C	D	E	F	G	H	I	J
1	Assignment	Miles	Deliveries	Time						
2	1	100	4	9.3						
3	2	50	3	4.8						
4	3	100	4	8.9						
5	4	100	2	6.5						
6	5	50	2	4.2						
7	6	80	2	6.2						
8	7	75	3	7.4						
9	8	65	4	6						
10	9	90	3	7.6						
11	10	90	2	6.1						
12										
13	SUMMARY OUTPUT									
14										
15	*Regression Statistics*									
16	Multiple R	0.9507								
17	R Square	0.9038								
18	Adjusted R Square	0.8763								
19	Standard Error	0.5731								
20	Observations	10								
21										
22	ANOVA									
23		*df*	*SS*	*MS*	*F*	*Significance F*				
24	Regression	2	21.6006	10.8003	32.8784	0.0003				
25	Residual	7	2.2994	0.3285						
26	Total	9	23.9							
27										
28		*Coefficients*	*Standard Error*	*t Stat*	*P-value*	*Lower 95%*	*Upper 95%*	*Lower 99.0%*	*Upper 99.0%*	
29	Intercept	-0.8687	0.9515	-0.9129	0.3916	-3.1188	1.3813	-4.1986	2.4612	
30	Miles	0.0611	0.0099	6.1824	0.0005	0.0378	0.0845	0.0265	0.0957	
31	Deliveries	0.9234	0.2211	4.1763	0.0042	0.4006	1.4463	0.1496	1.6972	
32										

FIGURE 13.5 REGRESSION TOOL DIALOG BOX FOR THE BUTLER TRUCKING EXAMPLE

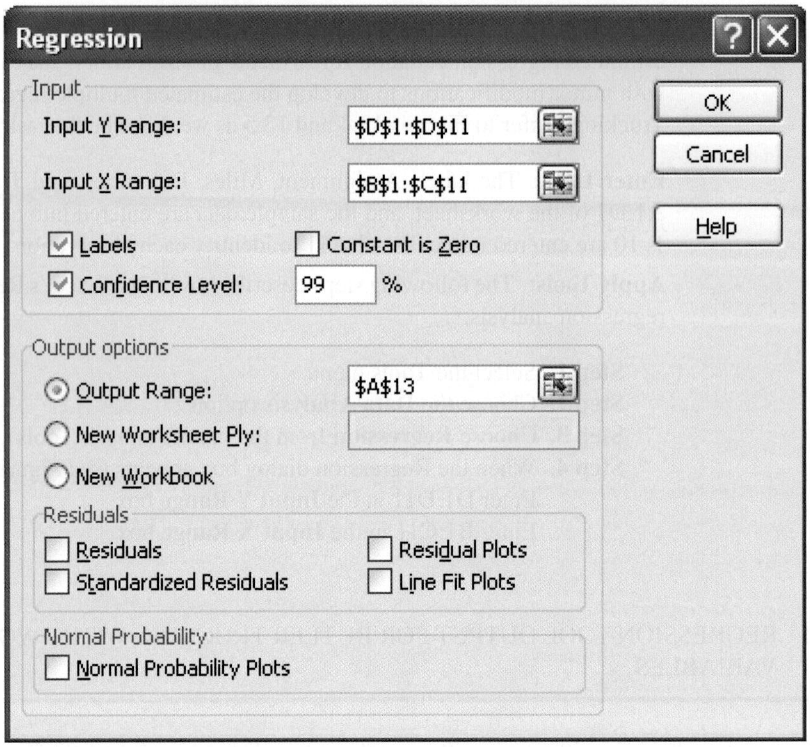

Select **Labels**
Select **Confidence Level**
Enter 99 in the **Confidence Level** box
Select **Output Range**
Enter A13 in the **Output Range** box (to identify the upper left corner of the section of the worksheet where the output will appear)
Click **OK**

In the Excel output shown in Figure 13.4 the label for the independent variable x_1 is Miles (see cell A30), and the label for the independent variable x_2 is Deliveries (see cell A31). The estimated regression equation is

$$\hat{y} = -.8687 + .0611x_1 + .9234x_2 \tag{13.6}$$

Note that using Excel's Regression tool for multiple regression is almost the same as using it for simple linear regression. The major difference is that in the multiple regression case a larger range of cells has to be provided in order to identify the independent variables.

In the next section we will discuss the use of the coefficient of multiple determination in measuring how good a fit is provided by this estimated regression equation. Before doing so, let us examine more carefully the values of $b_1 = .0611$ and $b_2 = .9234$ in equation (13.6).

Note on Interpretation of Coefficients

One observation can be made at this point about the relationship between the estimated regression equation with only the miles traveled as an independent variable and the equation that includes the number of deliveries as a second independent variable. The value of b_1 is not the same in both cases. In simple linear regression, we interpret b_1 as an estimate of the change in y for a one-unit change in the independent variable. In multiple regression analysis, this interpretation must be modified somewhat. That is, in multiple regression analysis, we interpret each regression coefficient as follows: b_i represents an estimate of the change in y corresponding to a one-unit change in x_i when all other independent variables are held constant. In the Butler Trucking example involving two independent variables, $b_1 = .0611$. Thus, .0611 hours is an estimate of the expected increase in travel time corresponding to an increase of one mile in the distance traveled when the number of deliveries is held constant. Similarly, because $b_2 = .9234$, an estimate of the expected increase in travel time corresponding to an increase of one delivery when the number of miles traveled is held constant is .9234 hours.

NOTES AND COMMENTS

In the appendix to this chapter we show how to use StatTools to perform multiple regression analysis for the Butler Trucking data. The regression analysis capabilities of StatTools are more comprehensive than those available using Excel's Regression tool.

Exercises

Note to student: The exercises involving data in this and subsequent sections were designed to be solved using Excel.

Methods

1. The estimated regression equation for a model involving two independent variables and 10 observations follows.

$$\hat{y} = 29.1270 + .5906x_1 + .4980x_2$$

   a. Interpret b_1 and b_2 in this estimated regression equation.
   b. Estimate y when $x_1 = 180$ and $x_2 = 310$.

2. Consider the following data for a dependent variable y and two independent variables, x_1 and x_2.

Exer2

x_1	x_2	y
30	12	94
47	10	108
25	17	112
51	16	178
40	5	94
51	19	175
74	7	170
36	12	117
59	13	142
76	16	211

a. Develop an estimated regression equation relating y to x_1. Estimate y if $x_1 = 45$.
b. Develop an estimated regression equation relating y to x_2. Estimate y if $x_2 = 15$.
c. Develop an estimated regression equation relating y to x_1 and x_2. Estimate y if $x_1 = 45$ and $x_2 = 15$.

3. In a regression analysis involving 30 observations, the following estimated regression equation was obtained.

$$\hat{y} = 17.6 + 3.8x_1 - 2.3x_2 + 7.6x_3 + 2.7x_4$$

a. Interpret b_1, b_2, b_3, and b_4 in this estimated regression equation.
b. Estimate y when $x_1 = 10$, $x_2 = 5$, $x_3 = 1$, and $x_4 = 2$.

Applications

4. A shoe store developed the following estimated regression equation relating sales to inventory investment and advertising expenditures.

$$\hat{y} = 25 + 10x_1 + 8x_2$$

where

$$x_1 = \text{inventory investment (\$1000s)}$$
$$x_2 = \text{advertising expenditures (\$1000s)}$$
$$y = \text{sales (\$1000s)}$$

a. Estimate sales resulting from a $15,000 investment in inventory and an advertising budget of $10,000.
b. Interpret b_1 and b_2 in this estimated regression equation.

5. The owner of Showtime Movie Theaters, Inc., would like to estimate weekly gross revenue as a function of advertising expenditures. Historical data for a sample of eight weeks follow.

Showtime

Weekly Gross Revenue ($1000s)	Television Advertising ($1000s)	Newspaper Advertising ($1000s)
96	5.0	1.5
90	2.0	2.0
95	4.0	1.5
92	2.5	2.5
95	3.0	3.3
94	3.5	2.3
94	2.5	4.2
94	3.0	2.5

a. Develop an estimated regression equation with the amount of television advertising as the independent variable.
b. Develop an estimated regression equation with both television advertising and newspaper advertising as the independent variables.
c. Is the estimated regression equation coefficient for television advertising expenditures the same in part (a) and in part (b)? Interpret the coefficient in each case.
d. What is the estimate of the weekly gross revenue for a week when $3500 is spent on television advertising and $1800 is spent on newspaper advertising?

6. In baseball, a team's success is often thought to be a function of the team's hitting and pitching performance. One measure of hitting performance is the number of home runs the team hits, and one measure of pitching performance is the earned run average for the team's pitching staff. It is generally believed that teams that hit more home runs and have a lower earned run average will win a higher percentage of the games played. The following data show the proportion of games won, the number of team home runs (HR), and the earned run average (ERA) for the 16 teams in the National League for the 2003 Major League Baseball season (*http://www.usatoday.com*, January 7, 2004).

MLB

Team	Proportion Won	HR	ERA	Team	Proportion Won	HR	ERA
Arizona	0.519	152	3.857	Milwaukee	0.420	196	5.058
Atlanta	0.623	235	4.106	Montreal	0.512	144	4.027
Chicago	0.543	172	3.842	New York	0.410	124	4.517
Cincinnati	0.426	182	5.127	Philadelphia	0.531	166	4.072
Colorado	0.457	198	5.269	Pittsburgh	0.463	163	4.664
Florida	0.562	157	4.059	San Diego	0.395	128	4.904
Houston	0.537	191	3.880	San Francisco	0.621	180	3.734
Los Angeles	0.525	124	3.162	St. Louis	0.525	196	4.642

a. Determine the estimated regression equation that could be used to predict the proportion of games won given the number of team home runs.
b. Determine the estimated regression equation that could be used to predict the proportion of games won given the earned run average for the team's pitching staff.
c. Determine the estimated regression equation that could be used to predict the proportion of games won given the number of team home runs and the earned run average for the team's pitching staff.
d. For the 2003 season San Diego won only 39.5% of the games they played, the lowest in the National League. To improve next year's record, the team is trying to acquire new players who will increase the number of team home runs to 180 and decrease the earned run average for the team's pitching staff to 4.0. Use the estimated regression equation developed in part (c) to estimate the percentage of games San Diego will win if they have 180 team home runs and have an earned run average of 4.0.

7. Designers of backpacks use exotic material such as supernylon Delrin, high-density polyethylene, aircraft aluminum, and thermomolded foam to make packs that fit comfortably and distribute weight to eliminate pressure points. The following data show the capacity (cubic inches), comfort rating, and price for 10 backpacks tested by *Outside Magazine*. Comfort was measured using a rating from 1 to 5, with a rating of 1 denoting average comfort and a rating of 5 denoting excellent comfort (*Outside Buyer's Guide,* 2001).

Backpack

Manufacturer and Model	Capacity	Comfort	Price
Camp Trails Paragon II	4330	2	$190
EMS 5500	5500	3	219
Lowe Alpomayo 90+20	5500	4	249
Marmot Muir	4700	3	249
Kelly Bigfoot 5200	5200	4	250
Gregory Whitney	5500	4	340
Osprey 75	4700	4	389
Arc'Teryx Bora 95	5500	5	395
Dana Design Terraplane LTW	5800	5	439
The Works @ Mystery Ranch Jazz	5000	5	525

a. Determine the estimated regression equation that can be used to predict the price of a backpack given the capacity and the comfort rating.
b. Interpret b_1 and b_2.
c. Predict the price for a backpack with a capacity of 4500 cubic inches and a comfort rating of 4.

8. Would you expect more reliable and better performing cars to cost more? *Consumer Reports* provided reliability ratings, overall road-test scores, and prices for affordable family sedans, midpriced family sedans, and large sedans (*Consumer Reports*, February 2008). A portion of the data follows. Reliability was rated on a 5-point scale from poor (1) to excellent (5). The road-test score was rated on a 100-point scale, with higher values indicating better performance. The complete data set is contained in the file named Sedans.

Sedans

Make and Model	Road-Test Score	Reliability	Price ($)
Nissan Altima 2.5 S	85	4	22705
Honda Accord LX-P	79	4	22795
Kia Optima EX (4-cyl.)	78	4	22795
Toyota Camry LE	77	4	21080
Hyundai Sonata SE	76	3	22995
.	.	.	.
.	.	.	.
.	.	.	.
Chrysler 300 Touring	60	2	30255
Dodge Charger SXT	58	4	28860

a. Develop an estimated regression equation that can be used to predict the price of the car given the reliability rating. Test for significance using $\alpha = .05$.
b. Consider the addition of the independent variable overall road-test score. Develop the estimated regression equation that can be used to predict the price of the car given the road-test score and the reliability rating.
c. Estimate the price for a car with a road-test score of 80 and a reliability rating of 4.

9. Waterskiing and wakeboarding are two popular water-sports. Finding a model that best suits your intended needs, whether it is waterskiing, wakeboading, or general boating, can be a difficult task. *WaterSki* magazine did extensive testing for 88 boats and provided a wide variety of information to help consumers select the best boat. A portion of the data they reported for 20 boats with a length of between 20 and 22 feet follows (*WaterSki*, January/February 2006). Beam is the maximum width of the boat in inches, HP is the horsepower of the boat's engine, and TopSpeed is the top speed in miles per hour (mph).

Boats

Make and Model	Beam	HP	TopSpeed
Calabria Cal Air Pro V-2	100	330	45.3
Correct Craft Air Nautique 210	91	330	47.3
Correct Craft Air Nautique SV-211	93	375	46.9
Correct Craft Ski Nautique 206 Limited	91	330	46.7
Gekko GTR 22	96	375	50.1
Gekko GTS 20	83	375	52.2
Malibu Response LXi	93.5	340	47.2
Malibu Sunsetter LXi	98	400	46
Malibu Sunsetter 21 XTi	98	340	44
Malibu Sunscape 21 LSV	98	400	47.5
Malibu Wakesetter 21 XTi	98	340	44.9

Make and Model	Beam	HP	TopSpeed
Malibu Wakesetter VLX	98	400	47.3
Malibu vRide	93.5	340	44.5
Malibu Ride XTi	93.5	320	44.5
Mastercraft ProStar 209	96	350	42.5
Mastercraft X-1	90	310	45.8
Mastercraft X-2	94	310	42.8
Mastercraft X-9	96	350	43.2
MB Sports 190 Plus	92	330	45.3
Svfara SVONE	91	330	47.7

    a.   Using these data, develop an estimated regression equation relating the top speed with the boat's beam and horsepower rating.

    b.   The Svfara SV609 has a beam of 85 inches and an engine with a 330 horsepower rating. Use the estimated regression equation developed in part (a) to estimate the top speed for the Svfara SV609.

10. The National Basketball Association (NBA) records a variety of statistics for each team. Four of these statistics are the proportion of games won (PCT), the proportion of field goals made by the team (FG%), the proportion of three-point shots made by the team's opponent (Opp 3 Pt%), and the number of turnovers committed by the team's opponent (Opp TO). The following data show the values of these statistics for the 29 teams in the NBA for a portion of the 2004 season (*http://www.nba.com*, January 3, 2004).

WEB file

NBA

Team	PCT	FG%	Opp 3 Pt%	Opp TO	Team	PCT	FG%	Opp 3 Pt%	Opp TO
Atlanta	0.265	0.435	0.346	13.206	Minnesota	0.677	0.473	0.348	13.839
Boston	0.471	0.449	0.369	16.176	New Jersey	0.563	0.435	0.338	17.063
Chicago	0.313	0.417	0.372	15.031	New Orleans	0.636	0.421	0.330	16.909
Cleveland	0.303	0.438	0.345	12.515	New York	0.412	0.442	0.330	13.588
Dallas	0.581	0.439	0.332	15.000	Orlando	0.242	0.417	0.360	14.242
Denver	0.606	0.431	0.366	17.818	Philadelphia	0.438	0.428	0.364	16.938
Detroit	0.606	0.423	0.262	15.788	Phoenix	0.364	0.438	0.326	16.515
Golden State	0.452	0.445	0.384	14.290	Portland	0.484	0.447	0.367	12.548
Houston	0.548	0.426	0.324	13.161	Sacramento	0.724	0.466	0.327	15.207
Indiana	0.706	0.428	0.317	15.647	San Antonio	0.688	0.429	0.293	15.344
L.A. Clippers	0.464	0.424	0.326	14.357	Seattle	0.533	0.436	0.350	16.767
L.A. Lakers	0.724	0.465	0.323	16.000	Toronto	0.516	0.424	0.314	14.129
Memphis	0.485	0.432	0.358	17.848	Utah	0.531	0.456	0.368	15.469
Miami	0.424	0.410	0.369	14.970	Washington	0.300	0.411	0.341	16.133
Milwaukee	0.500	0.438	0.349	14.750					

    a.   Determine the estimated regression equation that can be used to predict the proportion of games won given the proportion of field goals made by the team.

    b.   Provide an interpretation for the slope of the estimated regression equation developed in part (a).

    c.   Determine the estimated regression equation that can be used to predict the proportion of games won given the proportion of field goals made by the team, the proportion of three-point shots made by the team's opponent, and the number of turnovers committed by the team's opponent.

    d.   Discuss the practical implications of the estimated regression equation developed in part (c).

    e.   Estimate the proportion of games won for a team with the following values for the three independent variables: FG% = .45, Opp 3 Pt% = .34, and Opp TO = 17.

13.3 # Multiple Coefficient of Determination

In simple linear regression we showed that the total sum of squares can be partitioned into two components: the sum of squares due to regression and the sum of squares due to error. The same procedure applies to the sum of squares in multiple regression.

RELATIONSHIP AMONG SST, SSR, AND SSE

$$SST = SSR + SSE \qquad (13.7)$$

where

$$SST = \text{total sum of squares} = \Sigma(y_i - \bar{y})^2$$
$$SSR = \text{sum of squares due to regression} = \Sigma(\hat{y}_i - \bar{y})^2$$
$$SSE = \text{sum of squares due to error} = \Sigma(y_i - \hat{y}_i)^2$$

Because of the computational difficulty in computing the three sums of squares, we rely on computer packages to determine those values. The analysis of variance part of the Excel output in Figure 13.4 shows the three values for the Butler Trucking problem with two independent variables: SST = 23.9, SSR = 21.6006, and SSE = 2.2994. With only one independent variable (number of miles traveled), the Excel output in Figure 13.3 shows that SST = 23.9, SSR = 15.8713, and SSE = 8.0287. The value of SST is the same in both cases because it does not depend on $\hat{y}$, but SSR increases and SSE decreases when a second independent variable (number of deliveries) is added. The implication is that the estimated multiple regression equation provides a better fit for the observed data.

In Chapter 12, we used the coefficient of determination, $r^2 = SSR/SST$, to measure the goodness of fit for the estimated regression equation. The same concept applies to multiple regression. The term **multiple coefficient of determination** indicates that we are measuring the goodness of fit for the estimated multiple regression equation. The multiple coefficient of determination, denoted R^2, is computed as follows.

In the Excel Regression tool output the label R Square is used to identify the value of R^2.

MULTIPLE COEFFICIENT OF DETERMINATION

$$R^2 = \frac{SSR}{SST} \qquad (13.8)$$

The multiple coefficient of determination can be interpreted as the proportion of the variability in the dependent variable that can be explained by the estimated multiple regression equation. Hence, when multiplied by 100, it can be interpreted as the percentage of the variability in y that can be explained by the estimated regression equation.

In the two-independent-variable Butler Trucking example, with SSR = 21.6006 and SST = 23.9, we have

$$R^2 = \frac{21.6006}{23.9} = .9038$$

Therefore, 90.38% of the variability in travel time y is explained by the estimated multiple regression equation with miles traveled and number of deliveries as the independent variables. In Figure 13.4, we see that the multiple coefficient of determination is also provided by the Excel output; it is denoted by R Square = .9038 (see cell B17).

Figure 13.3 shows that the R Square value for the estimated regression equation with only one independent variable, number of miles traveled (x_1), is .6641. Thus, the percentage of the variability in travel time that is explained by the estimated regression equation increases from 66.41% to 90.38% when number of deliveries is added as a second independent variable. In general, R^2 always increases as independent variables are added to the model.

Adding independent variables causes the prediction errors to become smaller, thus reducing the sum of squares due to error, SSE. Because SSR = SST − SSE, when SSE becomes smaller, SSR becomes larger, causing R^2 = SSR/SST to increase.

Many analysts prefer adjusting R^2 for the number of independent variables to avoid overestimating the impact of adding an independent variable on the amount of variability explained by the estimated regression equation. With n denoting the number of observations and p denoting the number of independent variables, the **adjusted multiple coefficient of determination** is computed as follows.

If a variable is added to the model, R^2 becomes larger even if the variable added is not statistically significant. The adjusted multiple coefficient of determination compensates for the number of independent variables in the model.

ADJUSTED MULTIPLE COEFFICIENT OF DETERMINATION

$$R_a^2 = 1 - (1 - R^2)\frac{n-1}{n-p-1} \qquad (13.9)$$

For the Butler Trucking example with $n = 10$ and $p = 2$, we have

$$R_a^2 = 1 - (1 - .9038)\frac{10-1}{10-2-1} = .8763$$

Thus, after adjusting for the two independent variables, we have an adjusted multiple coefficient of determination of .8763. This value is provided by the Excel output in Figure 13.4 as Adjusted R Square = .8763 (see cell B18).

Exercises

Methods

11. In exercise 1, the following estimated regression equation based on 10 observations was presented.

$$\hat{y} = 29.1270 + .5906x_1 + .4980x_2$$

The values of SST and SSR are 6724.125 and 6216.375, respectively.
a.   Find SSE.
b.   Compute R^2.
c.   Compute R_a^2.
d.   Comment on the goodness of fit.

12. In exercise 2, 10 observations were provided for a dependent variable y and two independent variables x_1 and x_2; for these data SST = 15,182.9 and SSR = 14,052.2.
a.   Compute R^2.
b.   Compute R_a^2.
c.   Does the estimated regression equation explain a large amount of the variability in the data? Explain.

13. In exercise 3, the following estimated regression equation based on 30 observations was presented.

$$\hat{y} = 17.6 + 3.8x_1 - 2.3x_2 + 7.6x_3 + 2.7x_4$$

The values of SST and SSR are 1805 and 1760, respectively.
a. Compute R^2.
b. Compute R_a^2.
c. Comment on the goodness of fit.

Applications

14. In exercise 4, the following estimated regression equation relating sales to inventory investment and advertising expenditures was given.

$$\hat{y} = 25 + 10x_1 + 8x_2$$

The data used to develop the model came from a survey of 10 stores; for those data, SST = 16,000 and SSR = 12,000.
a. For the estimated regression equation given, compute R^2.
b. Compute R_a^2.
c. Does the model appear to explain a large amount of variability in the data? Explain.

15. In exercise 5, the owner of Showtime Movie Theaters, Inc., used multiple regression analysis to predict gross revenue (y) as a function of television advertising (x_1) and newspaper advertising (x_2). The estimated regression equation was

Showtime

$$\hat{y} = 83.2 + 2.29x_1 + 1.30x_2$$

The computer solution provided SST = 25.5 and SSR = 23.435.
a. Compute and interpret R^2 and R_a^2.
b. When television advertising was the only independent variable, $R^2 = .653$ and $R_a^2 = .595$. Do you prefer the multiple regression results? Explain.

MLB

16. In exercise 6, data were given on the proportion of games won, the number of team home runs, and the earned run average for the team's pitching staff for the 16 teams in the National League for the 2003 Major League Baseball season (*http://www.usatoday.com*, January 7, 2004).
a. Did the estimated regression equation that uses only the number of home runs as the independent variable to predict the proportion of games won provide a good fit? Explain.
b. Discuss the benefits of using both the number of home runs and the earned run average to predict the proportion of games won.

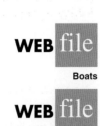
Boats

17. In exercise 9, an estimated regression equation was developed relating the top speed for a boat to the boat's beam and horsepower rating.
a. Compute and interpret and R^2 and R_a^2.
b. Does the estimated regression equation provide a good fit to the data? Explain.

NBA

18. Refer to exercise 10, where data were reported on a variety of statistics for the 29 teams in the National Basketball Association for a portion of the 2004 season (*http://www.nba.com*, January 3, 2004).
a. In part (c) of exercise 10, an estimated regression equation was developed relating the proportion of games won given the percentage of field goals made by the team, the proportion of three-point shots made by the team's opponent, and the number of turnovers committed by the team's opponent. What are the values of R^2 and R_a^2?
b. Does the estimated regression equation provide a good fit to the data? Explain.

Model Assumptions

In Section 13.1 we introduced the following multiple regression model.

MULTIPLE REGRESSION MODEL

$$y = \beta_0 + \beta_1 x_1 + \beta_2 x_2 + \cdots + \beta_p x_p + \epsilon \qquad (13.10)$$

The assumptions about the error term ϵ in the multiple regression model parallel those for the simple linear regression model.

ASSUMPTIONS ABOUT THE ERROR TERM ϵ IN THE MULTIPLE REGRESSION MODEL $y = \beta_0 + \beta_1 x_1 + \cdots + \beta_p x_p + \epsilon$

1. The error term ϵ is a random variable with mean or expected value of zero; that is, $E(\epsilon) = 0$.
    Implication: For given values of $x_1, x_2, \ldots, x_p$, the expected, or average, value of y is given by

$$E(y) = \beta_0 + \beta_1 x_1 + \beta_2 x_2 + \cdots + \beta_p x_p \qquad (13.11)$$

Equation (13.11) is the multiple regression equation we introduced in Section 13.1. In this equation, $E(y)$ represents the average of all possible values of y that might occur for the given values of $x_1, x_2, \ldots, x_p$.

2. The variance of ϵ is denoted by σ^2 and is the same for all values of the independent variables $x_1, x_2, \ldots, x_p$.
    Implication: The variance of y about the regression line equals σ^2 and is the same for all values of $x_1, x_2, \ldots, x_p$.
3. The values of ϵ are independent.
    Implication: The value of ϵ for a particular set of values for the independent variables is not related to the value of ϵ for any other set of values.
4. The error term ϵ is a normally distributed random variable reflecting the deviation between the y value and the expected value of y given by $\beta_0 + \beta_1 x_1 + \beta_2 x_2 + \cdots + \beta_p x_p$.
    Implication: Because $\beta_0, \beta_1, \ldots, \beta_p$ are constants for the given values of $x_1, x_2, \ldots, x_p$, the dependent variable y is also a normally distributed random variable.

To obtain more insight about the form of the relationship given by equation (13.11), consider the following two-independent-variable multiple regression equation:

$$E(y) = \beta_0 + \beta_1 x_1 + \beta_2 x_2$$

The graph of this equation is a plane in three-dimensional space. Figure 13.6 provides an example of such a graph. Note that the value of ϵ shown is the difference between the actual y value and the expected value of y, $E(y)$, when $x_1 = x_1^*$ and $x_2 = x_2^*$.

FIGURE 13.6   GRAPH OF THE REGRESSION EQUATION FOR MULTIPLE REGRESSION
ANALYSIS WITH TWO INDEPENDENT VARIABLES

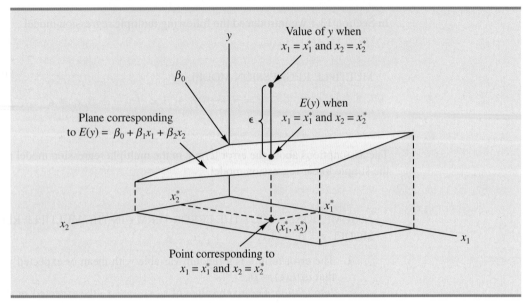

In regression analysis, the term *response variable* is often used in place of the term *dependent variable*. Furthermore, since the multiple regression equation generates a plane or surface, its graph is called a *response surface*.

(13.5) Testing for Significance

In this section we show how to conduct significance tests for a multiple regression relationship. The significance tests we used in simple linear regression were a t test and an F test. In simple linear regression, both tests provide the same conclusion; that is, if the null hypothesis is rejected, we conclude that $\beta_1 \neq 0$. In multiple regression, the t test and the F test have different purposes.

1. The F test is used to determine whether a significant relationship exists between the dependent variable and the set of all the independent variables; we will refer to the F test as the test for *overall significance*.
2. If the F test shows an overall significance, the t test is used to determine whether each of the individual independent variables is significant. A separate t test is conducted for each of the independent variables in the model; we refer to each of these t tests as a test for *individual significance*.

In the material that follows, we will explain the F test and the t test and apply each to the Butler Trucking Company example.

F Test

The multiple regression model as defined in Section 13.4 is

$$y = \beta_0 + \beta_1 x_1 + \beta_2 x_2 + \cdots + \beta_p x_p + \epsilon$$

The hypotheses for the F test involve the parameters of the multiple regression model.

$$H_0: \beta_1 = \beta_2 = \cdots = \beta_p = 0$$
$$H_a: \text{One or more of the parameters is not equal to zero}$$

If H_0 is rejected, the test gives us sufficient statistical evidence to conclude that one or more of the parameters is not equal to zero and that the overall relationship between y and the set of independent variables $x_1, x_2, \ldots, x_p$ is significant. However, if H_0 cannot be rejected, we do not have sufficient evidence to conclude that a significant relationship is present.

Before describing the steps of the F test, we need to review the concept of *mean square*. A mean square is a sum of squares divided by its corresponding degrees of freedom. In the multiple regression case, the total sum of squares has $n - 1$ degrees of freedom, the sum of squares due to regression has p degrees of freedom, and the sum of squares due to error has $n - p - 1$ degrees of freedom. Hence, the mean square due to regression (MSR) is SSR/p and the mean square due to error (MSE) is SSE/$(n - p - 1)$.

$$\text{MSR} = \frac{\text{SSR}}{p} \tag{13.12}$$

and

$$\text{MSE} = \frac{\text{SSE}}{n - p - 1} \tag{13.13}$$

As discussed in Chapter 12, MSE provides an unbiased estimate of σ^2, the variance of the error term ϵ. If H_0: $\beta_1 = \beta_2 = \cdots = \beta_p = 0$ is true, MSR also provides an unbiased estimate of σ^2, and the value of MSR/MSE should be close to 1. However, if H_0 is false, MSR overestimates σ^2 and the value of MSR/MSE becomes larger. To determine how large the value of MSR/MSE must be to reject H_0, we make use of the fact that if H_0 is true and the assumptions about the multiple regression model are valid, the sampling distribution of MSR/MSE is an F distribution with p degrees of freedom in the numerator and $n - p - 1$ degrees of freedom in the denominator. A summary of the F test for significance in multiple regression follows.

F TEST FOR OVERALL SIGNIFICANCE

H_0: $\beta_1 = \beta_2 = \cdots = \beta_p = 0$

H_a: One or more of the parameters is not equal to zero

TEST STATISTIC

$$F = \frac{\text{MSR}}{\text{MSE}} \tag{13.14}$$

REJECTION RULE

p-value approach: Reject H_0 if p-value $\leq \alpha$

Critical value approach: Reject H_0 if $F \geq F_\alpha$

where F_α is based on an F distribution with p degrees of freedom in the numerator and $n - p - 1$ degrees of freedom in the denominator.

Let us apply the F test to the Butler Trucking Company multiple regression problem. With two independent variables, the hypotheses are written as follows:

$$H_0: \beta_1 = \beta_2 = 0$$

$$H_a: \beta_1 \text{ and/or } \beta_2 \text{ is not equal to zero}$$

Figure 13.7 shows a portion of the Excel output shown previously in Figure 13.4 with miles traveled (x_1) and number of deliveries (x_2) as the two independent variables. In the analysis

FIGURE 13.7   PARTIAL EXCEL OUTPUT FOR THE BUTLER TRUCKING EXAMPLE WITH TWO
INDEPENDENT VARIABLES

	A	B	C	D	E	F	G	H	I
13	SUMMARY OUTPUT								
14									
15	*Regression Statistics*								
16	Multiple R	0.9507							
17	R Square	0.9038							
18	Adjusted R Square	0.8763							
19	Standard Error	0.5731							
20	Observations	10							
21									
22	ANOVA								
23		*df*	*SS*	*MS*	*F*	*Significance F*			
24	Regression	2	21.6006	10.8003	32.8784	0.0003			
25	Residual	7	2.2994	0.3285					
26	Total	9	23.9						
27									
28		*Coefficients*	*Standard Error*	*t Stat*	*P-value*				
29	Intercept	-0.8687	0.9515	-0.9129	0.3916				
30	Miles	0.0611	0.0099	6.1824	0.0005				
31	Deliveries	0.9234	0.2211	4.1763	0.0042				
32									
33									
34									
35									
36									

The *Significance F* value in cell F24 is the *p*-value used to test for overall significance.

The *p*-value in cell E30 is used to test for the individual significance of Miles.

The *p*-value in cell E31 is used to test for the individual significance of Deliveries.

Note: Rows 1–12 are hidden.

of variance part of the output, we see that MSR = 10.8003 and MSE = .3285. Using equation (13.14), we obtain the test statistic.

$$F = \frac{10.8003}{.3285} = 32.9$$

The label Significance F in cell F24 is used to identify the p-value in cell F24.

Note that the F value in the Excel output is $F = 32.8784$; the value we calculated differs because we used rounded values for MSR and MSE in the calculation. Using $\alpha = .01$, the p-value = 0.0003 in cell F24 indicates that we can reject $H_0: \beta_1 = \beta_2 = 0$ because the p-value is less than $\alpha = .01$. Alternatively, Table 4 of Appendix B shows that with two degrees of freedom in the numerator and seven degrees of freedom in the denominator, $F_{.01} = 9.55$. With $32.9 > 9.55$, we reject $H_0: \beta_1 = \beta_2 = 0$ and conclude that a significant relationship is present between travel time y and the two independent variables, miles traveled and number of deliveries.

As noted previously, MSE provides an unbiased estimate of σ^2, the variance of the error term ϵ. Thus, the estimate of σ^2 is MSE = .3285. The square root of MSE is the estimate of the standard deviation of the error term. As defined in Section 13.5, this standard deviation is called the standard error of the estimate and is denoted s. Hence, we have $s = \sqrt{MSE} = \sqrt{.3285} = .5731$. Note that the value of the standard error of the estimate appears in cell B19 of Figure 13.7.

TABLE 13.3 GENERAL FORM OF THE ANOVA TABLE FOR MULTIPLE REGRESSION WITH p INDEPENDENT VARIABLES

Source	Sum of Squares	Degrees of Freedom	Mean Square	F	p-value
Regression	SSR	p	$MSR = \dfrac{SSR}{p}$	$F = \dfrac{MSR}{MSE}$	
Error	SSE	$n - p - 1$	$MSE = \dfrac{SSE}{n - p - 1}$		
Total	SST	$n - 1$			

Table 13.3 is the general form of the ANOVA table for multiple regression. The value of the F test statistic and its corresponding p-value in the last column can be used to make the hypothesis test conclusion. By reviewing the Excel output for Butler Trucking Company in Figure 13.7, we see that Excel's analysis of variance table contains this information.

t **Test**

If the F test shows that the multiple regression relationship is significant, a t test can be conducted to determine the significance of each of the individual parameters. The t test for individual significance follows.

t TEST FOR INDIVIDUAL SIGNIFICANCE

For any parameter β_i

$$H_0: \beta_i = 0$$
$$H_a: \beta_i \neq 0$$

TEST STATISTIC

$$t = \frac{b_i}{s_{b_i}} \tag{13.15}$$

REJECTION RULE

p-value approach: Reject H_0 if p-value $\leq \alpha$

Critical value approach: Reject H_0 if $t \leq -t_{\alpha/2}$ or if $t \geq t_{\alpha/2}$

where $t_{\alpha/2}$ is based on a t distribution with $n - p - 1$ degrees of freedom.

In the test statistic, s_{b_i} is the estimate of the standard deviation of b_i. The value of s_{b_i} will be provided by the computer software package.

Let us conduct the t test for the Butler Trucking regression problem. Refer to the section of Figure 13.7 that shows the Excel output for the t-ratio calculations. Values of b_1, b_2, s_{b_1}, and s_{b_2} are as follows.

$$b_1 = .0611 \quad s_{b_1} = .0099$$
$$b_2 = .9234 \quad s_{b_2} = .2211$$

Using equation (13.15), we obtain the test statistic for the hypotheses involving parameters β_1 and β_2.

$$t = .0611/.0099 = 6.1717$$
$$t = .9234/.2211 = 4.1764$$

The t values in the Excel output are 6.1824 and 4.1763. The difference is due to rounding.

Note that both of these *t*-ratio values and the corresponding *p*-values are provided by the Excel output in Figure 13.7. Using $\alpha = .01$, the *p*-values of .0005 and .0042 on the Excel output indicate that we can reject H_0: $\beta_1 = 0$ and H_0: $\beta_2 = 0$. Hence, both parameters are statistically significant. Alternatively, Table 2 of Appendix B shows that with $n - p - 1 = 10 - 2 - 1 = 7$ degrees of freedom, $t_{.005} = 3.499$. Because $6.1717 > 3.499$, we reject H_0: $\beta_1 = 0$. Similarly, with $4.1763 > 3.499$, we reject H_0: $\beta_2 = 0$.

Multicollinearity

We use the term *independent variable* in regression analysis to refer to any variable being used to predict or explain the value of the dependent variable. The term does not mean, however, that the independent variables themselves are independent in any statistical sense. On the contrary, most independent variables in a multiple regression problem are correlated to some degree with one another. For example, in the Butler Trucking example involving the two independent variables x_1 (miles traveled) and x_2 (number of deliveries), we could treat the miles traveled as the dependent variable and the number of deliveries as the independent variable to determine whether those two variables are themselves related. We could then compute the sample correlation coefficient $r_{x_1 x_2}$ to determine the extent to which the variables are related. Doing so yields $r_{x_1 x_2} = .16$. Thus, we find some degree of linear association between the two independent variables. In multiple regression analysis, **multicollinearity** refers to the correlation among the independent variables.

To provide a better perspective of the potential problems of multicollinearity, let us consider a modification of the Butler Trucking example. Instead of x_2 being the number of deliveries, let x_2 denote the number of gallons of gasoline consumed. Clearly, x_1 (the miles traveled) and x_2 are related; that is, we know that the number of gallons of gasoline used depends on the number of miles traveled. Hence, we would conclude logically that x_1 and x_2 are highly correlated independent variables.

When the independent variables are highly correlated, it is not possible to determine the separate effect of any particular independent variable on the dependent variable.

Assume that we obtain the equation $\hat{y} = b_0 + b_1 x_1 + b_2 x_2$ and find that the F test shows the relationship to be significant. Then suppose we conduct a *t* test on β_1 to determine whether $\beta_1 \neq 0$, and we cannot reject H_0: $\beta_1 = 0$. Does this result mean that travel time is not related to miles traveled? Not necessarily. What it probably means is that with x_2 already in the model, x_1 does not make a significant contribution to determining the value of y. This interpretation makes sense in our example; if we know the amount of gasoline consumed, we do not gain much additional information useful in predicting y by knowing the miles traveled. Similarly, a *t* test might lead us to conclude $\beta_2 = 0$ on the grounds that, with x_1 in the model, knowledge of the amount of gasoline consumed does not add much.

To summarize, in *t* tests for the significance of individual parameters, the difficulty caused by multicollinearity is that it is possible to conclude that none of the individual parameters are significantly different from zero when an F test on the overall multiple regression equation indicates a significant relationship. This problem is avoided when there is little correlation among the independent variables.

A sample correlation coefficient greater than +.7 or less than −.7 for two independent variables is a rule of thumb warning of potential problems with multicollinearity.

Statisticians have developed several tests for determining whether multicollinearity is high enough to cause problems. According to the rule of thumb test, multicollinearity is a potential problem if the absolute value of the sample correlation coefficient exceeds .7 for any two of the independent variables. The other types of tests are more advanced and beyond the scope of this text.

If possible, every attempt should be made to avoid including independent variables that are highly correlated. In practice, however, strict adherence to this policy is rarely possible. When decision makers have reason to believe substantial multicollinearity is present, they must realize that separating the effects of the individual independent variables on the dependent variable is difficult.

NOTES AND COMMENTS

Ordinarily, multicollinearity does not affect the way in which we perform our regression analysis or interpret the output from a study. However, when multicollinearity is severe—that is, when two or more of the independent variables are highly correlated with one another—we can have difficulty interpreting the results of t tests on the individual parameters. In addition to the type of problem illustrated in this section, severe cases of multicollinearity have been shown to result in least squares estimates that have the wrong sign. That is, in simulated studies where researchers created the underlying regression model and then applied the least squares technique to develop estimates of β_0, β_1, β_2, and so on, it has been shown that under conditions of high multicollinearity the least squares estimates can have a sign opposite that of the parameter being estimated. For example, β_2 might actually be $+10$ and b_2, its estimate, might turn out to be -2. Thus, little faith can be placed in the individual coefficients if multicollinearity is present to a high degree.

Exercises

Methods

19. In exercise 1, the following estimated regression equation based on 10 observations was presented.

$$\hat{y} = 29.1270 + .5906x_1 + .4980x_2$$

Here SST = 6724.125, SSR = 6216.375, s_{b_1} = .0813, and s_{b_2} = .0567.
   a. Compute MSR and MSE.
   b. Compute F and perform the appropriate F test. Use $\alpha = .05$.
   c. Perform a t test for the significance of β_1. Use $\alpha = .05$.
   d. Perform a t test for the significance of β_2. Use $\alpha = .05$.

20. Refer to the data presented in exercise 2. The estimated regression equation for these data is

$$\hat{y} = -18.4 + 2.01x_1 + 4.74x_2$$

Here SST = 15,182.9, SSR = 14,052.2, s_{b_1} = .2471, and s_{b_2} = .9484.

   a. Test for a significant relationship among x_1, x_2, and y. Use $\alpha = .05$.
   b. Is β_1 significant? Use $\alpha = .05$.
   c. Is β_2 significant? Use $\alpha = .05$.

21. The following estimated regression equation was developed for a model involving two independent variables.

$$\hat{y} = 40.7 + 8.63x_1 + 2.71x_2$$

After x_2 was dropped from the model, the least squares method was used to obtain an estimated regression equation involving only x_1 as an independent variable.

$$\hat{y} = 42.0 + 9.01x_1$$

   a. Give an interpretation of the coefficient of x_1 in both models.
   b. Could multicollinearity explain why the coefficient of x_1 differs in the two models? If so, how?

Applications

22. In exercise 4, the following estimated regression equation relating sales to inventory investment and advertising expenditures was given.

$$\hat{y} = 25 + 10x_1 + 8x_2$$

The data used to develop the model came from a survey of 10 stores; for these data SST = 16,000 and SSR = 12,000.
   a. Compute SSE, MSE, and MSR.
   b. Use an F test and a .05 level of significance to determine whether there is a relationship among the variables.

23. Refer to exercise 5.

SELF test

   a. Use $\alpha = .01$ to test the hypotheses

$$H_0: \beta_1 = \beta_2 = 0$$
$$H_a: \beta_1 \text{ and/or } \beta_2 \text{ is not equal to zero}$$

   for the model $y = \beta_0 + \beta_1 x_1 + \beta_2 x_2 + \epsilon$, where

$$x_1 = \text{television advertising (\$1000s)}$$
$$x_2 = \text{newspaper advertising (\$1000s)}$$

   b. Use $\alpha = .05$ to test the significance of β_1. Should x_1 be dropped from the model?
   c. Use $\alpha = .05$ to test the significance of β_2. Should x_2 be dropped from the model?

24. *The Wall Street Journal* conducted a study of basketball spending at top colleges. A portion of the data showing the revenue ($ millions), percentage of wins, and the coach's salary ($ millions) for 39 of the country's top basketball programs follows (*The Wall Street Journal*, March 11–12, 2006).

WEB file

Basketball

School	Revenue	% Wins	Salary
Alabama	6.5	61	1.00
Arizona	16.6	63	0.70
Arkansas	11.1	72	0.80
Boston College	3.4	80	0.53
:	:	:	:
Washington	5.0	83	0.89
West Virginia	4.9	67	0.70
Wichita State	3.1	75	0.41
Wisconsin	12.0	66	0.70

   a. Develop the estimated regression equation that can be used to predict the coach's salary given the revenue generated by the program and the percentage of wins.
   b. Use the F test to determine the overall significance of the relationship. What is your conclusion at the .05 level of significance?
   c. Use the t test to determine the significance of each independent variable. What is your conclusion at the .05 level of significance?

25. *Barron's* conducts an annual review of online brokers, including both brokers that can be accessed via a Web browser, as well as direct-access brokers that connect customers directly with the broker's network server. Each broker's offerings and performance are evaluated in six areas, using a point value of 0–5 in each category. The results are weighted to obtain an overall score, and a final star rating, ranging from zero to five stars, is assigned to each broker. Trade execution, ease of use, and range of offerings are three of the areas evaluated. A point value of 5 in the trade execution area means the order entry and execution process flowed easily from one step to the next. A value of 5 in the ease of use area means that the site was easy to use

and can be tailored to show what the user wants to see. A value of 5 in the range offerings area means that all of the investment transactions can be executed online. The following data show the point values for trade execution, ease of use, range of offerings, and the star rating for a sample of 10 of the online brokers that *Barron's* evaluated (*Barron's,* March 10, 2003).

Brokers

Broker	Trade Execution	Use	Range	Rating
Wall St. Access	3.7	4.5	4.8	4.0
E*TRADE (Power)	3.4	3.0	4.2	3.5
E*TRADE (Standard)	2.5	4.0	4.0	3.5
Preferred Trade	4.8	3.7	3.4	3.5
my Track	4.0	3.5	3.2	3.5
TD Waterhouse	3.0	3.0	4.6	3.5
Brown & Co.	2.7	2.5	3.3	3.0
Brokerage America	1.7	3.5	3.1	3.0
Merrill Lynch Direct	2.2	2.7	3.0	2.5
Strong Funds	1.4	3.6	2.5	2.0

   a. Determine the estimated regression equation that can be used to predict the star rating given the point values for execution, ease of use, and range of offerings.

   b. Use the F test to determine the overall significance of the relationship. What is the conclusion at the .05 level of significance?

   c. Use the t test to determine the significance of each independent variable. What is your conclusion at the .05 level of significance?

   d. Remove any independent variable that is not significant from the estimated regression equation. What is your recommended estimated regression equation? Compare the R^2 with the value of R^2 from part (a). Discuss the differences.

NBA

26. In exercise 10 an estimated regression equation was developed relating the proportion of games won given the proportion of field goals made by the team, the proportion of three-point shots made by the team's opponent, and the number of turnovers committed by the team's opponent.

   a. Use the F test to determine the overall significance of the relationship. What is your conclusion at the .05 level of significance?

   b. Use the t test to determine the significance of each independent variable. What is your conclusion at the .05 level of significance?

(13.6) Using the Estimated Regression Equation for Estimation and Prediction

The procedures for estimating the mean value of y and predicting an individual value of y in multiple regression are similar to those in regression analysis involving one independent variable. First, recall that in Chapter 12 we showed that the point estimate of the expected value of y for a given value of x was the same as the point estimate of an individual value of y. In both cases, we used $\hat{y} = b_0 + b_1 x$ as the point estimate.

In multiple regression we use the same procedure. That is, we substitute the given values of $x_1, x_2, \ldots, x_p$ into the estimated regression equation and use the corresponding value of $\hat{y}$ as the point estimate. Suppose that for the Butler Trucking example we want to use the estimated regression equation involving x_1 (miles traveled) and x_2 (number of deliveries) to develop two interval estimates:

   1. A *confidence interval* of the mean travel time for all trucks that travel 100 miles and make two deliveries

   2. A *prediction interval* of the travel time for *one specific* truck that travels 100 miles and makes two deliveries

TABLE 13.4   THE 95% CONFIDENCE AND PREDICTION INTERVALS
FOR BUTLER TRUCKING

Value of x_1	Value of x_2	Confidence Interval		Prediction Interval	
		Lower Limit	Upper Limit	Lower Limit	Upper Limit
50	2	3.146	4.924	2.414	5.656
50	3	4.127	5.789	3.368	6.548
50	4	4.815	6.948	4.157	7.607
100	2	6.258	7.926	5.500	8.683
100	3	7.385	8.645	6.520	9.510
100	4	8.135	9.742	7.362	10.515

Using the estimated regression equation $\hat{y} = -.8687 + .0611x_1 + .9234x_2$ with $x_1 = 100$ and $x_2 = 2$, we obtain the following value of $\hat{y}$.

$$\hat{y} = -.8687 + .0611(100) + .9234(2) = 7.09$$

Hence, the point estimate of travel time in both cases is approximately seven hours.

To develop interval estimates for the mean value of y and for an individual value of y, we use a procedure similar to that for regression analysis involving one independent variable. The formulas required are beyond the scope of the text, but computer packages for multiple regression analysis will often provide confidence intervals once the values of x_1, $x_2, \ldots, x_p$ are specified by the user. In Table 13.4 we show the 95% confidence and prediction intervals for the Butler Trucking example for selected values of x_1 and x_2. Note that the interval estimate for an individual value of y is wider than the interval estimate for the expected value of y. This difference simply reflects the fact that for given values of x_1 and x_2 we can estimate the mean travel time for all trucks with more precision than we can predict the travel time for one specific truck.

Exercises

Methods

27. In exercise 1, the following estimated regression equation based on 10 observations was presented.

$$\hat{y} = 29.1270 + .5906x_1 + .4980x_2$$

   a. Develop a point estimate of the mean value of y when $x_1 = 180$ and $x_2 = 310$.
   b. Develop a point estimate for an individual value of y when $x_1 = 180$ and $x_2 = 310$.

28. Refer to the data in exercise 2. The estimated regression equation for those data is

$$\hat{y} = -18.4 + 2.01x_1 + 4.74x_2$$

   a. Develop a point estimate of the mean value of y when $x_1 = 45$ and $x_2 = 15$.
   b. Develop a 95% prediction interval for y when $x_1 = 45$ and $x_2 = 15$.

Applications

29. In exercise 5, the owner of Showtime Movie Theaters, Inc., used multiple regression analysis to predict gross revenue (y) as a function of television advertising (x_1) and newspaper advertising (x_2). The estimated regression equation was

$$\hat{y} = 83.2 + 2.29x_1 + 1.30x_2$$

a. What is the gross revenue expected for a week when $3500 is spent on television advertising ($x_1 = 3.5$) and $1800 is spent on newspaper advertising ($x_2 = 1.8$)?

b. Provide a 95% prediction interval for next week's revenue, assuming that the advertising expenditures will be allocated as in part (a).

30. In exercise 9 an estimated regression equation was developed relating the top speed for a boat to the boat's beam and horsepower rating.

a. Develop a point estimate of the mean top speed of a boat with a beam of 85 inches and an engine with a 330 horsepower rating.

b. The Svfara SV609 has a beam of 85 inches and an engine with a 330 horsepower rating. Develop a 95% prediction interval for the mean top speed for the Svfara SV609.

Boats

31. The Buyer's Guide section of the website for *Car and Driver* magazine provides reviews and road tests for cars, trucks, SUVs, and vans. The average ratings of overall quality, vehicle styling, braking, handling, fuel economy, interior comfort, acceleration, dependability, fit and finish, transmission, and ride are summarized for each vehicle using a scale ranging from 1 (worst) to 10 (best). A portion of the data for 14 Sports/GT cars is shown here (*http://www.caranddriver.com*, January 7, 2004).

WEB file

SportsCar

Sports/GT	Overall	Handling	Dependability	Fit and Finish
Acura 3.2CL	7.80	7.83	8.17	7.67
Acura RSX	9.02	9.46	9.35	8.97
Audi TT	9.00	9.58	8.74	9.38
BMW 3-Series/M3	8.39	9.52	8.39	8.55
Chevrolet Corvette	8.82	9.64	8.54	7.87
Ford Mustang	8.34	8.85	8.70	7.34
Honda Civic Si	8.92	9.31	9.50	7.93
Infiniti G35	8.70	9.34	8.96	8.07
Mazda RX-8	8.58	9.79	8.96	8.12
Mini Cooper	8.76	10.00	8.69	8.33
Mitsubishi Eclipse	8.17	8.95	8.25	7.36
Nissan 350Z	8.07	9.35	7.56	8.21
Porsche 911	9.55	9.91	8.86	9.55
Toyota Celica	8.77	9.29	9.04	7.97

a. Develop an estimated regression equation using handling, dependability, and fit and finish to predict overall quality.

b. Another Sports/GT car rated by *Car and Driver* is the Honda Accord. The ratings for handling, dependability, and fit and finish for the Honda Accord were 8.28, 9.06, and 8.07, respectively. Estimate the overall rating for this car.

c. Provide a 95% prediction interval for overall quality for the Honda Accord described in part (b).

d. The overall rating reported by *Car and Driver* for the Honda Accord was 8.65. How does this rating compare to the estimates you developed in parts (b) and (d)?

13.7 Categorical Independent Variables

The independent variables may be categorical or quantitative.

Thus far, the examples we have considered involved quantitative independent variables such as student population, distance traveled, and number of deliveries. In many situations, however, we must work with **categorical independent variables** such as gender (male, female), method of payment (cash, credit card, check), and so on. The purpose of this section is to show how categorical variables are handled in regression analysis. To illustrate the use and interpretation of a categorical independent variable, we will consider a problem facing the managers of Johnson Filtration, Inc.

TABLE 13.5   DATA FOR THE JOHNSON FILTRATION EXAMPLE

Service Call	Months Since Last Service	Type of Repair	Repair Time in Hours
1	2	electrical	2.9
2	6	mechanical	3.0
3	8	electrical	4.8
4	3	mechanical	1.8
5	2	electrical	2.9
6	7	electrical	4.9
7	9	mechanical	4.2
8	8	mechanical	4.8
9	4	electrical	4.4
10	6	electrical	4.5

An Example: Johnson Filtration, Inc.

Johnson Filtration, Inc., provides maintenance service for water-filtration systems throughout southern Florida. Customers contact Johnson with requests for maintenance service on their water-filtration systems. To estimate the service time and the service cost, Johnson's managers want to predict the repair time necessary for each maintenance request. Hence, repair time in hours is the dependent variable. Repair time is believed to be related to two factors, the number of months since the last maintenance service and the type of repair problem (mechanical or electrical). Data for a sample of 10 service calls are reported in Table 13.5.

Let y denote the repair time in hours and x_1 denote the number of months since the last maintenance service. The regression model that uses only x_1 to predict y is

$$y = \beta_0 + \beta_1 x_1 + \epsilon$$

Using Excel's Regression tool to develop the estimated regression equation, we obtained the partial Excel output shown in Figure 13.8. The estimated regression equation is

$$\hat{y} = 2.1473 + .3041 x_1 \tag{13.16}$$

At the .05 level of significance, the p-value of .0163 for the t (or F) test indicates that the number of months since the last service is significantly related to repair time. R Square $= .5342$ indicates that x_1 alone explains 53.42% of the variability in repair time.

To incorporate the type of repair into the regression model, we define the following variable.

$$x_2 = \begin{cases} 0 \text{ if the type of repair is mechanical} \\ 1 \text{ if the type of repair is electrical} \end{cases}$$

In regression analysis x_2 is called a **dummy** or *indicator* **variable**. Using this dummy variable, we can write the multiple regression model as

$$y = \beta_0 + \beta_1 x_1 + \beta_2 x_2 + \epsilon$$

Table 13.6 is the revised data set that includes the values of the dummy variable. Using Excel and the data in Table 13.6, we can develop estimates of the model parameters. The Excel Regression tool output in Figure 13.9 shows that the estimated multiple regression equation is

$$\hat{y} = .9305 + .3876 x_1 + 1.2627 x_2 \tag{13.17}$$

FIGURE 13.8 PARTIAL EXCEL OUTPUT FOR THE JOHNSON FILTRATION EXAMPLE WITH MONTHS SINCE LAST SERVICE CALL AS THE INDEPENDENT VARIABLE

The Excel regression output appears in a new worksheet because we selected New Worksheet Ply as the Output option in the Regression dialog box.

	A	B	C	D	E	F	G
1	SUMMARY OUTPUT						
2							
3	*Regression Statistics*						
4	Multiple R	0.7309					
5	R Square	0.5342					
6	Adjusted R Square	0.4759					
7	Standard Error	0.7810					
8	Observations	10					
9							
10	ANOVA						
11		*df*	*SS*	*MS*	*F*	*Significance F*	
12	Regression	1	5.5960	5.5960	9.1739	0.0163	
13	Residual	8	4.8800	0.6100			
14	Total	9	10.476				
15							
16		*Coefficients*	*Standard Error*	*t Stat*	*P-value*		
17	Intercept	2.1473	0.6050	3.5493	0.0075		
18	Months	0.3041	0.1004	3.0288	0.0163		
19							

At the .05 level of significance, the *p*-value of .0010 associated with the *F* test ($F = 21.3570$) indicates that the regression relationship is significant. The *t* test part of the printout in Figure 13.9 shows that both months since last service (*p*-value = .0004) and type of repair (*p*-value = .0051) are statistically significant. In addition, R Square = 0.8952 and Adjusted R Square = 0.8190 indicate that the estimated regression equation does a good job of explaining the variability in repair times. Thus, equation (13.17) should prove helpful in estimating the repair time necessary for the various service calls.

TABLE 13.6 DATA FOR THE JOHNSON FILTRATION EXAMPLE WITH TYPE OF REPAIR INDICATED BY A DUMMY VARIABLE ($x_2 = 0$ FOR MECHANICAL; $x_2 = 1$ FOR ELECTRICAL)

WEB file

Johnson

Customer	Months Since Last Service (x_1)	Type of Repair (x_2)	Repair Time in Hours (y)
1	2	1	2.9
2	6	0	3.0
3	8	1	4.8
4	3	0	1.8
5	2	1	2.9
6	7	1	4.9
7	9	0	4.2
8	8	0	4.8
9	4	1	4.4
10	6	1	4.5

FIGURE 13.9 PARTIAL EXCEL OUTPUT FOR THE JOHNSON FILTRATION EXAMPLE WITH MONTHS SINCE LAST SERVICE CALL AND TYPE OF REPAIR AS THE INDEPENDENT VARIABLES

	A	B	C	D	E	F	G
1	SUMMARY OUTPUT						
2							
3	*Regression Statistics*						
4	Multiple R	0.9269					
5	R Square	0.8592					
6	Adjusted R Square	0.8190					
7	Standard Error	0.4590					
8	Observations	10					
9							
10	ANOVA						
11		*df*	*SS*	*MS*	*F*	*Significance F*	
12	Regression	2	9.0009	4.5005	21.3570	0.0010	
13	Residual	7	1.4751	0.2107			
14	Total	9	10.476				
15							
16		*Coefficients*	*Standard Error*	*t Stat*	*P-value*		
17	Intercept	0.9305	0.4670	1.9926	0.0866		
18	Months	0.3876	0.0626	6.1954	0.0004		
19	Type	1.2627	0.3141	4.0197	0.0051		
20							

Interpreting the Parameters

The multiple regression equation for the Johnson Filtration example is

$$E(y) = \beta_0 + \beta_1 x_1 + \beta_2 x_2 \tag{13.18}$$

To understand how to interpret the parameters β_0, β_1, and β_2 when a categorical variable is present, consider the case when $x_2 = 0$ (mechanical repair). Using $E(y \mid \text{mechanical})$ to denote the mean or expected value of repair time *given* a mechanical repair, we have

$$E(y \mid \text{mechanical}) = \beta_0 + \beta_1 x_1 + \beta_2(0) = \beta_0 + \beta_1 x_1 \tag{13.19}$$

Similarly, for an electrical repair ($x_2 = 1$), we have

$$E(y \mid \text{electrical}) = \beta_0 + \beta_1 x_1 + \beta_2(1) = \beta_0 + \beta_1 x_1 + \beta_2 \tag{13.20}$$
$$= (\beta_0 + \beta_2) + \beta_1 x_1$$

Comparing equations (13.19) and (13.20), we see that the mean repair time is a linear function of x_1 for both mechanical and electrical repairs. The slope of both equations is β_1, but the y-intercept differs. The y-intercept is β_0 in equation (13.19) for mechanical repairs and $(\beta_0 + \beta_2)$ in equation (13.20) for electrical repairs. The interpretation of β_2 is that it indicates the difference between the mean repair time for an electrical repair and the mean repair time for a mechanical repair.

If β_2 is positive, the mean repair time for an electrical repair will be greater than that for a mechanical repair; if β_2 is negative, the mean repair time for an electrical repair will be less than that for a mechanical repair. Finally, if $\beta_2 = 0$, there is no difference in the mean repair time between electrical and mechanical repairs and the type of repair is not related to the repair time.

Using the estimated multiple regression equation $\hat{y} = .9305 + .3876x_1 + 1.2627x_2$, we see that .9305 is the estimate of β_0, .3876 is the estimate of β_1, and 1.2627 is the estimate of β_2. Thus, when $x_2 = 0$ (mechanical repair)

$$\hat{y} = .9305 + .3876x_1 \qquad \text{(13.21)}$$

and when $x_2 = 1$ (electrical repair)

$$\hat{y} = .9305 + .3876x_1 + 1.2627(1) \qquad \text{(13.22)}$$
$$= 2.1932 + .3876x_1$$

In effect, the use of a dummy variable for type of repair provides two estimated regression equations that can be used to predict the repair time, one corresponding to mechanical repairs and one corresponding to electrical repairs. In addition, with $b_2 = 1.2627$, we learn that, on average, electrical repairs require 1.2627 hours longer than mechanical repairs.

Figure 13.10 is the plot of the Johnson data from Table 13.6. Repair time in hours (y) is represented by the vertical axis and months since last service (x_1) is represented by the horizontal axis. A data point for a mechanical repair is indicated by an M and a data point for an electrical repair is indicated by an E. Equations (13.21) and (13.22) are plotted on the graph to show graphically the two equations that can be used to predict the repair time, one corresponding to mechanical repairs and one corresponding to electrical repairs.

FIGURE 13.10   SCATTER DIAGRAM FOR THE JOHNSON FILTRATION REPAIR DATA FROM TABLE 13.6

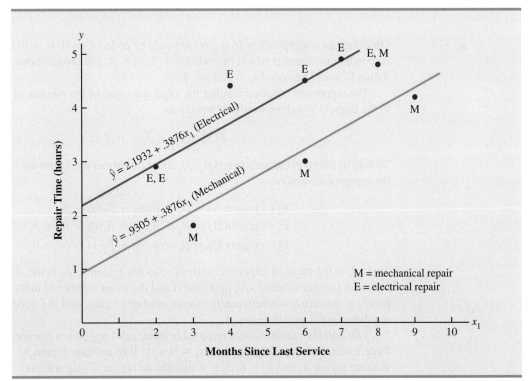

More Complex Categorical Variables

A categorical variable with k levels must be modeled using k − 1 dummy variables. Care must be taken in defining and interpreting the dummy variables.

Because the categorical variable for the Johnson Filtration example had two levels (mechanical and electrical), defining a dummy variable with zero indicating a mechanical repair and one indicating an electrical repair was easy. However, when a categorical variable has more than two levels, care must be taken in both defining and interpreting the dummy variables. As we will show, if a categorical variable has k levels, $k − 1$ dummy variables are required, with each dummy variable being coded as 0 or 1.

For example, suppose a manufacturer of copy machines organized the sales territories for a particular state into three regions: A, B, and C. The managers want to use regression analysis to help predict the number of copiers sold per week. With the number of units sold as the dependent variable, they are considering several independent variables (the number of sales personnel, advertising expenditures, and so on). Suppose the managers believe sales region is also an important factor in predicting the number of copiers sold. Because sales region is a categorical variable with three levels, A, B and C, we will need $3 − 1 = 2$ dummy variables to represent the sales region. Each variable can be coded 0 or 1 as follows.

$$x_1 = \begin{cases} 1 \text{ if sales region B} \\ 0 \text{ otherwise} \end{cases}$$

$$x_2 = \begin{cases} 1 \text{ if sales region C} \\ 0 \text{ otherwise} \end{cases}$$

With this definition, we have the following values of x_1 and x_2.

Region	x_1	x_2
A	0	0
B	1	0
C	0	1

Observations corresponding to region A would be coded $x_1 = 0$, $x_2 = 0$; observations corresponding to region B would be coded $x_1 = 1$, $x_2 = 0$; and observations corresponding to region C would be coded $x_1 = 0$, $x_2 = 1$.

The regression equation relating the expected value of the number of units sold, $E(y)$, to the dummy variables would be written as

$$E(y) = \beta_0 + \beta_1 x_1 + \beta_2 x_2$$

To help us interpret the parameters β_0, β_1, and β_2, consider the following three variations of the regression equation.

$$E(y \mid \text{region A}) = \beta_0 + \beta_1(0) + \beta_2(0) = \beta_0$$
$$E(y \mid \text{region B}) = \beta_0 + \beta_1(1) + \beta_2(0) = \beta_0 + \beta_1$$
$$E(y \mid \text{region C}) = \beta_0 + \beta_1(0) + \beta_2(1) = \beta_0 + \beta_2$$

Thus, β_0 is the mean or expected value of sales for region A; β_1 is the difference between the mean number of units sold in region B and the mean number of units sold in region A; and β_2 is the difference between the mean number of units sold in region C and the mean number of units sold in region A.

Two dummy variables were required because sales region is a categorical variable with three levels. But the assignment of $x_1 = 0$, $x_2 = 0$ to indicate region A, $x_1 = 1$, $x_2 = 0$ to indicate region B, and $x_1 = 0$, $x_2 = 1$ to indicate region C was arbitrary. For example, we could have chosen $x_1 = 1$, $x_2 = 0$ to indicate region A, $x_1 = 0$, $x_2 = 0$ to indicate region B, and $x_1 = 0$, $x_2 = 1$ to indicate region C. In that case, β_1 would have been interpreted as the mean difference between regions A and B and β_2 as the mean difference between regions C and B.

The important point to remember is that when a categorical variable has k levels, $k - 1$ dummy variables are required in the multiple regression analysis. Thus, if the sales region example had a fourth region, labeled D, three dummy variables would be necessary. For example, the three dummy variables can be coded as follows.

$$x_1 = \begin{cases} 1 \text{ if sales region B} \\ 0 \text{ otherwise} \end{cases} \qquad x_2 = \begin{cases} 1 \text{ if sales region C} \\ 0 \text{ otherwise} \end{cases} \qquad x_3 = \begin{cases} 1 \text{ if sales region D} \\ 0 \text{ otherwise} \end{cases}$$

Exercises

Methods

32. Consider a regression study involving a dependent variable y, a quantitative independent variable x_1, and a categorical variable with two levels (level 1 and level 2).
    a. Write a multiple regression equation relating x_1 and the categorical variable to y.
    b. What is the expected value of y corresponding to level 1 of the categorical variable?
    c. What is the expected value of y corresponding to level 2 of the categorical variable?
    d. Interpret the parameters in your regression equation.

33. Consider a regression study involving a dependent variable y, a quantitative independent variable x_1, and a categorical independent variable with three possible levels (level 1, level 2, and level 3).
    a. How many dummy variables are required to represent the categorical variable?
    b. Write a multiple regression equation relating x_1 and the categorical variable to y.
    c. Interpret the parameters in your regression equation.

Applications

34. Management proposed the following regression model to predict sales at a fast-food outlet.

$$y = \beta_0 + \beta_1 x_1 + \beta_2 x_2 + \beta_3 x_3 + \epsilon$$

where

$$x_1 = \text{number of competitors within one mile}$$
$$x_2 = \text{population within one mile (1000s)}$$
$$x_3 = \begin{cases} 1 \text{ if drive-up window present} \\ 0 \text{ otherwise} \end{cases}$$
$$y = \text{sales (\$1000s)}$$

The following estimated regression equation was developed after 20 outlets were surveyed.

$$\hat{y} = 10.1 - 4.2x_1 + 6.8x_2 + 15.3x_3$$

    a. What is the expected amount of sales attributable to the drive-up window?
    b. Predict sales for a store with two competitors, a population of 8000 within one mile, and no drive-up window.
    c. Predict sales for a store with one competitor, a population of 3000 within one mile, and a drive-up window.

35. Refer to the Johnson Filtration problem introduced in this section. Suppose that in addition to information on the number of months since the machine was serviced and whether

a mechanical or an electrical repair was necessary, the managers obtained a list showing which repairperson performed the service. The revised data follow.

WEB file

Repair

Repair Time in Hours	Months Since Last Service	Type of Repair	Repairperson
2.9	2	Electrical	Dave Newton
3.0	6	Mechanical	Dave Newton
4.8	8	Electrical	Bob Jones
1.8	3	Mechanical	Dave Newton
2.9	2	Electrical	Dave Newton
4.9	7	Electrical	Bob Jones
4.2	9	Mechanical	Bob Jones
4.8	8	Mechanical	Bob Jones
4.4	4	Electrical	Bob Jones
4.5	6	Electrical	Dave Newton

a. Ignore for now the months since the last maintenance service (x_1) and the repairperson who performed the service. Develop the estimated simple linear regression equation to predict the repair time (y) given the type of repair (x_2). Recall that $x_2 = 0$ if the type of repair is mechanical and 1 if the type of repair is electrical.

b. Does the equation that you developed in part (a) provide a good fit for the observed data? Explain.

c. Ignore for now the months since the last maintenance service and the type of repair associated with the machine. Develop the estimated simple linear regression equation to predict the repair time given the repairperson who performed the service. Let $x_3 = 0$ if Bob Jones performed the service and $x_3 = 1$ if Dave Newton performed the service.

d. Does the equation that you developed in part (c) provide a good fit for the observed data? Explain.

36. This problem is an extension of the situation described in exercise 35.

a. Develop the estimated regression equation to predict the repair time given the number of months since the last maintenance service, the type of repair, and the repairperson who performed the service.

b. At the .05 level of significance, test whether the estimated regression equation developed in part (a) represents a significant relationship between the independent variables and the dependent variable.

c. Is the addition of the independent variable x_3, the repairperson who performed the service, statistically significant? Use $\alpha = .05$. What explanation can you give for the results observed?

37. The National Football League rates prospects by position on a scale that ranges from 5 to 9. The ratings are interpreted as follows: 8–9 should start the first year; 7.0–7.9 should start; 6.0–6.9 will make the team as backup; and 5.0–5.9 can make the club and contribute. The following table shows the position, weight, time in seconds to run 40 yards, and ratings for 25 NFL prospects (*USA Today*, April 14, 2000).

	Position	Weight (pounds)	Time (seconds)	Rating
Cosey Coleman	Guard	322	5.38	7.4
Travis Claridge	Guard	303	5.18	7.0
Kaulana Noa	Guard	317	5.34	6.8
Leander Jordan	Guard	330	5.46	6.7
Chad Clifton	Guard	334	5.18	6.3
Manula Savea	Guard	308	5.32	6.1
Ryan Johanningmeir	Guard	310	5.28	6.0
Mark Tauscher	Guard	318	5.37	6.0
Blaine Saipaia	Guard	321	5.25	6.0

WEB file

Football

	Position	Weight (pounds)	Time (seconds)	Rating
Richard Mercier	Guard	295	5.34	5.8
Damion McIntosh	Guard	328	5.31	5.3
Jeno James	Guard	320	5.64	5.0
Al Jackson	Guard	304	5.20	5.0
Chris Samuels	Offensive tackle	325	4.95	8.5
Stockar McDougle	Offensive tackle	361	5.50	8.0
Chris McIngosh	Offensive tackle	315	5.39	7.8
Adrian Klemm	Offensive tackle	307	4.98	7.6
Todd Wade	Offensive tackle	326	5.20	7.3
Marvel Smith	Offensive tackle	320	5.36	7.1
Michael Thompson	Offensive tackle	287	5.05	6.8
Bobby Williams	Offensive tackle	332	5.26	6.8
Darnell Alford	Offensive tackle	334	5.55	6.4
Terrance Beadles	Offensive tackle	312	5.15	6.3
Tutan Reyes	Offensive tackle	299	5.35	6.1
Greg Robinson-Ran	Offensive tackle	333	5.59	6.0

a. Develop a dummy variable that will account for the player's position.
b. Develop an estimated regression equation to show how rating is related to position, weight, and time to run 40 yards.
c. At the .05 level of significance, test whether the estimated regression equation developed in part (b) indicates a significant relationship between the independent variables and the dependent variable.
d. Does the estimated regression equation provide a good fit for the observed data? Explain.
e. Is position a significant factor in the player's rating? Use $\alpha = .05$. Explain.
f. Suppose a new offensive tackle prospect who weighs 300 pounds ran the 40 yards in 5.1 seconds. Use the estimated regression equation developed in part (b) to estimate the rating for this player.

38. A 10-year study conducted by the American Heart Association provided data on how age, blood pressure, and smoking relate to the risk of strokes. Assume that the following data are from a portion of this study. Risk is interpreted as the probability (times 100) that the patient will have a stroke over the next 10-year period. For the smoking variable, define a dummy variable with 1 indicating a smoker and 0 indicating a nonsmoker.

Stroke

Risk	Age	Pressure	Smoker
12	57	152	No
24	67	163	No
13	58	155	No
56	86	177	Yes
28	59	196	No
51	76	189	Yes
18	56	155	Yes
31	78	120	No
37	80	135	Yes
15	78	98	No
22	71	152	No
36	70	173	Yes
15	67	135	Yes
48	77	209	Yes
15	60	199	No
36	82	119	Yes
8	66	166	No
34	80	125	Yes
3	62	117	No
37	59	207	Yes

a. Develop an estimated regression equation that relates risk of a stroke to the person's age, blood pressure, and whether the person is a smoker.
b. Is smoking a significant factor in the risk of a stroke? Explain. Use $\alpha = .05$.
c. What is the probability of a stroke over the next 10 years for Art Speen, a 68-year-old smoker who has blood pressure of 175? What action might the physician recommend for this patient?

Summary

In this chapter, we introduced multiple regression analysis as an extension of simple linear regression analysis presented in Chapter 12. Multiple regression analysis enables us to understand how a dependent variable is related to two or more independent variables. The regression equation $E(y) = \beta_0 + \beta_1 x_1 + \beta_2 x_2 + \cdots + \beta_p x_p$ shows that the expected value or mean value of the dependent variable y is related to the values of the independent variables $x_1, x_2, \ldots, x_p$. Sample data and the least squares method are used to develop the estimated regression equation $\hat{y} = b_0 + b_1 x_1 + b_2 x_2 + \cdots + b_p x_p$. In effect $b_0, b_1, b_2, \ldots, b_p$ are sample statistics used to estimate the unknown model parameters $\beta_0, \beta_1, \beta_2, \ldots, \beta_p$. Excel output was used throughout the chapter to emphasize the fact that computer software packages are the only realistic means of performing the numerous computations required in multiple regression analysis.

The multiple coefficient of determination was presented as a measure of the goodness of fit of the estimated regression equation. It determines the proportion of the variation of y that can be explained by the estimated regression equation. The adjusted multiple coefficient of determination is a similar measure of goodness of fit that adjusts for the number of independent variables and thus avoids overestimating the impact of adding more independent variables.

An F test and a t test were presented as ways to determine statistically whether the relationship among the variables is significant. The F test is used to determine whether there is a significant overall relationship between the dependent variable and the set of all independent variables. The t test is used to determine whether there is a significant relationship between the dependent variable and an individual independent variable given the other independent variables in the regression model. Correlation among the independent variables, known as multicollinearity, was discussed.

The chapter concluded with a section that showed how dummy variables can be used to incorporate categorical data into multiple regression analysis.

Glossary

Multiple regression analysis Regression analysis involving two or more independent variables.
Multiple regression model The mathematical equation that describes how the dependent variable y is related to the independent variables $x_1, x_2, \ldots, x_p$ and an error term ϵ.
Multiple regression equation The mathematical equation relating the expected value or mean value of the dependent variable to the values of the independent variables; that is, $E(y) = \beta_0 + \beta_1 x_1 + \beta_2 x_2 + \cdots + \beta_p x_p$.
Estimated multiple regression equation The equation that provides an estimate of the multiple regression equation based on sample data and the least squares method; it is $\hat{y} = b_0 + b_1 x_1 + b_2 x_2 + \cdots + b_p x_p$.
Least squares method The method used to develop the estimated regression equation. It minimizes the sum of squared residuals (the deviations between the observed values of the dependent variable, y_i, and the estimated values of the dependent variable, $\hat{y}_i$).
Multiple coefficient of determination A measure of the goodness of fit of the estimated multiple regression equation. It can be interpreted as the proportion of the variability in the dependent variable that is explained by the estimated regression equation.

Adjusted multiple coefficient of determination A measure of the goodness of fit of the estimated multiple regression equation that adjusts for the number of independent variables in the model and thus avoids overestimating the impact of adding more independent variables.

Multicollinearity The term used to describe the correlation among the independent variables.

Categorical independent variable An independent variable with categorical data.

Dummy variable A variable used to model the effect of categorical independent variables. A dummy variable may take only the value zero or one.

Key Formulas

Multiple Regression Model

$$y = \beta_0 + \beta_1 x_1 + \beta_2 x_2 + \cdots + \beta_p x_p + \epsilon \tag{13.1}$$

Multiple Regression Equation

$$E(y) = \beta_0 + \beta_1 x_1 + \beta_2 x_2 + \cdots + \beta_p x_p \tag{13.2}$$

Estimated Multiple Regression Equation

$$\hat{y} = b_0 + b_1 x_1 + b_2 x_2 + \cdots + b_p x_p \tag{13.3}$$

Least Squares Criterion

$$\min \Sigma(y_i - \hat{y}_i)^2 \tag{13.4}$$

Relationship Among SST, SSR, and SSE

$$\text{SST} = \text{SSR} + \text{SSE} \tag{13.7}$$

Multiple Coefficient of Determination

$$R^2 = \frac{\text{SSR}}{\text{SST}} \tag{13.8}$$

Adjusted Multiple Coefficient of Determination

$$R_a^2 = 1 - (1 - R^2)\frac{n-1}{n-p-1} \tag{13.9}$$

Mean Square Regression

$$\text{MSR} = \frac{\text{SSR}}{p} \tag{13.12}$$

Mean Square Error

$$\text{MSE} = \frac{\text{SSE}}{n-p-1} \tag{13.13}$$

F **Test Statistic**

$$F = \frac{\text{MSR}}{\text{MSE}} \tag{13.14}$$

t **Test Statistic**

$$t = \frac{b_i}{s_{b_i}} \tag{13.15}$$

Supplementary Exercises

39. The admissions officer for Clearwater College developed the following estimated regression equation relating the final college GPA to the student's SAT mathematics score and high-school GPA.

$$\hat{y} = -1.41 + .0235x_1 + .00486x_2$$

where

$$x_1 = \text{high-school grade point average}$$
$$x_2 = \text{SAT mathematics score}$$
$$y = \text{final college grade point average}$$

a.   Interpret the coefficients in this estimated regression equation.
b.   Estimate the final college GPA for a student who has a high-school average of 84 and a score of 540 on the SAT mathematics test.

40.   The personnel director for Electronics Associates developed the following estimated regression equation relating an employee's score on a job satisfaction test to his or her length of service and wage rate.

$$\hat{y} = 14.4 - 8.69x_1 + 13.5x_2$$

where

$$x_1 = \text{length of service (years)}$$
$$x_2 = \text{wage rate (dollars)}$$
$$y = \text{job satisfaction test score (higher scores}$$
$$\text{indicate greater job satisfaction)}$$

a.   Interpret the coefficients in this estimated regression equation.
b.   Develop an estimate of the job satisfaction test score for an employee who has four years of service and makes \$6.50 per hour.

41.   A partial computer output from a regression analysis using Excel's Regression tool follows.

	A	B	C	D	E	F	G
1	SUMMARY OUTPUT						
2							
3	*Regression Statistics*						
4	Multiple R						
5	R Square	0.923					
6	Adjusted R Square						
7	Standard Error	3.35					
8	Observations						
9							
10	ANOVA						
11		*df*	*SS*	*MS*	*F*	*Significance F*	
12	Regression		1612				
13	Residual	12					
14	Total						
15							
16		*Coefficients*	*Standard Error*	*t Stat*	*P-value*		
17	Intercept	8.103	2.667				
18	X1	7.602	2.105				
19	X2	3.111	0.613				
20							

a.   Compute the missing entries in this output.
b.   Using $\alpha = .05$, test for overall significance.
c.   Use the t test and $\alpha = .05$ to test $H_0: \beta_1 = 0$ and $H_0: \beta_2 = 0$.

42. Recall that in exercise 39, the admissions officer for Clearwater College developed the following estimated regression equation relating final college GPA to the student's SAT mathematics score and high-school GPA.

$$\hat{y} = -1.41 + .0235x_1 + .00486x_2$$

where

x_1 = high-school grade point average
x_2 = SAT mathematics score
y = final college grade point average

A portion of the Excel Regression tool output follows.

	A	B	C	D	E	F	G
1	SUMMARY OUTPUT						
2							
3	*Regression Statistics*						
4	Multiple R						
5	R Square						
6	Adjusted R Square						
7	Standard Error						
8	Observations						
9							
10	ANOVA						
11		*df*	*SS*	*MS*	*F*	*Significance F*	
12	Regression		1.76209				
13	Residual						
14	Total	9	1.88				
15							
16		*Coefficients*	*Standard Error*	*t Stat*	*P-value*		
17	Intercept	-1.4053	0.4848				
18	X1	0.023467	0.0086666				
19	X2	0.00486	0.001077				
20							

a. Complete the missing entries in this output.
b. Using $\alpha = .05$, test for overall significance.
c. Did the estimated regression equation provide a good fit to the data? Explain.
d. Use the t test and $\alpha = .05$ to test $H_0: \beta_1 = 0$ and $H_0: \beta_2 = 0$.

43. Recall that in exercise 40 the personnel director for Electronics Associates developed the following estimated regression equation relating an employee's score on a job satisfaction test to length of service and wage rate.

$$\hat{y} = 14.4 - 8.69x_1 + 13.5x_2$$

where

x_1 = length of service (years)
x_2 = wage rate (dollars)
y = job satisfaction test score (higher scores
indicate greater job satisfaction)

A portion of the Excel Regression tool output follows.

	A	B	C	D	E	F	G
1	SUMMARY OUTPUT						
2							
3	*Regression Statistics*						
4	Multiple R						
5	R Square						
6	Adjusted R Square						
7	Standard Error	3.773					
8	Observations						
9							
10	ANOVA						
11		*df*	*SS*	*MS*	*F*	*Significance F*	
12	Regression						
13	Residual		77.17				
14	Total		720				
15							
16		*Coefficients*	*Standard Error*	*t Stat*	*P-value*		
17	Intercept	14.4	8.191				
18	X1	-8.69	1.555				
19	X2	13.517	2.085				
20							

 a. Complete the missing entries in this output.
 b. Using $\alpha = .05$, test for overall significance.
 c. Did the estimated regression equation provide a good fit to the data? Explain.
 d. Use the *t* test and $\alpha = .05$ to test $H_0: \beta_1 = 0$ and $H_0: \beta_2 = 0$.

44. *SmartMoney* magazine evaluated 65 metropolitan areas to determine where home values are headed. An ideal city would get a score of 100 if all factors measured were as favorable as possible. Areas with a score of 60 or greater are considered to be primed for price appreciation, and areas with a score of below 50 may see housing values erode. Two of the factors evaluated were the recession resistance of the area and its affordability. Both of these factors were rated using a scale ranging from 0 (low score) to 10 (high score). The data obtained for a sample of 20 cities evaluated by *SmartMoney* follow (*SmartMoney,* February 2002).

WEB file

HomeValue

Metro Area	Recession Resistance	Affordability	Score
Tucson	10	7	70.7
Fort Worth	10	7	68.5
San Antonio	6	8	65.5
Richmond	8	6	63.6
Indianapolis	4	8	62.5
Philadelphia	0	10	61.9
Atlanta	2	6	60.7
Phoenix	4	5	60.3
Cincinnati	2	7	57.0
Miami	6	5	56.5
Hartford	0	7	56.2
Birmingham	0	8	55.7
San Diego	8	2	54.6
Raleigh	2	7	50.9

(Continued)

Metro Area	Recession Resistance	Affordability	Score
Oklahoma City	1	6	49.6
Orange County	4	2	49.1
Denver	4	4	48.6
Los Angeles	0	7	45.7
Detroit	0	5	44.3
New Orleans	0	5	41.2

a. Develop an estimated regression equation that can be used to predict the score given the recession resistance rating. At the .05 level of significance, test for a significant relationship.

b. Did the estimated regression equation developed in part (a) provide a good fit to the data? Explain.

c. Develop an estimated regression equation that can be used to predict the score given the recession resistance rating and the affordability rating. At the .05 level of significance, test for overall significance.

45. *Consumer Reports* provided extensive testing and ratings for 24 treadmills. An overall score, based primarily on ease of use, ergonomics, exercise range, and quality, was developed for each treadmill tested. In general, a higher overall score indicates better performance. The following data show the price, the quality rating, and overall score for the 24 treadmills (*Consumer Reports*, February 2006).

WEB file

Treadmills

Brand & Model	Price	Quality	Score
Landice L7	2900	Excellent	86
NordicTrack S3000	3500	Very good	85
SportsArt 3110	2900	Excellent	82
Precor	3500	Excellent	81
True Z4 HRC	2300	Excellent	81
Vision Fitness T9500	2000	Excellent	81
Precor M 9.31	3000	Excellent	79
Vision Fitness T9200	1300	Very good	78
Star Trac TR901	3200	Very good	72
Trimline T350HR	1600	Very good	72
Schwinn 820p	1300	Very good	69
Bowflex 7-Series	1500	Excellent	83
NordicTrack S1900	2600	Very good	83
Horizon Fitness PST8	1600	Very good	82
Horizon Fitness 5.2T	1800	Very good	80
Evo by Smooth Fitness FX30	1700	Very good	75
ProForm 1000S	1600	Very good	75
Horizon Fitness CST4.5	1000	Very good	74
Keys Fitness 320t	1200	Very good	73
Smooth Fitness 7.1HR Pro	1600	Very good	73
NordicTrack C2300	1000	Good	70
Spirit Inspire	1400	Very good	70
ProForm 750	1000	Good	67
Image 19.0 R	600	Good	66

a. Use these data to develop an estimated regression equation that could be used to estimate the overall score given the price.

b. Use $\alpha = .05$ to test for overall significance.

c. To incorporate the effect of quality, a categorical variable with three levels, we used two dummy variables, Quality-E and Quality-VG. Each variable is coded 0 or 1 as follows.

$$\text{Quality-E} = \begin{cases} 1 \text{ if quality rating is excellent} \\ 0 \text{ otherwise} \end{cases}$$

$$\text{Quality-VG} = \begin{cases} 1 \text{ if quality rating is very good} \\ 0 \text{ otherwise} \end{cases}$$

Develop an estimated regression equation that could be used to estimate the overall score given the price and the quality rating.

d. For the estimated regression equation developed in part (c), test for overall significance using $\alpha = .10$.

e. For the estimated regression equation developed in part (c), use the t test to determine the significance of each independent variable. Use $\alpha = .10$.

f. Estimate the overall score for a treadmill with a price of $2000 and a good quality rating. How much would the estimate change if the quality rating were very good? Explain.

46. A portion of a data set containing information for 45 mutual funds that are part of the *Morningstar Funds 500* for 2008 follows. The complete data set is available in the file named MutualFunds on the website that accompanies the text. The data set includes the following five variables:

Type: The type of fund, labeled DE (Domestic Equity), IE (International Equity), and FI (Fixed Income).

Net Asset Value ($): The closing price per share on December 31, 2007.

5-Year Average Return (%): The average annual return for the fund over the past 5 years.

Expense Ratio (%): The percentage of assets deducted each fiscal year for fund expenses.

Morningstar Rank: The risk adjusted star rating for each fund; Morningstar ranks go from a low of 1-Star to a high of 5-Stars.

MutualFunds

Fund Name	Fund Type	Net Asset Value ($)	5-Year Average Return (%)	Expense Ratio (%)	Morningstar Rank
Amer Cent Inc & Growth Inv	DE	28.88	12.39	0.67	2-Star
American Century Intl. Disc	IE	14.37	30.53	1.41	3-Star
American Century Tax-Free Bond	FI	10.73	3.34	0.49	4-Star
American Century Ultra	DE	24.94	10.88	0.99	3-Star
Ariel	DE	46.39	11.32	1.03	2-Star
Artisan Intl Val	IE	25.52	24.95	1.23	3-Star
Artisan Small Cap	DE	16.92	15.67	1.18	3-Star
Baron Asset	DE	50.67	16.77	1.31	5-Star
Brandywine	DE	36.58	18.14	1.08	4-Star
⋮	⋮	⋮	⋮	⋮	⋮

a. Develop an estimated regression equation that can be used to predict the 5-year average return given fund type. At the .05 level of significance, test for a significant relationship.

b. Did the estimated regression equation developed in part (a) provide a good fit to the data? Explain.

c. Develop the estimated regression equation that can be used to predict the 5-year average return given the type of fund, the net asset value, and the expense ratio. At the .05 level of significance, test for a significant relationship. Do you think any variables should be deleted from the estimated regression equation? Explain.

d. Develop an estimated regression equation that can be used to predict the 5-year average return given the type of fund, the expense ratio, and the Morningstar Rank. Using $\alpha = .05$, remove any independent variables that are not significant.

e. Use the estimated regression equation developed in part (d) to estimate the 5-year average return for a domestic equity fund with an expense ratio of 1.05% and a 3-Star Morningstar Rank.

47. The U.S. Department of Energy's Fuel Economy Guide provides fuel efficiency data for cars and trucks (*http://www.fueleconomy.gov*, February 22, 2008). A portion of the data for 311 compact, midsize, and large cars follows. The column labeled Class identifies the size of the car; Compact, Midsize, or Large. The column labeled Displacement shows the engine's displacement in liters. The column labeled Fuel Type shows whether the car uses premium (P) or regular (R) fuel, and the column labeled Hwy MPG shows the fuel efficiency rating for highway driving in terms of miles per gallon. The complete data set is contained in the file named FuelData.

WEB file

FuelData

Car	Class	Displacement	Fuel Type	Hwy MPG
1	Compact	3.1	P	25
2	Compact	3.1	P	25
3	Compact	3	P	25
.	.	.	.	.
.	.	.	.	.
.	.	.	.	.
161	Midsize	2.4	R	30
162	Midsize	2	P	29
.	.	.	.	.
.	.	.	.	.
310	Large	3	R	25
311	Large	3	R	25

a. Develop an estimated regression equation that can be used to predict the fuel efficiency for highway driving given the engine's displacement. Test for significance using $\alpha = .05$.

b. Consider the addition of the dummy variables ClassMidsize and ClassLarge. The value of ClassMidsize is 1 if the car is a midsize car and 0 otherwise; the value of ClassLarge is 1 if the car is a large car and 0 otherwise. Thus, for a compact car, the value of ClassMidsize and the value of ClassLarge is 0. Develop the estimated regression equation that can be used to predict the fuel efficiency for highway driving given the engine's displacement and the dummy variables ClassMidsize and ClassLarge.

c. Use $\alpha = .05$ to determine whether the dummy variables added in part (b) are significant.

d. Consider the addition of the dummy variable FuelPremium, where the value of FuelPremium is 1 if the car uses premium fuel and 0 if the car uses regular fuel. Develop the estimated regression equation that can be used to predict the fuel efficiency for highway driving given the engine's displacement, the dummy variables ClassMidsize and ClassLarge, and the dummy variable FuelPremium.

e. For the estimated regression equation developed in part (d), test for overall significance and individual significance using $\alpha = .05$.

Case Problem 1 Consumer Research, Inc.

Consumer Research, Inc., is an independent agency that conducts research on consumer attitudes and behaviors for a variety of firms. In one study, a client asked for an investigation of consumer characteristics that can be used to predict the amount charged by credit card users. Data were collected on annual income, household size, and annual credit card charges for a sample of 50 consumers. The following data are in the file named Consumer on the website that accompanies the text.

Consumer

Income ($1000s)	Household Size	Amount Charged ($)	Income ($1000s)	Household Size	Amount Charged ($)
54	3	4016	54	6	5573
30	2	3159	30	1	2583
32	4	5100	48	2	3866
50	5	4742	34	5	3586
31	2	1864	67	4	5037
55	2	4070	50	2	3605
37	1	2731	67	5	5345
40	2	3348	55	6	5370
66	4	4764	52	2	3890
51	3	4110	62	3	4705
25	3	4208	64	2	4157
48	4	4219	22	3	3579
27	1	2477	29	4	3890
33	2	2514	39	2	2972
65	3	4214	35	1	3121
63	4	4965	39	4	4183
42	6	4412	54	3	3730
21	2	2448	23	6	4127
44	1	2995	27	2	2921
37	5	4171	26	7	4603
62	6	5678	61	2	4273
21	3	3623	30	2	3067
55	7	5301	22	4	3074
42	2	3020	46	5	4820
41	7	4828	66	4	5149

Managerial Report

1. Use methods of descriptive statistics to summarize the data. Comment on the findings.
2. Develop estimated regression equations, first using annual income as the independent variable and then using household size as the independent variable. Which variable is the better predictor of annual credit card charges? Discuss your findings.
3. Develop an estimated regression equation with annual income and household size as the independent variables. Discuss your findings.
4. What is the predicted annual credit card charge for a three-person household with an annual income of $40,000?
5. Discuss the need for other independent variables that could be added to the model. What additional variables might be helpful?

Case Problem 2   Alumni Giving

Alumni donations are an important source of revenue for colleges and universities. If administrators could determine the factors that could lead to increases in the percentage of alumni who make a donation, they might be able to implement policies that could lead to increased revenues. Research shows that students who are more satisfied with their contact with teachers are more likely to graduate. As a result, one might suspect that smaller class sizes and lower student-faculty ratios might lead to a higher percentage of satisfied graduates, which in turn might lead to increases in the percentage of alumni who make a donation. Table 13.7 shows data for 48 national universities (*America's Best Colleges,* Year 2000 Edition). The column labeled Graduation Rate is the percentage of students who initially enrolled at the university and graduated. The column labeled % of Classes Under 20 shows the percentage of classes offered with fewer than 20 students. The column labeled Student-Faculty Ratio is the number of students enrolled divided by the total number of faculty. Finally, the column labeled Alumni Giving Rate is the percentage of alumni who made a donation to the university.

Managerial Report

1. Use methods of descriptive statistics to summarize the data.
2. Develop an estimated regression equation that can be used to predict the alumni giving rate given the number of students who graduate. Discuss your findings.
3. Develop an estimated regression equation that could be used to predict the alumni giving rate using the data provided.
4. What conclusions and recommendations can you derive from your analysis?

Case Problem 3   Predicting Winning Percentage for the NFL

NFLStats

The National Football League (NFL) records a variety of performance data for individuals and teams (*http://www.nfl.com*). Some of the year-end performance data for the 2005 season appear in the file named NFLStats. Each row of the data set corresponds to an NFL team, and the teams are ranked by winning percentage. Descriptions for the data follow:

WinPct	Percentage of games won
DefYds/G	Average number of yards per game given up on defense
RushYds/G	Average number of rushing yards per game
PassYds/G	Average number of passing yards per game
FGPct	Percentage of field goals
TakeInt	Takeaway interceptions; the total number of interceptions made by the team's defense
TakeFum	Takeaway fumbles; the total number of fumbles recovered by the team's defense
GiveInt	Giveaway interceptions; the total number of interceptions thrown by the team's offense
GiveFum	Giveaway fumbles; the total number of fumbles lost by the team's offense

Managerial Report

1. Use methods of descriptive statistics to summarize the data. Comment on the findings.
2. Develop an estimated regression equation that can be used to predict WinPct using DefYds/G, RushYds/G, PassYds/G, and FGPct. Discuss your findings.

TABLE 13.7   DATA FOR 48 NATIONAL UNIVERSITIES

Alumni

	State	Graduation Rate	% of Classes Under 20	Student-Faculty Ratio	Alumni Giving Rate
Boston College	MA	85	39	13	25
Brandeis University	MA	79	68	8	33
Brown University	RI	93	60	8	40
California Institute of Technology	CA	85	65	3	46
Carnegie Mellon University	PA	75	67	10	28
Case Western Reserve Univ.	OH	72	52	8	31
College of William and Mary	VA	89	45	12	27
Columbia University	NY	90	69	7	31
Cornell University	NY	91	72	13	35
Dartmouth College	NH	94	61	10	53
Duke University	NC	92	68	8	45
Emory University	GA	84	65	7	37
Georgetown University	DC	91	54	10	29
Harvard University	MA	97	73	8	46
Johns Hopkins University	MD	89	64	9	27
Lehigh University	PA	81	55	11	40
Massachusetts Inst. of Technology	MA	92	65	6	44
New York University	NY	72	63	13	13
Northwestern University	IL	90	66	8	30
Pennsylvania State Univ.	PA	80	32	19	21
Princeton University	NJ	95	68	5	67
Rice University	TX	92	62	8	40
Stanford University	CA	92	69	7	34
Tufts University	MA	87	67	9	29
Tulane University	LA	72	56	12	17
U. of California–Berkeley	CA	83	58	17	18
U. of California–Davis	CA	74	32	19	7
U. of California–Irvine	CA	74	42	20	9
U. of California–Los Angeles	CA	78	41	18	13
U. of California–San Diego	CA	80	48	19	8
U. of California–Santa Barbara	CA	70	45	20	12
U. of Chicago	IL	84	65	4	36
U. of Florida	FL	67	31	23	19
U. of Illinois–Urbana Champaign	IL	77	29	15	23
U. of Michigan–Ann Arbor	MI	83	51	15	13
U. of North Carolina–Chapel Hill	NC	82	40	16	26
U. of Notre Dame	IN	94	53	13	49
U. of Pennsylvania	PA	90	65	7	41
U. of Rochester	NY	76	63	10	23
U. of Southern California	CA	70	53	13	22
U. of Texas–Austin	TX	66	39	21	13
U. of Virginia	VA	92	44	13	28
U. of Washington	WA	70	37	12	12
U. of Wisconsin–Madison	WI	73	37	13	13
Vanderbilt University	TN	82	68	9	31
Wake Forest University	NC	82	59	11	38
Washington University–St. Louis	MO	86	73	7	33
Yale University	CT	94	77	7	50

3. Starting with the estimated regression equation developed in part (2), delete any independent variables that are not significant and develop a new estimated regression equation that can be used to predict WinPct. Use $\alpha = .05$.

4. Some football analysts believe that turnovers are one of the most important factors in determining a team's success. With Takeaways = TakeInt + TakeFum and Giveaways = GiveInt + GiveFum, let NetDiff = Takeaways − Giveaways. Develop an estimated regression equation that can be used to predict WinPct using NetDiff. Compare your results with the estimated regression equation developed in part (3).

5. Develop an estimated regression equation that can be used to predict WinPct using all the data provided.

Appendix   Multiple Regression Analysis Using StatTools

Butler

In this appendix we show how StatTools can be used to perform the regression analysis computations for the Butler Trucking problem. Begin by using the Data Set Manager to create a StatTools data set for these data using the procedure described in the Appendix in Chapter 1. The following steps describe how StatTools can be used to provide the regression results.

Step 1. Click the **StatTools** tab on the Ribbon
Step 2. In the **Analyses** group, click **Regression and Classification**
Step 3. Choose the **Regression** option
Step 4. When the StatTools—Regression dialog box appears,
    Select **Multiple** in the **Regression Type** box
    In the **Variables** section:
        Click the **Format** button and select **Unstacked**
        In the column labeled **I** select **Miles**
        In the column labeled **I** select **Deliveries**
        In the column labeled **D** select **Time**
    Click **OK**

The regression analysis output will appear in a new worksheet.

The StatTools—Regression dialog box contains a number of more advanced options for developing prediction interval estimates and producing residual plots. The StatTools Help facility provides information on using all of these options.

Statistical Methods for Quality Control

CONTENTS

STATISTICS *in* PRACTICE

DOW CHEMICAL*
FREEPORT, TEXAS

In 1940 the Dow Chemical Company purchased 800 acres of Texas land on the Gulf Coast to build a magnesium production facility. That original site has expanded to cover more than 5000 acres and holds one of the largest petrochemical complexes in the world. Among the products from Dow Texas Operations are magnesium, styrene, plastics, adhesives, solvent, glycol, and chlorine. Some products are made solely for use in other processes, but many end up as essential ingredients in products such as pharmaceuticals, toothpastes, dog food, water hoses, ice chests, milk cartons, garbage bags, shampoos, and furniture.

Dow's Texas Operations produce more than 30% of the world's magnesium, an extremely lightweight metal used in products ranging from tennis rackets to suitcases to "mag" wheels. The Magnesium Department was the first group in Texas Operations to train its technical people and managers in the use of statistical quality control. Some of the earliest successful applications of statistical quality control were in chemical processing.

In one application involving the operation of a dryer, samples of the output were taken at periodic intervals; the average value for each sample was computed and recorded on a chart called an $\bar{x}$ chart. Such a chart enabled Dow analysts to monitor trends in the output that might indicate the process was not operating correctly. In one instance, analysts began to observe values for the sample mean that were not indicative of a process operating within its design limits. On further examination of

Statistical quality control has enabled Dow Chemical to improve its processing methods and output.
© Dow Chemical Company USA.

the control chart and the operation itself, the analysts found that the variation could be traced to problems involving one operator. The $\bar{x}$ chart recorded after retraining of the operator showed a significant improvement in the process quality.

Dow Chemical achieves quality improvements everywhere statistical quality control is applied. Documented savings of several hundred thousand dollars per year are realized, and new applications are continually being discovered.

In this chapter we will show how an $\bar{x}$ chart such as the one used by Dow Chemical can be developed. Such charts are a part of statistical quality control known as statistical process control. We will also discuss methods of quality control for situations in which a decision to accept or reject a group of items is based on a sample.

*The authors are indebted to Clifford B. Wilson, Magnesium Technical Manager, The Dow Chemical Company, for providing this Statistics in Practice.

The American Society for Quality (ASQ) defines quality as "the totality of features and characteristics of a product or service that bears on its ability to satisfy given needs." In other words, quality measures how well a product or service meets customer needs. Organizations recognize that to be competitive in today's global economy, they must strive for a high level of quality. As a result, they place increased emphasis on methods for monitoring and maintaining quality.

Today, the customer-driven focus that is fundamental to high-performing organizations has changed the scope that quality issues encompass, from simply eliminating defects on a production line to developing broad-based corporate quality strategies. Broadening the scope of quality naturally leads to the concept of **total quality (TQ)**.

Total Quality (TQ) is a people-focused management system that aims at continual increase in customer satisfaction at continually lower real cost. TQ is a total system approach (not a separate area or work program) and an integral part of high-level strategy; it works horizontally across function and departments, involves all employees, top to bottom, and extends backward and forward to include the supply chain and the customer chain. TQ stresses learning and adaptation to continual change as keys to organization success.[1]

Regardless of how it is implemented in different organizations, total quality is based on three fundamental principles: a focus on customers and stakeholders; participation and teamwork throughout the organization; and a focus on continuous improvement and learning. In the first section of the chapter we provide a brief introduction to the three quality management frameworks: the Malcolm Baldrige Quality Award, ISO 9000 standards, and the Six Sigma philosophy. In the last two sections we introduce two statistical tools that can be used to monitor quality: statistical process control and acceptance sampling.

14.1 Philosophies and Frameworks

After World War II, Dr. W. Edwards Deming became a consultant to Japanese industry; he is credited with being the person who convinced top managers in Japan to use the methods of statistical quality control.

Two individuals who have had great influence on quality are Dr. W. Edwards Deming and Joseph Juran. These men helped educate the Japanese in quality management shortly after World War II. Although quality is everybody's job, Deming stressed that the focus on quality must be led by managers. He developed a list of 14 points that he believed represent the key responsibilities of managers. For instance, Deming stated that managers must cease dependence on mass inspection; must end the practice of awarding business solely on the basis of price; must seek continual improvement in all production processes and service; must foster a team-oriented environment; and must eliminate goals, slogans, and work standards that prescribe numerical quotas. Perhaps most important, managers must create a work environment in which a commitment to quality and productivity is maintained at all times.

Juran proposed a simple definition of quality: *fitness for use.* Juran's approach to quality focused on three quality processes: quality planning, quality control, and quality improvement. In contrast to Deming's philosophy, which required a major cultural change in the organization, Juran's programs were designed to improve quality by working within the current organizational system. Nonetheless, the two philosophies are similar in that they both focus on the need for top management to be involved and stress the need for continuous improvement, the importance of training, and the use of quality control techniques.

Many other individuals played significant roles in the quality movement, including Philip B. Crosby, A. V. Feigenbaum, Karou Ishikawa, and Genichi Taguchi. More specialized texts dealing exclusively with quality provide details of the contributions of each of these individuals. The contributions of all individuals involved in the quality movement helped define a set of best practices and led to numerous awards and certification programs. The two most significant programs are the U.S. Malcolm Baldrige National Quality Award and the International ISO 9000 certification process. In recent years, use of Six Sigma—a methodology for improving organizational performance based on rigorous data collection and statistical analysis—has also increased.

Malcolm Baldrige National Quality Award

The Malcolm Baldrige National Quality Award is given by the president of the United States to organizations that apply and are judged to be outstanding in seven areas: leadership; strategic planning; customer and market focus; measurement, analysis, and knowledge management; human resource focus; process management; and business results. Congress established the award program in 1987 to recognize U.S. organizations for their

---

[1]J. R. Evans and W. M. Lindsay, *The Management and Control of Quality*, 6th ed. (Cincinnati, OH: South-Western, 2005), pp. 18–19.

The U.S. Commerce Department's National Institute of Standards and Technology (NIST) manages the Baldrige National Quality Program. More information can be obtained at http://www.quality.nist.gov.

achievements in quality and performance and to raise awareness about the importance of quality as a competitive edge. The award is named for Malcolm Baldrige, who served as Secretary of Commerce from 1981 until his death in 1987.

Since the presentation of the first awards in 1988, the Baldrige National Quality Program has grown in stature and impact. Approximately 2 million copies of the criteria have been distributed since 1988, and wide-scale reproduction by organizations and electronic access add to that number significantly. For the eighth year in a row, a hypothetical stock index, made up of publicly traded U.S. companies that have received the Baldrige Award, outperformed the Standard & Poor's 500. In 2003, the "Baldrige Index" outperformed the S&P 500 by 4.4 to 1. At the 2003 Baldrige Award Ceremony, Bob Barnett, executive vice president of Motorola, Inc., said, "We applied for the Award, not with the idea of winning, but with the goal of receiving the evaluation of the Baldrige Examiners. That evaluation was comprehensive, professional, and insightful . . . making it perhaps the most cost-effective, value-added business consultation available anywhere in the world today."

ISO 9000

ISO 9000 is a series of five international standards published in 1987 by the International Organization for Standardization (ISO), Geneva, Switzerland. Companies can use the standards to help determine what is needed to maintain an efficient quality conformance system. For example, the standards describe the need for an effective quality system, for ensuring that measuring and testing equipment is calibrated regularly, and for maintaining an adequate record-keeping system. ISO 9000 registration determines whether a company complies with its own quality system. Overall, ISO 9000 registration covers less than 10% of the Baldrige Award criteria.

Six Sigma

In the late 1980s Motorola recognized the need to improve the quality of its products and services; their goal was to achieve a level of quality so good that, for every million opportunities, no more than 3.4 defects will occur. This level of quality is referred to as the six sigma level of quality, and the methodology created to reach this quality goal is referred to as **Six Sigma**.

An organization may undertake two kinds of Six Sigma projects:

- DMAIC (Define, Measure, Analyze, Improve, and Control) to help redesign existing processes
- DFSS (Design for Six Sigma) to design new products, processes, or services

In helping to redesign existing processes and design new processes, Six Sigma places a heavy emphasis on statistical analysis and careful measurement. Today, Six Sigma is a major tool in helping organizations achieve Baldrige levels of business performance and process quality. Many Baldrige examiners view Six Sigma as the ideal approach for implementing Baldrige improvement programs.

Six Sigma limits and defects per million opportunities   In Six Sigma terminology, a *defect* is any mistake or error that is passed on to the customer. The Six Sigma process defines quality performance as defects per million opportunities (dpmo). As we indicated previously, Six Sigma represents a quality level of at most 3.4 dpmo. To illustrate how this quality level is measured, let us consider the situation at KJW Packaging.

KJW operates a production line where boxes of cereal are filled. The filling process has a mean of $\mu = 16.05$ ounces and a standard deviation of $\sigma = .10$ ounces. In addition, assume the filling weights are normally distributed. The distribution of filling weights is shown in Figure 14.1. Suppose management considers 15.45 to 16.65 ounces to be acceptable quality

FIGURE 14.1   NORMAL DISTRIBUTION OF CEREAL BOX FILLING WEIGHTS
                WITH A PROCESS MEAN $\mu = 16.05$

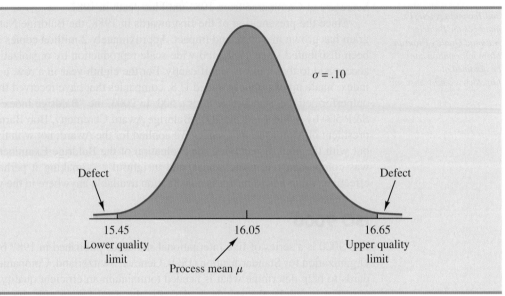

Using Excel,
NORMSDIST(6) −
NORMSDIST(−6) =
0.999999998.

limits for the filling process. Thus, any box of cereal that contains less than 15.45 or more than 16.65 ounces is considered to be a defect. Using Excel's NORMSDIST function it can be shown that 99.9999998% of the boxes filled will have between $16.05 - 6(.10) = 15.45$ ounces and $16.05 + 6(.10) = 16.65$ ounces. In other words, only .0000002% of the boxes filled will contain less than 15.45 ounces or more than 16.65 ounces. Thus, the likelihood of obtaining a defective box of cereal from the filling process appears to be extremely unlikely, because on average only 2 boxes in 10 million will be defective.

Motorola's early work on Six Sigma convinced them that a process mean can shift on average by as much as 1.5 standard deviations. For instance, suppose that the process mean for KJW increases by 1.5 standard deviations or $1.5(.10) = .15$ ounces. With such a shift, the normal distribution of filling weights would now be centered at $\mu = 16.05 + .15 = 16.20$ ounces. With a process mean of $\mu = 16.05$ ounces, the probability of obtaining a box of cereal with more than 16.65 ounces is extremely small. But how does this probability change if the mean of the process shifts up to $\mu = 16.20$ ounces? Figure 14.2 shows that for this case, the upper quality limit of 16.65 is 4.5 standard deviations to the right of the new mean $\mu = 16.20$ ounces.

Using Excel, 1 −
NORMSDIST(4.5) =
0.0000034.

Using this mean and Excel's NORMSDIST function we find that the probability of obtaining a box with more than 16.65 ounces is .0000034. Thus, if the process mean shifts up by 1.5 standard deviations, approximately $1,000,000(.0000034) = 3.4$ boxes of cereal per million boxes filled will exceed the upper limit of 16.65 ounces. Using Six Sigma terminology, the quality level of the process is said to be 3.4 defects per million opportunities. If management of KJW considers 15.45 to 16.65 ounces to be acceptable quality limits for the filling process, the KJW filling process would be considered a Six Sigma process. Thus, if the process mean stays within 1.5 standard deviations of its target value $\mu = 16.05$ ounces, a maximum of only 3.4 defects per million boxes filled can be expected.

Organizations that want to achieve and maintain a Six Sigma level of quality must emphasize methods for monitoring and maintaining quality. *Quality assurance* refers to the entire system of policies, procedures, and guidelines established by an organization to achieve and maintain quality. Quality assurance consists of two principal functions: quality engineering and quality control. The object of *quality engineering* is to include quality

FIGURE 14.2 NORMAL DISTRIBUTION OF CEREAL BOX FILLING WEIGHTS WITH A PROCESS MEAN $\mu = 16.20$

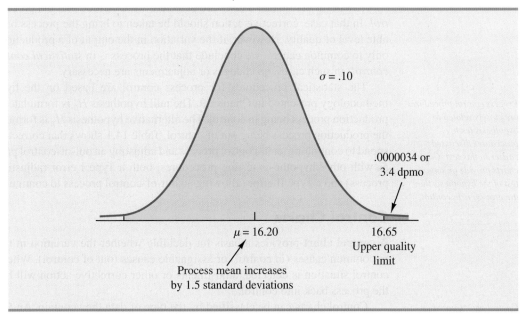

$\sigma = .10$

.0000034 or 3.4 dpmo

$\mu = 16.20$

16.65 Upper quality limit

Process mean increases by 1.5 standard deviations

in the design of products and processes and to identify quality problems prior to production. **Quality control** consists of a series of inspections and measurements used to determine whether quality standards are being met. If quality standards are not being met, corrective or preventive action can be taken to achieve and maintain conformance. In the next two sections we present two statistical methods used in quality control. The first method, *statistical process control,* uses graphical displays known as control charts to monitor a process; the goal is to determine whether the process can be continued or whether corrective action should be taken to achieve a desired quality level. The second method, *acceptance sampling,* is used in situations where a decision to accept or reject a group of items must be based on the quality found in a sample.

14.2 Statistical Control

In this section we consider quality control procedures for a production process whereby goods are manufactured continuously. On the basis of sampling and inspection of production output, a decision will be made to either continue the production process or adjust it to bring the items or goods being produced up to acceptable quality standards.

Continuous improvement is one of the most important concepts of the total quality management movement. The most important use of a control chart is in improving the process.

Despite high standards of quality in manufacturing and production operations, machine tools invariably wear out, vibrations throw machine settings out of adjustment, purchased materials contain defects, and human operators make mistakes. Any or all of these factors can result in poor quality output. Fortunately, procedures available to monitor production output help detect poor quality early, which allows for the adjustment and correction of the production process.

If the variation in the quality of the production output is due to **assignable causes** such as tools wearing out, incorrect machine settings, poor quality raw materials, or operator error, the process should be adjusted or corrected as soon as possible. Alternatively, if the variation results from **common causes**—that is, randomly occurring variations in materials, temperature, humidity, and so on, which the manufacturer cannot possibly control—the process does not need to be adjusted. The main objective of statistical process control is to determine whether variations in output are due to assignable causes or common causes.

Whenever assignable causes are detected, we conclude that the process is *out of control.* In that case, corrective action should be taken to bring the process back to an acceptable level of quality. However, if the variation in the output of a production process is due only to common causes, we conclude that the process is in *statistical control,* or simply *in control;* in such cases, no changes or adjustments are necessary.

The statistical procedures for process control are based on the hypothesis testing methodology presented in Chapter 9. The null hypothesis H_0 is formulated in terms of the production process being in control. The alternative hypothesis H_a is formulated in terms of the production process being out of control. Table 14.1 shows that correct decisions correspond to continuing an in-control process and adjusting an out-of-control process. However, as with other hypothesis testing procedures, both a Type I error (adjusting an in-control process) and a Type II error (allowing an out-of-control process to continue) are possible.

Process control procedures are closely related to hypothesis testing procedures discussed earlier in this text. Control charts provide an ongoing test of the hypothesis that the process is in control.

Control Charts

A **control chart** provides a basis for deciding whether the variation in the output is due to common causes (in control) or assignable causes (out of control). Whenever an out-of-control situation is detected, adjustments or other corrective action will be taken to bring the process back into control.

Control charts based on data that can be measured on a continuous scale are called variables control charts. The $\bar{x}$ chart is a variables control chart.

Control charts can be classified by the type of data they contain. An $\bar{x}$ **chart** is used if the quality of the output is measured in terms of a variable such as length, weight, temperature, and so on. In that case, the decision to continue or to adjust the production process will be based on the mean value found in a sample of the output. To introduce some of the concepts common to all control charts, let us consider some specific features of an $\bar{x}$ chart.

Figure 14.3 shows the general structure of an $\bar{x}$ chart. The center line of the chart corresponds to the mean of the process when the process is in control. The vertical axis measures $\bar{x}$ for the variable of interest. Each time a sample is taken from the production process, a value of the sample mean $\bar{x}$ is computed and a data point showing the value of $\bar{x}$ is plotted on the control chart.

The two lines labeled UCL and LCL are important in determining whether the process is in control or out of control. The lines are called the *upper control limit* and the *lower control limit,* respectively. They are chosen so that when the process is in control, there will be a high probability that the value of $\bar{x}$ will be between the two control limits. Values outside the control limits provide strong statistical evidence that the process is out of control and corrective action should be taken.

TABLE 14.1   DECISIONS AND STATES OF THE PROCESS

		State of Production Process	
		H_0 True Process in Control	H_0 False Process Out of Control
Decision	**Continue Process**	Correct decision	Type II error (allowing an out-of-control process to continue)
	Adjust Process	Type I error (adjusting an in-control process)	Correct decision

FIGURE 14.3   GENERAL STRUCTURE OF AN $\bar{x}$ CHART

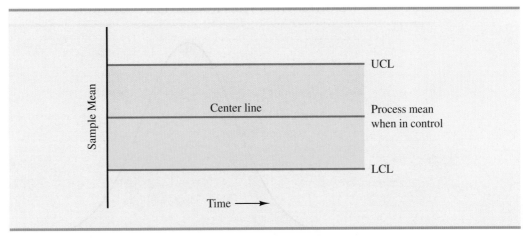

Over time, more and more data points ($\bar{x}$ values) will be added to the control chart. The order of the data points will be from left to right as the process is sampled. In essence, every time a point is plotted on the control chart, we are carrying out a hypothesis test to determine whether the process is in control.

In addition to the $\bar{x}$ chart, other control charts can be used to monitor the range of the measurements in the sample (R chart), the proportion of defective items in the sample (p chart), and the number of defective items in the sample (np chart). In each case, the control chart contains an LCL line, a center line, and a UCL line similar to the $\bar{x}$ chart in Figure 14.3. The major difference among the charts is what the vertical axis measures; for instance, in a p chart the vertical axis denotes the proportion of defective items in the sample instead of the sample mean. In the following discussion, we will illustrate the construction and use of the $\bar{x}$ chart, R chart, p chart, and np chart.

$\bar{x}$ Chart: Process Mean and Standard Deviation Known

We will use the KJW Packaging example introduced in Section 14.1 to illustrate the construction of an $\bar{x}$ chart. Recall that KJW operates a production line that fills cereal boxes. They designed the process so that when it is operating correctly—and hence the system is in control—the mean filling weight is $\mu = 16.05$ ounces and the process standard deviation is $\sigma = .10$ ounces. In addition, assume the filling weights (x) are normally distributed. The normal probability distribution of filling weights is shown in Figure 14.4.

The sampling distribution of $\bar{x}$, as presented in Chapter 7, can be used to determine the expected variation in $\bar{x}$ values for a process that is in control. Let us first briefly review the properties of the sampling distribution of $\bar{x}$. First, recall that $E(\bar{x})$, the expected value or mean of $\bar{x}$, is equal to μ, the mean filling weight when the production process is in control. For samples of size n, the formula for the standard deviation of $\bar{x}$, called the *standard error of the mean,* is

$$\sigma_{\bar{x}} = \frac{\sigma}{\sqrt{n}} \qquad (14.1)$$

In addition, because the filling weights (x) are normally distributed, the sampling distribution of $\bar{x}$ is normal for any sample size. Thus, the sampling distribution of $\bar{x}$ is a normal probability distribution with mean μ and standard deviation $\sigma_{\bar{x}}$. This probability distribution is

FIGURE 14.4 NORMAL PROBABILITY DISTRIBUTION OF CEREAL BOX FILLING WEIGHTS WHEN THE PROCESS IS IN CONTROL

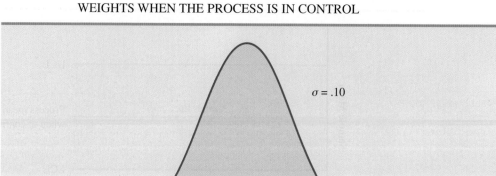

shown in Figure 14.5. Note that the sampling distribution of $\bar{x}$ has the same mean (16.05) as the probability distribution of individual filling weights.

The sampling distribution of $\bar{x}$ is used to determine what values of $\bar{x}$ are reasonable if the process is in control. The general practice in quality control is to define as reasonable any value of $\bar{x}$ that is within 3 standard deviations above or below the mean value μ. Recall from the study of the normal probability distribution that approximately 99.7% of the values of a normally distributed random variable are within ± 3 standard deviations of its mean value. Thus, if a value of $\bar{x}$ is within the interval $\mu - 3\sigma_{\bar{x}}$ to $\mu + 3\sigma_{\bar{x}}$, we will

FIGURE 14.5 SAMPLING DISTRIBUTION OF $\bar{x}$ FOR A SAMPLE OF n FILLING WEIGHTS

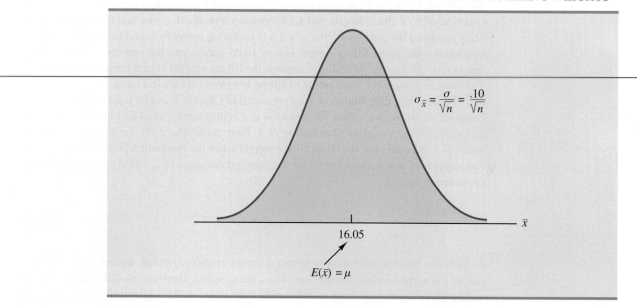

assume that the process is in control. In summary, then, the control limits for an $\bar{x}$ chart are as follows.

CONTROL LIMITS FOR AN $\bar{x}$ CHART: PROCESS MEAN AND STANDARD
DEVIATION KNOWN

$$UCL = \mu + 3\sigma_{\bar{x}} \qquad (14.2)$$
$$LCL = \mu - 3\sigma_{\bar{x}} \qquad (14.3)$$

Reconsider the KJW Packaging example with the normal probability distribution of filling weights shown in Figure 14.4 and the sampling distribution of $\bar{x}$ shown in Figure 14.5. Assume that a quality control inspector periodically selects a sample of six cereal boxes and uses the sample mean filling weight to determine whether the process is in control or out of control. Using equation (14.1), we find that the standard error of the mean is $\sigma_{\bar{x}} = \sigma/\sqrt{n} = .10/\sqrt{6} = .04$. Thus, with the process mean at $\mu = 16.05$, the control limits are UCL $= 16.05 + 3(.04) = 16.17$ and LCL $= 16.05 - 3(.04) = 15.93$. Figure 14.6 is a control chart showing the results of 10 samples taken over a 10-hour period. For ease of reading, the sample numbers 1 through 10 are listed below the chart.

Note that the mean for the fifth sample in Figure 14.6 shows that the process is out of control. The fifth sample mean is below the LCL, indicating that underfilling is occurring and that assignable causes of output variation are present. As a result, corrective action was taken at this point to bring the process back into control. The fact that the remaining points on the $\bar{x}$ chart are within the upper and lower control limits indicates that the corrective action was successful.

$\bar{x}$ Chart: Process Mean and Standard Deviation Unknown

In the KJW Packaging example, we showed how an $\bar{x}$ chart can be developed when the mean and standard deviation of the process are known before sampling. In many situations, the process mean and standard deviation must be estimated by using samples that are selected from the process when it is assumed to be operating in control. For instance, KJW might select a random sample of five boxes each morning and five boxes each afternoon for 10 days of operation. For

FIGURE 14.6 $\bar{x}$ CHART FOR THE CEREAL BOX FILLING PROCESS

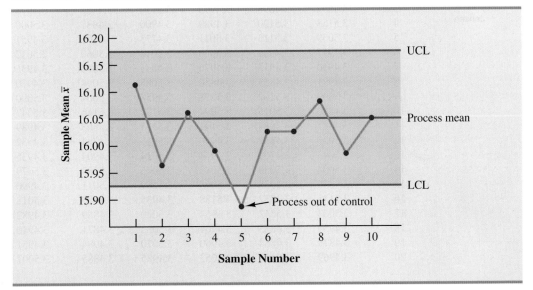

each subgroup, or sample, the mean and standard deviation of the sample are computed. The overall averages of both the sample means and the sample standard deviations can then be used to construct control charts for both the process mean and the process standard deviation.

In practice, it is common to monitor the variability of a production process by using the range instead of the standard deviation because the range is easier to compute. The range can then be used to provide good estimates of the process standard deviation; thus it can be used to construct upper and lower control limits for the $\bar{x}$ chart with little computational effort. To illustrate, let us consider the problem facing Jensen Computer Supplies, Inc.

Jensen Computer Supplies (JCS) manufactures 3.5-inch-diameter computer disks; they have just finished adjusting their production process so that it is operating in control. Suppose random samples of 5 disks are taken during the first hour of operation, during the second hour of operation, and so on, until 20 samples have been selected. Table 14.2 provides the diameter of each disk sampled as well as the mean $\bar{x}_j$ and range R_j for each of the samples.

The estimate of the process mean μ developed using k samples of size n is given by the overall sample mean.

OVERALL SAMPLE MEAN

$$\bar{\bar{x}} = \frac{\bar{x}_1 + \bar{x}_2 + \cdots + \bar{x}_k}{k} \qquad (14.4)$$

where

$$\bar{x}_j = \text{mean of the } j\text{th sample } j = 1, 2, \ldots, k$$
$$k = \text{number of samples}$$

TABLE 14.2   DATA FOR JENSEN COMPUTER SUPPLIES

Sample Number	Observations					Sample Mean $\bar{x}_j$	Sample Range R_j
1	3.5056	3.5086	3.5144	3.5009	3.5030	3.5065	.0135
2	3.4882	3.5085	3.4884	3.5250	3.5031	3.5026	.0368
3	3.4897	3.4898	3.4995	3.5130	3.4969	3.4978	.0233
4	3.5153	3.5120	3.4989	3.4900	3.4837	3.5000	.0316
5	3.5059	3.5113	3.5011	3.4773	3.4801	3.4951	.0340
6	3.4977	3.4961	3.5050	3.5014	3.5060	3.5012	.0099
7	3.4910	3.4913	3.4976	3.4831	3.5044	3.4935	.0213
8	3.4991	3.4853	3.4830	3.5083	3.5094	3.4970	.0264
9	3.5099	3.5162	3.5228	3.4958	3.5004	3.5090	.0270
10	3.4880	3.5015	3.5094	3.5102	3.5146	3.5047	.0266
11	3.4881	3.4887	3.5141	3.5175	3.4863	3.4989	.0312
12	3.5043	3.4867	3.4946	3.5018	3.4784	3.4932	.0259
13	3.5043	3.4769	3.4944	3.5014	3.4904	3.4935	.0274
14	3.5004	3.5030	3.5082	3.5045	3.5234	3.5079	.0230
15	3.4846	3.4938	3.5065	3.5089	3.5011	3.4990	.0243
16	3.5145	3.4832	3.5188	3.4935	3.4989	3.5018	.0356
17	3.5004	3.5042	3.4954	3.5020	3.4889	3.4982	.0153
18	3.4959	3.4823	3.4964	3.5082	3.4871	3.4940	.0259
19	3.4878	3.4864	3.4960	3.5070	3.4984	3.4951	.0206
20	3.4969	3.5144	3.5053	3.4985	3.4885	3.5007	.0259

WEB file

Jensen

For the JCS data in Table 14.2, $k = 20$ and the overall sample mean is $\bar{\bar{x}} = 3.4995$. This value will be the center line for the $\bar{x}$ chart. The range of each sample, denoted R_j, is simply the difference between the largest and smallest values in each sample. The average range for k samples is computed as follows.

> **AVERAGE RANGE**
>
> $$\bar{R} = \frac{R_1 + R_2 + \cdots + R_k}{k} \tag{14.5}$$
>
> where
>
> $$R_j = \text{range of the } j\text{th sample}, j = 1, 2, \ldots, k$$
> $$k = \text{number of samples}$$

For the JCS data in Table 14.2, the average range is $\bar{R} = .0253$.

In the preceding section we showed that the upper and lower control limits for the $\bar{x}$ chart are

$$\mu \pm 3 \frac{\sigma}{\sqrt{n}} \tag{14.6}$$

The overall sample mean $\bar{\bar{x}}$ is used to estimate μ and the sample ranges are used to develop an estimate of σ.

Hence, to construct the control limits for the $\bar{x}$ chart, we need to estimate μ and σ, the mean and standard deviation of the process. An estimate of μ is given by $\bar{\bar{x}}$. An estimate of σ can be developed by using the range data.

It can be shown that an estimator of the process standard deviation σ is the average range divided by d_2, a constant that depends on the sample size n. That is,

$$\text{Estimator of } \sigma = \frac{\bar{R}}{d_2} \tag{14.7}$$

The *American Society for Testing and Materials Manual on Presentation of Data and Control Chart Analysis* provides values for d_2 as shown in Table 14.3. For instance, when $n = 5$, $d_2 = 2.326$, and the estimate of σ is the average range divided by 2.326. If we substitute $\bar{\bar{x}}$ for μ and $\bar{R}/d_2$ for σ in equation (14.6), we can write the control limits for the $\bar{x}$ chart as

$$\bar{\bar{x}} \pm 3 \frac{\bar{R}/d_2}{\sqrt{n}} = \bar{\bar{x}} \pm \frac{3}{d_2\sqrt{n}} \bar{R} = \bar{\bar{x}} \pm A_2\bar{R} \tag{14.8}$$

Note that $A_2 = 3/(d_2\sqrt{n})$ is a constant that depends only on the sample size. Values for A_2 are also provided in Table 14.3. For $n = 5$, $A_2 = .577$; thus, the control limits for Jensen's $\bar{x}$ chart are

$$3.4995 \pm (.577)(.0253) = 3.4995 \pm .0146$$

Hence, UCL $= 3.514$ and LCL $= 3.485$.

Figure 14.7 shows the $\bar{x}$ chart for Jensen Computer Supplies. One can use the data in Table 14.2 and Excel's chart tools to construct the chart. The center line is shown at the

TABLE 14.3 FACTORS FOR $\bar{x}$ AND R CONTROL CHARTS

Observations in Sample, n	d_2	A_2	d_3	D_3	D_4
2	1.128	1.880	0.853	0	3.267
3	1.693	1.023	0.888	0	2.574
4	2.059	0.729	0.880	0	2.282
5	2.326	0.577	0.864	0	2.114
6	2.534	0.483	0.848	0	2.004
7	2.704	0.419	0.833	0.076	1.924
8	2.847	0.373	0.820	0.136	1.864
9	2.970	0.337	0.808	0.184	1.816
10	3.078	0.308	0.797	0.223	1.777
11	3.173	0.285	0.787	0.256	1.744
12	3.258	0.266	0.778	0.283	1.717
13	3.336	0.249	0.770	0.307	1.693
14	3.407	0.235	0.763	0.328	1.672
15	3.472	0.223	0.756	0.347	1.653
16	3.532	0.212	0.750	0.363	1.637
17	3.588	0.203	0.744	0.378	1.622
18	3.640	0.194	0.739	0.391	1.608
19	3.689	0.187	0.734	0.403	1.597
20	3.735	0.180	0.729	0.415	1.585
21	3.778	0.173	0.724	0.425	1.575
22	3.819	0.167	0.720	0.434	1.566
23	3.858	0.162	0.716	0.443	1.557
24	3.895	0.157	0.712	0.451	1.548
25	3.931	0.153	0.708	0.459	1.541

Source: Adapted from Table 27 of ASTM STP 15D, *ASTM Manual on Presentation of Data and Control Chart Analysis.* Copyright © 1976 American Society of Testing and Materials, Philadelphia, PA. Reprinted with permission.

overall sample mean $\bar{\bar{x}} = 3.499$. The upper control limit (UCL) is 3.514, which is 3 "sigma limits" above $\bar{\bar{x}}$. The lower control limit (LCL) is 3.485, which is 3 "sigma limits" below $\bar{\bar{x}}$. The $\bar{x}$ chart shows the 20 sample means plotted over time. Because all 20 sample means fall within the control limits, our assumption is confirmed that the data were collected during a period the process was in control. This chart can now be used to monitor the process mean on an ongoing basis.

R Chart

Let us now consider a range chart or **R chart** that can be used to control the variability of a process. To develop the R chart, we need to think of the range of a sample as a random variable with its own mean and standard deviation. The average range $\bar{R}$ provides an estimate of the mean of this random variable. Moreover, it can be shown that an estimate of the standard deviation of the range, denoted $\hat{\sigma}_R$, is

$$\hat{\sigma}_R = d_3 \frac{\bar{R}}{d_2}$$ (14.9)

FIGURE 14.7 $\bar{x}$ CHART FOR JENSEN COMPUTER SUPPLIES

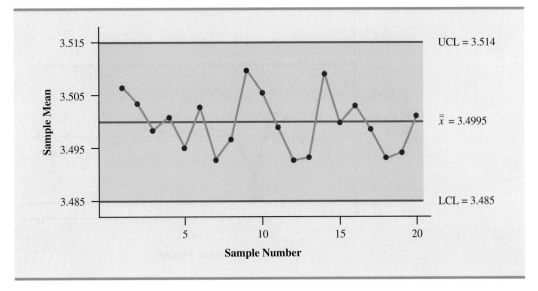

where d_2 and d_3 are constants that depend on the sample size; values of d_2 and d_3 are provided in Table 14.3. Thus, the UCL for the R chart is given by

$$\bar{R} + 3\hat{\sigma}_R = \bar{R} + 3d_3 \frac{\bar{R}}{d_2} = \bar{R}\left(1 + 3\frac{d_3}{d_2}\right) \tag{14.10}$$

and the LCL is

$$\bar{R} - 3\hat{\sigma}_R = \bar{R} - 3d_3 \frac{\bar{R}}{d_2} = \bar{R}\left(1 - 3\frac{d_3}{d_2}\right) \tag{14.11}$$

If we let

$$D_4 = 1 + 3\frac{d_3}{d_2} \tag{14.12}$$

$$D_3 = 1 - 3\frac{d_3}{d_2} \tag{14.13}$$

we can write the control limits for the R chart as

$$UCL = \bar{R}D_4 \tag{14.14}$$
$$LCL = \bar{R}D_3 \tag{14.15}$$

Values for D_3 and D_4 are also provided in Table 14.3. Note that for $n = 5$, $D_3 = 0$ and $D_4 = 2.114$. Thus, with $\bar{R} = .0253$, the control limits are

$$UCL = .0253(2.114) = .0535$$
$$LCL = .0253(0) = 0$$

FIGURE 14.8   *R* CHART FOR JENSEN COMPUTER SUPPLIES

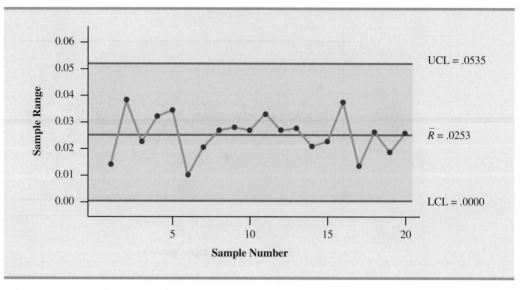

If the R chart indicates that the process is out of control, the $\bar{x}$ chart should not be interpreted until the R chart indicates the process variability is in control.

Figure 14.8 shows the *R* chart for Jensen Computer Supplies. The center line is shown at the overall mean of the 20 sample ranges, $\bar{R} = .0253$. The UCL is .0535 or 3 sigma limits above $\bar{R}$. The LCL is 0.0 or 3 sigma limits below $\bar{R}$. The *R* chart shows the 20 sample ranges plotted over time. Because all 20 sample ranges are within the control limits, we confirm that the process was in control during the sampling period.

Using Excel to Construct an *R* Chart and an $\bar{x}$ Chart

The $\bar{x}$ chart in Figure 14.7 and the *R* chart in Figure 14.8 can be constructed using Excel. Here we show how the data in Table 14.2 can be used to construct an *R* chart and an $\bar{x}$ chart using Excel. Figure 14.9 is an Excel worksheet containing the Jensen Computer Supplies data. The average value for the range is needed to compute the lower and upper control limits for the $\bar{x}$ chart. So we will construct the *R* chart first. Our approach will be to first develop a worksheet with the needed data. Then Excel's chart tools will be used to develop the *R* chart. A similar procedure is followed to construct the $\bar{x}$ chart. Figure 14.10 contains the data developed for the *R* chart. The formula worksheet is in the background; the value worksheet appears in the foreground.

Enter Data: The data for the diameter measurements for the 20 samples selected by Jensen Computer Supplies are contained in the worksheet in Figure 14.9. We will use the data in this worksheet to construct the worksheets shown in Figures 14.10 and 14.11. For future reference, the worksheet in Figure 14.9 is named Data. The only values entered directly into the worksheets in Figures 14.10 and 14.11 are the sample numbers 1–20 in column A, the headings in cells A1:E1, and the headings in cells C23 and C24.

Enter Functions and Formulas: The worksheet in Figure 14.10 contains the formulas needed to construct an *R* chart using Excel's chart tools. Here we describe how this worksheet was constructed. Column A contains the sample numbers 1–20 as noted. Column B contains the Excel formulas needed to compute the range for each sample from the data in cells B2:F21 of the Data worksheet shown in Figure 14.9. Excel's MAX and MIN functions are used. The cell references in the formulas are to cells in the Data worksheet; note that the worksheet name followed by an exclamation point must precede a cell reference when the

FIGURE 14.9   EXCEL DATA WORKSHEET FOR JENSEN COMPUTER SUPPLIES

	A	B	C	D	E	F	G
1	Sample	Observation 1	Observation 2	Observation 3	Observation 4	Observation 5	
2	1	3.5056	3.5086	3.5144	3.5009	3.5030	
3	2	3.4882	3.5085	3.4884	3.5250	3.5031	
4	3	3.4897	3.4898	3.4995	3.5130	3.4969	
5	4	3.5153	3.5120	3.4989	3.4900	3.4837	
6	5	3.5059	3.5113	3.5011	3.4773	3.4801	
7	6	3.4977	3.4961	3.5050	3.5014	3.5060	
8	7	3.4910	3.4913	3.4976	3.4831	3.5044	
9	8	3.4991	3.4853	3.4830	3.5083	3.5094	
10	9	3.5099	3.5162	3.5228	3.4958	3.5004	
11	10	3.4880	3.5015	3.5094	3.5102	3.5146	
12	11	3.4881	3.4887	3.5141	3.5175	3.4863	
13	12	3.5043	3.4867	3.4946	3.5018	3.4784	
14	13	3.5043	3.4769	3.4944	3.5014	3.4904	
15	14	3.5004	3.5030	3.5082	3.5045	3.5234	
16	15	3.4846	3.4938	3.5065	3.5089	3.5011	
17	16	3.5145	3.4832	3.5188	3.4935	3.4989	
18	17	3.5004	3.5042	3.4954	3.5020	3.4889	
19	18	3.4959	3.4823	3.4964	3.5082	3.4871	
20	19	3.4878	3.4864	3.4960	3.5070	3.4984	
21	20	3.4969	3.5144	3.5053	3.4985	3.4885	
22							

cells referenced are in another worksheet of the same workbook. The value worksheet shows that the ranges computed are the same as in Table 14.2. The AVERAGE function used in cell B22 computes the average of the ranges for the 20 samples.

In order to compute the LCL and UCL we must know D_3 and D_4. These values are obtained from Table 14.3 and placed into cells D23 and D24, respectively. The formulas in cells C2:C21 are identical; they compute the LCL by multiplying D_3 (cell D23) times the

FIGURE 14.10   EXCEL WORKSHEET SHOWING RANGE DATA AND COMPUTATION OF LCL, MEAN, AND UCL FOR AN *R* CHART

	A	B	C	D	E	F
1	Sample	R	LCL	Mean	UCL	
2	1	=MAX(Data!B2:F2)-MIN(Data!B2:F2)	=$D$23*$B$22	=$B$22	=$D$24*$B$22	
3	2	=MAX(Data!B3:F3)-MIN(Data!B3:F3)	=$D$23*$B$22	=$B$22	=$D$24*$B$22	
4	3	=MAX(Data!B4:F4)-MIN(Data!B4:F4)	=$D$23*$B$22	=$B$22	=$D$24*$B$22	
5	4	=MAX(Data!B5:F5)-MIN(Data!B5:F5)	=$D$23*$B$22	=$B$22	=$D$24*$B$22	
6	5	=MAX(Data!B6:F6)-MIN(Data!B6:F6)	=$D$23*$B$22	=$B$22	=$D$24*$B$22	
19	18	=MAX(Data!B19:F19)-MIN(Data!B19:F19)	=$D$23*$B$22	=$B$22	=$D$24*$B$22	
20	19	=MAX(Data!B20:F20)-MIN(Data!B20:F20)	=$D$23*$B$22	=$B$22	=$D$24*$B$22	
21	20	=MAX(Data!B21:F21)-MIN(Data!B21:F21)	=$D$23*$B$22	=$B$22	=$D$24*$B$22	
22	Mean(Rbar)	=AVERAGE($B$2:$B$21)				
23				D3	0	
24				D4	2.114	
25						

Note: Rows 7–18 (samples 6–17) are hidden.

	A	B	C	D	E	F
1	Sample	R	LCL	Mean	UCL	
2	1	0.0135	0.0000	0.0253	0.0534	
3	2	0.0368	0.0000	0.0253	0.0534	
4	3	0.0233	0.0000	0.0253	0.0534	
5	4	0.0316	0.0000	0.0253	0.0534	
6	5	0.0340	0.0000	0.0253	0.0534	
19	18	0.0259	0.0000	0.0253	0.0534	
20	19	0.0206	0.0000	0.0253	0.0534	
21	20	0.0259	0.0000	0.0253	0.0534	
22	Mean(Rbar)	0.0253				
23				D3	0.0000	
24				D4	2.1140	
25						

FIGURE 14.11   EXCEL WORKSHEET SHOWING $\bar{x}$ DATA AND COMPUTATION OF LCL, MEAN, AND UCL

	A	B	C	D	E	F
1	Sample	xbar	LCL	Mean	UCL	
2	1	=AVERAGE(Data!B2:F2)	=$B$22-$D$23*$D$24	=$B$22	=$B$22+$D$23*$D$24	
3	2	=AVERAGE(Data!B3:F3)	=$B$22-$D$23*$D$24	=$B$22	=$B$22+$D$23*$D$24	
4	3	=AVERAGE(Data!B4:F4)	=$B$22-$D$23*$D$24	=$B$22	=$B$22+$D$23*$D$24	
5	4	=AVERAGE(Data!B5:F5)	=$B$22-$D$23*$D$24	=$B$22	=$B$22+$D$23*$D$24	
6	5	=AVERAGE(Data!B6:F6)	=$B$22-$D$23*$D$24	=$B$22	=$B$22+$D$23*$D$24	
19	18	=AVERAGE(Data!B19:F19)	=$B$22-$D$23*$D$24	=$B$22	=$B$22+$D$23*$D$24	
20	19	=AVERAGE(Data!B20:F20)	=$B$22-$D$23*$D$24	=$B$22	=$B$22+$D$23*$D$24	
21	20	=AVERAGE(Data!B21:F21)	=$B$22-$D$23*$D$24	=$B$22	=$B$22+$D$23*$D$24	
22	Mean	=AVERAGE(B2:B21)				
23			A2	0.577		
24			Rbar	0.0253		
25						

	A	B	C	D	E	F
1	Sample	xbar	LCL	Mean	UCL	
2	1	3.5065	3.4849	3.4995	3.5141	
3	2	3.5026	3.4849	3.4995	3.5141	
4	3	3.4978	3.4849	3.4995	3.5141	
5	4	3.5000	3.4849	3.4995	3.5141	
6	5	3.4951	3.4849	3.4995	3.5141	
19	18	3.4940	3.4849	3.4995	3.5141	
20	19	3.4951	3.4849	3.4995	3.5141	
21	20	3.5007	3.4849	3.4995	3.5141	
22	Mean	3.4995				
23				A2	0.577	
24				Rbar	0.0253	
25						

Note: Rows 7–18 (samples 6–17) are hidden.

average range (cell B22). The formulas in cells D2:D21 are also identical; they provide the average range. Finally, the formulas in cells E2:E21 (also identical) compute the UCL by multiplying D_4 (cell D24) times the average range (cell B22).

In Figure 14.10 rows 7–18 are hidden. To construct the R chart you must first unhide rows 7–18.

Apply Tools: The following steps describe how to use Excel's chart tools to construct the R chart from the data in cells A2:E21 of Figure 14.10.

Step 1. Select cells A2:E21
Step 2. Click the **Insert** tab on the Ribbon
Step 3. In the **Charts** group, click **Scatter**
Step 4. When the list of scatter diagram subtypes appears,
  Click **Scatter with Straight Lines** (the chart in the lower left corner)
Step 5. In the **Chart Layouts** group, click **Layout 1**
Step 6. Select the **Chart Title** and replace it with **R Chart for Jensen Computer Supplies**
Step 7. Select the **Horizontal (Value) Axis Title** and replace it with **Sample Number**
Step 8. Select the **Vertical (Value) Axis Title** and replace it with **Sample Range**
Step 9. Right click the **Legend** (Series1—Series4) and click **Delete**

The resulting R chart will appear in the current worksheet. You will probably also want to resize the chart to satisfy your own preference. Just select the chart and move the drag handles until the chart looks the way you want it.

The procedure for constructing an $\bar{x}$ chart is similar. Figure 14.11 shows the worksheet developed to provide the data needed to construct an $\bar{x}$ chart. It is analogous to the worksheet developed for the R chart in Figure 14.10. One can use Excel's chart tools with this worksheet to construct the $\bar{x}$ chart shown in Figure 14.7. The steps followed are almost identical to those we just described for the R chart, so we will not repeat them here.

Control charts based on data indicating the presence of a defect or the number of defects are called attributes control charts. A p chart is an attributes control chart.

p Chart

Let us consider the case in which the output quality is measured in terms of the items being either nondefective or defective. The decision to continue or to adjust the production process will be based on $\bar{p}$, the proportion of defective items found in a sample of the output. The control chart used to monitor the proportion of defective items is called a p **chart**.

To illustrate the construction of a p chart, consider the use of automated mail-sorting machines in a post office. These automated machines scan the zip codes on letters and divert each letter to its proper carrier route. Even when a machine is operating properly, some letters are diverted to incorrect routes. Suppose that when a machine is operating correctly, or in a state of control, 3% of the letters are incorrectly diverted. Thus p, the proportion of letters incorrectly diverted when the process is in control, is .03.

The sampling distribution of $\bar{p}$, as presented in Chapter 7, can be used to determine the variation that can be expected in $\bar{p}$ values for a process that is in control. Recall that the expected value or mean of $\bar{p}$ is p, the proportion defective when the process is in control. With samples of size n, the formula for the standard deviation of $\bar{p}$, called the standard error of the proportion, is

$$\sigma_{\bar{p}} = \sqrt{\frac{p(1-p)}{n}} \qquad (14.16)$$

We also learned in Chapter 7 that the sampling distribution of $\bar{p}$ can be approximated by a normal probability distribution whenever the following two conditions are satisfied.

$$np \geq 5$$
$$n(1-p) \geq 5$$

Thus, if these two conditions are satisfied, the sampling distribution of $\bar{p}$ can be approximated by a normal probability distribution with mean p and standard deviation $\sigma_{\bar{p}}$. This distribution is shown in Figure 14.12.

To establish control limits for a p chart, we follow the same procedure we used to establish control limits for an $\bar{x}$ chart. That is, the limits for the control chart are set at 3 standard errors above and below the proportion defective when the process is in control. Thus, we have the following control limits.

CONTROL LIMITS FOR A p CHART

$$\text{UCL} = p + 3\sigma_{\bar{p}} \qquad (14.17)$$
$$\text{LCL} = p - 3\sigma_{\bar{p}} \qquad (14.18)$$

FIGURE 14.12 SAMPLING DISTRIBUTION OF $\bar{p}$

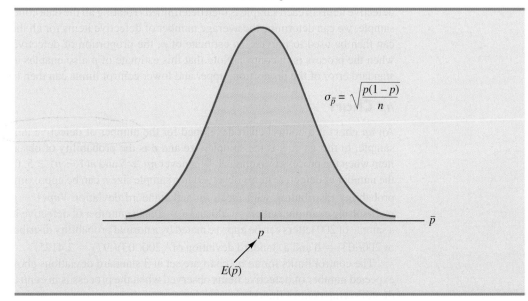

$$\sigma_{\bar{p}} = \sqrt{\frac{p(1-p)}{n}}$$

$\bar{p}$

p

$E(\bar{p})$

FIGURE 14.13   *p* CHART FOR THE PROPORTION DEFECTIVE IN A MAIL-SORTING PROCESS

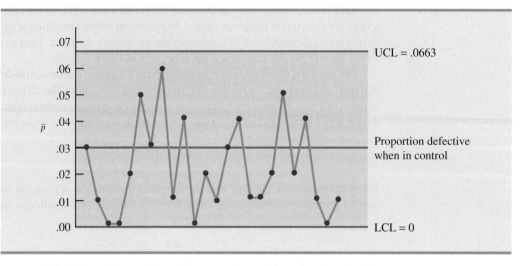

With $p = .03$ and samples of size $n = 200$, equation (14.16) shows that the standard error is

$$\sigma_{\bar{p}} = \sqrt{\frac{.03(1 - .03)}{200}} = .0121$$

Hence, the control limits are UCL $= .03 + 3(.0121) = .0663$ and LCL $= .03 - 3(.0121) = -.0063$. Whenever equation (14.18) provides a negative value for LCL, LCL is reset to zero in the control chart.

Figure 14.13 is the control chart for the mail-sorting process. The points plotted show the sample proportion defective found in samples of letters taken from the process. All points are within the control limits, and the sorting process shows no evidence of being out of control. In fact, the *p* chart indicates that the process should continue to operate.

If the proportion of defective items for a process that is in control is not known, that value is first estimated by using sample data. Suppose, for example, that *k* different samples, each of size *n*, are selected from a process that is in control. The fraction or proportion of defective items in each sample is then determined. Treating all the data collected as one large sample, we can determine the average number of defective items for all the data; that value can then be used to provide an estimate of *p*, the proportion of defective items observed when the process is in control. Note that this estimate of *p* also enables us to estimate the standard error of the proportion; upper and lower control limits can then be established.

np **Chart**

An *np* **chart** is a control chart developed for the number of defective items observed in a sample. In this case, *n* is the sample size and *p* is the probability of observing a defective item when the process is in control. Whenever $np \geq 5$ and $n(1 - p) \geq 5$, the distribution of the number of defective items observed in a sample size *n* can be approximated by a normal probability distribution with mean *np* and standard deviation $\sqrt{np(1 - p)}$. Thus, for the mail-sorting example, with $n = 200$ and $p = .03$, the number of defective items observed in a sample of 200 letters can be approximated by a normal probability distribution with a mean of $200(.03) = 6$ and a standard deviation of $\sqrt{200(.03)(.97)} = 2.4125$.

The control limits for an *np* chart are set at 3 standard deviations above and below the expected number of defective items observed when the process is in control. Thus, we have the following control limits.

CONTROL LIMITS FOR AN *np* CHART

$$\text{UCL} = np + 3\sqrt{np(1 - p)} \qquad (14.19)$$

$$\text{LCL} = np - 3\sqrt{np(1 - p)} \qquad (14.20)$$

For the mail-sorting process example, with $p = .03$ and $n = 200$, the control limits are UCL $= 6 + 3(2.4125) = 13.2375$ and LCL $= 6 - 3(2.4125) = -1.2375$. Because equation (14.20) provides a negative value for LCL, it is reset to zero in the control chart. Hence, if the number of letters diverted to incorrect routes is 14 or more, the process is concluded to be out of control.

The information provided by an *np* chart is equivalent to the information provided by the *p* chart; the only difference is that the *np* chart is a plot of the number of defective items observed, whereas the *p* chart is a plot of the proportion of defective items observed. Thus, if we were to conclude that a particular process is out of control on the basis of a *p* chart, the process would also be concluded to be out of control on the basis of an *np* chart.

Interpretation of Control Charts

Control charts are designed to identify when assignable causes of variation are present. Managers must then authorize action to eliminate the assignable cause and return the process to an in-control state.

The location and pattern of points in a control chart enable us to determine, with a small probability of error, whether a process is in statistical control. A primary indication that a process may be out of control is a data point outside the control limits, such as point 5 in Figure 14.6. Such a point is statistical evidence that the process is out of control; in such cases, corrective action should be taken as soon as possible.

In addition to points outside the control limits, certain patterns of the points within the control limits can be warning signals of quality control problems. For example, assume that all the data points are within the control limits but that a large number of points are on one side of the center line. This pattern may indicate that an equipment problem, a change in materials, or some other assignable cause has led to a shift in quality. Careful investigation of the production process should be undertaken to determine whether quality has changed.

Even if all points are within the upper and lower control limits, a process may not be in control. Trends in the sample data points or unusually long runs above or below the center line may also indicate out-of-control conditions.

Another pattern to watch for in control charts is a gradual shift, or trend, over time. For example, as tools wear out, the dimensions of machined parts will gradually deviate from their designed levels. Gradual changes in temperature or humidity, general equipment deterioration, dirt buildup, or operator fatigue may also result in a trend pattern in control charts. Six or seven points in a row that indicate either an increasing or decreasing trend should be cause for concern, even if the data points are all within the control limits. When such a pattern occurs, the process should be reviewed for possible changes or shifts in quality. Corrective action to bring the process back into control may be necessary.

NOTES AND COMMENTS

1. Because the control limits for the $\bar{x}$ chart depend on the value of the average range, these limits will not have much meaning unless the process variability is in control. In practice, the *R* chart is usually constructed before the $\bar{x}$ chart; if the *R* chart indicates that the process variability is in control, then the $\bar{x}$ chart is constructed.

2. The *p* and *np* control charts can also be constructed using Excel's chart tools. For instance, to develop a *p* chart, start by organizing the data for $\bar{p}$, LCL, mean, and UCL in a worksheet similar to Figures 14.10 or 14.11. Then use the chart tools in the same way we did earlier to construct an *R* chart.

Exercises

Methods

1. A process that is in control has a mean of $\mu = 12.5$ and a standard deviation of $\sigma = .8$.
    a. Construct an $\bar{x}$ chart if samples of size 4 are to be used.
    b. Repeat part (a) for samples of size 8 and 16.
    c. What happens to the limits of the control chart as the sample size is increased? Discuss why this change is reasonable.

2. Twenty-five samples, each of size 5, were selected from a process that was in control. The sum of all the data collected was 677.5 pounds.
    a. What is an estimate of the process mean (in terms of pounds per unit) when the process is in control?
    b. Develop the control chart for this process if samples of size 5 will be used. Assume that the process standard deviation is .5 when the process is in control and that the mean of the process is the estimate developed in part (a).

3. Twenty-five samples of 100 items each were inspected when a process was considered to be operating satisfactorily. In the 25 samples, 135 items were found to be defective.
    a. What is an estimate of the proportion defective when the process is in control?
    b. What is the standard error of the proportion if samples of size 100 will be used for statistical process control?
    c. Compute the upper and lower control limits for the control chart.

4. An in-control process sampled 20 times with a sample of size 8 resulted in $\bar{\bar{x}} = 28.5$ and $\bar{R} = 1.6$. Compute the upper and lower control limits for the $\bar{x}$ and R charts for this process.

Applications

5. Temperature is used to measure the output of a production process. When the process is in control, the mean of the process is $\mu = 128.5$ and the standard deviation is $\sigma = .4$.
    a. Construct an $\bar{x}$ chart if samples of size 6 are to be used.
    b. Is the process in control for a sample providing the following data?

    | 128.8 | 128.2 | 129.1 | 128.7 | 128.4 | 129.2 |

    c. Is the process in control for a sample providing the following data?

    | 129.3 | 128.7 | 128.6 | 129.2 | 129.5 | 129.0 |

6. A quality control process monitors the weight per carton of laundry detergent. Control limits are set at UCL = 20.12 ounces and LCL = 19.90 ounces. Samples of size 5 are used for the sampling and inspection process. What are the process mean and process standard deviation for the manufacturing operation?

7. The Goodman Tire and Rubber Company periodically tests its tires for tread wear under simulated road conditions. To study and control the manufacturing process, 20 samples, each containing three radial tires, were chosen from different shifts over several days of operation; the data collected are shown below. Assuming that these data were collected when the manufacturing process was believed to be operating in control, develop the R and $\bar{x}$ charts.

Sample	Tread Wear*		
1	31	42	28
2	26	18	35
3	25	30	34
4	17	25	21
5	38	29	35
6	41	42	36
7	21	17	29
8	32	26	28
9	41	34	33
10	29	17	30
11	26	31	40
12	23	19	25
13	17	24	32
14	43	35	17
15	18	25	29
16	30	42	31
17	28	36	32
18	40	29	31
19	18	29	28
20	22	34	26

Tires

*Hundredths of an inch

8. Over several weeks of normal, or in-control, operation, 20 samples of 150 packages each of synthetic-gut tennis strings were tested for breaking strength. A total of 141 packages of the 3000 tested failed to conform to the manufacturer's specifications.
   a. What is an estimate of the process proportion defective when the system is in control?
   b. Compute the upper and lower control limits for a p chart.
   c. With the results of part (b), what conclusion should be drawn about the process if tests on a new sample of 150 packages find 12 defective? Do there appear to be assignable causes in this situation?
   d. Compute the upper and lower control limits for an np chart.
   e. Answer part (c) using the results of part (d).
   f. Which control chart would be preferred in this situation? Explain.

9. An automotive industry supplier produces pistons for several models of automobiles. Twenty samples, each consisting of 200 pistons, were selected when the process was known to be operating in control. The numbers of defective pistons found in the samples follow.

8	10	6	4	5	7	8	12	8	15
14	10	10	7	5	8	6	10	4	8

   a. What is an estimate of the proportion defective for the piston manufacturing process when it is in control?
   b. Construct a p chart for the manufacturing process, assuming each sample has 200 pistons.
   c. With the results of part (b), what conclusion should be drawn if a sample of 200 has 20 defective pistons?
   d. Compute the upper and lower control limits for an np chart.
   e. Answer part (c) using the results of part (d).

(14.3) Acceptance Sampling

In acceptance sampling, the items of interest can be incoming shipments of raw materials or purchased parts as well as finished goods from final assembly. Suppose we want to decide whether to accept or reject a group of items on the basis of specified quality characteristics. In quality control terminology, the group of items is a **lot**, and **acceptance sampling** is a statistical method that enables us to make an accept-reject decision based on a sample of items from the lot.

Acceptance sampling has the following advantages over 100% inspection:
1. Usually less expensive
2. Less product damage due to less handling and testing
3. Fewer inspectors required
4. Provides only approach possible if destructive testing must be used

The general steps of acceptance sampling are shown in Figure 14.14. After a lot is received, a sample is selected for inspection. The results of the inspection are compared to specified quality characteristics. If the quality is satisfactory, the lot is accepted and sent to production or shipped to customers. If the quality is not satisfactory, the lot is rejected. Managers must then decide on the disposition of the lot. In some cases, the decision may be to keep the lot and remove the unacceptable or nonconforming items. In other cases, the lot may be returned to the supplier at the supplier's expense; the extra work and cost placed on the supplier can motivate the supplier to provide high-quality lots. Finally, if the rejected lot consists of finished goods, the goods must be scrapped or reworked to meet acceptable quality standards.

The statistical procedure of acceptance sampling is based on the hypothesis testing methodology presented in Chapter 9. The null and alternative hypotheses are stated as follows.

$$H_0: \text{Good-quality lot}$$
$$H_a: \text{Poor-quality lot}$$

FIGURE 14.14   ACCEPTANCE SAMPLING PROCEDURE

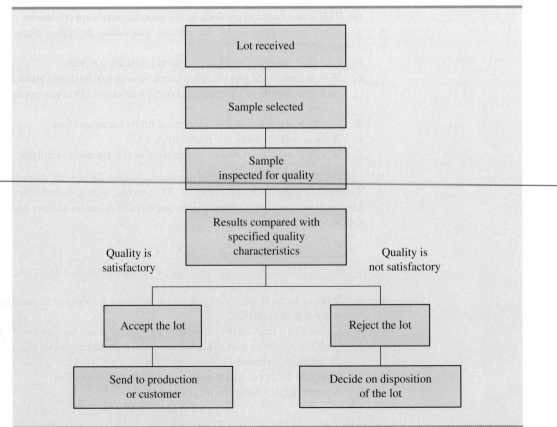

TABLE 14.4   OUTCOMES OF ACCEPTANCE SAMPLING

	State of the Lot	
	H_0 True Good-Quality Lot	H_0 False Poor-Quality Lot
Accept the Lot	Correct decision	Type II error (accepting a poor-quality lot)
Reject the Lot	Type I error (rejecting a good-quality lot)	Correct decision

Decision

Table 14.4 shows the outcomes of the hypothesis testing procedure. Note that correct decisions correspond to accepting a good-quality lot and rejecting a poor-quality lot. However, as with other hypothesis testing procedures, we need to be aware of the possibilities of making a Type I error (rejecting a good-quality lot) or a Type II error (accepting a poor-quality lot).

Because the probability of a Type I error creates a risk for the producer of the lot, it is known as the **producer's risk**. For example, a producer's risk of .05 indicates a 5% chance that a good-quality lot will be erroneously rejected. Because the probability of a Type II error creates a risk for the consumer of the lot, it is known as the **consumer's risk**. For example, a consumer's risk of .10 means that there is a 10% chance that a poor-quality lot will be erroneously accepted and thus used in production or shipped to the customer. Specific values for the producer's risk and the consumer's risk can be controlled by the person designing the acceptance sampling procedure. To illustrate how to assign risk values, let us consider the problem faced by KALI, Inc.

KALI, Inc.: An Example of Acceptance Sampling

KALI, Inc., manufactures home appliances that are marketed under a variety of trade names. However, KALI does not manufacture every component used in its products. Several components are purchased directly from suppliers. For example, one of the components that KALI purchases for use in home air conditioners is an overload protector, a device that turns off the compressor if it overheats. The compressor can be seriously damaged if the overload protector does not function properly; therefore, KALI is concerned about the quality of the overload protectors. One way to ensure quality would be to test every component received; this approach is known as 100% inspection. However, to determine proper functioning of an overload protector, the device must be subjected to time-consuming and expensive tests, and KALI cannot justify testing every overload protector it receives.

Instead, KALI uses an acceptance sampling plan to monitor the quality of the overload protectors. The acceptance sampling plan requires that KALI's quality control inspectors select and test a sample of overload protectors from each shipment. If very few defective units are found in the sample, the lot is probably of good quality and should be accepted. However, if a large number of defective units are found in the sample, the lot is probably of poor quality and should be rejected.

An *acceptance sampling plan* consists of a sample size n and an acceptance criterion c. The **acceptance criterion** is the maximum number of defective items that can be found in the sample and still indicate an acceptable lot. For example, for the KALI example let us suppose that a sample of 15 items will be selected from each incoming shipment or lot. Furthermore, suppose that the manager of quality control states that the lot can be accepted only if no defective items are found. In this case, the acceptance sampling plan established by the quality control manager is $n = 15$ and $c = 0$.

This acceptance sampling plan is easy for the quality control inspector to implement. The inspector simply selects a sample of 15 items, performs the tests, and reaches a conclusion based on the following decision rule.

- *Accept the lot* if zero defects are found.
- *Reject the lot* if one or more defects are found.

Before implementing this acceptance sampling plan, the quality control manager wants to evaluate the risks or errors possible under the plan. The plan will be implemented only if both the producer's risk (Type I error) and the consumer's risk (Type II error) are controlled at reasonable levels.

Computing the Probability of Accepting a Lot

The key to analyzing both the producer's risk and the consumer's risk is a what-if type of analysis; that is, we assume that a lot has some known percentage of defective items and compute the probability of accepting the lot for a given sampling plan. By varying the assumed percentage of defective items, we can examine the effect of the sampling plan on both types of risks.

Let us begin by assuming that in a large shipment of overload protectors 5% of the overload protectors are defective. For a shipment or lot with 5% of the items defective, what is the probability that the $n = 15$, $c = 0$ sampling plan will lead us to accept the lot? Because each overload protector tested will be either defective or nondefective and because the lot size is large, the number of defective items in a sample of 15 has a *binomial probability distribution*. The binomial probability function, which was presented in Chapter 5, follows.

BINOMIAL PROBABILITY FUNCTION FOR ACCEPTANCE SAMPLING

$$f(x) = \frac{n!}{x!(n-x)!} p^x (1-p)^{(n-x)}$$

(14.21)

where

$$n = \text{sample size}$$
$$p = \text{proportion of defective items in the lot}$$
$$x = \text{number of defective items in the sample}$$
$$f(x) = \text{probability of } x \text{ defective items in the sample}$$

For the KALI acceptance sampling plan, $n = 15$; thus, for a lot with 5% defective ($p = .05$), we have

$$f(x) = \frac{15!}{x!(15-x)!} (.05)^x (1 - .05)^{(15-x)}$$

(14.22)

Using equation (14.22), $f(0)$ will provide the probability that, in the sample, zero overload protectors will be defective and the lot will be accepted. In using equation (14.22), recall that $0! = 1$. Thus, the probability computation for $f(0)$ is

$$f(0) = \frac{15!}{0!(15-0)!} (.05)^0 (1 - .05)^{(15-0)}$$

$$= \frac{15!}{0!(15)!} (.05)^0 (.95)^{15} = (.95)^{15} = .4633$$

TABLE 14.5 PROBABILITY OF ACCEPTING THE LOT FOR THE KALI EXAMPLE
WITH $n = 15$ AND $c = 0$

Percent Defective in the Lot	Probability of Accepting the Lot
1	.8601
2	.7386
3	.6333
4	.5421
5	.4633
10	.2059
15	.0874
20	.0352
25	.0134

We now know that the $n = 15$, $c = 0$ sampling plan has a .4633 probability of accepting a lot with 5% defective items. Hence, a corresponding probability of rejecting a lot with 5% defective items is $1 - .4633 = .5367$.

Excel's BINOMDIST function can also be used to compute these probabilities. See Chapter 5.

In Table 14.5 we show the probability that the $n = 15$, $c = 0$ sampling plan will lead to the acceptance of lots with 1%, 2%, 3%, . . . defective items. The probabilities in the table were computed by using $p = .01$, $p = .02$, $p = .03$, . . . in the binomial probability function (14.21).

With the data in Table 14.5, a graph of the probability of accepting the lot versus the percent defective in the lot can be drawn as shown in Figure 14.15. This graph, or curve, is called the **operating characteristic (OC) curve** for the $n = 15$, $c = 0$ acceptance sampling plan.

FIGURE 14.15 OPERATING CHARACTERISTIC CURVE FOR THE $n = 15$, $c = 0$
ACCEPTANCE SAMPLING PLAN

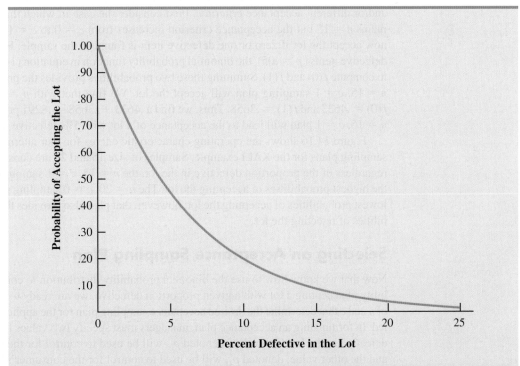

FIGURE 14.16 OPERATING CHARACTERISTIC CURVES FOR FOUR ACCEPTANCE SAMPLING PLANS

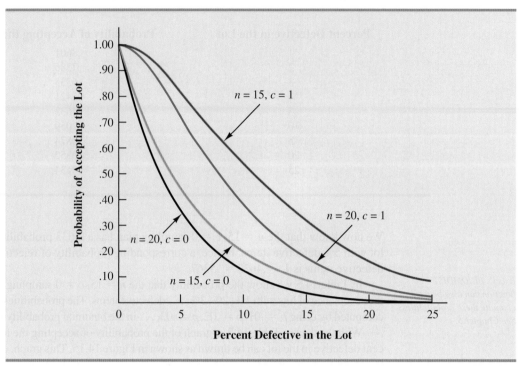

Perhaps we should consider other sampling plans, ones with different sample sizes n and/or different acceptance criteria c. First consider the case in which the sample size remains $n = 15$ but the acceptance criterion increases from $c = 0$ to $c = 1$; that is, we will now accept the lot if zero or one defective item is found in the sample. For a lot with 5% defective items ($p = .05$), the binomial probability function in equation (14.21) can be used to compute $f(0)$ and $f(1)$. Summing these two probabilities provides the probability that the $n = 15$, $c = 1$ sampling plan will accept the lot. We find that with $n = 15$ and $p = .05$, $f(0) = .4633$ and $f(1) = .3658$. Thus, we find a $.4633 + .3658 = .8291$ probability that the $n = 15$, $c = 1$ plan will lead to the acceptance of a lot with 5% defective items.

Figure 14.16 shows the operating characteristic curves for four alternative acceptance sampling plans for the KALI example. Samples of size 15 and 20 are considered. Note that regardless of the proportion defective in the lot, the $n = 15$, $c = 1$ sampling plan provides the highest probabilities of accepting the lot. The $n = 20$, $c = 0$ sampling plan provides the lowest probabilities of accepting the lot; however, that plan also provides the highest probabilities of rejecting the lot.

Selecting an Acceptance Sampling Plan

Now that we know how to use the binomial probability distribution to compute the probability of accepting a lot with a given proportion defective, we are ready to select the values of n and c that determine the desired acceptance sampling plan for the application being studied. In formulating an acceptance plan, managers must specify two values for the proportion defective in the lot. One value, denoted p_0, will be used to control for the producer's risk, and the other value, denoted p_1, will be used to control for the consumer's risk.

FIGURE 14.17 OPERATING CHARACTERISTIC CURVE FOR $n = 15$, $c = 0$ WITH $p_0 = .03$ AND $p_1 = .15$

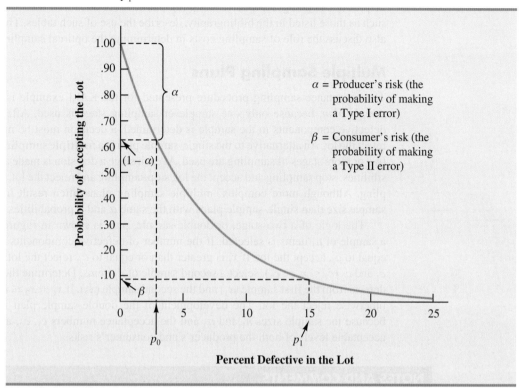

In showing how this formulation can be done, we will use the following notation.

α = the producer's risk; the probability that a lot with p_0 defective will be rejected

β = the consumer's risk; the probability that a lot with p_1 defective will be accepted

Suppose that for the KALI example, the managers specify that $p_0 = .03$ and $p_1 = .15$. From the OC curve for $n = 15$, $c = 0$ in Figure 14.17, we see that $p_0 = .03$ provides a producer's risk of approximately $1 - .63 = .37$, and $p_1 = .15$ provides a consumer's risk of approximately .09. Thus, if the managers are willing to tolerate both a .37 probability of rejecting a lot with 3% defective items (producer's risk) and a .09 probability of accepting a lot with 15% defective items (consumer's risk), the $n = 15$, $c = 0$ acceptance sampling plan would be acceptable.

Suppose, however, that the managers request a producer's risk of $\alpha = .10$ and a consumer's risk of $\beta = .20$. We see that now the $n = 15$, $c = 0$ sampling plan offers a better-than-desired consumer's risk but an unacceptably large producer's risk. The fact that $\alpha = .37$ indicates that 37% of the lots will be erroneously rejected when only 3% of the items in them are defective. The producer's risk is too high, and a different acceptance sampling plan should be considered.

Using $p_0 = .03$, $\alpha = .10$, $p_1 = .15$, and $\beta = .20$ in Figure 14.16 shows that the acceptance sampling plan with $n = 20$ and $c = 1$ comes closest to meeting both the producer's and the consumer's risk requirements. Exercise 13 at the end of this section will ask you to compute the producer's risk and the consumer's risk for the $n = 20$, $c = 1$ sampling plan.

As shown in this section, several computations and several operating characteristic curves may need to be considered to determine the sampling plan with the desired producer's and consumer's risks. Fortunately, tables of sampling plans are published. For example, the American Military Standard Table, MIL-STD-105D, provides information helpful in designing acceptance sampling plans. More advanced texts on quality control, such as those listed in the bibliography, describe the use of such tables. The advanced texts also discuss the role of sampling costs in determining the optimal sampling plan.

Multiple Sampling Plans

The acceptance sampling procedure presented for the KALI example is called a *single-sample plan,* because only one sample or sampling stage is used. After the number of defective components in the sample is determined, a decision must be made to accept or reject the lot. An alternative to the single-sample plan is a **multiple sampling plan**, in which two or more stages of sampling are used. At each stage a decision is made among three possibilities: stop sampling and accept the lot, stop sampling and reject the lot, or continue sampling. Although more complex, multiple sampling plans often result in a smaller total sample size than single-sample plans with the same α and β probabilities.

The logic of a two-stage, or double-sample, plan is shown in Figure 14.18. Initially a sample of n_1 items is selected. If the number of defective components x_1 is less than or equal to c_1, accept the lot. If x_1 is greater than or equal to c_2, reject the lot. If x_1 is between c_1 and c_2 $(c_1 < x_1 < c_2)$, select a second sample of n_2 items. Determine the total number of defects from the first sample (x_1) and the second sample (x_2). If $x_1 + x_2 \leq c_3$, accept the lot; otherwise reject the lot. The development of the double-sample plan is more difficult because the sample sizes n_1 and n_2 and the acceptance numbers c_1, c_2, and c_3 must meet acceptable levels of both the producer's and consumer's risks.

NOTES AND COMMENTS

1. The use of the binomial probability distribution for acceptance sampling is based on the assumption of large lots. If the lot size is small, the hypergeometric probability distribution is the appropriate distribution.

2. In the MIL-STD-105D sampling tables, p_0 is called the acceptable quality level (AQL). In some sampling tables, p_1 is called the lot tolerance percent defective (LTPD) or the rejectable quality level (RQL). Many of the published sampling plans also use quality indexes such as the indifference quality level (IQL) and the average outgoing quality limit (AOQL). The more ad-

   vanced texts listed in the bibliography provide a complete discussion of these other indexes.

3. In this section we provided an introduction to *attributes sampling plans.* In these plans each item sampled is classified as nondefective or defective. In *variables sampling plans,* a sample is taken and a measurement of the quality characteristic is taken. For example, for gold jewelry a measurement of quality may be the amount of gold it contains. A simple statistic such as the average amount of gold in the sample jewelry is computed and compared with an allowable value to determine whether to accept or reject the lot.

Exercises

Methods

10. For an acceptance sampling plan with $n = 25$ and $c = 0$, find the probability of accepting a lot when the defect rate is 2%. What is the probability of accepting the lot if the defect rate is 6%?

11. Consider an acceptance sampling plan with $n = 20$ and $c = 0$. Compute the producer's risk for each of the following cases.
    a. The lot has a defect rate of 2%.
    b. The lot has a defect rate of 6%.

FIGURE 14.18   A TWO-STAGE ACCEPTANCE SAMPLING PLAN

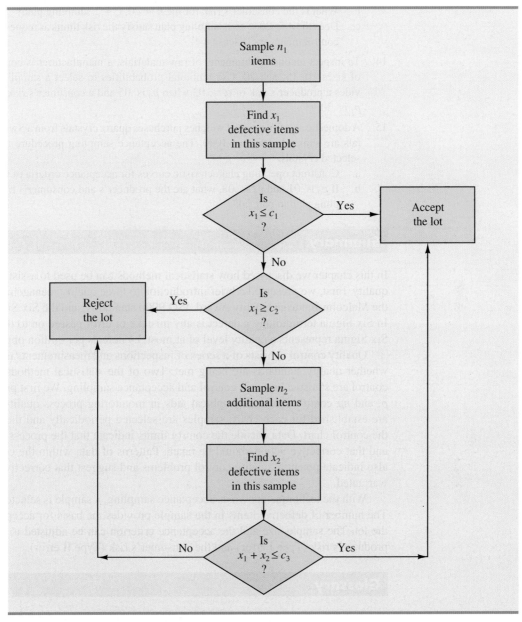

12.   Repeat exercise 11 for the acceptance sampling plan with $n = 20$ and $c = 1$. What happens to the producer's risk as the acceptance number c is increased? Explain.

Applications

13.   Refer to the KALI example presented in this section. The quality control manager requested a producer's risk of .10 or less when p_0 was .03 and a consumer's risk of .20 or less when p_1 was .15. Consider the acceptance sampling plan based on a sample size of 20 and an acceptance criterion of $c = 1$. Answer the following questions.

    a. What is the producer's risk for the $n = 20$, $c = 1$ sampling plan?

    b. What is the consumer's risk for the $n = 20$, $c = 1$ sampling plan?

    c. Does the $n = 20$, $c = 1$ sampling plan satisfy the risk limits as requested by the quality control manager? Discuss.

14. To inspect incoming shipments of raw materials, a manufacturer is considering samples of sizes 10, 15, and 20. Use binomial probabilities to select a sampling plan that provides a producer's risk of $\alpha = .03$ when p_0 is .05 and a consumer's risk of $\beta = .12$ when p_1 is .30.

15. A domestic manufacturer of watches purchases quartz crystals from a Swiss firm. The crystals are shipped in lots of 1000. The acceptance sampling procedure uses 20 randomly selected crystals.

    a. Construct operating characteristic curves for acceptance criteria of 0, 1, and 2.

    b. If p_0 is .01 and $p_1 = .08$, what are the producer's and consumer's risks for each sampling plan in part (a)?

Summary

In this chapter we discussed how statistical methods can be used to assist in the control of quality. First, we presented a brief introduction to three quality management frameworks: the Malcolm Baldrige Quality Award, ISO 9000 standards, and the Six Sigma philosophy. In Six Sigma terminology a defect is any mistake or error passed on to the customer, and Six Sigma represents a quality level of at most 3.4 defects per million opportunities.

Quality control consists of a series of inspections and measurements used to determine whether quality standards are being met. Two of the statistical methods used in quality control are statistical process control and acceptance sampling. We first presented the $\bar{x}$, R, p, and np control charts as graphical aids in monitoring process quality. Control limits are established for each chart; samples are selected periodically and the data plotted on the control chart. Data outside the control limits indicate that the process is out of control and that corrective action should be taken. Patterns of data within the control limits can also indicate potential quality control problems and suggest that corrective action may be warranted.

With the technique known as acceptance sampling, a sample is selected and inspected. The number of defective items in the sample provides the basis for accepting or rejecting the lot. The sample size and the acceptance criterion can be adjusted to control both the producer's risk (Type I error) and the consumer's risk (Type II error).

Glossary

Total quality (TQ) A people-focused management system that aims at continual increase in customer satisfaction at continually lower real cost.

Six Sigma A methodology used to provide a level of quality so good that for every 1 million opportunities, no more than 3.4 defects will occur. This level of quality is referred to as the Six Sigma level of quality.

Quality control A series of inspections and measurements used to determine whether quality standards are being met.

Assignable causes Variations in process outputs that are due to factors such as machine tools wearing out, incorrect machine settings, poor-quality raw materials, operator error, and so on. Corrective action should be taken whenever assignable causes are detected.

Common causes Normal or natural variations in process outputs that are due purely to chance. No corrective action is necessary when output variations are due to common causes.

Control chart A graphical tool used to help determine whether a process is in control or out of control.

$\bar{x}$ **chart** A control chart used to monitor the mean value of a variable such as a length, weight, temperature, and so on.

R **chart** A control chart used to monitor the variability of a process.

p **chart** A control chart used to monitor the proportion of defective items generated by a process.

np **chart** A control chart used to monitor the number of defective items generated by a process.

Lot A group of items such as an incoming shipment of raw materials, a shipment of purchased parts, or a batch of finished goods from final assembly.

Acceptance sampling A statistical procedure in which the number of defective items found in a sample is used to determine whether a lot should be accepted or rejected.

Producer's risk The risk of rejecting a good-quality lot; a Type I error.

Consumer's risk The risk of accepting a poor-quality lot; a Type II error.

Acceptance criterion The maximum number of defective items that can be found in the sample and still indicate an acceptable lot.

Operating characteristic (OC) curve A graph showing the probability of accepting the lot as a function of the percent defective in the lot. This curve can be used to determine whether a particular acceptance sampling plan meets both the producer's and the consumer's risk requirements.

Multiple sampling plan A form of acceptance sampling in which more than one sample or stage is used. On the basis of the number of defective items found in a sample, a decision will be made to accept the lot, reject the lot, or continue sampling.

Key Formulas

Standard Error of the Mean

$$\sigma_{\bar{x}} = \frac{\sigma}{\sqrt{n}} \tag{14.1}$$

Control Limits for an $\bar{x}$ Chart: Process Mean and Standard Deviation Known

$$\text{UCL} = \mu + 3\sigma_{\bar{x}} \tag{14.2}$$
$$\text{LCL} = \mu - 3\sigma_{\bar{x}} \tag{14.3}$$

Overall Sample Mean

$$\bar{\bar{x}} = \frac{\bar{x}_1 + \bar{x}_2 + \cdots + \bar{x}_k}{k} \tag{14.4}$$

Average Range

$$\bar{R} = \frac{R_1 + R_2 + \cdots + R_k}{k} \tag{14.5}$$

Control Limits for an $\bar{x}$ Chart: Process Mean and Standard Deviation Unknown

$$\bar{\bar{x}} \pm A_2\bar{R} \tag{14.8}$$

Control Limits for an *R* Chart

$$\text{UCL} = \bar{R}D_4 \tag{14.14}$$
$$\text{LCL} = \bar{R}D_3 \tag{14.15}$$

Standard Error of the Proportion

$$\sigma_{\bar{p}} = \sqrt{\frac{p(1-p)}{n}} \qquad (14.16)$$

Control Limits for a p Chart

$$\text{UCL} = p + 3\sigma_{\bar{p}} \qquad (14.17)$$
$$\text{LCL} = p - 3\sigma_{\bar{p}} \qquad (14.18)$$

Control Limits for an np Chart

$$\text{UCL} = np + 3\sqrt{np(1-p)} \qquad (14.19)$$
$$\text{LCL} = np - 3\sqrt{np(1-p)} \qquad (14.20)$$

Binomial Probability Function for Acceptance Sampling

$$f(x) = \frac{n!}{x!(n-x)!} p^x (1-p)^{(n-x)} \qquad (14.21)$$

Supplementary Exercises

16. Samples of size 5 provided the following 20 sample means for a production process that is believed to be in control.

95.72	95.24	95.18
95.44	95.46	95.32
95.40	95.44	95.08
95.50	95.80	95.22
95.56	95.22	95.04
95.72	94.82	95.46
95.60	95.78	

  a. Based on these data, what is an estimate of the mean when the process is in control?
  b. Assuming that the process standard deviation is $\sigma = .50$, develop an $\bar{x}$ control chart for this production process. Assume that the mean of the process is the estimate developed in part (a).
  c. Are any of the 20 sample means outside the control limits?

17. Product filling weights are normally distributed with a mean of 350 grams and a standard deviation of 15 grams.
  a. Develop the control limits for samples of size 10, 20, and 30.
  b. What happens to the control limits as the sample size is increased?
  c. What happens when a Type I error is made?
  d. What happens when a Type II error is made?
  e. What is the probability of a Type I error for samples of size 10, 20, and 30?
  f. What is the advantage of increasing the sample size for control chart purposes? What error probability is reduced as the sample size is increased?

18. Twenty-five samples of size 5 resulted in $\bar{\bar{x}} = 5.42$ and $\bar{R} = 2.0$. Compute control limits for the $\bar{x}$ and R charts, and estimate the standard deviation of the process.

19. The following quality control data for a manufacturing process at Kensport Chemical Company show the temperature in degrees centigrade at five points in time during a manufacturing cycle. The company is interested in using control charts to monitor the temperature of its manufacturing process. Construct the $\bar{x}$ and R charts. What conclusions can be drawn about the quality of the process?

Sample	$\bar{x}$	R	Sample	$\bar{x}$	R
1	95.72	1.0	11	95.80	.6
2	95.24	.9	12	95.22	.2
3	95.18	.8	13	95.56	1.3
4	95.44	.4	14	95.22	.5
5	95.46	.5	15	95.04	.8
6	95.32	1.1	16	95.72	1.1
7	95.40	.9	17	94.82	.6
8	95.44	.3	18	95.46	.5
9	95.08	.2	19	95.60	.4
10	95.50	.6	20	95.74	.6

20. The following data were collected for the Master Blend Coffee production process. The data show the filling weights based on samples of 3-pound cans of coffee. Use these data to construct the $\bar{x}$ and R charts. What conclusions can be drawn about the quality of the production process?

WEB file

Coffee

	Observations				
Sample	1	2	3	4	5
1	3.05	3.08	3.07	3.11	3.11
2	3.13	3.07	3.05	3.10	3.10
3	3.06	3.04	3.12	3.11	3.10
4	3.09	3.08	3.09	3.09	3.07
5	3.10	3.06	3.06	3.07	3.08
6	3.08	3.10	3.13	3.03	3.06
7	3.06	3.06	3.08	3.10	3.08
8	3.11	3.08	3.07	3.07	3.07
9	3.09	3.09	3.08	3.07	3.09
10	3.06	3.11	3.07	3.09	3.07

21. Consider the following situations and comment on whether the sample results might cause concern about the quality of the process.
   a. A p chart has LCL = 0 and UCL = .068. When the process is in control, the proportion defective is .033. Plot the following seven sample results: .035, .062, .055, .049, .058, .066, and .055. Discuss.
   b. An $\bar{x}$ chart has LCL = 22.2 and UCL = 24.5. The mean is μ = 23.35 when the process is in control. Plot the following seven sample results: 22.4, 22.6, 22.65, 23.2, 23.4, 23.85, and 24.1. Discuss.

22. Managers of 1200 different retail outlets make twice-a-month restocking orders from a central warehouse. Past experience shows 4% of the orders contain one or more errors such as wrong item shipped, wrong quantity shipped, and item requested but not shipped. Random samples of 200 orders are selected monthly and checked for accuracy.
   a. Construct a control chart for this situation.
   b. Six months of data show the following numbers of orders with one or more errors: 10, 15, 6, 13, 8, and 17. Plot the data on the control chart. What does your plot indicate about the order process?

23. An n = 10, c = 2 acceptance sampling plan is being considered; assume that p_0 = .05 and p_1 = .20.
   a. Compute both the producer's and the consumer's risks for this acceptance sampling plan.
   b. Would the producer, the consumer, or both be unhappy with the proposed sampling plan?
   c. What change in the sampling plan, if any, would you recommend?

24. An acceptance sampling plan with $n = 15$ and $c = 1$ was designed with a producer's risk of .075.
    a. Was the value of p_0 equal to .01, .02, .03, .04, or .05? What does this value mean?
    b. What is the consumer's risk associated with this plan if p_1 is .25?

25. A manufacturer produces lots of a canned food product. Let p denote the proportion of the lots that do not meet the product quality specifications. An $n = 25$, $c = 0$ acceptance sampling plan will be used.
    a. Compute points on the operating characteristic curve when $p = .01, .03, .10,$ and .20.
    b. Plot the operating characteristic curve.
    c. What is the probability that the acceptance sampling plan will reject a lot that has .01 defective?

Appendix   Control Charts Using StatTools

Jensen

In this appendix we show how StatTools can be used to construct an $\bar{x}$ chart and an R chart for the Jensen Computer Supplies data in Figure 14.9. Begin by using the Data Set Manager to create a StatTools data set for these data using the procedure described in the appendix in Chapter 1. The following steps describe how StatTools can be used to provide both control charts.

Step 1. Click the **StatTools** tab on the Ribbon
Step 2. In the **Analyses** group, click **Quality Control**
Step 3. Choose the **X/R Charts** option
Step 4. When the StatTools—Xbar and R Control Charts dialog box appears,
    Select **X-Bar/R Chart** in the **Chart Type** box
    In the **Variables** section, select **Observation 1, Observation 2, Observation 3, Observation 4,** and **Observation 5**
Click **OK**

An $\bar{x}$ chart similar to the one in Figure 14.7 will appear. It will be followed by an R chart similar to the one in Figure 14.8.

APPENDIXES

Appendix A: References and Bibliography

General

Freedman, D., R. Pisani, and R. Purves. *Statistics,* 4th ed. W. W. Norton, 2007.

Hogg, R. V., and A. T. Craig. *Introduction to Mathematical Statistics,* 6th ed. Prentice Hall, 2004.

Hogg, R. V., and E. A. Tanis. *Probability and Statistical Inference,* 7th ed. Prentice Hall, 2005.

Miller, I., and M. Miller. *John E. Freund's Mathematical Statistics with Applications,* 7th ed. Prentice Hall, 2003.

Moore, D. S., and G. P. McCabe. *Introduction to the Practice of Statistics,* 5th ed. Freeman, 2005.

Probability

Hogg, R. V., and E. A. Tanis. *Probability and Statistical Inference,* 7th ed. Prentice Hall, 2005.

Ross, S. M. *Introduction to Probability Models,* 9th ed. Elsevier, 2006.

Wackerly, D. D., W. Mendenhall, and R. L. Scheaffer. *Mathematical Statistics with Applications,* 7th ed. Duxbury Press, 2007.

Sampling

Cochran, W. G. *Sampling Techniques,* 3rd ed. Wiley, 1977.

Deming, W. E. *Some Theory of Sampling.* Dover, 1984.

Hansen, M. H., W. N. Hurwitz, W. G. Madow, and M. N. Hanson. *Sample Survey Methods and Theory.* Wiley, 1993.

Kish, L. *Survey Sampling.* Wiley, 1995.

Levy, P. S., and S. Lemeshow. *Sampling of Populations: Methods and Applications,* 3rd ed. Wiley, 1999.

Scheaffer, R. L., W. Mendenhall, and L. Ott. *Elementary Survey Sampling,* 6th ed. Duxbury Press, 2005.

Experimental Design

Box, E. P., J. S. Hunter, and W. G. Hunter. *Statistics for Experimenters,* 2nd ed. Wiley, 2005.

Cochran, W. G., and G. M. Cox. *Experimental Designs,* 2nd ed. Wiley, 1992.

Hicks, C. R., and K. V. Turner. *Fundamental Concepts in the Design of Experiments,* 5th ed. Oxford University Press, 1999.

Kempthorne, O., and K. Hinkelmann. *Design and Analysis of Experiments, Introduction to Experimental Design, Vol. 1,* 2nd ed. Wiley, 2007.

Kempthorne, O., and K. Hinkelmann. *Design and Analysis of Experiments, Vol. 2,* Wiley, 2005.

Montgomery, D. C. *Design and Analysis of Experiments,* 6th ed. Wiley, 2004.

Winer, B. J., K. M. Michels, and D. R. Brown. *Statistical Principles in Experimental Design,* 3rd ed. McGraw-Hill, 1991.

Wu, C. F. Jeff, and M. Hamada. *Experiments: Planning, Analysis, and Parameter Optimization.* Wiley, 2000.

Regression Analysis

Belsley, D. A., E. Kuh, and R. Welsch. *Regression Diagnostics: Identifying Influential Data and Sources of Collinearity,* Wiley, 2004.

Belsley, D. A. *Conditioning Diagnostics: Collinearity and Weak Data in Regression.* Wiley, 1991.

Chatterjee, S., and B. Price. *Regression Analysis by Example,* 3rd ed. Wiley, 1999.

Draper, N. R., and H. Smith. *Applied Regression Analysis,* 3rd ed. Wiley, 1998.

Graybill, F. A., and H. Iyer. *Regression Analysis: Concepts and Applications.* Duxbury Press, 1994.

Keith, T. Z. *Multiple Regression and Beyond.* Allyn & Bacon, 2005.

Kleinbaum, D. G., L. L. Kupper, and K. E. Muller. *Applied Regression Analysis and Other Multivariate Methods,* 4th ed. Duxbury Press, 2007.

Kutner, M. H., J. Neter, R. Lewis, D. Shier, and J. Butler. *Applied Linear Statistical Models,* 5th ed. McGraw-Hill, 2004.

Mendenhall, M., and T. Sincich. *A Second Course in Statistics: Regression Analysis,* 6th ed. Prentice Hall, 2003.

Quality Control

Deming, W. E. *Quality, Productivity, and Competitive Position.* MIT, 1982.

Evans, J. R., and W. M. Lindsay. *Managing for Quality and Performance Excellence,* 7th ed. South-Western, 2007.

Gryna, F. M., R. Chua, and J. Defeo. *Juran's Quality Planning & Analysis for Enterprise Quality,* 3rd ed. McGraw-Hill, 2005.

Ishikawa, K. *Introduction to Quality Control.* Kluwer Academic, 1991.

Montgomery, D. C. *Introduction to Statistical Quality Control,* 5th ed. Wiley, 2004.

Appendix B: Tables

TABLE 1 CUMULATIVE PROBABILITIES FOR THE STANDARD NORMAL DISTRIBUTION

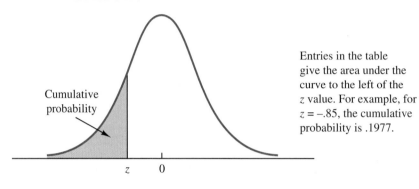

Cumulative probability

Entries in the table give the area under the curve to the left of the z value. For example, for $z = -.85$, the cumulative probability is .1977.

z	.00	.01	.02	.03	.04	.05	.06	.07	.08	.09
−3.0	.0013	.0013	.0013	.0012	.0012	.0011	.0011	.0011	.0010	.0010
−2.9	.0019	.0018	.0018	.0017	.0016	.0016	.0015	.0015	.0014	.0014
−2.8	.0026	.0025	.0024	.0023	.0023	.0022	.0021	.0021	.0020	.0019
−2.7	.0035	.0034	.0033	.0032	.0031	.0030	.0029	.0028	.0027	.0026
−2.6	.0047	.0045	.0044	.0043	.0041	.0040	.0039	.0038	.0037	.0036
−2.5	.0062	.0060	.0059	.0057	.0055	.0054	.0052	.0051	.0049	.0048
−2.4	.0082	.0080	.0078	.0075	.0073	.0071	.0069	.0068	.0066	.0064
−2.3	.0107	.0104	.0102	.0099	.0096	.0094	.0091	.0089	.0087	.0084
−2.2	.0139	.0136	.0132	.0129	.0125	.0122	.0119	.0116	.0113	.0110
−2.1	.0179	.0174	.0170	.0166	.0162	.0158	.0154	.0150	.0146	.0143
−2.0	.0228	.0222	.0217	.0212	.0207	.0202	.0197	.0192	.0188	.0183
−1.9	.0287	.0281	.0274	.0268	.0262	.0256	.0250	.0244	.0239	.0233
−1.8	.0359	.0351	.0344	.0336	.0329	.0322	.0314	.0307	.0301	.0294
−1.7	.0446	.0436	.0427	.0418	.0409	.0401	.0392	.0384	.0375	.0367
−1.6	.0548	.0537	.0526	.0516	.0505	.0495	.0485	.0475	.0465	.0455
−1.5	.0668	.0655	.0643	.0630	.0618	.0606	.0594	.0582	.0571	.0559
−1.4	.0808	.0793	.0778	.0764	.0749	.0735	.0721	.0708	.0694	.0681
−1.3	.0968	.0951	.0934	.0918	.0901	.0885	.0869	.0853	.0838	.0823
−1.2	.1151	.1131	.1112	.1093	.1075	.1056	.1038	.1020	.1003	.0985
−1.1	.1357	.1335	.1314	.1292	.1271	.1251	.1230	.1210	.1190	.1170
−1.0	.1587	.1562	.1539	.1515	.1492	.1469	.1446	.1423	.1401	.1379
−.9	.1841	.1814	.1788	.1762	.1736	.1711	.1685	.1660	.1635	.1611
−.8	.2119	.2090	.2061	.2033	.2005	.1977	.1949	.1922	.1894	.1867
−.7	.2420	.2389	.2358	.2327	.2296	.2266	.2236	.2206	.2177	.2148
−.6	.2743	.2709	.2676	.2643	.2611	.2578	.2546	.2514	.2483	.2451
−.5	.3085	.3050	.3015	.2981	.2946	.2912	.2877	.2843	.2810	.2776
−.4	.3446	.3409	.3372	.3336	.3300	.3264	.3228	.3192	.3156	.3121
−.3	.3821	.3783	.3745	.3707	.3669	.3632	.3594	.3557	.3520	.3483
−.2	.4207	.4168	.4129	.4090	.4052	.4013	.3974	.3936	.3897	.3859
−.1	.4602	.4562	.4522	.4483	.4443	.4404	.4364	.4325	.4286	.4247
−.0	.5000	.4960	.4920	.4880	.4840	.4801	.4761	.4721	.4681	.4641

TABLE 1   CUMULATIVE PROBABILITIES FOR THE STANDARD NORMAL
DISTRIBUTION (*Continued*)

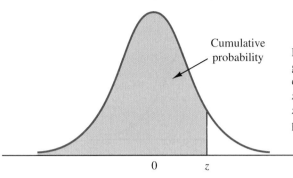

Cumulative
probability

Entries in the table
give the area under the
curve to the left of the
z value. For example, for
z = 1.25, the cumulative
probability is .8944.

0   *z*

z	.00	.01	.02	.03	.04	.05	.06	.07	.08	.09
.0	.5000	.5040	.5080	.5120	.5160	.5199	.5239	.5279	.5319	.5359
.1	.5398	.5438	.5478	.5517	.5557	.5596	.5636	.5675	.5714	.5753
.2	.5793	.5832	.5871	.5910	.5948	.5987	.6026	.6064	.6103	.6141
.3	.6179	.6217	.6255	.6293	.6331	.6368	.6406	.6443	.6480	.6517
.4	.6554	.6591	.6628	.6664	.6700	.6736	.6772	.6808	.6844	.6879
.5	.6915	.6950	.6985	.7019	.7054	.7088	.7123	.7157	.7190	.7224
.6	.7257	.7291	.7324	.7357	.7389	.7422	.7454	.7486	.7517	.7549
.7	.7580	.7611	.7642	.7673	.7704	.7734	.7764	.7794	.7823	.7852
.8	.7881	.7910	.7939	.7967	.7995	.8023	.8051	.8078	.8106	.8133
.9	.8159	.8186	.8212	.8238	.8264	.8289	.8315	.8340	.8365	.8389
1.0	.8413	.8438	.8461	.8485	.8508	.8531	.8554	.8577	.8599	.8621
1.1	.8643	.8665	.8686	.8708	.8729	.8749	.8770	.8790	.8810	.8830
1.2	.8849	.8869	.8888	.8907	.8925	.8944	.8962	.8980	.8997	.9015
1.3	.9032	.9049	.9066	.9082	.9099	.9115	.9131	.9147	.9162	.9177
1.4	.9192	.9207	.9222	.9236	.9251	.9265	.9279	.9292	.9306	.9319
1.5	.9332	.9345	.9357	.9370	.9382	.9394	.9406	.9418	.9429	.9441
1.6	.9452	.9463	.9474	.9484	.9495	.9505	.9515	.9525	.9535	.9545
1.7	.9554	.9564	.9573	.9582	.9591	.9599	.9608	.9616	.9625	.9633
1.8	.9641	.9649	.9656	.9664	.9671	.9678	.9686	.9693	.9699	.9706
1.9	.9713	.9719	.9726	.9732	.9738	.9744	.9750	.9756	.9761	.9767
2.0	.9772	.9778	.9783	.9788	.9793	.9798	.9803	.9808	.9812	.9817
2.1	.9821	.9826	.9830	.9834	.9838	.9842	.9846	.9850	.9854	.9857
2.2	.9861	.9864	.9868	.9871	.9875	.9878	.9881	.9884	.9887	.9890
2.3	.9893	.9896	.9898	.9901	.9904	.9906	.9909	.9911	.9913	.9913
2.4	.9918	.9920	.9922	.9925	.9927	.9929	.9931	.9932	.9934	.9936
2.5	.9938	.9940	.9941	.9943	.9945	.9946	.9948	.9949	.9951	.9952
2.6	.9953	.9955	.9956	.9957	.9959	.9960	.9961	.9962	.9963	.9964
2.7	.9965	.9966	.9967	.9968	.9969	.9970	.9971	.9972	.9973	.9974
2.8	.9974	.9975	.9976	.9977	.9977	.9978	.9979	.9979	.9980	.9981
2.9	.9981	.9982	.9982	.9983	.9984	.9984	.9985	.9985	.9986	.9986
3.0	.9986	.9987	.9987	.9988	.9988	.9989	.9989	.9989	.9990	.9990

TABLE 2 *t* DISTRIBUTION

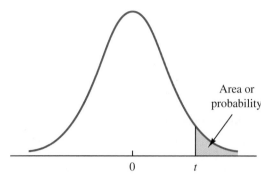

Area or probability

Entries in the table give *t* values for an area or probability in the upper tail of the *t* distribution. For example, with 10 degrees of freedom and a .05 area in the upper tail, $t_{.05} = 1.812$.

Degrees of Freedom	Area in Upper Tail					
	.20	.10	.05	.025	.01	.005
1	1.376	3.078	6.314	12.706	31.821	63.656
2	1.061	1.886	2.920	4.303	6.965	9.925
3	.978	1.638	2.353	3.182	4.541	5.841
4	.941	1.533	2.132	2.776	3.747	4.604
5	.920	1.476	2.015	2.571	3.365	4.032
6	.906	1.440	1.943	2.447	3.143	3.707
7	.896	1.415	1.895	2.365	2.998	3.499
8	.889	1.397	1.860	2.306	2.896	3.355
9	.883	1.383	1.833	2.262	2.821	3.250
10	.879	1.372	1.812	2.228	2.764	3.169
11	.876	1.363	1.796	2.201	2.718	3.106
12	.873	1.356	1.782	2.179	2.681	3.055
13	.870	1.350	1.771	2.160	2.650	3.012
14	.868	1.345	1.761	2.145	2.624	2.977
15	.866	1.341	1.753	2.131	2.602	2.947
16	.865	1.337	1.746	2.120	2.583	2.921
17	.863	1.333	1.740	2.110	2.567	2.898
18	.862	1.330	1.734	2.101	2.552	2.878
19	.861	1.328	1.729	2.093	2.539	2.861
20	.860	1.325	1.725	2.086	2.528	2.845
21	.859	1.323	1.721	2.080	2.518	2.831
22	.858	1.321	1.717	2.074	2.508	2.819
23	.858	1.319	1.714	2.069	2.500	2.807
24	.857	1.318	1.711	2.064	2.492	2.797
25	.856	1.316	1.708	2.060	2.485	2.787
26	.856	1.315	1.706	2.056	2.479	2.779
27	.855	1.314	1.703	2.052	2.473	2.771
28	.855	1.313	1.701	2.048	2.467	2.763
29	.854	1.311	1.699	2.045	2.462	2.756
30	.854	1.310	1.697	2.042	2.457	2.750
31	.853	1.309	1.696	2.040	2.453	2.744
32	.853	1.309	1.694	2.037	2.449	2.738
33	.853	1.308	1.692	2.035	2.445	2.733
34	.852	1.307	1.691	2.032	2.441	2.728

TABLE 2   *t* DISTRIBUTION (*Continued*)

Degrees of Freedom	Area in Upper Tail					
	.20	**.10**	**.05**	**.025**	**.01**	**.005**
35	.852	1.306	1.690	2.030	2.438	2.724
36	.852	1.306	1.688	2.028	2.434	2.719
37	.851	1.305	1.687	2.026	2.431	2.715
38	.851	1.304	1.686	2.024	2.429	2.712
39	.851	1.304	1.685	2.023	2.426	2.708
40	.851	1.303	1.684	2.021	2.423	2.704
41	.850	1.303	1.683	2.020	2.421	2.701
42	.850	1.302	1.682	2.018	2.418	2.698
43	.850	1.302	1.681	2.017	2.416	2.695
44	.850	1.301	1.680	2.015	2.414	2.692
45	.850	1.301	1.679	2.014	2.412	2.690
46	.850	1.300	1.679	2.013	2.410	2.687
47	.849	1.300	1.678	2.012	2.408	2.685
48	.849	1.299	1.677	2.011	2.407	2.682
49	.849	1.299	1.677	2.010	2.405	2.680
50	.849	1.299	1.676	2.009	2.403	2.678
51	.849	1.298	1.675	2.008	2.402	2.676
52	.849	1.298	1.675	2.007	2.400	2.674
53	.848	1.298	1.674	2.006	2.399	2.672
54	.848	1.297	1.674	2.005	2.397	2.670
55	.848	1.297	1.673	2.004	2.396	2.668
56	.848	1.297	1.673	2.003	2.395	2.667
57	.848	1.297	1.672	2.002	2.394	2.665
58	.848	1.296	1.672	2.002	2.392	2.663
59	.848	1.296	1.671	2.001	2.391	2.662
60	.848	1.296	1.671	2.000	2.390	2.660
61	.848	1.296	1.670	2.000	2.389	2.659
62	.847	1.295	1.670	1.999	2.388	2.657
63	.847	1.295	1.669	1.998	2.387	2.656
64	.847	1.295	1.669	1.998	2.386	2.655
65	.847	1.295	1.669	1.997	2.385	2.654
66	.847	1.295	1.668	1.997	2.384	2.652
67	.847	1.294	1.668	1.996	2.383	2.651
68	.847	1.294	1.668	1.995	2.382	2.650
69	.847	1.294	1.667	1.995	2.382	2.649
70	.847	1.294	1.667	1.994	2.381	2.648
71	.847	1.294	1.667	1.994	2.380	2.647
72	.847	1.293	1.666	1.993	2.379	2.646
73	.847	1.293	1.666	1.993	2.379	2.645
74	.847	1.293	1.666	1.993	2.378	2.644
75	.846	1.293	1.665	1.992	2.377	2.643
76	.846	1.293	1.665	1.992	2.376	2.642
77	.846	1.293	1.665	1.991	2.376	2.641
78	.846	1.292	1.665	1.991	2.375	2.640
79	.846	1.292	1.664	1.990	2.374	2.639

TABLE 2   *t* DISTRIBUTION (*Continued*)

Degrees of Freedom	Area in Upper Tail					
	.20	**.10**	**.05**	**.025**	**.01**	**.005**
80	.846	1.292	1.664	1.990	2.374	2.639
81	.846	1.292	1.664	1.990	2.373	2.638
82	.846	1.292	1.664	1.989	2.373	2.637
83	.846	1.292	1.663	1.989	2.372	2.636
84	.846	1.292	1.663	1.989	2.372	2.636
85	.846	1.292	1.663	1.988	2.371	2.635
86	.846	1.291	1.663	1.988	2.370	2.634
87	.846	1.291	1.663	1.988	2.370	2.634
88	.846	1.291	1.662	1.987	2.369	2.633
89	.846	1.291	1.662	1.987	2.369	2.632
90	.846	1.291	1.662	1.987	2.368	2.632
91	.846	1.291	1.662	1.986	2.368	2.631
92	.846	1.291	1.662	1.986	2.368	2.630
93	.846	1.291	1.661	1.986	2.367	2.630
94	.845	1.291	1.661	1.986	2.367	2.629
95	.845	1.291	1.661	1.985	2.366	2.629
96	.845	1.290	1.661	1.985	2.366	2.628
97	.845	1.290	1.661	1.985	2.365	2.627
98	.845	1.290	1.661	1.984	2.365	2.627
99	.845	1.290	1.660	1.984	2.364	2.626
100	.845	1.290	1.660	1.984	2.364	2.626
∞	.842	1.282	1.645	1.960	2.326	2.576

TABLE 3   CHI-SQUARE DISTRIBUTION

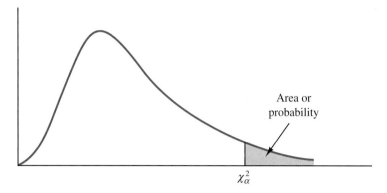

$$\chi_\alpha^2$$

Area or probability

Entries in the table give χ_α^2 values, where α is the area or probability in the upper tail of the chi-square distribution. For example, with 10 degrees of freedom and a .01 area in the upper tail, $\chi_{.01}^2 = 23.209$.

Degrees of Freedom	Area in Upper Tail									
	.995	.99	.975	.95	.90	.10	.05	.025	.01	.005
1	.000	.000	.001	.004	.016	2.706	3.841	5.024	6.635	7.879
2	.010	.020	.051	.103	.211	4.605	5.991	7.378	9.210	10.597
3	.072	.115	.216	.352	.584	6.251	7.815	9.348	11.345	12.838
4	.207	.297	.484	.711	1.064	7.779	9.488	11.143	13.277	14.860
5	.412	.554	.831	1.145	1.610	9.236	11.070	12.832	15.086	16.750
6	.676	.872	1.237	1.635	2.204	10.645	12.592	14.449	16.812	18.548
7	.989	1.239	1.690	2.167	2.833	12.017	14.067	16.013	18.475	20.278
8	1.344	1.647	2.180	2.733	3.490	13.362	15.507	17.535	20.090	21.955
9	1.735	2.088	2.700	3.325	4.168	14.684	16.919	19.023	21.666	23.589
10	2.156	2.558	3.247	3.940	4.865	15.987	18.307	20.483	23.209	25.188
11	2.603	3.053	3.816	4.575	5.578	17.275	19.675	21.920	24.725	26.757
12	3.074	3.571	4.404	5.226	6.304	18.549	21.026	23.337	26.217	28.300
13	3.565	4.107	5.009	5.892	7.041	19.812	22.362	24.736	27.688	29.819
14	4.075	4.660	5.629	6.571	7.790	21.064	23.685	26.119	29.141	31.319
15	4.601	5.229	6.262	7.261	8.547	22.307	24.996	27.488	30.578	32.801
16	5.142	5.812	6.908	7.962	9.312	23.542	26.296	28.845	32.000	34.267
17	5.697	6.408	7.564	8.672	10.085	24.769	27.587	30.191	33.409	35.718
18	6.265	7.015	8.231	9.390	10.865	25.989	28.869	31.526	34.805	37.156
19	6.844	7.633	8.907	10.117	11.651	27.204	30.144	32.852	36.191	38.582
20	7.434	8.260	9.591	10.851	12.443	28.412	31.410	34.170	37.566	39.997
21	8.034	8.897	10.283	11.591	13.240	29.615	32.671	35.479	38.932	41.401
22	8.643	9.542	10.982	12.338	14.041	30.813	33.924	36.781	40.289	42.796
23	9.260	10.196	11.689	13.091	14.848	32.007	35.172	38.076	41.638	44.181
24	9.886	10.856	12.401	13.848	15.659	33.196	36.415	39.364	42.980	45.558
25	10.520	11.524	13.120	14.611	16.473	34.382	37.652	40.646	44.314	46.928
26	11.160	12.198	13.844	15.379	17.292	35.563	38.885	41.923	45.642	48.290
27	11.808	12.878	14.573	16.151	18.114	36.741	40.113	43.195	46.963	49.645
28	12.461	13.565	15.308	16.928	18.939	37.916	41.337	44.461	48.278	50.994
29	13.121	14.256	16.047	17.708	19.768	39.087	42.557	45.722	49.588	52.335

TABLE 3   CHI-SQUARE DISTRIBUTION (*Continued*)

Degrees of Freedom	Area in Upper Tail									
	.995	.99	.975	.95	.90	.10	.05	.025	.01	.005
30	13.787	14.953	16.791	18.493	20.599	40.256	43.773	46.979	50.892	53.672
35	17.192	18.509	20.569	22.465	24.797	46.059	49.802	53.203	57.342	60.275
40	20.707	22.164	24.433	26.509	29.051	51.805	55.758	59.342	63.691	66.766
45	24.311	25.901	28.366	30.612	33.350	57.505	61.656	65.410	69.957	73.166
50	27.991	29.707	32.357	34.764	37.689	63.167	67.505	71.420	76.154	79.490
55	31.735	33.571	36.398	38.958	42.060	68.796	73.311	77.380	82.292	85.749
60	35.534	37.485	40.482	43.188	46.459	74.397	79.082	83.298	88.379	91.952
65	39.383	41.444	44.603	47.450	50.883	79.973	84.821	89.177	94.422	98.105
70	43.275	45.442	48.758	51.739	55.329	85.527	90.531	95.023	100.425	104.215
75	47.206	49.475	52.942	56.054	59.795	91.061	96.217	100.839	106.393	110.285
80	51.172	53.540	57.153	60.391	64.278	96.578	101.879	106.629	112.329	116.321
85	55.170	57.634	61.389	64.749	68.777	102.079	107.522	112.393	118.236	122.324
90	59.196	61.754	65.647	69.126	73.291	107.565	113.145	118.136	124.116	128.299
95	63.250	65.898	69.925	73.520	77.818	113.038	118.752	123.858	129.973	134.247
100	67.328	70.065	74.222	77.929	82.358	118.498	124.342	129.561	135.807	140.170

TABLE 4   *F* DISTRIBUTION

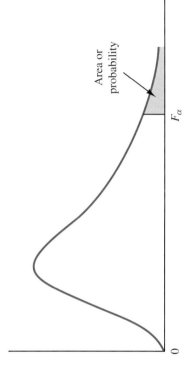

Entries in the table give F_α values, where α is the area or probability in the upper tail of the *F* distribution. For example, with 4 numerator degrees of freedom, 8 denominator degrees of freedom, and a .05 area in the upper tail, $F_{.05} = 3.84$.

Denominator Degrees of Freedom	Area in Upper Tail	Numerator Degrees of Freedom																	
		1	2	3	4	5	6	7	8	9	10	15	20	25	30	40	60	100	1000
1	.10	39.86	49.50	53.59	55.83	57.24	58.20	58.91	59.44	59.86	60.19	61.22	61.74	62.05	62.26	62.53	62.79	63.01	63.30
	.05	161.45	199.50	215.71	224.58	230.16	233.99	236.77	238.88	240.54	241.88	245.95	248.02	249.26	250.10	251.14	252.20	253.04	254.19
	.025	647.79	799.48	864.15	899.60	921.83	937.11	948.20	956.64	963.28	968.63	984.87	993.08	998.09	1001.40	1005.60	1009.79	1013.16	1017.76
	.01	4052.18	4999.34	5403.53	5624.26	5763.96	5858.95	5928.33	5980.95	6022.40	6055.93	6156.97	6208.66	6239.86	6260.35	6286.43	6312.97	6333.92	6362.80
2	.10	8.53	9.00	9.16	9.24	9.29	9.33	9.35	9.37	9.38	9.39	9.42	9.44	9.45	9.46	9.47	9.47	9.48	9.49
	.05	18.51	19.00	19.16	19.25	19.30	19.33	19.35	19.37	19.38	19.40	19.43	19.45	19.46	19.46	19.47	19.48	19.49	19.49
	.025	38.51	39.00	39.17	39.25	39.30	39.33	39.36	39.37	39.39	39.40	39.43	39.45	39.46	39.46	39.47	39.48	39.49	39.50
	.01	98.50	99.00	99.16	99.25	99.30	99.33	99.36	99.38	99.39	99.40	99.43	99.45	99.46	99.47	99.48	99.48	99.49	99.50
3	.10	5.54	5.46	5.39	5.34	5.31	5.28	5.27	5.25	5.24	5.23	5.20	5.18	5.17	5.17	5.16	5.15	5.14	5.13
	.05	10.13	9.55	9.28	9.12	9.01	8.94	8.89	8.85	8.81	8.79	8.70	8.66	8.63	8.62	8.59	8.57	8.55	8.53
	.025	17.44	16.04	15.44	15.10	14.88	14.73	14.62	14.54	14.47	14.42	14.25	14.17	14.12	14.08	14.04	13.99	13.96	13.91
	.01	34.12	30.82	29.46	28.71	28.24	27.91	27.67	27.49	27.34	27.23	26.87	26.69	26.58	26.50	26.41	26.32	26.24	26.14
4	.10	4.54	4.32	4.19	4.11	4.05	4.01	3.98	3.95	3.94	3.92	3.87	3.84	3.83	3.82	3.80	3.79	3.78	3.76
	.05	7.71	6.94	6.59	6.39	6.26	6.16	6.09	6.04	6.00	5.96	5.86	5.80	5.77	5.75	5.72	5.69	5.66	5.63
	.025	12.22	10.65	9.98	9.60	9.36	9.20	9.07	8.98	8.90	8.84	8.66	8.56	8.50	8.46	8.41	8.36	8.32	8.26
	.01	21.20	18.00	16.69	15.98	15.52	15.21	14.98	14.80	14.66	14.55	14.20	14.02	13.91	13.84	13.75	13.65	13.58	13.47
5	.10	4.06	3.78	3.62	3.52	3.45	3.40	3.37	3.34	3.32	3.30	3.324	3.21	3.19	3.17	3.16	3.14	3.13	3.11
	.05	6.61.	5.79	5.41	5.19	5.05	4.95	4.88	4.82	4.77	4.74	4.62	4.56	4.52	4.50	4.46	4.43	4.41	4.37
	.025	10.01	8.43	7.76	7.39	7.15	6.98	6.85	6.76	6.68	6.62	6.43	6.33	6.27	6.23	6.18	6.12	6.08	6.02
	.01	16.26	13.27	12.06	11.39	10.97	10.67	10.46	10.29	10.16	10.05	9.72	9.55	9.45	9.38	9.29	9.20	9.13	9.03

TABLE 4 *F* DISTRIBUTION (*Continued*)

		Numerator Degrees of Freedom																	
Denominator Degrees of Freedom	Area in Upper Tail	1	2	3	4	5	6	7	8	9	10	15	20	25	30	40	60	100	1000
6	.10	3.78	3.46	3.29	3.18	3.11	3.05	3.01	2.98	2.96	2.94	2.87	2.84	2.81	2.80	2.78	2.76	2.75	2.72
	.05	5.99	5.14	4.76	4.53	4.39	4.28	4.21	4.15	4.10	4.06	3.94	3.87	3.83	3.81	3.77	3.74	3.71	3.67
	.025	8.81	7.26	6.60	6.23	5.99	5.82	5.70	5.60	5.52	5.46	5.27	5.17	5.11	5.07	5.01	4.96	4.92	4.86
	.01	13.75	10.92	9.78	9.15	8.75	8.47	8.26	8.10	7.98	7.87	7.56	7.40	7.30	7.23	7.14	7.06	6.99	6.89
7	.10	3.59	3.26	3.07	2.96	2.88	2.83	2.78	2.75	2.72	2.70	2.63	2.59	2.57	2.56	2.54	2.51	2.50	2.47
	.05	5.59	4.74	4.35	4.12	3.97	3.87	3.79	3.73	3.68	3.64	3.51	3.44	3.40	3.38	3.34	3.30	3.27	3.23
	.025	8.07	6.54	5.89	5.52	5.29	5.12	4.99	4.90	4.82	4.76	4.57	4.47	4.40	4.36	4.31	4.25	4.21	4.15
	.01	12.25	9.55	8.45	7.85	7.46	7.19	6.99	6.84	6.72	6.62	6.31	6.16	6.06	5.99	5.91	5.82	5.75	5.66
8	.10	3.46	3.11	2.92	2.81	2.73	2.67	2.62	2.59	2.56	2.54	2.46	2.42	2.40	2.38	2.36	2.34	2.32	2.30
	.05	5.32	4.46	4.07	3.84	3.69	3.58	3.50	3.44	3.39	3.35	3.22	3.15	3.11	3.08	3.04	3.01	2.97	2.93
	.025	7.57	6.06	5.42	5.05	4.82	4.65	4.53	4.43	4.36	4.30	4.10	4.00	3.94	3.89	3.84	3.78	3.74	3.68
	.01	11.26	8.65	7.59	7.01	6.63	6.37	6.18	6.03	5.91	5.81	5.52	5.36	5.26	5.20	5.12	5.03	4.96	4.87
9	.10	3.36	3.01	2.81	2.69	2.61	2.55	2.51	2.47	2.44	2.42	2.34	2.30	2.27	2.25	2.23	2.21	2.19	2.16
	.05	5.12	4.26	3.86	3.63	3.48	3.37	3.29	3.23	3.18	3.14	3.01	2.94	2.89	2.86	2.83	2.79	2.76	2.71
	.025	7.21	5.71	5.08	4.72	4.48	4.32	4.20	4.10	4.03	3.96	3.77	3.67	3.60	3.56	3.51	3.45	3.40	3.34
	.01	10.56	8.02	6.99	6.42	6.06	5.80	5.61	5.47	5.35	5.26	4.96	4.81	4.71	4.65	4.57	4.48	4.41	4.32
10	.10	3.29	2.92	2.73	2.61	2.52	2.46	2.41	2.38	2.35	2.32	2.24	2.20	2.17	2.16	2.13	2.11	2.09	2.06
	.05	4.96	4.10	3.71	3.48	3.33	3.22	3.14	3.07	3.02	2.98	2.85	2.77	2.73	2.70	2.66	2.62	2.59	2.54
	.025	6.94	5.46	4.83	4.47	4.24	4.07	3.95	3.85	3.78	3.72	3.52	3.42	3.35	3.31	3.26	3.20	3.15	3.09
	.01	10.04	7.56	6.55	5.99	5.64	5.39	5.20	5.06	4.94	4.85	4.56	4.41	4.31	4.25	4.17	4.08	4.01	3.92
11	.10	3.23	2.86	2.66	2.54	2.45	2.39	2.34	2.30	2.27	2.25	2.17	2.12	2.10	2.08	2.05	2.03	2.01	1.98
	.05	4.84	3.98	3.59	3.36	3.20	3.09	3.01	2.95	2.90	2.85	2.72	2.65	2.60	2.57	2.53	2.49	2.46	2.41
	.025	6.72	5.26	4.63	4.28	4.04	3.88	3.76	3.66	3.59	3.53	3.33	3.23	3.16	3.12	3.06	3.00	2.96	2.89
	.01	9.65	7.21	6.22	5.67	5.32	5.07	4.89	4.74	4.63	4.54	4.25	4.10	4.01	3.94	3.86	3.78	3.71	3.61
12	.10	3.18	2.81	2.61	2.48	2.39	2.33	2.28	2.24	2.21	2.19	2.10	2.06	2.03	2.01	1.99	1.96	1.94	1.91
	.05	4.75	3.89	3.49	3.26	3.11	3.00	2.91	2.85	2.80	2.75	2.62	2.54	2.50	2.47	2.43	2.38	2.35	2.30
	.025	6.55	5.10	4.47	4.12	3.89	3.73	3.61	3.51	3.44	3.37	3.18	3.07	3.01	2.96	2.91	2.85	2.80	2.73
	.01	9.33	6.93	5.95	5.41	5.06	4.82	4.64	4.50	4.39	4.30	4.01	3.86	3.76	3.70	3.62	3.54	3.47	3.37
13	.10	3.14	2.76	2.56	2.43	2.35	2.28	2.23	2.20	2.16	2.14	2.05	2.01	1.98	1.96	1.93	1.90	1.88	1.85
	.05	4.67	3.81	3.41	3.18	3.03	2.92	2.83	2.77	2.71	2.67	2.53	2.46	2.41	2.38	2.34	2.30	2.26	2.21
	.025	6.41	4.97	4.35	4.00	3.77	3.60	3.48	3.39	3.31	3.25	3.05	2.95	2.88	2.84	2.78	2.72	2.67	2.60
	.01	9.07	6.70	5.74	5.21	4.86	4.62	4.44	4.30	4.19	4.10	3.82	3.66	3.57	3.51	3.43	3.34	3.27	3.18
14	.10	3.10	2.73	2.52	2.39	2.31	2.24	2.19	2.15	2.12	2.10	2.01	1.96	1.93	1.91	1.89	1.86	1.83	1.80
	.05	4.60	3.74	3.34	3.11	2.96	2.85	2.76	2.70	2.65	2.60	2.46	2.39	2.34	2.31	2.27	2.22	2.19	2.14
	.025	6.30	4.86	4.24	3.89	3.66	3.50	3.38	3.29	3.21	3.15	2.95	2.84	2.78	2.73	2.67	2.61	2.56	2.50
	.01	8.86	6.51	5.56	5.04	4.69	4.46	4.28	4.14	4.03	3.94	3.66	3.51	3.41	3.35	3.27	3.18	3.11	3.02
15	.10	3.07	2.70	2.49	2.36	2.27	2.21	2.16	2.12	2.09	2.06	1.97	1.92	1.89	1.87	1.85	1.82	1.79	1.76
	.05	4.54	3.68	3.29	3.06	2.90	2.79	2.71	2.64	2.59	2.54	2.40	2.33	2.28	2.25	2.20	2.16	2.12	2.07
	.025	6.20	4.77	4.15	3.80	3.58	3.41	3.29	3.20	3.12	3.06	2.86	2.76	2.69	2.64	2.59	2.52	2.47	2.40
	.01	8.68	6.36	5.42	4.89	4.56	4.32	4.14	4.00	3.89	3.80	3.52	3.37	3.28	3.21	3.13	3.05	2.98	2.88

Numerator Degrees of Freedom

Denominator Degrees of Freedom	Area in Upper Tail	1	2	3	4	5	6	7	8	9	10	15	20	25	30	40	60	100	1000
16	.10	3.05	2.67	2.46	2.33	2.24	2.18	2.13	2.09	2.06	2.03	1.94	1.89	1.86	1.84	1.81	1.78	1.76	1.72
	.05	4.49	3.63	3.24	3.01	2.85	2.74	2.66	2.59	2.54	2.49	2.35	2.28	2.23	2.19	2.15	2.11	2.07	2.02
	.025	6.12	4.69	4.08	3.73	3.50	3.34	3.22	3.12	3.05	2.99	2.79	2.68	2.61	2.57	2.51	2.45	2.40	2.32
	.01	8.53	6.23	5.29	4.77	4.44	4.20	4.03	3.89	3.78	3.69	3.41	3.26	3.16	3.10	3.02	2.93	2.86	2.76
17	.10	3.03	2.64	2.44	2.31	2.22	2.15	2.10	2.06	2.03	2.00	1.91	1.86	1.83	1.81	1.78	1.75	1.73	1.69
	.05	4.45	3.59	3.20	2.96	2.81	2.70	2.61	2.55	2.49	2.45	2.31	2.23	2.18	2.15	2.10	2.06	2.02	1.97
	.025	6.04	4.62	4.01	3.66	3.44	3.28	3.16	3.06	2.98	2.92	2.72	2.62	2.55	2.50	2.44	2.38	2.33	2.26
	.01	8.40	6.11	5.19	4.67	4.34	4.10	3.93	3.79	3.68	3.59	3.31	3.16	3.07	3.00	2.92	2.83	2.76	2.66
18	.10	3.01	2.62	2.42	2.29	2.20	2.13	2.08	2.04	2.00	1.98	1.89	1.84	1.80	1.78	1.75	1.72	1.70	1.66
	.05	4.41	3.55	3.16	2.93	2.77	2.66	2.58	2.51	2.46	2.41	2.27	2.19	2.14	2.11	2.06	2.02	1.98	1.92
	.025	5.98	4.56	3.95	3.61	3.38	3.22	3.10	3.01	2.93	2.87	2.67	2.56	2.49	2.44	2.38	2.32	2.27	2.20
	.01	8.29	6.01	5.09	4.58	4.25	4.01	3.84	3.71	3.60	3.51	3.23	3.08	2.98	2.92	2.84	2.75	2.68	2.58
19	.10	2.99	2.61	2.40	2.27	2.18	2.11	2.06	2.02	1.98	1.96	1.86	1.81	1.78	1.76	1.73	1.70	1.67	1.64
	.05	4.38	3.52	3.13	2.90	2.74	2.63	2.54	2.48	2.42	2.38	2.23	2.16	2.11	2.07	2.03	1.98	1.94	1.88
	.025	5.92	4.51	3.90	3.56	3.33	3.17	3.05	2.96	2.88	2.82	2.62	2.51	2.44	2.39	2.33	2.27	2.22	2.14
	.01	8.18	5.93	5.01	4.50	4.17	3.94	3.77	3.63	3.52	3.43	3.15	3.00	2.91	2.84	2.76	2.67	2.60	2.50
20	.10	2.97	2.59	2.38	2.25	2.16	2.09	2.04	2.00	1.96	1.94	1.84	1.79	1.76	1.74	1.71	1.68	1.65	1.61
	.05	4.35	3.49	3.10	2.87	2.71	2.60	2.51	2.45	2.39	2.35	2.20	2.12	2.07	2.04	1.99	1.95	1.91	1.85
	.025	5.87	4.46	3.86	3.51	3.29	3.13	3.01	2.91	2.84	2.77	2.57	2.46	2.40	2.35	2.29	2.22	2.17	2.09
	.01	8.10	5.85	4.94	4.43	4.10	3.87	3.70	3.56	3.46	3.37	3.09	2.94	2.84	2.78	2.69	2.61	2.54	2.43
21	.10	2.96	2.57	2.36	2.23	2.14	2.08	2.02	1.98	1.95	1.92	1.83	1.78	1.74	1.72	1.69	1.66	1.63	1.59
	.05	4.32	3.47	3.07	2.84	2.68	2.57	2.49	2.42	2.37	2.32	2.18	2.10	2.05	2.01	1.96	1.92	1.88	1.82
	.025	5.83	4.42	3.82	3.48	3.25	3.09	2.97	2.87	2.80	2.73	2.53	2.42	2.36	2.31	2.25	2.18	2.13	2.05
	.01	8.02	5.78	4.87	4.37	4.04	3.81	3.64	3.51	3.40	3.31	3.03	2.88	2.79	2.72	2.64	2.55	2.48	2.37
22	.10	2.95	2.56	2.35	2.22	2.13	2.06	2.01	1.97	1.93	1.90	1.81	1.76	1.73	1.70	1.67	1.64	1.61	1.57
	.05	4.30	3.44	3.05	2.82	2.66	2.55	2.46	2.40	2.34	2.30	2.15	2.07	2.02	1.98	1.94	1.89	1.85	1.79
	.025	5.79	4.38	3.78	3.44	3.22	3.05	2.93	2.84	2.76	2.70	2.50	2.39	2.32	2.27	2.21	2.14	2.09	2.01
	.01	7.95	5.72	4.82	4.31	3.99	3.76	3.59	3.45	3.35	3.26	2.98	2.83	2.73	2.67	2.58	2.50	2.42	2.32
23	.10	2.94	2.55	2.34	2.21	2.11	2.05	1.99	1.95	1.92	1.89	1.80	1.74	1.71	1.69	1.66	1.62	1.59	1.55
	.05	4.28	3.42	3.03	2.80	2.64	2.53	2.44	2.37	2.32	2.27	2.13	2.05	2.00	1.96	1.91	1.86	1.82	1.76
	.025	5.75	4.35	3.75	3.41	3.18	3.02	2.90	2.81	2.73	2.67	2.47	2.36	2.29	2.24	2.18	2.11	2.06	1.98
	.01	7.88	5.66	4.76	4.26	3.94	3.71	3.54	3.41	3.30	3.21	2.93	2.78	2.69	2.62	2.54	2.45	2.37	2.27
24	.10	2.93	2.54	2.33	2.19	2.10	2.04	1.98	1.94	1.91	1.88	1.78	1.73	1.70	1.67	1.64	1.61	1.58	1.54
	.05	4.26	3.40	3.01	2.78	2.62	2.51	2.42	2.36	2.30	2.25	2.11	2.03	1.97	1.94	1.89	1.84	1.80	1.74
	.025	5.72	4.32	3.72	3.38	3.15	2.99	2.87	2.78	2.70	2.64	2.44	2.33	2.26	2.21	2.15	2.08	2.02	1.94
	.01	7.82	5.61	4.72	4.22	3.90	3.67	3.50	3.36	3.26	3.17	2.89	2.74	2.64	2.58	2.49	2.40	2.33	2.22

TABLE 4 *F* DISTRIBUTION (*Continued*)

Denominator Degrees of Freedom	Area in Upper Tail	Numerator Degrees of Freedom																	
		1	2	3	4	5	6	7	8	9	10	15	20	25	30	40	60	100	1000
25	.10	2.92	2.53	2.32	2.18	2.09	2.02	1.97	1.93	1.89	1.87	1.77	1.72	1.68	1.66	1.63	1.59	1.56	1.52
	.05	4.24	3.39	2.99	2.76	2.60	2.49	2.40	2.34	2.28	2.24	2.09	2.01	1.96	1.92	1.87	1.82	1.78	1.72
	.025	5.69	4.29	3.69	3.35	3.13	2.97	2.85	2.75	2.68	2.61	2.41	2.30	2.23	2.18	2.12	2.05	2.00	1.91
	.01	7.77	5.57	4.68	4.18	3.85	3.63	3.46	3.32	3.22	3.13	2.85	2.70	2.60	2.54	2.45	2.36	2.29	2.18
26	.10	2.91	2.52	2.31	2.17	2.08	2.01	1.96	1.92	1.88	1.86	1.76	1.71	1.67	1.65	1.61	1.58	1.55	1.51
	.05	4.23	3.37	2.98	2.74	2.59	2.47	2.39	2.32	2.27	2.22	2.07	1.99	1.94	1.90	1.85	1.80	1.76	1.70
	.025	5.66	4.27	3.67	3.33	3.10	2.94	2.82	2.73	2.65	2.59	2.39	2.28	2.21	2.16	2.09	2.03	1.97	1.89
	.01	7.72	5.53	4.64	4.14	3.82	3.59	3.42	3.29	3.18	3.09	2.81	2.66	2.57	2.50	2.42	2.33	2.25	2.14
27	.10	2.90	2.51	2.30	2.17	2.07	2.00	1.95	1.91	1.87	1.85	1.75	1.70	1.66	1.64	1.60	1.57	1.54	1.50
	.05	4.21	3.35	2.96	2.73	2.57	2.46	2.37	2.31	2.25	2.20	2.06	1.97	1.92	1.88	1.84	1.79	1.74	1.68
	.025	5.63	4.24	3.65	3.31	3.08	2.92	2.80	2.71	2.63	2.57	2.36	2.25	2.18	2.13	2.07	2.00	1.94	1.86
	.01	7.68	5.49	4.60	4.11	3.78	3.56	3.39	3.26	3.15	3.06	2.78	2.63	2.54	2.47	2.38	2.29	2.22	2.11
28	.10	2.89	2.50	2.29	2.16	2.06	2.00	1.94	1.90	1.87	1.84	1.74	1.69	1.65	1.63	1.59	1.56	1.53	1.48
	.05	4.20	3.34	2.95	2.71	2.56	2.45	2.36	2.29	2.24	2.19	2.04	1.96	1.91	1.87	1.82	1.77	1.73	1.66
	.025	5.61	4.22	3.63	3.29	3.06	2.90	2.78	2.69	2.61	2.55	2.34	2.23	2.16	2.11	2.05	1.98	1.92	1.84
	.01	7.64	5.45	4.57	4.07	3.75	3.53	3.36	3.23	3.12	3.03	2.75	2.60	2.51	2.44	2.35	2.26	2.19	2.08
29	.10	2.89	2.50	2.28	2.15	2.06	1.99	1.93	1.89	1.86	1.83	1.73	1.68	1.64	1.62	1.58	1.55	1.52	1.47
	.05	4.18	3.33	2.93	2.70	2.55	2.43	2.35	2.28	2.22	2.18	2.03	1.94	1.89	1.85	1.81	1.75	1.71	1.65
	.025	5.59	4.20	3.61	3.27	3.04	2.88	2.76	2.67	2.59	2.53	2.32	2.21	2.14	2.09	2.03	1.96	1.90	1.82
	.01	7.60	5.42	4.54	4.04	3.73	3.50	3.33	3.20	3.09	3.00	2.73	2.57	2.48	2.41	2.33	2.23	2.16	2.05
30	.10	2.88	2.49	2.28	2.14	2.05	1.98	1.93	1.88	1.85	1.82	1.72	1.67	1.63	1.61	1.57	1.54	1.51	1.46
	.05	4.17	3.32	2.92	2.69	2.53	2.42	2.33	2.27	2.21	2.16	2.01	1.93	1.88	1.84	1.79	1.74	1.70	1.63
	.025	5.57	4.18	3.59	3.25	3.03	2.87	2.75	2.65	2.57	2.51	2.31	2.20	2.12	2.07	2.01	1.94	1.88	1.80
	.01	7.56	5.39	4.51	4.02	3.70	3.47	3.30	3.17	3.07	2.98	2.70	2.55	2.45	2.39	2.30	2.21	2.13	2.02
40	.10	2.84	2.44	2.23	2.09	2.00	1.93	1.87	1.83	1.79	1.76	1.66	1.61	1.57	1.54	1.51	1.47	1.43	1.38
	.05	4.08	3.23	2.84	2.61	2.45	2.34	2.25	2.18	2.12	2.08	1.92	1.84	1.78	1.74	1.69	1.64	1.59	1.52
	.025	5.42	4.05	3.46	3.13	2.90	2.74	2.62	2.53	2.45	2.39	2.18	2.07	1.99	1.94	1.88	1.80	1.74	1.65
	.01	7.31	5.18	4.31	3.83	3.51	3.29	3.12	2.99	2.89	2.80	2.52	2.37	2.27	2.20	2.11	2.02	1.94	1.82
60	.10	2.79	2.39	2.18	2.04	1.95	1.87	1.82	1.77	1.74	1.71	1.60	1.54	1.50	1.48	1.44	1.40	1.36	1.30
	.05	4.00	3.15	2.76	2.53	2.37	2.25	2.17	2.10	2.04	1.99	1.84	1.75	1.69	1.65	1.59	1.53	1.48	1.40
	.025	5.29	3.93	3.34	3.01	2.79	2.63	2.51	2.41	2.33	2.27	2.06	1.94	1.87	1.82	1.74	1.67	1.60	1.49
	.01	7.08	4.98	4.13	3.65	3.34	3.12	2.95	2.82	2.72	2.63	2.35	2.20	2.10	2.03	1.94	1.84	1.75	1.62
100	.10	2.76	2.36	2.14	2.00	1.91	1.83	1.78	1.73	1.69	1.66	1.56	1.49	1.45	1.42	1.38	1.34	1.29	1.22
	.05	3.94	3.09	2.70	2.46	2.31	2.19	2.10	2.03	1.97	1.93	1.77	1.68	1.62	1.57	1.52	1.45	1.39	1.30
	.025	5.18	3.83	3.25	2.92	2.70	2.54	2.42	2.32	2.24	2.18	1.97	1.85	1.77	1.71	1.64	1.56	1.48	1.36
	.01	6.90	4.82	3.98	3.51	3.21	2.99	2.82	2.69	2.59	2.50	2.22	2.07	1.97	1.89	1.80	1.69	1.60	1.45
1000	.10	2.71	2.31	2.09	1.95	1.85	1.78	1.72	1.68	1.64	1.61	1.49	1.43	1.38	1.35	1.30	1.25	1.20	1.08
	.05	3.85	3.00	2.61	2.38	2.22	2.11	2.02	1.95	1.89	1.84	1.68	1.58	1.52	1.47	1.41	1.33	1.26	1.11
	.025	5.04	3.70	3.13	2.80	2.58	2.42	2.30	2.20	2.13	2.06	1.85	1.72	1.64	1.58	1.50	1.41	1.32	1.13
	.01	6.66	4.63	3.80	3.34	3.04	2.82	2.66	2.53	2.43	2.34	2.06	1.90	1.79	1.72	1.61	1.50	1.38	1.16

Appendix C: Summation Notation

Summations

Definition

$$\sum_{i=1}^{n} x_i = x_1 + x_2 + \cdots + x_n \tag{C.1}$$

Example for $x_1 = 5$, $x_2 = 8$, $x_3 = 14$:

$$\sum_{i=1}^{3} x_i = x_1 + x_2 + x_3$$
$$= 5 + 8 + 14$$
$$= 27$$

Result 1

For a constant c:

$$\sum_{i=1}^{n} c = \underbrace{(c + c + \cdots + c)}_{n \text{ times}} = nc \tag{C.2}$$

Example for $c = 5$, $n = 10$:

$$\sum_{i=1}^{10} 5 = 10(5) = 50$$

Example for $c = \bar{x}$:

$$\sum_{i=1}^{n} \bar{x} = n\bar{x}$$

Result 2

$$\sum_{i=1}^{n} cx_i = cx_1 + cx_2 + \cdots + cx_n$$
$$= c(x_1 + x_2 + \cdots + x_n) = c\sum_{i=1}^{n} x_i \tag{C.3}$$

Example for $x_1 = 5$, $x_2 = 8$, $x_3 = 14$, $c = 2$:

$$\sum_{i=1}^{3} 2x_i = 2\sum_{i=1}^{3} x_i = 2(27) = 54$$

Result 3

$$\sum_{i=1}^{n} (ax_i + by_i) = a\sum_{i=1}^{n} x_i + b\sum_{i=1}^{n} y_i \tag{C.4}$$

Example for $x_1 = 5$, $x_2 = 8$, $x_3 = 14$, $a = 2$, $y_1 = 7$, $y_2 = 3$, $y_3 = 8$, $b = 4$:

$$\sum_{i=1}^{3} (2x_i + 4y_i) = 2 \sum_{i=1}^{3} x_i + 4 \sum_{i=1}^{3} y_i$$

$$= 2(27) + 4(18)$$

$$= 54 + 72$$

$$= 126$$

Double Summations

Consider the following data involving the variable x_{ij}, where i is the subscript denoting the row position and j is the subscript denoting the column position:

		Column		
		1	**2**	**3**
Row	**1**	$x_{11} = 10$	$x_{12} = 8$	$x_{13} = 6$
	2	$x_{21} = 7$	$x_{22} = 4$	$x_{23} = 12$

Definition

$$\sum_{i=1}^{n} \sum_{j=1}^{m} x_{ij} = (x_{11} + x_{12} + \cdots + x_{1m}) + (x_{21} + x_{22} + \cdots + x_{2m})$$

$$+ (x_{31} + x_{32} + \cdots + x_{3m}) + \cdots + (x_{n1} + x_{n2} + \cdots + x_{nm}) \qquad \text{(C.5)}$$

Example:

$$\sum_{i=1}^{2} \sum_{j=1}^{3} x_{ij} = x_{11} + x_{12} + x_{13} + x_{21} + x_{22} + x_{23}$$

$$= 10 + 8 + 6 + 7 + 4 + 12$$

$$= 47$$

Definition

$$\sum_{i=1}^{n} x_{ij} = x_{1j} + x_{2j} + \cdots + x_{nj} \qquad \text{(C.6)}$$

Example:

$$\sum_{i=1}^{2} x_{i2} = x_{12} + x_{22}$$

$$= 8 + 4$$

$$= 12$$

Shorthand Notation

Sometimes when a summation is for all values of the subscript, we use the following shorthand notations:

$$\sum_{i=1}^{n} x_i = \sum x_i \qquad \text{(C.7)}$$

$$\sum_{i=1}^{n} \sum_{j=1}^{m} x_{ij} = \sum \sum x_{ij} \qquad \text{(C.8)}$$

$$\sum_{i=1}^{n} x_{ij} = \sum_{i} x_{ij} \qquad \text{(C.9)}$$

Chapter 1

2. a. 10

  b. 5

  c. Categorical variables: Class and Fuel Type
  Quantitative variables: Cylinders, City MPG, and Highway MPG

  d.

Variable	Measurement Scale
Class	Nominal
Cylinders	Ratio
City MPG	Ratio
Highway MPG	Ratio
Fuel Type	Nominal

3. a. Average for city driving = 182/10 = 18.2 mpg

  b. Average for highway driving = 261/10 = 26.1 mpg
  On average, the fuel efficiency rating for highway driving is 7.9 mpg greater than the average for city driving

  c. 3 of 10 or 30% have four-cylinder engines

  d. 7 of 10 or 70% will run on regular fuel

4. a. 7

  b. 5

  c. Categorical variables: State, Campus Setting, and NCAA Division
  Quantitative variables: Endowment ($ billions) and % Applicants Admitted

6. a. Quantitative

  b. Categorical

  c. Categorical

  d. Quantitative

  e. Categorical

8. a. 1015

  b. Categorical

  c. Percentages

  d. No

  e. .10(1015) = 101.5
  Since the percentage reported was reported as 10%, values of 97 to 106 will all provide a value of 10%. Thus, the best we can say is that the number of respondents who said the Federal Bank is doing a good job is between 97 and 106.

10. a. Quantitative; ratio

  b. Categorical; nominal

  c. Categorical; ordinal

  d. Quantitative; ratio

  e. Categorical; nominal

12. a. All visitors to Hawaii

  b. Yes

  c. First and fourth questions provide quantitative data
  Second and third questions provide categorical data

13. a. Quantitative

  b. Time series

  c. Federal spending ($ trillions)

  d. Federal spending appears to be increasing over time

14. a. Graph with a time series line for each manufacturer

  b. Toyota surpasses General Motors in 2006 to become the leading auto manufacturer

  c. A bar chart would show cross-sectional data for 2007; bar heights would be GM 8.8, Ford 7.9, DC 4.6, and Toyota 9.6

16. a. Product taste tests and test marketing

  b. Specially designed statistical studies

18. a. 36%

  b. 189

  c. Categorical

20. a. 43% of managers were bullish or very bullish, and 21% of managers expected health care to be the leading industry over the next 12 months

  b. The average 12-month return estimate is 11.2% for the population of investment managers

  c. The sample average of 2.5 years is an estimate of how long the population of investment managers think it will take to resume sustainable growth

22. a. The population consists of all customers at the chain's stores in Charlotte, North Carolina

  b. Some of the ways the grocery store chain could use to collect the data are
  • Customers entering or leaving the store could be surveyed
  • A survey could be mailed to customers who have a shopper's club card
  • Customers could be given a printed survey when they check out
  • Customers could be given a coupon that asks them to complete a brief online survey; if they do, they will receive a 5% discount on their next shopping trip

24. a. Correct

  b. Incorrect

  c. Correct

  d. Incorrect

  e. Incorrect

Chapter 2

2. a. .20

   b. 40

   c/d.

Class	Frequency	Percent Frequency
A	44	22
B	36	18
C	80	40
D	40	20
Total	200	100

3. a. $360° \times 58/120 = 174°$

   b. $360° \times 42/120 = 126°$

   c.

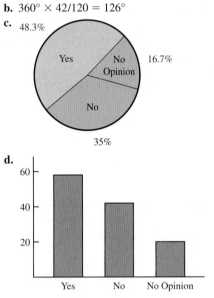

   d.

4. a. Categorical

   b.

TV Show	Frequency	Percent Frequency
L&O	10	20
CSI	18	36
Trace	9	18
DH	13	26
Total	50	100

   d. *CSI* had the largest; *DH* was second

6. a.

Network	Frequency	Percent Frequency
ABC	15	30
CBS	17	34
FOX	1	2
NBC	17	34

   b. CBS and NBC tied for first; ABC is close with 15

7.

Rating	Frequency	Relative Frequency
Outstanding	19	.38
Very good	13	.26
Good	10	.20
Average	6	.12
Poor	2	.04

Management should be pleased with these results: 64% of the ratings are very good to outstanding, and 84% of the ratings are good or better; comparing these ratings to previous results will show whether the restaurant is making improvements in its customers' ratings of food quality

8. a.

Position	Frequency	Relative Frequency
P	17	.309
H	4	.073
1	5	.091
2	4	.073
3	2	.036
S	5	.091
L	6	.109
C	5	.091
R	7	.127
Totals	55	1.000

   b. Pitcher

   c. 3rd base

   d. Right field

   e. Infielders 16 to outfielders 18

10. a.

Rating	Frequency
Excellent	20
Good	101
Fair	528
Bad	244
Terrible	122
Total	1015

   b.

Rating	Percent Frequency
Excellent	2
Good	10
Fair	52
Bad	24
Terrible	12
Total	100

   d. 36% of adults in the United States think the Federal Bank is doing a bad or a terrible job in handling the credit problems. Only 12% think the Federal Bank is doing a good or excellent job.

e. Overall, adults in Spain are very pessimistic about the Bank's ability to handle the credit problems as compared to adults in the United States

12.

Class	Cumulative Frequency	Cumulative Relative Frequency
≤19	10	.20
≤29	24	.48
≤39	41	.82
≤49	48	.96
≤59	50	1.00

14. b/c.

Class	Frequency	Percent Frequency
6.0–7.9	4	20
8.0–9.9	2	10
10.0–11.9	8	40
12.0–13.9	3	15
14.0–15.9	3	15
Totals	20	100

15. a/b.

Waiting Time	Frequency	Relative Frequency
0–4	4	.20
5–9	8	.40
10–14	5	.25
15–19	2	.10
20–24	1	.05
Totals	20	1.00

c/d.

Waiting Time	Cumulative Frequency	Cumulative Relative Frequency
≤4	4	.20
≤9	12	.60
≤14	17	.85
≤19	19	.95
≤24	20	1.00

e. 12/20 = .60

16. a.

Salary	Frequency
150–159	1
160–169	3
170–179	7
180–189	5
190–199	1
200–209	2
210–219	1
Total	20

b.

Salary	Percent Frequency
150–159	5
160–169	15
170–179	35
180–189	25
190–199	5
200–209	10
210–219	5
Total	100

c.

Salary	Cumulative Percent Frequency
Less than or equal to 159	5
Less than or equal to 169	20
Less than or equal to 179	55
Less than or equal to 189	80
Less than or equal to 199	85
Less than or equal to 209	95
Less than or equal to 219	100
Total	100

e. There does not appear to be a lot of skewness in the data
f. 15%

18. a. Lowest $180; highest $2050

b.

Spending	Frequency	Percent Frequency
$0–249	3	12
250–499	6	24
500–749	5	20
750–999	5	20
1000–1249	3	12
1250–1499	1	4
1500–1749	0	0
1750–1999	1	4
2000–2249	1	4
Total	25	100

c. The distribution shows a positive skewness
d. Majority (64%) of consumers spend between $250 and $1000; the middle value is about $750; and two high spenders are above $1750

20. a.

Income	Frequency	Percent Frequency
1300–3299	19	47.5
3300–5299	12	30.0
5300–7299	2	5.0
7300–9299	5	12.5
9300–11299	2	5.0
Total	40	100.0

b. 5.0 + 12.5 + 5.0 = 32.5%
d. The data are skewed to the right
e. 47.5 + 30.0 = 77.5% earned less than $5,300,000

22.
```
5 | 7  8
6 | 4  5  8
7 | 0  2  2  5  5  6  8
8 | 0  2  3  5
```

23. Leaf unit = .1
```
 6 | 3
 7 | 5  5  7
 8 | 1  3  4  8
 9 | 3  6
10 | 0  4  5
11 | 3
```

24. Leaf unit = 10
```
11 | 6
12 | 0  2
13 | 0  6  7
14 | 2  2  7
15 | 5
16 | 0  2  8
17 | 0  2  3
```

25.
```
 9 | 8  9
10 | 2  4  6  6
11 | 4  5  7  8  8  9
12 | 2  4  5  7
13 | 1  2
14 | 4
15 | 1
```

26. a.
```
1 | 0  3  7  7
2 | 4  5  5
3 | 0  0  5  5  9
4 | 0  0  0  5  5  8
5 | 0  0  0  4  5  5
```

b.
```
0 | 5  7
1 | 0  1  1  3  4
1 | 5  5  5  8
2 | 0  0  0  0  0
2 | 5  5
3 | 0  0  0
3 | 6
4 |
4 |
5 |
5 |
6 | 3
```

28. a.
```
2 | 14
2 | 67
3 | 011123
3 | 5677
4 | 003333344
4 | 6679
5 | 00022
5 | 5679
6 | 14
6 | 6
7 | 2
```

b. 40–44 with 9

c. 43 with 5

d. 10%; relatively small participation in the race

29. a.

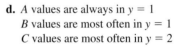

		1	2	Total
	A	5	0	5
x	B	11	2	13
	C	2	10	12
Total		18	12	30

b.

		1	2	Total
	A	100.0	0.0	100.0
x	B	84.6	15.4	100.0
	C	16.7	83.3	100.0

c.

		1	2
	A	27.8	0.0
x	B	61.1	16.7
	C	11.1	83.3
	Total	100.0	100.0

d. A values are always in $y = 1$
B values are most often in $y = 1$
C values are most often in $y = 2$

30. a.

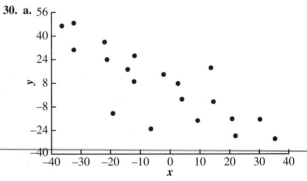

b. A negative relationship between x and y; y decreases as x increases

32. a.

	Household Income ($1000s)					
Education Level	Under 25	25.0– 49.9	50.0– 74.9	75.0– 99.9	100 or more	Total
Not H.S. Graduate	32.70	14.82	8.27	5.02	2.53	15.86
H.S. Graduate	35.74	35.56	31.48	25.39	14.47	30.78
Some College	21.17	29.77	30.25	29.82	22.26	26.37
Bachelor's Degree	7.53	14.43	20.56	25.03	33.88	17.52
Beyond Bach. Deg.	2.86	5.42	9.44	14.74	26.86	9.48
Total	100.00	100.00	100.00	100.00	100.00	100.00

15.86% of the heads of households did not graduate from high school

b. 26.86%, 39.72%

c. Positive relationship between income and education level

34. a.

Fund Type	0–9.99	10–19.99	20–29.99	30–39.99	40–49.99	50–59.99	Total
DE	1	25	1	0	0	0	**27**
FI	9	1	0	0	0	0	**10**
IE	0	2	3	2	0	1	**8**
Total	**10**	**28**	**4**	**2**	**0**	**1**	**45**

b.

Fund Type	Frequency
DE	27
FI	10
IE	8
Total	45

c.

5-Year Average Return	Frequency
0–9.99	10
10–19.99	28
20–29.99	4
30–39.99	2
40–49.99	0
50–59.99	1
Total	45

d. The right margin shows the frequency distribution for the fund type variable and the bottom margin shows the frequency distribution for the 5-year average return variable

e. Higher returns are associated with International Equity funds and lower returns are associated with Fixed Income funds

36. b. There is some indication that higher 5-year returns are associated with higher net asset values

38. a.

Row Labels	15–19	20–24	25–29	30–34	35–39	Total
1–3	0	6	72	46	4	128
3–5	3	56	86	0	0	145
5–7	23	14	1	0	0	38
Total	**26**	**76**	**159**	**46**	**4**	**311**

b. Higher fuel efficiencies are associated with smaller displacement engines and lower fuel efficiencies are associated with larger displacement engines

d. The scatter diagram shows that larger displacement engines are associated with lower fuel efficiencies

e. The scatter diagram. It is easier to see the relationship between the two variables using the scatter diagram

40. a.

Response	Frequency	Percent Frequency
Accuracy	16	16
Approach shots	3	3
Mental approach	17	17
Power	8	8
Practice	15	15
Putting	10	10
Short game	24	24
Strategic decisions	7	7
Total	100	100

b. Poor short game, poor mental approach, lack of accuracy, and limited practice

42. a.

SAT Score	Frequency
750–849	2
850–949	5
950–1049	10
1050–1149	5
1150–1249	3
Total	25

b. Nearly symmetrical

c. 40% of the scores fall between 950 and 1049
A score below 750 or above 1249 is unusual
The average is near or slightly above 1000

44. a.

Population	Frequency	Percent Frequency
0.0–2.4	17	34
2.5–4.9	12	24
5.0–7.4	9	18
7.5–9.9	4	8
10.0–12.4	3	6
12.5–14.9	1	2
15.0–17.4	1	2
17.5–19.9	1	2
20.0–22.4	0	0
22.5–24.9	1	2
25.0–27.4	0	0
27.5–29.9	0	0
30.0–32.4	0	0
32.5–34.9	0	0
35.0–37.4	1	2
Total	50	100

c. High positive skewness

d. 17 (34%) with population less than 2.5 million
29 (58%) with population less than 5 million
8 (16%) with population greater than 10 million
Largest 35.9 million (California)
Smallest .5 million (Wyoming)

46. a. High Temperatures

```
1 |
2 |
3 | 0
4 | 1 2 2 5
5 | 2 4 5
6 | 0 0 0 1 2 2 5 6 8
7 | 0 7
8 | 4
```

b. Low Temperatures

```
1 | 1
2 | 1 2 6 7 9
3 | 1 5 6 8 9
4 | 0 3 3 6 7
5 | 0 0 4
6 | 5
7 |
8 |
```

c. The most frequent range for high is in 60s (9 of 20) with only one low temperature above 54
High temperatures range mostly from 41 to 68, while low temperatures range mostly from 21 to 47
Low was 11; high was 84

d.

High Temp	Frequency	Low Temp	Frequency
10–19	0	10–19	1
20–29	0	20–29	5
30–39	1	30–39	5
40–49	4	40–49	5
50–59	3	50–59	3
60–69	9	60–69	1
70–79	2	70–79	0
80–89	1	80–89	0
Total	20	Total	20

48. a.

Level of Support	Percent Frequency
Strongly favor	30.10
Favor more than oppose	34.83
Oppose more than favor	21.13
Strongly oppose	13.94
Total	100.00

The results show support for a higher tax. Note that 64.93% of the respondents said they strongly favor or favor more than oppose a higher tax on higher carbon emission cars.

b.

Country	Percent Frequency
Great Britain	20
Italy	19
Spain	21
Germany	21
United States	19
Total	100

c. Converting the entries in the crosstabulation into column percentages provides the following results:

	Country				
Support	Great Britain	Italy	Spain	Germany	United States
Strongly favor	31.00	31.96	45.99	19.98	20.98
Favor more than oppose	34.04	39.04	32.01	36.99	32.06
Oppose more than favor	23.00	17.99	13.98	24.03	26.96
Strongly oppose	11.96	11.01	8.03	18.99	20.00
Total	100.00	100.00	100.00	100.00	100.00

The level of support among European countries appears to be different than the level of support in the United States

50. a. Row totals: 247; 54; 82; 121
Column totals: 149; 317; 17; 7; 14

b.

Year	Freq.	Fuel	Freq.
1973 or before	247	Elect.	149
1974–79	54	Nat. Gas	317
1980–86	82	Oil	17
1987–91	121	Propane	7
Total	504	Other	14
		Total	504

c. Crosstabulation of column percentages

Year Constructed	Fuel Type				
	Elect.	Nat. Gas	Oil	Propane	Other
1973 or before	26.9	57.7	70.5	71.4	50.0
1974–1979	16.1	8.2	11.8	28.6	0.0
1980–1986	24.8	12.0	5.9	0.0	42.9
1987–1991	32.2	22.1	11.8	0.0	7.1
Total	100.0	100.0	100.0	100.0	100.0

d. Crosstabulation of row percentages

Year Constructed	Fuel Type					
	Elect.	Nat. Gas	Oil	Propane	Other	Total
1973 or before	16.2	74.1	4.9	2.0	2.8	100.0
1974–1979	44.5	48.1	3.7	3.7	0.0	100.0
1980–1986	45.1	46.4	1.2	0.0	7.3	100.0
1987–1991	39.7	57.8	1.7	0.0	0.8	100.0

52. a. Crosstabulation of market value and profit

Market Value ($1000s)	Profit ($1000s)				
	0–300	300–600	600–900	900–1200	Total
0–8000	23	4			27
8000–16,000	4	4	2	2	12
16,000–24,000		2	1	1	4
24,000–32,000		1	2	1	4
32,000–40,000		2	1		3
Total	27	13	6	4	50

b. Crosstabulation of row percentages

Market Value ($1000s)	Profit ($1000s) 0– 300	300– 600	600– 900	900– 1200	Total
0–8000	85.19	14.81	0.00	0.00	100
8000–16,000	33.33	33.33	16.67	16.67	100
16,000–24,000	0.00	50.00	25.00	25.00	100
24,000–32,000	0.00	25.00	50.00	25.00	100
32,000–40,000	0.00	66.67	33.33	0.00	100

c. A positive relationship is indicated between profit and market value; as profit goes up, market value goes up

54. b. A positive relationship is demonstrated between market value and stockholders' equity

Chapter 3

2. 16, 16.5

3. Arrange data in order: 15, 20, 25, 25, 27, 28, 30, 34

$i = \dfrac{20}{100}(8) = 1.6$; round up to position 2

20th percentile = 20

$i = \dfrac{25}{100}(8) = 2$; use positions 2 and 3

25th percentile $= \dfrac{20 + 25}{2} = 22.5$

$i = \dfrac{65}{100}(8) = 5.2$; round up to position 6

65th percentile = 28

$i = \dfrac{75}{100}(8) = 6$; use positions 6 and 7

75th percentile $= \dfrac{28 + 30}{2} = 29$

4. 59.73, 57, 53

6. a. Marketing: 36.3, 35.5, 34.2
Accounting: 45.7, 44.7, no mode

b. Marketing: 34.2, 39.5
Accounting: 40.95, 49.8

c. Accounting salaries are approximately $9000 higher

8. a. $\bar{x} = \dfrac{\Sigma x_i}{n} = \dfrac{3200}{20} = 160$

Data in order: 100, 105, 105, 110, 115, 115, 120, 120, 120, 130, 140, 150, 155, 160, 180, 195, 230, 235, 255, 360

Median (10th and 11th positions)

$\dfrac{130 + 140}{2} = 135$

Mode = 120 (appears three times)

b. $i = \dfrac{25}{100}(20) = 5$; use 5th and 6th positions

$Q_1 = \dfrac{115 + 115}{2} = 115$

$i = \dfrac{75}{100}(20) = 15$; use 15th and 16th positions

$Q_3 = \dfrac{180 + 195}{2} = 187.5$

c. $i = \dfrac{90}{100}(20) = 18$; use 18th and 19th positions

90th percentile $= \dfrac{235 + 255}{2} = 245$

90% of the tax returns cost $245 or less. 10% of the tax returns cost $245 or more.

10. a. .4%, 3.5%
b. 2.3%, 2.5%, 2.7%
c. 2.0%, 2.8%
d. optimistic

12. Disney: 3321, 255.5, 253, 169, 325
Pixar: 3231, 538.5, 505, 363, 631
Pixar films generate approximately twice as much box office revenue per film

14. 16, 4

15. Range $= 34 - 15 = 19$
Arrange data in order: 15, 20, 25, 25, 27, 28, 30, 34

$i = \dfrac{25}{100}(8) = 2; Q_1 = \dfrac{20 + 25}{2} = 22.5$

$i = \dfrac{75}{100}(8) = 6; Q_3 = \dfrac{28 + 30}{2} = 29$

IQR $= Q_3 - Q_1 = 29 - 22.5 = 6.5$

$\bar{x} = \dfrac{\Sigma x_i}{n} = \dfrac{204}{8} = 25.5$

x_i	$(x_i - \bar{x})$	$(x_i - \bar{x})^2$
27	1.5	2.25
25	−.5	.25
20	−5.5	30.25
15	−10.5	110.25
30	4.5	20.25
34	8.5	72.25
28	2.5	6.25
25	−.5	.25
		242.00

$s^2 = \dfrac{\Sigma(x_i - \bar{x})^2}{n - 1} = \dfrac{242}{8 - 1} = 34.57$

$s = \sqrt{34.57} = 5.88$

16. a. Range $= 190 - 168 = 22$

b. $\bar{x} = \dfrac{\Sigma x_i}{n} = \dfrac{1068}{6} = 178$

$s^2 = \dfrac{\Sigma(x_i - \bar{x})^2}{n - 1}$

$= \dfrac{4^2 + (-10)^2 + 6^2 + 12^2 + (-8)^2 + (-4)^2}{6 - 1}$

$= \dfrac{376}{5} = 75.2$

c. $s = \sqrt{75.2} = 8.67$

d. $\dfrac{s}{\bar{x}}(100) = \dfrac{8.67}{178}(100\%) = 4.87\%$

18. a. 38, 97, 9.85

    b. Eastern shows more variation

20. *Dawson:* range = 2, $s = .67$
    Clark: range = 8, $s = 2.58$

22. a. Freshmen: \$1285; Seniors: \$433; Yes

    b. Freshmen: \$1720; Seniors: \$352

    c. Freshmen: \$404; Seniors: \$131.5

    d. Freshmen: \$367.04; Seniors: \$96.96

    e. Freshmen

24. *Quarter-milers:* $s = .0564$, Coef. of Var. = 5.8%
    Milers: $s = .1295$, Coef. of Var. = 2.9%

26. .20, 1.50, 0, −.50, −2.20

27. Chebyshev's theorem: *at least* $(1 - 1/z^2)$

    a. $z = \dfrac{40 - 30}{5} = 2$; $1 - \dfrac{1}{(2)^2} = .75$

    b. $z = \dfrac{45 - 30}{5} = 3$; $1 - \dfrac{1}{(3)^2} = .89$

    c. $z = \dfrac{38 - 30}{5} = 1.6$; $1 - \dfrac{1}{(1.6)^2} = .61$

    d. $z = \dfrac{42 - 30}{5} = 2.4$; $1 - \dfrac{1}{(2.4)^2} = .83$

    e. $z = \dfrac{48 - 30}{5} = 3.6$; $1 - \dfrac{1}{(3.6)^2} = .92$

28. a. 95%

    b. Almost all

    c. 68%

29. a. $z = 2$ standard deviations

    $1 - \dfrac{1}{z^2} = 1 - \dfrac{1}{2^2} = \dfrac{3}{4}$; at least 75%

    b. $z = 2.5$ standard deviations

    $1 - \dfrac{1}{z^2} = 1 - \dfrac{1}{2.5^2} = .84$; at least 84%

    c. $z = 2$ standard deviations
    Empirical rule: 95%

30. a. 68%

    b. 81.5%

    c. 2.5%

32. a. −.67

    b. 1.50

    c. Neither an outlier

    d. Yes; $z = 8.25$

34. a. 76.5, 7

    b. 16%, 2.5%

    c. 12.2, 7.89; no

36. 15, 22.5, 26, 29, 34

38. Arrange data in order: 5, 6, 8, 10, 10, 12, 15, 16, 18

    $i = \dfrac{25}{100}(9) = 2.25$; round up to position 3

$Q_1 = 8$

Median (5th position) = 10

$i = \dfrac{75}{100}(9) = 6.75$; round up to position 7

$Q_3 = 15$

5-number summary: 5, 8, 10, 15, 18

40. a. 619, 725, 1016, 1699, 4450

    b. Limits: 0, 3160

    c. Yes

    d. No

41. a. Arrange data in order low to high

    $i = \dfrac{25}{100}(21) = 5.25$; round up to 6th position

    $Q_1 = 1872$

    Median (11th position) = 4019

    $i = \dfrac{75}{100}(21) = 15.75$; round up to 16th position

    $Q_3 = 8305$

    5-number summary: 608, 1872, 4019, 8305, 14138

    b. IQR = $Q_3 - Q_1 = 8305 - 1872 = 6433$

    Lower limit: $1872 - 1.5(6433) = -7777.5$

    Upper limit: $8305 + 1.5(6433) = 17,955$

    c. No; data are within limits

    d. 41,138 > 27,604; 41,138 would be an outlier; data value would be reviewed and corrected

    e.

42. a. 66

    b. 30, 49, 66, 88, 208

    c. Yes; upper limit = 146.5

44. a. 18.2, 15.35

    b. 11.7, 23.5

    c. 3.4, 11.7, 15.35, 23.5, 41.3

    d. Yes; Alger Small Cap 41.3

45. b. There appears to be a negative linear relationship between x and y

    c.

x_i	y_i	$x_i - \bar{x}$	$y_i - \bar{y}$	$(x_i - \bar{x})(y_i - \bar{y})$
4	50	−4	4	−16
6	50	−2	4	−8
11	40	3	−6	−18
3	60	−5	14	−70
16	30	8	−16	−128
40	230	0	0	−240

$\bar{x} = 8$; $\bar{y} = 46$

$s_{xy} = \dfrac{\Sigma(x_i - \bar{x})(y_i - \bar{y})}{n - 1} = \dfrac{-240}{4} = -60$

The sample covariance indicates a negative linear association between x and y

d. $r_{xy} = \dfrac{s_{xy}}{s_x s_y} = \dfrac{-60}{(5.43)(11.40)} = -.969$

The sample correlation coefficient of $-.969$ is indicative of a strong negative linear relationship

46. b. There appears to be a positive linear relationship between x and y

  c. $s_{xy} = 26.5$

  d. $r_{xy} = .693$

48. $-.91$; negative linear relationship

50. b. .9098

  c. Strong positive linear relationship; no

52. a. 3.69

  b. 3.175

53. a.

f_i	M_i	$f_i M_i$
4	5	20
7	10	70
9	15	135
5	20	100
25		325

$$\bar{x} = \frac{\Sigma f_i M_i}{n} = \frac{325}{25} = 13$$

  b.

f_i	M_i	$(M_i - \bar{x})$	$(M_i - \bar{x})^2$	$f_i(M_i - \bar{x})^2$
4	5	-8	64	256
7	10	-3	9	63
9	15	2	4	36
5	20	7	49	245
25				600

$$s^2 = \frac{\Sigma f_i(M_i - \bar{x})^2}{n - 1} = \frac{600}{25 - 1} = 25$$

$$s = \sqrt{25} = 5$$

54. a.

Grade x_i	Weight w_i
4 (A)	9
3 (B)	15
2 (C)	33
1 (D)	3
0 (F)	0
	60 credit hours

$$\bar{x} = \frac{\Sigma w_i x_i}{\Sigma w_i} = \frac{9(4) + 15(3) + 33(2) + 3(1)}{9 + 15 + 33 + 3}$$

$$= \frac{150}{60} = 2.5$$

  b. Yes

56. 3.49, .94

58. a. 1800, 1351
  b. 387, 1710
  c. 7280, 1323
  d. 3,675,303, 1917
  e. High positive skewness
  f. Using a box plot: 4135 and 7450 are outliers

60. a. 2.3, 1.85
  b. 1.90, 1.38
  c. Altria Group 5%
  d. $-.51$, below mean
  e. 1.02, above mean
  f. No

62. a. \$670
  b. \$456
  c. $z = 3$; yes
  d. Save time and prevent a penalty cost

64. a. 215.9
  b. 55%
  c. 175.0, 628.3
  d. 48.8, 175.0, 215.9, 628.3, 2325.0
  e. Yes, any price over 1308.25
  f. 482.1; prefer median

66. b. .9856, strong positive linear relationship

68. a. 817
  b. 833

70. a. 60.68
  b. $s^2 = 31.23$; $s = 5.59$

Chapter 4

2. $\dbinom{6}{3} = \dfrac{6!}{3!3!} = \dfrac{6 \cdot 5 \cdot 4 \cdot 3 \cdot 2 \cdot 1}{(3 \cdot 2 \cdot 1)(3 \cdot 2 \cdot 1)} = 20$

ABC	ACE	BCD	BEF
ABD	ACF	BCE	CDE
ABE	ADE	BCF	CDF
ABF	ADF	BDE	CEF
ACD	AEF	BDF	DEF

4. b. (H,H,H), (H,H,T), (H,T,H), (H,T,T), (T,H,H), (T,H,T), (T,T,H), (T,T,T)

  c. $\frac{1}{8}$

6. $P(E_1) = .40$, $P(E_2) = .26$, $P(E_3) = .34$
  The relative frequency method was used

8. a. 4: Commission Positive—Council Approves
    Commission Positive—Council Disapproves
    Commission Negative—Council Approves
    Commission Negative—Council Disapproves

9. $\dbinom{50}{4} = \dfrac{50!}{4!46!} = \dfrac{50 \cdot 49 \cdot 48 \cdot 47}{4 \cdot 3 \cdot 2 \cdot 1} = 230,300$

10. a. Use the relative frequency approach. The percent tells us that 94 out of 100 Morehouse students graduate with debt.

$P(\text{Debt}) = .94$

b. Use the relative frequency approach. Five of the 8 schools have over 60% of their students graduating with debt.

$P(\text{School with over 60\%}) = 5/8 = .625$

c. Use relative frequency approach.

$P(\text{School with average debt} > \$30{,}000) = 2/8 = .25$

d. $P(\text{No debt}) = 1 - .72 = .28$

e. This is a weighted average; 72% graduate with an average debt of $32,980 and 28% graduate with an average debt of $0

$$\text{Mean debt per student} = \frac{.72(\$32{,}980) + .28(\$0)}{.72 + .28}$$
$$= \$23{,}745.60$$

12. a. 3,478,761

b. 1/3,478,761

c. 1/146,107,962

14. a. ¼

b. ½

c. ¾

15. a. $S = \{$ace of clubs, ace of diamonds, ace of hearts, ace of spades$\}$

b. $S = \{$2 of clubs, 3 of clubs, . . . , 10 of clubs, J of clubs, Q of clubs, K of clubs, A of clubs$\}$

c. There are 12; jack, queen, or king in each of the four suits

d. For (a): 4/52 = 1/13 = .08
For (b): 13/52 = 1/4 = .25
For (c): 12/52 = .23

16. a. 36

c. ⅙

d. ⁵⁄₁₈

e. No; $P(\text{odd}) = P(\text{even}) = \frac{1}{2}$

f. Classical

17. a. (4, 6), (4, 7), (4, 8)

b. .05 + .10 + .15 = .30

c. (2, 8), (3, 8), (4, 8)

d. .05 + .05 + .15 = .25

e. .15

18. a. $P(0) = .02$

b. $P(4 \text{ or more}) = .82$

c. $P(0, 1, \text{ or } 2) = .11$

20. a. .108

b. .096

c. .434

22. a. .40, .40, .60

b. .80, yes

c. $A^c = \{E_3, E_4, E_5\}$; $C^c = \{E_1, E_4\}$;
$P(A^c) = .60$; $P(C^c) = .40$

d. (E_1, E_2, E_5); .60

e. .80

23. a. $P(A) = P(E_1) + P(E_4) + P(E_6)$
$= .05 + .25 + .10 = .40$
$P(B) = P(E_2) + P(E_4) + P(E_7)$
$= .20 + .25 + .05 = .50$
$P(C) = P(E_2) + P(E_3) + P(E_5) + P(E_7)$
$= .20 + .20 + .15 + .05 = .60$

b. $A \cup B = \{E_1, E_2, E_4, E_6, E_7\}$;
$P(A \cup B) = P(E_1) + P(E_2) + P(E_4) + P(E_6) + P(E_7)$
$= .05 + .20 + .25 + .10 + .05$
$= .65$

c. $A \cap B = \{E_4\}$; $P(A \cap B) = P(E_4) = .25$

d. Yes, they are mutually exclusive

e. $B^c = \{E_1, E_3, E_5, E_6\}$;
$P(B^c) = P(E_1) + P(E_3) + P(E_5) + P(E_6)$
$= .05 + .20 + .15 + .10$
$= .50$

24. a. .05

b. .70

26. a. .48

b. .64

c. .36

d. .76

28. Let $B = $ rented a car for business reasons
$P = $ rented a car for personal reasons

a. $P(B \cup P) = P(B) + P(P) - P(B \cap P)$
$= .540 + .458 - .300$
$= .698$

b. $P(\text{Neither}) = 1 - .698 = .302$

30. a. $P(A \mid B) = \dfrac{P(A \cap B)}{P(B)} = \dfrac{.40}{.60} = .6667$

b. $P(B \mid A) = \dfrac{P(A \cap B)}{P(A)} = \dfrac{.40}{.50} = .80$

c. No, because $P(A \mid B) \neq P(A)$

32. a.

	Yes	No	Total
18 to 34	.375	.085	.46
35 and older	.475	.065	.54
Total	.850	.150	1.00

b. 46% 18 to 34; 54% 35 and older

c. .15

d. .1848

e. .1204

f. .5677

g. Higher probability of No for 18 to 34

33. a.

	Reason for Applying			
	Cost/			
	Quality	Convenience	Other	Total
Full-time	.218	.204	.039	.461
Part-time	.208	.307	.024	.539
Total	.426	.511	.063	1.000

b. A student is most likely to cite cost or convenience as the first reason (probability = .511); school quality is the reason cited by the second largest number of students (probability = .426)

c. $P(\text{quality} \mid \text{full-time}) = .218/.461 = .473$

d. $P(\text{quality} \mid \text{part-time}) = .208/.539 = .386$

e. For independence, we must have $P(A)P(B) = P(A \cap B)$; from the table
$P(A \cap B) = .218, P(A) = .461, P(B) = .426$
$P(A)P(B) = (.461)(.426) = .196$
Because $P(A)P(B) \neq P(A \cap B)$, the events are not independent

34. a.

	On Time	Late	Total
Southwest	.3336	.0664	.40
US Airways	.2629	.0871	.35
JetBlue	.1753	.0747	.25
Total	.7718	.2282	1.00

b. Southwest Airlines

c. .7718

d. US Airways, Southwest

36. a. .7921

b. .9879

c. .0121

d. .3364, .8236, .1764
Don't foul Reggie Miller

38. a. .70

b. .30

c. .67, .33

d. .20, .10

e. .40

f. .20

g. No; $P(S \mid M) \neq P(S)$

39. a. Yes, because $P(A_1 \cap A_2) = 0$

b. $P(A_1 \cap B) = P(A_1)P(B \mid A_1) = .40(.20) = .08$
$P(A_2 \cap B) = P(A_2)P(B \mid A_2) = .60(.05) = .03$

c. $P(B) = P(A_1 \cap B) + P(A_2 \cap B) = .08 + .03 = .11$

d. $P(A_1 \mid B) = \dfrac{.08}{.11} = .7273$

$P(A_2 \mid B) = \dfrac{.03}{.11} = .2727$

40. a. .10, .20, .09

b. .51

c. .26, .51, .23

42. $M = $ missed payment
$D_1 = $ customer defaults
$D_2 = $ customer does not default
$P(D_1) = .05, P(D_2) = .95, P(M \mid D_2) = .2, P(M \mid D_1) = 1$

a. $P(D_1 \mid M) = \dfrac{P(D_1)P(M \mid D_1)}{P(D_1)P(M \mid D_1) + P(D_2)P(M \mid D_2)}$

$= \dfrac{(.05)(1)}{(.05)(1) + (.95)(.2)}$

$= \dfrac{.05}{.24} = .21$

b. Yes, the probability of default is greater than .20

44. a. .47, .53, .50, .45

b. .4963

c. .4463

d. 47%, 53%

46. a. .26

b. .40

c. 1249

48. a. 315

b. .29

c. No

d. Republicans

50. a. .76

b. .24

52. b. .2022

c. .4618

d. .4005

54. a. .49

b. .44

c. .54

d. No

e. Yes

56. a. .25

b. .125

c. .0125

d. .10

e. No

58. a.

	Young Adult	Older Adult	Total
Blogger	.0432	.0368	.08
Nonblogger	.2208	.6992	.92
Total	.2640	.7360	1.00

b. .2640

c. .0432

d. .1636

60. a. .40

b. .67

Chapter 5

1. a. Head, Head (H, H)
Head, Tail (H, T)
Tail, Head (T, H)
Tail, Tail (T, T)

b. $x = $ number of heads on two coin tosses

c.

Outcome	Values of x
(H, H)	2
(H, T)	1
(T, H)	1
(T, T)	0

d. Discrete; it may assume 3 values: 0, 1, and 2

2. **a.** x = time in minutes to assemble product
   b. Any positive value: $x > 0$
   c. Continuous

3. Let Y = position is offered
   N = position is not offered
   a. $S = \{(Y, Y, Y), (Y, Y, N), (Y, N, Y), (Y, N, N), (N, Y, Y),$
   $(N, Y, N), (N, N, Y), (N, N, N)\}$
   b. Let N = number of offers made; N is a discrete random
   variable
   c.

Experimental Outcome	(Y, Y, Y)	(Y, Y, N)	(Y, N, Y)	(Y, N, N)	(N, Y, Y)	(N, Y, N)	(N, N, Y)	(N, N, N)
Value of N	3	2	2	1	2	1	1	0

4. $x = 0, 1, 2, \ldots, 9$

6. **a.** $0, 1, 2, \ldots, 20$; discrete
   b. $0, 1, 2, \ldots$; discrete
   c. $0, 1, 2, \ldots, 50$; discrete
   d. $0 \le x \le 8$; continuous
   e. $x > 0$; continuous

7. **a.** $f(x) \ge 0$ for all values of x
   $\Sigma f(x) = 1$; therefore, it is a valid probability
   distribution
   b. Probability $x = 30$ is $f(30) = .25$
   c. Probability $x \le 25$ is $f(20) + f(25) = .20 + .15 = .35$
   d. Probability $x > 30$ is $f(35) = .40$

8. **a.**

x	$f(x)$
1	3/20 = .15
2	5/20 = .25
3	8/20 = .40
4	4/20 = .20
	Total 1.00

   b.
   $f(x)$

   c. $f(x) \ge 0$ for $x = 1, 2, 3, 4$
   $\Sigma f(x) = 1$

10. **a.**

x	1	2	3	4	5
$f(x)$	.05	.09	.03	.42	.41

    b.

x	1	2	3	4	5
$f(x)$	.04	.10	.12	.46	.28

    c. .83
    d. .28
    e. Senior executives are more satisfied

12. **a.** Yes
    b. .15
    c. .10

14. **a.** .05
    b. .70
    c. .40

16. **a.**

y	$f(y)$	$yf(y)$
2	.20	.4
4	.30	1.2
7	.40	2.8
8	.10	.8
Totals	1.00	5.2

    $E(y) = \mu = 5.2$

    b.

y	$y - \mu$	$(y - \mu)^2$	$f(y)$	$(y - \mu)^2 f(y)$
2	−3.20	10.24	.20	2.048
4	−1.20	1.44	.30	.432
7	1.80	3.24	.40	1.296
8	2.80	7.84	.10	.784
			Total	4.560

    $Var(y) = 4.56$
    $\sigma = \sqrt{4.56} = 2.14$

18. **a/b.**

x	$f(x)$	$xf(x)$	$x - \mu$	$(x - \mu)^2$	$(x - \mu)^2 f(x)$
0	0.04	0.00	−1.84	3.39	0.12
1	0.34	0.34	−0.84	0.71	0.24
2	0.41	0.82	0.16	0.02	0.01
3	0.18	0.53	1.16	1.34	0.24
4	0.04	0.15	2.16	4.66	0.17
Total	1.00	1.84			0.79

    $E(x)$ ↑ $Var(x)$ ↑

    c/d.

y	$f(y)$	$yf(y)$	$y - \mu$	$(y - \mu)^2$	$y - \mu^2 f(y)$
0	0.00	0.00	−2.93	8.58	0.01
1	0.03	0.03	−1.93	3.72	0.12
2	0.23	0.45	−0.93	0.86	0.20
3	0.52	1.55	0.07	0.01	0.00
4	0.22	0.90	1.07	1.15	0.26
Total	1.00	2.93			0.59

    $E(y)$ ↑ $Var(y)$ ↑

    e. The number of bedrooms in owner-occupied houses is
    greater than in renter-occupied houses; the expected
    number of bedrooms is $2.93 - 1.84 = 1.09$ greater,
    and the variability in the number of bedrooms is less
    for the owner-occupied houses

20. **a.** 430
    b. −90; concern is to protect against the expense of a big
    accident

22. a. 445
   b. \$1250 loss

24. a. Medium: 145; large: 140
   b. Medium: 2725; large: 12,400

25. a.

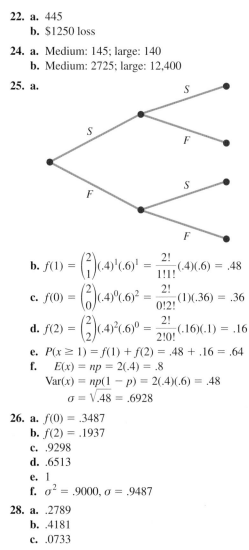

b. $f(1) = \binom{2}{1}(.4)^1(.6)^1 = \dfrac{2!}{1!1!}(.4)(.6) = .48$

c. $f(0) = \binom{2}{0}(.4)^0(.6)^2 = \dfrac{2!}{0!2!}(1)(.36) = .36$

d. $f(2) = \binom{2}{2}(.4)^2(.6)^0 = \dfrac{2!}{2!0!}(.16)(.1) = .16$

e. $P(x \geq 1) = f(1) + f(2) = .48 + .16 = .64$

f. $E(x) = np = 2(.4) = .8$
   $\text{Var}(x) = np(1 - p) = 2(.4)(.6) = .48$
   $\sigma = \sqrt{.48} = .6928$

26. a. $f(0) = .3487$
   b. $f(2) = .1937$
   c. .9298
   d. .6513
   e. 1
   f. $\sigma^2 = .9000, \sigma = .9487$

28. a. .2789
   b. .4181
   c. .0733

30. a. Probability of a defective part being produced must be .03 for each part selected; parts must be selected independently
   b. Let D = defective
      G = not defective

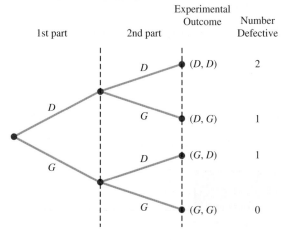

1st part	2nd part	Experimental Outcome	Number Defective
D	D	(D, D)	2
D	G	(D, G)	1
G	D	(G, D)	1
G	G	(G, G)	0

c. Two outcomes result in exactly one defect
d. $P(\text{no defects}) = (.97)(.97) = .9409$
   $P(1 \text{ defect}) = 2(.03)(.97) = .0582$
   $P(2 \text{ defects}) = (.03)(.03) = .0009$

32. a. .90
   b. .99
   c. .999
   d. Yes

34. a. .2262
   b. .8355

36. a. .1897
   b. .9757
   c. Yes
   d. 5

38. a. $f(x) = \dfrac{3^x e^{-3}}{x!}$
   b. .2241
   c. .1494
   d. .8008

39. a. $f(x) = \dfrac{2^x e^{-2}}{x!}$
   b. $\mu = 6$ for 3 time periods
   c. $f(x) = \dfrac{6^x e^{-6}}{x!}$
   d. $f(2) = \dfrac{2^2 e^{-2}}{2!} = \dfrac{4(.1353)}{2} = .2706$
   e. $f(6) = \dfrac{6^6 e^{-6}}{6!} = .1606$
   f. $f(5) = \dfrac{4^5 e^{-4}}{5!} = .1563$

40. a. $\mu = 48(5/60) = 4$
   $f(3) = \dfrac{4^3 e^{-4}}{3!} = \dfrac{(64)(.0183)}{6} = .1952$
   b. $\mu = 48(15/60) = 12$
   $f(10) = \dfrac{12^{10} e^{-12}}{10!} = .1048$
   c. $\mu = 48(5/60) = 4$; expect four callers to be waiting after 5 minutes
   $f(0) = \dfrac{4^0 e^{-4}}{0!} = .0183$; the probability none will be waiting after 5 minutes is .0183
   d. $\mu = 48(3/60) = 2.4$
   $f(0) = \dfrac{2.4^0 e^{-2.4}}{0!} = .0907$; *the probability of no interruptions in 3 minutes is .0907*

42. a. $f(0) = \dfrac{7^0 e^{-7}}{0!} = e^{-7} = .0009$
   b. probability $= 1 - [f(0) + f(1)]$
   $f(1) = \dfrac{7^1 e^{-7}}{1!} = 7e^{-7} = .0064$
   probability $= 1 - [.0009 + .0064] = .9927$

c. $\mu = 3.5$

$$f(0) = \frac{3.5^0 e^{-3.5}}{0!} = e^{-3.5} = .0302$$

probability $= 1 - f(0) = 1 - .0302 = .9698$

d.
probability $= 1 - [f(0) + f(1) + f(2) + f(3) + f(4)]$
$\qquad = 1 - [.0009 + .0064 + .0223 + .0521 + .0912]$
$\qquad = .8271$

44. a. $\mu = 1.25$
  b. .2865
  c. .3581
  d. .3554

46. a. $f(1) = \dfrac{\dbinom{3}{1}\dbinom{10-3}{4-1}}{\dbinom{10}{4}} = \dfrac{\left(\dfrac{3!}{1!2!}\right)\left(\dfrac{7!}{3!4!}\right)}{\dfrac{10!}{4!6!}}$

$\qquad = \dfrac{(3)(35)}{210} = .50$

  b. $f(2) = \dfrac{\dbinom{3}{2}\dbinom{10-3}{2-2}}{\dbinom{10}{2}} = \dfrac{(3)(1)}{45} = .067$

  c. $f(0) = \dfrac{\dbinom{3}{0}\dbinom{10-3}{2-0}}{\dbinom{10}{2}} = \dfrac{(1)(21)}{45} = .4667$

  d. $f(2) = \dfrac{\dbinom{3}{2}\dbinom{10-3}{4-2}}{\dbinom{10}{4}} = \dfrac{(3)(21)}{210} = .30$

48. a. .5250
  b. .8167

50. $N = 60, n = 10$
  a. $r = 20, x = 0$

$$f(0) = \frac{\dbinom{20}{0}\dbinom{40}{10}}{\dbinom{60}{10}} = \frac{(1)\left(\dfrac{40!}{10!30!}\right)}{\dfrac{60!}{10!50!}}$$

$$= \left(\frac{40!}{10!30!}\right)\left(\frac{10!50!}{60!}\right)$$

$$= \frac{40 \cdot 39 \cdot 38 \cdot 37 \cdot 36 \cdot 35 \cdot 34 \cdot 33 \cdot 32 \cdot 31}{60 \cdot 59 \cdot 58 \cdot 57 \cdot 56 \cdot 55 \cdot 54 \cdot 53 \cdot 52 \cdot 51}$$

$$\approx .01$$

  b. $r = 20, x = 1$

$$f(1) = \frac{\dbinom{20}{1}\dbinom{40}{9}}{\dbinom{60}{10}} = 20\left(\frac{40!}{9!31!}\right)\left(\frac{10!50!}{60!}\right)$$

$$\approx .07$$

  c. $1 - f(0) - f(1) = 1 - .08 = .92$
  d. Same as the probability one will be from Hawaii; in part (b) it was equal to approximately .07

52. a. .5333
  b. .6667
  c. .7778
  d. $n = 7$

54. a.

x	1	2	3	4	5
$f(x)$	.24	.21	.10	.21	.24

  b. 3.00, 2.34
  c. Bonds: $E(x) = 1.36$, $\text{Var}(x) = .23$
     Stocks: $E(x) = 4$, $\text{Var}(x) = 1$

56. a. .0596
  b. .3585
  c. 100
  d. 9.75

58. a. .9510
  b. .0480
  c. .0490

60. a. 240
  b. 12.96
  c. 12.96

62. .1912

64. a. .2240
  b. .5767

66. a. .4667
  b. .4667
  c. .0667

Chapter 6

1. a.

  b. $P(x = 1.25) = 0$; the probability of any single point is zero because the area under the curve above any single point is zero
  c. $P(1.0 \le x \le 1.25) = 2(.25) = .50$
  d. $P(1.20 < x < 1.5) = 2(.30) = .60$

2. b. .50
  c. .60
  d. 15
  e. 8.33

4. a.

b. $P(.25 < x < .75) = 1(.50) = .50$
c. $P(x \le .30) = 1(.30) = .30$
d. $P(x > .60) = 1(.40) = .40$

6. a. .125
   b. .50
   c. .25

10. a. .9332
   b. .8413
   c. .0919
   d. .4938

12. a. .2967
   b. .4418
   c. .3300
   d. .5910
   e. .8849
   f. .2389

13. a. $P(-1.98 \le z \le .49) = P(z \le .49) - P(z < -1.98)$
   $= .6879 - .0239 = .6640$
   b. $P(.52 \le z \le 1.22) = P(z \le 1.22) - P(z < .52)$
   $= .8888 - .6985 = .1903$
   c. $P(-1.75 \le z \le -1.04) = P(z \le -1.04) - P(z < -1.75) = .1492 - .0401 = .1091$

14. a. $z = 1.96$
   b. $z = 1.96$
   c. $z = .61$
   d. $z = 1.12$
   e. $z = .44$
   f. $z = .44$

15. a. The z value corresponding to a cumulative probability of .2119 is $z = -.80$
   b. Compute $.9030/2 = .4515$; the cumulative probability of $.5000 + .4515 = .9515$ corresponds to $z = 1.66$
   c. Compute $.2052/2 = .1026$; z corresponds to a cumulative probability of $.5000 + .1026 = .6026$, so $z = .26$
   d. The z value corresponding to a cumulative probability of .9948 is $z = 2.56$
   e. The area to the left of z is $1 - .6915 = .3085$, so $z = -.50$

16. a. $z = 2.33$
   b. $z = 1.96$
   c. $z = 1.645$
   d. $z = 1.28$

18. $\mu = 30$ and $\sigma = 8.2$
   a. At $x = 40$, $z = \dfrac{40 - 30}{8.2} = 1.22$
   $P(z \le 1.22) = .8888$
   $P(x \ge 40) = 1.000 - .8888 = .1112$
   b. At $x = 20$, $z = \dfrac{20 - 30}{8.2} = -1.22$
   $P(z \le -1.22) = .1112$
   $P(x \le 20) = .1112$
   c. A z value of 1.28 cuts off an area of approximately 10% in the upper tail
   $x = 30 + 8.2(1.28)$
   $= 40.50$

A stock price of $40.50 or higher will put a company in the top 10%

20. a. .0885
   b. 12.51%
   c. 93.8 hours or more

22. a. .7193
   b. $35.59
   c. .0233

24. a. 200, 26.04
   b. .2206
   c. .1251
   d. 242.84 million

26. a. .5276
   b. .3935
   c. .4724
   d. .1341

27. a. $P(x \le x_0) = 1 - e^{-x_0/3}$
   b. $P(x \le 2) = 1 - e^{-2/3} = 1 - .5134 = .4866$
   c. $P(x \ge 3) = 1 - P(x \le 3) = 1 - (1 - e^{-3/3})$
   $= e^{-1} = .3679$
   d. $P(x \le 5) = 1 - e^{-5/3} = 1 - .1889 = .8111$
   e. $P(2 \le x \le 5) = P(x \le 5) - P(x \le 2)$
   $= .8111 - .4866 = .3245$

28. a. .5624
   b. .1915
   c. .2461
   d. .2259

29. a.

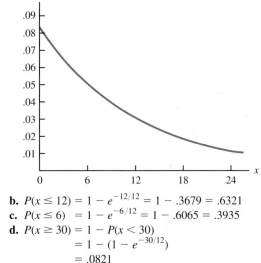

   b. $P(x \le 12) = 1 - e^{-12/12} = 1 - .3679 = .6321$
   c. $P(x \le 6) = 1 - e^{-6/12} = 1 - .6065 = .3935$
   d. $P(x \ge 30) = 1 - P(x < 30)$
   $= 1 - (1 - e^{-30/12})$
   $= .0821$

30. a. 50 hours
   b. .3935
   c. .1353

32. a. $f(x) = 5.5e^{-5.5x}$
   b. .2528
   c. .6002

34. a. $3780 or less
   b. 19.22%
   c. $8167.50

36. a. 3229
 b. .2244
 c. $12,382 or more

38. a. .0228
 b. $50

40. a. 38.3%
 b. 3.59% better, 96.41% worse
 c. 38.21%

42. $\mu = 19.23$ ounces

44. a. $\frac{1}{7}$ minute
 b. $7e^{-7x}$
 c. .0009
 d. .2466

46. a. 2 minutes
 b. .2212
 c. .3935
 d. .0821

Chapter 7

1. a. AB, AC, AD, AE, BC, BD, BE, CD, CE, DE
 b. With 10 samples, each has a $\frac{1}{10}$ probability
 c. B and D because the two smallest random numbers are .0476 and .0957

2. Elements 2, 3, 5, and 10

3. The simple random sample consists of New York, Detroit, Oakland, Boston, and Kansas City

4. Step 1. Generate a random number for each company
 Step 2. Sort with respect to random numbers and select the first three companies

6. a. finite
 b. process
 c. process
 d. finite
 e. process

7. a. $\bar{x} = \dfrac{\Sigma x_i}{n} = \dfrac{54}{6} = 9$

 b. $s = \sqrt{\dfrac{\Sigma(x_i - \bar{x})^2}{n - 1}}$

 $\Sigma(x_i - \bar{x})^2 = (-4)^2 + (-1)^2 + 1^2 + (-2)^2 + 1^2 + 5^2$
 $= 48$

 $s = \sqrt{\dfrac{48}{6 - 1}} = 3.1$

8. a. .50
 b. .3667

9. a. $\bar{x} = \dfrac{\Sigma x_i}{n} = \dfrac{465}{5} = 93$

b.

x_i	$(x_i - \bar{x})$	$(x_i - \bar{x})^2$
94	+1	1
100	+7	49
85	−8	64
94	+1	1
92	−1	1
Totals 465	0	116

$$s = \sqrt{\frac{\Sigma(x_i - \bar{x})^2}{n - 1}} = \sqrt{\frac{116}{4}} = 5.39$$

10. a. .45
 b. .15
 c. .45

12. a. .10
 b. 20
 c. .72

15. a. The sampling distribution is normal with:

$$E(\bar{x}) = \mu = 200$$

$$\sigma_{\bar{x}} = \frac{\sigma}{\sqrt{n}} = \frac{50}{\sqrt{100}} = 5$$

For $+5$, $(\bar{x} - \mu) = 5$,

$$z = \frac{\bar{x} - \mu}{\sigma_{\bar{x}}} = \frac{5}{5} = 1$$

Area $= .8413 - .1587 = .6826$

 b. For ± 10, $(\bar{x} - \mu) = 10$,

$$z = \frac{\bar{x} - \mu}{\sigma_{\bar{x}}} = \frac{10}{5} = 2$$

Area $= .9772 - .0228 = .9544$

16. 3.54, 2.50, 2.04, 1.77
 $\sigma_{\bar{x}}$ decreases as n increases

18. a. Normal with $E(\bar{x}) = 51,800$ and $\sigma_{\bar{x}} = 516.40$
 b. $\sigma_{\bar{x}}$ decreases to 365.15
 c. $\sigma_{\bar{x}}$ decreases as n increases

19. a.

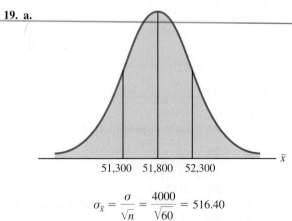

51,300   51,800   52,300

$$\sigma_{\bar{x}} = \frac{\sigma}{\sqrt{n}} = \frac{4000}{\sqrt{60}} = 516.40$$

At $\bar{x} = 52{,}300$, $z = \dfrac{52{,}300 - 51{,}800}{516.40} = .97$

$P(\bar{x} \le 52{,}300) = P(z \le .97) = .8340$

At $\bar{x} = 51{,}300$, $z = \dfrac{51{,}300 - 51{,}800}{516.40} = -.97$

$P(\bar{x} < 51{,}300) = P(z < -.97) = .1660$

$P(51{,}300 \le \bar{x} \le 52{,}300) = .8340 - .1660 = .6680$

Using Excel:
= NORMDIST(52300,51800,516.40,TRUE)-
    NORMDIST(51300,51800,516.40,TRUE) = .6671

b. $\sigma_{\bar{x}} = \dfrac{\sigma}{\sqrt{n}} = \dfrac{4000}{\sqrt{120}} = 365.15$

At $\bar{x} = 52{,}300$, $z = \dfrac{52{,}300 - 51{,}800}{365.15} = 1.37$

$P(\bar{x} \le 52{,}300) = P(z \le 1.37) = .9147$

At $\bar{x} = 51{,}300$, $z = \dfrac{51{,}300 - 51{,}800}{365.15} = -1.37$

$P(\bar{x} < 51{,}300) = P(z < -1.37) = .0853$

$P(51{,}300 \le \bar{x} \le 52{,}300) = .9147 - .0853 = .8294$

Using Excel:
= NORMDIST(52300,51800,365.15,TRUE)-
    NORMDIST(51300,51800,365.15,TRUE) = .8291

20. a. Normal with $E(\bar{x}) = 17.5$ and $\sigma_{\bar{x}} = .57$
  b. .9198
  c. .6212

22. a. Using table: .4246, .5284, .6922, .9586
  b. Higher probability with a larger sample size

24. a. Normal with $E(\bar{x}) = 95$ and $\sigma_{\bar{x}} = 2.56$
  b. Using table: .7580; using NORMDIST: .7595
  c. Using table: .8502; using NORMDIST: .8494
  d. Part (c) because of the larger sample size

26. a. $n/N = .01$; no
  b. 1.29, 1.30; little difference
  c. Using table: .8764

28. a. $E(\bar{p}) = .40$

$\sigma_{\bar{p}} = \sqrt{\dfrac{p(1 - p)}{n}} = \sqrt{\dfrac{(.40)(.60)}{200}} = .0346$

Within $\pm .03$ means $.37 \le \bar{p} \le .43$

Using table: $z = \dfrac{\bar{p} - p}{\sigma_{\bar{p}}} = \dfrac{.03}{.0346} = .87$

$P(.37 \le \bar{p} \le .43) = P(-.87 \le z \le .87)$

$= .8078 - .1922$

$= .6156$

Using Excel:
=NORMDIST(.43,.40,.0346,TRUE)-
    NORMDIST(.37,.40,.0346,TRUE) = .6141

b. Using table: $z = \dfrac{\bar{p} - p}{\sigma_{\bar{p}}} = \dfrac{.05}{.0346} = 1.44$

$P(.35 \le \bar{p} \le .45) = P(-1.44 \le z \le 1.44)$

$= .9251 - .0749$

$= .8502$

Using Excel:
=NORMDIST(.45,.40,.0346,TRUE)-
    NORMDIST(.35,.40,.0346,TRUE) = .8516

30. a. Using table: .6156; using NORMDIST: .6175
  b. Using table: .7814; using NORMDIST: .7830
  c. Using table: .9488; using NORMDIST: .9490
  d. Using table: .9942; using NORMDIST: .9942
  e. Higher probability with larger n

31. a.

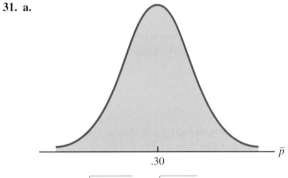

$\sigma_{\bar{p}} = \sqrt{\dfrac{p(1 - p)}{n}} = \sqrt{\dfrac{.30(.70)}{100}} = .0458$

The normal distribution is appropriate because $np = 100(.30) = 30$ and $n(1 - p) = 100(.70) = 70$ are both greater than 5

b. $P(.20 \le \bar{p} \le .40) = ?$

$z = \dfrac{.40 - .30}{.0458} = 2.18$

$P(.20 \le \bar{p} \le .40) = P(-2.18 \le z \le 2.18)$

$= .9854 - .0146$

$= .9708$

Using Excel:
=NORMDIST(.40,.30,.0458,TRUE)-
    NORMDIST(.20,.30,.0458,TRUE) = .9710

c. $P(.25 \le \bar{p} \le .35) = ?$

$z = \dfrac{.35 - .30}{.0458} = 1.09$

$P(.25 \le \bar{p} \le .35) = P(-1.09 \le z \le 1.09)$

$= .8621 - .1379$

$= .7242$

Using Excel:
=NORMDIST(.35,.30,.0458,TRUE)-
    NORMDIST(.25,.30,.0458,TRUE) = .7250

32. a. Normal with $E(\bar{p}) = .66$ and $\sigma_{\bar{p}} = .0273$
  b. Using table: .8584; using NORMDIST: .8571
  c. Using table: .9606; using NORMDIST: .9608
  d. Yes, standard error is smaller for youth population
  e. Using table: .9616; using NORMDIST: .9618

34. a. Normal with $E(\bar{p}) = .56$ and $\sigma_{\bar{p}} = .0248$
   b. Using table: .5820; using NORMDIST: .5800
   c. Using table: .8926; using NORMDIST: .8932

36. a. Normal with $E(\bar{p}) = .76$ and $\sigma_{\bar{p}} = .0214$
   b. Using table: .8384; using NORMDIST: .8390
   c. Using table: .9452; using NORMDIST: .9455

38. Thoroughbreds, The Marker, Officers Club, SeaBlue, Crickets

40. a. Normal with $E(\bar{x}) = 115.50$ and $\sigma_{\bar{x}} = 5.53$
   b. Using table: .9298; using NORMDIST: .9292
   c. Using table: $z = -2.80$, .0026; using NORMDIST: .0025

42. a. 707
   b. .50
   c. Using table: $z = \pm 1.41$, .8414; using NORMDIST: .8428
   d. .9544

44. a. 625
   b. .7888

46. a. Normal with $E(\bar{p}) = .28$ and $\sigma_{\bar{p}} = .0290$
   b. Using table: $z = \pm 1.38$, .8324; using NORMDIST: .8322
   c. Using table: $z = \pm .69$, .5098; using NORMDIST: .5096

48. a. Using table: $z = \pm 1.59$, .8882; using NORMDIST: .8900
   b. Using table: $z = +1.99$, .0233; using NORMDIST: .0232

50. a. 48
   b. Normal, $E(\bar{p}) = .25$, $\sigma_{\bar{p}} = .0625$
   c. .2119

Chapter 8

2. Use $\bar{x} \pm z_{\alpha/2}(\sigma/\sqrt{n})$
   a. $32 \pm 1.645(6/\sqrt{50})$
      32 ± 1.4; 30.6 to 33.4
   b. $32 \pm 1.96(6/\sqrt{50})$
      32 ± 1.66; 30.34 to 33.66
   c. $32 \pm 2.576(6/\sqrt{50})$
      32 ± 2.19; 29.81 to 34.19

4. 54

5. a. $1.96\sigma/\sqrt{n} = 1.96(5/\sqrt{49}) = 1.40$
   b. 24.80 ± 1.40; 23.40 to 26.20

6. 8.1 to 8.9

8. a. Population is at least approximately normal
   b. 3.1
   c. 4.1

10. a. \$113,638 to \$124,672
   b. \$112,581 to \$125,729

c. \$110,515 to \$127,795
d. Width increases as confidence level increases

12. a. 2.179
   b. -1.676
   c. 2.457
   d. -1.708 and 1.708
   e. -2.014 and 2.014

13. a. $\bar{x} = \dfrac{\Sigma x_i}{n} = \dfrac{80}{8} = 10$

   b. $s = \sqrt{\dfrac{\Sigma(x_i - \bar{x})^2}{n-1}} = \sqrt{\dfrac{84}{7}} = 3.46$

   c. $t_{.025}\left(\dfrac{s}{\sqrt{n}}\right) = 2.365\left(\dfrac{3.46}{\sqrt{8}}\right) = 2.9$

   d. $\bar{x} \pm t_{.025}\left(\dfrac{s}{\sqrt{n}}\right)$
      10 ± 2.9 (7.1 to 12.9)

14. a. 21.5 to 23.5
   b. 21.3 to 23.7
   c. 20.9 to 24.1
   d. A larger margin of error and a wider interval

15. $\bar{x} \pm t_{\alpha/2}(s/\sqrt{n})$
   90% confidence: $df = 64$ and $t_{.05} = 1.669$
   $19.5 \pm 1.669\left(\dfrac{5.2}{\sqrt{65}}\right)$
   19.5 ± 1.08 (18.42 to 20.58)
   95% confidence: $df = 64$ and $t_{.025} = 1.998$
   $19.5 \pm 1.998\left(\dfrac{5.2}{\sqrt{65}}\right)$
   19.5 ± 1.29 (18.21 to 20.79)

16. a. 1.69
   b. 47.31 to 50.69
   c. Fewer hours and higher cost for United

18. a. 22
   b. 3.8014
   c. 18.20 to 25.80
   d. Larger n next time

20. $\bar{x} = 22$; 21.48 to 22.52

22. a. 3.348%
   b. 2.40% to 4.29%

24. a. Planning value of $\sigma = \dfrac{\text{Range}}{4} = \dfrac{36}{4} = 9$

   b. $n = \dfrac{z_{.025}^2\sigma^2}{E^2} = \dfrac{(1.96)^2(9)^2}{(3)^2} = 34.57$; use $n = 35$

   c. $n = \dfrac{(1.96)^2(9)^2}{(2)^2} = 77.79$; use $n = 78$

25. a. Use $n = \dfrac{z_{\alpha/2}^2\sigma^2}{E^2}$

   $n = \dfrac{(1.96)^2(6.84)^2}{(1.5)^2} = 79.88$; use $n = 80$

b. $n = \dfrac{(1.645)^2(6.84)^2}{(2)^2} = 31.65$; use $n = 32$

26. a. 18
b. 35
c. 97

28. a. 328
b. 465
c. 803
d. n gets larger; no to 99% confidence

30. 81

31. a. $\bar{p} = \dfrac{100}{400} = .25$

b. $\sqrt{\dfrac{\bar{p}(1 - \bar{p})}{n}} = \sqrt{\dfrac{.25(.75)}{400}} = .0217$

c. $\bar{p} \pm z_{.025}\sqrt{\dfrac{\bar{p}(1 - \bar{p})}{n}}$

$.25 \pm 1.96(.0217)$
$.25 \pm .0424$; .2076 to .2924

32. a. .6733 to .7267
b. .6682 to .7318

34. 1068

35. a. $\bar{p} = \dfrac{281}{611} = .4599$ (46%)

b. $z_{.05}\sqrt{\dfrac{\bar{p}(1 - \bar{p})}{n}} = 1.645\sqrt{\dfrac{4599(1 - .4599)}{611}} = .0332$

c. $\bar{p} \pm .0332$
$.4599 \pm .0332$ (.4267 to .4931)

36. a. .23
b. .1716 to .2884

38. a. .1790
b. .0738; .5682 to .7158
c. 354

39. a. $n = \dfrac{1.96^2 p^*(1 - p^*)}{E^2}$

$n = \dfrac{1.96^2(.156)(1 - .156)}{(.03)^2} = 562$

b. $n = \dfrac{2.576^2(.156)(1 - .156)}{(.03)^2} = 970.77$; use $n = 971$

40. .0267, .8333 to .8867

42. a. .0442
b. 601, 1068, 2401, 9604

44. a. 4.00
b. 29.77 to 37.77

46. a. 122
b. $1751 to $1995
c. $172.316 billion
d. Less than $1873

48. a. 14 minutes
b. 13.38 to 14.62
c. 32 per day
d. Staff reduction

50. 37

52. 176

54. a. .2844 to .3356
b. .7987 to .8413
c. Margin of error is larger when $\bar{p}$ is closer to $\frac{1}{2}$

56. a. .8273
b. .7957 to .8589

58. a. 1267
b. 1509

60. a. .3101
b. .2898 to .3304
c. 8219; no, this sample size is unnecessarily large

Chapter 9

2. a. $H_0: \mu \leq 14$
$H_a: \mu > 14$
b. No evidence that the new plan increases sales
c. The research hypothesis $\mu > 14$ is supported; the new plan increases sales

4. a. $H_0: \mu \geq 220$
$H_a: \mu < 220$

5. a. Rejecting $H_0: \mu \leq 56.2$ when it is true
b. Accepting $H_0: \mu \leq 56.2$ when it is false

6. a. $H_0: \mu \leq 1$
$H_a: \mu > 1$
b. Claiming $\mu > 1$ when it is not true
c. Claiming $\mu \leq 1$ when it is not true

8. a. $H_0: \mu \geq 220$
$H_a: \mu < 220$
b. Claiming $\mu < 220$ when it is not true
c. Claiming $\mu \geq 220$ when it is not true

10. a. $z = \dfrac{\bar{x} - \mu_0}{\sigma/\sqrt{n}} = \dfrac{26.4 - 25}{6/\sqrt{40}} = 1.48$

b. Using normal table with $z = 1.48$: p-value = $1.0000 - .9306 = .0694$
Using Excel: p-value = $1 - \text{NORMSDIST}(1.48)$
$= .0694$
c. p-value $> .01$, do not reject H_0
d. Reject H_0 if $z \geq 2.33$
$1.48 < 2.33$, do not reject H_0

11. a. $z = \dfrac{\bar{x} - \mu_0}{\sigma/\sqrt{n}} = \dfrac{14.15 - 15}{3/\sqrt{50}} = -2.00$

b. p-value = $2(.0228) = .0456$
c. p-value $\leq .05$, reject H_0
d. Reject H_0 if $z \leq -1.96$ or $z \geq 1.96$
$-2.00 \leq -1.96$, reject H_0

12. a. .1056; do not reject H_0
b. .0062; reject H_0
c. ≈ 0; reject H_0
d. .7967; do not reject H_0

14. a. .3844; do not reject H_0

b. .0074; reject H_0
c. .0836; do not reject H_0

15. a. $H_0: \mu \geq 1056$
$H_a: \mu < 1056$

b. $z = \dfrac{\bar{x} - \mu_0}{\sigma/\sqrt{n}} = \dfrac{910 - 1056}{1600/\sqrt{400}} = -1.83$

p-value $= .0336$

c. p-value $\leq .05$, reject H_0; the mean refund of "last-minute" filers is less than \$1056

d. Reject H_0 if $z \leq -1.645$
$-1.83 \leq -1.645$; reject H_0

16. a. $H_0: \mu \leq 895$
$H_a: \mu > 895$

b. .1170

c. Do not reject H_0

d. Withhold judgment; collect more data

18. a. $H_0: \mu = 4.1$
$H_a: \mu \neq 4.1$

b. -2.21, .0272

c. Reject H_0

20. a. $H_0: \mu \geq 32.79$
$H_a: \mu < 32.79$

b. -2.73

c. .0032

d. Reject H_0

22. a. $H_0: \mu = 8$
$H_a: \mu \neq 8$

b. .1706

c. Do not reject H_0

d. 7.83 to 8.97; yes

24. a. $t = \dfrac{\bar{x} - \mu_0}{s/\sqrt{n}} = \dfrac{17 - 18}{4.5/\sqrt{48}} = -1.54$

b. Degrees of freedom $= n - 1 = 47$
Area in lower tail is between .05 and .10
p-value (two-tail) is between .10 and .20
Using Excel: p-value $=$ TDIST(1.54,47,2) $= .1303$

c. p-value $> .05$; do not reject H_0

d. With $df = 47$, $t_{.025} = 2.012$
Reject H_0 if $t \leq -2.012$ or $t \geq 2.012$
$t = -1.54$; do not reject H_0

26. a. Between .02 and .05; using Excel: p-value $=$
TDIST(2.10,64,2) $= .0397$; reject H_0

b. Between .01 and .02; using Excel: p-value $=$
TDIST(2.57,64,2) $= .0125$; reject H_0

c. Between .10 and .20; using Excel: p-value $=$
TDIST(1.54,64,2) $= .1285$; do not reject H_0

27. a. $H_0: \mu \geq 238$
$H_a: \mu < 238$

b. $t = \dfrac{\bar{x} - \mu_0}{s/\sqrt{n}} = \dfrac{231 - 238}{80/\sqrt{100}} = -.88$

Degrees of freedom $= n - 1 = 99$

p-value is between .10 and .20
Using Excel: p-value $=$ TDIST(.88,99,1) $= .1905$

c. p-value $> .05$; do not reject H_0
Cannot conclude mean weekly benefit in Virginia is less than the national mean

d. $df = 99$, $t_{.05} = -1.66$
Reject H_0 if $t \leq -1.66$
$-.88 > -1.66$; do not reject H_0

28. a. $H_0: \mu \geq 9$
$H_a: \mu < 9$

b. Between .005 and .01
Using Excel: p-value $=$ TDIST(2.50,84,1) $= .0072$

c. Reject H_0

30. a. $H_0: \mu = 600$
$H_a: \mu \neq 600$

b. Between .20 and .40
Using Excel: p-value $=$ TDIST(1.17,39,2) $= .2491$

c. Do not reject H_0

d. A larger sample size

32. a. $H_0: \mu = 10{,}192$
$H_a: \mu \neq 10{,}192$

b. Between .02 and .05
Using Excel: p-value $=$ TDIST(2.23,49,2) $= .0304$

c. Reject H_0

34. a. $H_0: \mu = 2$
$H_a: \mu \neq 2$

b. 2.2

c. .52

d. Between .20 and .40
Using Excel: p-value $=$ TDIST(1.22,9,2) $= .2535$

e. Do not reject H_0

36. a. $z = \dfrac{\bar{p} - p_0}{\sqrt{\dfrac{p_0(1 - p_0)}{n}}} = \dfrac{.68 - .75}{\sqrt{\dfrac{.75(1 - .75)}{300}}} = -2.80$

p-value $= .0026$
p-value $\leq .05$; reject H_0

b. $z = \dfrac{.72 - .75}{\sqrt{\dfrac{.75(1 - .75)}{300}}} = -1.20$

p-value $= .1151$
p-value $> .05$; do not reject H_0

c. $z = \dfrac{.70 - .75}{\sqrt{\dfrac{.75(1 - .75)}{300}}} = -2.00$

p-value $= .0228$
p-value $\leq .05$; reject H_0

d. $z = \dfrac{.77 - .75}{\sqrt{\dfrac{.75(1 - .75)}{300}}} = .80$

p-value $= .7881$
p-value $> .05$; do not reject H_0

38. a. $H_0: p = .64$
   $H_a: p \neq .64$

   b. $\bar{p} = 52/100 = .52$

   $$z = \frac{\bar{p} - p_0}{\sqrt{\dfrac{p_0(1 - p_0)}{n}}} = \frac{.52 - .64}{\sqrt{\dfrac{.64(1 - .64)}{100}}} = -2.50$$

   Area = .4938
   p-value = $2(.0062) = .0124$

   c. p-value $\leq .05$; reject H_0
   Proportion differs from the reported .64

   d. Yes, because $\bar{p} = .52$ indicates that fewer believe the supermarket brand is as good as the name brand

40. a. .2702

   b. $H_0: p \leq .22$
   $H_a: p > .22$
   p-value ≈ 0; reject H_0

   c. Helps evaluate the effectiveness of commercials

42. a. $\bar{p} = .15$

   b. .0718 to .2218

   c. Houston proportion is different

44. a. $H_0: p \leq .51$
   $H_a: p > .51$

   b. p-value = $1 - \text{NORMSDIST}(2.80) = .0026$

   c. reject H_0

46. a. $H_0: \mu = 16$
   $H_a: \mu \neq 16$

   b. .0286; reject H_0
   Readjust line

   c. .2186; do not reject H_0
   Continue operation

   d. $z = 2.19$; reject H_0
   $z = -1.23$; do not reject H_0
   Yes, same conclusion

48. a. $H_0: \mu \leq 119{,}155$
   $H_a: \mu > 119{,}155$

   b. .0047

   c. Reject H_0

50. $t = -.93$
   p-value between .20 and .40
   Using Excel: p-value = TDIST(.93,31,2) = .3596
   Do not reject H_0

52. $t = 2.26$
   p-value between .01 and .025
   Using Excel: p-value = TDIST(2.26,31,1) = .0155
   Reject H_0

54. a. $H_0: p \leq .50$
   $H_a: p > .50$

   b. .64

   c. .0026; reject H_0

56. a. $H_0: p \leq .80$
   $H_a: p > .80$

   b. .84

   c. .0418; reject H_0

58. $H_0: p \geq .90$
   $H_a: p < .90$
   p-value = .0808
   Do not reject H_0

Chapter 10

1. a. $\bar{x}_1 - \bar{x}_2 = 13.6 - 11.6 = 2$

   b. $z_{\alpha/2} = z_{.05} = 1.645$

   $$\bar{x}_1 - \bar{x}_2 \pm 1.645\sqrt{\frac{\sigma_1^2}{n_1} + \frac{\sigma_2^2}{n_2}}$$

   $$2 \pm 1.645\sqrt{\frac{(2.2)^2}{50} + \frac{(3)^2}{35}}$$

   $2 \pm .98$ (1.02 to 2.98)

   c. $z_{\alpha/2} = z_{.05} = 1.96$

   $$2 \pm 1.96\sqrt{\frac{(2.2)^2}{50} + \frac{(3)^2}{35}}$$

   2 ± 1.17 (.83 to 3.17)

2. a. $z = \dfrac{(\bar{x}_1 - \bar{x}_2) - D_0}{\sqrt{\dfrac{\sigma_1^2}{n_1} + \dfrac{\sigma_2^2}{n_2}}} = \dfrac{(25.2 - 22.8) - 0}{\sqrt{\dfrac{(5.2)^2}{40} + \dfrac{(6)^2}{50}}} = 2.03$

   b. p-value = $1.0000 - .9788 = .0212$

   c. p-value $\leq .05$; reject H_0

4. a. $\bar{x}_1 - \bar{x}_2 = 85.36 - 81.40 = 3.96$

   b. $z_{.025}\sqrt{\dfrac{\sigma_1^2}{n_1} + \dfrac{\sigma_2^2}{n_2}}$

   $$1.96\sqrt{\frac{(4.55)^2}{37} + \frac{(3.97)^2}{44}} = 1.88$$

   c. 3.96 ± 1.88 (2.08 to 5.84)

6. p-value = .015
   Reject H_0; an increase

8. a. 1.08

   b. .2802

   c. Do not reject H_0; cannot conclude a difference exists

9. a. $\bar{x}_1 - \bar{x}_2 = 22.5 - 20.1 = 2.4$

   b. $df = \dfrac{\left(\dfrac{s_1^2}{n_1} + \dfrac{s_2^2}{n_2}\right)^2}{\dfrac{1}{n_1 - 1}\left(\dfrac{s_1^2}{n_1}\right)^2 + \dfrac{1}{n_2 - 1}\left(\dfrac{s_2^2}{n_2}\right)^2}$

   $$= \frac{\left(\dfrac{2.5^2}{20} + \dfrac{4.8^2}{30}\right)^2}{\dfrac{1}{19}\left(\dfrac{2.5^2}{20}\right)^2 + \dfrac{1}{29}\left(\dfrac{4.8^2}{30}\right)^2} = 45.8$$

   c. $df = 45$, $t_{.025} = 2.014$

   $$t_{.025}\sqrt{\frac{s_1^2}{n_1} + \frac{s_2^2}{n_2}} = 2.014\sqrt{\frac{2.5^2}{20} + \frac{4.8^2}{30}} = 2.1$$

   d. 2.4 ± 2.1 (.3 to 4.5)

10. a. $t = \dfrac{(\bar{x}_1 - \bar{x}_2) - 0}{\sqrt{\dfrac{s_1^2}{n_1} + \dfrac{s_2^2}{n_2}}} = \dfrac{(13.6 - 10.1) - 0}{\sqrt{\dfrac{5.2^2}{35} + \dfrac{8.5^2}{40}}} = 2.18$

b. $df = \dfrac{\left(\dfrac{s_1^2}{n_1} + \dfrac{s_2^2}{n_2}\right)^2}{\dfrac{1}{n_1 - 1}\left(\dfrac{s_1^2}{n_1}\right)^2 + \dfrac{1}{n_2 - 1}\left(\dfrac{s_2^2}{n_2}\right)^2}$

$= \dfrac{\left(\dfrac{5.2^2}{35} + \dfrac{8.5^2}{40}\right)^2}{\dfrac{1}{34}\left(\dfrac{5.2^2}{35}\right)^2 + \dfrac{1}{39}\left(\dfrac{8.5^2}{40}\right)^2} = 65.7$

Use $df = 65$

c. $df = 65$, area in tail is between .01 and .025; two-tailed p-value is between .02 and .05
Exact p-value = .0329

d. p-value $\le$ .05; reject H_0

12. a. $\bar{x}_1 - \bar{x}_2 = 22.5 - 18.6 = 3.9$ miles

b. $df = \dfrac{\left(\dfrac{s_1^2}{n_1} + \dfrac{s_2^2}{n_2}\right)^2}{\dfrac{1}{n_1 - 1}\left(\dfrac{s_1^2}{n_1}\right)^2 + \dfrac{1}{n_2 - 1}\left(\dfrac{s_2^2}{n_2}\right)^2}$

$= \dfrac{\left(\dfrac{8.4^2}{50} + \dfrac{7.4^2}{40}\right)^2}{\dfrac{1}{49}\left(\dfrac{8.4^2}{50}\right)^2 + \dfrac{1}{39}\left(\dfrac{7.4^2}{40}\right)^2} = 87.1$

Use $df = 87$, $t_{.025} = 1.988$

$3.9 \pm 1.988\sqrt{\dfrac{8.4^2}{50} + \dfrac{7.4^2}{40}}$

3.9 ± 3.3 (.6 to 7.2)

14. a. $H_0\colon \mu_1 - \mu_2 \ge 0$
$H_a\colon \mu_1 - \mu_2 < 0$

b. -2.41

c. Using t table, p-value is between .005 and .01
Exact p-value = .009

d. Reject H_0; conclude salaries of staff nurses are lower in Tampa

16. a. $H_0\colon \mu_1 - \mu_2 \le 0$
$H_a\colon \mu_1 - \mu_2 > 0$

b. 3 points higher for midpriced family sedans

c. Using t table, p-value is greater than .20
Exact p-value is .2671

d. p-value $>$ .05; we cannot reject H_0.

18. a. $H_0\colon \mu_1 - \mu_2 \le 0$
$H_a\colon \mu_1 - \mu_2 > 0$

b. 1.186 points higher for Dunlop SP60 tires

c. Exact p-value = .000

d. The population mean rating for Dunlop SP60 tires is greater than the population mean rating for Michelin tires.

19. a. 1, 2, 0, 0, 2

b. $\bar{d} = \Sigma d_i / n = 5/5 = 1$

c. $s_d = \sqrt{\dfrac{\Sigma(d_i - \bar{d})^2}{n - 1}} = \sqrt{\dfrac{4}{5 - 1}} = 1$

d. $t = \dfrac{\bar{d} - \mu}{s_d / \sqrt{n}} = \dfrac{1 - 0}{1/\sqrt{5}} = 2.24$

$df = n - 1 = 4$
Using t table, p-value is between .025 and .05
Exact p-value = .0443
p-value $\le$ .05; reject H_0

20. a. 3, -1, 3, 5, 3, 0, 1

b. 2

c. 2.08

d. 2

e. .07 to 3.93

21. $H_0\colon \mu_d \le 0$
$H_a\colon \mu_d > 0$

$\bar{d} = .625$
$s_d = 1.30$

$t = \dfrac{\bar{d} - \mu_d}{s_d / \sqrt{n}} = \dfrac{.625 - 0}{1.30/\sqrt{8}} = 1.36$

$df = n - 1 = 7$
Using t table, p-value is between .10 and .20
Exact p-value = .1080
p-value $>$ .05; do not reject H_0

22. $.10 to $.32

24. $t = 1.32$
Using t table, p-value is greater than .10
Exact p-value = .1142
Do not reject H_0

26. a. $t = -.60$
Using t table, p-value is greater than .40
Exact p-value = .5633
Do not reject H_0

b. $-.103$

c. .39; larger sample size

28. a. $\bar{\bar{x}} = (156 + 142 + 134)/3 = 144$

$\text{SSTR} = \sum_{j=1}^{k} n_j(\bar{x}_j - \bar{\bar{x}})^2$

$= 6(156 - 144)^2 + 6(142 - 144)^2 + 6(134 - 144)^2$
$= 1488$

b. $\text{MSTR} = \dfrac{\text{SSTR}}{k - 1} = \dfrac{1488}{2} = 744$

c. $s_1^2 = 164.4$, $s_2^2 = 131.2$, $s_3^2 = 110.4$

$\text{SSE} = \sum_{j=1}^{k} (n_j - 1)s_j^2$

$= 5(164.4) + 5(131.2) + 5(110.4)$
$= 2030$

d. $MSE = \dfrac{SSE}{n_T - k} = \dfrac{2030}{18 - 3} = 135.3$

e.

Source of Variation	Sum of Squares	Degrees of Freedom	Mean Square	F	p-value
Treatments	1488	2	744	5.50	.0162
Error	2030	15	135.3		
Total	3518	17			

f. $F = \dfrac{MSTR}{MSE} = \dfrac{744}{135.3} = 5.50$

From the F table (2 numerator degrees of freedom and 15 denominator), p-value is between .01 and .025

Using Excel, the p-value corresponding to $F = 5.50$ is .0162

Because p-value $\leq \alpha = .05$, we reject the hypothesis that the means for the three treatments are equal

30. a. $H_0\colon \mu_1 = \mu_2 = \mu_3 = \mu_4 = \mu_5$
H_a: Not all the population means are equal

b. Yes; p-value $= .0000$

32. a.

Source of Variation	Sum of Squares	Degrees of Freedom	Mean Square	F	p-value
Treatments	1200	2	600	43.99	.0000
Error	600	44	13.64		
Total	1800	46			

Significant relationship

34. a.

Source of Variation	Sum of Squares	Degrees of Freedom	Mean Square	F	p-value
Treatments	4560	2	2280	9.87	.0006
Error	6240	27	231.11		
Total	10800	29			

b. Significant relationship

36. No significant relationship: p-value $= .2104$

38. p-value $= .0931$; at the .05 level of significance we cannot reject the null hypothesis that the mean drying times for the four paints are equal

40. a. 412
b. 267.79
c. 412 ± 267.79

42. a. $H_0\colon \mu_1 - \mu_2 \leq 0$
$H_a\colon \mu_1 - \mu_2 > 0$

b. $t = .60$, $df = 57$
Using t table, p-value is greater than .20
Exact p-value $= .2754$
Do not reject H_0

44. a. 15 (or \$15,000)
b. 9.81 to 20.19
c. 11.5%

46. Significant relationship; p-value $= .0061$
48. Significant difference; p-value $= .0000$
50. Significant relationship; p-value $= .0340$

Chapter 11

1. a. $\bar{p}_1 - \bar{p}_2 = .48 - .36 = .12$

b. $\bar{p}_1 - \bar{p}_2 \pm z_{.05}\sqrt{\dfrac{\bar{p}_1(1 - \bar{p}_1)}{n_1} + \dfrac{\bar{p}_2(1 - \bar{p}_2)}{n_2}}$

$.12 \pm 1.645\sqrt{\dfrac{.48(1 - .48)}{400} + \dfrac{.36(1 - .36)}{300}}$

$.12 \pm .0614 \ (.0586 \text{ to } .1814)$

c. $.12 \pm 1.96\sqrt{\dfrac{.48(1 - .48)}{400} + \dfrac{.36(1 - .36)}{300}}$

$.12 \pm .0731 \ (.0469 \text{ to } .1931)$

2. a. $\bar{p} = \dfrac{n_1\bar{p}_1 + n_2\bar{p}_2}{n_1 + n_2} = \dfrac{100(.28) + 140(.20)}{100 + 140} = .2333$

b. $z = \dfrac{\bar{p}_1 - \bar{p}_2}{\sqrt{\bar{p}(1 - \bar{p})\left(\dfrac{1}{n_1} + \dfrac{1}{n_2}\right)}}$

$= \dfrac{.28 - .20}{\sqrt{.2333(1 - .2333)\left(\dfrac{1}{100} + \dfrac{1}{140}\right)}} = 1.44$

p-value $= 2(1 - .9251) = .1498$
c. p-value $> .05$; do not reject H_0. We cannot conclude that the two population proportions differ.

3. a. Professional Golfers: $\bar{p}_1 = 688/1075 = .64$
Amateur Golfers: $\bar{p}_2 = 696/1200 = .58$
Professional golfers have the better putting accuracy

b. $\bar{p}_1 - \bar{p}_2 = .64 - .58 = .06$
Professional golfers make 6% more 6-foot putts than the very best amateur golfers

c. $\bar{p}_1 - \bar{p}_2 \pm z_{.025}\sqrt{\dfrac{\bar{p}_1(1 - \bar{p}_1)}{n_1} + \dfrac{\bar{p}_2(1 - \bar{p}_2)}{n_2}}$

$.64 - .58 \pm 1.96\sqrt{\dfrac{.64(1 - .64)}{1075} + \dfrac{.58(1 - .58)}{1200}}$

$.06 \pm .04 \ (.02 \text{ to } .10)$

The confidence interval shows that professional golfers make from 2% to 10% more 6-foot putts than the best amateur golfers

4. a. $H_0\colon p_w \leq p_m$
$H_a\colon p_w > p_m$

b. $\bar{p}_w = .3699$

c. $\bar{p}_m = .3400$

d. p-value $= .1093$

Do not reject H_0

6. a. $H_0: p_1 - p_2 = 0$
$H_a: p_1 - p_2 \neq 0$

b. .28

c. .26

d. .3078, do not reject

8. a. $H_0: p_1 - p_2 = 0$
$H_a: p_1 - p_2 \neq 0$

b. .13

c. p-value $= .0404$

10. a. $H_0: p_1 - p_2 = 0$
$H_a: p_1 - p_2 \neq 0$

b. .27, .17

c. p-value ≈ 0

Difference is significant

11. a. Expected frequencies: $e_1 = 200(.40) = 80$
$e_2 = 200(.40) = 80$
$e_3 = 200(.20) = 40$

Actual frequencies: $f_1 = 60, f_2 = 120, f_3 = 20$

$$\chi^2 = \frac{(60 - 80)^2}{80} + \frac{(120 - 80)^2}{80} + \frac{(20 - 40)^2}{40}$$

$$= \frac{400}{80} + \frac{1600}{80} + \frac{400}{40}$$

$$= 5 + 20 + 10 = 35$$

Degrees of freedom: $k - 1 = 2$
$\chi^2 = 35$ shows p-value is less than .005
p-value $\leq .01$; reject H_0

b. Reject H_0 if $\chi^2 \geq 9.210$
$\chi^2 = 35$; reject H_0

12. $\chi^2 = 15.33, df = 3$
p-value less than .005
Reject H_0

13. $H_0: p_{ABC} = .29, p_{CBS} = .28, p_{NBC} = .25, p_{IND} = .18$
H_a: The proportions are not
$p_{ABC} = .29, p_{CBS} = .28, p_{NBC} = .25, p_{IND} = .18$
Expected frequencies: $300(.29) = 87, 300(.28) = 84$
$300(.25) = 75, 300(.18) = 54$
$e_1 = 87, e_2 = 84, e_3 = 75, e_4 = 54$
Actual frequencies: $f_1 = 95, f_2 = 70, f_3 = 89, f_4 = 46$

$$\chi^2 = \frac{(95 - 87)^2}{87} + \frac{(70 - 84)^2}{84} + \frac{(89 - 75)^2}{75}$$

$$+ \frac{(46 - 54)^2}{54} = 6.87$$

Degrees of freedom: $k - 1 = 3$
$\chi^2 = 6.87$, p-value between .05 and .10
Do not reject H_0

14. $\chi^2 = 29.51, df = 5$
p-value is less than .005
Reject H_0

16. a. $\chi^2 = 12.21, df = 3$
p-value is between .005 and .01
Conclude difference for 2003

b. 21%, 30%, 15%, 34%
Increased use of debit card

c. 51%

18. $\chi^2 = 16.31, df = 3$
p-value less than .005
Reject H_0

19. H_0: The column variable is independent of the row variable

H_a: The column variable is not independent of the row variable

Expected frequencies:

	A	B	C
P	28.5	39.9	45.6
Q	21.5	30.1	34.4

$$\chi^2 = \frac{(20 - 28.5)^2}{28.5} + \frac{(44 - 39.9)^2}{39.9} + \frac{(50 - 45.6)^2}{45.6}$$

$$+ \frac{(30 - 21.5)^2}{21.5} + \frac{(26 - 30.1)^2}{30.1} + \frac{(30 - 34.4)^2}{34.4}$$

$$= 7.86$$

Degrees of freedom: $(2 - 1)(3 - 1) = 2$
$\chi^2 = 7.86$, p-value between .01 and .025
Reject H_0

20. $\chi^2 = 19.77, df = 4$
p-value less than .005
Reject H_0

21. H_0: Type of ticket purchased is independent of the type of flight
H_a: Type of ticket purchased is not independent of the type of flight

Expected frequencies:

$e_{11} = 35.59$ $e_{12} = 15.41$
$e_{21} = 150.73$ $e_{22} = 65.27$
$e_{31} = 455.68$ $e_{32} = 197.32$

Ticket	Flight	Observed Frequency (f_i)	Expected Frequency (e_i)	$(f_i - e_i)^2/e_i$
First	Domestic	29	35.59	1.22
First	International	22	15.41	2.82
Business	Domestic	95	150.73	20.61
Business	International	121	65.27	47.59
Full-fare	Domestic	518	455.68	8.52
Full-fare	International	135	197.32	19.68
Totals		920		$\chi^2 = 100.43$

Degrees of freedom: $(3 - 1)(2 - 1) = 2$
$\chi^2 = 100.43$, p-value is less than .005
Reject H_0

22. a. $\chi^2 = 7.95$, $df = 3$
  p-value is between .025 and .05
  Reject H_0
  b. 18 to 24 use most

24. a. $\chi^2 = 10.60$, $df = 4$
  p-value is between .025 and .05
  Reject H_0; not independent
  b. Higher negative effect on grades as hours increase

26. a. 6448
  b. $\chi^2 = 424.6674$
  p-value ≈ 0
  Reject H_0
  c. Italy

28. $\chi^2 = 3.01$, $df = 2$
  p-value is greater than .10
  Do not reject H_0; 63.3%

30. a. p-value ≈ 0; reject H_0
  b. .0468 to .1332

32. a. .35, .47
  b. .0163 to .2237
  c. Yes

34. $\chi^2 = 8.04$, $df = 3$
  p-value between .025 and .05
  Reject H_0

36. $\chi^2 = 4.64$, $df = 2$
  p-value between .05 and .10
  Do not reject H_0

38. $\chi^2 = 42.53$, $df = 4$
  p-value is less than .005
  Reject H_0

40. $\chi^2 = 23.37$, $df = 3$
  p-value is less than .005
  Reject H_0

42. a. $\chi^2 = 12.86$, $df = 2$
  p-value is less than .005
  Reject H_0
  b. 66.9, 30.3, 2.9
  54.0, 42.0, 4.0

44. $\chi^2 = 7.75$, $df = 3$
  p-value is between .05 and .10
  Do not reject H_0

Chapter 12

1. a.

y
14
12
10
8
6
4
2
0
  0   1   2   3   4   5   x

b. There appears to be a positive linear relationship between x and y

c. Many different straight lines can be drawn to provide a linear approximation of the relationship between x and y; in part (d) we will determine the equation of a straight line that "best" represents the relationship according to the least squares criterion

d. Summations needed to compute the slope and y-intercept:

$$\bar{x} = \frac{\Sigma x_i}{n} = \frac{15}{5} = 3, \quad \bar{y} = \frac{\Sigma y_i}{n} = \frac{40}{5} = 8,$$

$$\Sigma(x_i - \bar{x})(y_i - \bar{y}) = 26, \quad \Sigma(x_i - \bar{x})^2 = 10$$

$$b_1 = \frac{\Sigma(x_i - \bar{x})(y_i - \bar{y})}{\Sigma(x_i - \bar{x})^2} = \frac{26}{10} = 2.6$$

$$b_0 = \bar{y} - b_1\bar{x} = 8 - (2.6)(3) = 0.2$$

$$\hat{y} = 0.2 - 2.6x$$

e. $\hat{y} = .2 + 2.6x = .2 + 2.6(4) = 10.6$

2. b. There appears to be a negative linear relationship between x and y
  d. $\hat{y} = 68 - 3x$
  e. 38

4. a.

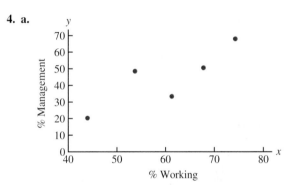

b. There appears to be a positive linear relationship between the percentage of women working in the five companies (x) and the percentage of management jobs held by women in each company (y)

c. Many different straight lines can be drawn to provide a linear approximation of the relationship between x and y; in part (d) we will determine the equation of a straight line that "best" represents the relationship according to the least squares criterion

d. Summations needed to compute the slope and y-intercept:

$$\bar{x} = \frac{\Sigma x_i}{n} = \frac{300}{5} = 60, \quad \bar{y} = \frac{\Sigma y_i}{n} = \frac{215}{5} = 43,$$

$$\Sigma(x_i - \bar{x})(y_i - \bar{y}) = 624, \quad \Sigma(x_i - \bar{x})^2 = 480$$

$$b_1 = \frac{\Sigma(x_i - \bar{x})(y_i - \bar{y})}{\Sigma(x_i - \bar{x})^2} = \frac{624}{480} = 1.3$$

$$b_0 = \bar{y} - b_1\bar{x} = 43 - 1.3(60) = -35$$

$$\hat{y} = -35 + 1.3x$$

e. $\hat{y} = -35 + 1.3x = -35 + 1.3(60) = 43\%$

6. c. $\hat{y} = 1.8395 + .0084x$
  e. 11.9%

8. c. $\hat{y} = -6745.44 + 149.29x$

 d. 4003

10. c. $\hat{y} = 359.2668 - 5.2772x$

 d. \$254

12. c. $\hat{y} = -8129.4439 + 22.4443x$

 d. \$8704

14. b. $\hat{y} = 28.30 - .0415x$

 c. 26.2

15. a. $\hat{y}_i = .2 + 2.6x_i$ and $\bar{y} = 8$

x_i	y_i	$\hat{y}_i$	$y_i - \hat{y}_i$	$(y_i - \hat{y}_i)^2$	$y_i - \bar{y}$	$(y_i - \bar{y})^2$
1	3	2.8	.2	.04	−5	25
2	7	5.4	1.6	2.56	−1	1
3	5	8.0	−3.0	9.00	−3	9
4	11	10.6	.4	.16	3	9
5	14	13.2	.8	.64	6	36
				SSE = 12.40		SST = 80

$$\text{SSR} = \text{SST} - \text{SSE} = 80 - 12.4 = 67.6$$

 b. $r^2 = \dfrac{\text{SSR}}{\text{SST}} = \dfrac{67.6}{80} = .845$

 The least squares line provided a good fit; 84.5% of the variability in y has been explained by the least squares line

 c. $r_{xy} = \sqrt{.845} = +.9192$

16. a. SSE = 230, SST = 1850, SSR = 1620

 b. $r^2 = .876$

 c. $r_{xy} = -.936$

18. a. The estimated regression equation and the mean for the dependent variable:

$$\hat{y} = 1790.5 + 581.1x, \quad \bar{y} = 3650$$

 The sum of squares due to error and the total sum of squares:

$$\text{SSE} = \Sigma(y_i - \hat{y}_i)^2 = 85,135.14$$

$$\text{SST} = \Sigma(y_i - \bar{y})^2 = 335,000$$

 Thus, SSR = SST − SSE

$$= 335,000 - 85,135.14 = 249,864.86$$

 b. $r^2 = \dfrac{\text{SSR}}{\text{SST}} = \dfrac{249,864.86}{335,000} = .746$

 The least squares line accounted for 74.6% of the total sum of squares

 c. $r_{xy} = \sqrt{.746} = +.8637$

20. a. $\hat{y} = 12.0169 + .0127x$

 b. $r^2 = .4503$

 c. 53

22. a. $\hat{y} = -745.480627 + 117.917320x$

 b. $r^2 = .7071$

 c. $r_{xy} = +.84$

23. a. $s^2 = \text{MSE} = \dfrac{\text{SSE}}{n-2} = \dfrac{12.4}{3} = 4.133$

 b. $s = \sqrt{\text{MSE}} = \sqrt{4.133} = 2.033$

 c. $\Sigma(x_i - \bar{x})^2 = 10$

$$s_{b_1} = \dfrac{s}{\sqrt{\Sigma(x_i - \bar{x})^2}} = \dfrac{2.033}{\sqrt{10}} = .643$$

 d. $t = \dfrac{b_1 - \beta_1}{s_{b_1}} = \dfrac{2.6 - 0}{.643} = 4.04$

 From the t table (3 degrees of freedom), area in tail is between .01 and .025

 p-value is between .02 and .05

 Using Excel, the p-value corresponding to $t = 4.04$ is .0272

 Because p-value $\leq \alpha$, we reject H_0: $\beta_1 = 0$

 e. $\text{MSR} = \dfrac{\text{SSR}}{1} = 67.6$

$$F = \dfrac{\text{MSR}}{\text{MSE}} = \dfrac{67.6}{4.133} = 16.36$$

 From the F table (1 numerator degree of freedom and 3 denominator), p-value is between .025 and .05

 Using Excel, the p-value corresponding to $F = 16.36$ is .0272

 Because p-value $\leq \alpha$, we reject H_0: $\beta_1 = 0$

Source of Variation	Sum of Squares	Degrees of Freedom	Mean Square	F	p-value
Regression	67.6	1	67.6	16.36	.0272
Error	12.4	3	4.133		
Total	80	4			

24. a. 76.6667

 b. 8.7560

 c. .6526

 d. Significant; p-value = .0193

 e. Significant; p-value = .0193

26. a. $s^2 = \text{MSE} = \dfrac{\text{SSE}}{n-2} = \dfrac{85,135.14}{4} = 21,283.79$

$$s = \sqrt{\text{MSE}} = \sqrt{21,283.79} = 145.89$$

$$\Sigma(x_i - \bar{x})^2 = .74$$

$$s_{b_1} = \dfrac{s}{\sqrt{\Sigma(x_i - \bar{x})^2}} = \dfrac{145.89}{\sqrt{.74}} = 169.59$$

$$t = \dfrac{b_1 - \beta_1}{s_{b_1}} = \dfrac{581.08 - 0}{169.59} = 3.43$$

 From the t table (4 degrees of freedom), area in tail is between .01 and .025

 p-value is between .02 and .05

 Using Excel, the p-value corresponding to $t = 3.43$ is .0266

 Because p-value $\leq \alpha$, we reject H_0: $\beta_1 = 0$

b. $MSR = \dfrac{SSR}{1} = \dfrac{249{,}864.86}{1} = 249{,}864.86$

$F = \dfrac{MSR}{MSE} = \dfrac{249{,}864.86}{21{,}283.79} = 11.74$

From the F table (1 numerator degree of freedom and 4 denominator), p-value is between .025 and .05

Using Excel, the p-value corresponding to $F = 11.74$ is .0266

Because p-value $\le \alpha$, we reject $H_0: \beta_1 = 0$

c.

Source of Variation	Sum of Squares	Degrees of Freedom	Mean Square	F	p-value
Regression	249,864.86	1	249,864.86	11.74	.0266
Error	85,135.14	4	21,283.79		
Total	335,000	5			

28. They are related; p-value $= .000$

30. Significant; p-value $= .002$

32. a. $\hat{y} = 6.1092 + .8951x$
  b. Significant relationship
  c. $r^2 = .82$; a good fit

34. a. $\hat{y} = 80.0 + 50.0x$
  b. p-value $\le \alpha$; reject $H_0: \beta_1 = 0$
  c. p-value $\le \alpha$; reject $H_0: \beta_1 = 0$
  d. p-value $= .000$

36. b. There appears to be a negative linear relationship between the two variables
  c. $\hat{y} = 2044.38 - 28.35$ Weight
  d. Significant relationship
  e. .77; a good fit

37. a. $s = 2.033$
$\bar{x} = 3, \Sigma(x_i - \bar{x})^2 = 10$

$s_{\hat{y}_p} = s\sqrt{\dfrac{1}{n} + \dfrac{(x_p - \bar{x})^2}{\Sigma(x_i - \bar{x})^2}}$

$= 2.033\sqrt{\dfrac{1}{5} + \dfrac{(4 - 3)^2}{10}} = 1.11$

  b. $\hat{y} = .2 + 2.6x = .2 + 2.6(4) = 10.6$
$\hat{y}_p \pm t_{\alpha/2}s_{\hat{y}_p}$
$10.6 \pm 3.182(1.11)$
10.6 ± 3.53, or 7.07 to 14.13

  c. $s_{ind} = s\sqrt{1 + \dfrac{1}{n} + \dfrac{(x_p - \bar{x})^2}{\Sigma(x_i - \bar{x})^2}}$

$= 2.033\sqrt{1 + \dfrac{1}{5} + \dfrac{(4 - 3)^2}{10}} = 2.32$

  d. $\hat{y}_p \pm t_{\alpha/2}s_{ind}$
$10.6 \pm 3.182(2.32)$
10.6 ± 7.38, or 3.22 to 17.98

38. a. 8.7560
  b. 30.07 to 57.93
  c. 9.7895
  d. 12.85 to 75.15

40. a. $s = 145.89, \bar{x} = 3.2, \Sigma(x_i - \bar{x})^2 = .74$
$\hat{y} = 1790.5 + 581.1x = 1790.5 + 581.1(3) = 3533.8$

$s_{\hat{y}_p} = s\sqrt{\dfrac{1}{n} + \dfrac{(x_p - \bar{x})^2}{\Sigma(x_i - \bar{x})^2}}$

$= 145.89\sqrt{\dfrac{1}{6} + \dfrac{(3 - 3.2)^2}{.74}} = 68.54$

$\hat{y}_p \pm t_{\alpha/2}s_{\hat{y}_p}$
3533.8 $\pm$ 2.776(68.54)
3533.8 $\pm$ 190.27, or \$3343.53 to \$3724.07

  b. $s_{ind} = s\sqrt{1 + \dfrac{1}{n} + \dfrac{(x_p - \bar{x})^2}{\Sigma(x_i - \bar{x})^2}}$

$= 145.89\sqrt{1 + \dfrac{1}{6} + \dfrac{(3 - 3.2)^2}{.74}} = 161.19$

$\hat{y}_p \pm t_{\alpha/2}s_{ind}$
3533.8 $\pm$ 2.776(161.19)
3533.8 $\pm$ 447.46, or \$3086.34 to \$3981.26

42. a. \$11,740 to \$14,420
  b. \$9300 to \$16,860
  c. Yes
  d. Any deductions exceeding the \$16,860 upper limit

44. a. $\hat{y} = -6.76 + 1.755x$
  b. $r^2 = .713$; good fit
  c. 31.8 to 60
  d. 6.3 to 85.5; not much value

45. a. $\bar{x} = \dfrac{\Sigma x_i}{n} = \dfrac{70}{5} = 14, \bar{y} = \dfrac{\Sigma y_i}{n} = \dfrac{76}{5} = 15.2,$

$\Sigma(x_i - \bar{x})(y_i - \bar{y}) = 200, \Sigma(x_i - \bar{x})^2 = 126$

$b_1 = \dfrac{\Sigma(x_i - \bar{x})(y_i - \bar{y})}{\Sigma(x_i - \bar{x})^2} = \dfrac{200}{126} = 1.5873$

$b_0 = \bar{y} - b_1\bar{x} = 15.2 - (1.5873)(14) = -7.0222$

$\hat{y} = -7.02 + 1.59x$

  b.

x_i	y_i	$\hat{y}_i$	$y_i - \hat{y}_i$
6	6	2.52	3.48
11	8	10.47	-2.47
15	12	16.83	-4.83
18	20	21.60	-1.60
20	30	24.78	5.22

  c.

With only five observations, it is difficult to determine whether the assumptions are satisfied; however, the plot does suggest curvature in the residuals, which would indicate that the error term assumptions are not satisfied; the scatter diagram for these data also indicates that the underlying relationship between x and y may be curvilinear

46. a. $\hat{y} = 2.32 + .64x$

  b. No; the variance does not appear to be the same for all values of x

47. a. Let x = advertising expenditures and y = revenue
  $\hat{y} = 29.4 + 1.55x$

  b. SST = 1002, SSE = 310.28, SSR = 691.72
  $$MSR = \frac{SSR}{1} = 691.72$$
  $$MSE = \frac{SSE}{n-2} = \frac{310.28}{5} = 62.0554$$
  $$F = \frac{MSR}{MSE} = \frac{691.72}{62.0554} = 11.15$$
  From the F table (1 numerator degree of freedom and 5 denominator), p-value is between .01 and .025
  Using Excel, p-value = .0206
  Because p-value $\leq \alpha = .05$, we conclude that the two variables are related

  c.

x_i	y_i	$\hat{y}_i = 29.40 + 1.55x_i$	$y_i - \hat{y}_i$
1	19	30.95	−11.95
2	32	32.50	−.50
4	44	35.60	8.40
6	40	38.70	1.30
10	52	44.90	7.10
14	53	51.10	1.90
20	54	60.40	−6.40

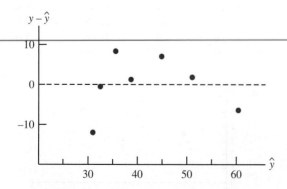

  d. The residual plot leads us to question the assumption of a linear relationship between x and y; even though the relationship is significant at the $\alpha = .05$ level, it would be extremely dangerous to extrapolate beyond the range of the data

48. b. Yes

50. No. Regression or correlation analysis can never prove that two variables are causally related.

52. The purpose of testing whether $\beta_1 = 0$ is to determine whether or not there is a significant relationship between x and y. However, rejecting $\beta_1 = 0$ does not necessarily imply a good fit.

54. a. $\hat{y} = -2.9874 + .9113x$
  b. $42.58
  c. Significant
  d. Yes; $r^2 = .7694$

56. a. $\hat{y} = 10.528 + .9534x$
  b. Since the p-value corresponding to $F = 47.62 = .0001 < \alpha = .05$, we reject $H_0: \beta_1 = 0$
  c. The 95% prediction interval is 28.74 to 49.52 or $2874 to $4952
  d. Yes, since the expected expense is $3913

58. a. A negative linear relationship appears to be reasonable
  b. $\hat{y} = 8.0978 - .3442x$
  c. Since the p-value corresponding to $F = 419.67$ is .0022 $< \alpha = .05$, we reject $H_0: \beta_1 = 0$
  d. $r^2 = .711$. The estimated regression equation explained 71.1% of the variability in y; this is a reasonably good fit
  e. The 95% confidence interval is 5.195 to 7.559 or approximately 5.2 to 7.6 days

60. a. $\hat{y} = 5.8470 + 0.8295x$
  b. Since the p-value corresponding to $F = 57.42$ is .000 $< \alpha = .05$, we reject $H_0: \beta_1 = 0$
  c. 84.65 points
  d. The 95% prediction interval is 65.35 to 103.96

62. a. $\hat{y} = -0.4710 + .0000387x$
  b. Since the p-value = 0.0384 is less than $\alpha = .05$, the relationship is significant
  c. $r^2 = .217$. The least squares line does not provide a very good fit
  d. The 95% confidence interval is .7729 to .9927

Chapter 13

2. a. The estimated regression equation is
  $\hat{y} = 45.0594 + 1.9436x_1$
  An estimate of y when $x_1 = 45$ is
  $\hat{y} = 45.0594 + 1.9436(45) = 132.52$
  b. The estimated regression equation is
  $\hat{y} = 85.2171 + 4.3215x_2$
  An estimate of y when $x_2 = 15$ is
  $\hat{y} = 85.2171 + 4.3215(15) = 150.04$
  c. The estimated regression equation is
  $\hat{y} = -18.3683 + 2.0102x_1 + 4.7378x_2$
  An estimate of y when $x_1 = 45$ and $x_2 = 15$ is
  $\hat{y} = -18.3683 + 2.0102(45) + 4.7378(15) = 143.16$

4. a. $255,000

5. a. The Excel output is shown in Figure D13.5a
   b. The Excel output is shown in Figure D13.5b
   c. It is 1.6039 in part (a) and 2.2902 in part (b); in part (a) the coefficient is an estimate of the change in revenue due to a one-unit change in television advertising expenditures; in part (b) it represents an estimate of the change in revenue due to a one-unit change in television advertising expenditures when the amount of newspaper advertising is held constant
   d. Revenue = 83.2301 + 2.2902(3.5) + 1.3010(1.8)
   $\phantom{\text{Revenue}}$ = 93.59 or $93,590

6. a. $\hat{y} = .3540 + .0009$ HR
   b. $\hat{y} = .8647 - .0837$ ERA
   c. $\hat{y} = .7092 + .0014$ HR $- .1026$ ERA
   d. .551

8. a. $\hat{y} = 31054.2597 - 1328.7218$ Reliability
   b. $\hat{y} = 21312.9147 + 136.6908$ Score $-$ 1446.3449 Reliability
   c. $26,463

10. a. $\hat{y} = -1.2207 + 3.9576$ FG%
   b. .04
   c. $\hat{y} = -1.2346 + 4.8166$ FG% $- 2.5895$ Opp 3 Pt% + .0344 Opp TO
   e. .6372

12. a. $R^2 = \dfrac{\text{SSR}}{\text{SST}} = \dfrac{14,052.2}{15,182.9} = .926$

   b. $R_a^2 = 1 - (1 - R^2)\dfrac{n-1}{n-p-1}$

   $ = 1 - (1 - .926)\dfrac{10-1}{10-2-1} = .905$

c. Yes; after adjusting for the number of independent variables in the model, we see that 90.5% of the variability in y has been accounted for

14. a. .75
   b. .68

15. a. $R^2 = \dfrac{\text{SSR}}{\text{SST}} = \dfrac{23.435}{25.5} = .919$

   $R_a^2 = 1 - (1 - R^2)\dfrac{n-1}{n-p-1}$

   $ = 1 - (1 - .919)\dfrac{8-1}{8-2-1} = .887$

   b. Multiple regression analysis is preferred because both R^2 and R_a^2 show an increased percentage of the variability of y explained when both independent variables are used

16. a. No, $R^2 = .1532$
   b. Using both independent variables provides a better fit

18. a. $R^2 = .5638$, $R_a^2 = .5114$
   b. The fit is not very good; but it does explain over 50% of the variability in y

19. a. $\text{MSR} = \dfrac{\text{SSR}}{p} = \dfrac{6216.375}{2} = 3108.188$

   $\text{MSE} = \dfrac{\text{SSE}}{n-p-1} = \dfrac{507.75}{10-2-1} = 72.536$

   b. $F = \dfrac{\text{MSR}}{\text{MSE}} = \dfrac{3108.188}{72.536} = 42.85$

   p-value (2 degrees of freedom numerator and 7 denominator) = .0001
   Because the p-value $\leq \alpha = .05$, the overall model is significant

FIGURE D13.5a

Regression Statistics	
Multiple R	0.8078
R Square	0.6526
Adjusted R Square	0.5946
Standard Error	1.2152
Observations	8

ANOVA

	df	SS	MS	F	Significance F
Regression	1	16.6401	16.6401	11.2688	0.0153
Residual	6	8.8599	1.4767		
Total	7	25.5			

	Coefficients	Standard Error	t Stat	P-value
Intercept	88.6377	1.5824	56.0159	2.174E-09
Television Advertising ($1000s)	1.6039	0.4778	3.3569	0.0153

FIGURE D13.5b

Regression Statistics	
Multiple R	0.9587
R Square	0.9190
Adjusted R Square	0.8866
Standard Error	0.6426
Observations	8

ANOVA

	df	SS	MS	F	Significance F
Regression	2	23.4354	11.7177	28.3778	0.0019
Residual	5	2.0646	0.4129		
Total	7	25.5			

	Coefficients	Standard Error	t Stat	P-value
Intercept	83.2301	1.5739	52.8825	4.57E-08
Television Advertising ($1000s)	2.2902	0.3041	7.5319	0.0007
Newspaper Advertising ($1000s)	1.3010	0.3207	4.0567	0.0098

c. $t = \dfrac{b_1}{s_{b_1}} = \dfrac{.5906}{.0813} = 7.26$

p-value (7 degrees of freedom) = .0002
Because the p-value $\leq \alpha = .05$, β_1 is significant

d. $t = \dfrac{b_2}{s_{b_2}} = \dfrac{.4980}{.0567} = 8.78$

p-value (7 degrees of freedom) = .0001
Because the p-value $\leq \alpha = .05$, β_2 is significant

20. a. Significant; p-value = .0001
b. Significant; p-value = .0000
c. Significant; p-value = .0016

22. a. SSE = 4000, MSE = 571.43,
MSR = 6000
b. Significant; p-value = .0078

23. a. $F = 28.38$
p-value (2 degrees of freedom numerator and
1 denominator) = .0019
Because the p-value $\leq \alpha = .01$, reject H_0
b. $t = 7.53$
p-value = .0007
Because p-value $\leq \alpha = .05$, β_1 is significant and x_1
should not be dropped from the model
c. $t = 4.06$
$t_{.025} = 2.571$

With $t > t_{.025} = 2.571$, β_2 is significant and x_2 should
not be dropped from the model

24. a. $\hat{y} = -.6820 + .0498$ Revenue $+ .0147$ %Wins
b. Significant; p-value = .001
c. Revenue is significant; p-value = .0007
%Wins is significant; p-value = .0063

26. a. Significant; p-value = .0000
b. All of the independent variables are significant

28. a. 143.15
b. Using StatTools, the 95% prediction interval is 111.16
to 175.16

29. a. See Excel output in Figure D13.5b
$\hat{y} = 83.2 + 2.29(3.5) + 1.30(1.8) = 93.555$
or $93,555
b. Using StatTools, 91.774 to 95.401, or $91,774 to
$95,401

30. a. 49
b. 44.815 to 52.589

32. a. $E(y) = \beta_0 + \beta_1 x_1 + \beta_2 x_2$
where $x_2 = \begin{cases} 0 \text{ if level 1} \\ 1 \text{ if level 2} \end{cases}$
b. $E(y) = \beta_0 + \beta_1 x_1 + \beta_2(0) = \beta_0 + \beta_1 x_1$
c. $E(y) = \beta_0 + \beta_1 x_1 + \beta_2(1) = \beta_0 + \beta_1 x_1 + \beta_2$

d. $\beta_2 = E(y \mid \text{level 2}) - E(y \mid \text{level 1})$

β_1 is the change in $E(y)$ for a one-unit change in x_1 holding x_2 constant

34. a. $15,300

    b. $\hat{y} = 10.1 - 4.2(2) + 6.8(8) + 15.3(0) = 56.1$

    Sales prediction: $56,100

    c. $\hat{y} = 10.1 - 4.2(1) + 6.8(3) + 15.3(1) = 41.6$

    Sales prediction: $41,600

36. a. $\hat{y} = 1.8602 + 0.2914 \text{ Months} + 1.1024 \text{ Type} - 0.6091 \text{ Person}$

    b. Significant; p-value $= .0021 < \alpha = .05$

    c. Person is not significant

38. a. $\hat{y} = -91.7595 + 1.0767 \text{ Age} + .2518 \text{ Pressure} + 8.7399 \text{ Smoker}$

    b. Significant; p-value $= .0102 < \alpha = .05$

    c. 95% prediction interval is 21.35 to 47.18 or a probability of .2135 to .4718; quit smoking and begin some type of treatment to reduce his blood pressure

40. b. 67.39

42. a.

Regression Statistics	
Multiple R	0.9681
R Square	0.9373
Adjusted R Square	0.9194
Standard Error	0.1298
Observations	10

ANOVA

	df	SS	MS	F	Significance F
Regression	2	1.7621	0.8810	52.3053	6.17838E-05
Residual	7	0.1179	0.0168		
Total	9	1.88			

	Coefficients	Standard Error	t Stat	P-value
Intercept	−1.4053	0.4848	−2.8987	0.0230
XI	0.0235	0.0087	2.7078	0.0303
X2	0.0049	0.0011	4.5125	0.0028

    b. Significant

    c. Yes

    d. Both significant

44. a. $\hat{y} = 50.6095 + 1.5621 \text{ RecRes}$; significant

    b. Not that good; $r^2 = .4315$

    c. $\hat{y} = 33.4848 + 1.8998 \text{ RecRes} + 2.6108 \text{ Afford}$; significant

46. a. $\hat{y} = 4.9090 + 10.4658 \text{ FundDE} + 21.6823 \text{ FundIE}$

    b. $R^2 = .6144$; reasonably good fit

    c. $\hat{y} = 1.1899 + 6.8969 \text{ FundDE} + 17.6800 \text{ FundIE} + 0.0265 \text{ Fund Asset Value (\$)} + 6.4564 \text{ Expense Ratio (\%)}$

    Net Asset Value (%) is not significant and can be deleted

    d. $\hat{y} = -4.6074 + 8.1713 \text{ FundDE} + 19.5194 \text{ FundIE} + 5.5197 \text{ Expense Ratio (\%)} + 5.9237 \text{ 3StarRank} + 8.2367 \text{ 4StarRank} + 6.6241 \text{ 5StarRank}$

    e. 15.28%

Chapter 14

2. a. 5.42

    b. UCL = 6.09, LCL = 4.75

4. *R chart:*

UCL $= \bar{R}D_4 = 1.6(1.864) = 2.98$

LCL $= \bar{R}D_3 = 1.6(.136) = .22$

$\bar{x}$ chart:

UCL $= \bar{\bar{x}} + A_2\bar{R} = 28.5 + .373(1.6) = 29.10$

LCL $= \bar{\bar{x}} - A_2\bar{R} = 28.5 - .373(1.6) = 27.90$

6. 20.01, .082

8. a. .0470

    b. UCL = .0989, LCL = −0.0049 (use LCL = 0)

    c. $\bar{p} = .08$; in control

    d. UCL = 14.826, LCL = −0.726 (use LCL = 0)

    Process is out of control if more than 14 defective

    e. In control with 12 defective

    f. *np* chart

10. $f(x) = \dfrac{n!}{x!(n-x)!} p^x(1-p)^{n-x}$

When $p = .02$, the probability of accepting the lot is

$$f(0) = \frac{25!}{0!(25-0)!}(.02)^0(1-.02)^{25} = .6035$$

When $p = .06$, the probability of accepting the lot is

$$f(0) = \frac{25!}{0!(25-0)!}(.06)^0(1-.06)^{25} = .2129$$

12. $p_0 = .02$; producer's risk $= .0599$

$p_0 = .06$; producer's risk $= .3396$

Producer's risk decreases as the acceptance number c is increased

14. $n = 20, c = 3$

16. a. 95.4

    b. UCL = 96.07, LCL = 94.73

    c. No

18.

	R Chart	*x̄* Chart
UCL	4.23	6.57
LCL	0	4.27

Estimate of standard deviation = .86

20.

	R Chart	*x̄* Chart
UCL	.1121	3.112
LCL	0	3.051

22. a. UCL = .0817, LCL = −.0017 (use LCL = 0)

24. a. .03

   b. $\beta = .0802$

Microsoft Excel 2007, part of the Microsoft Office 2007 system, is a spreadsheet program that can be used to organize and analyze data, perform complex calculations, and create a wide variety of graphical displays. We assume readers of this primer are familiar with basic Excel operations such as selecting cells, entering formulas, copying, and so on. But we do not assume readers are familiar with Excel 2007 or the use of Excel for statistical analysis.

The purpose of this primer is twofold. First, we provide an overview of Excel 2007 and discuss the basic operations needed to work with Excel 2007 workbooks and worksheets. Second, we provide an overview of the tools that are available for conducting statistical analysis with Excel. These include Excel functions and formulas which allow users to conduct their own analyses and add-ins that provide more comprehensive analysis tools.

Excel's Data Analysis add-in, included with the basic Excel system, is a valuable tool for conducting statistical analysis. In the last section of this primer we provide instructions for installing the Data Analysis add-in. Other add-ins have been developed by outside suppliers to supplement the basic statistical capabilities provided by Excel. In the last section we also discuss StatTools, a commercially available add-in developed by Palisade Corporation.

Overview of Microsoft Excel 2007

A workbook is a file containing one or more worksheets.

When using Excel for statistical analysis, data is displayed in workbooks, each of which contains a series of worksheets that typically include the original data as well as any resulting analyses, including charts. Figure 1 shows the layout of a blank workbook created each time Excel is opened. The workbook is named Book1, and consists of three worksheets named Sheet1, Sheet2, and Sheet3. Excel highlights the worksheet currently displayed (Sheet1) by setting the name on the worksheet tab in bold. To select a different worksheet simply click on the corresponding tab. Note that cell A1 is initially selected.

The wide bar located across the top of the workbook is referred to as the Ribbon. Tabs, located at the top of the Ribbon, provide quick access to groups of related commands. There are eight tabs: Home; Insert; Page Layout; Formulas; Data; Review; View; and Add-Ins. Each tab contains a series of groups of related commands. Note that the Home tab is selected when Excel is opened. Figure 2 displays a portion of the Home tab. Under the Home tab there are seven groups of related commands: Clipboard; Font; Alignment; Number; Styles; Cells; and Editing. Commands are arranged within each group. For example, to change selected text to boldface, click the Home tab and click the Bold button in the Font group.

Figure 3 illustrates the location of the Office Button, the Quick Access Toolbar, and the Formula Bar. When you click the Office Button, Excel provides a list of workbook options such as opening, saving, and printing (worksheets). The Quick Access Toolbar allows you to quickly access these workbook options. For instance, the Quick Access Toolbar shown in Figure 3 includes an Open button 📂 that can be used to open files without having to first click the Office Button. To add or remove features on the Quick Access Toolbar click the Customize Quick Access Toolbar button ⬇ on the Quick Access Toolbar.

FIGURE 1   BLANK WORKBOOK CREATED WHEN EXCEL IS OPENED

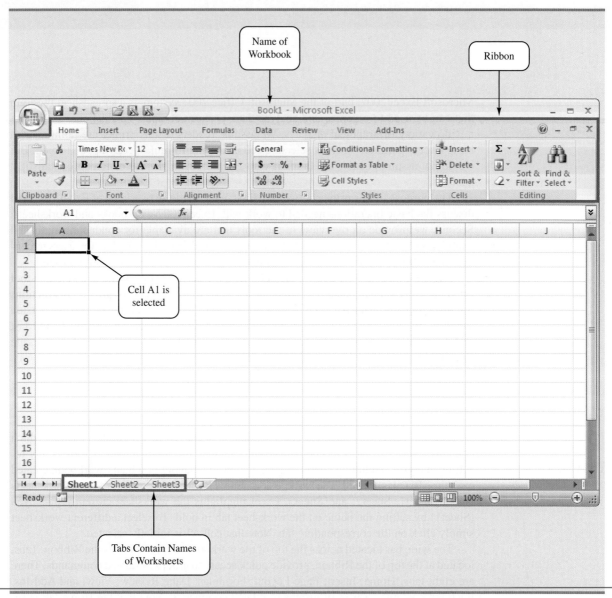

The Formula Bar contains a Name box, the Insert Function button f_x, and a Formula box. In Figure 3, "A1" appears in the Name box because cell A1 is selected. You can select any other cell in the worksheet by using the mouse to move the cursor to another cell and clicking or by typing the new cell location in the name box. The Formula box is used to display the formula in the currently selected cell. For instance, if you had entered $=A1+A2$ into cell A3, whenever you select cell A3 the formula $=A1+A2$ will be shown in the Formula box. This feature makes it very easy to see and edit a formula in a particular cell. The Insert Function button allows you to quickly access all of the functions available in Excel. Later we show how to find and use a particular function.

FIGURE 2   PORTION OF THE HOME TAB

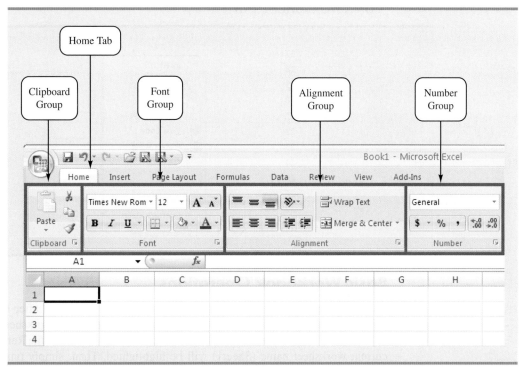

FIGURE 3   EXCEL 2007 OFFICE BUTTON, QUICK ACCESS TOOLBAR, AND FORMULA BAR

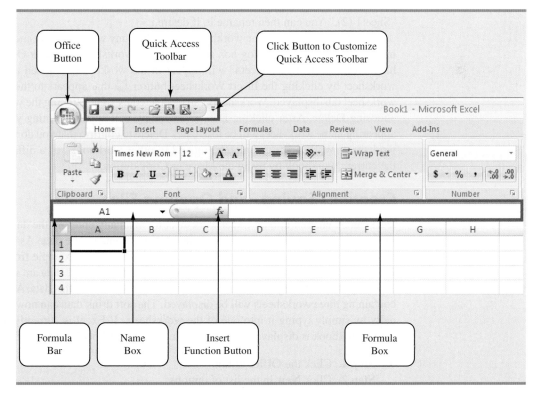

FIGURE 4   WORKSHEET OPTIONS OBTAINED AFTER RIGHT-CLICKING ON A WORKSHEET TAB

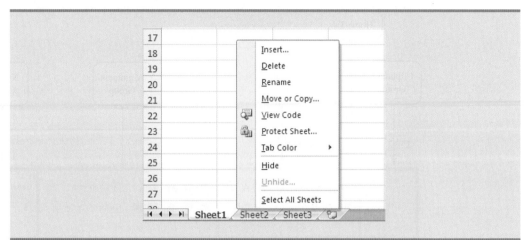

Basic Workbook Operations

Figure 4 illustrates the worksheet options that can be performed after right-clicking on a worksheet tab. For instance, to change the name of the current worksheet from "Sheet1" to "Data," right-click the worksheet tab named "Sheet1" and select the Rename option. The current worksheet name (Sheet1) will be highlighted. Then, simply type the new name (Data) and press the Enter key to rename the worksheet.

Suppose that you wanted to create a copy of "Sheet1." After right-clicking the tab named "Sheet1," select the Move or Copy option. When the Move or Copy dialog box appears, select Create a Copy and click OK. The name of the copied worksheet will appear as "Sheet1 (2)." You can then rename it, if desired.

To add a worksheet to the workbook, right-click any worksheet tab and select the Insert option; when the Insert dialog box appears, select Worksheet and click OK. An additional blank worksheet titled "Sheet4" will appear in the workbook. You can also insert a new worksheet by clicking the Insert Worksheet button ⬚ that appears to the right of the last worksheet tab displayed. Worksheets can be deleted by right-clicking the worksheet tab and choosing Delete. After clicking Delete, a window will appear warning you that any data appearing in the worksheet will be lost. Click Delete to confirm that you do want to delete the worksheet. Worksheets can also be moved to other workbooks or a different position in the current workbook by using the Move or Copy option.

Creating, Saving, and Opening Files

Data can be entered into an Excel worksheet by manually entering the data into the worksheet or by opening another workbook that already contains the data. As an illustration of manually entering, saving, and opening a file we will use an example from Chapter 2 involving data for a sample of 50 soft drink purchases. The original data are shown in Table 1.

Suppose you have just opened Excel and want to work with this data. A blank workbook containing three worksheets will be displayed. The soft drink data can now be entered manually by simply typing it into one of the worksheets. If Excel is currently running and no blank workbook is displayed, you can create a blank workbook using the following steps:

Step 1. Click the **Office** button
Step 2. Click **New** in the list of options

TABLE 1   DATA FROM A SAMPLE OF 50 SOFT DRINK PURCHASES

Coke Classic	Sprite	Pepsi
Diet Coke	Coke Classic	Coke Classic
Pepsi	Diet Coke	Coke Classic
Diet Coke	Coke Classic	Coke Classic
Coke Classic	Diet Coke	Pepsi
Coke Classic	Coke Classic	Dr. Pepper
Dr. Pepper	Sprite	Coke Classic
Diet Coke	Pepsi	Diet Coke
Pepsi	Coke Classic	Pepsi
Pepsi	Coke Classic	Pepsi
Coke Classic	Coke Classic	Pepsi
Dr. Pepper	Pepsi	Pepsi
Sprite	Coke Classic	Coke Classic
Coke Classic	Sprite	Dr. Pepper
Diet Coke	Dr. Pepper	Pepsi
Coke Classic	Pepsi	Sprite
Coke Classic	Diet Coke	

Step 3. When the New Workbook dialog box appears:
Select **Blank and recent** under **Templates**
Double click **Blank Workbook**

A new workbook containing three worksheets labeled Sheet1, Sheet2, and Sheet3 will appear.

Suppose we want to enter the data for the sample of 50 soft drink purchases into Sheet1 of the new workbook. First, we enter the label "Brand Purchased" into cell A1; then, we enter the data for the 50 soft drink purchases into cells A2:A51. As a reminder that this worksheet contains the data, we will change the name of the worksheet from "Sheet1" to "Data" using the procedure described previously. Figure 5 shows the data worksheet we have just developed.

Before doing any analysis with these data, we recommend that you first save the file; this will save you from having to reenter the data in case something happens that causes Excel to close. To save the file as an Excel 2007 workbook using the filename SoftDrink we perform the following steps:

Keyboard shortcut: To save the file, press CTRL+S

Step 1. Click the **Office** button
Step 2. Click **Save** in the list of options
Step 3. When the **Save As** dialog box appears:
In the **Save in** box select the location where you want to save the file
Type the filename **SoftDrink** in the **File name** box
Click **Save**

Excel's Save command is designed to save the file as an Excel 2007 workbook. As you work with the file to do statistical analysis you should follow the practice of periodically saving the file so you will not lose any statistical analysis you may have performed. Simply follow the procedure described above using the Save command.

Sometimes you may want to create a copy of an existing file. For instance, suppose you would like to save the soft drink data and any resulting statistical analysis in a new file

FIGURE 5   WORKSHEET CONTAINING THE SOFT DRINK DATA

	A	B	C	D	E	F
1	**Brand Purchased**					
2	Coke Classic					
3	Diet Coke					
4	Pepsi					
5	Diet Coke					
6	Coke Classic					
7	Coke Classic					
8	Dr. Pepper					
9	Diet Coke					
10	Pepsi					
11	Pepsi					
12	Coke Classic					
13	Dr. Pepper					
14	Sprite					
15	Coke Classic					
16	Diet Coke					
17	Coke Classic					
18	Coke Classic					
19	Sprite					
20	Coke Classic					
50	Pepsi					
51	Sprite					
52						
53						
54						
55						

Note: Rows 21–49 are hidden.

named "SoftDrink Analysis." The following steps show how to create a copy of the Soft-Drink workbook and analysis with the new filename, SoftDrink Analysis.

Step 1. Click the **Office** button
Step 2. Position the mouse pointer over **Save As**
Step 3. Click **Excel Workbook** from the list of options
Step 4. When the **Save As** dialog box appears:
In the **Save in** box select the location where you want to save the file
Type the filename **SoftDrink Analysis** in the **File name** box
Click **Save**

Once the workbook has been saved, you can continue to work with the data to perform whatever type of statistical analysis is appropriate. When you are finished working with the file simply click the Close Window button ✖ located at the top right-hand corner of the Ribbon. To access the SoftDrink Analysis file at another point in time you can open the file by performing the following steps:

Step 1. Click the **Office** button
Step 2. Click **Open** in the list of options

Step 3. When the Open dialog box appears:
In the **Look in** box select the location where you previously saved the file
Enter the filename **SoftDrink** in the **File name** box
Click **Open**

The procedures we showed for saving or opening a workbook begin by clicking on the Office Button to access the Save and Open commands. Once you have used Excel for awhile you will probably find it more convenient to add these commands to the Quick Access Toolbar.

Using Excel Functions

Excel 2007 provides a wealth of functions for data management and statistical analysis. If we know what function is needed, and how to use it, we can simply enter the function into the appropriate worksheet cell. However, if we are not sure what functions are available to accomplish a task or are not sure how to use a particular function, Excel can provide assistance.

Finding the Right Excel Function

To identify the functions available in Excel, click the **Formulas** tab on the Ribbon and then click the **Insert Function** button in the **Function Library** group. Alternatively, click the *fx* button on the formula bar. Either approach provides the **Insert Function** dialog box shown in Figure 6.

FIGURE 6   INSERT FUNCTION DIALOG BOX

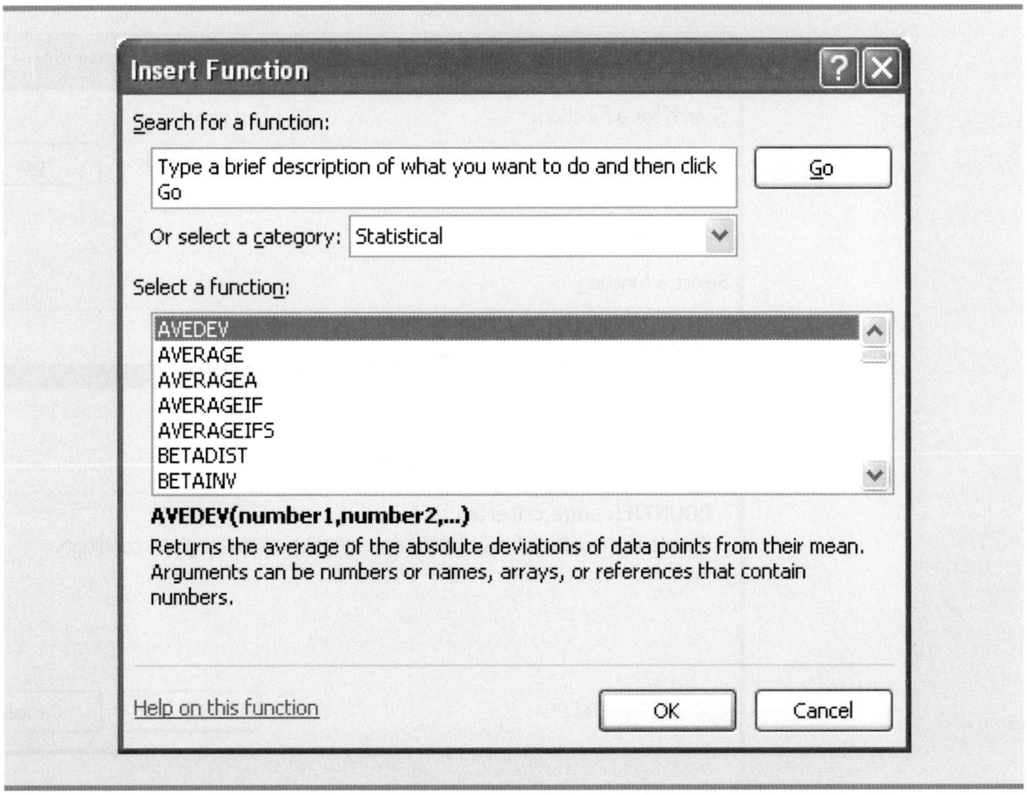

The **Search for a function** box at the top of the Insert Function dialog box enables us to type a brief description of what we want to do. After doing so and clicking **Go**, Excel will search for and display, in the **Select a function** box, the functions that may accomplish our task. In many situations, however, we may want to browse through an entire category of functions to see what is available. For this task, the **Or select a category** box is helpful. It contains a drop-down list of several categories of functions provided by Excel. Figure 6 shows that we selected the **Statistical** category. As a result, Excel's statistical functions appear in alphabetic order in the Select a function box. We see the AVEDEV function listed first, followed by the AVERAGE function, and so on.

The AVEDEV function is highlighted in Figure 6, indicating it is the function currently selected. The proper syntax for the function and a brief description of the function appear below the Select a function box. We can scroll through the list in the Select a function box to display the syntax and a brief description for each of the statistical functions that are available. For instance, scrolling down farther, we select the COUNTIF function as shown in Figure 7. Note that COUNTIF is now highlighted, and that immediately below the Select a function box we see **COUNTIF(range,criteria)**, which indicates that the COUNTIF function contains two arguments, range and criteria. In addition, we see that the description of the COUNTIF function is "Counts the number of cells within a range that meet the given condition."

If the function selected (highlighted) is the one we want to use, we click **OK**; the **Function Arguments** dialog box then appears. The Function Arguments dialog box for the COUNTIF function is shown in Figure 8. This dialog box assists in creating the appropriate

FIGURE 7   DESCRIPTION OF THE COUNTIF FUNCTION IN THE INSERT FUNCTION DIALOG BOX

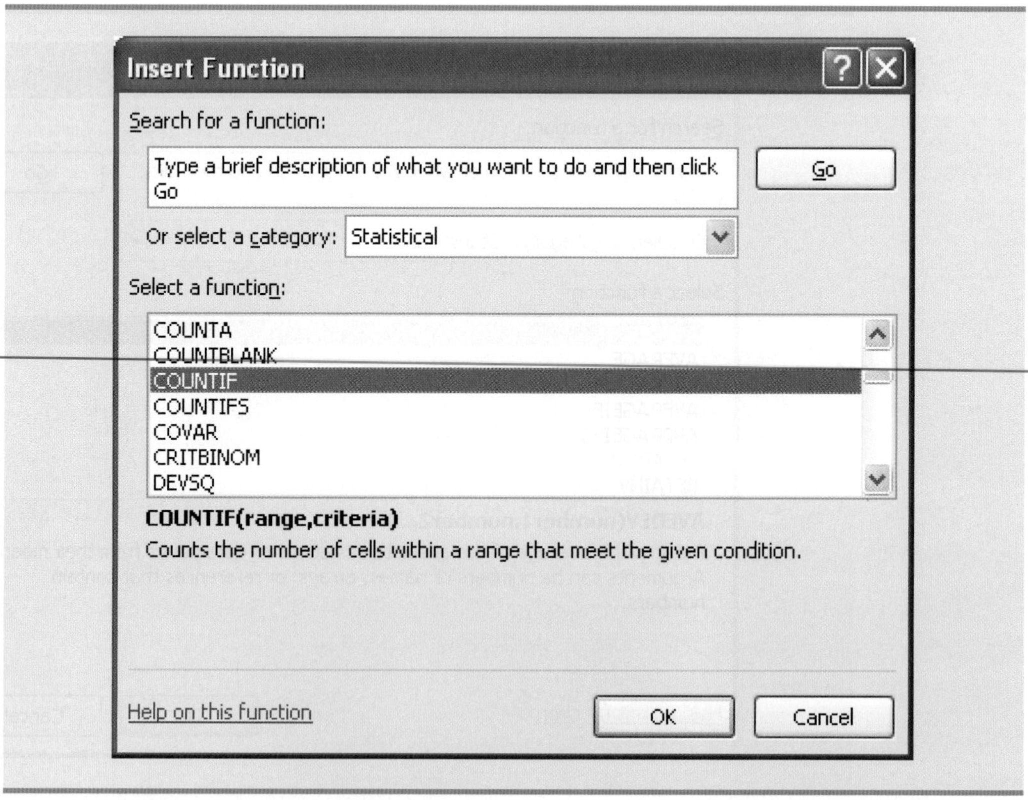

FIGURE 8   FUNCTION ARGUMENTS DIALOG BOX FOR THE COUNTIF FUNCTION

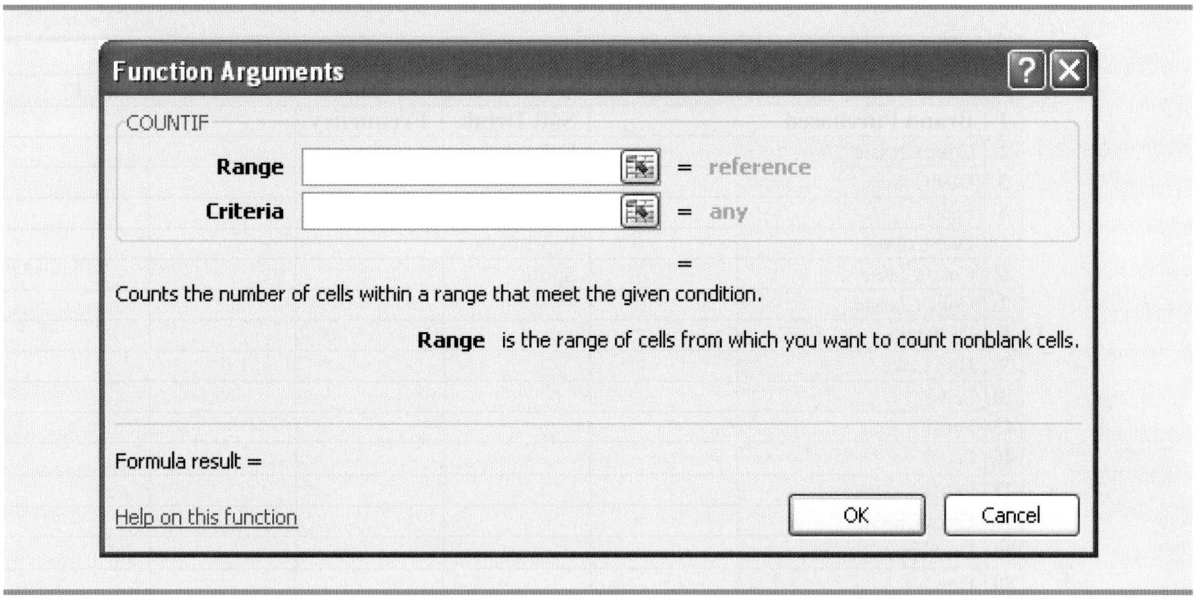

arguments for the function selected. When finished entering the arguments, we click OK; Excel then inserts the function into a worksheet cell.

Inserting a Function into a Worksheet Cell

We will now show how to use the Insert Function and Function Arguments dialog boxes to select a function, develop its arguments, and insert the function into a worksheet cell.

Suppose we want to construct a frequency distribution for the soft drink purchase data in Table 1. Figure 9 displays an Excel worksheet containing the soft drink data and labels for the frequency distribution we would like to construct. We see that the frequency of Coke Classic purchases will go into cell D2, the frequency of Diet Coke purchases will go into cell D3, and so on. Suppose we want to use the COUNTIF function to compute the frequencies and would like some assistance from Excel.

Step 1. Select cell D2
Step 2. Click f_x on the formula bar
Step 3. When the Insert Function dialog box appears
Select **Statistical** in the **Or select a category** box
Select **COUNTIF** in the **Select a function** box
Click **OK**
Step 4. When the **Function Arguments** dialog box appears (see Figure 10):
Enter $A$2:$A$51 in the **Range** box
Enter C2 in the **Criteria** box (At this point, the value of the function will appear on the next-to-last line of the dialog box. Its value is 19.)
Click **OK**
Step 5. Copy cell D2 to cells D3:D6

The worksheet then appears as in Figure 11. The formula worksheet is in the background; the value worksheet appears in the foreground. The formula worksheet shows that

FIGURE 9 EXCEL WORKSHEET WITH SOFT DRINK DATA AND LABELS FOR THE FREQUENCY DISTRIBUTION WE WOULD LIKE TO CONSTRUCT

	A	B	C	D	E	F
1	Brand Purchased		Soft Drink	Frequency		
2	Coke Classic		Coke Classic			
3	Diet Coke		Diet Coke			
4	Pepsi		Dr. Pepper			
5	Diet Coke		Pepsi-Cola			
6	Coke Classic		Sprite			
7	Coke Classic					
8	Dr. Pepper					
9	Diet Coke					
10	Pepsi					
45	Pepsi					
46	Pepsi					
47	Pepsi					
48	Coke Classic					
49	Dr. Pepper					
50	Pepsi					
51	Sprite					
52						

FIGURE 10 COMPLETED FUNCTION ARGUMENTS DIALOG BOX FOR THE COUNTIF FUNCTION

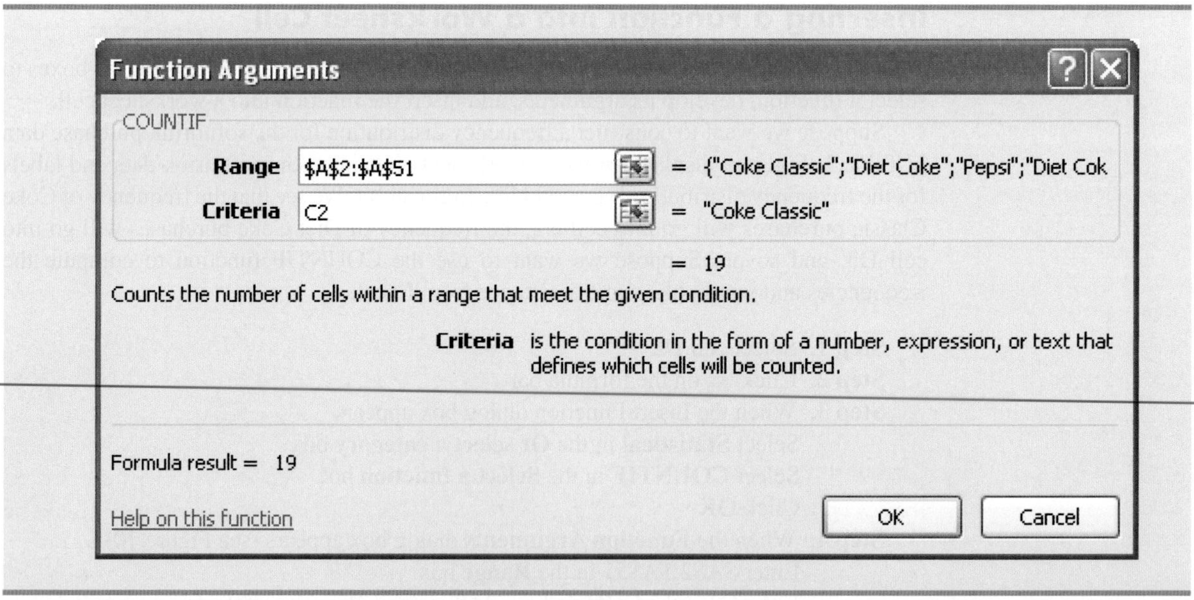

the COUNTIF function was inserted into cells D2:D6. The value worksheet shows the proper class frequencies as computed.

We illustrated the use of Excel's capability to provide assistance in using the COUNTIF function. The procedure is similar for all Excel functions. This capability is especially helpful if you do not know what function to use or forget the proper name and/or syntax for a function.

FIGURE 11   EXCEL WORKSHEET SHOWING THE USE OF EXCEL'S COUNTIF FUNCTION
TO CONSTRUCT A FREQUENCY DISTRIBUTION

	A	B	C	D	E
1	**Brand Purchased**		**Soft Drink**	**Frequency**	
2	Coke Classic		Coke Classic	=COUNTIF($A$2:$A$51,C2)	
3	Diet Coke		Diet Coke	=COUNTIF($A$2:$A$51,C3)	
4	Pepsi		Dr. Pepper	=COUNTIF($A$2:$A$51,C4)	
5	Diet Coke		Pepsi-Cola	=COUNTIF($A$2:$A$51,C5)	
6	Coke Classic		Sprite	=COUNTIF($A$2:$A$51,C6)	
7	Coke Classic				
8	Dr. Pepper				
9	Diet Coke				
10	Pepsi				
45	Pepsi				
46	Pepsi				
47	Pepsi				
48	Coke Classic				
49	Dr. Pepper				
50	Pepsi				
51	Sprite				
52					

	A	B	C	D	E
1	**Brand Purchased**		**Soft Drink**	**Frequency**	
2	Coke Classic		Coke Classic	19	
3	Diet Coke		Diet Coke	8	
4	Pepsi		Dr. Pepper	5	
5	Diet Coke		Pepsi-Cola	13	
6	Coke Classic		Sprite	5	
7	Coke Classic				
8	Dr. Pepper				
9	Diet Coke				
10	Pepsi				
45	Pepsi				
46	Pepsi				
47	Pepsi				
48	Coke Classic				
49	Dr. Pepper				
50	Pepsi				
51	Sprite				
52					

Using Excel Add-Ins

Excel's Data Analysis Add-In

Excel's Data Analysis add-in, included with the basic Excel package, is a valuable tool for conducting statistical analysis. Before you can use the Data Analysis add-in it must be installed. To see if the Data Analysis add-in has already been installed, click the Data tab on the Ribbon. In the Analysis Group you should see the Data Analysis command. If you do not have an Analysis Group and/or the Data Analysis Command does not appear in the Analysis Group, you will need to install the Data Analysis add-in. The steps needed to install the Data Analysis add-in are as follows:

Step 1. Click the **Office Button**
Step 2. Click **Excel Options**
Step 3. When the Excel Options dialog box appears:
Select **Add-Ins** from the list of options (on the pane on the left)
In the **Manage** box, select **Excel Add-Ins**
Click **Go**

Step 4. When the Add-Ins dialog box appears:
Select **Analysis ToolPak**
Click **OK**

Outside Vendor Add-Ins

One of the leading companies in the development of Excel add-ins for statistical analysis is Palisade Corporation. In this text we use StatTools, an Excel add-in developed by Palisade. StatTools provides a powerful statistics toolset that enables users to perform statistical analysis in the familiar Microsoft Office environment.

In the appendix to Chapter 1 we describe how to download and install the StatTools add-in and provide a brief introduction to using the software. In several appendices throughout the text we show how StatTools can be used when no corresponding basic Excel procedure is available or when additional statistical capabilities would be useful.

Typically the add-ins offered with textbooks are designed primarily for classroom use. StatTools, however, was developed for commercial applications. As a result, students who learn how to use StatTools will be able to continue using StatTools throughout their professional career.

Index